INTERMEDIATE ACCOUNTING

VOLUME 1

SEVENTH EDITION

Thomas H. Beechy
Schulich School of Business
York University

Joan E. Davison Conrod
Faculty of Management
Dalhousie University

Elizabeth J. Farrell
Schulich School of Business
York University

Ingrid McLeod-Dick
Schulich School of Business
York University

Intermediate Accounting
Volume 1
Seventh Edition

The Internet addresses listed in the text were accurate at the time of publication. The inclusion of a Web site does not indicate an endorsement by the authors or McGraw-Hill Ryerson, and McGraw-Hill Ryerson does not guarantee the accuracy of the information presented at these sites.

ISBN-13: 978-1-25-910801-3

ISBN-10: 1-25-910801-5

1 2 3 4 5 6 7 8 9 0   TCP   1 9 8 7 6

Printed and bound in Canada.

Care has been taken to trace ownership of copyright material contained in this text; however, the publisher will welcome any information that enables them to rectify any reference or credit for subsequent editions.

Portfolio and Program Manager: Karen Fozard

Product Manager: Keara Emmett

Executive Marketing Manager: Joy Armitage Taylor

Product Developer: Lindsay MacDonald

Senior Product Team Associate: Stephanie Giles

Supervising Editor: Jessica Barnoski

Photo/Permissions Editor: Photo Affairs, Inc.

Copy Editors: Karen Rolfe & Rodney Rawlings

Plant Production Coordinator: Sarah Strynatka

Manufacturing Production Coordinator: Emily Hickey

Cover Design: Mark Cruxton

Cover Images: (Globe and money) © Vstock LLC/Getty Images RF; (Skyscrapers) © Arpad Benedek/Getty Images RF; (Canadian flag) © BjArn Kindler/Getty Images RF; (Tablet, pen, keyboard) © John Lamb/Getty Images RF

Interior Design: Jodie Bernard

Page Layout: MPS

Printer: Transcontinental Printing Group

About the Authors

Thomas H. Beechy, York University

Thomas H. Beechy is Professor Emeritus of Accounting at the Schulich School of Business, York University. He also is the Schulich Director of International Academic Development. Professor Beechy holds degrees from the George Washington University (BA), Kellogg School of Management at Northwestern University (MBA), and Washington University (DBA). Professor Beechy was employed as a case writer for the Kellogg School, following which he taught at Illinois Institute of Technology for 10 years. He has been a professor at York University since 1971, teaching in BBA, MBA, IMBA and EMBA programs. Professor Beechy has been a leader in Canadian accounting education, emphasizing the importance of prescriptive case analysis for developing students' professional judgement. He has been an active researcher and advocate in Canadian in both business and nonprofit financial accounting realms.

Joan E. Davison Conrod, Dalhousie University

Joan Davison Conrod is a Professor of Accounting in the Rowe School of Business at Dalhousie University. Her teaching excellence has been recognized through awards such as the 2013 3M National Teaching Fellowship, the Dalhousie University Alumni Award for Teaching Excellence, and the AAU Distinguished Teacher award. Joan is an active member of the University community and has served on the Dalhousie University Senate and the Board of Governors. She is a past president of the Canadian Academic Accounting Association. Joan has a lengthy history of involvement in professional accounting education, a contributing factor in her FCPA designation. She taught financial and managerial accounting courses to professional accounting students across Canada, but particularly in Atlantic Canada, for 20 years. She has served on CA education committees at the local, regional, and national levels. Her publications include the text *Advanced Financial Reporting* for CPA—Canada, and a variety of case material and other publications.

Elizabeth J. Farrell, York University

Elizabeth J. Farrell is an adjunct professor and has taught at the Schulich School of Business for many years. She was awarded her FCPA, FCA from the Institute of Chartered Accountants of Ontario in 2013. In recognition of her excellence in teaching, she was awarded the Seymour Schulich Award for Teaching Excellence in 1999, 2003, and 2010 and was nominated for the award in 2004, 2005, 2006, 2007, 2008, 2012, and 2015. She was awarded the John Peace teaching faculty award in 2001 and 2012. She has taught financial accounting courses for over 20 years. Liz served as assistant coordinator of the Institute of Chartered Accountants of Ontario's School of Accountancy, where she also had served as a seminar leader for many years. She served as a member of the competency map committee. She has taught executive development courses for the Schulich Executive Education Centre (SEEC), as well as professional development courses for the CPA Ontario and for CPA firms. In addition to being a co-author of *Intermediate Accounting*, she has worked on an accounting case analysis software package; study guides; an IFRS Property, Plant, and Equipment, Intangible Assets and Impairment professional development course; *IFRS - Leases; ASPE—A Comparison to IFRS*; Researching and Documenting an Accounting Issue; and a variety of case material and other publications. She was one of the lead authors for the assurance elective module for the CPA PEP program. She also serves as a Board member for a not-for-profit organization.

Ingrid McLeod-Dick, York University

Ingrid McLeod-Dick is an adjunct professor and has taught at the Schulich School of Business for many years in its BBA, MBA, and EMBA programs. In recognition of her excellence in teaching, she received the John Peace part-time faculty teaching award in 2000 and was nominated for the Seymour Schulich Award for Teaching Excellence in 2000 to 2007 and 2012. She was awarded her FCA from the Ontario Institute of Chartered Accountants in 1994. Ingrid also served as a seminar leader for many years for the Institute of Chartered Accountants of Ontario's School of Accountancy. She currently teaches professional development courses for the ICAO. Her publications include the IFRS Financial Presentation and Disclosure course, and she is a contributing author to *Guides to International Financial Reporting Standards in Canada*, as well as a variety of case material for the PEP program for CPA Canada.

Brief Table of Contents—Volume 1

Chapter 1	The Framework for Financial Reporting	1
Chapter 2	Accounting Judgements	37
Chapter 3	Statements of Income and Comprehensive Income	84
Chapter 4	Statements of Financial Position and Changes in Equity; Disclosure Notes	147
Chapter 5	The Statement of Cash Flows	221
Chapter 6	Revenue Recognition	301
Chapter 7	Financial Assets: Cash and Receivables	387
Chapter 8	Cost-based Inventories and Cost of Sales	452
Chapter 9	Long-lived Assets	517
Chapter 10	Depreciation, Amortization, and Impairment	587
Chapter 11	Financial Instruments: Investments in Bond and Equity Securities	657
Appendix	Fundamentals: The Accounting Information Processing System (AIS)	747
	Compound Interest Tables and Formulae	819
	Index	Available Online

Table of Contents—Volume 1

Chapter 1   **The Framework for Financial Reporting**   **1**

Introduction   1

Accounting Standards in Canada   2

Objectives of Financial Reporting   8

External-User Objectives   11

Preparer Motivations   15

Conflicting Objectives   18

Required Financial Statements under IFRS   19

Summary of Key Points   21

Key Terms   22

Case 1-1   23

Case 1-2   24

Case 1-3   24

Technical Review   26

Assignments   30

Chapter 2   **Accounting Judgements**   **37**

Introduction   37

Categories of Accounting Concepts   38

Ethical Professional Judgement—Part 1   40

Underlying Assumptions   40

Qualitative Criteria   44

Elements of Financial Statements and Recognition   48

Measurement   54

Ethical Professional Judgement—Part 2   58

Summary of Key Points   63

Key Terms   64

Case 2-1   65

Case 2-2   66

Case 2-3   67

Technical Review   68

Assignments   72

Chapter 3   **Statements of Income and Comprehensive Income**   **84**

Introduction   84

Nature of Income	85
General Presentation Format	87
Income Tax Allocation	96
Asset Disposals, Discontinued Operations, and Restructuring	97
Summary of Key Points	117
Key Terms	117
Review Problem 3-1	118
Review Problem 3-2	122
Case 3-1	123
Case 3-2	124
Case 3-3	125
Technical Review	128
Assignments	133

Chapter 4	**Statements of Financial Position and Changes in Equity; Disclosure Notes**	**147**
	Introduction	147
	Statement of Financial Position	148
	Purpose and Limitations	152
	Specific SFP Items	155
	Statement of Changes in Equity	158
	Accounting Changes	164
	Disclosure Notes	167
	Summary of Key Points	177
	Key Terms	178
	Review Problem 4-1	179
	Review Problem 4-2	181
	Review Problem 4-3	183
	Case 4-1	184
	Case 4-2	185
	Case 4-3	188
	Technical Review	189
	Assignments	194

Chapter 5	**The Statement of Cash Flows**	**221**
	Introduction	221
	Interpretation Issues	234
	Analyzing More Complex Situations	236
	Disclosure of Cash Flows for Interest, Dividends, and Income Tax	246
	Summary of Adjustments in Operating Activities	251

Summary of Key Points   253

Key Terms   254

Review Problem 5-1   254

Case 5-1   258

Case 5-2   260

Case 5-3   261

Technical Review   264

Assignments   268

Appendix: Spreadsheet Method   297

Summary of Key Points   300

Chapter 6   **Revenue Recognition**   **301**

Introduction   301

Definitions   302

The Revenue Recognition Process   303

General Revenue Recognition Principle   303

Contract Costs   306

Transfer of Goods and Services at a Single Point in Time   307

Transfer of Goods and Services over Time   316

Long-Term Contracts Measured over Time   319

Licensing Fees   326

Measurement of Consideration   327

Multiple Goods and Service Contracts   330

Accounting for Losses on Long-Term Contracts   334

Non-monetary Transactions   339

Interest and Dividend Income   346

Choosing a Revenue Recognition Policy   346

Revenue on the Cash Flow Statement   348

Summary of Key Points   352

Key Terms   354

Review Problem 6-1   354

Review Problem 6-2   358

Review Problem 6-3   363

Case 6-1   363

Case 6-2   365

Case 6-3   368

Case 6-4   369

Technical Review   370

Assignments   373

Chapter 7	**Financial Assets: Cash and Receivables**	**387**
	Introduction	387
	Financial Assets	388
	Cash and Cash Equivalents	389
	Accounts Receivable	392
	Transfer of Receivables	399
	Notes Receivable	404
	Foreign Currency Receivables	411
	Statement of Cash Flows and Disclosure	411
	Summary of Key Points	416
	Key Terms	417
	Review Problem 7-1	417
	Case 7-1	420
	Case 7-2	421
	Case 7-3	422
	Technical Review	426
	Assignments	429
	Appendix: Bank Reconciliation	446
	Summary of Key Points	451
Chapter 8	**Cost-based Inventories and Cost of Sales**	**452**
	Introduction	452
	Right to Recovery Assets	454
	Cost-based Inventories	454
	Applying Lower-of-Cost-or-NRV Valuation	460
	Other Issues for Cost-based Inventories	463
	Inventory Estimation Methods	466
	Reporting Issues	470
	Summary of Key Points	474
	Key Terms	475
	Review Problems 8-1	475
	Review Problems 8-2	477
	Review Problems 8-3	477
	Case 8-1	479
	Case 8-2	480
	Case 8-3	482
	Technical Review	484
	Assignments	489
	Appendix: Periodic versus Perpetual Systems	508

Chapter 9	**Long-lived Assets**	**517**
	Introduction	517
	Categories of Long-lived Assets	517
	Valuation of Long-lived Assets	518
	Recognition of Property, Plant, and Equipment	519
	Cost of Property, Plant, and Equipment	523
	Biological Assets	532
	Intangible Assets—Elements of Cost	532
	Specific Intangible Assets	534
	Goodwill	538
	Derecognition of Long-lived Assets	541
	Long-lived Assets on the Statement of Cash Flows	543
	Presentation and Disclosure	544
	Summary of Key Points	551
	Key Terms	552
	Review Problem 9-1	553
	Case 9-1	555
	Case 9-2	556
	Case 9-3	557
	Technical Review	559
	Assignments	563
	Appendix 1: Investment Property	580
	Summary of Key Points	583
	Appendix 2: Government Assistance	583
	Summary of Key Points	586
Chapter 10	**Depreciation, Amortization, and Impairment**	**587**
	Introduction	587
	Review of Definitions—Depreciation and Amortization	588
	Accounting Policy—Choice of Method	590
	Depreciation and Amortization Methods	594
	Component Depreciation Accounting	599
	Additional Depreciation or Amortization Issues	601
	Impairment of Long-lived Assets	604
	Disclosure Requirements	611
	Statement of Cash Flows	616
	Summary of Key Points	619
	Key Terms	620
	Review Problem 10-1	621

	Case 10-1	622
	Case 10-2	624
	Case 10-3	625
	Technical Review	627
	Assignments	631
	Appendix 1: Capital Cost Allowance	648
	Summary of Key Points	651
	Appendix 2: Revaluation Model	651
	Summary of Key Points	656
Chapter 11	**Financial Instruments: Investments in Bond and Equity Securities**	**657**
	Introduction	657
	Investment Objectives	658
	Categories and Classification of Passive Investments	659
	Categories and Classification of Bond Investments	660
	The Amortized Cost (AC) Method	661
	The Fair-Value-through-Other-Comprehensive-Income-Bond Method (FVOCI-BOND)	671
	Classification and Accounting of Passive Share Investments	676
	Passive Share Investments: The Fair-Value-through-Profit-or-Loss Method (FVTPL)	677
	Estimating Fair Value	684
	Categories and Classification Criteria for Strategic Investments	691
	The Equity Method	693
	Consolidation	698
	Reclassification	700
	Disclosure and SCF Requirements	702
	Looking Ahead	705
	Accounting Standards for Private Enterprises	708
	Summary of Key Points	714
	Key Terms	715
	Review Problem 11-1	715
	Case 11-1	718
	Case 11-2	719
	Case 11-3	721
	Case 11-4	723
	Technical Review	725
	Assignments	729

Appendix   **Fundamentals: The Accounting Information
                    Processing System (AIS)**   **747**

                    Accounts, Transaction Recording, and Financial Statements   747

                    The Impact of Technology   750

                    The Accounting Cycle   750

                    Subsidiary Ledgers   768

                    Special Journals   768

                    Worksheets   773

                    Summary of Key Points   777

                    Key Terms   778

                    Review Problem   778

                    Technical Review   784

                    Assignments   787

                    Compound Interest Tables and Formulae   **819**

                    Index   **Available Online**

Preface

Welcome to the complex Canadian GAAP reporting environment! The vast majority of Canadian public companies prepare financial statements that comply with International Financial Reporting Standards (IFRS), as set by the International Accounting Standards Board (IASB) and contained in the *CPA Canada Handbook, Part I*. In contrast, Canadian private companies may choose to comply with either IFRS or Canadian Accounting Standards for Private Enterprise (ASPE), as contained in the *CPA Canada Handbook, Part II*. These two sets of GAAP are similar in many respects but quite different in other respects. This duality presents a huge challenge to accountants, managers, and financial statement users.

Clearly, accounting standards are ever expanding, and change is the norm; you might find the expanding universe of accounting knowledge to be intimidating. Intermediate accounting is the essential course for developing both the technical skills and the professional judgement that you need to succeed. We believe that neither technical knowledge nor professional judgement is sufficient on its own; it is the blend of the two that represents the value added by a professional accountant.

So that is what *Intermediate Accounting* will do for you: provide complete, appropriate technical knowledge while also developing your professional judgement. Both these elements are described in the broad range of topics in this book. We clearly explain the standards, identify patterns, explore the impact of alternatives on users and uses of financial statements, and look forward to further changes that are on the horizon. Throughout this book, we stress the importance of ethical standards—an accountant must learn to recognize and respond appropriately in potentially challenging situations.

In selecting material to include in this book, we have assessed the realities of Canadian business practice and the choices that are currently available. We have a distinctly Canadian agenda, looking at the issues that matter in Canadian business. We are clear in our treatment of the body of knowledge. Our coverage does not get bogged down in the (sometimes twisted) past history of a given issue, nor does it speculate needlessly on what might or might not happen in the future. Our emphasis is on preparing you to apply the standards now in place, providing an overview of some expected changes, and moving to develop the necessary judgemental skills to apply those standards wisely and effectively. These same judgemental skills will serve you equally well even when standards change in the future, as they undoubtedly will.

After you master the contents of *Intermediate Accounting*, you will be able to account for the wide range of events and transactions found in this unique and challenging economic environment. We are proud that this book is now in its seventh edition. Many thousands of students have started their substantive study of the corporate reporting environment with this book. In addition, many people have supported the evolution of this book over the last 25 years, and we are very grateful for their encouragement and continued goodwill.

IFRS and ASPE

A Canadian agenda means that we all must master international standards. Every chapter is based first and foremost on IFRS. Differences between ASPE and IFRS are explained in a separate section, to provide clarity regarding one set of standards as compared with the other. Assignment material reflects both IFRS and ASPE so that applications reflect the dual GAAP environment.

Technical Knowledge

Accountants have to be able to account for things! The seventh edition provides a level of expertise that must become part of every accountant's body of knowledge: how to record a receivable, capitalize a lease, account for a pension, or prepare a statement of cash flows. Some of the transactions that we must account for are very complex, and the specific rules must be mastered. An affinity for numbers is important.

Professional Judgement

Professional judgement, it is often said, is the hallmark of a profession. There are often different ways to account for the same transaction. Professional accountants must become expert at sizing up the circumstances and exercising judgement to determine the appropriate accounting policy for those circumstances.

Once an accounting policy has been established, management almost always must make accounting measurement estimates before the numbers can be recorded. Accounting estimates require the exercise of professional judgement.

Professional judgement is not acquired overnight. It is nurtured and slowly grows over a lifetime. In this book, we begin the development process by explicitly examining the variables that companies consider when evaluating their options, and the criteria that accountants use to make choices. Many opportunities to develop and improve judgement are provided in the case material.

Accuracy

The text has been extensively reviewed and proofread prior to publication. Chapter material has been reviewed by professional accountants. All assignment materials have been solved independently by multiple individual "assignment checkers" in addition to the authors. Nevertheless, errors may remain, for which we accept full responsibility. If you find errors, please email the authors at **j.conrod@dal.ca, efarrell@schulich.yorku.ca,** or **ing.mcleod@sympatico.ca**. Your help will be greatly appreciated.

Topical Review Identifying Key Changes

Chapter 1

The book starts by exploring the multiple accounting frameworks in use in Canada for public companies and private companies—IFRS standards for public companies, IFRS or ASPE or DBA for private companies. The chapter then explores the issue of international comparability and the difference between nations in their acceptance of IFRS—whether a nation adopts, adapts, or harmonizes with IFRS. While companies in different countries may use IFRS, the financial reports still embed significant differences that arise from differences in nations' economic, business, and sometimes even religious practices.

After establishing the multiple GAAP frameworks, our attention turns to the basis of application of any framework. Before we can make judgements on choosing accounting policies and making accounting estimates, we must understand the many possible (and often conflicting) objectives underlying a company's financial reporting. Thus, the second major theme of the first chapter is how the many different factors and influences shape a company's financial reporting. This is fundamental material that supports professional judgement.

Chapter 1 has been extensively revised and rewritten for this edition, with new exhibits to further clarify the material.

Chapter 2

The primary focus of Chapter 2 is on the accounting choice process, emphasizing underlying assumptions, qualitative characteristics, and measurement methods. Having set the basic reporting framework in Chapter 1, Chapter 2 further develops the theme of professional judgement. This chapter explains the basic assumptions underlying financial reporting and then moves on to develop the qualitative characteristics that must be considered when developing professional approaches to accounting issues.

Ethical issues are strongly emphasized in this chapter, as they are throughout the book. After discussing the broad recognition issues for revenue and expense, the chapter then sets out the elements of financial reporting. The increased incidence of fair value measurement within IFRS requires that the traditional distinction between "revenue" and "gains" be modified.

By the end of Chapter 2, all of the factors and elements underlying the exercise of professional judgement have been laid out and clarified. These factors and elements underlie the professional judgements that students must make as they move through the text, particularly in the case material at the end of each chapter.

Chapter 3

Chapter 3 discusses the nature of income and the difference between the economic and accounting concepts of income. The statement of comprehensive income is explained, and emphasizes the distinction between operating income and comprehensive income. The general presentation approach is explained, along with format variations that are accepted in practice.

Chapter 3 contains the book's primary discussion of asset disposals, discontinued operations, and restructuring. Discontinued operations is just one part of a broader issue of asset disposals. We have introduced asset disposals in this chapter to provide a clearer context for understanding discontinued operations. We discuss and provide examples of all forms of asset disposals, including abandonment, sales of individual assets, sale of asset groups, and discontinued operations. Because asset disposals are often connected with restructurings, we also present the criteria and reporting requirements for restructuring plans as well as the requirements for reporting constructive obligations that frequently accompany restructurings.

The chapter ends with a discussion of ASPE and the ways in which the reporting requirements for private enterprises using ASPE differ from enterprises reporting under IFRS.

Chapter 4

This chapter begins with a general discussion of the purpose and limitations of the statement of financial position. This discussion includes an explanation of the different ways in which the assets, liabilities, and shareholders' equity can be presented, depending on the individual regional practice.

Specific individual items on the statement are then discussed. IFRS requires certain items to be reported on the face of the statement but does not prescribe a specific format.

The next section discusses and illustrates the statement of changes in equity. We illustrate that the statement of changes in equity (SCE) includes not only the "normal" shareholder accounts (e.g., share equity and retained earnings) but also each of the various components of other comprehensive income.

In the fourth section, we have expanded the overview of accounting changes, including changes in estimate, changes in accounting policy, and error correction. Accounting changes are pervasive, and this section prepares students to understand accounting changes as they move through the specific topics that comprise the rest of the book. A full discussion of accounting changes is reserved for the end of the book, Chapter 21 (in Volume Two).

The final section is a discussion of disclosure notes. This section reflects the current disclosure requirements of IFRS, including related party transactions, segment reporting, contingencies, and guarantees.

Chapter 5

The statement of cash flows (SCF) is dealt with in sequence, as a primary financial statement. The chapter deals with the mechanics of statement preparation, using both a format-free approach and the T-account method. The journal-entry-based worksheet approach is included in an appendix. Coverage is linked to the reporting example of International Forest Products, to emphasize IFRS presentation issues and judgemental presentation choices. Presentation of investment revenue cash flow, interest, and dividends paid is discussed and illustrated in a separate section. Statement of cash flows (SCF) issues are reviewed in every subsequent chapter of the text book. And, new in this edition, there is a comprehensive SCF review at the end of Volume Two.

Chapter 6

Revenue is one of the most judgemental areas of accounting policy choice and new standards requiring a contract-based approach must be adopted by 2018 although earlier adoption is permitted. For the seventh edition of the book, this chapter reflects the new standard for revenue recognition under IFRS and specifically outlines the five criteria required for revenue recognition. A consistent approach is used to apply these criteria to determine the appropriate revenue recognition for various types of transactions. Specifically, the chapter provides examples of revenue transactions, including sales with rights of return or warranty agreements, bill and hold arrangements, consignments, and licensing fees. Transactions involving multiple deliverables are explained, with examples of loyalty point programs and franchisee fees provided. In accounting for long-term contacts, examples illustrate contracts requiring revenue to be recognized at a single point in time and contracts requiring revenue to be recognized over time.

Biological assets and agricultural produce are also discussed in the chapter. Barter transactions and exchanges of similar and dissimilar goods or services are important but challenging aspects of accounting. The chapter puts these transactions into a broader context and illustrates, based on IFRS, just how each of the various types of non-monetary exchanges should be measured and reported.

The chapter also details the revenue recognition standard under ASPE, which is now different than under IFRS. ASPE still requires an earning-based approach be used for revenue recognition. Significant differences are explained and examples provided where necessary. In addition, there is a brief discussion on the accounting treatment of related party transactions and non-monetary transactions under ASPE.

Chapter 7

This chapter now deals with two important financial instruments: cash and receivables. Coverage of payables has been shifted to Volume Two. Classification and valuation decisions are central to the coverage of cash and receivables. New to this edition are the new impairment guidance and revised financial asset classifications in IFRS 9. Important topics, such as foreign currency translation (a must, in this age of globalization) and the IFRS rules governing the transfer of receivables, are incorporated. Material on bank reconciliations is in an Appendix, and coverage of present and future value calculations is available online on Connect, as is a more extensive set of compound interest tables.

Chapter 8

This chapter conforms to the IFRS approach applying lower of cost and market valuation methods wherein the IFRS defines "market" as net realizable value. Also, we explain the process for writing inventory back up if NRV recovers before the inventory is sold.

This chapter provides focus on many accounting issues with respect to inventory: items to include or exclude, lower of cost or NRV valuation, onerous contracts, errors, and estimation techniques.

Inventory valuation raises the possibility of unethical behaviour. Therefore, the chapter includes discussion of the ethical issues surrounding inventory valuation and accounting.

Chapters 9 and 10

Accounting for fixed assets and intangible assets is challenging in the IFRS context. There are three possible models to consider depending on the type of asset: the fair value model, the revaluation model, and the cost model. Also, component accounting and depreciation add complexities to the accounting for fixed assets. Impairment testing and reversals will create more volatility in earnings using IFRS. These chapters systematically look at acquisition, amortization, impairment, and disposal considering both the IFRS and ASPE. The appendices cover the complexities related to investment property, government assistance, capital cost allowance, and the revaluation model.

Chapter 11

This chapter reflects coverage of IFRS 9, effective in 2018 but available for early adoption. Accounting for passive investments, including amortized cost, fair value through profit and loss, and fair value through other comprehensive income are explained and illustrated for bond and equity investments. Accounting for investment revenue and impairment is also discussed with many numeric examples provided. The classification of strategic investments based on the level of control and influence is examined as related to associates, joint arrangements and subsidiaries. The accounting methods for strategic equity investments including cost, equity method, and consolidation are briefly addressed. Both policy and numeric issues are thoroughly explored. The chapter includes a number of helpful diagrams and figures to help clarify the roadmap through this complex territory. ASPE alternatives are very different in this area, and the choices are documented, described and illustrated where necessary.

Volume One Appendix—Fundamentals: The Accounting Information Processing System (AIS)

The Appendix reviews the accounting cycle from the original transaction to the journals, trial balance, and preparation of financial statements. Examples of adjusting journal entries are discussed as well as subsidiary ledgers and worksheet applications. Extensive examples are used to illustrate the accounting cycle.

Chapters 12 and 13

There are two chapters on liabilities to start Volume Two. Chapter 12 deals with operating payables, as well as notes payable and provisions. The chapter includes some examples of liability measurement that require discounting. We hope that this shorter chapter is an appropriate way to start off a new term! This chapter fully reflects IFRS and ASPE standards in the area.

Chapter 13 delves into long-term debt, using bonds as an example. The chapter relies on discounted cash flow models for liability measurement, accompanied by the effective-interest method of amortization. Straight-line amortization is illustrated in the ASPE section. Various valuation and measurement complexities are covered, including the effect of upfront fees and derecognition scenarios. This chapter includes a section on the capitalization of borrowing costs.

Chapter 14

This chapter deals with straightforward shareholders' equity issues. Multicolumn presentation of the shareholders' equity statement, consistent with International Accounting Standard 1 (IAS 1), is completely incorporated. Classification and presentation of amounts in accumulated other comprehensive income, (e.g., from fair-value-through-other-comprehensive-income [FVTOCI] investments, and certain foreign currency gains/losses) is included, and is supported by assignment material. Summary charts have been incorporated, where appropriate.

Chapter 15

One major topic in this chapter is classification: debt versus equity, compound financial instruments, and the like. Classification is based on the substance of a financial instrument rather than its legal form. A major section covers the IFRS approach to share-based payments, emphasizing the estimates needed for measurement and forfeitures. Basic patterns for option accounting are established. Finally, the material on derivative instruments is included in this chapter. While many of the complexities of derivatives are appropriately left to advanced accounting courses, this introduction is vital. We think that the material is clear and understandable, at an appropriate level for Intermediate courses.

Chapters 16 and 17

Accounting for income tax remains two separate chapters, to acknowledge that many instructors prefer to spend two blocks of time on this most challenging area. The Chapter 16 material establishes a three-step process for typical situations. The focus of Chapter 17 remains accounting for the tax effect of losses—carrybacks and carryforwards. This is difficult material for students, but the Chapter 17 problems incorporate the prior-chapter material and allow solid reinforcement of the steps associated with tax accounting. The ASPE section explains the taxes payable method that is available for private enterprises.

Chapter 18

The chapter itself deals with the current IFRS lease accounting requirements. The new lease accounting standard requres all leases longer than one year to be capitalized, although classes of low-value assets can be excluded. This new standard will not become effective before 2019. Accordingly, the new lease standard is presented in the Appendix, supported by appropriate assignment material.

Chapter 19

Pensions and other post-retirement benefits are highly complex arrangements, with correspondingly complex accounting treatment. The current IFRS standard is emphasized, wherein three elements are identified and recorded. ASPE coverage is included. This chapter also includes an example of accounting for other post-retirement benefits and appropriate coverage of defined contribution plans, since the latter are gaining in popularity.

Chapter 20

Earnings per share material includes an explanation of basic and diluted earnings per share (EPS). IFRS terminology is used throughout. The procedural steps associated with organizing a complex EPS question are emphasized to provide more comfort and support in this complicated area. There are a variety of useful summary figures and tables.

Chapter 21

Accounting policy changes and error corrections require restatement of one or more prior years' financial statements. Restatement is surely an important topic, given the number of fraud-based restatements reported in the public press in recent years. Also, the ongoing changes in accounting standards means that companies must often restate their accounts. This chapter deals with the theory and mechanics related to such restatement, reflecting current IFRS standards.

Chapter 22

The text concludes with a review of financial statement analysis and emphasizes the importance of accounting policy choice and disclosure in the analysis of published financial statements. The chapter provides an in-depth discussion related to the type of information to gather specifically to assist with the analysis. Each of the ratios described in the chapter are calculated for the same sample company, and the results are analyzed, taking into consideration the entity's business and industry. There is an extensive case illustration, showing restatements, which demonstrates the importance of accounting policy choice.

Volume Two Appendix—Statement of Cash Flows

SCF topics have been explained in each chapter of the text, and students have had assignment material to reinforce each topic. However, some instructors prefer to end the course with a comprehensive review of SCF topics, as review and reinforcement. This Appendix gathers material that will support this approach. The Appendix is based on a T-account analysis, and has an appropriate range of assignment material.

Pedagogical Walkthrough

Introduction

Each chapter has an introduction that explains the objectives of the chapter in narrative form.

Concept Review

Throughout each chapter concept review questions are included. Students can stop and think through the answers to these basic questions, covering the previously explained material. This helps comprehension and focus! Answers to these questions can be found online on Connect.

CONCEPT REVIEW

1. What is the definition of "current" for current assets and current liabilities?
2. Why might some of a company's major "assets" not appear on the SFP?
3. What interpretive problems arise from the fact that the financial statements of public companies are consolidated?

Figures and Tables

Where appropriate, chapter material is summarized in figures and tables to establish the patterns and help reinforce material.

EXHIBIT 6-1

THE REVENUE RECOGNITION PROCESS

Performance complete, but conditional right to consideration	Received consideration but performance not yet completed	Performance complete and unconditional right to consideration
Goods and services transferred but receipt of consideration is conditional (e.g., delivering another distinct performance obligation)	Payment received (or receivable) before goods and services are transferred	Goods and services transferred and unconditional right to consideration
⬇	⬇	⬇
DR Contract Asset/Accrued Receivable CR Revenue	DR Accounts Receivable (or Cash) CR Contract Liability/Unearned Revenues	DR Accounts Receivable (or Cash) CR Revenue
⬇	⬇	
Conditions are met and now unconditional right to consideration	Performance is completed (goods and services are transferred)	
DR Accounts Receivable/Cash CR Contract Asset/Accrued Receivable	DR Contract Liability/Unearned Revenue CR Revenue	

Ethical Issues

Many chapters discuss accounting issues that raise ethical concerns. These concerns are highlighted in the chapter. Where ethical issues are particularly problematic, we have included a separate "Ethical Issues" section to help students focus on the ethical aspects of policy choice.

Ethics assignment material has also been incorporated into the case material. Essentially, when an accountant makes a recommendation on a contentious choice of accounting policy, ethics are tested. Students exercise true-to-life ethical judgement when they have to make a tough judgement call and recommend an accounting policy that is "good" for one group but "bad" for another. These ethical overtones are highlighted in the case solutions to help instructors draw them out in discussion and evaluation.

ETHICAL ISSUES

Choice of accounting policy must be based on the facts, the user environment, and the competitive situation. Policies chosen to manipulate certain measurements, or foster erroneous conclusions by financial statement users, are not acceptable. However, accountants must be aware of the implications of choosing a certain policy. A decision to capitalize costs, and amortize them over the period of use instead of immediate expensing, will effectively transfer the cash outflow out of operating activities and show the outflow under investing activities.

Accounting Standards for Private Enterprises

At the end of each chapter, there is a section that expands on essential items to understand for Accounting Standards for Private Enterprise (ASPE) in Canada. These sections include numeric examples, where appropriate. The ASPE sections provide students and instructors with a detailed, but easy-to-use guide to these important standards.

Accounting Standards for Private Enterprises

Balance Sheet

Canadian ASPE continues to use the title *balance sheet*, but use of that title is not required. *Statement of financial position* remains an acceptable alternative. The general format of the balance sheet is the same as for IFRS. *CPA Canada Handbook, Part II*, section 1521, contains a list of items that should be "separately presented." Some of these will usually appear on the face of the balance sheet, but some may be disclosed in the notes. The only items in the list that do not specifically appear in IFRS are:

- Prepaid expenses
- Obligations under capital leases
- Asset retirement obligations

Looking Forward

Standards are constantly evolving and changing! To help keep abreast of forthcoming probable changes, at the end of each chapter we provide a discussion of key anticipated changes in IFRS and/or ASPE standards.

Relevant Standards

At the end of each chapter, we provide a comprehensive list of the IASB and ASPE standards that are relevant to the material in that chapter. We have not quoted the standards directly in chapter material, and we have not provided paragraph references to either the IASB publications or *CPA Canada Handbook*. This omission is intentional—the two sources are harmonized but may use different words. Also, the IASB makes "annual improvements" that change the wording of some standards. Our focus is on the application of standards, not the technicalities of the wording.

RELEVANT STANDARDS

CPA Canada Handbook, Part I (IFRS):

- IAS 1, Presentation of Financial Statements
- IAS 8, Accounting Policies, Changes in Accounting Estimates and Errors
- IAS 24, Related Party Disclosures
- IAS 10, Events after the Reporting Period
- IAS 37, Provisions, Contingent Liabilities and Contingent Assets
- IFRS 8, Operating Segments

Summary of Key Points

A summary of key points concludes each chapter. This provides a list of the key ideas and reinforces the chapter material.

Key Terms

Each chapter concludes with a list of key terms used and explained in the chapter.

Review Problems

From Chapter 3 onward, we provide at least one self-study review problem, with the solution. This provides an opportunity to practise the primary aspects of that chapter's content.

Cases

More than 60 cases are included in *Intermediate Accounting*, and there is at least one new case in every chapter in the seventh edition. The cases portray realistic situations, usually with multiple financial reporting implications. Students must put themselves into the situation and grapple with the facts to arrive at the most appropriate accounting policies for the circumstances. A blend of professional judgement and technical skills is needed to respond to a case. Case coverage is not limited to "one chapter" bites but often integrates material learned to date. For those trying to build a base of professionalism, the use of cases consistently over the term is highly recommended. Cases can be assigned for class debriefing, class presentations, or written assignments.

Technical Review

In this edition, we have added five new Technical Review exercises at the end of each chapter, preceding the somewhat more demanding assignment material. These Technical Review Exercises are directive, brief, and quantitative and encourage students to ensure they understand the chapter's basic quantitative aspects. We have provided ten such exercises in total in each chapter (except in the introductory chapters) these are more conceptual than numerical in nature, and technical review is not the focus.

Assignment Material

There is an extensive range of assignment material at the end of each chapter. The assignments provide the opportunity to "learn by doing."

The Technical Review Exercises, in addition to a wealth and variety of assignments, are available online on Connect; the Connect logo identifies these questions. The Connect problems allow web-based iterations of the problem for assessment, immediate feedback, and extra practice.

★

Stars accompany each assignment to indicate length, with one star indicating a shorter assignment and three stars indicating a longer assignment.

To help students practise on their own, we have selected a few assignments from each chapter and put their solutions online. These selected assignments are highlighted by the icon in the margin.

Excel® templates for selected assignments provide an introduction to basic spreadsheet applications. These assignments are identified with the icon in the margin and are available online.

Market Leading Technology

connect

Learn without Limits

McGraw-Hill Connect® is an award-winning digital teaching and learning platform that gives students the means to better connect with their coursework, with their instructors, and with the important concepts that they will need to know for success now and in the future. With Connect, instructors can take advantage of McGraw-Hill's trusted content to seamlessly deliver assignments, quizzes and tests online. McGraw-Hill Connect is the learning platform that continually adapts to each student, delivering precisely what they need, when they need it, so class time is more engaging and effective. Connect makes teaching and learning personal, easy, and proven.

Connect Key Features:

SmartBook®

As the first and only adaptive reading experience, SmartBook is changing the way students read and learn. SmartBook creates a personalized reading experience by highlighting the most important concepts a student needs to learn at that moment in time. As a student engages with SmartBook, the reading experience continuously adapts by highlighting content based on what each student knows and doesn't know. This ensures that he or she is focused on the content needed to close specific knowledge gaps, while it simultaneously promotes long-term learning.

Connect Insight®

Connect Insight is Connect's new one-of-a-kind visual analytics dashboard—now available for instructors—that provides at-a-glance information regarding student performance, which is immediately actionable. By presenting assignment, assessment, and topical performance results together with a time metric that is easily visible for aggregate or individual results, Connect Insight gives instructors the ability to take a just-in-time approach to teaching and learning, which was never before available. Connect Insight presents data that helps instructors improve class performance in a way that is efficient and effective.

Simple Assignment Management

With Connect, creating assignments is easier than ever, so instructors can spend more time teaching and less time managing. Instructors can:

- Assign SmartBook learning modules;
- Draw from a variety of text-specific Technical Review Exercises, Assignments, and test bank questions to assign online;
- Edit existing questions and create their own questions; and
- Streamline lesson planning, student progress reporting, and assignment grading to make classroom management more efficient than ever.

Smart Grading

When it comes to studying, time is precious. Connect helps students learn more efficiently by providing feedback and practice material when they need it, where they need it. Instructors can:

- Automatically score assignments, giving students immediate feedback on their work and comparisons with correct answers;
- Access and review each response; manually change grades or leave comments for students to review;
- Track individual student performance—by question, assignment or in relation to the class overall—with detailed grade reports;
- Reinforce classroom concepts with practice tests and instant quizzes; and
- Integrate grade reports easily with Learning Management Systems including Blackboard, D2L, and Moodle.

Instructor Library

The Connect Instructor Library is a repository for additional resources to improve student engagement in and out of the class. It provides all the critical resources instructors need to build their course. Instructors can:

- Access Instructor resources;
- View assignments and resources created for past sections; and
- Post their own resources for students to use.

Acknowledgements

Our initial draft of this edition was reviewed by several colleagues with expertise in IFRS. Our manuscript benefited significantly from the comments and suggestions from Judy Cumby, FCPA, FCA, Marisa Morriello, CPA, CA, and Jessica Di Rito. Many other reviewers had contributed valuable comments on the previous editions, which informed our decisions about coverage and approach for the seventh edition.

We are grateful to the team members who exhaustively checked the assignment material and the solutions, including Eric McTaggart; Amy Pike; Li Chen; Jessica Di Rito, CPA, CA; Marcella Agustina; Marisa Morriello, CPA, CA; Balpreet Singh; and Cara Chesney, CA. The residual errors are our responsibility, but these expert individuals have significantly improved our accuracy. A special thanks to Karla Benata.

We appreciate the permissions granted by the following organizations to use their problem and case material:

- The Chartered Professional Accountants of Canada;
- The Chartered Professional Accountants of Ontario;
- The Atlantic School of Chartered Accountancy;
- The American Institute of Certified Public Accountants; and
- Brookfield Asset Management Incorporated.

We are grateful to the people at McGraw-Hill Education who guided this manuscript through the development process. We appreciate the support of Keara Emmett, our Product Manager; Lindsay MacDonald, our Product Developer; and the production team, led by Crystal Shortt and including Jessica Barnoski, Sarah Strynatka, and Emily Hickey, who have all contributed in significant ways to this final product. And, of course, Karen Rolfe and Rodney Rawlings, copy editors, have become welcome and active partners in this enterprise.

On a personal level, we would like to thank our friends and family members for their support and encouragement throughout the lengthy process of bringing this book to fruition, especially, in Toronto—Brian McBurney; in Halifax—Andrew, Yen, Meredith, and Daniel Conrod; in Richmond Hill—Ed Farrell, Catherine, Michael, and Megan Farrell; and in Collingwood—Michael Dick and Kenneth Dick.

CHAPTER 1

The Framework for Financial Reporting

INTRODUCTION

Air Canada (AC) is a large international airline. The company has more than 300 aircraft and operates flights not only throughout Canada but also over an extensive international network. About 36% of its revenue is from flights in Canada, while 64% is from international flights, including those to the United States.

AC is a public company with 286 million common shares outstanding. Its two classes of shares are traded on the Toronto Stock Exchange (TSX). Most of the shares are owned by Canadian investors, but many are owned by investors in the United States and other countries. The company has about 24,000 employees and innumerable creditors around the world. Many organizations and individuals have a significant interest in it, whether as shareholders, employees, lessors, debt holders, government regulators, or customers. As a public company, AC must issue general-purpose financial statements for the use of its many current and potential stakeholders.

In contrast, Porter Airlines Inc. is a regional airline based in Toronto. It has far fewer planes than Air Canada. Porter is a wholly-owned subsidiary of a privately held company named Porter Aviation Holdings Inc. It almost certainly holds privately negotiated debt, although the sources and amount of the financing are not public information; as a private company, Porter is under no obligation to disclose its financial details. The company's shareholders and creditors can obtain the information they need directly from the company.

For accounting, the significant difference between AC and Porter is not in their relative sizes, but in their status as public versus private companies. AC's financial statements must be prepared using **International Financial Reporting Standards (IFRS)**, which constitute Part I of the *CPA Canada Handbook*. Porter, in contrast, has a choice: it may *choose* to be guided by Canadian **Accounting Standards for Private Enterprises (ASPE)** in Part II of the *Handbook*, rather than by IFRS.

Regardless of whether a company is public or private, financial reporting will be strongly affected by (1) entity-specific financial reporting objectives and (2) management's accounting judgements. A company's financial reporting objectives and judgements will have a major impact on the company's reported financial results.

This chapter begins with an overview of the Canadian approach to business enterprise financial reporting in Canada. Then it discusses the objectives of financial reporting and how different objectives can affect financial reporting, even in public companies.

ACCOUNTING STANDARDS IN CANADA

As you already know from your introductory study of accounting, there are two related sets of financial reporting standards for Canadian business enterprises: International Financial Reporting Standards (IFRS) and Accounting Standards for Private Enterprises (ASPE). The two sets are contained in the *CPA Canada Handbook* as *Part I* and *Part II*, respectively.

Non–publicly accountable private enterprises can choose between IFRS and ASPE. The choice depends on management's reporting objectives and on the needs (and demands) of their financial statement users, primarily the providers of both debt and equity capital.

Authoritative Source of Canadian Standards

The accounting standard–setting body in Canada is the **Accounting Standards Board (AcSB)**, an independent body of the Chartered Professional Accountants of Canada (CPA). The authority of the CPA comes from the corporations acts of the federal and provincial governments. Each corporations act, including the federal *Canadian Business Corporations Act* (CBCA), requires auditors to report in accordance with generally accepted accounting principles (GAAP), and GAAP are defined in the regulations as compliance with the recommendations of the *CPA Canada Handbook*.

The GAAP requirement for public companies is enforceable by the provincial securities commissions, which are responsible for enforcing the reporting standards for companies traded in their province. In the case of Air Canada, the primary regulatory agency is the Quebec Securities Commission (Autorité des marchés financiers) because Air Canada is based in Montreal. Since AC is traded on the TSX, the Ontario Securities Commission also has strong jurisdiction.

The AcSB had, for many decades, maintained Canadian standards by regular revisions and additions to the *CPA Canada Handbook*. With the rapid acceptance of IFRS around the world, the AcSB had to decide whether to maintain a separate standard-setting process or adopt IFRS. After extensive deliberation, the AcSB decided to follow a two-pronged approach for Canadian enterprises:

1. Public companies and other publicly accountable enterprises must use *International Financial Reporting Standards* (IFRS) for financial reporting for all reporting periods beginning on or after 1 January 2011. To meet legal requirements for corporate reporting, all of the IFRS standards are included in the *CPA Canada Handbook, Part I*. Canada is an endorser jurisdiction, which means the AcSB must approve IFRS standards before they are considered Canadian GAAP.
2. Private non–publicly accountable enterprises have a choice between two options:
   a. Full IFRS, just as for public companies; or
   b. Canadian Accounting Standards for Private Enterprises (ASPE), as prescribed in the *CPA Canada Handbook, Part II*.

Although the sources for public versus private company standards differ, the content of the two sets of standards is substantially parallel. However, the private-company standards are somewhat less complex, put less reliance on fair-value measurements, and have far fewer disclosure requirements.

IFRS Overview

Organization

International standards are developed and issued by the **International Accounting Standards Board (IASB)**, which is based in London, England. The IASB's oversight body is the not-for-profit IFRS Foundation, based in the U.S. state of

Delaware. The IASB comprises 14 experts "with an appropriate mix of recent practical experience in setting accounting standards, in preparing, auditing, or using financial reports, and in accounting education." The members are appointed by the IFRS Foundation.

In October 2015, the IASB website listed 14 members, consisting of two members at large, three from North America, three from Europe, four from Asia/Oceania, one from Africa, and one from South America. Board members have international experience in accounting/auditing practice, accounting standard setting, and investment analysis; the IFRS Foundation emphasizes "broad geographic diversity" for membership.

The national representation of the IFRS Foundation is rather similar to that of the IASB, although its membership is somewhat broader: of its 22 trustees, six are from each of Asia, Europe, and North America; one is from each of Africa and South America; and two are from the rest of the world.

Adopt, Adapt, or Converge?

The hope of the IFRS (and of many international corporations) is that all countries will use IFRS as their reporting standard for publicly accountable enterprises. In reality, it is not so simple. Actually there are three different approaches in use, the usage depending on the regulatory environment in each nation:[1]

1. *Adopt.* When a country adopts IFRS, use of the country's pre-existing public company GAAP is ended, and IFRS is substituted. When Canada initially "adopted" IFRS in 2011, all standards were adopted into the *CPA Canada Handbook* without modification.

2. *Adapt.* Under this approach, a country uses IFRS, but not before reviewing each standard for suitability in that specific national environment. If the national regulatory body (often, the legislature) deems a particular IFRS to be unsuitable in some respect, then the standard is altered, such as by deleting one or more specific aspects of the standard before approving it for use in that country. Thus, the standards are *adapted* to the perceived national environment. This is the approach used in the European Union (EU), where all standards must be approved by the EU parliament before they go into effect.

3. *Converge.* Under a convergence approach, a national standard setter revises its own standards to reduce the differences from an international standard, for example by "harmonizing" or converging standards on such topics as inventory accounting or revenue recognition. This is the approach used by such disparate countries as the United States. In the case of the United States, the FASB and IFRS work directly together to reduce differences between their standards. Indeed, it is fair to say that the IFRS may modify some of its draft standards to be closer to the U.S. standards rather than the other way around.

Translations and Authority

The IASB prepares translations of IASs and IFRSs into many other languages, but these translations are not authoritative. Worldwide, only the English version of IFRS is authoritative. In case of dispute, the English version must prevail. This is an issue because different languages have different linguistic practices and vocabularies. Other languages might not have exactly equivalent phraseology. Despite this precaution, since the companies in other countries will use the local-language version of IFRS, the outcome from applying IFRS might still be rather different from that in English-speaking countries.

In Canada, however, there is an authoritative French version, since the standards must say the same thing in both English and French. CPA Canada prepares its own French translations (as it always has done for Canadian standards). The IASB now uses the CPA Canada translations as its own French-language standards.

Accounting Standards for Canadian Publicly Accountable Enterprises

A **publicly accountable enterprise (PAE)** is any company that either (1) has securities (debt or equity, or both) issued to the public or is in the process of issuing them or (2) is a for-profit private enterprise that holds assets in a fiduciary capacity for a broad group of outsiders as one of its primary businesses.

---

1. Stephen A. Zeff and Christopher W. Nobes, "Has Australia (or Any Other Jurisdiction) 'Adopted'" IFRS?" *Australian Accounting Review*, no. 53, vol. 20, Issue 2 (2010).

A **fiduciary enterprise** is any organization that acts in a trusteeship capacity for members of the general public. Examples are investment funds, mutual funds, pension funds, savings institutions, privately owned banks, credit unions, and other deposit-taking organizations; many such enterprises and organizations are private in the sense that they have no securities outstanding in public hands.

As well, governmental business enterprises must disclose their financial performance and thus are PAEs, regardless of whether they are intended to earn a profit. Examples are Canada Post, VIA Rail, Toronto Transit Commission, and the many port authorities across Canada. Government business enterprises are usually known as **Crown corporations**.

In this book, we will use *public company* or *public enterprise* to indicate any type of publicly accountable enterprises, rather than encumber the text with excessive repetition.

Choice of GAAP

Although IFRS is the normal reporting requirement for Canadian public corporations, the shares of some Canadian corporations are heavily traded in the United States. To enhance the acceptability of its shares in the U.S. financial markets, a Canadian company may choose to follow U.S. GAAP. The use of U.S. standards is accepted by the Ontario Securities Commission (OSC) and the TSX for trading in Canada, thanks to a mutual-recognition agreement between the Securities Exchange Commission (SEC) and the OSC. Conversely, if a Canadian corporation uses Canadian GAAP and its securities are traded in the U.S. financial markets, the SEC will accept IFRS-based reporting.

Although there is an SEC–OSC mutual recognition agreement, it is fairly rare for a Canadian company to use U.S. GAAP. Some Canadian U.S. GAAP users are listed on the New York Stock Exchange (NYSE). However, as of 2015, only 82 Canadian companies were listed on the NYSE, and only a minority of those companies use U.S. GAAP. Hence, do not get distracted by this rarely used alternative. The basic reporting requirement for Canadian public companies is IFRS.

IFRS is the normal reporting requirement for lists on other securities exchanges around the world. Therefore, Canada's adoption of IFRS makes it relatively easy for Canadian public companies to list on foreign exchanges.

Legal and Regulatory Requirements

In some special industries, such as investment funds, chartered banks, and regulated enterprises (e.g., telephone or cable companies), the normal provisions of IFRS may be supplemented by legal requirements. Canada's chartered banks, for example, are governed by Canada's *Bank Act*. IFRS still prevails, however, except for certain rare instances in which legal or regulatory requirements may take precedence.

Reporting Currency

Canadian companies do not always prepare their financial statements in Canadian dollars. Under IFRS, a company should report in its **functional currency**, which is the currency in which most of a company's transactions are conducted. For example, if a Canadian company has most of its transactions in U.S. dollars, all non–U.S. currency flows and values are translated into U.S. dollars. Normally, such a company would also adopt the U.S. dollar as the company's **presentation currency**—the currency in which the financial statements are presented. IFRS requires an enterprise to disclose its presentation currency at the top of each financial statement.

For example, in the notes to its 2014 financial statements, Montreal-based Bombardier Inc., a manufacturer of airplanes (BA) and railroad equipment (BT), explains its use of U.S. dollars as follows:

> **Foreign currency translation**
>
> The consolidated financial statements are expressed in U.S. dollars, the functional currency of Bombardier Inc. The functional currency is the currency of the primary economic environment in which an entity operates. The functional currency of most foreign subsidiaries is their local currency, mainly the U.S. dollar in BA, and the euro, pound sterling, various other Western European currencies, and the U.S. dollar in BT.

Do not get confused between reporting in U.S. dollars and reporting using U.S. GAAP. There is no necessary relationship between the presentation currency and the reporting GAAP. This is illustrated by the reporting practices of three major Canadian companies:

- Barrick Gold Corporation reports in Canadian GAAP but U.S. dollars.
- Hydro One Inc. reports in U.S. GAAP but Canadian dollars.
- Lululemon Athletica Inc. reports in U.S. GAAP and U.S. dollars.

Accounting Standards for Canadian Private Enterprises

A **private enterprise** is one that neither issues debt or equity securities *to the public* nor is in the process of doing so, and also does not hold assets in a fiduciary capacity as one of its primary businesses. All of the company's shares are held privately and cannot be offered for sale on the open market. Usually, the shares are all owned by the members of a single family and sometimes by senior executives as well. However, other investors can be involved. The fact that "outsiders" own part of the stock does not affect its status as a private enterprise.

The suppliers of capital to a private corporation are assumed to be either insiders or sophisticated investors who do not need the special protection given to members of the general public who may buy shares on the open market.

Private companies provide financial statements for a limited group of users, including managers, shareholders, taxation authorities, lenders, and other creditors. These users are presumed to have access to the information that they need, either as owners and/or managers or as bankers/creditors. Financial statements must also accompany each corporation's income tax form; tax authorities can demand additional information as well.

Canadian private companies have three financial statement reporting choices:

1. IFRS, the same as public companies;
2. Canadian ASPE, as prescribed in the *CPA Canada Handbook, Part II*; or
3. Tailored accounting policies, known as a *disclosed basis of accounting*.

A private company is often referred to as an **SME**, which stands for **small and medium-sized enterprises**. In some countries, accounting standards for SMEs are limited to companies below a certain size threshold of revenue, capital, or employees. However, some of Canada's largest corporations are private corporations (e.g., McCain Foods Ltd. and Bata Shoes—both companies have multi-billion-dollar annual revenues). Therefore, the SME appellation has never been used to refer to private-company accounting standards in Canada. There are no size thresholds. The choice between following IFRS versus Canadian ASPE is unaffected by a Canadian private corporation's size.

Using IFRS

A private company may wish to use IFRS instead of following private-company Canadian standards because it competes with public companies for capital.

Despite the inability to sell shares to the public, private corporations can obtain substantial capital through **private placements**. A *private placement* is arranged by direct negotiation with the one or more suppliers of capital. Private capital suppliers include pension funds, investment funds, private equity investment companies, and major banks. In Canada, almost all major debt financing for both public and private corporations is by means of private placements.

Private placements also are a source of equity financing for private companies. Securities issued in a private placement cannot be publicly traded, and therefore a private company remains outside the jurisdiction of the securities acts and securities regulators.

Even though private companies' shares are not publicly traded, management may choose to use IFRS so that the company's financial statements can be more easily compared with those of public companies. This is not simply a matter of competing for financing in Canada—for a large company, the competition for funds is international. A large private Canadian corporation is competing for debt and equity funds against companies from the United States, Europe, Asia, South America, and so on. To compete for capital effectively, an important financial reporting objective for a private company may be to issue financial statements comparable with those issued by public companies worldwide.

Other reasons a private enterprise may choose to use IFRS are:

- The company is a subsidiary of a parent that reports on the basis of IFRS.
- The company may be considering issuing shares to the public in the foreseeable future and wishes to establish a pattern of IFRS compliance in the financial statements that it must submit as part of the company's prospectus.

- The company's controlling shareholders may intend to sell the company in the near future. Using IFRS may enhance the financial statements' credibility to prospective public-company acquirors.

Using ASPE

Most Canadian corporations are private, not public, companies. The AcSB has long recognized that private companies are unnecessarily burdened by the complex standards designed for public companies. Thus, upon adopting IFRS, the AcSB had to decide how to reduce the financial reporting burden for private companies. One alternative was to adopt the IASB's simplified version of IFRS for SMEs. An advantage of using IFRS-SME is that a nation does not need to maintain an accounting standard-setting structure of its own. Australia, for example, has gotten out of the business of accounting standard setting and adopted IFRS-SME as its reporting requirement for private enterprises.

The other alternative was to continue home-grown standards as an option for Canadian private companies. After all, only a tiny proportion of Canadian corporations are public. By using Canada-specific standards instead of tying private companies to international standards, the AcSB would be better able to adapt private company reporting to the Canadian legal, regulatory, and capital environments.

After considering the alternatives, the AcSB opted to maintain national standards. The pre-existing standards in the *CPA Canada Handbook* were simplified by removing some of the reporting requirements that are less appropriate for private companies. Canadian accounting standards for private enterprises are based less on fair values and more on historical cost, and the disclosure requirements are less onerous. Cost/benefit tradeoff is an important consideration in ASPE.

As a result of continuing use of the *CPA Canada Handbook* instead of IFRS-SME, many private companies found that there was little change in their reports when they converted to ASPE, in contrast to the major impacts on Canadian public companies in 2011 when they adopted IFRS.

Using a Disclosed Basis of Accounting

In practice, private enterprises are not bound by GAAP unless an external user (such as a major lender) requires the company to use them. While many private companies do abide by all accounting standards, many others deviate from the standards in one or more respects. The deviation is usually to make the statements more useful for specific users or to coincide with the income tax treatment of specific items. For example, a company may prepare statements to satisfy contractual requirements, such as compliance with the requirements of a major loan.

When non-GAAP accounting policies are used, the company is said to be reporting on a **disclosed basis of accounting (DBA).** The description of DBA will normally be included in the accounting policy note to the financial statements, and the auditor's opinion (if any) will refer to the fact that the financial statements have been prepared in accordance with the accounting principles described in the accounting policy note.

Be cautious! We are not suggesting that a company can toss out all of GAAP. Deviations from GAAP are usually limited to just certain policies (e.g., using tax-based capital cost allowance [CCA] instead of accounting depreciation), except for very small companies that report on what is essentially a modified accrual basis. A Canadian company using a DBA cannot also state that they are using GAAP.

Learning Multiple Sets of Standards

Canada is using different accounting standards for public and private enterprises. Other countries are using yet other sets of standards (e.g., IFRS-SME). Does this mean we all have to learn two or three different sets of standards? Not really.

IFRS is the biggie—the one all professional accountants and investment managers around the world must understand. As your career takes you around the world, whether as a professional accountant, a financial expert, a private investor, or a company manager, you should be highly knowledgeable about IFRS.

On the other hand, most Canadian private companies will use ASPE, with fewer disclosure requirements and less reliance on fair values. Although these are two different sets of GAAP, they are very similar in many respects. The AcSB is unlikely to let Canadian ASPE deviate very far from the general principles and practices prescribed by IFRS. In fact, every time a new standard is issued in IFRS the private advisory committee considers whether it should be adopted in ASPE. Again, cost/benefit tradeoff is key and the standard in ASPE may be much simpler.

Thus, there is a lot of convergence between ASPE and IFRS. Private-company GAAP can be regarded mainly as simplifying exceptions to IFRS rather than as a substantially different body of standards. Many of the principles and practices of international standards had already been incorporated into Canadian standards before the 2011 changeover to IFRS, although there were still many significant differences.

This book will discuss IFRS in the main text of each chapter. At the end of each chapter, we will explain the ways Canadian ASPE differs from IFRS.

The Issue of Comparability

The point of establishing IFRS is not only to promote multiple exchange listings but also to greatly improve comparability between companies based in different countries. Previously, it was quite difficult to compare the financial statements of companies based in different countries. Even relatively minor differences between U.S. and Canadian reporting caused difficulties for analysts. To compare companies between more radically different standards (e.g., German versus United Kingdom) required detailed knowledge of both countries' accounting standards.

But now that both Germany and the United Kingdom use IFRS for their consolidated statements, comparisons should be straightforward, right? Unfortunately, no. The financial reporting of any company is strongly affected by its national environment. There are differences between countries regarding legal requirements, economic environment, political environment, regulation, and ways of doing business.

In the United States and Canada, the principal focus of general-purpose statements is on residual earnings for the shareholder. Other countries may put more emphasis on other stakeholder groups or have different cultural practices. For example:

- Many countries base income tax on reported earnings; taxable income is equal to accounting income. Income tax minimization therefore becomes a dominant financial reporting objective.
- Corporations in Sweden are expected to provide information about social responsibility and environmental protection in their annual reports. Accounting information relating to these issues is highlighted in financial reporting.
- German financial reporting puts strong emphasis on creditor protection. The tendency is to understate earnings and to provide for income reserves that have no correspondence in IFRS or Canadian ASPE.
- Many countries emphasize employee protection. Information on employee compensation and benefits must be disclosed in considerable detail, in contrast to Canadian and U.S. practice, where only limited information about employee compensation and benefits is reported in the financial statements—only broad totals are provided.
- Companies that follow Muslim practice do not enter into lending relationships. Instead, banks and other sources of financing enter into equity-based arrangements. Therefore, amounts that would be reported as interest expense in Canadian will be reported as dividends in companies based on Muslim principles.
- The "consolidated" statements of large Japanese conglomerates do not include the bulk of their related companies, because there is no "parent" company. Each company within the large group holds just a small share (e.g., 1%–3%) of each other company. At least 60% of the shares are held within the group (called a *keiretsu*), and yet no company "controls" any others. Thus, there is no comparison between the consolidated financial statements of General Motors (which includes all of its subsidiaries) and those of Mitsubishi or Toyota (which include only controlled foreign subsidiaries).

International comparisons of financial statements are fraught with hazard because of the many differences that arise. For example, a very high debt load is usually viewed in North America as a bad sign, while low debt is usually a sign of good management. In Germany and Japan, however, low debt indicates that the banks have no confidence in the company—banks will support only strong companies, and thus strong companies are able to access high levels of debt.

CONCEPT REVIEW

1. What is the difference between a public corporation and a private corporation? Which type is dominant in the Canadian economy?
2. How can private corporations obtain capital from outside investors without becoming public companies?
3. Why would a Canadian private enterprise choose to use IFRS instead of ASPE?

OBJECTIVES OF FINANCIAL REPORTING

Is XYZ Corporation making a profit or a loss this year? Well, that depends on how you measure it! To prepare the financial statements, managers and accountants have to make many judgements. They must:

1. Choose appropriate measurement methods (i.e., accounting policies); and
2. Make suitable accounting estimates.

To help users understand the financial statements and the approximate nature of the information they contain, managers must also decide what additional information to disclose in both the statements and the notes.

As we will see throughout this book, management's choice of accounting policy and disclosure are constrained by the requirements of IFRS (for public companies) and Canadian ASPE (for private companies). Nevertheless, management must make policy choices in some areas and many estimates in applying the standards. A fairly small change in an estimate can have a very substantial impact on the company's reported results. Indeed, variations in a number of small estimates, such as from optimistic to pessimistic, can sometimes turn a profit into a loss, and vice versa. We will discuss this crucial issue of estimation more extensively later.

To exercise judgement, the accountant must have *criteria* against which to measure the suitability of alternatives. The most fundamental criteria for deciding on policies, estimates, and disclosures are the **objectives of financial reporting** for the specific reporting enterprise or organization.

To be useful to the users, the financial statements must convey information that is useful for their decision purposes. These purposes may vary widely, and information suitable for one purpose might not be suitable for another.

Financial statements often have direct economic impacts for either the enterprise or its stakeholders, or both. For example:

- Reported earnings may be used as the basis for employee profit sharing and/or management bonuses.
- Accounting methods may increase or decrease a corporation's income tax liability.
- The reported level of accounts receivable and inventories affects the level of financing provided by a bank through an operating line of credit.
- Reported earnings and reported net asset value affect the permitted return in regulated industries, such as cable companies and electric utilities.
- Various reported numbers in the financial statements may trigger a default on loan requirements, which are known as **covenants**.
- In partnerships, cooperatives, and mutual insurance companies, the reported financial results affect the financial rewards of the partners, members, and policyholders.

In addition, many users' decisions are *evaluative* ones that may not have immediate economic impacts, but do affect users' perceptions of the reporting enterprise and affect their relationship with (or stake in) the enterprise:

- Lenders evaluate the cash flow potential of a borrower to assess the ability of the borrower to service the loan (i.e., to pay the interest and principal as they come due).
- Income tax authorities evaluate the financial statements to see whether the information a corporation is reporting to its owners is compatible with (but not necessarily the same as) the information it is reporting to the Canada Revenue Agency (CRA).
- Employees evaluate an employer's ability to pay higher compensation (or the validity of employer requests for reductions in compensation).
- Shareholders assess management's ability to conduct the affairs of the enterprise.
- Security analysts evaluate public companies' performance and issue recommendations to buy, hold, or sell shares.
- Regulators evaluate a rate-regulated enterprise to see if the enterprise's earnings are reasonable.

To establish each enterprise's financial objectives, management must consider many aspects of the company and the users of its financial statements. Exhibit 1-1 illustrates the forces that shape a company's financial reporting objectives:

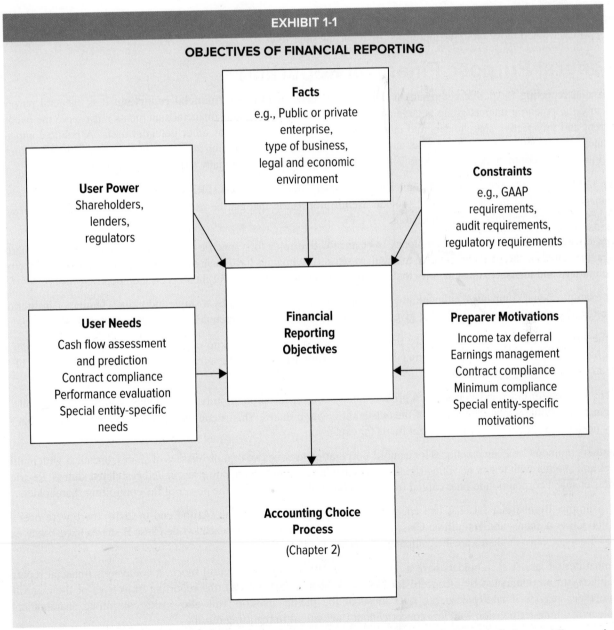

EXHIBIT 1-1

OBJECTIVES OF FINANCIAL REPORTING

Facts
e.g., Public or private enterprise,
type of business,
legal and economic environment

User Power
Shareholders,
lenders,
regulators

Constraints
e.g., GAAP requirements,
audit requirements,
regulatory requirements

User Needs
Cash flow assessment and prediction
Contract compliance
Performance evaluation
Special entity-specific needs

Financial Reporting Objectives

Preparer Motivations
Income tax deferral
Earnings management
Contract compliance
Minimum compliance
Special entity-specific motivations

Accounting Choice Process
(Chapter 2)

- The *facts* of the company's operations—for example, the sources of its capital; whether it is a public or private enterprise; the length of its operating cycle; the volatility (and predictability) of its revenues and costs.

- The financial reporting *constraints* facing the company—for example, whether an audit is required; whether the audit report must have an unqualified opinion; whether there are regulatory or statutory requirements to meet.

- The *power* of the users—for example, the ability of users such as securities regulators, major lenders, or shareholders to enforce their needs over those of other users or the managers.

- The needs of the financial statement *users*—for example, cash flow prediction; contract compliance; management performance.

- The motivations or objectives of the *preparers* (i.e., the managers)—for example, to minimize current taxes payable; to reveal as little about the company as possible; to show a smooth growth in earnings.

Before identifying the appropriate reporting objectives in a specific situation, the enterprise's facts and constraints must be taken into account. If the facts and the constraints allow an alternative, the needs of users and the motivations of preparers can be identified and ranked in order of priority. Obviously, ethics are very important: you cannot just do whatever you want to achieve the objectives of the users! The cases at the end of each chapter will give you practice in identifying company-specific facts and constraints.

We will begin our discussion of financial reporting standards with a quick overview of *general purpose financial reporting*, after which we will move on to the more specific reporting objectives.

General Purpose Financial Reporting

Financial reporting for public companies is described as **general purpose financial reporting**. It is "general purpose" because the potential interest group is large and diverse. A public company's financial statements must serve the needs of current and prospective shareholders and other suppliers of capital, as well as other potential users. A public company's financial statements users can be anyone, anywhere. Public-company accounting standards have been developed to protect the interests of economic decision makers who are dependent solely on a company's financial statements.

The IASB focuses on the supplier of capital as the primary user group. The IFRS *Conceptual Framework for Financial Reporting* states that the objective is to provide useful information that can be used by "existing and potential investors, lenders and other creditors" in their decisions.

In practice, "general purpose" is too imprecise to be an effective guide for a specific enterprise. While the financial reporting objectives cited by the IASB are a guide to standard setting, companies have their own, more specific reporting objectives. Accountants and managers must identify the appropriate reporting objectives for their specific company.

For example, some companies, although publicly listed, are really controlled by a single individual, family, or institutional investor. The group of voting shares that gives control to a small group of shareholders is called a **control block**.

In the *Financial Post*'s annual listing of Canada's 500 largest corporations, known as the FP500, approximately half the companies are public. Of the public companies, however, well over half have control blocks. Only about 20% in the FP500 list are "widely held public companies."

Usually, a control block exists because a private, family-controlled corporation has issued shares to the public, while the original shareholders retain a majority of the outstanding *voting* shares. This is common in Canada for companies that find they need to "go public" to raise sufficient funds for expansion.

Another common Canadian practice is for a public corporation to issue two or more classes of shares, one class with multiple votes and another with few or no voting rights. Shares that have limited voting power are called **restricted shares**. Restricted shares enable a corporation to raise capital from the public without impairing the power of the controlling shareholders.

For example, Bombardier Inc. has two classes of common shares outstanding. At the end of 2014, there were over 314 million Class A shares and 1.4 million Class B. Class A shares have 10 votes each, while Class B shares have 1 vote each. The holders of Class A shares are the company's founding family.

Bombardier's Class A shareholders have a *control block*. When there is a control block, a company's financial reporting is unlikely to be dominated by a concern for the public shareholder. Instead, the reporting objectives of the controlling shareholder may well take precedence over those of the public investor. This allows the controlling shareholders to implement a long-term vision with less concern about fluctuations in reporting results.

When there is a control block, managers may focus primarily on satisfying the controlling shareholder—the needs and perceptions of other shareholders and lenders can become secondary. Alternatively, management may be especially concerned about meeting the requirements of a large major supplier of debt capital, such as a pension fund.

Users

"Users" can be grouped into two categories—(1) external users and (2) preparers:

- **External users** include all nonmanagement users of the financial statements, such as investors, creditors, and employees.
- **Preparers** consist of the managers who make decisions in the three judgemental aspects of applying accounting standards—accounting policy, estimates, and disclosure—as well as the accountants who participate in and carry out those decisions by incorporating them into the accounts.

A manager is a *preparer* but may also be a *user* in a different role. A chief financial officer (CFO) of a large corporation is a preparer of the corporation's consolidated statements. On the other hand, that same CFO will use the financial statements of different business units and subsidiaries to evaluate their performance.

In Exhibit 1-1, each of the two boxes labelled "User Needs" and "Preparer Motivations" contains a summary listing of the primary financial reporting objectives. This list is by no means comprehensive, because entity-specific objectives often arise. Remember, we are discussing the financial reporting objectives, not the business objectives.

Ethical Issues

Accountants are part of the preparer group, because they carry out the accounting and reporting decisions of management. Ethical issues can arise. Some accountants have gone to jail because they followed accounting instructions (or strong "hints") from senior executives that resulted in financial misrepresentation.

A professional accountant, whether internal or external (e.g., an auditor), must be prepared to resist management's pressure to misstate financial results, even if it leads to dismissal. It is bad to be temporarily unemployed, but it is far worse to be convicted of a crime. At the end of the day the financial statements need to be "fair."

EXTERNAL-USER OBJECTIVES

Assessing and Predicting Cash Flows

A financial reporting objective that has received much attention in both the professional and the academic accounting literature is that of *cash flow assessment and prediction*—investors and creditors are interested in predicting the ability of the company to earn sufficient income and generate sufficient cash flows in the future to be able to pay the company's obligations and to provide a return to shareholders.

Bankers and creditors need to assess a business's ability to generate enough cash through its normal operations to be able to pay interest and to repay debt principal. The shareholders of public companies may also be interested in cash flow prediction, because in theory share value is derived from the present value of the perpetual stream of future dividend payments. To the extent that earnings are retained instead of being paid out as dividends, the reinvested earnings increase the asset base and should generate increased cash flow (and increased dividends) in the future.

Assessment versus Prediction

There is a subtle but important difference between the assessment of *current* cash flows and the prediction of *future* cash flows. To assess current cash flows, the nonmanagement financial statement user wants to understand the cash inflows and outflows of the enterprise in the current period. Normally, the user puts special emphasis on the *cash flow from operating activities* to assess the entity's ability to generate cash. The availability of other sources of financing is also important, as is the disposition of those funds: *How much cash is the company generating or raising externally, and what is the company doing with that money?*

Cash flow *prediction* requires extrapolating the current cash flow into future years. Users must make assumptions to do this, and accounting can help this process by measuring and/or disclosing the company's commitments to future cash flows (e.g., forthcoming lease and loan payments).

As all accountants are well aware, a company's operating cash flow for a year is very different from its earnings for that year. In the long run, however, earnings are the result of cash flows. Revenues and expenses arise from cash flows but differ from the actual cash flows to the extent that accountants engage in the processes of *accrual accounting* and *interperiod allocation* to estimate earnings. Financial analysts and bankers, too, are aware of the difference.

Earnings Quality

Creditors and analysts who attempt to assess and predict future cash flows tend to prefer earnings measures that are supported by operating cash flows. For this reason, analysts often use the reported *cash flow from operating activities* to calculate *cash flow per share* for public companies. They compare the operating cash flow per share with the earnings per share.

If there is a high degree of correlation between the two measures, the company has **high-quality earnings**. If the two measures differ significantly, the company is said to have **low-quality earnings**. The perceived quality of earnings is good when the relationship between operating cash flow and net income is fairly stable.

Sometimes a company will report positive earnings but negative cash flow from operations; this situation is not viewed kindly by analysts because it suggests that management may be manipulating earnings through accruals and interperiod allocations.

Effect on Financial Reporting Choices

What impact does an objective of cash flow prediction have on financial reporting? The consequences of adopting cash flow prediction as a primary reporting objective include:

- Accounting policies are chosen that tend to reduce interperiod allocations. For example, costs that could be capitalized and amortized depending on management's estimates (e.g., development costs) or accounting policies (e.g., the numeric threshold for capitalization) may be expensed instead, so that the impact on earnings (as an expense) will coincide with the cash flow.

- Full disclosure of future cash flow commitments is given in the notes. A great deal of leeway is permitted in disclosing future commitments of various kinds. Under a cash flow reporting objective, the choice is to provide fuller disclosure of future cash flows, and particularly to alert users to probable future changes in cash flows (positive or negative).

When cash flow assessment and prediction is the primary objective, financial reporting policies are chosen that provide the clearest indication of the cash flows underlying reported earnings. Accrual accounting and interperiod allocation are still used, but their use is restricted to those instances in which there is little or no choice, such as amortization of capital assets for profit-oriented enterprises.

Income Tax Deferral

A very common objective, particularly for private companies, is that of **income tax deferral** (also known as income tax *minimization*). Since there is a time value of money, why pay taxes this year if they can be delayed until next year? The cash saved by reducing this year's income tax bill can be invested to earn a return or can be used to service debt or pay dividends. A company has better things to do with its money than pay income taxes, if the payment might legitimately be delayed to a later year.

Financial Reporting versus Income Tax Reporting

Canada Revenue Agency (CRA) is an agency of the federal government that interprets and enforces the nation's federal tax laws. The *Income Tax Act* and the CRA have procedures and reporting requirements whose primary purpose is to collect taxes efficiently and effectively. At times, the government also uses tax law to attain specific social or economic objectives that Parliament considers important, such as encouraging investment in research and development.[2]

The overall aim of the *Income Tax Act* is to collect tax revenue. In general, the act provides for taxation when cash is flowing, so that revenues are usually taxed when they have been substantively realized and costs are deducted from taxable revenue when they are incurred. Taxation principles tend to emphasize cash flows because those flows normally can be measured

---

2. For example, in 2007, the government provided incentive for investment by permitting highly accelerated CCA for new investments in equipment and machinery, an incentive that was renewed in 2011 and again 2013. Instead of amortizing over 14 years, companies were permitted to amortize over as little as three years.

quite clearly. There are exceptions to this emphasis in assessing taxable income, of course. For example, the taxation of revenue is often affected by the revenue recognition policy used by the business, which may differ significantly from the revenue cash flow. Nevertheless, tax law and tax regulations generally steer clear of interperiod allocations and subjective estimates.

The general principle of taxing on the basis of cash flows has an impact on the tax treatment of expenses. Expenses may be recognized for tax purposes quite differently from their accounting treatment. This is particularly true for costs that are viewed as assets for financial reporting purposes but as expenses by CRA, such as development costs, pension costs, and long-term leases.

Similarly, the Canadian *Income Tax Act* has specific requirements for amortizing the cost of capital assets—the capital cost allowance (CCA). CCA is unrelated to depreciation or amortization expense for financial reporting purposes. Nevertheless, private companies may choose to amortize their capital assets on the same basis as CCA is calculated to simplify their financial reporting.

CRA does not require a corporation (or the owners of proprietorships and partnerships) to use the same reporting principles for tax as for accounting, or vice versa. However, corporations must attach their annual financial statements to their tax return. One of the basic parts of the corporate income tax form is a reconciliation of reported pre-tax accounting income to reported taxable income. The corporation must make it clear just what accounting differences caused any discrepancy between the net earnings reported to its shareholders and the taxable income reported to CRA. This is the principle of *exception reporting* as applied to the taxable income calculation.

Tax-Book Conformity

When corporations adopt the same accounting practices for financial reporting as for tax reporting, this is known as *tax-book conformity*. Many accountants believe that disclosure of variations between tax and book reporting on the tax return acts as a "red flag" for CRA and invites a tax audit.

Therefore, although there is no requirement in Canada (unlike in some other countries, such as Germany and Japan) that tax reporting be identical to financial reporting, tax treatment of items may have an impact on financial reporting. The impact is most likely to be observed for revenue; CRA generally takes a dim view of a corporation's recognizing revenue in the income statement while deferring revenue recognition for tax purposes.

Tax Deferral versus Tax Evasion

When we discuss tax deferral, we are not talking about *cheating* on income taxes. There is some flexibility in the timing of reporting certain revenues and expenses on the corporate income tax return. To a limited extent, a company can affect the amount of tax that it pays through its selection of accounting policies. The use of legitimate options for reducing a company's current taxable income is known as *tax deferral* or *tax minimization*. In contrast, deliberate misstatement on the tax return is *tax evasion*, which is fraud.

Effect on Financial Reporting Choices

If a company wishes to minimize the amount of taxes it pays, it will adopt accounting policies that tend to:

- Delay the recognition of revenue to the extent permitted by the *Income Tax Act*, particularly for long earnings cycles; and
- Speed the payment of expenses that can legitimately be deducted for tax purposes.

Why wouldn't every company attempt to reduce its income tax bill? The reason is that if the company adopts accounting policies that reduce taxable income, those policies may also reduce reported net income.

This might be a problem for managers whose compensation is tied to book income. A lower book income may also lead to a poorer performance evaluation and hence reduced promotion possibilities for managers. Furthermore, many executive compensation packages include significant amounts of stock options. Anything that lowers the firm's stock price will lower the value of those options.

As a result of the impact on reported earnings, income tax deferral is more likely to be an objective for private corporations and, to a lesser extent, for public corporations that have a strong family control block. The owner-managers of these types of corporations have independent sources of information about the company, and their bankers are usually kept closely informed about the activities of the corporation.

A tax-deferral objective is in the best interests of bankers and creditors, but they must recognize that reported earnings under a tax deferral objective will *look* poorer, even though the cash flow will actually be better. In contrast, public corporations are likely to put less emphasis on tax deferral because their managers are more concerned about external stakeholder perceptions of the company's earnings ability.

Contract Compliance

External users often use financial statements as the basis for assessing whether an enterprise has complied with contract provisions. The most common type of financial statement contracting is for debt, particularly with bank loans and with issues of bonds (both publicly issued and privately placed). Debt contracts or agreements usually have provisions that require companies to maintain a certain level of performance, such as:

- Maximum debt-to-equity ratio;
- Maximum percentage of dividend payout;
- Minimum times-interest-earned ratio; and/or
- Minimum level of shareholders' equity.

These provisions are known as covenants or **maintenance tests**. If a company fails to meet the covenants, the lender (or trustee, in the case of publicly issued bonds) has the right to call the loan and force immediate repayment. Since the debtor seldom will be able to satisfy the call for repayment, the company is forced into reorganization or receivership.

Shareholders' agreements in private corporations also usually contain provisions that affect the valuation of shares if a shareholder decides to sell her or his shares. Since there is no public market for the shares of private corporations, there is no easily identifiable market price. In theory, the value of shares is a function of future earnings (and cash flow) and of the fair value of the corporation's net assets. In practice, most shareholders' agreements stipulate that the price is based on historical earnings and on net asset book values.

Effect on Financial Reporting Choices

Accounting policy choices and accounting estimates can have a significant effect on the ratios used in debt agreements and for share valuation in shareholders' agreements. For example, electing to use straight-line depreciation instead of accelerated depreciation for buildings and equipment will result in relatively higher earnings, higher shareholders' equity, lower debt-to-equity ratio, and higher times-interest-earned ratio (calculated as income before interest and taxes, divided by interest).

Therefore, some debt agreements (particularly in private placements) specify what accounting policies must be used for calculating the ratios. When specific policies are stipulated in the debt agreement, management's ability to select policies to enhance the ratios is restricted.

Similarly, the share valuation components of private company shareholders' agreements often contain specific provisions concerning the valuation of net assets. These provisions are not constrained by GAAP and therefore may be more suitable to the needs of the shareholders for a fair valuation of their shares than would a GAAP-based valuation.

Stewardship

A question commonly asked by lenders and investors is "What did they do with my money?" A *steward* is someone responsible for managing an enterprise on behalf of someone else. The word originally applied to the person who managed large household estates on behalf of the owners. **Stewardship reporting** focuses on showing the financial statement reader just how the resources entrusted to management's care were managed. Transparency is important—full disclosure should exist and the financial affairs should be transparent. It is a very important objective for not-for-profit organizations. Financial reporting should not be complicated by a large number of allocations that obscure the operating results for the year.

Effect on Financial Reporting Choices

The objective of stewardship is reflected in two ways: (1) minimization of interperiod allocations and (2) full disclosure.

Interperiod allocations make it difficult for financial statement readers to see how management is managing the funds entrusted to its care. For example, some types of expenditures can be either expensed immediately or capitalized (as an asset) and amortized. A stewardship objective would lead to expensing rather than capitalization.

In addition, the company may choose to provide more than the minimum mandatory disclosures concerning the company's financial position. The role of stewardship is especially clear in the case of mutual fund reporting, where the investment activity of the organization is fully reported every year to satisfy investors' natural inquisitiveness about the nature of the fund's investments and the level of investment activity during the year.

Performance Evaluation

Financial statement readers often use the statements to evaluate management performance. The common use of bonus schemes for managers that are based on reported earnings attests to the widespread use of financial statements for this purpose.

Performance evaluation is a reporting objective that benefits not only external users but also managers themselves. Managers are users of financial statements to (1) evaluate their own performance and (2) evaluate the performance of the managers of subsidiaries and other, related companies in a corporate family of companies.

Effect on Financial Reporting Choices

To be useful for performance evaluation, financial statements should, as much as possible, reflect the basis on which management decisions are made. For example, suppose a cruise line builds and introduces a new ship. Substantial costs are involved in set-up costs for a new ship. These costs are essential to successful operation of the ship. If performance evaluation is a reporting objective, these costs are carried as work-in-progress inventory to be matched against the revenue they are intended to enhance. If, instead, cash flow prediction were the dominant objective, it would be preferable for the costs to be expensed when incurred.

Managers are fully aware of the performance evaluation objective of financial statements, and managers of widely held public companies are apt to be quite sensitive to the earnings impacts of accounting policy choices. Therefore, managers have strong motivation to select accounting policies and make accounting estimates that will enhance their apparent performance. The issue of management motivations in financial accounting policy selection is important and is the subject of the next section.

Role of Auditor

One area that needs to be clarified is the role of the auditor. Auditors are not users of the financial statements; they are independent of the company and they provide an opinion on whether the statements are "fair" and conform with GAAP.

CONCEPT REVIEW

1. What type of company is *required* to issue general purpose financial statements?
2. Explain the difference between *assessing* cash flows and *predicting* cash flows.
3. What is meant by *high-quality earnings*?
4. Since all companies would like to reduce the amount of income taxes they pay, why isn't *income tax minimization* always the primary objective of financial reporting?
5. What is a *control block*?

PREPARER MOTIVATIONS

The needs of external financial statement users are vital to developing appropriate financial reporting objectives for each specific enterprise. However, managers (i.e., preparers) have their own objectives or motivations that influence their selection of accounting policies and their accounting estimates. These motivations often conflict with external users' objectives and may dominate the accounting choice process if external users lack the power to enforce the dominance of their objectives. This section will briefly discuss the most common preparer motivations.

Earnings Management

Income Smoothing (even out income)

Managers often like to show a smooth record of earnings, free of annoying peaks and valleys. Widely fluctuating earnings are an indication of volatility and business risk, and managers often do not want investors or creditors to perceive the company as risky. Thus, managers have strong motivation to show a smooth upward trend in earnings, year after year.

Income can be smoothed by taking advantage of the opportunities available for spreading both revenues and costs over several periods. The capitalize-and-amortize approach beloved by many managers is a reflection of wide acceptance of the income-smoothing motivation. In recent years, accounting standards have been revised to reduce the options for the capitalize-and-amortize approach, but the opportunity still exists in some contexts.

Accounting estimates provide the most fertile territory for income smoothing. By edging various accounting estimates up or down within a feasible range, management can often significantly affect net income. Remember that net income is a residual. Relatively small changes in estimates for revenues and expenses, such as the amount of accruals, the estimate of bad debts, or the writedown of inventory, can have a significant impact on this residual.

For example, suppose that a company's net income is 10% of total revenue. If total expenses are decreased by 1% through adjustments in estimates, the net income will increase by 10% (i.e., from 10% to 11% of revenue), a significant change in most investors' eyes. Thus, shifting of earnings from one period to another is quite feasible.

The impact of accounting estimates is still largely invisible to the external user. IFRS has increased disclosure requirements for many estimates and even requires some sensitivity analysis, as we shall see in later chapters. Nevertheless, there are still many areas where management is not required to provide disclosure of estimates used; their impact is simply impounded in the numbers to which they relate.

Maximizing Earnings

Maximization of net income is one of the most common management motivations, particularly in public companies. This motive stems from three powerful concerns:

1. To make it easier to comply with debt covenants and to provide a margin of safety between the covenant requirements and the reported numbers (i.e., to keep lenders from getting worried);
2. To positively influence users' judgements when they evaluate the performance of management (i.e., to help managers keep their jobs and to enhance their public standing); and
3. To enhance managers' compensation in the many corporations in which management compensation is tied to either net income or stock price performance (or both).

These concerns are particularly relevant for the managers of public companies, because ownership is dispersed and there is a general concern on the part of the shareholders and the board of directors about the share price. Managers believe, with good reason, that share prices are affected by reported earnings.

There is a belief that investors in an efficient public market are able to "see through" accounting manipulations intended to maximize earnings. However, this ability may be effective only in the short run. In the long run, the information necessary to make adjustments for accounting policy differences usually disappears from view.

For example, the effects of a change in depreciation methods (such as asset life or depreciation method) are "transparent" for one year, but there is no way an investor can adjust for the effect of the change in following years. There is no evidence that shareholders are able to "see through" complex earnings maximization objectives over the long run.

Minimizing Earnings

Instead of *maximizing* reported earnings, management may wish to *minimize* reported earnings as an ongoing endeavour. In addition to the possible objective of minimizing income taxes, management may strive to reduce earnings for any of the following reasons:

- To avoid public criticism of earnings that might be viewed as "excessive";
- To avoid attracting competitors into a very profitable business;
- To discourage hostile takeover bids;
- To avoid the scrutiny of regulators or politicians; or
- To discourage large wage claims by employees or to justify management initiatives for wage reductions and cutbacks.

Accounting policies that *maximize* earnings include early revenue recognition and delayed expense recognition. Accounting policies for *minimizing* earnings are just the opposite: delay revenue recognition, but expense every cost as soon as possible.

The "Big Bath"

Sometimes, a corporation will elect to *maximize a loss* in one year as part of a longer-run strategy to *maximize earnings*. The philosophy is that if there will be an operating loss anyway, they might as well take advantage of the opportunity to load as many losses into that year as possible (this is known as "taking a **big bath**" or "taking a big hit").

It is not at all unusual to see a corporation (in a bad year) announcing changes to accounting estimates that increase the total loss, including substantial writedowns of investments and impairments of capital assets. If a company writes down its capital assets, less depreciation will be charged to expense in future years, thereby enhancing *future* earnings. This motivation has been diminished somewhat for public companies by Canada's move to IFRS because, in certain circumstances, IFRS requires assets to be written back up if fair value recovers in future years (as we will see in Chapter 10), but it will still be management's judgement that decides whether asset values have "permanently" recovered or not.

Another ploy is to make a substantial provision (charged to expense) for the estimated amount of future liabilities, such as site restoration costs. If these liabilities turn out to have been overestimated, the company will be able to report a *gain* in future periods when the excess provision is "returned" to earnings.

Minimum Compliance

Minimum compliance is the motivation of managers to reveal the as little information as possible while still complying with GAAP.

Minimum compliance may be a motivation for managers in a public company, because management does not wish to give outsiders any more information about the company than absolutely necessary. Managers might wish, for example, to maintain confidentiality about their business activities to keep competitors in the dark.

Minimum compliance is usually equated with *minimum cost* of providing accounting information. However, the buyers and sellers of public companies' shares may value a company's shares at a lower level if they feel that the company is giving less than full disclosure about its operations and financial position. Minimum compliance may save accounting and auditing costs but may bear a cost in reduced share prices and increased cost of capital.

Expanded Disclosure

The opposite of minimum compliance might be called **expanded disclosure**. Management may wish to disclose a great deal of information not required by GAAP. The motivation might be simply to indicate that the company and its management are "good corporate citizens" with nothing to hide and who wish to provide the most informative financial statements possible. Sometimes expanded disclosure is motivated by the expected concerns of specific stakeholders.

For example, a company that might be accused of polluting the environment may choose to disclose its environmental record and its efforts to curb pollution and/or clean up an already-polluted environment. By providing additional disclosure, management may hope to forestall criticism of the company's pollution-control efforts.

In other situations, a company might provide expanded voluntary disclosures to reassure the capital markets that the company is a good investment. For example, management may include information on product demand in the financial statement notes or in management's discussion and analysis, such as (1) the value of current contracts for a service company, (2) the order backlog for a manufacturer, or (3) environmental protection initiatives for a company publicly perceived as a high polluter.

CONFLICTING OBJECTIVES

Virtually every enterprise, public or private, will have more than one financial reporting objective. For example, a company may want to maximize earnings, minimize income taxes, and maintain high-quality earnings. Each of these might be desirable on its own, but they conflict. Minimizing income taxes conflicts with earnings maximization, while both may conflict with showing high-quality earnings (i.e., earnings that correspond closely with cash flow from operations).

Once a company's objectives have been identified, they have to be prioritized: which is most important, which is second most important, and so forth. Only then, where the facts allow a choice, can accounting choices of policy, estimates, and disclosures be made.

In the real world, accounting requires constant exercise of judgement. Despite the apparent "precision" of the numbers in financial statements, accounting reports are always approximations of the underlying economic phenomena.

ETHICAL ISSUES

External users' needs and managers' motivations often conflict. Managers are aware of users' objectives, and therefore managers may attempt to present the best picture of the corporation's operations and financial position. The resolution of this conflict depends on general concepts of fair presentation and often presents an ethical dilemma for management, the company's accountants, and auditors.

The investigation of the events underlying the collapse of a major U.S. Internet provider provides an example of an accountant who held her ground in the face of senior management pressure to make an unethical "estimate":

> In an … effort to reduce costs, Sullivan [the CFO] directed General Accounting to reduce the Wireless division's expense for line costs by $150 million. When General Accounting called Delores DiCicco, Vice President of Wireless Finance, requesting her to reduce her line costs, she was surprised because there was no support for the entry. Even after Yates [Director, General Accounting] made several follow-up calls, asking her to make the journal entry following Sullivan's instructions, DiCicco firmly refused. In response, Sullivan told DiCicco that she should make the entry because she would eventually find $150 million in savings from disputed billings. … Still refusing, she argued that she would not book the entry until she found the savings. As a consequence, the requested journal entry was prepared in General Accounting.[3]

CONCEPT REVIEW

1. Why is it important to establish the financial reporting objectives for a company?
2. Give an example of how the reporting objectives of a public company might differ from those of a private corporation.
3. How might a shareholders' agreement influence a company's financial reporting objectives?
4. Why might the objectives of financial statement users conflict with the motivations of managers?

---

3. "Behind Closed Doors at WorldCom: 2001," *Issues in Accounting Education* (February 2004). Copyright © 2004 American Accounting Association. Full text of American Accounting Association articles available at http://aaahq.org/pubs.cfm. See also *the Report of Investigation by the Special Investigative Committee of the Board of Directors of WorldCom Inc.* by Beresford et al., March 31, 2003. Retrieved May 14, 2013, from http://fl1.findlaw.com/news.findlaw.com/hdocs/docs/worldcom/bdspcomm60903rpt.pdf

REQUIRED FINANCIAL STATEMENTS UNDER IFRS

Chapters 3, 4, and 5 describe the various financial statements in detail. Under IFRS, a complete set of financial statements consists of the following:

1. Statement of financial position;
2. Statement of comprehensive income, consisting of:
    a. statement of profit or loss;
    b. statement of other comprehensive income;
3. Statement of changes in equity;
4. Statement of cash flows; and
5. A set of notes comprising a summary of significant accounting policies and other explanatory information.

Some general observations:

- All statements should be *comparative* statements, with both the current and the preceding year's amounts presented in comparative columnar format.
- *The statement titles shown above are not mandatory.* For example, the commonly used title of "balance sheet" can be used instead of "statement of financial position." Also, "statement of profit or loss" is primarily a European convention. Titles such as "income statement" and "statement of earnings" are quite acceptable.
- The statement of comprehensive income is a two-step statement that can instead be shown as two individual statements: (1) an income statement and (2) a statement of comprehensive income that begins with net income as its first line. If the two-statement format is used, the two statements must be presented in immediate succession.

Looking Forward—Whither the United States?

A major exception in all this harmonization is the United States. The United States Financial Accounting Standards Board (FASB) and the IASB have been working to reduce and eventually eliminate differences between the two sets of standards, a process known as the *convergence project*. The ultimate goal is to have just one set of standards or (more likely) two sets of consistent standards.

In 2010, the U.S. SEC reconfirmed its support for the convergence project, stating that:

> The Commission continues to believe [in] a single set of high-quality globally accepted accounting standards and that this goal is consistent with our mission of protecting investors, maintaining fair, orderly, and efficient markets, and facilitating capital formation. As a step toward this goal, we continue to encourage the convergence of US GAAP and IFRS and expect that the differences will become fewer and narrower, over time, as a result of the convergence project.[4]

In this statement, the SEC is not saying that IFRS will be an acceptable reporting standard for U.S. companies, but only that U.S. GAAP and IFRS should be "converged" to eliminate or sharply reduce the differences.

In July 2012, the SEC issued a 137-page staff report on the practicalities of incorporating IFRS into the U.S. financial reporting system.[5] This was an extensive study of the practical aspects of moving to IFRS, including the burden of conversion, the lack of investor understanding, and the inconsistency of application in various countries, as we have mentioned above.

Although the report contains no conclusions or recommendations on whether the United States should fully accept IFRS, there seem to be sufficient serious concerns about the wisdom of such a move. It seems highly unlikely that the United States will ever grant control of accounting standards to a "foreign" institution, no matter how closely involved the FASB may be in its deliberations.

4. Securities and Exchange Commission, Release no. 33-9109, pp. 1–2. http://www.sec.gov (go to "Regulatory Actions"; "Other Commission Orders, Notices, and Information"; "33-9109").
5. Office of the Chief Accountant, United States Securities and Exchange Commission, "Work Plan for the Consideration of Incorporating International Financial Reporting Standards into the Financial Reporting System for U.S. Issuers." Retrieved May 14, 2013, from http://www.sec.gov/spotlight/globalaccountingstandards/ifrs-work-plan-paper-052611.pdf

The following quote from the most recent SEC Draft Strategic Plan (2014–2018) indicates a change in direction by the SEC:

> Promote high-quality accounting standards: The SEC will continue to promote the establishment of high-quality accounting standards by independent standard setters in order to meet the needs of investors. In overseeing the Financial Accounting Standards Board (FASB), the SEC will strengthen and support the FASB's independence and maintain the focus of financial reporting on the needs of investors. Due to the increasingly global nature of the capital markets, the agency will work to promote higher quality financial reporting worldwide and will consider, among other things, whether a single set of high-quality global accounting standards is achievable.[6]

There have been recent examples in which the decision has been made that U.S. standards will not be converged with IFRS. The new lease standard and final revisions for financial instruments are not converged.

As for those foreign companies (including Canadian) listed on U.S. stock exchanges, the SEC already accepts IFRS-based financial statements from non-U.S. companies. Therefore, the move to IFRS has greatly simplified reporting for Canadian companies cross-listed on the NYSE or NASDAQ, even if the United States never fully accepts IFRS for reporting by domestically based public corporations.

Accounting Standards for Private Enterprises

Objectives of Financial Reporting

The AcSB defines the objective of financial statements in a very similar manner to how the IASB does. The emphasis clearly is on investors and creditors. Although the AcSB's definition refers to other users, the intended "other users" are advisors to investors and creditors, such as security analysts, financial advisors, and bond rating agencies. The AcSB specifically states that:

> It is not practicable to expect financial statements to satisfy the many and varied information needs of all external users of information about an entity. [ASPE 1000.09]

Required Financial Statements

Canadian Accounting Standards for Private Enterprises (ASPE) have a somewhat simpler set of financial statements:

1. Balance sheet (i.e., statement of financial position);
2. Income statement (*not* a statement of *comprehensive* income);
3. Statement of changes in retained earnings (*not* changes in all share equity balances);
4. Statement of cash flows; and
5. Disclosure notes.

Chapters 3, 4, and 5 explain the differences between IFRS and ASPE for each type of statement.

Presentation Currency

ASPE does not specify a presentation currency. The concept of *functional currency* does not appear in ASPE. Nevertheless, companies that have a functional currency other than the Canadian dollar will

---

6. Securities and Exchange Commission, "Draft Strategic Plan 2014–2018." Retrieved Oct. 10, 2015 from https://www.sec.gov/about/sec-strategic-plan-2014-2018-draft.pdf

generally report on the basis of that currency. Thus, companies involved in products priced in U.S. dollars will normally report in U.S. dollars. This includes international transportation companies, computer game developers, software developers, gold producers, dealers in diamonds and other precious stones, and so forth.

Canadian subsidiaries of foreign parents may report in the parent's currency, although they may provide "convenience translations" into Canadian dollars for the benefit of their Canadian lenders and creditors.

RELEVANT STANDARDS

CPA Canada Handbook, Part I (IFRS):

- IASB, *Conceptual Framework for Financial Reporting*, Chapter 1
- IAS 1, *Presentation of Financial Statements*

CPA Canada Handbook, Part II (ASPE):

- Section 1000, *Financial Statement Concepts*
- Section 1400, *General Standards of Financial Statement Presentation*

SUMMARY OF KEY POINTS

1. General purpose financial statements are intended to serve the needs of economic decision makers who have no direct or special access to a corporation's financial information.
2. A publicly accountable enterprise is one that either (1) has issued securities (debt or equity) to the general public and therefore must abide by the regulations of the securities commissions in the jurisdiction(s) in which its securities are traded or (2) holds assets in a fiduciary capacity for a broad group of outsiders as one of its primary businesses.
3. In Canada, all publicly accountable enterprises must report in accordance with International Financial Reporting Standards (IFRS). International standards are set forth in the *CPA Canada Handbook, Part I*.
4. IFRS are developed by the International Accounting Standards Board (IASB). IFRS is the set of financial reporting standards that many nations have adopted or adapted for their public companies. All major securities exchanges around the world accept financial statements prepared on the basis of IFRS for nonresident companies, which increases the likelihood of a company being listed on multiple exchanges.
5. The vast majority of Canadian corporations are private corporations. Many are very small enterprises, while many others are subsidiaries of foreign parent corporations. Many large public Canadian corporations have a control block owned by an individual or a family. A private corporation's shareholders and lenders are presumed to have access to the information they need.
6. Canadian private corporations have three choices for financial reporting: (1) IFRS, (2) Canadian Accounting Standards for Private Enterprises (ASPE), or (3) a disclosed basis of accounting. Large private companies that compete for capital internationally may choose to use IFRS to present financial statements that are directly comparable with those of public companies.

7. ASPE is maintained by the CPA Canada Accounting Standards Board (AcSB) and is set forth in the *CPA Canada Handbook, Part II.*

8. It is impossible to impose a single, dominant objective on financial reporting. The objectives of financial reporting must be determined with reference to each specific organization's environment and its stakeholders, and with regard to the users' decisions that the financial statements are intended to facilitate.

9. The reporting objective taken by the IASB for developing IFRS is to present information that will assist lenders, creditors, and shareholders in making their economic decisions.

10. Cash flow prediction is a financial reporting objective that is often appropriate for lenders, creditors, and shareholders. Financial stakeholders need to predict a corporation's ability to generate cash flow from operations and to service debt or to pay dividends. Under a cash flow objective, revenues and expenses are recognized in a way that corresponds (on an accrual basis) with cash flow.

11. Income tax minimization is another very common objective, especially for private corporations. Public corporations are less likely to have this as a primary objective, because they may be more concerned about the perceptions of other users of the statements than about saving taxes in the short run. An income tax minimization objective leads to delayed revenue recognition and faster expense recognition.

12. Financial statement readers often use the statements to assess the corporation's adherence to contract requirements, such as those in loan agreements and shareholders' agreements.

13. A major reporting objective is that of performance evaluation. Statements that have been prepared to facilitate the evaluation of management's performance will use reporting policies that coincide as closely as possible with the basis for management's operating decisions.

14. Managers are the preparers of financial statements. Managers often have motivations that stem from their desire to influence the decisions of external users, particularly those of public companies. Managers may be tempted to adopt accounting policies and make accounting estimates that tend to maximize reported earnings, minimize earnings, smooth earnings, or show compliance with contract provisions such as loan covenants.

15. The motivations of preparers often conflict with the financial reporting objectives that are appropriate for external users in a particular situation. Accountants must use their professional judgement to try to reconcile such conflicts ethically and to avoid issuing financial statements that contain biased measurements.

Key Terms

Accounting Standards Board (AcSB)

accounting standards for private enterprises (ASPE)

big bath

control block

covenants

Crown corporations

disclosed basis of accounting (DBA)

expanded disclosure

external users

fiduciary enterprise

functional currency

general purpose financial reporting

high-quality earnings

income tax deferral

International Accounting Standards Board (IASB)

International Financial Reporting Standards (IFRS)

low-quality earnings

maintenance tests

minimum compliance

objectives of financial reporting

preparers

presentation currency

private enterprise

private placements

publicly accountable enterprise (PAE)

restricted shares

shareholders' agreements

small and medium-sized enterprises (SME)

stewardship reporting

CASE 1-1

NORTH AND SOUTH

James North and Leanne South have operated a small gardening centre and landscaping business for the past 10 years. Their business is incorporated as a private corporation. Since there is no market price for their shares, their shareholder agreement states that in the event a shareholder decides to buy or sell their shares the amount will be based on four times shareholders' equity. The company has a December 31 year-end.

For the past year, Leanne has been managing all operations and making all accounting policy decisions, as James decided he wanted a career change and went back to school. Last week they met for coffee, and James mentioned he wanted to invoke the shareholders' agreement. He felt it unfair that Leanne was doing all the work but not getting all the profits. He has no intention of returning to the business; he loves school and is in fact contemplating setting up his own advertising agency. Besides, he said, on a personal note he needs the money to pay back his school loans and set himself up in his new career.

Leanne has been happy with being able to make all the decisions and wants to buy James out rather than get a new partner. She has negotiated with their bank to obtain a loan with a personal guarantee to make the buyout. She is a little nervous, however, about the risk of having a lot of debt.

You have been the accountant for the business since they started. You know both the owners well. This morning you had your usual year-end meeting with the bookkeeper to go over anything new so you can start to prepare their financial statements. The following are notes from your meeting:

1. During the year, a significant amount of inventory of garden gnomes and animal statues were written off. They had been sitting in the gardening centre for the past two years with only a few being sold each year. The bookkeeper said that Leanne thought it was time to write off their bad decision in investing in that inventory.
2. The business has never offered a warranty to go along with their trees and shrubs. All their competitors offer a one-year money-back guarantee. If a shrub or tree dies within a year of purchase, the money is refunded. Leanne decided in the fall it was time to implement a similar policy. The bookkeeper was told by Leanne to recognize warranty expense and set up an estimated liability based on their past history that approximately 5% from the sales of all trees and shrubs this year would need to be replaced based on her best guess.
3. Another decision made this year by Leanne was to finally invest in some new computer equipment in the gardening centre. A new computer system was installed that keeps track of all sales in the stores, on-line ordering, inventory values, and all sorts of information Leanne feels will be very useful for future decisions on the direction the business should take. The other assets in the business all use straight-line depreciation. Leanne feels that since computer equipment can get obsolete very quickly it would be more appropriate to use declining balance, and proposes a 40% rate with full depreciation in year 1.

You have a meeting with Leanne at the end of the week to discuss the new accounting policies she has proposed. James was invited to the meeting but he has a class on that date that he cannot miss.

Required:

Prepare briefing notes for your discussion with Leanne. Consider if the proposed policy is appropriate, consider valid alternatives, and provide a recommendation for each policy.

CASE 1-2

RICHARD PLOUGHWRIGHT

Andriana Bessemer, a sole practitioner in a rural area, is working in her office when one of her most important clients, Richard Ploughwright, walks in. He operates one of the largest dairy farms in the region.

"Sorry to barge in like this, but I've just been across the street to see my banker. He suggested that I ask you to explain some matters that affect my financial statements. You'll recall that I need to renew my loans every year. The new bank manager isn't very happy with the way my previous statements have been prepared. He has requested that I make some changes to my statements this year before he processes my loan renewal.

"The new manager wants me to switch from the cash basis of accounting to the accrual basis. I don't quite understand how that will help either him or me. The cash basis provides me with the information I need to evaluate my performance for the year—after all, what I make in a year is the cash left over and in the bank at the end of the year after tending my cattle, selling my milk, and maintaining my dairy barns and equipment. That ending amount is what I use to pay my taxes and the bank. I know the income tax people will accept either the cash or the accrual basis from farmers, so why the change?

"Also, he now wants me to value all of my cattle at market value. I can't see the benefit of that, because I'll never sell cattle that are still productive. Anyway, some of the cattle are for breeding, not for milking.

"I know I have to give the bank manager what he wants, but I'd really appreciate knowing why I must make these changes. After all, they are just going to increase your bill, which already seems rather high to me, so it'll be an extra cash drain for me."

Required:

Assume the role of Andriana Bessemer. Respond to Mr. Ploughwright.

CASE 1-3

MILTON KIDD

Sander Persaud is an audit manager for a national public accounting firm. Every summer, the firm recruits several university students as interns. One such intern is Milton Kidd, a high-performing student who has just finished his third year of university and is majoring in accounting.

As a test of Milton's understanding of accounting, Sander has assigned him the task of reviewing three of the firm's recently acquired clients. He has asked Milton to give him a report in which he points out any significant differences between the three clients and the implications of those differences for the clients' financial reporting, with a ranking of importance for each client. He wants the report on his desk by the end of the day.

Brief descriptions of the new clients follow.

Breeze Inc.

Breeze Inc. is a new entrant into the mobile phone market. The company is incorporated in Ontario and is establishing a new network, initially covering only the "Quebec City to Windsor" corridor, which includes the cities of Montreal, Ottawa, and Toronto. This heavily populated corridor encompasses more than half the Canadian population and generates about 60% of the national GDP.

Since mobile phones use public airwaves, entrance to that market is strictly limited and is controlled by the national telecommunications regulator, the Canadian Radio-television and Telecommunications Commission (CRTC). The CRTC has regulatory power over many aspects of Breeze Inc.'s operations but does not control or limit the profits (or potential profits) of the company. Breeze Inc. entered the market as one of the winners of competitive bidding when the CRTC made new licences available.

A new network requires intensive infrastructure investment, both financial and intellectual. Breeze is being assisted by Telyu, a Japanese telecom company that operates a very advanced network in Japan. The cooperation agreement provides that Breeze will pay Telyu a fee of 2% of all revenue arising from Internet traffic on Breeze's network. That is, the fee does not apply to voice traffic, ordinary text messages, sales of handsets, revenue from advertising messages, or any other tangential revenue.

Breeze Inc. has a 12-member board of directors. Three of the seats are reserved for nominees from Fenzal Partners, an Egyptian venture capital firm that provided most of the financing for Breeze Inc., mostly in the form of a private placement of nonvoting preferred shares but also via some secured debt. The other nine members are Canadian, including the chair of the board.

The company is a private company that has no intention of becoming a public company in the foreseeable future.

Saturn Software Systems Ltd. (SSS)

Saturn Software Systems Ltd. (SSS) designs large-scale custom software programs for health management and social agencies, both private and provincial. The company has been in existence for about eight years. Demands on the company's resources have increased significantly in the past couple of years due to an increasing recognition among health care and social agencies that they need better computer-based client management systems. The company is owned equally by the two former university classmates, Rejean and Klaus, who founded the company.

SSS has been profitable from the beginning, but the increase in business has begun to strain the company's resources. SSS has tripled its staff over the past two years, thereby more than tripling the company's costs, both payroll and other, related costs. The company has been perpetually short of cash, because contracts-in-progress have grown much more quickly than finished projects.

This year, SSS's owners turned to the venture capital unit of a large Canadian public pension fund for financial support. SSS issued a new class of convertible nonvoting preferred shares to the fund. The dividends on the preferred shares must be paid before Rejean and Klaus can declare any dividends to themselves. Also, the fund has approval rights over any salary increases for the owners.

SSS has negotiated a substantial line of credit with the Sterling Bank of Canada. The credit line has restrictions on salary and dividend levels, as well as a requirement for prior approval of any additional debt financing.

Rejean and Klaus are not wealthy. They have put their heart and soul into SSS since its founding and are strongly committed to the success of the company and the welfare of their employees, all of whom enjoy a profit-sharing plan.

International Auto Parts Ltd. (IAP)

IAP is an Ontario-based manufacturer of auto parts originally known as Magnum Manufacturing Corporation. The company started more than 20 years ago and slowly built up business by supplying parts to the "Big 3" U.S. automobile companies. A major recession in the industry caused IAP to almost collapse, but it was saved by a substantial injection of capital by the founding family.

The additional capital not only saved the company but also enabled it to begin acquiring other small auto parts companies in the southern Ontario and Northern Michigan regions that had suffered near-collapse. As the auto industry recovered and sales rose, so did the fortunes of Magnum. The name was changed to International Auto Parts to reflect its dual-country nature, and also because the company's senior managers envision expansion (and acquisitions) in Europe, as well as linkages with emerging auto companies in China. Over the past two years,

IAP was able to obtain contracts to supply parts to the North American plants of two non–North American auto makers, one from Japan and one from South Korea.

IAP is a private, family-owned company with a significant level of debt financing through investment funds and, to a lesser extent, through Canadian and U.S. banks. However, the owners recognize that to continue expansion through acquisitions they will need to tap the public financial markets. An IPO (initial public offering) is definitely an expectation within another two or three years, depending on the state of the market. IAP plans to apply for a listing on the Toronto Stock Exchange in conjunction with an IPO.

Required:

Assume that you are Milton Kidd. Prepare the report for Sander Persaud.

TECHNICAL REVIEW

connect

TR1-1 Chapter Overview:

Indicate whether each statement is true or false:

1. The IASB has authority for setting Canadian accounting standards.
2. All Canadian corporations must comply with international accounting standards.
3. Most public Canadian corporations are listed on the Toronto Stock Exchange.
4. IFRS must be used for the financial statements of every Canadian public corporation.
5. The objective of general purpose financial reporting is to serve the information needs of a wide variety of users, including lenders, shareholders, employees, and regulators.
6. The primary objective of financial accounting is to reveal all information about an enterprise's financial performance.
   xf
7. If a corporation has a restrictive bond covenant that specifies a minimum times-interest-earned ratio, the corporation's management will be motivated to pick discretionary accounting policies that maximize income.
8. Income tax law has no impact on the accounting choices made by management.
9. The presence of a control block can have an impact on a public company's choice of accounting policies.
10. Any Canadian company that uses U.S. GAAP must prepare its statements in U.S. dollars.

connect

TR1-2 Chapter Overview:

Indicate whether each statement is true or false:

1. IFRS and the *CPA Canada Handbook, Part II*, have equal status in Canada for financial reporting.

2. In a private corporation, the needs of external users have no impact on the company's financial reporting objectives.

3. Canadian companies must always prepare their annual financial statements in Canadian dollars.

4. Canadian accounting standards are governed by the *Canada Business Corporations Act*.

5. The debt and equity securities of a private company cannot be traded on public exchanges. Therefore, private companies have no external sources of financing.

6. A company may take a big bath in a loss year if management wishes to maximize future earnings.

7. A public company may not use a disclosed basis of accounting for external public financial reporting.

8. When an enterprise's primary reporting objective is cash flow assessment, the enterprise will use a cash basis of reporting rather than an accrual basis.

9. Any Canadian company may use IFRS.

10. The IASB cannot require transnational corporations to use IFRS.

connect

TR1-3 Acronyms:

The language of accounting is littered with acronyms, abbreviations for common organizations or phrases. Match the phrase or organization on the left with its abbreviation.

Phrase or Organization	Abbreviation
1. International Accounting Standards Board	A. AcSB
2. Accounting Standards for Private Enterprises	B. SEC
3. Accounting Standards Board	C. CPA
4. International Financial Reporting Standards	D. OSC
5. Toronto Stock Exchange	E. IFRS
6. Ontario Securities Commission	F. ASPE
7. CPA Canada	G. FASB
8. Securities and Exchange Commission	H. DBA
9. Financial Accounting Standards Board	I. TSX
10. Disclosed Basis of Accounting	J. IASB

connect

TR1-4 IFRS or ASPE:

Indicate whether the use of IFRS or ASPE is required or more likely for the following entities:

	IFRS	ASPE
1. Bank	——	——
2. Private company two shareholders	——	——
3. Public company	——	——

4. Mutual fund   ____   ____
5. Private company wholly owned subsidiary   ____   ____
   public company

Mc Graw Hill Education connect

TR1-5 IFRS or ASPE:

Indicate whether the use of IFRS or ASPE is required or more likely for the following entities:

	IFRS	ASPE
1. Private bank	____	____
2. Private company many shareholders	____	____
3. Private company major competitor public company	____	____
4. Government business enterprise	____	____
5. Private company intending to go public	____	____

Mc Graw Hill Education connect

TR1-6 Disclosed Basis of Accounting

Indicate whether each statement is true or false. If the statement is false, provide a brief explanation of why it is false.

1. A disclosed basis of accounting is GAAP.
2. An audit opinion can be provided on a disclosed basis of accounting.
3. A disclosed basis of accounting is used to provide more useful information for the users.
4. Note disclosure is required if a disclosed basis of accounting is used.
5. A public company can use a disclosed basis of accounting.

Mc Graw Hill Education connect

TR1-7 GAAP and Reporting Currency:

Indicate whether each statement is true or false. If the statement is false, provide a brief explanation of why it is false.

1. A private company based in Canada must follow the recommendations of the *CPA Canada Handbook*.
2. A company that reports in U.S. dollars must use U.S. accounting standards.
3. A company cannot report under Canadian accounting standards unless it uses Canadian dollars as the unit of presentation in its financial statements.
4. A Canadian company listed on the TSE may use U.S. accounting standards.

5. All companies listed on the NYSE must use U.S. accounting standards.

connect

TR1-8 GAAP and Reporting Currency:

Indicate whether each statement is true or false. If the statement is false, provide a brief explanation of why it is false.

1. The U.S. SEC will accept financial statements from U.S.-listed foreign companies in their home-country accounting standards.
2. Every country that accepts IFRS commits to using the full set of standards.
3. A Canadian private enterprise does not have access to outside investors if it uses Canadian ASPE.
4. Under Canadian ASPE, a company must report in its functional currency.
5. A private Canadian company that is a subsidiary of a U.K. parent company may not report in British pounds sterling unless the pound is also its functional currency.

connect

TR1-9 Users and Objectives:

Match the user with the most likely objective.

User	**Objective**
1. Bank	A. Stewardship
2. Small private company	B. Income tax deferral
3. Not-for-profit organization	C. Cash flow prediction
4. Management	D. Contract compliance
5. Shareholders with agreement	E. Performance evaluation

connect

TR1-10 Required Financial Statements:

Indicate whether each statement is required in IFRS or in ASPE, or in both.

	IFRS	ASPE	Both
1. Statement of Financial Position	——	——	——
2. Statement of Comprehensive Income	——	——	——
3. Income Statement	——	——	——
4. Statement of Retained Earnings	——	——	——
5. Cash Flow Statement	——	——	——
6. Statement of Changes in Shareholders' Equity	——	——	——

ASSIGNMENTS

 A1-1 IASB Standard Setting:

The IASB is the standard-setting body for IFRS. Anyone who uses financial statements should understand the process by which standards are set.

Required:

Consult the IASB website (http://www.ifrs.org). Click "Standards development," then "Standard-setting process." Describe the process of standard setting in your own words, including some information about each step in the process.

 A1-2 International Comparisons:

You have recently attended a conference on behalf of your manager. One speaker from a large bank, Mr. Stearns, stated:

> With the advent of international accounting standards, we now can easily compare the financial results of companies across borders when we are choosing high-quality companies to invest in. We no longer have to struggle with different accounting in different countries. Now, when we compare the "net income" line on an earnings statement from Japanese company with one from a British company, we can be confident that the net incomes are comparable because both companies are using IFRS.

Required:

Write a memo to your manager discussing the issues raised by this speaker.

 A1-3 Accounting Choices:

For each of the situations listed below, state what judgements and/or estimates are necessary when preparing financial statements at each business's fiscal year-end of 31 January:

1. Due to no snow fall in December, a ski store has an unexpectedly large inventory of unsold skiis.
2. One of Sukkor Corporation's major clients has gone into creditor protection. The client accounts for 40% of Sukkor's outstanding accounts receivable. Sukkor has filed a court claim against the client (along with other unsecured creditors), but a loss of somewhere between 20% and 35% of the receivable is likely.
3. IMF Inc. has been sued by another company for trademark infringement. The other company has won a lower-court judgement against IMF for $1.5 million. IMF is appealing the decision to a higher court. IMF's lawyers are confident that IMF will win the appeal.
4. Innovative Ltd. develops new products and technologies. They have a project under development. For the project there is a working prototype and the hope is to have a finished product by early next year. Staff are currently exploring the potential markets for this product. The company has been experiencing financial difficulty this year.

5. Pacific Alliance has just finished producing a new children's computer-animated motion picture for DVD distribution. The total accumulated production cost is $3.4 million. Pacific Alliance has signed a distribution agreement with a major supplier of educational materials, including DVDs. Normally, Pacific Alliance's earlier movies of the same general type have a sales life of about three years—slow to start, then increasing acceptance, followed by market saturation and obsolescence.

★ ★ A1-4 Effect of Accounting Policies:

A private company has two debt covenants in place:

a. *Maximum debt-to-equity ratio.* Current and long-term liabilities, excluding future income taxes, are divided by total shareholders' equity.

b. *Minimum times-interest-earned ratio.* Income before interest and taxes is divided by total interest expense.

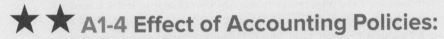

if both A or B ratios will be affected or wan't

Required:

For each of the accounting policy choices listed below, indicate which ratio(s), if any, would be affected, and whether the policy would increase or decrease the ratio.

change income statement

1. Depreciation method is straight-line, rather than declining-balance. *B*
2. Costs that might either be deferred and written off or expensed immediately are expensed immediately.
3. Interest expense might be measured using straight-line amortization for the debt discount; alternatively, the effective interest rate method might be used. The straight-line method results in lower interest expense in the early years and is the chosen policy.
4. An issue of preferred shares that has the characteristics of debt (guaranteed cash flows to the investor) is reclassified from equity to debt.
5. Warranty expense is accrued as sales are made, rather than expensing it as warranty claims are paid.
6. Revenue is recorded as goods are delivered, rather than when cash is later collected.

★ A1-5 Reporting Alternatives:

For each of the situations below, explain whether the company can use its preferred basis of accounting:

1. A Great Lakes shipping company based in Thunder Bay, Ontario, wishes to use U.S. dollars as its presentation currency. Shipping on the Great Lakes is always priced in U.S. dollars. The company prefers to use IFRS rather than U.S. GAAP. The company is registered with the SEC and its common shares are listed on the NYSE.

2. The wholly owned Canadian subsidiary of a U.K. carpet manufacturer is primarily a sales arm, importing and selling carpets manufactured by its parent company. The parent wants the subsidiary to use U.K. GAAP (which is IFRS-compliant) instead of the *CPA Canada Handbook* recommendations for private companies. The parent also wants the subsidiary's financial statements to be expressed in British pounds sterling.

3. A private Ontario-based auto parts manufacturer has rapidly expanding operations in Germany, India, and Russia. The company is negotiating with private investors to issue a new class of restricted-voting common shares. Because of the increasing globalization of the company, management wants to use IASB standards to facilitate possible future listings on the Frankfurt stock exchange.

4. An expanding publicly owned airline corporation is soliciting substantial new investment from private equity funds. One potential investor has requested that the corporation submit special private financial statements that do not follow certain recommendations of IFRS.

A1-6 Non-IFRS Situations:

A manager of a medium-sized private company recently asked for your advice on the following:

> I'm very confused about whether I should continue to use ASPE or change to IFRS. I need to make a recommendation to the Board next week on what we should do. Our bank is a Canadian one and we have a debt-to-equity ratio. Our two major competitors in the market place are public companies. We have no desire to go public in the near future, but the owners have been talking about possibly selling the business within the next five years.

Required:

Respond to the manager's concern, and be sure to provide support for both sides and a recommendation.

A1-7 Reporting Situations:

Four different unrelated Canadian corporations are described below:

1. Privately owned Vancouver-based Moonburst Coffee Ltd. imports coffee beans from around the world, but mainly from South America. The company roasts and packages the coffee and distributes it to several B.C. retail grocery stores under its own Moonburst label. Moonburst owns and operates 47 retail coffee shops in British Columbia and has franchised 16 coffee shops in Seattle, Washington. Currently, the company is in negotiations with a large Canada-wide supermarket chain to supply coffee under the chain's private-label brand, Chairman's Choice. To supply the chain, Moonburst will have to drastically increase its purchasing and processing capacity. To finance its expanded operations, Moonburst's owners are negotiating with four private investment firms for new equity. Three of the potential investment firms are based in the United States; the fourth firm is a large Canadian pension fund.

2. Pangal Inc. is a steel-fabricating company based in Hamilton, Ontario. The company is listed on the TSX. The controlling shareholder, Nataraj Pangal, holds shares entitling him to 51% of the voting rights. Seventy percent of Pangal's output is sold to U.S. manufacturers and builders (in U.S. dollars), although contracts with non-American manufacturers are under negotiation and are expected to account for an increasing proportion of sales in future years. Pangal is considering the possibility of registering with the SEC and applying for a U.S. exchange listing.

3. Economics International (EI) is a Toronto-based consulting company. EI provides consulting services to European companies that have operations in Canada and in the United States. EI bills its clients in the currency of their home country, primarily in euros and pounds sterling. Some billings are in the Scandinavian currencies as well. About half of EI's consultants are based in Canada; the others are located in London and Brussels. EI's shares are owned by the consultants; to become a *senior* consultant, a consultant must make a substantial equity investment in EI.

4. Chorus Entertainment Corporation's (CEC) head office is in Montreal, while its executive offices are in Los Angeles. CEC's main operations are in Los Angeles, although CEC does maintain an animation studio in Vancouver and operates a sound stage in Toronto. CEC is privately owned, but it raises additional financing almost exclusively in the United States and through its industry contacts in Los Angeles.

Required:

For each of the four companies, discuss the most appropriate accounting standards to use: IFRS, U.S. GAAP, Canadian ASPE, or DBA. Also indicate the most appropriate presentation currency for each company.

A1-8 Reporting Situations:

The reporting situations of two different companies are described below:

1. Stardust Explorations Incorporated (SEI) is seeking significant new financing for a gold and diamond mining venture in northern Ontario. In their search for new financing, company directors have been visiting Australia, South Africa, China, and India. The directors have met some resistance because Stardust's financial statements are based on Canadian private-company standards and use the Canadian dollar as the unit of measure in the company's financial statements. Gold and diamonds are valued internationally in U.S. dollars.

2. Private shareholders have invested significant amounts of money in Class B shares of privately owned Fish Incorporated (FI). FI is a family owned business that recently issued Class B shares to raise additional capital for expansion. The family owns Class A shares that have 10 votes per share and the Class B shares have one vote per share. FI has been reporting in accordance with ASPE. Now, however, the Class A shareholders would like for FI to begin reporting on a near-cash basis, recognizing all except capital expenditures as expenses and delaying revenue recognition until the revenue has been realized as cash. FI's management fears that such a change in accounting policy will prevent the company from receiving an unqualified audit report. Also, the company worries that while the company is expanding this change will mean that the company will have a loss instead of a profit for this year. FI management is concerned with possible repercussions from the company's Class B shareholders.

Required:

For each of the two companies, recommend and justify an accounting approach that is appropriate under its particular circumstances.

A1-9 Objectives of Financial Reporting:

The *CPA Canada Handbook* in both Part I and Part II sets out the objectives of general purpose financial statements, but companies and their managers have objectives that relate to their specific circumstances. Explain how managers' objectives impact the choice of accounting policies and the exercise of judgement. Explain differences, if any, between private and public companies' managers' objectives.

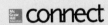 connect

A1-10 Impact of Differing Objectives:

Privately owned BlueScreen Corporation is primarily a retailer of computer equipment for individuals and small business. The effective cost of computer equipment and peripherals, at both the retail and manufacturing levels, has been declining rapidly for many years and shows every sign of continuing that decline.

The company also develops software intended for small business applications—that is, for companies with up to 500 employees. The software is sold in BlueScreen's own stores as well as through the company website. However, most sales come through general software distributors (e.g., Download.com).

For sales through the distributors, purchasers can obtain a 30-day limited-feature trial by paying an initial fee equal to 10% of the retail price of the software. If the customer decides to buy after 30 days, the trial fee is credited to the total cost of the purchase. On average, about two-thirds of the trials result in final purchase. Software development is a continuous process, including updates of existing software.

Some of BlueScreen's accounting issues are as follows:

1. What inventory methods should be used for retail merchandise in its stores and warehouses.
2. How the software development cost should be accounted for.
3. How the company should account for tangible capital assets, such as the warehouse building (which it owns), stores (which are leased), and store fixtures.
4. All of the company's personnel—retail, managerial, and software development—are sent annually to professional development programs to keep their skills at the cutting edge of performance. The company spends many millions of dollars on these programs every year.
5. The company opens an average of 20 new stores every year. About five stores are closed every year.

Required:

Using the chart below, indicate the accounting policies the company should choose for each of these issues under each of three *different* primary financial reporting objectives:

1. Earnings maximization
2. Cash flow prediction
3. Earnings minimization

Issue	Earnings Maximization	Cash Flow Prediction	Earnings Minimization
1			
2			
3			
4			
5			

★ ★ A1-11 Accounting Policy Disagreement:

You have been hired as the assistant in the finance department of a medium-sized publicly traded firm. Realizing the importance of accounting to your new duties, you have recently completed an intensive introductory course in financial accounting. On this course, you learned that research costs are expensed during the period in which they are incurred but that if certain criteria are met development costs should be treated as an asset and amortized over their projected benefit period.

Over the prior two years, your company's R&D unit had achieved an important breakthrough in electronic copying. This year, the company spent a substantial amount of money to develop a revolutionary new type of copying equipment and bring it to a marketable stage.

Your superior, Matta Hari, wishes to treat the development costs as an expense in the current year rather than deferring and amortizing them. After all, she argues, the costs have already been incurred and the cash spent, and she would prefer that future earnings from the sale of the equipment not be burdened by amortization of the development cost. She also points out that the company's primary lender, one of the Big 5 Canadian banks, is particularly interested in assessing the company's cash flow.

Ms. Hari has asked you to research the issue and submit a written report to her on this issue by tomorrow morning.

You have researched your firm's past practice in this area and reread the relevant accounting standard. Although your firm has not previously experienced the level of research and development expenses associated with the present project, past practice in your firm has been to expense these costs. Your reading of the accounting standard confirms what you recall from your course—that development expenditures should be capitalized and amortized if certain criteria have been met.

Required:

Explain the status of GAAP to this manager. Be sure to distinguish between general purpose and special purpose financial statements.

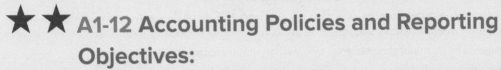

A1-12 Accounting Policies and Reporting Objectives:

Entities may have a variety of corporate reporting objectives specific to their circumstances, such as:

a. Assessing and predicting cash flows;

b. Minimizing current income taxes;

c. Complying with restrictive covenants (specifically, debt covenants that specify minimum levels of shareholders' equity); and

d. Evaluating management's performance.

Required:

For each of the accounting policies listed below, indicate which objectives of corporate reporting are best served. Each policy may serve more than one objective.

1. Capitalize and amortize development costs.

2. Disclose potential lawsuits against the company.

3. Defer expenses to match them against revenue generated from the activity.

4. Delay recognizing revenue as long as possible.

5. Write off goodwill.

A1-13 Policy Choice:

Marcon Properties Ltd. is a diversified private company that owns approximately 60 retail properties that the company has operated as discount department stores. These stores are small, stand-alone properties that Marcon owns outright, although most properties are heavily mortgaged. In 20X1, the company decided, due to increasing losses from retail operations, that all discount department stores should be closed and properties converted to rental units. This process was successfully started in 20X1, with 22 of 60 properties signed to long-term rental agreements with tenants. It is now the end of 20X1, and all retail operations have ceased. There are 38 properties currently sitting vacant. Marcon believes that it can successfully lease the remaining properties over the next 9 to 23 months.

For the 20X1 fiscal year, an accounting policy issue has come up in relation to the vacant properties—whether the properties should be depreciated during the period they sit vacant prior to rental. Those in favour of recording depreciation point out that the properties continue to deteriorate during the period in which they are idle and that depreciation is meant to allow for obsolescence, not just wear and tear. Those who favour suspension of depreciation point out that amortization should be matched with the rental revenue that the properties will generate in the future.

Marcon is reporting a positive net income in 20X1, generated from a variety of other activities.

Required:

Explain which accounting policy you would expect to be adopted in the following independent circumstances. Note that in some circumstances, the company will be indifferent as to the policy chosen.

1. Marcon is a public company and wants to show a smooth upward earnings trend.
2. Marcon has a team of senior managers who are compensated with a cash bonus based on a percentage of annual net income. Senior managers will choose the accounting policy.
3. Marcon is a private company, financed 60% through debt and 40% through equity, and has debt covenants that specify minimum debt-to-equity and return on assets (net income divided by total assets).
4. Marcon is managed by its major shareholders, who wish to minimize income tax payments.
5. Marcon's controlling shareholders are not directly involved in the business, and they wish to use the financial statements as a method to evaluate the stewardship and performance of managers.
6. Marcon has a team of senior managers who are compensated with a cash bonus based on a percentage of annual income. Assume *for this part only* that the company will report a loss in 20X1 from other sources and that managers will not receive any bonus this year.

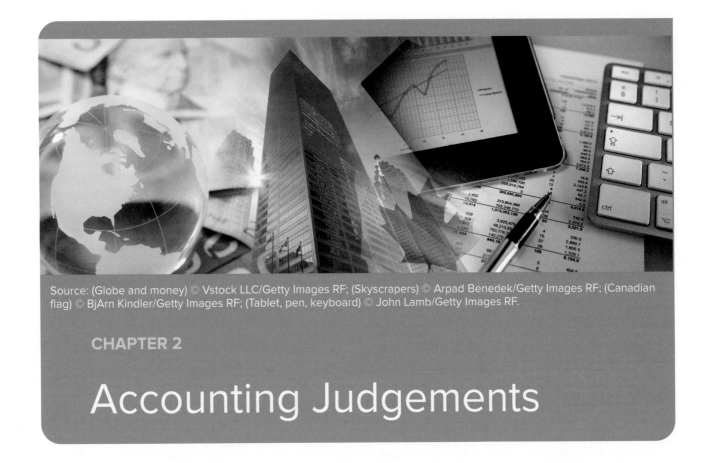

Source: (Globe and money) © Vstock LLC/Getty Images RF; (Skyscrapers) © Arpad Benedek/Getty Images RF; (Canadian flag) © BjArn Kindler/Getty Images RF; (Tablet, pen, keyboard) © John Lamb/Getty Images RF.

CHAPTER 2

Accounting Judgements

INTRODUCTION

In 2011 and 2012, the former senior managers of a once-prominent Canadian electronics company, Nortel Networks Corporation, were under attack in court for allegedly manipulating earnings through the use of "accounting reserves." The preliminary results for one quarter showed a potential profit. The senior managers then sent queries to the financial managers of their worldwide subsidiaries. The queries were about whether the subsidiaries had any accounting reserves in those subsidiaries that might be reversed or "unwound." After the subsidiaries reported back with suggested adjustments, head office made adjusting entries that turned the prospective profit into a loss. A similar process was used in subsequent quarters that then turned a preliminary loss into a profit, triggering generous bonuses for the executives.

The issue in the court case was whether the executives intentionally manipulated earnings to trigger their bonuses. The defence was that in making the end-of-quarter adjustments, the company was simply following the accounting practice of adjusting estimates at the end of each accounting period.

This action ultimately ended with the company going bankrupt and still has implications today. It was not until 2015 that the Ontario Supreme Court and the U.S. Bankruptcy Court issued judgements for the distribution of assets by creditors.

Accounting estimates are, by definition, approximations. Theoretically, estimates are based on the facts of the situation and expectations about the future. But how well can we predict the future? Corporate loan loss predictions in 2007 certainly did not take into account the financial system meltdown that occurred in 2008 and could not possibly have done so. Hindsight does not mean that a prior estimate was incorrect.

Accounting choice is often a matter of professional judgement, but exercising that judgement can be difficult and contentious. The previous chapter pointed out that management's selection of reporting objectives can significantly affect both earnings and the statement of financial position. Within any accounting model and with any sets of reporting objectives, accounting estimates play a major role. Indeed, it has been suggested that net income should not be stated as a single number but, instead, should be a median number within a range—for example, "Net income for the year is $4.2 million, plus or minus $1.8 million." The range is due to different feasible reporting practices and accounting estimates.

This chapter explains the underlying assumptions of our accounting model and discusses the qualitative criteria needed to provide useful information. These criteria are useful guides to standard setters when they develop accounting standards. They are also guidelines for management when they adopt accounting policies and make accounting estimates. As we will continue to emphasize through this text, accounting is full of estimates—virtually every amount on a company's financial statements is the result of multiple estimates.

What we call "generally accepted accounting principles" (GAAP) is really a collection of assumptions, objectives, and measurement concepts leading to an accumulation of accounting practices and accounting standards. We lump these all together and call them GAAP. In this chapter, we will analyze the different components of GAAP to get a clearer picture of the structure of accounting principles and how they are applied.

CATEGORIES OF ACCOUNTING CONCEPTS

The general body of accounting concepts (or principles—the "P" in GAAP) consists of three different categories: *underlying assumptions*, *qualitative criteria*, and *measurement methods*. We can describe these as follows:

- **Underlying assumptions** form the foundation upon which all accounting measurement rests. For example, the accounting principle of *going concern* (also called *continuity*) is an underlying assumption.

- **Qualitative characteristics** are the criteria that, *in conjunction with the organization's reporting objectives, facts, and constraints, are used to evaluate the possible measurement options* and choose the most appropriate measurement methods *for a given situation*. The principles of comparability and understandability are examples of qualitative criteria.

- **Measurement methods** are the various ways in which financial position and the results of operations can be reported. The accounting principles of fair value and realizable value are examples of measurement methods, both of which are based on the underlying assumption of continuity.

Measurement methods are *how* transactions and events are measured and reported; qualitative criteria are *why* they are measured that way, provided the underlying assumptions are valid in the particular situation.

For example, historical cost is a widely used measurement method in which assets are reported at their acquisition cost. Historical cost (a *measurement method*) is commonly used because it is perceived as more verifiable (a *qualitative criterion*) than other, alternative measurement methods. But the use of historical cost depends on the reporting enterprise's continuity as a functioning entity (an *underlying assumption*).

To set standards and to understand the accounting choice process, we must clearly differentiate between underlying assumptions, qualitative characteristics, and measurement methods.

For example, *historical cost* is not a fundamental concept of financial accounting, but *verifiability* is. Without a high degree of verifiability provided by historical cost, accounting reports would have less credibility, and accounting would not serve its most basic objective of conveying useful information. But there are many situations in which historical cost is not the appropriate measurement method, situations in which fair value is both highly verifiable and more *relevant* (which is another qualitative criterion).

Limitations of the Concepts

The financial statement concepts established by standard setters pertain to general purpose financial statements. Statements prepared for a *specific* use may well have attributes different from those described in the International Financial Reporting Standards (IFRS) concepts. Since one of the primary purposes of defining the concepts is to help standard setters determine appropriate policies for wide application, their focus on general purpose financial statements is appropriate. *But it also means that there are exceptions to the applicability of the concepts and conclusions!*

Structure of Accounting Policy Choice

To construct financial statements for a particular enterprise, we must:

- Consider the facts and constraints for the organization;
- Determine the objectives of financial reporting;
- Make sure that the underlying assumptions are valid;
- Measure the elements of financial statements using situation-specific measurement methods that satisfy the qualitative criteria; and
- Prepare the financial statements.

The process is illustrated in Exhibit 2-1. Chapter 1 discussed the forces that shape an organization's financial reporting objectives. This chapter will focus on the concepts that interact when we make accounting choices for measurement and reporting:

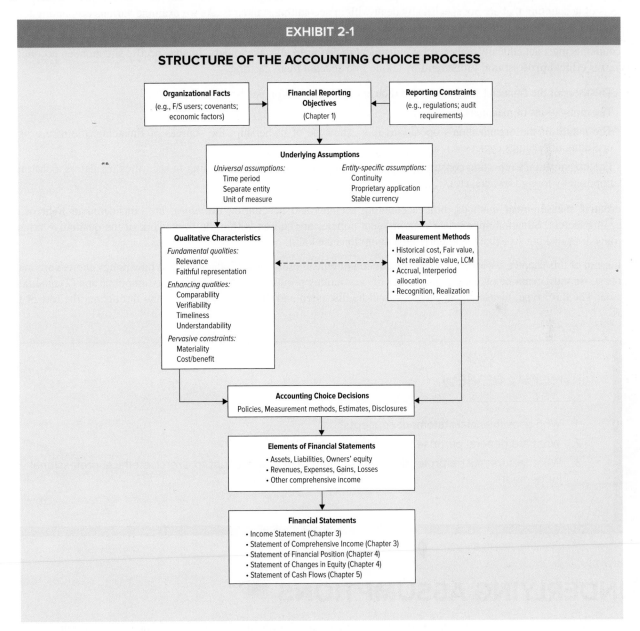

EXHIBIT 2-1

STRUCTURE OF THE ACCOUNTING CHOICE PROCESS

1. Underlying assumptions
2. Qualitative criteria

3. Accounting choices
   a. Financial statement elements
   b. Recognition and realization
   c. Measurement methods

ETHICAL PROFESSIONAL JUDGEMENT—PART 1

The process of making (or recommending) choices in accounting is the process of exercising **professional judgement**. Professional judgement is pervasive in accounting; accounting standards frequently refer to the exercise of professional judgement. Indeed, one of the differentiating characteristics of IFRS and Accounting Standards for Private Enterprises (ASPE), in contrast to those of our Financial Accounting Standards Board (FASB) cousins south of the border, is that they rely a great deal on professional judgement in preference to stipulating rigid rules. As well, judgement is pervasive in many aspects of accounting that are not specifically dealt with in accounting standards. As we examine various accounting topics throughout this text, we will emphasize their judgemental aspects.

Accountants must act ethically and exercise judgement to be fair to all stakeholders. In any specific situation, an accountant exercises **ethical professional judgement** by taking into account many factors:

- The users of the financial statements, and their *specific* information needs;
- The motivations of managers;
- The nature of the organization's operations (e.g., the type of ownership, the sources of financing, the nature of its operating or earnings cycle, etc.); and
- The organization's reporting constraints, if any (e.g., audit requirements, reporting to securities regulators, constraints imposed by foreign owners, etc).

Alternative measurement methods, both accounting *policies* and accounting *estimates*, are considered in light of the foregoing factors. Situation-appropriate measurement policies are chosen within the framework of the qualitative criteria, but only after making sure that the underlying assumptions are valid.

At the end of this chapter, we will return to a discussion of ethical professional judgement and how policy choices are made. But first, we must examine two of the three types of "accounting principles": (1) underlying assumptions and (2) qualitative criteria. The third type, measurement methods, will be discussed and illustrated topic by topic throughout the rest of this book.

CONCEPT REVIEW

1. Who uses financial statement concepts?
2. What are general purpose financial statements?
3. What factors must a professional accountant take into account to exercise ethical professional judgement?

UNDERLYING ASSUMPTIONS

Underlying assumptions provide the foundation of GAAP for for-profit enterprises, as shown in Exhibit 2-1. The going-concern assumption is the only one specifically identified in the conceptual framework. Six basic assumptions significantly affect the recording, measuring, and reporting of accounting information. The assumptions can be grouped into two categories: (1) **universal assumptions** that are essential to making financial reports feasible and meaningful and (2) **entity-specific assumptions** that are very common but actually depend on an individual entity's reporting circumstances:

Universal assumptions:

1. *Time period.* Meaningful information can be assembled and reported for a time period that is less than the enterprise's life span.
2. *Separate entity.* The enterprise can be accounted for and reported independent of its owners and other stakeholders.
3. *Unit of measure.* The results of the enterprise's operations can be measured meaningfully in monetary terms.

Entity-specific assumptions:

1. *Proprietary approach.* The results of operations for a profit-oriented enterprise's operations should be reported from the viewpoint of its owners.
2. *Continuity.* The enterprise will continue in operation for a reasonable future period; also known as the *going-concern assumption.*
3. *Stable currency.* The value of the measurement currency (e.g., the Canadian dollar) does not change from year to year; the enterprise has generated a profit if its revenues are higher than the measurement basis (e.g., historical cost or fair value) of the resources used.

At times one or more of the entity-specific assumptions are not valid, in which case GAAP is not appropriate and might be useless or highly misleading if used.

Universal Assumptions

Time Period

The operating results of any business enterprise cannot be known with certainty until the company has completed its life span and ceased doing business. In the meantime, decision makers need timely information. The **time-period assumption** states that it is feasible to provide useful information in shorter periods while the enterprise is still functioning instead of only at the end.

Although the reporting period varies, one year is the standard. Some companies use a calendar year, and others use a fiscal year-end that coincides with the low point in business activity over a 12-month period. Some businesses (such as retail stores and movie chains) report on a 52-week basis because their activity cycle is weekly (with an occasional 53-week year to catch up with the calendar). In addition, companies also report summarized financial information on an interim basis, usually quarterly for public reporting or monthly for internal purposes.

Separate Entity

The **separate-entity assumption** means each specific, identifiable business entity is considered an accounting unit separate and apart from its owners and from other entities. It says that accounting, in essence, can draw a boundary around the business unit and account only for the business's activities, independently of the affairs of the owner(s).

This may be quite artificial. For example, an enterprise carried out as a corporation may be inseparable from its owner if it has a single shareholder who is the owner-manager and who mingles business and personal finances. The same is true for sole proprietorships and partnerships (for which each partner's share of the partnership income is included in each partner's individual tax return).

The accountant must be aware of the relationship between the business and its owner(s) and must take care to portray this relationship realistically. For example, loans by a controlling shareholder to the corporation are usually, in substance, equity infusions. These have the legal form of debt and are classified as such in the financial statements. However, lenders routinely insist that such loans be subordinated (i.e., made secondary) to their own loans and reclassify the shareholder loan as equity when performing any analysis of the company. The accountant must strive to disclose the nature of the shareholder loan so that any external user is able to understand that there is a special relationship between the creditor and the debtor.

This separate-entity accounting "boundary" does not necessarily correspond with the legal and tax status of an entity. Partnerships and sole proprietorships do not share the legal or tax status of separate entities; in law and in taxation, they are viewed as an extension of their owners. Partners and nonincorporated sole proprietors are fully liable for the debts of the business—the personal assets of the owners cannot legally be isolated from the business. There is no separate tax return for the partnership or sole proprietorship. Only one tax return is filed, by the individual proprietor or by each of the partners.[1]

Unit of Measure

The **unit-of-measure assumption** means that the results of a business's economic activities can be reported in terms of a standard monetary unit throughout the financial statements. Simply stated, the assumption is that it is possible to prepare meaningful financial statements for an enterprise because everything of relevance can be measured using the dollar (or euro, or yen) as the unit of measure. Money amounts are thus the language of accounting. The common unit of measure enables dissimilar items, such as the cost of a tonne of coal and the amount of an account receivable, to be aggregated into a single total.

Unfortunately, the use of a standard monetary unit for measurement purposes poses a dilemma. If financial statements are to be meaningful, they must include complete relevant information to enable a user to make informed decisions. The unit-of-measure assumption implies that *if it cannot be measured, it cannot be reported*, and, by extension, that *if it cannot be reported, it cannot be used for decision making by external users*. Because of the unit-of-measure assumption, many important aspects of a modern business's operations are not included in the financial statements, such as:

- The value of in-house intellectual capital;
- Some environmental impacts of the company's operations; and
- The value of customer goodwill and "human capital" (i.e., employees).

Many companies attempt to fill this information void with nonfinancial information, but its quality and consistency are often questionable. Another shortcoming is that supplementary information is not subject to audit.

Entity-Specific Assumptions

Proprietary Concept

The proprietary assumption is one of the fundamental assumptions of financial reporting for business accounting. An organization's financial condition and results of operations are reported from the point of view of the owners, or *proprietors*. All other claims on the assets are liabilities, and all payments other than those to the owners are expenses. Returns to owners are returns on capital and are not expenses. This is the dominant view of a business enterprise—all outsiders are paid off, and the owners keep the residual wealth.

Continuity

The **continuity assumption** is also known as the **going-concern assumption**. Under the continuity assumption, the business entity is expected to continue operations into the future. This does not assume perpetual life but does assume that the business will continue to operate long enough to recover (or use up) the assets now in its possession and repay its outstanding liabilities. Financial statement preparers must assess the entity's ability to continue as a going concern, considering all available information.

Two occasions in which the continuity assumption is not valid are (1) when a business is a limited-life venture and (2) when a business is in financial difficulty and is expected to be shut down or liquidated. In these circumstances, many commonly used measurement methods are not appropriate.

The continuity assumption provides a conceptual basis for many of the measurement methods used in accounting. For example, asset measurement assumes that the business's capital assets will be used up over their lifetime, which gives rise to the process of depreciation. If the entity is about to be ended, financial statements cannot be prepared on a going-concern basis—assets and liabilities will be valued at their net realizable value, not at their amortized carrying value.

The continuity assumption also justifies the classifications used in accounting. Assets and liabilities, for example, are classified as either current or long-term on the basis of this assumption. If continuity is not a safe assumption, the distinction between current and long-term loses its significance; all assets and liabilities become current.

---

1. Limited liability partnerships (LLP) are an exception. These normally are professional service partnerships, particularly public accounting firms and legal firms that are not permitted to incorporate. Partners in LLPs, by definition, have limited personal liability for the firm's liabilities.

Stable Currency Assumption

The monetary unit of measure is often compared to a ruler, by which the dimensions of a business and its operations are measured. But unlike a ruler, which is always the same length, the value of a currency changes over time. The relative value of a currency can be measured in two ways:

1. In relation to the value of other currencies (its *exchange rate*); or

2. In relation to the amount of goods and services that it will buy (its *purchasing power*).

These two relative values are related. As the general purchasing power of a currency declines, its value in relation to currencies that have constant purchasing power also declines. A decline in the general level of purchasing power is a condition of *inflation*. Over time, the relative values of currencies of different nations will adjust to maintain their relative purchasing powers; this is known as maintaining **purchasing power parity**.

To keep operating successfully, any enterprise has to preserve its capital investment. This is the concept of **capital maintenance**. Annual profit can be measured only after keeping the same level of net assets from the beginning to the end of the year (excluding transactions with shareholders).

Usually, accounting is performed under the assumption that every dollar of revenue and expense has the same value, regardless of whether it was a 1950 dollar, a 1980 dollar, or a 2010 dollar. Dollars of different vintages are accounted for without regard to the fact that some have greater purchasing power than others. We call these **nominal dollars**, unadjusted for their purchasing power (inflation).

The assumption of an absolutely stable dollar is not correct, but it is used because inflation in most developed countries has been relatively modest. Unfortunately, over time, even modest annual rates of inflation can cause large cumulative changes in purchasing power. For example, Cdn$100 spent in 1970 is equivalent in purchasing power to Cdn$500 spent in 2010.

Alternative Capital Maintenance Approaches

There are two approaches to capital maintenance:

- Financial capital maintenance
  - Measured in nominal monetary units; or
  - Measured in units of constant purchasing power; and
- Physical capital maintenance.

We normally assume that the dollar is stable and does not change significantly from year to year. In contrast, **constant dollar capital maintenance** explicitly recognizes that not all dollars are created equal. If prices are rising (i.e., there is inflation), a dollar of capital at the end of the year is not worth as much as a dollar at the beginning of the year. Therefore, the enterprise must keep more nominal dollars invested in capital at the end of the year just to stay even, or to have *maintained* capital.

The **physical capital maintenance** concept recognizes that the prices of individual goods and services change at different rates and in different directions, some going up and some down. A company's capital is invested in productive assets. The key to capital maintenance is that a company must be able to maintain the same level of service or *productivity*, not simply the equivalent dollars of investment.

Physical capital maintenance is a misnomer because the point is not to maintain the *physical* capacity but, rather, the *productive* capacity. No one would strive to maintain exactly the same computers, for example—they would maintain the computing *capacity*.

IFRS accepts both nominal dollar and physical/productive capacity capital maintenance concepts. The physical capacity concept may be used in regulatory situations. A good example is telecommunication companies. Telecom Italia, for example, uses physical capacity maintenance for its cellular phone network because its rates are regulated to maintain capacity plus a permitted maximum rate of return. Since the cost of electronic equipment keeps declining, the cost of maintaining capacity is not stable—it declines, which leads to lower rates for customers.

The apparently universal dominance of nominal dollar maintenance is somewhat misleading. Nominal dollar maintenance relies on historical cost as the basis of measurement. As accounting standards increasingly move toward fair values, the measurement of earnings incorporates more value changes. Changes in asset values reflect the expected productivity of those assets. Thus, the more we move to fair-value reporting (as in the investment and real estate markets), the more we are unconsciously using productive/physical capital maintenance.

Example

To illustrate these possible assumptions, assume that an item of inventory is purchased for $1,000, held for one year and then sold for $1,500. Inflation during the period was 10%. It would cost $1,350 to replace the item in inventory at the end of the period, because supplier price has increased. Under each of the three capital maintenance concepts, the profit under each method would be reported as shown in Exhibit 2-2.

EXHIBIT 2-2

CAPITAL MAINTENANCE CONCEPTS

Capital Maintenance	Measure of Profit	Commentary
Nominal dollar financial capital maintenance	$1,500 − $1,000 = **$500**	Profits are reported after historical costs in nominal dollars are recovered.
Constant dollar financial capital maintenance	$1,500 − ($1,000 × 1.10) = $1,500 − $1,100 = **$400**	Profits are reported after inflation, ensuring that the purchasing power of the original investment is maintained.
Physical (productive capacity) capital maintenance	$1,500 − $1,350 = **$150**	Profits are reported only after the entity keeps enough capital to replace assets used.

CONCEPT REVIEW

1. Why may the separate-entity assumption be artificial for a small corporation with a single shareholder?
2. When might the continuity assumption not be valid?
3. What is the proprietary concept?
4. Which underlying assumption is not appropriate in a country that suffers triple-digit annual inflation?

QUALITATIVE CRITERIA

Qualitative criteria are needed to establish accounting policies, as indicated in Exhibit 2-1. Many attempts to develop, clarify, and/or codify these criteria have been made, beginning way back in 1966.[2] The various conceptual frameworks have varied in detail, but they all reflect the same general ideas and qualitative hierarchy.

The discussion below will follow the IFRS *Conceptual Framework for Financial Reporting* (see Chapter 3). Exhibit 2-3 presents a summary of the most recent IASB version of qualitative criteria.

---

2. See *A Statement of Basic Accounting Theory* (American Accounting Association, 1966); *Statement of Financial Accounting Concepts No. 2: Qualitative Characteristics of Accounting Information* (Financial Accounting Standards Board, May 1980); and *Corporate Reporting: Its Future Evolution* (Canadian Institute of Chartered Accountants, 1980).

EXHIBIT 2-3

QUALITATIVE CHARACTERISTICS OF ACCOUNTING INFORMATION

Fundamental Characteristics	**Enhancing Characteristics**
Relevance (*the primary characteristic*)	Comparability (*the goal*)
Predictive value	Consistency (*the means*)
Confirmatory (*or* feedback) value	Verifiability, as:
Faithful representation	Representation of economic phenomena
Completeness	Application of a measurement method
Neutrality	Timeliness
Freedom from material error	Understandability

Pervasive constraints

Materiality

Cost/benefit

Based on Chapter 3 of the IASB *Conceptual Framework for Financial Reporting*, "Qualitative Characteristics of Useful Financial Information."

Source: The International Accounting Standards Board, © 2012.

Fundamental Qualities

Relevance

Relevance is the most important qualitative characteristic, because it means that accounting information must be useful for decisions. Relevance refers to the capacity of accounting information to make a difference to the external decision makers who use financial reports. It relates to the objectives of financial reporting. Chapter 1 pointed out that accounting choices made when cash flow prediction is the primary reporting objective are not necessarily the same as those made when performance evaluation is the primary objective.

Two qualities that contribute to relevance are *predictive value* and *confirmatory value*:

1. **Predictive value**. Accounting information should be helpful to external decision makers by increasing their ability to make predictions about the outcome of future events. Decision makers working from accounting information with little or no predictive value are merely speculating intuitively.
2. **Confirmatory value**. This is also known as **feedback value**. Accounting information should be helpful to external decision makers who are confirming past predictions or making updates, adjustments, or corrections to predictions.

Faithful Representation

Information is reliable if users can depend on it as a sufficiently accurate measure of what it is intended to measure. Accounting information should represent what it purports to represent and should report the economic substance of transactions. This characteristic is known as **faithful representation**.

An important aspect of faithful representation is **substance over form**. As an example of accountants' efforts to portray substance over form, consider a company that leases a computer system. The legal form of the contract is a rental agreement, which would seem to suggest that payments made by the company should simply be reported as rent expense with no other financial statement impact.

However, suppose that the accountant discovers that this company decided to lease the computer instead of buying one outright with money borrowed from a bank. The lease term covers the entire expected useful life of the computer, cannot be cancelled by the company, and provides a full return of the cost of the computer plus a profit margin (in the form of interest) to the lessor. Now it looks as though, *in substance*, the company has acquired property rights over the computer, far more than a simple rental contract would imply. In substance, it owns full rights to the use of the asset and is financing it with a lease agreement. Thus, to reflect *substance over form*, and to faithfully represent the substance of the transaction, the asset and the obligation should be shown on the balance sheet of the lessee; the subsequent statements of comprehensive income (SCIs) should reflect both depreciation of the computer and interest on the liability.

Faithful representation is closely related to the concept of reliability but has three additional subcomponents: *completeness*, *neutrality*, and *freedom from material error*:

- **Completeness**: To ensure that information faithfully represents the economic events or financial elements it is purporting to measure, the information must not mislead or deceive. Information must give a faithful picture of the facts and circumstances involved, as a city map should accurately represent the layout of a city. If some important streets are omitted, the map is far less useful than it could be because it lacks completeness.

- **Neutrality**: Financial reports are neutral if they do not influence a user's decisions or judgements to achieve a specific intended outcome. This characteristic is also known as *freedom from bias*. Accounting information is biased if the measurements result in consistent overstatements or understatements of the items being measured.

  The concept of neutrality is sometimes taken to mean that reported accounting information should not influence economic decisions. This view does not make sense, because if information does not affect economic decisions, it is irrelevant and thus useless. Lack of neutrality means the deliberate misstatement or exaggeration of information to influence decisions in a predetermined direction.

- **Freedom from material error**: Faithful representation does not imply "accuracy" in the sense that the measurement is completely free from error. Most accounting measurements are inherently uncertain, and that is why they are *estimates*. Estimates must be based on appropriate inputs and must reflect the best available information; biased estimates defeat faithful representation. If the extent of approximation is too great, measurements should be accompanied (in the notes) by an explanation of the degree of uncertainty. If statements are free from bias, overstatements and understatements must not exist, including any that may be introduced under the guise of "conservatism."

ETHICAL ISSUES

Preparers of financial reports should not attempt to induce a predetermined outcome or a particular mode of behaviour. For example, a set of financial statements should not be made to look "rosy" to influence potential investors to purchase a company's shares. Thus, there is a potential conflict between management's financial reporting objectives (or motivations) and the accountant's ethical professional responsibility.

Enhancing Qualities

Comparability

Comparability is a factor when considering the relationship between two pieces of information. There are two aspects of comparability—*consistency*, which entails using the same accounting policies from year to year within a firm, and *uniformity*, which means that companies with similar transactions and similar circumstances use the same accounting treatments.

Consistency involves applying accounting concepts and principles from period to period in the same manner. There is a presumption that an accounting principle, once used, should not be changed. However, if consistency is carried too far, it adversely affects relevance. A change to a preferred accounting principle is permitted, even if it seemingly impairs consistency. The apparent conflict is usually resolved by retrospective restatement of financial statements to reflect the new policy, with appropriate note disclosure.

The principle of **uniformity** is a goal for which standard setters strive. The concept is that various companies should use the same accounting methods for the same economic events and phenomena. Companies' financial statements can be most readily compared with each other only when they use similar accounting policies and methods.

Verifiability

If knowledgeable and independent observers can measure an economic event and arrive at generally the same result, the measurement is said to be verifiable. There are two aspects to **verifiability** in the IFRS framework:

- The accounting measure is a reasonable measure of the economic event, without material error or bias; and
- Independent observers, *using the same measurement methods*, would reach substantially the same conclusion.

The first aspect relates to faithful representation—that the measurement actually represents what it is supposed to. The second aspect is that the calculation or measurement can be replicated or reproduced by independent observers; this is the essence of the auditor's function.

Timeliness

Accounting information should be reported soon enough for it to be useful for decision making. Like the daily news, stale financial information has less impact. Lack of **timeliness** reduces relevance.

Understandability

Information must be understandable to be useful to users in their decision-making process. **Understandability** does not mean that all information has to be reduced to the lowest common level or simplified so that the least sophisticated investor can understand it. Investors and creditors should have a reasonable understanding of business and economic activities, and also of accounting, and they are expected to study the information with reasonable diligence. Those investors and creditors who lack expertise are presumed to have obtained professional advice.

Pervasive Constraints

Materiality

The term **materiality** is used to describe the significance of an item. Something is said to be material if its omission or misstatement would be likely to influence or change a user's decision. Essentially, it does not matter how an *immaterial* item is accounted for, because errors or omissions relating to them would not lead to different decisions.

Materiality may be created either by the relative size of an item or by its nature. Regarding size, an essentially arbitrary limit of a small percentage (e.g., ranging from 3% to 7%) of income from continuing operations or of assets is frequently used to measure materiality. However, even a much smaller amount might affect investor or creditor perceptions.

For example, the auditors of Toronto-based Nortel Networks Ltd. insisted that the company disclose the reversal of "accounting reserves" of $80 million in its interim statements, even though the company had assets of $15.7 billion and quarterly revenue of $2.4 billion in the quarter. Such a small amount is only 0.3% of revenue and 0.005% of assets. The reason for the auditor's insistence was that the company's quarterly net earnings amounted to only $97 million. The reversal, which is a managerial judgement, amounted to 82% of the reported earnings.[3]

For an example of the nature of an item giving rise to materiality, assume that a large company with a $500,000 materiality limit discovered a $100,000 payment that might have been a bribe. This item, immaterial dollar-wise, would have to be brought to the attention of the audit committee of the board of directors for further action because of its questionable legality.

The Cost/Benefit Tradeoff

The concept of **cost/benefit effectiveness** holds that any accounting measurement or disclosure should result in greater benefits to the users than it costs to prepare and present. Benefits should exceed costs.

In standard setting, this is a very difficult concept to implement, since the benefits of an individual accounting standard are very vague, while the costs of compliance are very real. Furthermore, the costs are borne by the companies, while the benefits are usually enjoyed by the external users. The cost/benefit perceptions of standard setters and of the preparers of

3. "Nortel Executives Clashed with Auditors, Trial Told," *The Globe and Mail*, 24 May 2012, p. B2.

financial statements do not always coincide, with the result that some standards enjoy less than full compliance, even by public companies.

For private companies not bound by a GAAP constraint, the cost/benefit trade-off is very pragmatic. In particular, if there are no external users of a private company's financial statements (other than the Canada Revenue Agency [CRA]), no benefit is to be derived from incurring higher accounting costs. Commonly, such companies will use accounting methods that coincide with their tax treatment, even though they may not be compliant with GAAP—for example, calculating depreciation/amortization expense on the same basis as capital cost allowance (the tax method of depreciation).

Canadian accounting standards acknowledge this cost/benefit threshold by providing a somewhat simpler version of GAAP called ASPE, as we described in the previous chapter. ASPE enables private companies to follow simpler accounting policies in some areas, as we will see throughout this textbook.

Tradeoff between Enhancing Qualitative Characteristics

Enhancing characteristics often require the emphasis of one characteristic over another. For example, *timeliness* might have to be reduced to increase the degree of *verifiability*, or vice versa. If financial statements were delayed until all the future events that affect them were to come to pass, measurements would be far more verifiable. Uncollectible accounts, warranty reserves, and useful lives of depreciable assets would not have to be estimated and verifiability would increase.

On the other hand, the timeliness of the financial statements would suffer, and thus the statements would lack relevance. The relative importance of the characteristics changes from situation to situation and requires the exercise of professional judgement.

The extent of tradeoffs is, in itself, subjective. This is particularly apparent in the standard-setting process, where there is often vigorous debate about what is *relevant* and what is *measurable*. The concerns of the auditing profession often show up in the presence of standards that seem to emphasize verifiability. The historical cost measurement convention often seems to override what many observers perceive to be the relevance of other highly objective measurements.

CONCEPT REVIEW

1. How does relevance relate to financial reporting objectives?
2. Does the criterion of understandability mean that every person should be able to understand the financial statements?
3. What are the four *enhancing* qualities of accounting information?
4. Why must there often be tradeoffs between different enhancing qualitative characteristics?

ELEMENTS OF FINANCIAL STATEMENTS AND RECOGNITION

The building blocks of financial statements are called *elements*. **Elements** are the different *classes* of items in financial statements, as shown in the first column of Exhibit 2-4. The first three elements (assets, liabilities, and owners' equity/ net assets) relate directly to the statement of financial position; the next three elements (revenues/gains, expenses/ losses, and other comprehensive income [OCI]) relate directly to the statement of comprehensive income (SCI) but are derived from the definitions of assets and liabilities. The definitions of these six elements are particularly important, because they provide the basis for deciding whether to recognize the results of a transaction or event in the financial statements.

EXHIBIT 2-4	
ELEMENTS OF FINANCIAL STATEMENTS[*]	
Recognized	**Elaboration**
Statement of Financial Position (Discussed in Chapter 4)	

1. An **asset** is recognized in the statement of financial position (SFP) when:
  a. It is a resource controlled by the entity that arose as the result of past events;
  b. It is probable that the future economic benefits will flow to the entity; and
  c. The asset has a cost or value that can be measured reliably.
	If the entity has an expenditure that is *unlikely* to result in future economic benefits, it must be recognized as an *expense*, not as an asset.
	An entity will make some expenditures that are *likely* to result in future economic benefits, for example, research costs, but the future benefits cannot be measured with a sufficient degree of reliability to satisfy the definition of an asset; therefore, they must be recognized as an expense.

2. A **liability** is recognized in the SFP when:
  a. It is a present obligation arising from past events;
  b. It is probable that an outflow of resources embodying economic benefits will result from the settlement of the obligation; and
  c. The amount at which the settlement will take place can be measured reliably.
	Normally, a liability is not recognized for executory contracts in which neither side of the contract has performed the actions required by the contract.
	If circumstances require recognition of such a liability, recognition of a liability requires a balancing recognition of related asset(s) or expense(s).

3. **Owners' equity** (or **net assets**) is the residual of assets minus liabilities.	While total equity is a residual, it includes individual categories of items, such as various types of share capital, retained earnings, and individual components of other comprehensive income (OCI).
Statement of Comprehensive Income (Discussed in Chapter 3)	

4. **Income** (including both revenues and gains) is an increase in future economic benefits that can be measured reliably with a sufficient degree of certainty, by way of:
  1. Inflows or enhancements of assets; and/or
  2. Reductions of liabilities.
	An essential characteristic of income is that it is an increase in the entity's net assets as the result of the company's operating activities, and *not* from **(a)** capital transactions, **(b)** the settlement of monetary liabilities, or **(c)** the sale of capital assets or investment assets.

5. **Expenses** (and **losses**) are decreases in future economic benefits that can be measured reliably and that result from the income-generating activities of an entity, by way of:
  1. Decrease in assets (by outflows or amortization); and/or
  2. Increase in liabilities.
	The essential characteristic of an expense or loss is that it must be incurred in conjunction with the company's income-generating process. Expenditures that do not qualify as expenses are treated either as assets, as OCI, or as distributions to owners.

6. **Other comprehensive income (OCI)** comprises increases and decreases in net assets that are: 1. Specifically excluded from net income by IFRS; or	Components of OCI are the results of transactions with nonowners that are specifically excluded by IFRS from the measurement of profit or loss and must be included in OCI. Each type of item is a separate category of shareholders' equity, even though it does not reflect transactions with shareholders.

> 2. Do not reflect transactions with owners in their capacity as owners.
>
> *Based on the IASB's *Conceptual Framework for Financial Reporting*, Chapter 4: "Recognition of the Elements of Financial Statements."
>
> Source: The International Accounting Standards Board, © 2011.

Elements of the Statement of Financial Position

Assets and Liabilities

Assets and liabilities are central to the definitions, since all other definitions are *derived from* asset and liability definitions. That is, owners' equity equals assets minus liabilities. Revenues and gains are defined as increases in assets or decreases in liabilities; expenses and losses are decreases in assets or increases in liabilities. Obviously, the definitions emphasize the statement of financial position and the assets and liabilities it comprises.

The definitions of assets and liabilities include three components and embody three time frames:

1. An asset involves a *future benefit* (e.g., through a direct future cash flow or through its use in generating a future cash flow), and a liability entails a future sacrifice (either a payment of cash or performance of service).

2. The reporting enterprise has a clear *present right* to the asset or obligation for the liability.

3. The asset or liability arose as the result of a *past transaction* or event.

Owners' Equity

Owners' equity is a residual. It is not measured directly but is the difference between assets and liabilities. Thus it represents the enterprise's net assets. Primarily, owners' equity captures the results of transactions between the enterprise and its shareholders in their capacity as shareholders. This excludes non-share-related activities and transactions. There is nothing to stop a shareholder from having normal business transactions with the enterprise, but the results of those transactions must not be confused with the shareholder's role as an owner.

However, in addition to capturing the results of shareholders' ownership transaction, owners' equity also includes items of OCI. These items reflect changes in net assets that do not qualify for recognition as components of revenue or expense. Thus, owners' equity includes the net impact of all changes in assets and liabilities, regardless of whether they have been recognized in net income (profit or loss).

Elements of the Statement of Comprehensive Income

The IASB uses the term **income** to mean all increases in net assets that are flowing into the enterprise as the result of the operating activities of the company. The framework does not distinguish between "revenues" and "gains."

In general, **gains** are increases in net assets that arise from two sources:

*   Peripheral or incidental activities, such as sales of individual assets or income from investments; and

*   Remeasurement of asset or liabilities, such as increases in the value of fair-valued assets (e.g., marketable investments or investment properties).

These distinctions are widely used in practice, but there is really no absolute rule about what we call *revenue* and what we call *gains*. Some companies will report all types of income as "revenue," whether from operating activities, peripheral items, or remeasurements.

The distinction between expenses and losses is similarly indefinite. **Expenses** normally relate to the ordinary activities of the company; **losses** relate to peripheral activities or downward remeasurements. But again, many companies will report all expenses and losses together in a single category.

For the ordinary operations of the company, revenues and expenses must be reported separately, not netted. However, gains and losses from peripheral activities may be reported "net"—gains net of related (or similar) expenses, and losses net of related income. For example, companies will usually report a net gain or loss from temporary investments. Income tax expenses can never be netted against gains or losses, however.

OCI includes only certain specific changes in net assets as prescribed by individual IFRS standards. Management does not have an option about whether to report such items in the net income (or "profit or loss") section of the statement or in the OCI section.

Recognition

Recognition is the process of measuring and including an item in the financial statements. A *recognized* item is given a title and numerical value. Recognition applies to all financial statement elements in all accounting entities.

Disclosure (i.e., information reported in the notes to the financial statements) is not the same as recognition. A *recognized* element is reported on the face of the financial statements and is directly incorporated into earnings and net asset measurements. By contrast, *disclosed* information is there for financial statement readers to use if they wish and if they can figure out what to do with it. Disclosure is not a substitute for recognition.

In Exhibit 2-4, each element contains the same two basic criteria:

- The item's cost or value can be measured reliably; and
- The future benefit will flow to (or from) the reporting entity, either in the future or in the current reporting period.

Therefore, we can summarize the recognition process with three questions to be resolved:

- Does the item seem to be a financial statement element within the broad context of financial reporting?
- Does the item have a suitable basis of measurement, and can the amount be measured reliably?
- For assets and liabilities, is it probable that the economic benefits will be received or given up—that is, realized?

It seems obvious that financial statement elements are the things measured in financial statements—this is the first criterion. Next comes *measurability*. If an item cannot be measured, it cannot be recognized, even if it has a high probability of being realized. To be measurable, there must be both a basis of measurement (e.g., historical cost or fair value) and a reasonable estimate of the amount. *Probability* is the final criterion. It is entirely possible that an item that meets the first two recognition criteria will not be recognized because of failure of the last criterion—probability of realization (Exhibit 2-5).

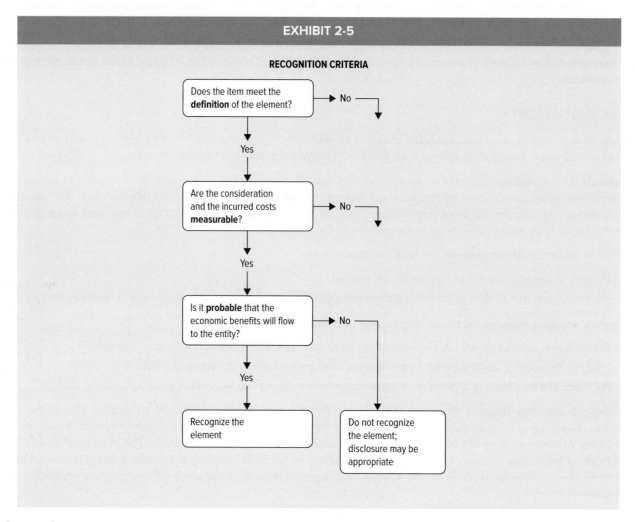

EXHIBIT 2-5

RECOGNITION CRITERIA

Commitments

Suppose a company signs a three-year contract to hire a special consultant; the contract is noncancellable. Should the company recognize a liability? The company has committed to a cash outflow over the next three years, and the contract is noncancellable, but although a contract has been signed, there will not be a *transaction* until the consultant performs the contracted work. A liability does not arise until one of the parties to the contract has actually performed the contracted service or delivered the contracted product.

Therefore, the **commitment** would be viewed as an **executory contract**—a contract wherein neither party has yet fulfilled the requirements of the contract—and would not be recognized.

Recognition versus Realization

Recognition means that an item is recorded in the accounts. **Realization** is the process of converting an asset, liability, or commitment into a cash flow. Revenues are *recognized* when a credit sale is made but not *realized* until the receivable has been collected. Once realization has occurred, recognition *must* occur because there has been a cash flow impact that cannot be ignored in the accounts. For example:

- A customer pays in advance for goods yet to be produced and delivered; since the cash has been received (*realized*), it must be *recognized*. Revenue will not yet have been earned; the offsetting credit is to recognize unearned revenue.
- A company pays a retainer to a lawyer who will be acting on the company's behalf in the next fiscal year; the cash outflow triggers *realization*, which requires *recognition* of a prepaid expense.

However, recognition often occurs prior to realization. For example:

- A liability for a purchase of inventory is *recognized* when the goods are received—the offset is to recognize inventory as an asset. *Realization* occurs when the creditor is paid.
- A change in the value of cash held in a U.S.-dollar bank account is *recognized* at the balance sheet date—the offset is to a gain or loss account, depending on the direction of the change in value. *Realization* of the gain or loss occurs only when the U.S. dollars are converted to Canadian dollars.

The Accrual Concept

When we *recognize* assets and liabilities that have not yet been *realized* as a cash flow, we are using **accruals**. In contrast, when we have *realized* costs and receipts by a cash outflow or inflow, we use **deferrals** to delay their recognition as expenses and revenues. For example:

Cash Timing	Results In:
Cash received after revenue recognition is appropriate	Accrued revenue (asset) (e.g., a receivable)
Cash received before revenue recognition is appropriate	Deferred revenue (liability) (e.g., unearned revenue)

When we recognize the effects of transactions and events prior to their realization, we are using the *accrual concept*. The accrual concept says that we recognize transactions when they occur. Cash flow may well happen in this period or in a different period.

In interperiod allocation, amounts originally recognized as assets are transferred to (i.e., *recognized* as) expense, and amounts recorded as liabilities are transferred to the income statement as revenue (or as reduction of expense).

Expense Recognition and "Matching"

Matching is "the simultaneous or combined recognition of revenues and expenses that result directly and jointly from the same transaction or other events."[4] Assets such as inventory are recognized in the same period as is the revenue from sale of a product. Interperiod allocation (e.g., depreciation) is a prime example of matching. The reason for depreciation and amortization is to match the costs of long-lived assets to the revenue generated by their use in productive activity.

An alternative approach to joint measurement of revenues and expenses is via the increases and decreases in net assets—assets minus liabilities, which we can call the **net asset principle of revenue/expense recognition**. When we generate revenue, we increase net assets by recording cash received or accounts receivable. The increase in net assets indicates that revenue has been earned. However, to fulfill our obligation to earn that revenue, we must use assets, such as inventory and cash, as well as long-lived assets, such as equipment, and we incur liabilities for labour and materials. These decreases in net assets (i.e., decreases in assets and increases in liabilities) are the expenses we recognize in the same period as we recognize the revenue. Thus, matching is achieved, but the rationale is based on changes in assets and liabilities rather than on the concept of matching.

As a long-lived asset, such as equipment, is used up, its future usefulness decreases. For most assets, we do not try to measure the actual decrease in an asset's value; instead, we make an assumption that the remaining service potential has declined, signalling that an expense should be recognized. Thus, we can justify interperiod allocation as an estimation of assets consumed rather than under the rubric of matching.

Be careful, though—some expenses related to long-term assets are recognized only when the measurable value of the asset has actually declined. An example is purchased goodwill, which is expensed only when its value has been demonstrably *impaired*.

Illustration of Net Asset Principle

To illustrate the net asset principle, assume that a home appliance is sold for cash with a 100% warranty on parts and labour in effect for 12 months from date of sale.

---

4. "Recognition of the Elements of Financial Statements," ¶4.50, *Conceptual Framework for Financial Reporting*, Chapter 4. IASB 2011.

The cash from the sale is recognized as an asset immediately; the offset for this increase in net assets is revenue. Immediate costs (i.e., inventory) are recognized, but they are already consumed and have no future benefit. Therefore, those costs are recognized as expenses. These expenses include the costs of manufacturing and assembling the unit and the shipping and direct selling expenses incurred.

To fully measure the change in net assets, though, the estimated future liability implicit in honouring the warranty should also be recognized, even though the actual warranty cost may not be known until the next year. At the end of the year in which the sale occurs, the warranty expense should be estimated and recorded and thus recognized. In this way, the warranty expense is recognized in the same period as the revenue to which it is related, even though the cash may be expended at a later time.

You may notice that the net result of this example of the net asset principle is the same as would result under the matching concept—the estimated warranty cost is recognized in the same period as the sale that generated the probable estimated liability.

Professional Judgement

The measurement of cost and the timing of expense recognition are matters that require a great deal of professional judgement. Almost all expense items in the income statement are the result of several interrelated judgements and estimates. Many of the following chapters in this book discuss issues of revenue and expense recognition at some length. Each chapter deals with recognition in the context of specific accounting issues, such as inventories, capital assets, leases, pensions, income tax, and so forth.

Cash Flow Is Central

Before leaving the concepts of realization and recognition, we must stress that accounting recognition always relates to realized cash flows—past, present, and future. The recognition issue is always one of fitting the actual (or predicted) cash flows into time periods through a complex system of accruals and interperiod allocations. If actual cash flows deviate from those that we presumed in recognizing revenues and expenses, we must adjust our accounts. *At no time can accounting recognize financial statement elements that are not based on actual or predicted cash flows.*[5]

CONCEPT REVIEW

1. What is the difference between accounting *realization* and *recognition*?
2. What is the difference between *accrual* and *interperiod allocation*?
3. What are the three criteria that must be met to justify recognition of an item in the financial statements?

MEASUREMENT

Measurement is the process of determining the amount at which an item is recognized in the financial statements. Measurement is integral to accounting choice, as indicated in Exhibit 2-1. In your introductory financial accounting course, you learned to use concepts of historical cost, net realizable value (NRV), lower-of-cost-and-NRV, and fair value. These concepts form the basis of the more specific measurement methods you will learn in the following chapters of this book.

Measurement methods encompass not only the process of attaching a number to a specific asset or a liability but also income measurement. The process of income measurement involves both (1) the initial measurement of a financial statement element and (2) the disposition or recognition of that measurement as it moves through the financial statements. IFRS recognizes that many measurement bases are possible. The primary measurement ones used in IFRS are:

---

5. There is one exception—the expense recorded for employee stock options is hypothetical and is never substantiated by actual cash flows. You will not
    have to bother with this until Volume Two, though.

1. Historical cost
2. Current cost
3. Present value
4. Fair value

There are variations and alternatives within each approach.

Historical Cost

The **historical cost convention** specifies that acquisition cost be used for initial accounting recognition, especially for asset acquisitions. The cost principle assumes that assets are acquired in business transactions conducted at arm's length—that is, transactions between a buyer and a seller are at a fair market value prevailing at the time of the transaction.

The cost of the asset is based on the *value of the consideration given up*. If an asset is acquired via some means other than cash, **consideration** is whatever the buyer gives the seller as payment. For noncash transactions conducted at arm's length, the cost principle assumes that the fair value of the resources *given up* in a transaction provides reliable evidence for the valuation of the item acquired. This may be the amount of money paid, the market value of common shares issued, or the present value of debt assumed in the transaction.

Sometimes, though, it is difficult to value the consideration given up, and then the fair market value of the assets *received* is referred to as a more reliable indicator. For example, if a company receives widely traded common shares valued at $50,000 in payment for land appraised at $60,000, the value of the shares should be used as the value of the consideration, since its value is less subjective than the appraised value of the land. Noncash or barter transactions are discussed in more detail in later chapters.

The historical cost convention provides guidance primarily at the initial acquisition date. Once acquired, the original cost basis of long-lived assets is then subject to amortization, depletion, depreciation, impairment, or writeup.

Current Cost

Current cost is what it would cost to replace an asset or, more precisely, to replace its productive capacity. Current cost is used primarily under the physical capital maintenance concept, as we discussed earlier in this chapter. It also is sometimes used for rate-setting purposes in regulated enterprises. There are several ways of measuring current cost, such as:

- Cost of acquiring a similar asset of similar remaining productivity (and age) on an established used-asset market. Motor vehicles are a good example of an asset type that can readily be measured this way.
- Cost of currently acquiring a similar asset, then deducting an estimated amount for depreciation. This measurement method is commonly called *depreciated replacement cost*.
- Applying a price index to a class of assets, when an appropriate index is available through either public sources or a productivity index maintained by the entity itself. This approach is useful when the company has a very large number of similar or identical assets, either inventory items or common tools or equipment such as computers and printers.

Current cost does not have much application in the normal run of business enterprise in North America, where financial capital maintenance is virtually ubiquitous.

Current cost and historical cost are usually identical at the time that an asset is acquired. However, this is not always the case if assets are acquired through an exchange of assets. We will discuss asset exchanges in Chapter 6.

Realizable Value

Historical cost and current cost are *entry values*—the cost of acquiring an asset. In contrast, **realizable value** is an *exit value*—what can be recovered when an asset is disposed of. For liabilities, it is the **settlement value**, or what it would cost to pay off the liability.

Realizable value has several variations, depending on the circumstances. You already are familiar with such concepts as lower-of-cost-and-NRV for inventory. You also know that a realizable value depends on whether an asset sale is forced (such as by bankruptcy) or is a sale in due course without pressure to sell.

The same is true of liabilities. The sacrifice required to settle a liability may be higher if it is settled prior to its maturity date. Or if settlement is delayed, the sacrifice may be either higher or lower than its face value or nominal amount. The true settlement price might be higher due to prepayment penalties or late-payment penalties; it might be lower due to changes in interest rates or due to a creditor's accepting less than full face value if the entity is in financial distress.

Present Value

Present value is the value of a future asset or liability with its interest component removed—its discounted value. Present value is the normal measurement method used for financial assets and liabilities with a maturity of more than one year after the SFP date. The present value may be fixed by contract, such as by the interest rate built into a mortgage. Alternatively, the present value might be an approximation based on expected future rates of return, such as in pension accounting.

A present value can be either an entry value or an exit value. When we initially record a long-term receivable, we discount it by using the current interest rate at the transaction date. The resulting present value is an entry value because it recognizes the interest rate at the time of the transaction.

However, suppose that a year later, we sell that receivable to another company. The buyer will be willing to pay only an amount based on the current rates of interest at the transaction date. If the current rate is higher than the historical rate, for example, the buyer will pay less to buy the receivable because its present value has gone down. That present value, based on the current interest rate, is an exit value (and also the realizable value).

Not all liabilities that appear to be financial liabilities are subject to present value reporting, however. A prime example is the balance of deferred income taxes, which is explicitly exempted from discounting by both IFRS and ASPE.

Fair Value

Fair value is a current measurement of the value of an asset or liability at the reporting date. It can be either an *entry value* or an *exit value*, which means that it could be measured as current cost, present value, or realizable (or settlement) value. *Fair value* is a slippery term—when using it, one must be very careful to understand what it means in any particular situation. Of course, fair value is always better than unfair value, which would be any value that violates the fundamental qualitative criteria of faithful representation and relevance.

Accounting standards have tended to define "fair value" in varying ways. To resolve confusion and to provide a comprehensive approach to fair valuation, the IASB issued IFRS 13 to be applied with any standard that permits or requires fair values with a few scope exemptions.

Fair value is the price that would be received to sell an asset or paid to transfer a liability in an *orderly transaction* between market participants at the measurement date. An **orderly transaction** is one in which neither the buyer nor the seller is under undue pressure to enter the transaction. That means the buyer does not have a special urgency to acquire the asset, and the seller does not have any strong pressure to sell, such as bankruptcy.

Although fair value has a relatively simple theoretical value, it can be very difficult to measure. Therefore, the IASB established a three-level *hierarchy* for measuring fair value:

- *Level 1.* Quoted prices in active markets for identical assets;
- *Level 2.* Prices for similar assets or that can be derived from observable market data; and
- *Level 3.* Values derived by indirect valuation techniques, not verifiable by direct observation of market data.

These levels are stated in the order of priority. A reporting entity should not use an indirect method of measuring value if it is determinable directly. For example, quoted prices for an investment should be used, if available, and not an indirect valuation based on the prices of similar investments. It also should be a *current* price, not a forecasted price nor a historical average.

An asset should be valued in its *principal or most advantageous market*. For example, many corporations have art collections. These can be of great value, but the value of each piece will often depend on what market it is being offered in. A painting by Vancouver artist Joe Average is likely to bring a better price in his home market rather than in a market where he is unknown, so Vancouver would probably be the principal market for his work.

An asset also should be measured at its **highest and best use**. That is, if an asset has several possible uses, the valuation should be based on its most advantageous use. Sometimes this means to use the asset by itself, on a stand-alone basis. But sometimes it means combining it with other assets. For example, a conveyor system might not have much value on its own, and would probably have a much higher value when used in the right type of production or distribution facility.

Fair value should not be adjusted for transaction costs. If an entity decides to sell an asset, the transaction costs are an expense in the period of the sale; estimated transaction costs should not be deducted from the fair value reported on the SFP prior to the sale.

Level 1—Direct Observation

This is the easiest measurement to understand. Level 1 uses quoted prices in active markets for identical items. For example, if Leslie Corporation holds common shares of Air Canada, the value of those shares at the end of Leslie's reporting year can easily be verified by looking at Air Canada's share price on the Toronto or New York stock exchanges. Brokerage fees (which are transaction costs) would not be deducted.

Level 2—Indirect Observation

If there are no quoted prices in active markets for identical items, the next-best alternative is to use a close approximation. The prices of similar assets can be used as the basis for estimation, or a price can be derived from observable market data.

For example, suppose Leslie Corporation is a private equity firm that has invested in Ordeal Ltd. debt securities that were issued in a private placement. That is, the debt is all privately held and not traded publicly. There is no quoted market price, and thus level 1 valuation cannot be used.

However, Ordeal does have another debt issue that is publicly traded. Leslie can use the price for the publicly traded debt securities as the basis for estimating the fair value of the debt securities that it holds. Leslie may need to adjust the price to take into account any difference in the characteristics of the private versus public debt, but the resulting fair value will be a reasonable estimate.

Level 3—Unobservable Values

If the fair value of an asset (or liability) cannot be observed, either directly (level 1) or indirectly (level 2), what then? Level 3 identifies types of "unobservable inputs" that should be used to estimate the fair value. The term "unobservable" is rather unfortunate, because if it cannot be observed, how can it be measured? However, the real point is that other measures can be used that are based on how potential buyers would determine what price to pay if they were to buy it.

For example, suppose Leslie Corp. owns some suburban land adjacent to its manufacturing plant. The company reports the land by the fair-value method as an investment property. Every piece of real estate is unique; the value of Leslie Corporation's land is estimated on the basis of several factors, such as:

- Property valuations in the broader region;
- Accessibility to highways and rail lines;
- Access to municipal services, such as water and sewage;
- Zoning restrictions;
- The probability of getting zoning changes to permit higher-value uses; and
- Interest rates.

Although the land could be valued on its basis as a stand-alone piece of real estate, that probably is not its highest and best use. The land most likely is more valuable to Leslie Corp. than it would be to most other users because it is adjacent to Leslie's current facilities. Even if Leslie went out of business, the combination of the vacant land and Leslie's currently used land could make the entire site especially valuable to another user or to a developer.

Obviously, fair values determined by level 3 methods will have less *faithful representation* than fair values determined on the basis of levels 1 or 2. But if levels 1 and 2 cannot be used, level 3 estimates will be more *relevant* to the decision needs of users than historical cost; this is an application of qualitative criteria in accounting measurement. Since level 3 is more subjective, a reconciliation of the beginning and ending balance is required for items measured using level 3. This allows a user to see if changes are due to items going in and out of level 3 or due to estimates.

The Crucial Importance of Estimates

Accounting practice requires seemingly endless estimates. Virtually every item on the SFP contains estimates, and which flow through to the SCI, affecting net income and comprehensive income. They are required because, by definition, every asset or liability involves future benefit or future sacrifice—otherwise, they could not be reported on the SFP.

Perhaps the most tenuous of all estimates are those made for possible future liabilities. Pension costs are an outstanding example; those costs will not be realized until many years in the future but they must be estimated in the current period. Some future liabilities have an even greater level of approximation, such as estimates for future cleanup or environmental remediation costs. Others include potential liabilities under patent or licence litigation.

The reason we stress the importance of estimates is that fairly minor changes of estimates can trigger significant changes in earnings. Many academic research papers have established that companies about to go public tend to adjust their accruals in the immediately preceding period to "enhance" their apparent earnings potential. Indeed, some executives have been accused of intentionally manipulating earnings through adjustments in "reserves" often referred to as "cookie jars"—anticipated future costs—that shifted profits from one period to another.

CONCEPT REVIEW

1. What is the difference between an entry value and an exit value?
2. Determining fair values usually requires several estimates. What qualitative criteria underlie accounting standards' requirement for estimated fair values in certain situations rather than historical cost, which requires no estimation?
3. What are the three levels of fair-value measurement?
4. What is meant by *highest and best use*?

ETHICAL PROFESSIONAL JUDGEMENT—PART 2

The Problem of Earnings Targets

The managers of public companies are under strong pressure to achieve *earnings expectations* or **earnings targets**. There are two sources of earnings targets: (1) the company's own projected earnings for the current fiscal period and (2) financial analysts' independent projections. When numerous financial analysts are following a company, the average of analysts' predictions is often cited in the financial news as the target for management to achieve. Stock markets can react quite violently to "missed" targets, wherein the company's reported earnings fall below expectations. The reaction is particularly adverse when management is faced with the possibility of missing its own publicly announced earnings target.

Faced with this pressure to achieve targets, management is often tempted to use relatively small "adjustments," which can fall into two categories: (1) changes in measurement and (2) adjustments to reserves.

Measurement Variability

Measurement is a significant issue for those financial statement elements that are measured at fair value. Significant conflict can arise between the various qualitative criteria unless the basis of measurement is quite clear. Some fair values are reasonably obtainable, such as those at the first level of the fair-value hierarchy. Others, however, are much more subjective.

For example, as we will discuss in Chapter 9, management may choose to use the fair-value method for qualifying land and buildings (investment property), which requires annual revaluations. There are various ways of estimating the fair value of land and buildings. If appraisals are used for land and buildings, different appraisers will make different estimates of fair value. Management may be tempted to use the estimate that helps the company achieve its earnings target. Valuations should be undertaken to enhance users' decisions but not to influence them one way or the other. Unhappily, maintaining objectivity in such situations is easier said than done.

Management must be alert to the possibility of introducing bias into fair-value measurements, either intentionally or subconsciously. When these measurements pertain to major assets or classes of assets, rather small variations in estimate can have a significant impact on net income when fair-value changes are recognized in earnings, as they usually are.

Reserves Variability

What are **reserves**? IFRS uses the term *reserves* only in reference to items in equity, such as "reserve for plant expansion."

In common practice, however, the term is often used for estimated liabilities that appear on the company's financial statements and that underlie reported expenses. At the simpler end, they include allowances such as the bad debt allowance, the estimated warranty liability, or an allowance for inventory obsolescence.[6]

At the more complex end of the range are such items as the estimated receivable asset for tax loss carryforwards and the estimated liability for asset restoration costs. Major companies have many such provisions in their balance sheets; a fairly modest adjustment can have a significant impact on reported earnings.

In the Introduction to this chapter, we cited the charges faced by former executives of Nortel Networks Corp. The allegation was that management used "reserves" to manipulate profits.[7] Estimates are always subject to debate and different interpretations. There is always more than one feasible or justifiable number for an estimate. The issue is: Which came first, the estimate or the profit goal? Even then, it is not so simple. In weak economic times, estimates are likely to reflect a pessimistic view, while the reverse is true in boom times. Thus, the influence of current events clearly affects estimates.

ETHICAL ISSUES

Exercising Professional Judgement

Accountants can find themselves in great difficulty if they carry out the demands of management to adjust earnings to match predictions. Indeed, prosecutors prosecute the accountants first, hoping they then will testify against their bosses. An ethical accountant will resist "orders" to manipulate estimates to achieve a desired result. Many chief accountants have, indeed, shown such strength and have emerged with their reputations intact (and not in jail).

Professional judgement permeates the work of a professional accountant and requires the ability to build accounting measurements that take into account:

- The objectives of financial reporting in each particular situation;
- The facts of the business environment and operations; and
- The organization's reporting constraints (if any).

The result of properly applied ethical professional judgement is fair financial information. Failure of ethical professional judgement may result in false or misleading information. Think about the steps required to apply professional judgement in an ethical fashion. The building blocks for accounting choice were illustrated in Exhibit 2-1.

1. The first judgement, upon which all else is built, is to determine the objectives of financial reporting for the specific reporting entity. There are usually multiple objectives, and the objectives must be ethically and appropriately prioritized to be able to resolve conflicts between them when decisions about specific accounting policies or estimates must be made. To develop the financial reporting objectives, we must first consider important facts and constraints:

---

6. Nortel Networks reversed an allowance for inventory obsolescence by $25.5 million, thereby creating a gain, to offset another loss item. However, the company argued that $25.5 million was immaterial in the context of the $1 billion reserve for obsolete inventory. See "Accounting Change Not a Material Sum, Nortel Trial Hears," The Globe and Mail, 12 April 2012, p. B3.

7. For example, see "Use of Accounting Reserves Out in Open, Defence Suggests," The Globe and Mail, 29 March 2012, p. B3.

a. The facts of the organization's operations and its economic environment must be determined to understand just what is to be measured. For example: Who are the users of the entity's financial statements? Is the entity bound by restrictive covenants or other contractual requirements? Is compensation based on accounting measures, such as net income?

b. The reporting constraints must be determined. Is the reporting enterprise a publicly accountable enterprise, bound by the reporting constraints of the securities commissions or regulators? Is it a private company that uses the financial statements only for its owner(s) and for income tax purposes? Is an audit required? If an audit is required (or desired by management), is a "clean" audit opinion necessarily needed? Can the enterprise report on the basis of disclosed (or tailored) accounting policies rather than IFRS or ASPE?

2. The underlying assumptions must be tested. In preparing the financial statements for the vast majority of Canadian business organizations, the normal underlying assumptions of continuity, nominal dollar financial capital maintenance, proprietary approach, and so forth are quite valid. But they cannot be taken for granted, and their appropriateness in the specific reporting situation must be evaluated.

3. Once the objectives have been discerned and prioritized, the facts and constraints determined, and the underlying assumptions evaluated, only then should the measurement choices or accounting policies be considered.

4. The measurement method must be consistent with the objectives, facts, and constraints. The measurement choices are further tempered by the qualitative criteria, especially in the realm of recognition. When should revenues be recognized? When should costs incurred or committed be recognized? When costs are recognized, should they be recognized as assets or as expenses? If they are recognized as assets, when should they be transferred to expense? There are many ethical decisions to be made. Faithful representation may conflict with relevance, and both verifiability and understandability come into play.

5. The measurement and recognition criteria lead to the financial statement elements, which then are classified in a manner appropriate to the industry and consistent with the operational activities of the enterprise. The result is, finally, the financial statements themselves. To be appropriate for the specific reporting situation, the final financial statements must satisfy the specific reporting objectives at the foundation of the whole pyramid.

6. The ethical requirements are met if the financial statements are a fair representation of the underlying business activity.

Looking Forward

An Exposure Draft was issued by the IASB in May 2015 for the Conceptual Framework. It addresses the areas of measurement, financial performance including the use of OCI, presentation and disclosure, derecognition, and the reporting entity.

One of the areas addressed in the Exposure Draft was the role of prudence (conservatism). Revisions to the conceptual framework in 2010 removed the term *prudence* as a qualitative characteristic; it was replaced with *neutrality*. The Exposure Draft proposes to reintroduce the term *prudence* as one aspect of the characteristics in providing useful information. Prudence supports neutrality, in that assets and income are not overstated and expenses not understated.

CONCEPT REVIEW

1. List three different possible measurement bases for inventory.
2. How is the concept of matching usually applied to period costs?
3. Does full disclosure mean that all available information is provided in the disclosure notes?

Accounting Standards for Private Enterprises

Objectives and Qualitative Characteristics

The ASPE conceptual framework is very similar to that of IFRS. Some of the wording is different, and the positioning of the various qualitative characteristics differs, but overall there is no significant difference.

Financial statement objectives are "to communicate information that is useful to investors, creditors and other users" concerning the economic resources of an entity, and changes in those resources during the reporting period. A related objective also is to assess the entity's economic performance.

ASPE's qualitative characteristics are shown in Exhibit 2-6. You will observe that while the arrangement (and some of the wording) is different from that of IFRS, the substance is the same. The overall constraints of materiality and cost/benefit also apply within the ASPE framework.

EXHIBIT 2-6	
ASPE QUALITATIVE CHARACTERISTICS	
Principal Qualitative Characteristics	**Pervasive Constraints**
Understandability	Cost/benefit
Relevance	Materiality
Predictive value and feedback value	
Timeliness	
Reliability	
Representational faithfulness	
Verifiability	
Neutrality	
Conservatism	
Comparability	

Source: *CPA Canada Handbook, Part II*, Section 1000, © Chartered Professional Accountants of Canada, 2015.

The one difference between the frameworks of ASPE and IFRS is that ASPE includes the characteristic of conservatism as one component of reliability. The traditional understanding of conservatism is that when there is measurement uncertainty, amounts should be recorded that tend to lower earnings and/or net assets. However, ASPE discourages this traditional conservatism. Indeed, ASPE interprets conservatism as an avoidance of optimistic amounts rather than favouring a downward bias:

When uncertainty exists, estimates of a conservative nature attempt to ensure that assets, revenues and gains are not overstated and, conversely, that liabilities, expenses and losses are not understated. (¶1000.18d)

Financial Statement Elements

An explanation of the ASPE definitions of assets and liabilities is shown in Exhibit 2-7. The ASPE definitions are parallel to those of IFRS; although wording varies somewhat, there is no substantive difference. Similarly, the definition of equity is the same—equity is the excess (deficiency) of assets over (under) liabilities.

EXHIBIT 2-7
ASPE DEFINITIONS OF ASSETS AND LIABILITIES

Assets	Liabilities
a. An asset is a resource acquired as the result of past events;	a. A liability is a present obligation or responsibility to others that arises from past events;
b. The entity can control access to the benefits; and	b. The duty or responsibility obligates the entity and leaves it little or no discretion to avoid it; and
c. The asset contributes directly or indirectly to future benefits that result in net cash flows.	c. In the future, the entity will be required to transfer or use assets, provide services or yield other economic benefits, at a specified or determinable date, on occurrence of a specified event, or on demand.

Regarding liabilities, ASPE makes it clear that while an obligation must arise from past events, the obligation should be reported as a liability whether or not it is legally enforceable. A constructive or equitable obligation (e.g., environmental remediation not specifically legally required) is a liability, even if it may not be legally enforceable. "An equitable obligation is a duty based on ethical or moral considerations" (¶1000.30).

On the income statement (not SCI, since there is no "other comprehensive income" in ASPE) a definition difference is that ASPE draws a distinction between (1) revenues and expenses, which arise from the normal business activities of the entity and (2) gains and losses, defined as arising from peripheral or incidental transactions and events. IFRS makes no such distinction—income is income, whether called revenue or a gain and whether from normal operations or from unusual transactions or activities.

Measurement

Unlike IFRS, ASPE specifically cites historical cost as the primary basis of measurement. "Other bases" are listed as replacement cost (i.e., current cost in IFRS), realizable value, and present value. Curiously, fair value is not mentioned as a basis. However, the "financial instruments" section of ASPE is only partially harmonized with IFRS and requires some degree of fair-value measurement. We will examine those specific differences later in the book.

Overall, the measurement methods in ASPE are basically the same as those in IFRS, although they are not necessarily applied the same way. As we proceed through the following chapters, we will point out specific differences between IFRS and ASPE concerning measurement requirements.

ASPE permits only nominal dollar capital maintenance. Neither constant dollar nor productive capacity are acceptable capital maintenance approaches for Canadian private enterprises using ASPE.

Since the use of fair value is limited in ASPE, the standards do not include a standard for fair-value measurement or the fair value hierarchy.

RELEVANT STANDARDS

CPA Canada Handbook, Part I (IFRS):

- IASB, *Conceptual Framework for Financial Reporting*
- IFRS 13, *Fair Value Measurement*

CPA Canada Handbook, Part II (ASPE):

- Section 1000, *Financial Statement Concepts*

SUMMARY OF KEY POINTS

1. Accounting principles consist of three different sets of concepts: (1) underlying assumptions, (2) qualitative criteria, and (3) measurement methods.

2. *Underlying assumptions* include the basic postulates that make accounting measurements possible (such as *time period*, *separate entity*, and *unit of measure*), as well as underlying measurement assumptions that usually, but not always, are true in a given reporting situation. These measurement assumptions include *proprietary approach*, *continuity*, and *nominal dollar financial capital maintenance*.

3. There are two feasible alternatives to nominal dollar financial capital maintenance. One is constant dollar financial capital maintenance, in which the purchasing power of the capital investment is maintained rather than simply the nominal number of dollars invested. The other is physical (or productive) capital maintenance, in which sufficient capital is maintained to achieve the same level of productivity.

4. *Qualitative criteria* are the criteria used in conjunction with an enterprise's financial reporting objectives to determine the most appropriate measurement methods to use in that particular reporting situation.

5. A fundamental qualitative criterion is that of *relevance*; relevance should be determined with reference to the users of the financial statements and the resulting financial reporting objectives. Relevance is enhanced if information is timely and has both predictive and confirmatory (i.e., feedback) value.

6. A second fundamental qualitative criterion is *faithful representation*, which means that an accounting measurement should be a sufficiently accurate measure of the reality of whatever it is measuring and should reflect economic substance. The attributes of faithful representation include *completeness*, *neutrality*, and *freedom from material error*.

7. *Neutrality* means that information is not biased in a way that would influence users' decisions in a particular direction. It does *not* mean that the information has no impact on users' decisions. For example, *conservatism* may not be used as a justification for overstating liabilities or understating assets. Accounting information should be unbiased.

8. Enhancing qualities are those that improve the quality of accounting information and/or its usefulness. Enhancing qualities include *comparability*, *verifiability*, *timeliness*, and *understandability*.

9.   Users are presumed to have a reasonable knowledge of financial reporting to interpret or understand accounting information. Financial statements are not prepared for naive or unsophisticated users.

10. *Materiality* and *cost* are *pervasive constraints* that underlie all accounting information. Information will be reported if it is *material*, meaning that the information has the capacity to influence users' decisions. The constraint of *cost* indicates that the cost of preparing accounting information should not outweigh its benefit to users.

11. There are tradeoffs among the enhancing qualitative characteristics. For example, verifiability of reported collectible accounts receivable may be improved by waiting to find out how many accounts seem uncollectible, but timeliness would be diminished because the information would be delayed.

12. The *elements of financial statements* are the six types of accounts that appear on the statement of financial position and the statement of other comprehensive income: assets, liabilities, owners' equity, income, expenses (and losses), and other comprehensive income.

13. The IFRS asset and liability definitions require (1) a *future* benefit or sacrifice and (2) a reliably measurable cost, value, or settlement amount.

14. Initial accounting *recognition* occurs when the effects or results of a transaction or event are first measured and assigned to an account or *element*. To be recognized, or recorded, an item must meet the element definition, be measurable, and be probable.

15. *Recognition* is the process of measuring and including an item or event in the financial statements. *Realization* is the process of converting an asset, liability, or commitment into a cash flow.

16. *Realization* occurs when a cash flow occurs. Realization often occurs after recognition but can never occur prior to recognition because the cash flow forces recognition if it has not occurred previously.

17. The accrual concept relates to the recognition of receivables when the right to receive cash arises and to the recognition of liabilities when the obligation is created. Accrual does not refer to subsequent matching and interperiod allocations.

18. *Measurement* is the process by which numbers are attached to events and items that are reported in the financial statements.

19. *Measurement methods* are the various ways that the results of transactions and events can be reported in the financial statements. Measurement conventions include historical cost, the revenue recognition convention, expense recognition, and full disclosure. Measurement methods also encompass the process of earnings measurement.

20. Accounting is full of choices. Financial statements are constructed from the financial statement elements that have been recognized using measurement methods that optimize the qualitative characteristics and that are based on the appropriate underlying assumptions. The organization's reporting constraints and the facts of its business and environment all impact on the choice of accounting policy. The result is information that best satisfies the objectives of financial reporting in any given situation. This series of related decisions constitutes *ethical professional judgement in accounting*.

Key Terms

accruals

asset

capital maintenance

commitment

comparability

completeness

confirmatory value

consideration

consistency

constant dollar capital maintenance

continuity assumption

cost/benefit effectiveness

current cost

deferrals

earnings targets	owners' equity
elements	physical capital maintenance
entity-specific assumptions	predictive value
ethical professional judgement	present value
executory contract	professional judgement
expenses	proprietary concept
fair value	purchasing power parity
faithful representation	qualitative characteristics
feedback value	realizable value
freedom from material error	realization
gains	recognition
going-concern assumption	relevance
highest and best use	reserves
historical cost convention	revenue
income	separate-entity assumption
liability	settlement value
losses	substance over form
matching	timeliness
materiality	time-period assumption
measurement	underlying assumptions
measurement methods	understandability
net asset principle of revenue/expense recognition	uniformity
net assets	unit-of-measure assumption
neutrality	universal assumptions
nominal dollars	verifiability
orderly transaction	
other comprehensive income	

CASE 2-1

SYMPOSIUM

You have recently being asked to participate in a symposium at an accounting conference. One of the sessions at the conference is discussing concerns with the conceptual framework. You have been provided with a number of questions ahead of time so that you can be prepared for the debate.

1. The first discussion topic relates to prudence. Prudence (conservatism) was dropped from the conceptual framework when it was amended in 2010. Are we not still conservative in accounting policies? Provide some specific examples. The Exposure Draft recommends reintroduction of the term *prudence*, stating that it supports neutrality. The new definition of *prudence* would be the concern that assets and income not be overstated and expenses not beunderstated. Do you agree?

2. The second discussion topic relates to the question of how to measure assets and liabilities. What are the pros and cons of the use of historical costs compared to current values? Which method is more relevant for the statement of financial position compared to the income statement for users? Are certain types of assets more suited to the use of current values?

3. The final discussion topic relates to other comprehensive income (OCI) and comprehensive income. What is a concern with OCI and comprehensive income? Do you think OCI is useful? If so, in which situations?

Required:

In preparation for the symposium prepare notes to address the questions that might be asked concerning the conceptual framework.

CASE 2-2

AEROTRAVEL INC.

James Ehnes has recently completed his second year of accounting studies. He has just been hired as a summer intern at the auditing firm of Hetu & Fauré. He feels fortunate to have landed an internship in such a prestigious firm. His supervisor, Venus Yang, has handed him a lengthy description of the operations of AeroTravel Inc. (ATI) and has asked James to prepare a report in which he outlines the significant accounting policies that arise in this company. She also wants James's recommendations on how the company should account for the revenues and expenses relating to ATI's provision of services, as well as the balance sheet ramifications of his recommendations.

James knows that the purpose of this exercise is to test his understanding of the complex relationships underlying revenue and expense recognition. After reading through the description several times, he makes the following notes:

- ATI is a public company that operates loyalty reward plans for a wide range of clients involved in the travel business, including airlines, hotels, and package tour operators. It sells *loyalty units* to the clients, who, in turn, reward their customers or members with those loyalty units when they buy the clients' services or products. Clients' customers and members can then acquire products or services through ATI either for free or at a reduced price by using their loyalty points.

- ATI derives its cash inflows by selling loyalty units in bulk to each client. Each client then issues the points to the members of the client's loyalty plan. ATI receives payment directly from client companies for the loyalty units sold to the clients for their members.

- Loyalty plan members redeem loyalty units through ATI for rewards of travel, merchandise, or other services. ATI buys the airline seats, merchandise, or services from the vendor to provide the tangible rewards to members. For example, if a member of a client airline's loyalty plan books reward travel, ATI must buy the seat from the airline.

- The largest client is Trans-National Airways, which accounts for over 60% of ATI's business.

- Every year, Trans-National is required by contract to buy a pre-established quantity of AeroTravel Miles from ATI.

- Conversely, every year ATI is required by the same contract to buy a minimum quantity of reward travel seats on Trans-National and its affiliates.

- The estimated redemption value of loyalty units outstanding (i.e., those sold by ATI to its clients but not yet redeemed) are stated as deferred revenue on ATI's year-end SFP. Not all loyalty units are redeemed. ATI has not estimated the amount that will not be redeemed.

- When the company revises its estimated redemption rate at the end of a fiscal year, the company restates that year-end's balance of deferred revenue.

- In limited circumstances, ATI sells loyalty units directly to client plan members (rather than through the client company), such as to client plan members who wish to top up their point balance just enough to claim a desired reward.
- AIT also derives fees from client companies for direct marketing, for sales promotion, and for designing, developing, and administering loyalty programs for both existing and new client companies.

Required:

Ms. Yang wants the report on her desk first thing tomorrow morning. Assume you are James Ehnes. Prepare the report.

CASE 2-3

DUBOIS LTD.

Dubois Ltd. is a Vancouver-based private company established 30 years ago. Until very recently, all 16 of the shareholders have been relatives of the founder, Blanche Dubois. The company has been profitable in most years. In recent years, however, it has become obvious that the company needed a capital infusion to remain competitive in the face of increased international competition; Dubois required substantial investment in more modern facilities and processes.

To obtain the needed funds, the Dubois board of directors sought private investment from nonfamily sources. After negotiating with several potential investors, the board approved an investment by The Mangle Group, a private equity investment cooperative. After issuing the new shares to Mangle, the Dubois family members hold 65% of the outstanding common shares, with Mangle holding the remaining 35%.

The company holds a substantial line of credit with the Canadian subsidiary of a London-based international bank. The credit line is secured by a lien on all of the Dubois assets, based on 75% of accounts receivable, 60% of inventory, and 50% of buildings and equipment. The bank has been willing to maintain the credit line as long as the collateral is adequate and as long as Dubois is able to liquidate (i.e., fully pay off) the credit line at least once each calendar year.

In past years, the external auditor has given Dubois a qualified audit opinion, because the company did not use a systematic depreciation method for its buildings. Instead, the company's policy was to obtain an independent assessment of its buildings. If the assessment was less than the buildings' book value, Dubois would record an "impairment" charge. The company's chief financial officer, Colleen Bissau, argues that the value of the building is much more relevant to the bank than an arbitrary "depreciated book value," and thus Dubois's method is more appropriate under the circumstances.

As a condition of its investment, The Mangle Group insists that Dubois obtain a "clean" (unqualified) audit opinion in the future so that Dubois's financial statements are more comparable with those of other companies in which Mangle has invested.

Following the Mangle investment, Dubois continues to be a private company. Dubois Ltd. reports on the basis of ASPE.

You have been approached by Ms. Bissau to advise the company's board of directors on how Dubois Ltd.'s financial reporting objectives and criteria for measurement methods might have changed from past years following the new equity investment, and how they might change in the future if the company issues shares to the public.

Required:

Prepare the report for Ms. Bissau.

TECHNICAL REVIEW

■ connect

TR2-1 Underlying Assumptions:

Indicate whether each of the following statements is true or false:

1. The continuity assumption states that a business entity will last long enough for its assets to be used up and its liabilities settled.

2. The entity basis of reporting is the same as consolidated reporting, wherein all resources under the control of the shareholders of the parent company are combined into financial statements for the entire economic entity.

3. Under the proprietary assumption, financial statements are prepared from the point of view of the enterprise's owners.

4. The unit-of-measure assumption states that it is meaningful to express the affairs of an enterprise in currency units.

5. Because of the continuity assumption, it is impossible to prepare meaningful financial statements for a bankrupt company.

■ connect

TR2-2 Underlying Assumptions:

Indicate whether each of the following statements is true or false:

1. Nominal dollar capital maintenance assumes that earnings are distributable once the dollar level of investment has been maintained.

2. Nominal dollar financial capital maintenance is the only feasible basis for measuring earnings for a modern diversified business corporation.

3. The separate-entity assumption means that there must be no financial transactions between the business entity and its owners, except for the payment of dividends.

4. The continuity assumption means that it is feasible to prepare corporate financial statements at any point over the continuity of time.

5. The time-period assumption means that it is feasible to prepare meaningful annual financial statements, even though the entity still has many unfulfilled transactions outstanding.

■ connect

TR2-3 Qualitative Characteristics:

Explain how the fundamental qualitative characteristics apply in each of the following situations:

1. A company acquires land in exchange for shares, but the shares are lightly traded and cannot be easily valued. The most recent trades have fluctuated widely. The company proposes to use its own internal expert's appraisal for the land.

2. A significant economic downturn occurs just as a company is preparing to issue its financial statements, three months after year-end. Because of the downturn, the collectibility of its quite substantial accounts receivable is in doubt. The company's CFO proposes that the company delay the issuance of the financial statements for another two or three months, until the collectibility of the accounts becomes clearer.

3. The CEO of a major biotechnology company wishes to show the company's important internally generated assets on the balance sheet. She is concerned that financial statement users are deprived of relevant information when they assess the earnings potential of the firm. She proposes that the assets be measured and reported by computing the discounted future cash flows that will occur from their use.

4. A company uses many assets that were acquired through long-term rental contracts. The easiest way to measure the cost is by treating the monthly rent as an expense. However, the company's auditor insists that the leases be shown on the balance sheet as though the assets had been bought and a liability taken on, despite the significant number of estimates that will be necessary to report it that way.

connect

TR2-4 Concepts Identification:

In the blanks provided to the left below, enter the letters of the underlying assumption, measurement method, qualitative criteria, or constraint most closely associated with the statements. Some letters may be used more than once and some may not be used at all.

A. Separate-entity assumption	G. Matching
B. Continuity assumption	H. Historical cost
C. Materiality	I. Unit-of-measure assumption
D. Time-period assumption	J. Faithful representation
E. Cost/benefit	K. Verifiability
F. Revenue recognition	L. Full disclosure

_____ 1. Any accounting method is acceptable for small items that will not change users' decisions.

_____ 2. Assumes that all financial statement elements can be meaningfully described in dollar terms.

_____ 3. Long-term assets that increase in value are not normally written up in the financial statements.

_____ 4. Assets and earnings should be neither understated nor overstated.

_____ 5. The estimated future cost of fulfilling warranties that may not arise until two years into the future are accrued in the period of the sale.

____   6.   It is not necessary to use a complex accounting method for minor items that are highly unlikely to improve the decisions of financial statement users.

____   7.   It must be possible to numerically confirm all amounts reported in the body of the financial statements.

____   8.   The various costs associated with a revenue transaction may be deferred until the revenue is earned.

____   9.   The personal transactions of owners should be kept separate from transactions of the business.

____   10.   Significant recognized and many nonrecognized items should be fully described in the notes to the financial statements.

____   11.   Enables historical cost, rather than liquidation values, to be used.

____   12.   Enables measurement of the income and financial position of entities at regular intervals.

connect

TR2-5 Capital Maintenance:

Oundjian Corporation recently sold inventory for $140,000. The goods had originally cost $94,000. Inflation during the period was 5%. The goods could be replaced from their long-time supplier for $115,000. For simplicity, assume that there are no other costs of doing business.

Required:

1.   Calculate a measure of accounting income, consistent with:
   a.   Nominal dollar financial capital maintenance
   b.   Constant dollar financial capital maintenance
   c.   Physical capital maintenance, in nominal dollars

2.   Assume in each case in requirement 1 that the company collected revenue in cash and paid out 100% of net income in dividends to owners. Calculate the remaining cash balance. Explain the significance of the remaining cash flow in each case.

3.   If the company were planning to replace the inventory, which capital maintenance concept allows it to keep enough money to accomplish this with no further investment or borrowing?

4.   Which capital maintenance concept is dominant in Canada? Which one(s) is (are) acceptable under IFRS?

connect

TR2-6 Capital Maintenance:

At the beginning of 20X5, its first year of business, Marsalis Ltd. invested $64,000 in inventory and $300,000 in equipment. Total sales were $160,000. Of the initial inventory purchases, $25,000 remained in inventory at the end of the period. Marsalis depreciated the equipment by 20% straight-line, taking a full year's depreciation in 20X5.

The replacement cost of the inventory, both that sold and that remaining in year-end inventory, had decreased by 10% by the end of the year. The replacement cost of the equipment, however, had increased by 3% over the year.

Required:

Determine the net income (using only the costs indicated above), under each of the following assumptions:

1. Nominal dollar capital maintenance
2. Physical capital maintenance

TR2-7 Measurement Methods:

Which measurement method would be most appropriate for the following items: historical cost, fair value, lower of cost and net realizable value, net realizable value, or present value?

1. Inventory
2. Shares in a public company
3. Land
4. Lease (finance/capital lease)
5. Long-term receivable

Required:

Identify the most appropriate measurement method for each item.

TR2-8 Measurement Methods:

Which measurement method would be most appropriate for the following items: historical cost, fair value, lower of cost and net realizable value, net realizable value, or present value?

1. Inventory
2. Derivative
3. Building
4. Bond
5. Note receivable (2 years)

Required:

Identify the most appropriate measurement method for each item.

TR2-9 Fair-Value Measurement:

Identify the level in the hierarchy that would be most appropriate for measuring the following items using the fair-value hierarchy:

	Level 1	Level 2	Level 3
1. Shares in a public company	____	____	____
2. Land	____	____	____
3. Patent	____	____	____
4. Beef cattle	____	____	____
5. Unique machinery	____	____	____

Required:

Identify the most appropriate value of the hierarchy to measure each item.

 connect

TR2-10 Fair-Value Measurement:

Identify the level in the hierarchy that would be most appropriate for measuring the following items using the fair value hierarchy:

	Level 1	Level 2	Level 3
1. Shares in a private company	____	____	____
2. Building	____	____	____
3. Patent	____	____	____
4. Pigs (hogs)	____	____	____
5. Shares in public company	____	____	____

Required:

Identify the most appropriate value of the hierarchy to measure each item.

ASSIGNMENTS

★ A2-1 Relevance versus Faithful Representation:

Tannino Ltd. is a private investment company that manages investments for a group of about 30 wealthy individuals. The company is owned and managed by two experienced investment managers, each of whom owns

50% of the shares. The company merges all of its clients' money into a single investment fund. At the end of each period, the investors' investment accounts are increased or decreased by the percentage gain or loss for the entire investment fund.

A majority of the investments are in publicly traded companies, but a significant portion are invested in real estate (land and buildings) and in private companies as (quite speculative) venture capital. The company is preparing its financial statements for its first fiscal year ended 31 December 20X4. The two owner-managers are discussing the proper method of reporting the company's investment portfolio. On the one hand, they wish to present the most useful and relevant information to their investors, as well as to the bank that provides some debt financing. On the other hand, they are concerned about the faithful representation of the reported asset values for various parts of the investment portfolio.

Required:

Discuss the tradeoff between relevance and faithful representation for reporting the asset value of each of these various types of investments: (1) publicly traded securities, (2) real estate, and (3) venture capital in start-up businesses. Your discussion must be relevant to Tannino's specific situation.

★ A2-2 Relevance and Faithful Representation:

Accounting measurements are enhanced by the presence of the qualities of predictive value, feedback value, comparability, verifiability, timeliness, freedom from bias, and faithful representation. For each of the following, indicate the quality demonstrated:

1. The value assigned to equipment is checked by referring to the original invoice.

2. Predictions concerning this year's income, issued 12 months ago, are compared with the actual results to assess the accuracy of the prediction.

3. Past trends are used to forecast this year's sales.

4. An outside expert is retained to assess the value of the recorded amounts for tangible and intangible capital assets.

5. Adjustments are made to financial statements that both increase and decrease net income despite the manager's preference to report lower net income.

6. Financial statements are issued four weeks after the year-end, even though this requires the use of estimates for some elements.

7. Preferred shares that have to be repaid on a given date are classified as a liability despite their legal status as equity.

8. The company releases estimates of operating results for the coming year, based on its budgets.

9. Cash received in advance of work done is recorded as a liability, unearned revenue.

10. Lawyers provide an estimate of the company's potential liability for product defects.

★ A2-3 Questions on Principles:

For each of the following situations, indicate whether you agree or disagree with the practice described, list *one* accounting concept/assumption/qualitative criteria/measurement method that is related to the situation (either followed or violated), and indicate how it is related:

1. Inventory that the company paid $450 for is carried on the balance sheet at $620 because it can be easily sold for $620.

2. The Book Printer Ltd. has an operating cycle of three years. It takes three years to have a book written, published, and marketed. The company, therefore, produces financial statements every three years.

3. WLZ Co. must estimate and record a warranty liability and has obtained three estimates—one for $75,000, one for $92,000, and one for $106,000. The company records $75,000.

4. Cambria Corporation has purchased a rare manuscript wanted by the major shareholder, whose passion is antiquities. The manuscript is kept at the shareholder's house for his sole use but is carried on the company's books as a long-term investment.

5. Elocom Ltd. has an account receivable *from* Maddox Ltd. for $40,000, and an account payable *to* Maddox Ltd. for $37,000. Elocom shows a net account receivable of $3,000, and no accounts payable, on its balance sheet.

6. Darlington Designs Ltd. has not fixed a $5,000 error in inventory accounting because it would have a trivial effect on cost of goods sold and net income.

A2-4 Questions on Principles:

If the following statements are true, write "True" after the statement. However, most are false. For a false statement, write "False," and *briefly* indicate why the statement is false.

1. Full disclosure involves telling financial statement users everything about the company's transactions.
2. Matching means that revenue is matched to the time period in which the enterprise does the work.
3. The continuity assumption means that a manufacturing company will stay in business long enough to use or sell its inventory.
4. The proprietary approach is the reason that dividends declared are classified on the retained earnings statement rather than on the income statement.
5. A liability is something owed by a company.
6. Relevance suffers when market values are included in the financial statements.
7. To preserve comparability, accounting policies may never be changed.
8. Human capital is not recorded because of the nominal dollar capital assumption.
9. Materiality is based only on the relative size of the item.

A2-5 Application of Principles:

The following list of statements poses conceptual issues:

a. The business entity is considered separate and apart from its owners for accounting purposes.
b. A transaction is always recorded in such a way as to reflect its legal form.
c. It is permissible for a company to use straight-line depreciation, even though the rest of the industry uses declining-balance, because the company believes straight-line better reflects the pattern of benefits received from these assets.
d. All details of transactions must be disclosed in the notes to the financial statements.
e. The lower-of-cost-and-net realizable value method must be used in valuing inventories.
f. The cost principle relates only to the income statement.
g. Revenue should be recognized only when cash is received.
h. Accruals and deferrals are necessary because of the separate-entity assumption.
i. Revenue should be recognized as late as possible and expenses as early as possible.

Required:

1. Indicate whether each statement is correct or incorrect.
2. Identify the principle(s) posited.
3. Provide a brief discussion of its (their) implications.

 A2-6 Realization versus Recognition:

For each of the following transactions, indicate the point at which (1) the initial transaction is recognized and (2) the financial statement element is realized:

1. Inventory is purchased on credit on 1 August and is received on 14 August. It is paid for on 12 September.
2. A customer buys a product on credit on 13 November and takes immediate delivery, promising to pay on 1 February of the following year.
3. Expected warranty claims on products sold are accrued as the sales are made. Warranty claims are made at the end of the subsequent fiscal year. A cash payment is made to the customer at the beginning of the year following the claim.
4. A customer orders a custom-built machine and pays when the order is placed on 20 February. The machine is delivered on 10 March.
5. The company uses a substantial amount of electricity. The electric utility issues bimonthly bills (i.e., one every two months) three weeks following the two-month usage period.
6. A sale on credit is completed on 20 January; the product is delivered on 1 February. Payment is received on 1 March.

 A2-7 Recognition of Elements:

In each of the following situations, identify the element or elements, if any, that would appear in financial statements. If no element is recognized, give the reason.

1. Unpaid gas bill.
2. A patent on a new invention that the market is unknown.
3. Training courses taken by employees at the company's expense.
4. Authorized but unissued common shares of a company that will likely be issued for cash next year.
5. A partially completed consulting project for a client.
6. The expenses of a lawsuit against the company.
7. Customer goodwill as indicated by a high percentage of satisfied return customers
8. A reputation for high-quality products.
9. Cash received from a customer for work to be done next year.
10. A Mercedes-Benz limousine leased for the company CEO.

connect

 A2-8 Elements of Financial Statements:

Financial statement elements have specific definitions. To the right, some important aspects of the definitions are listed. Match the aspects with the elements by entering appropriate letters in the blanks. More than one letter can be placed in a blank.

Element of Financial Statement	Important Aspect of the Definition of the Element
A. Assets	_____ 1. Using up of assets or incurrence of liabilities
B. Liabilities	_____ 2. Probable future economic benefits
C. Owners' equity/net assets	_____ 3. Enhancement of assets or settlements of liabilities
D. Revenues obtained by an entity	_____ 4. Residual interest in assets after deducting liabilities
E. Expenses	_____ 5. Increases in net assets from peripheral or incidental activities
F. Gains	_____ 6. Changes in net assets from peripheral or incidental transactions of the entity
G. Losses	_____ 7. Future sacrifices arising from past transactions
H. None of the above	_____ 8. Results from the entity's ongoing major or central operation

 connect

★ A2-9 Questions on Principles:

For each of the following circumstances, give the letter item(s) indicating the accounting principle involved. Some letters may be used more than once, and some may not be used at all.

A. Continuity
B. Freedom from bias
C. Comparability
D. Cost/benefit effectiveness
E. Full disclosure
F. Historical cost
G. Relevance
H. Nominal dollar financial capital maintenance

I. Matching
J. Proprietary
K. Faithful representation
L. Revenue recognition
M. Separate entity
N. Time period
O. Unit of measure

1. Financial statements are prepared from the point of view of the owners.
2. A note describing the company's possible liability in a lawsuit is included with the financial statements, even though no formal liability exists at the balance sheet date.
3. Marketable securities are valued at market value.

4. The personal assets of partners are excluded from the partnership balance sheet, even though they are pledged as security for partnership loans.

5. A retail store uses estimates rather than a complete physical count of its inventory for purposes of preparing monthly financial statements.

6. Goodwill is recorded in the accounts only when it arises from the purchase of another entity.

7. An entity reports a $50 profit after buying a unit of inventory for $100 and selling it for $150, even though the cost to replace the unit has escalated to $112 due to inflation.

8. An advance deposit on a sale contract is reported as unearned revenue.

9. Accounting policies chosen for revenue recognition are the same as those of the entity's major competitors.

10. Capital assets are amortized over their useful lives.

★ A2-10 Identification of Accounting Principles:

In each of the following cases, indicate the principle that appears to have been violated:

Case A   For its factory equipment, Unrequited Love Inc. used accelerated depreciation in 20X2; straight-line in 20X3; and accelerated in 20X4.

Case B   Aaronist Ltd. sold a tract of land on credit by accepting a $55,000, two-year, non-interest-bearing note. The land account was credited (and notes receivable was debited) for $55,000. The going rate of interest was 10%.

Case C   JED Inc. always issues its annual financial report nine months after the end of the annual reporting period to ensure greater accuracy.

Case D   Idiomatic Inc. always recognizes its sales revenue when received in cash.

Case E   RBJ Corporation records interest income only on the payment dates.

Case F   Loran Co. includes among its financial statement elements an apartment building owned and operated by the owner of the company.

Case G   Adam Ltd.'s CEO refuses to permit the company to use notes or supplementary schedules in its financial reports because he believes that the financial statements are self-explanatory.

★ A2-11 Revenue Recognition:

Which of the following events would normally cause revenue recognition, assuming use of accrual accounting and transfer of title on delivery?

1. Collection of cash from a customer 30 days after the product is delivered.

2. Collection of cash from a customer 30 days before the product is delivered.

3. Delivery of a magazine as part of a prepaid 12-month subscription.

4. Inventory that cost $40,000 is known to have a replacement value of $67,000.

5. Collection of cash for a nonrefundable deposit.

6. Goods are delivered to a customer with an invoice price of $26,000; the customer is notoriously slow in paying.

A2-12 Recognition and Elements:

Indicate if each of the following items would be recognized in TelCan Ltd.'s financial statements for 20X3 and, if so, what elements would be recognized. For any items that would not be recognized, explain the reason for nonrecognition.

1. TelCan issued a purchase order to buy inventory early in the following year.
2. TelCan's share price has decreased from $50 to $45 on the stock exchange.
3. The month of December has passed, and tenants occupying space in TelCan's building have not yet paid the rent. TelCan's rental agent believes that payment is reasonably assured.
4. TelCan sold the right to use its international industrial trademark to a Taiwanese computer manufacturer for the next five years.
5. TelCan experienced decreases in the value of cash deposits held in U.S. dollars because of a stronger Canadian dollar.
6. TelCan invested in employee training costs to improve the company's future productivity.
7. TelCan's major competitor has liquidated and gone out of business. The company has purchased the competitor's customer list.
8. TelCan has a reasonably reliable estimate of the future cost of reaching a settlement on a pending patent infringement lawsuit.

 A2-13 Application of Principles:

The independent auditor of Fluidity Inc. found the following situations:

a. The company uses the straight-line method of measuring depreciation on manufacturing machinery, even though it knows that a method based on actual usage would provide better matching, more accurate income determination, and thus better information for financial statement users. However, the company uses the straight-line method because of the level of data needed to implement a usage method. The method is significantly cheaper to calculate and provides a stable net income.
b. For inventory valuation, Fluidity switched from FIFO to weighted-average cost and then back to FIFO for the same items during a five-year period.
c. Fluidity does not provide information about future contracts, called the "order backlog," in its financial statements. Such disclosure is quite common in the industry.
d. Fluidity follows a policy of depreciating plant and equipment on the straight-line basis over a period of time that is 50% longer than the historic use of similar equipment.
e. In its annual financial statements, the company reports interest expense as the *net* amount of interest expense less interest revenue. The amounts are very small, relative to the scale of Fluidity's business activities.

Required:

1. Identify and briefly explain the accounting principle directly involved in each situation.
2. Indicate what, if anything, the company should do in the future by way of making any changes in accounting policy.

 A2-14 Application of Principles:

An examiner's close inspection of the annual financial statements and the accounting records revealed that Mawani Inc. may have violated some accounting principles. The examiner questioned the following transactions:

a. Merchandise purchased for resale was recorded as a debit to inventory for the invoice price of $80,000 (accounts payable was credited for the same amount); terms were 2/10, n/30. Ten days later, Mawani Inc. paid the account at the net amount due, $78,400 ($80,000 less the 2% discount). The $1,600 discount was credited to revenue. The purchased goods were still shown in inventory at $80,000 at year-end.

b. Mawani Inc. recorded equipment depreciation expense of $227,000 as a debit to retained earnings and a credit to the equipment account.

c. Routine repairs on equipment were recorded as follows: debit equipment, $500; credit cash, $500.

d. The company sustained a $96,000 storm damage loss during the current year. The company had no insurance. Mawani Inc. reported the loss as follows:

Statement of retained earnings—storm loss	$24,000
Statement of financial position (liabilities): Deferred charge—storm loss	$72,000

e. Mawani's balance sheet showed accounts receivable of $95,000. This amount included a $42,000 three-year loan to the company president. The maturity date of the loan was not specified.

Required:

1. For each transaction, identify the inappropriate treatment and the principle(s) violated, if any.

2. Give the original entry that should have been made or the appropriate reporting.

Mc Graw Hill ▪ **connect**

★ ★ A2-15 Implementation of Principles:

Carleton Builders Ltd. recorded the following summarized transactions during the current year:

a. The company originally sold and issued 100,000 common shares. During the current year, 94,000 of these shares were outstanding and 6,000 were repurchased from the shareholders and retired. Near the end of the current year, the board of directors declared and paid a cash dividend of $8 per share. The dividend was recorded as follows:

Retained earnings	800,000	
Cash ($8 × 94,000)		752,000
Dividend income ($8 × 6,000)		48,000

b. Carleton Builders Ltd. purchased a machine that had a list price of $90,000. The company paid for the machine in full by issuing 10,000 common shares (market price = $8.50). The purchase was recorded as follows:

Machine	90,000	
Share capital ($8.50 × 10,000)		85,000
Gain on purchase of equipment		5,000

c. Carleton needed a small structure for temporary storage. A contractor quoted a price of $769,000. The company decided to build the structure itself. The cost was $542,000, and construction required three months. The following entry was made:

Buildings—warehouse	769,000	
Cash		542,000
Revenue from self-construction		227,000

d. Carleton owns a plant located on a river that floods occasionally. A severe flood occurred during the current year, causing an uninsured loss of $97,000 (measured as the amount spent to repair the flood damage). The following entry was made:

Retained earnings, flood loss	97,000	
Cash		97,000

e. On 28 December, the company collected $76,000 cash in advance for merchandise to be shipped in January. The company's fiscal year-end is 31 December. This transaction was recorded on 28 December as follows:

Cash	76,000	
Sales revenue		76,000

Required:

1. For each transaction, determine which accounting principle (if any) was violated.
2. Explain the nature of the violation.
3. In each instance, indicate how the transaction should have been originally recorded.

★ ★ A2-16 Implementation of Principles:

The bookkeeper for Branford Ltd. has drawn up a financial statement on 31 December 20X1. Some of the items on the draft balance sheet are as follows:

Cash	$400,000	Consists of 300,000 Canadian dollars in the bank, plus 100,000 Hong Kong dollars held in cash. The HK$ were received in full payment for a consulting assignment recorded as revenue in 20X1.
Marketable securities	$900,000	Represents the cost of a temporary investment in the common shares of another company.
Accounts receivable	$500,000	Recorded as revenue in December 20X1 for a customer order that had not been shipped by year-end.

Contract liability	$ 100,000	The amount of a contract with a construction firm for modifications to Branford Ltd.'s office space, expected to be undertaken in early 20X2.
Other liabilities	$ 1	Recorded as a result of a contractual (long-term) requirement to repair the roof of an office building that Branford rents for an advertising sign. The sign is to be removed and the roof repaired in January 20X2, at an estimated cost of $75,000.

Upon further inquiry, you discover that at 31 December 20X1, the Canadian dollar is worth HK$7.5. You also ascertain that the value of the marketable securities was $987,000 at 20X1 year-end.

Required:

1. Indicate what change, if any, you would make in reporting each of the preceding items.
2. In each case, discuss the accounting principle involved.

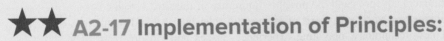 A2-17 Implementation of Principles:

In ASPE if the contingent loss (lawsuit) is reasonably measurable and likely to be incurred, the amount is accrued in the financial statements. If the amount is not measurable or is not likely to be incurred, then the potential loss is disclosed but not recorded. Also, if the probability of payment cannot be determined (is not estimable) the possibility of a loss is disclosed but not recorded.

For example, this policy can be directly applied to lawsuits. If a company is being sued by a disgruntled ex-customer, and the matter is before the courts, there can be a long delay in dispute resolution. A company will record a loss from the lawsuit prior to the court decision only if an amount, if any, of the court-ordered award can be predicted, *and* it appears likely that the company will lose the lawsuit or agree to a settlement. If an amount is not recorded, the existence of the lawsuit is explained in the disclosure notes.

Required:

1. List the recognition criteria.
2. Explain the accounting policy for contingent losses with reference to the recognition criteria in ASPE.

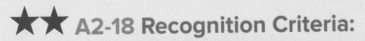 A2-18 Recognition Criteria:

Consider each of the following independent situations:

Case A   The value of Coca-Cola's trademark has been estimated as billions of dollars. Yet, even though Coca-Cola reports over $12 billion of goodwill and other intangible assets, none of this reported value relates to the Coca-Cola trademark, which is unrecognized in the accounts despite its substantial commercial value.

Case B   Air Canada purchases Aeroplan Miles® from Groupe Aeroplan Inc., a separate corporation. Air Canada is an Aeroplan partner providing certain Air Canada's customers with Aeroplan Miles®, which can be redeemed by customers for air travel or other rewards acquired by Aeroplan.

Under the CPSA, the companies' joint agreement, Aeroplan purchases passenger tickets from Air Canada to meet its obligation for the redemption of Aeroplan Miles® for air travel. The proceeds from the sale of passenger tickets to Aeroplan are included in advance ticket sales. Revenue related to these passenger tickets is recorded in passenger revenues when transportation is provided.

For Aeroplan Miles® earned by Air Canada customers, Air Canada purchases Aeroplan Miles® from Aeroplan in accordance with the terms of the CPSA. The cost of purchasing Aeroplan Miles® from Aeroplan is accounted for as a sales incentive and charged against passenger revenues when the points are issued, which occurs upon the qualifying air travel being provided to the customer.

Case C   Calgary-based Suncor Energy Inc. explores and develops sites within the Alberta oil sands. The company will be responsible for restoring the sites in the future. At 31 December 2011, the company reported an estimate of $3.43 billion in decommissioning and restoration costs. The following explanation appears in Suncor's disclosure notes (Note 4—Significant Accounting Estimates and Judgements):

Decommissioning and Restoration Costs

The company recognizes liabilities for the future decommissioning and restoration of exploration and evaluation assets and property, plant and equipment. These provisions are based on estimated costs, which take into account the anticipated method and extent of restoration, technological advances and the possible future use of the site. Actual costs are uncertain and estimates can vary as a result of changes to relevant laws and regulations, the emergence of new technology, operating experience, prices and closure plans. The expected timing of future decommissioning and restoration may change due to certain factors, including reserve life. Changes to assumptions related to future expected costs, discount rates and timing may have a material impact on the amounts presented.

Required:

For each of the preceding situations, discuss the issues relating to the recognition (or nonrecognition) of relevant elements in each company's financial statements.

★★ **A2-19 Implementation of Principles:**

Consider the following five reporting situations:

Case A   The financial statements of Raychem Corporation included the following note:

During the current year, plant assets were written down by $8,000,000. This writedown will reduce future expenses. Depreciation and other expenses in future years will be lower, and as a result this will benefit profits of future years.

Case B   During an audit of the Silvona Co., the audit manager observed that certain liabilities, such as income taxes, seemed to be overstated. Also, some potentially obsolete inventory items seemed to be undervalued, and the tendency was to expense rather than capitalize as many items as possible. Management states that "the company has always taken a very conservative view of the business and its future prospects." Management suggests that it does not wish to weaken the company by reporting any more earnings or paying any more dividends than absolutely necessary because it does not expect business to continue to be good. Management points out that the lower valuations for assets do not cost the company anything but do create reserves for "hard times."

Case C   There was no comment on or explanation of the fact that Simone Ltd. changed its inventory method from FIFO (first-in, first-out) to average cost at the beginning of the current reporting period. A large changeover difference was involved, and there was no retrospective restatement.

Case D   Current assets amounted to $314,000 and current liabilities $205,000; the balance sheet of Nelta Corporation reported a single amount: "Working capital, $109,000."

Case E   In 20X1, Tryler Corporation switched its inventory method for financial reporting from LIFO (last-in, first-out) to FIFO due to a change in accounting standards that prohibits LIFO. Tryler publicly explained, "Our major competitors have consistently used the FIFO method. Therefore, the reported loss for 20X1 and the restated profit for 20X0 are on a comparable basis as to inventory valuation with competitors." The impact on opening balances is not material.

Required:

Analyze each of the preceding situations and indicate which accounting principles, as described in this chapter, are applicable in each situation.

Source: (Globe and money) © Vstock LLC/Getty Images RF; (Skyscrapers) © Arpad Benedek/Getty Images RF; (Canadian flag) © BjArn Kindler/Getty Images RF; (Tablet, pen, keyboard) © John Lamb/Getty Images RF.

CHAPTER 3

Statements of Income and Comprehensive Income

INTRODUCTION

Maple Leaf Foods Inc.'s 2014 consolidated statements of net earnings shows five earnings (loss) subtotals before arriving at the amount for net earnings: (1) gross margin, (2) loss from continuing operations before restructuring and other related costs, change in fair value of non-designated interest rate swaps, and other income (expense), (3) interest and income taxes from continuing operations, (4) income taxes from continuing operations, and (5) loss from continuing operations.

Similarly, Bombardier Inc. also shows multiple subtotals on its consolidated statements of income before arriving at the final amount for net earnings for the period: (1) gross margin, (2) earnings before interest and income taxes (EBIT), and (3) earnings before income tax expense (EBT).

In contrast, Canadian Tire Corporation shows only two earnings subtotals on its consolidated statements of income: (1) gross margin and (2) income before income taxes—prior to the final amount for net income.

This chapter explains the various aspects of earnings and how they are displayed on the statement of comprehensive income (SCI). The chapter also explains what is not necessarily shown on the statement, such as major categories of expense.

This chapter focuses on the display of revenues, expenses, gains, and losses after they have been recorded. Accounting standards require that certain items of information be reported on the income statement or in the notes or sometimes the entity has a choice. In general, however, the level of information provided in the profit or loss section of the SCI is left largely to the discretion of management, as is the style of presentation.

One item that requires special classification in the income statement is the reporting of discontinued operations. The main body of this chapter will conclude with a section on "discontinued operations" as well as other types of asset disposals.

Finally, as with all of the following chapters, we will end by explaining the income statement reporting requirements for private entities using ASPE.

NATURE OF INCOME

"Income" Terminology

The word "income" often is used to mean quite different things in accounting usage, as well as in everyday language. However, in IFRS, **income** means *all* amounts flowing into the entity through operations. IAS 1 (*Presentation of Financial Statements*) states:

> An entity shall recognise all items of income and expense in a period in profit or loss unless an IFRS requires or permits otherwise. (¶88)

"Income" in this sentence means *revenue* and *gains*, while "profit or loss" means *net income*. This can be a little confusing, because we commonly use *income* for ancillary sources of revenue such as *interest income*.

Largely because of this confusion, most Canadian companies avoid the use of "income" and instead use *revenue* and "earnings." IFRS adopts the European tradition and refers to net income as "profit or loss." Although IFRS does not use the word "earnings" when defining revenue, it is nevertheless useful for avoiding confusion and is consistent with other common terminology, such as retained *earnings* and *earnings per share*.

The moral of this story is to be careful about what people mean when they say "income." Do they mean all sources of gain, or *revenue*, or *net income* (e.g., *earnings* or *profit or loss*) or *comprehensive income* (a topic discussed shortly)?

Accounting versus Economic Income

An economist defines income as a *change in wealth*, whether or not that change in wealth has been realized. Suppose that a company owns a parcel of land for which it paid $10,000 several years ago. A new highway has just been built next to the property, and several individuals have offered to pay $125,000 to $150,000 for the land. The firm has not yet agreed to sell. An economist would say that an increase in wealth has occurred because the land is worth more than historical cost. The wealth increase is called **economic income**, and it is based on an *events approach* rather than on a *transactions approach* to measuring profit or loss.

Using the transaction approach, an accountant would not recognize such an increase in wealth as income. Only if the land is sold to another party in an arm's-length transaction would the accountant recognize the increase in wealth as income. This is **accounting income**, based on the transactions approach.

Historically, accounting had been based strictly on the transactions approach and the historical cost measurement principle. Changes in value were recognized only when there was a transaction that *realized* the change in value. The only exceptions to the transaction approach occurred in the writedown or downward valuation of items, such as obsolete inventory and capital assets (both tangible and intangible).

Accounting standards under IFRS are moving more toward the concept of economic income. Accounting now recognizes not only value changes realized through transactions, but also certain types of value changes that have not been realized. A prime example is the reporting of financial assets and liabilities, many of which are reported on the statement of financial position (SFP) at fair values. Reporting based on fair values leads to accounting recognition of value changes as either realized or unrealized income. Another example is the option to use the fair-value model for investment property and the revaluation model for property, plant, and equipment and certain intangibles.

But only some value changes are recognized and reported. Many other value changes, such as increases in the value of inventory, are not normally recognized in accounting. Therefore, accounting income is still quite different from economic income.

Comprehensive Income

Comprehensive income is defined as all changes to owners' equity that are *not* the result of transactions with the owners (i.e., the shareholders) in their capacity as owners. For example:

- The issuance of new shares, repurchase of outstanding shares, and the payment of dividends are examples of transactions with shareholders solely *in their capacity as owners* and will be reported as changes in equity, not as part of comprehensive income.

- In contrast, selling goods or services to a shareholder is a transaction with the shareholder that is *not* part of the relationship with the shareholder as an owner; it is a transaction with the shareholder as a customer and will be reported as part of comprehensive income.

The concept of comprehensive income has two objectives:

- To eliminate all direct entries to shareholders' equity except those resulting from transactions with the shareholders; and
- To differentiate between (1) those value changes recognized both in net assets and in profit or loss and (2) those recognized in net assets (on the SFP) but not in the current year's earnings or net income.

There are two categories of comprehensive income:

1. Periodic profit or loss (also known as *net income* or *earnings*); and
2. Other comprehensive income (OCI).

The IASB permits two slightly different reporting formats:

- A continuous **statement of comprehensive income (SCI)** that starts with revenue, goes down to a total for net profit or loss (or "earnings") after tax and then continues to the items of *other comprehensive income*; or
- Two separate statements consisting of (1) a statement of profit or loss and (2) an SCI that begins with profit or loss as the first line.

When separate statements are prepared, the SCI must immediately follow the income statement in the company's financial statement presentation.

Classification

Which items affecting net assets should be included in the computation of profit or loss and reported in the income statement? Or, to look at it another way, what items should be *excluded* from profit or loss and reported as a component of OCI?

The vast majority of items (other than transactions with owners) are included in profit or loss. In accounting terminology, this is the *all-inclusive* approach to earnings reporting—very few transactions or events are shown outside profit or loss.

Nevertheless, some items are excluded from profit or loss. One type of item is reported in retained earnings, while the other three types are reported in OCI:

- Cumulative changes to retained earnings that are the result of (1) changes in accounting policies or (2) corrections of errors in prior periods. The retrospective effects of changes and corrections are reported as *changes to retained earnings*. Our detailed discussion of accounting changes occurs much later in this book, in Chapter 21.
- Certain specified changes in value are *recognized* in the SFP under IFRS but have not yet been *realized*. For the most part, these are value changes (1) that will be recognized in income only if and when realized or (2) that will be matched by an offsetting gain or loss in a future period. These items are reported in OCI. For example, revaluation of property, plant, and equipment discussed in Chapter 10 and revaluation financial assets discussed in Chapter 11.
- When companies have operations in foreign countries, the subsidiaries' financial statements must be converted to the parent's presentation currency so that they can be consolidated. The process is more complicated that it sounds, because changes in exchange rates create an accounting gain or loss. This gain or loss has no economic significance; it is the mechanical result of the conversion process. Therefore, it is reported as an item of OCI.

- Currently, IFRS requires that net actuarial gains and losses and other remeasurements relating to pension plans be reported as an item of OCI. Essentially, this is necessary to get the SFP to balance!

Other than these four types of value changes, the results of all transactions and all *recognized* value changes are reported in the profit or loss portion of the SCI.

We will explore the components of OCI as we go through the following chapters. For now, just accept that these nonowner changes in net assets are *excluded* from profit or loss but need to be reported somewhere since our debits must equal our credits—that "somewhere" is in the SCI as items of *other comprehensive income*. The rest of this chapter will focus on the "profit or loss" (or "net income" or "earnings") section of the SCI.

CONCEPT REVIEW

1. What different meanings are often accorded to the term "income"?
2. Explain the difference between accounting income and economic income.
3. What general types of changes in assets and liabilities are *not* reported as part of net income? Where are such excluded items reported?

GENERAL PRESENTATION FORMAT

IFRS prescribes little detail for either the content or the format of the SCI except for the clear division between *profit or loss* and *OCI*. Companies are quite free to use various presentation formats, as long as they do report those items specifically required by the various accounting standards.[1]

Line Items Required for Profit or Loss Section

In reporting a company's net earnings, IFRS requires a company to show the following minimum line items:

- Revenues, either (1) separated into categories, such as sales revenue, finance revenue, and investment income, or (2) shown in aggregate with note disclosure of the various income sources;
- Finance costs (which includes interest expense);
- The enterprise's share of earnings from associated companies and/or joint ventures accounted for using the equity method;
- Income tax expense on continuing operations;
- Profit or loss on discontinued operations, net of tax;
- Net earnings; and
- Earnings per share.

This is a really short list! Note that it does not even mention any expense items except for finance cost and income tax expense.

There are three important additional disclosures that must appear either on the face of the SCI or in the notes:

- The amount of inventory charged to expense;
- Depreciation and amortization expense; and
- Employee benefits expense, which includes wages and salaries, payroll taxes, heath care costs, post-retirement benefits, and so forth.

---

1. This situation may or may not change. The IASB has been working on a revised framework for financial reporting for several years but with no end in sight.

Whether these items are shown on the face of the SCI or in a disclosure note depends on the presentation format, as we shall see in the next section.

Notwithstanding the list of required disclosures, materiality plays an important role. If particular items of income or expense are material, they must be disclosed either on the face of the SCI or in the notes.

IFRS requires that items of profit and loss be reported on a continuous basis. That is, the statement should start with revenues, and then other items should be subtracted (or added) to obtain net earnings. This might seem obvious, but in some countries (including Canada), it used to be possible to show gross revenue, then draw a line, and skip to "earnings except the undernoted," which then included the few specific items required by accounting standards; in some countries, it was even possible to avoid disclosing revenue. But not under IFRS.

Alternative Formats of the Income Statement

IFRS specifies two alternative formats that may be used for the "profit or loss" section of the SCI:

1. Classification by *nature of expense*; and
2. Classification by *function within the enterprise,*

Classification by *nature* of expense will classify expenses on the basis of input costs—what the money was spent on. Classification by *function* is an output-based presentation—what the expenditure was used for.

By Nature of Expense

Exhibit 3-1 shows the consolidated SCI for Air Canada. Air Canada classifies expenses by *nature*. It shows the expense incurred for each type input cost, such as fuel, maintenance, depreciation. The "required" expense categories are all reported on the face of the statement, with details explained in the disclosure notes.

EXHIBIT 3-1		
AIR CANADA		
Consolidated Statement of Operations		

CONSOLIDATED STATEMENT OF OPERATIONS

For the year ended December 31

(Canadian dollars in millions except per share figures)		**2014**	**2013**
Operating revenues			
Passenger	Note 20	$ 11,804	$ 11,021
Cargo	Note 20	502	474
Other		966	887
Total revenues		**13,272**	**12,382**
Operating expenses			
Aircraft fuel		3,747	3,534
Wages, salaries and benefits		2,282	2,247
Benefit plan amendments	Note 9	—	(82)
Capacity purchase agreements		1,182	1,123

Airport and navigation fees		1,031	983
Aircraft maintenance		728	632
Sales and distribution costs		672	613
Depreciation, amortization and impairment		543	578
Ground package costs		377	327
Aircraft rent		313	318
Food, beverages and supplies		309	289
Communications and information technology		204	190
Other		1,069	1,011
Total operating expenses		**12,457**	**11,763**
Operating Income		**815**	**619**
Non-operating income (expense)			
Foreign exchange loss		(307)	(120)
Interest income		39	32
Interest expense		(322)	(397)
Interest capitalized		30	46
Net financing expense relating to employee benefits	Note 9	(134)	(208)
Fuel and other derivatives	Note 17	(1)	37
Other		(15)	(7)
Total non-operating expense		(710)	(617)
Income before income taxes		**105**	**2**
Income taxes	Note 12	—	8
Net income		**$ 105**	**$ 10**
Net income attributable to:			
Shareholders of Air Canada		100	6
Non-controlling interests		5	4
Net income		**$ 105**	**$ 10**
Net income per share attributable to shareholders of Air Canada	Note 15		

Basic earnings per share	$ 0.35	$ 0.02
Diluted earnings per share	$ 0.34	$ 0.02

The accompanying notes are an integral part of the consolidated financial statements.

Source: Air Canada, 2014 audited annual financial statements, page 4, www.sedar.com, posted 11 February 2015.

Note the column for note references—a company must cross-reference each line item (when relevant) to the disclosure notes where the reader can find more detailed information. For example, Note 20 will disclose the various sources of revenue within each major category of passenger and cargo.

By Function within the Enterprise

Bombardier presents its operating results classified by function. While Air Canada shows its total employee cost (classified by nature) on the face of its SCI, Bombardier's employee costs will be included in each of the major functional categories of cost of sales, SG&A, and R&D.

When a company reports on the basis of function, required information, such as employee benefit expense and amortization and depreciation expense, is shown in the notes to the financial statements. For example, in Note 10, Bombardier reports employee benefit costs totalling $5,893 million (for 2014); depreciation and amortization are reported in Note 19 (property, plant, and equipment) and Note 20 (intangible assets).

Bombardier's presentation is in two statements rather than one continuous statement. Exhibit 3-2 shows the consolidated statement of income, while Exhibit 3-3 shows the consolidated SCI. As required by IFRS, the SCI immediately follows the statement of income in Bombardier's financial statements (and annual report).

Bombardier uses common abbreviations for the various components of the income statement, including:

- SG&A—sales and general and administrative expense
- R&D—research and development
- EBIT—earnings before interest and income tax
- EBT—earnings before income tax
- NCI—non-controlling interest (an explanation follows below)

These abbreviations are familiar to any knowledgeable financial statement user and do not really need to be spelled out. Remember, accounting standards assume that financial statement readers are not naive; users are expected to have a reasonable level of accounting sophistication.

The abbreviations in the SCI are as follows:

- OCI—other comprehensive income
- AFS—assets available for sale
- CCTD—cumulative currency translation difference
- NCI—non-controlling interest (an explanation follows below)

EXHIBIT 3-2			

BOMBARDIER INC.

Consolidated Statements of Income

For the fiscal years ended December 31

(in millions of U.S. dollars, except per share amounts)	Notes	2014	2013
Revenues		$ 20,111	$ 18,151
Cost of sales	16	17,534	15,658
Gross margin		2,577	2,493
SG&A		1,358	1,417
R&D	6	347	293
Share of income of joint ventures and associates	34	(89)	(119)
Other expense	7	38	9
Special items	8	1,489	(30)
EBIT		(566)	923
Financing expense	9	249	271
Financing income	9	(75)	(119)
EBT		(740)	771
Income taxes	11	506	199
Net income (loss)		$ (1,246)	$ 572
Attributable to			
Equity holders of Bombardier Inc.		$ (1,260)	$ 564
NCI		14	8
		$ (1,246)	$ 572
EPS (in dollars)	12		
Basic and diluted		$ (0.74)	$ 0.31

The notes are an integral part of these consolidated financial statements.

Source: Bombardier Inc., or its subsidiaries, 2014 audited annual financial statements, page 109, www.sedar.com, posted 12 February 2015.

EXHIBIT 3-3			

BOMBARDIER INC.

Consolidated Statements of Comprehensive Income

For the fiscal years ended December 31

(in millions of U.S. dollars)

	Note	2014	2013

Net income (loss) $		$	**(1,246)**	$ 572
OCI				
Items that may be reclassified to net income				
Net change in cash flow hedges				
Foreign exchange re-evaluation			**17**	(6)
Net gain (loss) on derivative financial instruments			**(389)**	26
Reclassification to income or to the related nonfinancial asset[1] [2]			**216**	(32)
Income taxes			**37**	6
			(119)	(6)
AFS financial assets				
Net unrealized gain (loss)			**7**	(5)
CCTD				
Net investments in foreign operations			**(146)**	36
Net gain (loss) on related hedging items			**4**	(15)
			(142)	21
Items that are never reclassified to net income				
Retirement benefits				
Remeasurements of defined benefit plans[3]			**(646)**	911
Income taxes	21		**(45)**	(87)
			(691)	824
Total OCI			**(945)**	834
Total comprehensive income (loss)		$	**(2,191)**	$ 1,406
Attributable to		$	**(2,198)**	$ 1,399
Equity holders of Bombardier Inc.				
NCI			**7**	7
		$	**(2,191)**	$ 1,406

[1]Include $97 million of loss reclassified to the related nonfinancial asset for fiscal year 2014 ($10 million of gain for fiscal year 2013).

(2)$196 million of net deferred loss is expected to be reclassified from OCI to the carrying amount of the related nonfinancial asset or to income during fiscal year 2015.

(3)Include net actuarial gains (losses).

The notes are an integral part of these consolidated financial statements.

Source: Bombardier Inc., or its subsidiaries, 2014 audited annual financial statements, page 110, www.sedar.com, posted 12 February 2015.

Non-controlling Interest

A consolidated income statement includes the revenues and expenses of both the parent company and the subsidiaries it controls. However, the parent may control a subsidiary without owning all of its shares. When the parent owns less than 100% of a subsidiary's shares, the shares held by others outside the consolidated entity are known as the **non-controlling interest (NCI)**.

In a consolidated income statement, the net income amount includes *all* of the revenues and expenses of the parent and the subsidiary. However, the parent corporation's shareholders are not entitled to the benefit of that full amount (e.g., through dividends from the parent). Therefore, the final net income figure must be allocated proportionately to the controlling interest and the non-controlling interest.

In Exhibit 3-2, Bombardier for the year ended 31 December 2014 allocates $14 million profit to NCI even though they have a consolidated net loss of $1,246 million to NCI. This presentation format is required by IFRS.

Earnings per Share

A company must disclose its earnings per share (EPS), both basic and diluted, at the end of the income statement or, if the company is using a continuous statement of earnings and comprehensive income, at the end of the SCI. Both basic and diluted EPS must be shown. A company also must disclose the weighted average number of shares used in the EPS calculations, but this disclosure can be in the notes rather than on the face of the statement. EPS is the only ratio required by public companies.

The **weighted average number of shares** is a simple calculation. For example, if a company had 10,000 shares outstanding at the beginning of the year and then issued another 6,000 at the beginning of the fourth quarter (and thus outstanding for just three months), the weighted average would be $10,000 + (6,000 \times 3/12) = 11,500$.

Basic EPS is the total net income divided by the weighted average of common shares outstanding during the year. Bombardier (see Exhibit 3-2) shows EPS of ($0.74) for 2014, as against $0.31 for 2013.

Diluted EPS is computed by using the weighted average of all shares that would have been outstanding if all conversion privileges had been exercised by the holders of convertible bonds, preferred shares, and so forth. While basic EPS is useful for historical comparisons, diluted EPS is forward-looking—what will happen if conversion rights are exercised?

If the company reports any *discontinued operations* (which we shall discuss shortly), EPS must be reported in three steps:

- EPS (basic and diluted) for continuing operations
- EPS (basic and diluted) for discontinued operations
- Total EPS (basic and diluted)

Air Canada (see Exhibit 3-1) has basic EPS and diluted EPS, while Bombardier (see Exhibit 3-2) just has one number for basic and diluted because they are the same.

Note that EPS is based on *earnings attributable to shareholders of the parent corporation*. For Air Canada, EPS is based on the $100 million attributable to the shareholders of Air Canada, not on the $105 million total earnings.

EPS is *not* based on comprehensive income, because, by definition, the items included in OCI are not part of earnings in the reporting period, even though they might "recycle" into earnings in future periods. Items reported in OCI in this period will be recognized in earnings and EPS only when reported in earnings in a subsequent period.

Single-Step versus Multiple-Step Income Statements

Single-Step

IFRS makes no prescription for the set-up of the income statement. An income statement always starts with revenue, subtracts and adds things, and concludes with net income (or net earnings, or profit or loss). Theoretically, a company can display a single section for all "revenue and other income," followed by another single section for all "expenses and losses" (including income taxes), concluding with net income. This format is known as a **single-step statement**. There is just one step—*revenues* minus *expenses* equals *net income*.

In practice, a strict single-step income statement is extremely rare. All companies are required to segregate gains and losses of discontinued operations from net earnings (or loss) from continuing operations, as we will explain later in this chapter. As well, almost every company will segregate income tax expense from other expenses. Thus, a pure single-step statement is a rare sight indeed.

Multiple-Step

In contrast to a single-step income statement, most companies provide some sort of **multiple-step statement**, in which subtotals are presented after each section that presents certain types of income (or gain) and/or expense (or loss). IFRS encourages companies to provide additional line items, headings, and subtotals that are relevant to an understanding of the company's financial performance.

Both Air Canada and Bombardier Inc. use a multiple-step format. Air Canada (see Exhibit 3-1) has its first subtotal as "operating income," which includes the effect of all operating revenue and operating expenses (except income tax). In contrast, Bombardier (see Exhibit 3-2) draws its first subtotal for "gross margin." Gross margin is a common subtotal for manufacturing and mercantile entities, but it is optional.

Both companies present amounts for:

- Earnings before interest and taxes (EBIT); and
- Earnings before income taxes (EBT).

These subtotals are reported by many companies, but they are certainly not required. It is perfectly acceptable to simply include both interest expense and income tax expense as line items within the general expense category. Also, many companies will segregate **unusual items**, which are usually gains and losses that are not a part of normal earnings; such companies might highlight a subtotal labelled *earnings before unusual items*.

The IASB has expressed some displeasure with multiple subtotals such as "earnings before unusual items" and EBIT. It is concerned that these "non-GAAP" measures of earnings suggest there are several ways of measuring earnings, that is, by ignoring certain items of expense on the basis that they are nonrecurring or unusual.

The IASB's concern is that the qualitative criterion of *faithful representation* requires that all factors affecting profitability for a period should be taken into account in profitability analysis, both for feedback value and for predictive value. Unusual items are a fact of life for all entities, especially for large companies.

One item that does require special attention is *discontinued operations*. The results of operations that have been discontinued (e.g., sold) during the reporting period are relevant for measuring profit or loss for the period but are irrelevant as a basis for predicting future earnings. Thus, if a company reports discontinued operations, additional subtotals *must* be provided both before and after discontinued operations—(1) earnings from continuing operations after tax and (2) earnings after discontinued operations net of tax.

Other Comprehensive Income

Exhibit 3-3 shows Bombardier's consolidated SCI. Bombardier presents a separate SCI following the statement of income. When separate statements are prepared, the first line of the SCI *must* be the net income shown on the last line of the income statement. The format is straightforward:

- Net income/earnings/profit
- The items of OCI, segregated into two general categories:

- Items that may be reclassified to earnings in a later period
- Items that will never be reclassified to earnings

- The total comprehensive income allocated to the company's shareholders and NCI (if any)

As we noted earlier, there is no EPS calculation because "earnings" does not include items of OCI.

Bombardier's items in the first section (those that may be reclassified to net income) involve unrecognized (in earnings) foreign exchange changes, cash flow hedges for foreign exchange commitments, changes related to available for sale financial assets, and cumulative currency translation difference. The first two lines for cash flow hedges are changes for 2014; the third line is the reclassification (known as *recycling*) of prior years' amounts to income (i.e., moved from OCI to the income statement), while the fourth line represents the net income tax relating to the first three lines. Confusing? Well, do not worry about it now. You will have plenty of opportunity to fathom this mystery much later in your course.

"CCTD," which means "cumulative currency translation difference," is a little unusual on when it would be reclassified. It arises because Bombardier has investments in foreign subsidiaries, but the Canadian dollar equivalent of those investments keeps changing as currencies fluctuate. It is really just a mechanical outcome of the consolidation process, and it would get reclassified to net income only if and when the parent company sells or shuts down one or more foreign subsidiaries.

Available for sale assets is a category for financial instruments in IAS 39. This category does not exist anymore with the new standard IFRS 9 discussed later in Chapter 11.

Only one item appears in Bombardier's "never reclassified" section, and that is "Net actuarial gains (losses)" relating to employees' pensions. Two other items that would be reported in this section are (1) revaluation surpluses and (2) fair-value adjustments to certain types of financial instruments. Bombardier has neither of these items.

Net Income or Comprehensive Income?

If you are trying to understand a company's earnings, what is the "correct" measure of a company's earnings? IFRS seems to give us at least three options: (1) earnings after tax from continuing operations, (2) net income, or (3) comprehensive income.

The only EPS figures that IFRS requires are those based on net income, both before and after discontinued operations. There is no calculation of comprehensive income per share. Nevertheless, some financial analysts are beginning to emphasize comprehensive income rather than net income because they want to include all gains and losses in their calculations.

Including all of OCI in a periodic earnings analysis is unwise. As you go through the following chapters, you will come to understand the nature of the various items that flow through (or stay in) OCI. OCI is a mixed bag into which IFRS puts changes arising from valuations that we do not quite know what else to do with. One of those changes (translation of investment in foreign subsidiaries) is a purely mechanical result of the consolidation process; some others have more economic substance but relate to future periods, not the current period.

CONCEPT REVIEW

1. What are the two sections of the SCI? Explain the nature of the items that go into each section.
2. What components of net earnings are *required* by international accounting standards?
3. How might interest expense on long-term debt be presented differently in a single-step as opposed to a multiple-step income statement?

INCOME TAX ALLOCATION

Intraperiod Tax Allocation

As the name implies, income tax allocation is the process of allocating a company's total income tax expense to various categories within the financial statements of any reporting period. If an item is shown *net of related tax*, it means that the tax consequences of the item have been determined and the reported amount is shown after these tax effects have been adjusted for.

Determining this amount is the process of **intraperiod tax allocation**. *Intra* means that the allocation is within the period and within the SCI and the components of shareholders' equity. The total amount of income tax expense (or benefit) must be reported along with the components to which they relate:

- Continuing operations;
- Discontinued operations;
- Items of other comprehensive income; and
- Other components of shareholders' equity.

For example, you can see in Exhibit 3-3 that Bombardier allocated income tax effects relating to each individual component of OCI. Intraperiod tax allocation also applies to the *cumulative effect of a retrospective change in accounting policy*, shown in the statement of changes in equity discussed in our next chapter.

The crucial aspect is that net earnings from continuing operations should include only that portion of a company's total income tax expense that relates directly to continuing operations.

Interperiod Tax Allocation

A different aspect of reporting income taxes in the financial statements is known as *interperiod tax allocation*, although accounting standards consider it a form of liability recognition rather than tax allocation. **Interperiod tax allocation** is the allocation of a company's income tax liability to different reporting periods, which is covered in depth in Chapter 16.

Although we will not discuss interperiod allocation in depth here, you will see its results on most financial statements as amount for "deferred taxes" (or "future income taxes," which means the same thing). IFRS uses "deferred," which is what we will use in this book. You will often see a line for *deferred* (or *future*) *taxes* on either the face of the income statement or in the disclosure notes, as well as one or two lines on the SFP. The income statement usually shows only one line for income tax expense (or benefit), but that amount is almost always composed of two components:

- Current income tax (or benefit); and
- Deferred (or future) income tax (or benefit).

Usually, the components are shown in a note rather than on the face of the SCI.

"Current income tax" is the amount paid (or payable) to the government on taxable earnings in the current year. The amount of deferred income tax expense is not payable for current operations, nor is it a liability to the government. Instead, it reflects the possible impact of certain items of revenue and/or expense on future years' income taxes.

Some items of revenue and expense are taxed in one year but included in accounting earnings in a different year. When that happens, the current tax expense reflects only revenues and expenses actually reported (legally) on the company's income tax return. The calculation for deferred income taxes is intended to reflect the taxes that *would have been paid* if the company had reported exactly the same items of revenue and expense on the tax return as it reports on the income statement.

By far the most common source of deferred tax expense (and liability) arises from the difference between (1) capital cost allowance (CCA) for tax purposes and (2) accounting depreciation and amortization expense. For a company following IFRS, it is almost impossible to avoid this difference.

If you see a deferred tax *gain* on the income statement (and an asset on the SFP), it almost always reflects the probable future benefits from tax loss carryforwards.

If this seems confusing, we are not surprised. Do not worry about it now. You will have plenty of time to worry about it next semester, when you get to Chapters 16 and 17. The important point now is simply that the *deferred income tax expense does not represent a current cash flow.* Also, the deferred tax liability on the SFP does not mean that the company actually owes that amount to the government.

ASSET DISPOSALS, DISCONTINUED OPERATIONS, AND RESTRUCTURING

Sometimes a company decides to make significant changes in the way it operates. There are many reasons for making changes: for example, to cut costs and restore profitability, to make the company's production more efficient, or to meet competitive threats.

When a company decides that it can improve its operations, it can take several different approaches:

1. Shut down or abandon a part of its operations, laying off the employees, and selling some of the company's operating assets;
2. Significantly reorganize the company's operations, but continue in the same businesses, which usually includes the disposal of at least one major asset or a group of assets; or
3. Sell a major business line as an operating unit (i.e., as a going concern) to the highest bidder, thereby transferring the operation to the buyer intact and as a functioning unit, which is known as a *discontinued operation*.

These are not really distinct scenarios but points along a continuum, as shown in Exhibit 3-4. Many reorganizations and restructurings involve a combination of these approaches. The following sections will explain the accounting treatment of the different types of disposals.

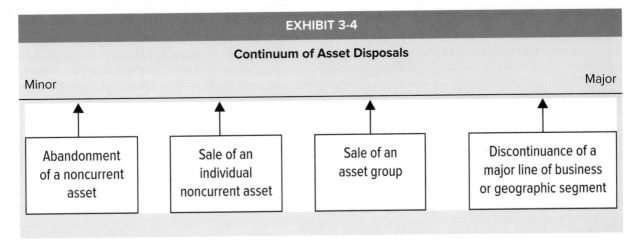

EXHIBIT 3-4

Continuum of Asset Disposals

Minor — Major

| Abandonment of a noncurrent asset | Sale of an individual noncurrent asset | Sale of an asset group | Discontinuance of a major line of business or geographic segment |

Asset Disposals

Business enterprises frequently change their business operations by shutting down factories or distribution centres, dropping products, or eliminating product lines. Usually, a company is continuing in the same line of business but has decided that it can obtain greater efficiencies and improve earnings or eliminate losses by getting rid of excess assets (and, unfortunately, employees).

For accounting purposes, we can identify two different scenarios for asset disposals:

1. Disposing of individual noncurrent assets; or
2. Disposing of several assets as a group.

Under IFRS, assets put up for sale are reclassified from *noncurrent* to *current* on the SFP. They are classified as current assets because the intent is to sell them rather than hold them for productive use.

Abandonment

An **abandoned asset** is an asset that a company continues to own but has permanently stopped using. Old mine sites, for example, are often abandoned, even though they still contain resources; the mine is abandoned because the cost of extraction is greater than the value of the resource mined.

An abandoned asset should *not* be reclassified as a current asset because there is no plan to sell it. Depreciation stops, and the asset is written down to its **recoverable amount**, which is the higher of the *value in use* and **fair value less the cost to sell** the asset. If there is no fair value less cost to sell, the asset is written down to zero.

The asset is subject to impairment tests as long as the company owns it. If an impairment test reveals that an abandoned asset's value has *increased*, the asset should be written up, but not to more than its original carrying value at the time of abandonment (net of any depreciation or amortization expense that would have been taken). The increase in value is recognized as a gain on the company's income statement. Impairment testing will be discussed in depth in Chapter 10.

An *abandoned* asset is not the same as an **idle asset**, which is an asset that the company is not using, but only at the moment. In a recession, for example, many companies temporarily shut down factories, but they have not abandoned those assets. Idle assets continue to depreciate and are accounted for as productive assets, even though they are currently not producing.

Selling Individual Assets

A company may decide to put an individual asset, or series of individual assets, on the market for sale.

Current asset

If the asset is a *current* asset, no special treatment is necessary as long as the carrying value of the asset does not exceed its recoverable amount. If the recoverable amount is less than the carrying value, a writedown is necessary; the loss will be reported in operating expenses.

An example of a current asset to be disposed of is inventory of a discontinued product line. The inventory's recoverable amount may have been higher than its carrying cost in the normal course of business, but the recoverable amount will probably be less once the inventory is declared surplus. The inventory will most likely be sold to a clearance company at a price well below its carrying value. Thus, it must be written down to its recoverable amount. The amount of any writedown is recognized in operating expenses.

Noncurrent asset

Often, a company will put one or more individual *noncurrent* assets, such as a warehouse building, up for sale. The asset had been classified as a capital asset, but once it is removed from productive use and put on the market, it is subjected to an impairment test and written down to recoverable amount, if that amount is lower than carrying value. The asset may then be classified as a **held-for-sale asset**if it meets the necessary conditions. A held-for-sale asset is shown on the SFP as a current asset. When the asset is reclassified, depreciation or amortization ceases because it is no longer being held as a productive asset with future benefit beyond its recoverable amount.

Conditions for *held-for-sale* classification for a noncurrent asset

Before an asset can be classified as "held-for-sale," two conditions must be satisfied:

1. The asset is available for immediate sale in its present condition; and
2. The asset's sale is *highly probable*, which means satisfying five requirements:

   - The price being asked for the asset must be reasonable, relative to the asset's current condition and fair value;
   - An active program to find a buyer must have been started;
   - Management must be committed to selling the asset;
   - It is unlikely that the offer to sell will be withdrawn or that the terms of the offer will be changed significantly; and
   - The sale is expected to take place within one year of the asset's being reclassified as "held-for-sale."

Let's think of a couple of situations wherein an asset might not be available for sale immediately in its present condition. If a company was locked into a supply contract that went beyond the reporting date and they needed to fulfill that contract before they could sell the asset, it would not be available immediately for sale. If a company plans to sell their manufacturing facility, but prior to sale some renovations need to be completed to comply with the safety code but are not completed by the reporting date, it will not be available for sale in its present condition. Events or circumstances may delay the sale beyond one year. If the delay is beyond the control of the company, the asset can continue to be shown as a current asset.

ETHICAL ISSUES

The reason for the conditions for reclassifying an asset as held-for-sale is to prevent managers from reclassifying assets as "current" for a short period and then reversing that decision later. For example, a company might have a lending covenant that requires a minimum current ratio. If these restrictions were not in place, an unethical manager could temporarily reclassify a *noncurrent* asset to *current*, claiming that it is held-for-sale, just to meet the current ratio requirement, and then reclassify it back to noncurrent after the reporting date had passed. Clearly, there is an ethical issue involved in the "held-for-sale" classification.

The "held-for-sale" two-step

There are two steps to recording a noncurrent asset as held-for-sale:

1. A noncurrent asset intended for sale must first be "remeasured" to the lower of its carrying value and its fair value less costs to sell.
2. After remeasurement, the asset can be declared "held-for-sale" and classified as a current asset, provided the five conditions listed above are satisfied.

In general, when any noncurrent asset is written down, the loss is reported as part of that period's net income. If the recoverable amount of the written-down asset increases later, the increase in value is reported in profit or loss as a gain. When a company writes up the asset, the writeup is limited to the extent of any prior writedowns, including any impairments recorded prior to the asset's classification as held-for-sale. It is important to note that assets are only written down when classified as held-for-sale; they are not written up to fair value if that is higher than the carrying amount.

Example

Suppose that in early September 20X4, near the end of the company's third fiscal quarter, Finagle Ltd. (a public company) completes installation of new package-handling equipment in its distribution centre in downtown Montreal. The old equipment is still serviceable but is not as efficient as Finagle's new equipment.

Finagle contacts a major industrial resale firm and requests that the firm put the old equipment on the market for sale. The resale firm believes that it can get a quick sale, because many start-up companies in the Montreal area can use serviceable low-cost package-handling equipment. Finagle therefore wishes to reclassify the equipment as held-for-sale.

The original cost of the equipment was $500,000; accumulated depreciation to the date of disuse (i.e., September 20X4) was $240,000, leaving a carrying value of the old equipment of $260,000. The resale firm estimates that the old equipment is worth about $250,000 on the resale market; the firm will charge 20% commission on the sales price. The commission is the "cost to sell." Therefore, the recoverable amount (fair value less cost to sell) is $200,000 (i.e., $250,000 × 80%). The process is as follows:

1. The accumulated depreciation to the date of abandonment will be offset against the original cost of $500,000, leaving a net book value of $260,000 in the equipment account:

Accumulated depreciation	240,000	
Equipment		240,000

2. Finagle will "remeasure" the old equipment by writing it down to $200,000, reporting the $60,000 loss in profit or loss:

| Loss on equipment held-for-sale | 60,000 | |
| Equipment | | 60,000 |

3. Finagle then reclassifies the equipment from a noncurrent asset to current asset:

| Equipment held-for-sale (current asset) | 200,000 | |
| Equipment (noncurrent asset) | | 200,000 |

This series of entries will (1) reclassify the equipment as a current asset at its net recoverable amount and (2) record the $60,000 writedown as a loss to be included in net income. Of course, these entries can be combined into a single compound entry:

Equipment held-for-sale (current asset)	200,000	
Accumulated depreciation	240,000	
Loss on equipment held-for-sale	60,000	
Equipment (noncurrent asset)		500,000

In December 20X4, a sudden economic crisis has the effect of freezing the capital market; few new companies are able to get going. The resale firm advises Finagle that the equipment now can probably be sold for no more than $180,000. Consequently, Finagle writes down the equipment to the new lower estimated recoverable amount: $180,000 × 80% = $144,000. The loss of $56,000 (i.e., $200,000 − $144,000) is reported in Finagle's income statement with the following entry:

| Loss on equipment held-for-sale | 56,000 | |
| Equipment held-for-sale | | 56,000 |

In March 20X5, the Canadian financial market begins to recover as the nation finds that the banking and financial system is still sound. The resale firm now begins aggressively marketing the equipment, asking a selling price of $260,000. For Finagle's first-quarter financial reports, under IFRS the company remeasures the equipment and writes it up to $208,000, disclosing the gain as a component of profit or loss:

| Equipment held-for-sale | 64,000 | |
| Gain (recovery) on equipment held-for-sale | | 64,000 |

In July 20X5, the beginning of Finagle Ltd.'s third quarter, the asset is sold for $270,000. The resale firm collects its 20% commission and remits the remaining $216,000 to Finagle. Since the carrying value at the end of the second quarter was $208,000, the company recognizes a gain of $8,000:

Cash	216,000	
Equipment held-for-sale		208,000
Gain on sale of equipment		8,000

In this example, Finagle met all five conditions for reclassifying the asset as held-for-sale:

*   The asking price is realistic, according to expert opinion (i.e., the resale firm);
*   An active program of sale was started;
*   Management is committed to selling the asset;

- It is unlikely that management will withdraw or significantly change the terms of the offer to sell; and
- There is a reasonable expectation of selling it within a year.

Even though it took longer than a year to sell the equipment, the cause of the delay (a general economic financial crisis) was beyond the control of management.

Declassification as "held-for-sale"

Declassification as held-for-sale occurs when a noncurrent asset no longer satisfies the held-for-sale criteria. The company may have changed its mind about selling the asset, or market conditions may have changed so that sale is no longer "highly probable." If that happens, the asset must be restored to its original classification at the lower of:

1. Its net recoverable amount at the date of the decision not to sell; and
2. What its carrying value would have been if the asset had not been reclassified in the first place, that is, if depreciation had continued as usual.

Effectively, this is the lower-of-cost-and-market rule.

Disposal Groups

A **disposal group** is a group of assets being sold together in a single transaction. A disposal group can consist of both current and noncurrent assets, such as a combination of buildings, equipment, and inventory. As well, a disposal group can include liabilities that are specifically related to the assets in the group, such as a mortgage liability on a building.

Normally, a disposal group is an operating part of the business. For example, a company may decide to sell its warehousing operation to a third party that may be able to operate it more efficiently or at lower cost—this is a form of outsourcing, but with the basic working unit developed by the company and sold to an outside specialist. In this example, the disposal group of assets may include a building, equipment, land, inventory, supplies, and accounts payable.

When a company decides to sell a group of assets, the same general procedure is followed as we described above for a single noncurrent asset:

1. Initially, before classification as a held-for-sale asset, each individual asset and liability in the group is remeasured using the appropriate measurement rules for that item. In other words, the group is not remeasured as a whole, but by its individual components.
2. When the group is classified as held-for-sale, the assets of the group *as a whole* are reported separately as a current asset; the liabilities are reported separately from the company's other liabilities. The group's liabilities cannot be offset against the group assets in the SFP.
3. Future revaluations or remeasurements are based *on the group as a whole*. Individual asset values do not matter, because the group will be sold as a whole for a single price.[2]

As with sales of single assets, decreases and subsequent recoveries in recoverable amount are reported in net income; recoveries are limited to the amount of any previous impairment losses. Also, depreciation (or amortization) stops at the date that the group is classified as held-for-sale.

There are two categories of disposal groups:

1. Asset groups that are stand-alone groups, such as the example of a warehousing operation cited above; and
2. Asset groups that are part of a *discontinued operation*.

The following sections will explain the special treatment given to discontinued operations.

---

2. There are some exclusions from the statement that all of the items in the group are valued together as a group. The exclusions are "scoped out" items specified in IFRS 5, such as deferred taxes and some financial assets. We need not bother with these details at this point.

Discontinued Operations

Although all the types of asset sales we have described above might theoretically be viewed as discontinued operations of some sort, the term "discontinued operations" has a quite specific meaning in accounting. The distinction is important, because discontinued operations are given special recognition in both the SCI (profit or loss section) and the SFP.

One of the primary functions of the SCI is to provide a basis for investors and others to predict future earnings. If a company is selling a significant revenue-generating part of the company, that sale will have a material impact on predicting future earnings. Therefore, operating results of a discontinued operation are segregated so that financial statement users will not expect the revenues and earnings relating to this unit to continue into the future. The segregation happens not only in the year in which the discontinuance decision is made but also for the prior year's comparative income statement.

Similarly, the assets and liabilities of a discontinued operation are segregated on the balance sheet. The assets of a discontinued operation are held-for-sale *current assets* under IFRS. Amortization is discontinued, and the *assets* are remeasured at their fair value less costs to sell. Liabilities are *not* remeasured except as may be required for financial instruments, which are discussed much later in this book.

Definition

When a company decides to terminate some part of its operations, the first financial reporting issue is whether the termination fits the definition of a "discontinued operation."

To qualify as a discontinued operation, a disposal group must be a *cash-generating unit* of the business that constitutes a major line of business or a significant geographic segment. IFRS 5 defines a **cash-generating unit** as a "group of assets that generates cash flows that are largely independent of the cash inflows from other assets or groups of assets." In other words, it has to be a unit that generates revenue from its own operations and that can be sold as an operating unit.

IFRS 5 defines a **discontinued operation** as *an operating segment* of a company that either (1) has been sold or (2) is held-for-sale. The "held-for-sale" requirement means that all of the conditions listed in the previous section for disposal of assets and asset groups must be satisfied—an active program to find a buyer, a reasonable asking price based on fair value, expectation of sale within the next year, etc. It is important to note that if the held-for-sale criteria are not met the asset cannot be a discontinued operation.

A crucial aspect of a discontinued operation is that the operation must be *separable* from the rest of the enterprise. That is, the operation must not be so well integrated with the other (continuing) operations that its cash flows cannot be separately identified.

Under IFRS, the special reporting requirements for discontinued operations should be applied only upon the discontinuance of major business segments. The special category of discontinued operations should not be cluttered with the disposal of relatively minor lines of business. Only the big ones matter, because their discontinuance can have a significant impact on the decisions of financial statement users. As well, this limitation to major portions of a company's operations ties into the *segment reporting* required in the disclosure notes, as we shall discuss in the next chapter.

There is one caveat, however. To qualify as a discontinued operation (or disposal group), the proceeds of the sale must be recovered mainly through a sale transaction, rather than through continuing use. Thus, a company cannot "sell" part of its operations to a third party and then continue to operate the unit and collect the sales price through revenue from the operation.

An operation is reported as discontinued when management has made the decision and has begun the process of selling it or shutting it down. It is quite likely that a plan of discontinuance will be begun in one fiscal year and finished in the next. Almost certainly, any discontinuance plan will extend over more than one public company's quarterly reporting period. Therefore, an operation that is reported as discontinued may, in fact, still be in operation at the end of the fiscal period.

The past tense "discontinued" should not be taken too literally. Remember the one-year future time horizon. An operation that is *expected* to be sold or shut down within the next year is still reported as discontinued.

Example

Suppose that an automobile manufacturer also manufactures buses. The bus business is a separate division of the larger company, with separate responsibility and reporting lines within the company and with separately measurable revenues and expenses. The manufacturer decides to sell its entire bus-manufacturing operation. In that case, the bus operation qualifies as a *discontinued operation* for accounting purposes.

To continue one step further, suppose that the automobile manufacturer decides to sell one of its brands, much as Ford Motor Co. sold its Volvo line of cars to Chinese auto maker Geely. Even if Ford retained all of the factories that had made cars under the Volvo brand (and used those factories for other products), the sale of the brand is the discontinuance of a cash-generating unit because the cash flows relating to the Volvo brand will be transferred to the new owner.

Purpose-Bought Subsidiaries

Occasionally a company will buy another company with the sole purpose of reselling it at a higher price. The practice of buying an asset only in order to resell it is known as **flipping** the asset. When the newly acquired company is purchased, it is reported as a discontinued operation from the date of its acquisition since the buyer's intent is to sell it.

Reporting Discontinued Operations

Statement of Comprehensive Income

The results of discontinued operations should be reported in the SCI as a single line item *after* earnings from continuing operations. The results of discontinued operations should appear in the profit or loss section of the statement, *not* in OCI.

There are two broad components of the total amount reported as net earnings (or net loss) on discontinued operations:

- The net profit or loss, net of related income taxes, from operating the discontinued operation to the date of disposal or the end of the reporting period, if the disposal is not complete by year-end; and
- Writedowns of asset carrying values to *fair value less cost to sell*, and all realized gains or losses on disposal to the extent not previously recognized, net of related income taxes.

Thus, the single amount consists of (1) operating profits or losses plus (2a) completed sales, gains, and losses on assets or asset disposal groups sold and (2b) uncompleted sales, writedowns to fair value less costs to sell for assets not yet sold. All amounts are *net of related income taxes*.

We will discuss the measurement of writedowns when we get to Chapter 10. The measurement criteria for disposing of a discontinued operation are the same as for disposing of an asset or an asset disposal group. For now, just bear in mind that the net profit or loss from discontinued operations is a combination of the current year's operating revenues and expenses plus the gains and losses on disposal, including any appropriate reduction of assets' book value to their fair value less costs to sell.

Statement of Financial Position

On the SFP, the accounting basis of the assets (and related liabilities) is changed:

- The assets are reclassified as held-for-sale and are reported as a single current asset line item, labelled *assets of discontinued operations held for sale*; and
- Liabilities are reclassified as a single current liability item labelled *liabilities related to discontinued operations*.

This is a significant change in status. When a long-lived asset is reclassified as "held-for-sale," its carrying value must be reduced to its fair value less costs to sell. Of course, if the cost-basis carrying value of the asset is below fair value less costs to sell, there will be no writedown. Also, once long-lived assets are reclassified as held-for-sale, amortization stops.

In summary, the effects on the SFP are:

- Depreciation and amortization ceases, effective on the date of the discontinuance decision.
- Current assets are carried at lower of cost and fair value less costs to sell except for those reported at fair value under IFRS, such as marketable equity securities.
- Capital assets (tangible and intangible) are carried at lower of amortized cost and fair value less costs to sell.
- All assets are grouped and shown as a single "held-for-sale" current asset.
- Liabilities continue to accrue and are shown as a single current liability item.

Disclosure

In the notes to the financial statements, the company should provide a description of the facts and circumstances leading to the disposal or expected disposal, along with the expected manner and timing of the disposal.

As well, the components of the single amount of net gain or loss from discontinued operations reported in the income statement should be disclosed. The components can be shown in the income statement, but companies will almost always put these details in the disclosure notes. The disclosed components should be:

- The revenue, expense, and pretax profit (or loss) of the discontinued operation;
- The income tax amount related to the pretax profit or loss;
- The gain or loss recognized on the remeasurement of assets and liabilities to fair value less costs to sell; and
- The income tax relating to the remeasurement gain or loss.

If the disposal is not finalized during the current fiscal year, there will be additional revenues, expenses, gains, and losses between the beginning of the following year and the date that the disposal is completed. Those amounts will be reported in that following period, when they are recognized, and must not be anticipated by any accruals in the year that the decision to discontinue was made. Subsequent-year adjustments must be reported separately as *discontinued operations* and not "hidden" in other revenues and expenses.

Adjusting Comparative Statements

As we have seen, when a business segment is discontinued, the operating results for that segment are segregated from operations that will continue into the future. To improve comparability, the operating results of that segment should also be reclassified from continuing operations to discontinued operations in prior periods' income statements.

Reclassifying prior periods' results will enable financial statement readers to see more clearly the impact of this period's discontinued operations and thus to better analyze results of operations that are continuing beyond the current year-end.

Illustration

The board of directors of Pacific Eastern Corporation (PEC), a large consumer products company, approved a plan to sell its Automatic Transmission Diagnostic Centres division at a board meeting on 30 August 20X1. The division is a cash-generating unit of PEC. PEC engaged professional business valuators to appraise the fair value of the division's assets, and solicited competitive bids from prospective buyers for the division. PEC then engaged the consultancy firm of KGMP to assist with the bidding and selling process. At 31 December 20X1, the following information is available:

- From 1 January 20X1 through 30 August 20X1, the division earned $7 million before tax.
- From 1 September through 31 December 20X1, the division earned an additional $2 million before tax.
- The evaluators estimate that the fair value less costs to sell of the division's net assets is $40 million; this is $5 million less than the $45 million carrying value on PEC's books.
- The bidding process closes on 31 January 20X2. Final negotiations and preparation for sale are expected to extend to at least the end of April, after which date PEC expects to have no continued interest in the division.
- PEC managers estimate that due to uncertainty surrounding the fate of the division, the division will probably lose $4 million between 1 January 20X2 and the closing date of the sale.
- PEC managers expect to receive a total purchase price of at least $50 million when the deal is finalized.
- PEC will have to pay a 5% commission to KGMP on any sale.
- PEC's marginal income tax rate is 30%.

The disposal of this division qualifies for reporting as a *discontinued operation* in 20X1 because the sale has been properly authorized, the division is a separate and separable division of the company, a plan is in place to actively sell the division, PEC will have no interest in the cash flows or operations after the sale, and the other criteria cited above appear to have been met.

The next issue is what amount should be reported in the discontinued operations section of PEC's 20X1 financial statements. The total reported amount on the income statement will be a net gain of $1,400,000, consisting of the following components (which should be reported in a disclosure note):

Earnings from operations for 20X1, before income tax ($7 m + $2 m)	$9,000,000
Reduction in carrying value of the assets to estimated fair value	(5,000,000)
5% commission to be paid on the estimated asset fair value less costs to sell of $40 million (i.e., the estimated *cost to sell*)	(2,000,000)
Income tax expense related to all of the above [($9 m − $5 m − $2 m) × 30%]	(600,000)
Total gain (loss) on discontinued operations, net of tax, 20X1	$1,400,000

The gain of $1,400,000 is the division's profit, adjusted for the asset impairment and the cost to sell the division. The anticipated operating loss for 20X2 is not included, nor is the estimated gain or loss arising from the final sale.

Suppose that in 20X2, the division is sold to an Australian company for $53 million, minus the 5% commission and minus estimated additional income tax expense of $3 million. The net amount to be shown in PEC's 20X2 earnings is:

Sales price, gross	$53,000,000
Less carrying value of assets sold (net of cost to sell, recognized in 20X1)	(40,000,000)
Sales commission not previously recognized [($53 m − $40 m) × 5%]	(650,000)
Income tax expense not previously recognized	(3,000,000)
Profit on discontinued operation, 20X2	$ 9,350,000

Distinction between asset groups and discontinued operations

The major difference in accounting for discontinued operations (as contrasted with other asset group disposals) is that both (1) gains and losses from disposals and (2) operating profit or loss are segregated and reported below earnings from continuing operations. In contrast, the gains and losses from other asset disposal groups continue to be reported as part of earnings from continuing operations, even though some companies may choose to segregate them as "unusual" items.

Disclosure Example

Exhibit 3-5 shows the lower portion of the income statement for Maple Leaf Foods Inc. as well the disclosure note relating to discontinued operations. Maple Leaf's statement of earnings presents EPS in the three-step format described earlier in this chapter—separately for continuing operations, discontinued operations, and total. Also, note that "Note 21" includes two components in deriving the net earnings from discontinued operations: (1) the net earnings for the period during which it operated plus (2) the gain on disposal. Both these components must be disclosed.

EXHIBIT 3-5

MAPLE LEAF FOODS INC.

Reporting Illustration—Discontinued Operations

Extract from the consolidated statements of earnings:

Loss from continuing operations	25	$	(213,813)	$	(141,425)
Earnings from discontinued operations			925,719		653,588
Net earnings		$	711,906	$	512,163
Attributed to:					
Common shareholders		$	709,931	$	496,310
Non-controlling interest			1,975		15,853
		$	711,906	$	512,163
Earnings per share attributable to common shareholders:	26				
Basic and diluted earnings per share		$	5.03	$	3.55
Basic and diluted earnings (loss) per share from continuing operations		$	(1.51)	$	(1.01)
Weighted average number of shares (millions)			141.2		139.9

25. DISCONTINUED OPERATIONS

Canada Bread Co., Ltd.

On May 23, 2014, Grupo Bimbo, S.A.B. de CV. of Mexico ("Grupo Bimbo") acquired the 90.0% of issued and outstanding shares of Canada Bread owned by the Company, by way of a statutory plan of arrangement under the Business Corporations Act (Ontario) (the "Arrangement"). The Company received proceeds of $1,647.0 million for its 90.0% interest in Canada Bread, resulting in a pre-tax gain of $997.0 million for the twelve months ended December 31, 2014. Upon the sale of the business, the net assets of Canada Bread have been derecognized from assets held for sale. For the twelve months ended December 31, 2014 and 2013, the Canada Bread operations have been classified as discontinued operations on the Consolidated Statements of Net Earnings, and are presented as part of Bakery Products Group for segmented reporting.

Olivieri Fresh Pasta and Sauce Business

On November 25, 2013, the Company sold substantially all the net assets of its Olivieri fresh pasta and sauce business ("Olivieri"), a component of the Bakery Products Group, to Catelli Foods Corporation. The purchase price was finalized during March 2014. The final net proceeds were $115.8 million, including a pre-tax adjustment in 2014 of $1.9 million and the final gain on sale was $77.6 million. The adjustment to the gain on disposal and its related tax impact is recognized as part of the results of discontinued operations for the twelve months ended December 31, 2014.

Rothsay By-product Recycling Business

On October 28, 2013 the Company sold substantially all of the net assets of its Rothsay animal by-product recycling operations ("Rothsay"), a component of the Agribusiness Group, to Darling International Inc. for net proceeds of $628.5 million, resulting in pre-tax gain of $526.5 million recognized for the year ended December 31, 2013. During the twelve months ended December 31, 2014, the Company recorded an adjustment to the gain on disposal of $5.1 million relating to additional transaction costs incurred associated with the sale.

Following is a summary of earnings from discontinued operations:

Years ended December 31,	Note	2014				2013			
		Canada Bread	Olivieri	Rothsay	Total(i)	Canada Bread	Olivieri	Rothsay	Total
Sales		$ 567,861	$ —	$ —	$ 567,861	$ 1,453,586	$78,407	$ 206,194	$ 1,738,187
Cost of goods sold		439,710	—	—	439,710	1,148,633	64,749	138,959	1,352,341
Gross margin		$ 128,151	$ —	$ —	$ 128,151	$ 304,953	$13,658	$ 67,235	$ 385,846
Selling, general, and administrative expenses		80,322	—	—	80,322	180,744	11,327	5,674	197,745
Operating Earnings before the following:		$ 47,829	$ —	$ —	$ 47,829	$ 124,209	$ 2,331	$ 61,561	$ 188,101
Restructuring and other related costs		(2,612)	—	—	(2,612)	(17,953)	—	—	(17,953)
Gain on disposal of discontinued operations(ii)(iii)		996,994	—	—	996,994	—	79,424	526,477	605,901
Adjustment of prior gain on disposal of		—	(1,866)	(5,135)	(7,001)	—	—	—	—

discontinued operations[iv]

Other income (expense)	6,341	87	—	6,254	**(1,582)**	—	—	**(1,582)**
Earnings (loss) before interest and income taxes from discontinued operations	$ 782,390	$ 588,125	$ 81,755	$ 112,510	**$ 1,033,628**	**$ (5,135)**	**$(1,866)**	**$ 1,040,629**
Interest expense and other financing costs	1,012	42	—	970	**786**	—	—	**786**
Earnings (loss) before income taxes from discontinued operations	$ 781,378	$ 588,083	$ 81,755	$ 111,540	**$ 1,032,842**	**$ (5,135)**	**$(1,866)**	**$ 1,039,843**
Income taxes	127,790	87,433	11,699	28,658	**107,123**	**(1,242)**	**(140)**	**108,505**
Net earnings (loss) from discontinued operations	$ 653,588	$ 500,650	$ 70,056	$ 82,882	**$ 925,719**	**$(3,893)**	**$ (1,726)**	**$ 931,338**
Attributed to:								
Common shareholders	$ 637,832	$500,650	$62,805	$ 74,377	**$ 923,744**	**$(3,893)**	**$(1,689)**	**$ 929,326**
Non-controlling interest	15,756	—	7,251	8,505	**1,975**	—	**(37)**	**2,012**
	$ 653,588	$500,650	$70,056	$ 82,882	**$ 925,719**	**$(3,893)**	**$ (1,726)**	**$ 931,338**

26

Earnings per share from discontinued operations attributable to common shareholders:

	2014	2013
Basic and diluted earnings per share from discontinued operations	$ 6.54	$ 4.56
Weighted average number of shares (millions)	141.2	139.9

(i) *The Rothsay and Olivieri operations were sold during 2013.*

(ii) *Included in the gain on disposal of discontinued operations is $8.5 million of stock compensation expenses for the year ended December 31, 2014.*

(iii) *Gain, net of tax, attributable to common shareholders $894.5 million (2013: $515.9 million) for the year ended December 31, 2014.*

(iv) *Adjustment of prior gain on disposal of discontinued operations includes $2.5 million (2013: $0.0 million) of stock-based compensation granted during 2014.*

In order to accurately represent the continuing and discontinuing operations sales and cost of goods sold, certain intercompany eliminations have been reversed in the amounts presented above and in the statement of net earnings for all periods presented.

	2014			2013			
Twelve months ended December 31,	**Canada Bread**	**Olivieri**	**Total(i)**	Canada Bread	Olivieri	Rothsay	Total
Operating cash flows	**$ (41,059)**	**$ 160**	**$ (40,899)**	$184,333	$ 4,143	$ 67,601	$ 256,077
Financing cash flows(ii)	**(246,583)**	**—**	**(246,583)**	(51,145)	—	—	(51,145)
Investing cash flows	**1,584,833**	**(468)**	**1,584,365**	(23,170)	115,578	616,268	708,676
Net cash flows	**$ 1,297,191**	**$(308)**	**$1,296,883**	$ 110,018	$ 119,721	$683,869	$ 913,608

(i) *The Rothsoy operation was sold during 2013, and had no cash flows for 2014.*

(ii) *Includes intercompany dividends that are eliminated on consolidation.*

Source: Maple Leaf Foods Inc., 2014 audited annual financial statements, page 4, www.sedar.com, posted 31 March 2015.

Restructuring

Restructurings are a fairly common phenomenon in most lines of business. If a company does not restructure its operations from time to time, it is likely to get out of date and begin to falter.

Companies often develop plans for major restructuring. Those plans may involve any or all of the disposal options that we have already discussed as well as significant additional costs. Restructuring usually requires relocation costs, retooling costs, training costs, and so forth. A particularly important aspect of most reorganizations involves the employees. Frequently, the employee group is reduced, sometimes quite drastically, obligating the company to provide severance pay and other termination benefits such as counselling services.

Definition of a Restructuring Plan

Restructurings show up frequently in financial statements. This is partially due to the rather restrictive guidelines for reporting discontinued operations, as we discussed above. If an operational change does not qualify under IFRS as a discontinued operation, it often ends up being reported as a restructuring. However, restructuring has its own definition and requirements under IFRS. IAS 37 defines a **restructuring plan** as a plan that has two characteristics:

1. The program must be planned and controlled by management; and
2. The program must significantly alter:
    a. The manner in which the business is conducted, and/or
    b. The scope of business in which the company is engaged.

Take special note of the words "significantly alter." The IFRS does not want companies to clutter up their financial reporting by treating minor operational adjustments as restructurings. Only major alterations in an entity's operations may be reported as restructurings under IFRS. Major restructurings should be a flag to investors and creditors to expect a change in the nature of the entity's operations and therefore the earnings and cash flows in future periods.

The definition of a restructuring plan is one thing; it is quite another to decide (1) *what* costs can be recognized and (2) *when* they can be recognized. The costs to be recognized must only be direct expenditures arising from the restructuring plan, and they must not be related to the ongoing or continuing activities of the company.

For example, suppose a communications company has decided to restructure its mobile phone manufacturing facilities. Some employees will be let go, with severance pay and supplemental benefits. Those costs are clearly direct expenditures arising from the restructuring plan. However, other affected manufacturing employees will be retrained and relocated to other divisions of the company. Those costs cannot be included as costs of the restructuring because the employees will still be employed by the company.

The *future* costs of a formal restructuring plan can be recognized in the financial statements only if the future expenditures are a *constructive obligation*.

Definition of a Constructive Obligation

A **constructive obligation** is a liability of uncertain timing and amount that will arise in the future as a result of an entity's present or past practices and actions. Without the guidance of accounting standards, any company could set up a provision for future costs arising from current or past decisions. Indeed, in past years, many companies did set up "provisions" for poorly defined future costs of restructuring and other potential costs. It is easy for a company to *say* it is going to take certain actions, but it is something different to follow through. Without strong limitations on a company's ability to establish such provisions or "reserves," management might be strongly tempted to use these provisions as a way of manipulating profits by subsequent "adjustments" to the projected costs.

For example, it is not unusual for a company's management to announce that it will lay off thousands of employees, but then either not lay anyone off or lay off significantly fewer people. While that outcome is good for the employees, it is not good enough to merit recognition of severance costs when the announcement is made.

Therefore, in order for a constructive obligation to exist, the company must not only have publicly communicated the restructuring plan in detail, it must also have taken specific actions to implement the plan. One example of specific action is reaching agreement with the affected employee group for early retirements, layoffs, retraining, and terminations. Such an agreement would identify the employees affected, specify the timing of the various actions, and provide a reliable estimate of the costs.

Exhibit 3-6 shows a flowchart for deciding when a *provision for restructuring costs* can be recognized. If any step is not satisfied, the company cannot recognize the estimated future expense or the future liability as a provision in its financial statements—the restructuring plan should only be disclosed in the notes.

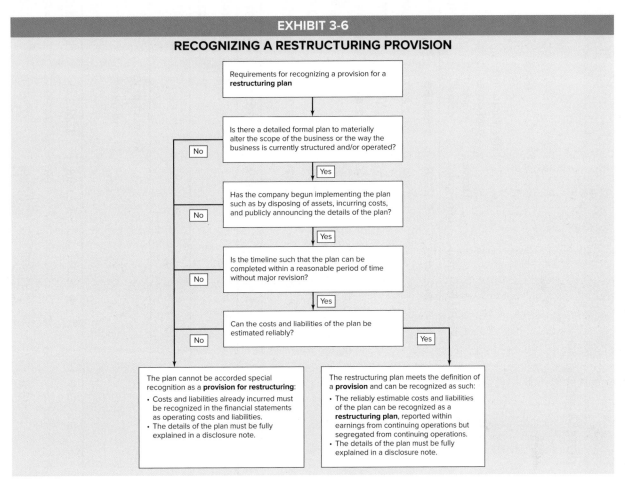

EXHIBIT 3-6

RECOGNIZING A RESTRUCTURING PROVISION

Provision for Restructuring Cost

A **provision** is *a reliably estimable liability for a probable cost that will arise due to a past action*. As you can see, the definition of a provision is derived from defining and recognizing the liability rather than the cost. This approach is in line with the definitions of financial statement elements that we discussed in Chapter 2. An expense arises from an increase in liabilities—thus, a restructuring cost is recognized in the income statement because the increase in liabilities (the constructive obligation) triggers recognition of an expense.

Since a provision must be based on reliable estimates, it follows that costs that cannot be reliably estimated must be excluded from the provision. Other costs can be added to the provision as they become reliably estimable. That means that not all of the costs for a restructuring plan will be recognized as a liability and as an expense in the first period. Both newly estimated costs and revisions of previously recognized costs will show up in the income statements throughout the years of restructuring, as well as in later years as payments are actually made (e.g., for separation payments).

One final important point—restructuring costs are reported as an expense under *continuing operations* in the profit or loss section of the SCI. The only exception arises when the restructuring plan will include the discontinuance of a major segment of the business or a geographic area of operations. Then, only the discontinued operation will be reported *below* the line for "earnings from continuing operations" while other restructuring costs will be reported as expenses *above* that line.

Disclosure Example

A good example of restructuring is provided by the annual financial statements of Maple Leaf Foods Inc.

Exhibit 3-7 shows the Maple Leaf's disclosure note for restructuring that appeared in the company's 2014 financial statements.

EXHIBIT 3-7

NOTE 14—PROVISIONS

14. PROVISION

	Notes	Legal	Environmental	Lease make-good	Restructuring and other related costs[i]	Total
Balance at December 31, 2013		$ 561	$12,603	$ 4,736	$ 56,556	$ 74,456
Charges		2,191	—	2,134	52,667	56,992
Reversals		—	—	—	(7,751)	(7,751)
Cash payments		(502)	(177)	—	(32,474)	(33,153)
Non-Cash Items		—	—	—	(2,091)	(2,091)
Foreign currency translation		—	(80)	104	193	217
Transfer to liabilities associated with assets held for sale	8	—	(1,316)	(2,517)	(6,959)	(10,792)
Balance at December 31, 2014		$ 2,250	$ 11,030	$ 4,457	$ 60,141	$ 77,878
Current						$ 60,443
Non-current						17,435
Total at December 31, 2014						$ 77,878

		Legal	Environmental	Lease make-good	Restructuring and other related costs[i]	Total
Balance at December 31, 2012		$ 741	$ 16,071	$ 6,098	$ 29,225	$ 52,135
Charges		—	—	83	74,393	74,476
Reversals		(43)	(3,148)	(1,769)	(7,365)	(12,325)

Cash payments	(137)	(314)	—	(37,667)	(38,118)
Non-cash items	—	—	—	(2,231)	(2,231)
Foreign currency translation	$ —	$ (6)	$ 324	$ 201	$ 519
Balance at December 31, 2013	$ 561	$12,603	$ 4,736	$ 56,556	$ 74,456
Current					$ 54,853
Non-current					19,603
Total at December 31, 2013					$ 74,456

(i) *For additional information on restructuring and other related costs, see the table below.*

	Severance	Site closing and other cash costs	Retention	Total restructuring and other related costs
Balance at December 31, 2013	**$ 27,824**	**$ 12,124**	**$ 16,608**	**$ 56,556**
Charges	32,098	4,306	16,263	52,667
Reversals	(5,125)	(67)	(2,559)	(7,751)
Cash payments	(13,215)	(4,723)	(14,536)	(32,474)
Non-cash Items	(4,015)	3,153	(1,229)	(2,091)
Foreign currency translation	(29)	222	—	193
Transfer to liabilities associated with assets held for sale	(2,765)	(2,691)	(1,503)	(6,959)
Balance at December 31, 2014	**$ 34,773**	**$ 12,324**	**$ 13,044**	**$ 60,141**

Source: Maple Leaf Foods Inc., 2014 audited annual financial statements, note 14, www.sedar.com, posted 31 March 2015.

CONCEPT REVIEW

1. Explain the difference between an *idle* asset and an *abandoned* asset. What is the accounting treatment for an asset that a company is abandoning?
2. What are the two necessary conditions that must be satisfied for a noncurrent asset to be reclassified as *held-for-sale*?
3. What is a *disposal group*? How is a disposal group reported on the SFP?
4. Define a *cash-generating unit*. Why must a *discontinued operation* be a cash-generating unit?
5. What is the reporting objective of the special treatment given to *discontinued operations*?

Looking Forward

In 2011, the IASB began the process of reconsidering the conceptual framework, including the role of comprehensive income and the use of non-GAAP performance measures. Respondents to a 2011 survey raised a number of issues concerning the SCI, such as the basic nature of comprehensive income and OCI, a lack of clarity between the roles of profit or loss and OCI in measuring an enterprise's performance, and a perception that OCI has become a dumping ground for controversial items.

In March 2013, the IASB released an early draft of a series of discussion papers on possible changes to the conceptual framework. One paper addresses issues that have been raised about the SCI. It attempts to set out a set of principles by which to improve the reporting framework. The goal is to improve the measurement of *financial performance*, but it concedes that IFRS does not define the term.

One major suggestion is that only two general types of items should be reported in OCI: (1) bridging items and (2) mismatched remeasurements. The paper also raises the question of whether the term *comprehensive income* should be replaced by a more understandable one.

Interestingly (and perhaps a bit frighteningly), some hold that there should be no differentiation between profit or loss and OCI. That is, the subtotal of profit and loss should be eliminated and only one final amount should be shown for comprehensive income.

Don't hold your breath waiting for the outcome. Discussions on changes to the conceptual framework take a long time to work through. Nevertheless, clearly a lot of discomfort has been expressed by both preparers and users with the present content of OCI, particularly those with items that are never recycled into profit or loss.

The following tables provide a summary of provisions recorded in respect of restructuring and other related costs as at December 31, 2014, and December 31, 2013, all on a pre-tax basis.

Accounting Standards for Private Enterprises

Comprehensive Income

There is no SCI in Canadian ASPE; only an income statement should be provided. The concept of *other comprehensive income* does not exist in ASPE. Instead:

- Net income after taxes is transferred directly from the income statement to retained earnings (or via the statement of changes in retained earnings, if a separate statement is prepared);

- Unrealized foreign exchange translation gains or losses related to a foreign subsidiary (a component of OCI under IFRS) are reported as a separate component of shareholders' equity; and
- Any other nonearnings items that affect shareholders' equity are reported in shareholders' equity, as appropriate.

Under ASPE, *consolidated* financial statements are not required. The statements of a private enterprise are not issued to the public, and users are presumed to be knowledgeable. If a user wants consolidated statements, he or she can request them (or, in the case of a major provider of capital such as an institutional investor, insist on them).

Format

- ASPE does not specify a format other than the obvious fact that it should begin with "revenue" and end with "net income." There is no requirement for basing the expense disclosure on the "functional" versus the "nature of expense" approach that is required by IFRS.
- ASPE requires just one subtotal in the statement, and that is for "income or loss before discontinued operations." Other subtotals are permitted, but none are required.
- As with IFRS, discontinued operations are reported separately after earnings from continuing operations, net of income tax.

Thus, the default position for ASPE is a single-step statement to derive earnings from continuing operations, followed by a line for discontinued operations net of income tax. Otherwise, subject to the line item requirements below, items may be listed in whatever arrangement the company chooses.

Line Items

In general, all of the line items required by IFRS are also required under ASPE, *except* for information relating to total employee expenses, which is *not required*. Additional detail on some items is required:

- The amounts of major categories of revenue recognized
- The amount of inventories recognized as expense
- Income from investments should be disclosed not only in total but also broken down into earnings from:
  - Nonconsolidated subsidiaries;
  - Investments measured using the equity method;
  - All other investments measured at cost; and
  - All other investments carried at fair value.
- The amount of exchange gain or loss included in net income
- The amount of gain or loss recognized on long-lived assets (including disposal groups) disposed of or reclassified as held-for-sale
- Separately, the amounts charged for:
  - Amortization of property, plant, and equipment;
  - Impairment losses on property, plant, and equipment;
  - Amortization of intangible assets;
  - Impairment losses on goodwill; and
  - Impairment losses on intangible assets.
- Net gains and losses recognized on financial instruments
- Share-based compensation and other share-based payments
- Separately, interest expense related to:

  – Current liabilities;
  – Long-term liabilities; and
  – Capital lease obligations.

- Unusual revenues, expenses, gains and losses that are not normal business activities of the enterprise
- Government assistance credited directly to income
- Income taxes on continuing operations
- Net income (loss) after taxes relating to discontinued operations

While this might look like a long list, it is really not very significantly different from IFRS. Most of this detail is shown in the notes rather than on the face of the income statement.

Held-for-Sale Assets

IFRS classifies held-for-sale assets as current because the expectation is that they will be sold within one year. In contrast, ASPE continues to classify the assets as current or noncurrent, depending on their nature. The only exception is when a noncurrent asset is sold prior to the date of completion of the financial statements and the proceeds from the sale are expected within the next year. Note that this reclassification as "current" does *not* require the asset to be sold prior to the year-end but only prior to finalizing the year's financial statements.

When a company writes down an asset and classifies it as held-for-sale, any subsequent increase in value is recognized in net income only to the extent that the asset had been written down *after* its classification. The asset's initial remeasurement before its reclassification becomes the upper limit.

Restructuring

ASPE does not specifically deal with restructuring. However, the general concepts underlying the recognition of constructive obligations would still apply for private enterprises.

Earnings per Share

Earnings per share amounts are not required. Indeed, EPS is not even mentioned in ASPE. The reason is that private companies are very closely held, often by just one person or one family, and there is no widespread share ownership or fluctuating number of outstanding shares as in a public company. Dilution of earnings is not an issue.

RELEVANT STANDARDS

CPA Canada Handbook, Part I (IFRS):

- IAS 1, Presentation of Financial Statements
- IAS 8, Accounting Policies, Changes in Accounting Estimates and Errors
- IAS 37, Provisions, Contingent Liabilities and Contingent Assets
- IFRS 5, Non-current Assets Held-for-Sale and Discontinued Operations

CPA Canada Handbook, Part II (ASPE):

- Section 1520, Income Statement
- Section 3475, Disposal of Long-Lived Assets and Discontinued Operations

SUMMARY OF KEY POINTS

1. Public companies must report *comprehensive income*, which has two components: (1) profit or loss (i.e., net income) and (2) *other comprehensive income*. OCI generally includes value changes that have been recognized in the SFP but are excluded from periodic earnings, either temporarily or permanently.

2. Comprehensive income can be presented either in one continuous statement or in two consecutive statements with net income as the final line of the profit or loss statement (i.e., income statement) and also as the first line of the SCI, which must follow immediately on the same page.

3. Companies can report expenses in the profit and loss section either by *nature of expense* or by *function*. Under either presentation approach, two compulsory expense disclosures are (1) depreciation and amortization expense and (2) the cost of employee benefits.

4. Both IFRS and ASPE require a subtotal for net earnings from continuing operations (net of income tax). IFRS encourages companies to provide information, headings, and other subtotals that will help the financial statement reader understand the company's financial performance.

5. Income taxes must be allocated over two dimensions: *intraperiod*, which is within the financial statements of a reporting period, and *interperiod*, which allocates the income tax burden to the current and future years.

6. Intraperiod tax allocation apportions income taxes to current operations, discontinued operations, items of OCI, and transactions involving share capital.

7. Interperiod tax allocation apportions income tax to current and future operations. Tax relating to future operations is *deferred* (or *future*) income tax and is the result of differences between asset and liability bases for tax and accounting purposes. Deferred tax does not represent a currently payable liability (or asset), and it cannot be reported on the SFP as a current liability (or asset) under IFRS.

8. When a company discontinues use of a noncurrent asset or a group of noncurrent and current assets, those assets may be abandoned or put up for sale. Amortization stops and the assets are remeasured to net recoverable amount. If sale is highly probable, the assets can be reclassified as held-for-sale current assets.

9. Held-for-sale assets are subject to impairment tests. If the recoverable amount declines, they must be written down. If the value subsequently increases, they should be written up, but not higher than the original "remeasured" value after considering any depreciation that would have been taken.

10. The gains or losses resulting from the sale or abandonment of an operating segment, whose activities represent a separate major line of business, must be reported, net of income tax effects, as a separate component of income, positioned after income from continuing operations.

11. Companies often restructure their operations to match their operations with the market and remain efficient and effective. When management establishes a formal restructuring plan and takes action to put it into effect, it may be appropriate for the company to establish a provision for restructuring cost. The provision is based on the obligations the company undertakes in conjunction with the restructuring, such as for employee severance pay and related costs.

Key Terms

abandoned asset

accounting income

basic EPS

cash-generating unit

comprehensive income

constructive obligation

declassification as held-for-sale

diluted EPS

discontinued operation	non-controlling interest (NCI)
disposal group	provision
economic income	recoverable amount
fair value less the cost to sell	restructuring plan
flipping	single-step statement
held-for-sale	statement of comprehensive income (SCI)
idle asset	unusual items
income	weighted average number of shares
interperiod tax allocation	
intraperiod tax allocation	
multiple-step statement	

Review Problem 3-1

The following information is taken from the adjusted trial balance of Killian Corp. at 31 December 20X5, the end of Killian's fiscal year:

Account	Amount
Sales revenue	$1,000,000
Service revenue	200,000
Interest revenue	30,000
Gain on sale of capital asset	100,000
Cost of goods sold[1]	630,000
Selling, general, and administrative expense[2]	170,000
Interest expense	20,000
Loss on sale of long-term investment	10,000
Loss from earthquake damage	200,000
Loss on sale of assets of discontinued business segment	60,000
Loss on operations of discontinued business segment	10,000

[1]Consists of depreciation of $30,000, employee wages and benefits of $40,000, and $580,000 of merchandise purchases less $20,000 increase in inventory.

[2]Includes depreciation of $35,000 and employee wages and benefits of $90,000.

Other information:

a.   The income tax rate is 30% on all items.

b.   There were 100,000 common shares outstanding throughout the year. No preferred shares are outstanding.

c.   Assume that the capital cost allowance deductible for tax purposes is equal to the depreciation expense shown on the income statement.

Required:

Prepare in good form:

1. A single-step SCI by nature of expense
2. A single-step SCI by function within the enterprise
3. A multiple-step SCI by function within the enterprise

REVIEW PROBLEM 3-1—SOLUTION

1. Single-step income statement, by nature of expense:

KILLIAN CORPORATION

Statement of Comprehensive Income

For the year ended 31 December 20X5, in Canadian dollars

Revenues and gains:	
Sales revenue	$1,000,000
Service revenue	200,000
Interest revenue	30,000
Gain on sale of capital asset	100,000
Total revenue and gains	1,330,000
Expenses and losses:	
Cost of merchandise purchased, less increase in inventory	560,000
Employee wages, salaries, and benefits	130,000
Depreciation	65,000
Other operating expenses	45,000*
Interest expense	20,000
Loss on sale of long-term investment	10,000
Loss from earthquake damage	200,000
Income tax expense on continuing operations [see computations below]	90,000
Total expenses and losses	1,120,000
Income from continuing operations	210,000
Loss from discontinued operation (net of $21,000 income tax)	(49,000)
Net income and comprehensive income	$ 161,000
Earnings per share:	
Income from continuing operations	$ 2.10
Income (loss) from discontinued operations	(0.49)
Net income	$ 1.61

*($630,000 + $170,000) − ($560,000 + $130,000 + $65,000) = $45,000.

Computation of income tax expense:

Total revenues		$1,330,000
Expenses from continuing operations, before income taxes:		
Merchandise cost	$560,000	
Employee cost	130,000	
Depreciation	65,000	
Other operating expenses	45,000	
Interest expense	20,000	
Loss on sale of long-term investment	10,000	
Earthquake damage	200,000	1,030,000
Taxable income		300,000
Tax rate		30%
Income tax expense on continuing operations		$ 90,000

2. Single-step income statement, by function:

KILLIAN CORPORATION

Statement of Comprehensive Income

For the year ended 31 December 20X5, in Canadian dollars

Revenues and gains:	
Sales revenue	$1,000,000
Service revenue	200,000
Interest revenue	30,000
Gain on sale of capital asset	100,000
Total revenue and gains	1,330,000
Expenses and losses:	
Cost of goods sold	630,000
Selling, general, and administrative expense	170,000
Interest expense	20,000
Loss on sale of long-term investment	10,000
Loss from earthquake damage	200,000
Income tax expense on continuing operations (see computations below)	90,000
Total expenses and losses	1,120,000
Income from continuing operations	210,000
Loss from discontinued operation (net of $21,000 income tax)	(49,000)

Net income and comprehensive income		$ 161,000

Earnings per share:

Income from continuing operations		$ 2.10
Income (loss) from discontinued operations		(0.49)
Net income		$ 1.61

Computation of income tax expense:

Total revenues		$1,330,000

Expenses from continuing operations, before income taxes:

Cost of goods sold	$630,000	
Selling, general, and administrative expenses	170,000	
Interest expense	20,000	
Loss on sale of long-term investment	10,000	
Earthquake damage	200,000	1,030,000
Taxable income		300,000
Tax rate		30%
Income tax expense on continuing operations		$ 90,000

3. Multiple-step income statement, by function:

KILLIAN CORPORATION

Income Statement

For the year ended 31 December 20X5

Sales revenue		$1,000,000
Cost of goods sold		630,000
Gross margin		370,000
Operating expenses:		
Selling, general, and administrative expenses		170,000
Income from continuing operations before the undernoted		200,000
Other revenues and gains:		
Service revenue	200,000	
Interest revenue	30,000	
Gain on sale of capital asset	100,000	330,000
Other expenses and losses:		
Interest expense	(20,000)	
Loss on sale of long-term investment	(10,000)	(30,000)

Income from continuing operations before unusual item	500,000
Unusual item: Loss from earthquake damage	(200,000)
Income from continuing operations before income tax	300,000
Income tax expense	90,000
Income from continuing operations	210,000
Loss from discontinued operations (net of $21,000 income tax)	(49,000)
Net income and comprehensive income	$ 161,000
Earnings per share:	
Income (loss) from continuing operations	$ 2.10
Income (loss) from discontinued operation	(0.49)
Net income	$ 1.61

Alternative arrangements of the information above the income from continuing operations line are allowed for all formats. In single-step statements, there is commonly a subtotal for *income from continuing operations before income tax*. In multiple-step statements, other revenues and other expenses are commonly combined into a single category of *other revenues and expenses* instead of being shown in two categories.

The amount of earnings from continuing operations should be identical in every presentation, as should all of the items below that subtotal.

Review Problem 3-2

In August 20X5, TLC Printing Ltd. installed a new six-colour printing press to enable the company to produce high-quality posters and handbills in high volume at low cost. The new printer replaced a four-colour printer that had been purchased in 20X0 for $550,000. Accumulated depreciation on the old printer amounted to $230,000 through the end of July 20X5.

TLC's management put the older printer up for sale through Like-New Inc., a used-equipment dealer. The asking price was $320,000, an amount that the dealer had evaluated the old printer to be worth on the open market. The dealer was confident of obtaining a fairly quick sale as there always were new start-ups in the commercial printing business. Upon sale, the dealer will retain a sales commission of 10%.

At the end of 20X5, the dealer informed TLC that due to innovations in high-speed laser printers, the market for standard four-colour presses had declined. The dealer advised that a more likely resale price would be $290,000, although the public asking price would be retained at $320,000.

On 4 February 20X6, the dealer sold the printer to a corporation that wished to establish its own in-house printing capability. The sales price was $310,000.

Required:

Prepare the journal entries necessary to record for foregoing information in TLC's accounting records.

REVIEW PROBLEM 3-2—SOLUTION

a. 31 August 20X5—Offset the accumulated depreciation against the original historical cost:

Accumulated depreciation	230,000	
Equipment		230,000

The equipment now has net book value of $320,000.

b. 31 August 20X5—Remeasure the equipment to the lower of carrying value ($320,000) and its fair value less cost to sell ($320,000 − $32,000 = $288,000; $320,000 − $288,000 = $32,000):

Loss on equipment held-for-sale	32,000	
Equipment		32,000

The old printer's book value now is $320,000 − $32,000 = $288,000, which is the estimated net sales value.

c. 31 August 20X5—Reclassify the printer from a noncurrent asset to current asset:

Equipment held-for-sale (current asset)	288,000	
Equipment (noncurrent asset)		288,000

31 December 20X5—Write down the equipment to the new lower estimated recoverable amount: $290,000 × 90% = $261,000. The loss of $27,000 (i.e., $288,000 − $261,000) is reported in TLC's income statement with the following entry:

Loss on equipment held-for-sale	27,000	
Equipment held-for-sale		27,000

d. 4 February 20X6—Record the sale for a net amount (less $31,000 commission) of $279,000:

Cash	279,000	
Equipment held-for-sale		261,000
Gain on sale of equipment		18,000

CASE 3-1

INTERNATIONAL CORP.

International Corp. (IC) is a large Canadian company that has operations around the world that are very diverse. In the past few years they have acquired a number of different companies in a variety of businesses. They have decided this year that it is time to reorganize their operations by amalgamating similar businesses, shutting down operations that are not efficient, and upgrading to new facilities. IC has a December 31 year-end.

You, CPA, have recently been hired as an accounting policy advisor. Your first job is to prepare a report for your manager identifying how the following events should be accounted for and the impact on the financial statements.

After the reorganization is complete IC hopes to issue shares to the public, so they are concerned about any impact on EPS. In addition, IC has financing from both Canadian and international banks with covenants based on a maximum debt to equity ratio.

Your manager provided you with a summary from the last board of directors meeting of the following sales that have been approved as part of the reorganizing. The company is in the process of trying to find a buyer for these assets.

1. IC plans to sell its head office building and relocate to a larger new building that will meet the needs of their expanded organization. The existing building will continue to be used until February of next year when the new building is expected to be completed.

2. IC plans to sell one of their manufacturing facilities and discontinue that product line, as sales have been low the past few years. Any uncompleted customer orders will be transferred to the buyer. The sale is anticipated within the next year.

3. IC has been operating their own power-generating facilities for the past few years. They have decided to exit that operation entirely, as the cost of generating power for their manufacturing facilities was higher than buying power from hydro. The facility was only for IC's own use, not to sell to others. The sale requires government approval, which could take up to two years once a firm commitment has been made by a buyer. It is anticipated that a buyer will commit within the next year because the facility is being put up for sale at a deeply discounted price.

4. In November IC announced plans to sell their research facility and move into a new building that has the latest technology and is ready for immediate occupancy. Prior to the sale, renovations need to be completed on the research facility to bring the standards up to the current building code. It is anticipated that these renovations will be completed within the next three months.

5. IC stopped using one of their manufacturing facilities in October of this year due to low demand for the products. Operations have ceased until demand recovers, at which time IC will resume production. The facility remains in workable condition.

Required:

Provide the requested report.

CASE 3-2

DELUCA SOLUTIONS INC.

Deluca Solutions Inc. is an Ontario-based manufacturer. The company is listed on the TSX, but the family of founder David Deluca retains control through multiple-voting shares. Deluca undertook modernization of its production facilities during fiscal year 20X4. As part of the modernization process, the following events have occurred:

1. Production equipment has been replaced by newer systems. The old equipment will be sold if a buyer can be found. The company has not yet identified a method for finding a likely buyer for the equipment. At the time its use was discontinued, the equipment had a carrying value of $1,000,000. Deluca's production manager estimates that it could be sold for about half that price, at best.

2. The company has discontinued using a small four-year-old building that has housed one part of a production process. Since the building is on Deluca's property, among the company's other buildings, it is not feasible to sell or rent it to an outside organization. However, it is quite possible that Deluca will find a

use for it in some future year. The building originally cost $3,000,000 to construct and is being depreciated on a straight-line basis over 20 years.

3. A warehousing conveyor system is being replaced. A buyer for the old system, including supplies and spare parts, is actively being sought so that it can be dismantled to make room for the new system. The warehousing manager estimates that the cost of dismantling the system will be about $600,000. The buyer will be responsible for installation. It is expected that the buyer will cover the cost of shipping, although the relative cost of shipping (depending on the distance to the buyer's facilities) will have an impact on the equipment's realizable value. The equipment has a carrying value on Deluca's books of $4,600,000; Deluca is asking $4,000,000 for the equipment, which is less than the $5,000,000 value estimated by the company that is supplying Deluca's new conveyor system.

4. Deluca has decided that its production and sales for the Eastern Canada area would be more efficient and effective if the company transferred all of its assets in that region to Irving Corp., an unrelated Halifax-based company. Deluca has negotiated to sell the assets to Irving for $1,250,000, effective 1 December 20X4. The equipment's current book value is $900,000. Effective 2 January 20X5, Irving will produce Deluca's products and maintain the inventory. It will manage the sales force for the eastern region, although all sales and accounts receivable will continue to be invoiced and collected by Deluca. Deluca will reimburse Irving Corp. for the cost of production and direct sales expense plus 50% of the gross margin.

5. The former employees in the Eastern Canada division were offered a choice of moving to the new Halifax owner or receiving six months of severance pay conditional on a promise not to seek employment from the new owner for at least one year. A survey of the affected employees indicated that 60% will elect to accept a transfer. The cost of severance pay for the other 40% is estimated to be $900,000, none of which will be paid out until after the end of the current fiscal year.

Deluca's general manager, Lindsey Adroit, is uncertain about how the financial aspects of these changes will affect the company's financial statements. The company has a substantial line of credit with the bank, but it is fully drawn upon, and the manager worries that the bank may reduce the credit line if the reorganization will have adverse effects on Deluca's financial statements.

You have recently been given a summer internship in Deluca's general accounting department. The manager is aware that you are enrolled in some higher-level accounting courses and would like you to prepare a report in which you summarize the reporting consequences of the company's reorganization activities.

Required:

Explain fully how each of these events should be accounted for by Deluca. What will be the impact on Deluca's financial statements for 20X4? As much as possible, specify the numerical effect on both the income statement and the SFP.

CASE 3-3

HOSPITALITY INC.

Hospitality Inc. (HI) is a holding company with wholly owned interests in the travel and entertainment industry. It is listed on the Toronto Stock Exchange and is subject to the reporting requirements of that exchange and of the Ontario Securities Commission. The company has four operating divisions:

1. Travel Adventures Inc. (TAI) is a travel services company. It sells vacation packages to vacation destinations, both at retail and at wholesale (i.e., to other travel agencies). TAI is incorporated in British

Columbia and operates 12 retail travel offices in the province. The company also sells its package vacations throughout Canada through agencies in other provinces.

2. Sunsation Inc. is a charter airline incorporated in Alberta that operates between Western Canada and various Caribbean and Central American vacation "sun destinations," and also to Hawaii. Sunsation's main customer is TAI. TAI buys bulk seat blocks on Sunsation's flights and resells them at retail (and at wholesale to other retail travel agencies). Sunsation also provides flights to sun destinations for an Alaska-based tour company. As a Canadian airline, Sunsation must operate the flights through Vancouver.

3. Elegance Ltd. is a hotel management company that manages hotels in the Caribbean, Costa Rica, and Mexico. Elegance is incorporated in the Cayman Islands—a "tax haven" that imposes no income taxes on corporations. Many (but not all) of TAI's tours are booked into Elegance's hotels.

4. Brookside Investments Corp. is a real estate company that owns and operates several commercial developments in Canada. It also owns some of the hotels managed by Elegance, including all the Mexican hotels TAI uses for its tour groups.

The senior executives of each of the operating divisions report directly to the senior executives of HI.

In mid-20X1, the North American economy entered a severe recessionary period. The recession caused a significant decline in the vacation travel business in late 20X1 and throughout 20X2. TAI was forced to cancel about 30% of its planned 20X1 tours due to lack of client bookings. The decline in vacation travel caused many airlines to reduce flight frequency. Sunsation was no exception. To make matters worse, the general decline in the travel business enabled All-Alaska Airways (AAA) to lease long-range jet aircraft at reduced rates and take over the charter services Sunsation had been operating from Alaska, because AAA had no need to stop in Vancouver on the way from Alaska to warmer climates.

The multiple effects of the decline in vacation travel caused a sharp drop in revenue from all of HI's business segments, although TAI and Sunsation were affected more drastically than Elegance and Brookside. Elegance, operating through management contracts, and Brookside, with its non-travel-related commercial developments in Canada, had less direct exposure to the travel slump.

The recession put HI's shares under extreme pressure, and two large HI shareholders demanded that the company "clean up its act" and put the company on sounder footing. Therefore, late in the third quarter of 20X2, HI's board of directors developed a restructuring plan, the major components of which are as follows:

Changes in Travel Adventures Inc.

Due to the slump in the travel business, HI's board decided to revamp TAI's operations. TAI announced its intention to close all but two of its retail travel offices, leaving only a single office each in Vancouver and Victoria. The company intended to significantly reduce the volume of personal travel counselling. Instead, the company would focus on corporate business travel and will also develop a stronger Internet presence for selling its tour packages. In December, HI publicly announced its intention to close 10 of its 12 offices in the first quarter of 20X3, offering transfers to some employees and generous severance packages to all full-time staff. Part-time employees would receive two weeks' pay after the offices close. TAI estimates the cost of severance packages at $1,340,000, although that amount had not been publicly announced.

TAI also contracted an Internet consultant to help the company develop a detailed request for proposals (RFP) for the planned website development. The RFP was expected to be issued in January 20X3, a development company retained in February, and a new on-line presence made public in March. HI budgeted $1.5 million for a full-featured website.

Sale of Hotel Properties

To generate some much-needed cash and to relieve HI of the burden of properties with negative cash flow, HI's board of directors decided to put the Mexican hotel group on the market. The Mexican hotels were owned by a wholly owned subsidiary of Brookside Investments Corp.

On 23 November 20X2, after conclusion of a 60-day open bidding period, the HI board accepted a purchase proposal from Lincoln Goodview Ltd. (LGL). LGL agreed to acquire all of Brookside's shares in the Mexican subsidiary for cash consideration of $250 million. LGL would acquire all the division's assets and assume all debt related to the Mexican properties. The purchase price was $250 million, based on the fair value of the hotel assets less the present value of the related mortgage debt. The transaction was contingent upon the completion of LGL's due diligence review of the Mexican hotel group's books. LGL's due diligence was expected to be completed in February 20X3. In the meantime, Brookside would continue to operate the hotels and will receive all monies until the sale was finalized, which was expected to occur in February 20X3, pending approval by the Mexican authorities.

The net book value of the division's real estate asset portfolio was $930 million on 23 November 20X2. The appraised fair value on 23 November was $1,240 million. At 31 December 20X2, the fair value of the portfolio was $1,360 million. The fair value of the related debt was $790 million on 23 November and $780 million on 31 December.

In 20X1, the Mexican hotel subsidiary had total revenues of $160 million and net income of $10 million. Revenue for 20X2 was expected to be $110 million, with a net operating loss of approximately $18 million.

LGL agreed to keep Elegance's management contracts for the Mexican hotels in place for at least two years.

Sale of Retail Mall

In July 20X2, HI realized that the company needed to improve its consolidated working capital position to satisfy a debt covenant. Therefore, HI asked Brookside to find a buyer for one of its major retail malls. After reviewing its portfolio, Brookside managers decided to put a fairly new retail mall in suburban Toronto on the market. The mall seemed to be a good prospect for sale, as it was located in a growing area populated mainly by fairly wealthy recent (incoming) immigrants from mainland China and was little affected by the recession. The mall had been constructed just three years ago and was carried on Brookside's books at $200 million, of which $15 million would have been charged to expense by the end of 20X2.

Because of the good future prospects for the region and the mall, Brookside decided to retain 51% interest in the mall and sell only 49%. Brookside retained a facilitator for the sale, promising a 5% commission. Although there was no publicly announced asking price, the facilitator let it be known that Brookside would entertain only offers of $100 million or higher.

Several real property developers in the United States and Canada expressed interest. However, in December 20X2, Brookside accepted an offer from a large pension fund for $123 million, conditional on the buyer's due diligence investigation. The buyer gave Brookside a 10% deposit. The tentative closing date was 15 April 20X3.

Required:

What are the reporting implications of these three transactions? Explain how each would be shown on HI's consolidated statements for the year ending 31 December 20X2. Be specific.

TECHNICAL REVIEW

TR3-1 Accounting Income versus Economic Income:

On 1 January 20X1, Tyler Trading Corp. was incorporated by Jim Tyler, who owned all the common shares. His original investment was $100,000. Transactions over the subsequent three years were as follows:

02 January 20X1	Purchased 20 units for resale at $5,000 each.
Throughout 20X1	Sold 12 units for an average of $8,000 each.
31 December 20X1	Remaining eight units have a selling market value of $6,000 each.
15 July 20X2	Bought six units for resale at $7,000 each.
Throughout 20X2	Sold nine units at an average of $12,000 each.
31 December 20X2	Remaining five units have a selling market value of $10,000 each.
Throughout 20X3	Sold all five remaining units at $9,000 each.

Required:

1. Calculate accounting income, based on transactions, for 20X1, 20X2, and 20X3. Assume FIFO.
2. Calculate economic income, based on events or changes in value, for 20X1, 20X2, and 20X3.
3. Compare total accounting income with total economic income, and explain your findings.
4. In what ways is accounting income superior to economic income? In what ways is economic income superior? Use the accounting principles from Chapter 2 to explain.

TR3-2 Comprehensive Income or Net Income?

Identify whether the following items belong in comprehensive income or net income.

	Comprehensive Income	Net Income
1. Unrealized gain FVOCI financial asset	_____	_____
2. Loss on sale of machinery	_____	_____
3. Interest expense	_____	_____
4. Non-controlling interest	_____	_____
5. Net actuarial loss pension plan	_____	_____

∎connect

TR3-3 Comprehensive Income Reclassified to Net Income or Not Reclassified?

Identify whether the following items in comprehensive income will be reclassified to net income or not reclassified.

	Reclassified	Not Reclassified
1. FVOCI financial asset	_____	_____
2. Foreign currency translation subsidiary	_____	_____
3. Cash flow hedges	_____	_____
4. Revaluation surplus	_____	_____
5. Net actuarial loss pension plan	_____	_____

∎connect

TR3-4 Comprehensive Income:

Acrimony Ltd. has the following balances in its general ledger on 31 December 20X8 (in thousands of Canadian dollars):

	Debit	Credit
Retained earnings, 31 December 20X7		$40,000
Sales revenue		18,000
Interest expense	$ 780	
Cost of sales	8,000	
Accumulated other comprehensive income, 31 December 20X7		1,350
Dividends paid	2,000	
Foreign currency gains and losses on 20X8 transactions		3,000
Income tax expense	1,120	
Selling and administrative expense	3,400	
Amortization on furniture and fixtures for 20X8	1,050	
Write-off of obsolete inventory	530	
Impairment of tangible capital assets	970	
Additional contributed capital		18,000
Loss on redemption of long-term debt	670	
Unrealized foreign currency translation loss on self-sustaining U.S. subsidiary for 20X8, net of $124 income tax	496	

Required:

Prepare, in good form, a statement of income and comprehensive income. Use a continuous format.

TR3-5 Format of Statement of Comprehensive Income:

The accounting records of Food Complex Ltd., a publicly listed company, showed the amounts below for the year ended 31 January 20X7, in millions of Canadian dollars. The company had 40 million common shares outstanding throughout the fiscal year.

Dr./(Cr.)	Retail	Wholesale	Dairy	Bakery	U.S.	Total
Sales revenue	$(390)	$(251)	$(45)	$(65)	$(67)	$(818)
Cost of inventory expensed	160	134	12	18	—	324
Employee cost	43	28	17	15	22	125
Other operating expense	16	14	8	13	27	78
Restructuring cost	5					5
Gain on sale of marketable securities						(8)
Interest expense						12
Depreciation expense						96
General advertising expense						21
General corporation administrative expense						33
Loss on discontinued operation	(21)					(21)
Loss on translation of U.S. subsidiary (OCI)						6
Income tax expense (including $5 tax recovery on discontinued operation)						20

Required:

Prepare two different versions of the SCI as follows:

1. By nature of income and expense
2. By function

TR3-6 Held-for-Sale Asset:

On 13 September 20X1, Nitish Corp.'s board of directors moved the company's operations into a newly constructed building and declared its old building available for sale. The original cost of the old building was $20 million; it was 40% depreciated. Other information is as follows:

a. On 15 September, a professional appraisal of the old building estimated its value as $10 million.

b. On 24 September, Nitish engaged a commercial property developer to place the building on the market for $10 million. Despite some softness in the market the developer expects to be able to sell the building within the next nine months. The developer charges a commission of 6% on final sale.

c. By 31 December, the commercial real estate market had "softened" considerably. Although the developer held the official asking price at $10 million, Nitish and the developer agreed they would consider offers as low as $8.5 million.

d. Despite receiving several "lowball" offers from prospective buyers over the first two months of 20X2, Nitish's management did not accept any of the offers.

e. By 31 March 20X2, the end of Nitish's first reporting quarter, the market had improved considerably. The developer relisted the property at $11.5 million, its newly appraised value.

f. On 27 April 20X2, Nitish's board accepted an offer of $11.7 million.

Required:

Prepare the appropriate general journal entries to record the information above.

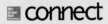

TR3-7 Disposal Group:

Drabinski Ltd. decided on 1 July 20X3 to dispose of an asset group consisting of land, a building, and equipment. An active plan of disposal is being carried out, and sale is highly probable within the following year. The assets' carrying values and estimated recoverable amounts at 1 July 20X3 are as follows:

	Cost	Carrying Value	Estimated Recoverable Amount
Land	$ 400,000	$ 400,000	$ 420,000
Building	2,700,000	1,500,000	900,000
Equipment	900,000	400,000	300,000
	$4,000,000	$2.300,000	$1,620,000

On 31 December 20X3, the net recoverable amount of the group is reliably estimated to be $1,640,000. On 1 April 20X4, the asset group is sold for $1,700,000, net of costs to sell.

Required:

Prepare journal entries that are appropriate to record the information above.

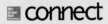

TR3-8 Discontinued Operation:

On 1 April 2015 Ski Inc. (SI) announced that it was going to sell its two ski clubs that were in Western Canada. The western market is very competitive for many ski clubs. SI has decided to focus only on clubs operating in Ontario and Quebec. It is currently looking for buyers. The asking prices are reasonable and real estate agents expect that the clubs will be sold before spring of next year. The carrying amount of the land is $50,000 but the fair market value is $750,000. The equipment, for example ski lifts and snow machines, has a carrying amount of $1,200,000 and a fair market value of $900,000. The two clubs had a loss of $15,000 for operations from January to the end of the ski season 31 March 2015.

Required:

What amount would be recorded as a gain or loss from discontinued operation (before tax)?

connect

TR3-9 EPS:

Identify each of the following statements as true or false.

1. All companies are required to provide basic and diluted EPS calculations.
2. Public companies are required to provide EPS calculations before and after a discontinued operation.
3. Basic EPS is total net income divided by market value of shares.
4. Private companies may provide EPS calculations.
5. EPS is the only ratio required for public companies.

connect

TR3-10 IFRS Compared to ASPE:

Identify each of the following statements as true or false.

1. ASPE and IFRS both require comprehensive income.
2. Held-for-sale assets are classified as current assets in ASPE and noncurrent assets in IFRS.
3. Both ASPE and IFRS may have non-controlling interest.
4. Private companies are required to provide EPS calculations.
5. Both ASPE and IFRS require a subtotal for net income or loss before discontinued operations.

ASSIGNMENTS

 A3-1 Accounting Income versus Economic Income:

Hoskins & Sells is a partnership that was established in March 20X6. If a partner decides to leave the partnership, the value of her or his partnership share will be determined by the net book value of the partnership's net assets at the end of the last-preceding fiscal year.

The following transactions and events occurred during 20X6, in thousands of dollars:

- Acquired land for $200 and constructed a building at a cost of $800. Hoskins expects to use the building productively for about 20 years, after which the company will sell the building and move to new premises. Hoskins will amortize the building at a declining-balance rate of 10% per year.
- Purchased furniture for $60. The useful life for the furniture is expected to be 10 years; it will be amortized on a straight-line basis, assuming no residual value.
- Had sales of $900 and operating and other expenses (excluding amortization) of $560.
- At the end of the year, fair value less costs to sell for the assets were as follows:
  - Land, $220
  - Building, $775
  - Furniture, $45

Required:

1. How much is Hoskins & Sells's accounting income?
2. Calculate the economic income.
3. If you were a partner in Hoskins & Sells, would you prefer for the partnership to report its earnings and value its net assets in accordance with accounting income or economic income? Explain.

★★ A3-2 Interpreting the Components of Income:

Excerpts from the statements of comprehensive income for Wild Adventures Ltd. for the years 20X2 through 20X4 are as follows:

(stated in millions of Canadian dollars)	20X4	20X3	20X2
Operating earnings from continuing operations, before unusual items and income tax	$50	$ 35	$15
Unusual items:			
Loss from writedown inventory	—	(40)	—
Gain on foreign exchange	—	—	25
Earnings (loss) from continuing operations, before tax	50	(5)	40
Income tax expense (recovery) on continuing operations	10	(1)	8
Earnings (loss) from continuing operations, after tax	40	(4)	32

Discontinued operations:			
Income (loss) from operations of discontinued segment, net of tax	—	(10)	5
Gain on disposal of discontinued segment, net of tax	20	—	—
Net earnings (loss)	$60	$ (14)	$37

Required:

1. Wild has experienced volatile earnings over the three-year period shown. Do you expect this to continue? Why or why not?

2. Net earnings increased from a loss of $14 million in 20X3 to a profit of $60 million in 20X4, a very substantial increase. Suppose the company's common share price increased only approximately 20% during the same period. Why might this be the case? Relate the 20% increase in share price to the components of net income.

3. Would you expect net income in 20X5 to be more or less than the amount reported in 20X4? More specifically, assuming no new unusual, nonrecurring items, what amount would you estimate net income to be in 20X5?

★ ★ A3-3 Income Statement Format:

The following items were taken from the adjusted trial balance of the Bremeur Corp. on 31 December 20X5. Assume an average 20% income tax on all items (including the divestiture loss). The accounting period ends 31 December. All amounts given are pre-tax and subject to the same income tax rate. Bremeur had 30,000 shares outstanding at the beginning of the year. On 31 August 20X5, an additional 9,000 shares were issued; at the end of 20X5, 39,000 shares were outstanding.

Sales revenue from continuing operations	$695,200
Revenue in business segment being discontinued	75,000
Rent revenue	2,400
Interest revenue	900
Gain on sale of investments	2,000
Distribution expenses	136,000
General and administrative expenses	110,000
Operating expenses in business segment being discontinued	78,000

Interest expense	1,500
Depreciation and amortization	6,000
Settlement of legal claim agains the company	10,000
Asset impairments, discontinued operation	12,000
Cost of goods sold	330,000
Operating loss of discontinued operation to disposal date, before income tax	75,000

Required:

1. Prepare a single-step income statement.
2. Prepare a multiple-step income statement.

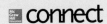

★ ★ ★ A3-4 Income Statement Formats:

The information below pertains to the operations of Montreal Retail Corp. for the year ended 31 December 20X6:

Cost of merchandise sold	$102,000
Inventory warehousing cost	20,000
Accounts payable	120,000
Sales revenue	525,000
Accumulated depreciation	140,000
Sales returns	5,000
Unearned revenue	2,000
Depreciation expense	50,000
Rent revenue	4,000
Employee wages, salaries, and benefits	100,000
Interest expense	6,000
Investment revenue	3,000
Loss on disposal of geographic segment	30,000
Earnings from discontinued geographic segment	20,000

Distribution expenses	106,000
General and administrative expenses	46,000
Loss on sale of noncurrent assets	13,000
Income tax expense	?
Fire loss	20,000

Additional information:

- Functional costs do not include depreciation or employee costs.
- Depreciation expense pertains 50% to warehousing cost, 30% to administrative costs, and 20% to distribution expense.
- Employee wages, salaries, and benefits pertain 20% to warehousing and merchandising, 50% to administrative costs, and 30% to distribution expense.
- The company's income tax rate is 20%. Assume that the tax rate pertains to all elements of revenue, expense, gain, and loss.

Required:

1. Prepare an income statement on a functional basis, in a single-step format.
2. Prepare an income statement on the basis of nature of expense, using a multiple-step format.

 **A3-5 Comprehensive Income:**

Quebecor Inc. is a major provider of cable services and also the owner of many newspapers. The company reported the following items in its 20X11 financial statements (in millions of Canadian dollars, except per-share amounts):

a.	Revenues	$4,206.6
b.	Cost of sales and selling and administrative expenses	2,864.9
c.	Non-controlling interest in earnings	182.0
d.	Financial expenses	322.9
e.	Dividends	12.8
f.	Income tax expense—continuing operations	141.9
g.	Change in unrealized gain on translation of net investments in foreign operations	1.6
h.	Restructuring of operations and impairment of assets	30.2
i.	Gain on translation of investments	1.6
j.	Reclassification to income of loss related to cash flow hedges (net of tax)	0.6
k.	Premium over book value paid on repurchased shares	23.1
l.	Diluted earnings per share from continuing operations	3.11

Required:

Identify whether each of the items above would be included in the SCI (1) as part of profit or loss, (2) as part of OCI, or (3) in the statement of changes in shareholders' equity.

★★ A3-6 Comprehensive Income, Intraperiod Tax Allocation:

Haliteck Corp. is based in Halifax. At the end of 20X4, the company's accounting records show the following items:

a. A $100,000 loss from hurricane damage.

b. Total sales revenue of $2,600,000, including $400,000 in the Decolite division, for which the company has a formal plan of sale.

c. Interest expense on long-term debt of $65,000.

d. Increase in fair value of marketable securities of $55,000.

e. Operating expenses of $2,100,000, including depreciation and amortization of $500,000. Of the total expenses, $390,000 (including $75,000 in depreciation and amortization) was incurred in the Decolite division.

f. Haliteck Corp. wrote down tangible capital assets by $35,000 during the year in order to reduce the Decolite division's assets to their estimated recoverable amount.

g. Haliteck has long-term debt denominated in U.S. dollars. Due to the weakening of the U.S. dollar during 20X4, the company has an unrealized gain of $20,000.

h. Haliteck has a subsidiary in France. The euro strengthened during the year, with the result that Norse had an unrealized gain of $15,000 on its net investment in the subsidiary.

i. Haliteck's income tax expense for 20X4 is $76,000. This amount is net of a tax recovery of $20,000 on the Decolite division and a $25,000 tax benefit from hurricane damage.

j. The company had 34,000 common shares outstanding at the beginning of the year; an additional 8,000 were issued on March 31.

Required:

Prepare a continuous SCI.

★★ A3-7 Asset Disposals:

Golf Inc. is a public company that has been in business since the 1980s. It owns and operates over 40 golf courses across Canada. It also owns and operates pro shops and dining facilities. On 1 November 20X4 GI announced it was going to sell three of its golf courses that were underperforming. They have had declining memberships over the past couple of years. GI is currently looking for a buyer. The asking prices are reasonable, and real estate agents expect that the courses will be sold before the spring of next year. The carrying amount of the land is $50,000 but the fair market value is $750,000. The equipment, for example golf carts, has a carrying amount of $600,000 and a fair market value of $450,000. GI has a December 31 year-end.

Required:

How would GI account for the disposal of the three golf courses? Explain the impact on the financial statements.

 **A3-8 Asset Disposals:**

Manufacturing Ltd. (ML) discontinued use of three assets during 20X2:

a. A specialized piece of equipment that originally cost $200,000 when purchased was shut down and placed in the far corner of the manufacturing facility on 30 June. It is being depreciated over 20 years on a straight-line basis. The carrying value (i.e., the net book value) was $50,000 at the beginning of 20X2. ML has no plans to use the equipment in the future since it was designed to produce a product MI has discontinued. Because the equipment is very specialized to the needs of MI and has no market to sell to, the salvage value is zero.

b. The company stopped using its product line B on 1 April 20X2 due to lack of demand for one of their products. Its use will be restored if and when demand picks up for that product. The product line's original cost was $660,000, and it was 60% depreciated on 1 January 20X2.

c. ML ceased to use a company-owned cargo plane on 30 September. The plane cost $7,000,000 and now has a carrying value of $2,400,000. The company plans to find a buyer as quickly as possible and has engaged a dealer to look for a buyer. The agent expects to find a buyer within the following six to eight months. The asking price is $2,000,000. The dealer will take a 3% commission on the sale.

Required:

How should each asset be reported on ML's 20X2 year-end balance sheet? Be specific as to classification and amount. Prepare journal entries to properly record the change of status of each asset.

 **A3-9 Disposal Group:**

Zhang Zinc Mines Ltd. decided on 1 April 20X8 to dispose of one of its mining properties in northern Ontario. The property consists of mineral rights (an intangible asset) and the on-site mining equipment. The mineral rights have a carrying value of $1,000,000 while the mining equipment has a net book value (after depreciation) of $400,000. Due to the currently depressed value of zinc on the world market, the value of the mineral rights is estimated to be $800,000. The recoverable amount of the mining equipment is very low, no more than $100,000, because most of the equipment is fixed to the property and cannot be moved at any reasonable cost. Zhang's board of directors has launched an active search for a resource company (or a speculator) to buy the mine; the board is confident of finding a buyer in no more than one year. As a public company traded on the TSX, Zhang must provide quarterly statements to the shareholders.

Required:

1. Prepare journal entries to recognize the mineral rights and equipment as a disposal group, including any reclassification entries, if necessary.

2. Assume that at 30 June (the end of the second quarter), the value of zinc has increased and the mineral rights are worth $1,150,000. Prepare any necessary journal entries to reflect the increase in value.

3. On 21 August (in the third quarter), Zhang signs a contract to convey all rights to the mine and the equipment to Rio Tonto Inc., an Australian-based mining company. The contract price is $1,350,000. Prepare the journal entry (or entries) to record the sale.

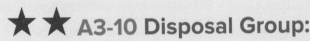 A3-10 Disposal Group:

Black Media Inc. owns and operates a large number of newspapers across Canada. On 1 October 20X5, the board of directors voted unanimously to dispose of one of those newspapers, *The Daily Con*. Black Media would continue to publish *The Daily Con* while a buyer was being sought. As Black Media was facing some financial problems, the board hoped for a quick sale. The newspaper was Black Media's sole holding in that city, and thus the newspaper's assets and liabilities could easily be transferred to a new owner. The board authorized an immediate search for possible buyers, and the company received several indications of interest by the end of 20X5. The net assets of *The Daily Con* can be summarized as follows:

	Carrying Values, 30 September 20X5			
	Cost	Accumulated Depreciation	Book Value	Estimated Recoverable Value
Cash			$ 10,000	$ 10,000
Accounts receivable			45,000	40,000
Inventory			55,000	45,000
Motor vehicles	700,000	400,000	300,000	150,000
Land	375,000	—	375,000	425,000
Building	1,250,000	1,000,000	250,000	300,000
Equipment and furnishings	225,000	175,000	50,000	40,000
Accounts payable	(60,000)		(60,000)	
				(60,000)
			$1,025,000	$1,005,000

Required:

1. Does the potential sale of *The Daily Con* qualify for treatment as a disposal group? Explain.

2. Give the appropriate entry or entries pertaining to *The Daily Con* on 1 October 20X5.

3. Assume that there is no change in recoverable amounts between 1 October and 31 December 20X5. Show how the year-end 20X5 SFP and SCI will be affected by the decision to sell *The Daily Con*.

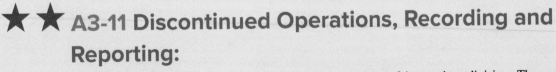 A3-11 Discontinued Operations, Recording and Reporting:

On 1 August 20X5, Graham Ltd. decided to discontinue the operations of its services division. The services division is not a separate corporation, but it is a major operating segment, financially and operationally. On 22 September 20X5, Graham closed a deal to sell the division to Frost Ltd. Frost will assume responsibility for the current liabilities (e.g., accounts payable and accrued liabilities) that pertain to the division. The facts pertaining to the sale are as follows:

Divisional assets, book values at 1 August 20X5 (cost of $475,000, less accumulated depreciation of $167,500)	$307,500
Division assets, estimated fair values at 1 August 20X5	275,000
Liabilities assumed by purchaser; fair value = book value	135,000
Purchase price paid by Frost Ltd.	235,000
Division revenue to 22 September 20X5	345,000
Division profit (before taxes) to 22 September 20X5	27,500
Commission fee paid to the business brokerage that facilitated the sale	40,000
Graham Ltd. marginal income tax rate	32%

On 31 December 20X5, the after-tax net income, including the services division, was $300,000.

Required:

1. Give the entries to record the (a) reclassification and (b) sale of the services division.
2. Complete the 20X5 income statement, starting with income from continuing operations, after tax.
3. Explain what other disclosures and/or reclassifications are necessary in the 20X4 comparative financial statements and notes.

connect

★ ★ ★ A3-12 Discontinued Operations:

Salamander Inc. is a food processing company that operates divisions in three major lines of food products: cereals, frozen fish, and candy. On 13 September 20X1, the board of directors voted to put the candy division up for sale. The candy division's operating results had been declining for the past several years due to intense competition from large international players such as Nestlé and Cadbury.

The board hired the consulting firm Atelier LLP to conduct a search for potential buyers. The consulting fee was to be 5% of the value of any sale transaction.

By 31 December 20X1, Atelier had found a highly interested buyer for the candy division, and serious negotiations were underway. The buyer was a food conglomerate based in Brazil; it offered $4.5 million cash.

On 25 February 20X2, after further negotiations, the Salamander's board accepted an enhanced Brazilian offer to buy the division for $4.7 million. The Salamander shareholders approved the sale on 5 March 20X2. The transfer of ownership took place on 31 March 20X2.

Salamander's income tax rate is 20%. Other information is as follows (before tax, in thousands of dollars):

	13 September 20X1		31 December 20X1
	Book Value	Fair Value	Fair Value
Candy division's net assets:			
Current assets	$ 910	$ 820	$ 740
Property, plant, and equipment (net)	4,400	3,200	3,400
Current liabilities	(900)	(900)	(900)
	$ 4,410	$3,120	$3,240
Net earnings (loss) of the candy division, net of tax:			
13 September to 31 December 20X1			450
1 January to 31 March 20X2			(560)

Required:

1. Prepare whatever journal entries are appropriate at 13 September 20X1, 31 December 20X1, 25 February 20X2, 5 March 20X2, and 31 March 20X2.

2. Assume that the after-tax earnings from continuing operations amounted to $5 million in 20X1. Prepare the lower section of the earnings section of the 20X1 SCI (in thousands of dollars).

★★★ A3-13 Disposal of Business Segment:

Loschiavo Ltd. (LL) has a 31 December fiscal year-end. LL disposed of its Computer Programming Group (CPG) on 31 July 20X3. CPG had a net loss (after taxes) of $18,850,000 in 20X3, to the date of disposal. The division was sold for $237,800,000 in cash plus future royalties through 31 May 20X4, which were guaranteed to be $10,000,000. The minimum guaranteed royalties were included in the computation of the 20X3 gain on the sale of the division. Actual royalties received in 20X4 were $15,000,000. Excerpts from comparative income statements found in the 31 December 20X4 financial statements are as follows:

	Year Ended 31 December	
(in millions of Canadian dollars)	20X4	20X3
Earnings (loss) from continuing operations	$(14.6)	$(52.8)
Discontinued operations:		
Earnings (loss) on operations, net of income taxes of $6.0	—	(18.8)
Gain on sale of discontinued operation (net of income taxes of $0.6 in 20X4 and $17.0 in 20X3)	2.2	91.2
Net income (loss) from discontinued operations	2.2	72.4
Net income (loss)	$(12.4)	$ (19.6)

Required:

1. Determine the net book value of CPG at the date of disposal.

2. Why does LL report a gain on the sale of the discontinued operation of $2.2 million in the year ending 31 December 20X4?

3. LL reports an after-tax loss from discontinued operations of $18.8 million for the year ending 31 December 20X3. Over what period was the loss accrued?

 A3-14 Restructuring:

Marcella Ltd. (ML) is a Northern Ontario–based manufacturer of building materials. In the fourth quarter of 20X1, ML's board of directors agreed with senior management that the company needed to restructure its operations so as to be more competitive, as competition from abroad was intensifying. Therefore, the board reviewed and accepted management's recommendations for the following series of actions:

a. Production of insulation products will cease. Instead, a western company will be contracted to supply insulation products that will be sold under ML's label. ML's insulation production equipment will be sold, assuming a buyer can be found; if no buyer can be found, the facilities will be scrapped. The current carrying value of the facilities is $1,800,000. ML's production manager estimates that the equipment could be sold for about $750,000, provided that ML paid the dismantling (estimated at $50,000) and shipping costs (which would depend on the location of the buyer).

b. The 12 employees currently involved exclusively in insulation production will be given eight weeks' severance pay. The average wage is $950 per week. Six other employees only partly involved in the insulation division will be assigned to other duties within the organization.

c. The production processes in the adhesives division will be modernized and streamlined. Computer-controlled mixing will be introduced for more consistent product quality. The upgrade has been priced at $2,200,000. Employee retraining will be required, which will cost an additional $180,000. The old equipment will be dismantled and the salvage sent for recycling.

By the end of 20X1, the employees of the insulation division had been notified of the outsourcing of insulation products and the planned shutdown of production. Management set 20 April 20X2 as the changeover to outsourcing. Of course, the restructuring plan had become public knowledge by that time, a development that was causing some agitation in the provincial government.

By 20X1 year-end, ML had entered into a contract for supplying the new computerized equipment for adhesives mixing; the value of the contract was $1,250,000 and ML had paid a 10% advance to the supplier. Other equipment (estimated to cost $620,000) had not yet been ordered, although a nonbinding memorandum of agreement had been reached with a supplier.

Required:

Assume that ML is a public company. How would the events described above be reported in its financial statements at the end of 20X1? Be specific.

 A3-15 Restructuring:

Leos Janacek is CEO and controlling shareholder of Mira Products Inc., a Vancouver-based company listed on the TSX. Mira's principal business is the manufacture of furniture for small children. The company has two product lines: (1) home furniture and (2) institutional furniture for schools, hospitals, daycare centres, and so forth. Home furniture is produced under contract by a manufacturer in Quebec and accounts for about 20% of the company's revenue. The institutional division operates two production facilities on its own, one in British Columbia and another in the Czech Republic. Institutional furniture accounts for a little over 70% of the company's revenue and 90% of its net earnings.

Twelve years ago, Mira had purchased the net assets of a Quebec company that manufactures a well-known line of stuffed animals known as PitaPets, which is also the name of the company. PitaPets has contributed less than 10% of Mira's revenue and a miniscule portion of earnings. PitaPets products are sold through different outlets than Mira's furniture product lines.

Mr. Janacek, with the concurrence of the Mira board of directors, has decided to restructure the company. He wants to modernize the Czech production facilities and sell PitaPets to obtain the necessary funds for modernization. Mira was never seriously involved in operating PitaPets, but had let the former owners continue to operate the firm with only broad overview by Mr. Janacek and his CFO.

Consequently, Mira Products Inc. took the following actions by the end of 20X4, the current fiscal year:

a. Through a broker, Mira reached agreement to sell the net assets of PitaPets to a U.S. company for $12 million cash, contingent on the buyer's due diligence inspection of PitaPets's books and operations. The closing date for the deal is set for 15 May 20X5. Mira will have to have responsibility for the employees of PitaPets, who will continue to work for that firm subject to any subsequent decisions made by PitaPets's new owners. The year-end 20X4 carrying value of PitaPets's net assets is $8.6 million.

b. Mira publicly announced to the business media (and to the employees) that the Czech operation would be upgraded. The announcement contained the following specifics:

   i. Negotiations for equipment modernization were underway with a German manufacturer. Mira had made a deposit of €1 million as an indicator of good faith, of which 90% is refundable if Mira and the manufacturer do not come to an agreement. The estimated equipment cost is €6.6 million. At the end of 20X4, the euro was worth C$1.40. The old equipment will be dismantled and taken away by the German manufacturer at no cost to Mira. The carrying value of the old equipment is €1.2 million.

   ii. Mira will provide retraining to affected employees in the Czech plant. Mira signed a €80,000 contract with a Czech training firm to deliver training over a three-week period once the new equipment is installed. The targeted installation date is 17 June 20X5.

   iii. Employees who are surplus to the Czech plant's needs after the modernization will be given six months' severance pay and assistance with finding a new position. The estimated cost of severance is €650,000. At the insistence of the Czech government, Mira deposited €150,000 toward the cost of the severance package in a special restricted account in a government bank.

Required:

Assume that Mira Products Inc. is a public company. How should this reorganization be reported in the company's financial statements for 20X4? Be specific.

★ ★ A3-16 Analytical—Statement Classification:

The following transactions have been encountered in practice. Assume that all amounts are material.

a. A company decided to put the assets of one product line up for sale (intended to be sold within next year) because management had decided to outsource production of that product to Mexico. The company established a plan of sale and engaged an industrial broker. The assets consisted of inventory with a carrying value of $80,000 and equipment with a carrying value of $840,000. The estimated recoverable amount was $60,000 for the inventory and $560,000 for the equipment, before deducting a 5% broker's commission.

b. A company suffered damages due to heavy snow accumulation and an ice storm that caused one of their warehouses to collapse amounting to $800,000. The company has had damages due to heavy winds ripping off the roof of one of their warehouses but never due to an ice and snow storm.

c. A company paid $225,000 damages assessed by the courts as a result of an injury to an employee while working on heavy machinery two years earlier.

d. A company sold a capital asset and recorded a gain of $50,000. The asset originally had a carrying value of $660,000 but had been written down to $500,000 in the prior year.

e. A major supplier of raw materials to a company experienced a prolonged strike. As a result, the company reported a loss of $250,000. This is the first such loss; however, the company has three major suppliers, and strikes are not unusual in the industry. With the economic downturn it is anticipated that more strikes are likely next year.

f. A Canadian company owns a majority of the shares of a publicly traded subsidiary in India. The shares have been held for a number of years and are viewed as long-term investments. During the past year, 10% of the shares were sold to meet an unusual cash demand. Additional disposals are not anticipated. In the process of translating the subsidiary's financial statements from rupees to the Canadian dollar, a translation adjustment arose from exchange rate changes that had occurred over the year.

Required:

For each of the foregoing transactions, explain how financial statement elements will be affected and how the results of the transactions and events should be reported in each company's year-end financial statements.

 connect

★ A3-17 ASPE—Income and Retained Earnings Statements:

The 31 December 20X2 year-end trial balance for Dynamics Ltd., a private company, showed the following account balances:

	Dr./(Cr.)
Retained earnings, 31 December 20X1	$(7,800,000)
Sales revenue	(8,400,000)
Dividend income from investments	(60,000)
Cost of sales	4,500,000
Impairment on discontinued plant assets, held-for-sale (before tax)	700,000
General, selling, and administrative expenses	1,800,000
Interest expense	95,000
Reduction in prior years' earnings due to change in accounting policy, cumulative to 31 December 20X1 (before tax)	310,000
Dividends declared, to be paid 15 January 20X3	600,000
Loss due to bankruptcy of major client	135,000

The company pays income tax at a rate of 20%.

Required:

Prepare an income statement and a statement of retained earnings for the year ended 31 December 20X2.

 **A3-18 ASPE—Restructuring, Ethics:**

Cayman Islands–based Harris Corp. is in the beauty industry. The company develops and produces a wide range of products for hair and skin care. The products are sold both at wholesale (through professional beauty supply stores) and retail (through various types of retail outlets and through hair and beauty salons and spas). Harris also owns a chain of hair styling salons that operate under the name Hair First. It has three subsidiaries, each operating in a single province—Ontario, Alberta, and British Columbia.

In 20X3, Harris's board of directors approved a restructuring plan with two principal components that are expected to be completed within the first six to eight months of 20X4:

a. To obtain additional working capital, Harris will sell the factory that produces the skin care products for $1.8 million to a new company being formed by the litigation attorney Harris retains for the many patent infringement cases that beset the industry. Harris will then lease the factory back on a year-by-year basis for $180,000 per year. If the attorney wishes to sell the building, Harris has the "right of first refusal" (i.e., Harris gets precedence over other potential buyers). Harris will continue to pay all costs associated with building maintenance and operation. The building originally cost $3 million to construct; its carrying value at the end of 20X3 is $1.3 million.

b. Due to intense competition in Ontario, Harris has decided to divest itself of the Ontario salons. It has reached a tentative deal to sell about 60% of the salons to a competitor for $2.4 million; the new owner will continue to operate those salons under the Harris brand, paying Harris a 2% royalty of all Harris products sold through the salons. The current carrying value of the salons (as a group) is $2.8 million. The remaining 40% of the salons will be closed and the staff laid off with four weeks' pay. Severance pay will amount to $600,000. Once all of the salons have been either sold or closed, the Ontario subsidiary will be liquidated and all funds will be transferred to Harris Corp. as the subsidiary's sole secured creditor.

Required:

1. How would these plans and events be reported in Harris's consolidated financial statements at the end of 20X1? Provide specific numbers, to the extent possible.
2. Comment on the ethical aspects of Harris Corp.'s plans.

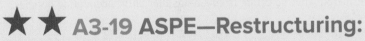 **A3-19 ASPE—Restructuring:**

Return to A3-15 and assume instead that Mira Products is a private company reporting in accordance with ASPE. How would the reorganization affect Mira's 20X4 financial reporting?

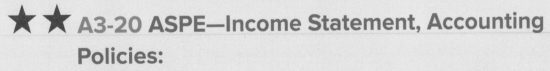 **A3-20 ASPE—Income Statement, Accounting Policies:**

You have been asked to prepare the financial statements for Neema Corp., a private Canadian corporation, for the year ended 31 December 20X4. The company began operations in early 20X4. The following information is available about its business activities during the year:

a. On 2 January, Neema issued no par common shares for $300,000.

b. On 3 January, machinery was purchased for $255,000 cash. It was estimated to have a useful life of 10 years and a residual value of $40,000. Management is considering using either the straight-line amortization method or the declining-balance method at twice the straight-line rate.

c. On 4 January, Neema purchased 20% ownership in a long-term investment, ABC Co., for $45,000. During the year, ABC paid dividends of $1,750 and earned net income of $8,000. Neema can use either the cost method or the equity method of accounting for its investment in ABC.

d. Inventory purchases for the year were, in order of acquisition:

Units	Unit Cost	Total Cost
50,000	$4.20	$ 210,000
80,000	4.25	340,000
30,000	4.30	129,000
15,000	4.40	66,000
175,000		$745,000

Neema uses a periodic inventory system. There were 25,000 units in ending inventory on 31 December. Management is considering whether to use FIFO or weighted average as the inventory accounting method.

e. Sales during the year were $1,500,000, of which 90% were on account and 10% for cash.

f. Management has estimated that approximately 1% of sales on account will be uncollectible. During the year, $1,035,000 was collected on accounts receivable. When management scrutinizes the year-end outstanding accounts, it estimates that approximately 6% of the accounts will prove uncollectible.

g. Additional operating expenses for the year were $550,000.

h. On 31 December, the company paid a $5,000 cash dividend on common shares.

i. On 31 December, accounts payable pertaining to operating expenses and inventory purchases totalled $154,000.

j. The cash balance on 31 December was $102,000.

Required:

1. Choosing from the alternative accounting policies described above, prepare a single-step income statement for the year ended 31 December 20X4 that will produce the lowest net income.

2. What ethical implications are to be considered when selecting from among alternative accounting policies?

(Source: [Adapted] © CGA-Canada. Reproduced with permission.)

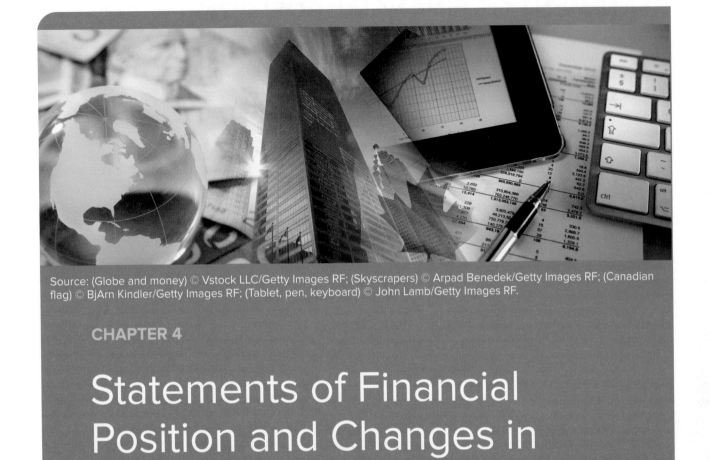

CHAPTER 4

Statements of Financial Position and Changes in Equity; Disclosure Notes

INTRODUCTION

Quebec-based CAE Inc. is the world's leading supplier of flight simulators and integrated training facilities for the civil aviation industry. In 2014, the company employed 8,000 people around the globe and operated in more than 160 sites in 35 countries. CAE's 2014 **statement of financial position (SFP)** showed total assets of $4.2 billion. Assets include current assets; property, plant, and equipment; finite-life intangible assets; intangible assets (with indefinite life); goodwill; investments; derivatives; and deferred income taxes. All $4.2 billion is captured by only 13 lines on the SFP. Yet these assets are reported on a variety of different measurement bases and give only a general overview of the company's asset position.

On the equities side (i.e., liabilities and shareholders' equity), CAE reported a total of about $2.8 billion of liabilities, comprising a variety of short-term and long-term liabilities. The company had shareholders' equity of $1.4 billion.

When assets and liabilities are shown in such a summarized manner, how can a financial statement reader know what underlies a large summary number, such as the $1.3 billion that CAE reports for capital assets? That is where the disclosure notes come in. CAE provided 53 pages of notes to the 2014 consolidated financial statements. The notes contain much of the detail that a user may seek to gain an understanding of the transactions.

This chapter gives a general introduction to the SFP—its format and content as well as the nature and content of the disclosure notes. The various types of assets, liabilities, and shareholders' equity accounts will be discussed extensively in the chapters that follow.

STATEMENT OF FINANCIAL POSITION

The **statement of financial position (SFP)** is a summary statement of the assets and liabilities of an organization at a single point in time. It is like a financial photograph. But every photograph is *static*—it may yield a detailed and seemingly precise portrait, yet a photograph taken a little later may appear quite different.

The SFP is widely known as the **balance sheet**, especially in North America. The naming practice has swung back and forth over the decades. While *balance sheet* has been the long-time favourite, there have been occasional attempts to require or persuade reporting entities to use *SFP*. Although *balance sheet* continues to be a valid title, we will use *statement of financial position* or *SFP* in the context of discussing International Financial Reporting Standards (IFRS), because that is the term used throughout IFRS. Canadian Accounting Standards for Private Enterprises (ASPE), however, continue to use *balance sheet*.

The amounts shown on the SFP are a combination of historical costs, partially amortized historical costs, discounted present values, fair values, and residuals. Many of a company's most important assets (and liabilities, to a lesser extent) are not shown on the SFP at all. Some examples of "missing" assets are the values of trademarks, customer loyalty, and intellectual capital. Liabilities shown on the SFP do not include such items as potential legal liabilities. We will discuss and illustrate all these issues as we move through the following chapters. In this chapter, we are concerned with the general format and presentation of the SFP rather than with the measurement of individual items, which is discussed in later chapters.

Items to Be Reported on the SFP

In Chapter 3, we saw that IFRS requires very little detail on the face of the income statement. In contrast, IFRS prescribes a minimum of 18 different line items to be shown on the face of the SFP, assuming they exist in the reporting company and are not immaterial. The full list is shown in Exhibit 4-1. This exhibit also indicates the chapters in this textbook in which each item is discussed in detail. Therefore, do not be alarmed if you do not know what some of these line items are. You will have ample opportunity to learn more about each of them later.

EXHIBIT 4-1
LINE ITEMS TO BE SHOWN ON THE SFP

Assets	Liabilities and Shareholders' Equity
Cash and cash equivalents (Ch. 5)	Trade and other payables (Ch. 12)
Assets held-for-sale (Ch. 3)	Provisions—e.g., restructuring (Ch. 3 & 12)
Trade and other receivables (Ch. 7)	Financial liabilities (Ch. 12, 13 & 18)
Inventories (Ch. 8)	Current tax liabilities (Ch. 16)
Biological assets—e.g., cows, timber (Ch. 6 & 8)	Deferred tax liabilities (Ch. 16 & 17)
Investments reported on the equity basis (Ch. 11)	Liabilities included in disposal groups classified as held-for-sale (Ch. 3)
Financial assets (Ch. 7)	
Intangible assets (Ch. 9 & 10)	Non-controlling interests in subsidiaries (Ch. 11)
Investment property—e.g., rental property (Ch. 9 & 10)	Issued capital and reserves (Ch. 14 & 15)
Property, plant, and equipment (Ch. 9 & 10)	

Classification and Presentation

IFRS permits two methods of classifying assets and liabilities on the SFP:

- On a current/noncurrent basis; or
- In order of liquidity, either decreasing or increasing.

Current/Noncurrent Presentation

The most common presentation format for Canadian companies is the current versus noncurrent classification. The definition of *current* depends on the operating cycle of the company. The **operating cycle** of a business is the average length of time from the expenditure of cash for inventory or raw materials, to the point of sale and the collection of accounts receivable. For most companies, the operating cycle is less than one year, but it might be longer than a year in some industries—for example, construction or wine making. Since the normal audited accounting period is one year, that is the lower limit on classifying assets and liabilities as current. Thus, we can define current items as follows:

- A **current asset** is one that is expected (or available) to be converted to cash or to be used in production within one year or the operating cycle, whichever is longer.
- A **current liability** is one that is due within one year or the operating cycle, whichever is longer.

If a company's operating cycle is longer than a year, the amount expected to be received or paid after 12 months should be disclosed. This post-12-month portion does not need to be shown as a separate line item on the SFP—note disclosure is adequate.

There is no requirement for any particular subclassification system within the current assets and current liabilities. Managers are trusted to use whatever headings and subtotals will help users to understand the company's operations.

Order of Presentation

IFRS does not prescribe the *order* of presentation within each of the current and noncurrent classifications, although an entity should be consistent from year to year in its form of presentation.

Current and noncurrent classification

When a current/noncurrent classification is used, the normal practice in Canada is that within each current and noncurrent SFP segment, assets are presented in the descending order of liquidity and liabilities in the descending immediacy of their demand on cash. Current assets start with cash and go down to the least liquid form of asset. Current liabilities start with notes payable (such as short-term bank loans) and proceed to estimated liabilities.

In many other countries, the order of presentation is reversed from the Canadian practice. The least liquid and longest-term assets are listed first, with increasing levels of liquidity. This format is used by the Canadian company Bright Path Learning Inc.

Presentation by liquidity

Some types of entities do not use a current/noncurrent classification at all, because it does not suit the nature of the entity's operations. Instead, all of the assets and liabilities are presented in order of liquidity (either descending or ascending). This format is generally used by financial institutions such as banks, investment companies, and insurance companies. An example, of a Canadian company that uses this format is Brookfield Asset Management Inc.

Again, a descending order of liquidity (most liquid to least liquid) is normally used in Canada, with the most liquid assets shown first, and the liabilities with the shortest maturity listed first. An ascending order is used in some other countries, however.

Other Regional Differences in Presentation

The two prescribed formats of (1) current/noncurrent and (2) order of liquidity apply to both the assets and liabilities, but that classification does not address other aspects of the SFP format. When using either of those two formats, there might still be differences in presentation.

In Canada, the overall format of the SFP is to present assets first (current, and then long-term), followed by liabilities and capital. However, companies in many countries use a reverse format. For example, the separate-entity SFP of Daimler AG (the manufacturer of Mercedes-Benz vehicles) shows assets first, but in ascending order of liquidity. Long-term assets are shown first, followed by current assets in ascending order of liquidity. Thus, "cash" is at the bottom rather than the top of the list of assets. On the other side, the presentation is from share capital down to "other liabilities." This style is common in Europe. Yet another alternative is to show equity and liabilities first and then long-term assets, followed by current assets.

While IFRS define the two alternative ways of sequencing items within each section, the standards do not prescribe any particular order of the sections themselves. This is due to long-standing practices; to achieve acceptance of the IFRS financial statement presentation standard, it was necessary to accommodate existing practices around the globe.

Example

Exhibit 4-2 presents the consolidated SFP for Bombardier Inc. Note that it has three columns. The third column is an opening balance sheet for the comparative period, which is required because they had a change in accounting policy. More on that issue later.

EXHIBIT 4-2

BOMBARDIER INC.

Consolidated Statements of Financial Position

BOMBARDIER INC.

CONSOLIDATED STATEMENTS OF FINANCIAL POSITION

As at

(in millions of U.S. dollars)

	Notes	December 31 2014	December 31 2013	January 1 2013
Assets		$ 2,489	$ 3,397	$ 2,557
Cash and cash equivalents	14			
Trade and other receivables	15	1,538	1,492	1,311
Inventories	16	7,970	8,234	7,540
Other financial assets	17	530	637	443
Other assets	18	592	626	564
Current assets		13,119	14,386	12,415
PP&E	19	2,092	2,066	1,933
Aerospace program tooling	20	6,823	6,606	4,770
Goodwill	20	2,127	2,381	2,316
Deferred income taxes	11	875	1,231	1,421
Investments in joint ventures and associates		294	318	311
Other financial assets	17	1,328	1,568	1,339
Other assets	18	956	807	670
Non-current assets		14,495	14,977	12,760
		$ 27,614	$ 29,363	$ 25,175
Liabilities	22	$ 4,216	$ 4,089	$ 3,310
Trade and other payables				
Provisions	23	990	881	1,000

Advances and progress billings in excess of long-term contract inventories	16	**1,698**	2,352	1,763
Advances on aerospace programs		**3,339**	3,228	3,053
Other financial liabilities	24	**1.010**	1,009	455
Other liabilities	25	**2,182**	2,227	2,212
Current liabilities		**13,435**	13,786	11,793
Provisions	23	**562**	584	608
Advances on aerospace programs		**1,608**	1,688	1,600
Long-term debt	26	**7,627**	6,988	5,360
Retirement benefits	21	**2,629**	2,161	2,999
Other financial liabilities	24	**602**	717	601
Other liabilities	25	**1,096**	990	957
Non-current liabilities		**14,124**	13,128	12,125
		27,559	26,914	23,918
Equity		**42**	2,426	1,211
Attributable to equity holders of Bombardier Inc.				
Attributable to NCI		**13**	23	46
		55	2,449	1,257
		$ 27,614	$ 29,363	$ 25,175
Commitments and contingencies	37			

The notes are an integral part of these consolidated financial statements.

Source: Bombardier Inc., or its subsidiaries, 2014 Audited annual financial statements, page 111, www.sedar.com, posted 12 February 2015.

IFRS requires an SFP for the beginning and end of each fiscal period being used for comparing financial performance. Financial performance for a period is assessed on the basis of an SFP at each end of the period, plus the statement of comprehensive income (SCI) and statement of cash flows (SCF) for the period. That is, in order to adequately compare Bombardier's 2014 performance with that of 2013, we need a beginning and ending SFP for each of the two years.

Line Items

IFRS specifies that the SFP should contain 18 specific line items, to the extent that the entity has a material amount of those items. Bombardier shows 26 line items, a somewhat more detailed listing than required, especially since the company does not have six of the items listed in Exhibit 4-1, such as held-for-sale assets, investment property, and biological assets.

You will notice that there are no subdivisions within each of the current and noncurrent classifications. This linear presentation is increasingly popular among corporations, since there is limited space for detail. However, entities are free to present greater detail in the form of additional line items, headings, and subtotals that may help the reader understand the company's financial position. For example, PP&E (property, plant, and equipment) could be expanded by listing the major categories on the face of the statement with a subtotal for PP&E.

Note References

Bombardier shows a "Note" reference number for every asset and liability on its SFP except for the three lines. The basic financial statements contain very little detail, as we have also seen in Chapter 3 for the income statement. Companies tend not to provide such levels of detail on the face of the SFP because the detail is provided in disclosure notes. Since a detailed disclosure note must be provided for PP&E, Bombardier does not list the components of PP&E on the face of the SFP.

The final note reference is just below the bottom line of the SFP. This reference, "Commitments and contingencies," tells financial statement users that the company has commitments and contingent liabilities that cannot be measured with sufficient reliability to be shown on the statement but that the user should be aware of.

We will explore the contents of the disclosure notes more fully in a later section of this chapter.

PURPOSE AND LIMITATIONS

The Purpose of the SFP

The basic purpose of the SFP is to provide an overview of the asset and liability structure of the entity. It is *only an overview*. The assets are measured by a variety of methods, including the fair value of most monetary assets, the fair values of some nonmonetary assets, the historical cost of most nonmonetary current assets, and the remaining unamortized historical cost of the company's nonmonetary assets.

Similarly, liabilities have several different measure bases, including monetary commitments, fair values, discounted present values, estimated constructive obligations, and allocation of potential future taxes (undiscounted). Thus, the SFP is definitely not a precise portrait of an entity's financial position; the measurements are full of estimates, approximations, and choices of accounting policy. Instead, it is a framework from which to begin analysis and interpretation.

The SFP and the disclosure notes can also provide some insight into the *risk profile* of a business and its *financial flexibility*. Are the company's assets old and fully amortized or relatively new? Are there sufficient liquid assets to cover the short-term monetary liabilities? Is the organization in a position to finance new activities with relative ease without incurring excessive debt? These are important questions that the SFP and its accompanying disclosure notes help address.

For example, Bombardier's cash resources and trade receivables amount to about $4.0 billion (i.e., $2.5 billion + $1.5 billion), which is not adequate to cover its short-term payables ("trade and other payables" plus "other financial liabilities") totalling $5.2 billion. Thus, the company's liquidity position appears to be weak.

Liquidity

Liquidity is evidence of a company's ability to pay short-term debts from its current assets and to meet short-term and long-term obligations. Creditors are obviously interested in assessing liquidity. Beyond this, equity investors are interested in liquidity because it affects dividend payments. Unions examine liquidity to establish bargaining positions. Employees are concerned with the company's continuing ability to pay wages. Liquidity is a major concern to many financial statement users.

While the SFP provides some information about actions and strategy over the year, the SCF contains more information about the investing and financing activities of the company; we will take a look at SCFs in Chapter 5.

Rates of Return

The SFP and the disclosure notes also provide data needed to determine *rates of return* and a variety of other ratios. One commonly used family of ratios is called **return on investment (ROI)**. ROI can be measured in different ways. The most basic measure is the entity's **return on assets (ROA)**: How much is the company earning on each dollar invested in assets?

Return ratios are very important to financial statement users, both lenders and equity investors, as they help determine the company's credit rating and share price. The figures used in ratio calculations will depend on the accounting policies chosen by the company, however, and therefore must be used with caution.

As well, return ratios work best for companies that have most of their assets on the SFP. Companies whose profitability is based mainly on unmeasured intangible assets may show a very high return on assets, but this is misleading, since the most important assets are not on the SFP. We will consider a different ROI ratio later in the chapter, following our discussion of the statement of changes in equity. Ratio analysis is discussed in more depth in Chapter 22.

Limitations of the SFP

Amounts Shown on the SFP Are the Result of the Company's Reporting Policies

Even within the constraints of GAAP, alternative accounting policies are acceptable. Many amounts shown on the SFP are the result of a company's chosen accounting policies; different policies will result in different SFP amounts. For example, a company's choice of depreciation policy (e.g., *straight-line* or *declining-balance*) will significantly affect the amounts shown for net capital assets, and thereby affect the amounts shown for total assets and for net assets (i.e., owners' equity). Ratios such as ROI and debt to equity will be affected.

The Typical SFP Includes Many Estimated Amounts

The amounts reported on the SFP are affected not only by accounting *policies* but also by accounting *estimates*. For example, the amounts shown for capital assets will be affected not only by the application of a given depreciation policy (such as straight-line) but also by the estimates used in applying the policy, such as each asset's useful life and estimated residual value. Other examples of estimates include the estimated loss from uncollectible receivables and the provision arising from warranties.

The impacts of estimates are difficult, sometimes impossible, for an external financial statement user to figure out. As we will see, companies must disclose the nature of measurement uncertainty that could affect financial statement elements. Although the *nature* of measurement uncertainty is disclosed, the potential variation that could be caused by using different estimates (from within a range of feasible estimates) is disclosed in only a few instances, particularly for some financial instruments. However, a public company may disclose more information about sensitivity to estimation error in the **management's discussion and analysis (MD&A)**.

The SCP Is Not Intended for Valuation Purposes

Many major items on many companies' SFP are reported at historical cost, which is not always a relevant attribute. Investors and creditors may be far more interested in market values or fair values. Fair-value reporting is only required for a very few items and an option for others. The items which may be reported at fair value include certain types of financial instruments, biological assets, some types of nonmonetary assets held-for-sale, and capital assets that the reporting enterprise chooses to remeasure at a fair value.

The amounts reported for major asset categories such as plant and equipment may be significantly different from fair-value or current replacement cost, given even a modest level of price changes. Individual companies are affected by this problem differently, depending on the date and rate of capital acquisitions, the rate of depreciation, and the level of specific price changes for the types of capital assets they use. Comparisons between companies can therefore be very misleading.

The historical-cost-based SFP can have particularly little relationship to market values when a company's assets are primarily intangible. At least tangible capital assets are valued at their fair value on the date of acquisition; the often-negligible *cost* of many *internally generated* intangible assets is not even close to their fair value. For example, a patent is often recorded only at the legal cost involved in registration. ROI and ratio comparisons are questionable in these circumstances.

Certain Assets and Liabilities Simply Do Not Appear on the SFP

For a financial statement element to be recognized, an item must (1) meet the definition of an element, (2) be measurable, and (3) have probable future cash flows. Assets that do *not* appear on the SFP include intangible assets acquired at no reliably measurable cost, such as brand names, customer loyalty, and the expertise and skill of the workforce. These assets may have substantial future benefit—usually future revenue cash flows—but they cannot be recognized, because the future cash flows specifically relating to these "assets" are not measurable.

Examples of recorded liabilities are (1) some types of lease commitments, (2) hazardous waste cleanups whose cost cannot be reliably estimated, and (3) other unrecognized commitments, such as purchase commitments. Measurement is usually the problem—things that cannot be reliably quantified are not recorded.

Numbers Are Consolidated

A company can be quite diversified. For example, Bombardier Inc. operates in four major sectors, each quite different from the others, with subsidiaries in Europe, Asia, and South America. It is not only diversified but also operates through a worldwide network of subsidiaries. Each of its many subsidiaries is a separate legal entity, with title to its own assets and its own obligations to fulfill. Each subsidiary will prepare its own separate-entity financial statements that will be used by its own creditors and by the income tax authorities in its resident country.

The process of consolidation combines the assets and liabilities of the Bombardier parent corporation with the assets and liabilities of all of its subsidiaries around the world. The result, consolidated financial statements, is an *accounting fiction*—because no legal entity comprises all those assets. Accounting is attempting to give shareholders a broad view of the resources under the *control* of the parent company. While consolidated statements do successfully portray the broad economic entity that goes under the name of Bombardier, most of those consolidated assets do not actually belong to the parent company, nor are most of them really obligations of the parent company.

Consolidated statements do not tell creditors what assets are available to satisfy their claims. A creditor, whether a trade supplier or a lender, has recourse only to the assets owned by the legal entity to which it has extended credit. Assets held by other corporations within the consolidated accounting group cannot be claimed. It is not unusual for one corporation in a consolidated group to go bankrupt while other corporations in the group remain healthy. The creditors of the bankrupt corporation would be out of luck if they based their lending decisions only on consolidated statements!

In Canada, public companies may issue separate-entity statements (i.e., nonconsolidated) to specific users such as banks and creditors, but they are not permitted to issue them publicly to shareholders or to the general public. Thus, as a Canadian company, Bombardier is permitted to issue the company's separate-entity statements only as *special purpose* statements when requested by individual users, such as the holders of the company's long-term debt. However, other countries, such as those in the European Union, either permit or require companies to issue separate-entity statements in addition to their general purpose financial statements.

CONCEPT REVIEW

1. What is the definition of "current" for current assets and current liabilities?
2. Why might some of a company's major "assets" not appear on the SFP?
3. What interpretive problems arise from the fact that the financial statements of public companies are consolidated?

SPECIFIC SFP ITEMS

Most of this book is devoted to examining financial statement elements: their recognition, valuation, and required disclosures. This overview of SFP items cannot replace the detailed study that lies ahead of you. Instead, try to gain an appreciation for the overall nature of SFP accounts and their related disclosures.

Assets

Most companies classify assets into the required minimum of two categories: (1) current assets and (2) noncurrent assets. Subcategories may be used if there are enough items to warrant a separate subcategory. The major categories and the items included therein are described below. Later chapters discuss each type of asset in more detail.

Current Assets

Cash and Cash Equivalents

Cash available for operating activities is a current asset. Accounts held for designated purposes (e.g., bond sinking funds) are long-term. Short-term, highly liquid investments are known as **cash equivalents** and usually are combined with the cash figure. Cash equivalents are defined as short-term (usually no longer than three months), interest-bearing investments, providing little risk of market value fluctuations.

Short-Term Investments

Short-term investments must be readily marketable *and* intended to be held only for the short term. Examples include investments in both debt and equity securities. As noted, some short-term debt investments are cash equivalents that companies group with the cash account. Those that do not qualify as cash equivalents are shown separately as short-term investments.

Trade and Other Receivables

Trade receivables (i.e., *accounts receivable*) and other receivables should be reported net of estimated uncollectible amounts. Notes and loans receivable within the next year, including those to shareholders, will be reported as current assets. Any receivables pledged as security for an obligation of the firm should be disclosed.

Inventories

Inventories usually are reported at the lower of cost and net realizable value. Fair value is normally defined as net realizable value for raw materials, work in process, and finished goods. In some sectors of the economy, inventories are valued at fair value (FV), whether FV is higher or lower than cost. An example is inventory of financial instruments held by investment companies (e.g., mutual funds or investment bankers) reported at market values.

Prepayments

Prepayments, or prepaid expenses, are cash outlays made in advance of receipt of service. Rent paid in May for the month of June is an example. A short-term prepayment should be classified as a current asset. Prepaid expenses are current assets because by paying cash in advance, the company's cash outlays for the coming reporting period are reduced. A long-term prepayment should be classified as a noncurrent asset.

Assets Held-for-Sale

The amount of any assets that are held-for-sale, that are part of a designated discontinued operation, or that make up an asset disposal group should be reported separately. Discontinued operations and disposal groups were discussed in Chapter 3.

Noncurrent Assets

Assets are noncurrent if:

1. Assets will not be used in the next operating cycle or within 12 months, whichever is longer; or
2. Management plans to retain the assets beyond the next year or operating cycle, whichever is longer.

Financial Assets

The principal types of financial assets are as follows:

- *Investments being held to maturity.* A company may invest in the long-term debt instruments of another company with the intent to hold the debt to maturity. This is common in Canada, as most corporate debt is privately placed and therefore is not available for trading. Investments held to maturity are normally reported at amortized cost. Amortization is calculated on the effective interest method, which will be discussed in Chapter 11. Any unamortized premium is added to the investment, and any unamortized discount is subtracted.

- *Long-term loans and receivables.* These are normally reported at amortized cost using the effective interest method, as with held-to-maturity investments.

- *Special funds.* Sometimes a company will set aside funds for long-term future use, either as required by contractual arrangements (e.g., compensating bank balances and nonregistered pension funds) or as directed by the company's board of directors (e.g., expansion funds, share retirement funds, and long-term savings deposits). Special funds are segregated from funds available for current operations. Funds may include cash, but usually the cash is invested in interest-bearing securities. Special funds are shown at their accumulated amount in the fund—contributions plus interest earned to date.

Strategic Investments

These are the reporting entity's investments in the shares of related companies, companies in which the reporting entity has significant influence over the related company's strategic operating policies. Such investments are carried at adjusted cost plus unremitted earnings, using the equity method (which we will discuss in Chapter 11).

Biological Assets

These are investments in living plants or animals, such as timber stands or cattle, during their period of growth. Biological assets with the exception of bearer plants, a later topic, are measured at fair value less estimated cost to sell.

Property, Plant, and Equipment

This category includes all property, plant, and equipment (PPE) used in the company's production or service process, either directly or indirectly. The category is also known as **tangible capital assets**. Historically, tangible capital assets have often been called **fixed assets** because of their relative permanence. A wide variety of terminology is found in practice.

PPE includes both (1) items that are depreciated, such as buildings, machinery, and office furniture and fixtures and (2) items not subject to depreciation, such as land. Tangible capital assets also include certain leased assets if the lease arrangement is capitalized (discussed in Chapter 18).

PPE is usually shown on the SFP at its net undepreciated amount—historical cost minus accumulated depreciation. However, if the recoverable amount of a capital asset has fallen below its net book value (or carrying value), the asset must be written down and a loss recognized in net income. If the recoverable amount increases in later years, the asset can then be written up again but only to the level that the carrying value would have been had no impairment loss been recognized (i.e., to the pre-writedown carrying value less additional depreciation that would have been taken).

A company can choose to use a *revaluation approach* for its PPE. Under this approach, the company can revalue individual assets to their fair value at the reporting date.

Investment Properties

Investment property includes any land and/or buildings that are held for rental or for capital appreciation. Investment properties cannot be owner-occupied. This category pertains mainly to real property development companies. Nevertheless, if any company holds property for rental or for capital appreciation, that property is accounted for as investment property. Investment properties can be reported either (1) on the cost basis with depreciation for buildings or (2) at fair value.

Intangible Assets

Intangible assets are long-lived assets that lack physical substance. Examples include brand names, copyrights, franchises, licences, patents, software, subscription lists, and trademarks. Intangible assets with limited lives are amortized and shown net of accumulated amortization on the SFP, with the accumulated amortization disclosed in the notes.

Some intangible assets are not amortized because they do not have a finite life span. Goodwill acquired by buying another business is one example.

Amortizable or not, all intangible assets are subjected to regular *impairment tests* to ensure they still have a value at least equal to their carrying value.

Liabilities

Most companies classify liabilities into two categories: (1) current liabilities and (2) noncurrent liabilities. Within noncurrent liabilities, the most common are (a) long-term financial liabilities, (b) deferred liabilities, and (c) accrued retirement benefits. The major categories and the items included therein are described below. Later chapters discuss each type of liability in more detail.

Current Liabilities

The current liabilities section of the SFP includes all obligations of the company due within one year or one operating cycle, whichever is longer. The following categories of current liabilities should normally be disclosed:

- Trade payables—amounts payable for goods and services that enter into the operating cycle of the business;
- Other current payables, such as accrued expenses for payroll and interest;
- Provisions for obligations that will be paid within the next year, either legally due or constructive obligations (such as a provision for restructuring costs, as discussed in Chapter 3);
- Income tax liabilities currently due;
- Financial liabilities other than those above, including short-term notes payable, short-term bank debt, and the current maturities of long-term debt; and
- Unearned revenue (such as rent collected in advance) that will be earned within the next year or operating cycle, whichever is longer.

Long-Term Liabilities

A **long-term liability** is an obligation that is due beyond the next operating cycle or during the next reporting year, whichever is longer. Typical long-term liabilities are bonds payable, long-term notes payable, pension liabilities, deferred long-term revenues from customers (e.g., "Advances on aerospace programs" on Bombardier's SFP, Exhibit 4-2), and long-term finance lease obligations.

Long-term liabilities will also include any part of a financial instrument that is debt in substance, even though the instrument may be described by the company as share equity. This type of financial instrument is discussed in Chapter 15.

Offsetting Assets and Liabilities

Normally, assets and liabilities should not be offset against one another. *Offsetting* or *netting* is a procedure by which a liability is subtracted from an asset, or vice versa, and the resulting net amount is disclosed. Such practice defeats the objective of full disclosure and could permit a business to show more favourable ratios. Offsetting is permissible only when:

- A legal right to offset exists; and
- The entity plans to settle the items on a net basis or at least simultaneously.

For instance, it may be permissible to offset a $5,000 overdraft in one bank account against another account reflecting $8,000 on deposit in that *same* bank, provided the bank can legally offset the two deposit accounts.

CONCEPT REVIEW

1. What is the difference between tangible and intangible long-term assets?
2. In what order are assets normally presented on a Canadian company's SFP?
3. What are the two necessary conditions for a liability to be offset by an asset?

STATEMENT OF CHANGES IN EQUITY

A company must include a *statement of changes in equity* as part of its complete set of financial statements. The **statement of changes in equity (SCE)** discloses the components of equity and the changes in each component during the reporting period. The SCE reconciles the beginning and ending balances of each component of shareholders' equity. Although *statement of changes in equity* is the title used in IFRS, many companies use the fuller (and perhaps more descriptive) title *statement of changes in shareholders' equity*. Either is completely acceptable.

Shareholders' equity accounts are derived from three sources:

- Accounts relating to transactions between the company and the shareholders such as (1) share issuance and redemption and (2) retained earnings;
- Components of *other comprehensive income (OCI)*; and
- Equity in the net assets that pertains to non-controlling shareholders of subsidiaries.

We will briefly explain each type of equity account in the following sections. Later chapters will explain each in more detail.

Contributed Capital

Share Capital

Share capital is the paid-in value or par value of the issued and outstanding preferred and common shares of the corporation. This amount is not available for dividend declarations.

Each share class should be reported at its paid-in amount, or, in the case of par value shares, at par value. Par value shares are found only in a very few provincial jurisdictions in Canada but may be found in other jurisdictions (e.g., in the United States).

Details of the terms and conditions of each class of share capital must be reported separately, including the number of shares authorized, issued, outstanding, and subscribed; also disclosed are conversion features, callability, preferences, dividend rates, and any other special features. Changes in share capital accounts during the period must be disclosed, along with outstanding options.

Share capital also will include any financial instrument (or the portion of a complex instrument) that might be described by the company as debt but that lacks the legal characteristics of debt. Financial instruments are discussed a little later in the chapter under "Specific Significant Disclosures."

Contributed Surplus

This is a subclassification of equity and includes shareholder-related transactions. **Contributed surplus** also is known as **additional paid-in capital**. Sources of contributed surplus are from transactions such as (1) the retirement of shares for less than the original amount paid in for the shares, (2) capital arising from donations from shareholders, (3) stock options when granted, and (4) changes in par value shares.

The entity must maintain a separate account for each type of contributed surplus on the books, but they all are combined into a single amount for the SFP. Or the SFP might just show one account for all equity. For each type of contributed surplus, details and changes during the period must be disclosed.

Equity Components of Debt Instruments

Corporations sometimes issue debt securities that have some characteristics of debt and other characteristics of equity. For example, a company may issue debt securities that require the company to pay interest in cash each year but are convertible into common shares at maturity at the holder's option. The interest obligation is legally binding and must be treated as a debt obligation, while the holder's conversion option has some characteristics of share equity. As a result, the proceeds of the debt issue are shown partially as debt and partially as equity. Accounting for these "complex instruments" is explained in Chapter 15.

Retained Earnings

Retained earnings is essentially a corporation's accumulated net earnings since the company's inception minus dividends paid out. In many corporations, retained earnings is the largest amount in the owners' equity section. A negative balance in retained earnings is called a *deficit* and usually arises when a company experiences continuing operating losses.

Retained Earnings Reserves

Retained earnings may be segregated into subclassifications called **reserves**. There are two types of reserves—*restrictions* and *appropriations*. Both are created by debiting retained earnings and crediting the reserve account. The point of a reserve is to restrict dividends. Regardless of their origin, restrictions and appropriations (and any changes in their balances) must be shown on the SCE (or in the notes).

Restrictions

A **restriction** is a reserve mandated by the provisions of a statute (i.e., by law), by contractual requirements, or by the bylaws of the corporation. Restrictions are rare in Canada, but they are common in some other countries (e.g., Germany) where "earnings reserves" are required by law. Restrictions may also be required by contract with lenders or bond holders so that a corporation's board of directors cannot freely declare dividends that may undermine the corporation's solvency.

Dividend restrictions usually exist to protect the interests of creditors, shareholders, or employees. They prevent management from paying out all earnings in good years and thereby leaving the company in bad financial state in poor years.

Appropriation

In contrast, an **appropriation** is a voluntary reserve created by the board of directors. Since an appropriation is a voluntary action of the board, the board can also reverse, reduce, or eliminate the appropriation at any time.

Appropriations announce the board's intention to designate a portion of assets for future use, such as for future plant expansion, or to provide for contingencies, such as a possible unfavourable outcome of a major lawsuit. However, an appropriation is not a substitute for a *provision* if the amount of a probable contingent liability is measurable.

When the need for a reserve has passed, the amount is returned to "unappropriated" retained earnings by reversing the entry that was made to create the reserve. *A reserve account is never debited directly for any reason.* For example, if an appropriation is created for plant expansion and the expansion occurs, the plant expansion is accounted for in the usual fashion, not by a direct charge to the retained earnings appropriation.

Items of Other Comprehensive Income

There are some changes in the reported value of net assets that standard setters do not want to appear in net income but that are reported instead as components of OCI. If value changes are not recognized in net income, their effect must be included elsewhere in shareholders' equity to make the SFP balance. A direct entry to retained earnings is not permitted because retained earnings should be directly affected by only two things: (1) net income and (2) other transactions with shareholders such as dividends. Only certain items identified in the standards are allowed to be included in OCI.

OCI is segregated into items that will be **recycled** or reclassified into earnings in future periods and items that will not be recycled.

The items that will be recycled include:

- Gains or losses on cash flow hedges;
- Gains or losses on financial assets (debt instruments) classified as FVOCI—Bonds; and
- The translation gain/loss on foreign subsidiaries.

The items that will not be recycled include:

- Changes in the revaluation surplus (if revaluation model is used);
- Actuarial gains or losses on defined-benefit pension plans;
- Gains or losses on equity instruments (shares) measured at FVOCI—Equity; and
- For financial liabilities designated at FVTPL the change in fair value due to credit risk.

We will explain the components of OCI as they arise in later chapters or in later accounting courses. For now, just bear in mind that the items listed in the "other comprehensive income" section of the statement of comprehensive income have not yet been recognized in earnings.

Non-controlling Interest in Subsidiaries

As we have emphasized, the financial statements of a public company are *consolidated*. Consolidated statements include 100% of the assets and liabilities of the parent plus 100% of those of its subsidiaries. However, sometimes the parent does not own 100% of the subsidiary. The amount *not* owned by the parent is called the **non-controlling interest** (also known as **minority interest**).

To make the parent's consolidated SFP balance, it is necessary to include an amount in equity to recognize the proportionate part of the subsidiary's net assets that are *not* owned by the parent. For example, suppose one company controls 80% of the shares of another company. The parent will combine 100% of the subsidiary's assets with the parent's assets, even though the parent holds only an 80% equity interest because the 80% ownership give the parent *control* over the subsidiary. The 20% equity of the outside shareholders must be reported on the right side of the statement to make it balance.

Non-controlling interest is shown as a component of consolidated equity but not as equity relating to the shareholders of the parent company. The NCI relates to the non-controlling shareholders' claim on the *subsidiaries'* net assets.

An example of non-controlling interest presentation can be seen in Exhibit 4-2. Bombardier's total shareholders' equity of $55 million is divided between $42 million relating to shareholders of the parent company and $13 million relating to non-controlling shareholders' claim on the net assets of Bombardier's subsidiary companies.

Reporting Example 1

Exhibit 4-3 shows Village Farms International Inc.'s consolidated SCE.

EXHIBIT 4-3

Village Farms International, Inc.
Consolidated Statements of Changes in Shareholders' Equity
For the Years Ended December 31, 2014 and 2013
(In thousands of United States dollars, except for shares outstanding)

	Number of Common Shares	Share Capital	Contributed Surplus	Accumulated Other Comprehensive Income	Retained Earnings	Total Shareholders' Equity
Balance at January 1, 2013	19,433,394	$ 24,850	$ 588	$ 55	$ 24,958	$ 50,451
Conversion of special shares to common shares	19,273,951	—	—	—	—	—

Share-based compensation (note 27)	—	—	161	—	—	161
Net income and comprehensive income	—	—	—	—	10,488	10,488
Balance at December 31, 2013	38,707,345	24,850	749	55	35,446	$ 61,100
Balance at January 1, 2014	38,707,345	24,850	749	55	35,446	61,100
Share-based compensation (note 27)	—	—	272	—	—	272
Cumulative translation adjustment	—	—	—	(265)	—	(265)
Net income and comprehensive income	—	—	—	—	(107)	(107)
Balance at December 31, 2014	38,707,345	$ 24,850	$ 1,021	$ (210)	$ 35,339	$ 61,000

Source: Village Farms International Inc., 2014 audited annual financial statements, page 4, www.sedar.com, posted 17 March 2015.

The statement is in two sections, the top section for 2013 and the lower section for 2014. The statement has six numerical columns, the first of which is the number of shares. In 2013, the company converted 19,273,951 special shares to common shares. Disclosure of share amounts is required, but the disclosure does not need to be in the SCE. The share information usually is disclosed in a note, especially for more complex capital structures.

The company has four types of shareholders' equity, each shown in individual columns: share capital, contributed surplus, accumulated other comprehensive income, and retained earnings. Note that Village Farms is reporting in U.S. dollars.

Reporting Example 2

Exhibit 4-4 presents the SCE for Bombardier Corporation. Unlike Village Farms International Inc., Bombardier presents the previous year's amounts first, followed by the most recent year (ending 31 December 2014). This style of presentation enables the company to show a continuous presentation, from 1 January 2013 through to 31 December 2013 and then through to 31 December 2014.

EXHIBIT 4-4

BOMBARDIER INC.

Consolidated Statements of Changes in Equity

For the fiscal years ended (in millions of U.S. dollars)

BOMBARDIER INC.
CONSOLIDATED STATEMENTS OF CHANGES IN EQUITY

For the fiscal years ended
(in millions of U.S. dollars)

| | Share capital | | Attributable to equity holders of Bombardier Inc. | | | Accumulated OCI | | | | | |
| | | | Retained earnings (deficit) | | | | | | | | |
	Preferred shares	Common shares	Other retained earnings	Remea-surement losses	Contributed surplus	AFS financial assets	Cash flow hedges	CCTD	Total	NCI	Total Equity
As at January 1, 2013	$347	$1,342	$2,239	$(2,794)	$109	$10	$(197)	$155	$1,211	$46	$1,257
Total comprehensive income											
Net income	—	—	564	—	—	—	—	—	564	8	572
OCI	—	—	—	824	—	(5)	(6)	22	835	(1)	834
	—	—	564	824	—	(5)	(6)	22	1,399	7	1,406
Options exercised	—	13	—	—	(3)	—	—	—	10	—	10
Dividends											
Common shares	—	—	(173)	—	—	—	—	—	(173)	—	(173)
Preferred shares	—	—	(32)	—	—	—	—	—	(32)	—	(32)
Capital distribution	—	—	—	—	—	—	—	—	—	(30)	(30)

Shares distributed - PSU plans	—	25	—	—	(25)	—	—	—	—	—	—
Share-based expense	—	—	—	—	11	—	—	—	11	—	11
As at December 31, 2013	$ 347	$ 1,380	$ 2,598	$ (1,970)	$ 92	$ 5	$ (203)	$ 177	$ 2,426	$ 23	$ 2,449
Total comprehensive income	—	—	(1,260)	—	—	—	—	—	(1,260)	14	(1,246)
Net income (loss)	—	—	—	(691)	—	7	(119)	(135)	(938)	(7)	(945)
OCI	—	—	(1,260)	(691)	—	7	(119)	(135)	(2,198)	7	(2,191)
Dividends											
Common shares	—	—	(160)	—	—	—	—	—	(160)	—	(160)
Preferred shares	—	—	(27)	—	—	—	—	—	(27)	—	(27)
Capital distribution	—	—	—	—	(2)	—	—	—	—	(17)	(17)
Shares distributed - DSU plans	—	1	—	—	—	—	—	—	(1)	—	(1)
Share-based expense	—	—	—	—	2	—	—	—	2	—	2
As at December 31, 2014	**$ 347**	**$ 1,381**	**$ 1,151**	**$ 2,661**	**$ 92**	**$ 12**	**$ (322)**	**$ 42**	**$ 42**	**$ 13**	**$ 55**

The notes are an integral part of these consolidated financial statements.

Source: Bombardier Inc., or its subsidiaries, 2014 audited annual financial statements, page 112, www.sedar.com, posted 12 February 2015.

This is a somewhat more complex example. Bombardier has both preferred and common shares, contributed surplus, retained earnings, and three types of OCI: AFS (i.e., available for sale) financial assets (IAS 39 now replaced by new categories discussed in Chapter 11), cash flow hedges, and CCTD, each of which is detailed in its own column. After the total column, the amounts relating to the non-controlling interest (NCI) are deducted, leaving the total equity attributable to the company's shareholders. Only the final total of the last two columns is reported on the face of the SFP (see Exhibit 4-2), which is all that IFRS requires.

ACCOUNTING CHANGES

We close the books at the end of each fiscal year. "Closing" means that we cannot reopen that year's accounts—the year is over. However, there are two circumstances in which, while we do not actually reopen the books, we do need to make changes to the financial statements of one or more prior years. This happens when:

1. Accounting standards have changed and we need to restate the financial results of one or more prior periods; or
2. We discover a material error in one or more prior periods, an error that must be corrected in those prior periods' financial statements.

In this section of the chapter, we will explain how these changes must be accounted for.

Changes in Accounting Policy

From time to time, a company changes an accounting policy that it has been using for a certain type of transaction or event. **Changes in accounting policy** can be either:

*   *Voluntary* when accounting policy options are available because management decides that its previous policy inadequately reflects the nature of the company's operations; or
*   *Compulsory* because new or changed accounting standards have come into effect that no longer permit the company's previous policy.

The International Accounting Standards Board (IASB) has regularly been introducing new standards or revisions to existing standards.

When a reporting entity changes an accounting policy, the historical comparability of the financial statements is reduced because the statements issued before the change in policy have been prepared on a different basis from those issued after the change. This lack of comparability can be overcome only if comparative amounts reported in prior years' statements are restated using the newly adopted principle. The resultant change in prior years' income also changes opening retained earnings in the current year.

For example, suppose that a company changes its inventory costing method in 20X2 to exclude storage costs that previously had been included in inventory cost. The change is due to the company's change to IFRS, which does not permit storage costs to be included as part of inventory cost. The company determines that the amount of storage costs included in the 20X1 ending inventory was $60,000. Since the 20X1 ending inventory had been subtracted in determining cost of goods sold for 20X1, an overstatement of inventory cost causes an understatement of cost of goods sold and an overstatement of net income. In 20X2, the 20X1 net income is in 20X2's opening retained earnings. To make the accounting policy change in 20X2, the company must reduce 20X2's opening inventory *and* opening retained earnings (net of income tax).

Assume an income tax rate of 30%. The cumulative effect of the change in accounting policy, net of applicable income taxes, is $60,000 × 70%, or $42,000. The entry in 20X2 to record the effect of the change in accounting policy is as follows:

Retained earnings—cumulative effect of change in accounting principle	42,000	
Deferred income tax liability	18,000	
Inventory—opening		60,000

The tax amount is deferred because the change is made for accounting purposes only—the tax return (and taxes payable) is not changed. We discuss this type of tax effect in Chapter 15.

The effect of a retrospective change in accounting policy is usually shown on the retained earnings statement as follows:

Opening retained earnings, as previously reported (assumed)	$400,000
Effect of change in accounting policy (net of tax)	(42,000)
Opening retained earnings, as restated	$358,000

The details of the nature and impact of the change would be provided in a disclosure note.

Occasionally, a new accounting standard permits *prospective treatment*. **Prospective treatment** means that the new policy is used for the current period and future periods, but past periods are left as is. This practice results in a loss of consistency, but it also avoids the necessity of digging into past records to determine exactly what the effect would be in prior years. Prospective treatment is also used as a practical matter when it is simply not feasible to reconstruct data for prior periods.

In other circumstances, the company can determine the impact of the change in accounting policy on opening balances in total but cannot reconstruct the detail needed to restate individual prior years. This will result in an adjustment to opening retained earnings, as illustrated, but no restatement of previous income statements. Again, practicalities force the use of less desirable disclosure of the effect of the new policy on prior years.

Changes in Accounting Estimates

A change in an accounting *estimate* is not the same as an accounting *error*. Errors are corrected retrospectively, while new estimates are always applied prospectively. A revised estimate is used for this year, and future years (or until revised again), but previous statements are *never* changed and retained earnings is not touched.

For example, we may discover in 20X6 that our estimate of the recoverable amount of year-end 20X4 inventory had been far too optimistic; the actual recoverable amount turned out to be significantly less than we had estimated. When we discover that fact, we are not finding an error; instead, we are finding that our 20X4 estimate had been incorrect. Therefore, the results of underestimating the year-end 20X4 inventory flow through to earnings in 20X3 and 20X4.

Prior-Period Error Corrections

Errors happen. They usually arise from classifying amounts and transactions incorrectly. When discovered, they must be corrected. This sometimes involves restating the financial statements of prior years, and thus changing prior income, which is summarized in retained earnings.

In the year that we discover the error, we must make a correcting adjustment. The adjustment is to the beginning-of-year retained earnings for the *cumulative* impact of the change to prior earnings, net of income tax. Thus, the opening retained earnings is *restated*.

Then, the comparative financial statements are adjusted to give effect to the correction. In effect, the transaction is backed out of the current income statement and into the appropriate prior year. A description of the error and its effect on the financial statements must be included in the disclosure notes.

Capital Transactions

The statement of changes in equity contains other increases and decreases in equity caused by capital transactions. Most capital transactions are share transactions. Since a corporation is dealing with itself (its owners) in share transactions, gains and losses caused by these transactions are not shown on the income statement because they are not arm's-length transactions.

For example, if a company repurchased common shares for cancellation, any gain or loss on the repurchase is not allowed to impact net income and would impact contributed surplus or retained earnings.

ETHICAL ISSUES

Usually, errors are accidental. However, some "errors" might be perceived as intentional—management might have been trying to affect reported results by misclassifying some transactions. Prosecutors allege that major public companies (such as Nortel, WorldCom, Enron, Live Entertainment, Philip Services, and Tyco) have in the past deliberately misstated their financial results.

In accounting terms, the cause of an error is irrelevant. All errors, innocent or not, are corrected in the same manner.

To illustrate the recording of a retrospective adjustment for an error correction, assume that a machine that cost the Bailey Retail Corp. $10,000 (with a ten-year estimated useful life and no residual value) was purchased on 1 January 20X2. Further, assume that the total cost was erroneously debited to an expense account in 20X2. The error was discovered on 29 December 20X5. A correcting entry would be required in 20X5. Assuming that any income tax effects are recorded separately, the entry would be as follows:

29 December 20X5:		
Machinery	10,000	
Amortization expense, straight-line (for 20X5)	1,000	
Accumulated amortization (20X2 through 20X5)		4,000
Retained earnings, error correction		7,000

The $7,000 retrospective adjustment corrects the 1 January 20X5 retained earnings balance on a pretax basis. The balance is understated by $7,000 before tax:

Understatement of 20X2 income ($10,000 – $1,000)	$9,000
Overstatement of 20X3 and 20X4 income ($1,000 × 2)	(2,000)
Net pretax understatement	$7,000

Assuming that the same error was also made on the income tax return, the entry to record the income tax effect of the error, assuming a 30% income tax rate, would be as follows:

Retained earnings, error correction ($7,000 × 30%)	2,100	
Deferred income tax liability		2,100

Appropriate reporting in the retained earnings column of the SCE is illustrated in Exhibit 4-5. Amounts other than the error correction are assumed.

EXHIBIT 4-5

BAILEY RETAIL CORPORATION

Statement of Changes in Equity (excerpt)

Year ended 31 December 20X5

(in thousands of Canadian dollars)

	Retained Earnings
Balance, 1 January 20X5, as previously reported	$ 378,800

Correction of error (net of income tax of $2,100) (Note 6)	4,900
Balance, 1 January 20X5, as restated	383,700
Net income	81,200
Cash dividends declared and paid during 20X5	(30,000)
Balance, 31 December 20X5	$434,900

Note 6. Error correction. During the year, the company discovered that a capital expenditure made in 20X2 was incorrectly expensed. This error caused net income of that period to be understated and that of subsequent periods to be overstated. The adjustment of $4,900 (after income tax of $2,100) corrects the error.

Other charges to retained earnings arise from share issue expenses, taxes resulting from a change in control or triggered by dividend payments to shareholders, and adjustments to retained earnings caused by a reorganization.

CONCEPT REVIEW

1. What types of items will appear on the statement of changes in equity?
2. What is the normal approach to accounting for a change in accounting policy?
3. How are errors in prior years corrected? How does this differ from the way we correct the results of accounting estimates made in prior years?

DISCLOSURE NOTES

Disclosure notes are an integral part of the financial statements and must be presented if the statements are to be complete. If the financial statements are audited, so are the notes.

Disclosure notes can adhere to minimal disclosure requirements or be far more extensive; this is management's decision based on corporate reporting objectives and the needs of user groups. Unlike the purely quantitative financial statements, disclosure notes can provide qualitative as well as quantitative information. Readers can then make their own assessment of the potential ramifications of the information presented. Notes are sometimes complex and highly technical.

It is important to remember that notes are not a substitute for proper measurement and financial statement reporting.

General Classification of Disclosure Notes

The objective of disclosure notes is to provide information that will help users understand the financial position and operating results of the company. However, bear in mind that financial statements, including the notes, are intended for sophisticated financial statement readers—people who have a good basis of understanding of both financial reporting and the operations of the company whose statements they are reading. Naive readers peruse financial statements at their own risk.

The most important functions of the disclosure notes are to:

- Give a quick overview of the nature of the business;

- Explain the accounting policies that the company is using, both in general and for each specific financial statement element;
- Forewarn of new standards that have been issued but not have not yet come into effect—the disclosure of each new standard should indicate the possible impact on the enterprise's financial reporting;
- Provide additional detail for individual financial statement elements, both as required by IFRS and as necessary to enable readers to understand the amounts presented;
- Provide information about commitments and contingencies;
- Identify major underlying assumptions and estimates; and
- Provide information not presented elsewhere in the financial statements but useful for understanding them.

The company should include cross-references to the notes from each financial statement item, as we have seen in the sample statements presented in Exhibits 4-2 and 4-3 and in Chapter 3. IFRS stipulates the general order in which the notes should appear.

Compliance Statement

The reporting enterprise should state that it is complying with IFRS. This is important, as there are multiple GAAPs in the *CPA Canada Handbook*. It is important for readers to understand which one is being used. For example, Bombardier states the following:

> **Statement of compliance**
>
> The Corporation's consolidated financial statements are expressed in U.S. dollars and have been prepared in accordance with IFRS, as issued by the IASB.[1]

Sometimes, this takes a somewhat different appearance than simply a flat statement of compliance. For example, Australian mining company Rio Tinto states:

> The Group's financial statements have been prepared in accordance with IFRS, as defined in note 1, which differs in certain respects from the version of IFRS that is applicable in Australia referred to as Australian Accounting Standards (AAS).[2]

This type of statement shows up in companies based in countries in which IFRS must be subject to legislative or regulatory approval. In the European Union (EU), for example, new IFRS become effective for EU companies only after they have been approved and adopted by the EU parliament.

Accounting Policies

A summary of accounting policies, starting with the compliance statement, should be presented prior to any notes on specific items. The accounting policy notes should include:

- Specific accounting chosen for each financial statement element, with any choices between acceptable alternatives that management made, such as FIFO (first-in, first-out) versus average cost inventory valuation;
- Any changes in accounting policies or new accounting standards that have or are about to come into effect; and
- The methods of applying these principles, including methods specific to the industry in which the company operates, as well as important judgements that are required.

---

1. *Bombardier Inc., or its subsidiaries, Annual Report*, page 114. Retrieved 13 November 2015, from http://ir.bombardier.com/en/financial-reports
2. *Rio Tinto 2011 Annual Report*, page 138. Retrieved 13 November 2015, from http://www.riotinto.com/ar2014/pdfs/ rio-tinto_2014-annual-report.pdf

New Accounting Standards

New accounting standards do not come into effect immediately. Companies need time to adjust their accounting procedures and information collection before they can apply new standards. When a new standard is issued, a reporting entity should alert financial statement readers to the fact that the standard will be coming into effect, the date at which it will be effective, and the potential impact on the company's financial reporting. Often, a company will end its disclosure of a new standard with a statement such as "implementation of this standard is not expected to have a material impact on our financial statements." In other instances, the impact can be quite substantial. Regardless of the possible impact, each new standard must be explained to the reader.

Additional Detail

As we have seen from the examples in this and the preceding chapter, financial statements are quite brief. Accounting standards require quite a bit of detailed information that does not appear on the face of the statements. Instead, the required detail is provided in individual notes relating to each item.

For example, on Bombardier Inc.'s 2014 SFP (see Exhibit 4-2), the company reports a single amount of $2,092 (million) for PPE. From disclosure note 19, we can learn that the total represents cost of $4,444 minus accumulated amortization of $2,352. The major components were buildings ($2,413 less $1,212 amortization) and equipment ($1,347 cost less $864 amortization). We also learn that PPE includes assets under finance lease ($243 less $91 amortization). Further, the company tells us that total amortization of $182 was charged against earnings in fiscal year 2014.

Bombardier leases some aircraft to other companies under operating leases. Those assets, amounting to $35 minus $14 amortization at year-end 2014, are included in Bombardier's PPE. Rental income during 2014 was $5 million.

Major Underlying Assumptions and Estimates

Sophisticated financial statement readers are generally aware of the large number of estimates that underlie amounts in the financial statements. Nevertheless, it is appropriate to call attention to **measurement uncertainty**—the extent to which errors in significant estimates can affect the financial statements. Disclosing the nature and extent of measurement uncertainty requires a description of the estimated amount, the amount recorded, and an indication of possible dollar change. Disclosure might also include key assumptions, ranges, and the sensitivity of the range to changes in assumptions.

The notes should indicate those assumptions that have a potentially significant impact on the financial statements. A reporting entity should explain the nature of each source of estimation uncertainty that might have a significant impact on the carrying value of assets and liabilities.

Bombardier makes several sensitivity disclosures in the notes to its 31 December 2014 statements. For example:

> A 1% increase in the estimated future costs to complete all ongoing production contracts would have decreased BT's gross margin for fiscal year 2014 by approximately $97 million. ...[3]

Bombardier's 2014 reported gross margin was $2,577, and thus a change in estimated costs would have reduced the margin by just 3.0%. This example indicates how crucial it is to make "fair" estimates!

Information Useful for Understanding the Statements

This can cover a wide range of information, such as:

- Contingencies
- Guarantees
- Segment reporting
- Related party transactions
- Economic dependence
- Unrecognized contractual commitments

---

3. From Note 4, page 127 of the 2014 annual report. "BT" refers to the company's rail transportation-division, which has numerous long-term contracts for rail systems in several parts of the world.

- Financial risk management objectives and policies
- Subsequent events

We will briefly explain some of these disclosures in the following section. Others will be dealt with in the following chapters.

Specific Significant Disclosures

Several disclosure requirements are significant enough to warrant separate discussion because they are either new or relatively complex.

Contingencies

A **contingency** is an event or transaction that will occur only if some other event happens. For example, a civil lawsuit poses a contingent gain for the plaintiff and a contingent loss for the defendant. However, the parties will not know whether they have a gain or a loss until the court reaches a decision.

Under IFRS, neither a contingent asset nor a contingent liability is recognized in the financial statements. Instead, the situation giving rise to the contingent event and its possible outcomes is described in the notes. When practicable, the note should also disclose a "best estimate" of its potential financial effect. It is then up to the users to assess the risks for themselves.

If and when a liability becomes *probable* rather than just *contingent*, the liability then should be recognized in the accounts as a *provision* (i.e., as a cost and a liability), as discussed in the previous chapter.

Guarantees

We are all familiar with a *guarantee* that relates to a product or service provided by the reporting enterprise. However, the concept of a guarantee goes beyond these simple (and usually estimable) warranty arrangements.

More broadly, a **guarantee** is an agreement by the reporting enterprise to pay compensation, to undertake to perform services, or to assume the obligation of another entity under certain conditions. Guarantees are really a type of *contingency*, but they are given special attention because they are so common in business affairs and because they can be the hidden elephant in a company's otherwise undisclosed contingent obligations.

For example, Bombardier Inc. sells small jets to regional airlines. The airlines often obtain debt or lease financing for the planes. To facilitate the sale, Bombardier will guarantee the debt by promising to pay the lender or lessor if the airline defaults on its obligations. In Bombardier's financial statements, the company describes the nature of these guarantees (along with other types of guarantees) in a disclosure note. This risk is discussed in note 37, "Commitments and Contingencies."

The company is able to quantify the extent of the risk—at 31 December 2014, the "maximum potential exposure" for credit risk from aircraft sales was $1,275 million. None of the amount appears as a liability in the company's SFP, however, because although the *exposure* is quantifiable, the actual amount of future liability is not predictable. Nevertheless, investors and creditors can see the maximum possible loss should the regional airline industry collapse. Bombardier also disclosed that "three regional airline customers accounted for 71% of the total maximum credit risk."

Other examples of guarantees that an entity should disclose include:

- A guarantee of debt of an affiliated corporation, such as a subsidiary;
- A promise to make good on nonperformance, such as when a subcontractor is unable to carry out the contracted services. This is known as a **performance guarantee**; or
- A promise to remedy any deficiency or shortfall of assets held by another entity. For example, a company may issue shares in payment for services received from another company, and guarantee that the value of the shares won't fall below a certain level. This is also known as **indemnification**.

When a company has given any guarantees, the nature and potential maximum amount of these guarantees should be disclosed in a separate disclosure note.

Segment Disclosures

Consolidated financial information may mask important trends, risks, and opportunities for a diversified company. Therefore, public companies are required to disaggregate their reported results by operating segment.

An **operating segment** has three characteristics:

1. It engages in business activities that may generate revenues and incur expenses;
2. There is discrete financial information available for the segment; and
3. Its operating results are reviewed regularly by the entity's "chief operating decision maker" (e.g., the CEO or the COO [chief operating officer]), who evaluates the segment's performance and makes resource allocation decisions.

Although there may be many operating segments under this definition, a **reportable segment** is one that meets at least one of the following tests:

- Its revenue to external customers is at least 10% of the company's total revenue; or
- Its assets are 10% or more of the company's total assets; or
- The absolute value of its profit or loss is 10% or more of the greater of the absolute amounts of:
  - The combined earnings of all operating segments that did not report a loss, or
  - The combined reported loss of all operating segments that reported a loss.

To illustrate this last condition, consider a company that has six operating segments:

Segment	Profit or (Loss)
A	$150,000
B	70,000
C	(100,000)
D	25,000
E	(60,000)
F	(20,000)

The sum of segments A, B, and D is $245,000. The sum of segments C, E, and F is $(180,000). The higher total is $245,000, and therefore the cut-off point for a reportable segment is $24,500. Since all segments except F have either a profit or a loss that is higher than $24,500, all but F are reportable segments.

Every public company must identify enough segments to explain 75% of its total revenue. If the total revenue of reportable segments does not add up to 75%, the company must report additional segments until the 75% threshold is met.

Once the reportable segments have been identified, the company must disclose selected information on each segment, including (1) revenue, (2) profit or loss, and (3) assets and liabilities. Other specific disclosures are required, too, such as interest revenue, interest expense, income tax expense, and depreciation and amortization.

The company must reconcile the disaggregated segment data to the numbers reported on the primary financial statements. As well, the company should disclose information about the geographic regions in which it operates. The data include (1) total revenue derived from each country in which the company operates and (2) the carrying value of noncurrent assets in each of those countries. Countries can be grouped into regions when individual countries do not account for a significant portion of business.

Segment disclosures can be quite long and complex if the company is involved in a large number of segments and geographic areas. Bombardier discloses two business segments—aerospace (BA) and rail transportation (BT). The 31 December 2014 segmented disclosures indicate, for example, that aerospace accounted for 52% of revenues.

The company reported geographic data for 11 countries individually and for an "other" category within each of Asia-Pacific, Europe, and "Other." The countries accounted for 73% of Bombardier's revenue and 93% of its capital assets.

Canada accounted for only 5% of Bombardier's consolidated revenue but 52% of the company's total assets.[4] Canada does not qualify as a reportable segment under the revenue criterion (10%) but does qualify on the basis of the high proportion of assets held in Canada.

---

4. In contrast, France accounted for a similar proportion of revenue (5.3%) but less than one percent of capital assets.

Related Party Transactions

When a firm engages in a transaction wherein one of the parties has the ability to influence the actions and policies of the other, the transaction is termed a **related party transaction**. Such transactions cannot be assumed to be at arm's length, because the conditions necessary for a competitive, free market interaction are not likely to be present. Related parties include management, individuals, and/or corporations with significant shareholdings; other corporations with common major shareholders; family members of related parties; and so on. There can be a large number of them!

If a company has had related party transactions during the reporting period, it should disclose the nature of the relationship and of the transactions, the amount of the transactions, and the amount of any outstanding balances including commitments.

A broader disclosure recommended by IAS 24 is that related party transactions should be made separately for a long list of categories, including associated companies, joint ventures in which the reporting entity is a participant, and key management personnel of the company or its parent company. Furthermore, a public company that is a subsidiary of another company should disclose who its parent is, if the parent is also a public company.

The disclosure of related party transactions is intended to alert financial statement readers to the existence of these relationships, either individual or corporate. The disclosures do not include any measurement of the fair value of transactions (as opposed to the recorded value of the transactions), and therefore there is little opportunity for readers to judge the impact of the non-arm's-length transactions on the reporting enterprise's financial statements.

The thrust of IAS 24 is *disclosure*. In contrast, ASPE has some explicit *measurement* requirements pertaining to the measurement basis of goods and services traded between related parties, as we will see in the ASPE section at the end of this chapter.

Economic Dependence

Segmented reporting is intended to alert financial statement readers to the company's vulnerability to economic changes in its various business segments and in its geographic exposure. An additional vulnerability arises when a company depends on the business of one large customer or a small group of major customers. An auto parts manufacturer may sell all of its output to a single large automobile manufacturer such as General Motors or Toyota. A medical research lab may perform all of its work under contract to a government health ministry. The company's continuance may depend on this customer's continued business. If the customer switches suppliers or goes bankrupt, the company may fail if it cannot quickly replace that business with new customers.

Financial statement readers need to know whether the company is highly dependent on one or a small group of customers. When a company is heavily dependent on certain few customers, this fact, and the volume of business involved, should be disclosed in the notes. The rule is that an entity must disclose each customer that represents 10% or more of the entity's revenue. It is not necessary to disclose who the customer is, although knowledgeable readers may well know from other sources or from their knowledge of the industry.

For example, in its 2014 annual report, Canadian auto parts manufacturer Magna International Inc. reported its economic dependence on six large automobile companies for 83% of its revenues (in millions of U.S. dollars) as shown in Exhibit 4-6.

EXHIBIT 4-6

MAGNA INTERNATIONAL INC.

Disclosure of Economic Dependence

[b] The following table aggregates external revenues by customer as follows:

	2014	2013	2012
General Motors	$ **6,734**	$ 6,394	$ 5,704
Fiat/Chrysler Group	**5,897**	5,137	4,637

Ford Motor Co.	**4,714**	4,450	3,848
BMW	**4,649**	4,882	4,100
Daimler AG	**4,262**	3,949	3,367
Volkswagen	**4,144**	4,047	3,835
Other	**6,241**	5,976	5,346
	$ 36,641	$ 34,835	$ 30,837

Source: Magna International Inc. audited annual financial statements, page 69, www.sedar.com, posted 5 March 2015.

Subsequent Events

What happens if the company unexpectedly sells a division soon after the end of the fiscal year? It is not an event of the past fiscal year, but shouldn't it be part of the report? Of course, users almost certainly would have learned about the event through the financial press or other sources—such news travels fast. But the financial statements must retain their credibility and relevance by reflecting up-to-date information. Therefore, disclosure is required for significant events that take place *after the end of the fiscal year*, but *before the date that the statements are completed*. The date that the entity's board of directors approves the statements is used as a cut-off date for reporting **subsequent events**.

There are two categories of subsequent events: (1) adjusting events and (2) nonadjusting events.

Adjusting events are those that occur after the year-end that require the company to make adjustments to the financial statements. Some events that take place *after* the year-end actually reflect economic conditions existing at the year-end; *these events must be recognized in the accounts*, and therefore are known as *adjusting events*. For example, if a major customer unexpectedly announces bankruptcy after the year-end, the accounts receivable relating to that customer at the year-end would be written down on the rationale that the customer was actually insolvent at the end of the fiscal year but this fact did not become known to the company until after the year-end.

This might seem to be the application of hindsight to financial reporting, but it really reflects a long-standing practice in financial reporting. The period between the year-end and the completion of the financial statements provides a reality check on the validity of many measurements, including uncollectible accounts, returns and allowances, and the net realizable value of inventory.

Other examples of adjusting events are (1) settlement of a court case related to events that took place before the reporting date and (2) evidence uncovered of asset impairment existing at the reporting date. Such events can be taken into account *in retrospect*, as part of the accounting estimation process that occurs at every financial reporting date.

Nonadjusting events are those that do not require modification of the year-end results. Examples of nonadjusting events are:

- A decline in the market value of an investment after the reporting date;
- An event that results in a loss, such as fire or flood;
- Issuance of debt or equity instruments that changed the common shares, or potential common shares, outstanding; and
- Announcing or commencing a restructuring.

These events will affect the financial statements in the following year in the year that they actually occur. When nonadjusting events are known before the issuance of the most recent year's statements, they should be communicated to the financial statement readers as part of the reporting exercise.

CONCEPT **REVIEW**

1. In general, what functions are served by disclosure notes?
2. Why might financial statement users want to see *segmented information*? What companies are required to disclose segmented information?
3. Define a *related party transaction*.
4. What is measurement uncertainty?
5. Explain the difference between *adjusting* and *nonadjusting* subsequent events.

Looking Forward

In November 2012, the IASB began looking into a wide range of issues on presentation, disclosure, and measurement. Among the issues on the IASB's Conceptual Framework agenda are a re-examination of the definitions of elements, definitions of liabilities, recognition principles, measurement principles, the distinction between equity and liability instruments, and measurements other than cost and fair value. In coming years, the Board is likely to issue new guidance on the format and presentation of items on the SFP. This project is ongoing.

Accounting Standards for Private Enterprises

Balance Sheet

Canadian ASPE continues to use the title *balance sheet*, but use of that title is not required. *Statement of financial position* remains an acceptable alternative. The general format of the balance sheet is the same as for IFRS. *CPA Canada Handbook, Part II*, section 1521, contains a list of items that should be "separately presented." Some of these will usually appear on the face of the balance sheet, but some may be disclosed in the notes. The only items in the list that do not specifically appear in IFRS are:

- Prepaid expenses
- Obligations under capital leases
- Asset retirement obligations

However, disclosure of these items is implicitly contained in the specific standards that deal with those topics.

ASPE does not require separate disclosure of three asset categories that are specifically required in IFRS:

- *Investment property* is included in land and buildings, as appropriate;
- *Agricultural produce and biological assets* are reported as inventory and/or tangible capital assets, as appropriate; and
- *Provisions* are reported as liabilities, either current or noncurrent, as appropriate.

Equity

Section 3251 of the *CPA Canada Handbook, Part II* requires the "presentation of equity and changes in equity." The components of equity are:

- Share capital
- Contributed surplus
- Retained earnings
- Reserves
- Non-controlling interests
- Other components of equity

Again, this list is essentially the same as under IFRS. "Other components of equity" is quite limited. One example of an "other component" is "foreign currency translation gain or loss" for a company that has one or more foreign operations (e.g., in the United States).

Bear in mind that ASPE contains no concept of "other comprehensive income," and therefore no accumulated other comprehensive income.

Changes in Equity

ASPE requires a company to "present separately [the] changes in equity for the period." There is no prescription for format. In practice, the core equity statement for a private enterprise is likely to be the statement of retained earnings, presented either separately or as a continuation of the income statement—a "statement of income and retained earnings." Information on other changes in equity are usually presented in a disclosure note rather than in a formal statement format.

Disclosure Notes

Accounting Changes

ASPE does not require disclosure of future accounting policy changes, only of actual accounting policies that have changed during the reporting period.

Segments

ASPE does not require segment disclosure.

Subsequent Events

Section 3820 covers subsequent events, including those that require adjustment and those that require only disclosure. Instead of the terms *adjusted events* and *nonadjusted events*, ASPE uses *existing* and *nonexisting*. The period is from the reporting date until the financial statements are fully drafted with no change expected and have been approved. The substance of the recommendations is the same.

Contingent Liabilities

Contingent liabilities are treated differently under ASPE. IFRS does not permit recognition of a contingent liability in the accounts until it becomes a *probable* liability, at which point it meets the IFRS definition as a provision. In contrast, ASPE is rather more specific by requiring that a contingent loss be recognized as an expense and a liability in the financial statements when:

- It becomes more likely than not that the company will become liable, and
- The amount of the future liability can be reasonably estimated.

Within the range of possible financial impacts, if one particular amount seems to be more likely than other estimates, that estimate should be accrued. In many cases, there will be no clear best estimate, in which case the lowest amount in the feasible range should be used.

ASPE contains no specific requirement for *provisions*. Instead, ASPE accomplishes the same goal via the recognition requirements for the probable outcomes of contingent liabilities. A good example is the liability for losses from a lawsuit, which is a *provision* under IFRS but would be a *recognized contingency* under ASPE. ASPE also has some estimated liabilities—for example, for warranties that would be called provisions in IFRS.

Related Party Transactions

ASPE makes a distinction between two types of transfers: (1) those in the normal course of business, such as a sale of merchandise, and (2) those not in the normal course of business, such as a transfer of property.

Related party transactions in the normal course of business must be recorded at the *exchange value* (which is the amount that changes hands between the two parties). In determining if the exchange is in the normal course of business, you would consider whether it is something the company would normally sell and whether the terms and conditions are similar to those used with other customers. That is, a regular sale of inventory that happened to be to a related company would be recorded at the exchange value, not carrying value.

Related party transactions not in the normal course of business need to consider other factors to determine measurement. The exchange amount is also used to value the transaction if (1) the transaction is monetary (i.e., if money changes hands), (2) the change of ownership interest is substantive, and (3) the exchange amount can be verified by independent evidence. Otherwise, the transaction must be recorded at *carrying value*, which is the *book value of the transferor*. Cost would be carrying value for inventory, net book value for capital assets, and so on. Carrying value is considered appropriate because no transaction of substance has taken place—a different related party simply owns the asset in question. If recorded at the carrying amount there is no impact on net income, only an equity impact!

Financial statement users tend to assume that all transactions are recorded at fair market value, and the presence of related party transactions may make the financial statements difficult to interpret. ASPE recommends the following disclosures:

- The nature of the relationship(s) involved;
- A description of the nature of the transactions, including the dollar amounts, and the measurement basis used;
- Any amounts due to or from related parties as of the reporting date, and the terms and conditions thereof;
- Any contingencies or contractual obligations with related parties; and
- The amount of any doubtful accounts, whether expensed or provided for, that pertain to related party transactions or balances.

RELEVANT STANDARDS

CPA Canada Handbook, Part I (IFRS):

- IAS 1, Presentation of Financial Statements
- IAS 8, Accounting Policies, Changes in Accounting Estimates and Errors
- IAS 24, Related Party Disclosures
- IAS 10, Events after the Reporting Period
- IAS 37, Provisions, Contingent Liabilities and Contingent Assets
- IFRS 8, Operating Segments

CPA Canada Handbook, Part II (ASPE):

- Section 1521, Balance Sheet
- Section 3251, Equity
- Section 3260, Reserves
- Section 3290, Contingencies
- Section 3820, Subsequent Events
- Section 3840, Related Party Transactions

SUMMARY OF KEY POINTS

1. The SFP provides information about an entity's assets, liabilities, and equities. The SFP, taken together with other financial statements, provides information useful to financial statement users for assessing an entity's financial position, risk profile, financial flexibility, liquidity, and rates of return.

2. The amounts reported on the SFP are a mix of historical costs and fair values, which may reduce its relevance for certain decisions. The specific amounts reported are the result of the company's reporting policies. The SFP also contains many estimates, excludes assets and liabilities that IFRS deems unrecognizable, and often consolidates financial data from very different types of industry segments. Financial statement users must proceed with caution.

3. Classification of SFP items is governed by accounting standards and industry norms and characteristics, but leaves much room for management judgement. Most, but not all, SFPs classify current assets and current liabilities to facilitate evaluation of short-term liquidity. Other classifications follow the major asset, liability, and equity groups. Elements are often highly condensed and summarized on the SFP.

4. Various SFP categories have specific display and disclosure requirements to meet accounting standards and users' expectations.

5. Companies following IFRS must provide a statement of changes in equity (SCE), also known as a statement of shareholders' equity. The SCE provides a columnar reconciliation that includes a column for each individual item of shareholders' equity. The major categories are (1) share capital accounts, (2) individual categories of OCI, (3) equity of non-controlling shareholders in consolidated subsidiaries, and (4) retained earnings.

6. Retained earnings may be subdivided by two types of *reserves*—restrictions and appropriations. Restrictions are created either by law or contract. Appropriations are created voluntarily by the board of

directors. Legal and contractual restrictions limit the amount that is available for dividends. In contrast, appropriations have no substantive effect; the board of directors can reverse them as easily as they are created.

7. Error corrections that affect the financial statements of prior periods are recorded (net of tax) as a change to opening retained earnings, and comparative statements are restated.

8. A change in accounting principle is normally applied retrospectively, the cumulative effect of the change being shown as an adjustment to opening retained earnings. Comparative financial statements should be restated. If this treatment is not feasible, only the cumulative effect is shown on the retained earnings statement. In certain circumstances, the change in principle is reflected prospectively. An accounting estimate is always changed prospectively.

9. Disclosure notes provide information regarding accounting policies, describe recognized and unrecognized items, and provide supplemental information regarding future cash flows and potential liabilities.

10. Important disclosures include segment disclosures, related party transaction data, economic dependence, subsequent events, contingencies and guarantees, and measurement uncertainty. Also, if a company's future is in doubt so that the continuity assumption might not apply, going-concern disclosures are needed.

Key Terms

additional paid-in capital	minority interest
adjusting events	nonadjusting events
appropriation	non-controlling interest
balance sheet	operating cycle
cash equivalents	operating segment
changes in accounting policy	performance guarantee
contingency	prospective treatment
contributed surplus	recycled
current asset	related party transaction
current liability	reportable segment
disclosure notes	reserves
fixed assets	restriction
guarantee	return on assets (ROA)
indemnification	return on investment (ROI)
intangible assets	statement of changes in equity (SCE)
investment property	statement of financial position (SFP)
liquidity	subsequent events
long-term liability	tangible capital assets
management's discussion and analysis (MD&A)	
measurement uncertainty	

Review Problem 4-1

The post-closing SFP accounts of Ibsen Icons Inc. at 31 December 20X3 are as follows:

Account	Debit	Credit
Cash (overdraft)		$ 3,500
Accounts payable		15,000
Deferred income tax liability		20,000
Common shares		40,000
Preferred shares		24,000
Long-term investment in common shares of Grieg Graphics Inc.	$ 14,000	
Accounts receivable	19,000	
Income taxes payable		10,000
Loan from shareholder, due 1 July 20X9		40,000
Land	120,000	
Leasehold improvements (net of amortization)	30,000	
Furniture and equipment (at cost)	90,000	
Accumulated depreciation, furniture, and equipment		30,000
Retained earnings—unappropriated		76,000
Deferred revenue		7,000
Notes receivable	7,500	
Goodwill	9,000	
Provision for restructuring costs (current)		9,000
Appropriation for plant expansion		11,000
Prepaid expenses	3,500	
Marketable securities available for sale	5,000	
Note payable to bank, due 15 October 20X4		25,000
Allowance for doubtful accounts		2,000
Supplies inventory	14,500	
	$312,500	$312,500

Required:

Prepare a classified SFP in good form.

REVIEW PROBLEM 4-1—SOLUTION

IBSEN ICONS INC.

Statement of Financial Position

31 December 20X3

Assets

Current assets:

Marketable securities		$ 5,000	
Notes receivable		7,500	
Accounts receivable	$19,000		
Less: allowance for doubtful accounts	2,000	17,000	
Supplies inventory		14,500	
Prepaid expenses		3,500	$ 47,500

Noncurrent assets:

Capital assets:

Land		120,000	
Furniture and equipment	90,000		
Less: accumulated depreciation	30,000	60,000	
Leasehold improvements (net)		30,000	
Goodwill		9,000	
		219,000	
Investment in Grieg Graphics Inc.		14,000	233,000
Total assets			$280,500

Liabilities and Shareholders' Equity

Liabilities:

Current liabilities:

Bank overdraft	$ 3,500	
Income taxes payable	10,000	
Bank note payable, due 15 October 20X4	25,000	
Accounts payable	15,000	
Provision for restructuring costs	9,000	
Deferred revenue	7,000	$ 69,500

Noncurrent liabilities:

Shareholder loan, due 1 July 20X9	40,000	
Deferred income tax liability	20,000	60,000
Total liabilities		129,500

Shareholders' equity:

Contributed capital:

Common shares	40,000	
Preferred shares	24,000	64,000

Retained earnings:

Appropriated for plant expansion	11,000	
Unappropriated	76,000	87,000
Total shareholders' equity		151,000
Total liabilities and shareholders' equity		$280,500

Capital assets could be separated into tangible and intangible categories. Deferred revenue and notes receivable are assumed to be within normal business practice for this company and therefore are classified as current.

Review Problem 4-2

On 1 January 20X5, the shareholders' equity for Svengali Controls Ltd. (SCL) included the following items (in thousands of dollars):

	Debit	Credit
Common shares		$12,000
Deficit	$250	
Preferred shares		2,500
Appropriation for plant expansion		1,000
Contributed surplus		250
Accumulated translation gain or loss on Mexican subsidiary		550

During the year ending 31 December 20X5, the following occurred:

a. Net income (after income tax) was $50,000.

b. Sixty thousand additional common shares were issued to existing shareholders for $50 each. The shares had no stated or par value.

c. The board of directors appropriated an additional $150,000 for plant expansion.

d. The company purchased and retired 1,000 of its preferred shares at their original issue price of $1,100 each. The shares had a stated value of $1,000 each, and had originally been issued to an institutional investor for $1,100 each.

e. SCL recorded a loss of $5,000 arising from a decline in the net asset value of the Mexican subsidiary due to a change in the exchange rate for the Mexican peso against the Canadian dollar.

Required:

1. Determine the amount of comprehensive income.
2. Prepare a statement of changes in equity for SIL for the year ended 31 December 20X5 in columnar format.

REVIEW PROBLEM 4-2—SOLUTION

1. Comprehensive income:

Net income	$50,000
Translation loss	5,000
Comprehensive income	$45,000

2. Statement of changes in equity, 31 December 20X5:

	Deficit	Appropriation for Plant Expansion	Translation Gain/ Loss	Contributed Surplus	Preferred Shares	Common Shares	TOTAL
Balances, 1 January 20X5	$(250)	$1,000	$550	$250	$2,500	$12,000	$16,050
Net income for 20X5	50						50
Change in translation gain/loss			(5)				(5)
Issuance of common shares						3,000	3,000
Redemption of preferred shares				(100)	(1,000)		(1,100)
Additional appropriation	(150)	150					

Balances, 31 December 20X5	$(350)	$ 1,150	$545	$150	$1,500	$15,000	$17,995

Note: There is no prescribed sequence of columns or rows, except for the beginning and ending balances.

Review Problem 4-3

Kanga Corp. had the following transactions and changes during the fiscal year ended 31 December 20X7:

a. On 15 October 20X7, the board of directors declared $2.5 million in dividends, to be paid on 15 November 20X7. The dividends were to be paid to shareholders of record as of 30 October.

b. Two thousand new preferred shares were issued to a private equity fund on 17 May at $72 per share. The stated value of the shares was $65. These were a new class of shares, not previously issued.

c. Kanga has a wholly owned subsidiary in Mexico. The subsidiary's reporting currency (i.e., for its own financial statements issued to creditors and regulators in Mexico) is the Mexican peso. When Kanga translated the year-end 20X7 financial statements to the Canadian dollar, its translated net investment had decreased from the beginning of the year, due to appreciation of the Canadian dollar, relative to the Mexican peso. The amount of the change was C$3.3 million.

d. On 15 March, Kanga redeemed $1.0 million outstanding debt securities for $0.9 million.

e. Near the end of 20X6 (the previous year), Kanga decided to discontinue its heavy maintenance division and began an active search for a buyer. It reported the division as a "discontinued operation" in its 31 December 20X6 financial statements. On 13 August 20X7, Kanga's management signed a binding agreement to sell the company's heavy maintenance division to Industrial Innovations Inc. (III). The net proceeds from the sale and transfer of the division to III were $1.2 million less than the carrying value of the division's net assets on Kanga's books at year-end 20X6.

f. On 31 December 20X7, Kanga's board of directors voted unanimously to reverse an appropriation of $15.2 million that had been established two years previously. The purpose of the appropriation was to reserve funds for plant expansion that the board now decided to postpone indefinitely.

g. When preparing the 20X7 financial statements, management (with consultation with the auditors) decided that, in hindsight, the company had been using overly optimist estimates of the useful lives of certain categories plant and equipment for the past five years. Therefore, management agreed to reduce those estimates to a more realistic level.

h. When preparing the 20X7 financial statements, the company discovered that certain items in the year-end 20X6 inventory had been overstated by $200,000.

Required:

Explain briefly how each of these items would be reported in the 31 December 20X7 comparative financial statements, if at all. Ignore income tax effects.

REVIEW PROBLEM 4-3—SOLUTION

a. Retained earnings is reduced by $2.5 million.

b. The total issue price at $72 per shares was $144,000. Of that total, $130,000 would be reported in the preferred shares account and $14,000 as contributed surplus in the statement of changes in equity. The total $144,000 would be shown in the financing section of the SCF.

c. The change of $3.3 million (OCI) would be reported as a loss in the "other comprehensive income" segment of the SCI, and as a reduction (debit) in the "translation adjustment" column in the statement of changes in equity.

d. The gain of $0.1 million is reported as gain (other income) in the profit and loss section of the SCI.

e. This $1.2 million loss is reported in the profit and loss section of the SCI, in the "discontinued operations" section.

f. The reversal will appear in the retained earnings column of the SCE. The amount would not appear on the 20X7 year-end SFP.

g. The changes in estimates will affect depreciation in 20X7 and following years. Previous years' statements will not be restated; changes in estimates are always applied forward and never in retrospect.

h. The $200,000 inventory overstatement will be corrected by adjusting opening retained earnings downward by $200,000 to correct for the resultant overstatement of 20X6 earnings; 20X7 earnings will be increased as a result. The year-end 20X6 comparative SFP and SCI also will be restated to correct the error.

CASE 4-1

PAINT INC.

Paint Inc. (PI) has been operating as a family-owned private company for the past 30 years. It started as a company manufacturing paint for sale in its own retail stores in Ontario. PI is known as a manufacturer of high-quality paint. Since then it has expanded with stores across Canada and recently started a decorating business. It has no desire to go public at this point in time and wants to keep accounting costs as low as possible.

With the recent real estate boom and new housing, the company has been very profitable for the past few years. PI has a loan with Canadian Bank. The bank requires audited financial statements and has a maximum debt-to-equity ratio.

You have recently been hired as an accounting consultant to assist PI's board of directors. You have been asked to develop appropriate accounting policies for events that have occurred during 20X5. The board has asked that you explain fully your analysis for your recommendations. PI has a 31 December year-end.

1. Individuals can purchase paint in the store or order on-line. If they order on-line they must pay by credit card. Contractors and real estate developers can purchase paint directly at the warehouse in bulk and receive a 15% to 25% discount depending on the quantity they purchase. They also have 30 days in which to pay. The paint provides a three-month money-back guarantee.

2. In the summer of 20X5, to encourage use of their new decorating services, PI offered customers a special deal. With the purchase of $200 of paint they received one hour of consulting advice from the decorator for free. Normally, the fee for the decorating service is $75 an hour. This deal was very popular with many customers purchasing additional services from the decorator beyond the one hour for free.

3. On 1 April 20X5, PI announced it was going to sell one of its older manufacturing facilities including all of the equipment. This facility will be replaced in a new location with a brand-new, fully computerized, state-of-the-art facility. The new facility will be operational in the spring of 20X6. Until that time PI will continue to manufacture in the existing facility. The facility has been listed at a reasonable price. The carrying amount of the facility and equipment is $1,000,000 with a fair value of $850,000. The land has a carrying amount of $200,000 and a fair value of $1,200,000.

4. In 20X5, PI traded a piece of excess land they owned for a potential new store for some manufacturing equipment for the new facility. The land had a carrying amount of $80,000, but three real estate appraisals estimated the fair value to be $500,000. The equipment was specially manufactured for PI and is unique.

5. In 20X5, PI sold a large quantity of paint to a board member who owns a new housing development. The paint was sold to the director for cash and the director was given a 25% discount and 30 days to pay.

6. In February 20X6, PI was informed that one of its building contractors went bankrupt and will not be able to pay an outstanding receivable of $80,000. This receivable was not considered in determining their allowance for bad debts for 20X5.

Required:

Prepare the report.

CASE 4-2

WONDER AMUSEMENTS LTD.

Wonder Amusements Ltd. (WAL) was incorporated over 40 years ago as an amusement park and golf course. Over time, a nearby city has grown to the point where it borders on WAL's properties. In recent years WAL's owners, who are all members of one family, have seen WAL's land values increase significantly. Majority shareholder Howard Smith owns 55% of the outstanding shares and is no longer active in WAL's day-to-day activities.

Last year Howard hired a new chief executive officer, Leo Titan. Leo has a reputation as an aggressive risk taker. Howard is committed to supporting Leo's plans and has the personal financial resources required to do so.

Eight months ago, WAL became the successful bidder for a new sports franchise, in conjunction with a minority partner. Under the terms of the franchise agreement, WAL is required to build a sports arena, which is currently being constructed. The arena is being built on a section of the amusement park. Another section of the amusement park is being relocated to ensure that the entrances to the arena are close to public transportation and parking. Consequently, some of the rides will be relocated. WAL is the sole owner of the arena at present.

The sports franchise is separately incorporated as Northern Sports Ltd. (NSL); WAL holds 75% of the shares in the company. Another bid is being prepared by NSL to obtain a second sports franchise so that the arena can be used more often. NSL will be required to lease space from WAL when the arena is completed, in about 22 months.

For the first two sports seasons, NSL will have to lease arena space from Aggressive Ltd. (AL). During this time, NSL does not expect to be profitable because:

- It may take time to build a competitive team;
- AL is charging a high rent and is not giving NSL a share of concession (e.g., hot dogs, drinks) revenue;
- AL cannot make the better dates (e.g., Saturday night) available to NSL to attract sports fans; and
- As a newcomer to the league, NSL is restricted with regard to the players available to it and the days of the week it can play in its home city.

Consequently, NSL has arranged to borrow funds from WAL and from others to finance costs and losses.

Your employer, Fabio & Fox, Chartered Accountants, has conducted the audit of WAL for several years. WAL has tended to be marginally profitable one year and then have losses the next. The company has continued to operate because the directors knew that the real estate holdings were becoming increasingly valuable. For purposes of financial statements WAL uses Canadian ASPE.

Leo is expected to oversee the expanded accounting and finance functions in the company. He has met with you and the partner in charge of the WAL audit and has discussed various issues related to the year ending 30 September 20X7. His comments are provided in Exhibit 1.

EXHIBIT 1

Notes from Discussion with Leo Titan

1. To build a road to the arena's parking lot, two holes of the 18-hole golf course will be relocated next spring. Costs of $140,000 are expected to be incurred this year in design, tree planting, ground preparation, and grass seeding to ready the area for next spring. These costs are to be capitalized as part of the golf course lands, along with related property taxes of $13,000 and interest of $15,000.

2. Approximately $600,000 will be required to relocate the rides currently on land needed for the arena. This amount is to be capitalized, net of scrap recovery on dismantled and redundant equipment of $60,000. Virtually all the rides were fully depreciated years ago.

3. In May 20X7, WAL acquired, for $4.25 million, all of the shares of an amusement park in a different city, when its land lease expired. The amusement park company was wound up and the equipment, rides, concessions, and other assets are being transported to WAL at a cost of $350,000. According to Leo, the estimated fair market value of WAL's net assets is $4.85 million, including liabilities of $1.20 million.

   WAL expects to spend approximately $400,000 in getting the assets in operating order and $500,000 on foundations and site preparations for the rides. Leo wants to "capitalize as much as possible."

4. To assist in financing the new ventures, WAL sold excess land to developers who intend to construct a shopping centre, office buildings, and expensive homes that will be adjacent to the golf course and away from the amusement park. The developers and WAL agreed to these terms:

Paid to WAL on 1 May 20X7	$ 6,000,000
To be paid to WAL on 1 March 20X8	10,000,000
To be paid to WAL on 1 March 20X9	8,000,000
	$24,000,000

   The land is to be turned over to the developers on or about 1 February 20X8, but the sale is to be reported in fiscal 20X7. The land was carried on WAL's books at $1.35 million; a pro-rata portion of the total land carrying value (at cost) will be allocated to the portion sold to the developers

5. An additional "contingent profit" will accrue to WAL if the developers earn a return on investment of more than 25% when they resell the newly constructed buildings. Leo wants a note to the 20X7 financial statements that describes the probability of a contingent gain.

6. The golf course has been unprofitable in recent years. However, green fees are to be raised and specific tee-off times will be allotted to a private club, currently being organized. Members of the private club will pay a nonrefundable entrance fee of $2,000 per member plus $100 per month for five years. The $2,000 is to be recorded as revenue on receipt. Approximately $350,000 is to be spent to upgrade the club facilities.

7. Leo wants to capitalize all costs of NSL on NSL's books until it has completed its first year of operations. In addition to the franchise fee, $20 million will have to be spent on the following:

Acquisition of player contracts	$ 12,000,000
Advertising and promotion	1,500,000
Equipment	3,200,000
Wages, benefits, and bonuses	6,800,000
Other operating costs	3,300,000
	26,800,000
Less revenue:	
Ticket sales	(6,000,000)
Other	(800,000)
	$20,000,000

The value of players can change quickly, depending upon their performance, injuries, and other factors.

8. The new sports arena will have private boxes in which a company can entertain groups of clients. The boxes are leased on a five-year contract basis, and they must be occupied for a fixed number of nights at a minimum price per night. To date, 12 boxes have been leased for $15,000 per box for a five-year period, exclusive of nightly charges. A down payment of $3,000 was required; the payments have been recorded as revenue.

9. Three senior officers of WAL, including Leo, receive bonuses based on income before income taxes. The three have agreed to have their fiscal 20X7 bonuses accrued in fiscal 20X8 along with their fiscal 20X8 bonuses. Actual payments to them are scheduled for January 20X9.

Source: The Canadian Institute of Chartered Accountants, © 2010.

You have been asked by the partner to prepare a report for him, which will be used for the next meeting with Leo. He would like you to discuss the accounting implications related to your discussion with Leo. The partner wants a thorough analysis of all important issues as well as support for your position.

In your review of documents, and as a result of various conversations, you have learned the following:

1. The arena will be mortgaged, but only for about 50% of its expected cost. Lenders are concerned about the special-use nature of the arena and whether it will be successfully rented for other events, such as concerts.

2. The mortgage lenders to WAL and the minority shareholders in NSL are both expected to want to see appraisals and financial statements before deciding whether to invest. Covenants will be required by the lenders to ensure that excessive expenditures are not undertaken and that cash is preserved.

3.   Leo does not intend to consolidate NSL until it is profitable. The investment in NSL will be reported on WAL's financial statements at cost. The WAL financial statements will be used for income tax purposes.

4.   WAL's minority shareholders are not active in the business and want quarterly financial statements to monitor progress and assess Leo's performance. The minority shareholders have all expressed concern over Leo's growth strategy over the past year. Most are approaching their retirement years and are relying on WAL to supplement their retirement income.

Required:

Prepare the report.

CASE 4-3

WPB LTD.

The management of WPB Ltd. has spent the past year reorganizing the company's business activities. WPB is a service provider to hospitals. Originally the company operated only in Canada, where hospital care is provided at government expense through public health care systems. After demonstrating successful operations, the company was invited by several African governments to extend its expertise to providing services on that continent, particularly as a result of the intense need for external support that arose from the ongoing AIDS crisis. The African operations were supported by the various nations' governments, with additional aid provided through the Stephan Louis Foundation. The Foundation requires WPB to provide audited financial statements each year as a condition for continuing its support.

WPB had been under pressure to decrease the cost of its services to hospitals as a result of severe budget pressure on the governments that bear the ultimate cost of hospital care. The company has consolidated some services, reduced its workforce, and sold some parts of its operations.

It is now 31 December 20X7, the end of the fiscal year. The vice-president of finance has requested your advice on the treatment of certain items in the company's financial statements. She has provided you with a description of the items about which she is uncertain (below), and she has requested that you prepare a report recommending appropriate financial statement presentation and note disclosure for each item, in accordance with international accounting standards.

Items of Concern

1.   In the last quarter of the year, we struck a deal with LaidLow Corp. to take over the ambulance service division that we had acquired in 20X4 from Asper Inc. for $12 million. The deal will not be finalized until 15 March 20X8, dependent on the results of LaidLow's due diligence inspection. We have operated the division as a separate unit, reporting directly to senior management. We struck the deal on 17 August 20X7. At that time, we estimated that the fair value of the division's assets was $24 million, of which $7 million is current assets, mainly billings receivable from the hospitals and other agencies for which we provided service. We estimated that the fair value of the $17 million noncurrent assets was $14 million at the end of the third quarter, 30 September 20X7, and we wrote the noncurrent assets down to that amount. Now, at 31 December, we have good reason to believe that the noncurrent assets are worth $16 million.

2. We also sold off some of our laboratory facilities to HealthCom Ltd. HealthCom paid the purchase price of $5 million in its shares. The value of the HealthCom shares at the end of 20X7 was $5.5 million. We do not intend to hold these shares over the long term.

3. Our facilities in the nation of Albageria were confiscated by the government after a coup, and we had to terminate our operations in that country. The facilities cost us $3 million to establish and were carried on our books at $2.7 million at the time of the confiscation. We estimated that the value of the facilities at the date of the confiscation was $4.3 million. We received compensation of $4.0 million from the Canadian federal government's Export Development Corporation (EDC), which had provided us with "political risk" insurance.

4. We have billings receivable of US$13 million from African countries (not including Albageria). The billings are in U.S. dollars. We have arranged hedges for 90% of that amount. The Canadian-dollar equivalent of the receivables at the time of billing was Cdn$14.4 million. At 31 December 20X7, the receivables were the equivalent of $15.3 million.

5. As the result of our restructuring activities during this past year, we estimate that we will have to make severance payments and give resettlement allowances of approximately $2.5 million during 20X8. The amount may vary up or down by $0.6 million, depending on whether our estimate of voluntary early retirements is correct.

6. We have guaranteed the operating lines of credit of several international agencies that cooperate with us in providing services abroad. The total amount of the guarantees varies, of course, because the draw on the credit lines fluctuates. At year-end 20X7, I would estimate that our total guarantees come to about $4.2 million. We do not expect any of these agencies to default on their credit obligations, however.

Required:

Prepare the report requested by the vice-president. Be sure to consider the impacts on all of the year-end 20X7 financial statements.

TECHNICAL REVIEW

connect

TR4-1 Financial Statement Classification:

The first list below shows the financial statements normally included in a company's annual financial statements. The second list shows some amounts that often appear in those financial statements.

A. SFP

B. Statement of comprehensive income—profit and loss section

C. Statement of comprehensive income—other comprehensive income section

D. Statement of cash flows

E.   Statement of changes in shareholders' equity

B, D, E   1.   Net income
_____   2.   Retained earnings (opening)
_____   3.   Translation gain/loss on foreign subsidiaries
_____   4.   Provision for restructuring costs
_____   5.   Cumulative translation gain or loss
_____   6.   Dividends declared, unpaid at year-end
_____   7.   Appropriation for factory reorganization
_____   8.   Loss on discontinued operation
_____   9.   Non-controlling interest in subsidiaries
_____   10. Investment property held-for-sale
_____   11. Cumulative effect of change in accounting policy
_____   12. Proceeds from issuance of common shares
_____   13. Unrealized gains/losses on hedge derivatives
_____   14. Deferred pension cost

Required:

Use the letters given in the first list to indicate the financial statement on which each item in the second list will appear. Some letters may be used more than once or not at all. The first item is completed for you as an example.

connect

TR4-2 Return Ratios:

Oleander Corp. had total assets of $1,200,000 on 31 December 20X3. At 31 December 20X4, total assets had increased to $1,400,000. Oleander's statement of changes in equity disclosed the following amounts at the beginning and end of 20X4:

	31 December 20X4	31 December 20X3
Class A shares	$345,000	$285,000
Class B shares	41,000	41,000
Contributed surplus	7,500	6,000
Translation reserve (OCI)	(15,000)	(17,000)
Hedge reserve (OCI)	(5,000)	(1,000)
Retained earnings	60,000	43,000
Total equity	$433,500	$357,000

The company's 20X4 statement of comprehensive income showed the following amounts:

Earnings from continuing operations, net of income tax	$53,000
Earnings (loss) from discontinued operations, net of income tax	(4,000)
Other comprehensive income	(2,000)
Comprehensive income	$47,000

Required:

Determine Oleander Corp.'s (1) return on assets and (2) return on invested capital for the year 20X4 based on net income.

connect

TR4-3 Change in Accounting Estimate:

Arboretum Ltd. has been depreciating its production equipment on a straight-line basis over ten years, taking a full year's depreciation in the year of acquisition and assuming no residual value at the end of the equipment's life. The company had invested $1,200,000 in the equipment at the beginning of 20X1. At the beginning of 20X4, the company decided to adjust the equipment's total useful life from ten years down to eight, but with an estimated residual value amounting to 5% of the equipment's original cost rather than zero.

Required:

How should this change be reported in Arboretum's comparative financial statements for 20X4? Determine the amount of depreciation expense to be shown for 20X4 and the comparative amount for 20X3.

connect

TR4-4 Error Correction:

In preparing the year-end financial statements for 20X7, the controller of Risk 'n Save Inc. discovered that the opening inventory for 20X6 had been overstated by $20,000. The company has a 20% income tax rate.

Required:

1. How will discovery of this error change the amounts previously reported on the company's SFP and SCI for the years prior to 20X7?

2. What will be the impact on the company's 20X7 reporting? Prepare a journal entry to correct the error at the end of 20X7, if needed.

connect

TR4-5 Accounting Changes:

A. Voluntary accounting policy change
B. Involuntary accounting policy change
C. Change in accounting estimate
D. Correction of an error
E. None of the above

_____   1.   This is the first year the company has incurred costs for development of a new product.

_____ 2.   It was determined that an employee had been stealing inventory from the warehouse and this was not discovered until after year-end. The fraud had been concealed by adjusting inventory records.

_____ 3.   Management decided to use the average cost for inventory instead of FIFO.

_____ 4.   The number of years used for straight-line amortization was changed from 10 to 12.

_____ 5.   Management decided to early adopt the revised *Handbook* section for financial instruments.

Required:

Use the letters given in the first list to indicate the type of accounting change appropriate for the examples on the second list.

connect

TR4-6   IFRS:

1. A contingent liability that is probable is accrued on the financial statements.

2. All accounting policy changes are retrospective adjustments.

3. All related party transactions are disclosed in the notes.

4. A company reporting using IFRS must have a note stating that the accounting policies are in compliance with the International financial reporting standards.

5. All events after the reporting date and before the financial statements are issued must be adjusted.

Required:

Indicate whether each statement is true or false.

connect

TR4-7   Segment Reporting:

Segment	Revenue	Profit	Assets
A	$ 80,000	$ 7,000	$ 30,000
B	350,000	3,000	120,000
C	340,000	17,000	108,000
D	100,000	3,000	22,000
E	135,000	9,000	60,000
F	550,000	60,000	350,000
G	90,000	11,000	50,000
H	95,000	10,000	30,000
Total	$1,740,000	$120,000	$770,000

Required:

Determine which segments are reportable segments.

connect

TR4-8 Subsequent Events:

Each of the following events occurred after year-end and before the financial statements were issued:

	Adjusting	Nonadjusting
1. Fire destroys warehouse.	_____	_____
2. Lawsuit settled initiated two years ago.	_____	_____
3. Existing customer went bankrupt.	_____	_____
4. New shares were issued.	_____	_____
5. Company initiated restructuring program.	_____	_____

Required:

Identify whether each event is an adjusting or a nonadjusting subsequent event.

connect

TR4-9 IFRS Compared to ASPE:

1. ASPE and IFRS both require note disclosure for related party transactions.
2. Future accounting policy changes are required note disclosure in IFRS only.
3. Both ASPE and IFRS require accrual of lawsuits that there is a 70% probability they will lose.
4. Contingent assets are not accrued in both IFRS and ASPE.
5. Both ASPE and IFRS require segmented reporting.

Required:

Indicate whether each statement is true or false.

connect

TR4-10 Related Party Transactions ASPE:

Identify if the following related party transactions in ASPE would be measured at the exchange amount (EA) or the carrying value (CV). The company sells computer equipment and software.

	EA	CV
1. Computer equipment sold to board member 5% standard discount.	____	____
2. Extra parcel of land sold to subsidiary from parent.	____	____

3. Building sold to board member and the price was determined by an external appraisal.   ____ ____

4. Computer equipment sold to wife of owner with 20% discount.   ____ ____

5. Office equipment sold to board member at a price agreed upon by owner and board member.   ____ ____

ASSIGNMENTS

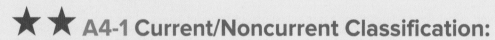 **A4-1 Current/Noncurrent Classification:**

Consider each of the following separate situations that arose in 20X1:

a. Corporation G invested $70,000 in corporate bonds as a short-term investment. The year-end 20X1 market value of the bonds is $63,000. The bonds are measured at fair value every reporting date in FVTPL.

b. Corporation A has the equivalent of C$200,000 cash in a bank in Elbonia. Elbonia's laws prohibit transferring the cash to the Canadian parent company. Corporation A has ongoing operations in Elbonia and uses the cash to run their operations in that country.

c. Corporation B received $85,000 from a customer as advance payment for a specialized piece of manufacturing equipment that is anticipated to be delivered in 20X3.

d. Corporation C has $800,000 in notes receivable from customers. The notes mature over a two-year period. The company normally sells its products on an instalment basis that requires payments over two years.

e. Corporation D received an advance payment of $50,000 for an event that will be held in 20x2.

f. Corporation H holds 10,000 shares in Theo Ltd. as a long-term investment; the shares cost $12 each. At year-end 20X1, the market value is $20 per share. The shares are not actively traded and are measured using fair value through OCI.

g. Corporation E has negotiated a two-year $600,000 loan from its bank to finance equipment. The bank will charge 6% interest per year, compounded. The loan will be repaid in a single lump sum in 20X3, including interest. The market rate of interest is 6%.

h. Corporation F has a major customer that recently went into receivership. As a result of an agreement among all creditors, Corporation F will receive payment on the customer's $200,000 outstanding account in equal instalments over a four-year period.

Required:

For each item indicate the amount(s) that will show as current and the amount(s) that will show as noncurrent in each company's 20X1 SFP. Or, if not shown, indicate why.

 A4-2 SFP/SCE Classification:

Dashall Ltd. has the following accounts in its year-end 20X7 trial balance:

a. Retained earnings.

b. Investment in shares of another company as a temporary use of cash to earn a return.

c. Deferred income tax asset.

d. Note payable for equipment, payable in equal instalments over two years.

e. Income tax payable.

f. U.S. deposit account held in a New York bank.

g. Inventory held in a bonded warehouse (i.e., protected against improper entry). The product needs to be aged for five years before being finished and released for sale.

h. Foreign currency translation gain on U.S. subsidiary.

i. Investment in the marketable equity securities of another company in which Dashall Ltd. has significant influence.

j. Decline in fair value of assets in a division that is being discontinued. A buyer for the division is actively being sought.

Required:

Explain how each item would be reported on Imposing Ltd.'s 20X7 SFP and/or statement of changes in equity.

A4-3 SFP/SCE Classification:

Abriel Ltd., a public company, has the following accounts in its year-end 20X5 trial balance:

a. Dividends payable.

b. Restricted cash balance in Abriel's bank, being held by the bank for a bank loan that will come due in early 20X7.

c. Loss on repurchasing Abriel shares from a minority shareholder; the shares have been cancelled.

d. Voluntary accounting policy change for inventory from FIFO to average cost.

e. Translation gain on converting the pound sterling financial statements of a UK subsidiary to Canadian dollars.

f. An empty warehouse not currently needed for storage.

g. Security deposits by customers who order custom-designed products; if a customer cancels an order, Abriel keeps the deposit.

h. Investment in marketable securities of an unrelated company; Abriel has held these securities for over two years but will sell when they need the cash.

i. Provision for restructuring costs; these estimated costs are mainly for employee severance pay and retraining costs. The restructuring will take place over the next two or three years.

j. A overdraft in one of Abriel's regional bank accounts; Abriel has more than sufficient funds in other accounts with the same bank.

Required:

Explain how each item would be reported on Imposing Ltd.'s 20X7 SFP and/or statement of changes in equity.

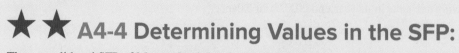

The consolidated SFP of Mutron Lock Inc. is shown below.

MUTRON LOCK INC.
Consolidated Statement of Financial Position
As of 31 December 20X5

Assets

Current assets

Cash and cash equivalents		$ 10,195
Marketable securities		a
Accounts receivable	$153,682	
Allowance for doubtful accounts	b	147,421
Inventories		201,753
Prepaid expenses		8,902
Total current assets		c

Noncurrent assets

Land		12,482
Building (net)		d
Equipment and machinery	195,467	
Accumulated depreciation	(103,675)	91,792
Total capital assets		261,056
Investments		14,873
Other assets		7,926
Total assets		$661,774

Liabilities and Shareholders' Equity

Current liabilities

Accounts payable	$ 85,476
Notes payable	e
Income taxes payable	6,421
Current portion of long-term debt	4,893
Accrued expenses	5,654
Total current liabilities	110,763

Long-term debt	122,004
Deferred income taxes	f
Total liabilities	g
Shareholders' equity	
Preferred shares, no par value (authorized 10,000 shares, issued 2,400 shares for $14,281)	h
Common shares, no par value (authorized 400,000 shares, issued 20,000 shares)	i
Total contributed capital	j
Retained earnings	206,471
Total Mutron Lock Inc. shareholders' equity	347,668
Non-controlling interest in subsidiaries	35,136
Consolidated shareholders' equity	382,804
Total liabilities and shareholders' equity	$ k

Required:

For each of items (a) through (k) in the SFP above, calculate the amount that should appear.

A4-5 Analyzing Data and Reporting on the SFP:

Akerman Techonology Corp. is preparing its SFP at 31 December 20X5. The following items are under consideration:

a. Rent received in advance for the first quarter of 20X6, $20,000.

b. Note payable, long-term, $100,000. This note was issued on 1 July 20X5 and will be paid in five equal instalments. The first instalment, $20,000, will be paid 1 January 20X6. Interest will accrue at the rate of 8% per annum.

c. $400,000 bonds payable bearing interest of 8% per annum, maturing 31 December 20X9. Unamortized premium amounted to $10,000 at the end of 20X5.

d. Long-term note payable, $250,000, issued on 30 June 20X2 and maturing 30 June 20X6. Interest at 8% must be paid 30 June each year.

e. Restriction for bond sinking fund, $20,000; this restriction is required by provisions of the bond agreement.

f. On 28 January 20X6, prior to finalizing the 20X5 statements, the company issued new preferred shares to a private equity fund for $1,400,000. The new shares increased the equity base of the company by almost 30%. The fund will be used to retire existing long-term debt and for new production processes.

Required:

Show, with appropriate captions, how each of these items should be reported on the 31 December 20X5 SFP. If amounts are not quantifiable, describe the appropriate reporting that would be followed when numbers are available. Round amounts to the nearest $100.

★ ★ A4-6 Financial Statement Classification:

Listed below are some financial statement classifications coded with letters and, below them, selected transactions and/or account titles.

Code	Financial Statement Classification
	Statement of Comprehensive Income
A	Earnings/loss from continuing operations
B	Earnings/loss from discontinued operations
C	Other comprehensive income
D	Earnings per share
	Statement of Financial Position
E	Current assets
F	Noncurrent assets
G	Current liabilities
H	Noncurrent liabilities
I	Shareholders' equity
	Statement of Changes in Shareholders' Equity
J	Beginning balance
K	An adjustment (addition to or deduction from) beginning balance
L	Change during the year—retained earnings
M	Change during the year—invested capital (not designated as a discontinued operation)
N	Change during the year—items of other comprehensive income
O	**Notes to the Financial Statements**

Response		Transaction or Account Title
A, E	0.	Accrued interest on long-term receivables
_____	1.	Provision for restructuring costs
_____	2.	Accrued liability for employee post-retirement benefits

_____ 3.   Factory equipment designated for sale

_____ 4.   Translation gain on self-sustaining foreign subsidiary

_____ 5.   Appropriation for plant expansion

_____ 6.   Payment of $30,000 additional income tax assessment on prior year's income

_____ 7.   Cash dividends declared; not yet paid

_____ 8.   Estimated amount to be collected from a lawsuit against a competitor for patent infringement

_____ 9.   Earnings from a subsidiary that was purchased with the explicit intent to resell it at a higher price

_____ 10.   Exchange loss on accounts receivable balances in euros; the euro balances are hedged

_____ 11.   Amount paid when the company purchased and retired some of its own common shares; the amount paid was in excess of the shares' original issue proceeds

_____ 12.   Earnings after income tax from a division held for sale

_____ 13.   Loss due to expropriation of a plant in a foreign country

_____ 14.   Change in the translated net investment in a U.S. subsidiary

_____ 15.   Interest paid during the year plus interest accrued on liabilities

_____ 16.   Dividends received on shares held as an investment

_____ 17.   Damages paid as a result of a lawsuit by an individual injured while shopping in the company's store; the litigation lasted three years

_____ 18.   Cumulative effect of a change in accounting policy

_____ 19.   A $100,000 bad debt is to be written off—the receivable had been outstanding for five years; the company estimates bad debts each year and has an allowance for bad debts

_____ 20.   Adjustment due to correction of an error during current year; the error was made two years earlier

Required:

For each transaction or account title, enter in the space provided one or more code letters to indicate how that item will appear on the statements, either directly or implicitly. The first item, "0," is shown as an example. Comment on any doubtful items.

★ ★ A4-7 Statement of Changes in Equity:

On 31 December 20X2, the balances of Argon Enterprises Inc.'s shareholders' equity accounts were as follows (all are credit balances):

Capital stock	$303,000
Contributed surplus	6,000
Retained earnings	121,000
Currency translation differences	1,500
Mark-to-market adjustments on available for sale investments	28,600
Cash flow hedges	2,100
Actuarial gains and losses	1,600
	$463,800

Argon's statement of comprehensive income for the year ending 31 December 20X3 showed the following amounts, from "net profit for the year" through "comprehensive income":

	31 December 20X3	31 December 20X2
Net profit for the year	$ 46,900	$ 62,100
Other comprehensive income (loss) net of applicable income tax:		
Currency translation differences	(4,500)	2,500
Mark-to-market adjustments on available for sale investments	(36,800)	7,200
Actuarial gains (losses)	2,100	(5,900)
Cash flow hedges	(500)	(150)
Total other comprehensive loss for the year	$(39,700)	$ 3,650
Comprehensive income for the year	$ 7,200	$65,750

Required:

Prepare a statement of changes in equity for Argon Enterprises Inc. for the year ended 31 December 20X3. The company declared no dividends during either 20X2 or 20X3.

★ ★ A4-8 Statement of Changes in Equity:

The Atlantic Refinery Corp. (ARC) is a public company headquartered in St. John's, Newfoundland. On 31 December 20X5, the post-closing trial balance included the following accounts (in thousands of Canadian dollars):

	Debit	Credit
Investment in Mongolian subsidiary	$72,000	
Provision for future site restoration		$ 34,000
Common shares		170,000
Translation differential from Mongolian subsidiary		12,000
Convertible bonds		85,000
Equity portion of convertible bonds		5,000
Contributed surplus—premium on common shares issued		35,000
Goodwill (from purchase of Mongolian subsidiary)	18,000	
Investment in shares of upstream affiliate	36,000	
Retained earnings		533,000
Trademarks	6,800	

The following transactions and events occurred during 20X6:

a. Net income amounted to $47 million.

b. The value of trademarks was written off after ARC lost a patent protection lawsuit.

c. An additional $1.5 million of convertible bonds was transferred from the debt portion to the equity portion.

d. An accounting policy was changed due to a new IFRS taking effect in 20X6; the effect of retrospective restatement was to reduce prior years' earnings by an aggregate amount of $31 million.

e. The future liability for site restoration was increased by $5 million.

f. Common shares with a stated value of $15 million were repurchased on the open market for $20 million and cancelled. The original issue price of the shares amounted to $18, of which $3 million had been credited to contributed surplus.

g. A new class of preferred shares was issued to a major public sector pension plan for $85 million to finance future development.

h. Dividends totalling $24 million were issued during the year. Of that amount, $6 million were declared on 24 December 20X6, payable to shareholders of record on January 15, 20X7.

i. The translated amount of ARC's investment in Mongolian subsidiary declined by $2 million due to a rise in the value of the Canadian dollar.

Required:

Prepare a statement of changes in equity for Atlantic Refinery Corp. for the year ended 31 December 20X6. Explain assumptions you need to make, if any. *Hint:* Not all of the accounts listed above are relevant to the SCE.

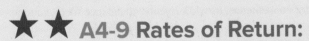

★ ★ A4-9 Rates of Return:

Refer to the data in A4-7. Assume that the assets of Argon Enterprises Inc. totalled $1,980,000 at the end of 20X1, $1,750,000 at year-end 20X2, and $2,120,000 at year-end 20X3.

Required:

1. Assume you are analyst for a private equity firm. Determine the following for each of 20X2 and 20X3:
    a. Return on assets
    b. Return on total shareholders' equity
    c. Return on invested capital

2. Explain the relevance and significance of these ratios for deciding whether or not your firm should invest in Argon Enterprises.

Hint: You will need to calculate the year-end 20X1 shareholders' equity and invested capital balances by working backward from the amounts given in A4-7.

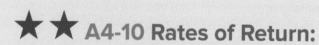

★ ★ A4-10 Rates of Return:

Po-Yen Devices Inc. and Kejia Computer Ltd. are competing businesses. Selected data from the financial statements for the two companies for the year ended 31 December 20X2 are shown below.

Year ended 31 December 20X2 (in thousands of Canadian dollars)	Po-Yen Devices	Kejia Computer
Sales revenue	$ 540,000	$270,000
Earnings from continuing operations, net of income tax	80,000	23,000
Net earnings, after income taxes	66,000	23,000
Comprehensive income	72,000	16,000
Current assets	$260,000	$ 110,000
Tangible capital assets, net	400,000	40,000
Total assets	$660,000	$ 150,000
Current liabilities	$ 120,000	$ 60,000
Long-term liabilities	360,000	—
Common shares	100,000	50,000
Retained earnings	80,000	40,000
Total liabilities and shareholders' equity	$660,000	$150,000
Number of common shares outstanding (thousands)	300,000	250,000

Required:

1. Compute the following ratios for both companies (for convenience, use 20X2 year-end balance sheet amounts instead of averages):
    a. Operating margin (i.e., earnings ÷ revenue)
    b. Return on assets

c. Return on shareholders' equity

d. Total debt-to-shareholders'

e. equity

2. Evaluate the two companies on the basis of the ratios you have calculated. Which company do you think is more profitable?

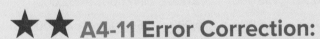

A4-11 Error Correction:

On 23 November 20X7, when engaged in preparing for the 20X7 fiscal year-end, the chief accountant of Harper Ltd. discovered two accounting errors in the 20X5 statements:

a. A government ministry had paid $4.5 million in partial settlement of an amount due for a large contract. The contract revenue had already been recognized. However, the payment was accidentally credited to contract revenue instead of to accounts receivable and was included in taxable income.

b. Inventory purchases of $2.4 million had inadvertently been charged to equipment, a capital asset account, and had been amortized by 10% for each of 20X5 and 20X6. The accounting amortization rate is the same as the CCA rate for tax purposes. The ending and beginning inventories had been properly stated. Therefore, the mistake caused cost of sales to be understated by $2.4 million and pretax earnings to be overstated by the same amount.

Harper's income tax rate is 20%.

Required:

1. Calculate the earnings correction that Harper must show in the 20X7 financial statements. Where will these amounts be disclosed?

2. Prepare a general journal entry to record the correction of each error.

connect

A4-12 Error Correction:

In May 20X5, the newly appointed controller of Butch Baking Corp. conducted a thorough review of past accounting, particularly of transactions that exceeded the company's normal level of materiality. As a result of his review, he instructed the company's chief accountant to correct two errors:

a. In 20X2, the company made extensive improvements to the baking process and installed a substantial amount of new equipment. The entire cost of the process improvements and equipment was accidentally charged to income as restructuring expense in 20X2. However, the equipment should have been capitalized and added to the factory equipment account. The cost of the equipment was $1,200,000. Butch depreciates its factory equipment on the straight-line basis over ten years. A full year's depreciation is charged in the year that equipment is acquired.

b. A year-end cut-off error occurred in 20X3. A large shipment of nonperishable supplies arrived from China on the last day of 20X3 and had been left in the shipping containers outside the main plant. As a result, the supplies were recorded as received in 20X4 and had not been included in the year-end 20X3 inventory count. The account payable also had not been recorded in 20X3. The supplies cost $160,000.

Like most companies, Butch Baking presents a five-year financial summary in its annual report. The 20X4 summary contained the following information (in thousands of dollars, except EPS):

	20X0	20X1	20X2	20X3	20X4
Gross revenue	$ 15,000	$ 16,000	$ 17,500	$ 17,000	$ 18,000
Net income	1,980	2,100	850	2,300	2,100
Total assets	140,000	155,000	148,000	147,000	152,000
Total liabilities	50,000	65,000	70,000	69,000	73,000
Net assets	90,000	90,000	78,000	78,000	79,000
Earnings per share*	$19.80	$21.00	$8.50	$23.00	$21.00

*100,000 shares outstanding.

Required:

1. Explain the impact of these two errors on the summary financial information.
2. Revise the financial summary.
3. Prepare the journal entry or entries necessary in 20X5 to correct the accounts as of 1 January 20X5.

★ A4-13 Change in Accounting Policy:

Hannam Co. decided to change from the declining-balance method of depreciation to the straight-line method effective 1 January 20X7. The following information was provided:

Year	Net Income as Reported	Excess of Declining-Balance Depreciation over straight-Line Depreciation
20X3*	$(30,000)	$5,000
20X4	35,000	15,000
20X5	22,500	12,500
20X6	52,500	7,000
*First year of operations.	80,000	39,500

The company has a 31 December year-end. The tax rate is 20%. No dividends were declared until 20X7; $20,000 of dividends were declared and paid in December 20X7. Income for 20X7, calculated using the new accounting policy, was $105,000.

Required:

Assuming that the change in policy was implemented retrospectively, present the retained earnings reconciliation that would appear in Hannam's 20X7 statement of changes in equity.

★ ★ A4-14 Change in Accounting Policy:

Moncton Developments Ltd. was established in early 20X2. During the first three years, the company followed the policy of expensing its development costs rather than capitalizing and amortizing them. It did so because in the early stages of the company's life, they felt there was no reasonable assurance that the development costs would meet the criteria for capitalization. However, Moncton's development activities turned out to be very successful. Therefore, the company decided in 20X4 to change its method of accounting for product development expenses from expensing such items to capitalizing them and amortizing them over the period of expected benefit.

To prepare for the change, the following data were gathered:

	20X4	20X3	20X2
Product development costs	$200,000	$150,000	$250,000
Depreciation and amortization, prior to change	70,000	70,000	60,000
Restated amortization, after policy change	120,000	110,000	90,000
Net income before income tax, old policy	840,000	770,000	300,000
Net income after income tax (at 30%), old policy	588,000	539,000	210,000
Earnings per share	$ 11.76	$ 10.78	$ 4.20

Moncton Developments has 50,000 common shares outstanding. The balance of retained earnings was $690,000 at 31 December 20X3. During 20X4, the company declared dividends of $50,000.

Required:

1. Determine the numerical impact of the policy change on net income and EPS for 20X2 and 20X3.
2. Prepare the retained earnings column (or section) of the 20X4 statement of changes in equity, giving appropriate treatment to the change in accounting policy.
3. Prepare an appropriate disclosure note.

A4-15 Note Disclosures:

Note disclosures provide the following information:

A. Explain the accounting policies that the company is using.
B. Provide additional detail for financial statement components.
C. Identify major underlying assumptions and estimates.
D. Provide information not presented elsewhere in financial statements but that is useful for understanding them.

Typical notes are:

B	a.	Description of income statement item, "discontinued operations"
___	b.	Amortization policy and amounts of accumulated amortization by asset class
___	c.	Revenue recognition policy
___	d.	Breakdown of the SFP amount shown for "other assets"
___	e.	Description of related party transactions
___	f.	Description of contingent loss that is not measurable
___	g.	Preferred share dividend rate
___	h.	Extent of reliance on major customers
___	i.	Sensitivity to variation in oil prices
___	j.	Description of subsequent event—fire in warehouse not relating to conditions before SFP date

_____ k.   Information on key operating segments of the business
_____ l.   Long-term debt note—interest rates, terms to maturity, five-year cash flow, market value
_____ m.   Breakdown of inventory into component parts and description of valuation method
_____ n.   Fair value of debt

Required:

For each note (a) to (n) above, indicate the type(s) of disclosure (letters A to D) provided. A note may provide more than one type of disclosure. The first one is done for you as an example.

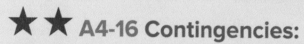 **A4-16 Contingencies:**

Unlimited Possibilities Ltd. (UPL) is finalizing the financial statements for 20X5. The company's managers are uncertain how each of the following events and situations should be reported:

a. UPL is the guarantor on a $10 million bank loan that was obtained by another company controlled by the same shareholders who control UPL. The amount of the guaranteed loan is a material amount for UPL.

b. UPL has a subsidiary in Japan. UPL has reached agreement to sell the Japanese subsidiary to a Taiwanese company, subject to approval by regulators in Japan. When the sale closes, UPL will realize a profit of $20 million as the purchase price is $20 million higher than the subsidiary's net book value. Approval is expected, but it will be at least six months before the regulators issue their final ruling.

c. An existing customer declared bankruptcy in February 20x6.

Required:

Discuss the appropriate reporting for each of these three items on UPL's 20X5 financial statements.

A4-17 Contingencies, Subsequent Events:

Zero Growth Ltd. has completed financial statements for the year ended 31 December 20X6. The financial statements have yet to be finalized or issued. The following events and transactions have occurred:

a. The office building housing administrative staff was damaged due to a hurricane on 15 January 20X7.

b. On 15 November 20X6, a customer sued the company for $1,000,000 based on a claim of negligence leading to personal injury; Zero is actively defending the suit and claims it is unfounded. Nothing has yet been recorded in the 20X6 financial statements in relation to this event.

c. On 1 February 20X7, The company received a $49,700 income tax reassessment for 20X5.

d. On 20 December 20X6, Zero applied for a bank loan to replace an existing line of credit. The loan was granted on 2 January 20X7. This event was not recorded in 20X6 or reported in the draft 20X6 financial statements.

e. The company has reinterpreted a legal agreement entitling it to commission revenue for the sale of a client's products. Zero Growth's interpretation would entitle it to an extra $60,000 over and above amounts recognized in 20X6. The amount has not been recorded in the accounts. The client was billed for this amount in 20X6 but has disagreed with Zero on the contract interpretation. Both parties have consulted their lawyers; resolution is not expected soon.

f. On 1 March 20X7, Zero Growth issued new common shares for cash. The new issue increased the total number of shares outstanding by 15%.

Required:

Discuss the appropriate accounting treatment for the contingencies and subsequent events described.

★ ★ A4-18 Subsequent Events:

Northern Switching Ltd. (NSL) is a manufacturer of digital switching equipment and systems. The company has total assets of approximately $784 million. Each of the following events occurred after the end of NSL's 20X8 fiscal year, but before the statements had been finalized:

a. NSL finalized an agreement to sell a major production facility to Cascade Cable Corporation for approximately $42 million cash. The sale includes buildings of approximately one million square feet, fixtures, equipment, and 63 acres of land. The property has an amortized cost of $28 million on NSL's draft 20X8 SFP.

b. NSL reached agreement with an international banking corporation for credit support for up to $23 million of new sales to customers abroad.

c. The company has a U.S. subsidiary. NSL (i.e., the parent company) signed a repayment guarantee on a $50 million line of credit that Citibank issued to the subsidiary.

d. Marketable securities held by NSL at 20X8 year-end, reported on the year-end draft SFP at their market value of $14 million, were sold for $12 million.

e. The CEO of Crisco Corporation, NSL's major competitor, accused a senior NSL executive of improperly accessing confidential information via an employee-only portal on Crisco's website and using that information for competitive advantage. Crisco said that the company will file a lawsuit to recover $76 million in damages. NSL vehemently denies the allegation.

Required:

Discuss what disclosure, if any, NSL should give to each of these events in its 20X8 financial statements.

★ ★ A4-19 Subsequent Events:

The auditor has completed her work on the financial statements of Leslie Kwok Inc. (LKI) for the year ended 31 December 20X7. The auditor signed her audit opinion on 5 March 20X8; LKI's board of directors has not yet approved the statements. The following transactions and events occurred after 31 December 20X7:

a. On 27 January, LKI entered into a long-term lease for a private airplane for the company president and CEO. The lease requires payments of US$75,000 per month for 60 months.

b. On 28 January, LKI acquired all of the shares of Phan Ltd. by issuing LKI shares in exchange. The acquisition more than doubled the size of LKI, and the former shareholders of Phan now have a majority of the votes in LKI.

c. On 15 February, the board of directors of LKI decided to discontinue a major segment of the company's business due to continuing losses and a change of strategy.

d. The Royal Toronto Bank extended a $25 million line of credit to LKI on 5 March.

e. One of the company's major customers declared bankruptcy on 22 March. The customer accounted for 30% of LKI's revenue in 20X7.

f. On 31 March, LKI reached an agreement with a major institutional investor to issue $250 million in secured debentures through a private placement.

g. A new board of directors was elected on 7 April.

h. On 10 April, the new directors cancelled the lease on the private airplane. The contract calls for a cancellation penalty of US$1 million.

Required:

Discuss how each item should be reported in LKI's 20X7 financial statements as a *subsequent event*, if at all.

 connect

★ **A4-20 Segment Disclosure:**

Union Carbolics Inc. has five operating segments. Segment operating data (in millions of Canadian dollars) for the year 20X6 are as follows:

Segment	Intersegment Sales	Sales to External Customers	Total Assets	Operating Profit (Loss)
Chemicals	$ 450	$ 1,500	$1,020	$ 90
Plastics	150	1,050	1,350	112
Adhesives	—	325	300	9
Solvents	—	275	255	(18)
Coatings	—	330	225	(21)
Totals	$600	$3,480	$3,150	$ 172

Required:

Identify which of these five segments are *reportable segments* under IFRS. Indicate the grounds on which you selected each identified segment.

★ ★ **A4-21 Segment Disclosure:**

The following disclosure note is from the 31 December 20X4 financial statements of Riconda Ltd.:

The company operates one operating segment, that being the design, manufacture, and sale of graphics and multimedia products for personal computers and consumer electronic devices.

	20X2	20X1	20X0
Sales			
Canada	$ 23,104	31,119	$ 41,175
U.S.	325,464	424,472	425,000
Europe	247,795	396,805	412,855
Asia-Pacific	441,446	430,669	307,320
Consolidated sales	$1,037,809	$1,283,065	$1,186,350
Product Sales			
Components	$ 81,083	$ 499,859	$ 390,238
Boards	548,053	778,015	796,112
Other	673	5,191	—

Consolidated sales	$1,037,809	$1,283,065	$1,186,350
Noncurrent Assets			
Canada	$ 54,162	$ 42,494	$ 36,590
U.S.	297,417	421,955	31,341
Europe	5,071	5,364	5,410
Asia-Pacific	706	919	1,051
Consolidated noncurrent assets	$ 357,356	$ 470,732	$ 74,392

Required:

1. What is the purpose of this disclosure note?
2. Evaluate the information presented. What does it tell you about the company's operations?
3. Review the requirements for segment disclosures. What information is lacking in the note above? Why?

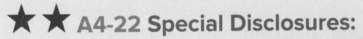

A4-22 Special Disclosures:

Respond to the specific questions in each of the two cases, below.

Case A   The following disclosure note is from the 31 October 20X2 financial statements of GreenWorld Ltd., a mining company:

> The preparation of the financial statements, in conformity with generally accepted accounting principles, requires management to make estimates and assumptions that affect the reported amounts of assets and liabilities and disclosure of contingent assets and liabilities at the date of the financial statements and the reported amounts of revenues and expenses during the reporting period. The most significant estimates are related to the physical and economic lives and the recoverability of mining assets, mineral reserves, site restoration and related obligations, commodity contracts and financial instruments, and income taxes. Actual results could differ from those estimates.

Required:

1. What is the purpose of this disclosure note?
2. How could this note be made more meaningful to the financial statement user?
3. List four other financial statement elements (not listed above) that are affected by estimates.
4. What sensitivity analysis might be required?

Case B   The following disclosure note is from the 31 December 20X2 financial statements of UMM Ltd., a software company:

> UMM has entered into an agreement with Vitech Ltd., a shareholder, with respect to acquiring certain rights to Vitech's software, technology, services, and other

benefits. In the current year, UMM acquired $200 (million) of specific software products from Vitech. These assets were recorded at the transaction price, which represents fair market value as determined by an independent appraisal. UMM has expensed $68 (million) in services received from Vitech in 20X2. Sales in 20X2 to Vitech amounted to $151 (million). These transactions were conducted in the normal course of business at prices established and agreed to by both parties.

Required:

1. What is the purpose of this disclosure note?
2. In general, what makes two parties related?
3. What measurement attribute has been used to record software assets, and revenues and expenses between these related parties? Comment.
4. What evidence has UMM gathered to support the value for software purchased?
5. What would be the difference if the company reported in ASPE compared to IFRS?

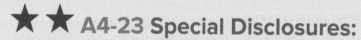 A4-23 Special Disclosures:

Respond to the specific questions in each of the two cases, below.

Case A   The following disclosure note appeared in the 31 December 20X5 financial statements of Dridell Corporation, a manufacturer of electronic equipment:

Dridell is exposed to liabilities and compliance costs arising from its past and current generation, management, and disposal of hazardous substances and wastes. As of 30 December 20X5, the accruals on the consolidated SFP for environmental matters were $20 million. Based on information available as of 31 December 20X5, management believes that the existing accruals are sufficient to satisfy probable and reasonably estimable environmental liabilities related to known environmental matters. Any additional liabilities that may result from these matters, and any additional liabilities that may result in connection with other locations currently under investigation, are not expected to have a material adverse effect on the business, results of operations, financial condition, and liquidity of Dridell. The company has a fund set up for all environmental matters.

Case B   The following disclosure note is from the 31 December 20X2 financial statements of Zing Ltd., a property developer:

On 7 January 20X3, the Corporation contracted to acquire 60 residential housing units from a third party for a purchase price of $2.8 million, cash. On 24 January 20X3, the Company issued 240,000 stock options to senior officers of the company. These options have a three-year vesting period, with one-third vesting on each anniversary date.

Required:

For each of these two disclosure notes, explain:

1. What is the purpose of the note?
2. What types of management estimates are implied by this disclosure?
3. What implications might this note have for the financial reporting in future years, if any?

★★★ A4-24 SFP Interpretation:

The SFP of Karmax Ltd. discloses the following assets:

KARMAX LTD.	
Statement of Financial Position (Extracts)	
Year ended 31 December 20X6	
(in thousands of Canadian dollars)	
Assets	
Current assets	
Cash	$ 710
Short-term investments	416
Accounts receivable	1,011
Inventory	2,600
Prepaid expenses	410
Total current assets	$ 5,147
Tangible capital assets, net	14,755
Intangible capital assets, net	984
Long-term investments	1,077
Total assets	$21,963

The following information has been established in relation to market values (amounts in thousands of dollars):

	Market Value	Source
Short-term investments	$416	Quoted stock market price
Inventory	$4,190	Karmax price list
Tangible capital assets	$20,000–$25,000	Real estate appraisal
Long-term investment	$3,000	(Note 1)
Intangible capital assets	$10,000	(Note 2)

Note 1

The long-term investment is an investment in the common shares of a company owned and operated by the two sons of Karmax's major shareholder. The Karmax investment is 25% of the outstanding shares. The long-term investment is accounted for using the equity method. The sons' company has never sold shares to a nonfamily investor, and the Karmax shareholder provided this estimate of value.

Note 2

Karmax holds patents on a successful consumer product, licensed to various manufacturers. Significant annual royalties are earned; the recorded SFP value consists of legal fees paid during patent infringement cases. The $10 million estimate of market value is based on discounted future cash flow.

Required:

Prepare a brief report that contains:

1. An analysis of the reliability of the various market value estimates as a good predictor of future cash flows; and

2. An assessment of the usefulness of the (primarily historical cost) SFP to:
   a. A banker making a lending decision.
   b. An investor evaluating return on investment.

★ ★ ★ A4-25 SFP Interpretation:

The SFP of a junior Canadian gold-mining company reports the following amounts (in $ thousands):

Assets

Current assets

Cash and cash equivalents	$ 8,260	
Accounts receivable, less allowance for doubtful accounts	20,338	
Taxes recoverable	200	
Inventories	20,800	
Prepaid expenses	500	
Investments (cost is equal to market value)	1,830	$ 51,928
Noncurrent assets		
Plant, equipment, and mine development costs, net		95,000
Goodwill		2,000
Total assets		$148,928

Liabilities and shareholders' quity

Current liabilities

Accounts payable and accrued liabilities	$ 6,550	
Royalties payable	560	$ 7,110
Noncurrent liabilities		
Liability for site restoration costs	2,280	
Convertible bonds	12,000	

Deferred income taxes	<u>1,830</u>	16,110
Shareholders' equity		
Share capital	100,000	
Contributed surplus	1,128	
Cumulative exchange adjustment	500	
Retained earnings	<u>23,000</u>	
	124,628	
Non-controlling interest	<u>1,080</u>	
Consolidated shareholders' equity		<u>125,708</u>
Total liabilities and shareholders' equity		<u>$148,928</u>

Required:

1. Explain the meaning of the following accounts:
    a. Mine development costs
    b. Goodwill
    c. Liability for future site restoration costs
    d. Deferred income tax
    e. Non-controlling interest
    f. Cumulative exchange adjustment
    g. Contributed surplus
2. What items on the above SFP would most likely be estimated? Explain.
3. For what assets would you expect the market value and book value to be the most different? Explain.
4. As a potential shareholder, what additional information would be relevant to any decision to acquire shares in this company? Why is this information not presented with the audited financial statements?

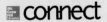

★ ★ A4-26 ASPE—Prepare an SFP:

The following trial balance was prepared by Vantage Electronics Corp., a Canadian private enterprise, as of 31 December 20X5. The adjusting entries for 20X5 have been made, *except* for any related to the specific information noted below.

VANTAGE ELECTRONICS	
Trial Balance	
31 December 20X5	
Cash	$15,000

Accounts receivable	15,000	
Inventories	17,000	
Equipment	22,400	
Land	6,400	
Building	7,600	
Prepaid expenses	1,100	
Accounts payable		$ 5,500
Note payable, 10%		8,000
Share capital, 2,500 shares outstanding		38,500
Retained earnings		32,500
Totals	$84,500	$84,500

Other information:

You find that certain errors and omissions are reflected in the trial balance:

a. The $15,000 balance in accounts receivable represents the entire amount owed to the company; of this amount, $12,400 is from trade customers and 5% of that amount is estimated to be uncollectible. The remaining amount owed to the company represents a long-term advance to its president.

b. Inventories include $1,000 of goods incorrectly valued at double their cost (i.e., reported at $2,000). No correction has been recorded. Office supplies on hand of $500 are also included in the balance of inventories.

c. When the equipment and building were purchased new on 1 January 20X0 (i.e., six years earlier), they had estimated lives of 10 and 25 years, respectively. They have been amortized using the straight-line method on the assumption of zero residual value, and depreciation has been credited directly to the asset accounts. Amortization has been recorded for 20X5.

d. The balance in the land account includes a $1,000 payment made as a deposit on the purchase of an adjoining tract. The option to buy it has not yet been exercised and probably will not be exercised during the coming year.

e. The interest-bearing note dated 1 April 20X5 matures 31 March 20X6. Interest on it has not been recorded for 20X5.

Required:

Prepare a balance sheet with appropriate captions and subcaptions. Show the computation of the ending balance in retained earnings.

 **A4-27 ASPE—Redraft a Deficient SFP:**

Rutgers e-Terminal Ltd. is a private corporation wholly owned by Mr. Adonis Rutgers. Mr. Rutgers also personally owns 40% of the common shares of a company named Princeton Corp. A further 20% of the Princeton common shares are held by Rutgers e-Terminal Ltd. The bookkeeper for Rutgers e-Terminal prepared the following SFP:

RUTGERS E-TERMINAL LTD.

Financial Situation

For the year ending 31 December 20X3

Short-Term Assets

Cash on hand	$ 600	
Cash in the Royal Dominion chequing account	15,200	
Overdraft in the ScotiaTrust chequing account	−3,800	
Accounts receivable (includes credit balances of $22,000)	52,600	
Automobile held for resale, fully depreciated (estimated market value, $10,000)	10,000	
Supplies on hand, at cost	1,800	
Inventory, at cost (estimated market value, $35,000)	37,900	
Final month's rent on office space (lease expires in 20X7)	3,000	
Investment in shares of subsidiary (market value, $150,000)	130,000	
		$247,300

Long-Term Assets

Furniture	40,000	
Warehouse	500,000	
Prepaid expenses	4,500	
Note receivable from customer (issued 5 March 20X1, due on Mr. Rutger's demand)	30,000	
Loan receivable from shareholder	120,000	694,500
Total financial assets		$941,800

Liabilities

Payable to suppliers	$175,300	
Amounts on purchase orders issued	50,000	
Reserve for depreciation on furniture	10,000	
Reserve for depreciation on warehouse	75,000	
Mortgage due to the Montreal National Bank	380,000	
Common shares of Rutgers e-Terminal held by Mr. Rutgers	150,000	
Accumulated surplus	101,500	
Total financial liabilities		$941,800

Required:

Prepare a corrected classified SFP, using appropriate terminology.

A4-28 ASPE—Redraft an SFP:

Prime Essentials Ltd. is a small private corporation. The owner plans to approach the bank for an additional loan or a line of credit to facilitate expansion. The company bookkeeper, after discussion with the owner of the company, has prepared the following draft SFP for the fiscal year ended 30 September 20X3, the company's first full year of operations:

PRIME ESSENTIALS LTD.

Statement of Financial Position

Year ended 30 September 20X3

Assets	
Cash in the bank	$ 12,000
Patent	30,000
Goodwill	50,000
Equipment	120,000
Amounts owed by customers	32,000
Stocks and bonds owned by the company	10,000
Total	$254,000
Financing Sources for Assets	
Amounts owed to suppliers	28,000
Amount owed to owner for automobile expenses	6,000
Amount owed to owner's brother-in-law	20,000
Amount owed to bank	26,000
Earnings accumulated in the business	27,000
Shares paid for by owner	60,000
Cash flow from used-up portion of equipment	24,000
Increases in value	63,000
Total	$254,000

The bookkeeper has provided some notes on the amounts included in the draft SFP:

a. The owner invested $60,000 of his own money to start the business.

b. The patent was purchased from the owner's brother-in-law for $17,000. The owner believes that the patent could easily be sold for $30,000, and probably more.

c. The equipment is being depreciated at the same rate as allowed for income tax. Depreciation represents a source of financing for the company because it is added back to net income and increases the operating cash flow.

d. The owner uses his personal automobile for occasional business errands. He estimates that the company owes him $6,000 for his use of the car.

e. Because the business has been profitable from the very first, the owner estimates that he could sell the company at a $50,000 premium, thereby almost doubling his initial investment after only one year.

f. The bank gave a five-year loan to the company, with the provision that the company had to maintain a 25% "compensating balance" in its cash account until the loan is repaid.

g. The company holds publicly traded shares in other companies. The value of these securities was $10,000 when the owner's brother-in-law gave them to the company as a loan on 1 April 20X3. On 30 September 20X3, their market value was $14,000. The company is free to sell the securities, but $10,000 plus one-half of any proceeds above $10,000 must be passed on to the brother-in-law. The brother-in-law also lent $10,000 cash to the company, repayable on demand.

h. One of the customers is a bit unsteady, financially. That customer owes $3,000.

Required:

Redraft the SFP. Provide an explanation for each change you make. Explain any note disclosures you think are needed.

★ ★ ★ A4-29 ASPE—Criticize and Redraft a Deficient SFP:

The most recent SFP of Blackstone Tire Corp., a private corporation, appears below:

BLACKSTONE TIRE CORPORATION
Statement of Financial Position
For the year ended 31 December 20X5

Assets			
Current			
Cash			$ 23,000
Short-term investments			10,000
Accounts receivable			15,000
Merchandise			31,000
Supplies			5,000
Shares of Wilmont Co. (not a controlling interest)			17,000
			$ 101,000
Investments			
Loan to shareholder			82,500
Tangible			
Building and land ($10,000)	$86,000		
Less: reserve for depreciation	40,000	46,000	
Equipment	$20,000		
Less: reserve for depreciation	15,000	5,000	51,000

Deferred

    Prepaid expenses   <u>5,000</u>

Total   <u>$239,500</u>

Debt and Capital

Current

Accounts payable	$16,000	
Reserve for future, deferred income tax	17,000	
Customers' accounts receivable with credit balance	<u>100</u>	$ 33,100

Fixed (interest paid at year-end)

Bonds payable, 8.5%, due 20X9	45,000	
Mortgage, 11%	<u>12,000</u>	57,000
Reserve for bad debts		900

Capital

Preferred shares, authorized and outstanding, 6,000 shares	50,000	
Common shares, authorized 10,000 shares	67,000	
Earned surplus	22,500	
Donated capital	<u>9,000</u>	<u>148,500</u>
Total		<u>$239,500</u>

Required:

1. List and explain in writing your criticisms of the above statement.
2. Prepare a complete SFP as far as possible, using appropriate format, captions, and terminology.

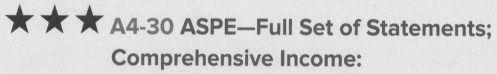

★ ★ ★ A4-30 ASPE—Full Set of Statements; Comprehensive Income:

Amana Cement Corp. is a private corporation controlled by Amin Amana. The company's adjusted trial balance and other related data at 31 December 20X5 are given below. Although the company uses some obsolete terminology, the amounts are correct.

AMANA CEMENT CORPORATION

Adjusted Trial Balance

31 December 20X5

Debit Balance Accounts

Cash	$ 38,600
Land (used for building site)	129,000
Cost of goods sold	150,000
Short-term securities, at market (cost, $32,000)	42,000
Investment in U.S. subsidiary	100,000
Goodwill	120,000
Merchandise inventory	29,000
Office supplies inventory	2,000
Patent	7,000
Operating expenses	55,000
Income tax expense	17,500
Impairment of patent	7,500
Prepaid insurance	900
Building (at cost)	150,000
Land (held for speculation)	75,000
Translation loss on U.S. subsidiary, 31 December 20X4	12,000
Accrued interest receivable	300
Accounts receivable (trade)	22,700
Note receivable, 10% (long-term investment)	30,000
Subscriber lists (net)	22,000
Prepayments to pension fund in advance of expensing (long-term)	26,000
Dividends declared in 20X5, payable in 20X6	15,000
Correction of error from prior year—no income tax effect	15,000
	$1,066,500

Credit Balance Accounts

Reserve for bad debts	$ 1,100
Accounts payable (trade)	15,000
Revenues	275,000

20X5 translation gain on U.S. subsidiary	15,000
Deferred income tax	47,500
Note payable (short-term)	12,000
Common shares, no par, 10,000 shares outstanding	170,000
Reserve for depreciation, building	90,000
Retained earnings, 1 January 20X5	202,500
Gain on new accounting policy	40,000
Accrued wages	2,100
Cash advance from customer	3,000
Accrued property taxes	800
Note payable (long term)	16,000
Rent revenue collected in advance	1,500
Bonds payable, 11% ($25,000 due 1 June 20X6)	175,000
	$1,066,500

Additional information (no accounting errors involved):

a. Merchandise inventory is based on FIFO, lower of cost and net realizable value.

b. The patent is subjected to an annual impairment test. The impairment for 20X5 has already been recorded.

c. Operating expenses as given include depreciation and interest expense, and revenues include interest and investment revenues.

d. The "cash advance from customer" was for a special order that will not be completed and shipped until March 20X6; the sales price has not been definitely established because it is to be based on cost (no revenue should be recognized for 20X5).

Required:

Prepare the following:

1. Income statement (including EPS)
2. Statement of retained earnings
3. SFP

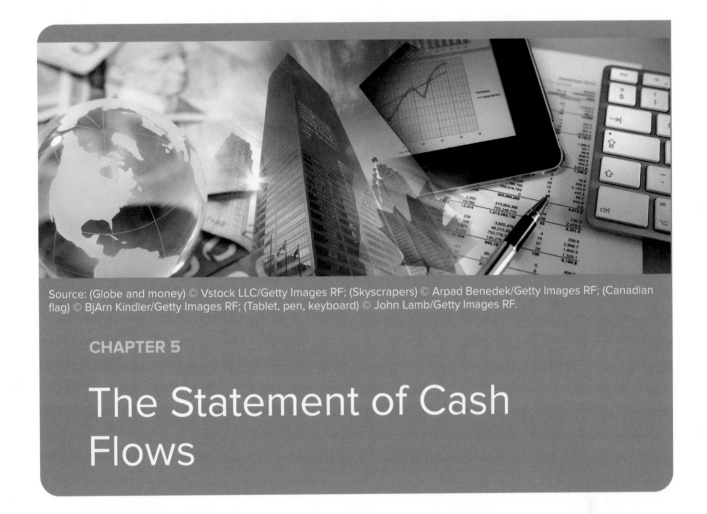

Source: (Globe and money) © Vstock LLC/Getty Images RF; (Skyscrapers) © Arpad Benedek/Getty Images RF; (Canadian flag) © BjArn Kindler/Getty Images RF; (Tablet, pen, keyboard) © John Lamb/Getty Images RF.

CHAPTER 5

The Statement of Cash Flows

INTRODUCTION

The statement of comprehensive income provides information about the results of operations. The statement of financial position includes information about the assets, liabilities, and equity of the company. What additional information can a statement of cash flows (SCF) provide?

Consider the 2014 financial statements of Prometic Life Sciences Inc., a vertically integrated biopharmaceutical company with a rapidly growing pipeline of drug candidates. The company had gross revenues of $23 million in 2014 and reported net earnings of $2.5 million. The statement of financial position shows total equity of $104 million and total assets of $203 million. Several asset and liability accounts show large changes in the year. What have been the company's major cash transactions during the year? An analyst could piece the changes together. Or the SCF could be consulted: it shows the cash effect of significant operating, investing, and financing decisions.

The SCF for Prometic shows that the $2.5 million net earnings actually represented significant cash outflows from operating activities of $25.9 million. Much of the difference is the result of non-cash gains, such as the gain from revaluation of an investment in another company, and a gain on a business combination. These items increased earnings but generated no cash during the period. The SCF shows that the company raised $28.9 million from the issuance of new common shares, and borrowed an additional $20 million. Prometic spent over $7.9 million on new capital assets. Thus, the cash implications of *strategic activity* during the year—negative cash flow from operations, but successfully raising new debt and equity financing—are *most obvious* from the SCF. This statement provides important, easily identifiable insights into the actions of the company that have immediate cash impact. The SCF unravels the accruals and deferrals needed in the other statements.

This chapter discusses the preparation and interpretation of the SCF. When individual categories of assets, liabilities, and shareholders' equity are covered in following chapters, the cash flow impact of each topic will be reviewed at the same time.

Objectives of the SCF

Companies are required to include the **statement of cash flows (SCF)** as an integral part of their financial statements. Historical cash flows are often used as an indicator of the amount, timing, and uncertainty of future cash flows. Cash inflows can be compared against cash outflows, such as loan repayments, replacement of capital assets, and payments to owners. Therefore, the objective of the SCF is to disclose the historical cash flows of the enterprise during the reporting period for both feedback and predictive purposes.

Classification and Organization

The SCF is classified on the basis of the type of cash flow:

- **Operating activities** are the principal revenue-producing activities of the enterprise and the related expenditures. The cash inflow from operations is measured as the cash received from customers or clients. Cash outflows are those disbursements for operating activities, such as cash paid for inventories, wages and salaries, and overhead costs. Cash flow is not accrual accounting, and cash from customers is different from revenue recognized, just as cash paid for expenses is different from expenses recognized on the statement of comprehensive income.

  Operating activities relate to *net earnings*, not *comprehensive income*. Net earnings comprise revenues and expenses. If the company has recognized specific amounts that are part of other comprehensive income, these transactions or events are not included in operating activities. Therefore, *net earnings is the reference point for operating activities on the SCF*.

- **Investing activities** are those activities that relate to long-term assets and investments that are not cash equivalents—essentially capital assets and investments. The acquisition and disposal of property, plant, and equipment, intangible assets, other assets, and investments[1] are all included in this section. Changes in (current) operating assets, such as inventory and accounts receivable, are included in operating activities. not investing activities.

- **Financing activities** relate to borrowings of the entity and contributed owners' equity. That is, financing activities are debt and equity cash flows. Changes in operating liabilities, such as accounts payable, are excluded from this section and included in operating activities.

Exhibit 5-1 lists some of the common transactions that fall into each category.

EXHIBIT 5-1	
EXAMPLES OF CASH FLOWS BY CATEGORY	
Operating Cash Flows	
Inflows	**Outflows**
Receipts from customers	Payments to suppliers
Advance deposits from customers	Wages and salaries paid to employees
Income tax refunds	Rent and insurance payments
	Income tax payments, related to any year
Investing Cash Flows	
Inflows	**Outflows**

---

1. Investments that are held for trading qualify as operating activity cash flows.

Cash received from sale of property, plant, and equipment	Payments to buy property, plant, and equipment, including capitalized interest
Cash received from sale of investment property	Payments to buy investment property
Cash from sale of debt or equity investments	Cash flows capitalized as intangible assets, such as:
Collection of principal on loans to others	• Legal fees • Development costs
	Purchase of investments in the form of debt or equity securities of others
	Loans extended to others

Financing Cash Flows

Inflows	**Outflows**
Net proceeds of issuing debt or equity securities	Repayment of principal on bonds or bank loans
Cash proceeds received from bank loans	Repurchase of the entity's own shares

Definition of "Cash"

On the SCF, cash is defined as cash, plus cash equivalents, less any temporary bank overdrafts.

1. Cash

Cash includes currency on hand, which is cash held for daily operating purposes in cash registers or petty cash funds. Cash also includes the amount that is held in the company's *current account(s)* with the bank, as long as these are due on demand, with no notice (delay before withdrawing funds) requirement.

2. Cash Equivalents

Cash is a nonproductive asset, and therefore companies strive to keep their immediately accessible cash balance at a minimum. Companies place their cash in term deposits, guaranteed investment certificates, certificates of deposit, or other money market instruments to earn interest. These investments are **cash equivalents** and are part of cash on the SCF if they meet two conditions:

- They are held for the purpose of meeting short-term cash commitments and not for investing or other reasons; and
- They are readily convertible into a known amount of cash and are subject to an insignificant risk of change in value. Investments with a very short maturity *at the time of purchase*, would qualify: Short maturity is suggested to be three months or less. There may be exceptional circumstances where a slightly longer term can be justified.
- Investments in common shares are excluded because they have no maturity date.

3. Overdrafts

Companies might be authorized by their lenders to have an **overdraft**, which is a negative balance in the bank current account. For example, suppose that a company begins the year with a balance of $10,000 in its current account. By the end of the year, the cash balance is completely used up and more—there is a negative balance, or an overdraft, of $15,000 in the current account. The change in cash for the year is not simply the decline in cash from $10,000 to zero, but is the change from a $10,000 asset to a $15,000 liability—a decrease of $25,000.

Bank overdrafts are included as a component of cash and cash equivalents *when the bank balance fluctuates from positive to negative on a regular basis.* That is, if the current account is always overdrawn, it is in substance a bank loan and not a cash equivalent. The current account must be regularly positive and then swing to overdraft status (and then back) to qualify as "cash." Furthermore, the overdrafts have to be repayable at any time that the bank demands payment.

Many companies rely on a **line of credit**, which is a preapproved short-term bank loan. The borrowing limit has been negotiated with the lender in advance. Lines of credit are often used to cover seasonal fluctuations in cash flows. However, lines of credit and other types of short-term bank loans (and a permanently overdrawn cash account) are normally viewed as financing activities and are *not* part of the cash definition.

Reconciliation

The components of cash and cash equivalents (including overdrafts) must be disclosed. The cash amount reported in the SCF must be reconciled to the equivalent items in the statement of financial position.

SCF Example

Exhibit 5-2 shows the SCF for International Forest Products Ltd. (Interfor), a Canadian company that produces wood products in British Columbia and in the U.S. Pacific Northwest for sale to markets around the world. Note that:

1. For all three categories, the cash flows can be either positive or negative. For example, investing activities include both cash outflows for purchase of property, plant, and equipment and cash inflows from disposal.

2. Positive and negative flows are *not* netted. For example, as shown, Interfor had a cash inflow of $480,487 in 2014 from new borrowing and also had a cash outflow of $421,059 to repay long-term debt.

3. The cash provided by operating activities is calculated *indirectly*, starting with *net earnings* of the period and then adjusting to cash flow. This is the most common presentation approach—we will discuss an alternative later in the chapter.

EXHIBIT 5-2

INTERNATIONAL FOREST PRODUCTS LTD.

Consolidated Statements of Cash Flows

(in thousands of Canadian dollars)

	2014	2013
Cash provided by (used in):		
Operating activities:		
Net earnings	$ 40,690	$ 42,239
Items not involving cash:		
Depreciation of plant and equipment	55,167	39,206
Depletion and amortization of timber, roads and other	28,912	23,061
Income tax expense (recovery)	(16,230)	555
Finance costs	8,915	9,069
Other assets	986	884
Reforestation liability	1,910	2,599
Other liabilities and provisions	(63)	6,612
Write-down of plant and equipment	20,468	—
Unrealized foreign exchange losses (gains)	2,191	(14)

Other income (expense)	46	(484)
	142,992	123,727
Cash generated from (used in) operating working capital:		
Trade accounts receivable and other	(8,628)	(9,667)
Inventories	15,083	(40,866)
Prepayments	1,236	493
Trade accounts payable and accrued liabilities	14,185	24,495
Income taxes paid	(3,077)	(652)
	161,791	97,530
Investing activities:		
Additions to property, plant and equipment	(48,922)	(33,038)
Additions to logging roads	(26,656)	(18,676)
Additions to timber and other intangible assets	(2,818)	(16,531)
Acquisitions	(124,421)	(120,407)
Proceeds on disposal of property, plant and equipment	1,926	2,089
Investments and other assets	(13)	(108)
	(200,904)	(186,671)
Financing activities:		
Issuance of share capital, net of share issue expenses	—	82,358
Interest payments	(7,122)	(7,142)
Debt refinancing costs	(757)	(1,460)
Additions to long term debt	480,487	326,738
Repayments of long term debt	(421,059)	(322,517)
	51,549	77,977
Foreign exchange gain on cash and cash equivalents held in a foreign currency	713	887
Increase (decrease) in cash and cash equivalents	13,149	(10,277)
Cash and cash equivalents, beginning of year	4,717	14,994
Cash and cash equivalents, end of year	$ 17,866	$ 4,717

Source: International Forest Products Limited, 2014 Annual Financial Statements, www.sedar.com, posted 12 February 2015.

Interpreting the Statement of Cash Flows

Interpretation involves examining the SCF for the major sources and uses of cash. The following questions must be considered, with professional judgement:

- Has operations provided cash or used cash?
- Why are earnings different than cash from operating activities? What are the major adjustments?
- What are the major investing activities that involved cash transactions?
- What are the major financing activities that involved cash transactions?
- How are these activities interrelated?
- Has cash, overall, increased or decreased for the period?

- How do the company's cash activities compare with those of prior years? With those of competitors?
- What accounting policy choice might affect classification of cash flows?

Since non-cash transactions are omitted from the SCF, it is important to review these transactions, included in the disclosure notes, to gather a complete picture of the company's strategic activities for the year. Only the cash transactions are included on the SCF.

Note that a company can report a loss and still have positive cash flows from operations. This commonly happens when net earnings include a large amount of depreciation of capitalized costs. Lenders may be quite willing to lend to such a company on the strength of the cash flow, despite the existence of losses, because they are convinced that there is adequate cash flow to pay the interest and principal.

Refer to the Interfor SCF in Exhibit 5-2. Interfor reported 2014 net earnings of $40,690 (all amounts in thousands), and cash flow from operating activities is positive, at $161,791. Depreciation and depletion expenses of $55,167 and $28,912, respectively, are added back—these expenses reduced earnings but did not require cash this period. Another major difference between cash generated by operating activities and earnings is the $15,083 inflow related to a decrease in inventory.

In investing activities, there were outflows of $48,922 for the purchase of property, plant, and equipment, and $26,656 for additions to logging roads. Acquisition of another timber company resulted in a cash outflow of $124,421. In financing activities, Interfor reported additional borrowing of $480,487, but also had debt repayment of $421,059. Overall, the cash balance increased by $13,149 this year, and the company ended the year with $17,866 in cash and cash equivalents.

CONCEPT REVIEW

1. What are the three categories of cash flows to be reported on the SCF?
2. What is the definition of cash on the SCF?
3. How does cash from operating activities differ from net earnings?

Basic Approach to Preparation

The statements of financial position and comprehensive income are prepared from the trial balance. Preparation of these statements involves classifying the general ledger accounts. The SCF, on the other hand, is a statement that is prepared by analyzing account balances and changes in balances. It is not enough, for example, to know by how much the equipment balance has changed over the course of an accounting period; one must analyze the sources of the accounting entries in the account. As a result, the SCF is usually a hand-prepared statement.

Analyzing Cash Flows

If the statement explains cash flows, it seems logical to start by analyzing the cash in and out of the cash account(s). The entries to the general ledger cash account are usually summary entries from subsidiary records such as specialized journals or cumulative transaction records. For example, it should be possible to see how much cash was received from customers by summarizing the debits to the cash account from the collections on accounts receivable and/or from the summary posting of the daily cash receipts; cash paid to employees for wages and salaries can be obtained by looking at the payroll accounts; and so on.

Unfortunately, direct analysis of the cash account is difficult and time-consuming. Therefore, the normal approach is to describe the cash activities by analyzing the changes in all of the *non-cash* accounts. Since one basic, indisputable characteristic of the statement of financial position (the balance sheet) is that it *balances*, cash flows can be determined by looking at the causes of the changes in all of the other accounts *except* cash (and cash equivalents). For example, it is possible to quickly determine how much cash was received from customers by taking the total sales revenue figure and adjusting that accrual-basis amount by the change in trade accounts receivable for the period. If the balance in accounts receivable went up, then the company received less cash than was recognized in sales for the period; if the accounts receivable balance went down, then the company received more cash than was recognized in sales.

A Simple Example

The data for preparing the SCF for Simple Ltd. are shown in Exhibit 5-3.

EXHIBIT 5-3		
SIMPLE LTD.		
Statement of Financial Position		
(in thousands) 31 December	**20X5**	**20X4**
Current assets:		
Cash	$ 35	$ 20
Short-term investments	20	70
Accounts receivable	110	125
Inventory	100	135
	$ 265	$ 350
Capital assets:		
Plant and equipment	1,100	1,000
Accumulated depreciation	(250)	(300)
	850	700
Total assets	$ 1,115	$1,050
Current liabilities:		
Bank loan	$ 65	$ 50
Accounts payable	100	125
	165	175
Long-term note payable	300	330
Shareholders' equity:		
Common shares	100	100
Retained earnings	550	445
	650	545
Total liabilities and shareholders' equity	$ 1,115	$1,050
SIMPLE LTD.		
Statement of Comprehensive Income		
Year ended 31 December 20X5		
Revenue:		
Sales revenue	$2,000	
Gain on sale of equipment	70	

		2,070
Operating expenses:		
Cost of goods sold		1,100
Other expenses		640
		1,740
Net earnings and comprehensive income		$ 330

SIMPLE LTD.

Statement of Changes in Equity

	Common Shares	Retained Earnings
Opening balance, 1 January 20X5	$ 100	$ 445
Net earnings and comprehensive income		330
Dividends declared		(225)
Closing balance, 31 December 20X5	$ 100	$ 550

Additional information:
   i. Other operating expenses include $200 of depreciation expense.
   ii. During the year, Simple sold equipment originally costing $310 for net proceeds of $130.

The cash account shows a change from $20 at the beginning of the year to $35 at the end, for a net increase of $15. However, there is a short-term investment account. Investigation shows that it meets the required criteria and can be classified as a cash equivalent investment. It is therefore included with cash, and the net change in the balance of cash and cash equivalents is a *decrease* of $35:

	Ending	Beginning	Change	
Cash balance	$ 35	$20	$ 15	increase
Short-term investments	20	70	(50)	decrease
Total	$55	$90		
Net increase (decrease) in cash and cash equivalents			$(35)	decrease

The SCF is shown in Exhibit 5-4. (The letters in the "key" column in Exhibit 5-4 refer to the explanations below.)

EXHIBIT 5-4		
SIMPLE LTD.		
Statement of Cash Flows		
Year ended 31 December 20X5	**Key**	
Operating activities:		
Net earnings	**(a)**	$330

Add (deduct) to reconcile net earnings to net operating cash flows:

Depreciation expense	(c)	200	
Gain on sale of equipment	(d)	(70)	
Decrease in accounts receivable	(e)	15	
Decrease in inventory	(f)	35	
Decrease in accounts payable	(g)	(25)	$485
Investing activities:			
Proceeds from sale of equipment	(d)	130	
Purchase of new equipment	(h)	(410)	(280)
Financing activities:			
Increase in current bank loan	(j)	15	
Dividends paid	(b)	(225)	
Reduction of long-term notes payable	(k)	(30)	(240)
Increase (decrease) in cash and cash equivalents			(35)
Cash and cash equivalents, 1 January			90
Cash and cash equivalents, 31 December			$ 55

To explain the flows that resulted in the net decrease of $35, all of the changes in the *non-cash* accounts are analyzed, starting with information from the statement of comprehensive income, the statement of changes in equity, and the *additional information*, as follows:

a. Net earnings of $330 is the basis for determining cash flow from operating activities. For this company, there are no items reported on other comprehensive income that would make net earnings different from comprehensive income. *If net earnings were different from comprehensive income, the SCF would still start with net earnings.*

The amount of net earnings is placed first in the operating activities section of the SCF. Net earnings, of course, includes all revenues and expenses, so starting with this number places all revenues in operating activities as inflows, and all expenses in operating activities as outflows. Net earnings is then reconciled to the *real* cash inflow and outflow for revenue and expenses.

b. Dividends of $225 were declared (and paid) during the year. This amount is placed in the financing section. Note that net earnings of $330 less dividends of $225 completely explain the $105 increase in retained earnings during the year.

c. *Additional information* reveals that operating expenses include $200 in depreciation. Since depreciation is an interperiod allocation of previous years' investment cash flows, its impact must be removed from net earnings. The $200 depreciation is *added back* to net earnings to eliminate the effect of this interperiod allocation.

d. *Additional information* reveals that equipment that originally cost $310 was sold for $130. The statement of comprehensive income also shows a gain from the sale of equipment amounting to $70. The following entry must have been made when the equipment was sold:

Cash	130	
Accumulated depreciation (to balance)	250	
Plant and equipment		310
Gain on sale of equipment		70

On the SCF, the $130 cash received is an investing activity; the $70 gain is eliminated (subtracted) from operating cash flow. The gain is eliminated for two reasons:

1. The sale of assets is not an operating activity but reflects a change in asset structure; the disposal of assets must be reported as an investing activity.

2. The gain does not measure the actual cash flow during the period, but instead it is the difference between the proceeds of the sale and the net book value of the asset. The net book value is the original expenditure for the asset, reduced by depreciation to date.

e. Accounts receivable decreased by $15 during the year. This means that customers paid more than the amount reported as sales. The $15 is added to net earnings in the operating section to restate the sales from an accrual to a cash basis.

f. Inventory decreased by $35. The change in inventory is a component of cost of goods sold (COGS). By definition, the beginning-of-year inventory was acquired in a previous period and not the current period. Therefore, a decrease in inventory indicates that less cash was paid for the goods than were sold during the year.

g. Accounts payable decreased by $25. The accounts payable adjustment is assumed to be primarily related to the inventory adjustment, since trade accounts payable relate largely to inventory purchases. This $25 decrease indicates that suppliers were paid more cash for goods and services than the company accrued during the period. The $25 decrease reduces the amount of cash from operating activities.

1. Plant and equipment increased by $100 during the year. However, this amount is the net result of both new investment and retirement of old equipment. From (d) (above), the disposal was $310. The amount of the 20X5 acquisition is determined as follows:

Beginning balance	$1,000
Original cost of equipment sold during the year	− 310
Equipment purchased during the year	+ ???
Ending balance	$ 1,100

The amount that makes the account balance is $410. This is an outflow for purchased equipment in the investing activities section.

h. Accumulated depreciation decreased by $50. Depreciation expense of $200 for 20X5 was added to this account, and accumulated depreciation on the equipment sold was $250. These two transactions combine to verify the $50 reduction and no additional entry to the SCF is needed.

i. The current bank loan increased by $15. This is a loan and not an overdraft; therefore, the loan is *not* included as a component of cash and cash equivalents. The increase in the loan is a source of financing and will go into the financing section of the SCF.

j. The long-term note payable decreased by $30. This represents a principal repayment and is an outflow in the financing activity section.

k. Common shares did not change during the period. There will be no item on the SCF relating to common shares.

The net result of entering all of these amounts in the SCF is that net decrease in cash of $35 is explained. In a disclosure note, the company will show the components of cash, that is, it will indicate that both cash and cash equivalents are included.

CONCEPT REVIEW

1. When the operating activities section starts with net earnings, why is depreciation added to derive cash flow from operating activities? Is depreciation a source of cash?

2. Explain why a gain on the sale of equipment is subtracted in the reconciliation of earnings and operating cash flows.

3. Why is the change in the balance of accounts receivable included in the SCF?

4. If salaries payable increases during the year, why does this imply that salary expense exceeds salary payments?

Presentation of Operating Activities

There are two approaches for presenting the cash provided by (used in) operating activities:

- *Indirect presentation.* The operating activities section begins with net earnings, and all interperiod allocations and accruals are reversed out of net earnings.
- *Direct presentation.* The revenues and expenses are each adjusted to a cash basis of reporting and listed directly.

In Exhibit 5-4, the indirect method of presentation is used. Operating activities begins with net earnings of $330 and is then adjusted for depreciation, the accounting gain on sale of equipment, and changes in the balances of the other current assets and current liabilities related to operating items.

Exhibit 5-5 shows the operating activities section of Simple Ltd.'s SCF, using the direct approach of presentation. The amounts are obtained as follows:

1. To convert from accrual-basis sales to cash received from customers, start with sales, and add the decrease in accounts receivable during the year ($15). This converts sales ($2,000) to cash received from customers ($2,015). This $15 adjustment is the same as adding the amount that customers owed at the beginning of the year ($125 opening balance) and subtracting the amount owing at the end of the year ($110 ending balance):

Sales, accrual basis	$2,000
Plus cash collected on opening accounts receivable	+ 125
Minus cash not collected at year-end	− 110
Cash received from sales during 20X5	$2,015

2. COGS requires two adjustments. The first is for the decrease in inventory of $35 during the year. Since inventory purchased in the previous year was used this year, the cash flow requirements for buying inventory were $35 less than the expense shown for COGS. Therefore, subtract the $35 decrease from the $1,100 expense to arrive at cash flow. Partially offsetting the decline in inventory is the decrease in accounts payable. The decrease in accounts payable of $25 indicates that more cash was expended to pay creditors (presumably, for inventory purchases and other expense components that make up COGS). Therefore, it is necessary to increase the expense by $25 to arrive at cash flow. The $1,090 cash flow for COGS is lower than the expense by $10.

3. Other operating expenses are decreased by the $200 depreciation. Items such as depreciation and the gain on sale of equipment are not cash flows and are omitted in the SCF under the direct presentation approach.

EXHIBIT 5-5
SIMPLE LTD.
Statement of Cash Flows

Sample of Direct Presentation of Operating Activities

Year ended 31 December 20X5

Operating activities:

Cash received from customers ($2,000 + $15)	(1)	$ 2,015
Operating expenses:		
Cash paid to suppliers ($1,100 − $35 + $25)	(2)	(1,090)
Cash paid for other operating expenses ($640 − $200)	(3)	(440)
Cash provided by operating activities		$ 485

Direct or Indirect?

The standard permits either the direct or the indirect method of reporting cash flows from operating, but enterprises are "encouraged" to report cash flows from operating activities using the direct method.

It is often argued that the direct approach is clearer to financial statement users because they do not have to untangle the adjustments made under the indirect approach. In particular, there is the concern that the indirect method encourages the idea that depreciation is a source of funds. The addback of depreciation is usually a large positive element in the operating section, and business people have often been heard to remark that they will be using their "depreciation funds" for certain projects. Of course, this is a mistaken impression, but the indirect presentation method certainly strengthens the myth.

Regardless of any possible advantages in clarity of using the direct approach, the indirect method of presentation has been, by far, the dominant approach in practice. There is certainly no trend toward the direct method.

Two-Step Indirect Presentation

A common refinement of the indirect method of presentation is a two-step approach. First, net earnings is adjusted for inter-period allocations and nonoperating amounts, and then it is adjusted for changes in other working capital accounts. Changes in working capital are often included as a single, summary amount, with the detail included in a disclosure note. The operating section of Simple Ltd.'s SCF is illustrated in Exhibit 5-6, using the two-step approach. (Interfor, in Exhibit 5-2, also uses a two-step approach.)

EXHIBIT 5-6
SIMPLE LTD.
SCF Operating Activities Two-Step Indirect Presentation

Year ended 31 December 20X5

Operating activities:	
Net earnings	$330
Plus (less) items not affecting cash:	
Depreciation	200
Gain on sale of equipment	(70)
	460
Changes in other working capital items:	
Decrease in accounts receivable	15
Decrease in inventory	35
Decrease in accounts payable	(25)
Cash provided by operating activities	$485

Note the subtotal of $460 after "items not affecting cash" in Exhibit 5-6. This subtotal is just a matter of convenience and has no special meaning.

Offsetting Transactions

Accounting standards emphasize that *offsetting should not occur in the SCF*. That is, gross cash receipts and gross cash payments must be reported separately for investing and financing activities.

Within the investing and financing activities of the enterprise, there are often transactions that, overall, have the effect of offsetting or partially offsetting each other. For example, if a company refinances its debt by retiring an outstanding bond issue and issuing new bonds, the *net* impact on the statement of financial position may be relatively minor. However, these activities demonstrate the company's ability to renew its capital structure. The cash flows associated with the refinancing should be disclosed separately and not offset, or netted.

Netting is permitted in limited circumstances. *If cash flows represent cash receipts and payments on behalf of a customer in relation to the activities of the customer, netting is appropriate.* For example, net cash flows would be reported if the company were a property management company that collected rent on behalf of a customer and turned that rent over to the customer, net of a management fee. Only the management fee is reported as a cash inflow.

Non-cash Transactions

Some transactions have a significant effect on the asset, liability, or equity structure of an entity without involving any direct cash flow at all. These non-cash transactions are economically similar to cash transactions *but are excluded from the SCF because no cash changes hands.* For example, settling a debt by issuing shares directly to the debt holder involves no cash but has the same effect as issuing the shares for cash and using the proceeds to settle the debt. As another example, an asset may be acquired without cash by entering into a mortgage or a long-term finance lease; the economic effect is the same as borrowing money to buy the asset.

Common types of non-cash transactions that are excluded from the SCF are:

- Retiring bonds through share issuance;
- Assuming finance lease obligations in exchange for leased assets;
- Converting preferred shares to common shares;
- Settling debt by transferring non-cash assets;
- Bond refinancing directly with existing bond holders;
- Converting bonds to common shares;
- Acquiring shares in another company in exchange for shares of the reporting enterprise; and
- Issuing a stock dividend, which increases common shares and decreases retained earnings.

At one point, non-cash transactions, such as those listed above, were included in the SCF as both an inflow and an outflow. However, the current reporting standard specifically *excludes non-cash transactions* from the SCF on the grounds that such transactions are not cash flows. For example, the acquisition of a building (an investing activity) acquired through a finance lease (a financing activity) would not be shown on the face of the SCF because there was no cash involved.

Note Disclosure

When a non-cash transaction is excluded from the SCF, it is included in a disclosure note to make sure financial statement users are informed about the transaction. This information is often part of other disclosure notes: property, plant, and equipment, common share disclosure, and so on. In our text assignments, a list of non-cash transactions should accompany a SCF to represent the note disclosure requirement.

Partial Cash Transactions

Sometimes an acquisition will take place in which part of the consideration is in cash and the remainder is a non-cash exchange. In this case, *the cash portion of the transaction* would be reported in the SCF while the non-cash portion would be omitted. For example, suppose that a building costing $4,000,000 is acquired by paying $1,000,000 cash and issuing a $3,000,000 long-term note to the vendor. The SCF would list only the $1,000,000 cash paid (as an investing activity), although the line item on the SCF should be referenced to the note that contains the details of the entire transaction.

Evaluation

In one sense, the exclusion of non-cash transactions provides an appropriate focus on cash flows. On the other hand, the total exclusion of non-cash transactions from the SCF seems to give precedence to form over substance. For example, the purchase of another company (i.e., a business combination) through an issue of shares would not be reported in the SCF, while the issuance of shares for cash and the use of the proceeds to buy the company *would be* reported in the SCF.

Debt Transactions

Sometimes the interest rate stated on a debt security is different from the market interest rate on the date of issuance. The true amount of interest must be *classified consistently with interest payments (operating or financing)* and the true principal *classified as financing*.

Examples

Consider the following examples:

1. A company borrows $100,000 and makes no annual payments of any kind but agrees to repay $125,000 in three years' time. The extra $25,000 is interest. In the SCF at maturity, $100,000 would be shown as a financing outflow and $25,000 is classified as an interest payment, in operating or financing.

2. A company issues a $1,000,000, 10% bond at a discount and receives $960,000 because market interest rates were higher than 10%. In the first year, interest paid is $100,000, but interest expense is $102,300 (amounts assumed), because interest expense includes discount amortization. On the SCF in the first year, financing activities show an inflow of $960,000 from the issuance of the bond, and the cash outflow for interest is $100,000. *Interest expense* has to be adjusted to *interest paid* by eliminating the $2,300 discount amortization. In the final year, when $1,000,000 is repaid, $960,000 is repayment of principal and $40,000 is classified as interest paid, making $140,000 ($40,000 plus the annual $100,000) as the cash outflow for interest in the final year.

3. A company retires a bond with a face value of $400,000 for $410,000. The discrepancy of $10,000 is a call premium, not directly related to interest. A loss of $10,000 is reported in earnings because of the retirement. In the SCF, the $10,000 loss is added back in operating activities as an adjustment to earnings. The $410,000 repayment is shown as a financing activity, an outflow of cash.

CONCEPT REVIEW

1. If the SCF lists "cash received from customers," is the direct or the indirect method used in operating activities?
2. A company acquires a $75,000 asset by entering into a finance lease. No down payment is needed. Is this transaction listed on the SCF? Explain.
3. If a company borrows $300,000, and later repays $350,000, what is the correct explanation and cash flow classification of the $50,000 discrepancy?

INTERPRETATION ISSUES

Quality of Earnings

Investment analysts sometimes refer to the **quality of earnings** of a company that they are analyzing. This concept relates the amount of net earnings to the amount of cash flow from operating activities. A company is said to have high quality of earnings when there is a close correspondence between *net earnings* and *cash flow from operations*, a relationship that persists over several years. It does not necessarily mean positive cash flow from operating activities. Instead, quality of earnings is present if, when earnings increase, cash flows also increase. When earnings decline, cash flows also decline. *Correlation* of the two numbers is considered to indicate higher quality of earnings.

In contrast, a company that reports earnings that are not closely related to cash flows is said to have low quality of earnings. In some companies, cash flows and earnings have an erratic relationship. For example, a company can have high earnings but a negative cash flow from operations because of soaring receivables or expanding inventories; this situation often makes analysts a bit nervous. The next year, earnings may be stable but cash flow may soar if receivables and inventory are trimmed. While this is a positive cash flow trend, it does not indicate a stable relationship between cash flow from operating activities and net earnings.

Effect of Accounting Policy Choices on the Statement of Cash Flows

One of the reasons that users like to see the SCF is that "cash doesn't lie." Many financial statement users work on the premise that managers and accountants have little room to manipulate cash flows.

However, companies may adopt accounting policies that have a significant and substantial effect on the measurement of net earnings and financial position. Management influences policy decisions and makes significant estimates for most assets and liabilities, which affect the related revenue and expenses. These policies and estimates are influenced by external events and are not entirely under the control of management, but management has considerable influence. The underlying cash flow is not changed by accounting policies and estimates.

It is reasonable to suggest, therefore, that the overall net cash flow for an accounting period is unaffected by accounting policy choices and estimates.

Policy and Cash Flow

A certain type of accounting policy decision affects the SCF by changing the classification of items on the SCF. This policy decision is whether to expense or *capitalize* one or more types of cost.

If expenditures of a certain category (i.e., development costs) are charged to expense, they will be included as a deduction in net earnings and therefore be part of operating cash flow. On the other hand, if those expenditures are capitalized, they will appear on the SCF as an *investing* activity. In subsequent years, amortization of capitalized costs is deducted in determining net earnings but is then added back to net earnings to derive cash flow from operating activities.

The result is that capitalized costs never enter into operating cash flow but will appear only as an investing activity. An organization that capitalizes and amortizes its development costs will show a consistently higher cash flow from operating activities than one that charges such costs to expense, all other things being equal.

ETHICAL ISSUES

Choice of accounting policy must be based on the facts, the user environment, and the competitive situation. Policies chosen to manipulate certain measurements, or foster erroneous conclusions by financial statement users, are not acceptable. However, accountants must be aware of the implications of choosing a certain policy. A decision to capitalize costs, and amortize them over the period of use instead of immediate expensing, will effectively transfer the cash outflow out of operating activities and show the outflow under investing activities.

CONCEPT REVIEW

1. If cash from operating activities increases as net earnings increase, and declines when net earnings declines, what does this imply about the quality of earnings?
2. If development costs are capitalized and amortized, how will they be reflected on the SCF? If they are expensed?

ANALYZING MORE COMPLEX SITUATIONS

T-Account Method

When preparing the SCF for Simple Ltd., we used an informal, ad hoc approach. We went down the statement of financial position and filled in the appropriate amounts in the SCF. In the process, we explained all of the changes in the non-cash accounts and thus indirectly explained all of the changes in the cash accounts.

While the informal approach is completely acceptable, in complex situations it is easy to lose track. Therefore, it is common to use some form of T-account approach, or a spreadsheet (see the Appendix to this chapter), to force some discipline on the process and to help ensure that relevant transactions are not overlooked. The method used to organize information does not affect the final SCF. A more formal approach is useful because it:

- Provides an organized format for documenting the preparation process;
- Facilitates review and evaluation by others;
- Provides proofs of accuracy; and
- Formally keeps track of the changes in statement of financial position accounts and ensures that all accounts are explained.

The T-accounts used in this approach are not actual ledger accounts. Rather, they are workspaces in account format used to accumulate the information necessary to prepare the SCF and to explain all account balance changes. The cash T-account accumulates all changes in cash (and cash equivalents) and is divided into three sections, corresponding to the three SCF categories.

Example

The comparative statement of financial position and the statement of comprehensive income for Ling Corp. are shown in Exhibit 5-7, along with some important supplementary information.

EXHIBIT 5-7		
LING CORP.		
Statement of Financial Position		
As at 31 December	**20X5**	**20X4**
Assets		
Current assets:		
Cash	$ 50,000	$ 36,000

Short-term liquid investments, two-month original term	10,000	34,000
Accounts receivable	84,000	70,000
Inventories	42,000	30,000
Prepaid expenses	15,000	11,000
	201,000	181,000
Fixed assets:		
Land	50,000	50,000
Plant and equipment	740,000	615,000
Accumulated depreciation	(260,000)	(215,000)
	530,000	450,000
Capitalized development costs	82,000	76,000
Long-term investments	92,000	70,000
Total assets	$905,000	$ 777,000

Liabilities and Shareholders' Equity

Current liabilities:		
Bank loan	$ 20,000	$ 5,000
Accounts payable	36,000	45,000
Dividends payable	10,000	5,000
	66,000	55,000
Long-term liabilities:		
Bonds payable	146,000	133,000
Deferred tax	27,000	24,000
Total liabilities	239,000	212,000
Shareholders' equity:		
Preferred shares	142,000	120,000
Common shares	230,000	180,000
Retained earnings	294,000	265,000
	666,000	565,000
Total liabilities and shareholders' equity	$905,000	$ 777,000

LING CORP.

Statement of Comprehensive Income

Year ended 31 December 20X5

Sales revenue	$ 960,000	
Gain on sale of equipment	4,000	
Operating expenses		$964,000
Cost of goods sold	597,000	

Interest expense	18,000	
Wages expense	131,000	
Other operating expenses	100,000	
Income tax expense	54,000	900,000
Net earnings and comprehensive income		$ 64,000

LING CORP.

Statement of Changes in Equity

	Preferred Shares	Common Shares	Retained Earnings
Opening balance, 1 January 20X5	$120,000	$ 180,000	$265,000
Issued shares	22,000	50,000	
Net earnings and comprehensive income			64,000
Dividends declared			(35,000)
Closing balance, 31 December 20X5	$142,000	$ 230,000	$294,000

Additional information:
1. Cost of goods sold includes depreciation of $65,000.
2. Other operating expenses include amortization of capitalized development costs of $5,000.
3. During 20X5, the corporation issued preferred shares with a market value of $22,000 in exchange for 1,000 common shares of THB Corp. The THB shares are being held as a long-term investment. Fair market value and cost are identical for long-term investments.
4. Old equipment was sold for $9,000; the original cost was $25,000.
5. Bonds with a face value of $20,000 were repurchased at par and retired.
6. Other operating expenses include a loss of $2,000 from liquidating the short-term investments. Net proceeds were $22,000.

From the statement of financial position, we can see that cash increased by $14,000 during the year. Short-term liquid investments, however, decreased by $24,000. Short-term liquid investments are *cash equivalents*, and thus the change in cash is really a decrease of $10,000.

There is no adjustment on the SCF for any gain or loss on sale of cash equivalent short-term investments. If the investments had not been cash equivalents, then the cash received would be an investing inflow of $22,000, and the loss on sale would be an add-back in the operating activities section. This is a total adjustment of $24,000. Since the investments are cash equivalents, all $24,000 is included in the change in cash, and no further recognition in the SCF is required.

	Ending	Beginning	Change	
Cash balance	$50,000	$36,000	$ 14,000	increase
Short-term investments	10,000	34,000	(24,000)	decrease
Total	$60,000	$70,000		
Net increase (decrease) in cash			$(10,000)	decrease

The task of the SCF is to explain the transactions that caused this decrease of $10,000 in cash and cash equivalents. As cash flows are identified by reconciling the individual asset, liability, and equity accounts, the offsetting cash effect is entered into the cash T-account.

T-Account Procedures

The starting point is to draw a simple T-account for each asset, liability, and equity account, including a single T-account for *cash and cash equivalents*. See Exhibit 5-8. The cash T-account has to be physically large; it is where all the information necessary for preparing the SCF will be accumulated. Within this T-account, three subsections are set up, one for each type of cash activity: operating, investing, and financing.

The second step is to insert in each T-account the beginning balance at the top, and the ending balance at the bottom. These are shown in green in Exhibit 5-8. Accuracy is critical. Alternatively, only the net change in the account may be used. This is a matter of personal preference.

The third step is to make reconciliation entries directly in the T-accounts that reconstruct the entries made during the year, including those made to cash. It is essential to cross-reference the entries so that it is straightforward to relate the different elements of a particular transaction. Generally, the place to start is with the reconciliation of retained earnings, because that is where net earnings for the year has been transferred. Net earnings is the top line in the operating activities section. Starting with net earnings also focuses attention on earnings and on the adjustments necessary to arrive at cash flow from operating activities.

Ling Corp.'s statement of changes in equity reveals that the change in retained earnings consists of two items: (1) net earnings and (2) dividends declared. The net $29,000 increase in the retained earnings balance came about as the result of $64,000 in net earnings and $35,000 in dividends declared. Therefore, the first reconciling entry is to enter net earnings:

a.

Cash: operating activities, net earnings	64,000	
Retained earnings		64,000

The second reconciling entry is to record the dividends declared:

b.

Retained earnings	35,000	
Cash: financing activities, dividends declared		35,000

These dividends have been declared and paid. If dividends are unpaid, dividends payable would be an account on the SFP, and the change in dividends payable would be an adjustment to the dividends line in the financing section of the SCF.

These entries are posted in the T-accounts. Observe that these entries recreate the original entries to (a) close net earnings into the retained earnings account and (b) to record the declaration of dividends. Dividends are debited to the retained earnings account in the T-accounts and credited to cash. The actual cash paid for dividends will be later calculated after including the change in the dividends payable account.

The rest of the reconciliation entries are as follows, considering first the list of items of additional information in Exhibit 5-7.

EXHIBIT 5-8

LING CORP.
T-Account Analysis
Cash and Cash Equivalents

Opening 70,000*

Operating Activities

a) Net earnings	64,000	f) Gain on sale	4,000
c) Depreciation	65,000	i) Increase in accounts receivable	14,000
d) Amortization	5,000	j) Increase in inventory	12,000
q) Deferred tax	3,000	k) Increase in prepaid expenses	4,000
		o) Decrease in accounts payable	9,000

Investing Activities

f) Sale of equipment	9,000	l) Purchased plant and equipment	150,000
		m) Increased capitalized development costs	11,000

Financing Activities

h) Issued bond	33,000	b) Dividends declared	35,000
n) Increased short-term bank loan	15,000	g) Repaid bond	20,000
p) Increased dividends payable	5,000		
r) Issued common shares	50,000		

Closing 60,000*

*Cash plus cash equivalent investments.

Accounts receivable

Op.	70,000		
i)	14,000		
Cl.	84,000		

Plant and Equipment

Op.	615,000		
l)	150,000	f)	25,000
Cl.	740,000		

Bank Loan

		Op.	5,000
		n)	15,000
		Cl.	20,000

Deferred Tax

		Op.	24,000
		q)	3,000
		Cl.	27,000

Inventories

Op.	30,000		
j)	12,000		
Cl.	42,000		

Accumulated Depreciation

		Op.	215,000
f)	20,000	c)	65,000
		Cl.	260,000

Accounts Payable

		Op.	45,000
o)	9,000		
		Cl.	36,000

Preferred Shares

		Op.	120,000
		e)	22,000
		Cl.	142,000

Prepaid Expenses

Op.	11,000		
k)	4,000		
Cl.	15,000		

Capitalized Development Costs

Op.	76,000		
m)	11,000	d)	5,000
Cl.	82,000		

Dividends Payable

		Op.	5,000
		p)	5,000
		Cl.	10,000

Common Shares

		Op.	180,000
		r)	50,000
		Cl.	230,000

Land

Op.	50,000		
Cl.	50,000		

Long-Term Investments

Op.	70,000		
e)	22,000		
Cl.	92,000		

Bonds Payable

		Op.	133,000
g)	20,000	h)	33,000
		Cl.	146,000

Retained Earnings

		Op.	265,000
b)	35,000	a)	64,000
		Cl.	294,000

c. Depreciation of $65,000 was expensed during the period. The entry is as follows:

Cash: operating activities, depreciation expense	65,000	
Accumulated depreciation		65,000

This entry is posted in the T-accounts, with the debit placed in cash, under *operating activities*.

d. Amortization of capitalized development costs amounting to $5,000 was recorded during the year. The entry is entered in the T-accounts:

Cash: operating activities, amortization expense	5,000	
Capitalized development costs		5,000

e. The company acquired a $22,000 long-term investment in another company's shares in exchange for Ling's own preferred shares. No cash changed hands, so this is an example of a non-cash transaction. Even though the transaction resulted in a material change in the asset and equity structure of the company, it will not be reported on the SCF. Details of the transactions will be disclosed in a note to the financial statements. The effects of the increase of $22,000 on long-term investments and on preferred shares are recorded in the asset and equity T-accounts, with no corresponding entry to cash:

Long-term investments	22,000	
Preferred shares		22,000

f. Old equipment was sold for $9,000; the original cost was $25,000. A gain of $4,000 was reported, so the net book value at the time of sale must have been $5,000. That is, the gain is the difference between net book value and cash. In a gain situation, net book value is lower than cash received. If net book value is $5,000 and original cost is $25,000, then accumulated depreciation on the asset sold therefore must have been $20,000. That is:

Proceeds from sale		$9,000
Net book value of the asset sold:		
Historical cost	$25,000	
Accumulated depreciation	?	5,000
Gain on sale		$4,000

The "?" must be $20,000. The entry for the sale is as follows:

Cash: investing activities, sale of equipment	9,000	
Accumulated depreciation	20,000	
Plant and equipment		25,000
Cash: operating activities, gain on sale		4,000

g. Bonds with a face value of $20,000 were repurchased and retired at par, since there is no gain or loss reported in earnings.

Bonds payable	20,000	
Cash: financing activities, bonds retired		20,000

The only other piece of *additional information* in Exhibit 5-7 is that other operating expenses include a loss of $2,000 on liquidation of short-term investments. The initial reaction may be to eliminate this by adding it back to operating activities and to record $22,000 as an investing activity inflow. However, the catch here is that the loss relates to a component of cash. Since short-term liquid investments are a cash equivalent and included within the definition of cash, the loss really did cause cash and cash equivalents to decrease by $2,000. This amount is appropriately included in net earnings. Therefore, *there is no adjustment for gains and losses incurred within the cash and cash-equivalent accounts*, including foreign currency exchange gains and losses.

h.   The reconciliation entries described above are those that result from the information provided in Exhibit 5-7. However, there have obviously been other transactions during the year that caused as-yet-unexplained changes in the asset, liability, and equity accounts. An example is that of bonds payable. The bonds payable account grew from $133,000 to $146,000 during the year, a net increase of $13,000. However, to have a net increase of $13,000 after the $20,000 retirement, the company must have issued $33,000 in new bonds during the year:

Cash: financing activities, bonds issued	33,000	
Bonds payable		33,000

Reconciliations, such as this one, for the bond issuance sometimes are referred to as *hidden entries*, because they become apparent only as the result of reconciling those changes that are known beforehand. That is, once the known elements are entered, as above, the remaining reconciliation entries are all balancing entries that simply record the change in each account that is required to explain the net change, *after* taking into consideration the reconciliation entries already made. Starting with the first non-cash account, accounts receivable, they are as follows:

i.

Accounts receivable	14,000	
Cash: operating activities		14,000

j.

Inventories	12,000	
Cash: operating activities		12,000

k.

Prepaid expenses	4,000	
Cash: operating activities		4,000

l.

Plant and equipment	150,000	
Cash: investing activities, purchase of equipment		150,000

The *net* increase of $125,000 in plant and equipment is due to acquisitions of $150,000 and the sale of equipment that originally cost $25,000.

m.

Capitalized development costs	11,000	
Cash: investing activities, investment in development costs		11,000

Since the net account increase was $6,000 *after* amortization, $11,000 must have been capitalized during the year.

n.	*Cash: financing activities*, increase in short-term bank loan	15,000	
	Bank loan		15,000

o.	Accounts payable	9,000	
	Cash: operating activities		9,000

p.

	Cash: financing, dividends	5,000	
	Dividends payable		5,000

The change in dividends payable does not affect operating cash flows because dividends are a financing cash flow for this company. The change in dividends payable is posted to the financing portion of the cash T-account and reduces the cash outflow for dividends. This is logical—dividends payable increased, and therefore comparatively less of the dividends declared were actually paid. The dividend paid is shown as one number on the SCF, calculated as dividends declared combined with the change in the dividends payable account.

q.

	Cash: operating activities	3,000	
	Deferred tax		3,000

The $3,000 increase in the liability account for deferred tax represents the part of income tax expense that was not paid in cash.

r.

	Cash: financing activities, common shares issued	50,000	
	Common shares		50,000

The increase in common shares is the result of new equity invested during the year.

Once all of the reconciliation entries are in the T-accounts, check for completeness by adding each T-account to make sure the beginning balance plus the reconciliation entries equals the ending balance. Then total the inflows and outflows in the cash account to ensure that it adds correctly.

The cash account in Exhibit 5-8 now contains all the information necessary for preparing the SCF. It is important to remember that Exhibit 5-8 is *not* the SCF in itself; it is only the data analysis that supports the SCF.

Statement of Cash Flows—Indirect Method

The SCF using the indirect approach for operating activities is shown in Exhibit 5-9. The indirect approach starts with net earnings, and makes all the adjustments necessary to convert from the accrual basis to the cash basis. The two-step approach shown in Exhibit 5-9 is the most common format. The non-cash transaction is listed as a disclosure note.

EXHIBIT 5-9		
LING CORP.		
Statement of Cash Flows (Indirect Approach)		
Year ended 31 December 20X5		
Operating activities:		
Net earnings	$ 64,000	
Adjustments for items not affecting cash:		
Depreciation of plant and equipment	65,000	
Amortization of development costs	5,000	
Gain on sale of equipment	(4,000)	
Deferred tax	3,000	
	133,000	
Changes in working capital amounts:		
Increase in accounts receivable	(14,000)	
Increase in inventory	(12,000)	
Increase in prepaid expenses	(4,000)	
Decrease in accounts payable	(9,000)	
Cash provided (used) by operating activities		$ 94,000
Investing activities:		
Acquisition of plant and equipment	(150,000)	
Investment in development costs	(11,000)	
Proceeds from sale of equipment	9,000	
Cash provided (used) by investing activities		(152,000)
Financing activities:		
Increase in short-term bank loan	15,000	
Issuance of bonds	33,000	
Retirement of bonds	(20,000)	
Common shares issued	50,000	
Dividends paid ($35,000 – $5,000)	(30,000)	
Cash provided (used) by financing activities		48,000
Increase (decrease) in cash and cash equivalents		$ (10,000)
Opening cash and cash equivalents		$ 70,000
Closing cash and cash equivalents		$60,000
Supplemental disclosures:		
Cash payment for interest		$ 18,000

Cash payment for income tax ($54,000 – $3,000)	$ 51,000

Disclosure note:

Preferred shares were issued for 1,000 shares of THB Corp., held as a long-term investment. The transaction was valued at $22,000.

Operating Activities—Direct Method

The operating activities section of the SCF can be presented using the direct method. The direct method may be prepared through the following steps:

1. Begin with the analysis of operating activities under the indirect method. Specifically, refer to the journal entry analysis (or the summary of adjustments to operating activities in the T-accounts in Exhibit 5-8).

2. Prepare a schedule to support the calculations for the direct method. This schedule should have three columns. In the first column, copy all profit and loss accounts, with all expenses and losses in brackets. This column should total to net earnings. (See Exhibit 5-10, first column.)

3. Copy all the adjustments collected in step 1 into the second column. Make sure the credit adjustments are in brackets. (See second column, Exhibit 5-10.) Sort the adjustments to the revenue or expense line to which they pertain. For example, accounts receivable is copied onto the revenue line, the adjustment for depreciation is on the COGS line, since the data state that depreciation is part of COGS, and so on.

4. Cross-add the schedule, entering cash flows in the third column. Note that non-cash items, such as depreciation and gains and losses, disappear as they are adjusted to zero.

5. Prepare the operating activities section of the SCF, using the numeric data from the third column, but changing the captions to appropriate cash flow descriptions, and then group cash flows, if that is considered desirable.

The final product is shown at the bottom of Exhibit 5-10. The $94,000 total cash from operating activities is the same as in Exhibit 5-9, but the presentation is different.

EXHIBIT 5-10				
LING CORP.				
Statement of Cash Flows Operating Activities Direct Method				
Year ended 31 December 20X5	**Profit and Loss Accounts**		**Adjustments (Letter References Refer to Prior Journal Entries)**	**Cash Flow**
Sales revenue	$960,000	i.	(14,000)	$946,000
Gain on sale of equipment	4,000	f.	(4,000)	0
Cost of goods sold	(597,000)	c.	65,000	(553,000)
		j.	(12,000)	
		o.	(9,000)	
Interest expense	(18,000)			(18,000)
Wages expense	(131,000)			(131,000)
Other operating expenses	(100,000)	d.	5,000	(99,000)
		k.	(4,000)	
Income tax expense	(54,000)	q.	3,000	(51,000)

| Net earnings and cash flow from operations | $ 64,000 | | $ 94,000 |

LING CORP.

Partial Statement of Cash Flows—Operating Activities

Year ended 31 December 20X5

Operating activities	
Cash received from customers	$946,000
Cash paid to suppliers ($553,000 + $99,000)	(652,000)
Cash paid to employees	(131,000)
Cash paid for interest	(18,000)
Cash paid for income tax	(51,000)
Cash from operating activities	$ 94,000

The investing and financing sections of the SCF are not dependent on the format chosen for the operating activities section and are not repeated here because they would be identical to those shown in Exhibit 5-9.

CONCEPT REVIEW

1. What is the effect on the SCF of selling a short-term investment, classified as a cash equivalent, at a $3,000 loss?
2. A company acquires a substantial amount of capital assets by issuing its own common shares to the vendor. What is the impact of this transaction on the SCF?
3. What section(s) of the SCF will be identical regardless of whether the direct or the indirect method of presentation is chosen?

DISCLOSURE OF CASH FLOWS FOR INTEREST, DIVIDENDS, AND INCOME TAX

Classification

Income Tax

In general, income tax should be shown in the operating activities section. However, there are times when tax is specifically related to investing or financing activities. In these cases, tax may be classified as investing or financing. For example, there are times when capital transactions, such as dividend distributions, attract specific taxes. It seems logical that the related tax be shown with the cash flow. *This classification decision is based on the transaction that causes the income tax and not on the judgement of management.*

Dividends Paid

Dividends paid have traditionally been classified in financing activities, as a voluntary payment to shareholders. Conceptually, classification in financing activities is appropriate if the company considers dividends paid to shareholders as an element related to obtaining financial resources. The reporting standard allows management to select an alternative classification of dividends as *operating activities*. This classification may be chosen to assist users in determining a company's ability to pay dividends out of operating cash flows.

Interest Paid

Interest paid has traditionally been classified in operating activities because interest is an expense in earnings. The reporting standard recognizes, though, that interest, like dividends, may be viewed as a element related to obtaining financial resources. Accordingly, the reporting standard allows interest to be classified as either an operating or a financing outflow. In Exhibit 5-2, Interfor classified interest paid of $7,122 in *financing activities*.

Capitalized Interest

Interest expense may be capitalized as part of the cost of various fixed assets and also investment properties. For example, if a company takes a year to construct a manufacturing facility, and interest of $600,000 is paid relating to money tied up in the project over this time, then the $600,000 is included in the cost of the asset and is not expensed. In this case, the $600,000 cash outflow is shown on the SCF in investing activities, with the acquisition of the manufacturing facility.

Dividends and Interest Received

Interest and dividend cash flows received also offer a particular classification challenge. Traditional practice has been to include these cash inflows in operating activities. That is, interest revenue and dividend revenue are part of net earnings and stay there in the SCF, adjusted for changes in related accounts such as interest receivable or dividends receivable, if needed. However, the reporting standard allows management to select an alternative classification and place these cash inflows in investing activities, to reflect the philosophy that cash is a return on investment decisions.

Summary

The management choice of classification of interest and dividends might be based on whether the payment is conceptually an operating item or whether it should be traced to its root cause of *investing* or *financing*. One concern is that management might pick classifications to portray a particular impression of operating cash flows or other key reporting metrics. Another concern is that financial statements may not be comparable with those of competitors. Financial statement users will have to proceed with caution when benchmarking.

The judgemental choices, and their rationale, can be summarized as follows:

Cash Flow	Operating Classification	Alternative SCF Classification
Interest received	*Operating activities*—interest received is judged to be part of operating decisions	*Investing activities*—interest received should be viewed as part of the evaluation of an investment decision
Interest paid[*]	*Operating activities*—interest paid is judged to be part of operating decisions	*Financing activities*—interest paid should be evaluated with the financing strategy
Dividends received	*Operating activities*—dividends received are judged to be part of operating decisions	*Investing activities*—dividends received should be viewed as part of the evaluation of an investment decision
Dividends paid	*Operating activities*—indicates the company's ability to pay dividends from operating cash flows	*Financing activities*—dividends paid should be evaluated with the financing strategy

> *Interest paid is an investing activity if capitalized on a qualifying asset such as fixed assets or investment properties.

Separate Disclosure Items

The reporting standard requires separate disclosure of cash flows associated with income tax, interest paid, interest received, dividends paid, and dividends received. This reporting requirement can be met by:

1. Using the direct method to show cash flows in the operating activities section of the SCF, which shows cash flows from each source; or

2. Using the indirect method of presenting cash flows in the operating activities section, *adding back the expense (deducting the revenue) and then listing the cash flows for the item separately.*

3. Reporting required cash flows as supplementary information (see Exhibit 5-8 for an example). This is not strictly in accordance with the reporting standard; but it is a common reporting practice.

Of course, the second approach makes the reconciliation in operating activities even more complex. In Exhibit 5-2, note that Interfor adjusts out the income tax recovery of $16,230 and adds back financing costs of $8,915 in the operating activities section and then deducts $3,077 of income tax paid in the operating activities section and interest payments of $7,122 in the financing section. The recovery/cost and cash flow numbers are not identical because of changes in deferred tax or interest payable, or other adjustments.

Reconciliation Method

To accomplish this disclosure though the indirect presentation approach (alternative 2, above), *basic account analysis does not change.* When *preparing* the SCF:

1. Add back the appropriate expenses and/or deduct revenues from net earnings.

2. Convert the revenue or expense to cash flow by applying the change in any related asset, liability, or equity account to the expense or revenue item. List the cash inflow or outflow in the SCF. *Do not relist on the SCF* any changes in payables, receivables, prepaids, and so on that were needed to convert this item from accrual to cash amounts.

Example

For RestCo, 20X2 net earnings are $1,925, after income tax expense of $670, interest expense of $350, and interest revenue of $180. Assume that prior analysis had produced an operating activities section of the SCF as follows:

Year ended 31 December 20X2	
Operating activities:	
Net earnings	$1,925
Plus (less) items not affecting cash:	
Depreciation	390
Increase in deferred tax liability	65
	2,380
Changes in other working capital items:	
Increase in interest receivable	(50)
Decrease in tax payable	(35)
Decrease in interest payable	(110)
Decrease in accounts payable	(75)

Cash provided by operating activities	$ 2,110

If the company were to show the cash flows for interest and tax in the operating activities section, the result would be as follows (items that have changed are highlighted):

Year ended 31 December 20X2	
Operating activities:	
Net earnings	$1,925
Plus (less) items adjusting net earnings:	
Depreciation	390
Interest expense	350
Income tax expense	670
Interest revenue	(180)
	3,155
Changes in other working capital items:	
Decrease in accounts payable	(75)
	3,080
Cash paid for income tax ($670 + $35 − $65)	(640)
Cash paid for interest ($350 + $110)	(460)
Cash received for interest ($180 − $50)	130
Cash provided by operating activities	$ 2,110

Note that the $2,110 cash flow from operating activities has not changed, but the presentation is different. Expenses and revenues related to interest and income tax have been added and subtracted in the top section. Cash outflows and inflows for interest and income tax are now listed at the bottom.

The cash outflow for income tax begins with tax expense of $670. It then incorporates the two adjustments to the original SCF that relate to tax expense: the $35 change in tax payable and the $65 change in deferred tax. A decrease in payables requires cash, so the outflow is *higher* than the expense; add the $35. Some of the expense will not be paid until the future, so the $65 increase in deferred tax *reduces* the outflow. The same logic applies to interest paid. The calculation begins with the $350 expense and *adds* the $110 reduction to the interest payable because it uses cash. For interest revenue, the increase in interest receivable means that some of the revenue is not received this year, so the cash inflow is $50 less than the $180 revenue.

In all cases, if the reconciling item relates to an item where cash is shown directly, the reconciling item is no longer listed separately on the SCF. Compared with the original SCF, the change in deferred tax and the changes in interest receivable, tax payable, and interest payable have been left off because they are individually incorporated in cash flow amounts.

Ling Corp. Example

The SCF for Ling Corp. in Exhibit 5-9 showed supplementary disclosure for the cash flow for interest and tax. If the company wished to continue to use the indirect presentation format in operating activities but show cash flows on the face of the SCF, the operating activities section would appear as follows (changed items are highlighted):

Year ended 31 December 20X5	
Operating activities:	
Net earnings	$64,000

Adjustments:	
Depreciation of plant and equipment	65,000
Amortization of development costs	5,000
Gain on sale of equipment	(4,000)
Interest expense	18,000
Tax expense	54,000
	202,000
Changes in working capital amounts:	
Increase in accounts receivable	(14,000)
Increase in inventory	(12,000)
Increase in prepaid expenses	(4,000)
Decrease in accounts payable	(9,000)
	163,000
Cash paid for interest	(18,000)
Cash paid for income tax ($54,000 − $3,000)	(51,000)
Cash provided (used) by operating activities	$94,000

As a final presentation alternative, remember that interest paid might be reclassified to the financing activities section.

Evaluation

Adding back these expenses and revenues and replacing them with their cash flows changes the operating activities from an indirect presentation to one that is partially indirect and partially direct. The direct method of presentation is far more logical, and it is clearer for financial statement readers. One might hope companies come to this realization and adopt the direct method of presentation. However, separate disclosure is the common reporting solution at this time.

CONCEPT REVIEW

1. What choices are available to classify dividends paid to shareholders on the SCF?
2. If a dividend payment of $50,000 to shareholders attracts $5,000 of tax for the company, what amount is shown as cash paid for dividends on the SCF?
3. If a company reported investment (interest) income of $320,000 and interest receivable increased by $18,000 during the year, how much cash was received from interest income?

SUMMARY OF ADJUSTMENTS IN OPERATING ACTIVITIES

To prepare the operating activities section of the SCF, it is necessary to convert accrual-basis earnings to the cash basis. There are certain types of adjustments that must be made to the accrual-basis earnings number. These are summarized as follows:

Type of Adjustment	Reason for Adjustment	Examples
The effects of cost/revenue allocations must be reversed	• Revenue or expense item has no related cash flow this period • Intent is to arrive at earnings as if the item were not included	• Add back depreciation and amortization of all kinds • Add back increase in deferred tax, deduct decrease in deferred tax • Add back bond discount amortization • Add back writedown of assets • Add back non-cash compensation expense from stock options • Deduct investment revenue under the equity method
Certain transactions, the net effects of which are included in net earnings, must be reclassified as investing or financing activities	Gain or loss on sale of fixed assets or bond retirement (in earnings) does not equal cash flow	• Add back losses • Deduct gains
Accruals must be "backed out" of various asset and liability accounts to determine cash inflows and outflows in operations	• Revenue or expense item has caused an asset or liability account because cash flow is before or after revenue or expense recognition • Asset or liability accounts must be directly related to a revenue or expense account (e.g., sales is related to accounts receivable)	• Change in accounts receivable, accounts payable, prepaid expenses, inventory, etc. • See chart below for direction of change
Expenses or revenues must be "backed out" of earnings to allow classification elsewhere	• Tax expense is added back, and then cash paid for tax is reported on a separate line in operating activities • Interest expense and interest and dividend revenue are "backed out," and then cash paid or received is listed as a	• Add back expenses • Deduct revenues • List cash flows

	separate line in the appropriate section of the SCF	

When adjustments must be made for changes in working capital accounts related to operations, the protocol is:

Change in Account Balance during the Year		
	Increase	**Decrease**
Asset (e.g., accounts receivable)	*Subtract* increase from net earnings	*Add* decrease to net earnings
Liability (e.g., accounts payable)	*Add* increase to net earnings	*Subtract* decrease from net earnings

Looking Forward

SCF issues are not now on the active agenda of either the IASB or the Canadian AcSB.

Accounting Standards for Private Enterprises

The SCF is required under Accounting Standards for Private Enterprises (ASPE) as part of a set of complete financial statements. The ASPE requirements for this statement are very similar to the IFRS presentation requirements, with the following differences:

1. Dividends paid *must* be classified as a financing activity.
2. Interest received and paid and dividends received *must* be classified in operating activities. There is no choice of alternative classification.
3. Cash flow from investment revenue, cash paid for interest, and cash paid for income tax must be *disclosed*. The disclosure can be accomplished through a note and is not needed on the face of the SCF.

RELEVANT STANDARDS

CPA Canada Handbook, Part I (IFRS):
- IAS 7, Statement of Cash Flows

CPA Canada Handbook, Part II (ASPE):
- Section 1540, Cash Flow Statement

SUMMARY OF KEY POINTS

1. Cash flow information discloses the historical pattern of cash flows in an enterprise for both feedback and predictive purposes. The information is used to predict future cash flows and to assess liquidity, the ability of a firm to pay dividends and obligations, the ability of a firm to adapt to changes in the business environment, the quality of earnings, and for other purposes.

2. The SCF classifies cash flows from operating activities, cash flows relating to investing activities, and cash flows relating to financing activities. In each category, *cash flow* includes both inflows and outflows.

3. Operating cash flows are related to the main revenue-producing activities of the business and are connected to the earnings process. Investing cash flows describe (long-term) capital asset and investment acquisitions and the proceeds from sale of these assets. Financing cash flows describe the sources of debt and equity financing and repayments of liabilities and equities, excluding liabilities directly relating to operations such as accounts payable.

4. The reporting basis for the SCF is the net cash position. The net cash position includes cash plus cash equivalent investments minus certain bank overdrafts. Cash equivalents include short-term liquid investments that are held for current needs and that bear little risk of change in value (maximum original three-month term).

5. Interpreting the SCF involves evaluating quality of earnings, major strategic sources and uses of cash, identifying trends, and benchmarking against industry norms.

6. There are two alternatives to present cash from operating activities—the direct and the indirect presentation methods. The indirect method reports operating activities by showing a reconciliation of net earnings with net cash flow from operating activities. Examples of adjustments are adding back depreciation, eliminating gains and losses, and adjusting for changes in operating working capital accounts. The direct method reports the cash inflows from the main classifications of revenues and cash outflows from the main classifications of expenses. Standard setters encourage companies to use the direct method but few Canadian companies use this formatting option.

7. In the investing and financing sections, gross cash flows are reported. Transactions are not offset, or netted, against other flows in the same category.

8. Non-cash transactions (e.g., acquiring plant assets with the vendor taking back a long-term note) are not shown as outflows and inflows on the SCF. These transactions must be described in the disclosure notes.

9. If debt is issued, only principal amounts are recorded in financing activities. Amounts that are in substance interest are classified consistently with interest expense.

10. Net cash flow is not affected by accounting policy choices or by management's accounting estimates. However, the reported cash flow from operations can be increased by capitalizing certain types of costs (e.g., development costs) because the costs are reclassified as investing activities and amortization has no effect on operating cash flows in future periods.

11. Cash paid for income tax, cash paid for interest, cash received for interest, and cash received for dividends must all be separately disclosed on the SCF. This can be accomplished through add-backs and deductions in the indirect presentation method in operating activities, or through use of the direct presentation method. Separate note disclosure is another commonly used solution.

12. Interest paid may be classified as an operating outflow or a financing outflow. The same two choices are available for dividends paid. Interest and dividends received may be classified as operating activities or investing activities. Once a classification alternative has been chosen, it must be applied consistently.

13. There are many approaches to preparing the SCF, including a format-free, ad hoc approach, T-accounts, and/or a worksheet. The same objectives apply to all—analyze transactions to identify all cash flows, reconciling items, and non-cash transactions.

Key Terms

capitalize

cash

cash equivalents

current account

financing activities

investing activities

line of credit

operating activities

overdraft

quality of earnings

statement of cash flows (SCF)

Review Problem 5-1

Phillies Corp. assembled the following information to prepare its 20X7 SCF:

Statement of Financial Position, 31 December	**20X7**	**20X6**
Cash	$ 62,000	$ 50,000
Temporary investments	—	150,000
Accounts receivable, net	80,000	60,000
Inventory	30,000	18,000
Equipment, net of accumulated depreciation	650,000	300,000
Goodwill	70,000	90,000
Total assets	$892,000	$668,000
Accounts payable	$ 63,000	$ 48,000
Salaries payable	50,000	60,000
Interest payable	9,000	6,000
Income tax payable	22,000	12,000
Mortgage payable	110,000	120,000
Bonds payable	250,000	200,000
Common shares	170,000	150,000
Retained earnings	218,000	72,000
Total liabilities and shareholders' equity	$892,000	$668,000

Statement of Comprehensive Income, year ended 31 December 20X7	
Sales	$820,000
Gain on insurance settlement	10,000
Cost of goods sold	(380,000)
Depreciation expense	(100,000)

Impairment of goodwill	(20,000)
Other expenses	(49,000)
Interest expense	(22,000)
Income tax expense	(73,000)
Net earnings and comprehensive income	$ 186,000

Additional information:

1. Phillies declared $40,000 in dividends in 20X7.
2. Equipment (cost $100,000, accumulated depreciation, $60,000) was destroyed by fire.
3. The temporary investments had a three-month term when they were first bought.
4. Goodwill was written down by $20,000 because of impairment.

Required:

1. Prepare the 20X7 SCF for Phillies Corp. Use the indirect method of presentation for the operating activities section. Phillies classifies dividends paid as a financing activity. Separate disclosure of cash paid for interest and income tax is not required.

2. Repeat the operating activities section of the SCF using the indirect method, showing cash flow for interest and income tax directly in the operating activities section of the SCF.

Use whichever method of preparation you feel most comfortable with (i.e., choose from among the format-free, T-account, or spreadsheet [see the Appendix to this chapter] methods). The suggested solution uses T-accounts.

REVIEW PROBLEM 5-1—SOLUTION

The T-account analysis appears below. Other approaches are equally valid—it is the result that matters. The actual SCF is shown at the end of this solution. Explanations for T-account entries are as follows:

a. Net earnings are $186,000. The T-account entry records net earnings.
b. Increase in accounts receivable; less cash was received from customers than was recognized as revenue.
c. Increase in inventories; more cash was paid for inventories than was recognized as COGS.
d. Increase in accounts payable; less was paid to trade creditors than was recognized as expense.
e. Depreciation expense was removed from operating expenses—a non-cash expense.
f. Goodwill impairment (expense) removed from operating expenses—another non-cash expense.
g. Salaries payable decreased, requiring more cash.
h. Adjustment to write off destroyed equipment and to record the insurance proceeds; $10,000 gain removed from operating earnings, and proceeds of $50,000 ($40,000 net book value disposed at a gain of $10,000) recorded as an inflow in the investing activities section.
i. Increase in interest payable, indicating that less cash was paid for interest than the amount of interest expense accrued.
j. Increase in bond payable, implying issuance of bond, in the absence of other information.
k. Increase in common shares implies issuance of additional shares, in the absence of evidence to the contrary.
l. Increase in income taxes payable; less tax paid than accrued.
m. Dividends declared *and paid* (i.e., there is no dividends payable account, so all must have been paid).
n. "Plug" entry to account for the otherwise unexplained change in the balance of the equipment account; the increase must have been due to the purchase of new equipment.
o. Decrease in mortgage payable implies repayment of mortgage, in the absence of other information.

T-Account Analysis

Cash and Cash Equivalents

Opening	200,000		
Operating Activities			
a) Net earnings	186,000	b) Accounts receivable	20,000
d) Accounts payable	15,000	c) Inventory	12,000
e) Depreciation expense	100,000	g) Salaries payable	10,000
f) Goodwill impairment	20,000	h) Gain on insurance settlement	10,000
i) Interest payable	3,000		
l) Income tax payable	10,000		
Investing Activities			
h) Insurance proceeds	50,000	n) Equipment bought	490,000
Financing Activities			
k) Issued common shares	20,000	m) Dividends paid	40,000
j) Bond issued	50,000	o) Mortgage repayment	10,000
Closing	62,000		

Accounts Receivable

Op.	60,000		
b)	20,000		
Cl.	80,000		

Accounts Payable

		Op.	48,000
		d)	15,000
		Cl.	63,000

Mortgage Payable

		Op.	120,000
o)	10,000		
		Cl.	110,000

Inventory

Op.	18,000		
c)	12,000		
Cl.	30,000		

Salaries Payable

		Op.	60,000
g)	10,000		
		Cl.	50,000

Bonds Payable

		Op.	200,000
		j)	50,000
		Cl.	250,000

Equipment, Net

Op.	300,000		
h)	60,000	e)	100,000
n)	490,000	h)	100,000
Cl.	650,000		

Interest Payable

		Op.	6,000
		i)	3,000
		Cl.	9,000

Goodwill

Op.	90,000		
		f)	20,000
Cl.	70,000		

Income Tax Payable

		Op.	12,000
		l)	10,000
		Cl.	22,000

Common Shares

		Op.	150,000
		k)	20,000
		Cl.	170,000

Retained Earnings

		Op.	72,000
m)	40,000	a)	186,000
		Cl.	218,000

Requirement 1

PHILLIES CORP.

Statement of Cash Flows

Year ended 31 December 20X7

Operating activities:		
Net earnings		$ 186,000
Adjustments:		
Depreciation expense	100,000	
Impairment of goodwill	20,000	
Gain on insurance settlement	(10,000)	110,000
		296,000
Plus (less) changes in non-cash working capital:		
Increase in accounts receivable	(20,000)	
Increase in accounts payable	15,000	
Increase in inventories	(12,000)	
Decrease in salaries payable	(10,000)	
Increase in interest payable	3,000	
Increase in income tax payable	10,000	(14,000)
		282,000
Investing activities:		
Insurance proceeds from equipment destroyed by fire	50,000	
New equipment purchased	(490,000)	(440,000)
Financing activities:		
Issuance of bonds	50,000	
Dividends paid	(40,000)	
Reduction of mortgage principal	(10,000)	
Issuance of common shares	20,000	20,000
Net increase (decrease) in cash		(138,000)
Opening cash and cash equivalents		200,000
Closing cash and cash equivalents		$ 62,000

Requirement 2

PHILLIES CORP.

Partial Statement of Cash Flows

Operating Activities

Year ended 31 December 20X7

Operating activities:		
Net earnings		$ 186,000
Adjustments:		
Interest expense	22,000	
Income tax expense	73,000	
Depreciation expense	100,000	
Impairment of goodwill	20,000	
Gain on insurance settlement	(10,000)	205,000
		391,000
Plus (less) changes in non-cash working capital:		
Increase in accounts receivable	(20,000)	
Increase in accounts payable	15,000	
Increase in inventories	(12,000)	
Decrease in salaries payable	(10,000)	(27,000)
Cash paid for interest ($22,000 – $3,000		364,000
increase in payable)		(19,000)
Cash paid for income tax ($73,000 –		
$10,000 increase in payable)		(63,000)
		$282,000

CASE 5-1

AURORA INC.

The owner of Aurora Inc., Cindy Hickey, has come to you, a public accountant, for advice.

"I am very worried about my business right now. My bank loan is at its maximum level, we have no cash, and my salary is backing up, unpaid. I don't know what has gone wrong, and what I can do about it. Please provide some advice!"

Hickey's company, Aurora, manufactures and distributes small, specialized boating items that have a good reputation and a stable market among pleasure boaters and fishers. She has been in business for ten years.

Cindy reports, "The company showed a profit again this year. I hired a new part-time manager during the year so I could spend less day-to-day time on the operation. He has been building up our asset base. We sold some investments, but made no new ones. We replaced some inefficient machinery, and purchased a vehicle to save on rental expenses.

"We sold old machinery that would not be able to meet the demand that our new manager is projecting. It had a cost of $9,600, and net book value of $3,800. I think the amount I took out of the company was in line with that of previous years, although my salary is backing up, unpaid. I can't afford that, I can tell you, but the company has no money to pay me.

"Our cash has dropped and we now owe a lot on a demand bank loan. I have some financial information for the year (Exhibit 1)."

EXHIBIT 1		
AURORA INC.		
Statement of Financial Position		
For the years ended December 31		
	20X5	**20X4**
Assets		
Cash	$ 500	$ 6,000
Accounts receivable	8,500	2,000
Inventory	11,200	3,700
Investments	20,000	32,000
Machinery	30,400	24,000
Accumulated depreciation, machinery	(6,400)	(8,000)
Vehicle	27,500	0
Accumulated depreciation, vehicle	(5,000)	0
	$86,700	$59,700
Liabilities and Shareholders' Equity		
Bank loan, payable on demand	$30,000	$ 0
Accounts payable	1,600	11,700
Salaries payable	5,300	2,200
Common shares	500	500
Retained earnings	49,300	45,300
	$86,700	$59,700

Selected information from the statement of earnings:

Net earnings	12,000	
Depreciation expense	9,200	

Rent expense	28,700
Loss on sale of machinery	(2,200)
Gain on sale of investments	3,600
Interest revenue	1,200
Interest expense	2,200
Income tax expense	2,750
Marketing expenses	14,300

"Can you explain what is happening with our cash flows? What should I do to get out of this hole?"

Required:

Respond to Cindy's request.

(Judy Cumby, used with permission.)

CASE 5-2

PURPLE LTD.

"Frankly, if we continue to grow, we will be out of business soon."

This was the glum assessment of Kathy Lin, President and CEO of Purple Ltd., a company that designs, manufactures, and retails women's fashion. Kathy has a 30-year history in the fashion business and has managed her own label for much of that time. In 20X0, she incorporated Purple, and the company grew rapidly. It was particularly known for its edgy fashion design, reasonable prices, and quick turnaround. Purple hires young designers and has established a highly efficient manufacturing and distribution system to place trendy clothes in stores ahead of her competition. Initially, designs had been sold only in Purple's own stores, but over the past two years, Purple began selling to larger chains. As a result, the scope of Purple has significantly increased as have revenues and profits. In fact, the company reported a loss of $1,345 in 20X0 but moved to earnings of $133 in 20X1, earnings of $2,580 in 20X2, and an impressive $6,245 in 20X3 (all figures in thousands). Sales had more than tripled over the past three years. Capital assets purchased over this period were $16,000 in 20X0, $9,500 in 20X2, and $8,000 in 20X3.

"We are pretty much out of cash, and I have bills to suppliers that are due. My banker will provide some cash, but not enough to keep up with this—and all that borrowing is getting expensive. I'm not sure how we can post such high earnings and be so broke. Can you explain this to me and help me with a plan to get out of this mess? I need good advice, fast."

You are an accounting professional in public practice and have provided business advice to Kathy in the past. You agree to meet with her on this issue tomorrow and now are preparing a draft report for discussion. You decide that calculating cash flows from operating activities is a good place to start (Exhibit 1).

EXHIBIT 1				
PURPLE LTD.				
Summarized Statement of Financial Position				
At 31 December (in thousands)	**20X3**	**20X2**	**20X1**	**20X0**
Cash	$ 320	$ 1,680	$ 4,210	$ 5,870
Accounts receivable	29,240	18,450	3,060	2,940
Inventory	41,970	32,970	25,760	22,800
Prepaid assets	1,566	1,211	1,087	1,004
Plant and equipment (net)	22,720	17,650	11,290	14,600
Other assets	3,650	1,540	2,970	1,340
Total	$99,466	$73,501	$48,377	$48,554
Liabilities				
Accounts payable and				
accrued liabilities	32,119	26,404	18,813	16,824
Short-term debt	35,566	24,929	13,276	14,675
Long-term debt	20,150	15,800	12,500	13,400
Equity				
Common shares	5,000	5,000	5,000	5,000
Retained earnings (deficit)	6,631	1,368	(1,212)	(1,345)
Total	$99,466	$73,501	$48,377	$48,554

Required:

Prepare the draft report for discussion.

CASE 5-3

HUM PRODUCTS LTD.

HUM Products Ltd. (HUM) is a consumer products company that designs, manufactures, markets, and distributes a diverse portfolio of products, primarily in the recreational and leisure segments. The products enjoy strong positive brand recognition and include such goods as bicycles, car seats, small boats, and strollers.

As a public Canadian company, HUM complies with IFRS. The company is currently evaluating alternative presentations for the SCF. You are an independent accounting professional, hired to provide some expertise in the area. Your charge from the CFO:

We'd like to take a fresh look at our SCF, with your help. We'd like to see what our SCF would look like if we used the direct method to present operating activities, rather than the indirect method that we have always used in the past. It would probably be helpful if your analysis also included an analysis of our strategic operating, investing, and financing decisions that are apparent from the SCF. I've provided you with the information you need [Exhibit 1]. You can piece it together from this, I expect. Document your assumptions and we'll review it together next week. We'd also like you to evaluate the alternatives for presenting dividends and interest paid in the operating versus financing sections: a demonstration of the alternatives, and the impact on our key reporting numbers, would be helpful. We also struggle with the accounting policy for our development costs; they're pretty steady from year to year, and we expense them. But that's a judgement call; we're evaluating the capitalization and amortization decision as well. Perhaps you should analyze that issue as well. We are meeting with the audit committee next week, and we need to present an analysis to them.

EXHIBIT 1

HUM PRODUCTS LTD.

Statement of Financial Position

As of 31 December (in thousands)	20X4	20X3
Assets		
Current assets		
Cash and cash equivalents	$ 19,600	$ 22,500
Accounts receivable	316,300	286,900
Inventories	508,500	322,400
Prepaid expenses	16,300	10,600
	860,700	642,400
Property, plant, and equipment, net	159,800	140,400
Intangible assets, net	368,900	276,400
Goodwill	540,200	540,200
	$1,929,600	$1,599,400
Liabilities		
Current liabilities		
Bank indebtedness	$ 4,400	$ 5,800
Accounts payable and accrued liabilities	380,900	325,900
Income tax payable	30,600	25,500
Current portion of long-term debt	8,900	63,000
	424,800	420,200
Long-term debt	450,700	162,900
Pension obligations	20,100	20,900

Deferred tax	111,800	109,700
	1,007,400	713,700
Shareholders' Equity		
Common shares	177,500	177,500
Retained earnings	744,700	708,200
	922,200	885,700
	$1,929,600	$1,599,400
For the year ended 31 December (in thousands)	**20X4**	**20X3**
Sales	$2,164,800	$ 1,792,500
Expenses		
Cost of sales	1,651,100	1,375,400
Selling, general, and administrative expenses	319,100	244,800
Depreciation	35,800	29,800
Amortization of intangibles	10,400	10,700
Development costs	10,900	9,000
Restructuring costs	700	14,600
Interest	21,200	23,800
	2,049,200	1,708,100
Earnings before income tax	115,600	84,400
Income tax		
Current	17,000	26,400
Deferred	2,100	(7,300)
	19,100	19,100
Net earnings and comprehensive income	$ 96,500	$ 65,300
Earnings per share		
Basic and diluted	$3.84	$2.60

Required:

Prepare a report that responds to the requests of the CFO.

TECHNICAL REVIEW

Note: **In all assignment questions, unless directed otherwise, assume that dividends paid are financing activities, and assume that interest paid and received and dividends received are operating transactions.**

connect

TR5-1 SCF—Cash Definition:

Selected accounts from the SFP of TMI Ltd. at 31 December 20X4 and 20X5 are presented below.

As at 31 December	20X5	20X4
Cash #1	$ 230,000	$ 20,000
Cash #2 (overdrawn at the end of 20X4)	15,000	(70,000)
Short-term investments (a cash equivalent)	300,000	—

Required:

Calculate the change in cash for the year.

connect

TR5-2 SCF—Cash from Operating Activities:

Selected accounts from the SFP of UVI Ltd. at 31 December 20X4 and 20X5 are presented below. UVI reported earnings of $407,000 in 20X5, and depreciation expense was $35,000.

As at 31 December	20X5	20X4
Accounts receivable	$160,000	$110,000
Inventory	200,000	240,000
Accounts payable	150,000	195,000
Short-term bank loan payable	75,000	102,000

Required:

Calculate cash from operating activities for 20X5.

connect

TR5-3 SCF—Cash from Operating Activities:

Selected accounts from the SFP of Tabby Ltd. at 31 December 20X7 and 20X6 are presented below. Tabby reported earnings of $125,000 in 20X7, and depreciation expense was $20,000.

As at 31 December	20X7	20X6
Prepaid insurance	$4,000	$16,000
Inventory	72,000	68,000
Rent payable	2,000	5,000
Pension liability	61,000	46,000

Required:

Calculate cash from operating activities for 20X7.

connect

TR5-4 SCF—Investing Activities:

Selected accounts from the SFP of Lexy Ltd. at 31 December 20X7 and 20X6 are presented below. During the year, equipment with an original cost of $200,000 and net book value of $85,000 was sold at a loss of $15,000. Other equipment was purchased for cash.

As at 31 December	20X7	20X6
Equipment	$400,000	$230,000
Accumulated depreciation, equipment	(170,000)	(150,000)
	230,000	80,000

Required:

List the items that would be included in the SCF from these accounts for 20X7. Include the appropriate section (operating, investing, or financing). Use the indirect method of presentation in the operating activities section.

connect

TR5-5 SCF—Investing Activities:

Selected accounts from the SFP of MNN Ltd. at 31 December 20X4 and 20X5 are presented below. Depreciation was $40,000 for equipment, $60,000 for buildings, and $75,000 for machinery. A new machine was purchased in 20X5, with 25% of the price paid in cash and the other 75% financed directly by the vendor through a long-term note. Other assets were purchased for cash.

As at 31 December	20X5	20X4
Equipment, net of accumulated depreciation	$530,000	$400,000
Buildings, net of accumulated depreciation	700,000	200,000
Machinery, net of accumulated depreciation	560,000	210,000

Required:

List the items that would be included in the SCF from these accounts for 20X5. Include the appropriate section (operating, investing, or financing). Use the indirect method of presentation in the operating activities section. Also list the non-cash item disclosure.

connect

TR5-6 SCF—Financing Activities:

Selected accounts from the SFP of Passen Ltd. at 31 December 20X8 and 20X7 are presented below. Passen reported earnings of $100,000 in 20X8. There was a stock dividend recorded, valued at $50,000 that reduced retained earnings and increased common shares.

There was also a cash dividend declared and common shares issued for cash.

As at 31 December	20X8	20X7
Cash dividends payable	$ 20,000	$ 12,000
Bonds payable	900,000	500,000
Common shares	400,000	100,000
Retained earnings	225,000	250,000

Required:

List the items that would be included in the SCF from these accounts for 20X8. Include the appropriate section (operating, investing, or financing). Use the indirect method of presentation in the operating activities section. List the non-cash item disclosure. Make logical assumptions about unexplained changes in accounts.

connect

TR5-7 SCF—Financing Activities:

Selected accounts from the SFP of Gentron Ltd. at 31 December 20X5 and 20X4 are presented below. Gentron declared $100,000 of cash dividends during the year, and purchased $200,000 of machinery in direct exchange for common shares.

As at 31 December	20X5	20X4
Preferred shares	$600,000	$400,000
Common shares	900,000	630,000
Retained earnings	940,000	780,000

Required:

List the items that would be included in the SCF from these accounts for 20X5. Include the appropriate section (operating, investing, or financing). Use the indirect method of presentation in the operating activities section. List the non-cash item disclosure. Make logical assumptions about unexplained changes in accounts.

■ connect

TR5-8 SCF—Financing Activities:

Selected accounts from the SFP of Norelco Ltd. at 31 December 20X4 and 20X5 are presented below. Norelco reported earnings of $280,000 in 20X5. There was a new $140,000 of notes payable this year that was direct financing (a note issued by the vendor) for a piece of machinery.

As at 31 December	20X5	20X4
Notes payable, long-term	$450,000	$700,000
Common shares	300,000	230,000
Retained earnings	610,000	540,000

Required:

List the items that would be included in the SCF from these accounts for 20X5. Include the appropriate section (operating, investing, or financing). Use the indirect method of presentation in the operating activities section. List the non-cash item disclosure. Make logical assumptions about unexplained changes in accounts.

■ connect

TR5-9 SCF—Cash Paid or Collected:

Information related to various financial statement elements is provided for two cases:

Case A Operating expenses were $500,000. Inventory increased by $72,000, accounts payable increased by $50,000, and prepaid rent decreased by $16,000.

Case B Sales revenue was $1,350,000. Accounts receivable decreased by $75,000 and unearned revenue increased by $46,000 during the year.

Required:

For each case, calculate the cash inflow or outflow related to the revenue or expense account.

■ connect

TR5-10 SCF—Cash Paid or Collected:

Information related to various financial statement elements is provided for three cases:

Case A   Interest expense was $26,400. Interest payable had an opening balance of $11,200 and a closing balance of $7,300. The discount on bonds payable was amortized by $2,200 during the year.

Case B   Interest revenue was $125,700. Interest receivable increased by $72,100 during the year.

Case C   Sales revenue was $794,300. Accounts receivable increased from $104,100 to $119,700 and unearned revenue decreased by $12,000 during the year.

Required:

For each case, calculate the cash inflow or outflow related to the revenue or expense account.

ASSIGNMENTS

Note: **In all assignment questions, unless directed otherwise, assume that dividends paid are financing activities, and assume that interest paid and received and dividends received are operating transactions. Use the indirect method of presentation in the operating activities section unless instructed otherwise.**

A5-1 Overview—SCF Classification:

The records of Neon Corp. provided the following data:

a.   Purchased capital asset for $340,000; paid cash.

b.   Depreciation expense, $134,000.

c.   Sold a capital asset for $68,000 cash; original cost, $180,000, accumulated depreciation, $140,000.

d.   Purchased capital asset for $340,000; signed a long-term note with the vendor for $300,000 and paid $40,000 in cash.

e.   Wages expense, $336,000; wages payable decreased, $20,000.

f.   Sales revenue, $2,600,000; accounts receivable decreased, $430,000.

g.   Borrowed $214,000 cash from the bank.

h.   Declared a cash dividend, $132,000; dividends payable decreased by $4,000.

i.   Paid a note payable, $300,000 principal plus $12,000 interest.

j.   Converted long-term bonds into common shares, $8,000,000.

Required:

The company uses the indirect method of presentation in the operating activities section. For each of the above items, give:

1.   The SCF category (operating, investing, financing), or indicate that the item is excluded from the SCF.

2.   List the items that would appear on the SCF for a–j, above.

A5-2 Overview—SCF Classification:

The main sections of the SCF are shown below with letter identification. Next, several transactions are given. Match the transactions with the SCF sections by entering one or more letters in each blank space. Assume loans and notes receivable are long-term investments not related to operating activities. State other assumptions or explanations, if needed.

Statement of Cash Flows:

A. Cash inflows (outflows) from operating activities (indirect method of presentation)

B. Cash inflows (outflows) from investing activities

C. Cash inflows (outflows) from financing activities

D. None of the above

Transactions:

_____ 1.   Payment of debt, 90% cash and 10% common shares issued

_____ 2.   Sale of land at a loss; proceeds will be received in the next fiscal year

_____ 3.   Decrease in rent payable

_____ 4.   Cash dividends declared but not paid

_____ 5.   Repurchase and retirement of common shares

_____ 6.   Stock dividend declared and distributed to common shareholders

_____ 7.   Proceeds from issuing bond payable

_____ 8.   Sale of plant assets at a loss

_____ 9.   Purchase of long-term investment

_____ 10. Purchase of a 30-day treasury bill with excess cash

_____ 11. Issuance of the company's own common shares, for cash

_____ 12. Acquisition of a building through a finance lease with no money changing hands at the inception of the lease

_____ 13. Acquisition of plant equipment assets; paid cash

_____ 14. Increase in prepaid expenses

_____ 15. Depreciation expense

A5-3 Overview—SCF Classification:

The records of Agricola Corp. provide information about transactions and events of the year. The company is preparing a SCF using the indirect presentation approach for operating activities.

a. Sold equipment for $172,000 cash; original cost, $720,000, accumulated depreciation, $420,000.

b. Repaid a bank loan, paying out $200,000 for principal and $24,000 for interest.

c. Issued common shares for equipment with a fair value of $1,340,000.

d. Paid a cash dividend, $100,000.

e. Recorded goodwill impairment of $80,000.

f. Issued common shares for cash, $1,250,000.

g. Bought land for $1,000,000; signed a long-term note with the vendor for $550,000 and paid $450,000 in cash.

h. Invested $100,000 of idle cash in a temporary investment with a 60-day term.

i. Sales revenue, $6,800,000; accounts receivable decreased, $290,000.

j. Invested $600,000 of idle cash in common shares of a public company. The shares will be sold in 30 days' time.

Required:

For each of the above items, list the item that would appear on the SCF, including its category (operating, investing, or financing) and amount. If the item is excluded from the SCF, list the required disclosure.

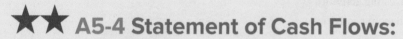 **A5-4 Statement of Cash Flows:**

The records of Rangler Paper Co. provided the selected data given below for the reporting period ended 31 December 20X5.

Statement of Financial Position Data

Paid cash dividend	$ 10,000
Established restricted construction cash fund (a long-term investment) to build a new building	60,000
Increased inventory of merchandise	14,000
Borrowed on a long-term note	25,000
Acquired five acres of land for a future site for the company; paid in full by issuing 3,000 shares of Rangler common shares, when the quoted market price per share was $15	45,000
Increase in prepaid expenses	3,000
Decrease in accounts receivable	7,000
Payment of bonds payable in full at book value	97,000
Increase in accounts payable	5,000
Cash from disposal of old operational assets (sold at book value)	12,000
Decrease in rent receivable	2,000

Statement of Comprehensive Income

Sales revenue	$400,000
Rent revenue	10,000
Cost of goods sold	(190,000)
Depreciation expense	(20,000)
Remaining expenses	(97,000)
Net earnings and comprehensive income	$103,000

Required:

Prepare the SCF. Use the indirect method for operations. Separate disclosure of cash paid for interest and income tax and investment income is not required. Group all changes in non-cash working capital in operations as one amount. Assume a beginning cash balance of $62,000.

 **A5-5 Statement of Cash Flows:**

Denton Corp.'s statement of financial position accounts as at 31 December 20X4 and 20X5 and information relating to 20X5 activities are presented below.

As at 31 December	20X5	20X4
Assets		
Cash	$ 230,000	$ 100,000
Short-term investments	300,000	—
Accounts receivable	510,000	510,000
Inventory	680,000	600,000
Long-term investments	200,000	300,000
Plant assets	1,700,000	1,000,000
Accumulated depreciation	(450,000)	(450,000)
Patent	90,000	100,000
Total assets	$3,260,000	$2,160,000
Liabilities and Shareholders' Equity		
Accounts payable and accrued liabilities	$ 825,000	$ 720,000
Short-term bank debt	325,000	—
Common shares	1,170,000	950,000
Retained earnings	940,000	490,000
Total liabilities and shareholders' equity	$3,260,000	$2,160,000

Information relating to 20X5 activities:

- Net earnings for 20X5 were $690,000.
- Cash dividends were declared and paid in 20X5.
- Equipment costing $400,000 and having a net book value of $150,000 was sold for $150,000.
- A long-term investment was sold for $135,000. There were no other transactions affecting long-term investments in the year.
- Short-term investments consist of treasury bills with an original term of three months.

Required:

Determine the following amounts for Denton for the year 20X5:

1. Net cash from operating activities (indirect method)
2. Net cash from investing activities
3. Net cash from financing activities

A5-6 Statement of Cash Flows:

The financial statements for Linked Ltd. are shown below:

Statement of Comprehensive Income		
For the year ended 31 December 20X5		
Sales revenue		$1,821,300
Investment revenue		37,500
Operating expenses, including cost of goods sold		793,200
Depreciation expense		105,000
Goodwill impairment		116,100
Administrative expenses		621,000
Interest expense		45,300
Gain on sale of investment		6,000
Income tax expense		73,800
Net earnings and comprehensive income		$ 110,400
Statement of Financial Position		
As of 31 December	**20X5**	**20X4**
Assets		
Cash	$ 82,500	$ 90,000
Accounts receivable	307,500	210,000
Merchandise inventory	694,200	630,000
Prepaid insurance	7,800	19,200
Investments	75,000	120,000
Land	270,000	270,000
Capital assets, net of accumulated depreciation	1,434,000	930,000
Goodwill, net of impairment	173,700	289,800
	$3,044,700	$2,559,000

Liabilities and Equity		
Accounts payable	$ 637,200	$ 567,000
Rent payable	22,500	15,000
Income tax payable	49,200	48,000
Bonds payable	1,110,000	900,000
Pension obligation	50,100	30,000
Common shares	972,000	810,000
Retained earnings	203,700	189,000
	$3,044,700	$2,559,000

During the year, the company purchased a capital asset valued at $30,000; payment was made by issuing common shares. Additional capital assets were acquired for cash. Changes in other accounts were typical transactions.

Required:

1. Prepare the SCF using the indirect method. Include required note disclosure of non-cash transactions. Omit the separate disclosure of cash flow for interest, investment income, and income tax.
2. Explain the company's cash transactions for the year, based on the SCF.

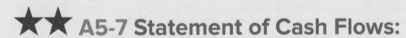

★★ A5-7 Statement of Cash Flows:

Grand Corp.'s 20X2 financial statements showed the following:

Sales		$421,050
Cost of goods sold	$ 160,000	
Depreciation	21,000	
Other operating expenses	62,950	
Income tax	36,200	
Loss on sale of equipment	2,550	
Gain on sale of investment	(1,600)	281,100
Net earnings and comprehensive income		$139,950

As at December 31	20X2	20X1
Cash	$ 56,900	$ 45,300
Accounts receivable	73,500	84,600
Inventory	154,000	144,500
Equipment	456,500	391,500
Less: accumulated depreciation	(189,500)	(188,500)

Investment	45,000	65,000
Total	$596,400	$542,400
Accounts payable	$ 50,900	$ 85,600
Income tax payable	8,150	5,800
Bonds payable	37,500	0
Common shares	252,000	252,000
Retained earnings	247,850	199,000
Total	$596,400	$542,400

Additional information:

During the year, equipment with an original cost of $82,000 was sold for cash.

Required:

1. Prepare the SCF, in good form. Include required note disclosure of non-cash transactions. Omit the separate disclosure of cash flow for interest, investment income, and income tax. Make logical assumptions regarding the nature of change in asset, liability, and equity accounts.

2. Explain the company's cash transactions for the year, based on the SCF.

★ A5-8 Presentation—Direct Method, Operating Activities:

Refer to the data in A5-6.

Required:

Prepare the complete SCF, in good form, using the direct method in the operating activities section. Include required note disclosure of non-cash transactions. Omit the separate disclosure of cash flow for interest, investment income, and income tax.

★★ A5-9 Presentation—Direct and Indirect, Operating Activities:

The statement of financial position, statement of comprehensive income, and additional information are given below for Supreme Co.

Statement of Financial Position

As at 31 December	20X5	20X4
Debits		
Cash	$ 44,900	$ 40,000
Accounts receivable	52,500	60,000
Merchandise inventory	141,600	180,000
Prepaid interest	1,200	2,400
Investments, long-term	—	30,000
Land	38,400	10,000
Capital assets	259,000	250,000
Patent (net)	1,400	1,600
	$539,000	$574,000
Credits		
Accumulated depreciation	$ 79,000	$ 65,000
Accounts payable	49,700	50,000
Wages payable	1,500	2,000
Income taxes payable	13,400	9,000
Bonds payable	50,000	100,000
Common shares	329,000	320,000
Retained earnings	16,400	28,000
	$539,000	$574,000

Statement of Comprehensive Income

For the year ended 31 December 20X5	20X5
Sales revenue	$399,100
Cost of goods sold	(224,400)
Depreciation expense	(14,000)
Patent amortization	(200)
Salary expense	(80,000)
Interest expense	(4,400)
Other expenses	(44,000)

Investment revenue	900
Gain on sale of investments	10,000
Income tax expense	(24,600)
Net earnings and comprehensive income	$ 18,400

Analysis of selected accounts and transactions:

a. Purchased capital asset, $9,000; payment by issuing 600 common shares.
b. Payment at maturity date to retire bonds payable, $50,000.
c. Sold the long-term investments for $40,000.
d. Reassessment for prior years' income taxes; paid during 20X5 and added to 20X5 tax expense, $6,600.
e. Purchased land, $28,400; paid cash.

Required:

1. Prepare the SCF, using the direct method in the operating activities section. Include a list of non-cash transactions that would be presented in the disclosure notes.
2. Prepare the operating activities section of the SCF using the indirect method in the operating activities section. Omit the separate disclosure of cash flow for interest, investment income, and income tax.

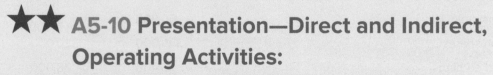

★★ A5-10 Presentation—Direct and Indirect, Operating Activities:

The following financial information is available for Chipmunk Inc. for the 20X3 fiscal year:

Statement of Financial Position		
As at 31 December	**20X3**	**20X2**
Cash	$ 10,000	$ 40,000
Receivables	440,000	360,000
Marketable securities	380,000	460,000
Inventory	1,462,000	1,264,000
Land	660,000	820,000
Building	2,080,000	2,240,000
Accumulated depreciation, building	(940,000)	(760,000)
Machinery	2,160,000	1,750,000
Accumulated depreciation, machinery	(438,000)	(424,000)
Goodwill	220,000	220,000

	$6,034,000	$5,970,000
Current liabilities	$ 512,000	$ 662,000
Bonds payable	2,000,000	2,000,000
Preferred shares	2,096,000	1,686,000
Common shares	1,130,000	1,000,000
Retained earnings	296,000	622,000
	$6,034,000	$5,970,000

Statement of Comprehensive Income

For the year ended 31 December 20X3

Sales	$3,368,000
Cost of goods sold	2,206,000
Gross profit	1,162,000
Depreciation	
Building	220,000
Machinery	150,000
Interest	230,000
Operating expenses	722,000
Selling expenses	80,000
Gain on sale of land	(44,000)
Loss on sale of machine	54,000
	1,412,000
Net earnings (loss) before income tax	(250,000)
Income tax recovery	108,000
Net earnings (loss) and comprehensive income (loss)	$ (142,000)

Additional information:

1. Marketable securities were sold at their carrying value. The marketable securities are not cash equivalents.
2. A partially depreciated building was sold for an amount equal to its net book value.
3. Cash of $80,000 was received on the sale of a machine.
4. Preferred shares were issued for cash on 1 March 20X3. Dividends of $100,000 were paid on the noncumulative preferred shares.
5. On 1 September 20X3, 50,000 common shares were purchased and retired for $110,000, their original issuance price. On 1 November 20X3, 130,000 common shares were issued in exchange for machinery and valued at $240,000.
6. Because of its loss, the company received a refund of taxes paid in prior years of $108,000.

Required:

1. Prepare the SCF, in good form. Use the indirect method for cash flows from operations. Omit the separate disclosure of cash flows for interest, investment income, and income tax. Include a list of non-cash transactions that would be presented in the disclosure notes.

2. Repeat the operating activities section of the SCF, using the direct method for cash flows from operations.

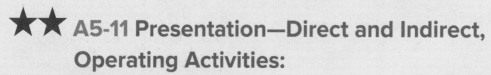 **A5-11 Presentation—Direct and Indirect, Operating Activities:**

The accounting records of Laurent Co. provided the following data:

Statement of Comprehensive Income	
For year ended 31 December 20X8	
Sales	$900,000
Cost of goods sold	(540,000)
Depreciation expense	(12,000)
Operating expenses	(192,000)
Net earnings and comprehensive income	$ 156,000

Statement of Financial Position		
At 31 December	20X8	20X7
Debits		
Cash	$102,000	$ —
Accounts receivable	54,000	57,000
Inventory	75,000	60,000
Investment, long-term	—	9,000
Capital assets	279,000	180,000
Total debits	$510,000	$306,000
Credits		
Bank overdraft	$ —	$ 15,000
Accumulated depreciation	42,000	30,000
Accounts payable	36,000	18,000
Short-term bank loan	12,000	9,000
Notes payable, long-term	108,000	60,000
Common shares	240,000	150,000
Retained earnings	72,000	24,000
Total credits	$510,000	$306,000

Other information:

a. Paid a $24,000 long-term note payable by issuing common shares.

b. Purchased capital assets that cost $99,000; gave a $72,000 long-term note payable and paid $27,000 cash.

c. Sold the long-term investment at cost, for cash.

d. Assume that unexplained differences in asset, liability, and equity accounts flow from logical sources.

Required:

1. Prepare the SCF, using the two-step indirect method of presentation for the operating activities section. Omit separate disclosure of cash paid for interest and income tax. Include a list of non-cash transactions that would be presented in the disclosure notes.

2. Prepare the operating activities section of the SCF using the direct method.

 # A5-12 Interpretation—Quality of Earnings:

Dromeda Ltd. has prepared the following comparison (in thousands):

31 December	20X5	20X4	20X3
Net earnings	$210	$670	$(145)
Cash flows from operating activities	535	560	510

The same information has been collected for Panel Corp.:

31 December	20X5	20X4	20X3
Net earnings	$210	$670	$(145)
Cash flows from operating activities	190	455	(50)

Required:

1. Which of the companies above illustrates higher quality of earnings? Explain.

2. Suggest four factors that would make cash flows from operating activities different from net earnings.

 # A5-13 Interpretation—Quality of Earnings:

Oakland Ltd. owns a chain of golf courses. Members sign multi-year membership packages, with increasing payments in later years of the contract. Revenue is recognized evenly over the membership term, regardless of the cash flow pattern. The operating activities section of the SCF for the past two years is as follows:

OAKLAND LTD.		
Statement of Cash Flows		
	20X3	**20X2**
Cash flows from operating activities		

Earnings for the period	$ 36,000	$ 31,500
Adjustment for:		
Depreciation and amortization	41,700	32,500
(Gains)/losses on sale of assets	(3,600)	(2,300)
Decrease/(increase) in accounts receivable	(4,200)	(3,300)
Increase/(decrease) in unearned revenue	7,400	61,100
Decrease/(increase) in other working capital accounts	(17,400)	(8,200)
Deferred income tax	9,300	6,900
Other	(1,000)	(700)
Net cash from operating activities	$ 68,200	$117,500

Required:

1. Does the above analysis suggest high quality of earnings? Explain.
2. Suggest two accounting policies that would contribute to lower quality of earnings, based on the adjustments above.

A5-14 Interpretation—Quality of Earnings:

Minex Corp. owns a number of mine sites, and is involved in exploration, extraction, and refining. Output is sold under long-term contracts, where prices are set, but extraction and exploration decisions are influenced by commodity prices. The operating activities section of the SCF for the past two years:

MINEX CORP.		
Statement of Cash Flows		
	20X3	**20X2**
Cash flows from operating activities		
Income (loss) for the period	$ (7,300)	$ 43,200
Adjustment for:		
Depreciation and depletion	11,300	42,400
Deferred development cost amortization	20,700	32,400
Decrease/(increase) in accounts receivable	(2,600)	(6,300)
Increase/(decrease) in unearned revenue	4,200	(53,300)
Decrease/(increase) in other working capital accounts	7,400	6,100
Deferred income tax	9,300	(17,100)
Other	1,700	(300)
Net cash from operating activities	$44,700	$ 47,100

Required:

1. Does the above analysis suggest high quality of earnings? Explain.
2. Suggest two accounting policies that would contribute to lower quality of earnings, based on the adjustments above.

★★ A5-15 Statement of Cash Flows—Indirect Method; Capital Assets:

Information related to capital assets is provided for three cases:

Case A	20X2	20X1
Capital assets	$660,000	$640,000
Accumulated depreciation	(340,000)	(380,000)
	320,000	260,000

The company sold an asset with an original cost of $120,000 at a loss of $8,000. Depreciation expense was $50,000. Other capital assets were acquired for cash.

Case B	20X2	20X1
Capital assets	$360,000	$320,000
Accumulated depreciation	(120,000)	(140,000)
	240,000	180,000

The company sold an asset with an original cost of $80,000 and a net book value of $20,000 for a gain of $4,000. Other capital assets were acquired for cash.

Case C	20X2	20X1
Capital assets	$1,200,000	$580,000
Accumulated depreciation	(320,000)	(220,000)
	880,000	360,000

The company sold an asset with an original cost of $160,000 and a net book value of $108,000 for a gain of $34,000. Capital assets of $400,000 were acquired by issuing a long-term note to the vendor for the full amount. Other capital assets were acquired for cash.

Required:

For each case, indicate the items and amounts that would appear on the SCF, along with their classification. Assume that the operating activities section reflects the indirect presentation format. Assume that unexplained account changes result from logical transactions.

A5-16 Statement of Cash Flows—Direct and Indirect:

Financial statements for Discovery Co. follow:

DISCOVERY CO.

Statement of Financial Position

As of 31 December	20X4	20X3
Assets		
Current assets:		
Cash	$ 37,000	$ 32,000
Accounts receivable	1,030,000	980,000
Inventory	840,000	761,600
Total current assets	1,907,000	1,773,600
Land	700,000	300,000
Plant and equipment	3,520,000	2,418,000
Less: accumulated depreciation	(1,781,600)	(1,756,000)
Patents	186,000	194,000
Total assets	$4,531,400	$2,929,600
Liabilities and Shareholders' Equity		
Liabilities:		
Current liabilities:		
Accounts payable	$ 580,000	$ 632,400
Salaries and wages payable	91,400	84,200
Income tax payable	213,800	198,600
Total current liabilities	885,200	915,200
Long-term debt	2,218,000	1,190,000
Total liabilities	3,103,200	2,105,200
Shareholders' equity:		
Common shares, no par	366,000	360,000
Retained earnings	1,062,200	464,400
Total shareholders' equity	1,428,200	824,400
Total liabilities and shareholders' equity	$4,531,400	$2,929,600

DISCOVERY CO.

Statement of Comprehensive Income

For the year ended 31 December 20X4		
Sales revenue		$7,400,000
Less expenses:		
Cost of goods sold	$4,082,000	
Selling and administrative expenses	1,090,000	
Depreciation and amortization	370,000	
Rent expense	30,000	
Miscellaneous expenses	284,000	
Total expenses		5,856,000
Other revenues and expenses:		
Interest expense	69,200	
Gain on sale of equipment	(12,000)	
Loss on debt retirement	22,000	79,200
Earnings before income tax		1,464,800
Income tax expense		623,600
Net earnings and comprehensive income		$ 841,200

Additional information:

a. The company sold equipment that had an original cost of $584,000 and a net book value of $247,600. Other equipment was purchased for cash. Patent amortization was $8,000.

b. Long-term debt with a face value of $800,000 was repaid during the year and other long-term debt was issued at a lower interest rate.

c. The company issued shares for land during the period. Other common shares were retired (bought back and cancelled) at book value.

d. Assume unexplained changes in accounts stem from logical transactions.

Required:

1. Prepare the SCF, using the indirect method. Use the two-step method for operations. Omit the separate disclosure of cash flows for interest, investment income, and income tax.

2. Prepare the SCF, using the direct method to present cash flows in the operating activities section.

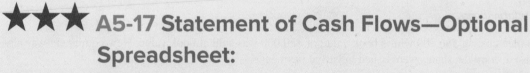

★★★ A5-17 Statement of Cash Flows—Optional Spreadsheet:

Shown below are the statements of comprehensive income, the comparative statements of financial position, and additional information useful in preparing the 20X5 SCF for Sells Co.

Statement of Comprehensive Income

For the year ended 31 December 20X5

Net sales	$ 300,000
Cost of goods sold	80,000
Gross margin	220,000
Depreciation expense	45,000
Amortization of intangibles	2,000
Other expenses	44,000
Interest expense	3,000
Income tax expense	65,000
Net earnings and comprehensive income	$ 61,000

Statement of Financial Position

As of 31 December	20X5	20X4
Cash	$ 32,000	$ 16,000
Accounts receivable	47,000	50,000
Other receivables	2,000	3,000
Inventory	32,000	30,000
Equipment	77,000	80,000
Accumulated depreciation	(5,000)	(6,000)
Intangibles, net	53,000	55,000
Total assets	$238,000	$228,000
Accounts payable	$ 60,000	$ 50,000
Income taxes payable	50,000	70,000
Interest payable	1,000	2,000
Bonds payable	—	32,000
Discount on bonds payable	—	(2,000)
Common shares	80,000	70,000
Retained earnings	47,000	6,000
Total liabilities and owners' equity	$238,000	$228,000

Additional information:

a.   Equipment costing $66,000 with a book value of $20,000 was sold at book value. New equipment was also purchased; common shares were issued in partial payment.

b. The bonds were repaid at maturity; $2,000 of bond discount was amortized in 20X5 prior to the maturity date.

Required:

Prepare the 20X5 SCF, indirect method, for Sells Co. Omit separate disclosure of cash paid for income tax and interest in the operating activities section. The solution to this assignment features an optional spreadsheet.

A5-18 Statement of Cash Flows, Partial:

The following selected information is available for Jones & Co. Ltd., for the year ended 31 December 20X8:

Statement of Comprehensive Income		
For year ended 31 December 20X8		
Sales	$1,200,000	
Gain on sale of equipment	9,000	$1,209,000
Cost of goods sold		750,000
Operating expenses, including $90,000 of depreciation		132,000
Loss on sale of land		30,000
Net earnings and comprehensive income		$ 297,000

Selected Asset, Liability, and Equity Accounts		
As of 31 December	**20X8**	**20X7**
Inventory	$ 112,000	$ 84,000
Equipment	1,100,000	920,000
Accumulated depreciation, equipment*	(644,000)	(632,000)
Land	400,000	500,000
Notes payable (long-term)*	(120,000)	(160,000)
Common shares*	(980,000)	(830,000)
Retained earnings*	(704,000)	(612,000)
*Brackets denote a credit balance.		

Other information:

1. Equipment with an original cost of $100,000 was sold for cash.
2. Other equipment was bought for cash.
3. There is no income tax expense.
4. Cash dividends were paid during the year as well as a $50,000 stock dividend that reduced retained earnings and increased common shares.

Required:

Present, in good form, the operating, investing, and financing section of the SCF for the year ended 31 December 20X8 as far as possible. Also list the non-cash transactions that would be separately disclosed. *Note:* You have not been provided with enough information (cash, other assets, and liabilities) to balance the SCF to the change in cash.

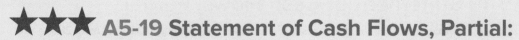

★★★ A5-19 Statement of Cash Flows, Partial:

Mackey Ltd. reported the following selected balances:

Account Title	20X4	20X3
Machinery	$283,900	$172,450
Accumulated depreciation, machinery*	(107,400)	(61,800)
Bonds payable*	(150,000)	(100,000)
Common shares*	(390,000)	(250,000)
Preferred shares*	(25,000)	(150,000)
Retained earnings*	(233,750)	(178,450)
*Brackets denote a credit balance.		

Other information:

1. There was a stock dividend of $25,000 on common shares and a cash dividend of $35,000.
2. Of the preferred shares, $50,000 were retired for cash, and $75,000 were converted into bonds payable.
3. Some common shares were issued for cash during the period.
4. Machinery with a net book value of $28,100 and an original cost of $48,650 was sold during the year at a loss of $1,050. Other machinery was purchased for cash.
5. Any unexplained change in the accounts should be assumed to be because of logical transactions.

Required:

List the items that would appear on the SCF for 20X4, considering the changes in the accounts above, and the other information. Organize your SCF appropriately (operating, investing, financing) and indicate whether each item is added or subtracted. Also list the non-cash transactions that would be separately disclosed. *Note:* You have not been provided with enough information (cash, other assets, and liabilities) to balance the SCF to the change in cash.

★★★ A5-20 Statement of Cash Flows:

The following data were provided by the accounting records of NewFort Ltd. at year-end, 31 December 20X9:

Statement of Financial Position

As of 31 December	20X9	20X8
Debits		
Cash	$ 21,000	$ 12,000
Accounts receivable	296,000	196,000
Inventory	362,000	393,000
Long-term investments	—	91,000
Property, plant, and equipment	1,196,000	960,000
Total debits	$1,875,000	$1,652,000
Credits		
Accumulated depreciation	$ 470,000	$ 576,000
Accounts payable	154,500	191,500
Interest payable	16,500	13,500
Deferred tax	71,000	47,000
Bonds payable	350,000	180,000
Common shares	480,000	250,000
Retained earnings	333,000	394,000
Total credits	$1,875,000	$1,652,000

Statement of Comprehensive Income

Year ended 31 December 20X9

Sales	$2,457,000
Cost of goods sold	(1,689,000)
Depreciation expense	(62,000)
Remaining expenses	(572,000)
Loss on sale of operating assets	(9,000)
Gain on sale of investments	36,000
Net earnings and comprehensive income	$ 161,000

Analysis of selected accounts and transactions:

a. Sold plant assets for cash; cost, $252,000; two-thirds depreciated.
b. Purchased plant assets for cash.
c. Purchased plant assets and exchanged unissued bonds payable of $190,000 in payment.
d. Sold the long-term investments for cash.
e. Retired bonds payable at maturity date by issuing common shares, $65,000.
f. Other changes in asset, liability, and equity accounts flow from logical sources.

Required:

1. Prepare the SCF, using the two-step indirect method to present the operations section. Omit separate disclosure of cash paid for interest and income tax in the operating activities section of the SCF. Include a list of non-cash transactions that would be presented in the disclosure notes.
2. Prepare the operating activities section of the SCF using the direct method.

 A5-21 Statement of Cash Flow—Optional Spreadsheet:

Todd Corp. reported the following in its 20X4 financial statements:

TODD CORP.

Statement of Comprehensive Income

For the year ended 31 December 20X4

Sales	$624,000
Cost of goods sold	(330,000)
Depreciation expense	(48,000)
Patent amortization	(1,800)
Remaining expenses	(106,200)
Net earnings and comprehensive income	$ 138,000

TODD CORP.

Statement of Financial Position

As of 31 December	20X4	20X3
Cash	$129,000	$ 90,000
Investments, short-term (common shares)	18,000	—
Accounts receivable	126,000	102,000
Inventory	90,000	60,000
Investments, long-term	60,000	—
Property, plant, and equipment (net)	354,000	360,000
Patent (net)	16,200	18,000
Other assets	42,000	42,000
Total	$835,200	$672,000
Accounts payable	$132,000	$ 72,000
Accrued expenses payable	52,200	—

Bonds payable	120,000	240,000
Common shares	267,000	210,000
Retained earnings	264,000	150,000
Total	$835,200	$672,000

Required:

1. Prepare the SCF using the indirect method. Assume that unexplained changes in the accounts are caused by logical transactions. Omit separate disclosure of cash paid for interest and income tax. The solution to this assignment features an optional spreadsheet.
2. Prepare the operating activities section of the SCF using the direct method.

 ## A5-22 Calculate Cash Flows—Interest and Income Tax:

Information related to various financial statement elements is provided for three cases:

Case A   Tax expense was $341,400. The deferred tax liability had an opening balance of $92,000 and a closing balance of $103,000. Income tax payable declined by $22,400 during the year.

Case B   Interest expense was $174,000. Discount amortization was $10,000 during the year. Interest payable had an opening balance of $11,000 and a closing balance of $13,400.

Case C   Interest revenue was $87,000. Interest receivable had an opening balance of $14,400 and a closing balance of $8,200.

Required:

For each case, calculate the cash inflow or outflow related to the revenue or expense.

 ## A5-23 Optional Presentation Alternatives, Direct Method:

The SCF for MacLaren Supplies Ltd., using the direct method of presentation for operating activities, is shown below.

MACLAREN SUPPLIES LTD.

Statement of Cash Flows

Year ended 31 December 20X5

Operating Activities	
Cash received from customers	$406,600
Cash paid for operating expenses	(306,300)
Cash paid for interest	(7,700)

Cash paid for income tax	(20,200)	
Cash received from investment income	4,900	
Cash from operating		$ 77,300
Investing Activities		
Sold long-term investment	36,000	
Purchased fixed assets	(28,400)	
Cash from investing		7,600
Financing Activities		
Dividends paid	(20,000)	
Bonds payable retired	(60,000)	
Cash used for financing		(80,000)
Net increase in cash during the year		4,900
Cash balance, beginning of the year		16,000
Cash balance, end of the year		$20,900

Required:

1. Some of the items included in operating activities, above, may be presented in other sections of the SCF. Explain the alternatives open to the company. What alternative is open for dividends paid, now in financing activities?

2. Redraft the SCF, classifying all items identified in requirement 1 into sections *other than* operating activities.

3. Return to the SCF as presented in the question. Redraft the SCF, classifying interest and dividends paid in operating activities.

4. Explain why companies might choose the presentations provided in requirement 2 or 3.

★★ A5-24 Optional Presentation Alternatives, Indirect Method:

The SCF for Wave Electronics Ltd., using the indirect method of presentation for operating activities, is shown below.

WAVE ELECTRONICS LTD.	
Statement of Cash Flows	
Year ended 31 December 20X2	
Operating activities:	
Net earnings	$ 28,200
Adjustments:	
Depreciation and amortization	14,200

Income tax expense	16,000	
Interest expense	23,500	
Dividend revenue	(6,800)	
Gain on sale of investments	(10,000)	
	65,100	
Changes in working capital:		
Decrease in accounts receivable	7,500	
Decrease in inventory	18,400	
Cash paid for interest	(24,000)	
Cash paid for income tax	(11,100)	
Cash received from dividend revenue	5,600	
Cash from operating		$61,500
Investing activities:		
Sold long-term investment	45,000	
Purchased fixed assets	(138,400)	
Cash for investing		(93,400)
Financing activities:		
Dividends paid	(20,000)	
Bonds payable issued	60,000	
Cash for financing		40,000
Net increase in cash during the year		8,100
Cash balance, beginning of the year		(1,300)
Cash balance, end of the year		$ 6,800

Required:

1. Some of the items included in operating activities, above, may be presented in other sections of the SCF. Explain the alternatives open to the company. What alternative is open for dividends paid, now in financing activities?

2. Redraft the SCF, reclassifying all items identified in requirement 1 into sections *other than* operating activities.

3. Return to the SCF as presented in the question. Redraft the SCF, classifying interest and dividends paid in operating activities.

4. Explain why the presentation prepared in requirement 2 or 3 may be preferable.

A5-25 Presentation of Interest and Tax, Indirect Method:

Return to the facts of A5-16.

Required:

1. Prepare the operating activities section of the SCF, using the indirect method of presentation but incorporating separate disclosure of income tax paid and interest paid within the operating activities section.
2. In what sections of the SCF could each of interest paid, investment revenue received, and dividends paid be classified?

 ## A5-26 Presentation of Interest and Tax, Indirect Method:

Return to the facts of A5-17.

Required:

1. Prepare the operating activities section of the SCF, using the indirect method of presentation, but incorporating separate disclosure of income tax paid and interest paid within the operating activities section.
2. In what sections of the SCF could each of interest paid, investment revenue received, and dividends paid be classified?

 ## A5-27 ASPE—Statement of Cash Flows:

Return to the facts of A5-24.

Required:

1. Prepare the operating activities section of the SCF incorporating ASPE classification and policy decisions. Include supplemental disclosure of interest paid, income tax paid, and dividend revenue received. Tax payable increased by $4,900, dividends receivable increased by $1,200, and prepaid interest increased by $500.
2. Explain the classification requirements that are different between ASPE and IFRS.

 ## A5-28 ASPE—Statement of Cash Flows:

The records of Koop Co. provided the following information for the year ended 31 December 20X8:

Statement of Comprehensive Income

For the year ended 31 December 20X8

Sales revenue	$ 360,000
Cost of goods sold	(262,000)
Depreciation expense	(20,000)
Insurance expense	(2,000)
Interest expense	(4,000)
Salaries and wages expense	(24,000)
Remaining expenses	(26,000)
Loss on sale of equipment	(4,000)
Income tax expense	(16,000)
Net earnings and comprehensive income	$ 2,000

Statement of Financial Position

As of 31 December	20X8	20X7
Cash	$ 122,000	$ 70,000
Accounts receivable	62,000	57,000
Inventory	31,000	20,000
Prepaid interest	2,800	4,800
Buildings and equipment	162,000	160,000
Accumulated depreciation	(42,000)	(40,000)
Land	162,200	80,200
Total	$500,000	$352,000
Accounts payable	$ 41,000	$ 36,000
Wages payable	4,000	8,000
Income tax payable	11,000	—
Notes payable, long-term	112,000	60,000
Common shares	286,000	200,000
Retained earnings	46,000	48,000
Total	$500,000	$352,000

Additional information:

a. Sold equipment for cash (cost, $30,000; accumulated depreciation, $18,000).
b. Purchased land, $40,000 cash.
c. Acquired land for $42,000 and issued common shares as payment in full.

d. Acquired equipment, cost $32,000; issued a $32,000, three-year, interest-bearing note payable.

Required:

Prepare the SCF, using the two-step indirect method. Analyze every account to ensure all changes are included. Assume unexplained changes are from logical sources. Include required note disclosure of non-cash transactions. Prepare separate disclosure of cash paid for interest and income tax, as is required by ASPE.

 A5-29 ASPE—Statement of Cash Flows:

You are presented with the following data from Jake Doyle Inc. for the year ended 31 December 20X1.

JAKE DOYLE INC.			
Statement of Financial Position			
As at 31 December			
	20X1	**20X0**	**Change**
Debits			
Cash	$ 41,000	$ 32,000	$ 9,000
Accounts receivable	256,000	196,000	60,000
Inventory	342,000	393,000	(51,000)
Long-term investments	—	71,000	(71,000)
Property, plant, and equipment	1,105,000	960,000	145,000
Total debits	$1,744,000	$1,652,000	
Credits			
Accumulated depreciation	$ 484,000	$ 576,000	$ (92,000)
Accounts payable	124,500	201,500	(77,000)
Interest payable	3,250	3,500	(250)
Income tax payable	49,550	47,000	2,550
Bonds payable	300,000	180,000	120,000
Common shares	300,000	250,000	50,000
Retained earnings	482,700	394,000	88,700
Total credits	$1,744,000	$1,652,000	

JAKE DOYLE INC.	
Statement of Comprehensive Income	
For the year ended 31 December 20X1	
Sales	$1,523,000
Cost of goods sold	(689,000)
Depreciation expense	(68,000)

Interest expense	(16,800)
Income tax expense	(55,000)
Other expenses	(457,200)
Loss on sale of operational assets	(7,200)
Gain on sale of investments	6,540
Net earnings and comprehensive income	$ 236,340

Additional information:

a. Sold property, plant, and equipment for cash. Cost of the assets was $236,000; net book value was $76,000.
b. Purchased equipment and exchanged unissued bonds payable of $120,000 in payment.
c. Purchased other equipment for cash.
d. Sold the long-term investments for cash.

Required:

1. Calculate cash paid for each of interest and income taxes. This is required under ASPE as separate disclosure.
2. Prepare the investing section of SCF and any disclosure notes for non-cash investing activities.

(Judy Cumby, used with permission.)

 **A5-30 Integrative Problem, Chapters 1–5:**

Account balances, taken from the ledger of Argot Flooring Ltd. as of 31 December 20X5, appear below.

Accounts payable	$280,000	Land	$ 398,000
Accounts receivable	632,000	General operating expenses	338,000
Accumulated depreciation, building equipment	42,000	Notes payable	232,000
Allowance for doubtful accounts	3,000	Notes receivable	120,000
Building and equipment	198,000	Property tax expense	3,200
Common shares	204,100	Cost of goods sold	1,042,000
Dividends declared	80,000	Cash	?
Deferred tax liability	116,700	Retained earnings, 1 January 20X5	806,400
Income tax expense[*]	334,600	Revenue	2,632,000
Interest revenue	5,000	Salaries expense	232,000
Inventory, 31 December 20X5	480,000	Store supplies inventory	12,400
		Unearned revenue	32,000

*Assume this amount is properly stated after all subsequent adjustments are considered.

Additional information:

1. Store supplies were counted at 31 December and found to be valued at $5,600.
2. Depreciation of building and equipment is over eight years with an expected salvage value of $10,000.
3. Property taxes of $3,200 were paid on 1 October 20X5 and relate to the year 1 October 20X5 to 30 September 20X6.
4. The note payable was issued on 1 November 20X5 and has an annual interest rate of 12%. Interest must be paid each 30 October along with $30,000 of principal. Interest payable has not been recorded.
5. The note receivable has been outstanding all year. Interest at 10% is collected each 1 June. The note is due 1 June 20X11. Interest receivable has not been recorded.
6. The allowance for doubtful accounts now has a $3,000 credit balance. Aging of accounts receivable indicates that $76,000 of the accounts are doubtful.
7. Unearned revenue represents an advance payment from a customer; 75% was still unearned at year-end.
8. At year-end, $10,000 (at retail value) of goods was shipped to customers, but the sale was not yet recorded. Correctly, the goods were not included in closing inventory. The revenue must be recorded.

Required:

1. Explain the meaning of GAAP.
2. Identify common objectives of financial reporting.
3. Prepare adjusting journal entries to reflect the additional information provided above.
4. Explain the following (a) through (d), and give an example of an adjusting journal entry in requirement 3 caused by each:
    a. Time-period assumption
    b. Continuity assumption
    c. Accrual concept
5. Prepare a multiple-step classified statement of comprehensive income, a statement of changes in equity, and a classified statement of financial position based on the adjusted accounts. There was no change in the common share account during the year. Use cash as a balancing figure on the SFP.
6. Assume that accounts have changed (*after the entries made in requirement 3*) as follows over the period:

Accounts receivable (net)	$41,900	decrease
Interest receivable	no change	
Inventory	136,000	increase
Store supplies inventory	8,000	decrease
Prepaid property tax	no change	
Buildings and equipment	40,000	increase
Accounts payable	75,000	increase
Interest payable	4,640	increase
Notes payable	232,000	increase

Deferred tax liability	26,400 increase
Unearned revenue	24,000 increase

Prepare the operating activities section of the SCF using the indirect method of presentation.

Begin the SCF with net earnings. Include separate disclosure of cash flows on the face of the SCF for interest paid and received and income tax paid.

APPENDIX

SPREADSHEET METHOD

The main body of this chapter pointed out that the analytical method used to derive the SCF is not important; what matters is the result. This chapter has illustrated two approaches—the ad hoc approach and the T-account approach. Another method that is popular, especially when complete documentation is important, is the spreadsheet approach. In essence, this approach puts the T-account data into columnar form.

SPREADSHEET PROCEDURES

To set up the spreadsheet, transfer the accounts and account balances from the statement of financial position to a four-column spreadsheet. Exhibit 5-A1 demonstrates the set-up for Ling Corp., based on the chapter example and data in Exhibit 5-7. The 20X4 asset, liability, and equity account balances are in the first column, and the 20X5 balances are in the last column. Reconciling entries are entered in the two middle columns.

EXHIBIT 5-A1

LING CORP.

Statement of Cash Flows Worksheet

Accounts	31 December 20X4	Key	Debit	Credit	Key	31 December 20X5
				Reconciliation		
Assets:						
Cash	$ 36,000	(s)	$ 14,000			$ 50,000
Short-term investments	34,000			$ 24,000	(s)	10,000
Accounts receivable	70,000	(i)	14,000			84,000
Inventories	30,000	(j)	12,000			42,000
Prepaid expenses	11,000	(k)	4,000			15,000

Land	50,000					50,000
Plant and equipment	615,000	(l)	150,000	25,000 (f)		740,000
Accumulated depreciation	(215,000)	(f)	20,000	65,000 (c)		(260,000)
Capitalized development costs	76,000	(m)	11,000	5,000 (d)		82,000
Long-term investments	70,000	(e)	22,000			92,000
Total assets	$777,000					$905,000
Liabilities and shareholders' equity:						
Bank loan	$ 5,000			15,000 (n)		$ 20,000
Accounts payable	45,000	(o)	9,000			36,000
Dividends payable	5,000			5,000 (p)		10,000
Bonds payable	133,000	(g)	20,000	33,000 (h)		146,000
Deferred tax	24,000			3,000 (q)		27,000
Preferred shares	120,000			22,000 (e)		142,000
Common shares	180,000			50,000 (r)		230,000
Retained earnings	265,000	(b)	35,000	64,000 (a)		294,000
Total equities	$777,000		$ 311,000	$311,000		$905,000

Components of the Statement of Cash Flows

Operating activities:

Net earnings	(a)	$ 64,000	
Non-cash items:			
Depreciation expense	(c)	65,000	
Amortization of development costs	(d)	5,000	
Gain on sale of equipment			$ 4,000 (f)
Working capital changes:			
Increase in accounts receivable			14,000 (i)
Increase in inventory			12,000 (j)
Increase in prepaid expenses			4,000 (k)
Decrease in accounts payable			9,000 (o)
Increase in deferred tax	(q)	3,000	$ 94,000

Investing activities:

Proceeds from equipment sold	(f)	9,000	
Purchase of plant and equipment			150,000 (l)

Development costs			_____	11,000	(m)	(152,000)
Financing activities:						
Dividends paid				35,000	(b)	
Increase in dividends payable	(p)	5,000				
Bonds retired				20,000	(g)	
Increase in short-term bank loan	(n)	15,000				
Bonds issued	(h)	33,000				
Common shares issued	(r)	50,000		_____		48,000
Subtotal			249,000	259,000		
Change in cash and cash equivalents	(s)	10,000		_____		$ (10,000)
			$259,000	$259,000		

The reconciling entries are exactly the same for the spreadsheet and the T-accounts. Refer to the chapter example for an explanation of the cross-referenced entries. One additional entry is needed on the spreadsheet to record the change in cash.

s. The final reconciling entry transfers the change in cash and cash equivalents to the lower spreadsheet section. The $14,000 increase in cash and the $24,000 decrease in short-term investments are reconciled as follows:

Cash	14,000	
Change in cash and cash equivalents	10,000	
Short-term liquid investments		24,000

Entering the net change into the lower part of the statement balances the inflows and outflows. Totalling the debit and credit columns in the upper part of the worksheet reveals that they are in balance (at $311,000). The total of the debit and credit columns is meaningless *except* for the important fact that they balance. Any imbalance would indicate a debit–credit imbalance in the reconciliation entries.

The lower section of Exhibit 5-A1 now contains all the information necessary for preparing the SCF. This SCF is shown in Exhibit 5-9 in the chapter.

A disadvantage of spreadsheets is the time it takes to format and to do all the adding and balancing. This can be counteracted by the use of electronic programs with macros and the like. Spreadsheets are commonly used in very complex situations or ones in which work has to be carefully documented so it can be reviewed.

SUMMARY OF KEY POINTS

1. The spreadsheet method is an alternative way to analyze information prior to preparing the SCF. The spreadsheet method is an analytical approach; it is *not* a method of presentation.

2. In setting up a spreadsheet, opening balances are entered in the first column of a four-column spreadsheet, and closing balances in the final column. Reconciling entries are entered in the middle two columns. Items that involve cash flow are collected at the bottom of the spreadsheet.

Source: (Globe and money) © Vstock LLC/Getty Images RF; (Skyscrapers) © Arpad Benedek/Getty Images RF; (Canadian flag) © BjArn Kindler/Getty Images RF; (Tablet, pen, keyboard) © John Lamb/Getty Images RF.

CHAPTER 6

Revenue Recognition

INTRODUCTION

Quebec-based CAE Inc. is the world's dominant manufacturer of flight simulators. Simulators are built for CAE's clients under long-term contracts that encompass design, engineering, and manufacturing. In addition, contracts may involve the provision of spare parts, maintenance, flight schools and other training services. Clearly, CAE's revenue-generating activities are numerous and complex. When should this revenue be recorded in earnings?

Revenue recognition is probably the most difficult single issue in accounting, largely because modern business activities can be very complex. Economic activity takes many months or many years to complete. In complex and long-term earnings processes, it is not at all obvious just when revenue should be recognized. As well, many "sales" actually involve the delivery of more than one product and/or service. How should the revenue for each component be measured and when should the revenue for each component be recognized?

This chapter will examine the nature of the earnings process and the various points at which revenue could be recognized, depending on the nature of the revenue-earning process. The chapter also deals with measuring the amount of revenue attached to separate activities.

All of the issues in revenue recognition have a direct impact on profit or loss measurement—a relatively small change in revenue recognition can have a major impact on earnings. Therefore, many ethical implications are associated with the choice of revenue recognition policies. This is an area in which judgement plays an important role.

To enhance comparability and reliability across all types of revenue transactions, accounting standard-setters have attempted to standardize and narrow revenue recognition choices by providing more explicit guidance. After many years of review and consultation, the IASB recently revised the standard for revenue recognition that will be effective for annual reporting periods beginning on or after 1 January 2018, with earlier adoption permitted. This chapter discusses revenue recognition under the new standards.

DEFINITIONS

Revenue and Expense

What is revenue? Revenue and expense are defined by changes in net assets (i.e., assets minus liabilities) that are not due to capital transactions with shareholders. As we pointed out in Chapter 2, IFRS defines revenue as follows:

- **Revenue** arises from (1) inflows of cash, increases in accounts receivable, or other increases in a business's assets, (2) settlements of its liabilities, or (3) a combination of the two. These inflows must be derived from delivering or producing goods, rendering services, or performing other activities that constitute a company's business operations over a specific period of time.
- Conversely, **expenses** arise from outflows of assets or increases in liabilities that result from delivering or producing goods, rendering services, or performing other activities that constitute a company's business operations over a specific period of time.

Revenues and expenses are reported on the SCI (statement of comprehensive income, or statement of profit or loss if a two-statement format is used), but their recognition is the result of changes that occur on the statement of financial position.

For example, suppose that a company sells merchandise on credit:

- Creating the account receivable increases assets. The increase is the result of an ongoing business operation, and therefore the increase in net assets constitutes *revenue*.
- Reducing inventory *decreases* assets. The reduction is the result of an ongoing business operation, and therefore the reduction in assets is an *expense*.

Thus, *revenue and expenses are defined by changes in net assets and liabilities arising from earnings-generating activities.* This is the asset–liability definitional approach to measuring earnings.

The increase in net assets is paramount; *revenue can be recognized only when net assets are increased as the result of a contractual relationship with a customer or client.*

Gains and Losses versus Revenue and Expense

Revenue and expenses, by definition, arise in the course of a company's ordinary business activities. As you know from Chapter 2, *gains and losses* are also included in earnings but have a different nature. They may or may not arise from a company's ordinary course of business.

A gain or loss can arise from either

- (1) peripheral transactions or events; examples are a gain on the sale of land or the sale of capital assets; or
- (2) transactions and events relating to the enterprise's principal lines of business; an example is remeasurement of assets to recoverable amounts.

Presentation

Gains and losses are often reported as a net amount—for example, the gain on sale of land is shown net of any related expenses. In contrast, revenue is reported at the **gross amount** with expenses listed separately.

Assume that a company sold a piece of land for $100,000. The land has a cost of $75,000. If the company was a developer whose normal business was land sales, revenue of $100,000 would be reported with cost of land sold reported at $75,000. If the sale of land was peripheral, a gain on sale of land for $25,000 would be reported. The bottom line is not affected, but presentation is different, and as a result revenue trends and patterns are different.

THE REVENUE RECOGNITION PROCESS

Economic Value Added

At a *conceptual* level, a firm earns revenue when it engages in activities that increase the value of an item or service. A company buys raw materials and supplies, and then employees perform services that change the raw materials into a product of higher value. The final product becomes worth more than the cost of its inputs in materials and labour. The difference between the input cost and the eventual value of the product (or service) is known as the **economic value added (EVA)**.

Suppose that an automobile parts manufacturer has a contract from Ford to produce automobile fenders. The manufacturer increases the value of sheet metal when it undertakes activities to cut, shape, and weld the sheet metal into fenders. Transporting completed fenders to a warehouse also adds value, because it makes the fenders available for delivery and use by Ford. The earnings process is fully completed when the fenders are sold and delivered to Ford in return for cash or a promise to pay cash. Paperwork must be completed and cash collected. Any deficient fenders must be fixed or replaced. All of these activities, and many more, are part of the earnings process.

Although added value is created throughout the earnings process, the impact on net assets is difficult to measure. *Accountants cannot recognize revenue and expenses until they become measurable.* Thus, the ability to measure the *impact on net assets* is essential. Relevance and representational faithfulness depend on reasonably accurate measurement of changes in assets and liabilities.

GENERAL REVENUE RECOGNITION PRINCIPLE

The Earnings-Based Approach

As noted earlier in the introduction to this chapter, the standards for recognizing and measuring revenue have recently undergone significant changes. Previously, revenue was recognized as "earned," using the **earnings-based approach.** Under standards in effect in prior years, revenue was recognized in the financial statements when:

(1)   Performance was complete and had been accepted by the customer;

(2)   Consideration, as well as any future costs, could be measured with reasonable assurance; and

(3)   Collection was reasonably assured.

As these earlier standards were difficult to implement and inconsistently applied across industries, the IASB (and FASB) began a joint project to update revenue recognition standards for principles that could be used for any type of revenue transaction, regardless of industry. The new standard requires companies to adopt a *contract-based approach*.

The Contract-Based Approach

The "contract basis" of reporting revenue is based on *enforceable rights and obligations* as contained in a contract between buyer and seller. In such a contract, the seller makes a commitment to transfer the goods and/or services to the buyer—the **performance obligation**. In return, the buyer agrees to pay some amount of **consideration**. Consideration is the dollar value, where usually, net assets increase, through an inflow of cash, a new accounts receivable, and so on. Less frequently, liabilities might be reduced as consideration, perhaps through forgiveness of debt.

The core principle of the **contract-based approach** *is that the seller recognizes revenue at the time there is a transfer of promised goods or services (performance is completed) to a buyer. The amount to be recognized is the expected amount of consideration for the transfer under the contract.*

This core principle sounds simple. Indeed, in many businesses, revenue recognition is not a major challenge. In other businesses, however, the challenge can be quite significant. There are two general issues:

1. *How is the SFP affected?* That is, accounting policy must dictate *when and how much* to recognize for any *contract assets*, *contract liabilities*, and accounts receivable on the statement of financial position; and

2. *How is the SCI affected?* Accounting policy must dictate *when and how much* to recognize as *revenue* in earnings.

Recognition on the Statement of Financial Position

From the perspective of the statement of financial position, as performance progresses during a contract, an asset or liability will arise depending on how much the customer has paid (if any) in comparison to how much work has been completed by the seller.

A **contract asset** results when the seller has transferred the good or service to the customer but has only a *conditional* right to the consideration dependent on some further future performance of another obligation (not the passage of time). As we will see, a *contract asset* differs from an *account receivable*; an account receivable is recorded once the transfer is complete and the entity has an *unconditional* right to be paid.

A **contract liability** arises when the customer has paid consideration, but the seller still has the obligation to transfer the goods and services. Other terms such as deferred or unearned revenue can also be used.

The diagram below (Exhibit 6-1) depicts how these accounts would be used under different situations.

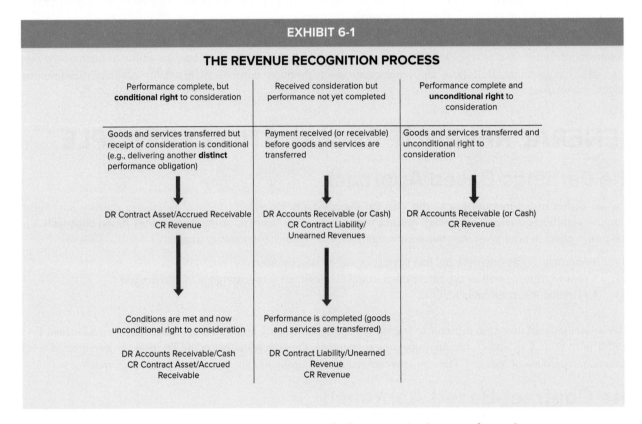

Recognition in the Statement of Comprehensive Income

As stated above, the seller recognizes revenue at the time there is a transfer of promised goods or services to a buyer.

When to recognize revenue can be very straightforward, for example when a customer takes delivery of all the goods on one date. In other cases, it can be complex.

How much revenue to recognize can also present problems. There are two potential problems:

- Assigning revenue to different parts of a complex contract, known as *separate performance obligations*; and
- Measuring the amount of revenue when the contract amount may vary throughout the contract or payments are made over a long period of time.

The complexities of these issues will be illustrated in later examples.

Contract-Based Revenue Recognition Requirements

In order to determine when revenue should be recognized, five steps must be addressed for each customer contract:

1. Identify the contract with the customer;
2. Identify separate performance obligations, if they exist.
3. Determine the overall transaction price;
4. Allocate the transaction price to the separate performance obligations; and
5. Determine when the performance obligation is satisfied and revenue can be recognized.

Refer to Exhibit 6-2, where the specific criteria for assessing each of these steps are listed. These criteria will be described in the sections that follow.

EXHIBIT 6-2		
THE FIVE STEPS FOR REVENUE RECOGNITION		
Step	**Description**	**Criteria to Be Met**
1. Identify the contract with the customer.	Contract: • Is written, oral, or implied by common business practice; and • Must be enforceable.	• Commercial substance exists; • Buyer and seller have approved the contract and are committed to perform; • Rights regarding transfer of goods and services can be identified; • Payment terms are specified; and • Collection of consideration is probable.
2. Identify separate performance obligations, if they exist.	Does the contract involve **separate and distinct** goods and services to be provided?	Separate and distinct when: • Customer can benefit from the good or service either on its own or with other readily available resources; and • Good or service is separately identifiable.
3. Determine the overall transaction price.	Consider discounts, rebates, incentives, penalties, variable consideration, and present value of future payments.	Two methods can be used: • Expected value method (using weighted probability of various outcomes); or • The most likely amount.
4. Allocate the transaction price to the separate performance obligations identified in step 2.	Pro-rate the price based on the *stand-alone value* of each separate performance obligation.	*Stand-alone value* can be determined: • As the price the item is separately sold for; • Estimated based on competitor's selling price; or

| 5. Determine when the performance obligation is complete and revenue can be recognized. | Completion occurs when **control** of the good or service is transferred to the customer. Control is the ability to direct the use, and obtain the benefits, of the good or service.

Note that completion can be at a single point in time or over a period of time. One of three specific criteria must be met to recognize revenue over time. When none of these are met, the contract revenue is recognized at a single point in time (by default). | • Estimated based on the cost plus margin approach.

In cases in which a stand-alone value cannot be determined for each obligation, the residual approach is acceptable.

Indications of transfer of control:
• Seller has right to payment;
• Legal title, physical possession, and/or significant risks and rewards have been transferred; and
• Customer has accepted the item. |

Collectability

Collectability refers to the customer's ability and intention to pay the consideration agreed to in the contract to ensure that the contract is valid. *The company must assess whether collection under the contract is probable when the consideration is due.* If this criterion is not met, the contract is seen not to be valid, and revenue cannot be recognized until consideration is received (effectively accounting for this transaction on a cash basis).

CONCEPT **REVIEW**

1. How is a *gain* different than a *revenue*?
2. What is the core principle of the contract-based approach to revenue recognition?
3. What accounts might appear on the statement of financial position with respect to a revenue contract prior to revenue recognition?
4. List the five steps to be assessed in determining when revenue should be recognized.

CONTRACT COSTS

Costs to Fulfill a Contract

If the costs to fulfill a contract cannot be classified as inventory, as property, plant, and equipment, or as an intangible asset, they are recognized as an asset called **contract costs**, as long as:

• The costs *relate directly to performance of that contract, generate or enhance resources used to satisfy the contract, and are expected to be recovered.* Examples are direct labour and materials and an allocation of other costs incurred for the contract including insurance, depreciation, supervisor salaries; or

- Those costs the customer has agreed to reimburse. Examples are photocopying expenses or travel expenses that will be added to an invoice on the completion of a consulting contract.

These contract costs will be expensed as the goods or services are transferred to the customer. If transfer takes place over time, the costs will be expensed using an amortization rate that is the same as the rate of transfer. The amortization rate must be reviewed at each reporting period to ensure that it still represents the pattern of transfer.

In addition, the contract cost asset will be tested for impairment. An impairment loss will result when the carrying cost of the asset exceeds the consideration to be received less remaining costs required to complete the contract. This loss can be subsequently reversed if the impairment conditions cease to exist.

Note that costs related to general and administration and wasted materials, labour and other resources, would be expensed immediately and not capitalized.

Costs to Obtain a Contract

Costs can also be incurred to initially obtain a contract. These types of costs can be recognized as an asset if they would not have been incurred otherwise and are expected to be recovered either directly from the customer or as part of the profit margin in the contract. The asset is amortized and tested for impairment as described above. For practical purposes, if the amortization period is likely to be less than one year, these costs are immediately expensed as incurred.

Example 1

RDI is an executive search firm that has been contracted to hire a new executive director for a client. RDI will recognize revenue on completion of the contract, which will end when the new executive director is selected. It will likely take about four months to complete the work. During this period, costs directly related to this contract will be reported as contract costs as they do not qualify as inventory. When the performance obligation is complete and revenue is recognized, these costs will be expensed. If there is a report date (a year-end for example) during this contract period, the contract costs will have to be assessed for impairment at that time.

Example 2

A software company entered into a contract to provide payroll services for a customer over a three year period. The company incurred initial costs required to integrate with the customer's computer systems so that it could build the appropriate platforms and software to prepare the weekly payroll. Costs of this initial set-up included: design $27,000; hardware $150,000; software $45,000; and testing and migration to the new platform $30,000. All of these costs relate to the fulfillment of the contract and are capitalized to contract costs. These total costs of $252,000 will be amortized on a monthly basis over the 36 months of the contract. They will also be tested for impairment to ensure they are still recoverable.

TRANSFER OF GOODS AND SERVICES AT A SINGLE POINT IN TIME

Revenue is recognized when control of the good or service is transferred. This can be over time or at a single point in time. If a contract does not meet one of the criteria to be recognized over time, then it is recognized at a single point in time. The specific criteria that must be met to recognize revenue over time are discussed in detail later in this chapter.

Recognition at Delivery

In many cases, revenue recognition is straightforward. For example, consider a simple transaction that involves the sale of goods in a retail store on 30 November. The item has a price tag of $100. At the checkout counter, the customer receives a bill that lists the item, its price, and the terms of the sale. Applying the five steps:

1. *Identify the contract with the customer.* By common business practice, the bill becomes the contract between the customer and the seller. The contract is for the seller to "deliver" the item to the customer. In return, the customer will pay the required amount.

2. *Identify separate performance obligations, if they exist.* In this example, only one performance obligation is required: the delivery of the goods to the customer.

3. *Determine the overall contract price.* The contract price is the $100 price tag on the item.

4. *Allocate the contract price to the separate performance obligations.* Since there is only one performance obligation, there is no need for this step.

5. *Determine when the performance obligation is satisfied and revenue can be recognized.* The performance obligation is complete once control of the item is transferred to the customer. This transfer takes place at the cash register, once the customer has paid the amount owing.

Based on the five steps, the revenue is recognized at the point in time when the item is delivered to the customer. On 30 November, revenue is credited for $100 and cash is debited for $100. Cost of goods sold is also recorded and inventory is reduced.

We can make this a little more complicated and add a new fact that the customer prepaid a deposit of $75 to hold the item on 29 October. The $75 represents a *contract liability* since the customer has paid some consideration, but the seller has not yet performed the obligation. On 29 October, the entry is as follows:

Dr. Cash	75	
Cr. Contract liability		75

On 30 November the customer now receives the item and pays the remaining $25. The performance obligation is now complete and the full amount of revenue is recognized. The entry on 30 November would be:

Dr. Cash	25	
Dr. Contract liability	75	
Cr. Revenue		100

Short-Term Service Revenue

Revenue from *short-term* services rendered is recognized when the services have been completed and accepted by the client. Services such as hairdressing, carpet cleaning, and repairs to equipment might be examples of these types of services that are transferred at the date of delivery. There is no great challenge to accounting for these services. More of a challenge arises when service is provided over a long period of time, which we will address later in this chapter.

Impact on Net Assets

Recall that revenue has been defined as *a change in net assets.* Exhibit 6-3 illustrates a situation in which a company buys inventory, customizes it, and then holds it until sold. It is sold on account and 30 days later the customer pays the agreed consideration. Exhibit 6-3 traces the appropriate entries if delivery is considered to be the date of transfer of control. Costs for customization and pre-delivery are added to the inventory account. When the item is delivered, the sales revenue is recognized (with an offsetting account receivable) and inventory (including the customization and pre-delivery costs) is expensed. Note that:

- Net assets (i.e., assets minus liabilities) are increased only at the date of transfer, which is the date of revenue recognition.
- Transactions before revenue recognition change assets: the change is in the *composition* of assets but not the *total* of net assets.
  - Inventory is distinct from the account receivable but both are assets.
- Transactions after revenue recognition likewise change the *composition* but not the *total* of net assets.

EXHIBIT 6-3

REVENUE RECOGNITION: IMPACT ON NET ASSETS

Data

15 January	Inventory purchased, $14,500.
17 January	Inventory repackaged and customized—labour and materials cost $2,250. Now ready for sale.
6 March	Inventory delivered to customer on account. Agreed-upon price, $28,000. Control is transferred to customer at the time of delivery.
30 April	Customer pays 100% of sales price.

Date	Revenue Recognized on Delivery		Effect on Net Assets
15 Jan.	Inventory	14,500	none
	Cash, A/P, etc.	14,500	
17 Jan.	Inventory	2,250	none
	Cash, A/P, etc.	2,250	
6 March	Accounts receivable	28,000	Increases net assets by $11,250
	Revenue	28,000	
	Cost of goods sold	16,750	
	Inventory	16,750	
30 April	Cash	28,000	none
	Accounts receivable	28,000	

On 6 March, when control is transferred on delivery, revenue is recognized at this single point in time.

This was a simple transaction involving the delivery of a good. The exact point of transfer of control can become more complicated when the customer has a right of return or the seller provides a warranty.

Sale with a Right of Return

In many industries, it is customary practice to allow customers to return unused products within a specified return period and receive a full refund or another type of product in exchange. In the textbook industry and manufacturing industries, for example, contract terms normally allow customers the right to return goods under certain conditions and over long periods of time after control has been transferred. From an accounting perspective, sales returns is a form of variable consideration.

Consequently, revenue can only be recognized to the extent that it is highly probable a reversal would not occur. Sales with a right of return can be accounted for as follows:

- *If the quantity of returns is reasonably predictable*, the company can recognize revenue at delivery for the estimated volume of goods that will not be returned. A liability representing the amount expected to be refunded on return must also be recorded at the time of the sale. An asset (with a corresponding adjustment to cost of goods sold) is recorded for the product expected to be returned when the liability is settled.

- *If returns are not predictable, revenue is deferred (as a contract liability) until the return situation is resolved.*

Example—Returns Predictable

Under contract, Rigour Corp. delivers 200 units to Customer A for $120 each on 1 March. Rigour's documented policy is to allow a customer to return any unused product within 60 days and receive a full refund. The cost of each product is $90. Based on historical experience, Rigour estimates that 3% of the units will be returned. Rigour expects that the returned products can be resold.

Five Steps

Applying the five steps:

1. *Identify the contract with the customer.* As noted, there is a contract between Rigour and the customer obligating Rigour to "deliver" 200 units, but also to "stand ready" to take back any unused product within 60 days of the sale.

2. *Identify separate performance obligations, if they exist.* There is one performance obligation requiring Rigour to deliver the 200 units.

3. *Determine the overall contract price.* The contract price is $24,000, as set in the contract.

4. *Allocate the contract price to the separate performance obligations.* Since there is only one performance obligation, there is no need for this step.

5. *Determine when the performance obligation is satisfied and revenue can be recognized.* The performance obligation is complete once control of the units is transferred to the customer. However, there is some uncertainty as to the number of units that might actually remain with the customer and not be returned. Until the 60-day period is over, Rigour can only estimate the number of units where the transfer of control is complete. From past experience, Rigour assumes that 6 (200 × 3%) units with a price of $720 ($120 × 6 units) and a cost of $540 ($90 × 6 units) will be returned.

Entries

Delivery of the 200 units to the customer constitutes transfer of control. Rigour estimates revenue to be the most likely consideration it will receive. This amount is $23,280, which represents 194 (200 units × 97%) products expected to be retained by the customer, multiplied by the price of $120 per unit. At the same time, a **refund liability** for the products expected to be returned will be reported at $720. This is based on 6 units expected to be returned (3% × 200 units) at a price of $120 per unit. A **right to recovery asset** for the cost of units expected to be returned will also be recorded as $540 (6 units at $90 each). This will result in a cost of goods sold equal to $17,460, which represents 194 units at $90 each. Below are the entries to record the sale on delivery to the customer:

1 March:		
Dr. Accounts receivable (200 × $120)	24,000	
Cr. Revenue		23,280
Cr. Refund liability		720
Dr. Cost of goods sold	17,460	
Dr. Right to recovery asset	540	
Cr. Inventory (200 × $90)		18,000

Once the return period has passed, any remaining amount in the refund liability and right to recovery asset accounts is recorded as revenue and expense. Assume that in the above example, there were only two units returned on 4 April and no additional products were returned by 29 April, the end of the return period. The entries:

4 April:		
Dr. Refund liability (2 × $120)	240	
Cr. Accounts receivable (or cash)		240
Dr. Inventory (2 × $90)	180	
Cr. Right to recovery asset		180
29 April:		
Dr. Refund liability (4 × $120)	480	
Cr. Revenue		480
Dr. Cost of goods sold (4 × 90)	360	
Cr. Right to recovery asset		360

Example—Returns Not Predictable

If, on the other hand, there is little or no historical knowledge available about product returns, or if returns have been volatile over the recent past, it will not be possible to predict the level of returns, and recognition of all of the revenue ($24,000) is delayed until the return period is over.

Assume the facts as in the prior example, except that returns are not predictable at 3%. In fact, what happens is that 160 units are kept by the customer, and 40 units are returned on April 29, the end of the return period. The inventory is derecognized in March with the entire cost of the units of $18,000 adjusted to right to recovery asset. The $24,000 account receivable would be entirely offset by a refund liability. On April 29, once the return period has expired and the performance obligation is satisfied, revenue and cost of goods sold are recognized.

Entries

1 March:		
Dr. Accounts receivable (200 × $120)	24,000	
Cr. Refund liability		24,000
Dr. Right to recovery asset	18,000	
Cr. Inventory (200 × $90)		18,000
29 April:		
Dr. Refund liability	24,000	
Cr. Accounts receivable (40 × $120)		4,800
Cr. Revenue (160 × $120)		19,200
Dr. Cost of goods sold (160 × $90)	14,400	
Dr. Inventory (40 × $90)	3,600	
Cr. Right to recovery asset		18,000

Summary

These points deserve emphasis:

- If the future returns can be quantified reliably, the sale is recorded on delivery and an estimate of the return liability accrued.
- If risk cannot be quantified reliably, the sale is recognized as revenue only after expiry of the return privilege. In this case, the entire consideration is shown as a return liability.

ETHICAL ISSUES

In the past, some managers have used questionable revenue recognition policies. For example, a now-defunct producer of farm equipment forced its dealers to accept excess inventory at the end of the year so that the manufacturer could show high sales revenue. However, there was an implicit, unwritten agreement that the manufacturer would take back the excess inventory in the following year and dispose of it elsewhere, such as in foreign markets, at a lower price if necessary. Similarly, some automobile manufacturers have been known to require dealers to accept the manufacturers' excess inventories at the end of the fiscal year.

Using the approach shown above, the right to return would be shown as a liability; it would not be fully recognized as revenue. This is intended to prevent improper revenue recognition. However, the "unwritten agreement" has to be clearly understood and reflected in the entries.

Sale with a Warranty or Service Agreement

Companies often provide a warranty with the sale of goods or services. The warranty may be in the form of assurance that the product will operate as intended and meet specifications. Warranties may also require the seller to provide certain service or repairs for a period of time. Such warranties and service agreements may be provided at no extra cost to the customer. In other cases, the customer must pay extra for the warranty or service agreement. *The nature of the warranty impacts how the warranty is recognized and measured at the time of sale.*

There are two approaches to accounting for a warranty or service agreement:

Approach	Use If:	Description
Cost deferral	The warranty is provided to give assurance that the product will meet agreed-upon specifications and the warranty is not sold separately. There is no distinct service provided.	Accrue the (reliably) *estimated costs* of the vendor's remaining performance obligation as a provision and an expense when revenue is recognized; future costs are charged to the warranty provision as they are incurred. The warranty provision is adjusted at each reporting period to reflect actual warranty cost experience.
Revenue deferral	The warranty provides the customer with future services in addition to product assurance, or the warranty can be purchased separately.	A proportionate part of the *sales revenue* is deferred as contract liability; the unearned revenue is recognized over time until the warranty or service agreement expires. Warranty or servicing costs are charged to expense as incurred. The proportion of revenue from *new* sales that is deferred is adjusted periodically to reflect actual cost experience, but there is no adjustment of deferred revenue already on the books other than through the passage of time until the warranty/service agreement expires.

The *revenue deferral method* includes an element of profit (or loss) in the warranty contract, which is the difference between warranty revenue and expenses paid to meet warranty claims. There is no such profit using the *cost deferral method*. The *revenue deferral method* is easier to apply in practice because it does not require periodic adjustment of existing balances. In contrast, the deferred warranty cost provision requires review and adjustment at each reporting date.

Example

On 6 March, Tudor Computers delivers a computer system to a buyer. The agreed-upon price is $28,000. Included in this price is a 12-month warranty that the system will be fixed or replaced if it does not perform to certain specifications and 25 hours of service to maintain the system over this period. The stand-alone price for the maintenance service is $2,250. The company also estimates that based on past experience, the warranty costs for defective product should be estimated at $3,900. Subsequently, 25 hours of service are performed, as expected, at a cost of $1,750, and warranty work results in expenditures of $3,700.

Five Steps

Applying the five steps:

1. *Identify the contract with the customer.* We assume that there is a contract between the buyer and the seller which has agreed upon price of $28,000 for the computer system, and which includes performance, warranty and service promises.

2. *Identify separate performance obligations, if they exist.* There are two performance obligations: to deliver the computer and to provide 25 hours of maintenance service. The warranty itself is not a separate obligation, because it deals with agreed-upon specifications and it is not sold separately.

3. *Determine the overall contract price.* The contract price is $28,000 as agreed to by the customer.

4. *Allocate the contract price to the separate performance obligations.* Using fair values, it is determined that $2,250 of the consideration is allocated to the service and $25,750 is allocated to the computer system including delivery.

5. *Determine when the performance obligation is satisfied and revenue can be recognized.* The performance obligation for the delivery of the computer system is complete once the customer accepts the computer. The service maintenance of 25 hours will be completed as the hours are provided. Cost deferral is used for the warranty as it is not sold separately.

Entries—Cost Deferral

The journal entries required are shown in the first column of Exhibit 6-4. Notice that the service revenue of $2,250 is deferred as a contract liability. When service is provided (over time), $2,250 revenue is eventually recognized, $1,750 of expense is also recognized and $500 of gross profit results. The warranty, on the other hand, results in a separate expense and provision that is recorded when the sale is recognized. When $3,700 of expenditures are required under the warranty, this is *not* expensed, but rather reduces the provision. The $200 unneeded provision is reversed at the end of the warranty period, resulting in an expense recovery.

EXHIBIT 6-4				
WARRANTY: COST DEFERRAL VERSUS REVENUE DEFERRAL				
Date	(a) Cost Deferral for Warranty		(b) Revenue Deferral for Warranty	
6 March	Accounts receivable	28,000	Accounts receivable	33,000	
	Revenue—sale of computer	25,750	Revenue—sale of computer	25,750
	Contract liability—service maintenance	2,250	Contract liability—service maintenance	2,250

				Contract liability—warranty		5,000
	Warranty expense	3,900				
	Provision for warranty		3,900			
Subsequently	Contract liability—service maintenance	2,250		Same entry		
	Revenue—service maintenance		2,250			
	Service expense	1,750		Same entry		
	Cash		1,750			
				Contract liability—warranty	5,000	
				Revenue—warranty		5,000
	Provision for warranty	3,700		Warranty expense	3,700	
	Cash		3,700	Cash		3,700
End of warranty period	Provision for warranty	200				
	Recovery of warranty expense		200			

Remember, it is *very* important that the warranty provision be measured correctly. The SFP must reliably reflect the obligations of the company. Detailed engineering studies and review of warranty experience are required to ensure that the provision is correctly valued. It can be increased (decreased) with additional expense (expense recovery) recognized if needed.

Entries—Revenue Deferral

Assume now that the contract is for $33,000 and includes the computers, a 12-month warranty that includes service and replacement as required, and 25 hours of service to maintain the system over this period. The stand-alone price for the maintenance service is $2,250. The maintenance warranty is sold separately and is valued at $5,000. Using fair values, the total contract value of $33,000 is allocated as follows: $25,750 to the computer system, $2,250 to the service agreement, and $5,000 to the warranty. This time, the warranty accounting follows the same pattern as the service agreement: initial unearned revenue (contract liability), followed by later warranty revenue and warranty expense.

In this case, if warranty expenses are projected to exceed unearned revenue, the contract is considered to be an *onerous contract* and a loss is recorded. This topic is considered in Chapter 12.

Delayed Revenue Recognition

Often, after-sale costs can be measured reliably for the company's sales as a whole, based on historical experience, even if the follow-up costs of individual sales might turn out to be quite substantial. For example, automobile manufacturers recognize revenue and accrue warranty expense using the cost deferral method when they sell cars, even though they might have to issue a *product recall* to fix design problems detected later. Recalls can be very expensive for the manufacturer.

But if potentially significant costs *cannot* be reliably estimated for the class of buyers as a whole, performance obligations have not been completed since there is still significant risk with the seller. In these circumstances, *no revenue can be recognized until the uncertainty is resolved.* (That is, step 5 in the revenue analysis structure would dictate no revenue being recognized.) This is highly undesirable for the seller, and thus considerable effort will be invested in estimating the warranty obligation!

Bill-and-Hold Arrangements

A **bill-and-hold arrangement** is a contract between a buyer and seller wherein the buyer is billed for a product, but the product is not delivered until some specific future point in time. Delivery is often at the buyer's request. This type of arrangement might be used if the buyer does not yet have the space or need for the product, but wishes to have guaranteed access to the product and thus the buyer is willing to sign a firm contract.

Example

An electronics dealer might agree to accept (and pay for) 10,000 units of a new cell phone, to be delivered at some points in time over the next six months, at the dealer's choice. The electronics dealer then has a guaranteed source of supply, but no price flexibility. The electronics dealer benefits from the transaction if demand for the new phone is expected to exceed the manufacturer's production capacity. When should the manufacturer recognize revenue?

As we have seen, revenue recognition is often triggered when the goods are delivered. However, in a bill and hold situation, revenue may be recognized before delivery if the buyer has *control of the units*. Control of the units shifts to the buyer when *all of the following* conditions are met:

- The reason for the bill-and-hold arrangement is substantive; that is, the customer has requested the arrangement;
- The buyer's inventory is separately identified as belonging to the buyer—that is, held apart from the seller's other inventory;
- The inventory is ready to be delivered; and
- The seller does not have the ability to use the product or sell to another customer and then replace it.

Only in these special situations can the seller recognize the revenue prior to the delivery of the product.

ETHICAL ISSUES

If revenue recognition prior to delivery was generally acceptable, companies could ask friendly customers to enter into bill-and-hold agreements so that the seller could recognize revenue on existing inventory. The agreements might provide various escape clauses so that the buyer could avoid the purchase requirements. Such clauses might give the buyer cancellation clauses, generous return rights, and the right to renegotiate the price. To avoid such abuses for revenue recognition, specific conditions have been established for revenue recognition prior to delivery to be acceptable.

Consignment Arrangements

Goods may be delivered to a customer (usually a dealer or a distributor), but held in a **consignment arrangement** if the seller retains control of the goods. No revenue is recognized at the time of delivery for consignment arrangements. Examples of indicators of a consignment arrangement include:

a. The entity still has control of the product until the occurrence of an event specified in the contract. The event might be the sale of the item to a customer of the dealer or the lapse of a certain period of time.

b. The entity has the ability to require the dealer to return the good or can transfer the good to another dealer.

c. The dealer has no unconditional obligation to pay the entity for the delivered product.

Example

Company A delivers goods to Dealer B and Dealer B is to sell the goods to the final customer C. How and when revenue is recognized will depend on which party has control of the goods and the terms and conditions of the contract. If Company A retains control until sale to the final customer C, this is a consignment arrangement. B likely has the ability to return the goods if not sold and has no obligation to pay for the goods. When B ultimately sells the goods to C, B *as an agent* can report as revenue only the fee or commission that it has earned. Company A will report the full sale price of the goods as revenue, because it was the party that transferred control to the final customer. The commission earned by B will be a cost to A. (In general, recall that a seller reports gross revenues if the company has control over the goods being sold.)

On the other hand, if B holds the goods, and can make product, pricing, location, and promotion decisions, B may in fact have control over the goods. B might have control even if B has the ability to return the goods. This would be a very different situation, and be accounted for as *a sale with the right of return,* as we have seen earlier. Accordingly, the nature of the contractual relationship between A and B has to be carefully analyzed.

CONCEPT REVIEW

1. Explain how revenue is recognized for a sales contract that has a right of return.
2. Explain the difference between cost deferral and revenue deferral for contracts that involve a warranty arrangement.
3. What criteria must be met before a bill-and-hold contract results in revenue recognition before delivery?
4. How is a consignment arrangement different from a sale with the right of return?

TRANSFER OF GOODS AND SERVICES OVER TIME

Not all revenue transactions result in a delivery of items at a single point in time. Some contracts last for a long period of time, making it difficult to assess when the performance obligation is completed and revenue can be recognized. Recognizing revenue from a long-term contract over several accounting periods poses some challenging measurement problems. However, the problems (and potential estimation errors) that are inherent in multiperiod recognition are offset by the relevance and timeliness of the information provided to financial statement readers. Thus, there is a tradeoff between the qualitative characteristics of *relevance* on the one hand, and *verifiability* on the other.

Performance Completed over Time

Revenue is recognized over time if *at least one of the following criteria* is met:

a. The *customer receives and consumes the benefits of the contract as it progresses.* This criterion would be true for a pure service contract, such as a cleaning contract, in which the receipt of the service coincides with the benefit of the service for the customer. For other performance obligations, the implications of transferring an uncompleted contract are reviewed. For instance, if another company took over an existing contract and there is no need to re-perform the services provided prior to the date of transfer, the seller has earned the right to payment for performance completed to date. In this case, the contract is satisfied over time.

b. The *customer controls the asset throughout the contract period* and the *seller is creating or improving that asset over time.* When does a customer control an asset? This would clearly be the case if the contract itself specifies that legal title of the project-in-process rests with the customer. A contract also might specifically state that if the contract is terminated early, the (incomplete) asset belongs to the customer (and another contractor would presumably be hired to complete the job). Thus, the customer is receiving the benefit of the work that has been completed to date. Any work done enhances the asset of the customer. Payments and /or inspection during the contract period also create opportunities for the customer to have control. *Contract terms must be carefully evaluated!*

c. The performance under the contract *yields an asset with no alternative use to the seller and the seller has a right to payment for work completed to date.* In other words, the work completed to date on a partially completed asset *cannot be sold* to another customer (either due to contractual limitations or without substantial rework). The contract may restrict any alternative use, or the asset may be too specialized that significant losses would be incurred to either sell or rework the asset for another customer.

Exhibit 6-5 provides a summary of these criteria.

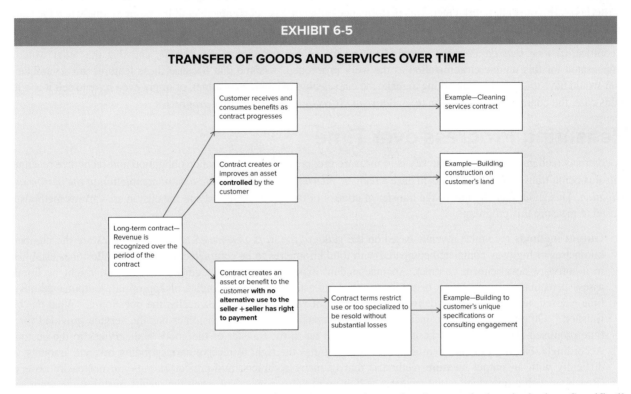

EXHIBIT 6-5

TRANSFER OF GOODS AND SERVICES OVER TIME

As mentioned, specific criteria must be met to recognize revenue over time, rather than at a single point in time. Specifically, the criteria examine three main factors: *Are the receipt and consumption of the services occurring simultaneously? Does the customer own the asset as it is being created at all times? Does the partially completed good or service have no alternative use?*

Once it is determined that revenue is to be recognized over time, the next challenge is measurement of the revenue. In other words, how do we take the *total consideration* and *spread it out over the term of the contract*? Below, we discuss the various measures that can be used.

Example 1

Consider a customer that enters into a three-year contract to receive cleaning services. The contract requires the customer to pay $75,000 at the beginning of each year. The seller initially recognizes the $75,000 as unearned revenue (a contract liability) and then records revenue evenly over the 12 months ($6,250 per month) assuming that the same type of cleaning services is provided each month. The cleaning services are *received and consumed at exactly the same time*, so the company has the right to compensation for these services transferred. The revenue is recognized over the term of the contract in this case, in accordance with criterion (a) above.

Example 2

Suppose a company has agreed to build a manufacturing plant for a customer on land owned by the customer. If the customer retains control of the partially built asset throughout the construction progress, then revenue is *recognized over time*, as the work is performed, in accordance with criterion (b) above. The manufacturing-plant-in-progress does not belong to the seller. Methods used to measure progress of completion and related revenue to be recognized for long-term projects will be discussed later in this chapter.

Example 3

A company has entered into a contract with Customer A to build a car, but there are no special characteristics that make this car unique. It is a standard inventory item and the seller can easily substitute it for another. Even if the car is partially complete, the seller could easily complete and sell this car to Customer B (i.e., it has an alternative use). In this case, none of criteria (a), (b), or (c) have been met. This performance obligation is not complete until the point in time when the vehicle is actually delivered to the customer.

In contrast, *assume that the contract specified some very unique features to this vehicle,* and that the seller would be compensated for this unique customization as the work proceeded. Assume that because these features are so unique the seller would have to do a lot of reworking to make the car saleable to another customer, or might even have to sell it at a loss. In this case, the contract meets criterion (c) and *revenue is recognized as the work progresses.*

Measuring Progress over Time

For contracts recognized over time, the key is to measure progress of the performance obligation and recognize revenue as control is being transferred. The goal is to have a realistic *measure of progress made toward completion of the performance obligation.* This should ideally mirror the transfer of control of the goods or services to the customer. Various methods can be used to measure this progress:

1. **Output methods** recognize revenue based on the *value of the work performed to date.* Examples are the number of kilometres of highway completed compared with total kilometres to be completed, or progress milestones established in a software development contract. An independent expert, such as an engineer or architect, might be hired to assess percentage-of-completion or achievement of milestones. Other examples of appropriate output methods are time elapsed, units produced or delivered, and survey of work completed. Basically, the question is "What has been finished?" Output measures also include the basic passage of time—the customer has the service provided for the time promised. The appropriate basis of measure will tie to the transfer of the goods and services to the customer. Accordingly, based on output measures, the seller also has the right to receive corresponding revenue amounts. The difficulty with an output measure method is that in many contracts, mid-project outputs are not easily observed. (Reaching such a milestone might trigger a billing point.) It is convenient when the results of milestone reports can also be used for financial reporting metrics.

2. **Input methods** recognize the revenue based on the *value of the effort performed to date relative to the total expected inputs to complete the obligation.* Examples are (1) costs incurred to date compared with total estimated costs for the project and (2) labour hours worked compared with total estimated labour hours required to complete the project. Other appropriate methods used to measure completion might be time elapsed and machine hours or other costs incurred to perform the work obligation in the contract. As long as control is transferred on a similar basis to that of the costs being incurred, input methods can be easier than output methods because measuring inputs is straightforward. In fact, if costs are incurred evenly over the contract, revenue can be recognized on a straight-line basis. The difficulty with this method is that costs incurred might not be linear with real progress, for example if there was wastage or failed initiatives.

Methods based on the passage of time are used when the performance is provided evenly over the contract. This results in a straight-line pattern of revenue recognition. Contracts in which services are provided evenly over a period of time is an example using this method.

Input versus Output Methods

Output measures, despite their subjectivity, seem to directly address the issue of the *degree of completion* and seem preferable. In particular, input measures can be misleading when a constant relationship between the input measure and transfer of control does not exist. For example:

- Cost overruns on projects might cause erroneous levels of completion to be estimated. These costs, which would include cost of wasted materials and labour, should ideally be immediately expensed and excluded from the input measures. Tracking inefficiencies is not simple, though.

- One-time, upfront expenditures for quantities of materials and supplies to be used during the construction period. These types of costs should be amortized based on usage rather than being expensed at the time of incurrence.

Despite their shortcomings, input measures are the most frequently used, because they are the most readily available.

Estimating Costs

When making cost estimates, only direct costs are included. Direct costs include:

- Direct labour and materials costs and all other costs that relate directly to the project, including design costs, costs of outsourcing, and fees charged by subcontractors;
- Costs that relate to contract activity in general and can be allocated to individual projects or contracts, such as equipment depreciation, insurance, and other construction overheads; and
- Any other costs that the client has contractually agreed to pay for.

General administrative overhead or selling costs are not included in estimated contract costs.

Obviously, the cost to complete is an estimate. It may be somewhat off the mark, because large-scale projects are often begun before the final design is even completed. Complications often arise during construction, and costs mount.

"Costs incurred to date" might seem like a definite figure. After all, the contractor must know how much has been spent on the project so far. But it really is an estimate. How much of the contractor's overhead is to be included in the costs assigned to the project, and how much is charged as a period cost? What proportion of purchased and/or contracted materials should be included in costs to date? If the contractor has ordered and delivered 5,000 tonnes of bricks for exterior sheathing, should the cost of those bricks be included in the costs to date when the bricks are purchased or should the cost be excluded until the bricks are actually used in construction of the building? Under IFRS, only the costs incurred to perform under the contract are used to measure performance to date. From the point of view of satisfying the obligation, only the bricks actually used in the construction of the building are included in the costs incurred to date.

Measurement Not Possible

If the company cannot measure progress with *reasonable assurance*, but expects to be able to recover the costs incurred to date, a revenue amount equal to costs can be recognized. This is commonly known as a **cost recovery** approach, and results in zero gross profit recognized until the contract is closed out. Of course, judgement plays an important role in determining whether the criterion of reasonable assurance can be met. Finally, in cases where the company lacks information to determine stage of completion and is not expected to be contractually able to recover the costs incurred to date, revenue is is not recognized until the contract is completed.

Examples

Some long-term services are really a series of short-term performances. Service contracts that provide the same type of service throughout the contract are recorded evenly over the life of the contract. For example, assume that an entity provides monthly payroll services to a customer. The contract is for six months and the customer pays a consideration of $24,000. As each payroll run is provided, it is being consumed immediately by the customer, and therefore meets the criteria to be recognized as time passes. The contract is really a series of monthly payroll runs, and falls neatly under an output measure of progress, as described above. The revenue will be recognized evenly over the six months, at $4,000 each month.

Similarly, consider the sale of a service contract on heating and air conditioning systems. The contract states that the service company will perform routine servicing of the system on a monthly basis as needed, providing whatever labour and materials are necessary without additional charge. Again, this contract is recorded with the passage of time *as an output measure* since the benefits are conferred and used at the same time and a proportionate part of the consideration is recorded as revenue month by month.

It is important to understand the extent of the estimates and approximations that underlie estimating the measurement of progress. Virtually every cost, revenue, and measurement calculation reflects not just one, but multiple estimates.

LONG-TERM CONTRACTS MEASURED OVER TIME

In some instances, a company enters into a long-term contract, one that requires economic activity that spans several fiscal years. Examples include construction contracts and development of large-scale custom software. Revenue from long-term contracts can be recognized at a single point in time or over time, depending on the terms and conditions. Earlier in the chapter the criteria for measurement over time were discussed. If the contract does not meet any one of these three criteria, then the revenue is recognized at a single point in time.

Measured over Time[1]

For a contract, revenue is measured over time if any one of these following criteria are met: *the customer receives and consumes the benefits simultaneously, the customer controls the asset under construction,* or *the asset created has no alternative use for the seller.* In this case, a measurement basis must be selected that is appropriate to estimate with reasonable assurance the progress toward completion of the contractual and the related right to the revenue. Measurement bases were also addressed earlier in the chapter.

Example

Ace Construction Corp. has entered into a $1.5 million contract to construct a building, starting construction on 1 February 20X1. The planned completion date is 1 August 20X3, and thus the contract spans three fiscal years for Ace. Initially, total costs to complete the contract are estimated at $1.35 million, so the contract is initially expected to generate gross profit of $150,000. Title to the asset under construction rests with the customer, even though the asset is incomplete; as a result, the contract's revenue is measured over time. For this example, Ace uses the costs incurred to date, an input measure, to assess the stage of completion for the contract.

The data shown in Exhibit 6-6 show the progress over the three-year construction period. The actual data for each of the three years become known as each year goes by. That is, in 20X1, Ace does not know the 20X2 or 20X3 information.

EXHIBIT 6-6			
ACE CONSTRUCTION CORPORATION			
Construction Project Fact Sheet, Three-Year Summary Schedule			
Contract Price: $1,500,000	**20X1**	**20X2**	**20X3**
1. Estimated total costs for project	$1,350,000	$1,360,000	$1,365,000
2. Costs incurred during current year	375,000	560,000	430,000
3. Costs incurred but not yet used for performance (will remain in contract costs) (represents cumulative amount in inventory)	25,000	35,000	—
4. Estimated costs to complete at year-end	1,000,000	460,000	—
5. Progress billings during year	300,000	575,000	625,000
6. Cumulative billings to date	300,000	875,000	1,500,000
7. Collections on billings during year	270,000	555,000	675,000
8. Cumulative collections to date	270,000	825,000	1,500,000

The total construction costs were originally estimated at $1,350,000, of which $375,000 were incurred in 20X1. However, of the $375,000 incurred, only $350,000 was actually used to complete performance. For example, the company might have purchased materials that have not yet been used on the building representing a cost of $25,000. These costs will remain in contract costs and not be expensed at the end of the year. In 20X2, another $560,000 in costs was incurred, bringing the total spent to $935,000 ($375,000 + $560,000). Again, there were materials not yet used of $35,000 on hand. Estimated total

---

1. Note that historically, the term "percentage of completion" has been used for this measurement over a period of time. Although this term is not specifically used in IFRS 15, the standard's guidance for methods that can be used to measure completion is consistent with the percentage of completion method.

project costs, including past and current costs but also all anticipated costs to complete the project, rose by $10,000 in 20X2, to $1,360,000. In 20X3, Ace finished the project and spent $430,000, bringing total costs to $1,365,000, another $5,000 higher than expected. Contract gross profit over the three years therefore drops from the original estimate of $150,000 to an actual gross profit of $135,000.

Construction companies do not wait until the end of the project to collect their money. Instead, **progress billings** are made throughout the duration of the project. The amount of progress billings is based on the contractor's need for cash to pay for materials and wages as the work is performed, as negotiated in the contract, and may need to be verified by an independent facilitator if required by the contract. Ace's contract allows progress billings of $300,000 in 20X1 and $575,000 in 20X2, with the balance to be billed when the project is complete.

Estimating Revenue

To establish the revenue and gross profit to be recognized in a given year:

- First, use *the relative proportion of the total costs that have been incurred to date to perform under the contract to total costs to be incurred to determine the cumulative percentage completed as of the end of the year.* Multiply this percentage by the contract price to determine *cumulative revenue to date.*
- Second, subtract revenue recognized in prior years, if any; the result is revenue for the current year.
- Recognize this amount of revenue, along with the costs incurred in the year, to determine gross profit for the year.

For Ace, year by year, the *cumulative estimated percentage-of-completion* and *cumulative revenue to date* would be:

	20X1	20X2	20X3
Cumulative costs incurred to date	$375,000	$ 935,000	$1,365,000
Costs not yet used on the project	(25,000)	(35,000)	
Costs used for performance to date	350,000	900,000	
Estimated total costs	1,350,000	1,360,000	1,365,000
Cumulative percent completed	26%	66%	100%
Revenue:			
20X1: $1.5 million × 26%; 66%; 100%	$390,000	$990,000	$1,500,000

The percentage completed is computed by dividing the estimate of *costs incurred to date* by the *estimated total costs*. For example, estimated total costs at the end of 20X1 ($1,350,000) equals costs incurred to date for performance ($350,000) plus estimated costs to complete at the end of 20X1 ($1,000,000). This percentage is multiplied by the $1.5 million contract value to determine cumulative revenue to date.

The percentages shown above have been rounded to the nearest full percentage point. The "exact" percentage for 20X2, to be precise, is 66.17647…%. But there is no point in calculating the percentage-of-completion to more than two digits. We are working with estimates here, and it is silly to be "precise" in calculating percentages that are based on approximations.

The second step is to subtract revenue previously recognized, and the result is revenue that is recognized in each specific year.

	20X1	20X2	20X3
Cumulative revenue (above)	$ 390,000	$990,000	$1,500,000
Less: Revenue previously recognized	—	(390,000)	(990,000)
Recognized revenue for the year	$390,000	$600,000	$ 510,000

Costs incurred are initially recognized as a contract costs asset account. Once the revenue is recognized, the appropriate amount of costs can be expensed. Any costs that have not been used for performance under the contract will remain in the contract cost account. Gross profit is the difference between revenue and the related costs expensed in the period:

	20X1	20X2	20X3	Total
Recognized revenue for the year (above)	$390,000	$600,000	$510,000	$1,500,000
Costs expensed in the current year for performance	350,000	550,000	465,000	1,365,000
Gross profit for the year	$ 40,000	$ 50,000	$ 45,000	$ 135,000

Recording

The entries to record the costs incurred on construction, the progress billings, and the collections are shown in Exhibit 6-7. In sequence:

- Costs incurred increase an asset account called *contract costs*; these costs are here temporarily until adjustment at year-end (or contract-end).
- Billings on contract increase accounts receivable, and are credited to an account, *contract liability*. The contract liability account is used temporarily until adjustment at year-end (or contract-end) for the amount of revenue that can now be recognized. (Remember that billings will be different from revenue recognized.)
- Cash received reduces accounts receivable.
- At year-end, in 20X1 and 20X2, or when the contract is completed in 20X3:
  - Revenue recognized is recorded through an entry that increases the *contract asset* account or reduces the *contract liability account* and increases revenue;
  - Contract liability is closed off to the *contract asset* account at least up to the amount of the revenue recognized; and
  - Costs recorded in contract costs that relate directly to the amount of performance under the contract to date are expensed.

EXHIBIT 6-7

JOURNAL ENTRIES—PERCENTAGE-OF-COMPLETION ACCOUNTING FOR LONG-TERM CONSTRUCTION CONTRACTS

	20X1		20X2		20X3	
To record costs of construction:						
Contract costs	375,000		560,000		430,000	
Cash, payables, etc.		375,000		560,000		430,000
To record progress billings:						
Accounts receivable	300,000		575,000		625,000	
Contract liability		300,000		575,000		625,000
To record cash received:						
Cash	270,000		555,000		675,000	
Accounts receivable		270,000		555,000		675,000
To recognize revenue for performance completed to date:						
Contract asset	90,000		25,000		115,000	
Contract liability	300,000		575,000		625,000	

Revenue—long-term contracts		390,000		600,000		510,000
To recognize costs related to revenue recognized to date:						
Construction costs	350,000		550,000		465,000	
Contract costs		350,000		550,000		465,000

Reporting Results

As a result of these entries:

- Costs incurred to date but not yet used to perform under the contract are kept in the contract cost account until they are used. This remaining amount would be tested for impairment at each reporting period to ensure they are still recoverable. If at any point it is determined that they are not, the amount would be immediately expensed.

- Accounts receivable will reflect the balance owing.

- As long as the revenue recognized to date is greater than the amount billed to date, the contract liability account will have a zero closing balance and there will be an amount in the contract asset. Conversely, if at any year-end date the cumulative billings are greater than the revenue recognized, the contract asset will be zero and there will be an outstanding balance in the contract liability account.

- The contract asset account will have a positive balance that represents the difference between revenue recognized and the contract liability (billings on the contract to date). For example, this is $90,000 for Ace in 20X1 ($390,000 of revenue less $300,000 for the contract liability). The contract asset represents Ace's financial interest in the construction contract—that is, the *value of the revenue recognized but not yet billed.* (There might also be a *contract liability* if the billings to date are higher than the cumulative revenue recognized to date.) By the end of the contract, the entire $1.5 million has been recognized as revenue and also billed, so the contract asset and the contract liability will always eventually be zero by the end of the contract.

Exhibit 6-8 gives a summary of the balances and recognized amounts for each of the three years.

EXHIBIT 6-8

FINANCIAL STATEMENT PRESENTATION—ACCOUNTING FOR LONG-TERM CONSTRUCTION CONTRACTS MEASURED OVER TIME

Year-End Amounts on SFP and SCI

	Years Ending 31 December		
	20X1	**20X2**	**20X3**
Statement of Financial Position:			
Current assets:			
Contract costs	$ 25,000	$ 35,000	$ 0
Accounts receivable	$ 30,000	$ 50,000	$ 0
Contract asset	$ 90,000	$ 115,000	$ 0
Statement of Comprehensive Income:			
Revenue from long-term construction contract	$390,000	$600,000	$510,000
Costs of construction	350,000	550,000	465,000
Gross profit	$ 40,000	$ 50,000	$ 45,000

Estimating Revenue

The contract price may also be an estimate. True, any long-term construction contract starts out with a contract price, but that initial contract price rarely ends up being the final revenue figure. Modifications, or **change orders**, may be made to the contract as it progresses. Careful analysis will have to be done to determine how these modifications impact the performance obligation and the amount of the consideration related to the contract.

Extent of Estimates

To summarize, in relation to a construction project:

- Estimated cost to complete will change each period;
- Costs incurred in the current period (to be used in the percentage calculation) involve judgement; and
- Estimated total revenue will change from period to period.

It is safe to say that the **percentage-of-completion method** is an approximation! It represents a tradeoff between conflicting qualitative characteristics—*verifiability* is sacrificed for *timeliness* and *relevance*.

Long-Term Contract—Recognized at a Single Point in Time

For a long-term contract in which *the transfer of the good or service is at a point in time*, revenue cannot be recognized until this transfer is complete. That is, if *the company controls the asset under construction* until it is delivered and accepted by the customer, revenue is recognized on delivery and acceptance. In this case all revenues and expenses are recognized in the final period when the performance obligation is completed. This is commonly referred to as the **completed-contract method**.

Contractor Control of the Asset

For example, Robotics Inc. has entered into a contract to build a robotic arm to be attached to a current manufacturing array. The contract outlines specific customer specifications as to size and weight and the contract also specifies that the customer will test the arm prior to acceptance. Robotics appears to have control over the asset under construction until inspection. In particular, the customer does not receive any benefits until the arm is actually installed. The contract states that if the contract is terminated early, the work-in-progress would still belong to Robotics and therefore, all of the work performed to date would have to be re-performed by another supplier. After acceptance, title will transfer to the customer, and the customer will pay at that time. Robotics is not entitled to any consideration until acceptance. There are no milestones to complete at which the company might be entitled to part of the consideration. Therefore, the revenue cannot be recognized over time, and would be recognized only on final acceptance.

Certain kinds of construction contracts also provide an example of revenue that must be recognized on completion, when the title transfers to the customer. Assume that a developer is constructing a house for a customer. The customer can pick from five different designs for the house, and make a few modifications, and will have some say on decorating items related to colour, tile, carpet, and hardwood floor. However, the choices are fairly limited. During the construction period, the developer has a large inventory of homes under construction. The developer retains ownership of the house until the home is complete and title can now be transferred to the customer. There is no transfer of risks and rewards, title, or physical possession until the house is complete and title is passed; therefore, this is the revenue recognition point.

Application

Under the completed-contract method, revenue is recognized when transfer of control of the asset takes place. Costs are not expensed until revenue is recognized. Costs are recorded in the work-in-progress inventory until the transfer is completed.

Example

Return to the Ace example in Exhibit 6-6. Assume now that revenue is only to be recognized once the contract is complete. Exhibit 6-9 shows the journal entries to record construction costs, billings, and cash collection.

EXHIBIT 6-9					
JOURNAL ENTRIES—LONG-TERM CONSTRUCTION CONTRACT RECOGNIZED AT A SINGLE POINT IN TIME					
	20X1		**20X2**		**20X3**
Construction-in-progress inventory	375,000		560,000		430,000
Cash, payables, etc.		375,000		560,000		430,000
Accounts receivable	300,000		575,000		625,000
Contract liability		300,000		575,000		625,000
Cash	270,000		555,000		675,000
Accounts receivable		270,000		555,000		675,000

Note that there are similarities with the entries shown for percentage-of-completion in Exhibit 6-7, *except* that the costs are accumulated in an inventory account and there is no entry at the end of each year to recognize construction revenue and construction expense in earnings. On the statement of financial position during the construction period, the *construction-in-progress inventory is reported as an asset*, total accumulated costs to date, and the *billings on contract are reported as a liability*. (See Exhibit 6-10 below.)

The accumulated balances at the end of the project in 20X3 are as follows:

Contract liability	$1,500,000
Construction-in-progress inventory	$1,365,000

When the contract is complete, the buyer accepts the project. *Only then are revenue and expenses recognized.* The accumulated amount of billings on contracts is recognized as revenue, and the accumulated amount of construction-in-progress inventory on completion of the contract is recognized as costs of construction. These two entries increase *net assets* and thereby recognize gross profit:

Contract liability	1,500,000	
Revenue from long-term contracts		1,500,000
Costs of construction	1,365,000	
Construction-in-progress inventory		1,365,000

Exhibit 6-10 gives a summary of the balances and recognized amounts for each of the three years.

Evaluation

For contracts requiring revenue be recognized at a single point in time, profit recognition is delayed. At the end of the contract, substantially all of the costs and revenues are known, although there may be some remaining costs that are roughly similar to warranty costs; these can be estimated and accrued.

EXHIBIT 6-10

FINANCIAL STATEMENT PRESENTATION—LONG-TERM CONSTRUCTION CONTRACT RECOGNIZED AT A SINGLE POINT IN TIME

Year-End Amounts on SFP and SCI

	Years Ending 31 December		
	20X1	**20X2**	**20X3**
Statement of Financial Position:			
Current assets:			
Accounts receivable	$ 30,000	$ 50,000	$ 0
Construction in progress—inventory	$ 375,000	$935,000	$ 0
Current liabilities:			
Contract liability	$ 300,000	$ 875,000	$ 0
Statement of Comprehensive Income:			
Revenue from long-term construction contract	$ 0	$ 0	$1,500,000
Costs of construction	0	0	1,365,000
Gross profit	$ 0	$ 0	$ 135,000

LICENSING FEES

Licensing arrangements allow a customer to use intellectual property, such as software, music, franchises, and trademarks. Licence agreements can be designed to either transfer a right to use the licence or a promise to provide access to the seller's intellectual property for a period of time. Revenue is recognized in one of two patterns, depending on whether the contract terms give the buyer *a right to use* or a *right to access* the intellectual property:

1. *Recognize revenue over time when the contract provides the customer the right to access intellectual property.* A right to access exits if: the seller will undertake activities that will change the intellectual property significantly; these rights expose the customer to positive and negative effects as a result of these changes; and these activities by the seller do not represent the transfer of goods or services to the customers. In other cases, the licence grants the buyer limited access to the seller's intellectual property for only a fixed period of time. For a right to access arrangements, revenue is recognized over the period of time covered by the licence.

2. *Recognize revenue at a point in time when the contract provides the customer the right to use the intellectual property.* In this case, the intellectual property will not be changed by the seller and, the customer can direct the use of this intellectual property immediately and gain substantial benefits from its use. The point in time occurs when the customer first can use the intellectual property. For example, the licensing fee for software that grants a right to use the software, would be recognized as revenue at a point in time, once the customer has installed and begins to use the software.

Note that even if the contract restricts the use of the intellectual property to a specified time period, geographical region, or use, these restrictions do not determine if the licence revenue is recognized over time or at a point in time.

Licences That Are Not Distinct

The discussion above relates to licences that are distinct from other goods or services. But in some cases, licences may be integral to the functioning of a tangible good or a related service. If this is the case, then they are not distinct from the related good or service and revenue will be recognized as the performance obligation related to the good or service is recognized. For example, an on-line service may only be accessible by a customer with the granting of a licence. In this case, the licence is part of providing the service and related revenue will be recognized over the period in which the customer uses the service.

CONCEPT REVIEW

1. Under what circumstances, must revenue be recognized over the term of the contract?
2. Explain the two methods used to determine progress over time.
3. Why might the use of input measures to measure progress in a contract lead to misleading information?
4. What estimates are required in order to measure progress of completion over time?
5. When would licence revenue be recognized for a contract that gives the customer the right to use the software over a five-year period?

MEASUREMENT OF CONSIDERATION

The third step in the five steps of revenue recognition is determining the overall contract price, the amount the company expects to be paid. In most cases, this amount will be quite obvious. In other cases, depending on the complexity of the customer contract, the consideration may vary. For example, if the customer is entitled to discounts or rebates depending on volume of product purchased, this might impact the final amount of cash received. Companies must estimate the amount of cash they expect to receive. Should the entity recognize the gross or the net amount of revenue in an agent–principal relationship? These considerations are addressed below.

Gross or Net Revenue?

To recognize and report revenue on its SCI, a company must be entitled to the full benefits of the increase in net assets. For example, consider an on-line auction company, Auction Inc. (AI) operating a website that lists items provided by the sellers and matches them with possible buyers. The seller sets the price and either accepts or rejects buyers' bids. Suppose an item is sold for $100 for which the site receives $5. What should AI report as revenue: the total amount of sales ($100) transacted through its website or only the commission ($5)?

If the full value of the sale is recorded, it would imply that the total sales value would increase AI's net assets. But AI has no control over the transaction prices. AI sets the commission and other fees it charges, but the price is set between the buyer and the seller. Therefore, AI is not entitled to the full benefits of the negotiated price, only to the commission. This is true even though the company collects the purchase price from the buyer and then passes on the proceeds, net of commission, to the seller. In this example, AI is an *agent* and will record revenue on a **net basis**.

Indicators that a company is actually *operating as an agent on behalf of another party* and that it is the other party's responsibility to fulfill the contract are the facts that the company:

- Bears no inventory risk at any time during the contract;
- Cannot change the price;

- Earns a commission; and
- Does not assume any credit risk.

In many cases, some of these indicators will be present and some absent. Professional judgment is required in the more complex cases to determine whether the company is acting as an agent. If the company has control of the goods or services for some period of time prior to the sale to the ultimate customer, the company is more likely acting as a *principal* and will record revenue at the **gross amount**.

Variable Consideration

Variable consideration is any amount of the consideration that is not fixed and can vary on the basis of certain terms of the contract. For example, variable consideration may arise with performance bonuses, penalties, price concessions, and customers' right to return products. In determining the amount of consideration under the contract, the seller must estimate the amount of the variable consideration using an expected value or more likely amount. This amount is included in the transaction price only if it is highly probable (i.e., likely to occur) that a significant amount will not later be reversed once the uncertainty is resolved. So the test is to determine whether the amount of variable consideration is highly likely to be received. If not, it should not be included in the price until the amount is known with certainty.

Example

On July 1, Casters Inc. enters into a contract with a customer to sell its Product X for $100 per unit. If the customer buys over 300 units over the next six months, Casters will provide a volume rebate effectively reducing the price to $85 per unit.

The consideration is therefore made up of a fixed amount of $85 and a variable amount of $15 per unit ($100 − $85). Based on past history, Casters does not believe that the customer will reach the 300 units. Casters believes there is a high probability that a significant revenue reversal (i.e., a reversal of $15) will not occur because the sales to this customer will not exceed 300 units, and therefore expects to be entitled to the $100 per unit. Casters then records revenue at $100 per unit.

Assume sales are as follows:

July 1	30 units
August	50 units
September	100 units
October	80 units

For July, August, and September, the company uses the $100 price per unit to recognize the sales and recorded revenue of $18,000 (180 × $100).

However, in October, judging from the customer purchase pattern, Caster concludes that on the basis of this new information, it is highly probable that the customer will reach 300 units prior to the end of the six-month contract and that a significant reversal of revenue will now occur. Accordingly, an adjustment is required to the price charged for the sales in July, August, and September, and October sales will be recognized at $85 per unit. The following entries are now required in October:

To adjust the unit price to $85 for the sales July to September:

Dr. Revenue (180 × $15)	2,700	
Cr. Accounts receivable		2,700
Dr. Account receivable (80 × $85)	6,800	
Cr. Revenue		6,800

Non-refundable Payments

Non-refundable upfront fees might be charged at the beginning of a contract. For example, initiation fees are often paid when you join a golf club. However, just because these fees are non-refundable does not mean they can be immediately recognized as revenue. The contract must be assessed to determine if the payment is related to a separate performance obligation or if it represents an advance payment for future goods and services. In either case, the fees received will be recognized initially as a contract liability and then as revenue when the *performance obligation* with respect to these fees is completed. In the case of a golf club, a new member paying an initiation fee has the ability to use the golf course generally over the rest of the member's life, as long as annual dues are paid. If the company determines that the member will be able to use the golf course for 35 years, the initiation fee is recognized evenly over this period.

Suppose that a client pays a non-refundable $100,000 lump sum to a law firm on 1 January. This payment guarantees that, for one year, the law firm will provide service as needed, *for extra compensation* over and above the $100,000. The law firm is committing to provide the client with *access* for $100,000, nothing more. This type of payment is commonly referred to as a *retainer*. The amount would be recorded as a contract liability when received, and then transferred to revenue month by month, as the revenue is earned evenly through the contract term. It doesn't matter whether the client actually required any service in a particular month, or whether the law firm was billing an extra $2 million in legal services rendered. The law firm *stood ready* to supply the service on demand as the contract requires, and thus the passage of time dictates revenue recognition.

In other cases, revenue recognition for a non-refundable upfront fee may be at *one point in time*. For example, think about a non-refundable upfront fee that relates to the transfer of goods to a customer. The transaction price (including the non-refundable upfront fee) will be recognized as revenue when the goods are delivered (at the point of transfer).

Every contract must be reviewed to see when the underlying performance obligations are complete and the related non-refundable upfront fees can be transferred from the contract liability to revenue.

Delayed Payment Contracts

Some contracts spread the cash paid by the buyer over future periods. For example, a $5 million contract may be payable $1 million a year for five years. If interest is charged over and above the $5 million (or on the outstanding balance), then this separate interest revenue is recognized as time passes. However, if the contract *appears to be interest-free*, the accountant must recognize *substance over form*, and acknowledge that there is no real economic truth to an interest-free contract. Interest is included in the $5 million price, and must be accounted for separately. This means that the amount of consideration is the *present value* of the *discounted cash flows*. The difference between the discounted amount and the gross amount is *imputed interest*, which is *recognized as time passes*. This is independent of the timing of the revenue recognition for the sale contract itself. (In practice, if the consideration is paid within a year, there is no need to present-value the cash flows.)

We will return to an examination of present value techniques in our discussion of notes receivable in Chapter 7. However, since discounting affects revenue recognition, we will provide a brief example here.

Example

A company delivers new manufacturing equipment on 1 January 20X1. The contract specifies that $4 million be paid on delivery and another $3 million is due on 1 January 20X3. Applying the five steps:

1. *Identify the contract with the customer.* We assume that there is a contract between the buyer and the seller that has an agreed-upon price of $7 million for the delivery of manufacturing equipment.

2. *Identify separate performance obligations, if they exist.* There is only one performance obligation: to deliver the equipment.

3. *Determine the overall contract price.* Although the contract price is $7 million in total, part of the payment will not be received for another two years. The $3 million must be discounted. Assuming that the appropriate discount rate is 6%, this has a present value of $2,670,000.[2] This results in the total consideration being $6,670,000, including the $4 million initial payment. There is also $330,000 ($3,000,000 − $2,670,000) of imputed interest involved in this contract.

---

2. Calculation of present value is as follows: $3,000,000/(1.06)^2$ More detail is provided in Chapter 7.

4. *Allocate the contract price to the separate performance obligations.* There is only one performance obligation for this contract, so this step is not needed.

5. *Determine when the performance obligation is satisfied and revenue can be recognized.* The performance obligation for the delivery of the manufacturing line is complete once the items are accepted by the customer on 1 January 20X1. This is when the $6,670,000 contract consideration is recognized.

Imputed interest of $330,000 is recognized as time passes.

Entries

On 1 January 20X1, revenue of $6,670,000 is recognized along with cash of $4 million and a long-term receivable of $2,670,000 as follows:

Dr. Cash	4,000,000	
Dr. Long-term receivable	2,670,000	
Cr. Revenue		6,670,000

In subsequent periods, the company will recognize interest revenue as time passes. The accounting treatment of discounted long-term receivables is illustrated in Chapter 7.

Non-cash Consideration

What happens when part or all of the consideration is not cash, but some other form of asset, good, or service? In these cases, the transaction price is determined to be the fair value of the non-cash consideration received. When it is impossible to determine the fair value of the consideration that is received, the company can use the estimated selling price of the goods or services being transferred. We will discuss non-monetary transactions later in this chapter.

MULTIPLE GOODS AND SERVICES CONTRACTS

A contract has **multiple deliverables** if it includes a *bundle of goods and/or services* in a single contract. Examples of different goods and/or services, which constitute *separate performance obligations*, are:

- Delivery of goods;
- Provision of a service;
- Providing a warranty;
- Granting licences for the use of intangible property
- Constructing, manufacturing, or developing an asset on behalf of a customer; and
- Granting options to the customer to receive additional goods or services at discounted prices.

Multiple deliverables make the timing and amount of recognition of revenue for the contract challenging. Refer again to Exhibit 6-2, which outlines the five-step process used for contract-based revenue recognition decisions:

- *Step 2* in the assessment of a contract requires an entity to determine if the contract is made up of more than one performance obligation. *Revenue is recognized for each separate performance obligation as the performance obligation is satisfied.*

- *Step 4* then requires the consideration to be allocated to each of these separate obligations.

Distinct Performance Obligations

First, let us examine step 2. When is there more than one performance obligation in a contract? Consider a software company that sells an advanced processing system to a client. The sales contract also includes three years of technical service, as well as periodic software updates at a reduced rate. There appear to be three distinct goods and services under this contract. The company has obligations to deliver (1) the processing system, (2) the updates, and (3) the technical services. Ideally, each promised good or service in such an agreement should be accounted for individually as a separate revenue-generating activity, provided that each is **distinct**. A good or service is *distinct* if both of the following criteria are met:

a. The customer can use the good or service on its own or with other resources that it can readily obtain (the good or service is capable of being distinct). For example, the good or service being sold separately by the seller would be evidence the item can be used on its own.

b. The seller's promise to deliver the good or service is separately identifiable from other items to be delivered in the contract. Examples of situations in which these items are separately identifiable are:

   - The contract's goods and services are not inputs used to produce or deliver a combined output to the customer;
   - A good or service does not modify another promised good or service in the contract;
   - A good or service is not highly dependent on, or highly integrated, with other goods and services promised in the contract.

Not distinct

The term "distinct" should not be taken too literally. In cases in which the products in the contract are *not distinct*, they will be treated as a single performance obligation. In this case, revenue would be recognized in one pattern only. If the goods and services are highly interrelated and integrated, or if significant customization of the bundle of goods and services is required, they are not distinct.

If a contract seems to have four different components but there is no separate sales market (stand-alone value) for *some* of them, those components should be combined with another component to form a single unit for accounting purposes.

Allocation of Consideration

Next, we move on to step 4. It is necessary to *allocate the consideration to the individual distinct items*. This allocation is calculated based on the **relative stand-alone value** of each good and service being delivered—that is, the fair value of that performance obligation when sold on its own. The stand-alone value is its selling price when sold alone. If this amount is not observable, the stand-alone value can be estimated using the following methods:

1. *Adjusted market assessment approach.* An entity estimates the price that a customer would have to pay for the good or service by reviewing competitors' prices for similar items and adjusting these prices accordingly for its own costs and margins.

2. *Expected cost plus margin approach.* An entity estimates the price by estimating costs and adding an appropriate margin.

3. *Residual value method.* An entity takes the total transaction price less the sum of observable stand-alone values for the other goods and services in the contract. However, this method can only be used if either of the following conditions exist:
   a. The entity sells the same good or service to different customers for a wide range of different selling prices; or
   b. A price for the good or service has not yet been established and has not been previously sold on a stand-alone basis.

Example 1

Allocation based on stand-alone selling prices

Suppose that on 20 December 20X4 Crease Computers Ltd. enters into a $900,000 contract with a customer to supply a sophisticated mainframe computer plus three years of regular service. Using the five steps as a framework:

1. *Identify the contract with the customer.* We assume that there is a contract between the buyer and the seller. The contract price is $900,000 for the mainframe plus the three-year service agreement.

2. *Identify separate performance obligations, if they exist.* There are two performance obligations: to deliver the mainframe and to provide three years of service. These are distinct because they are sold separately.

3. *Determine the overall contract price.* The contract price is $900,000 as agreed to by the customer.

4. *Allocate the contract price to the separate performance obligations.* The computer has a stand-alone selling price of $800,000 and the service is sold separately for $200,000. The total revenue will be allocated as follows (in thousands):

Revenue from sale of computer	$900[$800÷($800+$200)]	= $720
Revenue from service contract	$900[$200÷($800+$200)]	= 180
Total revenue		$900

5. *Determine when the performance obligation is satisfied and revenue can be recognized.* The performance obligation for the delivery of the mainframe is complete once the customer accepts. The service maintenance is completed over three years.

If the customer is paying for the entire contract at the outset and the computer is delivered to the customer on 20 December 20X4, the journal entry to record the sale will appear as follows:

20 December 20X4:		
Cash	900,000	
Revenue—sale of equipment		720,000
Contract liability		180,000

Since the delivery of the service will likely happen evenly over time, the revenue from the service contract will be recognized evenly over each of the following three years:

31 December 20X5, 20X6, and 20X7:		
Contract liability	60,000	
Revenue—service contracts		60,000

If the company does not sell each component separately, a stand-alone price might still be established by estimating the price competitors would normally charge for similar items or using a cost plus margin approach.

Example 2

Allocation when stand-alone prices are highly uncertain

In limited circumstances, the stand-alone price of one of the items may be highly uncertain and have a range of possible values. Examples of this would occur when the same item is sold to different customers for different prices or the company has not yet established a selling price for the item. In these circumstances, the stand-alone price can be estimated using the **residual approach**: the difference between the total contract consideration and the total of the stand-alone values of all the other items in the contract.

In the preceding example, if the value of the service contract is highly variable, Crease would allocate the $900,000 total consideration as $800,000 to the computer and the residual of $100,000 to the services.

Not distinct

Assume that Crease has another contract with a customer that includes software that will be highly customized for the specific needs of the company and services to transfer the customer data onto the new system. The software and services in this contract are integrated and the software cannot work without the services. These performance obligations are not distinct because they are so interrelated. The contract is therefore be recognized as a single performance obligation. Its revenue is recognized at the single point in time when the software is installed and the data transfer complete.

Examples of Multiple Deliverable Contracts

We now look at two common examples of contracts that have several performance obligations: customer loyalty programs and franchise fees.

Customer Loyalty Programs

Many companies have loyalty points programs to cement customer relationships, provide promotional opportunities, and track buyer behaviour. At the time of a sale, the customer not only receives the goods or service but also receives points that can be used toward future purchases. From the company's perspective then, two separate performance obligations are entered into at the time of sale: the delivery of the good or service and the right of the customer to use the points received toward a future sale.

Consider the following example: Drug Store Inc. (DSI) has a loyalty points program that awards one point for every $10 of goods purchased. During the month, the company sold $250,000 of goods in the store and awarded 2,500 points which can be redeemed and used toward future purchases. The stand-alone selling price for the goods sold is $250,000. Based on past experience, DSI expects that only 90% of the points will actually be redeemed. The stand-alone selling price of the points is $1 per point. Assuming 90% expected redemption, the value of the loyalty points is $2,250 (2,500 × $1.00 × 90%). The total of the two stand-alone values is $252,250 ($250,000 + $2,250).

Based on the relative stand-alone prices of the two separate performance obligations, the sales for the month would be reported as follows:

		Allocation of Consideration
Goods sold	[$250,000 ÷ ($252,250)] ×$250,000	$247,770
Points sold	[$2,250 ÷ ($252,250)] ×$250,000	2,230
Total		$250,000

Dr. Cash	$250,000	
Cr. Revenue		$247,770
Cr. Provision for loyalty program awards		2,230

Each year, the remaining points outstanding need to be assessed for redemption rates (known as "breakage") and adjusted accordingly. This provision will be covered again in Chapter 12.

Franchise Fees

Franchise fee arrangements are often complex, making revenue recognition decisions challenging.

Suppose that a doughnut chain (franchisor) "sells" one of its stores to an entrepreneur for an upfront franchise fee of $500,000 plus 2% of the store's gross revenues on a monthly basis. For this fee, the franchisor agrees to allow the entrepreneur to use its trade name and sell its product for 20 years. The franchisor also will provide market know-how as needed for five years, employee training, and all necessary equipment.

As we analyze the contract using the five-step approach, it is step 2, determining the distinct performance obligations of the franchisor, that is problematic. Stand-alone items must be identified, through research and investigation. It is determined that the rights to the trade name, product sale, and market experience cannot be separated and that in combination they are distinct from the training and equipment. This constitutes one performance obligation. Training and equipment are also sold separately and each has a stand-alone value. These are two more performance obligations, making three in total.

In step 4, the $500,000 is allocated to the three separate performance obligations and recognized as each of the separate performance obligations are dealt with. In this case, the training and equipment revenues are recognized on delivery when control is transferred. The right to use the trade name and market know-how is recognized with the passage of time (over the five years) commencing when the entrepreneur opens his business and starts to use them.

ACCOUNTING FOR LOSSES ON LONG-TERM CONTRACTS

When the costs exceed revenues and losses result in a contract, two situations are possible:

1. There is a loss in the current year, but the overall contract remains profitable.

2. The contract becomes unprofitable overall, and is thus an *onerous contract*.

Loss in the Current Year

Return to the Ace example in Exhibit 6-6, where revenue is recognized over time. Suppose Ace's costs incurred to the end of 20X2 are as shown, but the estimate to complete the contract has increased to $550,000. Total costs of $900,000 have already been incurred in 20X1 and 20X2. Therefore, the total estimated cost of completing the contract is now $1,450,000. The contract will still generate a gross margin of $50,000, so it is still a profitable contract overall.

Using the revised cost estimates at the end of 20X2, the completion percentage becomes 62%; $900,000 ÷ $1,450,000. The cumulative amount of revenue that will be reported at the end of 20X2 is $1,500,000 × 62% = $930,000.

Exhibit 6-11 shows the revised calculation. A loss is recorded for 20X2. In effect, the loss is caused by estimation errors in 20X1—the future costs to complete were estimated at too low a level, which caused too much gross profit to be recognized in 20X1. The impact of this corrects itself in the next year.

EXHIBIT 6-11			
CONTRACT MEASURED OVER TIME—LOSSES ON LONG-TERM CONTRACTS DUE TO CHANGES IN COST ESTIMATES			
Overall Profit; Loss in an Individual Year			
	20X1	**20X2**	**20X3**
Costs incurred to date for performance	$ 350,000	$ 900,000	$ 1,450,000
Estimated total costs	1,350,000	1,450,000	1,450,000
Percent completed	26%	62%	100%
Cumulative revenue recognized:			
$1.5 million × 26%; 62%; 100%	$ 390,000	$ 930,000	$ 1,500,000
Less: revenue previously recognized	—	(390,000)	(930,000)
Recognized revenue for the year	$ 390,000	$ 540,000	$ 570,000
Costs incurred during the year for performance	350,000	550,000	550,000
Gross margin (loss)	$ 40,000	$ (10,000)	$ 20,000

Overall Contract Loss—Onerous Contracts

A test must be done to see if the remaining performance obligation under a long-term contract is *onerous*, or *not profitable*. A contracted performance obligation is an **onerous contract** when the *consideration yet to be received* is less than the *lowest cost of settling the obligation*. This *lowest cost* is determined as the lower of:

1. The costs required to satisfy and complete the obligation; and
2. The amount the company would have to pay to cancel and exit the contract, if this is allowed.

When a contract represents an onerous contract, expected losses are recognized in the current year, before they are realized.

For example, assume that at the end of 20X4 there was $250,000 of remaining revenue in a contract, and expected costs to complete were $450,000. The contract will end in 20X5. The contractor investigates, and discovers that it would cost $625,000 to cancel the contract or have another contractor complete the work. Thus, $450,000 is the lowest-cost alternative. This is an onerous contract, because a loss of $200,000 is expected *in 20X5*. The $200,000 expected loss would be recorded *in 20X4*, with a credit recorded to a special provision (estimated liability) for onerous contracts. This is recorded in 20X4 as follows:

Loss on contract billings	200,000	
Provision for onerous contract		200,000

At each reporting date, this *onerous test* is updated and changes in the liability reported in profit or loss for the period. At the end of the contract, the onerous liability is **derecognized**, or eliminated in the books. Onerous contracts are also addressed in Chapter 12.

CONCEPT REVIEW

1. How is revenue measured when there are delayed payments?
2. What criteria are used to decide if a contract has more than one performance obligation?
3. Explain the relative value method.
4. When is a long-term contract an onerous contract?

Agricultural Produce and Biological Assets

IAS 41 gives special attention to agricultural produce and **biological assets**. Biological assets are unique in that they are living and growing assets owned by a company. Examples of biological assets are livestock (cattle, milk cows, and pigs) and plants. Some biological assets are **bearer plants**—that is, living plants that will be used for production and are expected to "bear produce" over more than one period and will likely be sold for scrap. Bearer plants are accounted for under IAS 16 (Property, Plant and Equipment) and are covered in Chapter 9. Biological assets that are not bearer plants are measured by the accounting standards using a *fair value approach*, because changes in fair values of these assets are seen to have a direct relationship with expected future economic cash flows.

Definitions

The basic definitions are as follows:

- *Biological assets* are living animals or plants (including trees, such as orchards and timberlands).
- **Agricultural produce** is the harvested product of a company's biological assets (e.g., wheat, fruit, milk, timber).
- *Harvest* involves separating the agricultural produce from the biological asset (e.g, picking apples in an orchard) or ending its life (e.g., cutting trees).
- *Products that are the result of processing after harvest* are products that have taken the agricultural produce and *done something else with it*, such as turning milk into butter or cheese, or grapes into wine. These items are classified as inventory.

Measurement

Biological assets and agricultural produce are only *recognized* when:

- The company controls the asset as the result of past events (i.e., planting crops or trees, or buying animals to raise to maturity);
- It is probable that the future economic benefits of the asset will flow to the reporting entity; and
- The asset's fair value can be reliably measured.

At each reporting date, the biological assets (other than bearer plants) are *measured at their fair value less costs to sell*. In cases where the fair value cannot be measured reliably at the time of initial recognition, the biological asset will be measured at cost less accumulated depreciation less accumulated impairment losses. *The change in value during the reporting period is recognized in earnings* for the year. Costs incurred during the period are recognized as expenses.

At the time of harvest, agricultural produce is valued at its fair value less costs to sell. This will become the cost of the item used for inventory valuation purposes. *Agricultural produce is not subsequently re-measured to a new fair value as the inventory valuation rules of lower of cost and net realizable value will apply.*

Reporting Example

As an example of biological assets, consider the following disclosures by Andrew Peller, a large Canadian winery:

Inventories

Inventories are valued at the lower of cost and net realizable value. Cost is determined on an average cost basis. The Company utilizes a weighted average cost calculation to determine the value of ending inventory (bulk wine and finished goods). Average cost is determined separately for import wine and domestic wine and is calculated by varietal and vintage year.

Grapes produced from vineyards controlled by the Company that are part of inventories are measured at their fair value less costs to sell at the point of harvest.

The Company includes borrowing costs in the cost of certain wine inventories that require a substantial period of time to become ready for sale.

Biological Assets

The Company measures biological assets, consisting of grape vines, at fair value less costs to sell. Agricultural produce, consisting of grapes grown on vineyards controlled by the Company, is measured at fair value less cost to sell at the point of harvest and becomes the basis for the cost of inventories after harvest.

Gains or losses arising from a change in fair value less costs to sell are included in the consolidated statement of earnings in the period in which they arise.

Fair Value of Biological Assets

Determining the fair value of grape vines involves making assumptions about how market participants assign the value of a vineyard between vines, land and other assets. Changes in the fair value of vines may occur as a result of changes in numerous factors, including vine health and expected future yields.

To estimate the fair value of controlled vines planted on leased land, discounted cash flows over the estimated remaining life of vines or the remaining lease term, whichever is shorter, were used. The fair value of vines on leased land reduces to $nil as the lease nears its expiration date. Assumptions used include the discount rate, expected yields, grape price trends, and annual growing cost trends.

To estimate the fair value of vines in the middle and later stages of development, the estimated fair value of mature vines was reduced by the net discounted cash outflows necessary to bring the vines to a fully developed state.

Actual amounts may vary from these assumptions and cause significant adjustments.

Fair Value of Grapes at the Point of Harvest

Where possible, the fair value of grapes at the point of harvest is determined by reference to local market prices for grapes of a similar quality and the same varietal. For grapes for which local market prices are not readily available, the average price of similar grapes is used. Actual amounts may vary from these assumptions and cause significant adjustments.

Source: Andrew Peller Limited, *2015 Annual Report*, Notes to Consolidated Financial Statements: p. 3, partial extract from Note 2, Summary of significant accounting policies; and p. 38, partial extract from Note 3, Critical accounting estimates and judgments, www.andrewpeller.com.

Peller reports its grapevines as biological assets. These assets are reported at fair value less costs to sell at each reporting period. Agricultural produce are the grapes grown on the vines controlled by Peller. Once the grapes are harvested, they are agricultural produce and are recognized at fair value less costs to sell as their deemed cost for inventory valuation.

Application

To illustrate accounting for biological assets, suppose that a farmer buys hogs for $150,000 at the end of 20X0. The purchase is recorded as a biological asset of $150,000, offset by the decline in cash.

During 20X1, the hogs are sheltered, fed, and otherwise cared for at a cost of $35,000. At the end of 20X1, the fair value less cost to sell of hogs of that age, type, and weight is $200,000. On the farmer's SFP, the biological asset "hogs" is written up by $50,000; the $50,000 gain is recognized in earnings as a "gain on biological asset—hogs." The $35,000 cost of caring for the hogs is charged as an expense. The net profit from raising hogs in 20X1 is $15,000.

Note that the increase in value is recorded as a gain, not as revenue. We usually reserve the term *revenue* for products that have been sold during the period rather than products held over the period. Regardless of what we call them, the increase in asset value is recognized in earnings because we've increased net assets. The resources expended to care for the hogs have decreased net assets, and therefore an expense has been recognized.

Further costs for raising the hogs of $55,000 are incurred in 20X2. That expenditure of resources will be recorded as an expense of the period. Near the end of 20X2, the hogs are slaughtered, an act that converts the hogs (as biological assets) to agricultural produce (as carcasses); the fair value less costs to sell at the time of slaughter for the carcasses is $300,000. On the 20X2 SFP, the classification of the asset has changed from biological assets (hogs) to inventory (carcasses). During the year, the value of hogs increased from $200,000 (at the beginning of 20X2) to $300,000 at the time of harvest. The net increase of $100,000 is reported in earnings as a gain on biological assets. The $55,000 cost of raising the hogs in 20X2 is charged to expense.

In 20X3, the hog carcasses are now part of inventory and valued at the *lower* of cost ($300,000 at the time of harvest) and net realizable value. As part of the processing, the carcasses are cut up into pork chops and processed into other pork products. Additional costs to process the inventory were $25,000. Finally, the pork products are sold in the commercial market for $400,000. The total cost of goods sold is $325,000 ($300,000 + $25,000). 20X3 earnings will show:

- Revenue from sale of pork products of $400,000; and
- Cost of goods sold of $325,000.

Exhibit 6-12 shows the financial statement effects of this series of events.

EXHIBIT 6-12

ILLUSTRATION OF BIOLOGICAL ASSET ACCOUNTING

(in thousands)

Year/Events	Gain or Revenue	Expense	Net Earnings	Y/E Balance, Biological Assets	Y/E Balance, Inventory
20X0:					
buy hogs	nil	nil	nil	150	nil
20X1:					
raise hogs	**Gain** $50	Costs to tend hogs $35	$ 15	+50 200	nil
20X2:					
(1) raise hogs;	**Gain** $100	Costs to tend hogs $55	$ 45	+100	
(2) convert to carcasses				−300 (transfer to inventory) 0	+300 300
20X3:					
(1) process into pork products in inventory				nil	+25 325
(2) sale of pork products	**Revenue** from sale of products $400	Cost of goods sold $325	$75		−325 0

Biological Assets Not Immediately Saleable

In the previous illustration, the biological asset (hogs) have a market price at various stages of maturity, which we used for valuation (i.e, the value changed from $150,000 to $300,000 as the hogs matured). These prices would be obtainable, and verifiable, in commodity markets with reference to the age and weight of livestock. Other biological assets do not have such reference prices.

For example, consider standing timber—that is, trees destined for harvest but still standing and growing. There is no market for immature trees that are not yet of a size to become lumber. However, there is a market for (mature) felled trees, or logs. The value of mature logs must be used to measure the net realizable value of the immature growing trees, but many adjustments are required.

Brookfield Asset Management Inc. states:

Sustainable resources consist of standing timber and other agricultural assets and are measured at fair value after deducting the estimated selling costs and are recorded in sustainable resources on the Consolidated Balance Sheets. Estimated selling costs include commissions, levies, delivery costs, transfer taxes and duties. The fair value of standing timber is calculated using the present value of anticipated future cash flows for standing timber before tax and terminal dates of 20 to 28 years. Fair value is determined based on existing, sustainable felling plans and assessments regarding growth, timber prices and felling and silviculture costs. Changes in fair value are recorded in net income in the period of change. The company determines fair value of its standing timber using external valuations on an annual basis.

(Brookfield Asset Management Inc. 2014 annual report, p. 91; www.brookfield.com)

To determine the fair value of their biological assets, Brookfield must look ahead to the saleability of that type of mature wood logs, adjusted for the current age of the trees, deduct felling and forestry costs, and then use discounting to present-value expected net future cash flows to the current year-end.

CONCEPT REVIEW

1. What is the difference between a biological asset, agricultural produce, and an inventory item?
2. How are biological assets valued?

NON-MONETARY TRANSACTIONS

Most transactions are based on a transfer of money. However, two entities can exchange assets, goods, or services without any money changing hands. Logically enough, these are called **non-monetary transactions**. Measurement issues can be quite significant for a non-monetary transaction if there is no obvious way to measure the value of the exchange.

Remember that **non-monetary assets**, such as inventory and capital assets, *do not have a value that is fixed in terms of dollars*, and their fair value can be subjective. **Monetary assets**, on the other hand, are assets whose value is fixed in terms of dollars. In addition to cash, monetary assets include receivables and investments in bonds.

Monetary transactions are those in which an exchange has one "side" primarily based on any *monetary asset*; non-monetary transactions lack this anchor. However, a transaction can be "non-monetary" and still have some small cash component. Relatively small amounts of cash might be used to equalize an exchange, to make up for agreed-upon differences in value of the non-monetary assets exchanged.

Valuation Alternatives

There are two general approaches to valuation of a non-monetary transaction:

- The **fair value method**, in which the asset or service acquired is valued on the basis of fair value, or
- The **book value method**, in which the asset or service acquired is valued at the carrying (book) value of the asset or service given up.

These alternatives are explored in the situations that follow.

Barter Transactions

Sometimes, two entities exchange (or **barter**) goods or services. Some exchanges involve similar goods while others involve dissimilar goods; the similarity/dissimilarity should be based on common sense and fairly obvious. The two categories are treated differently because the intent of the exchange is quite different.

Exchange of Similar Goods or Services

An exchange of goods of *similar nature* is treated as a straight exchange, valued at book value with *no revenue or expense* recognized.

Suppose that an oil company has ample supply of oil in storage in Ontario but is short of supply in Newfoundland. Another company has a reasonable supply in Newfoundland but is running low in Ontario. The two companies can agree to an exchange of a fixed and equal quantity of inventory, which is in the best interests of both. The ultimate sales are to customers in the two provinces. *The goods acquired are valued at the carrying value of the goods given up.* Assume that the Ontario inventory for the first company has a cost of $189,000 and a fair value of $265,000. No revenue or change in value is recorded, and the entry is:

Inventory—Newfoundland	189,000	
Inventory—Ontario		189,000

Exchange of Dissimilar Goods or Services

When the goods or services exchanged are dissimilar, the amount of revenue is measured at fair value, using the fair value of the consideration *received*. If the fair value of the consideration received cannot be determined, the fair value of the goods or services given up may be used to value the transaction. Establishing fair value often involves professional judgement.

For example, suppose that an accountant regularly prepares the tax return for a resort owner. Depending on the year and the amount of work involved, this has cost the resort owner between $1,000 and $2,000. For the past year, the resort business has been depressed and the resort company has very little cash. The accountant agrees to accept her payment in the form of an all-inclusive one-week vacation at the resort. Since the transfer is of dissimilar goods and services, the accountant should record revenue as the value of the vacation that she is receiving.

That raises a problem for her, however. Just what is the value of the vacation? There is the official list price, known in the hotel trade as the "rack rate," but rack rates are frequently discounted. Hoteliers discount heavily to attract business, based on the season and demand. The accountant searches on-line, and can find much cheaper rates, which seem more reasonable than the rack rate. But on-line prices vary significantly based on timing—school vacation and holiday weeks are more expensive weeks than shoulder season prices.

The hotelier has a similar problem. Effectively, he has sold a week's vacation and received a tax return as consideration. He must decide what value to assign to the accountant's services. After all, it might be a slow period for the accountant too, which is why she was willing to accept hotel accommodation instead of finding another client who will pay cash. It is a valuation challenge for both parties! There is no requirement for the two parties to the transaction to record a common value; each reaches her or his own decision about the value received.

Assume that the accountant has made her reservation for a week in March and has a firm reference point through an on-line quote for a $1,500 value. This is close to the amount she billed in cash last year for the tax return, something she knew when she agreed to the terms of the exchange. As a result, the amount seems reasonable to her. The entry is:

Prepaid vacation asset	1,500	
Revenue—tax return preparation		1,500

Exchanges of Capital Assets

Capital assets (including property, plant, equipment, and intangible assets) are often exchanged for other capital assets. For example, old equipment is traded in on the purchase of new equipment. These transactions do not give rise to *revenue*, but rather may generate *gains and losses*. Gains and losses are the appropriate classification because the exchange is peripheral and not part of customer-related revenue-generating activities. Again, the two alternative valuation approaches for the transaction are *fair value* versus *book value*.

Illustration of Valuation Alternatives

Assume that Company 1 and Company 2 decide to exchange assets. Since Company 1's asset is worth $40,000 versus the $45,000 for Company 2's asset, Company 1 will pay $5,000 to make the exchange even. This monetary amount is low in relation to the value of the transaction, so the transaction is still classified as non-monetary. The facts:

	Co. 1	Co. 2
Asset original cost	$76,400	$91,600
Accumulated depreciation	58,000	61,900
Net book value	$18,400	$29,700
Fair value of asset	$40,000	$45,000
Cash to change hands: $5,000, paid by Co. 1 to Co. 2		

Here are the two alternative ways to record the transaction on Company 1's books:

At Fair Value			At Book Value		
New asset	45,000		New asset**	23,400	
Accumulated depreciation, old	58,000		Accumulated depreciation, old	58,000	
Gain on exchange*		21,600	Cash		5,000
Cash		5,000	Old asset		76,400
Old asset		76,400			
*$40,000 – $18,400.					
**$5,000 + $18,400.					

Both entries record the disposal of the old asset, removing its original cost and accumulated depreciation from the books. Both record the $5,000 cash paid. But they differ significantly in the valuation of the new asset and recognition of a gain or loss.

Under fair value treatment, the new asset is recorded at its $45,000 fair value, and a gain is recorded as the difference between the $18,400 book value of the old asset and its fair value, or trade-in value—$40,000. Under the book value alternative, the new asset is recorded at a deflated value—the book value of the old asset, $18,400, plus $5,000 cash paid. No gain is recorded. There is quite a difference between $45,000 and $23,400, a valuation difference that affects earnings, assets on the SFP, and the level of depreciation expense in years to come.

Now we can consider the circumstances in which each method is acceptable.

Commercial Substance

As we saw above, accounting treatment of *barter transactions for goods and services* relied on a judgement of whether the exchanged items were similar. In contrast, accounting treatment of non-monetary exchanges of capital assets relies on a judgement of whether the transaction has *commercial substance*. That is:

Use the Fair-Value Method If:	Use the Book Value Method If:
• The transaction has *commercial substance*—the net present value or the configuration of cash flows is significantly altered by the exchange.	• The transaction has no *commercial substance*; the configuration of cash flows has not changed; or
	• The exchange has been in the ordinary course of business to facilitate a sale to a third party; or
	• Fair values cannot be determined; or
	• The exchange is a distribution to shareholders (part of a restructuring, spin-off, or liquidation).

Commercial substance exists if there is a significant change in the company's cash flows after the exchange. A transaction has commercial substance when:

- The configuration (i.e., the risk, timing, or amount) of the cash flows of the asset received differs significantly from the configuration of the cash flows of the asset given up; or
- The present value of the after-tax cash flow from use of the new asset is significantly different from that of the old asset. (The present value of the cash flows is called the "entity-specific value" of the asset.)

Significance is measured relative to the fair value of the assets exchanged, not to the overall operations of the company, and is a matter for professional judgement.

As stated above, certain circumstances dictate use of the book value method:

- If the transaction lacks commercial substance.
- The transaction is in the normal course of business and is part of a chain of transactions that will culminate in the transfer to a third party. For example, a parcel of assets might be assembled to meet contract requirements. Profit (or loss) will be recognized only when the sale to the eventual third party takes place.
- Fair values are not reliably determinable for either asset in the exchange. Undeterminable fair values exist when alternative measures of fair value are very different, or probabilities cannot be reliably assigned to different estimates in a range of fair values.
- The gain and loss is derived from transactions with shareholders in their role as shareholders. When the non-monetary transaction is a distribution to shareholders, the company receives nothing in return. These distributions should not trigger a gain or a loss and are recorded at book value.

Use of the book value approach in the absence of commercial substance is logical. If commercial substance is absent, there is no real difference in cash flows to the company "before" versus "after" the transaction. Companies should not be able to trade similar assets and record a gain or loss that has little economic substance.

Sources of Fair Values

Where do fair-value numbers come from? *Fair value* is ideally determined in an orderly market transaction, and is the price agreed to between market participants on the measurement date. Unfortunately, used equipment can be pretty thinly traded, and fair value can be difficult to establish. Here are some of the alternatives:

- Base fair value on prices actually observed in market transactions of identical assets; this is the ideal!
- Obtain quoted cash prices from suppliers of new and used assets. Remember, though, that the cash price is lower than the list price for many assets, and list price must be adjusted downward to cash price if this is the case.
- When a quoted cash price is unavailable, a company can invite bids for the asset to be exchanged. The highest reasonable bid for the asset in question is used as the fair value. However, this approach is not always appreciated by the companies that invest time and energy submitting quotes, only to discover that the asset wasn't really to be sold!
- Appraisal is another commonly used approach, although appraisals are notoriously subjective.
- Fair value can also be determined on the basis of prices for *similar* but not identical assets, adjusted for obvious differences such as age, operating efficiency, and capacity.
- A less reliable but commonly used alternative is published information on the average price of specific used assets, such as the *Kelley Blue Book* for automobiles.

As stated above, if fair value cannot be reliably determined for either of the assets in a swap, the book value method must be used.

Fair Value of Which Asset?

The general rule in the fair-value method for the exchange of capital assets is that the fair value of *the asset being given up* should be used to record the asset acquired. If, however, the fair value of the asset received is more clearly evident, this fair value should be used. (This is different from the valuation rule for barter transactions, explained above, in which the fair value of the good or service received is the primary reference point; instead, *capital assets start with the asset given up*.)

Sometimes, both fair values are known but they are not consistent with each other. Remember, two arm's-length companies would not trade assets unless the fair value of each was similar. Practical common sense should dictate measurement. For example, if an asset with a reported fair value of $25,000 was exchanged for an asset with a reported fair value of $32,000, and no cash changed hands, one of the fair values is clearly incorrect. *A determination must be made about which fair value is more reliable, and the valuation flows from there.*

Sometimes, one fair value is known but not the other. In this case, the exchange is valued at the known fair value, adjusted for cash paid. Consider the following cases:

	Case 1	Case 2	Case 3
Fair value of (old) asset given up	$44,000	$100,000	$73,000
Fair value of (new) asset received	50,000	?	?
Cash paid	10,000	4,000	—
Cash received	—	—	50,000

In Case 1, the values indicate some measurement uncertainty. The cash paid of $10,000 plus the fair value of the old asset of $44,000 equals $54,000, but the new asset is reportedly worth $50,000. In this situation, the two fair values must be assessed to see which is more reliable, and then *either*:

- The $50,000 is assessed to be the more reliable value, and is used to record the new asset, and therefore the "real" fair value of the old asset would be treated as $40,000, *or*
- The new asset is valued at $54,000, relying on the $44,000 fair value of the old asset.

In Case 2, the fair value of the new asset is unknown and its fair value must be implied by the value of the old asset, $100,000. However, the company also had to pay $4,000 to get the new asset, so the new one must have been worth $104,000.

In Case 3, the fair value of the new asset is again unknown. The old asset was worth $73,000, but the company received $50,000 in the exchange. Therefore, the new asset must have been worth $23,000.

Fair Market Value Cap

When non-monetary assets are exchanged and the book value method is used, the new asset is recorded at the book value of the old asset. However, *the highest value that can be recorded is the fair value of the acquired asset, regardless of other valuation rules.* This is known as the **fair market value cap**. For example, consider the following exchange (facts assumed), recorded at book value because the transaction lacked commercial substance.

New asset	97,000	
Accumulated amortization, old asset	56,000	
Old asset		153,000

The new asset is valued at $97,000, the book value of the old asset. Now, assume that there was reliable information available that indicated the fair value of the new asset was $80,000. This is the *maximum value* that can be used for the new asset, and the entry becomes:

New asset	80,000	
Accumulated amortization, old asset	56,000	
Loss on asset exchange ($97,000 – $80,000)	17,000	
Old asset		153,000

Of course, what is really implied in this situation is that the old asset was overvalued at the time of exchange, and was worth only $80,000 to the new owner, not its $97,000 book value. Overvaluation of assets is a failure in financial reporting, and should be caught prior to the exchange. A thorough review, every year, of depreciation methods and rates, coupled with an impairment review, should minimize this risk.

Examples of Non-monetary Asset Exchanges

The following information for Regina Corp. is used in the examples that follow:

Asset Transferred—Crane	
Original cost	$90,000
Accumulated depreciation, updated to date of exchange	$60,000

1. Transaction has commercial substance:
    a. *Fair values are determinable; no cash payment.* Assume that the crane has a fair value of $47,000 and is exchanged for a truck whose value is not more clearly measurable; no cash is paid or received. The book value of the crane is $30,000; therefore, a $17,000 gain is recognized. The entry is:

Equipment—truck	47,000	
Accumulated depreciation—crane	60,000	
Equipment—crane		90,000
Gain on disposal of the crane		17,000

    b. *Fair values are determinable; with cash payment.* Assume that the crane's fair value is not easily determinable, but that the truck has a fair value of $33,000. In addition, Regina receives $12,000 cash. The acquired truck is recorded at its fair value. The entry is:

Equipment—truck	33,000	
Cash	12,000	
Accumulated depreciation—crane	60,000	
Equipment—crane		90,000
Gain on disposal of the crane		15,000

c. *Fair values are not determinable*; *no cash payment*. Assume that neither fair value is reliably measurable. The acquired truck is recorded at the book or carrying value of the crane, the carrying value of the asset given up. There can be no gain or loss recognized on the transaction:

Equipment—truck	30,000	
Accumulated depreciation—crane	60,000	
Equipment—crane		90,000

2. Transaction does not have commercial substance:
   a. *Fair values are determinable; no cash payment.* Assume that the crane has a fair value of $47,000 and is exchanged for another crane whose fair value is not more reliably measurable. There is no cash payment. Because the transaction does not significantly affect Regina's cash flows, the acquired crane is recorded at the book value of the crane being given up. There can be no gain or loss recognized on the transaction:

Equipment—crane 2	30,000	
Accumulated depreciation—crane 1	60,000	
Equipment—crane 1		90,000

   b. *Fair values are determinable; with cash payment.* Assume that the old crane's fair value is not easily determinable, but that the new crane has a fair value of $33,000. In addition, Regina receives $12,000 cash. Since there is no commercial substance to the transaction, the acquired crane is recorded at the old crane's book value minus the cash received. The entry is:

Equipment—crane 2	18,000	
Cash	12,000	
Accumulated depreciation—crane 1	60,000	
Equipment—crane 1		90,000

   Whenever cash is involved in a transaction without commercial substance, the new asset is always recorded at the book value of the old asset, *minus any cash received or plus any cash paid*. Fair values are irrelevant. No gain or loss is recognized.

   c. *Fair values are determinable; with cash payment and fair-value cap.* Assume that the old crane's fair value is not easily determinable, but that the new crane has a fair value of $14,000. In addition, Regina receives $12,000 cash. Since there is no commercial substance to the transaction, the acquired crane is recorded at the old crane's book value minus the cash received ($18,000 = $30,000 book value less $12,000) to a maximum of $14,000. A loss of $4,000 is recorded. The entry is:

Equipment—crane 2	14,000	
Cash	12,000	
Accumulated depreciation—crane 1	60,000	

Loss on exchange of assets	4,000	
Equipment—crane 1		90,000

CONCEPT REVIEW

1. What is *commercial substance*? What is its significance?
2. When should the book value approach be used for recording non-monetary asset exchanges?

INTEREST AND DIVIDEND INCOME

Revenue by definition arises from a *contract with a customer* for goods and services that are part of the entity's normal operating activities. In some cases, the entity will receive other forms of *income* that are not part of its normal revenue-producing activities but still arise from a contract. Examples are rental income and interest income. These types of income are recognized as stipulated by the contract. *The most common pattern is to recognize these amounts as time passes.*

Other types of income do not arise from contract. For example, consider dividend income, which is the result of an intercorporate investment. Dividend income is subject to complex revenue recognition rules, depending on the classification of the investment that gave rise to the dividend. For a passive investment, IFRS 9 dictates that dividend income is recognized when all three of the following criteria are met:

- The entity has a right to receive the dividend;
- It is probable that economic benefits will flow to the entity; and
- The amount can be measured.

These are all topics for later chapters, including Chapters 7, 11 and 17.

CHOOSING A REVENUE RECOGNITION POLICY

This chapter has illustrated many different ways in which revenue can be recognized. Depending on the nature of a company's operations, the determination of the appropriate revenue recognition may be the single most pervasive and most difficult accounting policy choice. After all, revenue is the top line in the SCI and earnings is carefully watched by financial statement users!

Although there may seem to be many alternatives, revenue recognition policy is not really a free choice. The policy is, first and foremost, a function of the contractually based revenue activity of the enterprise. When there is more than one revenue-generating activity, there *may* be a different policy for each. For example, a retail company that engages in straightforward sales activity for cash or credit will probably recognize sales revenue at the point of delivery, while interest revenue on outstanding credit card balances will be recognized as time passes.

A revenue recognition policy must satisfy the core principle that revenue is recognized when *control of the goods or services is transferred to the customer and the performance obligation is satisfied.* This may occur over time if certain criteria can be met, or it will occur at a specific point in time. It is important to bear in mind that the act of revenue (and expense) recognition *increases (or decreases in the case of expenses) the net assets of the company.* This will occur when valid contract assets or receivables are correctly recognized on the statement of financial position.

ETHICAL ISSUES

Companies bring a variety of motives to the revenue recognition policy decision. Firms anxious to show increasing sales and profits have sometimes followed questionable and possibly even improper accounting procedures. A relatively innocent-looking example occurs when a firm records revenue for goods that have been ordered for a later delivery. For example, suppose a firm receives an order in December for goods that the customer desires to receive in mid-January, and agrees to pay for the goods by the end of December. Should the sale be recorded in December or January? We saw earlier in this chapter that these types of bill-and-hold transactions can be recorded prior to delivery *only if certain criteria are met.*

Even more problematic is a "sale" recorded for goods shipped to a customer that regularly purchases such goods in approximately the amounts shipped, but has not yet ordered them! There have also been cases wherein the invoices for goods shipped after the fiscal year-end are *backdated* to the current fiscal year in order to record them as sales in the earlier period. Yes, this really happens, but it's not acceptable, either ethically or under IFRS. Such actions are deliberate attempts to mislead users, tantamount to fraud.

One last example is misrepresenting the types of revenue and the related costs. In 2011 Hewlett-Packard (HP) acquired the software company Autonomy for US$11.1 billion. In November 2012, HP accused Autonomy of deliberately misrepresenting revenue on its financial statements that HP had used to determine the acquisition price. Specifically, HP reported that Autonomy had reported hardware sales as software sales as seen from the quote below:

> The mischaracterization of revenue from negative-margin, low-end hardware sales with little or no associated software content as "IDOL product," and the improper inclusion of such revenue as "license revenue" for purposes of the organic and IDOL growth calculations. ... The use of licensing transactions with value-added resellers to inappropriately accelerate revenue recognition, or worse, create revenue where no end-user customer existed at the time of sale. This negative-margin, low-end hardware is estimated to have comprised 10–15% of Autonomy's revenue[3].

Accounting standard-setters have developed criteria in an attempt to discourage the most egregious revenue recognition and disclosure practices. However, bear in mind that revenue recognition often involves a lot of estimates—expected consideration, allocation to the separate performance obligations, future costs, management intent, and customer acceptance (and returns). There is still a lot of flexibility for unscrupulous managers to manipulate revenue recognition. All accountants must be on guard!

Accounting Policy Presentation and Disclosure

The disclosure related to revenue is very extensive, reflecting not only its importance in determining earnings but also the fact that policy in this area is judgemental in many cases. Historically, revenue disclosures have been criticized by financial statement users, including regulators who have noticed that disclosures were commonly "boilerplate," generic disclosures copied from examples in accounting standards. Companies must provide *specific, helpful information* in the disclosure notes.

From Earnings

Companies must disclose the amount of revenue actually recognized in earnings. Revenue must also be segregated into different categories depending on its nature, timing, amount, and uncertainty. These categories might be by type of good or

---

3. "HP Alleges Fraud in Autonomy Deal; Takes $8.8 B charge" by Eric Savtiz, Forbes, November 20, 2012. http://www.forbes.com/sites/ericsavitz/2012/11/20/hp-alleges-fraud-in-autonomy-deal-takes-8-8b-charge/ retrieved November 21, 2012.

service, geography, customer type, length of contract, or distribution channels. Also included in earnings are any impairment losses recognized on receivables, contract assets, and contract costs.

From the SFP

SFP accounts related to revenue recognition include inventories, contract costs, contract assets, contract liabilities, receivables, and provisions for onerous contracts. Disclosure must provide the user with information on these specific accounts (reconciliation of opening and closing balances), information about contract balances, remaining performance obligations, and related information.

Policy and Estimates

Disclosure notes must deal with revenue recognition policy, but also describe the nature of revenue contracts with customers. The discussion must include such things as:

a. How the obligations are usually satisfied (When is revenue recognized? On shipment? When services are rendered?);

b. Significant payment terms including variable consideration or financing components;

c. The nature of the goods and services transferred;

d. Whether the entity acts as agent or principal;

e. Any other obligations such as returns, refunds, discounts, warranties, and so forth; and

f. For long-term contracts beyond one year, the amount of transaction price still to be allocated and when the related revenue will be recognized.

Critical estimates and decisions must be disclosed. For example, companies must indicate how performance is measured in cases where the contract revenue is recognized over time, and how the consideration is allocated when there is more than one performance obligation in the same contract. For onerous performance obligations, disclosure is required about the amount, the nature of the obligations, why it was concluded they were onerous, and when the company expects to complete them.

The spirit of good disclosure is not captured in long lists of required items. The key is to provide information designed to give the user insight into the nature, timing, and risk of the revenues and related cash flows.

REVENUE ON THE CASH FLOW STATEMENT

Accounting tends to recognize revenue at a particular point or with the passage of time in a more continuous earning cycle. On occasion, revenue recognition also coincides with the cash inflow, but that circumstance is quite rare. Usually, a company recognizes revenue prior to receiving the cash.

In order to report cash flow from operations, the accruals relating to revenue recognition must be removed. This has been demonstrated in Chapter 5.

If the *indirect* method is used for reporting cash from operations, the adjustments are made to the reported net income, the starting point for cash flow from operations. The primary adjustments are as follows:

*   Any increase in accounts receivable, notes receivable, or contract assets from customers must be deducted from net income; a decrease in these accounts is added.

*   Expenses that have been accrued (but not yet paid in cash) must be added back to net income; examples include warranty provisions.

*   Expenses that have been prepaid or set up as contract costs (i.e., paid in cash but not yet expensed) must similarly be deducted from net income; examples include direct materials not yet used in the performance of a contract.

*   Increases in contract liabilities must be added to net income; the cash has been received but revenue has not yet been recognized. Similarly, decreases in contract liabilities are subtracted from net income.

If the company uses the *direct* method of reporting cash from operations, the starting point is the amount of revenue as reported on the income statement (i.e., the profit or loss section of the statement of comprehensive income) adjusted as follows:

- Deduct increases in accounts receivable (and notes receivable) and contract assets from customers; decreases in those assets would be added to reported revenues, since more cash was received than had been reported as revenue.
- Add (deduct) any increase (decrease) in contract liabilities (representing deposits or other amounts prepaid by customers or unearned revenue).

Interest and dividends received may be classified on the cash flow statement as either operating or investing activities.

Expenses are adjusted by the amounts of changes in accrued expenses, prepaid expenses, and contract costs.

CONCEPT REVIEW

1. How is interest income recognized?
2. On the indirect cash flow statement, what adjustments are required for contract liabilities?

Accounting Standards for Private Enterprises

Revenue

The principles concerning revenue recognition under ASPE are very different than under IFRS. The Accounting Standards for Private Enterprises uses the *earnings-based approach* for revenue recognition. Revenue includes the sale of goods and the rendering of services that are the ordinary activities of the business in addition to dividend, interest, and royalty income.

Under ASPE, revenue is recognized when performance is satisfied and collection is assured. A seller can recognize revenue from the sale of goods and the rendering of services only when the seller's performance is complete. Completion means:

a. *Seller's performance is complete; seller has transferred the significant risks and rewards of ownership to the buyer.* The seller has delivered the goods or services and has no more significant risks; the seller also will not benefit from the goods or services in the future.

b. *The amount of revenue can be measured reliably.* There is no significant uncertainty about the amount of revenue to be received; there should be no revenue that is contingent on future events or performance, and the collectibility of amounts owing is reasonably assured.

c. *The benefit of the revenue will actually flow to the seller.* There is high probability that the seller will actually enjoy the economic benefits of the transaction.

d. *The seller can reliably measure all costs relating to the transaction, past and future.* There are no significant uncertainties about measuring the costs incurred in the past or any after-sale costs yet to be incurred in the future.

e. *The seller retains no continuing managerial involvement or control over the goods sold.* The seller cannot retain the right to affect the buyer's use of the product or service, and can retain no continuing interest in future benefits that are derived from the product.

Whichever is the last one of these criteria (a) to (e) to be satisfied is known as the ***critical event***. Revenue and directly related costs are recognized at the point of the critical event.

These criteria are very different from the contract-based approach adopted by IFRS, which recognizes revenue when control has been transferred and in which *control* is very clearly defined. Under IFRS, there are more definitive criteria to determine whether revenue is recognized over the term of the contract or at a specific point in time. The criteria are based on control being transferred and completion of the performance obligation. Under ASPE, the earnings-based approach uses criteria to determine when the critical event occurs and revenue is earned and recognized. As a result of these differences in the core principles and revenue criteria, there may be cases in which revenue for the same transaction will be recognized at different times and amounts under ASPE and IFRS.

IFRS recognizes contract costs, contract assets, and contract liabilities throughout the contract. Although there are differences in terminology, in many cases ASPE would similarly recognize assets for costs incurred to date on contracts not yet completed, as well as accrued revenue and unearned revenue.

Some specific examples of differences are as follows:

a. IFRS outlines specific criteria, one of which must be met in order to record the contract over time. As a result, if a contract does not meet any of these three criteria, the revenue is recognized at a single point in time. These criteria might dictate a different assessment of the critical event than under ASPE.

b. Regarding bill-and-hold arrangements, under ASPE the criteria to be met are:
    - The buyer has acknowledged the deferred delivery instructions;
    - Delivery is probable;
    - The buyer's inventory is separately identified as belonging to the buyer (i.e., held apart from the seller's other inventory);
    - The inventory is ready to be delivered; and
    - The customary payment terms apply to the invoice.

c. Concerning sales with warranties, IFRS has outlined specific guidance on when to treat a warranty as a cost deferral or a revenue deferral. Although ASPE does not provide this detailed guidance, revenue transactions with warranties would have similar treatment under ASPE and IFRS.

d. For sales with returns, similar to IFRS, if returns are estimable at the time of sale, the revenue is recorded along with an estimate for sales returns as a liability. Unlike under IFRS, there is no need to also set up a right to recovery asset for the cost of goods estimated to be returned. This entry would be recorded once the goods were actually received and put back into inventory. Under ASPE, if sales returns are not estimable, all of the revenue is deferred until the return situation is known (similarly to IFRS).

e. For customer loyalty programs, ASPE allows a choice of how to report the resulting liability: either as an accrued cost or as unearned revenue at the time of sale. Under IFRS, the liability is recorded as unearned revenue at the time of sale.

f. Onerous contracts do not need to be recognized under ASPE, although losses on long-term contracts should be recognized as they occur. The term *onerous contract* does not exist under ASPE, but the concept of recognizing losses as they occur is the same as under IFRS.

Revenue from service transactions and long-term contracts is usually recognized over time as the service is performed. For long-term contracts, revenue can either be recognized on the completed-contract method or as a percentage-of-completion basis depending on which method best correlates revenue to the work performed. Under ASPE, the completed contract method can only be used when performance is a single act (likely similar to IFRS), or when no reasonable estimate can be used to measure the stage of completion. Under both standards, consideration must be measurable. Under ASPE, the percentage-of-completion method results in an inventory item that is the difference between costs incurred to date plus profit margin less billings to date. Revenue transactions recognized using the completed-contract method result in the same entries under both ASPE and IFRS. But due to measurement and timing of performance completion, the amount of revenue recognized each period throughout the contract might be different under ASPE and IFRS.

Non-monetary Transactions

Under ASPE, if the non-monetary transaction has commercial substance, the transaction is reported at the fair value of either the asset given up or the asset received, depending on which value is more reliably measurable. In comparison, IFRS would use the fair value of the asset given up to determine the value of the transaction. (Only in cases wherein the asset received had a more reliable measure would it be used under IFRS.) The transaction is measured at the carrying value of the asset given up if there is no commercial substance, if neither of the items has a reliably measurable fair value, or if the transaction is a non-reciprocal transfer to the owners. This is similar to IFRS.

Under ASPE, for barter transactions in which non-cash consideration is received in return for goods and services, if the exchange has commercial substance, the fair value of the asset given up is used as discussed above. (Under IFRS, in cases in which there is an exchange of dissimilar goods and services, the fair value of the asset received is used to record the revenue.) If the exchange is in the ordinary course of business to facilitate a sale to a third party, the exchange is measured at the carrying value of the good or service given up (similar to IFRS).

Related Party Transactions

ASPE has specific guidance for **related party transactions**. Related parties exist when one party has the ability to exercise, directly or indirectly, control, joint control, or significant influence over the other. Similarly, two or more parties are also related when they are controlled, jointly controlled, or significantly influenced by the same party. Related parties also include management and immediate family members. Non-monetary transactions between related parties are measured at either the exchange amount or the carrying amount of the item given up. The **exchange amount** is the amount agreed on by the parties.

The following summarizes how non-monetary transactions between related parties are measured:

- *Commercial substance and normal course of business.* If the non-monetary exchange occurs between related parties and the transaction has commercial substance and is in the normal course of business, the exchange amount is used to record and measure the transaction.

- *Commercial substance but not in the normal course of operations.* If the non-monetary exchange between related parties has commercial substance but is not in the normal course of operations, it is measured at the exchange amount only when there is a change in ownership interests in the item exchanged and the exchange amount is supported by evidence.

- *No commercial substance and not in the normal course of operations.* If the non-monetary transaction has no commercial substance and is not in the normal course of business, the transaction is measured at the carrying value of the item given up.

- *Exchange of inventory items.* A non-monetary related party transaction that is an exchange of a good held-for-sale in the normal course of operations (e.g., inventory exchanges) to facilitate a sale to a customer is measured at the carrying amount of the asset given up (adjusted by the fair value of any monetary consideration).

Biological Assets

ASPE does not require biological assets to be carried at fair value less costs to sell. ASPE reports these assets at cost, and the lower of cost and NRV method is applied, consistently with other types of inventories.

Disclosure

Disclosure under ASPE is far less extensive than under IFRS. Under ASPE, the revenue recognition policy for each type of revenue transaction must be disclosed, including how multiple elements within a single contract and non-monetary sales are determined and valued. On the face of the income statement or in the notes, the major categories of revenue must be separately disclosed.

RELEVANT STANDARDS

CPA Canada Handbook, Part I (IFRS)

- IFRS 15 Revenue from Contracts with Customers
- IAS 41, Agriculture
- IAS 16, Property, Plant and Equipment
- IAS 38, Intangible Assets

CPA Handbook, Part II (ASPE):

- Section 3400, Revenue
- Section 3831 Non-monetary Transactions
- Section 3840 Related Party Transactions

SUMMARY OF KEY POINTS

1. Revenue arises from increases in net assets resulting from performance of the company's normal business activities. Expenses arise from decreases in net assets from the company's normal business activities. Gains and losses can arise from normal business activities or peripheral transactions.

2. Revenue is recognized using the contract-based approach. The contract outlines the seller's performance obligation to deliver goods and services and the consideration that the buyer agrees to pay. The seller recognizes revenue at the time the performance obligation is complete—that is, when the promised goods and services have been transferred to the customer. The amount of revenue is the consideration that the buyer has agreed to pay.

3. A five-step process is used to determine how and when revenue from a customer's contract will be recognized: (1) identifying the contract; (2) identifying separate performance obligations; (3) determining the contract price; (4) allocating the price to the separate performance obligations; and (5) determining when performance is complete and revenue is recognized.

4. Commission revenue must be reported at a net amount when the entity is acting as an agent. Indications of an agency relationship are that the entity does not have primary responsibility to fulfill the order, bears no inventory or credit risk, and has no influence on the price.

5. On the SFP, *contract assets, contract costs, and contract liabilities* will be reported as the contract progresses. Once revenue is recognized, accounts receivable or cash will be reported.

6. Completion of the performance obligation occurs when control of the promised goods and services is transferred to the customer. This may occur at a single point in time or over the term of the contract. Indications of the transfer of control are that the seller has a right to payment; legal title, physical possession, and/or significant risks and rewards are transferred; and the customer has accepted the product.

7. Revenue may be recognized at a single point of time on delivery or over a period of time. Transfer is completed over time if either (1) the customer receives and consumes the benefits of the contract simultaneously as the entity performs or (2) the customer controls the asset being created or enhanced throughout the contract or (3) the performance of the contract results in an asset with no alternative use to the seller.

8. Special accounting treatment is required for sales contracts with a right of return or warranties. In both cases, the amount of returns or warranty claims must be estimable in order to record the sale at the time of delivery, with the estimate of returns and warranties recorded as a liability. Bill-and-hold arrangements may be recognized as revenue prior to delivery only if certain criteria have been met.

9. *Output methods* and *input methods* can be used to measure the progress of a performance obligation over time. Output measures recognize revenue on the basis of the value of the work performed to date. Input measures recognize revenue on the basis of the value of the effort expended to date.

10. If consideration is received over a period longer than one year, the present value of the cash received must be used to determine the total value of the consideration. Interest revenue will be earned on this contract throughout the period of payment.

11. When a contract has *multiple deliverables*, the contract must be separated into individual performance obligations in which the goods and services to be delivered are *distinct*—that is, the customer has the ability to use the item separately on its own or with other resources that can be readily obtained *and* the seller's promise to deliver the good or service is separately identifiable from other goods and services in the contract. The *relative method* is used to allocate a contract's consideration into its separate performance obligations on the basis of stand-alone prices.

12. *Contract costs* directly related to the performance of a contract and recoverable are capitalized. Contract costs can include initial costs and fulfillment costs. These costs are expensed as goods and services are transferred to the customer and also tested for impairment.

13. Long-term contracts may complete the performance obligation over time or a single point in time. If over time, a measurement method using input or output measures is used to measure progress of completion.

14. Biological assets are living plants and animals and are measured at the fair value less costs to sell at each reporting period. Agricultural produce is measured at fair value less costs to sell at the time of harvest, which becomes the deemed cost for inventory.

15. The valuation of barter transactions depends on the types of goods or services being exchanged. Exchanges of *similar* goods and services are valued at the carrying value of the goods or services being given up. For *dissimilar* goods or services, the exchange is valued at the fair value of the items received, as is the nature of a sales transaction.

16. When non-monetary assets are exchanged and the transaction has commercial substance, the transaction is valued at fair market value and a gain or loss on the exchange is recorded. The transaction is valued at book value with no gain or loss if there is no commercial substance, the exchange is to facilitate a sale to a third party, when fair values are not available, or if the exchange is a distribution to owners. Nonetheless, an asset cannot be recorded at a value higher than fair value.

17. Revenue recognition policies must be chosen carefully and satisfy the core principle that revenue is recognized when control of the goods and services is transferred to the customer and the performance obligation is complete. There is extensive disclosure related to revenue recognition policies and critical estimates required in measuring revenues.

18. Cash flow from operations must be computed by adjusting revenue (or net income) for changes in accounts and notes receivable, contract assets, contract costs, and contract liabilities.

Key Terms

agricultural produce	gross amount
barter	input methods
bearer plants	licensing arrangements
bill-and-hold arrangement	monetary assets
biological assets	multiple deliverables
book value method	net basis
change orders	non-monetary assets
commercial substance	non-monetary transactions
completed-contract method	non-refundable upfront fees
consideration	onerous contract
consignment arrangement	output methods
contract asset	percentage-of-completion method
contract-based approach	performance obligation
contract costs	progress billings
contract liability	refund liability
cost recovery	related party transaction
derecognized	relative stand-alone value
distinct	residual approach
earnings-based approach	revenue
economic value added (EVA)	right to recovery asset
exchange amount	
expenses	
fair market value cap	
fair value method	

Review Problem 6-1

Cromax Corp. is a Canadian public company whose shares are listed on the TSX. The company has a December fiscal year-end. The following transactions and events occurred in 20X5. For each item review the five steps for revenue recognition and prepare the appropriate journal entries required to record the transactions. Assume all amounts are material.

1. Cromax has entered into a contract with Lukin Co. to deliver 1,000 switch boxes for a total amount of $150,000. Each box sells for $150 each and has a cost of $95. Cromax has stipulated in the contract that Lukin may return any of the items within 45 days and receive a full refund. On the basis of historical experience, Cromax estimates that 4% of the items will be returned. It also expects that any returns can be resold. Cromax delivered all the goods on 1 March, and Lukin accepted them. Then on 1 April, Lukin returned 30 items. On 18 April, Lukin paid the final balance owing.

2. On 1 June, Cromax signed a contract with Sigma Inc. to sell 1,000 printers for a total consideration of $600,000. Included in this price is an 18-month warranty that any printer will be fixed or replaced if it does not function in accordance with its specifications. From past experience with this type of product, Cromax predicts that warranty costs for deficiencies will be $50,000. Cromax delivered the goods on 15 June and Sigma paid the full

amount owing on 19 July. By the end of December, Cromax had incurred actual warranty costs related to this contract totalling $26,000.

3. Cromax entered into a contract with Almate Ltd. to deliver 250 photocopiers and provide two years of on-site service. The total contract consideration was $300,000. Cromax often sells individual photocopiers at a price of $1,100 each. The maintenance agreements are also sold separately, with a one-year maintenance cost being approximately $115 per photocopier. On 1 August, Cromax delivered the 250 photocopiers. At various times throughout August to December, Cromax sent its technicians to do regular maintenance on all the machines.

REVIEW PROBLEM 6-1—SOLUTION

1. Reviewing the five steps for revenue recognition:

Step 1: Identify the contract with the customer. As given in the problem, Cromax has an agreement with the customer obligating it to deliver 1,000 items to Lukin and to "stand ready" to accept any returns until 45 days after the date of delivery.

Step 2: Identify separate performance obligations. There is only one performance obligation and that is for Cromax to deliver the product to Lukin.

Step 3: Determine the overall contract price. The total contract consideration is $150,000.

Step 4: Allocate the price to the separate performance obligations. In this case, there is only one, as noted in step 2 above.

Step 5: Determine when the performance obligation is complete and revenue can be recognized. On 1 March all of the items were delivered and assumed accepted by Lukin. This is the point of the transfer of control and the point in time when revenue is recognized. However, there is still uncertainty about how many items will be returned before the 45-day period ends. Cromax estimates the amount of returns to be 4%, which is 40 (1,000 × 4%) items. Each item has a selling price of $150 and a related cost of $95.

The following journal entries are required:

1 March		
Dr. Accounts receivable (1,000 × $150)	150,000	
Cr. Revenue (960 × $150)		144,000
Cr. Refund liability (40 × $150)		6,000
Dr. Cost of goods sold (960 × $95)	91,200	
Dr. Right to recovery asset (40 × $95)	3,800	
Cr. Inventory (1,000 × $95)		95,000
1 April		
Dr. Refund liability (30 × $150)	4,500	
Cr. Accounts receivable (30 × $150)		4,500
Dr. Inventory (30 × $95)	2,850	
Cr. Right to recovery asset (30 × $95)		2,850
14 April (end of 45-day period from point of delivery)		
Dr. Refund liability (10 × $150)	1,500	
Cr. Revenue (10 × $150)		1,500

Dr. Cost of goods sold (10 × $95)	950	
Cr. Right to recovery asset (10 × $95)		950
18 April		
Dr. Cash (150,000 − 4,500)	145,500	
Cr. Accounts receivable		145,500

2. Reviewing the five steps for revenue recognition:

Step 1: Identify the contract with the customer. As given in the problem, Cromax has an agreement with the customer obligating it to deliver 1,000 printers along with a warranty promise if the printers do not work properly.

Step 2: Identify separate performance obligations. There is only one performance obligation and that is for Cromax to deliver the product to Sigma. The warranty is for assurance that the product will work to its specifications and is not a separate performance obligation.

Step 3: Determine the overall contract price. The total contract consideration is $600,000.

Step 4: Allocate the price to the separate performance obligations. In this case, there is only one performance obligation as noted in step 2 above.

Step 5: Determine when the performance obligation is complete and revenue can be recognized. On 15 June all of the items were delivered and assumed accepted by Sigma. This is the point of the transfer of control and the point in time when revenue is recognized. The costs estimated for any warranties must also be accrued at this point using the cost deferral method since this an assurance warranty.

The following journal entries are required:

15 June		
Dr. Accounts receivable (1,000 × $600)	600,000	
Cr. Revenue		600,000
Dr. Warranty expense	50,000	
Cr. Provision for warranty		50,000
19 July		
Dr. Cash	600,000	
Cr. Accounts receivable		600,000
31 December		
Dr. Provision for warranty	26,000	
Cr. Cash, accounts payable, etc.		26,000

At the end of December, the provision must also be reviewed to determine that the amount remaining of $24,000 ($50,000 − 26,000) is still correct. The amount may be revised up or down in accordance with this review.

3. Reviewing the five steps for revenue recognition:

Step 1: Identify the contract with the customer. As given in the problem, Cromax has an agreement with the customer obligating it to deliver 250 items to Almate and provide two years of maintenance.

Step 2: Identify separate performance obligations. It appears that there might be two performance obligations: one to deliver the goods and a second one to provide maintenance over a two-year period. We need to look to see if these goods and services are distinct. We are told that Cromax sells individual photocopiers for a price of $1,100 each. This would indicate a stand-alone price for the photocopiers. Cromax also provides separate maintenance agreements priced at $115 per photocopier per year which would be the stand-alone price for this service. These are distinct goods and services, and therefore there are two performance obligations.

Step 3: Determine the overall contract price. The total contract consideration is $300,000.

Step 4: Allocate the price to the separate performance obligations. There are two performance obligations and using their stand-alone prices, we can use the relative method to allocate the total consideration of $300,000 as seen below.

	Stand-Alone Values	Relative Calculation	Allocation of Consideration $
Revenue from sale of 250 photocopiers	250 × $1,100 = 275,000	275,000/332,500 × $300,000	248,120
Revenue from sale of two-year maintenance agreement	250 × $115 × 2 years = $57,500	57,500/332,500 × $300,000	51,880
Total	$332,500		$300,000

Step 5: Determine when the performance obligation is complete and revenue can be recognized. On 1 August all of the items were delivered and assumed accepted by Almate. This is the point of the transfer of control of the photocopiers and the point in time when revenue for the sale of the copiers is recognized. The maintenance contract is a two-year service contract. The services will be provided and consumed over the term of the contract. Consequently, the maintenance contract is recognized as unearned and will be recognized over the next 24 months commencing 1 August at $2,162 per month ($51,880/24)

The following journal entries are required:

1 August

Dr. Accounts receivable	300,000	
Cr. Revenue for sale of copiers		248,120
Cr. Contract liability—maintenance contract		51,880

Every month, Cromax would recognize the maintenance service revenue as follows: ($51,880/24 = $2,162 per month).

31 August, 30 September, 31 October, 30 November and 31 December

Dr. Contract liability—maintenance contract	2,162	
Cr. Revenue—maintenance services		2,162

Source: Atlantic School of Chartered Accountancy, © 2010.

Review Problem 6-2

Precision Punctual Construction Co. (PPCC) has agreed to build a ten-storey office building for Mountain Bank Ltd. on land owned by Mountain Bank. The contract calls for a contract price of $15,000,000 for the building, with progress payments being made by Mountain as the construction proceeds. The period of construction is estimated to be 30 months. The contract is signed on 1 February 20X5, and construction begins immediately. The building is completed and turned over to Mountain Bank on 1 December 20X7.

Data on costs incurred, estimated costs to complete, progress billings, and progress payments over the period of construction are as follows:

($ thousands)	20X5	20X6	20X7
Costs incurred this period and used for performance	$ 1,500	$ 7,875	$ 3,825
Costs incurred to date—all used for performance	1,500	9,375	13,200
Estimated costs to complete at year-end	10,500	3,125	0
Estimated total costs of project	12,000	12,500	13,200
Progress billings this period	1,200	6,000	7,800
Progress payments received this period	825	6,300	7,875

Required:

Part I

1. Assume that Mountain will own the building as it is being constructed. Show the entries to account for this project over the period of construction, assuming that PPCC recognizes this contract revenue over time.
2. Show the relevant SFP and SCI items for 20X5, 20X6, and 20X7 for PPCC.

Part II

1. Assume that PPCC controls the building during construction and title only transfers at the end of the project when the construction is complete. Show the entries to account for this project over the period of construction, assuming that PPCC recognizes the contract revenue at a single point in time—at delivery.
2. Show the relevant SFP and SCI items for 20X5, 20X6, and 20X7 for PPCC.

REVIEW PROBLEM 6-2—SOLUTION

Part I

1. The entries to record the construction of the building are as follows (in $ thousands):

Entries for 20X5:

a. *To record incurrence of construction costs:*

Contract costs (asset)	1,500	
Cash, payables, etc.		1,500

b. *To record progress billings:*

Accounts receivable	1,200	
Contract liability		1,200

c. *To record billing collections:*

Cash	825	
Accounts receivable		825

d. *To recognize revenue for percentage of completion and clear the contract liability account:**

Contract asset	675	
Contract liability	1,200	
Revenue from long-term contract		1,875

*The percentage of completion is the cost incurred
to date divided by total estimated project costs, or
$1,500 ÷ $12,000 = 12.5\%$. The total amount of
revenue recognizable to this point is $15,000 ×
12.5\% = $1,875$.

e. *To recognize construction costs related to revenue recognized:*

Construction costs	1,500	
Contract costs		1,500

Entries for 20X6:

a. *To record incurrence of construction costs:*

Contract costs	7,875	
Cash, payables, etc.		7,875

b. *To record progress billings:*

Accounts receivable	6,000	
Contract liability		6,000

c. *To record billing collections:*

Cash	6,300	
Accounts receivable		6,300

d. *To recognize revenue for percentage of completion:**

Contract asset	3,375	
Contract liability	6,000	
Revenue from long-term contract		9,375

*The percentage of completion is the cost incurred to date divided by total estimated project costs, or $9,375 ÷ $12,500 = 75%. The total amount of revenue recognizable to this point is $15,000 × 75% = $11,250. Since $1,875 was recognized in 20X5, the amount recognizable in 20X6 is $11,250 − $1,875 = $9,375.

e. *To recognize construction costs related to revenue recognized:*

Construction costs	7,875	
Contract costs		7,875

Entries for 20X7:

a. *To record incurrence of construction costs:*

Contract costs	3,825	
Cash, payables, etc.		3,825

b. *To record progress billings:*

Accounts receivable	7,800	
Contract liability		7,800

c. *To record billing collections:*

Cash	7,875	
Accounts receivable		7,875

d. *To recognize revenue for percentage of completion:**

Contract liability	7,800	
Contract asset		4,050
Revenue from long-term contract		3,750

*The project is completed; any remaining portion of the contract price not previously recognized as revenue should be recognized this period. In prior years, $1,875 + $9,375 = $11,250 was recognized; thus, $3,750 (i.e., $15,000 − $11,250) is recognized in 20X7. The contract asset account is now closed out on completion since all billings are now complete.

e. *To recognize construction costs related to revenue recognized:*

Construction costs	3,825	
Contract costs		3,825

2. Financial statement items (in $ thousands):

	31 Dec. 20X5	31 Dec. 20X6	31 Dec. 20X7
Statement of Financial Position			
Contract costs	$ 0	$ 0	0
Accounts receivable	$ 375	$ 75	0
Contract asset	$ 675	$4,050	0
Statement of Comprehensive Income			
Revenue from long-term contracts	$1,875	$9,375	$3,750
Cost of construction	(1,500)	(7,875)	(3,825)
Gross profit	$ 375	$ 1,500	$ (75)*

*This is an example of a current-year loss on a contract that is profitable overall.

Part II

1. The entries to record the construction of the building are as follows (in $ thousands):

Entries for 20X5:

a. *To record incurrence of construction costs:*

Construction in progress—inventory	1,500	
Cash, payables, etc.		1,500

b. *To record progress billings:*

Accounts receivable	1,200	
Contract liability		1,200

c. *To record billing collections:*

Cash	825	
Accounts receivable		825

Entries for 20X6:

a. *To record incurrence of construction costs:*

Construction in progress—inventory	7,875	
Cash, payables, etc.		7,875

b. *To record progress billings:*

Accounts receivable	6,000	
Contract liability		6,000

c. *To record billing collections:*

Cash	6,300
Accounts receivable	6,300

Entries for 20X7:

a. *To record incurrence of construction costs:*

Construction in progress—inventory	3,825	
Cash, payables, etc.		3,825

b. *To record progress billings:*

Accounts receivable	7,800	
Contract liability		7,800

c. *To record billing collections:*

Cash	7,875	
Accounts receivable		7,875

d. *To record the revenue at the end of the contract:*

Contract liability	15,000	
Revenue from long-term contracts		15,000

e. *To expense the costs at the end of the contract:*

Construction costs	13,200	
Construction-in-progress—inventory		13,200

2. Financial statement items (in $ thousands):

	31 Dec. 20X5	31 Dec. 20X6	31 Dec. 20X7
Statement of Financial Position			
Current assets			
Accounts receivable	$ 375	$ 75	0
Construction in progress—inventory	$1,500	$9,375	0
Current liabilities			
Contract liability	$1,200	$7,200	0
Statement of Comprehensive Income			
Revenue from long-term contracts	$ 0	$ 0	$15,000
Cost of construction	0	0	(13,200)
Gross profit	$ 0	$ 0	$ 1,800

Review Problem 6-3

Ocular Co. trades an electron microscope for new optical equipment and receives $30,000 cash as well. The old microscope had an original cost of $200,000 and has accumulated depreciation of $80,000 at the time of the trade. The old microscope has a fair value of $160,000 at trade-in time.

Required:

1. Assuming that the exchange does not have commercial substance, what entry is required to record the exchange?
2. Assuming that the exchange does have commercial substance, what entry is required to record the exchange?

REVIEW PROBLEM 6-3—SOLUTION

1. Since there is no commercial substance to the transaction, the new equipment is recorded at the book value of the old equipment, minus the cash received:

New optical equipment ($120,000 – $30,000)	90,000	
Accumulated depreciation—old equipment	80,000	
Cash	30,000	
Old Equipment		200,000

2. Since there is commercial substance, we start with determining the fair value of the asset that is given up. This appears to have a reliable fair value of $160,000. The new optical equipment will be recorded at $160,000 less the cash received of $30,000 for a net amount of $130,000. A gain on trade-in is reported of $40,000 representing the difference between the old equipment's fair value of $160,000 and its net book value of $120,000. If the fair value of the new equipment is known, we just have to be sure that its fair value is equal to or higher than the $130,000 recorded. If not, the new equipment would have to be recorded at the lower fair-value amount.

New optical equipment ($160,000 – $30,000)	130,000	
Accumulated depreciation—old equipment	80,000	
Cash	30,000	
Gain on trade-in		40,000
Old Equipment		200,000

CASE 6-1

SOLAR POWER INC.

Solar Power Inc. (SPI) is a public company manufacturing and distributing solar panels. It has been in existence for the past ten years, of which the last three have been as a public company. To date SPI has experienced good growth rates, slightly higher than industry averages. Historically, the company had only been a distributor of solar panels and solar power consulting. However, due to the high demand for solar panels and a potentially growing market in

Canada, management decided to open their own manufacturing facility in Canada. In order to finance this growth, the company obtained a bank loan. The maximum amount of the loan outstanding at any time cannot exceed three times the company's last 12 months' EBITDA (earnings before interest, taxes, depreciation, and amortization). The company is required to file interim statements with the banker so that EBITDA amount can be monitored.

SPI primarily sells two types of products: RHP-1 and CSP-2. RHP-1 products are solar panels that the company manufactures for residential use only. These products are sold primarily to individual home owners and home builders. The panels come in five different sizes suitable for installation on residential house roofs.

CSP-2 products are solar panels imported from a German supplier and sold to the commercial market for use on large commercial buildings. For these products, SPI acts as a distributor. The panels come in eight sizes. Both types of products can be installed either when the building is being constructed or any time after the completion of the building. The company sells all of the accessories required to install these panels.

SPI also provides services for installation and consulting. In most cases, installation is for the products SPI sells, although the company has started to provide installation services to other solar panel sellers in the industry. Consulting contracts are generally performed for companies looking for energy cost reduction solutions.

During 20X9, SPI entered into the following contracts:

1. On 16 March, SPI signed a contract with Sharone Co. for a total of $4 million. Sharone was building a new addition to its manufacturing facility and has decided to install solar panels to reduce its annual operating electricity costs. The contract price includes the CSP-2 solar panels, installation, a two-year warranty, and a five-year maintenance agreement that starts as soon as installation is completed. Separate selling prices for the panels and installation and a one-year maintenance contract are $3,200,000 for the panels and installation and $300,000 each year for the maintenance contract. Generally, the panels can be installed within four months of the date the contract is signed. A nonrefundable deposit of 10% of the contract is due on signing. Another 75% is due on delivery and installation. The remaining 15% is due six months or later after the installation date when all deficiencies have been resolved. Delivery and installation was completed on 31 August 20X9. The warranty is for assurance that the product will work within its specifications. SPI estimates that based on past experience, warranty costs will be approximately $150,000 on this size of contract. The company has recognized $3.4 million in revenue for 20X9.

2. On 5 May, SPI entered into a contract with Bakers Builders Inc. to supply RHP-1 panels. Bakers is a home builder that is currently building 3,000 homes that are energy-efficient. However, Baker does not want to take delivery until the panels are needed. Baker has agreed to be invoiced for all of the panels but will ask for delivery at different points in time for the next eight months. The total contract amount of $6,000,000 was invoiced to Baker on 15 May and Baker paid the full amount on 18 June. The panels specific to Baker's requirements are ready for delivery and have been set aside in a separate part of the warehouse. It is expected that there will be still 15% of the panels left to be delivered by the end of SPI's fiscal year-end. The company reported revenue of $5.1 million related to this contract in 20X9.

3. On 8 September, SPI entered into a unique agreement for the sale and installation of CSP-2 panels on the building of a local restaurant. The restaurant's owner, Fred Mason, is planning to sell most of the electricity generated by the panels back to the grid. As he currently does not have the cash flow to finance the upfront cost of the panels and installation, he has proposed that SPI receive an upfront payment of $50,000 when the panels are installed. The remaining amount will be paid as Mason receives credit for selling an excess power back to the grid for the next 24 months. Mason has proposed that he pay SPI 30% of the credit received from the power company. The amount would be determined monthly and immediately remitted to SPI for a period of two years from the date of installation. The normal selling price of this installation would have been $100,000, and management believes that this contract may yield $120,000 or more over the two-year period, although it has no history to support these estimates. The installation was completed on 10 October and the two-year period commenced on this date. SPI recorded a sale and related receivable of $120,000 in October. To date, SPI has received from Mason the upfront payment of $50,000 and a total of $5,700 from the sale of power back to the grid, which was recorded against the account receivable.

4. During 20X9, SPI entered into an arrangement with Solutions Co. to distribute its RHP-1 product in all of Solutions' retail stores. The contract specifies the following: (a) Solutions Co. will have some product on hand for demonstration purposes, which will be given at no cost; (b) once the customer decides to make a purchase, Solutions will call the order into SPI. Solutions will invoice the customer and be responsible for collection. Solutions will be required to remit to SPI on the date of invoice 85% of the sale proceeds; it may retain 15%. SPI will ship the product directly to the customer's home and install the product, if requested by the customer.

It is now one month before the fiscal 31 December 20X9 year-end. You have just been hired as an accounting manager responsible for the revenue reporting for the company. The CFO has asked you to prepare a memo outlining how SPI should recognize the revenue from these four contracts during 20X9. Particularly, the CFO wants you to identify the impact on the SFP and SCI and state how this will impact the amount of financing available.

Required:

Prepare the memo, as requested.

CASE 6-2

PRINCELY ENTERTAINMENT LTD.

Princely Entertainment Ltd. (PEL) is an interactive entertainment company for the mobile world. Frank Prince and his family members own the majority of the 4,000 shares, and have financed all growth through shareholder loans, equity investment, and retained earnings; lenders, historically, have been hesitant to become involved in this sector.

Currently, the company has three games it has developed and currently sells: Princely CRASH, Princely RATS, and Princely DOOM. Users access PEL games for free via their mobile devices and through social networks. PEL generates revenue primarily through sales of virtual items that can be used in the games, such as extra lives, boosters, and game content that enhance users' entertainment experience.

Princely CRASH has experienced viral growth in the past year, changing PEL from a marginal, home-grown company into an entity with far more potential. Frank is coming to understand that his company might be a takeover target for one of the larger players in this business, or even have the potential to go public itself if growth continues. PEL would require far more volume and breadth of games for a public offering to be feasible, however.

You, CPA, have just been hired as the first-ever professional accounting member of PEL's management team. You are VP Finance, but your position involves many different elements. The financial records have primarily been kept on a cash basis, but because of growth, Frank thinks it is time to revisit accounting policies and start getting audited statements that comply with ASPE or perhaps IFRS.

All revenue is received through direct deposit from Facebook© and PayPal©. Frank's wife, Ethel, keeps the accounting records, and is known for her attention to detail. Payroll is handled by a third-party service. Ethel prepares simple monthly financial statements for Frank based on cash received and paid. Unpaid bills are accrued at year-end for the preparation of the annual financial statements.

Frank has reviewed the cash-based revenue figures for 20X3 to date, per Exhibit 1. He explains that his expectations from hiring a professional accountant include having someone put the accounting policies in order and get the financial statements verified by external accountants. Frank is attentive to general business news, is involved with local business groups, and has some general awareness of specific accounting concepts. Frank asks that within the specific context of PEL, you explain the similarities and differences between Canadian Accounting

Standards for Private Enterprises (ASPE) and International Financial Reporting Standards (IFRS). Then, you are to identify the reporting issues facing PEL, and draft a report that sets out reporting policy alternatives and your recommendations. Based on your recommendations, you will have to recalculate revenue and any related balance sheet accounts.

Required:

Prepare the report requested.

EXHIBIT 1

REVENUE REPORT

Princely Entertainment Ltd., Nine Months Ended September 30, 20X3

(in 000s)

Refer to explanatory notes below.

	Refer to Notes:	Princely CRASH	Princely RATS	Princely DOOM	Total
Revenue—consumables	1,2	$ 2,245	$ 110	$ 260	$ 2,615
Revenue—durables	1,3	680	95	170	945
Revenue—virtual currency	1,4	180	5	30	215
					$3,775

Princely DOOM is a game that Frank purchased in 20X3 from its developer, in exchange for 250 common shares of PEL. The developer was working independently and had developed a highly viable game, but lacked the ability to scale it up. PEL has provided upgrades, added functionality, and integrated DOOM with the Princely playing platform. The game developer now works for PEL on salary, but is entitled to a royalty stream of 20% of revenue from this game for five years beginning in 20X3. The common shares (and DOOM) have been recorded at $1 in the accounts; Frank is not sure how to value this transaction or even whether it has to be recorded at all.

Note 1	All revenue represents cash received. There are no accounts receivable because items are paid up front through credit cards.
	Amounts "sold" through social media (Facebook©) have 30% deducted (a $10 sale results in $7 to PEL). Amounts through PayPal© have 3.5% deducted ($10 sale results in $9.65 to PEL). PEL reports $7.00 and $9.65 as revenue, respectively.
	Some players will access a game once, or only for a week or two. Others play for several years, upgrading to new versions as soon as they are made available. Statistics are kept on player retention. These statistics vary significantly among the three PEL games. The frequency of play is also very different from player to player, some playing hours per day and others playing for only brief

	periods per week. Some upgrades are more popular, and others seem to drive away players frustrated or disappointed with the changes.
	Overall, an average player will keep a PEL in-game character active for 5 to 8 months.
Note 2	Consumables are features used immediately in a game (e.g., rain, extra life, or health).
	Revenue amounts would be lower by the following amounts (in 000s) if revenue were recognized over the playing life of the in-game character rather than as cash is received:
	CRASH: $665
	RATS: 40
	DOOM: 50
Note 3	Durables are features that the in-game characters keep over their playing lives (e.g., stronger engines or tires, fences, and weapons).
	Revenue amounts would be lower by the following amounts (in 000s) if revenue were recognized over the playing life of the in-game character rather than as cash is received:
	CRASH: $315
	RATS: 10
	DOOM: 110
Note 4	Virtual currency is a new feature in 20X3.
	Virtual currency is paid for up front, banked in a player's account, and can be used for any item in the specific Princely game. It does not expire, but cannot be refunded. Past history in the on-line gaming industry indicates that 10% to 30% will be dormant and never utilized.
	Virtual currency issued this year is listed in the cash flow summary above, and totalled (in 000s) $215 for 20X3. "Banked," or unused, virtual currency for each game at September 30, 20X3 is:
	CRASH: $120
	RATS: 1
	DOOM: 20

(Judy Cumby, used with permission.)

CASE 6-3

TIME-LICE BOOKS LTD.

Time-Lice Books Ltd. (TLBL) is a well-established public company that publishes a wide variety of general interest nonfiction books. The company is incorporated under the *Canada Business Corporations Act*, and the heirs of Harold Lice, the firm's founder, hold 30% of the shares. The heirs do not take any active interest in the affairs of the company, but rely on the advice of their professional financial advisor, Mr. Jin-Shan Dai, in voting their shares. The remaining 70% of the shares are widely distributed and are traded on the TSX.

TLBL distributes about 25% of its books through retail booksellers (including on-line), but the bulk of the sales (75%) are made directly to customers by direct mail and Internet advertising. About half of the direct mail and Internet sales are for series of books, and the company has decided to review its accounting policy for this segment of the business. TLBL is also exploring the possibility of selling its books electronically for use on e-book readers.

A book series is a set of books on a particular topic. Rather than publishing all of the books at once, the approach is to issue one book at a time, at two-to-four-month intervals. Topics of some series that have recently begun are *Saving the Planet*, *Great Impressionist Artists*, *Time-Lice Guides to Home Maintenance*, and *Lives of Great Accountants* (a particularly popular series).

When TLBL decides to start a new series, the first step is to design an elaborate and expensive full-colour advertising brochure for the series. This brochure is then mailed to about two million homes in Canada, using TLBL's own mailing list plus purchased mailing lists. An electronic version of the brochure is also disseminated via the Internet. The first book of the series is offered free of charge to anyone who returns a postage-paid card or requests a copy via Internet.

While the sales campaign is going on, TLBL contracts writers to prepare the text of the first book in the series, and begins design of the book. However, actual production of the book does not occur until the direct sales campaign has ended and the number of copies needed has been determined from the returned postal cards and Internet requests.

The second book is produced about two months after the first has been mailed out, and it is sent to all those customers who received the first (free) volume. However, customers are then asked either to subscribe to the entire series at a fixed price or to return the second volume without charge. Company experience has been that, on average, 80% of the customers elect to subscribe and about 15% return the second book. The other 5% neither subscribe nor return the book, and TLBL takes no action against these subscribers except to send them a letter and to delete their names from its mailing lists. While 80% is the average subscription rate, the rate for specific series may vary anywhere from 70% to 85%.

Customers who do subscribe have a choice of paying for the entire series all at once or paying for each book (at a higher per-unit price) as it is sent. Roughly half of the customers elect each alternative, although there has been a trend toward advance payment via credit card or PayPal.

The advertising brochure and sales campaign is the largest single cost incurred. The writers of the books are under a fixed-fee contract with TLBL and do not receive royalties. The layout and design work on each volume is performed by TLBL's salaried designers. Although printing costs have been escalating sharply, the cost to print and bind each book has lately been about $5. The books are sold to customers at about $30 per copy. All customers may cancel their subscriptions at any time. The advance-payment subscribers must send a letter of cancellation, but few do so. The instalment subscribers may cancel simply by returning one of the volumes within 15 days of receipt, whereupon they are sent no more volumes in the series. At some point before the conclusion of the series, 20% to 30% of instalment subscribers cancel.

Required:

Evaluate the revenue and expense recognition alternatives for TLBL for the book series.

CASE 6-4

THOMAS TECHNOLOGIES CORP.

Thomas Technologies Corp. (TTC) is an engineering services company based in Calgary. The company's Class B common shares are listed on the Toronto Stock Exchange. The Class A common shares are all owned by Theodore Thomas, the company founder, and his immediate family. The Class A shares are multiple voting shares that assure that the Thomas family retains voting control over the company.

The company's shares have risen sharply in price over the past two years, driven mainly by the strength of the Alberta economy and the need for engineering services by the many resource and exploration companies based in Calgary. Stock analysts have been very enthusiastic about TTC shares and analysts have issued very favourable earnings forecasts for TTC's 20X4 year-end results.

In 20X4, TTC entered into special long-term contracts with two of its largest clients. The company's accounting staff recorded the transactions as directed by the TTC chief financial officer. The two transactions were as follows:

1. TTC entered into a three-year contract with Howard Ltd. to provide engineering services. The services would be rendered on an as-needed basis over the three years. The contract stated that Howard would pay $3 million to TTC during 20X4, $2 million during 20X5, and $1.6 million during 20X6. Howard paid for the first year's service as agreed. TTC recorded the payment as revenue for 20X4. The cost of services rendered by TTC to Howard is not separately tracked, but is part of the regular service provided by TTC to many clients.

2. TTC and Parker Inc. signed an agreement on 14 October 20X4. As one part of the agreement, TTC designed and built a special-purpose piece of equipment for Parker. Parker did not solicit bids from other manufacturers due to the close working relationship that has been established between Parker and TTC over the years, even though similar equipment might have been obtained for about 20% less from a heavy equipment manufacturer in Japan. The agreement provided that Parker would pay $5.6 million for the equipment. The equipment was delivered to Parker on 22 December 20X4. Parker paid 40% of the purchase price on 30 December, with a promise to pay the remaining 60% within the first 90 days of 20X5. The equipment cost TTC $3.4 million to construct. The agreement provided that Parker could not sell or otherwise convey the equipment to any other user.

In addition to the equipment sale, the agreement stipulated that Parker would pay $1.5 million per year for the next four years as a service contract with the first payment due within 120 days of delivery. The price is about 25% less than TTC would normally charge a client for that type of service.

TTC recorded revenue of $5.6 million for the equipment, and included $3.4 million in cost of services. The company also recorded the first year's service revenue by crediting $1.5 million to revenue and debiting accounts receivable—long-term. This revenue was matched by charging $1.0 million to cost of services (for the estimated cost of providing the service) and crediting an equal amount to estimated service liability.

It now is January 20X5. You are working for the audit firm of Andrew, Athens, and Argoyle on the annual audit of TTC. The audit manager is preparing to meet with the TTC CFO tomorrow morning. She has asked you to prepare a memorandum in which you set out your views on the accounting used by TTC for these two contracts, with a recommendation on whether or not to accept TTC accounting, and any alternatives that you propose.

Required:

Prepare the memorandum for your audit manager.

TECHNICAL REVIEW

connect

TR6-1 Net versus Gross:

Crane Inc. is an agent for Phillips Co. and negotiates sales contracts between Phillips and the final customer for heating and air conditioning units. By agreement, Crane is to receive a commission of 15% on each sale. During the last quarter, Crane negotiated sales of 100 furnaces for total sales of $60,000. The cost of each furnace is $37,000.

Required:

Calculate the amounts that would be recognized and reported by Phillips and Crane for the last quarter.

connect

TR6-2 Prepaid Deposits and Revenue Recognition:

Dress for Success is an upscale dress shop. On 15 August, Sally, a regular customer, came in and put a deposit down on two items: $50 on a dress and $100 on a suit. The deposit was in the amount of $150, which represented 20% of the total retail value of the clothes. On 21 August, Sally came in again to the store and decided to take the dress. She paid the remaining amount of $200 and took the dress home. On 2 September, she came in and paid the full amount remaining for the suit.

Required:

Prepare the journal entries that Dress for Success would use to record these transactions.

connect

TR6-3 Predictable Rights of Return:

Under contract, Sojourn Co. delivers 1,000 units to Customer A for $50 each on 1 April. Sojourn's documented policy is to allow a customer to return any unused product within 90 days and receive a full refund. The cost of each product is $35. On the basis of historical experience, Sojourn estimates that 4% of the units will be returned. Sojourn expects that the returned products can be resold.

Required:

Record the journal entries to be made by Sojourn on 1 April to recognize the sale.

■ connect

TR6-4 Warranty—Cost Deferral:

ELC Inc. sells all types of electronics with a one-year warranty for product assurance on all products sold. On 26 February, a customer came into the store and purchased a television for $1,250. The company estimates, from past experience, that warranty costs will be $150 for this product.

Required:

Prepare the journal entries that ELC would use to record this transaction.

■ connect

TR6-5 Licensing Fees:

Spreadsheets Made Easy (SME) is a company that designs and sells spreadsheet software. Corporate customers purchase licences for the number of users in their company who can access the software from their network at any time. The perpetual licences do not expire and can be easily reproduced by SME. SME has no additional obligations to fulfill with respect to this software. On 16 November 20X1, SME sold 50 licences to a customer for a total consideration of $50,000.

Required:

Prepare the journal entry that would be recorded by SME relating to this transaction.

■ connect

TR6-6 Output Measure:

CCS is a construction company that builds roads in the Northwest Territories (NWT). CCS uses the percentage-of-completion method and measures completion on the basis of kilometres completed. In November 20X9, CCS signed an agreement with the NWT government to build 50 kilometres of new road for a total cost of $40 million. The contract would likely take three years to complete and would start in the spring of 20X10. Over the next three years, 15 kilometres were completed in 20X10, 22 kilometres completed in 20X11, and 13 kilometres completed in 20X12.

Required:

Calculate the amount of revenue that would be recognized in 20X10, 20X11, and 20X12.

■ connect

TR6-7 Customer Loyalty Program:

Rock Gasoline decided to implement a customer loyalty point program. For each litre of fuel sold, the customer earns one point. The points can be accumulated and redeemed later for gas, products in the store, or a car wash. In May, Rock has sales of $60,000, which represents 48,000 litres. The fair value of all of the loyalty points awarded on these sales was $1,500.

Required:

Prepare the journal entry required to record the sales for May for Rock.

■ connect

TR6-8 Deferred Payments:

SorCo. Inc. has just entered into a sale agreement with a customer. The contract is for $1,100,000. However, the payments will be made as follows: 1 August 20X1 on date of delivery $500,000; 1 August 20X2 $300,000 and 1 August 20X3 $300,000. SorCo has estimated that the interest rate required for this customer is 7%.

Required:

Prepare the journal entry required to record the sale on 1 August 20X1 and the receipt of cash on 1 August 20X2 and 20X3.

■ connect

TR6-9 Multiple Deliverable:

Arrow Co. entered into a contract with a customer for $410,000. The contract is for the delivery of equipment and a three-year service maintenance contract for the equipment. Arrow sells separately the equipment for a selling price of $400,000, and the maintenance contract for three years for $50,000. The equipment was delivered on 1 June 1 20X1. Arrow has a 30 November year-end.

Required:

Prepare the journal entries required to record the revenue related to this contract during the period 1 June 20X1 to 30 November 20X1.

■ connect

TR6-10 Contract Costs:

In February, Huron Ltd. incurred costs to obtain a contract with a customer. The contract is for two years. The following costs were incurred:

Travel costs to meet with the customer	$10,000
Legal costs to write up the agreement	$5,000
Cost of meals	$7,000
Marketing materials used to promote the product	$2,500

Required:

Prepare the journal entry for these costs.

ASSIGNMENTS

 A6-1 Revenue Recognition—Gross or Net:

Each of the following situations is independent:

a. A company sells books through the Internet. The company obtains the books from the publishers and carries them in inventory for immediate shipment. Customer payment is by credit card.

b. An interior design company operates a showroom. Furniture manufacturers send samples of their products to the showroom for display. When a customer orders furniture, the company transmits the order to the manufacturer, and the manufacturer ships the products directly to the customer. Customers pay a deposit by cash or credit card, with the balance due (cash or credit card) when the product is delivered.

c. CanLight Ltd. is a company that sells electrical lighting fixtures. The fixtures are produced in China and shipped to CanLight by container ship. The producer pays shipping costs and retains title to the fixtures both while in transit and while they are in CanLight's inventory. CanLight markets and sells the fixtures to builders for inclusion in new construction. When a sale is made, CanLight delivers the fixtures to the building site and invoices the builder. When the builder pays the invoice, CanLight sends 70% of the cash to the producer by international bank transfer.

Required:

For each of the preceding situations, explain:

1. Whether the seller should report the gross amount of the sales transactions as revenue; and
2. Your basis for deciding whether to recognize gross or net revenue.

 A6-2 IFRS—Revenue Recognition:

For each of the following independent items, indicate when revenue should be recognized.

a. Interest on loans made by a financial institution, receivable in annual payments.

b. Interest on loans made by a financial institution, receivable in three years when the customer, who has an excellent credit rating, will make payment.

c. Recognition of revenue from the cash sale of airline tickets, when the travel purchased will occur in the next fiscal period.

d. Transportation of freight by a trucking company for a customer; the customer is expected to make payment in accordance with the terms of the invoice in 60 days.

e. Growing, harvesting, and marketing of Christmas trees; the production cycle is ten years.

f. Building houses in a subdivision, when the project will take two years to complete and each house must be individually sold by the contractor. The contractor owns each house until title is transferred to the new owner.

g. Building houses in a subdivision, when the project will take two years to complete and the contractor is building the houses under a contract from the local government. The local government owns the land and the homes as they are constructed.

h. Selling undeveloped lots for future retirement homes in a western province, with very low down payment and long-term payment contracts.

i. Sale of a two-year parking permit by a parking garage, with one-half the sale price received at the time of the sale, and the remainder to be received in equal monthly payments over the period of the permit.

j. A fixed-price contract with the government to design and build a prototype of a space arm; the costs to complete the project cannot be reliably estimated. The government owns the arm throughout the contract.

k. A silver-mining company produces one million ounces of silver but stores the silver in a vault and waits for silver prices to increase.

 **A6-3 IFRS—Revenue Recognition—Four Cases:**

The cases given below for 20X5 are independent of each other. In each, assume that the accounting period ends 31 December.

Case A On 31 December 20X5, Zulu Sales Co. sold a machine for $100,000 and collected $30,000 cash. The remainder plus 10% interest is payable 31 December 20X6. Zulu will deliver the machine on 5 January 20X6 at which time title is transferred. The buyer has an excellent credit rating.

Case B On 17 April 20X5, the law firm of Pearlstein and Wolf received $30,000 from a client. The payment was a retainer for legal services to be provided, as needed, from 1 May 20X5 though 30 April 20X6. During 20X5, additional work was provided to the client and billed accordingly.

Case C On 15 November 20X5, Victor Cement Co. sold a tonne of its product for $500. The cement was delivered on that date. Victor agreed that the buyer could pay for the product with three units of its own merchandise commonly sold for $200 each. The buyer promised to deliver the merchandise around 31 January 20X6.

Case D On 2 August 20X5, Remer Publishing Co. collected $720 cash for a three-year subscription to a monthly magazine, *Investor's Stock and Bond Advisory*. The first issue will be mailed to subscribers in December 20X5.

Required:

Write a brief report covering the following for each of the four situations:

1. When revenue should be recognized.
2. Any entry that should be made on the transaction date.
3. An explanation of the reasoning for your responses to requirements 1 and 2.

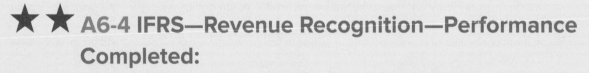 **A6-4 IFRS—Revenue Recognition—Performance Completed:**

Each of the following situations is independent of the others:

a. Rory Inc. is a manufacturer of windows. Rory primarily sells to residential builders who take delivery of the windows only when the house is at the stage at which the windows can be immediately installed. Consequently, builders will order the total number of windows in the various shapes and sizes needed for an entire season. The builder will be invoiced as the order is completed and the windows put into a separate section of the warehouse and tagged with the customer name. But the windows will not be delivered until requested by the customer. The completed order is held in Rory's warehouse and shipped as the requests are received. Payment is made 60 days after the invoice date.

b. Heckinger Inc. manufactures customized equipment used in the paper packaging industry. Customers can pick from a variety of "sections" to build a customized piece of machinery. It takes about nine months to build these machines. However, even though the machines are "customized," they can be easily modified at any time during the production phase for another customer, since the sections are standard and easily disassembled if required. The contract outlines which standard sections will be required and how they will be assembled for the final machine, the amount of the consideration to be paid, and that the customer will take title on delivery and inspection of the machinery. Payment is due after delivery and inspection.

c. Nevo Corp. develops customized software for clients related to inventory management. Nevo starts with the customer specifications and then writes the software based on these requirements. It takes about 18 months to complete the project from concept and specifications through programming, debugging, and testing. Included in the contract are installation, on-site testing, training, and two years' upgrade and service (which commences after the training is complete). Customers make progress payments throughout the contract as certain milestones are achieved. A contract outlines the specifications for the software; a project plan for installation, testing, training, upgrades, and service; the milestones to be achieved; and the consideration to be paid. Nevo also sells ongoing upgrade and service agreements separately to customers, but installation, testing, and training are not offered separately, since these are customized to the specific customer's software.

Required:

For each situation, assess the five steps, and determine when revenue is recognized and how costs and payments should be accounted for.

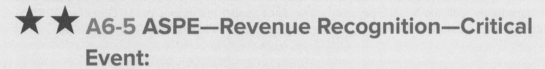

★ ★ A6-5 ASPE—Revenue Recognition—Critical Event:

Luke Windows Ltd. manufactures custom-made windows for homes. The company deals directly with some individual customers, but mainly does business with contractors that are building tract housing under contract with a developer—that is, a real property development company that is constructing a large number of houses in a single new development.

For tract housing, Luke bids on the contract according to specifications given by the developer. The costs of preparing the bid are not substantial, but they are not insignificant either. If Luke wins the contract, the company then sets up a production line in the factory to manufacture the windows according to specifications. As the windows are finished, they are stored in Luke's factory temporarily, until the contractor is ready to receive them. When they are delivered to the building site (usually in batches, not all together), the contractor is responsible for any damage or breakage that occurs. Also, the contractor is responsible for proper installation.

The houses are built (and sold) in batches. The sales from one batch help the developer to finance the next batch. After each batch of houses is finished and has been standing empty through a few rain or snow storms, the developer inspects for any failure in design, construction, or installation. If all is satisfactory, the developer authorizes payment for that part of the development. Payment is made to the contractor, which then is responsible for paying Luke. In the unlikely event that the contractor does not pay Luke, Luke can establish a lien on the houses that requires the developer (or the new owners who have purchased the houses) to satisfy Luke's claim.

Depending on the size of the housing development, the entire project from bid preparation to final collection can take anywhere from two to five years. Each batch of houses is usually completed within about 18 months. However, Luke's construction and delivery of the windows for a batch seldom takes more than two months.

Required:

1. From the information given, identify the point at which Luke should recognize revenue from windows for tract housing. Explain your reasoning.

2. Using the revenue recognition point identified in requirement 1, explain how Luke should account for costs and revenues related to this project over time.

★ ★ ★ A6-6 IFRS—Revenue Recognition:

Shawinegan Development Co. (SDC) conducts research and development on specific projects under contract for clients; SDC also conducts basic research and attempts to market any new products or technologies it develops.

In January 20X4, scientists at SDC began research to develop a new industrial cleaner. During 20X4, $3,160,000 of costs were incurred in this effort. Late in July 20X5, potentially promising results emerged in the form of a substance the company called Scourge. Costs incurred through the end of July 20X5 were $1,540,000. At this point, SDC attempted to sell the formula and rights to Scourge to Pride and Glory Industries Ltd. (PGIL), for $16,000,000. PGIL, however, was reluctant to sign before further testing was done. It did wish to have the first option to acquire the rights and formulas to Scourge if future testing showed the product to be profitable. SDC was very confident that Scourge would pass further testing with flying colours. Accordingly, the two companies signed an option agreement that allowed PGIL to acquire the formulas and rights to Scourge any time before 31 December 20X6. Testing costs on the product incurred by SDC for the remainder of 20X5 amounted to $1,800,000.

On 6 March 20X6, PGILG exercised its option and agreed to purchase the formulas and rights to Scourge for $16,000,000. The formula was to be completed and delivered within 18 months.

On 2 January 20X7, SDC delivered the formulas and samples of Scourge to PGIL. On that date, PGIL paid $6,400,000 immediately with the balance payable in four equal annual instalments on 31 December 20X7 to 20X10. Additional testing costs incurred by SDC during 20X6 amounted to $540,000; in 20X7, $260,000.

Required:

1. When should revenue be recognized by SDC from its work on Scourge? Why? Apply the five steps for revenue recognition.
2. Assume that the total costs of $7,300,000 actually incurred by SDC over the years 20X4 to 20X7 had been accurately estimated in 20X4. Determine the amount of revenue and expense that should be recognized each year from 20X7 to 20X10. The appropriate discount rate for the credit risk associated with this customer is 6%. Prepare journal entries related to revenue recognition for 20X6 to 20X10 assuming revenue is recognized at the point of delivery.

Note that the $3,160,000 *research* costs must be expensed in all alternatives to comply with accounting standards for research costs. *Development* costs may be deferred if appropriate.

★ ★ ★ A6-7 ASPE—Entries for Critical Events:

Maypole Industries imports goods from Taiwan and resells them to domestic Canadian markets. Maypole uses a perpetual inventory system. A typical transaction stream follows:

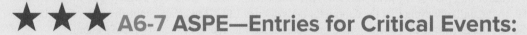

18	July	Purchased goods for $456,000.
24	August	Goods repackaged and ready for sale. Cost incurred, $60,000.
10	September	Goods delivered to customer. Agreed-on price, $712,000.
22	November	Customer paid.

Required:

1. Prepare journal entries assuming the following critical events:
   a. Delivery to customer
   b. Cash receipt
   c. Preparation of goods for resale
2. Explain the circumstances under which each of these methods would be appropriate.

★ ★ A6-8 IFRS—Revenue Recognition:

Dominum Corp. is a mining company that mines, produces, and markets teledine, a common mineral substance. The mineral is mined and produced in one large batch per year, as the mine is accessible only for a brief period in the summer due to severe weather conditions at the mine site. Dominum has an advance purchase contract with one customer that takes all of Dominum's output each year. The agreement allows the customer to return defective product for up to 60 days from the date of delivery. Transactions in 20X6 were:

30	August	186,000 tonnes of teledine ore removed from mine, at a cost of $4,300,000.
30	September	All of the ore refined to 115,000 tonnes of teledine, at a cost of $640,000. A deposit is received from the customer for $1,350,000 (10% of the contract amount).
15	October	All of the teledine delivered to the customer, total contract price, $13,500,000. At this point, 50% of the contract amount is received. Dominum estimates, from historical experience, that 7% of the goods might be returned.
25	November	Five percent of the teledine is returned for full credit; ore had been improperly refined and the teledine was unusable; customer given full credit for $675,000 and the unusable teledine scrapped.
		No other returns are anticipated.
30	November	Customer fully paid the final amount owing.

Required:

1. Assess the five steps for revenue recognition and determine when the performance obligation is complete. Prepare all the journal entries to record these events.

2. If the customer instead asked for Dominum to hold onto 30% of the production until the customer asked for delivery, how would the journal entries in requirement 1 change?

★ ★ A6-9 IFRS—Return Policy:

Carnegie Corp. commissions, produces, and sells books through faith-based nonprofit organizations. The books are sold on the basis that a maximum of 50% of the quantity purchased can be returned within six months. The contract with the customer outlines the amount of consideration and the return policy and that payment is due within 30 days of the end of the return period. Carnegie has a good historical record of the proportion of books returned, on average. On 1 June, Carnegie sold $25,000 worth of books. On 15 August, $4,000 were returned, and on 3 October, an additional $5,500 were returned. The payment for the balance owing was received on 20 December. The cost of the books is 65% of the selling price. All of the returns are put back into inventory and can be resold.

Required:

1. Assess the five steps and determine when revenue should be recognized.
2. Prepare the appropriate journal entries that are required for the described transactions.

★ ★★ A6-10 ASPE—Unconditional Right of Return:

McLaughlin Novelty Corp. developed an unusual product, electric clip-on eyeglass wipers. McLaughlin felt the product would appeal to hikers, joggers, and cyclists who engaged in their sports in rainy climates. Because retail establishments were skeptical about the market appeal of the product, McLaughlin sold the product with a declining unconditional right of return for up to ten months, with 10% of the right-of-return amount of the purchase expiring every month for ten months. Thus, after the retailer had the product for one month, only 90% could be returned. After two months, only 80% could be returned, and after ten months, the right of return was fully expired.

McLaughlin had no basis for estimating the amount of returns. Consistent with the terms McLaughlin offered its customers, all retailers paid cash when purchasing the clip-on-eyeglass wipers but received cash refunds if goods were returned. McLaughlin had its first sales of the product in September 20X5. Sales for the remainder of the year, and returns prior to 31 December 20X5, were as follows:

Month of Sale	Units Sold	Sales Price	Monthly Sales	Units Returned
September	10,000	$10	$100,000	2,500
October	12,000	10	120,000	1,000
November	15,000	12	180,000	1,000
December	11,000	12	132,000	0
Totals	48,000		$532,000	4,500

Each unit of product costs McLaughlin $6 to produce.

Required:

1. Show the journal entries to record the four months of sales transactions, including the deferral of gross margin. Prepare one summary entry.

2. Show a summary entry to record the returns in 20X5.

3. Compute the amount that McLaughlin can record as (realized) sales for 20X5. How much is gross margin? Record the revenue recognition entry.

4. For the above transactions, total returns in all of 20X6 were as follows:

Month of Sale	Units Returned
September	1,000
October	2,000
November	2,500
December	4,000

Show the entries to record the returns in 20X6 and to record sales revenue and cost of sales from the 20X5 shipments of this product.

A6-11 IFRS—Licensing Fees:

GoRight Inc. (GRI) is a franchisor who sells the rights to its trademark to franchisees. The franchisee pays an upfront, nonrefundable deposit of $1,000. This amount is used to cover the expenses for GRI preforming a check on the franchisee's background and credentials, interviews and preparation of the agreement is the franchisee is accepted. This takes only about four days to complete. If the franchisee passes this screening, a contract is signed with GRI. The contract states that for consideration of $150,000, the franchisee will have the right to use the trademark for a period of three years. The three-year period commences at the beginning of the month the contract is signed. At the end of the period, the contract can be extended for another two years on payment of an agreed-upon amount. The franchisee may pay the $150,000 in three instalments starting on the date the contract is signed. (The upfront fee is part of the $150,000 total.) In other words, on signing of the contract, $50,000 is due, and then another $50,000 is paid in the next 30 days and the final $50,000 payment is due in 60 days (from the date of signing the contract). Failure to pay the amounts on time will forfeit the franchisee's right to use the trademark. If a franchise is revoked, GRO will retain an amount equal to 5% of the total $150,000 to cover administrative costs incurred and the remaining amounts received are refunded. In 20X4, GRI signed 20 contracts with various franchisees as detailed below. GRI has a December year-end.

	Number of Licence Agreements Signed	Amount Paid to Date $	Payments Not Yet Received
April 20X4	3	450,000	0
July 20X4	8	1,200,000	50,000 (note 1)
October 20X4	5	700,000	
November 20X4	4	400,000	200,000
Total	20	2,750,000	250,000

Note 1: All franchisees made their payments on time, except for one who owed his last payment of $50,000. The rights to this franchise were revoked in November 20X4.

Required:

1. Determine when revenue should be recognized for the sale of the franchise fees.
2. Give the required entries for 20X4 for each month.
3. Give the related balances that would be reported on the 20X4 income statements and SFP.

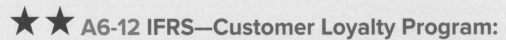

★ ★ A6-12 IFRS—Customer Loyalty Program:

Beaver Ltd. is a retail company that sells sporting goods. It has a customer loyalty program that allows customers to earn points based on sales made. These points can be accumulated and used for future purchases. One customer loyalty point is awarded for every $1 of purchases. During March 20X4, the company recorded sales of $1,725,000 to customers who were accumulating points. The stand-alone value of these goods sold was $1,725,000. Beaver has also determined that each point has a fair value of $0.017. The loyalty account had a balance of $870,000 at the beginning of March. During the month of March, customers used 1,200,000 points to purchase goods in the store.

Required:

Prepare the entries for the above transactions for the month of March 20X4.

★ ★ A6-13 IFRS—Warranty—Two Accounting Methods:

On 30 April 20X2, Neuman Ltd. sells a product to a customer for $600,000. The product carries a one-year assurance warranty. Neuman management estimates that the probable cost of fulfilling the warranty will be $50,000. Between 1 May and 31 December 20X2, the actual warranty cost was $20,000. On 31 December 20X2, management decides that the probable additional warranty cost will be no more than $13,000. Between 1 January and 30 April 20X3, the additional cost was $11,000.

Required:

1. Prepare the entries concerning the sale and the warranty for 30 April 20X2 through 30 April 20X3.
2. Assume instead that the warranty now includes service and is sold separately with a stand-alone value of $75,000. The product has a stand-alone value of $580,000 and the total contract is $600,000. Prepare the relevant journal entries for 30 April 20X2 through 30 April 20X3.

★ ★ A6-14 IFRS—Warranty—Two Accounting Methods:

Chapnik Equipment Corp. (CEC) produced custom-designed machinery for a long-time customer. The direct cost to produce the machinery was $1.4 million. CEC sold the equipment to the customer for $2.0 million. The machinery was delivered, installed, and tested during September 20X1. At the end of September, the customer declared satisfaction with the machinery and signed a formal declaration of acceptance. CEC guaranteed the equipment for a full two years after acceptance, agreeing to correct any defects or operational problems that might occur before 30 September 20X3.

At the time of the sale, CEC management estimated that the eventual warranty cost would be no more than $100,000, since CEC had considerable experience with this general type of machinery. Subsequent experience was as follows:

a. Repair costs during the remainder of 20X1 amounted to $25,000.

b. At the end of 20X1, CEC managers decided that the total warranty cost might be as much as $130,000 by the end of the warranty period.

c. During 20X2, total warranty costs amounted to $40,000.

d. At the end of 20X2, management revised their estimate of remaining warranty cost to just $20,000.

e. Additional warranty costs during 20X3 (i.e., up to the end of the warranty period) were $15,000.

Required:

Prepare the entries concerning the sale and the warranty that the company would make from 30 September 20X1 through 30 September 20X3 under each of the following two assumptions:

1. Assume that warranty cost is in the form of an assurance.

2. Assume instead that CEC also sells the warranty as a separate service. The total contract is still for $2 million. The stand-alone value of the machinery and warranty are $150,000 and $1,900,000, respectively.

 # A6-15 IFRS—Multiple Deliverables:

BigBoy Equipment Inc. sells heavy-duty forklift trucks. Model 217A has a stand-alone price of $140,000. BigBoy offers to sell the 217A inclusive of a three-year service contract for $180,000.

Required:

Prepare a journal entry to record the sale of one Model 217A forklift truck plus service contract for $180,000 assuming:

1. A comparable service contract is sold separately for $60,000. BigBoy uses the relative stand-alone value method for multiple deliverables.

2. The service contract has a variable stand-alone value ranging from $35,000 to $60,000 and BigBoy uses the residual value method.

 # A6-16 ASPE Multiple Deliverables:

Dominion Mobile Inc. provides cellular phone services. The company conducts a special sales campaign in which new subscribers will get a high-end cell phone for only $100 if they sign a 36-month contract that has a service fee of $100 per month. Thus, the total price of the cell phone plus 36 months of service is $3,700.

The company normally sells the phone for $1,000. Current subscribers pay $60 per month for comparable service but are not permitted to take advantage of the $100 cell phone offer.

Required:

Determine how a customer contract for $3,700 should be recognized.

 # A6-17 IFRS—Biological Assets and Agricultural Produce:

Timber Resource Inc., a forestry company, owns timber resources in northern Quebec. The company produces lumber from these resources. During 20X3, the company cut trees into logs with a fair market value of $600,000. The selling costs estimated at the time were 5% of fair value. At the end of the year, about 20% of these logs have not yet entered production. The 80% that have entered production required $175,000 of production costs to produce lumber into fixed cut lengths that are now available for sale to various customers. By the end of the year, 40% of the lumber was still on hand and ready for sale. There was no work-in-progress at the year-end. Fair-value information for assets owned at the year-end is provided below:

	Timber	Logs	Lumber
Fair value at end of 20X2	$8,900,000	$110,000	$295,000
Fair value at end of 20X3	$9,350,000	$125,000	$310,000

Costs to sell are estimated to be 5% for timber, 5% for logs and 7% for lumber.

Required:

1. Prepare the journal entries to record the transactions during 20X3 as well as any entries needed to adjust year-end balances.
2. Show relevant balances in the SCI and SFP related to the above transactions.

★ A6-18 IFRS Biological Assets and Agricultural Produce:

Refer to the following list of various products:

a. yarn

b. lumber

c. sheep

d. eggs

e. grapes

f. trees

g. frozen omelets

h. wool

i. chickens

j. logs (felled trees)

Required:

1. In this list, identify those items that may qualify as biological asset, agricultural produce, and inventory. In addition, match up the biological asset with its agricultural produce and its processed inventory.
2. Explain how each of the three types of assets—biological asset, agricultural produce, and inventory—is recognized and reported.

A6-19 IFRS Percentage-of-Completion Method and Completed-Contract Method:

Star Construction Corp. has a contract to construct a building for $10,950,000. The building is controlled by the customer throughout the term of the contract. Total costs to complete the building were originally estimated at $8,850,000. Construction commenced on 4 February 20X5. Actual costs were in line with estimated costs for 20X5 and 20X6. In 20X7, actual costs exceeded estimated costs by $150,000.

Total construction costs incurred in each year were as follows:

20X5	$2,700,000
20X6	$4,500,000
20X7	$1,800,000

Billings each year were as follows:

20X5	$2,300,000
20X6	$4,900,000
20X7	$3,750,000

Required:

1. Calculate the revenues and gross profit for the construction project for each of the three years assuming the company uses inputs to measure progress.

2. Prepare the journal entries for revenue recognition for each year and for contract completion in 20X7.

3. Prepare the journal entries for revenue recognition for each year and for contract completion in 20X7, if the customer did not take control of the asset until the building was fully constructed and title transferred.

(Source: [Adapted] © CGA-Canada. Reproduced with permission.)

★ ★ A6-20 IFRS Construction Contract:

Thrasher Construction Co. was contracted to construct a building for $975,000. The building is owned by the customer throughout the contract period. The contract provides for progress payments. Thrasher's accounting year ends 31 December. Work began under the contract on 1 July 20X5, and was completed on 30 September 20X7. Construction activities are summarized below by year:

20X5   Construction costs incurred during the year, $180,000; estimated costs to complete, $630,000; progress billings during the year, $153,000; and collections, $140,000.

20X6   Construction costs incurred during the year, $450,000; estimated costs to complete, $190,000; progress billing during the year, $382,500; and collections, $380,000.

20X7   Construction costs incurred during the year, $195,000. Because the contract was completed, the remaining balance was billed and later collected in full per the contract.

Required:

1. Give Thrasher's journal entries to record these events. Assume that percentage of completion is measured by the ratio of costs incurred to date divided by total estimated construction costs.

2. Provide the balances that would be shown on the SCI and SFP for this contract for each year.

3. Now assume that the building is owned by Thrasher throughout the construction period and title is transferred to the customer only once the building is fully constructed. Prepare the journal entries required to record the events from 20X5 to 20X7. Also calculate the balances that would be shown on the SCI and SFP for this contract for each year.

 A6-21 ASPE Construction Contract:

Buildit Corp. was contracted to construct a building for $1,600,000. The contract provided for progress payments. Buildit's accounting year ends 31 December. Work began under the contract on 1 March 20X3, and was completed on 30 November 20X5. Construction activities are summarized below by year:

20X3   Construction costs incurred during the year, $470,000; estimated costs to complete, $830,000; progress billings during the year, $380,000; and collections, $290,000.

20X4   Construction costs incurred during the year, $700,000; estimated costs to complete, $210,000; progress billing during the year, $990,000; and collections, $870,000.

20X5   Construction costs incurred during the year, $195,000. Because the contract was completed, the remaining balance was billed and later collected in full per the contract.

Required:

1. Give Buildit's journal entries to record these events. Assume that percentage of completion is measured by the ratio of costs incurred to date divided by total estimated construction costs.
2. Provide the balances that would appear on the income statement and balance sheet for this contract for each year.

 A6-22 Asset Exchanges—Five Situations:

Consider each of the following independent situations:

a. GYT Co. exchanges a machine that cost $4,000 and has accumulated amortization of $2,560 for a similar machine. GYT also receives $25 in the exchange. The fair market value of the old asset is $750. The fair market value of the new asset is $725. There is no commercial substance to the transaction.
b. FST Co. exchanges a machine that cost $4,000 and has accumulated amortization of $3,560 for a similar machine. FST also receives $25 in the exchange. The fair market value of the old asset is $750. The fair market value of the new asset is $725. There is no commercial substance to the transaction.
c. LKC Co. pays $250 and exchanges a machine that cost $3,000 and has accumulated amortization of $1,900 for a similar machine. The fair market value of the old asset is undeterminable. The fair market value of the new asset is $690. The transaction has commercial substance.
d. HRT Co. pays $250 and exchanges a machine that cost $2,000 and has accumulated amortization of $1,400 for a similar machine. The fair market value of the old asset is $435. The fair market value of the new asset is $680. The transaction has commercial substance.
e. AML Co. pays $500 and exchanges a machine that cost $9,000 and has accumulated amortization of $8,400 for a similar machine. The fair market value of the new asset is $1,580. The transaction has commercial substance.

Required:

For each situation, determine:

1. The value at which the acquired asset will appear on the company's statement of financial position.

2. The amount of gain or loss that will be recorded on the company's statement of comprehensive income.

(Judy Cumby, adapted.)

★ ★ A6-23 ASPE Asset Exchanges—Four Situations:

Ricardo Heavy Hauling has some earth-moving equipment that cost $432,000; accumulated amortization is $288,000. Ricardo traded equipment with another construction company. The fair value of Ricardo's old equipment is estimated to be $225,000, and the fair value of the equipment being acquired is estimated to be $285,000. Four different possible scenarios are presented below:

a. The new equipment will perform essentially the same tasks as the old equipment. The estimate of the fair value of the new equipment is the more reliable of the two estimates. The exchange is a straight swap and no cash changes hands.

b. The new equipment has very different functions than the old equipment. The new equipment will permit Ricardo to attract new business that it had previously been unable to obtain. The fair-value estimate of the new equipment is the more reliable of the two estimates. The exchange is a straight swap and no cash changes hands.

c. In addition to exchanging its old equipment, Ricardo pays $24,000 cash. The characteristics of Ricardo's operating cash flows will change as a result of the exchange. The fair value of the old equipment is the more reliable estimate.

d. Assume the same facts as in (c) above, except that the exchange will not significantly alter Ricardo's cash flows.

e. A large truck, which cost Company A $100,000 ($60,000 accumulated depreciation), has a market resale value of $70,000. The truck is traded to a dealer, plus a cash payment of $20,000, for a new truck that will perform essentially the same services as the old truck, but will look a lot nicer to the customers. The new truck has a list price of $95,000, although discounts of 3% to 4% may be negotiable.

f. Rochester Shipping Co. received a new ferry that has a normal purchase price of $1.30 million. In exchange, the company gave the vendor a parcel of land and a building located on the waterfront. The market value of the land and building is $1.15 million. The land cost $300,000; the building cost $700,000 and is 30% depreciated. The vendor will use the land and building to operate a maintenance facility. The new ferry will enable Rochester Shipping to launch a new ferry service across Lake Ontario. The ferry was available because the buyer for whom it had been built went bankrupt and was unable to take delivery. The boat remained unsold for two years before Rochester was able to negotiate the exchange. Because the boat had been dormant for so long, it needed some upgrading and maintenance. Rochester agreed to pay for the necessary work, which was estimated to cost $350,000.

Required:

For each scenario, prepare the journal entry to record the exchange.

★ ★ A6-24 SCF Impact

XYZ Co. had a variety of revenue transactions during the year. Below are the balances on the SFP related to its revenue transactions.

	Closing Balance 20X8	Closing Balance 20X9
	$	$
Accounts receivable	675,000	890,000
Contract costs	128,000	172,000
Contract liabilities	457,000	525,000
Provision for warranties	24,000	35,000

Required:

Using the information in the table, explain the effects that the revenue transactions would have on the SCF, assuming the company uses the indirect method.

 ## A6-25 Revenue and Expense Recognition:

Pewter Publishing Co. (PPC) prepares and publishes a monthly newsletter for an industry in which potential circulation is limited. Because information provided by the newsletter is available only piecemeal from other sources and because no advertising is carried, the subscription price for the newsletter is relatively high. To increase circulation, PPC recently purchased a contact list from the industry's trade association for $110,000. PPC then engaged in a campaign to increase circulation. The campaign involved extensive use of long-distance telephone calls to industry members on the list who were not current subscribers. The telephone cost of the campaign was $38,000, plus salary payments to individuals who made the calls amounting to $51,000.

As a direct result of the campaign, new one-year subscriptions at $175 each generated revenue of $294,100. New three-year subscriptions at $450 each generated revenue of $224,700, and new five-year subscriptions at $625 each generated $187,500. Cancellations are rare, but when they occur, refunds are made on a half-rate basis (e.g., if a subscriber has yet to receive $100 worth of newsletters, $50 is refunded).

The subscription campaign was conducted during August 20X0. New subscriptions began with the October 20X0 issue of the monthly newsletter. The company's accounting year ends 31 December.

Required:

Identify the specific accounting issues involved in recognizing revenue and costs for PPC. Calculate the related assets, liabilities, revenue, and expenses that would be reported by the company for 20X0 on its SFP and SCI.

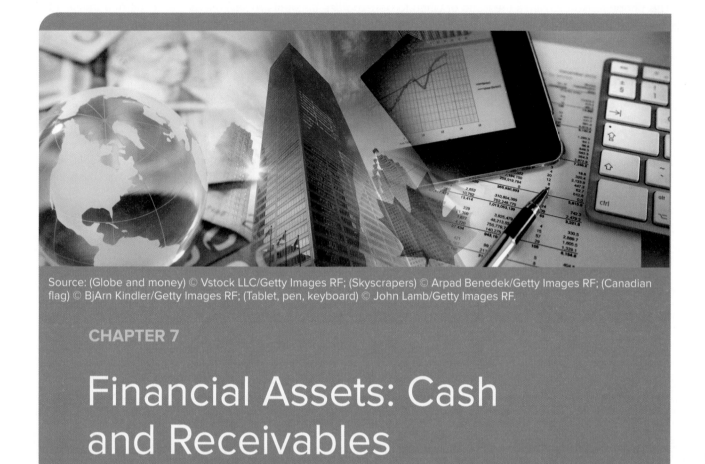

Source: (Globe and money) © Vstock LLC/Getty Images RF; (Skyscrapers) © Arpad Benedek/Getty Images RF; (Canadian flag) © BjArn Kindler/Getty Images RF; (Tablet, pen, keyboard) © John Lamb/Getty Images RF.

CHAPTER 7

Financial Assets: Cash and Receivables

INTRODUCTION

One objective of financial reporting is to provide information to allow financial statement users to assess the financial position of an entity. Levels of current financial assets are critical when assessing the *liquidity* and viability of an operation. For example, consider Aastra Technologies Ltd., a Canadian public company involved in developing and marketing products and systems for accessing communication networks, including the Internet. The company was recently purchased by Mitel Networks Corp. Prior to the purchase at the end of the 2012 fiscal year, the statement of financial position (SFP) reported $100,965 (thousand) in cash and $159,260 (thousand) in accounts receivable out of total assets of $524,837. That is, these two assets alone represented 50% of total assets. At the end of 2014 those same two accounts represented only 27% of Mitel Networks Corp.'s total assets. Correct measurement and presentation of these assets is important to the company's overall financial picture.

This chapter explores accounting principles for the recognition, measurement, and reporting of several critical financial assets: cash, accounts receivable, and notes receivable. This material is based on IFRS 9, effective in 2018, with early adoption permitted. Financial instruments that are investments are discussed in Chapter 11.

This chapter deals with both presentation issues and valuation. The financial instruments discussed in this chapter are initially recorded at fair value, which is the exchange amount. This is *book value,* or *cost.* The recorded value is maintained, subject to allowances that reduce various receivables for factors such as bad debts, cash discounts, and sales allowances. Receivables must reflect the present value of future cash flows. Accordingly, *amortized cost* is the valuation approach when the time value of money is a factor in valuation. In some circumstances, these financial assets might be remeasured to a (new) fair value at a later year-end date.

This chapter also examines the issue of when to *derecognize* accounts receivable as the result of a transaction called a *transfer*, which can be accounted for as a sale of the receivables or as a loan, depending on the terms of the transfer.

Most students will already be familiar with present value calculations. If practice is needed, a review is included on Connect.

FINANCIAL ASSETS

Financial assets comprise a wide range of financial statement elements, including cash, accounts/notes receivable, many investments, and derivatives. In this chapter, the discussion of financial assets is limited to cash and accounts/notes receivables. These elements are financial assets because they are either:

1. Cash; or
2. A contractual right to receive cash from another entity.

Cash obviously qualifies as a financial asset. Accounts/notes receivable represent the contractual right to receive cash. This cash claim has been fixed through a transaction, such as the sale of goods or services, or borrowing. In contrast, balances, such as inventories and capital assets, are not financial assets, even though they eventually will be converted into cash because their cash value is not known with certainty in advance. The amount of cash to be obtained from nonfinancial assets will depend on future market conditions.

Financial assets include balances that represent assets to be received in a *determinable* amount of cash. An example of a *determinable* amount is a cash deposit held in foreign currency. The foreign currency cash deposit (or a foreign account receivable) represents a claim to cash, whose value in Canadian dollars is *determinable* from the current exchange rate.

Monetary Items

Financial assets are, by their nature, **monetary items**. Cash is a monetary item and so are receivables because they represent a claim to cash *where the amount is fixed by contract or agreement*. Like financial assets, monetary items have two key aspects: cash must be involved, and the amount of cash must be fixed (or determinable) by contract or agreement.

Classification

Accounting standards require that companies classify each financial asset. All financial assets are initially recognized at the *transaction value,* which is *fair value* on that date. This is then the *cost* of the financial instrument. *Classification then determines the subsequent measurement of the financial asset.* The asset may be carried at cost or amortized cost, or the asset may have to be remeasured to fair value at each reporting date:[1]

Classification	Summarized Classification Criteria	Initial Valuation	Subsequent Valuation
1. Amortized cost	Two conditions must be met: 1. Objective is to hold financial asset to collect contractual cash flows; and 2. Contractual cash flows are solely principal and interest	Fair value, which is the transaction value and establishes the cost of the financial instrument; ADD Transaction costs, if any	Cost or amortized cost

---

1. Reflects content of IFRS 9, effective 2018, with early adoption allowed.

2. Fair value through other comprehensive income (FVOCI)	Two conditions must be met: 1. Objective is to hold financial asset to collect contractual cash flows and eventually sell; and 2. Contractual cash flows are solely principal and interest	Fair value, which is the transaction value and establishes the cost of the financial instrument; ADD Transaction costs, if any	Amortized cost information in income statement and the difference between fair value and amortized cost in OCI
3. Fair value through profit or loss (FVTPL)	All other financial assets Assets that meet the amortized cost criteria can nonetheless be classified as FVTPL if: a. Loans and receivables will be sold in the short term; and b. Management wishes to avoid an accounting mismatch (related/hedged financial instruments are FVTPL)	Fair value, which is the transaction value and establishes the cost of the financial instrument and any transaction costs are expensed	Fair value; gains and losses from change in fair value in earnings

CASH AND CASH EQUIVALENTS

Classification of Cash

Cash is measured at fair value in the FVTPL category, and if fair value changes, any gain or loss is included in earnings. Cash balances are not ordinarily subject to such fair-value fluctuations, so this classification decision presents few challenges. If fair value were to change, however, because of foreign currency fluctuations and so on, any change in fair value is recorded as a gain or loss in earnings.

Cash Equivalents

Cash equivalents are items that can readily be converted to cash. On the SFP, cash and cash equivalents are often lumped together, appropriately described.

Cash equivalents are limited to investments that are highly liquid and have little risk of price fluctuation—**money market instruments**—but not investments in common shares. Cash equivalents are usually classified as FVTPL.

The most common examples of cash equivalents are **treasury bills** (**T-bills**), **guaranteed investment certificates** (**GICs**), **commercial paper** (short-term notes receivable from other companies), and money market funds. To be classified as a *cash equivalent*, the term of these investments must be *short*—90 days maximum at the acquisition date—to minimize possible price fluctuations caused by interest rate changes or market conditions.

Asset-backed commercial paper

Of course, the unexpected can happen. In the liquidity crunch that spiked in 2007, some short-term **asset-backed commercial paper (ABCP)** turned out to be highly risky because the issuers lacked liquid resources to repay. ABCP is a short-term investment instrument secured by assets, such as trade receivables or mortgage receivables. In this case, cash equivalents that should have been subject to very little price fluctuation turned out to be the cause of large losses.

Under a court-supervised restructuring program, pools of ABCP held as cash equivalents by many companies were replaced with notes receivable of varying maturities. The investor companies would then have to reclassify these investments as FVTPL financial instruments, now long-term investments, valued at their (lower) fair value. With hindsight, the risk of these investments was such that they should not have been classified as cash equivalents.

Overdrafts

An **overdraft** is a negative bank account balance. Overdrafts occur when the dollar amount of cheques honoured by the bank exceeds the account balance. An overdraft is reported as a separate current liability on the SFP despite the fact that it may be classified with cash on the statement of cash flows (SCF). Netting with other cash accounts is not allowed on the SFP.

However, if a depositor overdraws an account but has positive balances in other accounts *with that same bank*, it is appropriate to net the negative and positive balances on the SFP as long as:

- The bank has the legal right to offset, which is usual; and
- The company *plans to settle the overdraft in this way*—by a transfer from one of the other accounts.

Accounts with different financial institutions may never be netted against each other, since they fail the first condition above.

Compensating Balances

A **compensating balance**, or a *restricted balance*, is a minimum balance that must be maintained in a depositor's account as support for a separate loan borrowed by the depositor. Companies might consider such compensating balances as long-term assets and therefore not include them in the current cash account because they are not currently available for use. However, the practice is often to include these balances in cash and disclose the restrictions in notes to the financial statements. The same approach is used for any cash held offshore that has usage restrictions imposed by a foreign country; the amounts are typically included in cash and restrictions are disclosed.

Foreign Currency

The Canadian dollar value of cash holdings in foreign currency fluctuates with changes in the relevant exchange rate. To arrive at the Canadian dollar equivalent, it is necessary to multiply the amount of foreign currency by the *current exchange rate*. Gains and losses are included in earnings.

For example, assume that DGF Group Ltd. has a U.S. bank account, with US$4,500 on deposit at year-end. The money was received as a result of a cash sale that took place when the exchange rate was US$1.00 = Cdn$0.80, and was recorded at a Canadian dollar amount of 3,600:

Cash, U.S. dollars [$4,500 × $0.80]	3,600	
Sales		3,600

At the end of the year, the exchange rate is US$1.00 = Cdn$0.75. The current Canadian dollar equivalency must be established:

Exchange loss	225	
Cash, U.S. dollars [$4,500 × ($0.80 − $0.75)]		225

Of course, foreign cash holdings could be converted to the current exchange rate every time the rate changes, but this is a lot of extra work, and valuation is usually important only at reporting dates. The cash is included on the SFP at the 31 December exchange rate, $0.75, or $3,375.

Internal Control Over Cash

The need to safeguard cash is crucial. Cash can be stolen in a lot of creative ways in addition to simply being physically picked up; for example, cheques can be issued to fictitious suppliers. The risk of theft is directly related to the ability of individuals to access the accounting system and obtain custody of cash. Firms address this problem through an **internal control system**, which is a planned organizational design meant to protect all assets and the integrity of the information system. A sound internal control system for cash increases the likelihood that the reported values for cash and cash equivalents are accurate and may be relied on by financial statement users.

A fundamental principle of internal control is *division of duties*—the person who handles cash must not also be responsible for the books. This is called "segregation of duties." The functions of cash handling and record keeping must be separated, so it will be difficult to embezzle cash unless two people agree together (or *collude*) to take the money. Internal control is built largely on the principle that dishonest collusion is significantly less likely than individual action.

ETHICAL ISSUES

If the bookkeeper handles cash, it is both possible and occasionally tempting for him or her to set cash aside for personal use and cover up the cash shortage by making a fictitious entry in the books. In a large enterprise, quite a large amount of cash (in personal terms) can go missing before anyone starts to notice it. Modest embezzlement may unfortunately go undetected for years. A robust internal control system will reduce any such opportunities.

Bank Reconciliation as Internal Control

By comparing the bank account to the cash general ledger account, the company can ensure that the books are being kept accurately. The **bank reconciliation** provides the correct cash balance for the SFP and information for adjusting entries. A bank reconciliation analyzes the firm's cash account versus the bank's reported cash amount to ensure that transaction recording is complete and accurate. Since cash forms a part of so many transactions, *the accuracy of the cash account is often a good surrogate for the accuracy of other accounts.* Thus, the bank reconciliation is an important internal control. Of course, it is crucial that the individual who is in charge of cheques and/or deposits is not also in charge of the bank reconciliation since it would be too easy to cover up something. It is not appropriate for individuals to check their own work; there is no segregation of duties.

Bank Reconciliation Adjustments

A bank reconciliation begins with the two cash balances (bank and book), lists the specific items that are different between those balances, and ends with the true cash balance, as follows:

Adjustments to the Bank Balance	Adjustments to the Book Balance (Adjustments to Be Journalized)
Starting point: Cash balance per the bank statement	*Starting point:* Balance per the books
Add: Outstanding deposits	*Add:* Deposits recorded by the bank but not yet recorded by the company (e.g., customers that paid by direct deposit)
Deduct: Outstanding cheques	*Deduct:* Charges recorded by the bank but not yet recorded by the company (e.g., expenses paid by direct transfer and not yet recorded on the books, service charges, customers' cheques returned NSF [not sufficient funds])
Add or deduct: Bank errors in recording transactions	*Add or deduct:* Company errors in recording transactions
Ending point: Adjusted cash balance	*Ending point:* Adjusted cash balance

The adjustments to the book balance usually represent transactions processed by the bank that the company has not yet recorded or transactions that the company has improperly recorded. These items are journalized to establish the accuracy of the accounting records. Bank reconciliations are illustrated in the Appendix to this chapter.

Reporting

Cash and cash equivalents are reported as the first asset on the SFP. Companies are required to show the components of cash, which they often do in conjunction with the statement of cash flows. Others provide a breakdown in the disclosure notes. For instance, Bombardier Inc., in its 31 December 2014 financial statements, provides disclosure of the components of its cash account (in thousands):

14. CASH AND CASH EQUIVALENTS

Cash and cash equivalents were as follows, as at:

	December 31, 2014	December 31, 2013	January 1, 2013
Cash	$ 997	$ 1,475	$ 916
Cash equivalents			
Term deposits	796	762	656
Money market funds	696	1,160	985
Cash and cash equivalents	$ 2,489	$ 3,397	$ 2,557

See Note 30 - Credit facilities for details on covenants related to cash and cash equivalents.

Source: Bombardier Inc., or its subsidiaries, 2014 Audited annual financial statements, page 140, www.sedar.com, posted 12 February 2015

CONCEPT REVIEW

1. What is the definition of a financial asset?
2. What are the two categories of financial assets that relate to cash and receivables, and how is each category valued?
3. What is the valuation problem for cash that is denominated in a foreign currency?
4. What is the basic principle of internal control?
5. Why is it necessary to perform regular bank reconciliations?

ACCOUNTS RECEIVABLE

Classification of Accounts Receivable

As financial assets, accounts and notes receivable are usually in the *amortized cost* category. They are initially recognized at the transaction value, which is fair value on the transaction date. They are subsequently measured at amortized cost (AC), subject to valuation allowances. If the company has a business model of collecting contractual cash flows and eventually selling rather than holding, they would be classified as FVOCI. They are classified as FVTPL if they are part of an actively traded portfolio or were part of a hedging arrangement.

Accounts receivable are called *trade accounts receivable*, if they are amounts owed by customers for goods and services sold in the firm's normal course of business. These receivables are supported by sales invoices or other documents rather than by formal written promises to pay. *Notes receivable* are also amounts receivable but are usually supported by formal promissory notes. *Nontrade receivables* arise from many other sources, such as tax refunds, contracts, investments, finance receivables, sale of assets, and advances to employees. Receivables may be current or noncurrent assets, depending on the expected collection date.

Individual accounts receivable for customers with credit balances (from prepayments or overpayments) are reclassified and reported as liabilities on the SFP if they are material. Credit balances should not be netted against other accounts receivable, but netting is a common practice if the amounts are small (i.e., immaterial).

Valuation Allowances

The receivable balance is meant to be an approximation of the cash that will be collected. Say a company has $2,000,000 in accounts receivable at the end of 20X8. This may not be the amount of money it will actually collect. Usually, adjustments have to be made at year-end to reduce receivables to *net realizable value*, for things such as:

- Cash discounts;
- Sales returns and allowances; and
- Allowance for doubtful accounts.

Cash Discounts

Companies frequently offer a cash discount, or sales discount, for payment received within a designated period. Cash discounts are used to increase sales, encourage early payment by the customer, and increase the likelihood of collection. Sales terms might be 2/10, n/30, which means that the customer is given a 2% cash discount if payment is made within 10 days from sale; otherwise, the full amount net of any returns or allowances is due in 30 days. Theoretically, the sale and the receivable should be recorded at the lowest cash price, or the net amount after deducting the discount. This would be $980 for a $1,000 sale, if the discount for prompt payment is 2%. In practice, though, sales are usually recorded gross because it is easier to relate the account receivable to the (gross) invoice if they are the same amount. The entry on sale, for the gross method is:

Accounts receivable	1,000	
Sales revenue		1,000

The entry on collection is:

Cash	980	
Sales discounts (a contra account to sales)	20	
Accounts receivable		1,000

Under the gross method, if material cash discounts are expected to be taken on outstanding accounts receivable at year-end, an adjusting entry is required to *decrease net sales* and to *reduce net accounts receivable* to the estimated amount collectible. To illustrate, assume that the $2 million of accounts receivable mentioned above all have terms of 2/10, n/30, and are recorded gross. Management expects 60% of these accounts to be collected within the discount period. There is no balance in an allowance account. The adjusting entry on 31 December 20X8 is:

Sales discounts [$2,000,000 × 2% × 60%]	24,000	
Allowance for sales discounts		24,000

The sales discounts account is a contra account to sales, and reduces sales to the net amount. The allowance for sales discounts account is a contra account to accounts receivable and reduces accounts receivable to the net cash value. If there had been a $3,000 credit balance in the allowance account prior to this entry, the entry would have been made for $21,000 ($24,000 − $3,000).

During 20X9, the allowance can then be used to absorb the discounts taken when payment is made. The following entry would be recorded, assuming that the estimates were correct:

Allowance for sales discounts	24,000	
Cash	1,176,000	
Accounts receivable [$2,000,000 × 60%]		1,200,000

Alternatively, and more commonly, the sales discounts account can be directly debited each time customers use discounts during the year, and the allowance can be adjusted up or down at the end of each reporting period.

Sales Returns and Allowances

Return privileges are frequently part of a comprehensive marketing program required to maintain competitiveness. Sales returns are significant amounts in some industries, including retailing and book publishing. Of course, if returns are material and unestimable, sales revenue cannot be recorded until after the uncertainty is resolved. If returns can be estimated, the company does not recognize revenue for the items it estimates will be returned. This issue was discussed in Chapter 6.

Allowance for Doubtful Accounts

When sales are on account, some amount of uncollectible receivables is generally inevitable. Firms attempt to develop a credit policy that is neither too conservative (leading to excessive lost sales) nor too liberal (leading to excessive uncollectible accounts). Past records of payment and the financial position of customers are key factors to consider.

An amount of uncollectible accounts must be recognized so that accounts receivable and earnings are not overstated. This is a form of asset valuation that is a common theme in financial reporting: Assets may not be overvalued. Because accounting recognition criteria require companies to anticipate a writedown before actually giving up on a particular account, the writedown is made to an allowance account, called the **allowance for doubtful accounts**, or the *allowance for uncollectible accounts*. This allowance is a contra account to accounts receivable that represents the portion of outstanding receivables whose collection is doubtful. Estimated uncollectibles are recorded in bad debt expense, an operating expense usually classified as a selling expense.

For example, if this company estimates that $120,000 of the $2,000,000 in receivables will not be collected, and the existing credit balance in the allowance account is $12,000, the adjusting entry is as follows:

Bad debt expense	108,000	
Allowance for doubtful accounts [$120,000 − $12,000]		108,000

Available information

On initial recognition of the receivable the company is required to estimate the expected lifetime credit losses for the receivable. In making this allowance the company considers the credit losses over the lifetime of the receivable. This allowance is remeasured at every reporting date.

Write-Off and Recovery

Two other events must be considered:

1. The write-off of a specific receivable; and
2. The collection of an account previously written off.

The adjusting entry for bad debt expense creates the allowance for doubtful accounts for future uncollectible accounts. When specific accounts are determined to be uncollectible, they are removed from the accounts receivable and that part of the allowance is no longer needed. The bad debt estimation entry had previously recognized the estimated economic effect of future uncollectible accounts. Thus, write-offs of specific accounts do not further reduce net assets unless they exceed the estimate.

For example, the following entry is recorded by a company deciding not to pursue collection of R. Knox's $1,000 account:

Allowance for doubtful accounts	1,000	
Accounts receivable, R. Knox		1,000

This write-off entry affects neither earnings nor the net amount of accounts receivable outstanding. The write-off entry changes only the components of net accounts receivable, not the net amount itself (amounts assumed):

	Before Knox Write-Off	After Knox Write-Off
Accounts receivable	2,000,000	$1,999,000
Allowance for doubtful accounts	(120,000)	(119,000)
Net accounts receivable	$1,880,000	$1,880,000

When amounts are received on account after a write-off, the write-off entry is reversed to reinstate the receivable and cash collection is recorded. Assume that R. Knox is able to pay $600 on account some time after the above write-off entry was recorded, but no additional payment is expected. These entries are required:

Accounts receivable, R. Knox	600	
Allowance for doubtful accounts		600
Cash	600	
Accounts receivable, R. Knox		600

The net effect of these two entries is to increase cash and *reinstate* the allowance for doubtful accounts to the extent of the cash recovery. The reason for reinstating the allowance is that since $600 cash was collected, the writedown of $1,000 was excessive; the writedown should have been for only $400. The adjustment of $600 to the allowance will have a direct (or indirect) effect on the amount of bad debt expense recorded in the next year.

Reporting

The SFP presentation of net accounts receivable provides focus on the realizable cash amount. In our example, the net balance is $2,000,000 less the $24,000 allowance for cash discounts, less the $9,000 allowance for sales returns, and less the $120,000 allowance for doubtful accounts. This is reported as follows:

Accounts receivable, net	$1,847,000

While allowances do not have to be shown separately on the SFP, the allowance for doubtful accounts, in particular, must be included in the disclosure notes. The itemized changes in the allowance from the beginning to the end of the year are also disclosed.

Bombardier Inc. reports the following information in its 2014 annual report (in thousands):

15. TRADE AND OTHER RECEIVABLES

Trade and other receivables were as follows, as at:

	Total	Not past due	Past due but not impaired[3] less than 90 days	Past due but not impaired[3] more than 90 days	Impaired[4]
December 31, 2014[1][2]					
Trade receivables, gross	**$ 1,453**	**$ 717**	**$ 238**	**$ 381**	**$ 117**
Allowance for doubtful accounts	**(39)**	**—**	**—**	**—**	**(39)**
	1,414	$ 717	$ 238	$ 381	$ 78
Other	124				
Total	**$ 1,538**				
December 31, 2013[1][2]					
Trade receivables, gross	$ 1,430	$ 796	$ 194	$ 359	$ 81
Allowance for doubtful accounts	(44)	—	—	—	(44)
	1,386	$ 796	$ 194	$ 359	$ 37
Other	106				
Total	$ 1,492				
January 1, 2013[1][2]					
Trade receivables, gross	$ 1,256	$ 813	$ 204	$ 200	$ 39
Allowance for doubtful accounts	(34)	—	—	—	(34)
	1,222	$ 813	$ 204	$ 200	$ 5
Other	89				
Total	$ 1,311				

[1] Of which $355 million and $475 million are denominated in euros and other foreign currencies, respectively, as at December 31, 2014 ($465 million and $411 million, respectively, as at December 31, 2013 and $396 million and $356 million, respectively, as at January 1, 2013).

[2] Of which $419 million represents customer retentions relating to long-term contracts as at December 31, 2014 based on normal terms and conditions ($392 million as at December 31, 2013 and $240 million as at January 1, 2013).

[3] Of which $525 million of trade receivables relates to BT long-term contracts as at December 31, 2014, of which $376 million were more than 90 days past due ($509 million as at December 31, 2013, of which $353 million were more than 90 days past due and $335 milllion as at January 1, 2013, of which $190 million were more than 90 days past due). BT assesses whether these receivables are collectible as part of its risk management practices applicable to long-term contracts as a whole.

(4) Of which a gross amount of $71 million of trade receivables are individually impaired as at December 31, 2014 ($73 million as at December 31, 2013 and $34 million as at January 1, 2013).

See Note 30 - Credit facilities for details on covenants related to cash and cash equivalents.

Source: Bombardier Inc., or its subsidiaries, 2014 Audited annual financial statements, page 140, www.sedar.com, posted 12 February 2015.

Valuation of the Allowance for Doubtful Accounts

The previous section illustrated that when an allowance for doubtful accounts is established, the entry increases bad debt expense and increases the allowance. The expected lifetime credit losses are estimated for the receivable on initial recognition. These credit losses are reviewed every reporting date.

Aging Method

In reassessing the expected credit losses each reporting date, an aging method is often used. This approach begins with the reported value of accounts receivable. Accounts receivable are examined item by item, *or aged, or* analyzed statistically. This will determine net realizable value and the value of an appropriate allowance. The allowance is then increased *to* this amount, *which involves adjusting for the opening balance.* This is called the **aging method**, because accounts receivable are usually aged to provide a basis for the allowance.

This method emphasizes the net realizable value of accounts receivable and uses historical data to estimate the percentage of accounts receivable expected to become uncollectible over the lifetime of the receivables. Exhibit 7-1 illustrates Rally's aging schedule and the application of the collection loss percentages. The $177,500 receivable balance is divided into four age classifications with a collection loss percentage applied to each age category. This percentage is usually based on past experience. Rally's collection loss *percentages* (logically) increase with the age of the accounts because when accounts are collected, good accounts are removed from each category, and what is left is more likely to be uncollectible.

EXHIBIT 7-1

RALLY COMPANY

Accounts Receivable Aging Schedule

31 December 20X2

Customer Account	Balance 31 Dec. 20X2	Age of Account Balance			
		Current	31–60 days	61–90 days	Over 90 days
Denk	$ 500	$ 400	$ 100		
Evans	900	900			
Field	1,650		1,350	$ 300	
Harris	90			30	$ 60
King	800	700	60	40	
Zabot	250	250			

Total	$177,500	$110,000	$31,000	$29,500	$7,000
Percent estimated uncollectible		0.2%	1.0%	8.0%	40.0%
Amount estimated uncollectible		$ 220	$ 310	$ 2,360	$2,800

Total amount to include in allowance: $220 + $310 + $2,360 + $2,800 = $5,690

The estimated net realizable value of accounts receivable is $171,810 ($177,500 − $5,690); in this case, a reasonable approximation.

The general condition of the economy, the economic health of specific customers, and the seller's credit policy and collection effort affect the rate of account write-offs. Over time, this rate changes, necessitating adjustment to the percentages applied to aged receivables. If the unused balance in allowance for doubtful accounts is found to increase each year, the estimate of uncollectibles can be decreased to reflect actual experience. Alternatively, if the allowance is inadequate, future estimates will increase.

FVOCI Classification

In the event that the business model is not to hold receivables to maturity, they would be classified as FVOCI financial instruments. This would not usually be the case since typically receivables have a short period until maturity. However, if this is the case, they are accounted for using amortized cost then fair value is determined at each reporting date after initial recognition. The difference between amortized cost and fair value are reported in OCI until the receivable is derecognized. At that point any realized gain or loss is recycled or recognized in net income. Specifically, if the receivables are to be sold to a third party (see the section on transfers of receivables later in the chapter), then they would be classified as FVOCI.

FVTPL Classification

Various receivables may sometimes be classified as FVTPL financial instruments. If this is the case, they are valued at fair value at reporting dates after initial recognition. Management may designate certain loans and receivables as FVTPL. This might be appropriate, for example, if various hedging strategies were in place, and management wished to have both the hedged asset and the hedged liability in the same category for valuation purposes. When an asset is carried at fair value, fair value is remeasured at reporting dates, and gains and losses are recorded in earnings.

Speeding Cash Flow from Sales

Credit Card Transactions

In the past, many retail stores offered credit to customers—in fact, some built a business primarily on offering credit (e.g., consider People's Credit Jewellers, now usually just called People's). Now, most retailers prefer to accept third-party credit cards and receive their money upfront, letting the customers owe the credit card company. Retailers are charged a fee by the credit card company, which is a percentage of the total sale, but prefer this arrangement because they avoid bad debts, there is no delay in receiving cash, and they hope that customers will spend more when they can charge their purchases. There are not many cash-only businesses these days; retail customers expect to be able to use credit cards.

Other retailers have expanded their credit-granting operations into separate credit card companies. These operations earn profits by charging interest on overdue accounts. Their largest expenses are the cost of funds (interest) and bad debts.

Assume that a merchant has $2,000 in credit card sales. The credit card company deducts a commission for its services and the money is electronically transferred. Assuming that the fee is 2%, the appropriate entry is as follows:

Cash	1,960	
Credit card fees expense [$2,000 × 2%]	40	
Sales		2,000

The merchant does not always receive the cash immediately. Sometimes, for low-volume credit card sales, the merchant must accumulate credit card sales in batches. These documents are deposited with a bank acting as agent for the credit card company. The company receives its money by direct deposit after the request is reviewed and processed.

Debit Card Transactions

Most merchants accept debit cards. The primary difference between a debit card and a credit card is from the point of view of the customer: A debit card will remove the transaction amount immediately from the customer's bank account, while a credit card is paid when due. The merchant has to go through the same motions for debit cards as with credit cards: An agreement must be negotiated with the sponsoring financial institution for a fee (again a percentage of the transaction amount) and payment terms. All transactions are authorized through automated point-of-sale systems, and the merchant receives the cash immediately through direct deposit.

Loans Secured by Accounts Receivables

If a company has a $100,000 account receivable from a creditworthy customer that will not pay for 45 days, how can the company get cash sooner? One alternative is to encourage the customer to pay sooner, and a variety of policies are usually explored to speed collection. Then what? One common course of action is to go to a financial institution and borrow money using the account receivable as collateral.

This is not very complicated on the books: A loan is recorded, and interest expense is accrued as time passes. When the account is collected, the financial institution is repaid. Assets pledged as collateral are disclosed in the financial statements. Of course, it is less common to make credit arrangements for one receivable at a time: The overall balance of accounts receivable, and usually inventory, too, are used to secure working capital loans. These current loans payable are a relatively permanent part of the capital structure for most companies.

CONCEPT REVIEW

1. Why is it necessary to establish an allowance for doubtful accounts?
2. What other allowances, in addition to doubtful accounts, might be necessary to value accounts receivable correctly?
3. What is the purpose of an aging schedule?
4. Name two ways to speed collection of sales revenue.

TRANSFER OF RECEIVABLES

Derecognition of accounts receivable simply means that the accounts are taken off the SFP. This automatically happens when cash is collected because the company has no further right to cash flow from the contract. However, derecognition can be far more complex.

Accounts receivable can be *transferred* to another party to speed cash flow. One example of a transfer is *factoring,* where individual accounts receivable are passed over to a financial institution, which then collects from the customer. This is a common business arrangement in certain industries. A transfer might be a far more complex transaction, where accounts receivable are bundled together and sold as a portfolio to a financial institution subject to certain guarantees and administrative functions. This is also called a **securitization**.

Agreements to transfer receivables are made either:

- On a **notification basis**—customers are directed to remit to the new party holding the receivables, the finance company; or

- On a **non-notification basis**—customers continue to remit to the original seller, which then, in turn, remits to the finance company.

Receivables can be transferred with recourse or without recourse. **Recourse** means that the finance company can come back to the company that sold the account receivable for payment if the account turns out to be uncollectible. Recourse arrangements often allow the company to replace defaulted receivables with "good ones" in the event of default.

Alternative Accounting Treatments

A transfer of accounts receivable may be recorded as a sale or a borrowing, depending on the terms of the transfer, as we will see below. The two accounting alternatives are described as follows:

1. A *sale/derecognition*. The accounts receivable come off the books of the selling company and a financing fee is recognized. This represents *derecognition* of the accounts receivable.

2. A *borrowing*. The accounts receivable are left on the books of the selling company, and the amount received from the finance company is recorded as a loan until the customer actually pays. Payment by the customer triggers derecognition of the account receivable and repayment of the loan.

To illustrate a transfer recorded as a sale, consider the following case. Largo Inc. (the **transferor**), now has a large volume of accounts receivable on its books. Largo sells $200,000 of its accounts receivable on 15 August 20X2. The buyer is a finance company (the **transferee**). The finance company charges a 12% financing fee. The entry to record the transfer as a *sale*, which *derecognizes* the accounts receivable, is:

Largo Incorporated			Finance Company		
Cash	176,000*		Accounts receivable	200,000	
Finance expense	24,000**		Deferred financing revenue***		24,000
Accounts receivable		200,000	Cash		176,000
*$200,000 − (12% × $200,000)					
**12% × $200,000; expensed immediately					
***Deferred and recognized in earnings over the collection period.					

This looks relatively straightforward. Accounts receivable can be sold, like any other asset! Now, what if an identical transaction was recorded as a *borrowing*?

Largo Incorporated			Finance Company		
Cash	176,000		Note receivable	200,000	
Discount on note payable	24,000		Discount on note receivable*		24,000
Note payable		200,000	Cash		176,000
*Recognized in earnings as time passes.					

Note that the accounts receivable stay on Largo's books and are joined by a loan. The discount on the loan is amortized to finance/interest expense and revenue over the life of the note. This transfer was on a non-notification basis. When the receivables are collected by Largo, the money is remitted to the finance company, and the note is repaid:

Largo Incorporated			Finance Company		
Cash	200,000				
Accounts receivable		200,000			
Notes payable	200,000		Cash	200,000	
Cash		200,000	Notes receivable		200,000
Finance expense*	24,000		Discount on notes receivable	24,000	
Discount on notes payable		24,000	Finance revenue*		24,000
*Recognized in earnings as time passes.					

Evaluation

The sale/derecognition alternative effectively uses a journal entry to *net off* the loan against the assets being financed, with the difference recorded as an expense. That is, the receivables come off the books, the loan never goes on the books, and as a result, both assets and liabilities are lower. The SFP may suggest a different business model—fewer receivables and less debt—than really exists. Certain key financial ratios, such as debt/equity, the current ratio, and return on assets, would also be affected. Furthermore, an analyst attempting to determine the period of time between when inventory is purchased and cash collected from customers (sometimes called the *cash-to-cash cycle*) might be misled. As a result, many analysts use note disclosure information on recorded transfers to reinstate transferred accounts receivable and recognize related notes payable before performing ratio analysis, although this is difficult to do accurately. Chapter 22 will give you a taste of these kinds of adjustments.

ETHICAL ISSUES

The sale/derecognition alternative may reflect genuine business realities. Risk of delayed collection or noncollection may be appropriately transferred or shared, and the core business activities are all that remains. On the other hand, derecognition may be an attempt to portray the business cycle in a more favourable light for investors or creditors. Derecognition is appropriate only when it reflects economic reality.

Derecognition has been subject to significant scrutiny in financial markets because many financial institutions, especially in the United States, transferred and derecognized large portfolios of mortgage receivables. When residential real estate markets in the United States crumbled during the period between 2006 and 2008, these mortgage receivables had high default rates. Various legislative initiatives made *the transferor* assume responsibility for losses in some cases despite contractual terms to the contrary. Thus, the risks of receivables that had been derecognized came back to the transferor. In other cases, the transferee was significantly destabilized because of the transfers.

Criteria for Classification

The criteria for establishing whether a transfer qualifies for derecognition have changed several times over the last decade and are still under review. The most recent set of standards makes it more difficult for a transfer to qualify for derecognition, and thus derecognition will become less commonly recorded. Borrowing treatment will prevail. The challenge for standard setters is that the terms of transfer contracts are both ingenious and aggressive and are often structured to allow sale/derecognition treatment.

Classification is assessed at the level of the consolidated entity. That is, before making any accounting policy decisions, all subsidiaries and special purpose entities (SPEs) (see section below) must be added in, and then only transfers that go *outside the complete economic entity* are considered. Furthermore, a decision has to be made as to whether the criteria are applied to all or part of a financial asset. Then, derecognition would be allowed if and only if *BOTH the following tests are met*:

Test 1: The account receivable is transferred.

The account receivable is considered to be transferred if:

1. *The rights to the cash flows from the asset have been completely transferred.* This is the simplest case—a clean sale, and the transferee (the finance company) has the right to all cash flows and accepts all the risks. The transferor (the company, or vendor) is no longer involved in any way. Since the finance company would expect to be compensated for accepting such risk, a transfer that met this condition would be expensive for the company.

2. *The transferor (the company, or vendor) retains the contractual rights to the cash flows but assumes a contractual obligation to pay the cash flows to the transferee (the finance company).* In this contractual obligation, the terms must represent a "real" transfer of the original account receivable. The terms must require that:

    a. There is no obligation to pay the finance company unless cash is actually received from the accounts receivable;

    and

    b. The company is not permitted to use the original accounts receivable for collateral in another transaction or sell the accounts receivable to another party;

    and

    c. The cash flows from the original account receivable must be passed on to the finance company without material delay.

Test 2: The risks and rewards of ownership are passed to another party.

The risks and rewards of ownership are considered to be passed to another party if:

1. The company's exposure to variability in the amounts and timing of cash flow are different before versus after the transfer; and

2. If transfer of risks and rewards is not clear-cut, then the company must assess control over the receivables; if control has not been retained, then this is an indication that risks and rewards have passed. For example, if the receivables can be resold by the transferee without the consent of the transferor, then derecognition is appropriate because the transferor has no effective control over the receivables and the risks and rewards of ownership have been passed to the transferee.

Clearly, these two tests are highly detailed and quite restrictive. This will limit the cases for which a transfer can be recorded as a sale.

Examples

The complexity of these arrangements, with their extensive call and put options, makes accounting in this area very specialized. This discussion only scratches the surface. Two examples follow.

Case 1

Transfer recorded as a sale/derecognition. Assume that Largo sells $200,000 of accounts receivable to a finance company with no recourse on 15 August 20X2. The parties agree that uncollectible accounts will amount to $3,000; that is, the transferee is expecting to be able to collect only $197,000 of accounts receivable. If loan losses are higher or lower, the fact that there is no recourse to Largo means that the transferee will have losses or gains. The negotiated $3,000 amount is already in the allowance for doubtful accounts of Largo. The financing fee is 15%.

Assume that conditions are met to record this transfer as a sale/derecognition, and the accounts receivable will be derecognized. That is, there has been a transfer (Test 1) and the risk and rewards of ownership have passed (Test 2). The difference between the book value of receivables transferred and cash received from the finance company is recognized immediately as an expense.

Cash {$200,000 − $3,000 − [15% × ($200,000 − $3,000)]}	167,450	
Allowance for doubtful accounts*	3,000	
Finance expense [15% × ($200,000 − $3,000)]	29,550	
Accounts receivable		200,000
*Debit to bad debt expense if not already part of allowance estimate.		

Largo receives $197,000, the net "good" receivables balance, less the (hefty) $29,550 financing fee on $197,000. The allowance for doubtful accounts is reduced.

Case 2

Transfer recorded as a borrowing. In a transfer recorded as a borrowing, the receivables stay on the books, and a loan is recorded. The transferor recognizes the difference between the assets received from the finance company and the book value of the receivables as interest *over the term of the loan*. This is in contrast to the sale/derecognition example, in which the financing fee was immediately recognized as an expense. Assume the same facts as Case 1, except that Largo accepts recourse and also retains the option to repurchase the receivables. This means that Largo has not transferred the risks and rewards of ownership, and fails Test 2. The transaction is recorded as a borrowing as follows:

Cash {$200,000 − $3,000 − [15% × ($200,000 − $3,000)]}	167,450	
Discount on payable to finance company [15% × ($200,000 − $3,000)]	29,550	
Payable to finance company		197,000

The discount account is a contra account to the payable to finance company account and represents the total interest expense to Largo. The discount account is amortized as interest expense over the loan term using the effective interest method. Largo records sales adjustments, such as sales discounts and returns, as they occur and reduces the receivable from the customer and payable to the finance company as customers remit cash. No adjustment is made for bad debts because the allowance is already appropriate. Write-offs would be recorded when the facts dictate. At the end of the arrangement, Largo must pay any outstanding balance on the payable, whether or not customers have remitted on time.

It is worth noting that the payable to the finance company must be shown as a current liability on the SFP and may *not* be netted with the related accounts receivable. Netting is appropriate only when there is a legal right to net, *and* intent to net. While intent is present in this case, there is no legal right to net, and the balances must be shown as the separate elements they really are.

Allowance for Bad Debts

Review the entry for Case 1 again, and note that the allowance for bad debts was debited because of the $3,000 of problematic accounts transferred. *If the allowance was inadequate, bad debt expense might be debited.* Similarly, when the transaction is recorded as a loan, there might be an additional allowance of $3,000 set up, with a corresponding debit to bad debt expense, if the allowance were deemed inadequate at this time. However, this decision to acknowledge additional bad debt expense need not be part of the transfer transaction. The adequacy of the allowance is reviewed regularly in the reporting cycle, based on aging and transfer of accounts receivable does not have to disturb this routine.

Disclosure

Companies are required to disclose information to allow financial statement users to understand the relationship between transferred financial assets that are still on the SFP and the related liabilities. In addition, information must be provided to assess the nature and risks associated with derecognized financial assets. An example of disclosure of transfer of accounts might appear as follows:

In the 2016 fiscal year, the Company completed a new trade accounts receivable securitization agreement with a financial institution that requires the sale of trade accounts receivable be recorded as a sale from an accounting perspective and accordingly trade accounts receivable sold under these agreements are derecognized on the consolidated statement of financial position at 31 December 2016 and 2015. Under these agreements, the Company retains a very limited recourse obligation for delinquent accounts receivable. The agreements expire in 2018.

At 31 December 2016, trade accounts receivable under these agreements amounted to $508.6 million (2015, 530.4 million). In return for the sale of these receivables, the Company received cash of $502.3 million (2015, $525.1) on the settlement date.

Transfer of Accounts Receivable to a Special Purpose Entity

Another structure that may be used for the transfer of accounts receivable involves a **special purpose entity** (SPE). This is a separate entity that carries out a specific part of a company's business but is not legally controlled by the company; the SPE has a separate shareholder group. Often, the "parent' company owns no shares of the SPE at all. The SPE holds the accounts receivable as assets, using them as security for loans from outside investors. However, the transactions typically involve the parent company continuing to hold the *financial risk* of the receivables and loans, through contractual arrangements. The parent company would also gain benefits if the collection operations are profitable.

The use of SPEs may be a legitimate and low-cost way to segregate a particular kind of asset, and raise money using these assets as collateral. SPEs might also be used to manipulate financial reporting and keep accounts receivable and liabilities off the company's SFP. To avoid manipulation, there are accounting standards that require SPEs to be consolidated, despite the fact that the parent company owns no shares in the SPE. **Consolidation** involves combining the financial statements of the two companies. If the SPE is consolidated, the receivables and loan balances would come back onto the parent's SFP. After that, any transfer arrangement *with third parties* can be evaluated to see if derecognition is the correct accounting treatment.

Consolidation is considered appropriate when the parent company has power over the SPE, from whatever source, plus the parent has the right (or exposure to) to *variable returns* from the activities of the SPE, *and* the ability to use power over the SPE to affect returns. If the operations of the SPE are conducted for the primary benefit of the parent company, it seems obvious that irrespective of share ownership, the SPE is part of the parent's economic entity and should be consolidated. Consolidation of SPEs is covered in depth in advanced accounting courses.

CONCEPT REVIEW

1. What does *derecognition* mean?
2. What financial statement ratios will be especially affected by a derecognition entry?
3. Why is the allowance for doubtful accounts part of a derecognition entry?
4. What is an SPE, and how can it be used to transfer accounts receivable?

NOTES RECEIVABLE

Notes receivable may arise from loans and also from normal sales, extension of the payment period of accounts receivable, exchanges of long-term assets, and advances to employees. Notes are a written promise to pay a specified amount at a specified future date (or a series of amounts over a series of payment dates). Some notes formalize **collateral security** for the lender. Collateral security represents assets of the borrower that the secured lender can seize if the note goes into default. The examples in this chapter illustrate the accounting treatment for both the note receivable and the note payable, since they are mirror images.

Compared with accounts receivable/payable, notes receivable/payable usually provide:

- Extended payment terms;
- More security and a solid legal footing for the payments;
- A formal basis for charging interest; and
- Negotiability.

Valuation

Notes receivable and payable are initially valued at fair value, which is the exchange value of the date of initial recognition. Fair value is established *using the effective interest method. If the note carries a stated interest rate equal to market interest rates, or has a very short term, then valuation issues are immaterial and stated values are used.* When the stated and market interest rates are different, and the term is more than a year (i.e., not short), then present values must be used to establish initial fair value. Similar to accounts receivable, an allowance for expected credit losses is established on initial recognition.

Terminology

The borrower is the *maker* of the note and the lender is the *payee*. The **face value**, or **maturity value**, is the dollar amount stated on the note. The face value is the amount, excluding interest, payable at the end of the note term, unless the note requires that principal repayments be made according to an instalment schedule. The total interest over the life of the note equals the difference between total cash inflows and cash outflows.

Notes may be categorized as **interest-bearing** or **non-interest-bearing** notes. Interest-bearing notes specify the interest rate to be applied to the face amount in computing interest payments. Non-interest-bearing notes do not state an interest rate but command interest through the difference between cash lent and (higher) cash repaid. Notes receivable with stated interest rates below market rates may be used by companies as a sales incentive.

Interest-bearing notes, in turn, can be divided into two categories according to the type of cash payment required: (1) notes whose cash payments are interest only, except for the final maturity payment and (2) notes whose cash payments are *blended*, and include both interest and principal. Actually, there are an unlimited number of principal and repayment options. Payment schedules are not limited to those used in the examples below.

The **stated interest rate** in a note may not equal the market rate prevailing on obligations involving similar credit rating or risk. The **market interest rate** is the rate accepted by two parties for loans of equal profile. The loans must have identical amounts, with identical credit risk, terms, and conditions for the rate to be appropriate.

If the rate is not given, but the value of the transaction is known, the rate can be determined by equating the present value of the cash flows called for in the note to the market value of the transaction. The rate can be determined with a computer program or calculator that determines the correct rate iteratively—that is, by trial and error.

Effective Interest Method

The effective interest method requires that the *market rate is used to value the note and the transaction. The market rate is also used to measure interest revenue or expense. The stated rate is used to determine the cash interest payments.* If an interest rate differential between the market and stated rates is not material, it can be ignored. This might be true when the term is less than one year.

Example 1: Interest-Bearing Note

On 1 April 20X2, Lionel Company sold merchandise for $12,000 to Baylor Company and received a two-year, 4% note. Interest is payable each 31 March, and the principal is payable at the end of the second year. *The stated and market interest rates are equal.* The entry to record the sale is as follows:

Lionel			Baylor		
1 April 20X2			1 April 20X2		
Note receivable	12,000		Inventory (1)	12,000	
Sales (1)		12,000	Note payable		12,000
(1) If this were a loan transaction instead of a sale, Lionel and Baylor would pay or receive cash					

Accounting for this note is very simple because the 4% interest rate charged is also the market rate. Cash interest received equals interest revenue recognized over the terms of the note, as indicated in the remaining entries. The computation for interest assumes months of equal length; in practice, interest is accrued by day if it is material.

31 December 20X2 and 20X3—Adjusting entries					
Lionel			**Baylor**		
Interest receivable	360[*]		Interest expense	360	
Interest revenue		360	Interest payable		360
*$12,000 × 4% × 9/12					

31 March 20X3 and 20X4—Interest payments					
Lionel			**Baylor**		
Cash	480		Interest payable	360	
Interest receivable		360	Interest expense	120	
Interest revenue		120[*]	Cash		480
*$12,000 × 4% × 3/12					

31 March 20X4—Payment at maturity					
Lionel			**Baylor**		
Cash	12,000		Note payable	12,000	
Note receivable		12,000	Cash		12,000

Example 2: Different Market and Stated Rates

Assume the same facts for the Lionel and Baylor $12,000 sale as illustrated in Example 1. This time, though, while the stated rate on the note is 4%, the market interest rate is assumed to be 10%. Assume also that the inventory sold does not have a readily determinable market value. To value the transaction, it is necessary to calculate the present value of the note, including both principal and interest:

Present value of maturity amount: $12,000(P/F, 10%, 2) =	$ 9,917
Present value of the nominal interest payments: $480(P/A, 10%, 2) =	833
Present value of the note at 10%	$10,750

Notes are recorded at gross (face) value plus a premium or minus a discount amount (the gross method), or at the net present value (the net method). The two methods are illustrated below.

1 April 20X2:				
	Gross		**Net**	
For Lionel Company				
Note receivable	12,000		10,750	
Discount on note receivable		1,250		—
Sales (1)		10,750		10,750
For Baylor Company				
Inventory (1)	10,750		10,750	
Discount on note payable	1,250			—
Note payable		12,000		10,750
(1) If this were a loan transaction instead of a sale, Lionel and Baylor would pay or receive cash				

Under either method, the net book value of the note is $10,750, the present value. The discount account is a contra account to notes receivable or payable. Since the note is disclosed net of its discount on the SFP, the two methods are identical in presentation. In the remaining parts of the example, only the gross method will be illustrated, as it is more comparable with accounting for bonds payable, which you will see in Chapter 13. However, both recording conventions are common in practice.

In each year of the note, the market rate of interest is applied to the beginning balance of the net note receivable to compute interest. This approach, called the **effective-interest method**, results in a constant rate of interest throughout the life of the note. The calculations may be organized in a table:

(1) Opening Net Liability/ Receivable	(2) Interest Expense/ Revenue 10% Market Rate (1) × 10%	(3) Interest Paid/Received 4% Stated Rate $12,000 × 4%	(4) Discount Amortization (2) – (3)	(5) Closing Net Liability/ Receivable (1) + (4)
$10,750	$1,075	$480	$595	$11,345
$11,345	1,135	480	655	12,000

The net notes receivable and payable balance is always the present value of remaining payments. For example, the $11,345 balance is the present value on 31 March 20X3, of the remaining payment (principal plus interest), a payment that is due on 31 March 20X4.

$12,480(P/F, 10%, 1) = $11,345

If the fiscal year corresponded with the dates of the note, the interest and payment information from this table would correspond directly to the interest entry, that is:

Hypothetical full year entry—31 March 20X3:					
Lionel			**Baylor**		
Cash	480		Interest expense	1,075	
Discount on note receivable	595		Discount on note payable		595
Interest revenue		1,075	Cash		480

Since the fiscal year is different from the dates of the note, accruals must be made that also include discount amortization. In this case, the year-end is 31 December, or 9/12 of the year. The entries at the end of the fiscal year are as follows:

31 December 20X2:					
Lionel			**Baylor**		
Interest receivable ($12,000 × 4% × 9/12)	360		Interest expense	806	
			Discount on note payable		446
Discount on note receivable	446		Interest payable		360
Interest revenue ($10,750 × 10% × 9/12)		806			

Entries on cash payment:

31 March 20X3:					
Lionel			**Baylor**		
Cash ($12,000 × 4%)	480		Interest expense	269	
Discount on note receivable	149		Interest payable	360	
Interest receivable		360	Discount on note payable		149
Interest revenue			Cash		480
($10,750 × 10% × 3/12)		269			

In the second year of the note:

31 December 20X3:					
Lionel			**Baylor**		
Interest receivable	360		Interest expense	851	
Discount on note receivable	491		Discount on note payable		491
Interest revenue			Interest payable		360
($11,345 × 10% × 9/12)		851			

Entries on cash payment:

31 March 20X4:					
Lionel			**Baylor**		
Cash ($12,000 × 4%)	480		Interest expense	284	
Discount on note receivable	164		Interest payable	360	
Interest receivable		360	Discount on note payable		164
Interest revenue			Cash		480
($11,345 × 10% × 3/12)		284			

After the 31 March 20X5 entry, the net notes receivable and payable balance is $12,000, the face value. The discount account balance is zero, and the note is paid.

31 March 20X4:					
Lionel			**Baylor**		
Cash	12,000		Note payable	12,000	
Note receivable		12,000	Cash		12,000

Straight-Line Measurement of Interest Expense/Revenue

Another approach to measuring interest, the straight-line method, amortizes an equal amount of discount each period. The straight-line method produces the same interest amount each period but shows a varying rate of interest period by period (i.e., "interest ÷ note" will vary). It is less accurate for this reason and is not permitted under IFRS standards. This method is allowed in ASPE. This method is much simpler and may yield results that are not materially different from the effective interest method. In this example, the straight-line method results in discount amortization of $625 ($1,250 ÷ 2 years) and interest revenue or expense of $1,105 ($625 + $480) in both years.

Example 3: Blended Payments

Consider a 10%, $4,000, two-year note receivable of Vancouver Sea Lines that requires interest to be paid on its face value. This is an interest-bearing note, and the annual interest of $400 ($4,000 × 10%) is due at the end of each year of the note term. The $4,000 face amount is due at the end of the second year. In total, $800 of interest is required over the term of the note. In notes of this type, the original principal is not decreased by the yearly payment.

Now assume instead that Vancouver's note requires blended payments, involving *two equal* annual amounts due at the end of each year. These payments *each* contain some interest and some principal in the amount necessary to extinguish the receivable. The payment is computed as follows:

$4,000 = Present value of an annuity = Payment ÷ (P/A, 10%, 2)

$4,000 ÷ (P/A, 10%, 2) = Payment

$2,305 = Payment (rounded)

Payment	Interest Component	Principal Component
1	$400 ($4,000 × 10%)	$1,905 ($2,305 − $400)
2	210 ($4,000 − $1,905) × 10%	2,095 ($2,305 − $210)
	$ 610	$4,000

Total interest for the second type of note ($610) is less than for the first note ($800) because part of the first payment of $2,305 is a principal payment, which reduces the principal on which interest is paid in the second period. Vancouver would record the note and its payments as follows:

Initial entry:		
Note receivable	4,000	
Cash (etc.)		4,000
First payment:		
Cash	2,305	
Interest revenue		400

Note receivable		1,905
Second payment:		
Cash	2,305	
Interest revenue		210
Note receivable		2,095

Sometimes, blended payment notes may not include an explicit disclosure of the interest rate. The implicit interest rate must be calculated before the transaction can be recorded. For example, assume that on 30 June 20X5, a firm sells equipment with a cash price of $10,000 and receives in exchange a note receivable that requires a payment of $6,000 on 30 June 20X6, and another $6,000 on 30 June 20X7. The note does not explicitly mention interest, but $2,000 of interest is implicit in the note ($6,000 × 2) − $10,000. The interest rate is computed using the present value of an annuity as follows:

$$\$10,000 = \$6,000 \times (P/A, i, 2)$$
$$\$10,000 \div \$6,000 = 1.66667 = (P/A, i, 2)$$

A calculator equipped for present value tells us that $i = 13.066\%$. This rate should be comparable with the rate incurred by the debtor on similar financing.

Impairment

Notes receivable will be an asset only if the maker of the note pays—both principal and interest are to be considered in this regard. Revenue cannot be recognized—that is, interest cannot be accrued—unless it is collected or collectible.

Similar to accounts receivables discussed above, the expected credit losses for notes receivable must be determined on initial recognition. However, accounts receivable usually involve a short period of time. Notes receivables may span a far longer period of time.

On initial recognition, an allowance is established for any expected credit losses. This allowance is reviewed each reporting period. If a significant increase in credit risk occurs then the expected lifetime credit losses must be estimated and are recognized. This allowance is reviewed each reporting period.

Transfer of Notes Receivable

Rather than hold a note receivable to maturity, a company may transfer notes receivable, a transaction that may be recorded as a borrowing or as a sale/derecognition. For a discussion of the related issues on transfers, refer to "Transfer of Receivables."

CONCEPT REVIEW

1. What is the effective interest method?
2. What is a low-interest loan? How is it valued?
3. What happens to the discount on a note receivable over time?
4. What is a blended payment?

FOREIGN CURRENCY RECEIVABLES

If a company has accounts or notes that are receivable or payable in foreign currencies, they must be *restated to Canadian dollars* at the current exchange rate at the year-end date. When the receivable is first recorded, the then-current exchange rate is used. For example, suppose that Talud Ltd. has a sale to a customer in Europe for €10,000 when the exchange rate was €1 = $1.25. The sale would be recorded as follows:

Accounts receivable (€10,000)	12,500	
Sales (€10,000 × $1.25)		12,500

The receivable is stated (or *denominated*) in euros, not in dollars. The sale is recorded at the Canadian dollar–equivalent of the European sales price. However, when the European company pays the account, it will pay €10,000, not $12,500. The cash receipt must be recorded at the current exchange rate. Suppose that the customer pays the €10,000 when the exchange rate is €1 = $1.19. Talud will receive only $11,900 in Canadian currency when it converts the cash. The exchange loss is recognized in current-period earnings.

Cash (€10,000 × $1.19)	11,900	
Foreign exchange gains and losses	600	
Accounts receivable		12,500

Exchange Gain or Loss

The difference between the Canadian equivalent of the receivable and of the cash receipt is charged to an *exchange gain or loss* account. Exchange gains and losses are netted in this account, and the net balance is reported in earnings. It is important to understand that changes in the exchange rate following the initial transaction *do not affect the amount initially charged or credited to sales*. In the Talud example above, the sales account is not affected by the subsequent exchange rate change.

Similarly, if inventory or capital assets (such as equipment) are purchased in a foreign currency, changes in the exchange rate between the date of purchase and the date of payment will not affect the originally recorded value of the asset. *Historical cost is determined by the exchange rate at the date of the purchase transaction.* Subsequent gains and losses on the outstanding monetary balance are recognized directly and immediately in earnings.

Year-End

Assume instead that at Talud's year-end date, the receivable (recorded at $12,500) is still outstanding. The receivable must be translated to the then-current exchange rate. If the exchange rate at the year-end date is €1 = $1.30, the value of the account receivable will be $13,000 (€10,000 × $1.30). The increase of $500 in the Canadian equivalent of the €10,000 balance would be recorded as follows:

Accounts receivable ($13,000 − $12,500)	500	
Foreign exchange gains and losses		500

STATEMENT OF CASH FLOWS AND DISCLOSURE

SCF

The statement of cash flows is designed to explain the change in cash and cash equivalents over the period and as a result is the major element of disclosure related to cash. Components of cash as defined on the SCF (i.e., cash equivalents, if any) must be reconciled to the SFP. The change in accounts and notes receivable is an adjustment in operating activities to reconcile earnings to cash flow from operating activities. If notes receivable arise from investing activities rather than operating activities, then the change in this account would be classified in investing activities on the SCF.

Disclosure

Accounting standards require disclosure of information that will allow users to evaluate the significance of financial instruments in an evaluation of financial position and performance. Financial instrument disclosure is extensive; this recap provides the highlights only. Companies must disclose the following:

1. The *carrying amounts* for financial instruments in each category. For some categories, this is amortized cost or cost. For others, carrying value is fair value.

2. Regardless of what is used for carrying value, disclosure must be made of fair value, and a description provided of the methods used to estimate fair value. For many of the financial instruments in this chapter, cost and fair value are identical.

3. When a financial instrument has been valued at fair value, details about the change in fair value are required, in addition to the maturity value and methods used to assess fair value and its components.

4. The important components of each financial statement category. For example, receivables from outside customers are shown separately of receivables from related parties, receivables for tax refunds, and so on.

5. Collateral for accounts/notes receivable, along with the terms and condition of use.

6. A reconciliation of the changes in any allowance for credit losses (bad debts), and an analysis of past due accounts that have not been written down or for which no bad debt allowance has been provided.

7. Extensive disclosure that allows the financial statement users to evaluate the effect of netting arrangements (i.e., transfer of receivables that has resulted in derecognition). This essentially involves disclosing the major terms of the transaction(s).

8. Various revenue and expense amounts must be disclosed separately, including interest income.

9. Information on *credit risk, liquidity risk,* and *market risk,* as appropriate. As part of this, objectives, policies and processes for managing risk must be disclosed. Such disclosure is extensive and includes both qualitative and quantitative elements. Disclosure of interest rates and terms of receivables would be included as a matter of course.

Example

As an example of disclosure of carrying and fair value, consider the following extract from the 2014 Bombardier Inc. 2014 annual financial statements. Note in addition to this extract the methods to determine fair value are described in a separate note as well as the level of the hierarchy that is used to measure the financial instrument. Note that since IFRS 9 is not effective until 2018 most entities continue to use the existing standard IAS 39. In the extract below Bombardier is using IAS 39. The presentation of the trade and other receivables would be consistent with IFRS 9.

Looking Ahead

The financial instrument standards have been under constant review and revision since they were finalized in June 2014.

NOTE 13 FINANCIAL INSTRUMENTS

Carrying amounts and fair value of financial instruments

The classification of financial instruments and their carrying amounts and fair value of financial instruments were as follows as at:

December 31, 2014
Financial assets

| | FVTP&L | | | | Total carrying | |
	HFT	Designated	AFS	Amortized[1] cost	DDHR	value	Fair value
Cash and cash equivalents	$ 2,489	$ —	$ —	$ —	$ —	$ 2,489	$ 2,489
Trade and other receivables	—	—	—	1,538	—	1,538	1,538
Other financial assets	43	578	330	422	485	1,858	1,869
	$ 2,532	$ 578	$ 330	$ 1,960	$ 485	$ 5,885	$ 5,896

Source: Bombardier Incorporated, 2014 Annual Financial Statements, page 138 of annual report, www.sedar.com, posted 12 February 2015.

Accounting Standards for Private Enterprises

The ASPE requirements for cash, accounts receivable, and notes receivable are largely similar to IASB standards. The following differences are noted:

- In terms of classification, *CPA Canada Handbook, Part II* requirements specify that any cash held in a foreign country that is subject to restrictions, and cannot be used for general purposes, is not classified as cash. Under IASB standards, this restriction is simply disclosed in the notes and does not affect cash classification.

- Measurement of accounts receivables and notes receivables would be at amortized cost or elected to measure at fair value. If measured at fair value the changes every reporting period would be recognized in net income.

- Impairment testing for notes receivables would not require an allowance for the expected credit losses on initial recognition. Instead, factors that indicate impairment would be assessed at the end of each reporting period. If there was an indication of impairment, the carrying amount of the notes receivables would be compared to the higher of present value of the discounted future cash flows expected to be generated by the notes. This is the amount that would be realized by selling the notes plus the amount received by exercising any collateral. If impaired, the carrying amount of the notes receivables would be reduced directly or by using an allowance account.

- With respect to the classification of a transfer of accounts receivable (as a sale/derecognition or a borrowing), the ASPE approach focuses on surrender of control. That is, if the *transferee* has control over the receivables, the transferor will derecognize the accounts receivable. This is a different set of criteria than that established by the IASB, and thus a transaction that might result in derecognition for a private enterprise might be recorded as a borrowing by a company that complies with IASB standards.

- Required note disclosure under ASPE is far less onerous. For example, there is no requirement to show a continuity schedule for the allowance for doubtful accounts and significantly less disclosure for financial instruments in general.

- Amortization of a premium or discount on a note receivable or payable may be accomplished through the straight-line method. The effective interest method is not required.

Straight-Line Method

The straight-line method will amortize the discount on a note receivable to interest income over the life of the receivable, with the same dollar amount recognized each period. Interest revenue will therefore be measured as cash received plus discount amortization. While this is not consistent with the measurement model established through discounting, it is expedient. The following example will illustrate straight-line amortization.

Example: Straight-line amortization

On 1 April 20X2, Lee Co. sold merchandise for $7,000 to Vish Co. and received a two-year, 3% note. Interest is payable each 31 March, and the principal is payable at the end of the second year. *The market interest rate is 9%.* To value the transaction, it is (still) necessary to calculate the present value of the note, including both principal and interest:

Present value of maturity amount:	
$7,000(P/F, 9%, 2) =	$5,892
Present value of the nominal interest payments:	
$210(P/A, 9%, 2) =	370
Present value of the note at 9%	$6,262

The entry to record the sale is as follows:

1 April 20X2:		
Note receivable	7,000	
Discount on note receivable		738
Sales		6,262

Interest expense for each year can be organized in a table, with discount amortization of $369 ($738 ÷ 2) each year:

(1)	(2)	(3)	(4)	(5)
Opening Net Liability/ Receivable	Interest Expense/ Revenue Cash Paid + Discount Amortization (3) + (4)	Interest Paid/ Received 3% Stated Rate $7,000 × 3%	Discount Amortization Discount ÷ # of periods	Closing Net Liability/ Receivable (1) + (4)
$6,262	$579	$210	$369	$6,631
$6,631	579	210	369	7,000

Entries are identical in approach to those of the effective interest method.

Note, however, that the effective interest rate implied by interest revenue is 9.2% in the first year ($579 ÷ $6,262) and then 8.7% in the second year ($579 ÷ $6,631). This rate would be exactly 9%, and true to the substance of the transaction, if the effective interest method were used to measure interest revenue.

CONCEPT REVIEW

1. If a sale for €50,000 is finalized by a Canadian company when the exchange rate is €1 = $1.22, and paid by the customer when the exchange rate is €1 = $1.19, what Canadian dollar amount is recorded as a sale? What amount of cash is collected?
2. What is included in a continuity schedule for the allowance for doubtful accounts?
3. If the discount for three-year notes is $1,200, and the (annual) cash received is $600, how much is recorded as interest revenue if the straight-line method is used?

RELEVANT STANDARDS

CPA Canada Handbook, Part I (IFRS):

- IAS 1, Presentation of Financial Statements
- IAS 21, The Effects of Changes in Foreign Exchange Rates
- IAS 32, Financial Instruments: Presentation
- IAS 39, Financial Instruments: Recognition and Measurement
- IFRS 7, Financial Instruments: Disclosure
- IFRS 9, Financial Instruments
- IFRS 10, Consolidated Financial Statements

CPA Canada Handbook, Part II (ASPE):

- Section 1510, Current Assets and Current Liabilities
- Section 1651, Foreign Currency Translation
- Section 3856, Financial Instruments

SUMMARY OF KEY POINTS

1. Financial assets are those that are cash, or the contractual right to receive cash. Monetary items are those that will be paid or received in fixed or determinable amounts of money.

2. Cash is a financial asset. Cash equivalents, also financial assets, are certain kinds of short-term investments.

3. A bank reconciliation is an internal control mechanism. Reconciliation of the book balance to the correct cash balance provides the data for end-of-month adjusting entries for cash and provides insights as to the accuracy of recording.

4. In a bank reconciliation, adjustments to the bank are made for outstanding cheques and deposits, and bank errors. The book balance is adjusted for unrecorded items and errors.

5. Accounts receivable are financial instruments that are classified as amortized cost but may, in some circumstances, be classified as either FVOCI or FVTPL and carried at fair value. Doubtful accounts and cash discounts represent adjustments to the recorded value of receivables, which are necessary to provide an estimate of net realizable value.

6. The allowance for doubtful accounts is based on expected lifetime credit losses for accounts receivables.

7. Debit and credit card transactions may replace sales on account to speed the cash cycle. Accounts receivable can also be used as collateral for a loan to speed the cash cycle.

8. Accounts receivable can be transferred to a finance company to obtain immediate cash. The key accounting issue is whether the transfer of accounts receivable is treated as a sale/derecognition or borrowing. Derecognition is allowed if the accounts receivable are transferred, and if risks and rewards of ownership have genuinely passed to another party.

9. Notes receivable (and payable) that have low interest or no interest, and are longer than one year in duration, are recorded using the effective interest method. This method uses the present value of all cash payments to be received using an appropriate market rate of interest. Interest is based on the market interest rate and

the outstanding principal balance at the beginning of the period. On initial recognition the expected credit losses for the next 12 months are recorded.

10. Transactions that are denominated in a foreign currency are recorded at the exchange rate that exists at the transaction date. Monetary balances (i.e., cash and receivables) are restated to the exchange rate that exists on the year-end date. Foreign exchange gains and losses are recognized in earnings.

11. Extensive disclosure is required for financial instruments, including carrying value, fair value, details of contractual requirements, and continuity schedules for allowances, in addition to information on credit risk, liquidity risk, and market risk.

Key Terms

aging method

asset-backed commercial paper (ABCP)

allowance for doubtful accounts

bank reconciliation

cash equivalents

collateral security

commercial paper

compensating balance

consolidation

credit memo

debit memo

derecognition

effective-interest method

face value

financial assets

guaranteed investment certificate (GIC)

interest-bearing

internal control system

market interest rate

maturity value

monetary items

money market instruments

non-interest-bearing

non-notification basis

notification basis

overdraft

recourse

securitization

special purpose entity

stated interest rate (SPE)

transferee

transferor

Treasury bill (T-bill)

Review Problem 7-1

At the end of 20X5, three companies ask you to record journal entries in three different areas associated with receivables. The fiscal year of each company ends on 31 December.

1. *Mandalay Company—uncollectible accounts receivable.* Mandalay requests that you record journal entries for its bad debt expense and uncollectible accounts receivable in 20X5. Mandalay's 1 January 20X5 balances relevant to accounts receivable are as follows:

Accounts receivable	$400,000 (dr.)
Allowance for doubtful accounts	20,000 (cr.)

During 20X5, $45,000 of accounts receivable are judged to be uncollectible, and no more effort to collect these accounts will be made. Total sales for 20X5 are $1,200,000, of which $200,000 are cash sales; $900,000 was collected on account during 20X5.

Assuming that Mandalay ages its accounts receivables to estimate expected credit losses and uses 9% of total accounts receivable as its estimate of uncollectibles, provide the journal entries to record write-offs and bad debt expense for 20X5. Also, provide the 31 December 20X5 amount for net accounts receivable.

2. *Berkshire Company.—transfer of accounts receivable.* Berkshire requests that you record journal entries for accounts receivable transferred in 20X5:

> On 1 January 20X5, Berkshire transferred $45,000 of accounts receivable with no recourse to a finance company, on a notification basis. Bad debts are estimated to be $2,500, an amount that is already part of the allowance for doubtful accounts. The financing fee is 10%. Criteria for derecognition are met.

3. *White Mountain Company—accounting for long-term notes*: White Mountain requests that you record journal entries for a note it received in 20X5. On 1 January 20X5, White Mountain sold merchandise for $12,000 and received a $12,000, three-year, 6% note; 12% was the current market rate of interest at that time. Interest is paid annually at the end of each year, and the principal is due at the end of the third year. Provide journal entries from inception to final payment. Use the gross method to record the note.

REVIEW PROBLEM 7-1—SOLUTION

1. Mandalay Company

Summary entry for write-offs during 20X5:

Allowance for doubtful accounts	45,000	
Accounts receivable		45,000

Adjustment on 31 December 20X5:

Bad debt expense	65,950*	
Allowance for doubtful accounts		65,950

Calculation of adjustment:

Ending gross accounts receivable		$455,000
Required allowance balance ($455,000 × 9%)		$ 40,950
Allowance balance before adjustment for 20X5:		
Beginning balance, 1 January 20X5	$ (20,000)	
Write-offs during 20X5	45,000	25,000
Increase necessary to adjust balance		$ 65,950

Statement of financial position amounts at 31 December 20X5:

Accounts receivable	$455,000
Allowance for doubtful accounts	(40,950)
Net accounts receivable	$414,050

2. Berkshire Company

Cash ($45,000 − $2,500 − (10% × $42,500))	38,250	
Allowance for doubtful accounts	2,500	
Financing fee (10% × $42,500)	4,250	
Accounts receivable		45,000

3. White Mountain Company

Present value of note

$12,000 (P/F, 12%, 3)	$ 8,541
$720 (P/A, 12%, 3)	1,729
	$ 10,270

a. *1 January 20X5:*

Note receivable	12,000	
Sales revenue		10,270
Discount on note receivable		1,730

b. *31 December 20X5:*

Cash	720	
Discount on note receivable ($1,232 − $720)	512	
Interest revenue ($10,270 × 0.12)		1,232

c. *31 December 20X6:*

Cash	720	
Discount on note receivable ($1,294 − $720)	574	
Interest revenue ($10,270 + $512) × 0.12		1,294

d. *31 December 20X7:*

Cash	720	
Discount on note receivable	644	
Interest revenue ($10,270 + $512 + $574) × 0.12		1,364

e. *31 December 20X7:*

Cash	12,000	
Note receivable		12,000

CASE 7-1

MANUFACTURING INC.

Manufacturing Inc. (MI) is a public company that sells construction equipment to builders of primarily homes, office buildings, and highways. MI has been in operation for over 30 years. Up until this year the company has had profits with the real estate boom and large amounts of government funding for highway construction.

With the recent economic downturn MI has had to go to its bank for increased financing. The bank has imposed a minimum current ratio as well as a minimum balance that must be maintained in one of its accounts.

You have been recently hired as an accounting policy analyst to assist MI with its accounting policies. You have just finished meeting with Nancy who is the majority shareholder as well as CEO. Nancy had a lot of questions for you! You are trying to get a handle on what Nancy wants you to do and feeling a little overwhelmed at the moment. The following are comments made by Nancy at that meeting.

"This economic downturn has hit us really hard. We have had profits for a number of years and never worried about having enough cash on hand. Cash is critical in our business where the manufacturing of this specialized equipment can take a long period of time. In addition, our customers are really struggling to be able to invest in new machinery and pay their bills.

"I am very excited that you are able to join us and help out with a number of new situations that have arisen due to the economic downturn and possible solutions I have to solve our current cash crisis. Our bank has been very supportive but they are a little nervous about the economic downturn. I am not sure what, if anything, I need to do in the financial statements and notes about their recent covenant and restrictions. In addition, we have a number of bank accounts with our bank. Our line of credit has been in an overdraft position for over a year now. But we also have positive balances in our other accounts. All of these accounts are currently in cash and cash equivalents on our balance sheet. Is that okay?

"Some of our purchases for our manufacturing purchases are from the U.S. and we are required to pay in U.S. dollars. This has never been an issue for us before since the Canadian and U.S. dollar have been at par. As you know, with the recent economic downturn the Canadian dollar has been dropping in value and is currently at an all-time low and may continue to drop. What is the appropriate accounting for this drop in value and what impact will this have on our financial statements?

"Some customers who have been buying from us are having difficulty paying and are currently overdue. I know they will pay eventually and I want to help them out. What I have done is make their life a little easier by changing their accounts receivable to a note. This note allows them a two-year period to pay with an interest rate of 4% even though the current market rate is 8%. I have just taken the $500,000 of accounts receivable and reclassified them as a note receivable since I am sure they will pay. Is this okay?

"To get some extra cash I was considering selling some of my high quality receivables to a financial institution. I have $5,000,000 in these receivables. The financial institution will provide me with $4,800,000 in cash if I agree to make any payments that default. What would be the impact of this on my financial statements?

"One last thing: our head office was purchased a long time ago when real estate values were low. Currently, the carrying amount of that building is $520,000 but recent appraisals say it is worth $2 million. So I was thinking I could sell the building then immediately lease it back for its remaining useful life. What do you think of this idea? This could give me some much-needed cash and an immediate gain of $1.48 million on my financial statements.

"Sorry; I have to run to another meeting. Can you draft up a report on your preliminary ideas to all of my concerns? Thanks, and again we are so glad that you have become part of our team."

Required:

Prepare the requested report for Nancy.

CASE 7-2

MELVILLE CREDIT UNION

The Melville Credit Union has operated in small-town, rural Nova Scotia for the last 27 years. In the summer of 20X4, after decades of operation as a prosperous paper mill, the Lancaster Mersey Mill was abruptly shut down. Lancaster had been a major employer of many clients of Melville. In fact, of the 1,000 residents of the town in which Melville operates, over 320 were employed by Lancaster.

The following information relates to loans receivable of Melville as of 30 June 20X4:

	30 June 20X4	30 June 20X3
Loans receivable	$4,306,190	$3,164,000
Less: allowance for doubtful accounts	427,312	412,375
	$3,878,878	$2,751,625

Aging:

As of 30 June 20X3:

	Current	Over 30 days	Over 60 days	Over 120 days	Total
Loans receivable	$1,020,000	$872,000	$762,000	$510,000	$3,164,000

As of 30 June 20X4:

	Current	Over 30 days	Over 60 days	Over 120 days	Total
Loans receivable	$1,105,612	$632,000	$1,432,578	$1,136,000	$4,306,190

You, Karilyn Zinck, are in charge of the field work for the Melville audit. Melville has been a client of your firm for many years and has always received an unmodified audit report. Your audit senior reported the following discussion that took place between her and Colin Rodenizer, the chief accountant at Melville:

Audit Senior:	Colin, I noticed a lot of "for sale" signs on the houses as I drove here on my way to the Credit Union.
Colin:	Yes, sadly, that is true. Now that the mill has shut down many of our residents have decided to move. Well, many have lost their jobs and pretty much have to move.
Audit Senior:	How have house sales been going?
Colin:	Not really well, and the situation is getting worse by the day. We are now stuck with a number of homes ourselves, because we've had to foreclose on a number of mortgages that are not collectible. This is the first time this has happened in many years. I'm not sure how to account for these homes that we now own.
Audit Senior:	You would think that low interest rates and low property values would entice more sales.
Colin:	We hope that will help! Oh right, I'm also not sure what to do about the interest on these loans. Our system has been accruing interest on all of the loans receivable.

Required:

You are now working to identify the accounting issues that flow from the above information. You have scheduled a meeting with the audit partner tomorrow and decide, in advance of the meeting, to document the issues/areas of concern in a memo. The memo will include the quantitative impact of issues, to the extent possible.

(Tammy Crowell, used with permission)

CASE 7-3

MITRIUM CORP.

Mitrium Corp. is a large privately held company that manufactures frozen ice cream products, which are sold to large and small retailers across North America. The shares of this company are held by 12 individuals, some of them related and some of them not. Four of these shareholders are actively involved in the management of the company and are compensated with bonuses based on earnings. There are annual dividend payouts to provide some return to the remaining shareholders. The company has been prosperous in the past but the current retail grocery market, slowly being taken over by private-label goods, is proving a challenge for Mitrium. However, the company is actively engaged in manufacturing private-label goods and enjoys healthy sales and profit margins in several of its flagship products, which have strong brand recognition with the end consumer.

The VP Finance has come to you has come to you, a staff member, for commentary on two key financial ratios (Exhibit 1) based on the draft statement of financial position (Exhibit 2) for the most recent fiscal year. She has isolated these ratios because they are the subject of loan covenants. Specifically, one chartered bank provides the $6 million financing that appears as long-term debt on the statement of financial position. As part of this lending agreement, the current ratio on audited financial statements must not go below 2:1, and the debt-to-equity ratio must not go above 12:1. If either of these ratio requirements is violated, or if interest is not paid annually, the debt becomes payable on demand. The current ratio condition is not met in the financial statements, although it is very close. The VP Finance suspects that the draft financial statements will change based on the additional information she has provided to you (see Exhibit 2). Your task is to analyze this additional information and restate the ratios, providing any commentary or advice you feel is appropriate.

EXHIBIT 1

MITRIUM CORP.

Debt Covenant Ratios

Ratio	Definition	Calculation (Based on Draft Statements)
Current ratio	$\dfrac{\text{Current assets}}{\text{Current liabilities}}$	$\dfrac{\$2,360}{\$1,211} = 1.95$
Debt/equity	$\dfrac{\text{Total debt}}{\text{Total owners' equity}}$	$\dfrac{\$8,808}{\$867} = 10.2$

EXHIBIT 2

MITRIUM CORP.

Draft Statement of Financial Position 31 December 20X8

(in thousands)

Assets

Current assets:

Cash		$ 300	
Accounts receivable	$1,443		
Allowance for doubtful accounts	(12)	1,431	
Inventory		533	
Prepaid expenses		96	$2,360

Capital assets:

Property, plant, and equipment	7,293

Other assets — 22

Total assets — $9,675

Liabilities

Current liabilities:

Bank indebtedness	$ 405
Accounts payable and accrued liabilities	576
Current portion of long-term debt	230
Total current liabilities	$1,211

Long-term liabilities:		
Secured bank debt, 6%		1,442
Secured bank debt, floating interest rate		6,000
Deferred tax		155
Total liabilities		8,808
Owners' Equity		
Common share capital	583	
Retained earnings	284	
Total owners' equity		867
Total liabilities and owners' equity		$9,675

Additional information (all amounts in thousands):

At year-end, there was a balance of $22 in the cash account in the general ledger, a $300 bank balance less $278 in outstanding cheques. Cash is shown as the balance before outstanding cheques, which have been reclassified as accounts payable.

In 20X8, certain accounts receivable were transferred to a financial institution on a nonrecourse basis. The transfer was accounted for as a sale/derecognition of accounts receivable. An undivided percentage interest in the designated pool of receivables was transferred, with Mitrium retaining the right to repurchase the receivables and use them as collateral against the 6% bank loan. Servicing of the accounts receivable is done by Mitrium on a fee-for-service basis. At the end of the year, $210 of accounts receivable had been transferred. This transaction took place on 20 December and is expected to be of a 45-day duration. Mitrium recognized finance expense of $1.9 and reduced (debited) the allowance for doubtful accounts by $4 when the transfer was recorded. This was felt to be an accurate representation of the doubtful accounts in this account receivable population.

Of the remaining accounts receivable, $412 is receivable from one grocery chain, which is wholly owned by a shareholder of Mitrium. This account has been outstanding for some time, but Mitrium has had the shareholder personally pledge his share investment in Mitrium as security in the event of nonpayment. Activity in the account this fiscal year is:

Opening balance	$256
Sales	455
Payments on account	(341)
Interest accrued	42
Closing balance	$ 412

Of this amount, the $42 interest and $106 of sales are current and the remainder is over 90 days past due.

Mitrium instituted a sales discount program for all customers this year with the intent of speeding collections of accounts receivable. The discount program allows 1% of the invoice to be deducted if payment for the invoice is received by Mitrium within 10 business days of the invoice date. This program has been quite successful and Mitrium feels that its accounts receivable balances are lower this year as a result. However, since many of the company's highest credit rating customers use these discounts, Mitrium feels that the traditional noncollection percentage for current accounts receivable should likely triple this year. Other categories (30 days past due, etc.) are expected to be stable.

Sales data for the latter portion of December 20X8 are as follows:

Date: December 20X8	Business Day	Sales on Account (thousands)	Percentage Using Sales Discount as of 31 December
11	Yes	$53.4	54%*
12	Yes	71.2	53%*
13	Yes	68.9	61%*
14	Yes	56.7	45%*
15	Yes	48.1	24%
16–17	No	—	—
18	Yes	81.6	12%
19	Yes	41.3	14%
20	Yes	24.4	9%
21	Yes	22.2	12%
22	Yes	51.4	5%
23–26	No	—	—
27	Yes	10.4	4%
28	Yes	78.4	2%
29	Yes	46.4	0%
30–31	No	—	—

*Discount period now expired.

The allowance for doubtful accounts has not yet been addressed in the year-end financial statements. An aging of accounts receivable shows the following:

Status	Amount	Percentage Uncollectible*
Current	$ 424	3%
30 days past due	208	8%
60 days past due	231	10%
90+ days past due	580	40%
	$1,443	

*Based on prior experience. These percentages exclude the receivable from the grocery chain described above, which has not been included in the allowance in any prior year.

Required:

Prepare a report to the VP Finance that responds to her concerns. The tax rate is 40%.

TECHNICAL REVIEW

connect

TR7-1 Cash and Receivables:

1. Loans and receivables are classified according to their business model.
2. All notes receivables are measured at amortized cost.
3. Overdrafts can be netted against a positive balance in a bank account with any bank.
4. Gains and losses from translation foreign currency for cash are recognized in net income.
5. A common internal control over cash is segregation of duties.

Required:

Identify whether each statement is true or false.

connect

TR7-2 Cash and Cash Equivalents:

The following items would be included in cash and cash equivalents:

1. 2% investment in common shares public company.
2. 2% investment in common shares private company.
3. 60-day investment certificates.
4. Bank overdraft.
5. Commercial paper.

Required:

Identify whether each statement is true or false.

connect

TR7-3 Cash—Bank Reconciliation:

Vish Ltd. reported a cash balance of $36,000 in the general ledger, but the bank statement reported a balance of $27,900 at the end of September 20X9. You have ascertained that the bank cashed a cheque on this account, in the amount of $5,500, which was actually issued by Mish Ltd.; this was an error made by the bank. There was also an outstanding deposit of $4,900, an amount that was deposited by Vish at the end of September after the bank cut-off. Outstanding cheques were $2,500, and there was an error made by Vish's bookkeeper, who recorded a cheque to a supplier at $1,200 when it was really $2,100. Bank fees of $400 have not yet been recorded by Vish, and neither was a direct deposit of $1,100 by a customer, who paid Vish directly to Vish's bank account.

Required:

Prepare a bank reconciliation as of the end of September 20X9.

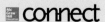

TR7-4 Accounts Receivable—Allowances:

The accounts of Quickly Company provided the following 20X4 information at 31 December:

Accounts receivable balance	$600,000 (dr.)
Allowance for sales discounts	5,500 (cr.)
Allowance for doubtful accounts	40,000 (cr.)

In fact, the allowance for sales discounts is not needed at the end of 20X5 and aging shows that the allowance for doubtful accounts should be $65,000.

Required:

1. Prepare journal entries to adjust all allowances.
2. By how much have these entries changed earnings?
3. What is the net balance of accounts receivable that will be included on the SFP?

connect

TR7-5 Accounts Receivable—Bad Debts:

The unadjusted net accounts receivable on the books of Elantra Ltd. as of 31 December 20X4 are as follows:

Accounts receivable	$100,000
Less: Allowance for doubtful accounts	10,000
	$ 90,000

40% of the accounts are current and 5% might not be collected, and the remainder is past due and 30% might not be collected.

Required:

Calculate the bad debt expense, the balance in the allowance for doubtful accounts, and the net accounts receivable on the SFP at the end of 20X4.

connect

TR7-6 Transfer of Receivables:

Hum Corp. has accounts receivable of $460,000. The company transfers these accounts receivable to a financial institution. There are no bad debts associated with these accounts receivable. Proceeds of $444,500 are received from the transfer. The transfer is on a non-notification basis, which means that the customers pay Hum, and Hum remits the cash to the financial institution. The customers pay $460,000 to Hum on schedule, and the cash remittance is forwarded to the financial institution.

Required:

Record all journal entries for the sequence of events assuming the transfer is recorded as a sale/derecognition of receivables.

connect

TR7-7 Transfer of Receivables:

Use information from TR7-6.

Required:

Record all journal entries for the sequence of events assuming the transfer is recorded as a borrowing.

connect

TR7-8 Notes Receivable:

Dharma, a public company, sold a piece of equipment at the beginning of Year 1, receiving a $10,000, two-year 2% note. Interest is paid at the end of each year. Market interest rates are assumed to be 10%.

Required:

1. Calculate the present value of the note receivable.
2. Prepare entries for the sale, interest revenue, and cash collection each year for two years.

connect

TR7-9 Notes Receivable:

Using the information from TR7-8 now assume the company is a private company and it has elected to use straight-line amortization.

Required:

1. Calculate the present value of the note receivable.
2. Prepare entries for the sale, interest revenue, and cash collection each year for two years.

connect

TR7-10 Impairment Receivables:

1. When initially recognized, accounts receivables are required to have a valuation allowance based on expected credit losses for their lifetime.

2. For a new company with no history of uncollectible accounts, receivables can be written off when they are determined uncollectible.

3. Aging of accounts receivable is often done to determine an allowance for doubtful accounts.

4. When initially recognized, notes receivables are required to have a valuation allowance based on expected credit losses for their lifetime.

5. In ASPE, impairment of notes receivables is considered only if there is objective evidence of a loss.

Required:

Identify whether each statement is true or false.

ASSIGNMENTS

 A7-1 Financial Assets:

The disclosure note of Big Products Ltd. showed the following (in millions):

	FVTPL	Amortized Cost	FVOCI	Total Carrying Value	Total Fair Value
Cash	$116	$ —	$ —	$116	$116
Cash equivalents	542	—	—	542	542
Accounts receivable	165	699	—	864	864
Notes receivable	—	—	210	210	210

Required:

1. Define financial instrument and financial asset.

2. With respect to cash, explain why the asset is classified as FVTPL. Under what circumstances would the fair value of cash change from the originally recognized value?

3. What is the definition of a cash equivalent?

4. With respect to accounts receivable, explain the difference between the accounting treatment of financial instruments classified as FVTPL and those classified as amortized cost. Why are some elements likely placed in one category versus the other?

5. Why are notes receivable in FVOCI instead of amortized cost?

 connect

★ A7-2 Accounts Receivable—Allowances:

The accounts of Polaris Company provided the following 20X5 information at 31 December 20X5:

Accounts receivable	$ 1,899,000 (dr.)
Allowance for sales discounts	23,500 (cr.)
Allowance for doubtful accounts	134,900 (cr.)
Total credit sales revenue during 20X5	23,589,000

Investigation showed the following:

a. Examination of an aging of accounts receivable showed that accounts of $106,200 previously provided for should be written off. Of the remaining balance, $216,000 was doubtful at year-end.

b. Estimated sales discounts inherent in the closing accounts receivable balance were $17,200. Terms of 1/10, n/45 were granted to customers. Accounts receivable were recorded gross, and the discounts taken were recorded when taken by the customers in a discounts account, reported contra to the sales account.

Required:

1. Prepare year-end adjusting entries with respect to accounts receivable and the related allowances.
2. Show how the net accounts receivable appear on the statement of financial position on 31 December 20X5.

★ A7-3 Accounts Receivable—Allowances and Entries:

The net accounts receivable on the books of GJY Corp. as of 1 January 20X3 are as follows:

Accounts receivable	$ 281,000
Less: Allowance for sales discounts	6,000
Allowance for doubtful accounts	20,650
	$254,350

During the year, the sales discount allowance is left unchanged, with discounts recorded directly in the sales discounts account. Allowances are adjusted at year-end. Summarized transactions during 20X3 are as follows:

a. Sales revenue was $620,000, of which 70% was on credit.

b. Customers paid off $492,500 of the outstanding accounts receivable. Of this reduction to the accounts receivable, $300,000 was paid in time to earn a 2% discount.

c. Accounts of $7,650 were written off at year-end.

d. There were recoveries of previously written-off accounts in the amount of $1,400.

e. At year-end, analysis of accounts receivable indicates that an allowance of $3,950 is needed for sales discounts.

f. At year-end, the allowance for doubtful accounts is increased by 1% of gross credit sales.

Required:

1. Prepare journal entries for the above transactions.
2. Show how the net accounts receivable appear on the statement of financial position on 31 December 20X3.
3. Do you have any concerns about the level of the allowance for doubtful accounts? Explain.

A7-4 Accounts Receivable—Allowances:

At 31 December 20X8, Small Ltd. reported gross accounts receivable of $2,481,800. Investigation showed the following:

a. The credit balance in the allowance for doubtful accounts was $182,400 after write-offs for the year but before any bad debt adjustment. Bad debt expense is based on a percentage of receivables. Based on the latest available facts, $280,000 will not be collected due to collection issues.
b. Terms of 1/10, n/30 were granted to all customers. Accounts receivable were recorded gross, and the discounts taken were recorded when taken by the customers in a discounts account, reported contra to the sales account. Estimated discounts inherent in the closing accounts receivable balance were $30,600. The allowance for sales discounts account was established at $29,800 last year and has not been adjusted since.

Required:

1. Prepare year-end adjusting entries with respect to accounts receivable.
2. Show how the net accounts receivable would appear on the statement of financial position on 31 December 20X8.

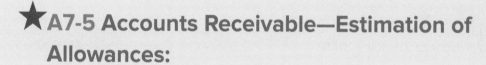 A7-5 Accounts Receivable—Estimation of Allowances:

Information related to accounts receivable is given:

At the beginning of the year, Health Products Corp. has a balance of $2,450,000 in accounts receivable and $220,000 in the allowance for doubtful accounts. Sales for the year were $19,300,000, of which 70% were on credit. Cash payments on account were $12,905,000. Sales returns were $340,000. Accounts of $107,600 were written off, but $32,900 was subsequently recovered and collected. This $32,900 cash payment was in addition to the collections previously mentioned. At year-end, a review indicated that 8% of outstanding accounts receivable were uncollectible, but that there was no risk of further sales returns.

Required:

Show how net accounts receivable would be reported on the statement of financial position, and calculate bad debt expense for the year.

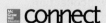

★ ★ A7-6 Accounts Receivable—Estimation of Allowances:

Information related to accounts receivable is given:

Mobile Technology Ltd. reported an unadjusted balance of accounts receivable of $1,285,000 at 31 December 20X3, along with a credit balance in the allowance for doubtful accounts of $83,100 and an allowance for sales discounts of $6,000. At year-end, the company determined that an allowance of $12,500 for sales discounts was needed. It also decided that $53,400 of accounts receivable were uncollectible and should be written off. Of the remaining receivables, it was determined that 40% were current, and of the remaining *net* current balance, an allowance for doubtful accounts of 3% of the net balance was needed. The remaining 60% of outstanding accounts receivable were past due and an allowance for doubtful accounts of 10% of the outstanding balance was needed.

Required:

Show how net accounts receivable would be reported on the statement of financial position, and calculate bad debt expense for the year.

★ ★ A7-7 Accounts Receivable—Estimation of Bad Debt Expense:

The accounts of Long Company provided the following 20X5 information at 31 December 20X5 (end of the annual period):

Accounts receivable balance, 1 January 20X5	$51,000
Allowance for doubtful accounts balance, 1 January 20X5	3,000
Uncollectible account to be written off during 20X5 (ex-customer Slo)	1,000
Cash collected on accounts receivable during 20X5	170,000

Estimates for bad debt losses:

a. Based on ending balance of accounts receivable, 8%.
b. Based on aging schedule (excludes Slo's account):

Age	Accounts Receivable	Probability of Noncollection
Less than 30 days	$28,000	2%
31–90 days	7,000	10
91–120 days	3,000	30
More than 120 days	2,000	60

Required:

1. Give the entry to write off customer Slo's long-overdue account.

2. Give all entries related to accounts receivable and the allowance account for the following two cases:

   Case A—Bad debt expense is based on the ending balance of accounts receivable

   Case B—Bad debt expense is based on aging

3. Show how the results of applying each case above should be reported in 20X5 earnings and on the 20X5 statement of financial position.

4. Briefly explain and evaluate each of the three methods used in Cases A and B.

5. On 1 August 20X6, customer Slo paid his long-overdue account in full. Give the required entries.

eXcel

★ ★ A7-8 Accounts Receivable—Allowance for Doubtful Accounts:

The accounting records of Sine.Com Ltd. provided the following for 20X9:

Balance in accounts receivable, 1 January 20X9	$ 90,000
Balance in accounts receivable, 31 December 20X9	120,000
Balance in allowance for doubtful accounts, 1 January 20X9	3,000 (cr.)
Accounts already written off as uncollectible during 20X9	5,500

a. Six percent of the uncollected accounts receivable at year-end will be uncollectible.

b. Aging of the accounts receivable at the end of the period indicated that 80% would incur a 2% loss, while the remaining 20% would incur a 10% loss.

Required:

1. For each of the two alternatives listed above, give the following:
   a. 20X9 adjusting entry
   b. Ending 20X9 balance in the allowance account
   c. An evaluation of the alternative

2. Explain which of the two alternatives you would recommend.

(Source: Atlantic School of Chartered Accountancy, used with permission.)

★ ★ A7-9 Accounts Receivable—Allowance for Doubtful Accounts:

Accounts receivable for Smith Ltd. were reported on the statement of financial position prepared at the end of 20X8, as follows:

Accounts receivable	$122,900	
Less: Allowance for doubtful accounts	3,530	$119,370

In 20X9, the following transactions took place:

Accounts written off	$2,150
Accounts previously written off but recovered	650

Additional information:

The company sells goods on account. At the end of the year, accounts receivable are aged and the following percentages are applied in arriving at an estimate of the charge for doubtful accounts.

	Estimated loss
Current accounts	0%
Accounts 1–2 months overdue	7%
Accounts 3–6 months overdue	20%
Accounts 7–12 months overdue	50%
Accounts more than 1 year overdue	95%

At the end of the year, most of the accounts receivable are current. However, the aging schedule (after write-offs and recoveries) shows the following:

Accounts 1–2 months overdue	$7,500
Accounts 3–6 months overdue	6,100
Accounts 7–12 months overdue	2,500
Accounts more than 1 year overdue	880

Required:

1. Give the entries required to record the transactions listed above and also to adjust the accounts.
2. Calculate the balance for accounts receivable and the related allowances as at 31 December 20X9, and show these accounts as they will appear on the statement of financial position.

★ ★ A7-10 Accounts Receivable—Alternatives for Allowance for Doubtful Accounts:

At 31 December 20X9, the end of the annual reporting period, the accounts of Huron Company showed the following:

a. Allowance for doubtful accounts, balance 1 January 20X9, $22,700 credit.
b. Accounts receivable, balance 31 December 20X9 (prior to any write-offs of uncollectible accounts during 20X9), $383,400.

c. Uncollectible accounts to be written off, 31 December 20X9, $19,800. These accounts are all in the "past due over 90 days" category.

d. Aging schedule at 31 December 20X9, showing the following breakdown of accounts receivable (prior to any write-offs of uncollectible accounts during 20X9):

Status	Amount
Not past due	$210,800
Past due 1–60 days	60,000
Past due over 60 days	89,100
Past due over 90 days	23,500

Required:

1. Give the 20X9 entry to write off the uncollectible accounts.

2. Give the 20X9 adjusting entry to record bad debt expense for each of the following independent assumptions concerning bad debt loss rates:
    a. On total receivables at year-end (after write-off), 4.2%.
    b. On aging schedule: not past due, 0.8%; past due 1–60 days, 1.8%; past due over 60 days, 11%, and past due over 90 days, 80%.

3. Show the amount that would be reported on the 20X9 statement of financial position relating to net accounts receivable for each assumption.

A7-11 Transfer of Accounts Receivable:

Belanger Ltd. reports a current ratio of 2-to-1 in its 20X2 financial statements. The statement of financial position shows current assets of $2,540,500 and current liabilities of $1,284,000. Accounts receivable are $745,900 of the current assets. Belanger is considering transferring $440,000 of the accounts receivable with a 90-day term to a financial institution. There are no bad debts associated with these accounts receivable. Proceeds of $421,200 are expected from the transaction.

Required:

1. What criteria must be met for the transfer of accounts receivable to qualify for derecognition?

2. Prepare the journal entry to record the transfer as (a) a sale/derecognition and (b) a borrowing.

3. Recalculate the current ratio reflecting first (a) and then (b) in requirement 2.

4. Why might a financial statement analyst restore transferred accounts receivable to the statement of financial position before performing a ratio analysis? What ratios other than the current ratio would be especially affected?

A7-12 Transfer of Accounts Receivable:

The following two cases are independent:

Case A Appa Apparel manufactures fine sportswear for many national retailers and frequently sells its receivables to financing companies as a means of accelerating cash collections. Appa transferred $600,000 of receivables from retailers to a financing company and has no control over, or continuing interest in, the accounts receivable. The receivables were transferred without recourse on a notification basis. The financing company charged 12% of the receivables total. There were no bad debts.

Required:

1. Should Appa record the transfer of receivables as a sale/derecognition or as a borrowing? Why?
2. Record all entries related to the transfer for Appa.

Case B Bappa Apparel manufactures fine sportswear for many national retailers and frequently sells its receivables to financing companies as a means of accelerating cash collections. Bappa transferred $600,000 of receivables from retailers to a financing company. The receivables were transferred with recourse on a notification basis. The financing company charged 8%. Bappa has no obligation to the financing company other than to pay the account of a retailer in the event of a default. However, Bappa retains legal control over the receivables, and the financing company may not sell the accounts receivable to a third party. There were no bad debts.

Required:

1. Should Bappa record the transfer of receivables as a sale/derecognition or as a borrowing? Why?
2. Record Bappa's entries related to the transfer.

A7-13 Transfer of Accounts Receivable:

On 1 April 20X5, XCourt Company transferred $75,000 of accounts receivable to Prima Finance Company to obtain immediate cash. Consider the two following independent circumstances.

Required:

1. The transfer agreement specified a price of $64,200 on a no-recourse, notification basis that effectively transferred legal control to Prima. Prima is permitted to resell the accounts receivables without permission from XCourt. Give the entry/entries that XCourt should make. The $10,800 reduction from face value represents a $6,800 financing fee and $4,000 of expected bad debts that are already in the allowance for doubtful accounts. Explain the basis for your response.
2. The transfer agreement specified a price of $70,000 on a with-recourse, notification basis. The $5,000 reduction from face value is related to expected bad debts, $2,000, and a $3,000 financing fee. The bad debt amount is already in the allowance for doubtful accounts. XCourt retained the right to repurchase the receivables; Prima is not permitted to resell the accounts receivable unless XCourt is given first refusal on the transaction. Give the entry/entries that XCourt should make.
3. Explain the difference to the statement of financial position between requirements 1 and 2.

A7-14 Transfer of Accounts Receivable:

Lincraft Corp. reports a current ratio of 3-to-1 in its 20X2 financial statements. The statement of financial position shows current assets of $3,116,500 and current liabilities of $1,040,100. Lincraft has accounts receivable of $1,267,300. The company transfers $970,000 of these accounts receivable to a financial institution. There are $33,600 of bad debts associated with these accounts receivable, an amount that is already in the allowance for doubtful accounts. Proceeds of $889,450 are received from the transfer. The transfer is on a non-notification basis, which means that the customers pay Lincraft and Lincraft then remit the cash to the financial institution. The customers pay $936,400 to Lincraft on schedule, $33,600 is written off to the allowance at the appropriate time, and the cash remittance is forwarded to the financial institution.

Required:

1. Record all journal entries for the sequence of events assuming:
    a. The transfer is recorded as a sale/derecognition; and

b. The transfer is recorded as a borrowing.

2. Calculate the current ratio, after the initial entry in requirements 1a and 1b, and comment on the result.

 Solution

 A7-15 Notes Receivable:

South Company, a public company, sells large construction equipment. On 1 January 20X5, the company sold North Company a machine at a quoted price of $120,000. South collected $40,000 cash and received a two-year note payable for the balance.

Required:

1. Give South's required entries for the two years, assuming an interest-bearing note, face value $80,000. (8% interest, simple interest, payable every 31 December.)

2. Assume that the market interest rate is still 8%. Give South's required entries for the two years, assuming a 2% interest-bearing note, face value $80,000. Prepare the entries based on the gross basis.

3. Compare the interest revenue and sales revenue under requirements 1 and 2.

4. Repeat requirement two above. Assume South is a private company that uses ASPE and has decided to use straight-line amortization.

 A7-16 Notes Receivable:

The following cases are independent:

Case A On 1 May 20X8, Jain Company sold merchandise to a customer and received a $110,000 (face amount), one-year, non-interest-bearing note. The going (i.e., market) rate of interest is 6%. Discounting must be used to value the transaction. The annual reporting period for Jain Co. ends on 31 December. The customer paid the note in full on its maturity date.

Case B On 15 April 20X8, Hall Company sold merchandise to a customer for $175,000, terms 2/10, n/30. The sale is recorded gross, at $175,000. Because of nonpayment by the customer, Hall agreed to accept a $175,000, 5%, 12-month note on 1 May 20X8 to replace the account receivable. This is a market interest rate. The annual reporting period ends 30 September. The customer paid the note in full on its maturity date.

Required:

For each case:

1. Give all entries related to the notes receivable through to maturity. Use the gross method to account for accounts and notes receivable.

2. List the items and amounts that will be reported on the 20X8 statement of comprehensive income and statement of financial position.

 A7-17 Notes Receivable:

MacWilliams Ltd. sold a $90,000 piece of machinery to a customer on 1 January 20X6, and took back a two-year, 2% note receivable. The customer has to pay interest every 31 December, but the $90,000 principal is due only after two years. Market interest rates are 6%.

Required:

1. What is the present value of the note receivable?
2. Record the sale/loan on 1 January 20X6, the interest each 31 December (two times) and the loan repayment on 31 December 20X7. Use the gross method to record the note.
3. Record the transaction, interest, and repayment on the books of the customer.

 connect

★ **A7-18 Notes Receivable:**

Bento Corp. took a $500,000 four-year, 4% note receivable from a customer in connection with a major sale transaction. The note required annual blended payments, to be paid at the end of each year. The market interest rate is 4%.

Required:

1. Calculate the required blended payment. Round to the nearest dollar.
2. Prepare a schedule that shows the annual interest and principal portion of the four payments.
3. Prepare journal entries to record the initial sale transaction and each payment.

 connect

★ ★ **A7-19 Notes Receivable:**

Cambria Ltd. took a $250,000 two-year note receivable from a customer in connection with a major inventory sale transaction on 1 January 20X5. The note required annual end-of-year interest payments of 4%, and the principal was due at the end of 20X6.

Required:

1. Prepare journal entries to record the initial sale transaction and each payment on the books of Cambria, assuming that the market interest rate is 4%.
2. Assume now that the market interest rate is 8%. Calculate the present value of the note, and prepare a schedule that shows the annual interest.
3. Prepare journal entries to record the initial sale transaction and each payment on the books of Cambria, consistent with requirement 2. Use the gross method to record the note.
4. What accounts are different between requirements 1 and 3? Explain.
5. Prepare journal entries to record the initial sale transaction and each payment on the books of the customer who bought inventory and owes the note, consistent with requirement 2.

connect

A7-20 Notes Receivable:

Omega Chemicals Ltd. took a $420,000 two-year note receivable from a customer in connection with a major sale transaction on 1 May 20X7. The note required annual 30 April interest payments of 3%, and the principal was due on 30 April 20X9. Omega has a 31 December year-end.

Required:

1. Prepare journal entries to record the initial sale transaction and each payment on the books of Omega, assuming that the market interest rate is 3%.

2. Assume now that the market interest rate is 5%. Calculate the present value of the note, and prepare a schedule that shows the interest for each year of the note receivable.

3. Prepare journal entries to record the initial sale transaction and each payment on the books of Omega, consistent with requirement 2. Use the gross method to record the note.

A7-21 Notes Receivable—Impairment:

On 1 January 20X5, Spencer Inc. sold merchandise (cost, $8,000; sales value, $14,000) to Bryden Inc. and received a non-interest-bearing note in return. The note requires $15,730 to be paid in a lump sum on 31 December 20X6.

On initial recognition of the note the expected credit losses were 0%. In February 20X6, Bryden requested that the terms of the note be modified so that the $15,730 payment be paid at the end of 20X11. Spencer refused Bryden's request.

During 20X6, however, news of Bryden's deteriorating financial condition prompted Spencer to reevaluate the collectibility of the note. Consequently, the modified terms requested by Bryden were accepted as of 31 December 20X6.

Required:

1. Prepare the entry to record the sale by Spencer, assuming a perpetual inventory system. Also prepare the 31 December 20X5 adjusting entry. Use the net method. You will need to establish the interest rate implicit in the original note.

2. Prepare the entry to record the impairment on 31 December 20X6. (Compare the book value of the note at 31 December 20X6 with the present value of the newly acknowledged cash flow stream using the same interest rate as in requirement 1. No interest revenue is accrued in 20X6.)

A7-22 Foreign Currency Receivables:

Grand Ltd. is a Canadian company that had the following transactions in 20X7:

a. Sold goods to a customer in Belgium on 25 November for 220,000 euros.

b. Sold goods to a U.S. customer on 25 November for US$80,000.

c. Sold goods on 1 December, to a British customer for 140,000 euros.

d. On 15 December, the customer in transaction (a) paid.

At year-end, the other two accounts receivable were still outstanding.

EXCHANGE RATES

Canadian Equivalencies	Euro	US$
25 November	1.55	1.02
1 December	1.61	0.98
15 December	1.42	1.01
31 December	1.47	1.03

Required:

Calculate the exchange gain or loss to be reported in 20X7, the accounts receivable on the 31 December 20X7 statement of financial position, and the sales revenue to be recorded from the transactions listed above.

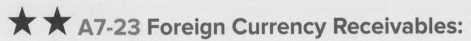 ## A7-23 Foreign Currency Receivables:

Johnston Ltd. had the following transactions in 20X5:

a. Sold goods on 1 June to a British customer for 140,000 euros with payment to be in four months.
b. Sold goods to a U.S. customer on 15 June for US$300,000; payment was due in one month.
c. Sold goods to a British customer on 15 July for 40,000 euros; settlement was to be in two months.
d. Received payment from the U.S. customer in (b) on 15 July.
e. Received payment from the British customer in (c) on 15 September.
f. Received payment from the British customer in (a) on 1 October.

EXCHANGE RATES:

Canadian Equivalencies	Euro	US$
1 June	1.45	1.07
15 June	1.40	1.11
15 July	1.42	1.09
15 September	1.36	1.03
1 October	1.32	1.06

Required:

Prepare journal entries for the above transactions.

 ## A7-24 Comprehensive:

April Ltd. reported various selected balances in its 31 December 20X7 unadjusted trial balance:

Accounts receivable	$1,800,000 dr.
Special accounts receivable	225,000 dr.

Accounts receivable—U.S.	116,000 dr.
Allowance for doubtful accounts	158,050 cr.
Allowance for sales discounts	45,000 cr.

The following transactions and events are noted:

1. An analysis of accounts receivable indicates that $800,000 are still in the discount period. An allowance of $80,000 is needed for sales discounts.

2. An analysis of accounts receivable indicated that $198,000 of accounts receivable should be written off. Of the remaining balance, 80% was current, and, after the allowance for sales discounts, approximately 5% was deemed doubtful. Of the 20% noncurrent, 75% was doubtful.

3. The U.S. account receivable was recorded when the exchange rate was $1.16. The exchange rate at year-end was $1.12.

4. The special account receivable was a single account receivable from a customer with an excellent credit rating that was transferred to a financial institution at a discount rate of 4% during the period. The cash collected from the financial institution was credited to an account called "Miscellaneous credits." Management has determined that this transaction was to be recorded as a sale/derecognition but has not yet made the necessary entry.

5. The company has a note receivable that has not yet been recorded. The note is a $70,000, three-year note that bears an interest rate of 4%. Interest is paid annually. The note was issued on 1 November 20X7 because of a sale. The market interest rate for accounts of this risk is 8%.

Required:

Provide journal entries to reflect the above items.

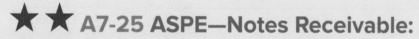

A7-25 ASPE—Notes Receivable:

Epsilon Ltd. accepted a $600,000 two-year note receivable from a customer in connection with a major inventory sale transaction on 1 January 20X5. The note required annual end-of-year interest payments of 2%, and the principal was due at the end of 20X6.

Required:

1. Assume that the market interest rate is 7%. Calculate the present value of the note, and prepare a schedule that shows the annual interest using the straight-line method of amortization.

2. Prepare journal entries to record the initial sale transaction and each payment on the books of Epsilon, consistent with requirement 1. Use the gross method to record the note.

3. Prepare a schedule that shows the annual interest using the effective interest method of amortization.

4. Compare interest revenue as calculated in requirements 1 and 3. Which is more accurate? Explain. What method(s) are permitted under ASPE? IFRS?

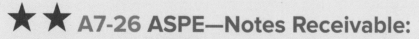

A7-26 ASPE—Notes Receivable:

Sumarah Corp. accepted a $450,000 two-year note receivable from a customer in connection with a major inventory sale transaction on 1 October 20X5. The note was interest-free, although market interest rates were in the range of 8%.

Required:

1. Can the company record a sale for $450,000? Explain.

2. Calculate the present value of the note, and prepare a schedule that shows the annual interest using the effective interest method. Prepare a second schedule using the straight-line method.

3. Compare the two alternate measures of interest revenue as calculated in requirement 2. Which is more accurate? Explain. What method(s) are permitted under ASPE? IFRS?

4. Prepare journal entries to record the initial sale transaction and each payment on the books of Sumarah, using the straight-line method. Use the gross method to record the note.

 A7-27 Bank Reconciliation (Appendix):

The August bank reconciliation for C&C Ltd.:

Balance per bank	$151,570
Plus: outstanding deposits	17,900
Less: Outstanding cheques ($11,245, $650, $1,570, $890, $120)	(14,475)
Cash, per general ledger	$154,995

September information, per books:

Opening balance: $154,995

Cash Receipts Journal		Cash Disbursements Journal	
Deposits:		**Cheques:**	
7 Sept.	$ 4,600	1030	$ 11,000
11 Sept.	42,500	1031	24,650
14 Sept.	17,800	1032	24,780
22 Sept.	13,400	1033	75
25 Sept.	21,600	1034	8,165
30 Sept.	13,210	1035	7,900
30 Sept.	1,750	1036	40,420
	$114,860		$116,990

September information, per bank:

Opening balance: $151,570

Deposits:	Cheques:
$ 17,900	$ 1,570
4,600	890
42,500	175 (cheque of C&S Co.)*

17,800		90 (service charges)
5,750 (direct deposit by customer on account)	11,000	
	24,780	
13,400	120	
21,600	9,700**	
$123,550	24,650	
	$72,975	

*Charged to this account in error

**For automobile; incorrectly recorded as $7,900 by company.

Required:

1. Prepare a bank reconciliation, in good form, at the end of September.
2. Prepare any adjusting journal entries required as a result of the reconciliation.

★★ A7-28 Bank Reconciliation (Appendix):

Ample Company carries its chequing account with Commerce Bank. The company is ready to prepare its 31 December bank reconciliation. The following information is available:

a. The 30 November bank reconciliation showed the following:
   i. Cash on hand (held back each day by Ample for change), $400 (included in Ample's Cash account).
   ii. Deposit in transit, #51, $2,000.
   iii. Cheques outstanding, #121, $1,000; #130, $2,000; and #142, $3,000.

b. Ample Company's cash account for December:

Balance, 1 December	$ 64,000
Deposits: #52—#55, $186,500; #56, $3,500	190,000
Cheques: #143—#176, $191,000; #177, $2,500; #178, $3,000; and #179, $1,500	(198,000)
Balance, 31 December (includes $400 cash held for change)	$ 56,000

c. Bank statement, 31 December:

Balance, 1 December	$ 67,600
Deposits: #51—#55	188,500
Cheques: #130, $2,000; #142, $3,000; #143—#176, $191,000	(196,000)
Account receivable collected for Ample Co.	6,720

Cash received from foreign customer: prepayment on order; not yet recorded by Ample Co.	10,000
NSF cheque, Customer Belinda	(200)
United Fund (automatic charitable donation per transfer authorization signed by Ample Co.)	(50)
Bank service charges	(20)
Balance, 31 December	$ 76,550

Required:

1. Identify by number and dollars the 31 December deposits in transit and cheques outstanding.
2. Prepare the 31 December bank reconciliation.
3. Prepare all journal entries.

 connect

★ ★ A7-29 Bank Reconciliation (Appendix):

The general ledger of Michelle Company Ltd. showed a cash balance of $25,160 on 31 December 20X2, while the bank showed a balance of $59,400. The following facts were available:

a. The bank collected $11,560 as a direct deposit for one of Michelle's customer as a payment on account. A $15 fee was charged by the bank for administration. Michelle has yet to record either of these amounts.

b. Michelle paid a utilities bill of $390 through direct transfer from its bank account but has not yet recorded the payment.

c. There was an outstanding deposit of $16,800 at the end of December.

d. The bank had charged a cheque of $2,600, written by Mitchell Corp., to Michelle's bank account. The bank has been contacted about the error, and will reverse the cheque in January.

e. A deposit of $1,300 from a customer on account was recorded by Michelle for $3,100. The bank noticed the error and deposited the correct amount of money, but the deposit is incorrectly recorded on Michelle's books.

f. Michelle's bank account shows a deposit of $22,000 in December, which is an increase in Michelle's bank loan. The amount has not been recorded by Michelle.

g. At the end of November, outstanding cheques were $8,185. This month, cheques were issued for $199,000, and cheques of $184,900 cleared the bank account.

Required:

1. Prepare a bank reconciliation, in good form, at the end of December 20X2.
2. Prepare any adjusting journal entries required as a result of the reconciliation.

 **A7-30 Bank Reconciliation (Appendix):**

Various information for Helix Company in relation to the cash account:

General Ledger:	
Balance, 1 April	$16,420
Plus: cash receipts journal	45,700
Less: cash disbursements journal	(42,980)
Balance, 30 April	$ 19,140

Information from the journals:

Cash Receipts Journal		Cash Disbursements Journal	
Deposits:		**Cheques:**	
4 April	$ 2,100	670	$ 440
5 April	13,550	671	16,100
19 April	650	672	1,180
26 April	23,800	673	450
30 April	5,600	674	12,600
		675	7,900
		Service charges	265
		676	4,045
	$45,700		$42,980

The March bank reconciliation:

Balance per bank	$ 19,730
Plus: Outstanding deposits	500
Less: Outstanding cheques ($450, $1,670, $1,355, $335)	(3,810)
Cash, per general ledger	$16,420

April information, per bank:

Opening bank balance	$ 19,730
Deposits: $500, $2,100, $13,550, $10,000 (loan from bank), $5,500 (direct deposit from customer for cash sale) $650, $23,800	56,100
Cheques: ($1,180, $12,600, $265 (service charges), $1,355, $4,900 (direct payment to supplier on account), $1,200 (interest), $450 (March cheque), $1,560 (direct payment for insurance), $4,450 (recorded in error as $4,045 in books; to supplier on account)	(27,960)
Closing bank balance	$47,870

Required:

1. Prepare a bank reconciliation in good form at the end of April.
2. Prepare any adjusting journal entries required as a result of the reconciliation that should be made at 31 December, based on your bank reconciliation.

APPENDIX

BANK RECONCILIATION

The purpose of a bank reconciliation is to ensure that transactions in both the company's cash account and the bank's cash account have been recorded accurately. This involves comparing every deposit and cheque/charge in both accounts. Items that are different are reconciling amounts, which may lead to adjusting entries.

Review the information in Exhibit 7A-1 for North Company.

EXHIBIT 7A-1

NORTH COMPANY

Information for Bank Reconciliation

30 June 20X8

Bank Statement Summary:

Opening balance, 1 June	$23,000
Deposits (see below)	12,600
Cheques and charges (see below)	(11,740)
Service fees	(100)
Ending balance, 30 June	$23,760

Deposits		Cheques and Charges			
1 June	$ 2,000	2 June #61	$1,000	17 June #65	$ 150
8 June	3,000	7 June #63	2,000	23 June #60	1,100
17 June	4,500	9 June #66	3,000	27 June #67	2,300
18 June	1,000*	14 June #64	1,420	29 June	250**
22 June	2,100	15 JuneNSF***	520		
Total	$12,600				$11,740

*Customer Franklin paid his outstanding account receivable through a direct deposit to North's bank account.

**Direct payment for utilities processed by bank.

***NSF: Customer Treetoe's $500 cheque, deposited on 1 June, was returned NSF; there was a $20 bank fee.

Balance per Books: *transactions recorded in the cash account in the general ledger:*

Opening balance, 1 June	$23,900
Deposits (see below)	12,300
Cheques (see below)	(12,970)
Closing balance, 30 June	$23,230

Deposits and cheques:

	Deposits				**Cheques**		
June 8	$ 3,000	#60	$1,100	#65	$ 150
June 17	4,500	#61	1,000	#66	3,000
June 22	2,100	#62	900	#67	2,100*
June 30	2,700	#63	2,000	#68	1,300
	$12,300	#64	1,420		
					$12,970

*This cheque was actually for $2,300 and was to a supplier, on account.

The bank reconciliation at 31 May:

Bank balance	$ 23,000
Add: deposit outstanding	$2,000
Deduct: cheque outstanding (#59)	($1,100)
Book balance	$23,900

The bank statement reported an ending $23,760 balance, and the cash account reflects an ending $23,230 cash balance. These figures are reconciled to $23,160, as shown in Exhibit 7A-2. Here are the steps to follow:

Step 1   Compare all deposits made in the bank account with those in the books. If there are differences, determine why. If the bank has processed something that should be on the books, adjust the book balance. If the bank has made errors or if deposits are in transit, adjust the bank balance. If the company has made errors, adjust the balance per the books. A careful bank reconciliation includes a comparison of the dates of deposits—there should be no delays in getting money to the bank. Deposits in transit from the prior month should clear in the first few days of the next month, and this month's deposits in transit should relate only to the last day or two.

Step 2   Compare all cheques and charges that went through the bank account to the cash disbursements journal. All cheques and direct payments that the bank processed should be in the cash disbursements journal this month or have been outstanding last month. Bank fees must be recorded on the books. If the bank has made errors or cheques are still outstanding, adjust the bank balance. If the bank has processed something that should be on the books, adjust the book balance. If the company has made errors, adjust the balance per the books. Again, watch for irregularities; cheques are usually cashed after only a short delay.

Step 3   Make journal entries for all adjustments *to the book balance*. The company must also inform the bank of any errors made by the bank so that they can be corrected before the end of next month.

EXHIBIT 7A-2

NORTH COMPANY BANK RECONCILIATION

30 June 20X8

Bank statement		
Ending bank balance, 30 June		$23,760
Additions:		
Deposits in transit, 30 June	2,700	
Deductions:		
Cheques outstanding 30 June(#59, $1,100; #62, $900; #68, $1,300)	(3,300)	(600)
Adjusted balance		$23,160
Book balance		
Ending book balance, 30 June		$23,230
Additions:		
Accounts receivable collected by bank		1,000
Deductions:		
NSF cheque, Treetoe, $500, plus $20 NSF fee	(520)	
Bank service charges	(100)	
Utility payment	(250)	
Error in recording cheque	(200)	(1,070)
Adjusted balance		$23,160

Adjustments

Review the bank reconciliation in Exhibit 7A-2 in detail. Examine the deposits and then the cheques/charges. When they are not identical, either the bank balance or the book balance has to be adjusted.

a. *Deposits.* For North Company, compare (cross off) the list of deposits in the bank versus those on the books (or last month's reconciliation.) Each item should be in both places. Circle the items that are in one place *or* the other, but not both, *or* if the items are for different amounts. These are the reconciling items.

The first deposit in the bank was the outstanding deposit from last month (see last month's bank reconciliation at the bottom of Exhibit 7A-1.) It was recorded in the books last month and now has cleared so it needs no adjustment. There is a $1,000 deposit made by a customer directly to the bank account. This should be recorded by the company and is added to the balance per the books.

All other deposits are identical until the end of the month, when there is a deposit of $2,700 in the books that is not in the bank. This is an outstanding deposit, made too late to be reflected in the bank statement. It is added to the bank balance in Exhibit 7A-2.

b. *Cheques and charges.* Compare cheques cleared through the bank account with cheques recorded in the books and the cheques that were outstanding last month. For North Company, compare (cross off) the two lists. Circle the items that are in one place or the other or are for different amounts. These are the reconciling items.

Outstanding cheques at the end of June are, first, *the outstanding cheques from last month that have not yet been cashed* and, second, any cheques written this month that have not been cashed. There are three such cheques, and they are subtracted from the bank balance in the reconciliation.

There was an NSF cheque returned from a deposit; this amount has reduced North's bank balance but is not recorded on the books. There was a $100 bank service charge that reduced North's bank balance. There was a $250 utilities payment put through the bank account; this is a direct payment, presumably preauthorized by the company. All these items must be recorded on the books and are recorded as reconciliation deductions *on the book side.*

Finally, one cheque was recorded correctly by the bank and incorrectly by North. Since this was the company's error, it affects the book balance. There must be an additional $200 reduction on the book side.

There were no bank errors in this example, but if there were, the adjustment would be made to the *bank side* of the reconciliation. For example, if the bank charged a cheque of a different company to this account, or charged too much in service fees, the bank balance would be adjusted and the bank notified to correct its error.

Book and bank balances are now reconciled to the same value, $23,160.

Balancing

But what if the two amounts are *not* equal? What if it did not work? Then, the reconciler gets to do it again … and again … until it does work! The nightmare is that a $10 difference is really a $10,000 error in one direction and a $10,010 error in the other direction! So the bank reconciliation really is expected to "work." Here are a couple of techniques to help find common errors:

1. If a reconciling item is deducted when it should have been added (or vice versa), the unreconciled amount will be *double* the item. Therefore, try dividing the unreconciled amount by 2, then look for an item of that amount. That is, if $170 is the unreconciled amount, look for an $85 item that is added when it should be subtracted, or vice versa.

2. Transposition errors are *always* divisible by 9. For example, if $5,012 was written as $5,102, the unreconciled amount will be $90. If $5,012 was written as $5,210, the error will be $198, which also is divisible by 9.

Of course, if there are multiple errors, these suggestions will not help much. In practice, after things have been very carefully reviewed a few times to make sure there is no possibility of large counterbalancing errors, small differences are written off to miscellaneous expense.

Adjusting Entries

Each of the reconciliation items on the book side requires an adjusting journal entry to correct the cash balance. *There are no entries in North's books for items that are reconciling items to the bank balance.*

A. *Account receivable collected by bank.* An account receivable for $1,000 was collected by the bank but was not recorded by North. Usually, the bank informs the company immediately, but if the item has not been recorded by month-end, it shows up as a reconciling item and is recorded at that time.

Cash	1,000	
Accounts receivable		1,000

B. *Not sufficient funds (NSF) cheque.* The $500 cheque from customer Treetoe, which was not supported by sufficient funds in Treetoe's chequing account, was returned to North by the bank. North had deposited the cheque, increased cash, and decreased accounts receivable, but the bank was unable to get any money from Treetoe's account. Again, the company is usually informed immediately so that it can pursue its delinquent customer. However, if there are delays, or the NSF cheque occurs late in the month, it is a reconciling item and will be recorded at that time. Note that the company will try to recover the bank fee charged as well as the original receivable.

Accounts receivable, Treetoe	520	
Cash		520

Is this really a bad debt? Treetoe might be delinquent, but no company will give up after only one try—it will create a receivable when an NSF cheque is received. The receivable may end up as part of the amount included in the allowance for doubtful accounts.

C. *Bank service charges and direct payments.* The bank debited North's account for $100 of bank charges in June. There was also a payment for $250 of utilities, a direct charge to the bank account. North deducts these amounts from the cash account as reconciling items and records an entry:

Miscellaneous expense (or Bank service charge expense)	100	
Utilities expense	250	
Cash		350

D. *Error in recording.* North recorded a $2,300 cheque in the cash disbursements journal as $2,100, debiting accounts payable and crediting cash for *too little.* The book balance of cash and accounts payable is now overstated by $200 ($2,300 − $2,100). North corrects the recording error as a reconciling item and makes an entry.

Accounts payable	200	
Cash		200

This entry corrects the cash disbursement amount and reduces the payable. Correction entries of this kind always either debit or credit the cash account, and the other side of the entry is made to whatever the first cheque was charged to: in this case, accounts payable. It helps to reconstruct the original (incorrect) entry.

Bank Debit and Credit Memos

Deposits and withdrawals may take place that are initiated by the bank or others rather than by the company. These show up on the bank statement as debit and credit memos and include items such as interest earned, cash collected by the bank from customers, and service charges. For a bank, a depositor's cash balance is a liability, the amount the bank owes to the company. A bank **debit memo** describes a transaction from the bank's point of view—a decrease in liability to the account holder. Therefore, a debit memo reports the amount and nature of a *decrease* in the company's cash account. A **credit memo** indicates an *increase* in the cash account. Since this debit-credit memo terminology is derived from the bank's point of view, it seems backward to the debit and credit convention in the company's cash account. This tends to create a little confusion.

SUMMARY OF KEY POINTS

1. To prepare a bank reconciliation, deposits and cheques/charges are compared between the bank account and the cash account in the general ledger. Where there are differences, there are reconciliation items.
2. Common adjustments to the bank balance in a bank reconciliation are outstanding cheques, outstanding deposits, and bank errors.
3. Common adjustments to the books in a bank reconciliation are deposits recorded by the bank but not yet in the books, charges recorded by the bank but not yet in the books, and recording errors made in the books.
4. Adjusting journal entries are prepared for the adjustments in a bank reconciliation that affect the books.

Source: (Globe and money) © Vstock LLC/Getty Images RF; (Skyscrapers) © Arpad Benedek/Getty Images RF; (Canadian flag) © BjArn Kindler/Getty Images RF; (Tablet, pen, keyboard) © John Lamb/Getty Images RF.

CHAPTER 8

Cost-based Inventories and Cost of Sales

INTRODUCTION

Inventories often represent the largest single current asset of manufacturing, wholesale, and retail companies. Inventory valuation simultaneously affects measurement of cost of sales (COS) and earnings. In today's competitive economic climate, inventory accounting methods and management practices are profit-enhancing tools. Enhanced inventory systems can increase profitability; poorly conceived systems can drain profits and put businesses at a competitive disadvantage.

Magna International Inc. is a global automotive supplier, with over 300 manufacturing operations and sales centres in 28 countries. In 2014, the company had $18.1 billion in assets, including $2.8 billion in inventory. However, cost of sales was many times this number, at $31.6 billion. This is indicative of the quick production cycle and efficient operations that have made Magna a global leader.

Good inventory and profit control depends on up-to-date, efficient, and reliable inventory accounting systems. Because of the volume of inventory transactions, and the subjective decisions involved, special care must be taken to avoid misstatement. No matter how sophisticated a company's electronic inventory systems may be, physical inventory still must be counted. Between counts, inventory amounts often are *estimated* for special reporting purposes, such as monthly or quarterly statements, or to test for possible "missing" inventory.

This chapter covers the accounting methods used to value and report inventories on the statement of financial position. Toward the end of this chapter, we will explain the two estimation methods: gross profit method and retail method. The topics of cost flow and perpetual inventory—discussed in introductory accounting textbooks—are included in the Appendix to this chapter, in case you need to refresh your memory.

Bases of Inventory Valuation

Recall from Chapter 6 that inventory is a **contract asset**. It has value because it will be sold to a customer.

Exhibit 8-1 shows the various classifications of inventory. For accounting purposes, there are two important bases for inventory valuation:

- Historical cost, subject to lower-of-cost-or-NRV (net realizable value) valuation; and
- Market value, either NRV or fair market value, depending on the type of inventory.

This chapter focuses on cost-based inventories.

EXHIBIT 8-1
TYPES OF INVENTORY

Inventories Based on Historical Cost

Classification	Measurement Basis
Right to recovery asset	Laid-down cost, net of rebates* (see Chapter 6)
Retail & wholesale	
Goods available for sale	Laid-down cost, net of rebates*
Manufacturing	
Raw materials	Laid-down cost, net of rebates†
Work-in-progress	Accumulated direct labour and materials costs + allocated manufacturing overhead to date†
Finished goods	Total accumulated direct labour and materials costs + allocated manufacturing overhead†
Supplies	Laid-down cost, net of rebates*
Long-term service contracts	
Work in progress	Direct labour and other direct costs + recoverable costs plus profits, if percentage of completion applies (see Chapter 6)§
Long-term contracts—construction	
Construction in progress	Total material, labour, and overhead cost to date§ plus profits, if percentage of completion is applied (see Chapter 6)

Inventories Based on Market Value

Classification	Measurement Basis
Biological assets related to agricultural activity and agriculture produce at point of harvest	NRV (see Chapter 6)
Agriculture and forest products, agricultural produce after harvest, and minerals at the point of extraction, if sale is assured	NRV when widely used in the industry; otherwise, the lower of cost or NRV (see Chapter 6)
Financial instruments held as inventory for trading (e.g., by	Fair market value minus cost to sell (see Chapter 7)

securities dealers or financial
institutions)

*Subject to lower-of-cost-or-NRV valuation.

†Subject to NRV valuation based on the selling price of finished goods.

§Subject to NRV valuation based on the finished contract price.

RIGHT TO RECOVERY ASSETS

In Chapter 6, we learned that, if a company sells a product that can be returned, a **right to recovery asset** is established. For example, special sales agreements exist in some industries that permit goods to be returned if not sold; this is common for sporting goods manufacturers and book publishers. The right to recovery asset is limited to the portion of a given shipment that is estimated to be returned. If returns are not estimable, the entire quantity is a right to recovery asset on the books of the vendor. Revenue recognition is delayed, in this case.

This is not inventory in the traditional sense, because the goods have been transferred to the customer. However, the right to recovery asset is an asset on the books of the vendor until the return window closes. The right to recovery asset is valued at cost or NRV, if NRV is lower than cost.

COST-BASED INVENTORIES

General Nature of Inventory

We typically think of inventories as tangible goods and materials, such as raw materials, work-in-process, finished goods, or merchandise held by retailers. Once the earnings process is complete, inventory is moved from asset to expense and is expensed in the same period as revenue is recognized. Depending on the nature of the company's business, inventory may include a wide range of costs incurred and held in an inventory account.

For example, a professional services firm, such as a software development company or a law firm, may accumulate the labour costs, and other expenditures, related to fulfilling a particular contract as "inventory" until the contract has been substantially completed and the criteria for revenue recognition have been met.

Items that may be fixed assets for one company may be inventory for another. Machinery, for example, is inventory for the manufacturer. Machinery becomes a fixed asset for the company that buys and uses the machinery. Even a building, during its construction period, may be an inventory item for the builder.

Cost-based Inventory Policy Issues

Since COS is often the largest single expense in measuring profit or loss, and since inventory is an integral part of current and total assets, accounting policies in this area can cause earnings and net assets to change significantly. There are four basic policy issues:

1. Items and costs to include in inventory;
2. Choice of accounting procedure: periodic versus perpetual systems;
3. Cost flow assumptions for measuring COS; and
4. Application of lower-of-cost-or-NRV valuations.

Strictly speaking, the choice of periodic or perpetual systems is a *procedural* choice rather than a *policy* choice, but the choice can affect financial reporting and thus should be viewed as an accounting policy choice.

This chapter focuses on the first two issues. Introductory accounting textbooks discuss **cost flow assumptions** and **periodic inventory systems** versus **perpetual inventory systems** quite extensively. Therefore, we have relegated these two topics to the Appendix of this chapter. If you need to refresh your knowledge, refer to the Appendix.

Items to Include in Inventory

Inventory includes all goods that are *both*:

1. Controlled by the company, regardless of their physical location; and
2. Intended for resale or use within the company.

These are not trivial requirements—at any time, a business may hold goods that it does not own, or it may own goods that it does not hold. Therefore, care must be taken to identify the goods that should be included in inventory.

Transfer of Control

Recall from Chapter 6 that the vendor (supplier, in our context) recognizes revenue when there has been a transfer of control, whether at one point in time or over time. We now consider the transaction from the customer's side—when the purchaser has control, the purchaser recognizes the inventory as an asset. Indications of control include:

1. The vendor's right to payment; and
2. The purchaser's legal title, physical possession, assumption of the significant risks and rewards of ownership, and the purchaser's acceptance of the asset.

Goods *purchased and in transit* are included in the purchaser's inventory if control has passed to the purchaser. Control, including passage of title, depends on the terms of the shipping contract. In some cases, title automatically transfers to the purchaser when the goods are given to the carrier (e.g., a trucking or railroad company). This is sometimes described as FOB (free on board) *shipping point*. In other cases, the seller has title until the carrier delivers the goods to the final customer. This is sometimes described as FOB *destination*. For international transactions, additional shipping arrangements include CIF (shipper bears responsibility for "Customs, Insurance, and Freight") and DPD (shipper is responsible for "Duty Paid and Delivered").

There are at least a dozen common shipping arrangements, so contracts must be carefully scrutinized to establish the point at which control is transferred from the vendor to the purchaser.

Goods that are owned by a company but are out on **consignment** (i.e., held by agents) should be included in inventory. Control has not passed, even though the goods are physically not with the company/vendor.

Goods that are sold to a customer, but subject to a **repurchase agreement**, are a right to recovery asset for the company/vendor. A repurchase agreement is a *form of return rights*. A repurchase agreement formally sets out the vendor's arrangement to sell to a customer, but buy back inventory items at a prearranged price if they are not resold by a certain date. The buyer usually pays all or most of the invoice cost of such inventory when the goods are delivered. If the goods are not sold, the vendor repurchases them. Control has not passed, because the risks of ownership remain with the vendor.

Legal ownership is a useful starting point to identify items that should be included in inventory; a strict legal determination of ownership does not automatically mean that those items should be included. The sales agreement, industry practices, and other evidence of intent should be considered.

Exclusions

Goods that are on hand must be *excluded* from inventory if they:

1. Are held for sale on commission or on consignment but owned by someone else, or
2. Have been received from a supplier but rejected and are awaiting return to the supplier for credit, or
3. Have been received from a supplier but are subject to a repurchase agreement with the supplier. *This is a right to recovery asset of the supplier, not inventory of the purchaser.*

Elements of Inventory Cost

The basic principle for measuring inventory cost is that the cost of inventories should include *all costs incurred to bring the inventories to their present location and condition*. The cost should be net of any discounts, rebates, or other concessions that effectively reduce the cost.

Raw Materials and Goods Purchased for Resale

In general, inventory cost is measured by the total cash equivalent outlay made to acquire the materials or goods. For goods intended for resale, the cost to prepare them for sale is also included. These costs include materials purchase cost and incidental costs incurred until the goods are ready for sale to the customer. Cost includes "freight-in" and other shipping costs incurred by the buyer, as well as customs charges and excise duties. The total of these costs is known as the **laid-down cost**. Sales taxes may or may not be included; as explained in the following section.

When freight charges and other incidental costs incurred in connection with the purchase of tangible inventory are part of laid-down cost, they should be attributed to the specific goods to which they pertain. However, specific identification often is impractical. For example, an individual supplier may ship many different types of inventory in a single shipment. Therefore, freight costs are commonly recorded in a special account, such as freight-in, which is allocated and added to inventory and to cost of goods sold for reporting purposes.

Certain other incidental costs often are not included in inventory valuation but are reported as separate expenses, even though they theoretically are a cost of goods purchased. Examples include insurance costs on goods in transit, material handling expenses, and import brokerage fees. These expenditures are usually not included in determining inventory costs because the cost of allocating them to specific purchased goods is not worth the benefit.

Storage, warehousing, and distribution costs are *not* normally included as an element of inventory cost. Although those costs are a necessary cost of inventory handling, they are treated as period costs and charged to expense when incurred. An exception arises when storage is a necessary part of the production process before further production or processing. Examples would be the storage costs for aging wine prior to its bottling, or holding cheese for maturation prior to packaging.

Companies in some industries regularly offer **cash discounts** on purchases to encourage timely payment from buyers. The intent is to speed cash inflow. Terms of 2/10, n/30, for example, means that if the invoice is paid within 10 days, a discount of 2% can be taken. Alternatively, the full balance, *n*, is due in 30 days. Most buyers make timely payments and take advantage of cash discounts because the savings are normally quite substantial.

Inventory must be recorded at the lowest available cash price, which is 98% of the invoice price in this example. *Lost discounts are a cost of financing and should not be included in inventory amounts.*

General, selling, and administrative (GS&A) expenses are never included as an element of inventory cost. GS&A costs are not directly related to the acquisition of inventory.

"Sales" Taxes

Two types of taxes that often are assessed on transactions are *sales tax* and *value-added tax*. There is an important difference that has an effect on how inventory cost is recorded:

- A merchant adds the amount of a **sales tax** to the price of goods thereby creating a liability for the seller because the tax must be remitted to the government. The buyer must absorb the full cost of the tax and it is part of inventory cost.
- A merchant adds the amount of a **value-added tax** (**VAT**) to the price of all goods sold regardless of the nature of the purchaser. The VAT collected creates a liability for the vendor. However, the purchaser also charges VAT on their goods sold. Only the net VAT is paid to the government. In other words, everyone along the entire supply chain is liable only for the net difference between the amount collected on sales and the amount paid on purchases. If more is paid on purchases than collected from sales, the company will receive a refund from the government. Only the final consumer bears the full amount of the tax.

In Canada, we have both types of taxes. There is a sales tax in some provinces, which is a **provincial sales tax** (**PST**) There is also a value-added tax, which is the federal **goods and services tax** (**GST**) in all provinces and territories. Several provinces have combined their PST with the federal GST to end up with a **harmonized sales tax** (**HST**). The HST is a value-added tax.

Our treatment of taxes paid on purchases depends on the type of tax:

- Sales taxes are not refundable and therefore are considered part of the laid-down cost for inventory.
- VAT (GST or HST) is not included in the cost of inventory because it is refundable. Instead it is debited to a "taxes payable" account to offset the VAT collected on sales revenue

Accounting for sales tax is covered in more detail in Chapter 12.

Borrowing Costs

Borrowing costs include interest paid, but also an allocation of initial costs to issue a loan contract and an allocation of any interest rate adjustment, such as a premium or discount. Borrowing costs are usually a period cost (an expense). However, any borrowing cost that is *directly attributable to the acquisition, construction, or production of a qualifying asset* forms part of the cost of that asset and must be capitalized. Qualifying assets are nonfinancial assets such as inventories, intangible assets, machinery, and office or manufacturing facilities.

Borrowing costs are to be capitalized if the inventory takes a substantial time to get ready for sale. There must be a time delay for construction, customization or shipping; borrowing costs related to this delay period qualify for capitalization. For example, if goods are purchased and the shipping time is lengthy, then borrowing costs must be capitalized for the shipping period. Inventory that is manufactured over a short period of time is not eligible for borrowing cost capitalization. Also, if goods are ready for resale when acquired, no borrowing costs can be capitalized. However, if goods are purchased and the shipping time is lengthy, then borrowing costs must be capitalized for the shipping period.

Borrowing costs need not be capitalized on inventory if the inventory is carried at fair value (biological inventories, for example), or if borrowing costs relate to inventories that are *manufactured in large quantities on a regular basis*. For these two cases, companies may choose whether to capitalize or not, depending on their reporting objectives and circumstances.

We return to the calculations associated with this accounting standard in Chapter 13.

Long-Term Service and Construction Contracts

A service company such as a law firm or a consulting company does not have physical inventory available for sale. Aside from some inventory of *supplies*, service inventory consists exclusively of **work-in-progress**, which is the accumulated cost of contract work performed to date. Construction contracts, as well, involve work-in-progress, which is the accumulated cost of a partially completed project.

There are two elements of cost:

- *Fulfillment costs.* These are the direct material costs associated with the project. Fulfillment costs also include the direct labour, or the costs of personnel who are directly engaged in providing the service, or building the asset, and also directly attributable allocated supervisory costs. Direct costs also include any material or equipment (e.g., special computer equipment or software) that is necessary to complete a particular contract. In fact, any cost that is recoverable from the customer falls into this category. Accordingly, if manufacturing overhead is directly recoverable, it is also included as a fulfillment cost.

- *Obtainment costs.* Obtainment costs are incremental costs incurred to obtain a customer contract, as, for example, a sales commission paid upfront. Obtainment costs also include costs that are explicitly chargeable to the customer, even if the contract is not obtained. In practical terms, if the customer contract is for less than 12 months, obtainment costs can be expensed.

The approaches for recognizing revenue from long-term contracts were explained in Chapter 6. *If percentage of completion method is used, the inventory amount includes the profit recognized to date.*

Inventory does not include general or administrative costs. General and administrative costs are recognized as period costs (expenses) when incurred.

Manufactured Goods

A manufacturing or producing company will normally have three types of inventory:

- *Raw materials*—the laid-down cost of raw materials and purchased small parts that will be used in production;
- *Work in progress*—the costs incurred on goods that are in production, but not yet finished; work in progress includes raw materials, direct labour, and an allocation of production overhead; and
- *Finished goods*—the cost of goods manufactured and ready for sale, including raw materials, direct labour, and allocated production overhead.

Production overhead should be allocated on the basis of *normal capacity*. **Normal capacity** is the operating level at which the factory is expected to operate most of the time, not full capacity, maximum capacity, or an abnormally low volume. You will study cost allocation systems in cost accounting courses, but the significant point for financial accounting is that the cost of inventory should *not* absorb all of the manufacturing costs if the manufacturing plant is operating below normal capacity. The costs of idle capacity are expensed as a period cost.

Standard costs may be used for inventory costing purposes, provided that the standards are based on normal capacity and are regularly reviewed and revised to ensure they are not materially different from actual cost.

Supplies Inventory

In addition to the inventory types described above, most companies also have an inventory of supplies. *Supplies* are items that are used in the productive activities of the company but that are either (1) used during production (e.g., lubricant for machinery) or (2) too small to try to keep track of individually, even though they may enter the product directly (e.g., adhesives, bolts, rivets, and small spare parts). Supplies inventories often are immaterial, and may be included in raw materials inventory.

Example

Consider the following example, and the analysis in the right column.

IAL Ltd. is finalizing its year-end inventory balance, and has collected the following information in the first two columns. What amounts are included in inventory?

Description	Inventory Value	Analysis
a. Goods counted in the physical inventory, including $4,100 in HST and $1,500 in import brokerage fees.	$36,000	$31,900 ($36,000 – $4,100) included as inventory; HST is refundable and not an element of inventory cost.
b. Gross invoice cost of goods received and included in inventory count but not yet paid for; IAL can deduct a 2% discount if the invoice is paid within 30 days of year-end.	6,000	$5,880 ($6,000 × .98) included as inventory; cost is determined after all available discounts.
c. Warehousing cost for inventory.	2,000	This is an expense, not a component of inventory cost.
d. Goods shipped to, and received by, a wholesale distributor; the distributor has the right to return up to 33% of the goods if they are not sold within three months; not included in inventory count.	9,000	This has been shipped and received; it is no longer in inventory. A right to recovery asset for at most $3,000 ($9,000 × 33%) should be set up; if past return history is consistent, a lower number might be justified.
e. Items included in inventory count that were in transit at year-end; they arrived from the supplier five days after the year-end and had been shipped FOB destination, where control transfers when the good arrive.	3,000	Not in inventory—the company does not have control at year-end.
f. Cost of goods on consignment to Big Box Inc. (including $2,000 commission that will be due to IAL if and when Big Box sells the goods).	10,000	Goods on consignment are controlled by the vendor, and must be included in inventory. The amount to include in inventory is $8,000 ($10,000 – $2,000), or cost.

g. Inventory that has been received by IAL and inspected but is being returned because of defects.	14,000	Excluded from inventory because the goods are being returned to the supplier.

Periodic or Perpetual Recording Method

Inventory cost may be measured by either a periodic inventory system or a perpetual inventory system. The essential difference between these two systems from an accounting point of view is the *frequency with which the cost flows are calculated*.

In a *periodic* system, the inventory is physically counted at least once each year and then the total inventory cost is calculated from cost records using the chosen cost flow policy (e.g., FIFO or weighted average cost).

In a *perpetual* system, inventory cost and COS is continuously updated for each purchase and sale. After each change in inventory quantities, the total cost of inventory and COS is recalculated, using the chosen cost flow policy.

Note that for accounting purposes, a perpetual system exists only when the total inventory cost is continually updated. In contrast, some companies use a perpetual system for *quantities only*, which often are linked to an automated purchasing system. The dollar cost is calculated only at the end of each accounting period. These quantity-only systems are not perpetual systems as far as accounting and financial reporting is concerned.

The Appendix to this chapter contains a more extensive discussion of this topic.

Cost Flow Assumptions

There are three cost flow assumptions that are acceptable for external reporting:

1. **Specific identification**;
2. **First-in, first-out (FIFO)**;
3. **Weighted average cost**.

Another cost flow assumption is **last-in, first-out (LIFO)**, but LIFO is not acceptable under IFRS.

The specific identification and FIFO methods are not affected by the decision to use periodic or perpetual inventory systems—the cost allocated to inventory and COS will be the same under each method. In contrast, average cost *is* affected by the inventory system. The Appendix to this chapter illustrates the details.

Specific identification is used only when inventory items are not ordinarily interchangeable. Specific identification is usually applied to special-order inventory items that are significantly unlike other items.

The most common inventory cost flow assumptions are (1) FIFO and (2) weighted average cost. Companies have leeway to pick the cost flow assumption that fits their circumstances.

CONCEPT REVIEW

1. Identify the accounting policy issues to be decided when accounting for inventory.
2. What are the three elements of cost that should be included in a manufacturer's finished-goods inventory cost?
3. What are obtainment costs versus fulfillment costs?

APPLYING LOWER-OF-COST-OR-NRV VALUATION

Most inventories are valued at the lower of *laid-down cost* or **net realizable value** (**NRV**). This test most often results in writedown when inventory is damaged or becomes obsolete, or when sales prices decline. If there is a recovery in a subsequent period for some reason, a writedown can be reversed.

Estimating Net Realizable Value

NRV is the estimated selling price in the normal course of business, minus (1) estimated costs of completion (if any) and (2) the estimated selling costs. For finished goods, there will be no costs of completion but there may be sales commissions or brokerage fees, and there may be special concessions (such as free shipping) that are necessary to close the sale. These costs must be subtracted from the year-end selling price to find NRV.

For example, suppose a retailer has an inventory consisting of a single line of office electronics products, all purchased during 20X2 at a cost of $150 per unit. The retail price was $200 at the time of acquisition. Late in the year, stiff competition in the electronics and office products market causes retail prices to drop significantly. At year-end, the retailer's remaining inventory can be sold in the normal course of business for no more than $160 per unit.

The year-end retail price of $160 is above the original unit cost of $150, but what is the NRV of the unit? To determine the NRV, the retailer must subtract any direct costs of making the sale. If the retailer pays a 15% commission to the salesperson, the $24 sales commission must be subtracted from the $160 sales price. The NRV is $160 − $24 = $136. The carrying value of the inventory must be written down from its historical cost of $150 to its NRV of $136, a loss of $14 per unit. This $14-per-unit loss must be reported in the retailer's 20X2 financial statements, the period during which the market price decline took place.

For work-in-process, NRV must incorporate the cost of completing the product or project, as well as any further costs to sell (e.g., commissions).

Raw materials and work-in-process inventories seldom are written down. That is because these inventories will be used in the production of finished goods. The recoverable cost of these items depends on the sales price of the finished good, not of the inventory item itself. If the final selling price is stable, the inventory item's cost may be fully recoverable and thus should not be written down. However, a writedown is required if any items of raw materials become obsolete and therefore will not be used or will not be used in the manner originally intended.

The determination of NRV is fairly straightforward in concept, but its application requires estimating (1) sales value (which can be difficult in a rapidly changing market) (2) costs of completion and sale, and (3) current or potential obsolescence.

Exceptions to Writedowns

There are two situations in which a writedown to lower of cost or NRV may not occur:

1. The amount of writedown does not necessarily depend on an inventory item's NRV at the reporting date. A writedown is always determined *after* the reporting date, when the financial statements are being prepared. A company takes a broader look at the cost/price situation around the reporting date. If it appears that the low NRV was a year-end anomaly and prices recovered thereafter, management may decide that it is not appropriate to write the inventory down.

2. The NRV is *not* the amount that could be obtained by selling the inventory to another party to dispose of (e.g., to a clearance house) unless such a sell-off is foreseen at the date on which the financial statements are finalized. The sales price of any item is the estimated selling price in the normal course of business. This principle is known as the *best and highest use* of the asset.

Aggregation

Normally, the lower-of-cost-or-NRV test is applied item-by-item. However, in some circumstances, it is acceptable to group related asset types and apply the NRV test for the group as a whole.

Aggregation is appropriate in limited circumstances. An example would be items of inventory relating to the same product line that have a similar purpose or end use, are produced and marketed in the same geographic region, and, on a practical level, cannot be evaluated separately. It is not appropriate to arbitrarily group all finished goods together, or all the inventories in a particular operating segment.

Exhibit 8-2 shows the application of each approach. Inventory is valued at $67,500, a loss of $3,500, if the individual approach is used. If valued in groups, inventory is reported at $69,000, a loss of $2,000.

EXHIBIT 8-2				
APPLICATION OF LOWER-OF-COST-OR-NRV VALUATION TO INVENTORY ITEMS OR GROUPS				
			Lower of Cost or NRV Applied to:	
Inventory Types	**Cost**	**NRV**	**Individual Items**	**Groups**
Group A:				
Item 1	$10,000	$ 9,500	$ 9,500	
Item 2	8,000	9,000	8,000	
	18,000	18,500		$ 18,000
Group B:				
Item 3	21,000	22,000	21,000	
Item 4	32,000	29,000	29,000	
	53,000	51,000		51,000
Total	$71,000	$69,500		
Inventory valuation under different approaches			$67,500	$69,000
Loss recorded				
($71,000 less $67,500 or $69,000)			$ 3,500	$ 2,000

The item-by-item basis produces the most conservative inventory value because units whose NRV exceeds cost are not allowed to offset items whose NRV is less than cost. This offsetting occurs to some extent when inventory is valued in groups. The more you aggregate, the less you write down.

The products in a single product line can be grouped together because they represent a "product" in the broad sense of a range of related products. For example, grouping would be appropriate if some products are sold at a loss to support the sales of products that are highly profitable.

Reversing Writedowns

What happens if the NRV goes back up after inventory has been written down? Prices may rise due to the failure of a major competitor, a shortage of supply, a change in the economic outlook, or many other reasons.

Suppose that an item of inventory is written down from $150 historical cost to $136 NRV in 20X2. In 20X3 the estimated $160 sales price goes up to $180. Sales commission remains at 15%, which is $27 on a sales price of $180. NRV has increased to $153: $180 − $27. The increase in NRV is $17 per unit (i.e., $153 − $136), but the reversal is limited to the amount of the original writedown, which was $14 per item. *Cost-based inventory cannot be written up above its historical cost.*

The writedown should be reversed by $14 for those items still in inventory, thereby restoring the unit inventory carrying value to $150.

In practice, reversals seldom occur. The normal expectation is that inventory will turn over within a year, and usually several times during a year. It is unlikely that written-down inventory will still be on the books a year later. If the inventory still is in stock, it probably will merit an additional writedown rather than a reversal due to obsolescence or due to inability to sell in the marketplace. Reversals are more likely to occur for shorter reporting periods, such as monthly or quarterly reporting.

Recording Writedowns—Using a Valuation Allowance

There are two methods of recording writedowns:

1. *Direct inventory reduction method.* The carrying value of individual inventory items is adjusted in the inventory accounts by the amount of any writedown. After adjustment, the inventory carrying values will show the NRV as the new carrying value. This method is possible only when NRV is applied to individual items.

2. *Inventory allowance method.* The writedown is not entered into the inventory accounts but is recorded separately in a contra inventory account, *allowance to reduce inventory to NRV*. The inventory remains at historical cost on the books but is reported on the SFP net of the valuation account. Assume that the company illustrated in Exhibit 8-2 had an existing allowance of $2,500 and decided to apply NRV by individual items. The entry would be as follows:

Holding loss on inventory	1,000	
Allowance to reduce inventory to NRV ($2,500 – $3,500)		1,000

In both methods, the amount of the writedown (and any reversal) is reported in earnings and included in a disclosure note; it must not be hidden in COS as once was common.

The direct reduction method is practical only if NRV has been applied item by item. Only then can individual inventory items be written down in the subsidiary records. If NRV has been applied to inventory groups, it is impossible to record the writedown to specific inventory items.

The valuation allowance method *must* be used when NRV is applied to groupings so that the detailed subsidiary inventory records will correspond with the balance in the inventory control account in the general ledger. However, the valuation allowance method is not limited to group writedowns; it may also be used when item-by-item lower of cost or NRV is applied.

A significant advantage to using a valuation allowance is that reversals can be handled very easily. If NRV rises after an initial writedown, only the allowance is adjusted; the inventory accounts themselves are not touched. In practice, the allowance method is the most common approach.

ETHICAL ISSUES

NRV valuations require estimations. Both the current selling price and the costs to complete and sell must be determined. In a stable market, these estimates may be straight-forward. In a volatile market, both estimates may require quite a lot of judgement.

The difficulty of estimating NRV allows room for income manipulation, especially if inventories are substantial. Inventory can be written down in one year and sold at a substantial profit in a later year. Sometimes this happens with no intent to mislead if weak market conditions and poor selling prices dictate writedowns. A subsequent price recovery may be unexpected.

In other cases, unethical decisions may drive high write-offs in a "big bath" scenario. Managers who receive bonuses based on earnings may be particularly motivated if earnings in the writedown year are below the level needed to trigger a bonus. In businesses with a thin profit margin, relatively small estimation errors can have a significant impact on reported earnings.

CONCEPT REVIEW

1. What is the definition of NRV?

2. In what situations can different items of inventory be aggregated and evaluated on the basis of lower of cost or NRV for the group as a whole?

3. What are the reasons for using a valuation allowance for inventory writedowns rather than using the direct inventory reduction method?

OTHER ISSUES FOR COST-BASED INVENTORIES

Damaged and Obsolete Inventory

While a NRV test will incorporate items that are damaged, shopworn, obsolete, or defective, it makes some sense to isolate these items in a separate inventory category, valued at NRV. This inventory is usually managed on a different basis than regular inventory, and account segregation assists reporting. This approach can also be used for trade-ins, or repossessed inventory.

To illustrate accounting for damaged inventory, assume that Allied Corp. suffers fire damage to 100 units of its regular inventory. The items, which originally cost $10 per unit (as reflected in the perpetual inventory records), were marked to sell before the fire for $18 per unit. No established "used or damaged" market exists. The company should value the item for inventory purposes at its NRV. Allied estimates that after cleaning and making repairs, the items would sell for $7 per unit; the estimated cost of the repairs for all the units is $150, and the estimated selling cost is 20% of the new selling price. Given these data, the total inventory valuation for the items is as follows:

Estimated sale price (100 × $7)		$700
Less: Estimated cost to repair	$150	
Estimated selling costs ($700 × 20%)	140	(290)
NRV for inventory		$ 410

Damaged inventory is segregated in a separate account as part of the writedown entry:

Inventory, damaged goods	410	
Loss from fire damage	590	
Inventory (100 × $10)		1,000

Onerous Contracts

To lock in prices and ensure sufficient quantities, companies often contract with suppliers to purchase a specified quantity of materials during a future period at an agreed unit cost. Some purchase commitments (contracts) are subject to revision or cancellation before the end of the contract period; others are not. Each case requires different accounting and reporting procedures. A loss must be accrued on a purchase contract when it is an **onerous contract**, and commits the company to a loss situation. The following criteria must be met for a loss and provision to be recorded:

- The purchase contract is not subject to revision or cancellation, *and*
- A loss is both likely and material, *and*
- The loss can be reasonably estimated.

Assume that the Bayshore Ltd. enters into a noncancellable purchase contract during October 20X2 that states, "During 20X3, 50,000 tanks of compressed chlorine will be purchased at $5 each," a total commitment of $250,000. At the end of 20X2 the current replacement cost of the chlorine is $240,000. Thus, a $10,000 loss is likely.

At the end of 20X2, the loss on the purchase commitment would be recorded as a loss and a **provision**, or estimated liability, as follows:

Estimated loss on onerous purchase commitment ($250,000 – $240,000)	10,000	
Provision for onerous purchase commitment		10,000

The estimated loss is reported in the profit and loss section of the 20X2 statement of comprehensive income, and the provision is a liability that is reported on the SFP. When the goods are acquired in 20X3, merchandise inventory (or purchases) is debited at the current replacement cost, and the provision account is debited. If, at the date of delivery, the replacement cost goes down further, to $235,000, the purchase entry would be as follows:

Materials inventory (or purchases)	235,000	
Provision for onerous purchase commitment	10,000	
Loss on onerous purchase commitment	5,000	
Cash		250,000

This treatment records the loss in the period when it became *likely*—$10,000 in 20X2 and an additional $5,000 in 20X3. Note that inventory is never recorded for more than its replacement cost at the date of acquisition, $235,000 in this example.

If there were a full or partial recovery of the purchase price, the recovery would be recognized in the period during which the recovery took place. Thus, if in 20X3 the materials had a replacement cost at date of delivery of $255,000, the purchase entry would be as follows:

Materials inventory (or purchases)	250,000	
Provision for onerous purchase commitment	10,000	
Recovery of loss on onerous purchase commitment		10,000
Cash		250,000

The loss recovery is reported in earnings.

Review the three criteria for accounting loss recognition listed above.

- What if the contract were cancellable? Then the loss is no longer likely, and the amount would not be accrued.
- What if the loss were not estimable? Recognition criteria are not met, and again no entry can be made.
- What if commodity prices are going up, not down? Then a loss is not likely, and no entry is appropriate.

Remember, gains never are recognized, although loss recoveries are. Disclosure of the contracts and terms is appropriate when the contracts are significant, or out of the ordinary, or when a loss is present that cannot be reasonably estimated.

Inventory Errors

In our discussion so far, we have focused mainly on the relationship between inventory and COS. Obviously, we will not get the correct COS if inventory calculations are incorrect.

But inventory interacts with more than just COS. Incoming inventory relates directly to accounts payable and purchases, while outgoing inventory relates directly to accounts receivable and revenue. Because of the sheer volume of transactions involving inventory, it takes special vigilance to avoid errors.

There may be some estimation errors in inventory, especially in lower-of-cost-or-market estimates, in work-in-process inventories relating to long-term contracts, or in estimation techniques, such as the retail inventory method (which we will discuss shortly). However, estimates are a fact of life in accounting. They may turn out to be wrong, *but they are not errors*—we just do the best we can with the information that we have at the time we exercise our professional judgement.

Other errors are errors of fact.

Cut-off Errors

A primary type of error is **cut-off errors**. "Cut-off" refers to the year-end closing of the books. When we reach the end of a fiscal period, we must draw a line between transactions at (1) the period just ending and (2) the start of the next period. In theory, this is a simple exercise. In practice, accurate cut-offs are both crucial and difficult.

Assuring proper cut-off is a major accounting (and auditing) control issue due to the high volume of activity and the need to coordinate all of the accounting activities that involve inventory. Think about a factory. New inventory is delivered almost continuously during every day, and finished goods are shipped to customers all day long. If the factory operates 24 hours a day, when do we stop counting for last year and start counting for next year? Consistency is crucial. If we say that the year-end inventory is the amount in our factories, warehouses, and offices at midnight on 31 December, we must use that same cut-off time each year and for each type of inventory. The physical count of inventory must be taken *as of* that specific time, even though inventory is flowing in and out of the factory while the physical count is taking place over the following days.

Counting inventory is only part of the problem. We must be sure that goods shipped on the closing days of the year have also been invoiced to the customers—revenue and accounts receivable must include last-minute shipments. Similarly, we must ensure that revenue has not been recorded for shipments that will not be made until the early days of the next year.

We also must ensure that no invoices were invoiced to customers prior to shipment of the goods. Unethical managers may be tempted to delay or accelerate shipments around year-end to manipulate earnings.

Counting Errors

Sometimes, inventory is simply miscounted. Parts of an inventory tally may go missing, or a storage area or facility (e.g., a small warehouse in a foreign country) may be overlooked when the physical inventory count is taken. Correcting this type of error is fairly straightforward.

Suppose that a company discovers in 20X7 that its 20X6 year-end inventory was overstated by $750,000. The error is discovered after its 20X6 financial statements were issued. An overstatement of ending inventory leads to an (1) understatement of COS, (2) overstatement of earnings, and (3) overstatement of retained earnings. Therefore, the correction in 20X7 will be recorded as follows:

Retained earnings	750,000	
Inventory (1 January 20X7)		750,000

When the 20X7 financial statements are prepared, the comparative 20X6 financial statements must be restated to show the correct inventory and earnings amounts. Errors are always corrected by restatement and never by showing special charges or credits in the SCI.

Self-correcting Errors

Some errors self-correct over time. Suppose that the 20X6 inventory overstatement is not discovered until 20X8. If the year-end 20X7 inventory was correct, then there will be no misstatement of earnings in 20X8 because both the beginning and ending inventories for 20X8 are correct. However, the reported earnings for both 20X6 and 20X7 will be misstated by the amount of the inventory error—$750,000 too high for 20X6 and $750,000 too low for 20X7. *No accounting entry is necessary in 20X8, but the prior years' statements will need to be restated.*

We mentioned accounting changes in Chapter 4, and later in the book, we have devoted a full chapter (Chapter 21) to accounting changes, including error correction.

INVENTORY ESTIMATION METHODS

Many companies, large and small, rely on the periodic inventory method. It is quite expensive to conduct inventory counts and therefore physical counts may be done only at the end of each fiscal year. What can be done when interim statements must be prepared?

The answer is quite simple: Inventory can be *estimated*. In a small business, the owner or inventory manager might be able to provide a reasonably accurate estimate. For larger businesses, a more formal calculation is made by using methods such as the *gross margin method* or the *retail inventory method*. It is important to understand that these are estimation methods. They necessarily introduce some level of unreliability to the financial results, a difficulty that is offset by providing more timely information.

Physical Count Required

Estimates of inventory cannot be used for audited annual financial statements—a physical count is required.

Gross Margin Method

The **gross margin method** (also known as the *gross profit method*) uses a constant gross margin to estimate inventory values based on current sales levels. The **gross margin rate** (i.e., gross margin ÷ sales) is estimated on the basis of recent past performance and is assumed to be reasonably constant in the short run. The gross margin method has two basic characteristics:

1. It requires the development of an *estimated gross margin rate* for different lines or products.
2. It applies the rate to *relevant groups of items*.

Estimating by Gross Margin Method

Estimating ending inventory by the gross margin method requires five steps, as illustrated in Exhibit 8-3:

EXHIBIT 8-3		
GROSS MARGIN METHOD		
	Known Data	**Estimated Results**[*]
Net sales revenue (base amount)	$10,000	$10,000
Cost of goods sold:		
Beginning inventory	$5,000	$5,000
Add: Purchases	8,000	8,000
Goods available for sale	13,000 (1)	13,000
Less: Ending inventory		7,000 (4)
Cost of sales		6,000 (3)
Gross margin		$ 4,000 (2)

*Computational steps:

(1) Gross margin rate (estimated as percent of sales based on last year's results) = 40%

Goods available for sale, above: $13,000

(2) Gross margin: $4,000 (i.e., $10,000 × 40%)

(3) Cost of sales: $6,000 ($10,000 − $4,000)

(4) Ending inventory $7,000 ($13,000 − $6,000)

Step 1 Estimate the gross margin rate on the basis of prior years' sales: gross margin rate = (sales − cost of sales) ÷ sales.

Step 2 Compute total cost of *goods available for sale* in the usual manner (beginning inventory plus purchases) based on actual data provided by the accounts.

Step 3 Compute the estimated gross margin amount by multiplying sales by the estimated gross margin rate.

Step 4 Compute COS by subtracting the computed gross margin amount from sales.

Step 5 Compute ending inventory by subtracting the computed COS from the cost of goods available for sale.

Uses of the Gross Margin Method

The gross margin method is used to:

- Test the reasonableness of an inventory valuation determined by some other means, such as a physical inventory count, or from perpetual inventory records. For example, assume the company in Exhibit 8-3 counted inventory, and got a figure of $10,000. The gross margin method provides an approximation of $7,000, which suggests that the physical count may be overvalued and should be examined.

- Estimate the ending inventory for interim financial reports prepared during the year when it is impractical to count the inventory physically and a perpetual inventory system is not used.

- Estimate the cost of inventory destroyed by an accident such as fire or storm. Valuation of inventory lost is necessary to account for the accident and to establish a basis for insurance claims and income taxes.

- Develop budget estimates of COS, gross margin, and inventory.

Limits on Accuracy

The accuracy of the gross margin method depends on whether or not gross margins really are fairly constant in the short run. If retail prices are slashed this year to spur consumer demand, or if theft has increased, the gross margin method will overstate earnings and inventory, perhaps significantly.

Similarly, the results will not be accurate if the product mix changes a lot in the current period. For example, if a company has traditionally sold about half its volume in a high-profit category, and half in a low-profit category, the historical gross profit margin will reflect this mix. In the current year, if volumes fall off in the high-profit side, the estimation method will produce inaccurate results.

Retail Inventory Method

The **retail inventory method** is often used by retail stores, especially stores that sell a wide variety of items. In such situations, perpetual inventory procedures may be impractical, and a complete physical inventory count is usually taken only once annually. The retail inventory method is appropriate when items sold within a department have essentially the same markup rate and articles purchased for resale are priced immediately. Two major advantages of the retail inventory method are (1) its ease of use and (2) reduced record-keeping requirements, compared with perpetual inventory systems.

The retail inventory method uses both *retail value* and *actual cost* data to:

1. Compute a ratio of cost to retail (referred to as the *cost ratio*);
2. Calculate the ending inventory at *retail value*; and
3. Convert that retail value to an estimated lower of cost or NRV by applying the computed cost ratio to the ending retail value.

Application of the retail inventory method requires that internal records be kept to provide data on:

- Sales revenue;
- Beginning inventory valued at both cost and retail;
- Purchases during the period valued at both cost and retail;

- Adjustments to the original retail price, such as additional markups, markup cancellations, markdowns, markdown cancellations, and employee discounts; and
- Other adjustments, such as interdepartmental transfers, returns, breakage, and damaged goods.

The retail inventory method differs from the gross margin method in that it uses a computed cost ratio, based on the actual relationship between cost and retail for the current period, rather than on historical ratio. The computed cost ratio is often an average across several different kinds of goods sold.

Estimating by Retail Inventory Method

The retail inventory method is illustrated in Exhibit 8-4. The steps are as follows:

Step 1   *Determine cost of goods available for sale at cost and retail.*

The total cost of goods available for sale during January 20X2 is determined to be $210,000 at cost and $300,000 at retail, as shown in Exhibit 8-4.

Step 2   *Compute the cost ratio (i.e., the ratio of cost to sales).*

The **cost ratio** is calculated by dividing the total goods available for sale at *cost* ($210,000) by the same items at *retail* ($300,000). In this example, the cost ratio is ($210,000 ÷ $300,000) = 0.70, or 70%, as shown in Exhibit 8-4. This is an *average cost* application of the retail method, because both beginning inventory and purchases are included in determining the cost ratio.

Step 3   *Compute closing inventory at retail (goods available for sale at retail, less sales).*

This is done by taking the total cost of goods available for sale at retail ($300,000) minus the goods that were sold in January ($260,000), resulting in the value of the ending inventory at retail ($40,000), as shown in Exhibit 8-4.

Step 4   *Compute ending inventory at cost.*

This is done by applying the cost ratio (70%), derived in (2), to the ending inventory at retail ($40,000), derived in (3). The result is an ending inventory of $28,000 at cost (i.e., $40,000 × 70%).

EXHIBIT 8-4		
RETAIL INVENTORY METHOD, AVERAGE COST		
	At Cost	**At Retail**
Goods available for sale:		
Beginning inventory	$ 15,000	$ 25,000
Purchases	195,000	275,000
Total goods available for sale (1)	$210,000	300,000
Cost ratio:		
$210,000 ÷ $300,000 = 70%; average, January 20X2 (2)		
Deduct January sales at retail		260,000 (3)
Ending inventory:		
At retail		$ 40,000
At cost ($40,000 × 70%)	$ 28,000 (4)	

Markups and Markdowns

The data used for Exhibit 8-4 assumed no changes in the sales price of the merchandise as originally set. Frequently, however, the original sales price on merchandise is changed, involving markups or markdowns. The retail inventory method requires that a careful record be kept of all changes to the original sales price because these changes affect the inventory cost computation. To apply the retail inventory method, it is important to distinguish among the following terms:

- **Original sales price**. Sale price first marked on the merchandise.
- **Markup**. The original or initial amount that the merchandise is marked up above cost. It is the difference between the purchase cost and the original sales price, and it may be expressed either as a dollar amount or a percentage of either cost or sales price.
- **Additional markup**. Any increase in the sales price above the original sales price. The original sales price is the base from which additional markup is measured.
- **Additional markup cancellation**. Cancellation of all, or some, of an additional markup.
- **Markdown**. A reduction in the original sales price.
- **Markdown cancellation**. An increase in the sales price (that does not exceed the original sales price) after a reduction in the original sales price markdown.

The definitions are illustrated in Exhibit 8-5. An item that cost $8 is originally marked to sell at $10. This item is subsequently marked up $1 to sell at $11, then marked down to a sales price of $7.

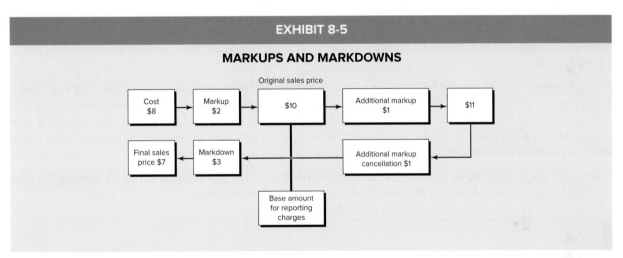

EXHIBIT 8-5

MARKUPS AND MARKDOWNS

Using the retail method, all additional markups, markup cancellations, markdowns, and markdown cancellations are included in the early calculations that determine goods available for sale, both at cost and at retail. However, to provide a conservative cost ratio that approximates lower of cost or NRV, the denominator of the cost ratio *excludes net markdowns*.

See the example in Exhibit 8-6. If all of the markups and markdowns had been included in the cost ratio, the cost ratio would have been 72% (i.e., $6,840 ÷ $9,500). Applying that ratio to the estimated inventory at retail would have given an estimated ending inventory of $720 at cost. However, when the $500 net markdowns (i.e., $600 markdowns minus $100 markdown cancellations) are *excluded* from the cost ratio, the cost ratio becomes 68.4% (i.e., $6,840 ÷ $10,000), thereby yielding a lower estimated ending inventory of $684. *This lower value approximates the lower of cost or NRV.*

EXHIBIT 8-6

RETAIL INVENTORY METHOD, LOWER OF COST OR NRV

	At Cost	At Retail
Goods available for sale:		
Beginning inventory	$ 550	$ 900
Purchases during period	6,290	8,900
Plus: additional markups during period		225
Less: additional markup cancellations		(25)

		$10,000
Less: markdowns		(600)
Plus: markdown cancellations		100
Total goods available for sale	$6,840	$ 9,500

Cost ratio (excluding net markdowns):

$6,840 ÷ $10,000 = 68.4%

Deduct:

Sales		(8,500)

Ending inventory:

At retail		$ 1,000
At cost, approximating lower of cost or NRV ($1,000 × 68.4%)	$ 684	

Uses of the Retail Inventory Method

Like the gross margin method, the retail inventory method is used to estimate the amount of the ending inventory at NRV and cost of goods sold.

The retail inventory method also can be quite useful if the entity regularly takes physical counts of inventory (e.g., monthly) and then converts the physical counts to a dollar value *at retail*. Remember, retail prices are much easier to determine on the selling floor than cost! The retail value can then be converted to cost by applying the retail inventory method without needing to know the costs of individual items. This derived inventory value may be used for interim reporting if sufficient evidence is accumulated to support the accuracy of the cost percentages.

Like the gross margin method, though, the retail inventory method is subject to estimation errors. Its accuracy depends on how carefully the company keeps track of data needed to develop accurate cost ratios.

CONCEPT REVIEW

1. Why would a company use an inventory estimation method?
2. What is the basic difference between the gross profit method and the retail inventory method?
3. Why are markdowns excluded from the cost ratio when the retail inventory method is used?

REPORTING ISSUES

Statement of Cash Flows

The amount of inventory expenditures that are included in cost of goods sold in any accounting period will be different from the amount that was spent to acquire inventory. The statement of cash flows (SCF) must show the cost of inventory *paid for*, not the cost of inventory *sold*.

If cash flow from operations is calculated by the indirect method, earnings must be adjusted by the change in inventory during the period:

- An *increase* in inventory means that the cash flow to purchase inventory was higher than the amount of expense reported as cost of goods sold—the increase must be subtracted from earnings to reflect higher cash outflow.

- A *decrease* in inventory means that the cash flow to acquire inventory was less than the amount of expense reported as cost of goods sold—the decrease must be added to earnings.

A further adjustment must be made for a manufacturing, resource, or service company. The COS (or cost of *services* provided) of such companies almost always includes non-cash expenses (e.g., depreciation on facilities or depletion on resources). Any depreciation that has been charged to inventory, whether to work-in-process or finished goods, must be added back to earnings when determining the cash flow from operations.

Inventory Disclosures

The following disclosures are required in the financial statements:

- The dollar amount of inventory that is recognized as expense for the period; normally, this is included as part of COS, cost of goods sold, or cost of services provided. The amount of inventory consumed must be disclosed;

- The major categories of inventory (e.g., raw materials, finished goods, contracts-in-progress, etc.);

- The basis for valuation for each inventory category (e.g., FIFO, weighted average cost, lower-of-cost-or-NRV, NRV);

- Amount of any NRV writedown recognized as expense in the period;

- The amount of any reversal of NRV writedowns, and the reasons for the reversal;

- The amount of inventories carried at fair value less the cost to sell (e.g., commodity inventories carried by dealers or brokers); and

- The carrying value of any inventories that have been pledged as collateral for liabilities.

Exhibit 8-7 shows New Flyer Industries Inc.'s inventory note disclosure for 2014. The company not only shows the year-end amounts of each category of inventory but also discloses the cost of inventories recognized as expense during the period, as required by IFRS. New Flyer recorded inventory writedowns in both fiscal years and reversed a previous writedown in 2014.

EXHIBIT 8-7

NEW FLYER INDUSTRIES INC.

Extracts from financial statements - Inventory

2 – SIGNIFICANT ACCOUNTING POLICIES

2.10 Inventories

Inventories are measured at the lower of cost and net realizable value. The cost of inventories is based on the first-in first-out principle, and includes expenditures incurred in acquiring the inventories, production or conversion costs and other costs incurred in bringing them to their existing location and condition. In the case of manufactured inventories and work in progress, cost includes an appropriate share of production overheads based on normal operating capacity. Net realizable value is the estimated selling price in the ordinary course of business, less the estimated costs of completion and selling expenses.

4. INVENTORIES

	December 28, 2014	December 29, 2013
Raw materials	$ 120,070	$ 108,166
Work in process	90,788	64,670
Finished goods	19,144	10,502
	$ 230,002	$ 183,338

	Fiscal 2014	Fiscal 2013
Cost of inventories recognized as expense and included in cost of sales	$ 1,262,781	$ 1,021,425
Write-down of inventory to net realizable value in cost of sales	3,077	1,682
Reversals of a previous write-down in inventory	335	—

Source: *2014 Consolidated Financial Statements of New Flyer Industries Inc.*, www.sedar.com, posted 18 March 2015.

ETHICAL ISSUES

As we stated in the Introduction to this chapter, inventory accounting has often been abused. By its nature, inventory accounting requires many judgements and estimates. These issues are particularly challenging in manufacturing, where more decisions must be made about whether a cost should be a part of inventory or an expense of the period.

Ethical issues also surround the year-end cut-off. Internal controls must be strong enough to resist unethical managers' attempts to manipulate income by accelerating or delaying the recording of shipments and sales invoices.

Assigning Costs to Inventory

Applying costs to the physical count, whether periodic or perpetual, requires careful tie-in. This is especially important when input costs change significantly during the period, such as for natural resources like oil, copper, and gold. Management may be tempted to be less than completely accurate in allocating overall purchase cost to inventory versus COS.

Accurate Cut-Off

It is essential to maintain a consistent and effective cut-off at the end of each reporting period. Cut-off errors, whether accidental or deliberate, can have a significant impact on earnings. Inventory shipments, sales recording, and accounts payable accounting must be carefully coordinated. Estimates such as damaged goods, missing inventory, probable returns, and cash discounts, offer additional opportunities for misstatement.

False Transactions

As past fraud cases have repeatedly illustrated, inventories can be used by senior managers to generate apparent earnings by creating complex fake transactions through nonexistent purchases and sales. It is very difficult for external audit procedures to detect fraud by senior executives; an underlying assumption of external auditing is that senior managers are not lying to the auditors.

However, internal auditors and accountants often become aware of suspicious transactions. It is the company accountant's responsibility to watch for suspicious account activity and to alert the board of directors' audit committee that something improper might be going on.

Writedowns

One very difficult ethical area is the use of inventory writedowns. The need for a writedown is a matter of judgement. Management may refuse to write down inventory, even in the face of slow-moving inventory and strong competitive pressures. Conversely, management may write down inventory prematurely. Management's decisions can be the result of an unintentionally inaccurate assessment of NRV or of a temporarily prevailing business mood. In either case, the writedown is legitimately motivated.

In other cases, however, management use inventory writedowns as a way of manipulating profit. This is a problem not only with inventory but also with fixed assets, as we shall discuss in Chapter 10. There have been many instances of management opposing demands by auditors to write down obviously obsolete inventory so as not to reduce earnings. There have been many other instances of management writing down inventories excessively in order to shift profits from the current year to a future year.

We have seen that lower-of-cost-or-NRV valuation requires many judgements. A primary issue is just how to measure NRV. How should the potential selling price be estimated? How can *costs to complete and sell* be estimated? What level of aggregation should be used? All of these questions are subject to significant estimation errors. The task of the accountant is to ensure that these questions are answered reasonably.

Conclusion

Inventory accounting raises many opportunities for improper accounting. Company accountants can get drawn into significant ethical dilemmas if they are not careful.

Looking Ahead

Inventory issues are not now on the active agenda of either the IASB or the Canadian ACsB.

Accounting Standards for Private Enterprises

Accounting for inventories under ASPE is substantially identical to IFRS. As in IFRS, LIFO is not permitted—inventory cost valuation methodology is the same. The few differences are as follows:

- Onerous contracts—The term *onerous contract* is not contained in ASPE. However, the effects of such contracts still should be recognized, as indicated in the chapter, but the term *onerous* is not used.
- **Writedowns**—ASPE does *not* require disclosure of the amounts of inventory writedowns.
- **Special inventories**—ASPE contains no special requirements for biological assets, agricultural produce, minerals, or mineral products. For *biological assets*, "existing practice" prevails, which essentially means the lower of cost or NRV both for products in growth and for products at the point of harvest.
- Presentation—ASPE specifies only the following disclosures:
  - Inventory accounting policies, including the cost method used;
  - The total carrying value of inventories, classified as is appropriate for the enterprise (i.e., as supplies, raw materials, work-in-progress, and finished goods); and
  - The amount of inventories recognized as expense during the period (which is similar to the IFRS requirement).

RELEVANT STANDARDS

CPA Canada Handbook, Part I (IFRS):

- IAS 2, Inventories
- IAS 41, Agriculture

CPA Canada Handbook, Part II (ASPE):

- Section 3031, Inventories

SUMMARY OF KEY POINTS

1. Inventories are assets that consist of material owned by the business and held either for future sale or for consumption in manufacturing or service provision. Inventories include raw materials, supplies, work-in-process (or progress), and finished goods or merchandise available for sale.

2. The cost of inventories includes all costs required to bring inventory to tits present location and condition but does not include inventory holding costs, such as insurance, storage, and distribution.

3. Work-in-process and finished-goods inventories of manufacturers should include raw materials, direct labour, and an allocation of manufacturing overhead determined on the basis of normal capacity.

4. All goods owned at the inventory date, including those out on consignment, should be counted and valued.

5. Either a periodic or a perpetual inventory system may be used to track inventory.

6. The only cost flow assumptions that are acceptable under both IFRS and ASPE for cost-based inventories are (1) specific identification, (2) weighted average cost, and (3) FIFO. Neither IFRS nor ASPE permits LIFO.

7. Net realizable value of inventory is measured as the current final sales price less costs to complete and to sell. If sales prices decline, NRV may be less than cost, in which case NRV, instead of historical cost, is used as the carrying value of inventory.

8. Raw materials and work-in-process inventories should be written down to NRV only if the cost cannot be recovered by the final selling price of the finished goods.

9. If the NRV of inventories goes up after it has been written down, the writedown should be reversed to the extent of the NRV recovery but never in excess of historical cost.

10. Lower-of-cost-or-NRV valuation is performed on an item-by-item basis, or, in limited circumstances, by groups of related or similar items.

11. When lower-of-cost-or-NRV valuation is conducted on an item-by-item basis, inventory writedowns can be recorded either directly in the inventory accounts or by using a valuation account; when lower-of-cost-or-NRV valuation is conducted by groups, the allowance method *must* be used for writedowns.

12. A company may enter into a purchase commitment that requires the buyer to purchase a minimum amount of goods at a fixed price. If prices decline, a loss on this onerous contract is recorded.

13. Inventory estimation methods may be used either when inventory valuations are needed for interim reporting or as a double-check on the reasonableness of physical inventory counts. They also can be used to test for the possible existence of fraud or theft.

14. The gross margin method is used to estimate inventory values when it is difficult or impractical to take a physical count of the goods. The method is most accurate when profit margins are stable.

15. The retail inventory method applies the ratio of actual cost to sales value with the ending inventory at sales value to estimate the inventory value. When net markdowns are excluded when calculating the cost ratio, the resulting valuation is an estimate of lower of cost or NRV.

16. Adequate inventory cut-off procedures at the end of each fiscal period are crucial because inventory affects not only the income statement (via COS) but also the balances of inventory, accounts receivable, and accounts payable.

17. The cash flow from operations is affected by (1) changes in inventory levels and (2) depreciation that has been included in the inventory.

18. Companies must report the dollar amount of inventories in various categories, valuation policies, the amount that has been recognized as expense in the reporting period, and writedowns and recoveries.

Key Terms

additional markup	net realizable value (NRV)
additional markup cancellation	normal capacity
borrowing costs	onerous contract
cash discounts	original sales price
consignment	periodic inventory system
contract asset	perpetual inventory system
cost flow assumptions	provincial sales tax (PST)
cost ratio	provision
cut-off errors	repurchase agreements
first-in, first-out (FIFO)	retail inventory method
goods and services tax (GST)	right to recovery asset
gross margin method	sales tax
gross margin rate	shrinkage
harmonized sales tax (HST)	special inventories
laid-down cost	specific identification
last-in, first out (LIFO)	value-added tax
markdown	weighted average cost
markdown cancellation	work-in-progress
markup	writedown

Review Problem 8-1

Dominion Vacuums Ltd. sells three general types of vacuum cleaners at retail. Each one is sold in both a basic model and a deluxe model. Information relating to the inventory at the end of 20X3 was as follows:

Inventory Type	No. of Units	Laid-Down Cost	Net Realizable Value
Upright models:			
Basic	20	$ 60	$ 70
Deluxe	10	75	90
Canister models:			
Basic	34	50	40
Deluxe	14	80	85
Shop-Vac models			
Basic	16	40	35
Heavy duty	22	120	150

Required:

1. Determine the total amount of ending inventory under each of the following two bases:
   a. For each individual model; and
   b. By type of model—upright, canister, and Shop-Vac.
2. Prepare the adjusting entry that will be necessary to reduce inventory to NRV under each of the two bases.

REVIEW PROBLEM 8-1—SOLUTION

1. The amount of inventory under each method is as follows:

Inventory Type	Units	Cost	NRV	a. Individual Item	b. General Type
		Inventory Value at:		**Lower of Cost or NRV Applied by:**	
Upright models:					
Basic	20	$1,200	$1,400	$1,200	
Deluxe	10	750	900	750	
		1,950	2,300		$1.950
Canister models:					
Basic	34	1,700	1,360	1,360	
Deluxe	14	1,120	1,190	1,120	
		2,820	2,550		2,550
Shop-Vac models:					
Basic	16	640	560	560	
Deluxe	22	2,640	3,300	2,640	
		3,280	3,860		3,280
Total		$8,050			
Inventory valuation				$7,630	$7,780

2. The adjusting entry under each method is as follows:

a. Using the individual item approach:

Holding loss on inventory	420	
Inventory		420
($8,050 − $7,630) = $420		

b. Grouping by model type:

Holding loss on inventory	270	
Allowance to reduce inventory to NRV		270
($8,050 − $7,780) = $420		

Review Problem 8-2

Super-Sell Inc. operates a discount store in downtown Edmonton. The store prepares financial statements monthly as required by Super-Sell's bank. A physical inventory is taken only on 31 January, the end of the fiscal year. Estimated inventory amounts are used for the monthly statements.

The 31 January inventory was $100,000. During February, Super-Sell purchased goods for sale amounting to $130,000. The average markup was 100% on cost. February sales revenue was $300,000.

Required:

Determine the estimated amount of inventory at 28 February using the gross margin method.

REVIEW PROBLEM 8-2—SOLUTION

Note that the 100% is the amount of *markup on cost, not the gross margin*. Goods costing $1 are marked for sale at $2.00. The gross margin percentage therefore must be computed as follows:

$1 ÷ $2 = 50%

- Cost of goods available for sale:

Opening inventory	$ 100,000
Purchases	130,000
Total	$230,000

- Sales amounted to $300,000. At a 50% gross margin, cost of goods sold was $150,000.
- Ending inventory = goods available for sale − cost of goods sold:

Ending inventory = $230,000 − $150,000 = $80,000

Review Problem 8-3

The inventory data for the Black Eagle Lounge Inc. for the beginning of June is shown below. Compute the inventory value at 30 June, using both perpetual inventory and periodic inventory approaches, under each of the following methods:

1. Specific cost identification
2. Weighted average cost
3. FIFO

> 1 June—no inventory on hand
>
> 2 June—bought one case of Red Hook Ale @ $10
>
> 13 June—bought one case of Red Hook Ale @ $16
>
> 24 June—sold one case of Red Hook Ale @ $20*
>
> 28 June—bought one case of Red Hook Ale @ $18
>
> *This case of Red Hook Ale was purchased on 13 June.

REVIEW PROBLEM 8-3—SOLUTION

At 30 June, there are two cases of ale on hand. The carrying value of the 30 June inventory is shown below under each method:

1. Specific cost identification:

> Periodic $(1 \times \$10) + (1 \times \$18) = \$28$
>
> Perpetual $(1 \times \$10) + (1 \times \$18) = \$28$

2. Weighted average cost:

> Periodic $[[(1 \times \$10) + (1 \times \$16) + (1 \times \$18)] \div 3] \times 2$ remaining
>
> $= \$14.67 \times 2 = \$29.34$
>
> Perpetual (moving average):

	Units		Total Inventory	
Average Bought (Sold)	Cost per Unit	Total Cost	Units	Cost
1	$10	$10	1	$10.00
1	16	26	2	13.00
(1)	(13)	13	1	13.00
1	18	31	2	15.50

3. FIFO:

> Periodic $(1 \times \$16) + (1 \times \$18) = \$34$
>
> Perpetual $(1 \times \$16) + (1 \times \$18) = \$34$

Comments:

- Under specific identification, *periodic* and *perpetual* always give the same result because the cost of each specific item sold is identified. Therefore, the same inventory amount is shown for both.

- Average cost yields different results under the periodic and perpetual methods because the numbers of items and their costs are averaged together differently under a moving average (perpetual) than under a historical tabulation of purchases (periodic).

- FIFO always yields the same result under both periodic and perpetual methods.

CASE 8-1

LOVE YOUR PET INC.

Love Your Pet, Inc. (LPI) is a pet food company located in rural Quebec. LPI has been operating for years as a distributor of pet food but in the last year has begun to manufacture raw dog food. In the current year, LPI has been certified by the Canadian Association of Raw Pet Food Manufacturers, (CARPFM). This organization believes that companion animals benefit greatly from a diet more closely related to their hereditary and biological makeup. Certification was completed in the third quarter. Sales of raw dog food literally doubled in the fourth quarter. Prices have been on the rise for raw meat used in production.

Dog food is primarily made from the organs of cattle, lamb, duck, or, in some cases, bison. LPI purchases its raw materials only from other companies that have received CARPFM certification. Accordingly, there are a limited number of suppliers that can provide raw materials as needed. Raw materials for manufacturing either raw dog food or dry dog food are turned over quickly to reduce spoilage. Raw foods are freeze-dried immediately once produced. Dry dog food is immediately packaged. Both freeze-dried and packaged raw food has a shelf life of one year if the product is unopened.

To meet CARPFM standards, LPI has made a significant investment in equipment, financed in part through an increased term loan plus a line of credit from its bank. The bank has tied the maximum line of credit amounts to 50% of inventory and 70% of accounts receivable.

You have been hired as the new controller for LPI. Your boss, Stuart Mack, needs guidance on proper treatment of several accounting issues, since the new arrangements with the bank will now necessitate an audit. LPI has not needed assurance on its financial statements in the past, and simply had a Notice to Reader prepared to assist with tax return preparation. LPI will be preparing its statements in accordance with IFRS.

Facts to note:

1. LPI sells bags of dry dog and cat food in its retail stores throughout Canada. Customers can collect stamps on an LPI frequent buyer card, and for every 10 similar bags purchased, LPI will provide an 11th bag for free. The price of a bag of dog food ranges between $15.00 and $70.00, depending on the size of the bag. This program has been in operation for the past two years. LPI has been tracking the extent of redemptions, and to date the program has attracted roughly 60% of customers who buy packaged dry food. This program is ignored in the accounting system—the product "given out for free" is simply expensed in the period it is distributed as part of cost of goods sold.

2. LPI has an agreement with a large farm in Quebec that gives LPI a rebate of 10% on purchases of raw meat as long as volume reaches a certain level. Volumes have been met, and in fact are increasing in every quarter since the agreement was signed. This rebate is paid to LPI in the quarter following purchases. LPI has always recorded this discount as a credit to cost of goods sold in the quarter received.

3. With the exception of direct materials and direct labour, all costs of operating the manufacturing operation are expensed in the period incurred.

4. LPI is a distributor of dry food for other suppliers. Recently, a manufacturer in the United States began a recall of several significant batches of its dry pet food products due to possible contamination with salmonella. There have been U.S. reports of some older small breed dogs dying after allegedly consuming this brand of dog food. The manufacturer has since gone out of business. Unfortunately, this product line had previously made up 20% of LPI's dry dog food sales. LPI had four months of inventory on hand, only some of which were from the recalled batches. However, all products from this supplier have been removed from the shelves and are essentially unsaleable because of concerns over pet health.

5. LPI has always used FIFO for all types of inventory, but Stuart is wondering if LPI should switch to the average cost method. A number of competitors use this method and he has asked you what the impact might be on gross margin and the current ratio as a result of the switch.

6. One of Stuart's friends, Carly Jetson, the owner of a local boutique holistic health store, has started a holistic line of rabbit food. LPI does not currently manufacture or sell rabbit food so Stuart has allowed Carly to have free shelf space for her product. Stuart pays Carly 80% of the retail price when the food sells.

Required:

Prepare a memo to Stuart in which you identify and analyze the accounting implications of each of these issues. Include a clear conclusion for the accounting treatment that should be adopted.

(Tammy Crowell, used with permission.)

CASE 8-2

ALLIANCE APPLIANCE LTD.

Alliance Appliance Ltd. (AAL) is an assembler and distributor of household appliances: kitchen equipment, washing machines, and driers. AAL assembles the appliances from components received mainly from Germany and some also provided by Japanese parts manufacturers.

AAL does not sell directly to end-users. The company's direct customers are retail appliance sales dealerships across Canada and, to a lesser extent, in the northern United States. Although the dealers sell primarily to homeowners, they also do contract work for institutional purchasers. Such institutional purchasers usually are real estate developers that are building new, or re-equipping existing apartment and condominium buildings. AAL works closely with such developers to meet their needs at a reasonable cost.

Alliance Appliance is based in Windsor, Ontario, where it operates its assembly plant and also has its principal warehousing facilities. The company has a second distribution centre in Vancouver for Western Canada.

AAL also has a distribution centre near Detroit, Michigan, to serve its customer base in the northern United States. The Michigan distribution centre is deemed essential for quick delivery to customers in the United States—rapid delivery is important, but shipments across the United States–Canada border can be delayed by security and customs procedures, which leads to a backup of shipments waiting to cross the border.

Each distribution centre stocks AAL's most popular models. High-end models, all customized models, and all orders from institutional purchasers are assembled (and customized, if necessary) to order in the company's Windsor assembly plant. Each distribution centre also stocks spare parts that can be shipped to firms that are licensed to repair AAL appliances either under warranty or post-warranty.

All of AAL's common shares are owned by the company's CEO, Douglas Beck, an engineer who migrated from Hungary to Canada 34 years ago and built up the business over three decades. Substantial external financing comes from two sources:

- International banking company HSBI provides ongoing banking services via operating loans secured by AAL's accounts receivable, inventory, and capital assets. HSBI also facilitates AAL's international transactions with the United States, Germany, and Japan.
- Toronto-based private equity firm Oxwell Inc. holds convertible preferred shares in AAL, shares that had been issued to provide financing for a plant upgrade in 20X3 and the 20X5 investment in the Michigan warehousing facility. These are voting shares that Oxwell can convert into common shares at any time.

As a Canadian private enterprise, AAL reports on the basis of ASPE. The company's annual financial statements are submitted to the AAL Board, to HSBI, and to Oxwell Inc. The Board and Oxwell also receive AAL's unaudited quarterly statements. HSBI does not receive the quarterly statements, but the bank requires a monthly update on the balance of accounts receivable and inventories because the bank's operating loans cannot exceed the sum of 75% of accounts receivable plus 50% of inventory.

It now is April 20X7. At some time over the next four or five years, Oxwell expects to convert its shares to common and then sell them to one or more investors. One potential option is that if the stock market is strong, Oxwell might choose to sell the shares through an initial public offering (IPO). If such an option were to be chosen, AAL would need to restate its accounts on the basis of IFRS. Even if other private investors acquire the Oxwell shares (i.e., instead of through an IPO), the potential pool of buyers would be increased if AAL used IFRS.

Therefore, in early 20X7, the AAL Board commissioned a review of how a change to IFRS would impact AAL's 20X6 financial reporting. AAL's CFO contacted Henry & Higgins, the company's auditors, and asked them to provide a well-qualified person to assess the impact of any change. In response to the request, H&H assigned a senior staff auditor, Maxwell Davies, to prepare a report that provides the information requested by AAL.

After extensive review of AAL's accounting records, Maxwell has assembled the following information that may be relevant to the assignment:

a. AAL uses the titles "Balance Sheet," "Statement of Income," "Statement of Cash Flows" and "Statement of Retained Earnings" for its primary financial statements.

b. The company's income statement has no subclassifications of expense items; all expenses (including income tax expense) are listed in summary fashion with no subtotals—just a final amount for "net income." The company does not report earnings-per-share amounts.

c. Preferred dividends paid to Oxwell Inc. are reported only in the retained earnings statement.

d. AAL provides a one-year full guarantee on its products when sold to the final user. The company estimates the approximate future cost of making good on the guarantees, an estimate that is adjusted at every year-end. AAL also guarantees the bank loans of the Michigan facility.

e. AAL has a high volume of foreign-currency transactions for purchases (in euros and in yen) and a somewhat lesser volume relating to sales and related costs in U.S. dollars. The foreign currency gains and losses (due to currency fluctuations between the transaction date and the payment or settlement date) are included as part of "finance expense" on the income statement.

f. The company has a three-year parts contract with the Canadian subsidiary of a Japanese company. The contract commits AAL to acquire 2,400 units per year of a certain type of washing machine motor at a cost of Cdn$150 each. The motors are manufactured in Japan. When the contract was entered into at the end of October 20X5, the value of the Japanese yen was increasing, and AAL management wished to protect the company from further price increases. During 20X6, however, the yen unexpectedly began to drop in value. As a result, identical motors are now available directly from Japan at a price equivalent to Cdn$130. AAL has attempted to reopen negotiations with the supplier but to no avail.

g. In 20X5, the company wrote down the carrying value of its entire inventory of 25-inch and 27-inch wall ovens due to increased consumer interest in 30- and 36-inch ovens. In late 20X6, however, company line managers reported that the builders of new high-rise centre-city condominium buildings were installing the narrower (i.e., "European design") ovens due to the small kitchen spaces in new buildings as well as to many downtown tenants' lack of interest in cooking.

h. During 20X6, AAL exchanged a disused building in the outskirts of Ottawa (previously a local distribution terminal, no longer in use) for an empty lot near its assembly plant. The acquired land will be used for parking for its delivery vans. AAL recorded the transaction at the value of the lot received because the value of the land was more reliably measurable than was the value of the building given up. The transaction had commercial value.

i. The Michigan distribution centre is legally owned by a wholly owned subsidiary of AAL. The subsidiary conducts its operations in U.S. dollars. The cumulative annual gains/losses on translating the net assets of the subsidiary from US$ to Cdn$ are reported as a separate component of shareholders' equity, as required by ASPE.

j. AAL ships its finished products from Windsor to Vancouver by train. In late 20X6, AAL's board of directors approved moving the Vancouver distribution centre to a location with better rail access. The move will occur in mid- to late-20X7. Therefore, in its 20X6 balance sheet, the company wrote down the soon-to-be-vacated building to its estimated recoverable value and reclassified it as a held-for-sale asset (long term).

Required:

Assume the role of Maxwell Davies, and prepare the report requested by AAL.

CASE 8-3

TERRIFIC TITLES INC.

Terrific Titles Inc. (TTI) is a major publisher of books for postsecondary education. TTI is a Canadian public corporation. One of TTI's major shareholders is Global Holdings PLC (GHC), a London-based media company.

In early 20X4, TTI's executives were preparing a bid to buy 80% of Truman Lorus Corp. of Canada (TLC). At present, all of TLC's common shares are owned by the company's CEO, Ashwin Joshee. If the sale goes through, Mr. Joshee will retain 20% and will continue as CEO and president of TLC for at least the following five years.

TLC is a niche publisher that evolved from Mr. Joshee's early endeavours in "vanity press," wherein authors self-publish their own books. Now, however, TLC has a strong line of business books for the college and university market. A particularly strong aspect of the business is the accounting line, including widely used titles such as *Indeterminate Accounting* (by the eminent authors Conchee and Beerod) and *Accounting Theory for Fun and Profit* (by Elizabeth Farroff). TTI is eager to acquire this line under the TLC imprint, provided that a reasonable price can be negotiated with Mr. Joshee. TTI's strategy is to acquire prominent high-quality publishing lines and expand them into international brands with the help of GHC, utilizing GHC's financial and market strengths.

Ian Fanwick is an accountant employed as an analyst by TTI's strategic development department. The department's executive director, Helen O'Malley, has asked Ian to prepare a report on certain accounting issues pertaining to TLC. She is concerned that TLC does not have adequate accounting controls in place, and she needs assurance that TLC's reported earnings and net assets are properly reported. She needs to know if any of the company's reported 20X3 numbers need to be adjusted before she finalizes TTI's bid for 80% of TLC's shares.

After receiving Ms. O'Malley's request, Ian visits TLC's head office in downtown Windsor, Ontario. The notes from his visit are as follows:

- Like other publishers, TLC ships to book retailers (including college and university bookstores) on terms of 2%/90 days, net/6 months. TLC pays normal shipping costs, usually via truck from TLC's Winnipeg warehouse. Air express for urgent orders is at the customer's cost unless the urgency is TLC's fault (e.g., out-of-stock, or delayed publication). The company also gives a free copy (known as a "comp," for *complimentary*) of a textbook to any faculty member who requests it, whether or not the book is adopted for his her or his course.

- Revenue is recorded when the books are shipped, FOB destination. The buyer is normally invoiced within 30 days of shipment. When a buyer pays within the 2% discount period, the discount is charged to interest expense.

- TLC accepts unlimited returns of unsold books within six months from the invoice date. In practice, as a small publisher, TLC accepts later returns, but only from colleges and universities to maintain good relationships with textbook selection committees. TLC does not accept returns of used or damaged books. Returned books are placed back in inventory at their original cost.

- Standard practice in the textbook business is that textbooks are never discounted by the publisher. Retailers usually add a 25% markup, although some "discount" booksellers apply a smaller markup. The usual author royalty is 15% of the wholesale price, split among the authors as designated by the publishing contract. Sales representatives receive a commission of 15% on all institutional sales. Overall, for all titles, 90% of sales are to colleges and universities.

- All costs associated with a given edition - development, supplementary materials, production and printing - are deferred into an inventory account. The cost is divided over the number of copies in the first press run, and expensed when those books are sold. Subsequent press runs bear only printing costs.

- Each successful textbook is revised once every three years. The time span between the start of revision and the release of the book is 12 to 20 months.

- TLC provides supplementary material to instructors free of charge. Supplemental material usually consists of instructors' manuals, solution manuals, and PowerPoint^{TM} presentations. These materials are essential for selling the books; no instructor would adopt a book that did not have the usual range of supporting resources. The cost of developing these materials is recorded as a deferred charge and amortized over the time span until the next revision—usually three years.

- Supporting resources are being provided online rather than by print, which provides cost savings for the publisher. TLC is not yet providing online resources for either the instructor or the students but plans to do so within the next two years. In 20X3, TLC spent $135,000 on developing an improved website to provide supplementary resources for both students and instructors for the company's various books. The improved website is not expected not go "live" until early 20X6, after a sufficient quantity of electronic resources has been developed. The development cost was recorded as an intangible asset.

- Due to an impending major change in accounting standards effective in 20X6, the only accounting textbook to go through the revision cycle in 20X3 was *Accounting Theory for Fun and Profit*, as it would not be significantly affected by the changes—the sixth edition of this book was released in January 20X4.

- About 75% of TLC's list will need to be issued in new editions by the end of 20X5 or the beginning of 20X6. TLC's acquisition editors are currently negotiating with authors for new editions, while the production department is lining up copy editors, technical checkers, typesetters, and so on, as well as blocking time at the printing presses and binderies—on average, it takes four to eight weeks to print and bind a book's print run, depending on the size of the run. Press runs are for 1,500 to 6,000 copies, depending on the book's popularity.

- After release of a new edition, a small inventory of that book's previous edition is kept in stock for one or two years to satisfy residual demand by instructors who do not wish to switch to the new edition. All other copies are sent for recycling after release of a new edition.

- TLC carries its inventory of books and supplementary instructor resources at cost. Inventory cost for each title includes all editorial and publishing costs for that edition plus an allocation of general overhead. The total inventory cost is then divided by the number of copies in the initial print run to determine the cost per unit.

Required:

Assume the role of Ian Fanwick. Prepare the report for Ms. O'Malley.

TECHNICAL REVIEW

connect

TR8-1 Right to Recovery Asset:

Pepper Ltd. delivers 500 units of product to Salt Corp. The sales price was $125 per unit, and Pepper's cost was $75 per unit. Pepper has agreed that Salt may return any unused product within 60 days and receive a full refund. Based on historical experience with Salt, Pepper estimates that 10% of the units will be returned, but Pepper will be able to resell any returned units.

Required:

1. What is the value of the right to recovery asset?
2. What value would you assign to the right to recovery asset if the units would have to be sold at a reduced price of $40 per unit?
3. How is a right to recovery asset different from inventory?

connect

TR8-2 Inventory Cutoff:

Max Petfood Ltd. is preparing an inventory listing for April 30, its fiscal year-end. The following items have been identified:

Description	Cost
Shipment from supplier, arrived in April 29, but inspected, found defective, and will be returned.	$43,200
Shipment from supplier, in transit April 30, arrived May 2, shipped FOB destination.	$16,900
Shipment from supplier, in transit April 30, arrived May 10, shipped FOB shipping point.	$5,300
Shipment to customer, shipped April 29, in transit April 30, FOB destination. Estimated shipping time is one week.	$22,600

Shipment to customer, shipped April 29, in transit April 30, FOB shipping point. Estimated shipping time is one week.	$33,100

Required:

Identify the items above that must be included in inventory of Max Petfood Ltd. as of April 30. Explain your reasoning in each instance.

connect

TR8-3 Cost of Inventory Item:

Yarn Imports Corp. is preparing an inventory listing, and is assigning a cost to inventory that arrived on December 29, two days before the end of the year. The following elements of potential cost have been identified:

Invoice price; the amount was prepaid when the goods were ordered because the supplier offered a 5% discount for payment up front. Goods were custom-manufactured for Yarn after the order date.
The invoice price was for $38,000, less 5%
HST on invoice price, $5,415
Interest on borrowed money between the time the deposit was paid and the goods were delivered, $510
Delivery charges, paid by the supplier, $1,100

Required:

Calculate the value to include in inventory of Yarn Imports Corp.

connect

TR8-4 Cost of Manufactured Item:

Meter Manufacturing Limited manufactures a component part in high volumes at a manufacturing facility in Hamilton, Ontario. The direct material cost for a unit is $12, direct labour is $18, and variable overhead is $22. Fixed manufacturing overhead for the facility is $1,450,000 per year. General and administrative costs are $950,000. The facility usually produces 200,000 units, but in the last year, because of the slowdown in the Canadian economy, has produced only 160,000 units.

Required:

Calculate the per unit cost of the component part.

connect

TR8-5 Inventory Holding Gains/Losses:

Arganon Ltd. had the following ending inventory balances for each of the past six years:

	Cost	Net Realizable Value
20X3	$ 0	$ 0
20X4	12,000	14,000
20X5	15,000	13,000
20X6	18,000	17,000
20X7	20,000	16,000
20X8	22,000	23,000

Required:

For each year, 20X4 through 20X8, determine the holding loss (gain) under lower-of-cost-or-NRV valuation.

connect

TR8-6 Lower of Cost or NRV:

Halicon Ltd. applies the lower of cost or NRV valuation to inventory. The company's inventory at the end of the year is as follows:

Inventory Classification	Quantity	Per Unit	
		Cost	Net Realizable Value
Class 1:			
Halicon basic models	50	$100	$120
Halican super models	30	150	140
Class 2:			
Private brand—regular	120	90	100
Private brand—deluxe	60	130	140
Private brand—super deluxe	40	200	150

Required:

Determine the amount of any adjustment that is required to inventory under each of the following valuation methods:

1. By individual type of item.

2. By class of inventory.

Mc Graw Hill **connect**

TR8-7 Damaged Inventory:

Purple Corp. had a fire sprinkler go off in a warehouse, damaging 800 units of its regular inventory. Information with respect to the units:

- Cost, $52 per unit
- Regular selling price, $89 per unit
- Estimated selling price once repaired, $42 per unit
- Estimated repair cost, $18 per unit
- Variable selling cost, $4 per unit

The company keeps perpetual inventory records

Required:

1. Determine the value to be assigned to each damaged unit.
2. Assume that the company segregates damaged inventory in a separate account. Provide the journal entry.

Mc Graw Hill **connect**

TR8-8 Onerous Contract:

In February 20X3, La Fondue Ltd. signed a two-year contract with a Quebec cheese supplier to provide a minimum of 1,000 kilograms of fine cheese for fondue at a fixed price of $20 per kilogram. By the end of September, La Fondue had purchased 650 kg at the agreed-upon price. By the end of October, the end of the fiscal year, the open market price of the cheese dropped to $17 per kg due to excess capacity in the dairy industry. On 27 November, La Fondue purchased 350 kg at the contract price of $20. The open market price was $18 at that time.

Required:

Prepare any journal entries that are necessary on La Fondue's books to record the events in October and November.

Mc Graw Hill **connect**

TR8-9 Gross Margin Method:

Tate Tasers Inc. is preparing interim financial statements for the quarter ending 31 March 20X1 and needs to estimate the value of inventory on hand at the end of the quarter. Physical inventory counts are taken only at the end of the fiscal year. The following information is available:

Beginning inventory	$ 400,000
Purchases	900,000
Sales	1,500,000
Sales returns	40,000
In-bound shipping on purchases	26,000
Out-bound shipping to customers	42,000
HST on purchases	117,000
HST on net sales	190,000
Import duties	40,000
Inventory storage costs	6,000

The average gross margin ratio is 30%.

Required:

Using the gross margin method, determine the cost of ending inventory and the cost of sales for the quarter.

connect

TR8-10 Retail Inventory Method:

Redux Ltd. estimates its quarterly inventory by the retail inventory method. The following data are available for the quarter ended 30 September 20X6:

	Cost	Selling Price
Inventory, 1 July 20X6	$362,000	$ 537,000
Markups		195,000
Markup cancellations		38,000
Markdowns		60,000
Markdown cancellations		23,000
Purchases	830,000	1,500,000
Purchase returns and allowances	16,000	25,000
Sales		1,680,000
Sales returns and allowances		80,000

Required:

Prepare a schedule to compute the estimated inventory at 30 September 20X6.

ASSIGNMENTS

★ A8-1 Inventory Cost—Items to Include in Inventory:

Rondo Ltd. (RL) is a wholesaler operation, with an active warehouse. Staff at RL have prepared a preliminary list of inventory, following its count on November 30.

a.	Goods counted in the physical inventory	$280,000
b.	Provincial sales tax on the amount in a.	22,400
c.	Federal GST on the amount in a.	16,800
d.	Goods that arrived from a supplier on December 2, shipped FOB shipping point on November 28	43,000
e.	Goods that were shipped to a customer on November 28, shipped FOB shipping point	51,000
f.	Goods that were on consignment with a customer but sold by the customer on December 10.	14,500
g.	Interest cost on goods in a, incurred during lengthy delivery period from supplier	1,600
h.	Goods that were in RL's warehouse on November 30, about to be shipped back to the supplier because of defects.	23,200
i.	Cost of operating and heating the warehouse facility for the year so that goods are available for sale when needed.	66,200
j.	Cost of freight to ship goods in a, from suppliers to RL, where RL is responsible for freight.	27,800
k.	Cost of freight to ship goods from RL to customers during the year, where RL is responsible for freight.	44,100

Required:

Determine the dollar amount of ending inventory.

 connect

★ A8-2 Inventory Cost—Items to Include in Inventory:

Digger Enterprises Ltd. has prepared the following information to support an inventory valuation as of 31 December 20X3 (in thousands of dollars):

a.	Physical count, 31 December 20X3	Cdn$60,000
b.	Advance payment for inventory due before year-end but not yet received	5,000

c.	HST (refundable) on inventory, not included in the above amounts	4,500
d.	California sales tax (not refundable) paid on part of the inventory that is included in physical count; this is the Canadian dollar equivalent	1,500
e.	Cost of items received from a supplier for testing, included in physical count; items are returnable after testing if they do not meet specifications	2,500
f.	Import excise tax paid on inventory acquired from a supplier in China; this is the Canadian dollar equivalent	2,000
g.	High-value inventory purchased and held in a bonded warehouse in California, not included in above count (Cdn$1.05 = US$1.00)	US$11,000

Required:

Determine the amount of ending inventory that should be reported on the company's SFP.

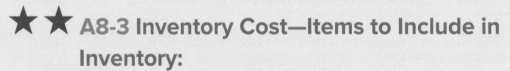

★ ★ A8-3 Inventory Cost—Items to Include in Inventory:

Gerard Ltd. reported inventory of $689,600 and accounts payable to suppliers of $456,300 for the year ended 31 December 20X6. The company has a periodic inventory system, and the inventory value given is the result of the physical count.

a. The inventory count took place on 31 December. Late in the day on 31 December, goods with a cost of $54,300 and a retail price of $98,500 were delivered to a customer. These goods had been counted earlier in the day and were included in the inventory count. The company did not record the sale until 3 January due to the New Year's break.

b. Goods from a supplier, in transit on 31 December, were neither counted nor recorded as a purchase and account payable as of 31 December. The goods, with a cost of $37,500, legally belonged to Gerard while they were in transit over the year-end.

c. Goods received from a supplier on 30 December were counted and included in inventory, but the invoice had not been recorded as a purchase or accounts payable by the end of December. The invoice was for $51,100.

d. On 4 January 20X7, a $5,000 bill for freight for the month of December was received. The freight was for goods bought from a supplier and delivered to the Gerard warehouse. None of these goods has been resold.

e. The inventory count was subsequently determined to include $21,900 of goods on consignment from a supplier; the goods have to be paid for only if they are sold to Gerard's customers.

f. Gerard had goods with a recorded cost of $12,700 that were properly recorded as a purchase and account payable, and counted in inventory. However, the goods were damaged and Gerard entered into negotiations with the supplier that resulted in a discount of $4,000 off the price. The negotiations were completed in early January 20X7.

g. Market value of remaining inventory *after* any adjustments appropriate for items (a)–(f), at NRV, was determined to be $605,000. The allowance to reduce inventory to NRV, unchanged for the end of the last fiscal period, was $32,200.

Required:

1. Calculate the correct balances for inventory (net) and accounts payable, as of 31 December 20X6.
2. Calculate the holding loss on inventory that will appear on the income statement for the year ended 31 December 20X6.

★ A8-4 Inventory Discounts and Rebates:

Majestic Stores Inc., a large Canadian publicly traded electronics dealer, buys large quantities of a flat-screen LCD television model that costs $500 and sells for $990. The supplier provides a rebate of $25 per set if Majestic buys 200 or more sets during the calendar year. Between 1 February and 1 December 20X1, Majestic purchased 150 sets, which were recorded in inventory at $75,000 (150 × $500). By 15 December, 130 of these units had been sold. On 15 December, Majestic ordered 50 more sets, FOB destination, for $500 each. Majestic received the sets on 22 December and promptly made a request for the rebate. Majestic sold an additional 40 sets by 31 January 20X2, the end of Majestic's fiscal year. The rebate cheque arrived on 20 February, after Majestic's accountants had closed the books.

The supplier provides terms of 2/10, n/30. The supplier paid a total of $1,760 in freight charges, including $375 paid in January for the last order of 50 sets.

Required:

1. Calculate the ending inventory value at 31 January 20X2. Majestic uses FIFO.
2. What entry should be made relative to the rebate on 31 January 20X2? Why?
3. What entry would be made on 20 February 20X2?

★ ★ A8-5 Inventory Policy Issues:

Consider each of the following independent situations:

Case A   Inventory was received and was recorded at the invoice price of $56,000. The goods had not been paid for at year-end. Consequently, a 2% discount for early payment was not taken.

Case B   In the lower-of-cost-or-market valuation at year-end, replacement cost was used as the definition of "market." The evaluation resulted in a writedown of $135,500. The company reports that although its supplier's prices were lower for certain products at year-end, thus causing the writedown, both its prices to its own customers and its direct selling costs had remained at constant levels.

Case C   Inventories costing $65,000, with a sales price of $97,000, were with a customer on consignment. These goods were excluded from the physical inventory count, and the $97,000 sale was recorded in the current fiscal year because final sale was reasonably assured—in the past, this customer has always been able to sell all the goods sent on consignment.

Case D   At the end of 20X4, Sino-India Inc. entered into a binding commitment to buy 150 units of a certain type of inventory at a cost of $16,000 per unit by the end of 20X7. In 20X5, the company bought 70 units, all of which were used in production. In 20X6 the company purchased 45 units and recorded them in inventory at $720,000 (i.e., 45 × $16,000). The market value per unit had been $17,000 during 20X4, dropped to $14,000 in 20X5, and rose again to $15,500 by the date of the 20X6 acquisition. It is now the end of 20X6.

Required:

For each situation, describe the accounting policy decision. Describe the impact that the chosen policy has had on earnings and the SFP. If the company's policy is not correct or if there is an alternate policy that should be considered, explain the alternative.

 A8-6 Lower of Cost or NRV:

Oporto Corp. produces and sells forklift trucks. Model 17A (the "Protex") has a list price of $140,000. The production cost for the 20 finished Protex units in inventory at the end of 20X4 was $120,000 per unit. Due to recent improvements in manufacturing flow, the cost of new production is expected to be $108,000 in the next year. The list price for the Protex will be reduced by $10,000 at the beginning of 20X5. The price reduction will reflect the reduced manufacturing cost and undercut the prices of generally comparable competing models made by other manufacturers. The Protex model often is sold below the list price; the actual discount varies by customer but is usually 10% less than list price for the regular industrial clients that comprise 40% of HMC's sales. Individual nonrepeat buyers receive smaller discounts, averaging about 3%. HMC's sales agents receive a 6% commission on the actual sales price. The buyer bears the cost of shipping.

Required:

1.   What value should be used for the lower-of-cost-or-NRV test? What amount of writedown is required?
2.   Assume that early in 20X5 the company sells five Protex units for $126,000 each. How much gross profit will be recorded, assuming that the company uses FIFO?

 A8-7 Lower of Cost or NRV—Income Effects:

Alomar Ltd. has been suffering the effects of strong price competition on a particular inventory item from an overseas company that has moved into Alomar's Canadian market. At the end of 20X4, Alomar management decided that the carrying cost (at historical value) of its year-end inventory was not recoverable and that Alomar would have to reduce its prices drastically to meet the competitor's prices. Management estimated that inventory currently carried at $40,000 (at historical cost) will have a NRV of only $32,000. Alomar normally priced its products at 50% above historical cost.

Early in 20X5, Alomar's competitor unexpectedly withdrew from the Canadian market because of financial difficulties in its home country. Consequently, Alomar restored the prices of its goods to full premarkdown selling price. By the end of 20X5, 60% of the inventory had been sold.

Required:

1.   Prepare the journal entry for 31 December 20X4 to write down the inventory to NRV. Use the direct writedown method.
2.   Prepare a summary journal entry to record the sale of the goods (and the cost of sales) in 20X5 and the writeup of remaining inventory.
3.   Suppose that Alomar's net income (after the writedown) was $100,000 in 20X4 and $120,000 in 20X5. What would each year's net income have been if Alomar had not written down the inventory?

★ ★ **A8-8 Lower of Cost or NRV—Direct Writedown versus Allowance Method:**

At the end of 20X5, Singh Inc. has four inventory items, two of which management believes should be written down. The cost and estimated NRVs of the items are as follows:

| | | Per Unit | |
	Quantity	Cost	NRV
Item A	100	$170	$160
Item B	260	80	90
Item C	150	140	100
Item D	200	100	120

Required:

1. Determine the amount by which the inventory should be written down if lower-of-cost-or-NRV valuation is applied item-by-item. Prepare the journal entry to record the writedown.

2. Items A and B are related, while Items C and D are related. Determine the inventory writedown if lower-of-cost-or-NRV valuation is applied by category. Prepare the journal entry to establish an inventory allowance.

3. Suppose that in 20X6, the NRV of Item A rises to $180 by the end of the year. Prepare journal entries to record the recovery in value, if feasible, under each of the two methods.

4. Explain the advantages and disadvantages of using an allowance instead of direct writedown.

★ ★ **A8-9 Lower of Cost or NRV—Allowance Method:**

At the end of 20X4, Sherpa Lighting Ltd. has a large stock of incandescent lighting fixtures that are becoming obsolete due to a new trend to low-energy fluorescent and LED lighting fixtures. The current inventory of incandescent fixtures has a cost of $170,000. The sales manager of Sherpa estimates that the inventory can be sold through the normal course of business over the next several reporting quarters for approximately $150,000. Sales personnel are given a 10% commission on sales. In addition, Sherpa will grant an additional 5% sales commission for sales of these almost-obsolete fixtures, intended to make up for the reduced sales prices as well as an additional incentive to sell them.

In early 20X5, Sherpa's production manager decided that the fixtures can be adapted to not only accept the new LED lighting but also compete quite effectively with new products coming on the market. During 2005, the fixtures are converted at a cost of $25,000. The sales manager estimates that after the conversion, the newly adapted inventory can be repriced to fetch $185,000 (before 10% sales commission) in the market.

Required:

Using the valuation allowance method, prepare the appropriate journal entries to record inventory adjustments at the end of each of 20X4 and 20X5.

Solution

★ ★ **A8-10 Lower of Cost or NRV—Allowance Method:**

The records of Loren Movers Ltd. contained the following inventory data:

| | | 20X1 | | 20X2 | |
		Cost	NRV	Cost	NRV
Category 1					
	Item A	$10,000	$ 9,000	$ 5,000	$ 3,000
	Item B	40,000	35,000	10,000	9,000
	Item C	25,000	33,000	45,000	52,000
		$75,000	$77,000	$60,000	$64,000
Category 2					
	Item D	$18,000	$16,500	$12,000	$ 10,500
	Item E	20,000	4,000	4,000	1,000
	Item F	42,000	42,000	56,000	54,000
		$80,000	$62,500	$72 000	$65,500

Required:

1. Calculate two different amounts that could justifiably be recorded as the allowance to reduce inventory to lower-of-cost-or-NRV at the end of 20X1.

2. Record the 20X1 lower-of-cost-or-NRV adjustments (if any) for each of the two amounts from requirement 1, using the valuation allowance method.

3. Record the 20X2 lower-of-cost-or-NRV adjustments (if any) under each of the two lower of cost or NRV methods, using the valuation allowance method.

 connect

★ ★ **A8-11 Lower of Cost or NRV—Two Ways to Apply:**

The information shown below relating to the ending inventory was taken at lower of cost or NRV from the records of Electronics Corp.:

Inventory Classification	Quantity	Per Unit	
		Cost	NRV
Keyboards			
Stock A	12	$94	$80
Stock B	20	76	70
Stock C	18	100	110
Hard drives			
Stock X	30	180	170
Stock Y	60	160	180
CD burners			
Stock D	60	76	66
Stock E	200	100	116

Required:

1. Determine the valuation of the above inventory at cost and at lower of cost or NRV, assuming application of lower-of-cost-or-NRV valuation by (a) individual items, and (b) classifications.

2. Give the entry to record the writedown, if any, to reduce ending inventory to lower of cost or NRV. Use the allowance method.

3. Of the two applications described in requirement 2 above, which one appears preferable in this situation? Explain.

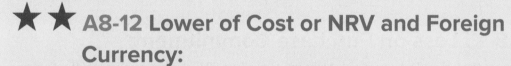

★ ★ A8-12 Lower of Cost or NRV and Foreign Currency:

Telma Ltd. is a public company incorporated in Alberta and traded on the Toronto Stock Exchange. In December 20X6, Telma management decided that cost exceeded NRV for a significant portion of the inventory. Consequently, the company wrote the Class A inventory down from $350,000 to $150,000 and the Class B inventory down from $425,000 to $325,000.

In June 20X7, the value of Class B inventory rose to $365,000. Half of the Class B was sold for $190,000 in November of that year.

In March 20X8, the Class A inventory was sold in bulk for a price of €100,000. At the time of the sale, €1 = Cdn$1.70. The buyer paid Telma's invoice one month later, when €1 = Cdn$1.62.

Required:

1. Prepare all entries, assuming that the direct writedown method is used for lower of cost or NRV.

2. Prepare all entries, assuming instead that the allowance method is used for lower of cost or NRV.

A8-13 Obsolete Inventory:

Olson Metrics Ltd. has been the dominant firm in its field. The company's most popular product has been the Model T, which carries a retail price of $350. The Model T costs $250 per unit to produce.

Recently, the company introduced a new version, Model A, priced at $380. When the Model A was released, Olson reduced the retail price of the remaining 1,000 units of Model T to $300. Despite the price reduction, the demand for the Model T dropped sharply. Therefore, Olson decided to sell 600 of the remaining units on consignment through FloorMart Inc. as a private label product at $220 per unit. FloorMart will collect a commission of 20% per unit. Olsen will lower the price of the remaining 400 units in inventory to $280.

Required:

Prepare any journal entry(ies) that are necessary to record the effects of the above information.

 A8-14 Purchase Commitment:

Pino Inc. is a BC-based wine producer. In anticipation of a particularly bounteous grape harvest and a potential problem in obtaining a sufficient volume of shipping crates, Pino entered into a noncancellable agreement with Lumber Products Ltd. to supply 200,000 wooden crates at a price of $24 per crate plus 7% PST and 5% GST. During the current fiscal year, Pino purchased 50,000 crates.

Near the end of the year, however, a restrictive tariff on the import of crates from the United States was lifted. Crates then became readily available from other suppliers for only $18 plus tax.

Required:

1. Prepare the journal entry to record the purchase of crates during the current fiscal year.
2. Prepare the journal entry to record the impact of the price drop. What conditions are necessary for Pino to recognize a loss on the contract?

 A8-15 Loss on Purchase Commitment:

During 20X7, Omega Corp. signed a contract with Alpha Inc. to purchase 20,000 subassemblies at $90 each during 20X8.

Required:

1. On 31 December 20X7, the end of the annual accounting period, the financial statements are to be prepared. Assume that the cost of the subassemblies is dropping and the total estimated current replacement cost is $1,700,000. Under what additional contractual and economic conditions would note disclosure only be required? Prepare an appropriate note.
2. What contractual and economic conditions would require accrual of a loss? Give the accrual entry.
3. Assume that the subassemblies are received in 20X7 when their replacement cost was $1,660,000. The contract was paid in full. Give the required entry, assuming the entry in requirement 2 was made, and a periodic inventory system is used.

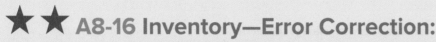 A8-16 Inventory—Error Correction:

On 31 December 20X5, Office Systems Ltd.'s books showed an ending inventory valuation of $490,000. The accounts for 20X5 have been adjusted and closed. Subsequently, the bookkeeper prepared a schedule that showed that the inventory should be $569,800, not $490,000.

a.	Merchandise in store (at 40% above cost)	$490,000
b.	Merchandise purchased, in transit (shipped FOB destination, estimated freight, not included, $800), invoice price	9,000
c.	Merchandise held for later shipment to Davis Electronics at sales price, 40% above cost (already billed to Davis Electronics)	16,800
d.	Merchandise out on consignment at sales price (cost, $12,000)	24,000
e.	Merchandise (office equipment) removed from the warehouse and now used in the company's marketing office (at cost)	20,000
f.	Merchandise out on approval, sales price = $10,000, cost = $4,000	10,000
	Total inventory as corrected	$569,800

Income tax rate = 30%

Required:

1. Review the items making up the list of inventory. Compute the correct ending inventory amount.
2. The income statement and SFP now reflect a closing inventory of $490,000. List the items on the income statement and SFP for 20X5 that should be corrected for the above errors; give the amount of the error for each item affected.

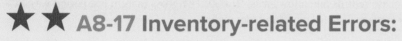 A8-17 Inventory-related Errors:

Flint Publishers Inc. prepared its draft 20X6 financial statements in February 20X7. The draft SCI showed earnings of $1,100,000. After the draft statements were prepared, but prior to their approval and release, the external auditors discovered several errors:

a. Inventory of $50,000 that was received from an offshore publisher on 29 December 20X6 (and included in the 31 December 20X6 physical inventory count) had not been recorded as an account payable until well into January 20X7.

b. The company had shipped books worth $240,000 to a distant customer FOB shipping point on 28 December 20X6. The revenue (and account receivable) was recorded by Flint on 4 January 20X7. However, the shipment was excluded from inventory so COS has been recorded.

c. Although the company's internal auditors had discovered a calculation error in the worksheets for the 31 December 20X6 physical inventory, the error was not yet corrected. Year-end 20X6 inventory actually should have been $100,000 greater than recorded and reported.

d. Books costing $160,000 were shipped to a large chain of bookstores in the final week of the fiscal year; a sale (and receivable) of $250,000 had correspondingly been recorded. However, the bookstore chain actually had accepted the books only on consignment.

Required:

1. What is the revised 20X6 earnings after correction of these errors?

 ★ ★ **A8-18 Inventory Errors:**

Case A   Internal auditors for Sandu Corp. discovered during 20X4 that finished goods inventory of $800,000 had been shipped to a customer on 30 December 20X3, the last working day of the year. The ending inventory for 31 December 20X3 had been properly stated on the basis of the year-end physical count. However, the sale was not recorded until 4 January 20X4, when sales revenue of $1,280,000 was recorded. Sandu uses a perpetual inventory system.

Case B   When the accounting staff of Zhang Ltd. was preparing the first-quarter 20X5 interim financial statements, they discovered an error in the 31 December 20X4 financial statements. Inventory costing $530,000 had been in transit and was not received until 4 January 20X5. The accounts payable department had recorded the purchase as an account payable on 28 December 20X4. Title to the inventory had passed to Zhang on 27 December, the date that the supplier had loaded the shipment onto the shipping company's trucks. Zhang uses a periodic inventory method.

Required:

1. What impact did the errors have on each company's financial statements?
2. What correcting entry should each company make when the error is discovered?

★ **A8-19 Gross Margin Method:**

You are auditing the records of Lin Corp. The company took a physical inventory under your observation. However, the valuations have not been completed. The records of the company provide the following data: sales, $400,000 (gross); returned sales, $17,500 (returned to stock); purchases (gross), $250,000; beginning inventory, $160,000; freight-in, $8,000; and purchase returns and allowances, $7,000. The gross margin last period was 25% of net sales; you anticipate that it will average 30% for the year under audit.

Required:

Estimate the cost of the ending inventory and the cost of sales using the gross margin method. Show all calculations.

 Solution

★ ★ **A8-20 Gross Margin Method:**

The manager of Seaton Books Ltd., a book retailer, requires an estimate of the inventory cost for a quarterly financial report to the owner on 31 March 20X5. In the past, the gross margin method was used because of the difficulty and expense of taking a physical inventory at interim dates. The company sells both fiction and nonfiction books. Due to their lower turnover rate, nonfiction books are typically marked up to produce a gross profit of 37.5%. Fiction, on the other hand, generates a 28.6% gross profit. The manager has used the average gross profit of 33.333% to estimate interim inventories.

You have been asked by the manager to estimate the book inventory cost as of 31 March 20X5. The following data are available from Seaton's accounting records:

	Fiction	Nonfiction	Total
Inventory, 1 January 20X5	$100,000	$ 40,000	$140,000
Purchases	600,000	200,000	800,000
Freight-in	5,000	2,000	7,000
Sales	590,000	160,000	750,000

Required:

(Round gross margin percentages to one decimal place.)

1. Using the average gross profit margin of 33.3%, compute the estimate of inventory as of 31 March 20X5, based on the method applied to combined fiction and nonfiction books.
2. Compute the estimate of ending inventory as of 31 March 20X5, based on the gross margin method applied separately to fiction and nonfiction books.
3. Which method is preferable in this situation? Explain.

 A8-21 Retail Inventory Method:

Hansard Ltd. estimates its quarterly inventory by the retail inventory method. The following data are available for the quarter ended 30 June 20X7:

	Cost	Selling Price
Inventory, 1 June	$452,000	$ 672,000
Markups		244,000
Markup cancellations		76,000
Markdowns		176,000
Markdown cancellations		86,000
Purchases	1,039,200	1,880,000
Purchase returns and allowances	18,000	32,000
Sales		2,100,000
Sales returns and allowances		100,000

Required:

1. Prepare a schedule to compute the estimated inventory at 30 June 20X7.

★ ★ A8-22 Retail Inventory Method:

Auditors are examining the accounts of Acton Retail Corp. They were present when Acton's personnel physically counted the Acton inventory; however, the auditors made their own tests. Acton's records provided the following data for the current year:

	At Retail	At Cost
Inventory, 1 January	$ 300,000	$180,500
Net purchases	1,453,000	955,000
Freight-in		15,000
Additional markups	31,000	
Additional markup cancellations	14,000	
Markdowns	8,000	
Employee discounts	2,000	
Sales	1,300,000	

Inventory at 31 December (per physical count valued at retail) = $475,000

Required:

1. Compute the ending inventory at lower of cost or NRV as an audit test of the overall reasonableness of the physical inventory count.
2. Note any discrepancies indicated. What factors should the auditors consider in reconciling any difference in results from the analysis?
3. What accounting treatment (if any) should be accorded the discrepancy?

★ ★ ★ A8-23 Gross Margin and Retail Inventory Methods:

The records of Diskount Department Stores Inc. provided the following data for 20X5:

Sales (gross)	$800,000
Sales returns	2,000
Additional markups	9,000
Additional markup cancellations	5,000
Markdowns	7,000

Purchases:	
At retail	850,000
At cost	459,500
Purchase returns:	
At retail	4,000
At cost	2,200
Freight on purchases	7,000
Beginning inventory:	
At retail	80,000
At cost	45,000
Markdown cancellations	3,000

1. Estimate the valuation of the ending inventory and cost of goods sold using the gross margin method. Last year's gross margin percentage was 51%.

2. Estimate the valuation of the ending inventory and cost of goods sold using the retail sales method, which approximates lower-of-cost-or-NRV valuation.

3. Which method is likely to be more accurate? Comment.

★ ★ ★ A8-24 Inventory Concepts—Recording, Adjusting, Closing, Reporting:

Gamit Ltd. completed the following selected (and summarized) transactions during 20X5:

a. Merchandise inventory on hand 1 January 20X5, $105,000 (at cost, which was the same as lower of cost or NRV).

b. During the year, purchased merchandise for resale at cost of $200,000 on credit, terms 2/10, n/30. Immediately paid 85% of the cash cost.

c. Paid freight on merchandise purchased, $10,000 cash.

d. Paid 40% of the accounts payable within the discount period. The remaining payables were unpaid at the end of 20X5 and were still within the discount period.

e. Merchandise that had a quoted price of $3,000 (terms 2/10, n/30) was returned to a supplier. A cash refund of $2,940 was received because the items were unsatisfactory.

f. During the year, sold merchandise for $370,000, of which 10% was on credit.

g. A television set caught fire and was damaged internally; it was returned by the customer. The set was originally sold for $600, of which $400 cash was refunded. The set originally cost the company $420. Estimates are that the set, when repaired, can be sold for $240. Estimated repair costs are $50, and selling costs are estimated to be $10.

h. Operating expenses (administrative and distribution) paid in cash, $120,000; includes the $10 (in thousands).

i. Excluded from the purchase given in (b) and from the ending inventory was a shipment for $7,000 (net of discount). This shipment was in transit, FOB shipping point at 31 December 20X5. The invoice had arrived.

j. Paid $50 cash to repair the damaged television set; see (g) above.

k. The ending inventory (as counted) was $110,000 at cost, and $107,000 at NRV. Income tax expense is $19,500. Income tax expense is $19,500.

Accounting policies followed by the company are as follows:

(1)   The annual accounting period ends 31 December.
(2)   A periodic inventory system is used.
(3)   Purchases and accounts payable are recorded net of cash discounts.
(4)   Freight charges are allocated to merchandise when purchased.
(5)   All cash discounts are taken.
(6)   Used and damaged merchandise is carried in a separate inventory account.
(7)   Inventories are reported at lower of cost or NRV, and the allowance method is used.

Required:

1. Give the entries for transactions (b) through (k).
2. Give the end-of-period adjusting entries.
3. Prepare a multiple-step SCI for 20X5. Assume that 20,000 common shares are outstanding.
4. Show how the ending inventory should be reported on the SFP at 31 December 20X5.

★★★ A8-25 Statement of Cash Flows:

Leander Corp. reported the following items in its 20X5 financial statements:

	20X5	20X4
From the SFP:		
Inventory, at lower of cost or market	$ 475,500	$ 420,500
Accounts payable	308,000	298,000
Estimated liability on noncancellable purchase commitments	4,000	—
From the SCI:		
Cost of goods sold*	$2,450,000	$2,050,300
Loss on purchase commitment	4,000	—
*Includes loss due to decline in market value		
From the notes:		

Inventories are carried at FIFO cost, net of an allowance to reduce finished goods inventory to the lower of cost or NRV of $32,500 (20X4, $23,000).

At year-end, the company has outstanding purchase commitments in the amount of $6,700 (20X4, $3,300). The market value of these goods is equal to, or exceeds, the purchase commitment cost except as accrued in the financial statements.

Required:

1. What items would appear on the cash flow statement as a result of the inventory transactions of the year? Assume the use of the indirect method of presentation in the operating activities section.

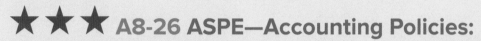

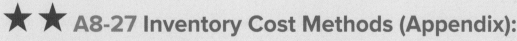 A8-26 ASPE—Accounting Policies:

The president of Aggressive Ltd. has come to you for advice. Aggressive is a newly established company with prospects for high growth. Decisions must soon be made concerning accounting policies for external financial reporting. The following information pertains to the company's first year of operations (in thousands of dollars):

Revenue	$48,000
Purchases	18,000
Closing inventory—FIFO	6,000
Closing inventory—average cost	4,800
Depreciation—straight line	2,400
Depreciation—declining balance	4,800
Development expense	2,400
Amortization of development over five years	480
Other expenses	5,000
Income tax rate	20%

Required:

1. Prepare a columnar income statement. In column 1, show net income assuming the use of FIFO, declining-balance depreciation, and expensing of development. In successive columns, show the individual impact of each of the following policy changes on net income:
    a. In column 2, average cost;
    b. In column 3, straight-line depreciation;
    c. In column 4, amortization of development; and
    d. In column 5, the combined effects of the alternatives presented separately in columns 2 through 4.
2. As president, which accounting policies would you choose? Explain.

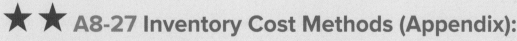 A8-27 Inventory Cost Methods (Appendix):

The inventory records of Acme Appliances Ltd. showed the following data relative to a food processor in inventory (the transactions occurred in the order given):

Transaction	Units	Unit Cost
1. Inventory	30	$19.00
2. Purchase	45	20.00
3. Sale	50	
4. Purchase	50	20.80
5. Sale	50	
6. Purchase	50	21.60

Required:

Compute the cost of goods sold for the period and the ending inventory, assuming the following (round unit costs to nearest cent):

1. Weighted average (periodic inventory system)
2. Moving weighted average (perpetual inventory system)
3. FIFO

★ ★ ★ A8-28 Inventory Cost Methods (Appendix):

The Yarn Store Inc. inventory records showed the following data relative to a particular item sold regularly (transactions occurred in the order given):

Transaction	Units	Unit Cost
1. Beginning inventory	3,000	$2.50
2. Purchase	27,000	2.60
3. Sales (at $6.5 per unit)	−10,500	
4. Purchase	9,000	2.75
5. Sales (at $6.75 per unit)	−24,000	
6. Purchase	4,500	3.00
7. Ending inventory	9,000	

Required:

1. Complete the following schedule (round unit costs to nearest cent and total costs of inventory to the nearest $5):

	Ending Inventory	Cost of Goods Sold	Gross Margin
a. FIFO			
b. Weighted average			
c. Moving weighted average			

2. Prepare journal entries, including year-end adjusting entries to establish ending inventory, if needed, for the two average calculations (b) and (c) above. Assume that the weighted average method is used with a periodic system and the moving weighted average method with a perpetual system.

3. Explain how your entries in (2) would be different if a standard cost system were used, with the standard cost established at $2.75 at normal capacity.

★ ★ ★ A8-29 Inventory Cost Methods (Appendix):

The records of Cordova Corp. showed the following transactions, in the order given, relating to the major inventory item:

	Units	Unit Cost
1. Inventory	3,000	$6.90
2. Purchase	6,000	7.20
3. Sale (at $15)	4,000	
4. Purchase	5,000	7.50
5. Sale (at $15)	9,000	
6. Purchase	11,000	7.66
7. Sale (at $18)	9,000	
8. Purchase	6,000	7.80

Required:

Complete the following schedule for each independent assumption (round unit costs to the nearest cent; show computations):

	Units and Amounts		
Independent Assumptions	Ending Inventory	Cost of Sales	Gross Margin
a. FIFO			
b. Weighted average, periodic inventory system			
c. Moving weighted average, perpetual inventory system			

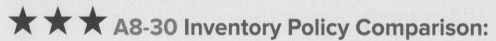

★ ★ ★ A8-30 Inventory Policy Comparison:

Carlton Inc. and Dennis Ltd. are two North American manufacturers of auto parts. The two firms use different inventory cost flow accounting policies. This question asks you to determine some of the differences due to the reporting. The two firms report the following selected information for 20X1:

	($ thousands)	
	Carlton Inc.	Dennis Ltd.
Earnings from continuing operations	$ (538)	$(3,432)
Cost of sales	24,803	71,826
Net earnings per share (continuing operations)	(2.22)	(7.21)
Assets (total)	43,076	174,429
Inventories	3,571	6,215
Total shareholders' equity	6,109	22,690
Comparative units sold: United States and Canada (millions)	1.661 units	3.114 units
Comparative units sold: Worldwide (millions)	1.866 units	5.346 units

CARLTON INC.

Note 1: Summary of Significant Accounting Policies

Inventories are valued at the lower of cost or NRV. The cost of approximately 41% and 49% of inventories at 31 December 20X1 and 20X0, respectively, is determined on a weighted average cost basis. The balance of inventory cost is determined on a first-in, first-out (FIFO) basis.

Note 2: Inventories and Cost of Sales

Inventories are summarized by major classification as follows (in thousands of dollars):

| | 31 December | |
	20X1	20X0
Finished products, including service parts	$1,192	$1,114
Raw materials, finished, production parts, and supplies	873	1,100
Work-in-process	1,476	911
Other	30	25
Total	$3,571	$3,150

If inventories valued by FIFO had instead been valued on a weighted average cost basis, inventory would have been $239 million and $208 million lower at 31 December 20X1 and 20X0, respectively (see Note 1). Total manufacturing cost of sales aggregated $24.81 million, and $24.13 million for 20X1 and 20X0, respectively.

DENNIS LTD.

Note 1: Accounting Policies (Inventory Valuation)

Inventories are stated at the lower of cost or market. The cost of substantially all North American inventories is determined by the weighted average cost method. The cost of the remaining inventories is determined substantially by the first-in, first-out (FIFO) method.

If FIFO were the only method of inventory accounting used by the company, inventories would have been $1,323 and $1,331 higher than reported at 31 December 20X1 and 20X0, respectively. The major classes of inventory at 31 December were as follows (in thousands of dollars):

	20X1	20X0
Finished products	$2,979.2	$3,628.2
Raw materials and work-in-process	2,800.9	3,025.7
Supplies	435.2	461.5
Total	$6,215.3	$ 7,115.4

Required:

1. Are prices rising or falling in the 20X1 supplier markets in which Dennis (and Carlton) buys? How do you know?

2. Compare Dennis's and Carlton's inventory levels and comment on the comparison.

3. Is it desirable to have similar companies using different inventory cost flow policies? If not, why do accounting standard setters not require uniformity?

APPENDIX

PERIODIC VERSUS PERPETUAL SYSTEMS

Periodic Inventory System

In a periodic inventory system, unit costs are applied to the ending inventory quantities to derive the ending inventory valuation. The costs are applied by using the specific cost flow assumption (e.g., FIFO or average cost). Cost of goods sold (or cost used in production or in a service contract) is determined by subtracting the ending inventory value from the cost of goods available for sale.

In a periodic system, purchases are debited to a purchases account, and end-of-period adjusting entries are made to close the purchases account, to close out beginning inventory, and to record the ending inventory as an asset (i.e., the ending inventory replaces the beginning inventory in the accounts). Additional accounts, for costs tracked separately (e.g., freight-in or customs duties) are also closed at this time. Finally, any contra accounts to purchases, such as accounts for purchase returns and allowances or purchase discounts, must also be closed.

Under a periodic system, COS is computed as a residual amount (beginning inventory plus net purchases less ending inventory) and, for all practical purposes, cannot be verified independently from an inventory count except by use of an estimation method, as we discussed in the main body of the chapter. The lack of verifiability is one reason that estimation methods may be used as a check.

Perpetual Inventory System

In a *perpetual inventory system*, both the quantities and costs of each receipt and each issue of an inventory item are recorded in the detailed inventory records to maintain an up-to-date perpetual inventory balance at all times. COS is recorded when each sale is made. The result of the perpetual system is verified at least once a year by physically counting the inventory and matching the count to the accounting records. Thus, the perpetual inventory system provides the units and costs of inventory and cost of goods sold at any time. The unit costs applied to each issue or sale are determined by the cost flow assumption used.

It is important to make a distinction between tracking the *physical flow* of goods and the *costing* of goods. Many companies maintain an ongoing record of physical flows as quantity information only. A continuous tracking of physical flows does not constitute a perpetual inventory system (from an accounting standpoint) unless the costs associated with those flows are simultaneously tracked. A good example is provided by some supermarkets that use automated scanners at checkout stations to keep track of physical inventory levels but assign accounting values to the physical flows only periodically.

Periodic versus Perpetual Systems—Illustration

To illustrate the periodic versus the perpetual systems, consider the following data for Lea Ltd.:

	Units	Unit Cost	Total
Beginning inventory	500	$4.00	$2,000
Purchases	1,000	4.00	4,000
Goods available for sale	1,500		$6,000
Less: Sales	900		

| Ending inventory, as calculated | 600 |
| Ending inventory, based on physical count | 580 |

Note that there should have been 600 units on hand, not 580; 20 must have been either damaged and discarded or stolen. The amount by which the physical count falls short of the expected level of inventory is generally (and euphemistically) referred to as shrinkage. However, it also is possible that the sales records are not completely accurate.

Based on the prior data, the computation of the COS yields the following amounts:

Beginning inventory (carried forward from the prior period): 500 × $4	$2,000
Merchandise purchases (accumulated in the purchases account): 1,000 × $4	4,000
Total goods available for sale during the period	6,000
Less: Ending inventory (quantity determined by a physical count): 580 × $4	2,320
Equals: Cost of sales (a residual amount)	$3,680

Periodic Recording

At the beginning of the year, the balance of the inventory account will be the $2,000 cost of the 500 units that were on hand. The entries to record the purchases and COS under a periodic inventory system are as follows:

To record purchases		
Purchases	4,000	
Accounts payable		4,000
To reallocate the cost of opening inventory and purchases		
Cost of sales	3,680	
Inventory (closing, per count)	2,320	
Inventory (opening)		2,000
Purchases		4,000

A variation on the second entry above is to explicitly recognize the shrinkage of 20 units as an expense, instead of hiding it in cost of goods sold:

Cost of sales (900 × $4)	3,600	
Inventory shrinkage expense (20 × $4)	80	
Inventory (closing, per count: 580 × $4)	2,320	
Inventory (opening)		2,000
Purchases		4,000

The inventory shrinkage expense will appear as an expense on the income statement. It may be included in COS if not material.

Under a periodic inventory system, the inventory is counted at least once a year. For interim financial statements, however, the amount of inventory may be estimated. If a perpetual record of only the physical units of inventory is maintained, then only the cost of that inventory needs to be estimated. If the company maintains no perpetual inventory count, then both the quantity and unit cost must be estimated.

Perpetual Recording

When a perpetual inventory system is used, detailed perpetual inventory records, in addition to the usual ledger accounts, are maintained for each inventory item, and an inventory control account is maintained in the general ledger. The perpetual inventory record for each item must provide information for recording receipts, issues, and balances on hand, both in units and in dollar amounts. With this information, the physical quantity and the valuation of goods on hand at any time are available from the accounting records. A physical count is made annually to compare the inventory on hand with the perpetual record and to provide data for any adjusting entries needed (errors and losses, for example).

When a difference is found between the perpetual inventory records and the physical count, the perpetual inventory records are adjusted to the physical count. In such cases, the inventory account is debited or credited as necessary for the correction, and COS is increased or decreased. The loss may be accumulated in a separate account, such as inventory shortages.

If there is a significant difference between the count revealed by the physical inventory and the quantity of inventory that the perpetual system says should be there, there can be only two reasons: (1) there is a problem with the perpetual system, or (2) someone is stealing the inventory. Prompt investigation and remedial action is required in either case.

In the Lea example above, the company began the year with 500 units in inventory, at a cost of $4 per unit. The purchase of 1,000 additional units is recorded as a debit to the inventory account (*not* to a purchases account):

Inventory (1,000 × $4)	4,000	
Accounts payable		4,000

When goods are sold, two entries are made; one to record the sale and the other to transfer their cost to COS. Assuming that Lea sells 900 units at a price of $10:

Accounts receivable (900 × $10)	9,000	
Sales revenue		9,000
Cost of sales (900 × $4)	3,600	
Inventory		3,600

The company will end the accounting period with an inventory balance of $2,400 (600 × $4). At the end of the year, a physical count would reveal only 580 units, and the additional expense would be recorded (it may also be recorded in a separate expense account):

Cost of sales	80	
Inventory ($2,320 – $2,400)		80

Thus at the end of the period, both the perpetual and periodic systems report identical inventory ($2,320) and COS ($3,680) amounts.

Choosing a Method

The choice of a periodic or a perpetual system is one of practicality—which method gives the best cost/benefit relationship?

A perpetual inventory system is especially useful when inventory consists of items with high unit values or when it is important to have adequate, but not excessive, inventory levels. Computer technology has made perpetual inventory systems far easier and much less expensive to maintain than was the case in manual systems. Thus, perpetual inventory systems are now widespread.

The choice of method depends on whether the company really needs to have *both* quantity information and cost information at its fingertips for control purposes:

- Does the company need to know exactly how many units it has at any point in time? If so, then it needs a perpetual system *for quantities* but not necessarily for costs. Point-of-sale computer terminals that read bar codes are very useful for maintaining quantity flow information but are not necessarily tied to the accounting records.
- Does the company need to know exactly how many units it has on hand, how old they are, *and how much they cost* on a regular basis (e.g., weekly or monthly)? The need for frequent interim financial statements will make perpetual tracking of costs more useful.

Bank operating lines of credit are often tied to the carrying value of receivables and inventory. If, for example, a company's bank is willing to lend up to 50% of the carrying value of the inventory, it is necessary to know at least monthly (and to report to the bank) the value of the inventory. In this case, a perpetual system makes sense. Also, full information on quantities and costs may be needed for insurance purposes. If a company has a fire in its warehouse or on the plant floor, how much inventory has been lost?

COST FLOW METHODS

At date of acquisition, inventory items are recorded at their cash equivalent laid-down cost. Subsequently, when an item is sold, net assets decline and expenses increase as a result of the transfer of the item's cost from inventory to cost of sales. The cost value assigned to the end-of-period inventory of merchandise and finished goods is an allocation of the total cost of goods available for sale between that portion sold (cost of sales) and that portion held as an asset for subsequent sale (ending inventory).

Each cost flow assumption gives a different result on the income statement and the SFP, since both cost of sales and inventory are affected by the chosen assumption. There is no difference in reporting the cash flow from operating activities, however.

The major cost flow methods are:

- Specific cost identification;
- Weighted average cost; and
- FIFO.

A numeric example of these three methods is shown below, applied to both perpetual and periodic systems.

Specific Identification

This method is, in theory, the most straightforward of all the methods. At the end of the year (periodic method) or on each sale (perpetual method) the specific units sold, and their specific cost, are identified to determine inventory and cost of sales. In the example in Exhibit 8A-1, there are 300 units left in closing inventory. Specific identification under a periodic system reveals that at the end of January, there are 100 units from the 9 January purchase, 100 units from the 15 January purchase, and 100 units from the 24 January purchase. The calculations are:

EXHIBIT 8A-1			
CHASE CONTAINER CORPORATION INVENTORY DATA			
Transaction Date	**Purchased**	**Units Sold**	**On Hand**
1 January—Inventory @ $1.00			200
9 January—Purchase @ $1.10	300		500
10 January—Sales		400	100
15 January—Purchase @ $1.16	400		500
18 January—Sale		300	200
24 January—Purchase @ $1.26	100		300

The costs to be allocated; goods available for sale:

Beginning inventory	200 × $1.00 =		$ 200	
Purchases	300 × $1.10 =	$330		
	400 × $1.16 =	464		
	100 × $1.26 =	126	920	
Cost of goods available for sale			$1,120	

The $1,120 is allocated between ending inventory and cost of sales, using one of the cost flow assumptions described.

Ending inventory = (100 × $1.10) + (100 × $1.16) + (100 × $1.26) = $110 + $116 + $126 = $352

Cost of sales = ($1,120 − $352) = $768

In practice, specific identification be inconvenient and/or difficult to establish just which items were sold and what their specific initial cost was. However, it is the method used when each product or service is unique (and substantial), such as for shipbuilding, special-order heavy equipment, custom software, construction contracts, consulting operations, and so forth.

Weighted Average Cost

A weighted average unit cost is computed by dividing the sum of the beginning inventory cost plus total current-period purchase costs by the number of units in the beginning inventory plus units purchased during the period. That is,

$$\text{Average cost} = \frac{\text{Opening Inventory+Purchases}}{\text{Units in opening inventory+Units purchased}}$$

Exhibit 8A-2 illustrates application of the weighted average method under a periodic system for the Chase Container Corporation using the data given in Exhibit 8A-1.

EXHIBIT 8A-2

CHASE CONTAINER CORPORATION

Weighted Average Inventory Cost Method, Periodic Inventory System

Goods Available	Units	Unit Price	Total Cost
1 January—Beginning inventory	200	$1.00	$ 200
9 January—Purchase	300	1.10	330
15 January—Purchase	400	1.16	464
24 January—Purchase	100	1.26	126
January—Total available	1,000		$1,120
Weighted average unit cost ($1,120 ÷ 1,000)		1.12	
Ending inventory:			
31 January (300 × $1.12)	300	1.12	$ 336
Cost of sales (700 × $1.12)	700	1.12	784[*]
Total cost allocated			$1,120

When the average cost method is used in a perpetual inventory system, a moving weighted average unit cost is used. *The moving weighted average provides a new unit cost after each purchase.* When goods are sold or issued, the moving weighted average unit cost at the time is used. Application of the moving weighted average concept in a perpetual inventory system is shown in Exhibit 8A-3, based on Exhibit 8A-2.

For example, on 9 January, the $1.06 moving weighted average cost is derived by dividing the total cost ($530) by the total units (500). The January ending inventory of 300 units is costed at the latest moving weighted average unit cost of $1.18 ($354 ÷ 300). The COS for the period is the sum of the sales in the total cost column, $766.

EXHIBIT 8A-3

CHASE CONTAINER CORPORATION

Moving Weighted Average Inventory Cost, Perpetual Inventory System

Dates	Purchases			Sales			Inventory Balance		
	Units	Unit Cost	Total Cost	Units	Unit Cost	Total Cost	Units	Unit Cost	Total Cost
1 January							200	$1.00	$ 200
9 January	300	$1.10	$330				500	1.06(a)	530
10 January				400	$1.06	$424	100	1.06	106

15 January	400	1.16	464					500	1.14(b)	570
18 January					300	1.14	342	200	1.14	228
24 January	100	1.26	126					300	1.18(c)	354
Ending inventory										$ 354
Cost of sales							$766			766
Total cost allocated										$1,120

(a) $530 ÷ 500 = $1.06

(b) $570 ÷ 500 = $1.14

(c) $354 ÷ 300 = $1.18

Moving weighted average requires a lot of calculating if it is done by hand; on a computerized system, moving weighted average cost is an easy method to use.

First-In, First-Out

The first-in, first-out (FIFO) method treats the first goods purchased or manufactured as the first units costed out on sale or issuance. *Goods sold (or issued) are valued at the oldest unit costs, and goods remaining in inventory are valued at the most recent unit cost amounts.* Exhibit 8A-4 demonstrates FIFO for the periodic system.

EXHIBIT 8A-4

CHASE CONTAINER CORPORATION

FIFO Inventory Costing, Periodic Inventory System

Beginning inventory (200 units at $1)	$ 200	
Add purchases during period (computed as in Exhibit 8A-1)	920	
Cost of goods available for sale		$1,120
Deduct ending inventory (300 units per physical inventory count):		
100 units at $1.26 (most recent purchase—24 January)	$ 126	
200 units at $1.16 (next most recent purchase—15 January)	232	
Ending inventory		358
Cost of sales		$ 762*

*Can also be calculated as 200 units on hand 1 January at $1 plus 300 units purchased 9 January at $1.10, plus 200 units purchased 15 January at $1.16.

Exhibit 8A-5 demonstrates the perpetual system. Using the perpetual system, a sale is costed out either currently throughout the period or each time there is a withdrawal. In Exhibit 8A-5, issues from inventory on 10 January and 18 January (FIFO basis) are costed out as they occur. FIFO always produces the same numeric results whether a periodic or perpetual system is used.

EXHIBIT 8A-5

CHASE CONTAINER CORPORATION

FIFO Inventory Costing, Perpetual Inventory System

	Purchases			Sales			Inventory Balance		
Dates	Units	Unit Cost	Total Cost	Units	Unit Cost	Total Cost	Units	Unit Cost	Total Cost
1 January	200	$1.00	$200						
9 January	300	1.10	330				200	1.00	200
							300	1.10	330
10 January				200	$1.00	$200			
				200	1.10	220	100	1.10	110
15 January	400	1.16	464				100	1.10	110
							400	1.16	464
18 January				100	1.10	110			
				200	1.16	232	200	1.16	232
24 January	100	1.26	126				200	1.16	232
							100	1.26	126
Ending inventory ($232 + $126)									$ 358
Cost of sales						$762			762
Total cost allocated									$1,120

Last-In, First-Out—The Banished Option

The last-in, first-out (LIFO) method of inventory costing matches inventory valued at the most recent unit acquisition cost with current sales revenue. When the cost of inventory is rising, LIFO attempts to give an approximation of *economic income* by recognizing that replacement inventory must be purchased at a cost closer to the most recent purchases rather than the oldest purchases, as under FIFO.

LIFO was most popular during periods of high inflation, even though the inventory account on the SFP was reported at the oldest stock (and prices). The lower, out-of-date inventory value on the SFP was tolerated to measure accounting income in a manner that is closer to economic income.

The IASB prohibited LIFO effective in 2005. The IASB argued (correctly) that LIFO is "inconsistent with the measurement of inventories for balance sheet purposes." The IASB believes that income should be measured only by changes in asset and liability accounts. LIFO gives the poorest approximation of inventory asset value compared with the other approaches, and thus it is not acceptable.

CONCEPT REVIEW

1. Explain the essential differences in accounting for inventories under the periodic and perpetual inventory systems.
2. Does the choice of periodic or perpetual system have any impact on the COS for a year? Explain.
3. Grocery stores usually use bar code scanners for ringing up prices at checkout. Does the use of bar code scanners necessarily mean that the store has a perpetual inventory system for measuring cost of sales?

Source: (Globe and money) © Vstock LLC/Getty Images RF; (Skyscrapers) © Arpad Benedek/Getty Images RF; (Canadian flag) © BjArn Kindler/Getty Images RF; (Tablet, pen, keyboard) © John Lamb/Getty Images RF.

CHAPTER 9

Long-lived Assets

INTRODUCTION

The main focus of this chapter is on the very broad category of long-lived assets—both tangible and intangible. Long-lived assets of many descriptions have future benefit to companies because they contribute to the revenue stream. For example, Maple Leaf Foods Inc., a producer of food products, reports hog and poultry stock (biological assets), in addition to the more classic tangible assets, such as land, buildings, machinery, equipment, and assets under construction. Intangible assets include computer software, trademarks, delivery routes, and goodwill. This is quite a diversified collection of assets!

Companies can report long-lived assets using three different models. Brookfield Asset Management Inc., which is a global asset management company, uses all three models for its long-lived assets. The company uses the *cost model* for intangibles and some items of property, plant, and equipment; the *revaluation model* for renewable power generating, utilities, transport, and energy assets; and the *fair-value model* for investment properties. Each of these models will have a very different impact on the financial statements. Within the structure established by accounting standards, companies must decide which measurement model to apply to long-lived assets.

This chapter will examine the issues surrounding the measurement and recording of long-lived assets, both tangible and intangible, and goodwill. The appendices to this chapter discuss the accounting for investment properties and government assistance. Chapter 10 continues this topic and deals with accounting for long-lived assets following acquisition, including amortization, impairment, revaluation, and also the fair-value model.

CATEGORIES OF LONG-LIVED ASSETS

Long-lived assets may be separated into five categories:

1. **Property, plant, and equipment**

An item of **property, plant, and equipment** can be defined as a *tangible item expected to be used for more than one period, and held for use in the production or supply of goods and services, or for rental to others, or for administrative purposes.*

Items of property, plant, and equipment are *tangible assets*. These assets have a physical presence; the word *tangible* means, literally, that the asset can be touched. Tangible assets include land, buildings, vehicles, equipment, furniture, leasehold improvements, and other such physical assets. Tangible assets also include long-lived property held to generate revenue through rental, such as office buildings, apartments, vehicles, and so on.

Property, plant, and equipment are not intended for sale in the ordinary course of business—if they were, they would be inventory. For example, a computer is an item of *property, plant, and equipment* to the company that buys and uses it, but it was *inventory* to the manufacturer that made it and to the dealer that sold it. It is not the asset itself that governs classification as property, plant, and equipment; it is the intended *use* of the asset that matters.

On the other hand, if an item of property, plant, and equipment is no longer needed, then it is reclassified as a *held-for-sale asset*. Sometimes, the reclassification is to *investment property*. Such assets are given a different classification on the SFP as discussed in Chapter 3.

2. **Investment property**

    Investment property is a unique classification for land and/or buildings that are held for rent (e.g., apartment buildings) or capital appreciation (e.g., vacant land held for future sale). Appendix 1 discusses accounting for investment property.

3. **Biological assets**

    Biological assets are living plants and animals. The accounting for these types of assets, when classified as inventory, was discussed in Chapter 6. Biological assets can also be long-lived assets.

4. **Intangible assets**

    Intangible assets are long-lived assets that *do not have a physical substance. Intangible assets are separately identifiable* and often arise from legal or contractual rights. These assets are held to generate revenue, and are not intended for sale in the ordinary course of business. They can be purchased or internally generated. Examples include customer lists, copyrights, patents, subscription lists, mineral rights, franchises, computer software, quotas, licenses, and trademarks.

5. **Goodwill**

    Goodwill is a category of its own, because it does not have physical substance (like an intangible asset) but it is not a *separately identifiable* asset (unlike an intangible asset.) Goodwill arises as a residual in the purchase of other assets acquired in a business combination. The superior earning potential of the purchased entity is assumed to be the reason that goodwill exists.

VALUATION OF LONG-LIVED ASSETS

There are three possible models used to value long-lived assets.

1. **Cost Model**

    Long-lived assets are normally recorded using the **cost model,** which records assets at cost. Accumulated depreciation and accumulated impairment losses are kept in a separate account; cost less these accumulated amounts is called **net book value**. Cost is the acquisition cost, plus all costs directly attributable to the acquisition, construction, development, installation, or betterment of the asset.

    Cost is usually the *fair value* at the date of purchase. That is, the asset is bought for its fair value as of the date of acquisition. As time passes, the fair value of the asset will change as the price for a comparable asset changes in the market, perhaps due to changes in technology and supply and demand forces. Since long-lived assets are held for lengthy periods of time, net book value and fair value may be quite different. The cost model does not attempt to reflect the current fair value of assets.

2. **Revaluation Model**

Companies can *choose* to use the revaluation model for the following long-lived assets:
    a. Property, plant, and equipment;
    b. Intangible assets with an active market; and/or
    c. Exploration and evaluation costs for mineral resources.
In all these cases, the *fallback choice is the cost model*.

The **revaluation model** uses fair value as its measurement base. Assets are revalued to fair value, with enough frequency that fair value is reasonably current. This might (or might not) require an annual valuation. In between valuations, the asset is recorded at the revalued amount less accumulated depreciation and accumulated impairment losses. The revaluation model, if adopted, must be used for an entire class of assets; it may not be applied to individual assets. The revaluation model is explained in Appendix 2 to Chapter 10.

A company might choose to adopt the revaluation model for long-lived assets when they are pledged as collateral for loans, and accordingly the fair value may be highly relevant to financial statement readers.

3. **Fair-Value Model**

Biological assets must be recorded at fair value, as long as fair value can be measured reliably. Changes in fair value are recorded in earnings.

Companies can *choose* to use the fair-value model for investment property. *The fallback choice is the cost model.*

Using the **fair-value model**, assets are revalued to fair value annually. This policy might be chosen if financial statement readers have a particular interest in the fair value of these assets.

One key difference between the fair-value model and the revaluation model is that fair value is determined every year. Depreciation is not recorded with the fair-value model. The fair-value model is discussed further in Appendix 1 to this chapter.

CONCEPT REVIEW

1. What are the five types of long-lived assets?
2. What is the difference between tangible and intangible long-lived assets?
3. What are the three valuation models used for measuring long-lived assets?

RECOGNITION OF PROPERTY, PLANT, AND EQUIPMENT

The purchase price for property, plant, and equipment is capitalized. **Capitalization** means that the expenditure is debited to an asset account. The alternative is to expense the amount.

In general, expenditures related to the acquisition of property, plant, and equipment are *capitalized* if:

a. There is a probable future economic benefit that will flow to the company, and
b. The cost of the asset can be measured reliably.

However, subsequent costs can be added to initial cost *only* if they will increase future economic benefits. Costs incurred to maintain the asset must be expensed.

Component Accounting

A unique consideration for recognition of property, plant, and equipment is **component accounting**. The definition of a component is driven by depreciation, which is discussed in Chapter 10. On initial recognition, *if an asset has significant components that depreciate at different rates, the asset is separated into these components.* A critical word here is *significant*! Not every part will be significant; similar items would be grouped.

For example, the cost of an aircraft might be segregated into the aircraft frame, the engine, cabin interior, and equipment. Each component is set up as a separate asset.

Assume that equipment is purchased for $47,000, and it consists of three components, which have separately identifiable values. When the equipment is purchased, the following entry is recorded:

Equipment component 1	1,000	
Equipment component 2	31,000	
Equipment component 3	15,000	
Cash		47,000

Components are separately depreciated.

Basket Purchase of Several Assets

Occasionally, several assets are acquired for a single lump-sum price that may be lower than the sum of the individual asset prices, to encourage the sale. In other cases, the assets are attached (e.g., land and building, vines and land in a winery). This type of acquisition is called a **basket purchase**, group purchase, or lump-sum purchase. A portion of the single lump-sum price must be allocated to each asset acquired. *Again, since they depreciate separately, they must be segregated on initial recognition.*

Any portion of the lump-sum price directly attributable to particular assets in the group is assigned in full to those assets. For example, land survey costs and back property taxes applicable to land are assigned *only to the land account.* Allocation of the remaining lump-sum price to each asset is necessary. Under the cost principle, the sum of the individual asset account balances at acquisition is limited to the lump-sum price.

Allocation is based on the relative fair values of the several assets involved. The company would determine the appropriate method of valuing the asset from the fair-value hierarchy in the standard for fair-value measurement discussed in Chapter 2. This value may be market prices for similar assets, current appraised values, or a present value of future net cash flows. The seller's book values are not relevant because they do not reflect the current value of the assets.

Each asset is valued according to the ratio of its value to the total value of the group; this valuation is called the *proportional method.*

To illustrate the proportional method, assume that $90,000 is the negotiated acquisition price paid for land, a building, and machinery. These assets are appraised individually. The best available indications of fair value are determined to be the following: land, $30,000; building, $50,000; and machinery, $20,000. This is a $100,000 total, purchased for $90,000.

The cost apportionment of the single lump-sum price and the entry to record the transaction are as follows:

	Appraised Asset Value	Apportionment of Cost	Apportioned Cost
Land	$ 30,000	30%* × $90,000	$27,000
Building	50,000	50% × $90,000	45,000

| Machinery | 20,000 | 20% × $90,000 | 18,000 |
| Total | $100,000 | | $90,000 |

*30% = $30,000 ÷ $100,000

The entry to record the basket purchase:

Land	27,000	
Building	45,000	
Machinery	18,000	
Cash		90,000

Spare Parts

Spare parts are included as a separate element of property, plant, and equipment. For an airplane, for example, spare aircraft and engine parts are a logical separate component element of equipment.

A unique type of spare part is *standby equipment*, which is often viewed as a backup in case of failure of a part. For example, a reliable source of power is critical in the utility industry, so the utility would own backup for key components, such as transformers, in case the original component fails.

Spare parts are not held for resale, so they are not inventory. However, if minor and immaterial, they may be included in inventory.

Subsequent Costs

After acquisition, many costs are incurred related to property, plant, and equipment. Examples include repairs, maintenance, betterments, replacement of major parts, and major inspections or overhauls. These expenditures may be expensed or capitalized, depending on their nature and the circumstances.

Maintenance and Ordinary Repairs

Day-to-day maintenance and ordinary repairs are expensed. Maintenance expenditures include lubrication, cleaning, adjustment, and painting incurred on a continuous basis to keep assets in usable condition. Ordinary repair costs include outlays for parts, labour, and related supplies that are necessary to keep assets in operating condition but do not add materially to the use of assets nor prolong their useful life significantly. If there are "surprise" repairs—the asset unexpectedly breaks down, or a flaw is discovered—these repairs do not enhance the expected longevity of the asset and are expensed.

On the other hand, if a machine is purchased, and the purchaser knows that it will have to be repaired prior to use, these initial repairs are capitalized. The assumption is that the price paid for the asset reflects the known repairs and modification.

Ordinary repairs usually involve relatively small expenditures but can be large expenditures, too. *Many expenditures related to long-lived assets are repairs.* Capitalization may look tempting at times; remember that expensing is the norm in this category!

Repairs cannot be accrued over time. For example, if a $1,200 repair is expected every three years, a company cannot record an expense (and a provision) of $400 per year. Instead, repair expense represents the amount actually spent during the year, even if that is "lumpy."

Additions

Additions are extensions, enlargements, or expansions of an existing asset. An extra wing or room added to a building is an example. Additions represent capital expenditures, and are recorded in the long-lived asset accounts at cost. Related work on the existing structure, such as shoring up the foundation for the addition or cutting an entranceway through an existing wall, is part of the cost of the addition and is also capitalized. The addition might be classified as a separate component, if its depreciation pattern were in some way different from the original asset.

Betterment

The replacement of a major component of an item of property, plant, and equipment is often referred to as a **betterment**.

Betterments may be *replacements* or *renewals*. A *replacement* is the substitution of a component of an item of property, plant, and equipment with one of comparable quality. For example, consider replacement of the seats in an airplane, or the replacement of the lining in the oven of a bakery. *Renewals* involve large nonrecurring expenditures, that increase the utility or the service life of the asset beyond the original estimate.

Betterments qualify as an asset, not an expense, because the *future economic benefits associated with the asset are enhanced.* The new component is a separate asset. Any net book value of the component that is being replaced is **derecognized**, or written off.

To illustrate, assume that a shingle roof with an original cost of $20,000 and now 80% depreciated, is replaced by a new fireproof tile roof costing $60,000. The two entries to record the betterment are as follows:

To remove old component accounts		
Accumulated depreciation, building component - roof ($20,000 × 80%)	16,000	
Loss on asset improvement	4,000	
Building component – roof (old roof)		20,000
To record cost of new component		
Building component - roof	60,000	
Cash		60,000

Major Inspection

Costs of **major inspections** are capitalized (e.g., the costs related to an inspection/overhaul of an airplane engine). Similar to the replacement of components, any remaining carrying amount from the previous inspection is derecognized.

CONCEPT REVIEW

1. What is component accounting?
2. Why is it necessary to allocate the overall cost of a basket purchase of assets to the individual assets in the basket?
3. What is the difference between accounting for repairs and for betterments?
4. What happens when a major part that has been recognized as a separate component is replaced in an asset?

COST OF PROPERTY, PLANT, AND EQUIPMENT

Elements of Cost

There is *normal practice* surrounding the typical kinds of costs that should be capitalized versus expensed in each category of property, plant, and equipment. Cost can include the purchase price, directly attributable costs, and dismantling or site restoration costs. Initial repairs and modifications *that are known at the time of purchase* are capitalized. Certain costs are never capitalized, such as start-up costs, relocation costs, and initial operating losses.

Review Exhibit 9-1 for common practices for property, plant, and equipment categories, such as buildings, machinery and equipment, land, and land improvements.

EXHIBIT 9-1
COMMON CAPITALIZATION PRACTICES: PROPERTY, PLANT, AND EQUIPMENT

Long-lived Asset	Capitalize
Buildings, purchased	• Purchase price, plus non-refundable sales tax • Cost of modifications
Buildings, constructed	• Architectural fees • Payments to contractors • Borrowing costs during construction • Cost of permits • Excavation costs • Legal fees, closing costs
Buildings, self-constructed	• As above, but costs are internal for labour, materials, and a reasonable apportionment of manufacturing overhead.
Machinery and equipment	• Invoice cost, net of discounts, plus non-refundable sales tax • Known or planned initial repairs and modifications • Taxes, freight, and duty • Borrowing costs during shipping or customization • Special platforms, foundations, other required installation costs but not training of staff to use the asset • Costs of building modifications necessary for installation • Site restoration costs
Land	• Cost of preparing asset for use, including testing • Purchase price

	• Back taxes on acquisition, paid to release title
	• Legal fees, closing costs
	• General land preparation costs, including grading, filling, draining, and surveying
	• Cost of removing structures and other obstructions, if land is acquired for development (proceeds from salvaged materials reduce the cost capitalized)
	• Special assessments for local government-maintained improvements, including streets, sidewalks, sewers, and streetlights
	• Property taxes, insurance, and other holding costs incurred on land not in current productive use (may be expensed on grounds of expedience and conservatism)
	• Landscaping and other property enhancements, if permanent
Land improvements	• Site restoration costs
	• Driveways, parking lots, fencing
	• Streets and sidewalks that the company must maintain
	• Landscaping, if not permanent

Careful analysis will show that each capitalized item creates some sort of future enhancement of cash flows. Often this results from the fact that the expenditure is required to get the long-lived asset into operation.

Note in particular the conventions surrounding land. Since land does not depreciate, but other tangible assets do, a decision to capitalize an amount in the land account means that there is no impact on earnings until the land is sold. In particular, note that land cost includes costs specifically related to obtaining clear title to the land, such as *legal fees and back property taxes*. Any expenditure associated with preparing the land for its intended use, such as *clearing existing structures and excavation*, is also capitalized to the land account.

Other expenditures, for elements that will wear out over time, are *components* and put in a separate land improvements account(s), and depreciated. These expenditures include non-permanent landscaping as well as fences and paving. Also included in the land improvements category are site restoration costs; the amount capitalized for site restoration costs is depreciated.

As you learned in the last chapter, a refundable value-added tax (HST, GST) is not part of the cost of an asset purchased. However, a non-refundable sale tax (PST) is part of the cost.

Borrowing Cost

As we learned in Chapter 8, borrowing costs include interest paid, but also an allocation of initial costs to issue a loan contract and an allocation of any interest rate adjustment, such as a premium or discount. Borrowing costs are usually expensed. However, any borrowing cost that is *directly attributable to the acquisition, construction, or production of a qualifying asset* forms part of the cost of that asset and must be capitalized. Qualifying assets include long-lived assets such as machinery, office or manufacturing facilities, and intangible assets.

Borrowing costs are to be capitalized *only if* the long-lived asset takes a substantial time to build, or prepare/customize for use. There must be a *time delay* for construction, customization, or shipping; borrowing costs related to this delay period must be capitalized.

We return to the calculations associated with the capitalization of borrowing costs in Chapter 13.

Safety or Environmental Expenditures

Involuntary costs incurred by the company for safety or environmental reasons are capitalized. Government action has initiated these expenditures, which makes them involuntary. If the upgrades are not completed, the company may not be able to continue operating. Examples include required environmental upgrades, such as "scrubbers" in smokestacks, and safety upgrades for sprinkler systems.

On the surface, these costs would appear to not meet the definition of an asset since there often is no future benefit from the expenditure on its own. For example, assume that a company must install a new sprinkler system to meet an enhanced fire code in a manufacturing operation. The sprinklers *on their own* do not provide an increased benefit, or future cash flow, to the company. However, the expenditure is capitalized because the future benefit is derived from the use of the asset as a whole. Without the sprinkler system, the building would be shut down.

Voluntary costs for environmental or safety reasons would be capitalized only if they had a future benefit on their own or enhanced the usefulness (enhanced the cash flow) of the asset. Otherwise, they would be expensed.

Self-constructed Assets

Many long-lived assets are not purchased, but rather are constructed by the company. The cost of a constructed asset is the sum of the expenditures—direct material, direct labour, and manufacturing overhead—relating to its construction. These costs may not reflect the fair value of the asset, even at the time of its creation. Remember, an asset such as a building may be constructed at a lower cost than if it were purchased, completed, from a third party.

For example, a utility employs its own personnel to extend transmission lines. All costs directly associated with the construction are capitalized to the transmission-line asset, but this is lower than the utility would pay to have an unrelated company build the line.

Overhead Cost

Overhead incurred during construction, *if it is directly attributable to the construction or development activity*, is included in the cost of self-constructed or self-developed assets. Overhead costs could include some portion of utility costs, depreciation and maintenance on equipment used, supervision, and so on. *Administrative costs are not eligible for capitalization.*

Many accountants contend that failure to allocate some portion of the overhead to self-construction projects causes an undervaluation of self-constructed assets. On the other hand, others argue that assets are often self-constructed during slack periods when the production facility and workers would otherwise be idle. Using this line of reasoning, no overhead should be capitalized because of the income-manipulation potential associated with this "make-work" project. Companies that want to show high asset values will tend to interpret "overhead" quite broadly and will allocate significant amounts of overhead cost to the project.

Incidental Revenues or Expenses

Any profits or losses from incidental operations that occur before or during construction are not capitalized. These are treated as a separate element in earnings. For example, a company might have demolished a building and decided to operate a parking lot on the land prior to beginning construction of a new facility. Any revenues and expenses from operating the parking lot are included in earnings.

Fair Market Value Cap

The actual cost of a self-constructed asset does not necessarily equal fair market value at the point of acquisition. Using the higher market value would result in recording a gain on construction. A company cannot record a gain as the result of expenditures! The lower construction cost is ultimately reflected in higher earnings because of lower depreciation expense in future years.

However, *the maximum value allowed for self-constructed assets is fair market value.* If total capitalized cost exceeds the market value of a similar asset of equal capacity and quality, the excess is recognized as a loss. Failure to do so carries forward cost elements that have no future benefit and causes overstated depreciation in future years.

Example—Self-constructed Asset

To illustrate the accounting for a self-constructed asset, assume that Kelvin Corp. completes a project to build a special piece of equipment with total construction costs as follows:

Material	$200,000
Labour	500,000
Incremental overhead	60,000
Applied overhead	40,000
Capitalized borrowing costs	100,000
Total	$900,000

Kelvin has recorded costs in an account called *equipment under construction*. If the asset's market value at completion equals or exceeds $900,000, the summary entry to record the completion of the project is:

Equipment	900,000	
Equipment under construction		900,000

Alternatively, if the asset's market value is only $880,000, the entry is:

Equipment	880,000	
Loss on construction of equipment	20,000	
Equipment under construction		900,000

Assume that staff must be trained to use the new equipment, which costs $3,500 in labour costs and material. Training cannot be capitalized.

Training expense	3,500	
Cash, wages payable, inventory, etc.		3,500

ETHICAL ISSUES

Expenditures might be capitalized and depreciated, or immediately expensed. If the company does not expense now, it will expense later. That is, capitalized costs, in almost all cases, are carried to earnings through depreciation. However, the two paths will provide different earnings and asset values throughout the life of the asset.

It is important to watch capitalization practices carefully—some firms, with a desire to maximize earnings or assets by deferring costs, seize the opportunity to try to defer lots of interesting things. Others wish to capitalize as little as possible. Remember, though, that the higher asset value generated is a base for future depreciation and potential impairment.

A company may prefer to expense rather than capitalize if cash flow prediction is a primary reporting objective. By including the expenditures in current expenses, a company achieves an earnings figure that is closer to the actual cash flow.

At the other end of the spectrum, some companies are very aggressive in their capitalization policies, seeking higher current earnings and long-lived assets, and accepting higher future depreciation. For example, a regulated public utility might capitalize as many costs as possible because the enterprise's permitted (i.e., regulated) profit is based on its regulated rate of return multiplied by the asset base. The higher the asset base, the larger is the profit it is entitled to earn.

Materiality plays a role in this area, as well. Small capital expenditures are often expensed on the basis that the more correct capitalization and depreciation would not produce results "different enough" to cause investors to make different decisions.

Long-lived Assets Financed with Low-Interest Debt

Sometimes, special payment terms for an asset stretch out over a long period. This presents no special accounting problem, unless the debt bears an interest rate that is lower than the market interest rate. Low-interest-rate terms are often offered as a sales incentive.

In such a case, the asset is recorded at the most objective amount, considering:

1. The cash equivalent price, or fair value, of the long-lived asset *if it were paid for immediately*, or
2. The present value of the future cash payments required by the debt agreement discounted at the prevailing (market) interest rate for that type of debt.

When a low-interest debt instrument is issued, it can be recorded *net* or *gross*.

- If recorded gross, the loan is recorded at its face value, and a discount is in a separate, contra account. The discount is the difference between the face value of the loan and its present value. The liability is always shown net of the discount on the SFP. The discount is amortized over the life of the loan, adjusting interest expense upward. Interest expense is the amount paid, plus a portion of the discount, so that interest expense reflects the true, market interest rate.

- If recorded net, the loan is recorded *at the present value of the liability*. The net liability is increased over the term of the debt, increasing interest expense each period.

Example

The following two cases illustrate the purchase of a long-lived asset with delayed payment terms.

Case A Assume that Cobb Corp. purchases equipment on 1 January 20X2, with a $600 cash down payment and a $1,000, one-year 12% note payable due on 31 December 20X2. *The stated interest rate is equal to the current market rate,* so the present value of the note equals its face value. There is no established fair value for the equipment.

The asset is recorded at the sum of the cash down payment plus the present value of the note, because the cash equivalent price of the asset is not available.

The present value of the note:

$$P = (\$1,000 + \$120) \times (P/F, 12\%, 1)$$
$$= \$1,120 \times .89286$$
$$= \$1,000$$

The recorded amount is:

$$\text{Equipment value} = \text{Cash down payment} + \text{Present value of note}$$
$$= \$600 + \$1,000 = \$1,600$$

Cobb's entries to record the asset and the note are as follows:

1 January 20X2

Equipment	1,600	
Cash		600
Note payable		1,000

Case B Assume instead that Feller Co. acquires a machine on 1 January 20X2, with a non-interest-bearing note that requires $8,615 to be paid on each of 31 December 20X2, 20X3, and 20X4. The note has no explicit interest, but the prevailing interest rate is 14% on liabilities of similar risk and duration. The face amount of the note is $25,845 ($8,615 × 3). The cash equivalent cost of the machine is unknown, and the asset is recorded at the present value of the three payments discounted at 14%.

P = $8,615 × (P/A, 14%, 3)

= $8,615 × 2.32163

= $20,000 (rounded)

Feller's entries to record the asset and the note are as follows, using the *net method.*

1 January 20X2

Net Method		
Equipment	20,000	
Note payable		20,000

Alternatively, the gross method can be used, where a separate discount and note payable are recorded in the accounts, even though they are shown net on the SFP:

1 January 20X2

Gross Method		
Equipment	20,000	
Discount to note payable (contra to note payable)	5,845	
Note payable		25,845

The discount of $5,845 ($25,845 − $20,000) on the note payable reduces the *net note payable balance* to the present value of the future cash flows ($20,000). The discount is amortized to interest expense over the life of the liability.

Site Restoration Costs or Decommissioning Liabilities

A company may have a legal requirement, either through legal statute or by contract, to incur site restoration or decommissioning costs when an asset (or group of assets) is retired.

For example,

- Companies often are required by law to restore mine sites to their original condition.
- Landfills must be covered, capped (e.g., with concrete), and perhaps landscaped when they are full.
- Companies that use rooftops for billboard advertising or for relay antennas usually are required by contract to physically remove billboards or antennas at the end of the contract and to repair the roofs as well.

A company may also have a history of site remediation in excess of legal requirements. If so, this creates an expectation in external stakeholder groups that such "excess" remediation will be carried out in the future as well. This is called a **constructive obligation**, a liability established through *past practice that creates an expectation by outsiders.*

Site restoration costs or **decommissioning obligations** are not expensed at the end of the asset's life, when the work is done. Instead, *they are recognized upfront as a (depreciable) asset and a liability.*

Accounting Practice

When a legal or constructive obligation exists, the cost of fulfilling that obligation must be recognized when the asset is acquired.

If the obligation arises at a later point in time, it is recognized at the time an obligation is known. For example, a mine is purchased, and site restoration costs are estimated and capitalized. After the mine has been operating for five years, legislation is amended and additional remediation is established. The site restoration asset is adjusted accordingly at the end of year 5.

The accounting requirements are as follows:

- Estimate the amount and the timing of future cash flows for the remediation activities under consideration;
- Calculate the **present value** of the cash flow at a pretax rate that reflects the risks related to that liability;
- Debit an asset (capitalize), and credit a provision for this present value amount;
- Over time, the asset must be depreciated;
- Over time, an expense must be recorded to reflect the increase to the liability because of the passage of time; and
- Amounts must be remeasured annually, and corrected.

Example—Initial Recognition

For example, suppose that on 2 January 20X0, Firkin Ltd. purchased equipment for $500,000 to install in a leased building. The company is legally required by the building lease to remove the equipment at the end of 10 years. The estimated cost of removal is $70,000.

To recognize the liability, the $70,000 must be discounted at an appropriate interest rate. Suppose that the pretax rate that reflects the risks is 5%. The future obligation must be discounted at 5% for 10 years:

P = $70,000 × (P/F, 5%, 10) = $70,000 × 0.61391 = $42,974

The asset purchase and the retirement obligation are recorded as follows:

To record the purchase of equipment		
Equipment	500,000	
Account payable (to equipment vendor)		500,000
To record the legal obligation to remove the equipment in the future		
Equipment	42,974	
Provision—decommissioning		42,974

The asset is recorded at $542,974.

Depreciation

Assuming that Firkin uses straight-line depreciation over a ten-year life with zero residual value, the initial book value will be depreciated at $54,297 per year. The depreciation is recorded exactly the same way as any other depreciation expense. For 20X0, the entry will be:

| Depreciation expense—equipment | 54,297 | |
| Accumulated depreciation—equipment | | 54,297 |

If the decommissioning obligation related to land instead of equipment, it would have been capitalized to a *land improvements* account and separately depreciated.

Interest

An expense must be recorded to reflect the increase to the liability because of the passage of time - that is, interest must be added. The retirement obligation was recorded at its present value. By the end of 10 years, the obligation must be $70,000 on Firkin's books, not $42,974. Therefore, Firkin must accrue an expense each year to build up the total obligation to $70,000. The increase is calculated using the same 5% interest rate as was used in the present value calculation. The increase is recognized as interest expense.

For 20X0, the accrual will be:

| Interest expense [$42,974 × 5%] | 2,149 | |
| Provision—decommissioning | | 2,149 |

At the end of 20X0, the book value of the obligation will be $42,974 + $2,149 = $45,123. For 20X1, the interest accrual will be $45,123 × 5% = $2,256. Each year's accrual is based on the accumulated obligation at the end of the preceding year.

Remeasurement

In addition to amortizing the cost and accruing interest on the obligation, Firkin must also adjust the amount of the obligation if there is a change in the amount or timing of the expected retirement obligation cash flows or a change in the discount rate to reflect current market rates. In Firkin's case, the timing could change if the lease term is extended, or if the estimated cost of removal changes. The current cost is quite likely to change from year to year as legislation, technology, and cost components change due to increasing or decreasing prices. We return to the complexities of this remeasurement in Chapter 12.

Long-lived Assets Acquired in Exchanges

Long-lived Assets Acquired in Exchange for Non-monetary Assets

Long-lived assets are often exchanged for other non-monetary assets. That is, assets are "swapped." Remember that monetary assets are those whose value is fixed in terms of dollars, such as cash and receivables. Non-monetary assets, such as inventory and long-lived assets, *do not have a value fixed in terms of dollars.*

Non-monetary transactions are any exchange of non-monetary assets, liabilities, or services for other non-monetary assets, liabilities, or services, or any exchange that has little or no monetary consideration involved. Valuation of the acquired asset is the substantive issue in non-monetary asset exchanges. This valuation determines whether a gain or loss is recognized.

The valuation alternatives and accounting for non-monetary exchanges of long-lived assets were explained in Chapter 6. A reminder that, in broad strokes:

1. If there is commercial substance to the exchange, then the new asset is recorded based on fair value.
2. If there is no commercial substance, or if fair value cannot be determined, then the new asset is recorded based on the net book value of the asset given up.

Long-lived Assets Acquired in Exchange for Equity Securities

When equity securities (e.g., common shares) are issued to acquire long-lived assets, this is another *non-monetary transaction.* For long-lived assets acquired in exchange for shares, *the fair value of the assets acquired* is used to value the transaction. The fair value of the shares is not used, unless the asset fair value cannot be measured reliably.

Donated Assets

Shareholders and other parties occasionally donate assets and services to corporations. For example, shareholders may donate valuable paintings to adorn the corporate boardroom. There is no cost to the company. They are obtained in a *non-reciprocal transfer*, which means that the company gives nothing in return (reciprocates with nothing.)

Does that mean that the assets need not be recognized? The SFP seems incomplete. On the other hand, why record depreciation for an asset that had no outlay cost to shareholders? *There is no specific IFRS guidance for donated assets to a corporation.*

In the not-for-profit world, where non-reciprocal exchanges with stakeholders are common, the following practices are required:

1. Record the asset at fair value, and credit a deferred revenue account.
2. Depreciate the asset.
3. Recognize revenue from the deferred revenue account in the same pattern as asset depreciation.

The result is that the SFP is complete, but bottom-line earnings reflect both an expense and an offsetting revenue.

In practice, some companies record the donated asset at fair value, and credit a contributed capital account in equity in the amount of the donation. They then trust that future depreciation of donated assets will be recognized along with revenue streams generated by the donated asset.

Example

To illustrate accounting for a donated asset, assume that a building (fair market value $400,000) and the land on which it is located (fair market value $100,000) are donated to Sui Ltd. A $5,000 legal and deed transfer cost for the land is borne by Sui, which records the donation as follows:

Building	400,000	
Land	105,000	
Cash		5,000
Contributed capital—donated assets		500,000

Government Assistance

Assets may be donated to a company from a government unit. In addition, to help fund the purchase or construction of property, plant, or equipment, government grants or forgivable loans might be available. A forgivable loan means that there is a loan from the government that will not have to be paid back as long as certain conditions are met. Conditions often involve employment levels over multiple years. Accounting for government assistance of various types is discussed further in Appendix 2 to this chapter.

CONCEPT REVIEW

1. In initial measurement of property, plant, and equipment, what costs are eligible for capitalization, and what kind of costs must be expensed immediately?
2. Under what circumstances can a company capitalize borrowing costs?

3. What is the difference in accounting for involuntary or voluntary costs related to safety or environmental costs?

4. When must a company record the present value of the expected cash outflows for asset retirement? How is the present value calculated?

BIOLOGICAL ASSETS

As you saw in Chapter 6, biological assets to the point of harvest are accounted for at fair value (less cost to sell), with the change in fair value included in earnings. At harvest, the asset becomes inventory, initially recorded at fair value, which is then treated as "cost" until the asset is sold.

A biological asset may be a long-term asset, as for example a stand of timber owned by a forestry company. The fair value of the timber would be assessed each reporting period, using models that incorporate market values, time to harvest, yield rates, and a myriad of other variables. Again, the change in fair value is included in earnings.

One exception to this are *bearer plants*, which are living plants that live for several periods, bearing fruit that is agricultural produce. Grape vines owned by wineries are an example of bearer plants. Bearer plants have a low probability of being sold as a biological asset, and would ordinarily be sold for scrap value, perhaps as firewood, at the end of their useful life. Bearer plants have been excluded from the accounting standard that requires fair-value accounting. (Remember, though, that the grapes themselves are a biological asset.)

One way to look at this classification is that biological assets are either:

1. *Consumable biological assets*, which will be turned to consumable inventory when mature (e.g., growing timber that is valued at fair value less cost to sell); or

2. *Bearer biological assets*, which are used to bear produce (e.g., grape vines that are recorded at cost.)

When biological assets are valued at fair value less cost to sell, there are significant estimates involved. To assist the users of the financial statements in understanding the nature of the valuation, major assumptions must be disclosed, as well as a continuity schedule that shows the opening and closing balance of the biological asset, as well as the changes in the account during the year, whether from harvest, increases from purchase, and gains and losses caused by the change in fair value.

INTANGIBLE ASSETS—ELEMENTS OF COST

Intangible assets are similar to property, plant, and equipment in that their cost is capitalized. If the intangible asset is purchased, then the purchase price is capitalized. Legal costs are a major part of the recorded cost of intangible assets. This includes the legal costs to register these assets, and also legal costs for successful defence of the restricted use of these assets (e.g., successful patent defence).

Costs related to introducing a new product or service (e.g., advertising) and conducting business in a new location (e.g., training) are expensed; they are not capitalized.

If the intangible asset is *internally generated*, rather than purchased, certain criteria must be met to qualify for capitalization. The cost of an internally generated intangible asset is the sum of the expenditures relating to its construction or development. Borrowing costs must be capitalized if the development timeline is lengthy.

Many intangible assets are internally generated or developed by the enterprise, and in fact are unique elements critical to the success of the enterprise. The cost assigned to these assets may well be very different from the fair value of the asset. In fact, cost and fair value may not be related at all; some very valuable intangibles may have been very inexpensive to create! Examples of internally developed intangibles include computer software, computer games, and information systems.

Refer to Exhibit 9-2 for the common capitalizable costs related to *specific intangibles* such as copyrights, trademarks, and franchise fees.

EXHIBIT 9-2
COMMON CAPITALIZATION PRACTICES: INTANGIBLE ASSETS

Patents	• Purchase price, transfer, and legal fees if bought from another entity • If internally generated, criteria must be met to justify capitalization • Development costs to internally develop a patented item; research costs are expensed • Legal and other necessary documentation costs to register the patent, if self-developed • Costs of a successful court defence (unsuccessful defences are expensed, along with the now-worthless patent)
Industrial design registrations (e.g., a five-year renewable registration of the shape, pattern, or ornamentation of a manufactured item)	• Acquisition and registration cost, as per patents • If internally generated, criteria must be met to justify capitalization • Successful defence costs, as per patents
Copyrights	• Acquisition and registration cost, as per patents • If internally generated, criteria must be met to justify capitalization • Successful defence costs, as per patents
Trademarks and trade names	• Acquisition cost, as per patents • If internally generated, criteria must be met to justify capitalization • Legal and other necessary documentation costs to register the trademark, if self-developed • Successful defence costs, as per patents
Brands	• Acquisition cost • If internally generated, cannot recognize
Customer lists	• Acquisition cost • If internally generated, cannot recognize
Publishing titles	• Acquisition cost • If internally generated, cannot recognize
Franchise rights	• Initial franchise fees, not related to annual volumes • Legal fees, closing costs

Internally developed intangibles	• Specific criteria must be met to justify capitalization
Leasehold improvements (alterations, improvements, or refurbishing of leased space)	• Invoice cost, installation costs
Resource exploration and evaluation costs	• Resource exploration and development costs incurred • Present value of site restoration costs
Computer software costs	• If internally generated, criteria must be met to justify capitalization
Website development costs	• If internally generated, criteria must be met to justify capitalization • Application and infrastructure costs capitalized • Graphics costs capitalized • Some content development capitalized, depending on longevity and nature

Internally generated or developed assets are subject to impairment tests, as are all assets. If fair value is below net book value, the asset must be written down.

SPECIFIC INTANGIBLE ASSETS

Internally Generated Intangibles

The criteria that must be met for any internally generated or developed intangible asset are:

1. First, the asset must be an *identifiable* intangible, which means that the intangible asset must be separable or able to be divided from an entity, or the asset must be caused by contractual or legal rights; and
2. Second, the recognition criteria must be met:
   a. The intangible asset must be controlled by the entity as a result of past transactions or events;
   b. Future economic benefits must flow from the intangible asset; for example, markets for the related product or the internal usefulness of the intangible asset must be clearly established; and
   c. The cost must be reliably measurable.

These criteria are an attempt to provide rigour over cost-deferral practices.

Ineligible Costs

Certain items are prohibited from being recognized as intangible assets. Costs would *not* meet capitalization criteria and therefore would be expensed as incurred.

Examples are internally generated brands, mastheads, publishing titles, and customer lists; these are simply not eligible for capitalization. If purchased from another party, these same items would be recognized as an intangible asset, since the purchase price indicates fair value.

Other costs that are not eligible for capitalization:

1. The costs of starting up a business (start-up costs);
2. Training;

3. Advertising and promotion; and

4. Costs of relocating or reorganizing all or part of an entity.

Research and Development

Broadly defined, *research and development* (R&D) includes the activities undertaken by firms to create new products and processes or to improve old ones and to discover new knowledge that may be of value in the future. For many firms, R&D is a very important part of ongoing activities and can be a significant expenditure. These expenditures are undertaken because the R&D effort is expected to more than pay for itself in the future by providing the firm with competitive, profitable products and processes.

Research costs are expensed. Development costs are capitalized, if certain recognition criteria are met. If the conditions are not met, development costs are expensed. Unfortunately, this means that significant research programs, which feed the economic health of the entity, are pure expense. It might mean that the firm's most valuable asset is not shown at all on the SFP and current-period expenses overstated.

Research versus Development

Research is defined as original and planned investigation undertaken with the hope of gaining new scientific or technical knowledge and understanding. Such investigation may or may not be directed toward a specific practical aim or application. *Development*, on the other hand, is the application of research findings or other knowledge into a plan or design for the production of new or substantially improved products and such before commercial production begins. Judgement is needed to differentiate research from development.

Accounting Requirements for Capitalization

Development costs for any internally generated intangible assets may be capitalized *after* certain specific criteria are met. Otherwise, development costs must be expensed. The following criteria must *all* be met for a development asset to be capitalized:

1. The asset must be proven to be technologically feasible so it will be available for sale or use;

2. Management must have the intent to complete and then produce and market, or use, the asset;

3. The entity must be able to use or sell the asset;

4. The probable future economic benefits for (or external market or internal usefulness) of the product or process is clearly established;

5. Adequate resources exist, or are expected to be available, to complete the project; and

6. Costs can be reliably measured.

The time line is important. For example, assume that $60,000 is spent on development expenses. The capitalization criteria are not met because financing is not available and the $60,000 is expensed. Then, financing is arranged and the firm spends an additional $10,000. Only $10,000 can be capitalized. Expenditures initially recognized as an expense may not subsequently be restated and capitalized if the criteria are met at a later date.

These criteria are subject to some potential for manipulation. Management plays a large role in assessing technological feasibility, future markets, and available resources. If management wishes to capitalize identifiable development costs for products or processes that the company is undertaking, it may be difficult to challenge the subjective information gathered.

Computer Software Costs

Computer software is often internally generated for either internal use, or developed to be sold as a product.

Classification of Computer Software

What kind of a long-lived asset is computer software? Is it tangible or intangible? If the software is integrated into an item of property, plant, and equipment, it is a separate component but accounted for as a tangible asset. *If not an integral part of a tangible asset, then computer software is classified as an intangible asset.*

Internally Generated Computer Software

Companies may develop software for use in the business or to be sold as a product. The criteria previously discussed for capitalization of an internally generated intangible asset would apply (i.e., the asset must be an identifiable intangible and the recognition criteria must be met.)

Own use

Companies that develop software for their own use are typically involved in expensive, large-scale systems and program development. Companies that develop large-scale systems will usually meet the capitalization criteria and will accordingly capitalize their software development costs. A common amortization period is three to five years.

However, many different measures of cost can be used, and there is significant variation in practice. For example:

1. Should all costs be capitalized, from the very beginning of the project, or should early feasibility and systems development studies be expensed?

2. Should only direct costs be capitalized, or should indirect and overhead costs also be capitalized?

There are no specific standards in this area, and there is diversity in practice.

Product to sell to others

Companies that develop software as a *product to sell to others* may have a somewhat different approach.

* Software product development has an initial period of feasibility testing to determine whether a proposed product is technically and financially feasible. Costs incurred during this period are viewed as research costs and are expensed.

* The six development cost criteria must be met in order for costs to be capitalized. Technological feasibility (and a defined product) is usually considered to be present only when a *working model* exists. Of course, other criteria must also be met (a market must exist, and there must be management intent and adequate resources to take the product to market, etc.) before development costs can be deferred.

* After capitalization criteria are met, costs are capitalized.

Comment

There is a lot of judgement involved in deciding whether the capitalization criteria have been met. Financial reporting objectives play a big role in the selection *and application* of accounting policies. The financial analyst community has tended to look unfavourably on software companies that capitalize a lot of their development costs. Therefore, software companies tend to be conservative when applying capitalization policies.

Website Development Costs

Companies spend material amounts to create websites. Websites may be used to promote or advertise products or services, replace traditional products or services, and/or sell things. A company may be a traditional enterprise with traditional marketing channels, or the company may base the business model on electronic transactions, or there might be a blend of both strategies.

How should the costs of website development be accounted for? Again, the listed criteria for internally developed intangible assets must be satisfied in order to support capitalization. That is, the asset must be identifiable, and the recognition criteria must be met.

Standard Interpretation Committee, SIC 32, breaks down website development costs into five areas:

Type of Website Expenditure	Accounting Policy Suggested; Capitalization Criteria Must Also Be Met
Costs incurred in the planning stage	Expense as incurred

Costs incurred for website application and infrastructure	Capitalize and amortize
Costs incurred to develop graphics	Capitalize and amortize
Costs incurred to develop content	Either expense or capitalize/amortize, depending on nature of content
Operating costs	Expense as incurred

What is the overall theme? If costs are very early in the process (planning), then there is nothing tangible as a website, and the costs must be expensed. After that, the question is always whether there is a long-term benefit from the expenditure. *Future benefits* support asset treatment, otherwise, the expense category wins.

One other small wrinkle is that if the website is used only for advertising, all expenditures are expensed.

Exploration and Evaluation Assets

Exploration and evaluation (E&E) assets relate to costs that oil and gas companies and mining companies incur in exploring and evaluating their resource properties. *Exploration and evaluation of mineral resources* is the process of seeking mineral deposits, oil, natural gas, and so on, after the entity has obtained legal rights to explore. This exercise also involves determination of the technical feasibility and commercial viability of these resources.

Much exploration is fruitless; that is the nature of the business. It is an expense.

After the exploration and evaluation stage, development of the site proceeds only if there is reasonable assurance that the site will generate enough revenue to recover costs. However, it can take years to develop a mine site or an oil field, and mineral prices can be volatile.

In order to account for expenditures in this area, costs are divided into three phases: pre-exploration and evaluation phase; exploration and evaluation phase; and post-exploration and evaluation phase.

Pre-Exploration and Evaluation Phase

Costs incurred prior to obtaining the legal right to explore are in the pre-exploration and evaluation phase. Costs in this stage are expensed, since before an entity obtains legal rights, it does not have access to any future benefits from that site. How can you have control over a future benefit if you do not even have the legal right to explore?

Exploration and Evaluation Phase

Once the legal right to mine or explore the property for resources has been obtained, the entity can capitalize costs until technical feasibility and commercial viability of the resource is reached. Examples of these activities could include acquisition costs for rights to explore the area, geological surveys and mapping, exploration, and test drilling of potential sites. Any removal or restoration costs for activities related to these mineral resources would be recognized. Of course, capitalization of costs would stop, and previously capitalized costs are written off, if the project was determined to be not technically feasible, or not commercially viable.

Post-Exploration and Evaluation Phase

After technical feasibility and commercial viability have been established, the same principles as property, plant, and equipment or intangibles apply to these costs. This phase is often referred to as *development and production*. Costs that are considered for property, plant, and equipment and intangible assets—materials and services, employee benefits, fees to register legal rights, interest costs, and other directly attributable costs—would be eligible for capitalization.

Successful Efforts Method

The accounting for post-exploration and evaluation costs described above applies what is known as the successful efforts method. The **successful efforts method** accumulates costs by site. When a site is been determined to be unproductive, costs are expensed. When a site is productive, the costs are segregated as a separate asset and amortized over their productive life.

Under the *successful efforts method*, unsuccessful efforts are written off *once they are determined to be unsuccessful*. The costs are initially capitalized, since the effort may last more than one reporting period and the results are not known, but the accumulated costs relating to that site are expensed when management gives up the effort. Note that this is a management decision; timing of that decision will determine which accounting period's earnings bear the cost.

This method requires management to segregate costs by site. There is flexibility in this regard; a site might be one project or several projects, linked by a common boundary. This choice is up to management, and likely reflects internal investment and site management practices. However, the choices may lead to a lack of comparability from one company to another; analysts and investors must have a keen sense of the projects underway and the way that the accounting standards are applied.

Full Cost Method

The alternative accounting for exploration and evaluation costs is the **full cost method**. The full cost method is not permitted under IFRS standards. The full cost method aggregates all expenditures in (potentially large) geographic or geological areas, again defined by management. If a particular site is discovered to be unproductive, its costs are not written off. The unsuccessful site remains part of the asset that relates to the overall geographic or geological area. The combined post-exploration and evaluation costs of *productive and unproductive* sites are carried forward as an asset, and amortized against the revenue generated by the successful sites. The method has fallen out of favour with standard setters because the cost of "dry holes" (unsuccessful sites) cannot be supported as an asset.

CONCEPT REVIEW

1. What is the difference between the research phase and the development phase for internally generated intangibles?
2. In general, when is it appropriate to capitalize costs in the development phase?
3. Is computer software always classified as an intangible asset?
4. Explain the successful efforts method of accounting for exploration and evaluation costs.

GOODWILL

Goodwill is a common intangible asset. It represents the value associated with favourable characteristics of a firm that result in earnings in excess of those expected from its identifiable assets. Goodwill is *internally generated* and *is recorded only when purchased*, along with identifiable tangible and intangible assets that constitute an operating unit. Goodwill typically cannot be separated from those identifiable assets. In the absence of an arm's-length transaction, it is difficult to measure the value of goodwill that a firm creates as it engages in business activities.

A few examples of factors that cause enhanced financial performance are:

- A superior management team;
- An outstanding sales organization;
- Especially effective advertising;
- Exceptionally good labour relations;
- An unusually good reputation for total quality; and
- A highly advantageous strategic location.

For accounting purposes, **goodwill** is the difference between the actual purchase price of an acquired firm or operation and the estimated fair market value of the identifiable net assets acquired (assets less liabilities, valued at fair value).

Measuring Goodwill

The value of goodwill is calculated indirectly in an acquisition of a business unit. The steps are as follows:

1. *Establish the cost of the acquisition.* This is the value of whatever the purchaser gives up to acquire the business unit. The cost is measured as any cash payment plus the fair value of shares or assets given to the seller, if any.

2. *Establish the fair value of all identifiable assets and liabilities assumed.* The fair value of the *net* assets acquired is the total fair value of the assets minus the total fair values of the liabilities:

> Fair value of tangible and identifiable intangible assets − Fair value of liabilities = Fair value of net assets acquired

3. *Cost less fair value of net identifiable assets is goodwill.* Goodwill is the excess purchase cost that cannot otherwise be assigned to specific assets or liabilities:

> Cost of acquisition (#1) − Fair value of net assets acquired (#2) = Goodwill

In completing Step 2, the purchaser would consider if there were any items acquired in the purchase that would meet the definition of an intangible asset and should be assigned a value instead of just allocating that amount to goodwill. Examples of the type of assets are provided in five categories:

- Marketing-related intangibles (e.g., an Internet domain name);
- Customer-related intangibles (e.g., a customer list);
- Artistic-related intangibles (e.g., a book);
- Contract-based intangibles (e.g., an employment contract); and
- Technology-based intangibles (e.g., computer software).

As discussed earlier, some intangibles can be recognized only when they are purchased and not when they are internally developed. For example, a customer list can be capitalized on purchase but would be expensed if internally developed.

The allocation of the purchase consideration between *other identifiable intangibles* and *goodwill* becomes critical when we get to the discussion of amortization and impairment in Chapter 10. We will see then that goodwill is not amortized but is tested for impairment, whereas the other intangibles, such as customer lists, would be amortized over their limited lifespan. As a result, this allocation of the purchase price has implications for earnings in subsequent years.

Example

Assume that Hotel Company is considering the acquisition of the net assets of Cafe Corp. Hotel obtains financial statements and other financial data on Cafe and estimates the fair value of Cafe's identifiable assets at $530,000 and the fair value of the liabilities at $400,000. See Exhibit 9-3.

EXHIBIT 9-3		
CAFE CORPORATION BALANCE SHEET BOOK VALUE AND FAIR VALUE		
As of 31 December 20X4	**Book Value**	**Fair Value**
Assets		
Cash	$ 30,000	$ 30,000
Receivables	90,000	85,000
Inventory	60,000	60,000

Other current assets	33,000	30,000
Plant and equipment (net)	220,000	235,000
Other assets	85,000	90,000
Total assets	$518,000	$530,000
Liabilities		
Short-term notes payable	$ 85,000	$ 85,000
Accounts payable	45,000	45,000
Provisions	30,000	30,000
Long-term debt	250,000	240,000
Total liabilities	410,000	400,000
Shareholders' equity	108,000	
Total liabilities and equities	$518,000	
Net assets at fair value		$130,000

The fair value column in Exhibit 9-3 shows that several assets have an estimated fair value different from their book value as reported in the published historical cost financial statements. Fair values include specific identifiable intangibles, such as customer lists.

The total fair value of Cafe's identifiable net assets is determined to be $130,000 ($530,000 total assets less liabilities of $400,000). Assume that Hotel negotiates a purchase price with the owners to acquire Cafe as of 31 December 20X4, for $202,000. Goodwill inherent in this price is $72,000, that is, the purchase price of $202,000 less current fair value of the identifiable net assets of $130,000. The entry Hotel makes to reflect the acquisition of Cafe's operations, at their *fair values*, is as follows:

Cash	30,000	
Receivables	85,000	
Inventory	60,000	
Other current assets	30,000	
Plant and equipment	235,000	
Other assets	90,000	
Goodwill	72,000	
Short-term notes payable		85,000
Accounts payable		45,000
Provisions		30,000
Long-term debt		240,000
Cash		202,000

Recording this $72,000 goodwill asset implicitly means that Hotel was willing to pay for anticipated superior earnings/cash flow from Cafe's operations. These superior results could be caused by a superior location, reputation for service or quality, and so on.

Do you *know* that goodwill is present, just because Hotel paid more than the fair value of the net assets? After all, Hotel may have been out-bargained by the old owners of Cafe. The $72,000 could be the result of an inflated price. Just because the price is arm's length does not mean that it is meaningful. Accountants always make the comfortable assumption that goodwill explains excess purchase price. But beware—the assets acquired are supposed to provide a return consistent with the existence of goodwill, or the goodwill does not, in substance, exist, and it would be impaired.

In the 1990s, many companies purchased Internet-based developing enterprises (the so-called "dot-com" companies) at prices that turned out to be exorbitant. There were very few identifiable assets in the acquired businesses, and therefore almost all of the purchase price was accounted for as goodwill. When the stock market for the dot-coms collapsed, any prospect of future earnings collapsed as well. Impairment write-offs followed quickly.

Negative Goodwill

When the fair market value of the identifiable net assets acquired is *higher* than the purchase price, the acquiring firm has made what is sometimes called a *bargain purchase*. Goodwill is negative, that is, **negative goodwill** has been created. Even though it would seem that the seller could benefit from selling the assets individually rather than selling the firm as a whole, such situations do occasionally occur. For example, the seller may be in financial difficulty and have an immediate cash need. Alternatively, the seller may not have the time or resources to take on the risks of selling the assets separately.

If there is negative goodwill, the fair value of the assets acquired are reassessed. Assets with subjective or uncertain fair values would be written down. For example, one of the items acquired in the purchase might be the intangible asset customer lists, where an estimate was made of fair value that could have a variance. This type of "soft asset" would be reassessed to see if a writedown is appropriate. *Any remaining excess after the reassessment is recognized immediately as a gain in earnings. This situation is rare.*

Form of Acquisition

In the previous example, one company bought the net assets of another company, and goodwill was directly recorded on the purchaser's books. In many acquisition transactions, the acquiring company buys the *shares* of the target company, which is then left to operate as before, only with new shareholders.

At *reporting dates*, the two sets of financial statements are combined, or *consolidated*, to produce a report of the economic activity of the combined entity. In consolidation, the assets of the target company are recorded at fair value at the date of acquisition, and the goodwill inherent in the purchase price is recorded. The nature of goodwill is identical, but the form of the transaction is different. Consolidation is a topic for an advanced accounting course.

DERECOGNITION OF LONG-LIVED ASSETS

Derecognition of long-lived assets occurs on disposal or when the asset will no longer provide future benefits to the company. The disposal of long-lived assets may be *voluntary* as a result of a sale, exchange, or abandonment; be *involuntary* as a result of a *casualty*, such as a fire, or storm; or be the result of *government action*, such as expropriation. Component accounting requires derecognition when separately recognized components are replaced.

Cost Model

If the asset to be disposed of is subject to depreciation, it is depreciated up to the date of disposal to update the recorded net book value. At the date of disposal, the original cost of the asset and its related accumulated depreciation are removed from the accounts.

The difference between the net book value of a long-lived asset and the amount received on disposal is recorded as a *gain* or *loss*. The gain or loss is segregated from ordinary earnings and reported separately.

Disposals that are not the choice of the company are called **involuntary conversions**. This may happen in a natural disaster or as the result of a government expropriation. Involuntary conversions result in gains or losses that are reported as *unusual items* in earnings.

To illustrate the disposal of a long-lived asset, assume that on 1 February 20X1, Brown Company paid $32,000 for office equipment with an estimated service life of five years and an estimated residual value of $2,000. Brown uses straight-line depreciation, by month, and sells the asset on 1 July 20X5, for $8,000. The entries for Brown, a calendar-year company, at date of disposal are as follows:

Depreciation expense ($32,000 − $2,000) × (1/5) × (6/12)	3,000	
Accumulated depreciation—equipment		3,000
Cash	8,000	
Accumulated depreciation—equipment	26,500	
($32,000 − $2,000) × (53 months used) ÷ (60 months total useful life)		
Equipment		32,000
Gain from disposal of equipment		2,500

Interpretation

The economic position of Brown is unaffected by the disposal. Brown received an asset worth $8,000 (cash) for an asset worth $8,000. *The gain arises because the net book value of the asset was not equal to fair value on the date of disposal.* Brown depreciated the equipment faster than it needed to. Notice that the net book value of $5,500 is $2,500 less than the fair value of $8,000 on the date of disposal.

If depreciation exactly reflected all changes in value, there would be no gain or loss from disposal. *The accounting gain in this example is a correction for excessive depreciation charges recognized before disposal.* In effect, the gain records a change in estimate.

If the asset is destroyed in an accident and was insured, then the entry will mirror the one recorded above. That is, the insurance proceeds will be received in cash, and the difference between cash and net book value will determine the gain or loss.

This approach is also used when an asset is abandoned or destroyed and was not insured, or when there are no proceeds. In this case, there is no debit to cash. The loss recognized equals the book value of the asset at disposal. For the Brown example, the loss recognized would be $5,500.

The costs of dismantling, removing, and disposing of plant assets are treated as reductions of any proceeds obtained from disposal. Therefore, the resulting gain is reduced, or the resulting loss is increased by these costs. If Brown incurs $500 in disposal costs, the net cash debit is $8,000 − $500, or $7,500, reducing the gain to $2,000 in the original example.

If site restoration costs had been accrued, monies would be spent at this point, and the provision would be debited.

Derecognition using the revaluation model is discussed in Appendix 2 in Chapter 10.

Replacement of Components

Component accounting requires an asset to be segregated into its major components. If a component is replaced, any remaining carrying amount of that part is derecognized at the time of replacement and recorded as a loss in earnings. The new component would then be recorded as an asset and depreciated. This was illustrated earlier in the chapter.

CONCEPT REVIEW

1. What is an involuntary conversion?
2. Why would a company dispose of a long-lived asset at a loss? Is the company necessarily in a worse position economically after doing so?

3. How would you interpret the gain on the disposal of a long-lived asset?

LONG-LIVED ASSETS ON THE STATEMENT OF CASH FLOWS

Investments in long-lived assets are shown as *investing activities* on the statement of cash flows (SCF), provided that the acquisition is for cash. If a long-lived asset is acquired in a non-cash transaction, the transaction will be described in the notes to the financial statements, but it would not be reported as part of the SCF because no cash was involved. If cash was only part of the consideration to acquire a long-lived asset, then only the cash portion will be shown.

Gains and Losses

Gains and losses on the sale of long-lived assets are non-cash items, from the viewpoint of operating activities. These are excluded from cash flow operations either through adjustment (indirect presentation) or omission (direct presentation). When an asset is sold for cash, what appears on the SCF is the amount of the proceeds (i.e., the cash actually received) for the asset. The proceeds are shown in the investing activities section as a cash *inflow*.

If a long-lived asset is disposed of through a non-cash transaction or exchange, the transaction will not appear on the SCF, but will be disclosed in the notes.

Cash Flow Reporting of Capitalized Costs

An interesting wrinkle to the issue of capitalizing instead of expensing certain costs is the impact that *the capitalization policy* has on the reporting of cash flows.

It is obvious that the accounting policy decision to capitalize or expense a cost will not affect actual cash flows. The cost has been incurred and either has been or will be paid in cash. The accounting policy choice is only of whether to put the cost on the balance sheet (as an asset) or in earnings (as an expense). Consider these differences in *cash flow reporting*, however:

- Costs that are accounted for as expenses are included in the cash flow from *operations*.
- Costs that are capitalized as assets are included in the *investing activities* section of the SCF.
- Depreciation on capitalized assets is deducted in determining earnings but is removed from cash flow from operations either by adding it back in the indirect approach, or leaving it out in the direct approach.

For example, assume that Lorimer Ltd. spends $100,000 on development costs during 20X2, and that earnings before deducting the development costs is $300,000. If the development costs are capitalized, they will be depreciated straight-line over the five years *following* their incurrence (i.e., from 20X3 through 20X7).

If Lorimer's management decides to expense the development costs (i.e., it decides that not all of the deferral criteria have been met), earnings for 20X2 is $200,000, and that amount is shown in the SCF as the cash flow from operations.

If the 20X2 costs are capitalized and depreciated, that $100,000 is shown as an investing activity outflow rather than being included in operations. Cash flow from operations therefore is reported as $300,000. In 20X3, $20,000 of the development costs (i.e., one-fifth) are depreciated and charged against earnings. In the operations section, however, depreciation is added back to earnings, and therefore the effect of the depreciation is removed. The result is that *if costs are capitalized, they will never affect reported cash flow from operations.*

ETHICAL ISSUES

A company that follows a policy of capitalizing as many expenditures as possible will, over time, show a consistently higher cash flow from operations than one that expenses those costs. While this may not fool a sophisticated user of the financial statements, management may choose to follow the capitalize-and-amortize approach consistently in an attempt to increase the company's apparent operating cash flow used to evaluate some debt covenants.

PRESENTATION AND DISCLOSURE

The major long-lived asset groups must be presented as separate line items on the SFP. That is, separate disclosure is needed for:

- Property, plant, and equipment;
- Goodwill;
- Biological assets; and
- Investment property

Other intangible assets may be aggregated and then presented as a separate line item.

Companies are required to disclose the cost of each major category of property, plant, and equipment and each class of intangibles either on the SFP or in the notes. Segregation by major asset category is important, as the various categories of long-lived assets are associated with different levels of business risk and may have dissimilar useful lives and amortization policies. Typically, tangible long-lived assets are shown as one net amount on the SFP, with the required detailed breakdown shown in the disclosure notes.

Extensive note disclosure is required by class, including measurement base, depreciation methods, useful lives or depreciation rates, gross carrying amount and accumulated depreciation, restrictions, expenditures related to construction, contractual commitments, and third-party compensation for impaired assets. In addition, a reconciliation of beginning balance of the carrying amount to the ending balance for the period is required, showing additions, assets held-for-sale, acquisitions in business combination, impairment losses, reversals of impairment losses, depreciation, net exchange differences due to foreign currency, and any other changes.

For example, Exhibit 9-4 contains the asset portion of the 2015 consolidated SFP for High Liner Foods Inc. High Liner is involved in the processing and marketing of prepared and packaged frozen seafood products. This SFP excerpt demonstrates the separate reporting for long-lived assets (e.g., property, plant, and equipment, intangible assets, and goodwill). Comparative figures have been excluded.

EXHIBIT 9-4

HIGH LINER FOODS INCORPORATED

Extract from 2015 Consolidated Balance Sheet

(in thousands of US dollars; comparative information and note references deleted)

January 3, 2015

ASSETS

Current:

Cash	$	1,044
Accounts receivable		81,772
Income taxes receivable		7,381
Other financial assets		4,139
Inventories		261,900
Prepaid expenses		2,568
Total current assets		**358,804**
Non-current:		
Property, plant and equipment		114,231
Deferred income taxes		3,372
Other receivables and miscellaneous assets		1,678
Intangible assets		100,218
Goodwill		126,510
Total non-current assets		**346,009**
Assets classified as held for sale		515
Total assets		**$ 705,328**

Source: High Liner Foods Incorporated 2015 Annual Financial Statements, www.sedar.com, posted 17 Feb 2016.

Exhibit 9-5 shows extracts from the significant accounting policy note as well as the specific note disclosure for property, plant, and equipment, and intangible assets. The accounting policy note explains the costs that are capitalized, as well as depreciation policy. Note 6 for property, plant, and equipment and note 5 for intangible assets illustrate the required reconciliations of the beginning and ending balances. (Comparative data and some detailed disclosure has been omitted.)

EXHIBIT 9-5

HIGH LINER FOODS INCORPORATED

Extracts from 2015 Disclosure notes

3. Significant Accounting Policies

PROPERTY, PLANT, AND EQUIPMENT

Property, plant and equipment

Items of property, plant and equipment are measured at cost less accumulated depreciation and accumulated impairment losses, if any. Cost includes expenditures that are directly attributable to the acquisition of the asset, including the present value of the expected cost for the decommissioning of the asset after its use, if the recognition criteria for a provision are met. The cost of self-constructed assets includes the cost of materials, direct labour, other costs directly attributable to bringing the assets to a working condition for their intended use, the costs of dismantling and removing the items and restoring the site on which they are located, and capitalized borrowing costs. Cost also may include transfers from OCI of any gain or loss on qualifying cash flow hedges of foreign currency purchases of property, plant and equipment. The cost of additions, including betterments and replacements of units of property, plant, and equipment are included in "Property, plant and equipment." The carrying amount of the replaced part is derecognized. The costs of the day-to-day servicing of property, plant and equipment are expensed as incurred.

When parts of an item of property, plant and equipment have different useful lives, they are accounted for as separate items (major components) of property, plant and equipment. An item of property, plant and equipment is derecognized upon disposal or when no future economic benefits are expected from its use. Any gain or loss on the derecognition of the asset is determined by comparing the proceeds from disposal with the carrying amount of property, plant and equipment, and is recognized on a net basis within the consolidated statement of income.

The estimated useful lives for the current and comparative periods are as follows:

Land and buildings	15-60 years
Furniture, fixtures and production equipment	10-25 years
Computer equipment	4-11 years

Depreciation is calculated on the depreciable amount, which is the cost of an asset, or other amount substituted for cost, less its residual value. Depreciation is recognized in income on a straight-line basis over the estimated useful lives of each major component part of an item of property, plant and equipment, since this most closely reflects the expected pattern of consumption of the future economic benefits embodied in the asset. Leased assets are depreciated over the shorter of the lease term and their useful lives unless it is reasonably certain that the Company will obtain ownership by the end of the lease term. Land is not depreciated.

Depreciation methods, useful lives and residual values are reviewed at each financial year-end and adjusted if appropriate.

Borrowing costs

Borrowing costs that are directly attributable to the acquisition, construction or production of an asset that necessarily takes a substantial period of time to get ready for its intended use or sale form pait of the cost of that asset. All other borrowing costs are expensed in the period they occur. Borrowing costs consist of interest and other costs that the Company incurs in connection with the borrowing of funds.

Intangible assets

Intangible assets acquired separately are measured on initial recognition at cost. The cost of intangible assets acquired in a business combination is its fair value as at the date of acquisition. Following initial recognition, intangible assets are carried at cost less any accumulated amortization and any accumulated impairment losses.

The Company's intangible assets consist of brands and customer relationships that have been acquired through a business combination.

The useful lives of intangible assets are assessed to be either finite or indefinite.

- Intangible assets with finite lives are amortized over their useful economic life and assessed for impairment whenever there is an indication that the intangible asset may be impaired.
- Intangible assets with indefinite useful lives are tested for impairment annually at the CGU level. Such intangibles are not amortized. The useful life of an intangible asset with an indefinite life is reviewed annually to determine whether indefinite life assessment continues to be supportable. If not, the change in the useful life assessment from indefinite to finite is made on a prospective basis.

The estimated useful lives of the Company's intangible assets for the current and comparative periods are as follows:

Brands	2-8 years
Customer relationships	25 years

| Indefinite lived brands | Indefinite, subject to impairment testing annually |

The amortization period and the amortization method for an intangible asset with a finite useful life are reviewed at least at each financial year-end. Changes in the expected useful life or the expected pattern of consumption of future economic benefits embodied in the asset are accounted for by changing the amortization period or method, as appropriate, and treated as changes in accounting estimates. The amortization expense on intangible assets with finite lives is recognized in the consolidated statement of income in the expense category consistent with the function of the intangible asset.

Gains or losses from derecognition of an intangible asset are measured as the difference between the net disposal proceeds and the carrying amount of the asset and are recognized in the consolidated statement of income when the asset is derecognized.

Goodwill

...

Goodwill is initially measured at cost, being the excess of the aggregate of the consideration transferred and the amount recognized for non-controlling interests, and any previous interest held, over the net identifiable assets acquired and liabilities assumed.

After initial recognition, goodwill is measured at cost less any accumulated impairment losses. For the purpose of impairment testing, goodwill acquired in a business combination is, from the acquisition date, allocated to each of the Company's CGUs that are expected to benefit from the combination, irrespective of whether other assets or liabilities of the acquiree are assigned to those units.

(Comparative numbers excluded)

5. Goodwill and intangible assets

Goodwill is tested for impairment annually (as at the first day of the Company's fourth quarter) or when circumstances indicate the carrying value may be impaired. The Company's impairment test for goodwill and intangible assets with indefinite useful lives was based on fair value less costs to sell at September 28, 2014. The method used to determine the Company's fair value less costs to sell uses a discounted cash flow model. The key assumptions used to determine the recoverable amount for the different CGUs for the most recently completed impairment calculations for fiscal 2014 and fiscal 2013 are discussed following the table below. The Company has not identified any indicators of impairment at any other date and as such has not completed an additional impairment calculation.

...

(Amounts in $000s)	Brands 2-8 Yrs	Customer relationships 25 Yrs	Land rights 15 Yrs	Indefinite lived brands	Total intangible assets	Goodwill	Total goodwill and intangible assets
Cost							
December 28, 2013	$ 6,216	$ 100,632	$ —	$ 14,611	$ 121,459	$ 111,999	$ 233,458
Additions from acquisitions	—	—	—	—	—	15,535	15,535
Translation adjustment of Canadian based assets	(51)	(127)	—	(48)	(226)	(1,025)	(1,251)
January 3, 2015	**$ 6,165**	**$ 100,505**	**$ —**	**$ 14,563**	**$ 121,233**	**$ 126,509**	**$ 247,742**
Accumulated amortization							
December 28, 2013	$ (2,296)	$ (13,469)	$ —	$ (441)	$ (16,206)	$ —	$ (16,206)
Amortization	(999)	(3,924)	—	—	(4,923)	—	(4,923)
Translation adjustment of Canadian based assets	48	67	—	—	115	—	115
January 3, 2015	**$ (3,247)**	**$ (17,326)**	**$ —**	**$ (441)**	**$ (21,014)**	**$ —**	**$ (21,014)**
Net carrying value							
December 28, 2013	$ 3,920	$ 87,163	$ —	$ 14,170	$ 105,253	$ 111,999	$ 217,252
January 3, 2015	**$ 2,918**	**$ 83,179**	**$ —**	**$ 14,122**	**$ 100,219**	**$ 126,509**	**$ 226,728**

...

(Comparative numbers excluded)

6. Property, plant and equipment

(Amounts in $000s)	Land and buildings	Furniture, fixtures, and production equipment	Computer equipment and vehicles	Total
Cost				
At December 28, 2013	$ 68,818	$ 65,606	$ 16,502	$ 150,926
Additions	16,658	8,500	2,917	28,075
Disposals	(603)	(1,839)	(172)	(2,614)
Effect of exchange rates	(1,752)	(1,783)	(714)	(4,249)
At January 3, 2015	**$ 83,121**	**$ 70,484**	**$ 18,533**	**$ 172,138**
Accumulated depreciation				
At December 28, 2013	$ (17,875)	$ (24,957)	$ (6,624)	$ (49,456)
Depreciation for the year	(2,838)	(7,552)	(1,484)	(11,874)
Disposals	501	1.379	145	2,025
Effect of exchange rates	1,073	829	348	2,250
Write-downs	—	(852)	—	(852)
At January 3, 2015	**$ (19,139)**	**$ (31,153)**	**$ (7,615)**	**$ (57,907)**
Carrying amounts				
At December 28, 2013	$ 50,943	$ 40,649	$ 9,878	$ 101,470
At January 3, 2015	**$ 63,982**	**$ 39,331**	**$ 10,918**	**$ 114,231**

Source: High Liner Foods Incorporated 2015 Annual Financial Statements, www.sedar.com, posted 17 Feb 2016.

CONCEPT REVIEW

1. Do all companies with goodwill have the asset listed on the SFP? Why is goodwill often not recorded?
2. How is goodwill calculated when net assets are bought?
3. What is negative goodwill, and how is it recorded on the SFP?
4. When there is a non-monetary exchange of assets, what will be recorded on the SCF?
5. Suppose that a company is very aggressive at capitalizing expenditures related to intangible assets. How will the capitalization of large amounts of expenditures affect the SCF, compared with a company that expenses many of the same types of expenditures?
6. What long-lived assets have to be shown separately on the SFP?

Looking Ahead

Long-lived assets are not now on the agenda of either the IASB or the Canadian AcSB.

Accounting Standards for Private Enterprises

There are many aspects to accounting for long-lived assets, and many different standards that govern accounting policy in this area. Overall, standards for publicly accountable enterprises are similar to accounting standards for private enterprises, but there are also many specific differences. Exhibit 9-6 summarizes some of the obvious areas where IFRS and ASPE standards are different.

EXHIBIT 9-6		
COMPARISON OF IFRS VERSUS ASPE FOR LONG-LIVED ASSETS		
Accounting Policy	**ASPE**	**IFRS**
Valuation rule for long-lived assets	Historical cost is normally used.	Historical cost is permitted. Another choice is permitted: *the revaluation model* can be applied for many long-lived assets, by class. The valuation rule under the revaluation model is fair value. The *fair-value model* can be used for investment properties.
Components	No standards requiring separate recognition of component parts of a long-lived asset.	Component parts are separately recognized.
Involuntary safety and environmental costs	Capitalize only if future benefit.	Costs must be capitalized to the asset.
Interest capitalization	Interest may be capitalized, but only interest on specific loans may be capitalized. If capitalized, note disclosure is required.	Borrowing costs on qualifying assets must be capitalized. Specific guidance provided on the calculation; includes specific and general borrowings.
Self-constructed assets	Incidental revenues and expenses are included in the costs of the constructed asset.	Incidental revenues and expenses are recognized in earnings.
Decommissioning obligations (asset retirement obligations)	Recognition of legal obligations on asset acquisition.	Recognition of legal and constructive obligations. Annual re-assessment for all estimates and discount rate.
Internally generated intangible assets	If expenditures meet criteria to capitalize development costs,	If expenditures meet criteria to capitalize development costs, must be capitalized.

	management accounting policy choice to capitalize or expense.	
Natural resources - post-exploration and evaluation costs	No standards; *management accounting policy choice* to use successful efforts or full cost.	Successful efforts accounting must be used; full cost is not permitted.

RELEVANT STANDARDS

CPA Canada Handbook, Part I (IFRS):

- IAS 16, Property, Plant, and Equipment
- IAS 23, Borrowing Costs
- IAS 37, Provisions, Contingent Liabilities and Contingent Assets
- IAS 38, Intangible Assets
- IAS 41, Agriculture
- IFRS 6, Exploration for and Evaluation of Mineral Resources
- IFRIC 1, Changes in Existing Decommissioning, Restoration and Similar Liabilities
- SIC-32, Intangible Assets—Web Site Costs

CPA Canada Handbook, Part II (ASPE):

- Section 1582, Business Combinations
- Section 3061, Property, Plant, and Equipment
- Section 3064, Goodwill and Other Intangible Assets
- Section 3110, Asset Retirement Obligations
- Section 3831, Non-monetary Transactions
- Section 3850, Interest Capitalized—Disclosure Considerations
- AcG–16, Oil and Gas Accounting—Full Cost

SUMMARY OF KEY POINTS

1. Long-lived assets include property, plant, and equipment; investment property; biological assets; intangible assets; and goodwill.
2. The three models used in valuation of long-lived assets are the cost model, the revaluation model, and the fair-value model. The most common model in practice is the cost model.
3. Costs for property, plant, and equipment are recognized if there is a probable future benefit and the cost can be measured reliably.
4. Component accounting requires that an asset is separated, and recorded, by significant components. If a component is replaced, the carrying amount of the original component is removed and recognized as a loss.

5. Assets acquired in a basket purchase must be individually valued using the proportional method.

6. Subsequent costs are typically repairs, which are expensed. If the expenditure is the replacement of a component, an addition, a betterment, or major inspection, the costs are capitalized.

7. Long-lived assets are recorded at cost, including cost to install assets and prepare them for use. Specific guidelines exist to aid in classification of expenditure for various asset categories, including buildings, self-constructed assets, machinery and equipment, land, and land improvements.

8. Borrowing costs are capitalized for eligible long-lived assets when there is a delay in acquisition or a delay for construction. Safety and environmental expenditures, when required by legislation, are capitalized.

9. Self-constructed assets are recorded at cost, which includes reasonable amounts of overhead and includes interest. Incidental revenues or expenses during construction period are recognized in earnings. Self-constructed assets may not be valued at an amount higher than fair value.

10. Long-lived assets purchased with low-interest debt are valued at the cash equivalent price or at the present value of the cash payments required.

11. If there is a legal requirement or constructive obligation to incur costs when an asset is retired, the present value of this is recorded as an asset and liability when the asset is acquired. As time passes, estimates are adjusted, the asset is depreciated, and the liability is increased through interest expense.

12. Biological assets, if long-lived, are recorded at fair value less cost to sell, with the change in fair value included in earnings. Disclosure is required for major assumptions and for the change in the asset account. Bearer plants are excluded from the requirement to be valued at fair value.

13. Specific intangible assets are recorded at cost, if purchased externally, or the cost to develop the asset, if internally generated. Legal costs are a major component of the cost of most intangible assets.

14. The practice of capitalizing some operating costs, such as training, promotion, and other start-up costs, is prohibited.

15. All costs in the research phase and many in the development phase must be expensed as incurred. Costs in the development phase or internally developed intangible assets may be capitalized if specific criteria, including marketability or economic value, are met. Since the criteria are based on management estimates, substantial variation in practice can arise.

16. Website development costs are subject to either capitalization or expensing, depending on the nature of the cost. Planning, some content costs, and all operating costs are expensed. Website application, infrastructure costs, and some content costs are capitalized. If a website is used solely for advertising, then all costs must be expensed.

17. Resource companies incur costs related to exploration and evaluation of their resource properties. Costs incurred prior to obtaining the legal right to explore must be expensed. Costs incurred after the legal right has been obtained are initially capitalized. Costs are written off if a site is determined to be not viable.

18. Goodwill is recognized on the purchase of another business unit. It is measured as the excess of acquisition cost over the fair value of identifiable net assets acquired.

19. When assets are sold or otherwise retired or disposed, the difference between proceeds, if any, and book value is the gain or loss on disposal. The gain or loss is, in substance, a correction of the recorded depreciation over the period that the asset was used.

20. On the SCF, cash expenditures to acquire long-lived assets and cash received on sale are reported as investing activities. Long-lived assets acquired in a non-cash exchange are not included on the SCF.

21. Different types of long-lived assets must be presented as separate line items on the SFP. Extensive note disclosure is required for long-lived assets, including assets, by major category, and the accumulated amortization for each category. In addition, reconciliations of beginning and ending balances are required for each class.

Key Terms

additions	**betterment**
basket purchase	**biological assets**

capitalization	involuntary conversions
component accounting	major inspection
constructive obligation	materiality
cost model	negative goodwill
decommissioning obligation	net book value
derecognition	non-monetary transactions
fair-value model	present value
full cost method	property, plant, and equipment
goodwill	revaluation model
gross	site restoration costs
intangible assets	spare parts
investment property	successful efforts method

Review Problem 9-1

The following four questions are independent.

1. *Plant asset cost classification.* Maldive Company completed the construction of a building. The following independent items are the costs and other aspects relevant to the purchase of the lot and construction:

Cash payments to contractor	$100,000
Total provincial nonrefundable sales tax on materials used in construction in addition to payments made to contractor	3,000
Cost of land (building site)	50,000
Gross cost to demolish old building on land	20,000
Proceeds from salvage of old building	5,000
Power bill for electricity used in construction	2,000
Interest on loans to finance construction	3,000
Net incidental profit from operating parking lot until construction started	5,000

What is the final recorded cost (i.e., carrying value) for *each* of the land and building?

2. *Accounting for debt incurred on acquisition.* The Round Wheel Barn Company purchases a tractor by making a down payment of $10,000. In addition, Round Wheel Barn signs a note requiring monthly payments of $2,000, starting one month after purchase and continuing for a total of 20 months. The contract calls for no interest, yet the prevailing interest rate is 2% per month on similar debts. What is the cost (and initial carrying value) of the asset? What is the interest expense that should be recognized for the month following purchase?

3. *Component.* After one-quarter of the useful life had expired on a component part of a piece of equipment with an original cost of $20,000 and no residual value, the component is unexpectedly replaced. The replacement component cost $30,000 and has no usefulness beyond that of the original component. What is the entry to record the replacement? Assume straight-line depreciation.

4. *Acquisition of intangibles.* Growth Company acquired Technology Company during the year and paid $2.5 million for the company. Growth obtained the following for its purchase price:

	Net Book Value	Fair Value
Inventory	$1,250,000	$1,300,000
Property, plant, and equipment	1,500,000	1,750,000
Liabilities	1,200,000	1,200,000

In addition, Growth obtained technology from projects in progress with an estimated value of $200,000. What is the journal entry to record the acquisition?

REVIEW PROBLEM 9-1—SOLUTION

1. Cost components of the land and building:

Land		Building	
Land cost	$50,000	Cash payments to	
Demolition	20,000	contractor	$100,000
Salvage proceeds	(5,000)	Sales tax on materials	3,000
		Power bill	2,000
		Capitalized loan interest	3,000
Total land cost	$65,000	Total building cost	$108,000

The incidental net revenues from operating the parking lot would be recognized in earnings.

2. The cost of the tractor is the present value of the monthly payment annuity:

$$P = \$10,000 + \$2,000(P/A, 2\%, 20) = \$42,703$$

Interest cost for the first month is the present value times the monthly interest rate:

$$\$32,703 \times 2\% = \$654$$

3. The new component is a replacement of an old component. The entries to remove the old component and substitute the new are as follows:

Loss on asset replacement	15,000	
Accumulated depreciation ($20,000 ÷ 4)	5,000	
Component #1		20,000
Component #1	30,000	
Cash		30,000

4. The acquisition of Technology Company would create goodwill of $450,000. Assets and liabilities are recorded at fair values.

Inventory	1,300,000	
Property, plant, and equipment	1,750,000	
Technology in progress	200,000	
Goodwill	450,000	
Cash		2,500,000
Liabilities		1,200,000

CASE 9-1

GLOWWORM INC.

"I cannot believe you have advised against an employee bonus this year," exclaimed Jessica Simpson, senior accountant of Glowworm Inc. (GI), as she stormed into the office of the GI chief financial officer on Monday morning. GI is a large, privately-owned manufacturing firm that reports in accordance with ASPE.

The CFO replied, "GI pays bonuses only when earnings before income tax exceed $1,000,000. Upon reviewing your draft income statement for the year ending 31 December 20X6, I was required to make several adjustments that reduced earnings before income taxes to $925,000. I am sorry Jessica; however, we cannot ignore GAAP!"

Required

Analyze the accounting issues presented in Exhibit 1 and, based on your conclusions, settle the argument between Jessica and the CFO.

EXHIBIT 1

GLOWWORM INC.

Additional information

Jessica's draft income statement reported earnings before tax of $1,220,000 and took into account the following issues:

1. GI's office building is located in a very "up and coming" location. Property values have been rising steadily and this trend is expected to continue. An independent appraisal recently appraised the building and found that the value has doubled since it was acquired by GI.

Jessica decided that reporting the building at a net book value that is less than the prior years' does not represent the economic reality of the situation. Therefore, she reversed the depreciation expense that had previously been recorded for 20X6:

| Accumulated depreciation - Building | 200,000 | |
| Depreciation expense | | 200,000 |

2. In January 20X6, GI received funding from the federal government for purposes of upgrading equipment to meet a higher standard of environmental responsibility. This grant of $50,000 was recorded in the accounts as follows:

| Cash | 50,000 | |
| Other revenue | | 50,000 |

The equipment, which cost $100,000 and has a useful life of 7 years, required GI to install a special platform for the equipment to sit on. The platform, which cost $13,000, was capitalized with the equipment. Due to the large size of the new equipment, existing equipment had to be removed and reinstalled in another area of the plant, which cost $6,000 and was expensed in the financial statements.

3. In late 20X5, a building that was no longer in use by GI was demolished. In early 20X6, the town started a petition calling for GI to clean up the land in order to maintain the beauty of the town and comply with community bylaws. Based on advice from a lawyer and to please the town citizens, GI made a public promise in early 20X6 to clean up and landscape the land by the end of fiscal 20X17. The estimated cost will be $40,000. This was reported in the financial statements as follows:

| Land | 40,000 | |
| Liability | | 40,000 |

No additional journal entries were recorded in relation to this situation.

(Laura Cumming, used with permission.)

CASE 9-2

WINERY INC.

Winery Inc. (WI) is a private corporation formed in 20X8. Prior to 20X8, WI had been operating as a partnership by the Verity family. Due to their success and desire to expand, they have made the decision to incorporate so that they will have additional sources of financing. They are just establishing their accounting policies for their first year-end as a corporation. Their previous financial statements as a partnership were used for filing their tax returns and management purposes. They were not audited or reviewed. WI is considering adopting GAAP for public companies to be comparable with its competitors.

WI grows grapes and produces wines in Ontario. The company also produces beer, spirits, and juices. It has a small store on the property where staff operate winery tours and sell wine. WI incorporated to raise additional capital to expand the operations by planting additional vines and expanding operations to produce organic wines.

In 20X8, WI obtained a bank loan with Big Bank. Previously, when WI operated as a partnership, the bank had provided a line of credit, and the owners had provided personal guarantees. The loan now has the personal guarantees removed, and instead the bank requires annual audited financial statements and has a financial covenant that stipulates a minimum current ratio.

You have recently been hired to develop new accounting policies for WI's 31 December year-end. Previously, the partnership used the cash basis of accounting. The owners know this will no longer be suitable for their corporation. You have been asked by the owners to discuss alternatives and provide recommendations on the appropriate accounting policies for events below that have occurred during 20X8.

1. WI spent $500,000 expanding its operations by planting new vines that were purchased in France. These vines are certified as being organic and will produce a red wine. The vines will produce grapes indefinitely as long as they are properly taken care of during the year.
2. WI obtained a winery licence during 20X8 from the Ministry. This licence allows WI to distribute wine in Western Canada. The licence does not have an expiry date.
3. Wine can take over two years to mature. Premium wine is stored in oak casks to age.
4. A customer can purchase WI's wine in the store at the winery, at the LCBO, or starting in 20X8 through WI's new website. WI invested $70,000 in acquiring software for its computer system. WI spent an additional $10,000 on the following costs to develop the website—consulting fees to a website consultant, graphics design, and costs for training employees on the use of a website and for the company's web domain.
5. A customer can become a member of WI's new wine club. To join the club, a $200 annual fee is paid. In return, the member is shipped one bottle of red wine and one bottle of white wine a month. If a member likes the wine, it can be ordered by the case through the website at a 10% discount. As part of the annual fee members receive a free subscription to *Wine Digest*, which could be purchased on its own.
6. Early in 20X8, WI's winemaker in error added too much yeast to the wine in the vats (large containers that the juice ferments in to make the wine). Initial tasting of samples from those vats indicates that the wine is spoiled. WI fired the winemaker, since the wine had a market value of $1 million. The winemaker has sued WI for wrongful dismissal.
7. Until the new vines are producing crops in 20X9, WI entered into an agreement to purchase grapes from Chile for production. To protect itself from foreign exchange fluctuations, WI entered into a hedge. If hedge accounting was elected, this would be a cash flow hedge.
8. WI received a forgivable loan of $1 million. This loan is forgiven if WI hires five additional employees for the next two years and produces a specified amount of organic fruit each season for use in its organic wines.

Required:

Prepare the requested report.

Part A: Assume that WI will adopt accounting standards for public companies.
Part B: Assume that WI will adopt accounting standards for private companies.

CASE 9-3

PENGUINS IN PARADISE

"The thing you have to understand is how these stage plays work. You start out with just an idea, but generally no cash. That's where promoters like me come in. We find ways of raising the money necessary to get the play written and the actors trained. If the play is a success, we hope to recover all those costs and a whole lot more, but cash flow is the problem. Since less than half of all plays make money, you cannot get very much money from banks.

"Take my current project, *Penguins in Paradise (PIP)*. You only have to look at the cash inflows to see how many sources I had to approach to get the cash. As you can see, most of the initial funding comes from the investors in the limited partnership. They put up their money to buy a percentage of the future profits of the play.

"The money that the investors put up is not enough to fund all the start-up costs, so you have to be creative. Take reservation fees, for example. You know how tough it is to get good seats for a really hot play. Well, *PIP* sold the right to buy great seats to some dedicated theatregoers this year for next year's performance. These amounts are nonrefundable, and the great thing is that the buyers still have to pay full price for the tickets when they buy them.

"Consider the sale of movie rights. Lots of good plays get turned into movies. Once the stage play is a success, the movie rights are incredibly expensive. My idea was to sell the movie rights in advance. *PIP* got a lot less money, but at least we got it upfront when we needed it.

"The other sources are much the same. We received the government grant by agreeing to have at least 50% Canadian content. We also negotiated a bank loan with an interest rate of 5% a year plus 1% of the gross revenue of the play, instead of the usual 16% annual interest a year. Even my fee for putting the deal together was taken as a percentage of the profit, so just about everybody has a strong interest in the play's performance."

Required:

Prepare a memo addressing the major financial accounting issues to be established by *PIP*. Include your recommendations. Do not prepare financial statements.

(Reprinted (or adapted) from Penguins in Paradise, with permission of Chartered Professional Accountants of Canada, Toronto, Canada. Any changes to the original material are the sole responsibility of the author (and/or publisher) and have not been reviewed or endorsed by the Chartered Professional Accountants of Canada.)

Summary of Cash Flows for the Period Ended 31 December 20X4
(in thousands of dollars)

Cash inflows:

Investor contributions to limited partnership	$6,000
Bank loan	2,000
Sale of movie rights	500
Government grant	50
Reservation fees	20
	8,570

Cash outflows:

Salaries and fees for rehearsal period	3,500
Costumes and sets	1,000
Miscellaneous costs	1,260
	5,760
Net cash inflows	$ 2,810

TECHNICAL REVIEW

connect

TR9-1 Lump-Sum Purchase:

Bell Inc. (BI) purchased a group of assets together from one of its competitors whose owner had recently decided to retire and stop operations. BI paid $500,000 for land, building, equipment, and a patent. Independent appraisals had been completed on all assets prior to the sale. These appraisals indicated the following fair values for the assets: land $250,000; building $225,000; equipment $75,000, and patent $50,000.

Required:

Give the entry to record the purchase; show computations.

connect

TR9-2 Capital versus Expense:

Lower Ltd. incurred the following expenditures:

Oil and filter change on delivery vehicle	$ 120
Repair to delivery vehicle after accident	3,500
Painting new delivery vehicle immediately after purchase	700
Repainting building hallway	2,200
Planting summer flowers outside administrative building	500

Required:

Which of the above items would be expensed versus capitalized?

connect

TR9-3 Elements of Cost:

Higher Ltd. purchased a large piece of earth-moving equipment for $5,000,000. The vehicle had six tires, each worth $100,000 and expected to last two years. This is the maximum value that should be allocated to tires. The reminder of the purchase cost, including incremental costs, was attributable 40% to the vehicle body, expected to last 6 years and 60% to the engine, expected to last 4 years. Other costs associated with the machine:

HST, 15% of $5,000,000 cost	$750,000
Delivery	12,200
Repair of incidental damage done during delivery	5,000
Servicing and tune-up to get the machine ready to use	14,000

Required:

Prepare the journal entry to record the equipment and the associated expenditures. Record all items on the list plus the $5,000,000 invoice price.

connect

TR9-4 Self-constructed Asset:

Mapleback Inc. recently completed construction of a new manufacturing facility. Prior to the approval of the building permits, the company operated a parking lot on the land. This parking lot had revenues, net of costs, of $50,000. Total construction costs were as follows:

Material	$300,000
Labour	600,000
Incremental overhead	120,000
General overhead	50,000
Interest costs	100,000
Cost of building permits	20,000

Required:

Provide the total amount of construction costs that would be capitalized to the cost of the building.

connect

TR9-5 Low-Interest Loan:

DesRosier Company acquires a machine on 1 January 20X6, with a non-interest-bearing note that requires $10,000 to be paid on 31 December 20X6 and again on 31 December 20X7. The note has no explicit interest, but the prevailing interest rate is 6% on liabilities of similar risk and duration. The cash equivalent cost of the machine is unknown.

Required:

Provide the journal entry to record the machine on 1 January 20X6. Use the net method to record the note payable.

connect

TR9-6 Decommissioning Obligation:

Manufacturing Incorporated (MI) purchased land on 1 January 20X2, which it started to operate as a gravel pit. The gravel pit will be operating for the next 20 years. At the end of the 20 years MI will be required to incur an estimated cost of $5 million to restore the land. This is required by government legislation. The interest rate that reflects the risks to MI is 8%.

Required:

1. Provide the journal entry for the restoration costs on 1 January 20X2.
2. Provide all required adjusting journal entries on 31 December 20X2.

■ connect

TR9-7 Research and Development:

Carlos Corp. recorded the following expenditures:

1. Engineering work to improve a product's design so it can be manufactured on a cost-effective basis
2. Salaries of scientists searching for a way to apply new research outcomes
3. Testing prototype products for effectiveness
4. Documenting the formulas associated with new research outcomes
5. Supervisors in a research lab

Required:

1. Classify each of the above items as research or development.
2. What accounting policy is applied to development expenditures?

■ connect

TR9-8 Website:

Wired Productions Ltd. uses its website for sales and client information. Costs incurred last year include:

Expenditure	Amount
Depreciation of computer equipment, connection, and utility cost	$35,000
Website maintenance and concept improvements	22,000
Graphics	12,000
Creation of content, expected to be valid for three years	24,000

Required:

Should each item above be expensed or capitalized?

■ connect

TR9-9 Goodwill:

Hendrie Inc. acquired the listed assets and liabilities of Smith Corp. for $1,250,000 cash on 1 January. The book values and fair values of the assets of Smith as of the date of acquisition were:

	Book Value	Fair Value
Accounts receivable	$150,000	$150,000
Inventory	225,000	350,000
Property, plant, and equipment	300,000	550,000
Land	200,000	400,000

In addition, Smith Corp. had liabilities totalling $320,000 at the date of acquisition and a customer list estimated to have a fair value based on discounted future cash flows of $75,000.

Required:

Prepare the journal entry necessary for Hendrie to record the acquisition.

connect

TR9-10 Disposal of Long-lived Assets:

O'Callaghan Inc. (OI) is in the highway construction business. OI's property, plant, and equipment account includes heavy construction equipment. The following transactions relate to the disposal of two of the company's pieces of equipment.

- Equipment One—OI decided to dispose of one of its pieces of heavy machinery and replace it with a newer, more efficient model. OI received $125,000 cash on the sale of the machine. At the date of the sale, the machine had a net book value of $60,000. The original cost of the equipment was $500,000.

- Equipment Two—OI recognizes the earth scoop separately from the rest of the piece of equipment, since it is a significant part that needs replacing. The scoop was replaced this year at a cost of $200,000. The scoop was depreciated separately. The net book value of the scoop at the date of replacement was $25,000. Its original cost was $110,000.

Required:

Provide the journal entry for the two pieces of equipment.

ASSIGNMENTS

 ## A9-1 Valuation Model:

For each of the following assets, assign the asset to a category of long-lived asset and identify the available choices for valuation models:

a. Rental apartment buildings
b. Manufacturing facility
c. Vacant land held for eventual sale
d. Vines in a winery
e. Agriculture quotas
f. Growing timber
g. Customer lists

 ## A9-2 Component Accounting:

AGT Ltd. has identified several assets:

a. Airplane
b. Wind farm
c. Manufacturing facility
d. Cruise ship
e. Hydro lines

Required:

1. For each asset, identify several possible components:
2. AGT has purchased an asset for $170,000; the asset has four components, each appraised at $50,000. Give the entry to record the purchase; show computations.

 ## A9-3 Lump-Sum Purchase:

Scarlett Inc. purchased a tract of land with an office building and equipment included. The cash purchase price was $900,000 plus $50,000 in fees connected with the purchase. The following data were collected concerning the property:

	Appraisal Value	Vendor's Book Value	Original Cost
Land	$220,000	$ 80,000	$ 80,000
Equipment	360,000	170,000	550,000
Office building	440,000	260,000	720,000

Required:

Give the entry to record the purchase; show computations.

 A9-4 Repairs and Other Expenditures:

Kettle Creek Inc. has various transactions in 20X6:

a. Plant maintenance was done at a cost of $70,400.

b. The entire manufacturing facility was repainted at a cost of $88,000.

c. The roof on the manufacturing facility was replaced at a cost of $132,400. At the same time, various upgrades were done to the electrical systems at a cost of $87,600. These upgrades to the electrical system were required to be in compliance with the current safety codes. Neither of these transactions increased the life of the manufacturing facility, although the safety of the facility was enhanced. The original roof was separately recorded as a component. It had a cost of $100,000 and accumulated depreciation of $96,000. Wiring was also a component, and had an original cost of $40,000, and was fully depreciated.

d. The company bought a piece of machinery at an auction at a price of $161,000. The machinery had an appraised value of $190,000, so the company was pleased to get this bargain. The company knew that the machine had to be painted and tuned up. HST of 14% was paid on the purchase price.

e. The machine was delivered to Kettle Creek's manufacturing facility. The freight bill was $3,200.

f. The machine was painted and tuned up, at a cost of $10,400. In the process of the tune-up, it was discovered that the machine needed additional unexpected repairs, which were done at a cost of $24,000.

Required:

Provide journal entries to record the transactions listed above. Justify your decisions. All items were acquired for cash.

 connect

★ A9-5 Acquisition Cost:

The following cases are independent.

Case A   Starling Ltd. bought a building for $1,060,000. Before using the building, the following expenditures were made:

Repair and renovation of building	$105,000
Construction of new paved driveway	27,500
Upgraded landscaping	4,200

Wiring	16,000
Deposits with utilities for connections	2,500
Sign for front and back of building, attached to roof	13,000
Installation of fence around property	14,000

Case B Lark Company purchased a $32,500 tract of land for a new manufacturing facility. Lark demolished an old building on the property and sold the materials it salvaged from the demolition. Lark incurred additional costs and realized salvage proceeds as follows:

Demolition of old building	$31,000
Routine maintenance (mowing) done on purchase	2,500
Proceeds from sale of salvaged materials	11,200
Legal fees	9,000
Title guarantee insurance	5,600

Required:

1. What balance would Starling report in the building account? List components separately.
2. What balance should Lark report in the land account? Land improvements?
3. If any items in the list above are excluded from the building and land accounts, indicate the appropriate classification.

★ ★ A9-6 Acquisition Cost:

GTT Company had the following transactions in 20X4:

a. On 1 January 20X4, a new machine was purchased at a list price of $22,500. The company did not take advantage of a 2% cash discount available upon full payment of the invoice within 30 days. Shipping cost paid by the vendor was $100. Installation cost was $300, including $100 that represented 10% of the monthly salary of the factory superintendent (installation period, two days). A wall was moved two metres at a cash cost of $550 to make room for the machine. The machine was considered to have two components; an engine valued at $900 (net) and the general machine for the balance of the cost.

b. On 1 January 20X4, the company purchased an automatic counter to be attached to a machine in use; the cost was $350. The estimated useful life of the counter was 7 years, and the estimated life of the machine was 10 years.

c. On 1 January 20X4, the company bought plant fixtures with a list price of $2,250, paying $750 cash and giving a one-year, non-interest-bearing note payable for the balance. The current interest rate for this type of note was 15%. Use the net method to record the note payable.

d. During January 20X4, the first month of operations, the newly purchased machine became inoperative due to a defect in manufacture. The vendor repaired the machine at no cost to GTT; however, the specially trained operator was idle during the two weeks the machine was inoperative. The operator was paid regular wages ($425) during the period, although the only work performed was to observe the repair by the factory representative.

e. During January 20X5, the company exchanged the electric motor on the machine in part (a) for a heavier motor and gave up the old motor and $600 cash. The market value of the new motor was $1,250. The parts list showed a $900 cost for the original motor, and it had been depreciated in 20X4 (estimated life, 10 years).

Required:

Prepare the journal entries to record each of the above transactions as of the date of occurrence. Explain and justify your decisions on questionable items. GTT uses straight-line depreciation.

A9-7 Expenditure Classification:

Consider each of the following items:

a. Cost of an oil change on the company's truck.
b. Cost of major brake replacement in a large piece of construction equipment that is expected to be completed every two years.
c. Lawyers' fees associated with a successful patent application.
d. Lawyers' fees associated with an unsuccessful patent application.
e. Cost for the development of a website used exclusively to advertise new products.
f. Cost of permits for building construction.
g. Cost to demolish an old building that is on a piece of land where a new building will be constructed.
h. Future costs to restore land used for mine at end of its useful life.
i. Costs required to remove asbestos in building to bring it up to new safety code.
j. Cost to excavate land to make it flat for a building site.
k. Cost of replacing tires in construction equipment expected to last two years.
l. Cost of installing a new roof on the company's building.
m. Cost to add new functions to a software package unique to the company.
n. Routine maintenance of website.

Required:

For each of the above items, give the name of the account to which the expenditure should be charged; that is, what account should be debited? Be specific.

★★★ A9-8 Asset Acquisition:

At 31 December 20X4, certain accounts included in the property, plant, and equipment section of Hint Corp.'s balance sheet had the following balances:

Land	$1,200,000
Buildings	2,600,000
Leasehold improvements	1,600,000
Machinery and equipment	3,200,000

During 20X5, the following transactions occurred:

a. Land site number 101 was acquired for $6,000,000. Additionally, to acquire the land, Hint paid a $360,000 commission to a real estate agent. Costs of $60,000 were incurred to clear the land. During the course of clearing the land, timber and gravel were recovered and sold for $32,000.

b. A second tract of land (site number 102) with a building was acquired for $1,200,000. The closing statement indicated that the land value was $800,000 and the building value was $400,000. Shortly after acquisition, the building was demolished at a cost of $80,000. A new building was constructed for $600,000 plus the following costs:

Excavation fees	$24,000
Architectural design fees	32,000
Building permit fee	8,000

The building was completed and occupied on 30 September 20X5.

c. A third tract of land (site number 103) was acquired for $3,000,000 and was put on the market for resale.

d. Extensive work was done to a building occupied by Hint under a lease agreement that expires on 31 December 20X14. The total cost of the work was $500,000, as follows:

	Cost	Useful Life Item (years)
Painting of ceilings	$ 20,000	1
Electrical work	180,000	10
Construction of extension to current working area	300,000	25
	$500,000	

The lessor paid half the costs incurred for the extension to the current working area.

e. During December 20X5, $240,000 was spent to improve leased office space.

f. A group of new machines was purchased subject to a royalty agreement, which requires payment of royalties based on units of production for the machines. The invoice price of the machines was $540,000, freight costs were $4,000, unloading costs were $6,000, and royalty payments for 20X5 were $88,000.

Required:

1. Prepare a detailed analysis of the changes in each of the following balance sheet accounts for 20X5:
    a. Land
    b. Buildings
    c. Leasehold improvements
    d. Machinery and equipment
    Disregard the related accumulated depreciation accounts.

2. What items would appear on the SCF in relation to the accounts in requirement 1?

(Source: Copyright 1994–2000 by the American Institute of Certified Public Accountants, Inc. All rights reserved. Reprinted with permission.)

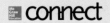

★ ★ A9-9 Self-constructed Asset:

Wonder Mountain Company operates a snow sports resort for skiers and snowboarders. The company has recently decided to replace an existing old chair lift with a new high-speed quad chair and expand the hill to allow for increased capacity. The old chair lift was a $725,000 asset on the books, 90% depreciated. The work was completed from April to November. Wonder Mountain incurred the following costs for the expansion:

Invoice price high-speed quad chair lift	$1,500,000
Costs to dismantle old chair lift	27,500
Cash received for sale used chair lift	150,000
Shipping costs for delivery	17,500
Landscape architect fees, grading expansion hill	6,000
Permit costs	4,000
Clearing trees/grading land for expansion	42,500
Installation of concrete bases for chair lift	90,000
Helicopter rental to install towers for chair lift	80,000
Labour installation ski lift	250,000
Training employees on maintenance and operation	7,500
Testing of chair lift	25,000
Interest costs on loan for construction	60,000
General overhead costs	30,000
Annual routine maintenance	45,000
Purchase tools required for annual maintenance	75,000

Required:

Calculate the total cost for each asset:

a. Land
b. Ski lift
c. Tools

★ ★ A9-10 Self-constructed Asset:

Casa Corp. needed a warehouse and maintenance facility on its company site, which already housed three manufacturing/storage facilities and the company head office. The lowest outside bid for the facility was $3,200,000. Casa believed that it could successfully construct the facility and have more control over the construction process. Accordingly, it began construction on company-owned land in 20X5. The facility was completed in 20X6. Costs related to the project have been accumulated in one account, "manufacturing facility":

Materials	$1,066,200
Subcontracted work (primarily electrical and plumbing)	345,900
Direct labour; idle plant workers assigned to construction tasks	455,800
Direct labour; construction workers hired specifically for this project	123,600
Plant foreman used for construction supervision; salary and benefits	34,900
Direct labour; plant maintenance workers assigned to construction tasks	53,200
Engineering and architectural services	216,700

Additional information:

a. Overhead is assigned in the plant to cover supplies used, electricity, occupation costs, maintenance, and so on in the production environment at a rate of $0.57 for every dollar of direct plant labour. This is reasonable for the warehouse project.

b. A loan was negotiated to cover the cash flow needed for construction. Interest of $75,900 was paid on this loan.

c. The administrative office handled the planning and paperwork related to the construction. The staff worked full-time on this for approximately six months, representing salary and benefit costs of $57,000.

d. The executive team (chief executive officer and chief financial officer of the company, primarily) devoted approximately 10% of their time to this project during construction. The compensation package for these two individuals was $320,000 for this period.

Required:

1. Prepare a schedule showing the costs that can be capitalized for the building. If any items are not capitalized, explain why not.

2. What, if anything, would change in your answer if the outside bid on this project had been $2,400,000? Explain.

3. Under what circumstances must loan interest be capitalized as part of the cost of self-constructed assets? Explain.

A9-11 Donated Assets:

Markus Company received two donations during the year. A long-term client donated a piece of artwork from his personal art collection to display in the company's entrance way as a thank-you for all of the years the company had completed work for him immediately. The artwork was appraised at $80,000. Markus also received a vacant building as a donation from the municipality, who no longer wanted to be responsible for operating costs. The building has a 20-year estimated remaining useful life ($50,000 residual value), which was recognized in the donation agreement. Transfer costs of $35,000 were paid by the company. The building originally cost $1,200,000, 10 years earlier. The building was recently appraised at $650,000 market value by the municipality's tax assessor. Anticipating occupancy within the next 10 days, the company spent $250,000 for repairs and internal rearrangements, and is expected to have value for 8 years. There are no unresolved contingencies about the building and Markus's permanent occupancy.

Required:

1. Give all entries for Markus related to (a) the donations, (b) the renovation, and (c) any depreciation at the end of the first year of occupancy, assuming that Markus records donations at fair value and uses straight-line depreciation.

2. What would appear on the SCF in relation to the transactions recorded in requirement 1?

3. What objections are raised concerning the accounting policy of capitalizing and depreciating a donated asset? Explain.

★★ A9-12 Long-lived Asset Accounting:

Fong Corp. reported various transactions in 20X2:

a. Equipment with an original cost of $32,500 and accumulated depreciation of $26,000 was deemed unusable and was sold for $250 scrap value.

b. A new machine was acquired for $37,850. The invoice was marked 2/10, n/30, but Fong did not pay in time to take advantage of the 2% discount for early payment and thus paid the gross amount of $37,850. Wiring was improved to accommodate the needs of the new machinery at a cost of $250. Related software to install in the machine required for operation was purchased for $1,500. Installation of the new machinery cost $1,250. There were no component parts with different useful lives, so the machine was recorded on one account.

c. Regular machine maintenance was carried out for $11,000.

d. A major overhaul was done on heavy machinery for a cost of $37,500. This overhaul is expected to be completed every five years.

e. The building roof was replaced during the period at a cost of $22,400 to improve the insulation in the building and save on heating costs. The old roof had been recorded as a separate component. It had an original cost of $10,200 and was three-quarters depreciated.

f. Two machines were acquired for a lump-sum amount of $26,900. One machine had an appraised value of $20,000 and the other, $10,000.

g. Land and building were acquired from a member of the board of directors in exchange for 325,000 of the company's own common shares. The land was appraised at $37,500 and the building, $200,000. The facility will be used for long-term storage. The market value of common shares has been around $1.25 per share this year, with weekly highs and lows ranging from $1.80 to $0.50, respectively.

h. The company spent $315,000 in a research lab program this year. It was successful in developing three new commercial projects, which represented $122,000 of the expenditures budget. Legal fees associated with the three successful projects amount to $27,500.

i. Fong paved its factory parking lot, previously a dirt lot, at a cost of $80,050.

Required:

Prepare journal entries to record the transactions listed above. State any assumptions made.

 connect

★ A9-13 Decommissioning Obligation:

Bruce Networks Ltd. (BNL) has a 10-year renewable lease contract with Open Ltd. (OL), the owner of a tall building in a major city. BNL is permitted to erect a transmission tower on the top of the building. BNL's contract with OL requires BNL to dismantle the tower if and when BNL discontinues its use. BNL expects to use the tower for only 10 years due to the rapid advance in transmission technology that is likely to render the tower obsolete in 10 years. The lease payments to OL are $375,000 per year.

BNL constructed the tower at the beginning of 20X6 at a cost of $4,200,000. BNL estimates that dismantling and removal of the tower will cost $360,000. The pre-tax interest rate that reflects risk is 6%. BNL plans to use straight-line depreciation; the company's policy is to take a full year's depreciation in the year of acquisition but none in the year of disposal.

Required:

1. Prepare the journal entry to record construction of the tower and the decommissioning cost obligation.
2. Prepare the necessary adjusting entries pertaining to the tower and the decommissioning cost obligation for each of the years ending 31 December 20X6 and 20X7. Assume that there is no change in the estimated cost of the tower's removal.

★ A9-14 Costs in Research and Development Phases:

Airfield Answers Corp. had several expenditures in 20X5:

a. Testing new plastic prior to use in commercial production
b. Redesign of prototype to improve performance
c. Testing electronic instrument components during their production
d. Study of the possible uses of a newly developed fuel
e. Start-up activities for the production of a newly developed jet
f. Construction of a prototype for a new jet model
g. Design of a new, more efficient wing for an existing airplane
h. Portion of vice-president's salary, related to the time spent managing the research lab
i. Experimentation to establish the properties of a new plastic just discovered
j. Current-period amortization taken on the company's laboratory research facilities
k. Salary of lab technician working on clinical trials of new drug

Required:

1. Explain the accounting policies required for costs in the research and development phases.
2. Which of the above expenditures are considered research? Development? Neither?

★ A9-15 Costs in Research and Development Phases:

Discoveries Ltd. (DL) is involved in research and development related to new processes to make manufacturing more efficient and environmentally friendly. The company has been working on a number of new projects for the past three years. On 31 October 20X5, the company was able to demonstrate the feasibility and potential markets for its latest project. In fact, it has a client that has already indicated it will purchase the technology for use in its manufacturing process when work is completed. DL has a 31 December year-end. It has incurred the following expenditures for this project:

Research costs expensed in 20X2 to 20X5	$4,400,000
Development costs incurred prior 31 Oct. 20X5	3,600,000
Development costs incurred 31 Oct. to 31 Dec. 20X5	2,400,000
Advertising costs to launch new product	1,600,000

Required:

1. Indicate how each expenditure should be accounted for and why.
2. How would your answer be different if there was no potential interest in the product at this time?

A9-16 Costs in Research and Development Phases:

Victor Medical Solutions Ltd. has a major scientific program underway, financed through an issuance of common shares. The program has an expected budget in excess of $55 million, and $17.9 million has been spent to date.

The program targets technology to reduce the chronic inflammation associated with cardiovascular disease. To successfully market an end-product from this project, the company has to meet rigorous testing standards established by government agencies. In Phase I testing, the product must be shown to be safe in animals. In Phase II testing, the product must be shown to be safe in humans. In rigorous Phase III testing, the product must be shown to be effective in treating the condition better than available treatments on the market, or show other advantages over available treatments (e.g., fewer side effects).

As a result of the scientific program, Victor has 12 compounds in Phase I testing, 3 in Phase II testing, and 1 compound in a 2,000-individual Phase III test. All costs to date for all projects have been expensed.

Required:

1. Explain the required accounting treatment of costs in the R&D phases.
2. Why are assets not established for research and many development initiatives?
3. Do you agree with Victor Medical Solutions' practice of expensing all costs for its scientific programs? What is the impact on its financial statements? How would you expect investors to react to the company's financial information?

A9-17 Costs of Software Development

Impact Systems Inc. has recently designed and developed its own payroll system intended for internal use. If there is a market, the company may also decide to sell it to outside companies. Work on this project was completed over an 18-month period. The following costs were incurred in development of the software:

Conceptual design work	$ 6,400
Evaluation and decision on alternative options	8,200
Evaluation and consideration software requirements for options	19,000
Final selection of option	4,600
Software design work	100,000

Software coding	56,000
Testing of software	24,000
Data conversion costs information from old system	16,600
Staff training on new software	4,200
Allocation of general and administrative costs	17,600
Ongoing software maintenance	9,000

Required:

1. Indicate how much would be accounted for as an intangible asset for software. Explain why a cost is included or not included.

2. Are software costs always classified as an intangible asset? Explain why or why not.

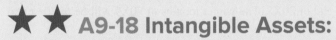

★ ★ A9-18 Intangible Assets:

Images Ltd. is a new company whose only operation is the development of a new kind of video camera that will link to home computers and easily allow image transfer. The camera will come with a program to allow editing, so customers can edit their home movies and, for example, airbrush pictures and alter backgrounds. The camera and software are protected by several patents and copyrights, but technology in the area is moving quickly, and competition is fierce from competing products with different technology.

By the end of 20X6, a prototype existed and was being used to solicit orders. The product itself is due out in the second quarter of 20X7, in time for the Christmas season, which represents the vast majority of the annual camera-buying volume.

In 20X6, various costs were incurred: design costs ($1,351,600), engineering costs ($489,200), software development costs ($397,500), and market research costs ($68,900). Administration costs amounted to $1,340,000. Interest on bank loans was $125,000. Legal costs to register patents and copyrights amounted to $164,400. In addition, manufacturing equipment costing $900,000 was purchased and installed. It was used briefly to manufacture the prototype in the second quarter of 20X6, but is primarily idle and will continue to be idle until the first quarter of 20X7. At that time, commercial production will begin.

Required:

Discuss classification of the various costs listed above. As part of your response, include a list of any additional information you would like to have.

★ ★ A9-19 Website Development:

Yucatan Tours Corp. (YTC) established a new division in 20X8. The mandate of this new division is to establish a presence in the growing luxury eco-tourism travel business. This division will offer, through a sophisticated website, on-line quotes and bookings for travel packages to a variety of ecologically interesting locations. The website will include ratings of the various packages, including video clips of locations and interviews with local experts. YTC will underwrite various packages or place clients with other operators, earning a commission. Initial market research indicates that there is a demand for objective information about travel opportunities and increased purchasing over the Internet.

In 20X8, YTC incurred the following costs in relation to the operation:

Manager salaries (half planning)	$492,000
Rented space	104,000
Software purchased	180,400
Consultant's fees—graphics design	143,600
Computer equipment purchased; four-year life	129,600
Operating costs—heat, power, etc.	84,200
Travel and research costs re: travel packages	111,600
Preparation of content	126,200
Promotion of website to customers	162,600

The website is just recently up and running at the end of 20X8. The winter months of 20X9 will be the first real test of the viability of the service.

Required:

1. Provide recommendations as to how to account for the expenditures listed above. Be specific.
2. How would your answer above be different if the website was used only for advertising and promotion of the company?

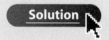

★ ★ A9-20 Intangible Assets:

Transactions during 20X5, the first year of the newly organized Nancy's Discount Foods Corp. (NDFC), included the following:

2 Jan.	Paid $12,000 lawyer's fees and other related costs to register the name and trademark of the company in various jurisdictions.
31 Jan.	Paid $5,500 for television commercials advertising the grand opening. This advertising increased customers' awareness of the company name and location.
1 Feb.	Paid $7,300 to an image consultant to create a logo and distinctive packaging.
1 May	Acquired a patent from an existing patent holder for $20,200. The patent will not be used in the operations of the corporation but rather will be held as a long-term investment to produce royalty revenue.
1 Oct.	Obtained a licence from the city to conduct operations in a specific location. The licence, which cost $12,000, runs for one year and is renewable.

1 Nov.	Acquired another business and paid, after analysis, $35,000 cash for its goodwill. Record only the goodwill.
31 Dec.	Paid $10,000 in legal fees in an unsuccessful patent defence related to the patent acquired on 1 May, which, as a result of the lawsuit, now appears to be questionable in its revenue-generating capacity.

Required:

Give the journal entry for each of the above transactions.

 connect

★ A9-21 Goodwill:

Purple Corp. purchased all of the listed assets and liabilities of Sudden Corp. for $1,600,000. The following assets and liabilities were purchased:

	Book Value	Fair Market Value
Accounts receivable	$ 140,000	$ 140,000
Inventory	168,000	256,000
Property, plant, and equipment (net)	820,000	1,040,000
Patent	0	276,000
Liabilities	(170,000)	(170,000)

Required:

1. What is the appropriate amount that would be recorded for goodwill?
2. Prepare the journal entry for the acquisition.

★ ★ A9-22 Goodwill:

During 20X4, the Pencil Corp. entered into negotiations to buy Stilo Company, finally agreeing on a final cash purchase price of $534,000. Pencil will acquire all assets and liabilities of Stilo effective 31 December 20X4, except for the existing cash balances of Stilo.

The 31 December 20X4 balance sheet prepared by Stilo is shown below in column (a), and the revised fair values added later by Pencil are shown in column (b).

STILO COMPANY BALANCE SHEET

At 31 December 20X4	(a) Book Values of Stilo Co.	(b) Fair Values assigned by Pencil Corp.
Assets		
Cash	$ 50,000	n/a
Accounts receivable (net)	106,000	$ 108,000
Inventory	320,000	180,000
Property, plant, and equipment (net)	618,000	570,000
Land	22,000	80,000
Franchise (unamortized balance)	38,000	42,000
Total	$1,154,000	
Liabilities and shareholders' equity		
Current liabilities	$ 74,000	74,000
Bonds payable	400,000	400,000
Shareholders' equity	680,000	n/a
Total	$1,154,000	

Required:

1. Compute the amount of goodwill purchased by Pencil.
2. Give the entry for Pencil to record the purchase of Stilo.

 A9-23 Disposal of Long-lived Assets:

Machinery that cost $192,000 on 1 January 20X1 was sold for $72,000 on 30 June 20X6. It was being depreciated over a 10-year life by the straight-line method, assuming its residual value would be $12,000.

A building that cost $1,700,000, residual value $100,000, was being depreciated over 20 years by the straight-line method. At the beginning of 20X6, when the structure was 8 years old, an additional wing component was constructed at a cost of $500,000. The estimated life of the wing considered separately was 15 years, and its residual value was expected to be $20,000.

The accounting period ends 31 December.

Required:

1. Give all required entries to record:
    a. Sale of the equipment, including depreciation to the date of sale.

b. The addition to the building: cash was paid.

c. Depreciation on the building and its addition after the latter has been in use for one year.

2. Show how the building and attached wing would be reported on a balance sheet prepared immediately after entry 1(c) was recorded.

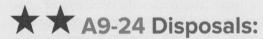 **A9-24 Disposals:**

Quispamsis Inc. (QI) recorded the following asset disposals during the year:

a. A computer system with an original cost of $47,600, 80% depreciated, was judged obsolete during the period and scrapped.

b. Automotive equipment, a large truck with an original cost of $101,600, 50% depreciated, was exchanged for a smaller truck. The smaller truck had a fair value of $50,000. The smaller truck will be used for the same general functions, but it is hoped that it will be more efficient and cost less money in gas. The larger used truck had a fair value of $46,000, and QI paid $4,000 in the exchange.

c. QI sold machinery with an original cost of $120,000 for $100,000 cash at the end of the year. It had held the machinery for three years. Originally, QI had planned to hold the machinery for eight years, and charged straight-line depreciation, with an estimate of a $20,000 salvage value. At the beginning of the second year, QI had spent $6,000 on routine maintenance of this machine. Recorded as a separate component, and depreciated over five years with no salvage, was a $10,500 special base for the machine to improve its efficiency. The base is now worthless. It had been held for three years.

d. A trademark, with a net book value of $24,000, representing primarily unamortized legal fees, was sold for $151,000 cash.

e. QI sold a piece of land with an original cost of $360,000 during the period. It accepted 20,000 common shares of the purchasing company, $60,000 in cash, and a five-year non-interest-bearing note that requires end-of-year payments of $100,000 per year for five years. The market interest rate is 7%. The purchaser's shares are widely traded in the stock market, and they have had a market value of about $4 per share in the last 12 months but have ranged from $1.10 to $5 in a volatile market. The land has been appraised a number of times over the years, with values ranging from $440,000 to $620,000.

Required:

1. Provide journal entries to record the disposal transactions listed above. Record the note receivable in part (e) using the net method.

2. What would appear in the investing activities section of the SCF as a result of each of these transactions?

 A9-25 Investment Property (Appendix)

Real Estate Company (REC) has a number of apartment buildings that it holds for rent. In addition, it is holding land for capital appreciation. REC will either sell the land if the price is right or use it to build additional rental property. This land has a fair value of $10,000 at the beginning of 20X8. During the year, further acquisitions were made of land totalling $110,000. REC disposed of an old apartment building with a carrying amount of $80,000, for $120,000. At the 20X8 year-end date, the fair value of the land had increased to $220,000, and the fair value of the apartment buildings had decreased by $50,000 due to a downturn in the real estate market.

Required:

1. What are the options available for recording the land and apartment buildings?

2. How would the changes be accounted for during the year under each option?

★ ★ A9-26 Investment Property (Appendix)

On 1 January 20X2, Rental Inc. purchased an apartment building. Apartments in this area are in high demand, and a wait list exists for potential tenants. The following costs were incurred for the purchase: cash $8,000,000; legal fees $1,200,000; and repairs and renovations $135,000. The fire code also required the installation of a new sprinkler system for $120,000. On 31 December 20X3, the fair value of the apartment building was estimated to be $10 million, and in 20X4, $11.5 million. In 20X5, a decision was made to add a new wing that allowed additional apartment units. The cost of this expansion was $5,000,000. On 31 December 20X5 the fair value of the apartment building was estimated to be $18 million. The building has a security system, and an apartment manager provides routine maintenance.

Required:

1. What are the options available for recording the land and apartment buildings?
2. Assuming the fair value model is selected, provide the journal entries for 20X2, 20X3, 20X4, and 20X5.

★ ★ A9-27 Government Assistance (Appendix):

On 1 July 20X4, Theriout Corp. acquired a manufacturing plant in Cape Breton for $1,750,000. The plant, employing 50 workers, began operation immediately and is expected to be in operation for 16 years with no residual value. In connection with the purchase, the following government assistance was received:

a. Theriout received a loan from the provincial government to help buy the assets, in the amount of $1,200,000. The loan need not be repaid as long as the plant operates for at least 10 years and employs an average of 25 people each year. Theriout is optimistic about the prospects for the plant but is aware of the high rate of business failure in Cape Breton.

b. Theriout received a subsidy for salary costs of $1,000,000 for the next two years as long as it meets the criteria in requirement (a) of hiring an average of 25 people per year.

Required:

1. Provide the entry to record the loan to purchase long-lived assets and the salary subsidy. Explain your choice of entry.
2. How much net depreciation expense on the manufacturing plant would be recorded in the year ended 31 December 20X4? Provide calculations.

★ ★ A9-28 Government Assistance (Appendix):

Gysbers Company has embarked on a two-year pollution-control program that will require the purchase of two smokestack scrubbers costing a total of $600,000. One scrubber will be bought in 20X5 and one in 20X6. These scrubbers qualify for an investment tax credit of 20%. In addition, the federal government will lend Gysbers $100,000 for each scrubber installed. Provided that emissions are reduced 95% by the end of 20X8, the loans will be forgiven. The federal funds are received when the expenditures are made. If the emission standards are not met, the loan will have to be repaid. In 20X5, it was impossible to predict the success that the company would have with the scrubbers.

Gysbers will depreciate the devices over 20 years, straight-line (no residual value), and will take a full year's depreciation in the year installed. The purchase and installation schedule is as follows:

		Cost
January 20X5	Scrubber 1	$300,000
January 20X6	Scrubber 2	300,000
Total		$600,000

Required:

1. Prepare journal entries to record the purchase of Scrubber 1 and Scrubber 2, and the receipt of the federal loans.
2. Prepare journal entries to record depreciation and amortization for the year ending 31 December 20X6.
3. Assume that after testing in early 20X9, it is found that the emissions have been reduced only 85%. After negotiations, it was agreed that 45% of the loan is repaid to the government in February 20X9. The balance of the loan will be forgiven at that time. Prepare the journal entries to record the repayment and reclassification in 20X9.

A9-29 Self-constructed Asset (ASPE):

Parks Inc. had recently completed construction of a new manufacturing facility. Prior to the approval of the building permits, the company operated a parking lot on the land. This parking lot had revenues, net of costs, of $130,000. Construction will take place over an 18-month period. Total construction costs were as follows:

Material	$640,000
Labour	1,100,000
Incremental overhead	240,000
General overhead	100,000
Interest costs on general loan	200,000
Cost of building permits	40,000

Required:

Provide the total amount of construction costs that would be capitalized to the cost of the building using ASPE. Indicate the items that are different as compared to IFRS.

A9-30 Expenditure Classification (ASPE):

Refer to the facts in A9-7.

Required:

For each of the above items, using ASPE, give the name of the account to which the expenditure should be charged; that is, which account should be debited? Be specific.

Indicate the items that are different as compared to IFRS.

APPENDIX 1

INVESTMENT PROPERTY

Investment property includes land and/or buildings that are rented out or held for capital appreciation. Major examples:

- Vacant land, held to resell, or
- An apartment building, earning rental income.

Property held for use in an active business, or held for administrative purposes, cannot be classified as investment property. For example, land used for a golf course, or a building that is the company's administrative office would not qualify as investment property.

A company could have a minor portion of the property being used or providing a service. For example, in an apartment building, one of the apartments in the building may be occupied by the apartment manager. In this case, this operating component would be considered insignificant, and the apartment building could still be classified as investment property.

In other cases, a building might be partly used by the company for its operation, and partly rented out. In this case, the building is partially a "normal" long-lived asset, and partially investment property.

Fair-Value Model

Assets that are classified as investment property may be recorded using the cost model, or *using the fair-value model*. If the fair-value model is adopted, it must be used for all investment property owned by the company; the fair-value method cannot be applied to selected investment property assets.

Application of the fair-value model is very simple:

- Initial recognition is similar to other items of property, plant, and equipment.
- The assets are remeasured at fair value at every reporting date. Fair value is assessed for the asset as a whole; components are not applied.
- Both increases and decreases in fair value are recognized in earnings in that period.
- The asset is not depreciated.

Transfers can occur between investment property and inventory or property, plant, and equipment if the use of the property changes. For example, if a rental building will now be used for the head office of the company, the building would change from investment property (fair-value model) to property, plant, and equipment (cost model or revaluation model).

Measuring Fair Value

Measuring fair value for investment property is not simple. Fair value is preferably measured by current prices in active markets for similar property in the same location and condition. Unfortunately, many investment properties are unique and reference prices may be difficult to obtain, even a reference price that can be adjusted and extrapolated for known differences in various properties. Failing a reference price, valuation models usually rest on discounted cash flow models, based on rental revenues and expected terminal values for the property. There are many, many assumptions involved in these estimation techniques.

In the fair-value hierarchy, it would be unusual to have a Level 1 fair value (current price for an identical property) available for an investment property; a discounted cash flow model would be a Level 3.

Example

To illustrate the accounting for investment property, assume that an apartment building met the classification as investment property. The building had a fair value in 20X1 of $1,000,000. Assume that at the next reporting date, fair value had increased to $1,250,000. The following entry would be recorded for the building:

Building ($1,250,000 – $1,000,000)	250,000	
Unrealized gain on change in fair value of investment property		250,000

The unrealized gain is reported in earnings.

Reporting Example

Exhibit 9A-1 provides an illustration from the 2014 annual report for Brookfield Asset Management Inc., where the fair-value model is used. Note that the 2014 change in fair value of investment properties was $3.3 billion. All fair value estimates are Level 3 and this note includes disclosure of major assumptions. There is extensive documentation in other disclosure notes surrounding significant estimates.

EXHIBIT 9A-1

BROOKFIELD ASSET MANAGEMENT INCORPORATED

Extract from Disclosure Notes, 2014 Annual Financial Statements

11. INVESTMENT PROPERTIES

The following table presents the change in the fair value of investment properties, all of which are considered Level 3 within the fair value hierarchy:

YEARS ENDED DECEMBER 31	2014	2013
(MILLIONS)		
Fair value at beginning of year	$ 38,336	$ 33,161
Additions	2,269	1,835
Acquisitions through business combinations	8,332	5,530
Disposals and reclassifications to assets held for sale	(4,800)	(1,908)
Fair value changes	3,266	1,031
Foreign currency translation	(1,320)	(1,313)
Fair value at end of year	$ 46,083	$ 38,336

Investment properties include the company's office, retail, multifamily, industrial and other properties as well as higher-and-better use land within die company's sustainable resource operations. Investment properties generated $3,679 million (2013 – $3,093 million) in rental income, and incurred $1,729 million (2013 – $1,302 million) in direct operating expenses.

Significant unobservable inputs (Level 3) are utilized when determining the fair value of investment properties. The significant Level 3 inputs include:

Valuation technique(s)	Significant unobservable input(s)	Relationship of unobservable input(s) to fair value
Discounted cash flow models	• Future cash flows primarily driven by net operating income	• Increases (decreases) in future cash flows increase (decrease) fair value
	• Discount rate	• Increases (decreases) in discount rate decrease (increase) fair value
	• Terminal capitalization rate	• Increases (decreases) in terminal capitalization rate decrease (increase) fair value
	• Investment horizon	• Increases (decreases) in the investment horizon increase (decrease) fair value

Key valuation metrics of the company's investment properties are presented in the following table on a weighted-average basis:

AS AT DECEMBER 31	Office		Retail		Multifamily, Industrial and Other		Weighted Average	
	2014	2013	**2014**	2013	**2014**	2013	**2014**	2013
Discount rate	**7.1%**	7.4%	**9.2%**	9.2%	**6.7%**	8.6%	**7.1%**	7.7%
Terminal capitalization rate	**6.0%**	6.3%	**7.2%**	7.6%	**7.3%**	7.5%	**6.1%**	6.6%
Investment horizon (years)	**10**	11	**10**	10	**10**	10	**10**	11

Source: Brookfield Asset Management Incorporated 2014 Annual Financial Statements, www.sedar.com, posted 27 March 2015.

Looking Ahead

Investment property is not now on the agenda of either the IASB or the Canadian AcSB.

Accounting Standards for Private Enterprises

 ASPE does not have a separate standard for investment property. The option of classifying assets as investment property and using the fair-value model is not an alternative. Investment property is accounted for using the cost model.

RELEVANT STANDARDS

CPA Canada Handbook, Part I (IFRS):

- IAS 40, Investment Property

CPA Canada Handbook, Part II (ASPE):

- No standard

SUMMARY OF KEY POINTS

1. Land and/or buildings can be classified as investment property and accounted for using the cost model or the fair-value model.
2. Investment property might be a component of a larger asset, such as a portion of a building.
3. The fair-value model records investment property at fair value every reporting date. Any changes in fair value are recognized in earnings. Using the fair-value model, the asset is not depreciated.

APPENDIX 2

GOVERNMENT ASSISTANCE

Assets sometimes are acquired with monetary assistance from various levels of governments. *Government grants* may be in the form of a *cash grant* or a *tax credit*.

Some monetary transactions with government are in the form of a standard (repayable) loan, or perhaps shares are issued to the government agency in exchange for cash or other assets. There is no special accounting for these transactions with government.

In other cases, accounting policy reflects *the substance of the government assistance*. In particular, consider the following three forms of government assistance used to purchase long-lived assets:

1. An outright cash grant.
2. An investment tax credit based on qualifying expenditures. For example, a company might get an 8% tax credit (reduction of taxes otherwise payable) for all amounts spent on new equipment (called an *eligible capital expenditure*).
3. A cash grant might be in the form of a *forgiveable loan*. The terms of the loan establish conditions; if the conditions are met, then the loan does not have to be repaid. For example, the firm might be required to maintain certain employment levels. If the conditions are not met, the firm may be required to repay the amounts received. If the conditions are met, the loan is forgiven at a certain point in time.

Accounting for Government Grants

Accounting standards require that government grants (both a cash grant and an investment tax credit) *toward the acquisition of property, plant, and equipment in any form* should be either:

1. *Deducted from the related assets* with any depreciation calculated on the net amount; or
2. *Recorded as deferred income that is recognized over the life of the asset.* The deferred income would be amortized to earnings on the same basis as the related depreciable assets are depreciated.

The choice allowed is really just a presentation issue; there is an identical impact on earnings. The major decision is that the government assistance is deferred with property, plant, and equipment, and recognized in earnings with depreciation.

If government assistance is in the form of a forgiveable loan, management must assess the conditions that are attached to the "loan." If the conditions are deemed likely to be met, the "loan" is recorded as a grant (above) and the conditions and unforgiven balance are disclosed in the notes. Should management's expectations prove wrong and the loan becomes repayable in the future, this event should be accounted for *in the period that conditions change*. That is:

1. The forgivable loan is treated similarly to a government grant when there is reasonable assurance that the conditions will be met; the "loan" element is disregarded.
2. The forgivable loan is treated as a loan if there is reasonable assurance that the conditions will NOT be met.

Usually, conditions are expected to be met and the loan is treated as a grant. Note disclosure is required of the criteria to be met to inform users.

Example

To illustrate accounting for a government grant, assume that machinery costing $100,000 was eligible for assistance of 30%. The machinery has a 10-year life with no salvage value. Because both the *net method* and *deferral method* of accounting are acceptable, both sets of journal entries are provided.

	Net Method		Deferral Method	
Record purchase:				
Machinery	100,000		100,000	
Cash		100,000		100,000
Record receipt of government assistance:				
Cash*	30,000		30,000	
Machinery		30,000		—
Deferred government grant		—		30,000

*Cash is debited if government assistance is in the form of money. If the assistance was an investment tax credit, taxes payable would be debited.

To record straight-line depreciation expense at the end of years 1 to 10:

	Net Method		Deferral Method	
Depreciation expense	7,000		10,000	
Accumulated depreciation		7,000		10,000
Deferred government grant	—		3,000	
Depreciation expense		—		3,000

The effect on earnings is the same under either method. The difference is on the SFP where, using the deferral method, the gross amount of the property, plant, and equipment would appear. The deferred government grant may be:

- Netted against the asset (as a contra account); or
- Shown under liabilities on the SFP.

Which method would you choose if you were trying to maximize assets to reassure creditors? Companies often prefer higher asset values.

Government assistance can have a major impact on cash flows. As a result, under either the net method or the deferral method, the cash flows reported on the SCF (as investment activities) will show separately the gross amount paid for the asset and the gross amount received for the government assistance.

Other Government Assistance

Before we leave government assistance, it is worth mentioning that government assistance can be obtained for a wide variety of purposes, not just the acquisition of property, plant, and equipment. *The purpose of the government assistance governs its accounting.* For example, if the assistance is to offset current expenses, then accounting for government assistance must reflect that fact and recognize government assistance in earnings when the related expenses appear. Companies would have a choice of netting the government assistance against the related expenses or recognizing as income in the current period. If assistance is for future expenses, then assistance should be deferred and recognized when the expenses are recognized.

For example, if a firm receives $100,000 in 20X4 to defray the cost of 20X5 payroll taxes, the amount would be deferred revenue in 20X4 and a revenue, or contra expense, in 20X5.

If there is a forgiveable loan to support operating expenses, and the conditions are likely to be met and the loan forgiven, the assistance is recognized over the period of operating expense assistance. For example, if the loan package was meant to provide four years of expense subsidy, then one-fourth of the amount would be recongnized in earnings each year.

Finally, government assistance may be the transfer of an asset (e.g., land for the use of the company at no cost). These non-monetary government grants may be recorded at fair value or the entity may record the asset at a nominal amount (e.g., $1).

Looking Ahead

Government assistance is not currently on the agenda of either the IASB or the Canadian AcSB.

Accounting Standards for Private Enterprises

ASPE and IFRS treat government assistance in the same way. However, ASPE requires non-monetary grants to be recorded at fair value. Recording at a nominal amount is not allowed.

RELEVANT STANDARDS

CPA Canada Handbook, Part I (IFRS):

- IAS 20, Accounting for Government Grants and Disclosure of Government Assistance
- IAS 41, Agriculture
- SIC-10, Government Assistance—No Specific Relation to Operating Activities

CPA Canada Handbook, Part II (ASPE):

- Section 3800, Government Assistance
- Section 3805, Investment Tax Credits

SUMMARY OF KEY POINTS

1. Government assistance for property, plant, and equipment, in the form of grants, forgivable loans, or tax credits, is amortized to earnings over the life of the related asset. On the SFP, the grant amount is shown in a separate deferred liability account or netted with the related asset.

2. Other government assistance is recognized in earnings when the related expenses, meant to be supported by the assistance, are also recognized.

CHAPTER 10

Depreciation, Amortization, and Impairment

INTRODUCTION

Sears Canada Inc. is a well-known Canadian retail operation, selling a broad range of goods and services. However, Sears is struggling in a challenging and competitive retail market. Stores have been closed and product lines revised. Property, plant, and equipment is a major asset category, reported on the 31 January 2015 SFP at $567.6 million. This represents 32% of total assets. During this fiscal year, the company reported $89.3 million of depreciation expense, and also an impairment loss of $162 million. Goodwill was written off to zero, and impairment reduced the carrying value of intangible assets, buildings and leasehold improvements, leased buildings, equipment, and fixtures. The impairment was triggered by a decrease in revenue, translating to a reduction in cash flow.

The primary emphasis in this chapter is on the *judgement* issues in depreciation, amortization, and impairment. Management chooses depreciation and amortization methods. As well, management assesses the future economic benefit of long-lived assets and goodwill and decides whether the assets should be written down as *impaired*. Management's many estimates and choices must be viewed in the context of financial reporting objectives as well as the more theoretical factors that influence choice. Depreciation methods are reviewed in the chapter, and the tax depreciation system, called capital cost allowance, is explained in Appendix 1.

There are occasions when the long-lived assets of a company may be written *up*. Previously impaired property, plant, and equipment; certain intangibles assets; and held-for-sale assets can be restored to their pre-writedown value in subsequent periods. The flexibility to write assets down and up, as long as reasonably justifiable at the time, gives managers flexibility in their quest to "manage earnings."

Finally, there are times when the assets of a company can be completely revalued, thereby establishing a new basis of accounting for those assets. The revaluation model is not widely found in Canadian practice, but it does exist as an alternative. The revaluation method is discussed in Appendix 2.

REVIEW OF DEFINITIONS—DEPRECIATION AND AMORTIZATION

Long-lived assets, both tangible and intangible, produce revenue through use rather than through resale. Long-lived assets represent quantities of *economic service potential* to be consumed over time in the earning of revenues.

Accounting principles call for recognizing an expense when the future economic benefit of an asset declines. For most long-lived assets, future benefit declines when the assets are used. Depreciation and amortization are an attempt to *recognize the declining future benefit* on a systematic and rational basis. *Depreciation and amortization are not intended to mimic the decline in market value of an asset—only its general pattern of declining future benefit.* The basic definitions are as follows:

- **Depreciation** is the periodic allocation of the cost of a *tangible asset* over its useful life.
- **Amortization** is the periodic allocation of the cost of an *intangible asset* over its useful life.
- **Depletion** may be used to describe depreciation of the costs of acquiring and developing natural resources.
- Residual value is the estimated *net recoverable amount from disposal or trade-in of the asset at the end of its estimated useful life with the company.* It is the portion of an asset's acquisition cost that is not consumed through use.
- **Depreciable amount** is total capitalized asset cost *minus* estimated residual value—the total amount of depreciation or amortization to be recognized over the useful life of the asset.
- **Net book value** (carrying value) is the total capitalized asset cost *minus* accumulated depreciation or amortization to date and *minus* any net impairment losses and reversals.
- Impairment is a write-down of a long-lived asset to its recoverable amount. Impairment arises when the fair value of an asset is less than its net book value.

Nature of Depreciation and Amortization

Depreciation and amortization are sometimes misrepresented. Depreciation and amortization are solely allocations of asset cost to expense. There are many misconceptions:

- Accumulated depreciation or amortization does not represent cash set aside for replacement of assets.
- Depreciation or amortization does not imply the creation of a separate cash fund for asset replacement.
- Depreciation or amortization does not measure the decline in market value during the period.

In everyday conversation, people often use *depreciation* to describe a decline in market value; for example, "A new car will depreciate by 25% as soon as you drive it off the dealer's lot." The accounting meaning of the term *depreciate* is quite different.

The Conceptual Basis of Depreciation or Amortization

The amount of depreciation or amortization recognized is not linked to the decline in an asset's utility or market value in a given period. However, the *inevitable, eventual* decline in value justifies periodic recognition of depreciation or amortization. The decline in utility of long-lived assets is caused by:

- Physical factors, mainly usage (wear and tear from operations, action of time and the elements, and deterioration and decay); and/or
- Obsolescence (the result of new technology).

Assets rendered obsolete are often in good condition and still capable of supplying the service originally expected of them. However, technological advances may have rendered their operating costs uneconomic. Obsolescence also occurs when facility expansion renders certain assets unusable under new operating conditions or when demand for the product or service supplied by the asset declines.

Technological change does not automatically mean that older equipment is obsolete, however. If the older equipment meets the *present needs* of the company, obsolescence is not a factor. For example, in the computer industry, new computer chips substantially increase computer speeds and capabilities. For many companies, continual upgrades to state-of-the art hardware are not cost effective. Older computers will still run required software, and they are not obsolete. Of course, software upgrades sometimes require hardware upgrades as well, and this is the point at which obsolescence becomes a factor.

Long-lived Assets Not Depreciated or Amortized

There are six asset categories that are not depreciated or amortized:

1. Land

Land is not at risk due to obsolescence, nor does it suffer from wear and tear. Therefore, land is not depreciated. We hope you find this intuitively appealing! Of course, if the land is a mining site, then the situation is far different, and depletion of the mineral resources contained in land would be recorded. In addition, if there are land improvements in a separate account, such as site restoration costs, these amounts are depreciated.

2. Investment Property

When the fair-value method is chosen to measure investment property, the property is adjusted to fair value every reporting date and not depreciated. Any changes in value are automatically accounted for, since they are reported in earnings each period. The fair-value method discussed in the Appendix to Chapter 9 is permitted for rental properties, although the cost method (which requires deprecation) is also permitted.

3. Held-for-Sale Assets

If a long-lived asset meets the criteria to be classified as a held-for-sale asset as discussed in Chapter 3, it is not being used in the business and therefore does not suffer from wear and tear. Therefore, these assets are not depreciated. All held-for-sale assets are tested for impairment at each reporting date.

4. Biological Assets

If an asset meets the definition of a biological asset, as discussed in Chapter 6, it is valued at net realizable value. Some biological assets are current assets, and some are long-lived. Biological assets are not depreciated. In fact, many biological assets increase in value (net realizable value) as they mature over time.

5. Intangible Long-lived Assets with an Indefinite Life

If an asset will continue to provide service over the foreseeable future without its future benefit being reduced, it has **indefinite life**. Intangible assets with an indefinite useful life are not be amortized.

For example, a trademark can legally and effectively be protected forever. If the product associated with the trademark has indefinite sales potential, the trademark would not be amortized. The value of the trademark does not decline with use. Indeed, in an economic sense, a trademark can increase in value the more it is used, as it becomes better known and trusted by customers.

"Indefinite" does not mean "infinite," however. Trademarks sometimes become outdated and must be updated or replaced. CBC and Air Canada have both updated or replaced their trademark designs in recent years. The old designs may have no more useful economic life, at which point they must be written down.

At some point, the situation might change, and the asset may decline in value. Some companies amortize the costs of acquiring or designing a trademark, even though the trademark has an endless legal life, because the company recognizes that the trademark may lose its effectiveness over time. Useful lives have to be reviewed annually, and if the useful life becomes limited, amortization of these assets must commence. Intangible assets that are not amortized must be reviewed for impairment on an annual basis.

6. Goodwill

The useful life of goodwill is assumed to be indefinite. Goodwill is not amortized but is subject to an annual review for impairment. We will discuss the goodwill impairment test later in this chapter.

ACCOUNTING POLICY—CHOICE OF METHOD

The only general requirement for a depreciation or amortization method is that it should be *rational and systematic;* most importantly, it needs to reflect the pattern of consumption of future economic benefits. The choices are:

1. *Based on equal allocation to each time period*—the **straight-line** (SL) method. Conceptually, this method is used when the loss of service potential is largely a function of time, or when the utilization of the asset is expected to be fairly constant over its useful life. Straight line also is generally used as a "default" method; if the company is not sure about what the usage pattern or future benefit decline will be, SL is the simplest method to use, and it is the most common method in practice.

2. *Based on inputs and outputs* (variable charge)—
   a. **Service-hours** (SH) method; or
   b. **Productive-output** (PO), or units-of-production, method.

   These methods are used when there is a physical capacity constraint; the more intensely the asset is used, the faster its future benefit declines. It also is used when the asset's utilization is apt to vary significantly from period to period and its utilization can be measured reliably, such as for equipment used in mining operations. These methods are sometimes called the *units-of-production* methods.

3. *Accelerated methods* (decreasing charge)—the **declining-balance** (or diminishing-balance) (DB) method. This is used particularly for assets that are subject to rapid obsolescence, such as computer equipment and software, or for assets that will see heavy use in the earlier years and lighter use in later years. Tax depreciation (CCA) is primarily a form of declining balance depreciation. See Appendix 1.

Conceptual Analysis

In theory, at least, the depreciation or amortization method should describe the pattern of consumption of future economic benefits—nature and use of the asset. For example, assume that a delivery truck has an estimated useful life of five years or 300,000 kilometres. Depreciation based on distance driven might yield a more accurate portrayal of *economic benefits used up* than depreciation based on useful life in years. Based on this reasoning, the methods based on usage appear to be the most logical unless obsolescence is a major factor, in which case straight-line is appealing.

However, GAAP allows choice with few guidelines: All methods are rational and systematic, and an evaluation of the nature of use of an asset can be subjective. Why are depreciation methods not narrowed down? In practice, the value produced by the use of one specific long-lived asset, or the extent to which its economic benefits are consumed in a period, is often impossible to determine with any degree of reliability. In fact, assets and other factors work together in complex business models. It is difficult to associate specifics with individual assets in many cases.

Therefore, as an allocation, depreciation is *incorrigible*—it cannot be supported or refuted without question. If it is impossible to establish one right way, *then all rational and systematic methods are equally acceptable*. Companies tend to let corporate reporting objectives, rather than pattern of use, dictate policy choice. This makes comparisons difficult.

Factors Influencing Choice

Some of the factors that dictate the choice of an accounting depreciation or amortization policy:

- *Nature and use of asset.* The pattern of consumption of future benefits is evaluated to establish the most logical depreciation or amortization pattern. The pattern of usage is often a good indicator of the pattern of consumption of future benefits or pattern of revenue generated.

- *Corporate reporting objectives.* On a situation-by-situation basis, it is important to analyze the various elements that drive reporting objectives. Is there a bonus based on earnings? Is the entity regulated? Is the entity subject to restrictive loan covenants governing debt-to-equity ratios, profitability, and so on? These factors have a powerful impact on the accounting policies chosen.

- *Industry norms.* Comparability is an important qualitative characteristic of financial reporting. Companies' financial statements are used by investors, creditors, and others to assess their performance relative to their competition. Using the same depreciation method helps. Some depreciation methods, such as units of production for natural resources, become generally accepted within an industry.

- *Parent company preferences.* Is the company a subsidiary of another company (the parent)? If so, its financial statements will be combined, or *consolidated*, at the end of the fiscal year. These consolidated financial statements are more meaningful if all constituents follow the same accounting policies, and thus the parent company often dictates key policies to its subsidiaries. Many Canadian companies are wholly owned subsidiaries of foreign parents (usually American). Those subsidiaries usually do what their parents tell them, which may include adopting accounting methods not widely used by Canadian-owned enterprises.

- *Simplified reporting.* Many smaller firms do not really care what amount of depreciation is booked but are interested in keeping their financial statements simple. Therefore, it seems logical to use an accounting policy that results in depreciation that is consistent with the required tax treatment. This is generally a form of declining-balance depreciation, as explained in Appendix 1 to this chapter.

- *Accounting information system costs.* The company must keep detailed information about acquisition costs, post-acquisition costs, useful life, residual value, and accumulated depreciation. Which system is the least complex? This may be a factor in policy choice.

The latitude in selection of depreciation methods and the variety of estimates of useful life and residual value are at odds with the uniformity and consistency objectives of financial reporting. The large dollar amount of depreciation expense reported, combined with the inherently arbitrary nature of depreciation, results in a potentially difficult comparison problem for financial statement users.

Unacceptable Methods

Sinking-fund depreciation is based on present value calculations, and has the opposite pattern as compared to a declining-balance method. That is, sinking-fund depreciation starts low, and ends high, with a steep rate of increase in later years. This method is not acceptable in practice.

Another method that is not acceptable, at least for tangible assets, is a **revenue-based depreciation model**. For example, assume an asset is expected to generate $1,000,000 of revenue over its life, and generates $350,000 in its first year. Using a revenue-based model, this translates to depreciation of 35% of the depreciable amount in this first year. Depreciation is meant to be a measure of the economic benefits used up, and *revenue is not an appropriate surrogate.* Revenue generally reflects factors other than just the consumption of the asset, such as sales market conditions.

However, for an intangible asset, this assessment that revenue is an inappropriate basis is a *rebuttable premise.* If a company can provide evidence that revenue generated and consumption of the intangible asset are strongly correlated, then a *revenue-based depreciation model* would be acceptable—for that intangible asset only.

Estimates Required

Depreciation or amortization methods require that the preparer make the following estimates:

1. Acquisition cost;
2. Useful life; and
3. Residual value.

Component accounting for property, plant, and equipment will require these estimates for each major component or part—not for the asset as a whole.

Acquisition Cost

At first glance, acquisition cost may appear to be a solid amount, not an estimate. In many cases, the cost of an asset is readily determinable. However, acquisition cost often can be an approximation because ancillary acquisition costs, such as excise taxes, shipping costs, and installation costs, either are estimated or ignored. Low-interest loans might be a factor, and site restoration costs as well—both of which require estimation of an appropriate discount rate. Thus, the measurement of "acquisition cost" is not always cut and dried.

Useful Life

An estimate of **useful life** for items of long-lived assets involves assumptions about potential obsolescence, intensity of use, and adequate maintenance. The useful life of an asset is often shorter than its economic life due to a management practice of replacing assets after a specified time frame. What is important is the consumption of future benefits, which considers many factors. For example, an asset may not be used during a strike, so it is idle. Should it be depreciated? While it is not used, it still may be growing obsolete. It is especially difficult to estimate the useful life of an intangible asset; the period of use or revenue generation must be estimated.

It is important to take a hard look at many factors for long-lived assets:

1. The expected use of the asset;
2. The legal life of an intangible asset (Exhibit 10-1) plus any renewal provisions;
3. The effects of economic factors, along with demand and competition;
4. Potential obsolescence;
5. The level of maintenance expenditures required; high maintenance implies an end to useful life;
6. The expected use of another asset or process that is related to the asset (e.g., a patent for a process versus the machinery that runs the process); and
7. The asset management policy of the company. For example, the company may have a corporate policy of disposing of an asset after a specific period of time.

EXHIBIT 10-1
LEGAL LIFE OF CERTAIN INTANGIBLE ASSETS

Patent	20 years from date granted; registration period is also covered
Industrial design	Five years; renewable for a further five years' registration
Trademark	15 years; renewable for infinite successive periods
Franchise	Unlimited unless specified in contract with franchisor
Copyright	Life of the author, plus 50 years

The estimate of useful life must be reviewed at every reporting date. Estimates of useful life change with new information and experience from the use of that asset. For example, a new technology could be introduced that changed the expected use of the asset. Because expectations have now changed, this would be treated as a change in an estimate and adjusted *prospectively*.

Residual Value

Residual value is the amount for which the asset will be sold at the end of its useful life with the company. Remember that, in order for the residual value to be positive, the asset must have a use to another party. It is at the end of its life with this company but may have some service potential for another company. It might not yet be scrap. Costs of dismantling, restoring, and disposing of the retired asset are netted with the expected proceeds. One of two cases holds:

1. The expected proceeds are higher than the costs expected. For example, if the estimated realizable value upon retirement of an asset is $2,500 and estimated dismantling and selling costs are $500, the net residual value is $2,000. This residual value is used in the depreciation formulas.

2. The costs expected are greater than the expected selling price. Remember, removal and site restoration costs can be material. These include all costs to dismantle and restore a property. These costs are particularly important for natural resources. For example, if estimated site restoration costs are $100,000, after which the site is expected to be sold for $20,000, the net is a *cost* of $80,000. *This amount is capitalized at its discounted present value, and then depreciated,* as outlined in Chapter 9. *It is not added or subtracted in the depreciation formulas.*

These estimates are reviewed every reporting date based on current prices.

In practice, the residual value for a tangible asset is often assumed to be zero. After all, the asset is at the end of its useful life with the company. An *intangible* asset usually has a residual value of zero. There must be an established market for similar intangible assets, or a specific sale agreement, to justify a residual value higher than zero.

If by some circumstance, *the residual value is higher than the asset's carrying amount* (net book value), then depreciation would be zero.

Depreciation or Amortization Period

Depreciation or amortization starts when an asset is in its intended condition and location and is available for use. Depreciation stops when the asset is retired. Some things to remember:

- The starting point is the same point in time at which initial costs would no longer be capitalized. For example, any borrowing costs would no longer be capitalized at this point, testing would be complete, and so on.
- When facilities are temporarily idle, straight-line and accelerated-method depreciation continues because these methods are based on the passage of time, not use. Items of property, plant, and equipment may become temporarily idle or retired from use for a period of time (e.g., during a strike) when the manufacturing facility and equipment are not being used. In that case, depreciation does not stop.
- If an input or output method is used, no depreciation is charged in a period of inactivity. Of course, the asset could still be impaired.
- Depreciation or amortization stops when a company permanently stops using the long-lived asset. At this point, the long-lived asset is derecognized (e.g., sold) or classified as a **held-for-sale** asset. At this point, if the fair value of the asset is less than its carrying value, the asset is written down to its fair value and a loss is recorded. Accounting for held-for-sale assets is discussed in Chapter 3.

Assets should not be depreciated or amortized below residual value under any method or system. Although declining-balance methods do not use residual value in calculating depreciation expense, *depreciation stops when the carrying value (net book value) is equal to residual value.*

Spare Parts

Major spare parts are a separate component of a long-lived asset and are depreciated separately. Spare parts are bought so that they are available when a long-lived asset breaks down. Depreciation of these parts does not begin until they are replaced in the asset and being used. Spare parts must be evaluated for impairment caused by poor condition or obsolescence.

Standby Equipment

A unique type of equipment is standby equipment that is ready for use as a backup and is rarely used. It is available for emergencies. Standby equipment is depreciated when ready for use, and depreciation continues even if the equipment is not used. The purpose of standby equipment is to "stand ready"— being available gives the equipment value to the firm. The expected pattern of consumption is most logically linked to the piece of equipment for which it is acting as backup.

CONCEPT REVIEW

1. What is the most popular method of depreciation or amortization?
2. Name three factors that influence management's choice of depreciation or amortization policy.
3. What estimates must be made before a long-lived asset can be depreciated or amortized?

DEPRECIATION AND AMORTIZATION METHODS

Exhibit 10-2 summarizes the depreciation or amortization formulas for four common methods. Each of the four depreciation or amortization methods will be illustrated in the following sections, using the data shown in Exhibit 10-3. Exhibit 10-4 shows depreciation or amortization schedules for the four methods.

EXHIBIT 10-2
DEPRECIATION OR AMORTIZATION FORMULAS

Straight-line (SL) method:

Annual SL depreciation or amortization = (Acquisition cost − Residual value) ÷ Estimated useful life in years

Service-hours (SH) method:

Depreciation rate per service hour = (Acquisition cost − Residual value) ÷ Estimated service life in hours

Annual service-hour depreciation = Depreciation rate per service hour × Hours of usage

Productive-output (PO) method:

Depreciation rate per unit of output = (Acquisition cost − Residual value) ÷ Estimated productive output in units

Annual productive-output depreciation = Depreciation rate per unit of output × Units produced

Declining-balance (DB) method:

Annual DB depreciation = (Acquisition cost − Accumulated depreciation) × DB rate; depreciation stops when net book value is equal to residual value

EXHIBIT 10-3
DATA USED TO ILLUSTRATE DEPRECIATION OR AMORTIZATION METHODS

Acquisition cost, 1 January 20X1	$ 6,600
Residual value	600
Estimated useful life:	
Years	5

Service hours	20,000
Productive output in units	10,000

Actual data:	Activity	Service Hours	Units Produced
	20X1	3,800	1,800
	20X2	4,000	2,000
	20X3	4,500	2,400
	20X4	4,200	1,800
	20X5	3,500	2,000
		20,000	10,000

EXHIBIT 10-4

DEPRECIATION OR AMORTIZATION SCHEDULES—FOUR METHODS

Straight-Line Method

Year	Amortization/ Depreciation Expense	Accumulated Depreciation/ Amortization	Cost	Net Book Value
1 January 20X1			$6,600	$6,600
31 December 20X1	$1,200	$1,200	6,600	5,400
31 December 20X2	1,200	2,400	6,600	4,200
31 December 20X3	1,200	3,600	6,600	3,000
31 December 20X4	1,200	4,800	6,600	1,800
31 December 20X5	1,200	6,000	6,600	600 (residual)
Total	$6,000			

Service-Hours Method

Year	Service Hours	Depreciation Expense	Accumulated Depreciation	Cost	Net Book Value
1 January 20X1				$6,600	$6,600
31 December 20X1	3,800	(3,800 × $.30) = $1,140	$1,140	6,600	5,460
31 December 20X2	4,000	(4,000 × $.30) = 1,200	2,340	6,600	4,260
31 December 20X3	4,500	(4,500 × $.30) = 1,350	3,690	6,600	2,910
31 December 20X4	4,200	(4,200 × $.30) = 1,260	4,950	6,600	1,650
31 December 20X5	3,500	(3,500 × $.30) = 1,050	6,000	6,600	600 (residual)
Total	20,000	$6,000			

Productive-Output Method

Year	Units Produced	Depreciation Expense	Accumulated Depreciation	Cost	Net Book Value
1 January 20X1				$6,600	$6,600
31 December 20X1	1,800	(1,800 × $.60) = $1,080	$1,080	6,600	5,520
31 December 20X2	2,000	(2,000 × $.60) = 1,200	2,280	6,600	4,320
31 December 20X3	2,400	(2,400 × $.60) = 1,440	3,720	6,600	2,880
31 December 20X4	1,800	(1,800 × $.60) = 1,080	4,800	6,600	1,800
31 December 20X5	2,000	(2,000 × $.60) = 1,200	6,000	6,600	600 (residual)
Total	10,000	$6,000			

Declining-Balance Method

Year	Depreciation Expense	Accumulated Depreciation	Cost	Net Book Value
1 January 20X1			$6,600	$6,600
31 December 20X1	(40% × $6,600) = $2,640	$2,640	6,600	3,960
31 December 20X2	(40% × $3,960) = 1,584	4,224	6,600	2,376
31 December 20X3	(40% × $2,376) = 950	5,174	6,600	1,426
31 December 20X4	(40% × $1,426) = 570	5,744	6,600	856
31 December 20X5	256[*]	6,000	6,600	600 (residual)
Total	$6,000			

[*]Should be 40% of $856, or $342, but limited to $256 so that net book value does not go below residual value.

Straight-Line Method

The straight-line (SL) method is based on the assumption that an asset provides equivalent service, or value in use, each year of its life. The SL method relates depreciation or amortization directly to the passage of time rather than to the asset's use, resulting in a constant amount of depreciation or amortization recognized per time period. The formula for computing periodic SL amortization, with its application to the asset in Exhibit 10-3, is:

Yearly SL depreciation or amortization

= (Acquisition cost − Residual value) ÷ Estimated useful life in years

= ($6,600 − $600) ÷ 5

= $1,200 per year

The SL method is logically appealing, and simple. It is especially appropriate for a tangible asset when the use of the asset is essentially the same each period, and repairs and maintenance expenditures are constant over the useful life. The method is less appropriate for assets whose decline in service potential or benefits produced relates not to the passage of time but rather to other variables, such as units produced or hours in service.

The SL method is the most popular method in practice, by far. Ease of use partially explains the method's popularity. It is also popular because it provides a stable, smooth depreciation or amortization pattern. A relatively low amount is expensed in the asset's first year, which allows firms to maximize earnings and net assets in the short run.

For intangible assets, SL amortization must be used if the pattern of economic benefits cannot be determined.

Methods Based on Units of Service

These depreciation methods associate periodic amortization with measurable use of long-lived assets. The units of service methods are most appropriate when production volumes vary greatly from period to period. These methods are rational and systematic *but can be applied only if the asset's utility is measurable in terms of service time or units of output* to reflect the pattern of consumption of the asset. These methods are not logical if obsolescence is a major factor in depreciation, because obsolescence occurs whether the asset is used or not. These methods would not normally be used for intangible assets.

Service-Hours Method

The service-hours (SH) method is based on the assumption that the appropriate depreciation is directly related to the amount of time the asset is in use.

Exhibit 10-4 illustrates the service-hours method for the life of the asset. Calculations are as follows:

Depreciation rate per service hour	= (Acquisition cost − Residual value) ÷ Estimated service life in hours
	= ($6,600 − $600) ÷ 20,000 = $0.30
Yearly SH depreciation, 20X1	= Depreciation rate per service hour × Hours used
	= $0.30 × 3,800 = $1,140

Productive-Output Method

The productive-output (PO) method is similar except that the number of units of output is used to measure asset use. A constant amount of depreciable cost is allocated to each unit of output as a cost of production, so annual depreciation amounts fluctuate with changes in the volume of output.

Exhibit 10-4 illustrates the PO method over the life of this asset. Calculations are as follows:

Depreciation rate per unit of output	= (Acquisition cost − Residual value) ÷ Estimated productive output in units
	= ($6,600 − $600) ÷ 10,000 = $0.60
Yearly PO depreciation, 20X1	= Depreciation rate per unit of output × Units produced
	= $0.60 × 1,800 = $1,080

The SH and PO methods can produce different results, depending on the ratio of machine-hours to units produced. For the asset under study, 2.11 machine-hours were required to produce one unit in 20X1 (3,800 ÷ 1,800), while in 20X2 that figure was reduced to 2.00 (4,000 ÷ 2,000), indicating a greater efficiency. The SH method, therefore, yielded slightly higher depreciation per unit of output in 20X1 than in 20X2.

This inconsistency might also arise when the running time of an asset varies without a corresponding effect in the output of service. For example, the increasingly heavy traffic in urban areas causes vehicles to run many more hours per week with no increase in their productive service.

If the yield ratio is constant, the two methods would produce identical results and the firm would choose the one that is easier to implement.

The PO method is commonly used to measure depletion of natural resources. For example, assume that a company incurs costs of $4,000,000 to lease, explore, and develop a mine site that is expected to produce two million tonnes of coal. The land can be sold for $500,000 after mining is finished. The depletion per tonne is $1.75: ($4,000,000 − $500,000) ÷ 2,000,000. Annual depletion is based on the actual production level. For these companies, mining equipment and even buildings are often also depreciated on a units-of-production basis.

Estimates

A significant difficulty in usage methods is an accurate estimate of total projected activity. But estimating total hours of service use, or tonnes of minerals in the ground is difficult, and subject to material error. Annual usage data is also needed to apply the method. Often, the extra cost of this data is not worth the effort.

Remember, too, that if usage is relatively constant, the result will not be materially different from the SL method.

Declining-Balance Method

A declining-balance (DB) method recognizes greater amounts of depreciation early in the useful life of tangible assets and lesser amounts later. A DB method is based on the assumption that newer assets produce more benefits per period because they are more productive and require less maintenance and repair. This method matches more of the acquisition cost against the revenue of these earlier periods when greater benefits are obtained. A smoother pattern of total annual operating expense is often the result because the sum of annual depreciation and maintenance expense is more constant than is likely with SL depreciation. Remember, this method must still reflect the pattern of consumption of the future benefits of the asset.

Declining-Balance Method

The declining-balance method is significantly different from other depreciation methods in two ways:

1. Residual value is not subtracted from cost when computing depreciation. It is still considered, but in a different way. *Declining-balance depreciation stops when the net book value of the asset is equal to residual value.*

2. The depreciation rate is applied to a declining (*net*) balance rather than to a constant cost.

How do companies arrive at a depreciation rate? A formula exists that can be used to find the rate that will reduce the book value of the asset to its estimated salvage value at the end of its estimated useful life, but the formula is rarely used in practice. Instead, firms may pick a fairly arbitrary rate, based on their assessment of useful life, on industry norms, or perhaps on corporate reporting objectives.

Another approach is to use the rates established by income tax regulations for capital cost allowance (CCA). CCA is mostly a declining-balance method but uses straight-line for some types of assets. CCA does not work in exactly the same way as declining-balance amortization, but if the same rates are used (and a half-year's depreciation is charged in the year of acquisition), the tax and book depreciation are often similar, and deferred income tax balances are minimized as a result. The CCA system is briefly described in Appendix 1 to this chapter. Tax-based rates often are used by private companies for simplicity. However, this practice is acceptable only if those rates reflected the pattern of consumption of the asset's life.

Another approach to determining the rate is called **double-declining balance** (DDB) depreciation, which uses a rate equal to twice the SL rate. For example, the asset in Exhibit 10-3 has a 20% straight-line rate (the reciprocal of the years of life; 1/5 = 20%), and so the DDB rate would be 40%. This is a fairly aggressive depreciation rate—40% of the capital cost would be written off in the first year. In comparison, if this long-lived asset is a piece of machinery, its CCA rate is set (in Class 8) at 20%.

In our example, the firm has chosen a 40% DB rate:

Annual DB depreciation	=	(Acquisition cost − Accumulated depreciation) × DB rate
20X1 DB depreciation	=	$6,600 × 40% = $2,640
20X2 DB depreciation	=	($6,600 − $2,640) × 40% = $1,584

See Exhibit 10-4 for the complete set of calculations.

Note, in particular, the last line, where depreciation expense *stops* when accumulated depreciation equals the $6,000 depreciable cost, leaving the $600 residual value intact. Thus, the maximum depreciation for 20X5 is $256 ($6,000 − $5,744) rather than the calculated $342 (40% of $856).

Estimates

Depreciation rates, which must be disclosed, should be reviewed by financial statement users to see if they are aggressive or not and if they reflect the pattern of consumption of an asset's life.

CONCEPT REVIEW

1. When is a company most likely to use a usage-based depreciation method?
2. What is *double* about DDB depreciation?
3. Why might a company want to use a depreciation method that coincides with tax-basis CCA?

COMPONENT DEPRECIATION ACCOUNTING

In Chapter 9, we introduced the concept of component accounting. This is the separation of an asset into separate significant parts. An asset is separated into components when the component parts are material, and depreciate at different rates. That is, any component that is *recognized separately* is also *depreciated separately*. Now, we examine this **component depreciation accounting**.

Information Required for Component Depreciation Accounting

The requirement for component depreciation accounting requires that a company obtain specific information and track this information in its information system. When a new asset is acquired, the company will need to determine the following information:

- Identification of significant major parts or components;
- For each significant major part or component;
  - Acquisition cost;
  - Residual value;
  - Useful life; and
  - Depreciation method and period.

Components may be grouped together to determine depreciation when they have a similar useful-life and method of depreciation.

If a major part is replaced or an unanticipated overhaul is required, the cost of the original major part or overhaul, and its accompanying accumulated depreciation, would be derecognized, or written off.

Example

Assume that a piece of earth-moving equipment has three components—tires, $645,000, including the recycling charge paid when the tires are disposed of, a frame valued at $1,300,000, and an engine valued at $2,100,000. Useful lives are 3 years for the tires, 8 years for the frame and 4 years for the engine. There are no salvage values. Each component has depreciation separately calculated and recorded. It is as if there were three separate assets. Using straight-line depreciation, depreciation calculations result in the following annual entry:

Depreciation expense	902,500	
Accumulated depreciation—tires ($645,000 ÷ 3)		215,000
Accumulated depreciation—frame ($1,300,000 ÷ 8)		162,500
Accumulated depreciation—engine ($2,100,000 ÷ 4)		525,000

There are no particular accounting complications to this practice; it is the same calculation, repeated over and over again. Record keeping is important, and can be tedious! Why is all the extra work for component depreciation necessary? When an asset is viewed as a whole, it does not reflect the pattern of consumption since some parts or components will be used up faster than others. The effect of this is lower depreciation than if the asset segregated into components.

Note that depreciation expense could be recorded as three separate expenses in the entry above, but is likely reported as one number and so has been recorded that way as well. Every company will have its own preferences in this regard. Accumulated depreciation must be tracked by each separate asset, though, because it is eliminated when the separate asset is derecognized.

Exhibit 10-5 illustrates the calculation of straight-line depreciation of one asset, assuming the asset was comprised of four major components, but had various quantities of each component.

EXHIBIT 10-5					
DATA FOR COMPONENT DEPRECIATION OF ASSET					
Component	Quantity	Original Unit Cost	Residual Value	Useful Life	Annual SL Depreciation
A	10	$50,000	$5,000	15 years	$3,000
B	4	20,000	4,000	10 years	1,600
C	6	7,000	600	8 years	800
D	20	3,000	0	3 years	1,000

Total asset acquisition cost: 10($50,000) + 4($20,000) + 6($7,000) + 20($3,000) = $682,000

Total depreciable cost: $682,000 − 10($5,000) − 4($4,000) − 6($600) = $612,400

Total annual depreciation: 10($3,000) + 4($1,600) + 6($800) + 20($1,000) = $61,200

CONCEPT REVIEW

1. Why is a long-lived asset segregated into components?
2. If a $100,000 asset is separated into two components, one at $70,000 (10-year life) and one at $30,000 (3-year life), what is the amount of depreciation expense in Year 2? Assume straight-line depreciation and no residual value.

ADDITIONAL DEPRECIATION OR AMORTIZATION ISSUES

Additional depreciation or amortization issues include fractional-year depreciation or amortization, depreciation related to asset retirement obligations, and group depreciation.

Fractional-Year Depreciation or Amortization

The calculations illustrated in Exhibit 10-4 assume that the company takes a full year of depreciation or amortization in the year that the asset was acquired. This seems logical in the specific example because the asset was assumed to have been purchased on 1 January. However, most long-lived assets are not placed in service at the beginning of a reporting period, nor do disposals occur neatly at the end of a year. Firms adjust for fractional periods in two different ways. Some compute the exact amount of depreciation or amortization for each fractional period, and others apply an accounting policy **convention**. A *convention* is a standardized shortcut.

Exact Calculation Approach

This approach computes the "precise" amount of depreciation or amortization for each fractional period. For example, assume that an asset costing $20,000 with a residual value of $2,000 and useful life of four years is placed into service on 11 April 20X1. The firm has a calendar-year reporting cycle. The asset in question is used only 265/365 of a year in 20X1. Rounded to the nearest month, this is 9/12 of the year. Under SL depreciation or amortization, the asset's fractional service period is applied to the annual depreciation or amortization amount, either by day or by month, as illustrated:

	By day	By month
Depreciation or amortization expense for 20X1	= ($20,000 − $2,000) ÷ 4 years	= ($20,000 − $2,000) ÷ 4 years
	× (265/365)	× (9/12)
	= $3,267	= $3,375
Depreciation or amortization expense for 20X2 through 20X4	= ($20,000 − $2,000) ÷ 4 years	= ($20,000 − $2,000) ÷ 4 years
	= $4,500 per year	= $4,500 per year
Depreciation or amortization expense for 20X5	= ($20,000 − $2,000) ÷ 4 years × (100/365) = $1,233	= ($20,000 − $2,000) ÷ 4 years × (3/12) = $1,125
Total depreciation for 20X1 through 20X5	$18,000	$18,000

($3,267 + $4,500 + $4,500 + $4,500 + $4,500 + $1,233), or
($3,375 + $4,500 + $4,500 + $4,500 + $4,500 + $1,125)

By Month The word *exact* should not be interpreted too literally. *The "exact" approach usually means that amortization or depreciation is calculated only to the nearest month.* Seldom will a company try to figure out amortization or depreciation to the exact day—what would be the benefit? You can see in the calculations that the difference is only $108 in 20X1 and again in 20X5. Amortization or depreciation involves selecting one from among many possible policies and applying it to amounts that are estimates. There is nothing less "precise" in accounting than depreciation or amortization, and therefore it makes no sense at all to try to be highly precise about a highly arbitrary number!

SH, PO, and DB Methods The SH and PO methods automatically adjust for fractions of a year. *The number of hours used or units produced in the partial-year period is applied to the depreciation rate in the normal manner. The number of hours used is lower because the asset is used for a shorter period.* No special calculations are required.

Using declining balance, the rate for the first year is simply the assumed annual rate times the fraction of the year during which the asset was owned. The first year's depreciation will be multiplied by 9/12. For the following years, the rate will be the normal 40% applied to the asset's net book value at the beginning of each year:

Recognized depreciation expense.

20X1 depreciation = $20,000 × 40% × 9/12 = $ 6,000

20X2 depreciation = ($20,000 − $6,000) × .40 = $ 5,600, etc.

Accounting Policy Convention Approach

To avoid tedious fractional-year depreciation or amortization, many firms adopt a policy convention. Conceptually, these conventions may not be ideal but consider the cost benefit tradeoff and make calculations and tracking far more straight-forward. Conventions may be applied only if the difference between an exact calculation and one of the conventions below is immaterial. *If a convention is chosen, it should be used consistently.*

Examples of conventions:

1. *Half-year convention.* Under this approach, a half-year's depreciation or amortization is charged on all assets acquired or disposed of during the year. The implicit assumption is that assets are acquired throughout the year and as a result are, on average, acquired in the middle of the year.

    Annual amortization or depreciation expense is the amortization or depreciation rate multiplied one-half.

    Given that depreciation or amortization is an approximation at best, this assumption is as good as any. This method also has the added convenience that it coincides with the convention used for income tax purposes in the year of acquisition.

2. *Full-first-year convention.* A full year's depreciation or amortization is charged to all assets that exist at the end of the year, including those acquired throughout the year. No depreciation or amortization is taken on assets disposed of during the year.

    This method bases depreciation or amortization expense on the ending balances. It is easily calculated without reference to transactions during the period. Since there is no amortization or depreciation in the year to sell, last-year fractional amortization or depreciation can be completely ignored.

3. *Final-year convention.* Annual depreciation or amortization is determined solely on the basis of the balance in the long-lived asset accounts at the *beginning* of the period. Assets disposed of during a period are depreciated or amortized for a full period, and assets purchased during a period are not depreciated or amortized that period. The underlying assumption is that assets are seldom fully productive when they are first put into service.

    In this method, depreciation or amortization expense is based solely on the *opening* balances in the asset accounts. The amount of depreciation expense for the year is determinable upfront. When pro-forma budgeted financial statements are prepared, the amount of depreciation or amortization is known with assurance, thereby avoiding unexpected (and uncontrollable) increases in overhead costs charged to operating divisions or departments.

    When a company has high capital expenditures and increasing asset bases, this method tends to lower the amount of depreciation or amortization taken each period, increasing earnings as compared to other conventions.

Depreciation Related to Asset Retirement Obligations

Land is not at risk due to obsolescence nor does it suffer from wear and tear. Therefore, land is not depreciated. With decommissioning costs related to land, the amount of the obligation is added to a land improvements account. This is often referred to as a *bump-up* to the related asset. The land improvements account is depreciated. Depreciation would occur over the period of benefit from the costs of the obligation.

Example

Assume that a company has a land account of $1,250,000, including legal fees and closure costs. The land is to be used as a storage site for 20 years, and then retired. There is $375,000 in a separate land improvements account, which represents the present value of site restoration costs, net of any salvage value.

Depreciation expense	18,750	
Accumulated depreciation—land improvements ($375,000 ÷ 20)		18,750

The present value of the site restoration costs is re-evaluated at the end of each year. However, depreciation is based on the opening amount in the account.

Group Depreciation

Unique features of certain tangible assets, as well as practical considerations, may cause firms to modify the application of standard deprecation methods. We call these adaptations "depreciation systems" because depreciation is calculated on a *group* of assets rather than on individual assets. This can dramatically reduce accounting costs. This group method is appropriate only when the assets are small, have no significant components, and have a short useful life. A good example of this type of asset would be tools, dyes, and patterns that would have very short useful lives. The approach used for these homogeneous assets is called **group depreciation**.

Group accounts work on the principle of averaging. When assets are accounted for individually, the estimated useful life for each asset is almost certain to be incorrect. For a group of assets as a whole, however, the law of averages can be applied. As long as the estimates are correct *on average*, the depreciation will be correct.

An advantage of a group system is that *no gains or losses are recorded on the routine disposals of assets*. Gains and losses on the disposal of individual assets really are the result of estimation errors in determining depreciation. Group methods, in contrast, offset the gains and losses within the asset group account, thereby eliminating any possibility of earnings manipulation through management's adroit timing of asset disposals.

Group systems are not only theoretically sound but also much easier for accounting purposes. When a company is accounting for many similar assets (which can easily involve thousands of units for assets such as tools and dyes), the record keeping for individual assets is an enormous burden, even in computerized systems. Group accounts do away with the need to maintain that level of detail and reflect an apt application of the cost/benefit constraint. Of course, the company must still maintain adequate *physical* control over each asset.

In the accounting records, there is one *control account* for each group of assets and one accumulated depreciation account is maintained. To apply this method:

- Debit the asset *control account* for each asset when it is purchased.
- Record annual depreciation based on the group rate.
- Credit the asset control account for the original cost of the item when it is sold, debit cash for the amount received, and debit accumulated depreciation to balance the entry.

Example

Assume that in 20X8 a company sells a tool that it had acquired in 20X7 for $1,000. The company received $200 from the sale of the asset. The asset is part of a group account that is depreciated at the rate of 50% per year, by the SL method. When the asset is disposed of, only two pieces of information are needed for recording the sale: (1) the original cost of the asset, and (2) the net proceeds from the sale. The sale is recorded as follows:

Accumulated depreciation—tools	800	
Cash	200	
Property, plant, and equipment—tools		1,000

This method is inconsistent with the tone and spirit of component depreciation. Remember that component depreciation breaks down assets into their component parts, worthy of separate recording and estimation. Group depreciation groups assets into a larger whole, lumping the estimates together. However, group depreciation is only acceptable when its results are not materially different from more precise approaches. Some companies have thousands of individual assets of a certain type, and practical measures are both justifiable and appropriate.

CONCEPT REVIEW

1. What information is required for implementing component depreciation when a new asset has been acquired by a company?
2. What is depreciated when there is a site restoration cost anticipated in the future?
3. What accounts are affected when there is a sale of an asset subject to a group depreciation approach?

IMPAIRMENT OF LONG-LIVED ASSETS

Long-lived assets will be reported as an asset for many years. The asset is reported at *net book value* if it depreciates over its limited life, or at *cost*, if it has an infinite life. However, an asset's real economic value to the enterprise may decline significantly over the years and may be less than its recorded value. *An asset may not be overvalued.* Therefore, it is important to critically examine long-lived assets and ask if they have an **impairment**: "Do these assets still have the ability to generate cash inflows commensurate with their net book value?"

A basic assumption underlying impairment tests is that the asset is intended to be used in the company's operations, through which its cost will be recoverable. If the cost is not recoverable through operations, the asset does not meet the definition of an asset and therefore must be written off.

It is important to understand that the impairment test is not typically made with reference to the current fair value of an asset. The current fair value is the value at which an asset can be sold, which implies that it is, in fact, available for sale. However, *assets that are listed as long-lived assets are explicitly not for sale.* These assets provide value to the operation through their ability to increase wealth through profitable operation.

An **impairment test** is the process of comparing the carrying value of an asset with its *recoverable amount*. If the asset's recoverable amount is less than its carrying value on the company's books, the asset has suffered impairment and is written down. The writedown is expensed; it is never charged directly to retained earnings. Impairment losses are often shown as a separate line item on the SCI, or may be part of a restructuring charge or discontinued operations, if circumstances warrant. *Reversal of impairment losses is allowed when the recoverable amount goes up. This is permitted for all long-lived assets except for goodwill.*

Impairment tests already are quite familiar to us, in the form of lower-of-cost-or-net realizable value valuations for inventory and for other short-term assets. However, accounting standards tend to use the term *impairment* only for long-lived assets. The process of testing for impairment is somewhat different between goodwill and other types of long-lived assets. Therefore, we will look at impairment tests separately for long-lived asset, and then goodwill.

Impairment testing below refers to the *cost model* for long-lived assets. The *revaluation model,* and the treatment of impairment within the revaluation model, is discussed in Appendix 2 to this chapter.

Review of Definitions—Impairment

The basic definitions in impairment testing are the following:

- **Impairment loss** is the amount by which the carrying amount of an asset or cash-generating unit exceeds its recoverable amount.
- **Cash-generating unit (CGU)** is the smallest group of assets that will generate cash inflows. These cash inflows must be largely independent of the cash flows of other assets or groups of assets.
- **Recoverable amount** is the *higher* of fair value less costs to sell and value in use.
- **Fair value less costs to sell** is the amount that could be received from the (present) sale of the asset between two knowledgeable, willing parties less the cost incurred for disposal.
- **Value in use** is the *discounted cash flow* (present value of cash inflows and cash outflows) derived from the use of the asset and (eventual) disposal.

Basic Steps in Impairment Testing of Long-lived Assets

In completing the impairment testing, the following steps are taken:

1. Identification of an asset or CGU;
2. Review of external and internal impairment indicators;
3. If required, annual impairment testing, which involves measurement of the recoverable amount; and
4. If impaired, record the impairment loss and allocate the impairment loss to various assets.

1. Identification of an Asset or Cash-generating Units

The impairment test is seldom applied to individual assets. After all, *assets function together* in a company to generate cash flows and earnings. Therefore, impairment tests normally are applied to CGUs—defined earlier as a *group of assets for which identifiable cash flows are largely independent* of the cash flows of other assets or groups of assets.

A CGU is the *lowest level* in a company at which it is possible to determine or identify the cash flows from a particular group of assets. For example, a company may have patents on several products and processes, all of which use the same facilities for production and administrative support. The production facilities are the CGU. If sales of one patented product are reduced because of a new product from a competitor, there may or may not be an impairment of the production facility—the impairment test is applied to the cash flows from all products from the production facility. The cash flow from the CGU is generated *by all of the assets working together to produce several products.*

Liabilities will be included in the group only when the recoverable amount could not be determined without including a specific liability. For example, a CGU might not be sold unless the buyer assumed the liabilities; examples are mortgage debt and asset retirement obligations.

2. Review of Impairment Indicators

Sometimes asset impairment is as plain as day, such as when a division's activities are significantly cut back, or if there is flood damage.

As a matter of course, though, impairment reviews are part of the decision making that surrounds preparation of the annual financial statements:

1. Intangible assets with indefinite lives and intangible assets not yet available for use *must be tested for impairment annually.*
2. For all other long-lived assets, both the internal and external impairment indicators must be assessed each reporting date. *These assets are tested for impairment only if there are impairment indicators.*

Examples of impairment indicators include:

- A significant adverse change in the technological, market, economic, or legal environment, such as a new product from a competitor that makes the company's product or processes obsolete;
- Physical damage to an asset, obsolescence, or a significant decline in market value of an asset;
- Evidence that the market value of the company as a whole (market capitalization) is less than recorded carrying values; and

- Plans to restructure an operation or leave assets idle.

If annual impairment testing is required, or an external or internal factor indicates possible impairment, then the CGU is tested for impairment.

3. Measurement of the Recoverable Amount

The impairment loss is the amount by which the carrying value of the CGU exceeds its recoverable amount. For example, if the net book value of all assets in the CGU is $1,000,000 and the recoverable amount is $650,000, the impairment loss is $350,000.

The recoverable amount is the *higher of fair value less costs to sell and value in use*. That is, if the fair value less costs to sell were $425,000, and value in use were $650,000, the $650,000 value in use is the *recoverable amount*. There are two alternative ways to define the recoverable amount because long-lived assets can recover their value from use in the business, or the assets could be sold for fair value. To determine these two amounts:

1. *Fair value less costs to sell* may be obtained from prices in an active market for the long-lived assets. However, long-lived assets are not often sold—especially in groups that constitute a CGU—and as a result there is no active market. One could try to piece together a fair value for the group by assembling market values for individual assets, and estimating depreciation, but that would involve many estimates and deny the synergy and productivity that is achieved when assets function together in an operating environment. Many times, fair value less cost to sell is not determinable, or might be determinable for one or two of the assets but not the CGU group.

2. *Value in use* calculates a value for the CGU using a valuation model. This valuation model is *expected present value*, using a probability-weighted discounted cash flow. It is a surrogate for fair value; a Level 3 fair value, referring back to the fair-value measurement hierarchy described in Chapter 2. Some of the required estimates:

   - An appropriate time horizon, generally not longer than five years, unless a longer time period can be justified;
   - Future cash inflows (revenue) from the asset in its current condition;
   - Future cash outflows necessary to generate inflow (revenue) from the asset, excluding finance costs and income tax;
   - Expected cash flows from disposal of the assets in the CGU, at the end of the time frame, including any remediation costs; and
   - Discount rate to use in the calculation of present value, which should be a market-based, risk-adjusted rate.

   Future cash flows must reflect the asset in its current condition, and may not be based on improvements or restructuring within the forecast period. Any growth rate applied to future cash flows must be steady.

   Of course, estimating future cash flows (and the probabilities attached to those cash flows) is not the job of the accountant. That is the task of management, with the assistance of professional business valuators. But once management estimates the fair value, the accountant must ensure that the parameters are reasonable.

4. Allocating the Impairment Loss

The impairment loss may relate to an individual asset, or to a group of assets in a CGU. If the loss relates to a specific asset, the carrying amount of the individual asset is reduced to the recoverable amount. The writedown must reduce the carrying value of the asset. The loss can be recorded by either:

1. Crediting the asset account, decreasing it; or
2. Crediting accumulated depreciation, increasing accumulated depreciation, but decreasing net carrying value.

Both approaches are found in practice.

To preserve historical cost as the measurement attribute for the asset, *we will generally credit accumulated depreciation, unless the asset is nondepreciable, in which case the asset is directly credited.* An impairment loss is recognized in earnings.

If the loss relates to a group of assets, then the loss is allocated first to goodwill, and then to the remaining component assets on a pro-rata basis. However, the allocation of an impairment loss should not reduce the carrying amount of an asset below the higher of:

1. The separate fair value less costs to sell, or its separate value in use, if either value can be readily determine; or

2. Zero. Clearly, an asset cannot be a negative number; zero is as low as it goes!

For example, suppose that an Internet service provider (ISP) shows a subscriber list as an asset, at cost, because the list was purchased from another company. An ISP subscriber list has a fairly readily determinable value because there is a reasonably active market. If the ISP is consistently losing money, it is probable that the company's assets are impaired. Nevertheless, that does not indicate that the subscriber list is impaired—another company may use it quite profitably. If an impairment loss is recognized, the carrying value of the subscription base should not be reduced below the higher of its fair value less costs to sell or value in use. Instead, a greater portion of the impairment loss should be allocated to the other long-lived assets, such as equipment and limited-life intangibles.

Example

Suppose that Justus Ltd. has the following assets in its recreational products group, which is a CGU:

	Carrying Value (thousands)
Land	$ 400
Building	640
Equipment	560
	$1,600

A change in the competitive environment suggests that the recoverable amount of this division may be less than its carrying value. Management conducts an impairment test and concludes that the recoverable amount based on the estimated discounted present value of the future cash flows of the asset group is $1,000. Fair value less costs to sell could not be determined for these assets. The recoverable amount is based on value in use for the CGU, and is $1,000. The impairment loss is $600—the excess of $1,600 carrying value over $1,000 recoverable amount.

The impairment loss must now be allocated to the long-lived assets. The "first try" will allocate the $600 impairment loss in proportion to its carrying value:

This result would be appropriate if there were no fair values available for individual assets. The impairment loss is recorded as follows:

Asset	Carrying Value	Proportion	Allocation of Impairment Loss	Adjusted Carrying Value
Land	$ 400	25%	$ 150	250
Building	640	40%	240	400
Equipment	560	35%	210	350
	$1,600	100%	$600	$1,000

Impairment loss	600	
Land		150
Building		240
Equipment		210

Now, let us assume that the fair value less disposal costs can be determined separately for land, although not for buildings or equipment. The fair value less cost to sell for land is $320. The allocation of impairment losses above *reduced the carrying value of land to $250. Land may not be reduced below $320*, its fair value less cost to sell. We must try again! This time, the

$600 loss is allocated first to land, in the amount of $80 ($400 versus $320), and then the remaining $520 impairment loss ($600 less $80) is allocated pro-rata to the remaining assets:

Asset	Carrying Value	Proportion	Allocation of Impairment Loss	Adjusted Carrying Value
Land	400	—	$ 80	320
Building	640	53%($640/$1,200)	276	364
Equipment	560	47%($560/$1,200)	244	316
	$1,600	100%	$600	$1,000
Total, building and equipment only	$1,200			

Notice the revised calculation of proportions—the percentage is now based on assets excluding land.

After an impairment loss has been recognized, estimates related to that asset should be reviewed, such as useful life, residual value, and depreciation method.

Reversal of Impairment Losses

When dealing with an impairment, *what goes down may go back up.* A *reversal* of an impairment loss is recorded if the fair value of the asset has recovered. Income will increase in the presence of an *impairment loss reversal.* Reversal is allowed for all impairments that affect long-lived assets, with the exception of goodwill. *A goodwill impairment is not reversed.*

The problem with reversing an impairment loss is that this provides yet another method by which management may be tempted to "manage" or smooth earnings—take an impairment loss when it is convenient and then restore it in a low-income year. To guard against such manipulation, accounting standards provide factors that must be assessed to trigger recognition of an impairment recovery. Logically, these are often opposite to the factors that indicate impairment. Examples of such circumstances include:

- A significant favourable change in the technological, market, economic or legal environment, such as a competitor leaving the market and increasing the market share for the company;
- Evidence that the economic performance of the asset is, or will be, better than expected;
- A significant increase in market value of an asset;
- Actions taken, or plans, to change the way the asset is used or restructure operations in a way that enhances cash flows.

Reversal of an impairment loss must result from an increase in the *value in use* of the asset or *fair value less costs to sell* of the asset.

Allocating the Reversal of an Impairment Loss

The reversal of an impairment loss may relate to an individual asset. The carrying amount of the individual asset is then written up, but cannot go higher than the *carrying value the asset would have reflected without the impairment.* This would be the carrying amount (net of depreciation or amortization) if no impairment loss had been previously recognized. This amount is not necessarily the pre-impairment value: it must be calculated, *including depreciation during the impairment period,* as we will see below. An impairment reversal is recognized in earnings.

If the reversal relates to all the assets of a CGU, the reversal is allocated to the assets *in proportion to their carrying values.* This reversal is allocated only to assets in the CGU that were decreased in recognizing previous impairment losses. If a reversal of an impairment loss is recognized, the carrying value of any particular asset may not be increased higher than the recoverable amount of that asset. Instead, a greater portion of the reversal of the impairment loss should be allocated to the other long-lived assets on a proportionate basis.

Let us return to our previous example, where we had an impairment loss of $600, which was allocated $150 to land, $240 to the building, and $210 to equipment (our first try, above, where no fair values could be determined for individual assets). One year has passed, and the competitive environment has improved sales and the recoverable amount of this division has increased. Management determines that the recoverable amount is now $1,400. Fair value less costs to sell could not be determined for these assets. The reversal of the impairment loss is $400—the excess of $1,400 recoverable amount over $1,000 carrying amount.

The reversal of the impairment loss must be allocated to the long-lived assets. The $400 impairment loss will be allocated to the assets in proportion to their carrying value:

Asset	Carrying Value	Proportion	Allocation of Reversal of Impairment Loss	Adjusted Carrying Value
Land	$ 250	25%	$ 100	350
Building	400	40%	160	560
Equipment	350	35%	140	490
	$1,000	100%	$400	$1,400

(Note that the carrying value would likely reflect depreciation, after the passage of time, and thus not be the post-writedown balances when an impairment reversal is recorded. We will leave this complication aside in the interest of clarity.)

Before this can be considered to be the correct allocation, it is necessary to calculate the carrying amount of the individual asset as they would have been *without the impairment*. Post-impairment reversal carrying values *cannot exceed this amount*. For the building, the pre-impairment value was $640 and the equipment was $560. Assuming straight-line depreciation; useful lives of 20 year and 10 years, respectively; and no residual values, the ceiling values are as follows:

Asset	Pre-Impairment Carrying Value (original value)	Depreciation – one year	Revised carrying value	Post-impairment reversal balance (above)
Land	$400	-	$400	$350
Building	$640	$32 ($640 ÷ 20)	$608	$560
Equipment	$560	$56 ($560 ÷ 10)	$504	$490

As you can see, the post-impairment reversal balances of $350, $560, and $490 are comfortably below the ceiling of $400, $608, and $504. The reversal therefore stands as allocated. If the revised carrying value were lower than the post-impairment reversal balance for any asset, *less of the reversal would be allocated to that asset*. More of the impairment reversal would be allocated to other assets. If all assets were at their limits, reversal, or a portion of the reversal, could not be recorded.

The reversal is recorded as follows:

Land	100	
Building	160	
Equipment	140	
Recovery of impairment loss		400

Goodwill Impairment

As we saw in Chapter 9, goodwill is measured as a residual, the excess of the purchase price paid for a unit over the fair value of its net assets on the acquisition date. Things to remember about goodwill impairment:

- Goodwill is not amortized, but like any intangible asset that is not amortized, *goodwill must be tested for impairment annually.*
- *Goodwill is assigned to the CGU to which it relates.*
- It is not possible to determine the fair value less cost to sell for the goodwill asset on its own. Goodwill is meaningful only as one of the assets of a CGU.
- Individual, identifiable assets within a CGU will be tested for impairment separately, before testing the entire CGU including goodwill. This test is based on individual fair value less cost to sell, if this amount is determinable. This will ensure that individual identifiable impairment losses are recognized before considering impairment of goodwill.
- The impairment test is similar to that described above for other assets, except that any impairment loss related to a CGU is assigned first to goodwill, and then to other assets on a pro-rata basis.
- A goodwill impairment is not reversed.

The key measuring unit for goodwill impairment is the *cash-generating unit*. Goodwill is allocated to the CGU to which it relates. The carrying amount of the CGU, including goodwill, is compared with the recoverable amount of the CGU. If the recoverable amount is above the carrying amount of the CGU, there is no impairment. If the recoverable amount is below the carrying amount, an impairment loss is recognized.

Example

Let us return to our previous example but now assume that the assets of the CGU include goodwill of $200, so the carrying value of assets has increased from $1,600 to $1,800.

Again, a change in the competitive environment suggests that the recoverable amount of this division may be less than its carrying value. Management conducts an impairment test, determining that the recoverable amount based on the estimated discounted present value of the future cash flows of the asset group is $1,000. Fair value less costs to sell could not be determined for any of these assets, including land. The impairment loss is $800—the excess of $1,800 carrying value over the $1,000 recoverable amount.

The impairment loss must be allocated to the long-lived assets. The $800 impairment loss will be allocated first to goodwill and then to the assets in proportion to their carrying value:

Asset	Carrying Value	Proportion (based on $1,600; excluding goodwill)	Allocation of Impairment Loss	Adjusted Carrying Value
Goodwill	$ 200		$200	$ 0
Land	400	25%	150 ($800 – $200) × 25%	250
Building	640	40%	240 ($800 – $200) × 40%	400
Equipment	560	35%	210 ($800 – $200) × 35%	350
	$1,800	100%	$800	$1,000

Reversal of Goodwill Impairment

Goodwill impairment is not reversed if there is an increase in the recoverable amount of a CGU. All other assets within the CGU would be increased by a proportionate basis, subject to the limit that an asset may not be written up to a value higher than its individual fair value less cost to sell, or its otherwise-depreciated value.

In our previous example, we had an impairment loss of $800. A change in the competitive environment has improved our sales, and our recoverable amount of this division is now $1,400, based on a discounted cash flow model. Fair value less costs to sell could not be determined for these assets. The reversal of the impairment loss is $400—the excess of $1,400 recoverable amount over $1,000 carrying amount.

The reversal of the impairment loss must be allocated to the long-lived assets. The $400 impairment loss will be allocated to the assets in proportion to their carrying value, *excluding goodwill*:

Asset	Carrying Value	Proportion (excluding goodwill)	Allocation of Reversal of Impairment Loss	Adjusted Carrying Value
Goodwill	$ 0		$ 0	$ 0
Land	250	25%	100	350
Building	400	40%	160	560
Equipment	350	35%	140	490
	$1,000	100%	$400	$1,400

Of course, goodwill has a carrying value of zero here, so it does not factor into the proportions. If, however, goodwill had been partially impaired in the original analysis and had, say, a carrying value of $100, it would still be excluded from the calculation of proportions. *No amount of reversal may be assigned to goodwill.*

A final reminder that this is the "first try" at assigning the impairment reversal. Before it is finalized, we must verify that the net book value, had the asset be depreciated and not impaired, is not a limiting factor. With reference to our prior calculation, this test is met in this example and the allocation of the impairment reversal is as shown above.

CONCEPT REVIEW

1. In general, when is it necessary to record an impairment of long-lived assets?
2. How is the recoverable amount determined for an impairment test?
3. Describe the steps followed to determine whether there has been an impairment of a long-lived asset.
4. What is unique about an impairment test for goodwill?

DISCLOSURE REQUIREMENTS

Not surprisingly, the requirement to disclose depreciation or amortization policy is front and centre in the disclosure requirements. If you are going to let companies pick a policy, it is crucial that financial statement readers be told about the choice. Thus, companies should disclose for each major category of depreciable long-lived assets:

- The depreciation or amortization method used, including the depreciation or amortization period or rate;
- The accumulated depreciation or amortization of each major category; and
- The amount of depreciation or amortization charged to earnings for the period.

If there has been an impairment or reversal of an impairment, the following is required:

- A description of the impaired asset or CGU and the facts and circumstances leading to the impairment;
- The amount of the impairment loss, and an indication of where it appears on the SCI if it is not presented separately;
- The amount of any reversal of impairment loss and an indication of where it appears on the SCI if it is not presented separately; and
- The method used for determining recoverable amount, including major assumptions.

Exhibit 10-6 shows an example of depreciation of property, plant, and equipment, amortization of intangible assets, and an impairment loss from the 2014 fiscal year of Sears Canada Inc. The company uses straight-line depreciation, and depreciates components separately. There was an impairment loss of $162 million recorded in the year, which affected various elements of property, plant, and equipment; intangibles; and goodwill. Goodwill balances were reduced to zero. There is extensive explanation of the impairment review, including the key assumptions made. There is also a continuity schedule for long-lived assets, which shows changes to the cost and accumulated depreciation of major asset categories. This allows depreciation and impairment amounts to be tied to specific categories.

EXHIBIT 10-6

SEARS CANADA INC. SELECTED NOTE DISCLOSURES FOR DEPRECIATION AND IMPAIRMENT

(ALL AMOUNTS FOR 2014 FISCAL YEAR, ENDED 31 JANUARY 2015)

Extracts from Significant Accounting Policy Note

2.8 Property; plant and equipment

Property, plant and equipment are measured at cost or deemed cost less accumulated depreciation and accumulated impairment losses. Costs include expenditures that are directly attributable to the acquisition of the asset. The cost of self-constructed assets includes site preparation costs, design and engineering fees, freight (only on initial freight costs incurred between the vendor and the Company), installation expenses and provincial sales tax (Saskatchewan. Manitoba and British Columbia), and is net of any vendor subsidies or reimbursements. An allocation of general and specific incremental interest charges for major construction projects is also included in the cost of related assets. Property, plant and equipment within one of the Company's Regina logistics centres have been classified as held for sale in the Consolidated Statements of Financial Position (see Note 29).

When the significant parts of an item of property, plant and equipment have varying useful lives, they are accounted for as separate components of property, plant and equipment. Depreciation is calculated based on the depreciable amount of the asset or significant component thereof, if applicable, which is the cost of the asset or significant component less its residual value. Depreciation is recognized using the straight-line method for each significant component of an item of property, plant and equipment and is recorded in "Selling, administrative and other expenses" in the Consolidated Statements of Net (Loss) Earnings and Comprehensive (Loss) Income. The estimated useful lives are 2 to 13 years for equipment and fixtures and 10 to 50 years for buildings and building improvements. The estimated useful lives, residual values and depreciation methods for property, plant and equipment are reviewed annually and adjusted, if appropriate, with the effect of any changes in estimates accounted for on a prospective basis.

Assets held under finance leases are depreciated over their expected useful lives on the same basis as owned assets or, where shorter, the term of the relevant lease, unless it is reasonably certain that the Company will obtain ownership by the end of the lease term.

The gain or loss arising on the disposal or retirement of an item of property, plant and equipment is determined as the difference between the proceeds from sale or the cost of retirement and the carrying amount of the asset, and is recognized in the Consolidated Statements of Net (Loss) Earnings and Comprehensive (Loss) Income.

For a discussion on the impairment of tangible assets, refer to Note 2.11. Property, plant and equipment are reviewed at the end of each reporting period to determine if there are any indicators of impairment.

2.11 Impairment of tangible assets and intangible assets with finite useful lives

At the end of each reporting period, the Company reviews property, plant and equipment, investment properties, intangible assets and goodwill for indicators of impairment. If any such indication exists, the recoverable amount of the asset is estimated in order to determine the extent of the impairment loss, if any. Where it is not possible to estimate the recoverable amount of an individual asset, the assets are then grouped together into the smallest group of assets that generate independent cash inflows from continuing use (the "cash generating unit" or "CGU") and a recoverable amount is estimated for that CGU. The Company has determined that its CGUs are primarily its retail stores.

Where a reasonable and consistent basis of allocation can be identified, corporate assets are also allocated to individual CGUs. Otherwise, they are allocated to the smallest group of CGUs for which a reasonable and consistent allocation basis can be identified.

If the recoverable amount of an asset or a CGU is estimated to be less than its earning amount, the asset or CGU will be reduced to its recoverable amount and an impairment loss is recognized immediately. If an impairment for a CGU has been identified, the impairment is first allocated to goodwill before other assets held by the CGU. Where goodwill is not part of a CGU, an impairment loss is recognized as a reduction in the carrying amount of the assets included in the CGU on a pro rata basis.

Where an impairment loss subsequently reverses (not applicable to goodwill), the carrying amount of the asset or CGU is revised to an estimate of its recoverable amount limited to the carrying amount that would have been determined had no impairment loss been recognized for the asset or CGU in pnor years. A reversal of an impairment loss is recognized immediately.

2.12 Impairment of goodwill

Goodwill was not amortized but was reviewed for impairment at least annually. For the purposes of impairment testing, goodwill was allocated to each of the Company's CGUs expected to benefit from the synergies of the combination.

CGUs to which goodwill had been allocated were tested for impairment annually, or more frequently when there was an indication that the unit may be unpaired. If the recoverable amount of the CGU was less than its carrying amount, the impairment loss was allocated first to reduce the carrying amount of any goodwill allocated to the CGU, and then to the other assets of the unit on a pro-rata basis, based on the carrying amount of each asset in the unit. Impairment losses for goodwill are not reversed in subsequent periods.

Extracts from Other Disclosure Notes

9. Property, plant and equipment and investment properties

The following is a continuity of property, plant and equipment:

(in CAD millions)	Land	Buildings and Leasehold Improvements	Finance Lease Buildings	Finance Lease Equipment	Equipment and Fixtures	Total
Cost or deemed cost						
Balance at February 2, 2013	$ 316.3	$ 1,387.1	$ 45.7	$ 3.5	$ 1,174.9	$ 2,927.5
Additions	—	26.1	1.4	0.9	33.3	61.7
Disposals	(75.7)	(248.9)	(2.6)	—	(78.3)	(405.5)
Net movement to assets held for sale[2]	(29)	(36.6)	—	—	(13.9)	(53.4)
Balance at February 1, 2014	$ 237.7	$ 1,127.7	$ 44.5	$ 4.4	$ 1,116.0	$ 2,530.3
Additions	0.2	1.0	—	0.1	28.5	29.8
Disposals	(9.5)	(42.3)	(3.0)	(3.5)	(8.5)	(66.8)
Balance at January 31, 2015	**$ 228.4**	**$ 1,086.4**	**$ 41.5**	**$ 1.0**	**$ 1,136.0**	**$ 2,493.3**
Accumulated depreciation and impairment						
Balance at February 2, 2013	$ 2.2	$ 770.3	$ 13.8	$ 2.0	$ 1,020.7	$ 1,809.0
Depreciation expense[1]	—	50.6	5.0	1.2	43.5	100.3
Disposals	—	(79.7)	(2.6)	—	(67.4)	(149.7)
Impairment (reversals) losses [1,2]	(2,2)	26.5	—	—	3.4	27.7
Net movement to assets held for sale [2]	—	(28.6)	—	—	(13.9)	(42.5)
Balance at February 1, 2014	**$ —**	**$ 739.1**	**$ 16.2**	**$ 3.2**	**$ 986.3**	**$ 1,744.8**
Depreciation expense[1]	—	35.9	3.8	0.8	36.4	76.9
Disposals	—	(18.2)	(3.0)	(3.5)	(7.1)	(31.8)
Impairment losses[1]	—	91.1	17.1	—	27.6	135.8
Balance at January 31, 2015	**$ —**	**$ 847.9**	**$ 34.1**	**$ 0.5**	**$ 1,043.2**	**$ 1,925.7**
Total property, plant and equipment						
Net balance at January 31, 2015	**$ 228.4**	**$ 238.5**	**$ 7.4**	**$ 0.5**	**$ 92.8**	**$ 567.6**
Net balance at February 1, 2014	$ 237.7	$ 388.6	$ 28.3	$ 1.2	$ 129.7	$ 785.5

Impairment loss

The Company conducted appraisals of certain land and building properties that it owned, with the assistance of independent qualified third party appraisers. The valuation methods used to determine fair value include the direct capitalization and discounted cash flow methods for buildings and the direct sales comparison for land.

During Fiscal 2014, the Company recognized an impairment loss of $68.3 million (2013: nil) on a number of Sears full-line and Corbeil stores, an impairment loss of $17.6 million (2013: $11.7 million) on a number of Sears Home stores and an impairment loss of $5.5 million (2013: nil) on a number of Hometown stores. The impairment loss was due to indicators (in particular a decrease in revenue or decrease in cash flows) that the recoverable amount was less than the carrying value. The recoverable amounts of the CGUs tested were based on the present value of the estimated cash flow, over the lease term plus two renewals for Sears full-line and Home stores and five years for Hometown stores, as this was management's best estimate of the useful life of the assets of these CGUs. A pre-tax discount rate of 10.8% was based on management's best estimate of the CGUs' weighted average cost of capital considering the risks facing the CGUs. The estimated cash flows for the CGUs described above assumed no future improvement in the CGUs' results, given their recent operating performance. If considered independently, a two percentage point change in the applied discount rate, a ten percentage point change in the estimated cash flows and a change in the number of renewal terms would have an insignificant impact on the amount of the reported impairment loss.

During Fiscal 2014, the Company undertook a comprehensive evaluation of its logistics network for current and future needs, given its changing warehousing requirements. Accordingly, the Company determined that the Montreal distribution centre ("MDC") may be considered for disposition. The Company determined the fair value of the MDC by engaging an independent qualified third party appraiser to conduct an appraisal of the property. The valuation methods used included the direct capitalization and discounted cash flow methods, and the direct sales comparison approach. A discount rate of 8.5% and a rate of mflation of 2.5% were applied to cash flow projections over a period of 10 years. The Company assessed various scenarios provided by the appraiser to determine a fair value. As a result of the carrying amount exceeding the recoverable amount of $44.3 million for the MDC, an impairment loss of $44.4 million (2013: $1.7 million) was included in "Selling, administrative and other expenses" in the Consolidated Statements of Net (Loss) Earnings and Comprehensive (Loss) Income.

The Company will continue to assess the recoverable amount of the CGUs at the end of each reporting period and adjust the carrying amount accordingly. To determine the recoverable amount of the CGUs, the Company will consider factors such as expected future cash flows, growth rates, capitalization rates and an appropriate discount rate to calculate the fair value or value in use as required.

The impairment loss of $135.8 million (2013: $27.7 million) was included in "Selling, administrative and other expenses" in the Consolidated Statements of Net (Loss) Earnings and Comprehensive (Loss) Income. Included in the impairment loss of $27.7 million during Fiscal 2013, was an impairment loss reversal relating to land of $2.2 million. The impairment loss reversal was a result of the proceeds received from the agreement to sell the Company's 50% joint arrangement interest in the Promenade de Drummondville property ("Drummondville"). See Note 11 for additional information.

The total impairment loss related to property, plant and equipment, goodwill and intangible assets and assets classified as held for sale included in Fiscal 2014 was $162.0 million (2013: $33.8 million). See Note 10 and Note 29 for additional information.

Source: Sears Canada Inc. 2014 Annual Financial Statements, www.sedar.com, posted 13 March 2015.

STATEMENT OF CASH FLOWS

Depreciation or amortization expense is an add-back to the operating activities section of the statement of cash flows (SCF). It is important to remember that depreciation or amortization is a little different from other expenses, because depreciation or amortization is a non-cash expense. Clearly, the company has to pay out cash or other resources to obtain the long-lived asset, but the timing of cash paid is likely to be a lot earlier than the expense.

Any writedowns of long-lived assets or reversals of writedowns, including impairment of goodwill, are a non-cash charge on the SCI. Like depreciation or amortization, they are added back to earnings in the operating activities section of the SCF.

ETHICAL ISSUES

The importance of accounting estimates has been emphasized throughout this book. Depreciation or amortization requires not only a choice of method but also estimates of useful life and residual value. A choice of method, once made, normally is not changed. The requirement that similar assets be depreciated or amortized by similar methods helps to maintain consistency in measurement.

However, over the life of a long-lived asset, it is quite possible for a company to change any or all of the asset's (1) depreciation or amortization method, (2) useful life, or (3) residual value. Changes in all estimates must be carefully scrutinized. If a company lengthens an asset's useful life, for example, is it really because the asset will be useful longer than expected, or is it because management seeks to improve the company's apparent profitability? Auditors can examine the rationale behind changes in management's estimates, but this scrutiny will have little effect unless the new estimates are quite obviously outside the feasible range.

There are two aspects that help limit the ability of management to act unethically in setting estimates relating to depreciation or amortization. One is that if the company's policies and estimates get out of line with industry practice, the nonconformity will be apparent to investors and bankers, especially those who deal often with a specific industry. Nonconformity will cause statement users to suspect management's motivations and investors will discount the stock price or lenders will be hesitant to extend loans. There is market discipline.

The second aspect is that investors take changes in accounting estimates into account—efficient markets are not fooled by accounting changes in the short run. Again, market discipline is a factor.

But still, there is cause for concern. Even subtle changes can have important long-term effects on earnings. Do investors really remember all of the past changes in management estimates when evaluating a company's performance? Furthermore, many covenants, bonuses, and other contracts are based on financial statement numbers, and are not adjusted for changes in estimates. As a result, these changes can have real cash flow implications for a firm.

Impairment

While depreciation or amortization estimates and revisions offer some scope for unethical behaviour, impairments offer a far more fertile area for bias, either intentional or unintentional. Impairment tests are based on estimates of fair values. In turn, fair value is based on estimates of *future* cash flows. By their nature, estimates of future cash flows cannot be verified. Managers may be pessimistic when they estimate future cash flows from an asset group, for example, because the company has not been successful at making its products profitable. Even when it is clear that the future cash flows of a CGU are in decline, management must estimate how quickly and how severe the decline will be.

Managers can hire professional appraisers to help estimate future cash flows and thus the fair value of assets and CGUs. Ideally, more than one appraiser is used. Professional appraisers are assumed to be essentially in agreement if their estimates of fair value are within 10% of each other. A variation of 10% in the fair value of an asset or CGU may not seem very significant. However, a relatively small variation in estimated fair value can have a major impact on earnings in the year of the writedown. The variation also affects the future earnings and EPS of the company by lowering depreciation or amortization after the writedown. Furthermore, management can write the asset back up again, partially or completely if the future cash flows turn out to be better than expected.

Writedowns can be a very effective tool for enabling managers to "manage" the company's reported earnings.

An additional facet relating to *goodwill* impairment tests is that the test is performed at the level of the CGU. By rearranging the organization's CGUs, the need to perform impairment tests on specific operating units can be eliminated.

In summary, the practices for depreciation or amortization and for impairment tests are not as objective and verifiable as they may seem at first glance. Auditors and financial statement users must be vigilant against manipulation of reported results, as must the senior accountants working within the company itself.

Looking Ahead

The IASB has a project titled "Goodwill and Impairment" on its list of *Assessment Stage* projects. Long-lived assets are not now on the agenda for the Canadian AcSB.

Accounting Standards for Private Enterprises

IFRS and ASPE standards are similar for depreciation and impairment; however, there are some differences to note.

ASPE uses the word *amortization* for all assets, including depreciation and depletion. IFRS standards explicitly use the word *depreciation* when referring to amortization of tangible long-lived assets, and *amortization* is used only for intangibles.

Component Depreciation

IFRS standards require component depreciation. ASPE, on the other hand, states that component depreciation should be done "if practicable." Many ASPE-compliant companies do not apply component depreciation.

Minimum Depreciation

IFRS standards have no requirement for a minimum amount of annual depreciation. Residual value and estimated useful life are relevant for determining the amount of depreciation, and an asset is not depreciated after net book value declines to residual value. Recall that residual value is the fair value less cost to sell *at the end of the asset's life with the company.*

Under ASPE, there is a dual calculation. Companies calculate two alternative depreciation expense amounts, and record the higher number:

- Cost less scrap value, over the entire life of the asset. **Scrap value** (also called salvage value) is the fair value less cost to sell *at the end of an asset's complete life*; versus
- Cost less residual value over the life of the asset with the company; this is the same as the IFRS calculation.

Example Assume that a company has a piece of equipment that cost $10,000. The company plans to keep it for 8 years and then sell it for $5,000. The asset itself is expected to have a total life of 12 years and then be sold for scrap, for $500. The two calculations:

- $792; ($10,000 cost – $500 scrap) ÷ 12 years
- $625; ($10,000 cost – $5,000 residual) ÷ 8 years

Depreciation is recorded at $792 under ASPE, the higher of the two values. Depreciation expense would be $625 under IFRS. Notice that the lower $625 value is caused by the fairly high residual value at the end of 8 years; management has estimated that the equipment will retain half its original cost as a residual value ($5,000 ÷ $10,000) despite the fact that the equipment is 2/3 of the way through its life (8 years ÷ 12 years).

This ASPE test is meant to provide a reality check on estimates; scrap value is usually negligible.

Determination of Impairment Losses

IFRS standards require companies to review impairment indicators at every reporting date. If a factor indicates impairment, then a *one-step test* is used to determine impairment. That is, the carrying amount of the long-lived asset or CGU is compared with the recoverable amount, which is the higher of value in use and fair value less costs to sell. If impairment exists then the asset is written down to its recoverable amount. The same approach is used for all long-lived assets, although the goodwill rules have some specifics that are unique to goodwill.

IFRS standards adopt the same impairment test for property, plant, and equipment; intangible assets; and goodwill. ASPE standards adopt one test for property, plant, and equipment and intangible assets that are amortized. There is a second approach used for intangible assets that are not amortized, and goodwill.

For property, plant, and equipment and intangible assets that are amortized, ASPE requires impairment testing only if there is a trigger, which is an event or circumstance that indicates impairment. A two-step test is used to determine impairment if there has been a triggering event:

1. First, the carrying value (net book value) is compared with the *undiscounted* cash flows from use and disposal (recoverable amount). If this test is failed, then impairment testing moves to the second step.

2. Second, if needed, the carrying amount is compared with *fair value*. If fair value is lower than carrying value, an impairment loss is recorded. Fair value is defined as the amount of the consideration that would be agreed upon in an arm's-length transaction between knowledgeable, willing parties who are under no compulsion to act.

This test is performed for *asset groups*, defined as the lowest level (smallest combination) of assets and liabilities for which identifiable cash flows are largely independent of the cash flows of other assets or groups of assets.

For *intangible assets with indefinite lives*, the impairment process is again set in motion by a triggering event. There is no two-step process, though. An impairment loss is recorded when the carrying amount is higher than *fair value,* as defined above.

Goodwill is tested for impairment as part of a *reporting unit*. The fair value of the reporting unit must be determined. Goodwill impairment is recognized when the carrying amount of the reporting unit as a whole, including goodwill, is higher than fair value.

A **reporting unit** is either an operating segment or one level below (referred to as a component). This is a unit for which discrete financial information is available and segment management regularly reviews the operating results. Components may be combined if they have similar economic characteristics.

Reversal of Impairment Losses

IFRS standards permit the reversal of impairment losses, other than goodwill impairment losses, which are not reversible. A reversal is caused by changed circumstances, causing an increase to the recoverable amount related to the long-lived asset.

ASPE does not permit reversal of any impairment losses related to long-lived assets.

Revaluation Accounting

IFRS allows use of the revaluation model. Under the revaluation model, routine revaluation (to fair value) of property, plant, and equipment is permitted. The use of the cost model is an *option* under IFRS, not a *requirement*.

ASPE, in contrast, does not permit use of the revaluation model.

Appendix 2 to this chapter contains an illustration of revaluation accounting.

RELEVANT STANDARDS

CPA Canada Handbook, Part I (IFRS):

- IAS 16, Property, Plant, and Equipment
- IAS 36, Impairment of Assets
- IAS 38, Intangible Assets
- IAS 40, Investment Property
- IFRS 5, Non-current Assets Held for Sale and Discontinued Operations

CPA Canada Handbook, Part II (ASPE):

- Section 3061, Property, Plant, and Equipment
- Section 3064, Goodwill and Intangible Assets
- Section 3063, Impairment of Long-lived Assets
- Section 3475, Disposal of Long-lived Assets and Discontinued Operations

SUMMARY OF KEY POINTS

1. Depreciation or amortization is a rational and systematic process of allocating depreciable or amortizable cost (acquisition cost less residual value) to the periods in which long-lived assets are used. Depreciation refers to items of property, plant, and equipment while amortization refers to intangible assets. Depreciation or amortization expense for a period does not represent the change in market value of assets, nor does it necessarily equal the portion of the asset's utility consumed in the period. Depreciation or amortization is justified on the basis of eventual decline in value, through physical wear and tear and obsolescence.

2. Goodwill, land, investment property, held-for-sale assets, biological assets, and intangible assets with an unlimited life are not depreciated or amortized.

3. Several methods of depreciation or amortization are rational and systematic and acceptable under GAAP: the straight-line (SL), service-hours (SH), productive-output (PO), and declining-balance (DB) methods. Factors affecting choice include individual corporate reporting objectives, information processing costs, a desire to minimize income tax temporary differences, industry norms, and parent company preferences.

4. Three factors contribute to the determination of periodic amortization expense: original acquisition cost and any capitalized post-acquisition costs, estimated residual value, and estimated useful life or productivity measured either in service hours or units of output. The key factor is that depreciation or amortization should reflect the pattern of consumption of future benefits.

5. For all methods, the estimated residual value is the minimum book value. Except for the declining-balance methods, depreciable or amortizable cost (cost minus residual value) is multiplied by a rate or fraction to determine periodic depreciation or amortization. Declining-balance depreciation is based on cost less accumulated depreciation and ceases when net book value equals residual value.

6. Component depreciation accounting is the depreciation of an asset by significant component parts.

7. For assets acquired during an accounting period, an accounting convention, such as the half-year convention, is usually used in practice.

8. The group depreciation system is an alternative to depreciation methods applied individually to assets. These systems save accounting costs and are justified under cost-benefit and materiality constraints.

9. Long-lived assets subject to depreciation or amortization must be reviewed for potential impairment. A loss is recognized when the recoverable amount is less than carrying value. The loss equals the difference between the asset's carrying value and the asset's recoverable amount. Recoverable amount is based on the higher of fair value less costs to sell and value in use (estimated future *discounted* cash flows).

10. An impairment test involves establishing cash-generating units, review of impairment indicators, measuring the recoverable amount, and allocating the impairment loss. Losses are allocated pro-rata for assets evaluated as part of a cash-generating unit. No asset may be written down to an amount less than its individual fair value less cost to sell.

11. Intangible assets not subject to amortization are written down to recoverable amount if their carrying value exceeds the recoverable amount.

12. Goodwill must be written down if the value is impaired. This is done by comparing the recoverable amount of a cash-generating unit (including goodwill) to its carrying value. If the recoverable amount is lower than the carrying value, then the impairment loss is allocated first to goodwill and then to other assets in the CGU.

13. Reversal of an impairment loss is permitted for all long-lived assets except for goodwill. Reversals are allocated pro-rata, except no asset may be written up to an amount that is greater than its individual fair value less cost to sell. An asset may not be written up to a value that is higher than its net book value would have been, had it been not previously impaired, but depreciated instead.

14. Depreciation or amortization is not a cash flow; the cash flow occurred when the long-lived asset was acquired. Depreciation and amortization and impairment writedowns are added back to earnings when cash flow from operations is determined on the statement of cash flows (SCF).

15. Companies must disclose the depreciation or amortization method chosen for major categories of long-lived assets, the depreciation or amortization period or rate, and the amount of depreciation or amortization charged to income for the period. Practices and assumptions used in impairment tests must be disclosed.

16. Standards for ASPE differ from IFRS in some ways: (1) ASPE permits but does not require component depreciation; (2) ASPE includes a minimum amortization test; (3) ASPE incorporates different impairment tests for tangible versus intangible assets, and uses a two-step impairment model for tangible assets where undiscounted cash flows are used as an assessment tool; (4) ASPE does not permit reversal of any impairment losses on assets; and (5) ASPE does not allow the revaluation method.

Key Terms

amortization

asset group

cash-generating unit (CGU)

component depreciation accounting

convention	indefinite life
declining-balance (DB) method	long-lived assets
depletion	net book value
depreciation	productive-output (PO) method
depreciable amount	recoverable amount
double-declining balance (DDB) method	reporting unit
fair value less costs to sell	residual value
group depreciation	revenue-based depreciation method
held-for-sale	scrap value
impairment	service-hours (SH) method
impairment loss	useful life
impairment loss reversal	value in use
impairment test	

Review Problem 10-1

The following cases are independent.

1. *Partial-year depreciation.* Whitney Corp. purchased equipment on 1 April 20X4 for $34,000. The equipment has a useful life of five years and a residual value of $4,000. The year-end is December 31. What is depreciation for 20X4 and 20X5, using declining-balance depreciation at a 40% rate and depreciating by month?

2. *Asset impairment.* Rancho Company purchases equipment on 1 April 20X3 for $34,000. The equipment has a useful life of five years, with a residual value of $4,000, and is depreciated using the straight-line method and the half-year convention. At the end of 20X5, Rancho suspects that the original investment in the asset will not be realized; the total remaining future cash inflows expected to be generated by the equipment, including the original residual value, amounts to $10,000 (undiscounted) and $8,000 (discounted). The equipment's fair value less costs to sell at 31 December 20X5 is $7,000. Determine whether the asset is impaired and, if so, the impairment loss at 31 December 20X5.

3. *Component depreciation.* Baja Company has a large asset that it just purchased that has a number of significant components. The company has determined that the straight-line method reflects the pattern of consumption of future benefits. Component A is a major spare part that had an original cost of $100,000 and a residual value of zero and an estimated life of five years. Component B is a major overhaul that had an original cost of $20,000 and a residual value of zero and an estimated life of two years. Component C is the frame of the asset that has an original cost of $185,000 and a residual value of $5,000 and an estimated life of 20 years. The remaining components grouped together that are insignificant have an original cost of $16,000 and a residual value of $1,000 and an estimated life of three years. What is the depreciation expense?

REVIEW PROBLEM 10-1—SOLUTION

1. Depreciation for 20X4: $34,000 \times 40\% \times 9/12 = $10,200

   Depreciation for 20X5: ($34,000 − $10,200) \times 40\% = $9,520

2. Book value of equipment at 31 December 20X5:

Cost	$34,000
Accumulated depreciation, 31 December 20X5: ($34,000 − $4,000) ÷ 5 × 2.5 years	15,000

Net book value	$19,000

The asset is impaired because the recoverable amount ($8,000) is lower than the carrying value ($19,000). The recoverable amount of $8,000 is the higher of the discounted future cash flow ($8,000) and fair value less costs to sell ($7,000). This is a loss of $11,000.

3. Depreciation for 20X5 = A ($100,000 − $0)/5 = $20,000

= B ($20,000 − $0)/2 = $10,000

= C ($185,000 − $5,000)/20 = $9,000

= D ($16,000 − $1,000)/3 = $5,000

The total depreciation for all components is $ 44,000.

CASE 10-1

BRIGHT LIGHTS LTD.

Bright Lights Ltd. (Bright) is a private company incorporated five years ago by a group of friends who had recently graduated with business or engineering degrees. The group is interested in innovative designs to meet a variety of lighting needs and has been working with photovaltaics technology (PV). PV is a clean, sustainable method of converting solar energy into direct current electricity. PV incorporates solar cells in panels; however, solar panels have been expensive in smaller applications to date. Bright is modifying PV technology to result in lower cost and relatively lightweight building integrated photovoltaics (BIP)—or solar panels—that can be installed on residential and commercial rooftops.

At this point, the beginning of 20X6, Bright is still in start-up mode, and has not commenced commercial production. The product is being fine-tuned and re-engineered to ensure it is cost-effective and meets output specifications. The SCI shows expenses but as yet no revenue; the company has an accumulated deficit. Great progress has been made, though, and the company has sufficient cash from loans and private equity infusion to reach the commencement of commercial operation in 20X7.

Bright's board of directors is in discussions with several potential investors who are interested in Bright's proprietary technology. Additional equity financing options are being explored because Bright is interested in lowering its cost of borrowing, which is 9%. These investors will be using ratios such the debt-to-equity ratio when assessing risk, and return on assets to assess profitability. While return on assets is not meaningful in the development stage, it will become important when operations commence. Shareholders' equity is currently a net positive number, despite accumulated losses, because of the encouraging but necessary level of equity investment to date.

It is now 25 February 20X6 and you, a CPA with a medium-sized public accounting firm, have been engaged to provide accounting advice to Bright for its 20X5 fiscal year. Although a private company, Bright reports under International Financial Reporting Standards (IFRS) so as to better meet the information needs of its potential investors. You know that, in general, technology companies hope to be takeover targets when their technology is desirable.

You have met with Bright's bookkeeper, Victoria Shugarue, who provided the information noted in Exhibit I. You realize that there are several accounting issues to discuss with respect to accounting policies for the 20X5 year-end. You decide to prepare a brief report to use as a basis for discussion with the audit committee, which will meet next week.

EXHIBIT I

BRIGHT LIGHTS LIMITED

Notes concerning accounting issues: 20X5 year-end

On January 1, 20X4 Bright acquired a building from the local municipality at a cost of $210,000. Also on that date, Bright received $50,000 in government assistance from the regional economic board to be used toward the purchase of the building. The building had a remaining useful life of 25 years in 20X4. Depreciation on the full building has been recorded on a straight-line basis in 20X4 and 20X5. There is a balance of $46,000 in a deferred government assistance account at 31 December 20X5 that represents the original $50,000 amount less the charges to reduce depreciation expense for two years.

Only 40% of the building is now used, because Bright is still in the development stage, but it will be large enough to support full-scale commercial development in 20X7. Manufacturing equipment is being rented on a modest scale, again consistent with development-stage activities. The entire operation will be scaled up and expanded for 20X7.

The 20X4 agreement with the municipality also provided Bright with access to land adjacent to the building. The land had been vacant for some time so Bright was able to obtain use of the land by agreeing to pay a nominal rent per year for 10 years. The municipality was pleased with the economic impact that will result when Bright advances its technology, begins production, and provides employment opportunities.

While use of solar panels provides a clean energy source, the manufacturing process generates wastewater that may contain hazardous compounds. This has not been an issue to date, but must be addressed for 20X7. Bright will follow regulatory guidelines to treat and properly dispose of any toxic contaminants generated in the manufacturing process.

Later in 20X6, Bright plans to install waste management tanks on the land rented from the municipality. To alleviate the loudly expressed concerns of the community, Bright announced a commitment to remove the waste management tanks before 31 December 20X13 and also promised to carry out significant enhancements to the land with the same time line. Tank removal and creation of a park and playground area are activities that are estimated to cost $90,000 in 20X13. By the end of 20X13, management of Bright is confident that technology will have moved on to either allow production without the hazardous compounds issue, or a different decontamination process will be available.

This announcement was made in early 20X4, and the plan was disclosed in the notes to the 20X4 financial statements. The $90,000 will be expensed when the money is spent.

Bright is spending large amounts of money to refine and re-engineer its technology and product lines to ensure they are cost-effective and meet output specifications. To date, all such expenditures have been expensed as research costs, but the question is whether expenditures can now be capitalized as a development asset for later amortization.

Required

Prepare the report.

(Judy Cumby, used with permission.)

CASE 10-2

ROCK GROUP LTD.

You were recently approached by one of your clients, Wendy Wonders, the chief financial officer of Rock Group Ltd. (RGL), a Canadian public company with a 31 December year-end. RGL manufactures and sells power precision hand tools and accessories, such as hammers and drills.

To complement RGL's existing products, RGL is interested in purchasing 100% of the common shares of Scrulox Screws Inc. (SSI), a private company reporting under Accounting Standards for Private Enterprises (ASPE).

SSI was identified as an acquisition target because of its complementary product offerings, extensive internally generated customer database, and overall strong financial results, including a consistent gross margin on all sales of 60%. As of 31 December 20X2, the carrying value of SSI's net assets, excluding the customer database, was $29 million (fair market value of $50 million), which includes two manufacturing plants with a carrying value of $11 million each (fair market value of $19 million each). SSI's customer database is estimated to have a fair market value of $0.8 million.

SSI's financial statements have never been audited. The purchase price for SSI is based on two times net income for its year ended 31 December 20X2, which currently is estimated at $52 million (2 × $26 million SSI preliminary net income).

It is now 1 April 20X3. You have met with Wally, SSI's bookkeeper and primary shareholder, to obtain additional information on SSI. Notes from this meeting are included in Exhibit 1.

EXHIBIT 1

NOTES FROM MEETING WITH SSI BOOKKEEPER

- In anticipation of being purchased by a public company, on 29 December 20X2, SSI signed a contract with a new controller, proficient in International Financial Reporting Standards (IFRS), and agreed to pay her $165,000 per year starting 1 February 20X3, her first day of work. Wally is excited to have a controller who will be able to teach him the fundamentals of IFRS!

- SSI's manufacturing plant in Barrie, Ontario, produces electric drills, with annual net cash flows of $10 million and manufacturing assets of $25 million. SSI management is committed to opening a new plant in Hamilton, Ontario, which will produce solar drills that power on solar energy and therefore do not require electricity. As a result, production at the Barrie plant will be adjusted to reflect the change, resulting in annual projected cash flows of $5 million expected for the next five years, after which the plant will be shut down.

- As the new plant is set to open in the future, no accounting entries have been recorded.

- To support the building of the new Hamilton plant, the Government of Ontario has provided SSI with $10 million to help with the cost of purchasing new manufacturing equipment and to support payroll costs of the various individuals directly involved in the construction project, including architects, construction workers, project managers, and those individuals indirectly involved in the project, such as marketing personnel who are promoting the new solar hammer.

- Wally recorded the receipt of the government funds as revenue. Wally notes that if the government grant was not received, SSI would be forced to obtain a bank loan to fund the construction at a costly interest rate of 8%.

- On 30 July 20X2, SSI made an $80,000 upfront payment to Print Inc. to print the new 20X3 SSI product catalogues, featuring the upcoming solar drill. The catalogues were delivered to SSI on 5

October 20X2 and will be distributed to the public in the spring of 20X3, at which point SSI will record an expense of $80,000.

- On 24 March 20X2 SSI's Estevan, Saskatchewan, plant was the victim of theft. As of the last inventory count on 31 December 20X1, the plant had $1.8 million worth of products. SSI's records indicate that sales from 1 January to 24 March were $1.48 million and during that same time, purchases were $1.3 million. SSI's insurance will cover the cost of the lost inventory once Wally has filed the claim. Wally is not sure how much inventory was lost and therefore has yet to record an entry.

- Adjacent to the Estevan plant, SSI owns a parcel of land that is currently vacant and held for undetermined future use. Due to the increasing population of Estevan, the land has been gradually increasing in value. To better reflect the true value of the land, Wally recorded the land at fair value on the balance sheet, increasing the carrying value from $1 million to $6 million.

Wendy would like you to review SSI's accounting under ASPE for the year ended 31 December 20X2 and provide your comments. For each significant transaction, she would also like to understand what alternatives and possible adjustment (if any) needs to be recorded to reflect the transaction under IFRS.

As this is the first acquisition of a company for RGL, Wendy is unsure of the initial and subsequent accounting for SSI by RGL.

Required:

Prepare a report that responds to Wendy Wonders' requests and concerns. Be specific and quantify, wherever possible.

(Alex Fisher)

CASE 10-3

ROAD SAFETY INC.

You have just been hired as an accounting advisor by Road Safety Inc. (RSI), a company that manufactures road safety equipment (e.g., crash barriers, traffic lights, and electronic information signs). RSI was founded in 20X4 and has grown rapidly over the last five years. In 20X7, the company had its first profit with annual sales of over $8 million, which is the highest level of sales in the company's history, and taxable income of $3 million.

RSI has needed to raise financing to develop a new product, "traffic sensors," which will identify traffic jams and warn motorists through the company's electronic information signs of problems and alternative routes. Part of the funding for product development has come from a bank loan. The bank requires an annual audit and specifies a maximum debt-to-equity ratio. At the end of 20X6, RSI was close to the maximum debt-to-equity ratio. This year will be the first year that RSI will have an audit completed.

You have just completed a meeting with the President of RSI, Nancy O'Callaghan. Nancy and other family members own all of the Class A common shares in RSI. They have 10 votes per share. During that meeting, she made the comments below. Nancy has requested that you draft a memo to her identifying alternative accounting policies as well as your overall recommendations for each issue.

"Our turnaround is for a large part due to the hiring of Tom, our new CEO. We were thrilled when he left our major competitor in January to join our team. He is such a valuable asset that we offered him a bonus of 10% of net income each year. Look at what he has accomplished! We are out of the red thanks to him. Besides increasing efficiency, he even had time to develop these new accounting policies.

"In the past all of our assets were recorded at cost and depreciated. Tom has just told us that we can recognize increases in some of these assets. For example, we have some vacant land that is just sitting there until we decide what to do with it. Also, we know our building used for administration and manufacturing has skyrocketed in value. Both can be shown at fair value, which is more relevant! And as an extra bonus, we will not need to record any depreciation on these assets. The bank will be very happy if we show higher values on our statement of financial position. And just think of how much stronger our earnings will be, which will make our family shareholders happy.

"We offer a minimum 10-year guarantee with our products. If something does not work, we will fix it within a minimum of 24 hours at no cost. Speed is critical, since our equipment saves lives. Our products are of such high quality we have few if any warranty costs. The warranty is not a stand-alone contract; it is just meant to ensure that our products work as planned. Tom decided to keep the accounting simple—when and if we do any work, we will record an expense.

"Another account Tom said not to worry about is that thing called *deferred taxes*. Whoever thought up that accounting rule? To keep life simple, income tax expense will equal the amount that we pay to the government for our taxes. On the other hand, when we can look good, Tom said we should take advantage of other options. We have past taxable losses of $2 million that Tom said we can record as an asset.

"We have never amortized or tested goodwill for impairment, since goodwill is being built up in our business, not used. In fact, Tom reassured me that it will never go down in value, since our business is continuing to grow. This year for the first time, on Tom's advice, we acquired another private company that provides additional products to add to our line. That increased our goodwill even more.

"To preserve our cash reserves, Tom obtained some needed computer technology for our traffic sensors by having RSI issue some Class B common shares. The value of these shares for the financial statements has yet to be determined. This computer technology is leading edge with nothing comparable in the marketplace.

"Some of our manufacturing machinery, especially the robotics equipment, is comprised of major parts that need to be replaced every few years. Major inspections and overhauls are also regular. Tom said we do not need to worry about that from an accounting point of view. That is just a business issue. Straight-line depreciation will be the simplest, and to minimize our information system costs, the machinery will just be depreciated based on the total carrying amount of the machinery."

Required:

Part A: Prepare the report for Nancy, assuming RSI will use IFRS.

Part B: Prepare the report for Nancy, assuming RSI will use ASPE.

connect

TR10-1 Depreciation Decision:

Benata Ltd. has the following assets:

a. Goodwill.

b. Trademark with a remaining life of ten years but renewable for an infinite period; expected to be used indefinitely.

c. Customer lists.

d. Machinery.

e. Land expected to be held for 20 years and then sold.

f. Site restoration costs with respect to the land in (e).

g. Buildings, accounted for using the revaluation method.

h. Rental property, accounted for using the fair- value method.

i. Vines (winery).

Required:

Which of the above assets are depreciated?

connect

TR10-2 Depreciation:

Manufacturing Inc. purchased a machine on 1 January 20X2 for $500,000. The estimated physical life of the machine is 15 years, but the estimated useful life to Manufacturing is 10 years. The equipment has an estimated residual value of $20,000. The equipment was ready for use on 1 January 20X2.

Required:

1. Calculate depreciation expense for 20X2 and 20X3 using the straight-line method.

2. Assume the machine is anticipated to produce 800,000 units. In 20X2 the machine produced 150,000 units and in 20X3 120,000 units. Calculate depreciation expense for 20X2 and 20X3 using the productive-output method.

3. Calculate depreciation expense for 20X2 and 20X3 using the declining-balance method using 40%.

connect

TR10-3 Depreciation Estimates:

Vert Ltd. purchased a vehicle on 1 January 20X8 for $34,000 and began to use it immediately. The estimated physical life of the vehicle is 20 years, but the estimated useful life to Vert is 10 years. The vehicle has an estimated residual value of $8,000. The vehicle is anticipated to be driven for 200,000 kilometres, and was driven 34,000 kilometres in 20X8 and 40,000 kilometres in 20X9.

Required:

1. Calculate depreciation expense for 20X8 and 20X9 using the straight-line method, units of production, and declining balance using a rate of 50%.

2. Repeat requirement 1 assuming that Vert decides that the useful life to Vert is 15 years, after which the residual value will be $4,000, and the total kilometres to be driven is now 300,000.

connect

TR10-4 Component Depreciation:

XYZ Inc. has a building it purchased for $400,000. It is estimated the building has a useful life of 25 years and zero residual value. The building has three major components. XYZ uses the straight-line method of depreciation.

Component	Unit Cost	Useful Life
A	$ 80,000	5 years
B	$120,000	10 years
C	$200,000	25 years

Required:

1. What is the amount of depreciation in year one? Provide the journal entry. Use a separate accumulated depreciation account for each component.

2. What would be the impact if component A was a major spare part that was replaced at the end of the fourth year instead of year five? The new major spare part had a cost of $100,000. Provide the journal entry.

connect

TR10-5 Fractional Depreciation:

Phillips Ltd. purchased a machine on 26 March 20X3 for $90,000 and began to use it immediately. The estimated useful life of the machine is 5 years, and it has an expected residual value of $10,000 at that time. Phillips uses straight-line depreciation.

Required:

1. Calculate annual depreciation for 20X3 through 20X8 assuming that depreciation is calculated to the nearest month.

2. Repeat requirement 1 using three accounting conventions:
    a. Half-year convention
    b. Full-first-year convention
    c. Final-year convention

3. Calculate the gain or loss on disposal assuming that the asset is unexpectedly sold for $6,000 at the end of 20X6, using net book value from requirement 1, and then from the three alternatives in requirement 2. Why is each amount different?

connect

TR10-6 Recoverable Amount:

Innovative Inc. has a piece of equipment with a carrying amount of $175,000. Technology has changed, indicating that the machine may be impaired. A new machine with updated technology could be purchased for $350,000. A used machine of similar vintage is listed on-line for $160,000. The estimated discounted cash flows from continuing to use the asset are $148,000. The undiscounted cash flows from the use of the asset are $180,000. The estimated value if the company sold the asset less commission costs is $155,000.

Required:

1. What is the recoverable amount?
2. What is the amount of impairment?

connect

TR10-7 Impairment:

Food Inc., a public company, has a machine that processes and packages tuna in oil. This machine cannot be used for any other purpose. The machine originally cost $100,000 and is being amortized on a straight-line basis over 20 years. The carrying amount of the machine on 31 December 20X2 is $20,000. Recent health studies have shown that due to contamination, eating tuna is bad for your health. Undiscounted cash flows for the machine are $22,000. Discounted cash flows for the machine are $17,000. The machine is unique; therefore, fair value cannot be determined.

Required:

1. Is the machine impaired? Provide the journal entry if there is impairment.
2. At the beginning of the following year new evidence comes out rebutting the evidence that tuna is bad for your health. In fact, studies have shown it is very healthy to eat fish. The company has also been able to package the tuna in water instead of oil. Can any previous impairment be reversed? If yes, provide the journal entry.

connect

TR10-8 Assigning Impairment to Assets:

Bovine Ltd. has the following assets in a CGU:

	Carrying Value (thousands)
Equipment	$ 600
Building	650
Land	700

Goodwill	550
	$2,500

The recoverable amount has been determined to be $1,500. The separate fair value less costs to sell for land is $600; no other assets could be separately valued.

Required:

1. Allocate the impairment loss to individual assets and calculate the net book value of each asset after the impairment.

2. Assume that the recoverable amount recovered to $1,800 in the subsequent year. Allocate the impairment reversal to individual assets and calculate the net book value of each asset after the impairment. The separate fair value less costs to sell for land remains at $600. There is no concern with a ceiling value when assigning the recovery to building or equipment.

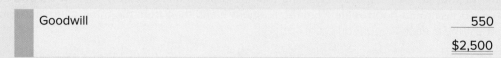

TR10-9 Minimum Depreciation Test:

Montonne Corp. is a private company that complies with ASPE. Montonne has a piece of equipment that cost $254,000. Its useful life to the company is estimated to be 15 years, after which it is expected to have a net residual value of $125,000. The equipment is expected to have a total life of 25 years and then would be useful only for scrap, for $2,500.

Required:

Calculate the two alternate measures of depreciation under ASPE, and indicate the amount that the company would record as expense.

TR10-10 CCA

Great George Ltd. purchased a group of equipment in December 20X8 for $100,000. In 20X9, the company sold one asset with an original cost of $25,000, for $6,000. It spent $40,000 on a new replacement piece of equipment. All equipment qualifies as a Class 8 asset (20%) for tax purposes.

Required:

Calculate CCA and the closing UCC balance for 20X8 and 20X9.

ASSIGNMENTS

★ A10-1 Depreciation Policy:

Nancy O'Callaghan, the president of Clean Enterprises, is proposing the following amortization policy for property, plant, and equipment:

> I want to keep things simple and minimize any deferred tax liabilities. I propose we use the CCA rates for declining-balance depreciation for all of our assets. These are the tax rules! I know that the equipment will last a longer period of time, but I prefer the fast write-off to be conservative.

Required:

Is this depreciation policy acceptable? Write a brief memo to the president explaining your position.

★ A10-2 Interpreting Depreciation Disclosures:

Portions of the 20X2 financial statements of Williams Company, a paint manufacturer, are reproduced below (in thousands of dollars):

Partial Income Statement for the year ended 31 December 20X2

Net sales	$2,266,732
Total expenses	2,079,455
Income before income tax	187,277
Income tax	64,611
Net income	$ 122,666

Note 1: Significant Accounting Policies

Property, Plant, and Equipment. Property, plant, and equipment is stated on the basis of cost. Depreciation is provided principally by the straight-line method. The major classes of assets and ranges of depreciation rates are as follows:

Buildings	2%–6%
Machinery	4%–20%
Furniture and fixtures	5%–20%
Automobiles and trucks	10%–33%

Note 16: Property, Plant, and Equipment Schedules

Cost	Beginning	Additions	Retirements	Other	Ending
Buildings	$191,540	$11,574	$ (960)	($7,185)	$194,969
Machinery	404,156	43,968	(16,319)	466	432,271

Total Accumulated Depreciation

	Beginning	Additions	Retirements	Other	Ending
Buildings	$ 62,843	$ 7,422	$ (769)	($4,951)	$ 64,545
Machinery	211,662	37,085	(12,302)	(845)	235,600

Required:

1. What method of depreciation is used by Williams?
2. What are the estimated useful lives of buildings owned by Williams?
3. What percentage of the useful life of buildings remains undepreciated, on average, at the end of the year?
4. What is the book value of machinery retired in the year?
5. Depreciation on buildings and machinery was what percentage of (a) total expenses and (b) pre-tax earnings?

A10-3 Valuation Models:

There are three valuation models described in Chapters 9 and 10:

a. Cost model
b. Revaluation model
c. Fair-value model

Required:

Explain the major differences among the models. Include an explanation of how depreciation and impairment is treated in each of these models.

A10-4 Depreciation or Amortization Policy:

The methods of depreciation or amortization demonstrated in the chapter include the following:

a. Straight-line
b. Productive-output
c. Declining-balance

Required:

Indicate the likely choice of depreciation or amortization method expected under each of the following circumstances:

a. The company has land as an asset. There is also an asset called land site restoration costs, which is an asset retirement obligation; the site restoration is expected to be completed in 10 years.

b. The company is a mining company and assets to be depreciated are mine exploration and evaluation costs.

c. The company has a number of intangible assets with a limited life span.

d. The company wishes to portray stable income and expense patterns over time.

e. The company has a backup transformer that is installed and ready to use, even though it may never be brought into operation.

f. The company wants to minimize bookkeeping costs by keeping allocation methods simple.

g. The company expects to use the asset heavily in initial years and less as it grows older.

h. The company expects to use the asset sporadically, but the asset will not wear out unless used.

i. Technological obsolescence is a significant factor in estimating the useful life of the asset.

j. The company wants to minimize its deferred tax liability balances.

k. The company is a subsidiary of a parent that uses straight-line depreciation.

A10-5 Amortization or Impairment:

Technology Inc. (TI) has the following intangible assets:

Case A   TI acquired a patent from another company that expires in 10 years. The purpose of the purchase was to eliminate competition for one of its top-selling products. Based on market surveys, the product will continue to have sales for at least the next eight years. TI intends to hold the patent but not manufacture the product.

Case B   TI acquired a second patent from another company that expires in 15 years. The company intends to manufacture the product. Based on market surveys, this product will have strong sales for at least the next 10 years or until another competitor enters the market with a similar product.

Case C   TI acquired a quota that can be renewed indefinitely at a minimal cost. TI's intention is to continue to renew the quota. These quotas are high in demand and very difficult to obtain.

Case D   TI has a registered trademark that it has used for 10 years for one of its top-selling products. TI intends to renew the trademark indefinitely.

Required:

Should the intangible assets be amortized or just tested for impairment? If amortized, what is the appropriate period? Support your response.

A10-6 Component Depreciation:

You have been asked to consider the following situations.

Case A   The company purchased a machine for $25,000 cash. The machine will probably have a useful life of 10 years but it has a component part that will need to be replaced every two and a half years. The cost to replace this part is $250.

Case B   The company purchased a second machine for $20,000 cash. The machine will probably have a useful life of 10 years but it has a component part that will need to be replaced every two years. The cost to replace this part is $4,000.

Case C   The company purchased a third machine for $50,000 cash. The machine will probably have a useful life of 10 years as long as it is given a major overhaul every three years; the overhaul will cost $12,500.

Required:

In each of the three cases, assess the need to apply component depreciation to the machine. That is, is the machine one asset, or should it be segregated into components, with each component depreciated separately?

A10-7 Standby Assets and Spare Parts:

You have been asked to explain the appropriate policy for depreciation for the following two cases for a major utility:

Case A   The utility has a number of transformers in its transformer stations that transform power from a high voltage to a lower voltage that is the required voltage for customers. To ensure that major customers that require a reliable source of power at all times (e.g., hospitals) have it, the utility installs two transformers. The first transformer is on-line continuously and has a useful life of 50 years. The second transformer is installed as a backup in case the first transformer fails. This is referred to as standby equipment. This means the hospitals will not lose their power supply. The second transformer is rarely used but is considered essential to customers that cannot afford to lose their power.

Case B   The utility has other customers for which it is not critical that they have a reliable source of power at all times. They can afford to have a short period of time without power while the transformer is replaced. Spare transformers are kept in the storage facility until they are needed for installation. These spare transformers are recorded as a long-lived asset, called spare parts. On installation, the utility replaces the existing transformer. The newly installed transformer then has a useful life of 50 years.

Transformers are not subject to obsolescence.

Required:

What is the appropriate accounting policy in these two unrelated cases?

A10-8 Depreciation Computation:

Mace Company acquired equipment that cost $36,000, which will be depreciated on the assumption that the equipment will last six years and have a $2,400 residual value. Component parts are not significant and need not be recognized and depreciated separately. Several possible methods of depreciation are under consideration.

Required:

1. Prepare a schedule that shows annual depreciation expense for the first two years, assuming the following (show computations and round to the nearest dollar):
    a. Declining-balance method, using a rate of 30%.
    b. Productive-output method. Estimated output is a total of 210,000 units, of which 24,000 will be produced the first year; 36,000 in each of the next two years; 30,000 the fourth year; and 42,000 the fifth and sixth years.
    c. Straight-line method.

2. Repeat your calculations for requirement 1, assuming a useful life of 10 years, and a declining-balance rate of 20% that reflects the longer life, but the same number of units of production. The residual value is unchanged. What conclusion can you reach by comparing the results of requirements 1 and 2?

3. What criteria would you consider important in selecting a depreciation method?

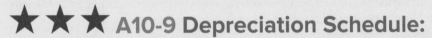

★ ★ ★ A10-9 Depreciation Schedule:

Quality Producers acquired factory equipment on 1 January 20X5, costing $156,000. Component parts are not significant and need not be recognized and depreciated separately. In view of pending technological developments, it is estimated that the machine will have a resale value upon disposal in four years of $32,000 and that disposal costs will be $2,000. The company has a fiscal year-end that ends on 31 December. Data relating to the equipment follow:

Estimated service life:

Years	4
Service-hours	20,000

Actual operation data:

Calendar Year	Service Hours
20X5	5,700
20X6	5,000
20X7	4,800
20X8	4,400

Required:

Round to the nearest dollar, and show computations.

1. Prepare a depreciation schedule for the asset that shows depreciation expense, accumulated depreciation, and net book value, using:
    a. Straight-line depreciation.
    b. Declining-balance depreciation, using a 40% rate.
    c. Service-hours depreciation.

2. Express straight-line depreciation as a percentage of original cost.

3. Explain whether:
    a. The rate of 40% was a good choice for declining-balance depreciation.
    b. The 20,000 estimate of total service hours was accurate.

 **A10-10 Analysis of Three Depreciation Methods—Maximize Earnings:**

On 1 January 20X5, Lee Company, a tool manufacturer, acquired new industrial equipment for $2 million. Component parts are not significant and need not be recognized and depreciated separately. The new equipment had a useful life of four years, and the residual value was estimated to be $220,000. The company estimates that the new equipment can produce 20,000 tools in its first year. Production is then estimated to decline by 2,000 units per year over the remaining useful life of the equipment.

The following depreciation methods are under consideration:

a. Declining-balance (50% rate)
b. Straight-line
c. Productive-output

Required:

Which depreciation method would result in maximum earnings for financial statement reporting for the three-year period ending 31 December 20X7? Prepare a schedule showing the amount of accumulated depreciation at 31 December 20X7, under each method selected. Show supporting computations in good form.

(Source: Copyright 1994–2000 by the American Institute of Certified Public Accountants, Inc. All rights reserved. Reprinted with permission.)

 A10-11 Identify and Recalculate Depreciation:

Beans Company purchased a special machine at a cost of $81,000 plus provincial sales tax of $6,480 (non-recoverable). Component parts are not significant and need not be recognized and depreciated separately. The machine is expected to have a residual value of $6,000 at the end of its service life.

To assist in preparing the journal entries for depreciation of this machine, your assistant prepared the following spreadsheet:

BEANS COMPANY			
Cost of asset			$87,480
Asset's residual value			6,000
Years of service life			4
Output in units	Year 1	1,400	
	Year 2	1,300	
	Year 3	1,000	
	Year 4	1,100	
Total expected output			4,800

	Method 1		Method 2		Method 3	
Year	Depreciation Expense	Accumulated Depreciation	Depreciation Expense	Accumulated Depreciation	Depreciation Expense	Accumulated Depreciation
1	$21,870	$21,870	$27,265	$27,265	$21,870	$21,870
2	16,403	38,273	25,318	52,583	21,870	43,740
3	12,302	50,575	19,475	72,058	21,870	65,610
4	36,905	87,480	21,422	93,480	21,870	87,480
Total	$87,480		$93,480		$87,480	

The spreadsheet includes statistics relating to the machine and calculates depreciation using three different methods—productive-output, straight-line, and declining-balance at a 50% rate. However, due to some carelessness, your assistant made at least one error in the calculations for each method.

Required:

1. Identify which method is the:
   a. Productive-output method
   b. Straight-line method
   c. Declining-balance method (50% rate)
2. Describe the error(s) made in the calculations for each method.
3. Recalculate depreciation expense for Year 2 under each method.

(Source: [Adapted] © CGA-Canada. Reproduced with permission.)

★ ★ ★ A10-12 Depreciation and Depletion— Schedule, Entries:

Gaspe Mining Corp. bought mineral-bearing land for $600,000. Engineers and geologists estimate that the site will yield 400,000 kilograms of economically removable ore. The land will have a net recoverable value of $80,000 after the ore is removed; this is the combination of site restoration costs and the resale value of the property.

To work the property, Gaspe built structures and sheds on the site that cost $160,000; these will last 10 years. Machinery that cost $144,000 was installed at the mine, and the added cost for installation was $3,000. This machinery should last 15 years; like that of the structures, the usefulness of the machinery is confined to these mining operations. For both structures and machinery, dismantling and removal costs when the property has been fully worked will approximately equal the value of the machinery at that time; therefore, Gaspe does not plan to use the structures or the machinery after the minerals have been removed.

In the first year, Gaspe removed only 12,000 kilograms of ore; however, production was doubled in the second year. It is expected that all of the removable ore will be extracted within eight years from the start of operations.

Required:

Prepare a schedule showing (1) unit and total depletion and depreciation and (2) net book value of the assets for the first and second years of operation. Use the productive-output method of depreciation for all assets.

★ ★ A10-13 Component Depreciation:

Boat Ltd. has a major asset that has just been purchased and has been segregated into the following significant components made up of spare parts and major inspections. Component D consists of a group of insignificant components lumped together with an average cost and useful life.

Component	Quantity	Original Unit Cost	Residual Value	Useful Life
A	2	$120,000	$5,000	12 years
B	1	40,000	0	3 years
C	5	8,000	500	6 years
D	10	2,000	0	2 years

Required:

1. Assuming straight-line is the appropriate method of depreciation, what is the amount of depreciation in year one?
2. What would be the impact if component B was a major spare part that was replaced at the end of the second year instead of the third year as originally predicted? The new major spare part has a value of $50,000. Prepare the journal entry that would be recorded when component B is replaced.

★ A10-14 Component Depreciation:

Earth Construction Inc. (ECI) bought a large piece of construction equipment at the beginning of 20X5.

- The construction equipment was a large piece of heavy equipment with an original cost of $1,200,000. This equipment was broken out into four components. The shell of the equipment is $400,000 and anticipated to last 10 years. The motor costs $360,000 and needs to have a major overhaul and inspection every three years. The tires cost $40,000 and need to be replaced every two years. The shovel at the front of the equipment costs $340,000 and needs to be replaced every five years. The remainder of the cost, $60,000, is made up of insignificant parts. These are grouped together and are replaced on average every two years.
- Expected residual value at the end of 10 years for the shell is $16,000. The residual value for the remaining components is zero.
- ECI uses straight-line depreciation for all construction equipment.

Required:

1. Calculate depreciation expense for 20X5, assuming a full year's worth of depreciation.
2. How would the amount of depreciation differ if the construction equipment was depreciated without breaking it into components?
3. What is the logic behind component accounting?

A10-15 Component Depreciation:

A large piece of equipment acquired on 1 January 20X5 by Kapadia Company has four major components for depreciation. Details regarding each component are given in the schedule below:

Component	Cost	Estimated Residual Value	Estimated Life (Years)
A	$200,000	$20,000	10
B	90,000	0	5
C	152,000	32,000	15
D	24,800	800	8

Required:

1. Calculate the depreciation for 20X5. Use the straight-line method, and one accumulated depreciation account for all components. Give the entry to record depreciation after one full year of use.

2. At the end of 20X6, it was necessary to replace component B, which was sold for $24,000. The replacement component cost $100,000 and will have an estimated residual value of $10,000 at the end of its estimated five-year useful life. Record the disposal and substitution, which was a cash acquisition.

3. Assume that the original machine was depreciated as a whole on a straight-line basis over 15 years with no residual value, and not broken into components. Provide the requested information in requirement 1.

 A10-16 Fractional Depreciation:

The following information relates to Riggs Corp.'s purchase of equipment on 15 June 20X7:

Invoice price	$420,000
Discount for early payment (if paid by 30 June)	$ 2,100
Shipping costs	$ 4,000
Installation	$ 3,000
Testing	$ 6,000

The equipment was installed and tested during the week of 22 June 20X7. Riggs paid the invoice price on 1 July 20X7. The equipment was ready for use on 30 June and put into production on 3 July 20X7. Riggs uses straight-line depreciation for the company's equipment and expects to use the asset for six years. Component parts are not significant and need not be recognized and depreciated separately. The estimated residual value is zero. The company's fiscal year-end is 31 December.

Required:

1. What is the book value of the equipment after installation?

2. Compute depreciation expense for 20X7, using the straight-line method, under each of the following assumptions:

a. Exact, to the closest month

b. Full first-year convention

c. Half-year convention

3. Why is depreciation not calculated to the nearest day under the exact method?

4. Calculate depreciation expense for both 20X7 and 20X8 under each of the methods in requirement 2, using declining-balance depreciation with a 33% rate.

★ ★ A10-17 Fractional Depreciation:

Jackson Company's records show the following machinery acquisitions and retirements during the first two years of operations:

| | Acquisition | | Retirement | |
Date	Cost of Machinery	Estimated Useful Life (years)	Acquisition Date	Original Cost
1 January 20X5	$200,000	10		
1 April 20X5	80,000	5		
1 December 20X6	10,000	10		
31 December 20X6			20X5*	$28,000

*Part of machinery acquired on 1 January 20X5.

Required:

1. Compute depreciation expense for 20X5 and for 20X6 and the balances of the machinery and related accumulated depreciation accounts at the end of each year, using straight-line depreciation. Machinery is depreciated according to the number of months of ownership in the year of acquisition or retirement. Assume no residual values. There are no sale proceeds upon retirement. Show computations and round to the nearest dollar. Set up separate columns in a schedule for machinery and for accumulated depreciation.

2. Compute depreciation expense for 20X5 and for 20X6 and the balances of the machinery and related accumulated depreciation accounts at the end of each year using straight-line depreciation. Machinery is depreciated for one-half year in the year of acquisition. Machinery that is retired is depreciated for one-half year in its year of retirement. Assume no residual values. There are no sale proceeds upon retirement. Show computations and round to the nearest dollar. Set up separate columns in a schedule for machinery and for accumulated depreciation.

3. Comment on the differences between requirements 1 and 2.

(Source: Copyright 1994–2000 by the American Institute of Certified Public Accountants, Inc. All rights reserved. Reprinted with permission.)

A10-18 Comprehensive Intangibles—Accounting and Amortization:

Bright Designs Ltd. began operations in 20X5 and, at the end of its first year of operations, reported a balance of $601,500 in an account called "intangibles." Upon further investigation, it is discovered that the account had been debited throughout the year as follows:

5 Jan.	Organization costs; legal fees. Economic life is indefinite.	$ 10,000
1 Feb.	Patent registration; legal fees re: patent with 20-year life to be used in research activities.	5,000
1 July	Operating expenses, first six months.	220,000
1 Aug.	Goodwill; excess of purchase price of an advertising company paid over tangible assets acquired.	160,000
10 Nov.	Copyright acquired; remaining legal life is 29 years but economic life is 10 years.	21,000
30 Nov.	Trademark registration; legal fees. The trademark is expected to have an indefinite economic life.	8,000
5 Dec.	Staff training costs; staff is expected to stay with the company for an average of three years; however, there are no employment contracts.	27,500
31 Dec.	Research costs incurred over the year; 40% of all research costs are properly classified as capitalizable development costs. The product developed will begin commercial production next year.	150,000
		$601,500

Required:

1. Prepare a correcting entry that reallocates all amounts charged to intangibles to the appropriate accounts. State any assumptions made.
2. Calculate amortization expense on intangible assets for 20X5. Straight-line amortization, to the exact month of purchase, is used. All residual values are expected to be zero.

 ## A10-19 Asset Impairment—Five Situations:

Each of the following five cases is independent:

a. Marlene Inc. produces several lines of office furniture. All of the furniture is sold through sales agents who sell the full array of lines. Each line is developed by the company internally, and the development costs are capitalized and amortized over 12 years. After several years of high revenue, one of Marlene's lines has recently suffered a significant sales decline. Marlene is considering shutting down production and discontinuing the line. About 40% of the development cost has not yet been amortized.

b. Antigonish Actuators Ltd. (AAL) has a production and sales division in northern Ontario. The divisional vice-president reports directly to the AAL CEO. AAL is decentralized, and the Northern Ontario division is one of several such divisions. The Northern Ontario division has operated at a loss for the past two years, and future prospects seem dim. The division has substantial property, plant, and equipment.

c. Canadian Wheels Corp. operates hardware and automotive stores throughout Canada. A few years ago, the company opened a series of stores in the northwestern United States. The new stores have not been doing well, and the company is thinking of selling them or shutting them down.

d. Capital Helicopter Services Corp. (CHSC) provides helicopter services for other corporations, mainly those in the resource industry that need extensive helicopter services for offshore oil and gas platforms, forestry operations, and otherwise inaccessible field operations. In addition, the company operates a separate division within Canada that manufactures airframe parts for manufacturers. This division is completely separate from the company's other operations and has a separate reporting line directly to the company's senior management. The division generates more than 10% of the company's overall revenues. However, the division has become only marginally profitable, and CHSC management has decided to sell the division and has put a plan for disposition in place.

e. Several years ago, Robertson Connectors Corp. (RCC) purchased the patents for a new type of connector. The new connector has enjoyed great success until recently. A competitor introduced a new product that is almost the same as RCC's product and that can be used interchangeably. RCC launched a patent infringement suit against the competitor, and RCC management was confident of success. In 20X4, however, the court ruled against RCC, thereby leaving the competitor free to continue its product. RCC management is considering whether to appeal the decision.

Required:

For each situation, explain whether an impairment test is necessary. If you need more information, explain what information you need and why you need it.

★ A10-20 Asset Impairment:

Softsweat Inc. is a software development company. It has several products on the market, including the widely used PlayMark animation software. The cash flows from PlayMark are clearly distinguishable within Softsweat. The company has recorded development costs of $2.8 million relating to PlayMark, which is being amortized on a straight-line basis over seven years. At the end of 20X5, the carrying value was $1,960,000. Softsweat maintains a separate account for accumulated amortization on PlayMark.

In 20X5, a large U.S. company, Macrosoftie, released a competing product that has been hailed as a substantial improvement over PlayMark. However, the competing product requires installation of a great deal of additional Macrosoftie software to make the new product run efficiently. In addition, the high price may delay its acceptance by some users.

Because of the new competition, Softsweat management decided that an impairment test should be performed. In January 20X6, as the 20X5 financial statements were being prepared, the company hired a professional business valuator. The valuator's appraisal was that the fair value of PlayMark at the end of 20X5 was $1,000,000.

Required:

1. Prepare the necessary adjusting journal entry to record the results of the impairment test.

2. Suppose that in 20X6, the Macrosoftie product was found to be unreliable and that the sales of PlayMark returned to almost their 20X4 level. The fair value of PlayMark therefore was $1,600,000 at the end of 20X6.
    a. What would the carrying value of the assets have been if the impairment had not been recorded?

b. How (if at all) would the increase in the recoverable amounts be recorded in Softsweat's financial statements for 20X6?

 A10-21 Asset Impairment:

Yuan Inc. has a large piece of machinery, and management has determined there is potential impairment. This piece of machinery has independent cash inflows. The following information relates to the machine:

- Net book value is $14 million.
- The machine could be sold for $6 million less a 10% commission.
- If the company was forced to sell immediately, the proceeds would likely be $5 million.
- If the machine continues to be used in production, it is anticipated to generate $3 million of cash flows for the next five years. It would require annual maintenance costs of $200,000 a year. The equipment could be sold for $100,000 at the end of the five years.
- Assume Yuan has a discount rate of 6%.

Required:

Is the machine impaired? If so, what is the amount of the impairment loss?

 A10-22 Asset Impairment:

The abrasives group of Chemical Products Inc. (CPI) has been suffering a decline in its business, due to new product introductions by competitors. At 31 December 20X5, the assets of the abrasives cash-generating unit are shown as follows (in millions) on the company's SFP:

	Cost	Accumulated Depreciation	Net Book Value
Equipment (10-year life)	400	$ 180	220
Fixtures (10-year life)	125	55	70
Patent rights (40-year life)	80	70	10
	$605	$305	$300

An impairment test indicates that the recoverable amount of the abrasives cash-generating unit's assets is $200 million. The assets are not separable—they must be operated or sold together as a group. No individual asset has a determinable individual fair value less cost to sell.

Required:

1. Prepare an adjusting journal entry to record the impairment.
2. What would be the net book value of the assets after one year if no impairment was recorded? Assume that straight-line depreciation is used.
3. After one year, the recoverable amount is reassessed because of changes in the competitive market, and is found to be higher than $200 million. Describe how the impairment reversal would be allocated to the various assets of the unit.

★★ A10-23 Goodwill Impairment:

Information has been collected regarding Orange Company's cash-generating unit that includes goodwill. At 31 December 20X5, the assets of the Orange Company's cash-generating unit are shown as follows (in millions) on the company's SFP:

	Cost	Accumulated Depreciation	Net Book Value
Goodwill	$ 800	$ 0	$ 800
Equipment	2,800	1,600	1,200
Building	4,200	1,200	3,000
Patent rights	400	160	240
	$8,200	$2,960	$5,240

An impairment test indicates that the recoverable amount assigned to the assets of this CGU is $3,600 million. The assets are not separable—they must be operated or sold together as a group.

Required:

1. Prepare an adjusting journal entry to record the impairment.
2. If the impairment was reversed, how would the reversal be accounted for among the assets in the cash-generating unit?

★ A10-24 Goodwill Impairment:

Information has been collected regarding Price Inc.'s cash-generating unit that includes goodwill. At 31 December 20X5, the assets of the Price's CGU are shown as follows (in millions):

	Cost	Accumulated Depreciation	Net Book Value
Goodwill	$ 4,000	$ 0	$ 4,000
Equipment	30,000	8,000	22,000
Land	16,000	0	16,000
Property	66,000	16,000	50,000
	$116,000	$24,000	$92,000

An impairment test indicates that the recoverable amount assigned to the assets of this CGU is $82,000 million. The assets are not separable—they must be operated or sold together as a group. However, land has an individual fair value less cost to sell of $14,000.

Required:

1. Prepare an adjusting journal entry to record the impairment.
2. If the impairment was reversed, how would the reversal be accounted for among the assets in the CGU?

 A10-25 Statement of Cash Flows:

Lindsay Ltd. reflected the following items in the 20X5 financial statements:

Income statement

Depreciation expense, machinery	$1,200,000
Amortization expense, patent	240,000
Loss on sale of machinery	100,000
Gain on sale of land	120,000

Balance sheet

Decrease in land account	$1,600,000
Increase in net patent account	260,000
Decrease in net machinery account	1,824,000

The only entry through the land account was a sale of land. The other accounts may reflect more than one transaction.

Required:

List the items that would appear on the statement of cash flows as a result of the above items. Indicate in which section each item would appear. Assume that the indirect method is used for the operating activities section. State any assumptions that you make.

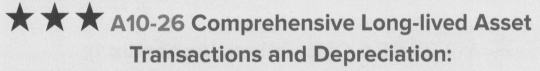 **A10-26 Comprehensive Long-lived Asset Transactions and Depreciation:**

MH Plumbing Inc. (MH) is the largest plumbing contractor in Moncton, Alberta. Information on selected transactions/events is given below:

a. On 15 January 20X2, MH purchased land and a warehouse building for $455,000. The land was appraised at $175,000, while the building was appraised at $375,000.

b. During January and February 20X2, MH spent $53,200 on the warehouse building, renovating it for its expected use as a storage and shipping facility.

c. MH used the warehouse building from February 20X2 until August 20X7. The building was expected to have a 20-year life and a residual value of $11,000.

d. In late August 20X7, MH traded the warehouse and land for another facility on the other side of town. The second facility was slightly larger. MH paid $33,750 to the vendor, and $19,800 in legal fees as a result of the transaction. The new warehouse was appraised at $425,000, and the new land at $180,000. This warehouse facility was expected to have a useful life of 18 years and a residual value of $7,800.

e. MH used the new warehouse facility from August 20X7 until February 20X9. At that time, a fire destroyed the warehouse. MH received $356,800 from the insurance company.

f. MH called for tenders for construction of a new warehouse building in March 20X9, but the lowest bid was $788,000. The company decided to self-construct and began in May 20X9. Monies spent were as follows:

Architect fees	$ 80,000
Removing debris from building site	13,400
Material cost for construction	245,800
Labour cost for construction	199,600
Parking lot	45,200
Specific overhead assigned to construction	24,800
Interest on loans related to construction	34,100

g. MH received a $100,000 investment tax credit in 20X9 as a result of the building activities, which reduced 20X9 taxes payable.

h. MH occupied its new warehouse in September 20X9. It was appraised at $650,000. It was expected to last for 25 years, and have a residual value of $20,000.

Required:

Prepare journal entries to record all transactions listed above, including annual depreciation to the end of 20X9. Record annual depreciation using a declining-balance method of 10% for buildings, and 5% for parking lots. MH records a full year of depreciation in the year of acquisition and no amortization in the year of disposal. Justify any decisions made with respect to accounting policy or application.

(Source: [Adapted] © CGA-Canada. Reproduced with permission.)

★★★ A10-27 CCA Calculations (Appendix 1):

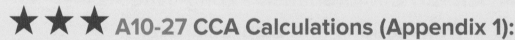

LaMar Company purchased several small pieces of equipment in May 20X5 for $300,000, which qualified as a Class 8 asset for tax purposes.

30 September 20X6	Sold equipment bought in 20X5 for $20,000; proceeds, $11,200
1 February 20X7	Sold equipment bought in 20X5 for $40,000; proceeds, $19,800
31 August 20X7	Bought Class 8 equipment for $25,000
16 November 20X8	Bought Class 8 equipment for $36,000

Required:

Calculate CCA and the closing UCC balance for 20X5 to 20X8.

A10-28 Revaluation Model (Appendix 2):

Real Estate Inc. (REI) has made the decision to use the revaluation model for its land. This is the only tract of land in this class. REI has a 31 December year-end. The following are independent situations.

Case A   REI purchased a tract of land in 20X1 for $100 million. At 31 December 20X1, the land was valued at $130 million.

Case B   REI purchased a tract of land in 20X1 for $140 million. At 31 December 20X1, the land was valued at $110 million. At 31 December 20X2, the land was valued at $160 million.

Case C   REI purchased a tract of land in 20X1 for $120 million. At 31 December 20X1, the land was valued at $170 million. At 31 December 20X2, the land was valued at $110 million.

Required:

1. For each case list the amounts, and direction, of the gains, gain reversals, losses, and loss reversals. Also indicate whether the amounts would be recorded as other comprehensive income or in earnings.

2. What would be different in your response to requirement 1 if the fair-value model was selected by REI?

A10-29 Asset Impairment (ASPE):

Refer to the facts in A10-21 and assume the company is following the accounting standards for private enterprises.

Required:

Is the machine impaired? If so, what is the amount of the impairment loss?

A10-30 Asset Impairment (ASPE):

Gardner Inc. manufactures products in two plants. One of the plants is an area where there has been a downturn in the market, and indications are that there has been potential impairment. Gardner has determined that the asset group includes land, building, equipment, and a mortgage. Management anticipates using the plant for the next 10 years. The net book values of the assets in the asset group are as follows:

Land	$ 60,000
Building	550,000
Equipment	210,000
Mortgage	(225,000)

Annual cash flows from continuing to operate the plant over the next 5 years are $50,000 a year. The plant would be demolished at the end of 5 years. The estimated net residual value of the land and equipment is $180,000. The appropriate discount rate for Gardner is 5%.

Gardner has considered selling the assets and using the cash to help open a new facility. The market value of the assets was estimated by appraisers to be $500,000 less a commission of 10%. The buyer would assume the mortgage.

Required:

1. Is the asset group impaired? If so, what is the amount of the impairment loss?

2. How would your response change if the expected annual cash flows were $100,000 each year for 5 years, with a $200,000 expected net residual value?

APPENDIX 1

CAPITAL COST ALLOWANCE

The *Income Tax Act* (ITA) does not allow the deduction of accounting depreciation or amortization expense in the determination of taxable income. Instead of depreciation or amortization, and depending on the type of expenditure involved, the taxpayer must either:

(1)   Deduct the expenditure from taxable income in the year that it is incurred; or
(2)   Use the form of depreciation or amortization mandated by the *Income Tax Act*.

There is no choice between these two treatments; the tax treatment is fact-based and depends on the type of expenditure (i.e., on the type of long-lived asset for accounting purposes).

Just because an expenditure (or group of expenditures) is classified as a long-lived asset for accounting purposes does not mean that Canada Revenue Agency (CRA) will view it as a capital asset. Many of the costs that are capitalized for accounting purposes are viewed as expenses for tax purposes. This is particularly true of a large number of expenditures that accountants tend to capitalize as intangible assets, particularly when they are self-developed assets, such as development costs.

Expenditures that are considered by the *Income Tax Act* to be capital assets are subject to depreciation or amortization for tax purposes, but the depreciation or amortization is completely independent of accounting depreciation or amortization. Under GAAP, depreciation or amortization is intended to allocate an asset's historical cost to the accounting periods in which the asset is used. In contrast, tax depreciation or amortization is geared to the economic goals of the federal government, which change in response to economic conditions and the fiscal policies of Parliament. For example, a federal budget might increase the CCA rate for manufacturing and processing equipment from 30% to 50% to encourage investment—not because 50% represents the pattern of economic benefit consumed.

The Capital Cost Allowance System

Tax depreciation or amortization is known as *capital cost allowance,* or *CCA*. Basically, the CCA system is a group depreciation method. CCA requires the grouping of assets into various CCA classes established by CRA regulations. An exception to the group requirement is that buildings that are held for rental (i.e., "income properties") are treated individually; each one is a separate "class."

Most classes provide a maximum rate of depreciation or amortization that approximates double-declining balance (DDB) depreciation or amortization, although some classes use the equivalent of straight-line (SL) depreciation or amortization. Classes and rates for some of the more common assets are shown in Exhibit 10A-1, with the prescribed maximum rate shown in parentheses for the declining-balance classes.

EXHIBIT 10A-1

SAMPLE CCA RATES

Asset Classes Using Declining-Balance CCA

Class 1 (4%)	Buildings or other structures, including component parts acquired after 1987
Class 8 (20%)	Tangible capital property and machinery or equipment not included in another class
Class 9 (25%)	Aircraft, including furniture, fittings or equipment attached, and their spare parts
Class 10 (30%)	Automobiles, vans, trucks, electronic data processing equipment and systems software, and timber-cutting equipment
Class 12 (100%)	Jigs, patterns, tools, utensils costing less than $200, linens, computer software (except systems software)
Class 29 (50%)	Manufacturing and processing equipment acquired after March 18, 2007 and before 2016

Asset Classes Using Straight-Line CCA

Class 13	Leasehold improvements (life of lease plus one renewal period; minimum five years, maximum 40 years)
Class 14	Patent, franchise, concession, or licence (life of asset) with a limited life

An important point is that the rates are *maximums*. A tax-paying company does not have to use the maximum rate and, in fact, does not need to deduct any CCA at all if the company chooses not to do so. CCA is an optional deduction.

Why would a company not want to deduct CCA? Because it is not making any taxable income! If a company's taxable income is insufficient to absorb all of the CCA, the CCA can be "saved" to be expensed against future earnings.

CCA cannot be doubled up in future years if skipped in a current year. The maximum percentage remains the same, *but the base on which CCA is calculated is higher* because the company did not take CCA in past years.

The basic rules for the capital cost allowance system can be explained (for most classes) as follows:

1. When assets are purchased, their purchase price (capital cost) is added to the balance of *unamortized capital cost*, or UCC, of the appropriate asset class. A separate accumulated CCA accounting is not kept. UCC is analogous to accounting *net book value*—the initial capital cost minus accumulated CCA.
2. When assets are sold, either (1) the proceeds or (2) the initial capital cost, *whichever is lower*, is deducted from the balance in that asset class.
3. A half-year of CCA is permitted in the year of acquisition. (i.e., the half-year convention, *applied to net additions*).
4. The maximum CCA deductible for a particular class is calculated as the closing balance of unamortized capital cost (UCC), multiplied by the CCA rate for that class, *adjusting for the half-year rule for any net additions to the class during the year.*

Exhibit 10A-2 provides an example of a calculation for CCA. Iles Machine Shop begins business in January 20X1 and purchases four lathes (class 8) for $5,000 each. A fifth lathe is purchased in 20X2 for $5,700. In 20X3, one of the original lathes is sold for $1,200 and is replaced with another lathe costing $6,500. In 20X4, one of the lathes is sold for $1,100.

EXHIBIT 10A-2		
EXAMPLE OF CALCULATING CAPITAL COST ALLOWANCE		
20X1 UCC opening balance		0
Additions (4 × $5,000)		$20,000
CCA for 20X1; ($20,000 × 20% × 1/2 year)		(2,000)
20X2 UCC opening balance		$18,000
Additions		5,700
CCA for 20X2; ($18,000 × 20%) + ($5,700 × 20% × 1/2)		(4,170)
20X3 UCC opening balance		$19,530
Additions	$6,500	
Proceeds on disposal	(1,200)	
Net additions		5,300
CCA for 20X3; ($19,530 × 20%) + ($5,300 × 20% × 1/2)		(4,436)
20X4 UCC opening balance		$20,394
Proceeds on disposal		(1,100)
CCA for 20X4; [($20,394 − $1,100) × 20%]		(3,859)
20X4 UCC closing balance		$ 15,435

When net asset additions take place, CCA on *the net addition is subject to the half-year convention* (see 20X2 and 20X3 in Exhibit 10A-2). However, when there is a net asset disposal, the entire amount is deducted prior to determining the CCA for the year (see 20X4 in Exhibit 10A-2).

The amount deducted on an asset disposal is the lower of (1) the proceeds and (2) the asset's original capital cost. Proceeds up to the original capital cost are credited to the asset pool. If the proceeds on sale are higher than the original capital cost, the excess is treated as a capital gain for tax purposes. It is possible (but unlikely) that high proceeds will drive the pool into a negative balance. If this happens, the negative unamortized capital cost (UCC) is reported as taxable income. More likely, though, proceeds up to capital cost are credited to the pool and just reduce the positive balance of UCC, and reduce the future CCA claimable in that class.

When *all* of the assets in a class are disposed of, any remaining balance is treated as follows:

- A positive UCC balance is deducted as a terminal loss in determining taxable income.
- A negative UCC balance is added to taxable income as *recaptured* CCA.

In effect, this treatment is similar to the gain or loss on disposal of plant assets on the assumption that either too little or too much amortization (i.e., CCA) was taken over the lives of the assets. Any proceeds received in excess of the assets' capital (original) cost are treated as a capital gain for tax purposes.

SUMMARY OF KEY POINTS

1. Accounting depreciation or amortization has no tax impact; depreciation or amortization of capital assets for tax purposes is governed by the *Income Tax Act* and regulations and is completely independent of accounting depreciation or amortization.

2. Income tax depreciation or amortization is called the *capital cost allowance (CCA)* system.

3. The CCA system groups capital assets into *classes* of assets of similar types. Except for certain buildings, which are each included in a separate, one-asset class, assets are not depreciated or amortized individually.

4. The ITA regulations specify a depreciation or amortization *rate* to be used for each class of asset; the rate is a maximum—a company can claim less CCA in any year if management so chooses, without losing the maximum deduction in future years.

5. The half-year rule is applied to net assets acquired during a taxation year.

6. Gains and losses are not recognized on the disposal of capital assets in a class, unless all of the assets in the class are disposed of. Proceeds on disposal of individual assets are credited to the asset class and reduce future CCA.

APPENDIX 2

REVALUATION MODEL

Historical cost has long been the generally accepted basis for reporting long-lived assets in Canada; the general use of fair values has not been a common practice.

The revaluation model is an alternative under IFRS to the cost model for property, plant, and equipment; intangible assets with an active market; and mineral reserves. The revaluation model is permitted but not required, and its use in practice is rare. The cost model is predominant; it is simple and less costly to maintain. The revaluation model is also less popular than the *fair-value model* that is an allowed alternative for investment property (as discussed in the Appendix to Chapter 9), likely because the fair-value attribute is more relevant to investment property financial statement users.

The highlights of the revaluation model:

- The revaluation model uses fair value as the basis of measurement. Revaluations are done regularly, but not annually. Revaluations must be performed often enough that fair value is not materially out-of-date.

- The revaluation model is applied by *class of assets*. For example, the revaluation model could be selected for the classes that include land and buildings, and the cost model could be selected for all other classes of assets. The revaluation method cannot be applied to only one asset in a class.

- Depreciation is recorded annually.

- In between revaluations, the asset is carried at its revalued amount less subsequent accumulated depreciation and subsequent accumulated impairment losses.

- When a revaluation occurs, either accumulated depreciation is eliminated, and the asset is restated to fair value, or the asset and accumulated depreciation are grossed up so that the net book value reflects fair value.

- Increases in fair value—gains—*and gain reversals*, are recorded as a component of other comprehensive income. Decreases in fair value greater than gains to date—losses—*and loss reversals*, are recorded in earnings. Losses and loss reversals are essentially analogous to impairments/ impairment reversals.

How Is Fair Value Determined?

Fair value is the base for the revaluation model. Therefore, to use this model, a company must be able to determine fair value. The fair-value hierarchy, discussed in Chapter 2, would provide guidance on fair-value measurement. The company might be able to reference an active market for long-lived assets to determine a reference price, or it might depend on discounted cash flow models. It would be rare to see a Level 1 fair value; most fair values would be Level 3, and dependent on internal information and estimates.

Management has a range of valuation methods or choices in estimating fair value. Some alternatives:

- Appraisals, where appropriate (e.g., for land and buildings);
- An estimate based on the present value of future cash flows; or
- An estimate based on depreciated replacement cost. For example, a specialized piece of machinery is 50% depreciated, and the replacement cost of a similar new machine is $100,000, so the fair value based on depreciated replacement cost would be $50,000.

Frequency of Revaluations

The frequency of revaluations depends on the volatility of the fair value of the asset. If the asset value changes frequently, revaluation may be completed every year. If the asset value is not very volatile, the revaluation could take place up to every five years. The revaluation period selected must be consistent unless the volatility of the fair value of the asset has changed.

Depreciation and Elimination of Accumulated Depreciation

Depreciation is recorded each year. If the asset is revalued for the year, deprecation is recorded prior to the revaluation. Then, the fair value is compared to the net book value after the current-year deprecation.

However, accumulated depreciation is eliminated or revised on revaluation. There are two methods of making the revaluation adjustment:

- *Method 1—Elimination Method:* The cost of the asset is restated to the fair value and the accumulated depreciation is eliminated. This is the more common method in practice and also the more simple method.
- *Method 2—Proportionate Method:* The original cost of the asset and the accumulated depreciation are restated proportionately (both grossed up or down) so the *net carrying amount* after revaluation equals fair value.

Changes in Fair Value

Debits and credits caused by revaluation may be recorded to other comprehensive income (OCI) or earnings. Classification depends on the direction of the change and the accumulated revaluation changes to date. The flowchart in Exhibit 10A-3 helps illustrate the impact of changes.

Terminology Keep in mind the difference between a *gain, a gain reversal, a loss, and a loss reversal*.

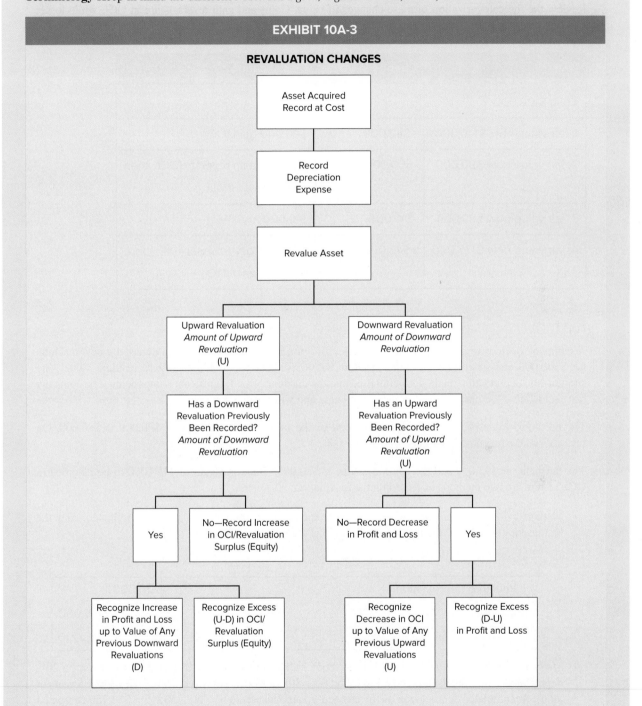

EXHIBIT 10A-3

REVALUATION CHANGES

Asset Acquired Record at Cost

Record Depreciation Expense

Revalue Asset

Upward Revaluation
Amount of Upward Revaluation
(U)

Downward Revaluation
Amount of Downward Revaluation

Has a Downward Revaluation Previously Been Recorded?
Amount of Downward Revaluation

Has an Upward Revaluation Previously Been Recorded?
Amount of Upward Revaluation
(U)

Yes

No—Record Increase in OCI/Revaluation Surplus (Equity)

No—Record Decrease in Profit and Loss

Yes

Recognize Increase in Profit and Loss up to Value of Any Previous Downward Revaluations
(D)

Recognize Excess (U-D) in OCI/Revaluation Surplus (Equity)

Recognize Decrease in OCI up to Value of Any Previous Upward Revaluations
(U)

Recognize Excess (D-U) in Profit and Loss

Example—Classification

Assume an asset is purchased for $100,000. (We will ignore deprecation in this case, for simplicity.) In the following four years, it has a fair value of $140,000, $90,000, $80,000, and then $125,000, respectively.

Review the the categorization of these changes in value. Gains and gain reversals are in OCI, while losses and loss reversals and in profit and loss:

Year	Change in Value	Classification
Cost; $100,000		
1; fair value now $140,000	+$40,000	$40,000 gain (OCI)
2; fair value now $90,000	-$50,000	$40,000 gain reversal (OCI), then $10,000 loss (P&L)
3; fair value now $80,000	-$10,000	$10,000 loss (P&L)
4; fair value now $125,000	+$45,000	$20,000 loss reversal (P&L) then $25,000 gain (OCI)

Example—Recording Alternatives

A company decides to use the revaluation model for a machine. On 1 January, it purchased a new machine for $100,000 and determined that the machine has a five-year useful life with zero residual value. The straight-line depreciation method is being used and the machine has no significant components. The company has decided that the machine has a volatile fair value and will revalue annually.

The net book value of the machinery at the end of the first year is $100,000 − $20,000 = $80,000. On revaluation, the machine has a fair value of $95,000.

The fair value is $95,000 and the net book value is $80,000. There is a gain of 4150,000 to be recorded in OCI. There are two methods of recording the revaluation:

- *Method 1—Elimination method:* The accumulated depreciation of $20,000 is eliminated, and the increase in the value of the machine of $15,000 is recorded in OCI.

Accumulated depreciation	20,000	
Machinery		5,000
OCI—revaluation surplus		15,000

- *Method 2—Proportionate method:* The net book value must be $95,000, and the asset must be 20% depreciated. The asset itself is $118,750 ($95,000 ÷.80), or ($95,000 ÷ 4 years left = $23,750 × 5 years in total). Accumulated depreciation on the grossed-up amount would be $118,750 ÷ 5 = $23,750 compared to $20,000; therefore, accumulated depreciation is adjusted by $3,750.

Machinery	18,750	
Accumulated depreciation		3,750
OCI—revaluation surplus		15,000

OCI Revaluation Surplus

The accumulated revaluation surplus is transferred to retained earnings when the asset is sold, or as the asset is used.

Note Disclosure

Not surprisingly, there is additional note disclosure required when the revaluation method has been selected by a company. Note disclosure is required for the following:

a. The date of the revaluation;

b. Whether or not an appraiser was used and, if so, the name and qualifications;

c. The methods used to determine fair value;

d. The amount of the revaluation surplus; and

e. For each class, the carrying amount of the asset if the cost model had been used.

Comparison to the Fair-Value Model

Some of the key differences between the *revaluation model* and the *fair-value model*, which was explained in an appendix to Chapter 9 are:

1. The fair-value model requires annual assessment of fair value, while the revaluation model requires less frequent revaluation;

2. There is no depreciation using the fair-value model but the revaluation model records depreciation in any year where fair values are not re-estimated;

3. All changes in fair value are part of earnings in the fair-value model, but the revaluation model uses OCI for gains and gain reversals. Losses and loss reversals are part of earnings in the revaluation model; and

4. The fair-value model is applicable to investment properties but the revaluation model can be applied to any class of long-lived asset that meets certain criteria.

RELEVANT STANDARDS

- *CPA Canada Handbook, Part I* (IFRS):
  - IAS 16, Property, Plant, and Equipment
  - IAS 38, Intangible Assets

SUMMARY OF KEY POINTS

1. The revaluation model is an alternative to the cost model for property, plant, and equipment; intangible assets with an active market; and mineral reserves. The revaluation model must be adopted for an entire class of assets.

2. Fair value is the base for the revaluation model and could be an appraisal or estimated fair value.

3. Revaluations are done with sufficient regularity that the carrying value of long-lived assets approximate for value; frequency of revaluation depends on the volatility of the fair value of the asset.

4. Depreciation is recorded every year.

5. The revaluation adjustment can be made using either the elimination or the proportionate method.

6. The revaluation can impact either earnings or OCI, depending on the direction of the change, and previous recorded changes in value. The OCI adjustments accumulate in an equity account called the *revaluation surplus*.

Source: (Globe and money) © Vstock LLC/Getty Images RF; (Skyscrapers) © Arpad Benedek/Getty Images RF; (Canadian flag) © BjArn Kindler/Getty Images RF; (Tablet, pen, keyboard) © John Lamb/Getty Images RF.

CHAPTER 11

Financial Instruments: Investments in Bond and Equity Securities

INTRODUCTION

The cash flow associated with an investment in the securities of another company can be straightforward. Such an investment is usually purchased for cash, produces an annual cash flow of interest or dividends that can be recorded as investment revenue, and is sold for cash. What can be so complicated?

The challenge is that investments are acquired for different purposes, and this distinction affects accounting policies. Notably, there are different approaches to valuation of the investment account and investment revenue.

The cost and fair value of an investment may be very different. Fair-value information might be far more relevant to a financial statement user and informative as long as fair value is objectively determinable with respect to securities markets. As a result, many investments that are financial instruments must be valued at fair value on the statement of financial position (SFP).

However, some investments are not held for resale, and fair value is less relevant. Long-term investments in voting shares may be used to establish a strategic intercompany relationship through which the investor corporation can control or significantly influence the operating and financing strategies of the investee. The carrying value of these investments will not reflect fair value. For example, Brookfield Asset Management Inc. shows an investment in Rouse Properties on its 2014 statement of financial position (SFP), carried at $408 million, but discloses that the fair value of this investment is $359 million.

What earnings should be reported for a strategic investment? Since the investor can control or influence the dividend policy of the investee, dividends are not the result of an arm's-length transaction, and the amount could be manipulated. The investor's share of the investee's earnings is more informative but is not cash flow. For example, in 2014 (Note 10 of the financial statements), Brookfield reported $1,345 million of investment revenue from all its strategic investments but then reported in the disclosure notes that cash distributions were quite different, at $674 million.

This chapter explores the alternatives and provides an overview of this complex area. Keep in mind, though, that many accounting programs devote an entire course to investment accounting, so this is only the proverbial tip of the iceberg! Standards are in transition in this area. This chapter reflects IFRS 9, effective in 2018, with early adoption permitted. Companion material based on IAS 39 is available on Connect.

INVESTMENT OBJECTIVES

Companies invest in the securities of other enterprises for a variety of reasons. Reasons for investments include:

- *Investment of idle cash.* Companies often have cash on hand that is not needed at present but will be needed in the future. Rather than allow idle cash to remain in a low-interest bank account, companies find money market investments with short terms that provide a higher return. These **cash equivalent** investments have low risk and are easily converted to cash.

  Other investments (not qualifying as cash equivalents) will generate return through interest or dividends but also may be sold at a gain if the market price has increased. These investments will likely be of higher risk and/or longer term, but the intent is still to sell the investment when money is needed for other activities and/or when the price is attractive.

- *Active investment portfolio.* Companies may own securities in a portfolio that is actively traded as part of the normal course of business, generally yielding a return because of price fluctuations or a dealer's margin. Such a portfolio might be used to offset, or hedge, gains or losses from other financial statement elements but might also be based on planned appreciation in various business sectors.

- *Long-term investments to generate earnings.* Some companies are active lenders, and have portfolios of loan assets. In other cases, resources are invested for the long term in securities to increase investment revenue. These investments are usually money market instruments (e.g., bonds), and the intent is to keep the investment to receive interest and principal cash flows.

- *Strategic alliances.* An investment, especially in voting shares, may establish or cement a beneficial intercompany relationship that will increase the profitability of the investing company, both directly and indirectly. Strategic decisions may be made to invest in suppliers, customers, and even competitors.

- *Legal frameworks.* Companies may choose to establish operations in one large company with numerous branches or organize activities in a set of smaller companies, all or partially controlled by a central holding company. This may be done for tax reasons, to allow outside shareholders a small stake in particular operations, to satisfy legal requirements in particular jurisdictions, and/or to limit potential liability claims to particular portions of the enterprise. The resulting corporate structure may be quite complex.

The investment can be a **passive** investment, meant primarily to increase investment revenue, or a **strategic** investment, meant to enhance operations in some way. Whether an investment is passive or strategic depends on the level of ownership and influence that an investor will have over the investee. Generally, investments where the investor has less than 20% ownership are passive investments. As such, all bond investments are passive. For share investments, since 20% and more ownership often gives the investor some influence over the decisions of the investee, these are strategic in nature. Ownership of 20% to 50% in an investee gives the investor significant influence over decisions of the investee. Ownership greater than 50% gives the investor control over the decisions of the investee.

Securities are **financial instruments**. *A financial instrument is any contract that gives rise to both a financial asset of one party and a financial liability or equity instrument of another party.* In the context of intercorporate investments, financial assets are defined as any contractual right to receive cash or another financial asset from another company or a contractual right that is the equity instrument of another entity. Investment in bond securities and share investments meet this definition.

CATEGORIES AND CLASSIFICATION OF PASSIVE INVESTMENTS

Passive investments include all bond investments and share investments where ownership does not give the investor any influence in the investee's decisions. Accounting alternatives for passive investments are summarized in Exhibit 11-1.

Overview of Alternatives for Passive Investments

As shown in Exhibit 11-1:

- An *investment in* a *bond instrument* of another entity can be classified as an amortized cost (AC) investment, fair-value-through-other–comprehensive-income-bonds (FVOCI-Bonds) or as a fair-value-through-profit-or-loss (FVTPL) investment.

- An *investment in common shares* of another company may be an FVTPL investment or a fair-value-through-other-comprehensive-income-equity (FVOCI-Equity) investment. If the investment in common shares is a strategic investment, it may be a subsidiary, an associate, or a joint arrangement.

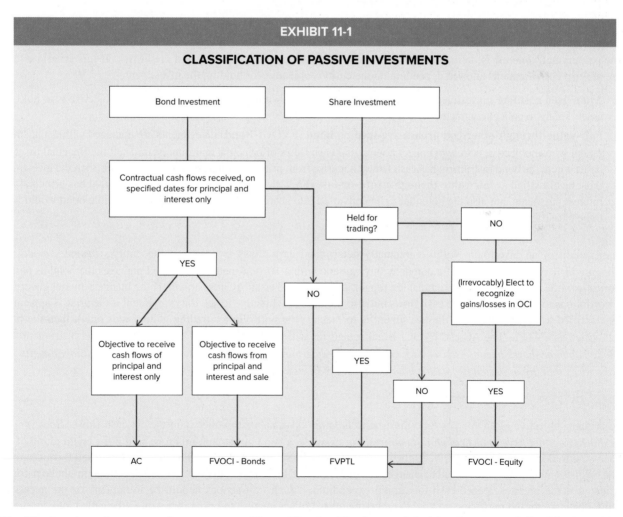

EXHIBIT 11-1

CLASSIFICATION OF PASSIVE INVESTMENTS

Classification depends on many factors, as we will see. The classifications and decision factors are defined in the sections that follow.

Initial Recognition

All investments are initially measured at fair value. This is the *acquisition cost* of the investment, appropriately measured, and is the *transaction value*. If there are transaction costs, these costs are also included in the investment cost, unless the investment is classified as an FVTPL investment, or a subsidiary, in which case transaction costs are expensed. The classification alternatives determine *subsequent* measurement of the asset's carrying value and investment revenue.

CLASSIFICATION AND ACCOUNTING OF BOND INVESTMENTS

Bond instruments are investments in bonds or loans that return principal and interest payments to the investor. The discussion below explains how the classification decision is made to the appropriate category and how the investments are accounted for.

Classification of Bond Investments

In determining the appropriate classification, the nature of the bond investment is important. Does the financial asset have contractual terms that give rise, on specified dates, to cash flows that are solely payments of principal and interest on the principal amount? *Interest* is defined as compensation for the time value of money and credit risk. If this criteria is met, there are two classifications allowed depending on the entity's objective for holding the investment.

1. **Amortized cost (AC)** investments must be held and managed within a business model whose objective is to hold the assets solely to collect contractual cash flows.

2. **Fair-value-through-other-comprehensive-income-bond (FVOCI-Bond)** investments are managed within a business model whose objective is to *both* collect contractual cash flows of principal and interest *and* sell the financial asset. In cases where the bond instrument has cash flows that arise from principal, interest, and other factors, then the investment must be classified as **fair-value-through-profit-or-loss (FVTPL)**. Consider a convertible bond that has principal and interest payments, but also the potential to be converted into shares. The investment in a convertible bond would have to be classified as FVTPL.

Classification of an investment with contractually determined cash flows is based on the entity's *business model for managing the asset.* For example, if a company buys a bond with a 10-year maturity date and manages the bond as part of a portfolio while interest and then principal are repaid, it is classified as an AC investment. If the business model governing the portfolio is to hold to receive the cash flows but also includes the directive to sell the investment if the price is appealing, it is classified as FVOCI-Bond. If the investment is to manage the portfolio for trading gains (sales only), then the bond is classified as FVTPL. The AC and FVOCI-Bond categories will include bonds and other money market instruments *but exclude common shares because shares lack contractually determined cash flows. Also excluded are bond investments that have returns that are impacted by factors other than just credit risk and interest rates.*

Objective of the AC Portfolio

The primary objective of an AC portfolio must be to *hold the investments* to collect contractual cash flows. *However, the investment does not have to be held until it matures.* For example, a bond investment might be sold if the credit rating of the issuer were to decline and no longer meets the investment policies set by the investor. The investor might sell the investment if the business model indicated a need to change the duration of the investment portfolio. The AC portfolio might be partially liquidated if the investor needed cash for capital expenditures. Such transactions should be infrequent, or the necessary overall objective for the portfolio—to hold the investments to collect interest and principal—might be called into question.

Investments in this category are measured at amortized cost. Interest, measured using the effective interest method, is recognized in profit or loss as earned.

ETHICAL ISSUES

Many financial statement measurements and classifications rest on the judgements and the representations of management. Auditors need to rely on management integrity and thus must evaluate this integrity. Auditors must be prudent and skeptical when reviewing management representations, which would include the objectives of an investment strategy. Management must demonstrate, through action, that the stated intent is real.

Fair-Value-through-Other-Comprehensive-Income-Bond Investments

The **fair-value-through-OCI-Bond (FVOCI-Bond)** category for bond investments covers investments that are managed within a business model whose objective is to both collect contractual cash flows of principal and interest and sell the financial asset. In this classification, sales of the assets will be more frequent than under the AC category. The investor might sell the asset to provide liquidity when needed or to match the maturities of financial liabilities that are funding the assets.

Investments in this category are revalued to fair value at each reporting period, with the unrealized gain or loss recognized in OCI. At the same time, interest earned (using the effective interest rate method) is recognized in profit or loss. The amounts allocated to OCI are accumulated in a separate equity reserve account (accumulated other comprehensive income, or AOCI) until the asset is sold. When the investment is sold, the amounts accumulated in OCI are reclassified to profit or loss.

Fair-Value-through-Profit-or-Loss Bond Investments

The **fair-value-through-profit-or-loss (FVTPL)** category covers bond investments that do not qualify as AC or FVOCI-Bond investments and investments that are not designated by management or circumstances to be in another category. Accordingly, *this category is a catch-all.*

Logically, an FVTPL investment is:

- An investment in bonds that is managed on a fair-value basis internally. This would be done in accordance with a documented risk management or investment strategy. Performance would be evaluated on a fair-value basis. In this category, the investment is *held for the purpose of resale*, or the investment is part of a portfolio of investments managed together for trading profit.
- An investment in bonds that should be subject to the FVTPL accounting rules (change in fair value in earnings) because doing so eliminates or significantly reduces a measurement or recognition inconsistency (called an "accounting mismatch.") This might occur if a related (hedged) financial instrument were required to be in the FVTPL category. Logically, related items should be treated equivalently so gains and losses offset.
- An investment that does not qualify as an AC or FVOCI-Bond investment because either:
  - The investment lacks the contractual cash flows necessary to allow it to be classified as an AC or FVOCI-Bond investment; or
  - It is a bond investment that is not managed to collect the contractual cash flows but, rather, held solely for resale.

Investments in this category are revalued to fair value each reporting date, with the change in fair value included in earnings. Techniques for estimating fair value (valuation models) are reviewed in a subsequent section.

Examples of accounting for the three different methods follow.

THE AMORTIZED COST (AC) METHOD

Using the amortized cost method, interest-bearing bond securities are recorded at cost, which is fair value on the date of acquisition. Fair value is the present value of the cash flow streams, discounted at the market interest rate. Any transaction costs, such as brokerage fees, are included in cost.

The amortized cost method for bond securities (AC) recognizes the following:

- The investment is originally recorded at cost. This is fair value on the purchase date.

- Transaction costs are *part of the cost of the investment*.
- Interest, using the effective interest rate method, is recorded as interest revenue.
- The investment is reported at amortized cost.
- Impairment losses for expected credit losses are recognized in profit or loss.
- When the investment is sold, the realized gain or loss is recognized in *the profit or loss*.

Accrued Interest

If the bond security is purchased between interest dates, accrued interest since the last interest payment date is paid by the new investor. Accrued interest is not part of investment cost but is recorded as interest receivable.

Accrued interest must be paid on acquisition because at each interest date, the *full periodic interest* is paid to whoever holds the securities regardless of how long they have been held. When bond securities are sold between interest dates, the seller collects accrued interest, which is recorded as interest revenue. For the new investor, the accrued interest is recorded separately from the cost of the security itself.

Note that interest calculations will be done by month in this text, but financial markets will make these adjustments counting by day.

Example—Purchase at Par

To illustrate the cost basis for a bond investment, assume that on 1 November 20X1, Able Company purchases face amount of $30,000 of Charlie Corporation 8% coupon bonds at 100 plus accrued interest. The bonds mature on 31 December 20X7. Interest is paid semi-annually on 30 June and 31 December. Able classifies this investment as an AC investment. Transaction costs are capitalized on acquisition.

Bond prices are quoted as percentages of the face value of the bond. A quote of 98 implies that a $30,000 face amount bond has a market price of $29,400. Able paid par, or 100, and so paid $30,000. The bond price is based on the present value of the cash flows, discounted at the market interest rate. The quoted price does not include accrued interest, which also must be paid to the seller of the bond.

Because the bond is purchased between interest dates, accrued interest must be paid by Able for the period 1 July to 31 October. The Able bond purchase occurred on 1 November, four months after the last interest payment on 30 June, and two months before the next payment at the end of December. Therefore, Able has to pay four month's interest *upfront*. When Able receives cash for six months' interest in December, interest revenue will net out to two months' interest earned.

Acquisition

The entry to record the acquisition is as follows:

Investment in Charlie Corporation bonds	30,000	
Accrued interest receivable ($30,000 × 8% × 4/12)	800	
Cash		30,800

Interest Revenue

When interest is received on 31 December, a portion of it represents the accrued interest recorded at the acquisition date:

Cash ($30,000 × 8% × 6/12)	1,200	
Interest revenue		400
Accrued interest receivable		800

Maturity

When an AC investment comes due, the investor receives the face value plus interest for a full six months, since maturity occurs on an interest date:

Cash	31,200	
Interest revenue		1,200
Investment in Charlie Corporation bonds		30,000

Sale

If the AC security is sold before maturity, the difference between book value at the time of the sale and the selling price (net of accrued interest), less commissions and other expenses, is recorded as a gain or loss.

Suppose on 31 March 20X2 Able Company sells its Charlie Corporation bonds at 105 plus accrued interest and incurs commissions and other expenses of $550. The cash received includes three months of accrued interest, or $600 ($30,000 × 8% × 3/12) plus the net proceeds from the bond itself, $30,950 (($30,000 × 105%), less $550 commissions). The gain on the sale is $950 because the proceeds of $30,950 are greater than the book value of $30,000.

The entry to record the sale is as follows:

Cash ($30,950 + $600)	31,550	
Interest revenue		600
Investment in Charlie Corporation bonds		30,000
Gain on sale of investment		950

Gains and losses on sale are recognized in earnings.

Amortization of Premium or Discount

What happens if bond securities are bought for an amount other than par value, for example, at 98 or 104? This is fair value and can be greater or less than the face amount of the bond because of interest rate differentials. The difference between fair value and par value is called a **premium** or **discount**. When fair value is higher than par value, the excess is called a *premium*. If fair value is less than par value, the difference is called a *discount*. The premium or discount must be amortized to interest revenue to properly measure the yield on the investment and also to bring the carrying value up (or down) to par value at maturity. Otherwise, interest revenue over the life of the investment is misstated, and a substantial gain or loss will be recognized at maturity.

Purchase Price

To ascertain fair value, the present value of the cash flows associated with the bond is calculated using the market interest rate as the discount rate. For example, assume that Marcus Corp. purchased Baker Company bonds when the market interest rate was 6%. The Baker bonds had a $500,000 maturity value, paid 5.5% interest semi-annually, and had a five-year life. The fair value is calculated as follows:

Principal $500,000 × (P/F, 3%, 10)	$372,045
Interest $13,750 × (P/A, 3%, 10)	117,290
Fair value (Present value)	$489,335

Both the principal of $500,000 and the semi-annual interest payments of $13,750 ($500,000 × 5.5% × 6/12) must be included in the present value calculation. Note that the discount rate used is 3%. This is the 6% market rate multiplied by 6/12 because payments and compounding are semi-annual. The number of periods is 10, which is the five-year life multiplied by two payments per year. Principal is a lump sum, and the interest amount is an ordinary annuity.

The fair value on this investment is $489,335, which is 0.97867 of face value ($489,335/ $500,000). This investment would therefore be quoted at a fair value of 97.867; *fair-value quotes in the bond market are based on a percentage of par value.* Acquisition would be recorded as follows:

Investment in bond securities: Baker bonds	489,335	
Cash		489,335

Since the bond will mature at $500,000, the $10,665 ($500,000 − $489,335) *discount* must be amortized to interest revenue over the life of the investment.

Amortization Methods

There are two methods of amortization, the **straight-line method** and the **effective-interest method**. The straight-line method is simpler, but the effective-interest method is preferable because it provides a constant yield on the recorded value of the investment. *IFRS standards require use of the effective-interest method.* (The straight-line method is allowed under ASPE and has been demonstrated in a later section of this chapter.)

Example: Effective-Interest Method

Using the effective-interest amortization method, interest revenue is measured using the market interest rate in effect when the bonds were issued. Each payment period, the investment carrying value is multiplied by the market interest rate to obtain interest revenue. The difference between cash received and interest revenue is the premium or discount amortization. The investment value changes by the amortization amount, and the investment book value changes to face value by maturity.

Effective-interest method calculations are illustrated in Exhibit 11-2 Note the following:

- The cash payment amount is constant each period, consistent with the terms of the bond. This is the stated (coupon) interest rate of 2.75% each six months, or 5.5% × 6/12.
- Interest revenue is a constant percentage of the bond carrying amount. To obtain interest revenue, multiply the bond's carrying value by the market interest rate. For example, the first amount is $14,680, or 3% of $489,335.
- Amortization is the difference between the cash payment and interest revenue. On the first line, this is $930, or $14,680 less $13,750.
- The bond carrying value grows each period by the amortization amount. On the first line, this is $489,335 plus $930, to equal $490,265.
- The bond carrying value increases to par value by the end of the 10-period amortization process.

EXHIBIT 11-2				
EFFECTIVE-INTEREST AMORTIZATION				
Period	Cash Payment	3% Interest Interest Revenue	Amortization	Bond Carrying Value
0				$489,335
1	$13,750	$14,680	$ 930	490,265
2	13,750	14,708	958	491,223
3	13,750	14,737	987	492,210
4	13,750	14,766	1,016	493,226
5	13,750	14,797	1,047	494,273
6	13,750	14,828	1,078	495,351
7	13,750	14,861	1,111	496,462
8	13,750	14,894	1,144	497,606

9	13,750	14,928	1,178	498,784
10	13,750	14,966[*]	1,216	500,000

[*]$14,964 + $2 rounding error

Interest revenue is recorded for the first period as follows:

Cash	13,750	
Investment in bond securities: Baker bonds	930	
Investment revenue: Interest		14,680

Purchase at Premium

Suppose Marcus paid *more* than the face of the bonds because the market interest rate was 4% when the bonds were purchased. In this case, the fair value would be:

Principal $500,000 × (P/F, 2%, 10)	$410,175
Interest $13,750 × (P/A, 2%, 10)	123,511
Fair value (Present value)	$533,686

The excess paid over the face amount is a *premium*. At acquisition, the bonds are recorded at $533,686, but over the period to maturity, the $33,686 premium is amortized, reducing the carrying amount (and reducing investment revenue below cash received) each year. Using the effective-interest method, the amortization table appears as in Exhibit 11-3. Only the first three interest periods have been included here. The table is constructed as for a discount situation except that the carrying value begins at a value *higher* than face value, the interest revenue is cash received *less* premium amortization, and the investment carrying value is *reduced* to face value over the life of the investment.

EXHIBIT 11-3				
EFFECTIVE-INTEREST AMORTIZATION				
Period	**Cash Payment**	**2% Interest Revenue**	**Amortization**	**Bond Carrying Value**
0				$533,686
1	$13,750	$10,674	$3,076	530,610
2	13,750	10,612	3,138	527,472
3	13,750	10,550	3,200	524,272
etc.				

The first interest payment is recorded as follows:

Cash	13,750	
Investment in bond securities: Baker bonds		3,076
Interest revenue		10,674

Loss Allowance and Impairment

The amount, timing, and riskiness of the cash flows expected to be received from an AC (or a FVOCI-Bond) bond security may change over time. In cases where the investee's credit risk has changed, the investee may become unable to pay the contractual amounts on the specified dates due to changes in its circumstances. Since AC and FVOCI-Bond investments are managed with an objective to receive these cash flows, IFRS requires that when expected cash flows differ from the contractual amounts, this loss in the value of the investment is recognized as a loss allowance. This is known as the **expected credit loss approach** for impairment assessment. Under this approach, it is not necessary for an event to trigger the recognition of a loss. Instead, at each reporting date, the credit risk of the investee is assessed and expected **credit losses** are recognized. Note that for bonds classified as FVTPL, there is no need for impairment losses to be recognized since the bond is adjusted to fair value at each reporting period with all gains and losses immediately recognized in net earnings.

The expected credit losses are the present value of all cash shortfalls over the life of the bond investment discounted at the effective interest rate determined at initial recognition. Cash shortfalls are the difference between the contractual cash flows and the cash flows now expected to be received. Both the timing and amount of these cash flows are considered. Impairment losses are still recognized in cases where the total amount of the contractual cash flows remains unchanged, but it will now take a longer period to collect. These expected credit losses represent the amount of the allowance for impairment loss that is then recognized at the end of each reporting period. Any change in the allowance for the period represents the impairment loss (or gain) recognized in net earnings for the year.

A bond investment is **credit-impaired** when one or more events have occurred that have a detrimental impact on the estimated future cash flows. If an investment is credit-impaired, then the allowance for expected credit losses is equal to the difference between the gross carrying amount of the investment (i.e., before the allowance) and the present value of the estimated future cash flows now expected, discounted at the original effective interest rate.

Determination of Allowance

A three-stage approach is used to measure the losses depending on how significant the change in credit risk is and whether a loss event has occurred. Exhibit 11-4 below depicts this approach.

The three stages of credit risk assessment are:

- Stage 1: If there is *no significant increase* in credit risk, then possible default events are considered for the next 12 months and expected credit losses determined. Interest revenue continues to be measured based on the original amounts (i.e., applying the effective interest rate to the gross carrying amount of the investment).

- Stage 2: If there is a *significant increase* in credit risk, then the credit losses expected for the life of the bond instrument are determined. Interest revenue continues to be measured based on the original amounts (i.e., applying the effective interest rate to the gross carrying amount of the investment).

- Stage 3: This stage occurs when there is a significant increase in credit risk and the investment is *credit-impaired* due to an adverse event. In calculating the allowance, it is similar to Stage 2 in that expected credit losses for the lifetime of the asset are estimated. The difference with this stage is that interest revenue is calculated based on the net amount (gross carrying amount less the allowance) using the original effective interest rate.

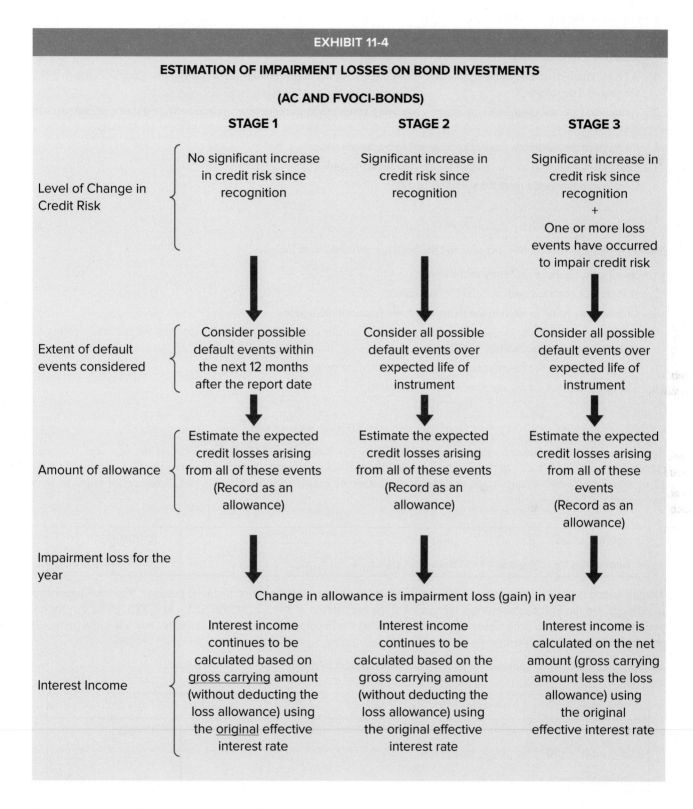

EXHIBIT 11-4

ESTIMATION OF IMPAIRMENT LOSSES ON BOND INVESTMENTS

(AC AND FVOCI-BONDS)

	STAGE 1	STAGE 2	STAGE 3
Level of Change in Credit Risk	No significant increase in credit risk since recognition	Significant increase in credit risk since recognition	Significant increase in credit risk since recognition + One or more loss events have occurred to impair credit risk
Extent of default events considered	Consider possible default events within the next 12 months after the report date	Consider all possible default events over expected life of instrument	Consider all possible default events over expected life of instrument
Amount of allowance	Estimate the expected credit losses arising from all of these events (Record as an allowance)	Estimate the expected credit losses arising from all of these events (Record as an allowance)	Estimate the expected credit losses arising from all of these events (Record as an allowance)
Impairment loss for the year	Change in allowance is impairment loss (gain) in year		
Interest Income	Interest income continues to be calculated based on <u>gross carrying</u> amount (without deducting the loss allowance) using the <u>original</u> effective interest rate	Interest income continues to be calculated based on the gross carrying amount (without deducting the loss allowance) using the original effective interest rate	Interest income is calculated on the net amount (gross carrying amount less the loss allowance) using the original effective interest rate

Indicators of Changes in Credit Risk

To make this assessment of changes in credit risk, the risk of default at the report date is compared to the risk of default at the time the investment was initially recognized. There are two levels of assessment; the first is for an increase in credit risk; and the second is whether a loss event has occurred. Some of the indicators that might be considered to assess credit risk in this assessment are:

1. Change in the price of credit risk;

2. Changes in credit risk for similar bonds with the same expected life;

3. Actual or expected changes in the bond's credit rating;

4. Adverse changes in the business, financial, technological, or economic conditions impacting the issuer's ability to make the required payments;

5. Actual or expected changes in the issuer's operating results such as reduced revenues, increased costs, or increases in debt levels;

6. Changes in the contractual cash flows agreed to by the investor;

7. Significant reduction in the value of underlying security; and

8. Contractual payments more than 30 days past due.

Indicators of Credit Impairment

Indicators that a loss event has occurred and the bond is credit-impaired include:

1. Significant financial difficulty of the issuer;

2. A breach of contract, such as default of payments;

3. Concessions being granted to the issuer due to its financial difficulties;

4. Adverse changes in the business, financial, technological, or economic conditions impacting the investee's ability to make the required payments;

5. It is probable that the issuer will enter bankruptcy creditor protection; or

6. The active market for the investment has disappeared.

Example: Impairment—No Significant Increase in Credit Risk

Review the facts of the Baker bond given above, originally purchased for $489,335. At the end of the first year, the gross carrying amount is $491,223 as per Exhibit 11-2 and there is no significant change in the credit risk. Assessing the next 12 months for possible default events, expected credit losses are estimated to be $10,000. An allowance for impairment is recognized for Year 1, as follows:

Impairment loss	10,000	
Allowance for impairment loss: Baker bonds		10,000

The allowance is shown as a *contra account* to the investment on the statement of financial position. The loss is reported in earnings. On the SFP, the investment is reported at the net balance of $481,223 ($491,223 − $10,000). (Note that for tax purposes, such losses are deductible only when realized, so the impairment loss is tax deductible only when the [reduced] payments are actually accepted.)

Note that interest revenue continues to be recognized as outlined in Exhibit 11-2 as shown below:

During Year 2,		
Cash	13,750	
Investment in bond securities: Baker bonds	987	
Interest revenue		14,737

Cash	13,750	
Investment in bond securities: Baker bonds	1,016	
Interest revenue		14,766

Example: Impairment—Significant Increase in Credit Risk

At the end of Year 2, the gross carrying amount of the bond is $493,226 (as per Exhibit 11-2) and the related allowance is $10,000 before the year-end assessment for impairment. It is now determined that there has been a significant increase in credit risk, and the expected credit losses for the lifetime of the investment are estimated to be $35,000. The allowance is adjusted to $35,000 with the following journal entry:

Impairment loss	25,000	
Allowance for impairment loss: Baker bonds		25,000

The Baker bonds are reported on the SFP at the net amount of $458,226 ($493,226 – 35,000). Interest revenue continues to be calculated based on the original amortization schedule similar to the above example.

Example: Impairment—Significant Increase in Credit Risk and a Loss Event

Assume at the end of Year 3, the credit risk has significantly increased due to Baker's poor operating results and defaulting on a payment. The expected future cash flows to be received on the bond are revised as follows:

EXHIBIT 11-5
PRESENT VALUE OF EXPECTED FUTURE CASH FLOWS

Period	Cash Payment	Present Value at 3%
Year 3		
Midyear Year 4	5,000	4,854
End of Year 4	5,000	4,713
Midyear Year 5	5,000	4,576
End of Year 5	5,000	4,442
End of Year 5 Final payment	450,000	399,819
Total present value of expected cash flows		$418,404

The present value of the expected cash flows based on these events, discounted at the original yield of 3%, is $418,404 (Exhibit 11-5). The difference between the gross amount and the revised discounted value is $76,947 ($495,351 – $418,404).

The impairment is recognized and the allowance is adjusted for this loss as follows:

Impairment loss (76,947 – 35,000)	41,947	
Allowance for impairment loss: Baker bonds		41,947

When the investment is credit-impaired, as in this case, the interest revenue for Year 4 and Year 5 will change. The effective interest rate of 3% is applied now on the net amount (net of the allowance) of $418,404. Exhibit 11-6 calculates the interest revenue to be recognized for the remainder of the term (assuming no further revisions in Year 5).

EXHIBIT 11-6
REVISED AMORTIZATION SCHEDULE

Period	Cash Payment	Present Value at 3%	Amortization	Carrying Value
Year 3	Revised to the net amount			418,404

Midyear Year 4	5,000	12,552	7,552	425,956
End of Year 4	5,000	12,779	7,779	433,735
Midyear Year 5	5,000	13,012	8,012	441,747
End of Year 5	5,000	13,253	8,253	450,000

The entries to record the interest revenue during Year 4 are:

Cash	5,000	
Investment in bond securities: Baker bonds	7,552	
Interest revenue		12,552

Cash	5,000	
Investment in bond securities: Baker bonds	7,779	
Interest revenue		12,779

Reversals

At each report date, the expected credit losses are assessed and discounted. Impairment losses may be reversed in cases where the expected amount and timing of cash flows change favourably. Since the impairment losses represent only cash shortfalls with the original contractual cash flows, reversal of impairment losses could never exceed accumulated impairment losses to date.

CONCEPT REVIEW

1. Under what circumstances is an investment in bonds classified as an AC investment? As a FVOCI-Bond investment? As a FVTPL investment?
2. A bond security is bought for $14,700, including $700 of accrued interest, and sold for $14,900, including $900 of accrued interest. Why is there no gain or loss on sale?
3. How is the fair value of a bond determined if it has a face value of $4 million and a quoted price of 98?
4. Is interest revenue on an AC investment necessarily equal to the cash entitlement? Explain.
5. When is an allowance for impairment recorded on bond investments?
6. Under what conditions would an impairment loss on an AC investment be reversed?

THE FAIR-VALUE-THROUGH-OTHER-COMPREHENSIVE INCOME-BOND METHOD (FVOCI-BOND)

The fair value method through OCI for bond securities (FVOCI-Bond) recognizes the following:

- The investment is originally recorded at cost. This is fair value on the purchase date.
- Transaction costs are *part of the cost of the investment*.
- Interest, using the effective-interest method, is recorded as interest revenue.
- The investment is reported at fair value on the statement of financial position. At the end of each reporting period, the investments are revalued to fair value, whether this is higher or lower than the existing balance in the investment account.
- *Holding gains or losses* are reported annually in *other comprehensive income*. The change is included on the statement of comprehensive income. The cumulative amount of such gains and losses is segregated in a separate equity reserve account (AOCI).
- Impairment losses for expected credit losses are recognized in profit or loss.
- When the investment is sold, the accumulated gains and losses in OCI are recycled out of this separate equity account *to the profit or loss* and holding gains or losses realized are reported in net earnings.

Example

YZone purchased on 1 December 20X5 a $100,000, 6%, eight-year Provincial Hydro bond that pays interest each 1 December and 1 June, at a price of $106,528, to yield 5%. Because the bond was purchased on an interest date, there was no accrued interest. There was also no commission paid. (Note that if commission had been paid, this would be included in the initial cost of the bond investment.) This investment is classified as FVOCI-Bond.

Investment in Provincial Hydro bonds	106,528	
Cash		106,528

The partial amortization schedule for this bond is shown in Exhibit 11-7.

EXHIBIT 11-7

EFFECTIVE-INTEREST AMORTIZATION

Period	Cash Payment	2.5% Interest Rate Interest Revenue	Amortization	Bond Carrying Value
1 Dec 20X5				$106,528
1 Jun 20X6	$3,000	$2,663	$ 337	106,191
1 Dec 20X6	3,000	2,655	345	105,846
1 Jun 20X7	3,000	2,646	354	105,492

Interest Revenue

Bond interest is accrued on 31 December using the effective-interest method.

Accrued interest receivable ($3,000 × 1/6)	500	
Interest revenue ($2,663 × 1/6)		444
Investment in Provincial Hydro bonds ($337 × 1/6)		56

Fair-Value Adjustment

At year-end, fair value is determined through reference to active market quotations. The bonds are trading at 107 and must be reflected in the financial statements at $107,000. An entry is made to record changes in fair value:

Investment in Provincial Hydro bonds ($107,000 − ($106,528 − $56))	528	
OCI-Holding gain: Provincial Hydro Bond		528

The 107 bond price is quoted exclusive of accrued interest, and *fair value is NOT adjusted for brokerage fees* that would have to be paid if the securities were actually sold.

Reporting

At the end of 20X5, the financial statements will reflect the following:

Specified items on the statement of financial position:

Assets:	
Investment, Provincial Hydro bonds	107,000

Equity:

Reserve Accumulated OCI–FVOCI-Bond investments	528

In net earnings:

Interest revenue	$444 (cr.)

In other comprehensive income:

Investments–FVOCI-Bond: Holding gains	528 (cr.)

Second Year

In 20X6, YZone receives interest on the Provincial Hydro bonds on 1 June and 1 December. YZone originally paid $106,528 for a yield to maturity of 5%. Although the carrying value was "topped up" to fair value at the end of Year 1, *the original measurements are used through the bond's life for interest revenue measurement.*

To record receipt of interest on 1 June (see Exhibit 11-7):

Cash	3,000	
Interest revenue ($2,663 × 5/6)		2,219
Investment in Provincial Hydro bonds ($337 × 5/6)		281
Accrued interest receivable (previously recorded)		500

To record receipt of interest on 1 December (see Exhibit 11-7):

Cash	3,000	
Interest revenue		2,655
Investment in Provincial Hydro bonds		345

The carrying value of the bond is now $106,374, which is the amortized amount of $105,846 from Exhibit 11-7 and the accumulated OCI of $528. On 1 December, the bond is sold for 109 less a broker's fee of $300.

Cash (($100,000 × 109%) − $300)	108,700	
OCI Reclassify holding gain	528	
Investment in Provincial Hydro bonds		106,374
Investment revenue: Gain on sale of investment		2,854

Note that the commission is netted with the proceeds, and effectively netted with the reported gain. *The commission is not separately expensed in a sale transaction.* Also notice that on sale of the investment, the amounts accumulated previously in OCI are reclassified to the profit or loss. As a result, the entire realized gain is recognized in net earnings.

Reporting

At the end of 20X6 the financial statements will reflect the following:

In earnings:

Interest revenue	$ 4,874 (cr.)
Investment revenue: Gain on sale of investment	2,854 (cr.)

In other comprehensive income:

Investment in FVOCI bond securities—Reclassification to profit or loss	$ 528 (dr.)

Impairment

Similar to AC investments, impairment losses arising from increased credit risk are reported in net earnings for FVOCI-Bond investments. In the above example, the assumption made is that all of the changes in fair value were due to changes in market interest rates and not the credit risk of Provincial Hydro. If this is not the case, then an impairment loss needs to be recognized.

Example—Impairment

Using the same information above, assume that at the 20X5 year-end, the Provincial Hydro bonds have a fair market value of 105 but YZone has determined that the credit risk related to these bonds has increased and estimated expected credit losses equal to $450. The following entry would be made:

Impairment loss	450	
OCI-Holding loss: Provincial Hydro bond	1,022	
Investment in Provincial Hydro bonds ($105,000 − ($106,528 − $56))		1,472

Notice that the carrying value of the bonds is still equal to the fair market value of $105,000. The impairment loss has been recognized in net earnings[1].

FAIR-VALUE-THROUGH-PROFIT-OR-LOSS METHOD FOR BOND INVESTMENTS

For bond investments classified as FVTPL, the following are recognized:

---

1. Technically the accumulated impairment losses are netted in OCI against total fair value changes.

- The investment is originally recorded at cost. This is fair value on the purchase date.
- Transaction costs, such as brokerage fees, are *immediately expensed*.
- Interest revenue on bond investments need not be separately reported and is included along with the fair-value adjustment as part of investment revenue.
- The investment is reported at fair value on the statement of financial position. At the end of each reporting period, the investment is revalued to fair value, whether this is higher or lower than the existing balance in the investment account.
- **Holding gains and losses**, defined as the difference between the existing balance in the investment account (the new fair value) and the prior investment account balance (the old fair value), are recorded in earnings. That is, earnings includes the change in value of the investment each year, whether **realized holding gains or losses** (realized through sale) or **unrealized holding gains or losses** (unrealized because the investment is still held).

Example

Assume YZone purchased on 1 December 20X5 a $100,000, 6%, eight-year Provincial Hydro bond that pays interest each 1 December and 1 June, at a price of $106,528, to yield 5%. Because the bond was purchased on an interest payment date, there was no accrued interest. There was also no commission paid. This investment is classified as FVTPL.

| Investment in Provincial Hydro bonds | 106,528 | |
| Cash | | 106,528 |

Interest Revenue

Bond interest is accrued on 31 December. (Note that the effective interest rate is not used for this classification.)

| Accrued interest receivable ($100,000 × 6% × 1/12) | 500 | |
| Investment revenue: Bonds ($100,000 × 6% × 1/12) , | | 500 |

Fair-Value Adjustment

At year-end, fair value is determined through reference to active stock market quotations. The bonds are trading at 107. This means that the bonds must be reflected in the financial statements at $107,000. An entry is made to record changes in fair value:

| Investment in Provincial Hydro bonds ($107,000 − $106,528) | 472 | |
| Investment revenue: Provincial Hydro bond—Holding gain: | | 472 |

The 107 bond price is quoted exclusive of accrued interest, and *fair value is NOT adjusted for brokerage fees* that would have to be paid if the securities were actually sold.

Reporting

At the end of 20X5 the financial statements will reflect the following:

Investments on the statement of financial position:

| Assets: | |
| Investment, Provincial Hydro bonds | 107,000 |

In earnings:

| Investment revenue: Provincial Hydro bonds ($500 + $472) | 972 (cr.) |

Second Year

In 20X6, YZone has further transactions with respect to its FVTPL bond investments. Interest on the Provincial Hydro bonds is paid on 1 June and 1 December. Note that the interest revenue can be recognized as part of investment revenue.

To record receipt of interest on 1 June:

Cash ($100,000 × 6% × 6/12)	3,000	
Investment revenue: Provincial Hydro bonds ($100,000 × 6% × 5/12)		2,500
Accrued interest receivable (previously recorded)		500

To record receipt of interest on 1 December:

| Cash ($100,000 × 6% × 6/12) | 3,000 | |
| Investment revenue: Provincial Hydro bonds (($100,000) × 6% × 6/12) | | 3,000 |

The carrying value of the bond is currently $107,000, which was the fair value of $107,000 at the end of year 1. The bond is sold on 1 December for 109, less a broker's fee of $300:

Cash (($100,000 × 109%) − $300)	108,700	
Investment in Provincial Hydro bonds (carrying value, $107,000)		107,000
Investment revenue: Provincial Hydro bonds		1,700

Note that the commission is netted with the proceeds, and effectively netted with the reported gain. *The commission is not separately expensed in a sale transaction.*

Reporting

At the end of 20X6 the financial statements will reflect the following:

In earnings:

| Investment revenue: Provincial Hydro bonds ($2,500 + $3,000 + $1,700) | $ 7,200 (cr.) |

Summary

Exhibit 11-8 summarizes the accounting methods available for bond investments.

EXHIBIT 11-8

ACCOUNTING FOR BOND INVESTMENTS

Summary of Accounting Methods

Method	Carrying Value on SFP	Investment Revenue	Unrealized Holding Gains and Losses	Realized Gains and Losses
Amortized cost (Bonds)	Amortized cost	Interest revenue—effective-interest method	—	Included in earnings; should be rare

Fair-value-through-other-comprehensive-income-bonds	Fair value	Interest income—effective-interest method	Included in other comprehensive income until sold; part of shareholders' equity as a separate reserve	Reclassify accumulated OCI amounts to net earnings in period of sale
Fair-value-through-profit-or-loss	Fair value	Interest revenue—may be shown separately or included with the holding gains and losses in Investment revenue	Included in earnings	Included in earnings; only the *annual change in value* in the year of sale

CLASSIFICATION AND ACCOUNTING OF PASSIVE SHARE INVESTMENTS

Equity instruments are investments in shares of other companies. The discussion below explains how the classification decision is made to the appropriate category for passive share investments and how the investments are accounted for.

Share Investments

In determining the correct classification for passive share investments, there are only two possible choices: FVTPL and FVOCI-Equity. The classification will depend on the reason for holding the shares. Share investments are generally classified as FVTPL, and under limited conditions management can elect to classify them as FVOCI-Equity. The criteria for these classifications are discussed below.

Fair-Value-through-Profit-or-Loss Share Investments

The **fair-value-through-profit-or-loss (FVTPL)** investment covers all passive share investments except those designated by management as FVOCI-Equity. This category includes:

- An investment in shares that is managed on a fair-value basis internally. This would be done in accordance with a documented risk management or investment strategy and performance evaluated on a fair-value basis. In this category, the investment is *held for the purpose of resale*, or the investment is part of a portfolio of investments managed together for trading profit.

- An investment in shares that should be subject to the FVTPL accounting rules (change in fair value in earnings) because doing so eliminates or significantly reduces a measurement or recognition inconsistency (called an "accounting mismatch.") This might occur if a related (hedged) financial instrument were required to be in the FVTPL category. Logically, related items should be treated equivalently so gains and losses offset.

Fair Value-through-Other-Comprehensive-Income-Equity Investments (FVOCI-Equity)

Only share investments that are not *held for trading* are eligible for this category. This category is determined by management designation; *any equity investment* that is designated by management as a **fair-value-through-other-comprehensive-income-equity (FVOCI-Equity) investment** is included. The process is as follows:

- Only equity investments can be FVOCI-Equity; investments in bonds or loans have their own classification FVOCI-Bonds as discussed earlier.
- The election to classify an investment as FVOCI-Equity must be made when the investment is initially recognized.
- The election to classify an investment as FVOCI-Equity is irrevocable.

Investments in this category are revalued to fair value each reporting date, with the change in fair value included in other comprehensive income (OCI). The cumulative amount is collected in a separate equity reserve account (accumulated other comprehensive income, or AOCI).

When the investment is sold, the AOCI amounts may remain in the separate equity reserve account or be transferred directly to another equity account, most logically to retained earnings. In either case, *any gain or loss on sale is permanently excluded from earnings.*

Investments are included in this category because the accounting treatment is considered desirable; that is unrealized gains and losses caused by an increase or decrease in fair value are isolated in equity and bypass earnings. The category might be desirable to manage earnings, but adds considerable complexity to the financial statements because unrealized amounts are part of comprehensive income and the equity reserve account.

PASSIVE SHARE INVESTMENTS: THE FAIR-VALUE-THROUGH-PROFIT-OR-LOSS METHOD (FVTPL)

Recognizing investments at fair value recognizes that financial statement users find fair value more relevant than the historical cost of the investment. Therefore, at reporting dates, the carrying value of an investment is adjusted to fair value. In the FVTPL method, gains and losses are included in earnings when the change in value is recognized, whether the gains and losses are *unrealized* or *realized through sale*. Dividend revenue is recorded during the year, as appropriate, and may be included in investment revenue along with the holding gains and losses.

For FVTPL investments:

- The investment is originally recorded at cost. This is fair value on the purchase date.
- Transaction costs, such as brokerage fees, are *immediately expensed.*
- Dividends on share investments are recorded as investment revenue when declared and need not be separately reported from the period holding gains and losses.
- The investment is reported at fair value on the statement of financial position. At the end of each reporting period, the investments are revalued to fair value, whether this is higher or lower than the existing balance in the investment account.

Holding gains and losses, defined as the difference between the existing balance in the investment account (the new fair value) and the prior investment account balance (the old fair value), are recorded in earnings. That is, earnings includes the change in value of the investment each year, whether realized holding gains or losses (realized through sale) or unrealized holding gains or losses (unrealized because the investment is still held).

Example

Assume that on 1 December 20X5, YZone bought 5,000 shares of Gerome Ltd., a public company, for $26.75 per share plus $1,200 in broker's fees. The investment is classified as FVTPL. *The commission is expensed for FVTPL investments on a purchase transaction.*

Investment in Gerome Ltd. shares (5,000 × $26.75)	133,750	
Commission expense	1,200	
Cash		134,950

Investment Revenue

Dividend revenue is recorded when declared. Gerome did not declare any dividends in 20X5.

Fair-Value Adjustment

At year-end, fair value is determined through reference to active stock market quotations. The Gerome shares are trading for $24.75. This means that the shares must be reflected in the financial statements at $123,750 (5,000 shares at $24.75). An entry is made to record changes in fair value:

Investment loss: Holding loss: Gerome Ltd. shares ($133,750 − $123,750)	10,000	
Investment in Gerome Ltd. shares		10,000

Note that *fair value is NOT adjusted for brokerage fees* that would have to be paid if the securities were actually sold.

Reporting

At the end of 20X5, the financial statements will reflect the following:

Investments on the statement of financial position:

Assets:	
Investment, Gerome Ltd. shares	$123,750

In earnings:

Investment loss: Gerome Ltd. shares	(10,000) (dr.)
Commissions expense	(1,200) (dr.)

Second Year

In 20X6, Gerome paid a $0.43 per share dividend in 20X6:

Cash (5,000 × $0.43)	2,150	
Investment revenue: Gerome Ltd. shares		2,150

The Gerome shares are still unsold at year-end. Their quoted share price is now $31.50, or a total of $157,500. Since the shares are currently recorded at $123,750, a holding gain is recorded:

Investment in Gerome Ltd. shares ($157,500 − $123,750)	33,750	
Investment revenue: Gerome Ltd. shares		33,750

Reporting

At the end of 20X6 the financial statements will reflect the following:

Investments on the statement of financial position:

Assets:	
Investment, Gerome Ltd. shares	$157,500

In earnings:

Investment revenue: Gerome Ltd. shares	35,900

Third Year

In 20X7, the Gerome shares are sold for $30.50 per share, or a total of $152,500 (5,000 × $30.50), less $1,700 in broker's fees:

Cash ((5,000 × $30.50) − $1,700)	150,800	
Investment revenue: Gerome Ltd. shares ($150,800 − $157,500)	6,700	
Investment in Gerome Ltd. shares		157,500

Again, the commission paid is netted with the proceeds. Overall, there has been a $17,050 gain on the shares: selling proceeds of $150,800 versus original cost of $133,750. This has been recognized as a $10,000 loss in 20X5, a $33,750 gain in 20X6, and a loss of $6,700 in 20X7.

Impairment

Adjusting to fair value at each reporting period automatically tracks any decrease in fair value through the financial statements and any subsequent recovery of fair value, so *no separate impairment test is needed.*

FAIR-VALUE-THROUGH-OTHER-COMPREHENSIVE-INCOME-EQUITY METHOD

The FVOCI-Equity method recognizes gains and losses through other comprehensive income (FVOCI-Equity) and is similar in structure to the previous example for FVTPL for the shares investment. The difference between the two fair-value methods lies in the entries to record dividend revenue, changes in value, and the entries on sale. Under FVOCI-Equity, changes in fair value are recorded in other comprehensive income and are permanently excluded from earnings. The cumulative gain or loss is recorded in an equity reserve. Dividend revenue is recognized in profit or loss in the year earned. This method may be applied only to *equity investments* that are irrevocably designated FVOCI-Equity on initial recognition.

For FVOCI-Equity investments:

- The investment is originally recorded at cost. This is fair value on the purchase date.

- Transaction costs are *part of the cost of the investment.*

- Dividends declared are recorded as investment revenue in profit or loss.

- At the end of each reporting period, the investments are revalued to fair value, whether this is higher or lower than the existing balance in the investment account. The investment is reported at fair value on the statement of financial position.

- *Holding gains or losses* are reported annually in *other comprehensive income.* The change is included on the statement of comprehensive income. The cumulative amount of such gains and losses is segregated in a separate equity reserve account (AOCI). The gains and losses *may be closed* out of this separate equity account *to another equity account* (most logically, retained earnings) when the investment is sold and the holding gains or losses are realized. Holding gains or losses may also be left permanently in the separate reserve account. This choice is up to the company.

Example

Assume that on 1 December 20X5, when YZone bought 5,000 shares of Gerome Ltd. for $26.75 per share plus $1,200 in broker's fees, the investment was classified as FVOCI-Equity.

Investment in Gerome Ltd. shares ([5,000 × $26.75] + $1,200)	134,950	
Cash		134,950

Note that transaction costs are capitalized and are not expensed.

Fair-Value Adjustment

At year-end, fair value is determined to be $24.75 per share, or a total of $123,750:

OCI: Holding loss: Gerome Ltd. shares ($134,950 – $123,750)	11,200	
Investment in Gerome Ltd. shares		11,200

The holding loss on the Gerome shares includes the write-off of the broker's fees that were capitalized on acquisition.

Reporting

Gains and losses caused by changes in fair value are not recorded in earnings but rather as an element of other comprehensive income and part of a separate equity account. The financial statements appear as follows:

On the statement of comprehensive income:

Net earnings (assumed)	$157,800
Other comprehensive income:	
Investment-FVOCI-Equity investments: Holding losses	(11,200)
Comprehensive income	$146,600

On the statement of changes in equity:

	AOCI: Equity Reserve: FVOCI-Equity Investments Holding (Loss) or Gain	Retained Earnings
Opening balance (assumed)	$ 0	$651,000
Comprehensive income	$(11,200) dr.	157,800
Closing balance	$(11,200) dr.	$808,800

On the statement of financial position:

Assets:	
Investment, Gerome Ltd. shares	$123,750
Equity:	
Retained earnings	808,800
Reserve: AOCI–FVOCI-Equity investments: holding loss	(11,200)

Second Year

In 20X6, Gerome paid a $0.43 per share dividend:

| Cash (5,000 × $0.43) | 2,150 | |
| Dividend revenue | | 2,150 |

Note that the FVOCI-Equity category dictates treatment of changes in fair value but *dividends are still investment revenue, which is reported in profit or loss.* The Gerome shares have a fair value of $157,500 at year-end.

| Investment in Gerome Ltd. shares ($157,500 − $123,750) | 33,750 | |
| OCI: Holding gain: Gerome Ltd. shares | | 33,750 |

Reporting

At the end of 20X6, the equity reserve includes the *cumulative amount* of holding gains and losses to date. The financial statements will reflect:

On the statement of comprehensive income:

Net earnings (assumed)	$ 177,100
Other comprehensive income:	
Holding gain on FVOCI investments	33,750
Comprehensive income	$210,850

On the statement of changes in equity:

	AOCI: Equity Reserve: FVOCI-Equity Investments Holding (Loss) or Gain	Retained Earnings
Opening balance	$ (11,200)	$808,800
Comprehensive income	33,750	177,100
Closing balance	$ 22,550	$985,900

On the statement of financial position:

Assets:	
Investment, Gerome Ltd. shares	$ 157,500
Equity:	
Retained earnings	$985,900

| Reserve: AOCI FVOCI Equity investments: holding gain | $22,550 |

To prove the $22,550 amount in equity, compare the original cost of the Gerome shares, $134,950, and their current fair value of $157,500. The result is $22,550.

Third Year

In 20X7, the Gerome shares are sold for $30.50 per share, less $1,700 in broker's fees:

Cash ((5,000 × $30.50) − $1,700)	150,800	
OCI: Holding loss: Gerome Ltd. shares	6,700	
Investment in Gerome Ltd. shares		157,500

The holding gains may remain permanently in the equity reserve. Alternatively, if the company wishes, the cumulative holding gains, which are now entirely realized, may be transferred to retained earnings:

OCI: Holding gains ($11,200 − $33,750 + $6,700)	15,850	
Retained earnings		15,850

Reporting

The financial statements will reflect the following:

On the statement of comprehensive income:

Net earnings (assumed)	$42,600
Other comprehensive income:	
Investments: FVOCI-Equity: Holding loss	(6,700)
Comprehensive income	$35,900

On the statement of changes in equity:

	AOCI: Equity Reserve: FVOCI-Equity Investments Holding (Loss) or Gain	Retained Earnings
Opening balance	$ 22,550	$ 985,900
Comprehensive income	(6,700)	42,600
Transfer to retained earnings on realization	(15,850)	15,850
Closing balance	$ 0	$1,044,350

On the statement of financial position:

Equity:	
Retained earnings	$1,044,350

Impairment

As for FVTPL investments, there is no separate impairment test needed because fair value is the measurement attribute, whether high or low.

Comparison

Both fair value methods report the share investment asset account on the statement of financial position at fair value. Both methods report dividends declared as investment revenue. Neither method requires an impairment test. The difference between the methods lies in the treatment of changes in fair value in earnings: These amounts are in earnings (and retained earnings) under FVTPL and excluded from earnings under FVOCI-Equity. Under FVOCI-Equity realized amounts may be transferred from the equity reserve to retained earnings, which means that the final destination can be the same.

Total earnings, however, will remain different between the two methods. Under FVTPL, increases and decreases in fair value will cause earnings to increase and decrease. Commissions and brokerage fees are immediately expensed, decreasing earnings. If investment fair values are volatile, inclusion of holding gains in earnings introduces volatility to earnings. Companies with FVTPL portfolios have registered concern about this volatility, and standard setters continue to grapple with these issues.

Under FVOCI-Equity, changes in fair value and commission/brokerage fees bypass earnings. Since both retained earnings and the equity reserve are in equity, total equity is not affected. *However, the level, pattern, and potential variability of earnings are different between the two methods.* Accordingly, the classification decision must be made carefully and thoughtfully by management.

Summary

Exhibit 11-9 summarizes the accounting methods for passive share investments.

EXHIBIT 11-9				
ACCOUNTING FOR PASSIVE SHARE INVESTMENTS				
Summary of Accounting Methods				
Method	**Carrying Value**	**Dividend Income**	**Unrealized Holding Gains and Losses**	**Realized Gains and Losses**
Fair-value-through-profit-or-loss	Fair value	Dividend revenue reported in profit or loss. May be separate or included with the holding gains and losses	Included in profit or loss	Included in profit or loss; only the *annual change in value* in the year of sale
Fair-value-through-other-comprehensive-income-equity	Fair value	Dividend revenue is reported in profit or loss	Included in other comprehensive income; part of shareholders' equity as a separate reserve	May be transferred to another equity account (retained earnings) when realized or may remain in separate reserve

CONCEPT REVIEW

1. Why might management choose to classify an equity investment as FVOCI-Equity instead of FVTPL?
2. Where are unrealized holding gains and losses recognized in the financial statements when investments are classified as FVOCI-Equity?
3. Can an investment in common shares be classified as an AC investment? Explain.
4. How are transaction costs, such as brokerage fees, accounted for if a share investment is classified as FVTPL? FVOCI-Equity?
5. A FVTPL share investment is bought for $10,000 and has a fair value of $14,000 at the end of the first year, $16,000 at the end of the second year, and then is sold for $21,000 in the third year. What amount of gain is recorded in profit or loss in the third year?
6. Assume that the same investment (as in number 5) is classified as a FVOCI-Equity investment. What amount of gain is recorded in profit or loss in the third year?

ESTIMATING FAIR VALUE

Since financial statements will reflect **fair value** for some investments, it stands to reason that fair value must be carefully estimated. After all, estimated fair value is not substantiated by the objective evidence of a transaction of the reporting entity. Fair value is defined as the *price that would be received to sell an asset in an orderly transaction between market participants at the measurement date.*

When there is an *active market for an identical investment,* quoted prices provide objective evidence of fair value. A fair value referenced to active markets has a high degree of validity, and is referred to as a Level 1 measure of fair value. Price quotes, whether from a stock exchange, dealer, broker, industry group, or pricing service, are an indication of actual transactions that have taken place at arm's length. The *bid price* is the appropriate measure, since it establishes the presence of a buyer (versus the *ask price,* which is offered by a vendor.)

If there is *no active market,* then *fair value must be estimated using a valuation technique* that incorporates all factors that market participants consider when establishing prices. For example, when trading is light, markets are not active. Recent bid prices may be acceptable if economic or firm-specific conditions have not changed. In particular, a recent price might not be relevant if significant events have taken place after the bid date.

Valuation models attempt to set a value that would have been valid in an arms-length transaction motivated by normal business considerations. Fair value can be inferred by referencing another "similar but not identical" transaction and then adjusting the market price for differences in term and risk. Discounted cash flow and option pricing models can also be used. The result is an *inferred fair value.* Such an estimate is referred to as a Level 2 measure of fair value. The reasonableness of any result must be carefully considered before the value can be used in the financial statements.

An estimate of fair value becomes less reliable when more estimates or adjustments have to be made. In the presence of extensive extrapolations, and unobservable data, a fair value is referred to as a Level 3 estimate. For example, if a discounted present value model is used that incorporates many internal estimates, the use of estimated *unobservable data* makes the resulting fair value a Level 3 estimate.

The following extracts from the 31 December 2014 financial statements of Brookfield Asset Management Inc. define the three fair value levels, show the portion of financial instruments valued at each level, and provide additional disclosure for Level 2 and Level 3 investments.

Partial Extract from Note 2—Significant Accounting Policies

i) Fair Value Measurement

Fair value is the price that would be received to sell an asset or paid to transfer a liability in an orderly transaction between market participants at the measurement date, regardless of whether that price is directly observable or estimated using another valuation technique. In estimating the fair value of an asset or a liability, the company takes into account the characteristics of the asset or liability if market participants would take those characteristics into account when pricing the asset or liability at the measurement date.

Fair value measurement is disaggregated into three hierarchical levels: Level 1, 2 or 3. Fair value hierarchical levels are directly based on the degree to which the inputs to the fair value measurement are observable. The levels are as follows:

Level 1 – Inputs are unadjusted, quoted prices in active markets for identical assets or liabilities at the measurement date.

Level 2 – Inputs (other than quoted prices included in Level 1) are either directly or indirectly observable for the asset or liability through correlation with market data at the measurement date and for the duration of the asset's or liability's anticipated life.

Level 3 – Inputs are unobservable and reflect management's best estimate of what market participants would use in pricing the asset or liability at the measurement date. Consideration is given to the risk inherent in the valuation technique and the risk inherent in the inputs in determining the estimate.

Further information on fair value measurements is available in Notes 6, 11, 12 and 13.

Partial Extract from Note 6—Fair Value of Financial Instruments

Fair Value Hierarchy Levels

Assets and liabilities measured at fair value on a recurring basis include $3,627 million (2013 – $2,729 million) of financial assets and $1,429 million (2013 – $1,089 million) of financial liabilities which are measured at fair value using unobservable valuation inputs or based on management's best estimates. The following table categorizes financial assets and liabilities, which are carried at fair value, based upon the fair value hierarchy levels:

(MILLIONS)	Dec. 31, 2014			Dec. 31, 2013		
	Level 1	Level 2	Level 3	Level 1	Level 2	Level 3
Financial assets						
Other financial assets						
Government bonds	$ 28	$ 69	$ —	$ 41	$ 138	$ —
Corporate bonds	768	159	—	20	299	—
Fixed income securities	57	39	773	44	55	113
Common shares and warrants	765	5	2,695	838	1	1.919
Loans and notes receivables	—	37	12	—	23	8
Accounts receivable and other	—	1,222	147	131	343	689
	$ 1,618	$ 1,531	$ 3,627	$ 1,074	$ 859	$ 2,729
Financial liabilities						
Accounts payable and other	$ —	$ 1,830	$ 92	$ 117	$ 1.046	$ 142
Subsidiary equity obligations	—	86	1,337	—	139	947
	$ —	$ 1,916	$ 1,429	$ 117	$ 1,185	$ 1,089

There were no transfers between Level 1, Level 2 and Level 3 in 2014 or 2013.

Fair values for financial instruments are determined by reference to quoted bid or ask prices, as appropriate. Where bid and ask prices are unavailable, the closing price of the most recent transaction of that instrument is used. In the absence of an active market, fair values are determined based on prevailing market rates for instruments with similar characteristics and risk profiles or internal or external valuation models, such as option pricing models and discounted cash flow analysis, using observable market inputs.

Level 2 financial assets and financial liabilities include foreign currency forward contracts, interest rate swap agreements, energy derivatives, and redeemable fund units.

The following table summarizes the valuation techniques and key inputs used in the fair value measurement of Level 2 financial instruments:

(MILLIONS) Type of asset/liability	Carrying value Dec. 31, 2014	Valuation technique(s) and key input(s)
Derivative assets/ Derivative liabilities (accounts receivable/ payable)	$ 1,222/ (1,830)	Foreign currency forward contracts – discounted cash flow model – forward exchange rates (from observable forward exchange rates at the end of the reporting period) and discounted at credit adjusted rate
		Interest rate contracts – discounted cash flow model – forward interest rates (from observable yield curves) and applicable credit spreads discounted at a credit adjusted rate
		Energy derivatives – quoted market prices, or in their absence internal valuation models corroborated with observable market data
Redeemable fund units (subsidiary equity obligations)	86	Aggregated market prices of underlying investments
Other financial assets	309	Valuation models based on observable market data

Fair values determined using valuation models (Level 3 financial assets and liabilities) require the use of unobservable inputs, including assumptions concerning the amount and timing of estimated future cash flows and discount rates. In determining those unobservable inputs, the company uses observable external market inputs such as interest rate yield curves, currency rates, and price and rate volatilities, as applicable, to develop assumptions regarding those unobservable inputs.

The following table summarizes the valuation techniques and significant unobservable inputs used in the fair value measurement Level 3 financial instruments:

(MILLIONS) Type of asset /liability	Carrying value Dec. 31, 2014	Valuation technique(s)	Significant unobservable input(s)	Relationship of unobservable input(s) to fair value
Fixed income securities	$ 773	Discounted cash flows	• Future cash flows	• Increases (decreases) in future cash flows increase (decrease) fair value
			• Discount rate	• Increases (decreases) in discount rate decrease (increase) fair value
Investment in common shares	1,297	Net asset valuation	• Forward exchange rates (from observable forward exchange rates at the end of the reporting period)	• Increases (decreases) in the forward exchange rate increase (decrease) fair value
			• Discount rate	• Increases (decreases) in discount rate decrease (increase) fair value
Warrants	1,398	Black-Scholes model	• Volatility	• Increases (decreases) in volatility increase (decrease) fair value

Limited-life funds (subsidiary equity obligations)	1,337	Discounted cash flows	• Future cash flows	• Increases (decreases) in future cash flows increase (decrease) fair value
			• Discount rate	• Increases (decreases) in discount rate decrease (increase) fair value
			• Terminal capitalization rate	• Increases (decreases) in terminal capitalization rate decrease (increase) fair value
			• Investment horizon	• Increases (decreases) in the investment horizon increase (decrease) fair value
Derivative assets/ Derivative liabilities (accounts receiveable/ payable)	147/(92)	Discounted cash flows	• Future cash flows	• Increases (decreases) in future cash flows increase (decrease) fair value
			• Forward exchange rates (from observable forward exchange rates at the end of the reporting period)	• Increases (decreases) in the forward exchange rate increase

		(decrease) fair value
	• Discount rate	• Increases (decreases) in discount rate decrease (increase) fair value

Further information on fair-value measurements is available in Notes 6, 11, 12 and 13.

Source: Brookfield Asset Management Inc., 2014, Audited Annual Financial Statements, page 92 and pages 111–112 , www.sedar.com, posted 27 March, 2015.

Fair Value Not Determinable

Fair value may not be determinable when there is no active market for the financial instrument *and valuation models are not considered to be accurate*. This might happen if there were a broad range of values, suggested by different techniques, or no reasonable reference transactions. This should not be a common situation. In these rare circumstances, the standard suggests that *cost be treated as though it were fair value*. Essentially, this means that the original cost of the investment is assumed to be fair value until a fair value can be determined.

The danger with this valuation approach is that fair value might be lower than cost, with the result that the asset is overvalued. Guidance is accordingly provided to help identify the conditions under which cost would not be a reasonable approximation of fair value. Usually, these are circumstances under which fair value is lower than cost. The investor is expected to consider a broad range of information that is available about the investee. Such information might include the performance of the investee in comparison with budget, technological risks, the health of the economy in general, the performance of competitors, any evidence of financial distress apparent in transactions with third parties, and any evidence of internal fraud or external litigation.

Fair Value in Distressed Markets

Through turbulent financial markets in 2007 and 2008, large financial institutions, particularly in the United States, recognized significant losses when they wrote down investments consisting of mortgage-backed securities. One issue was how to measure *fair value* for these investments. Some institutions might have been forced to "dump" comparable securities at short notice and at artificially low prices because of their internal financial constraints. These *actual transactions* then created reference prices for portfolios of investments in all financial markets and all companies.

Some claimed that these fair values were not realistic and that the reference prices forced writedowns that further exacerbated financial constraints.

As a result of these concerns, standard setters were put under considerable pressure to suspend the requirements for fair value accounting for these assets. The U.S. Financial Accounting Standards Board (FASB) not only made some concessions for U.S. financial institutions but also provided further guidance on measurement of fair value where markets were "not orderly." The changes were greeted with relief by some but triggered loud dismay from others, who consider fair values highly informative.

Other Issues—Investments Made in a Foreign Currency

Often, an investor will purchase equity or bond instruments that are priced in a foreign currency. The purchase price must be converted into Canadian dollars for recording on the Canadian investor's books and reporting in the investor's financial statements. To record the purchase, the exchange rate on the date of purchase is used.

Shares

For example, assume that LeBlanc Ltd. purchases an FVTPL investment, 20,000 shares of AllAm Inc., a U.S. corporation. The purchase price is US$65 per share, for a total of US$1,300,000. At the time of the purchase, the U.S. dollar is worth Cdn$1.07. The purchase would be recorded in Canadian dollars as follows:

Investment in AllAm Inc.	1,391,000	
Cash (US$1,300,000 × Cdn$1.07)		1,391,000

This entry establishes the cost of the investment to LeBlanc and will be the carrying value of the investment. Next year, if the fair value is US$68 per share and the exchange rate is $1.10, the fair value is a total of $1,496,000 (20,000 shares × $68 × $1.10). *No attempt is made to segregate the foreign exchange impact.* The entry to revalue the investment:

Investment in AllAm Inc. ($1,496,000 − $1,391,000)	105,000	
Investment revenue: Unrealized holding gain: AllAm shares		105,000

If this investment were FVOCI-Equity, the entire $105,000 revaluation amount would be recorded in OCI and the equity account, AOCI. Again, there is no separate treatment for the exchange gain or loss.

Bonds

An investment in foreign currency–denominated *bonds* must be restated at each reporting date to the equivalent amount in Canadian dollars, using the exchange rate at the reporting date (known as the spot rate). For all bond investments, *the exchange gain or loss is included in earnings as a separate element.*

For example, assume that LeBlanc Ltd. purchases an FVTPL investment, a U.S. $1,000,000 bond at par, when the U.S. dollar is worth Cdn$1.07. The purchase would be recorded:

Investment in bonds	1,070,000	
Cash (US$1,000,000 × Cdn$1.07)		1,070,000

At the end of Year 2, if the fair value is 102 and the exchange rate is $1.10, *both factors must be separately acknowledged in the entry.* Overall, the bond must be revalued to Cdn$1,122,000 (US$1,000,000 × Cdn$1.10 × 102). However, the exchange gain on the carrying value is $30,000. This is the newly translated par value, or $1,100,000 (US$1,000,000 × Cdn$1.10) versus the existing book value of $1,070,000. Then, there is a *holding gain* measured as the difference between the $1,100,000 versus fair value of $1,122,000:

Investment in bonds (Cdn$1,122,000 − Cdn$1,070,000)	52,000	
Foreign exchange gain (US$1,000,000 × (Cdn$1.10 − Cdn$1.07))		30,000
Investment revenue: Unrealized holding gain: bonds (Cdn$1,122,000 − Cdn$1,100,000)		22,000

That is, the bond is first adjusted to the current exchange rate, which creates an exchange gain or loss *in earnings*. Second, the bond is adjusted to fair value, which creates an unrealized holding gain, also included in earnings. *This is different than the investment in shares scenario*, where both the change in the exchange rate *and* the change in fair value create investment revenue. The distinction is important for classification but does not change reported earnings, since both gains are included in income for FVTPL investments.

For bonds classified as AC, the exchange gain or loss is calculated on the carrying amount (amortized cost) of the bond. The exchange gain or loss is reported in net earnings.

For bonds classified as FVOCI-Bonds, the exchange gain or loss on the amortized amount is recognized in profit or loss, and any other change to fair value is recognized in OCI.

CATEGORIES AND CLASSIFICATION CRITERIA FOR STRATEGIC INVESTMENTS

Overview of Alternatives for Strategic Investments

As shown in Exhibit 11-10, an investment in common shares for strategic purposes may be a subsidiary, an associate, or a joint arrangement.

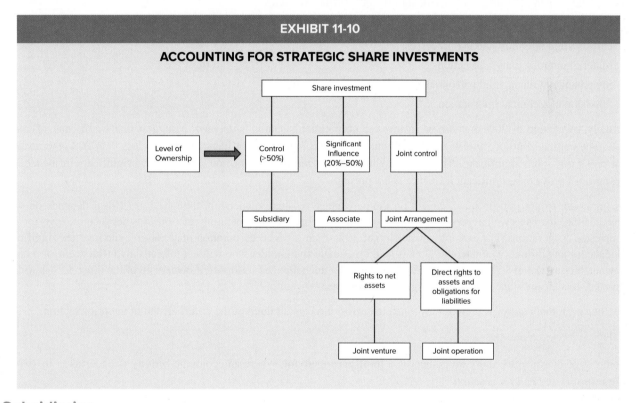

EXHIBIT 11-10

ACCOUNTING FOR STRATEGIC SHARE INVESTMENTS

Subsidiaries

A **subsidiary company** exists when the investor (**parent company**) has **control** over the investee. Control exists when the investor has:

1. Power over the investee; *and*
2. Exposure, or rights, to variable returns; *and*
3. The ability to use its power to affect the amount of the returns.

Percentage share ownership is a primary input to this decision, and control *should* exist if an investor owns a simple majority of voting shares, or 50% plus one vote, since this should establish the right to elect the majority of the board of directors. Control might exist with less than 50% of the shares if the investor has the practical ability to unilaterally direct the activities that affect investment return. Other indications of a subsidiary might be the power to elect or remove a majority of the board of directors or the ability to appoint or approve the investee's key management personnel.

Many corporations are "run" by a major shareholder who owns the largest single block of shares, perhaps because other shareholders are not active. If the block of shares owned by the major shareholder is less than 50% of the voting shares, then *accounting control* must be assessed, based on the facts of the situation. Could the other shareholders realistically gather enough power (through the support of enough voting shareholders) to control the company? If that scenario is far-fetched (all other shares are widely held by diverse and unorganized investors), then control may exist for the major shareholder. In other cases (shares are held by a small group of related investors who could easily cooperate to outvote the major shareholder), there is no control by that major shareholder. Control does not have to be exercised to exist, though: If a shareholder has voting control but has never exercised it, the shareholder still has control. The real test is if the investor could exercise control if desired, and a majority of voting shares confers this right.

Investment in Associates

An **associate** company exists when the investor company has the ability to exercise significant influence over the company. **Significant influence** is defined as the power to participate in financial and operating policy decisions of the investee, even though the investor does not control the investee. Significant influence can be obtained through several means and not just by equity investment. Possible evidence of significant influence includes:

- Representation on the board of directors;
- Participation in policy-making processes;
- Material intercompany transactions;
- Interchange of managerial personnel; or
- Provision of technical information.

Normally, ownership of 20% or more of an investee corporation's shares is deemed to suggest that significant influence exists. The burden of proof shifts at this line: If an investor *has* significant influence and owns less than 20%, the investor must prove *why* it has significant influence. If the investor has more than 20% and does *not* have significant influence, the investor must prove that significant influence *is not* present.

It is important to not put *too* much weight on the percentage of share ownership, though; a great deal depends on who owns the other shares as well as on the other (non-ownership) financial and operating relationships between the investor and the investee corporations. For example, ownership of 30% of an investee corporation may not give the investee significant influence (or any influence) if the other 70% is held by a single shareholder who will not tolerate any influence. Conversely, an ownership interest of 15% may give the investor virtually unchallenged influence if ownership of the other 85% is widely dispersed. It is the substance that matters, not the percentage ownership.

Note, however, that *control* is present only when the investor meets all three of the criteria listed in the prior section.

Joint Arrangement

Another type of strategic equity investment is a **joint arrangement**, where an economic activity is undertaken by two or more investors and *control is shared*.

Joint arrangements are distinct because of joint control, or *joint decision making*, regardless of ownership percentage. *There must be a contractual arrangement in these circumstances that gives joint control over the operation.* Joint control means that the investors must together agree on key decisions before they are implemented. This feature of joint control means that majority ownership, or even the right to appoint the majority of the board of directors, does not confer control.

Joint arrangements are quite common in mining operations and in oil and gas ventures. The investors all contribute something to exploration activities, and all share in any wealth generated. For example, a small mining company may have exploration rights over a property and agree to work the property with a larger joint arrangement partner. This large investor provides management, working capital, and capital assets in exchange for a certain percentage of the profits. However, key decisions over when and where to explore, when to put the property into commercial production, and so on are subject to *shared control established through a contract.*

Joint arrangements can be joint ventures or joint operations. The legal terms of the arrangement will dictate whether the joint arrangement is a joint venture or a joint operation. A **joint venture** (JV) exists when the investors have rights to *net assets* of the operation—that is, a residual equity (net assets) interest. The equity method (discussed below) is used for reporting joint ventures. A **joint operation** (JO) exists when the investors have *direct rights* to the assets and obligations for the liabilities of the arrangement. An investor in a joint operation includes in its financial statements, the financial statement elements (i.e. assets and liabilities) in which it holds a direct interest.

THE EQUITY METHOD

The equity method presents a radically different approach to measurement of investment revenue and investment valuation.

Equity Method

The **equity method** is used for associate companies and for joint ventures. Under the equity method:

- The original investment is recorded at its acquisition cost; this is initial book value and represents fair value on the purchase date.
- The investor's proportionate share of the investee's earnings (subject to certain adjustments) is recognized as investment revenue and as an increase to the investment account.
- Dividends are recorded as a decrease in the investment account and *not as investment revenue*. This reduces book value of the investment.
- When the investment is sold, the difference between proceeds and book value is recorded as a gain or loss on sale in earnings.

At any point in time, the equity method investment account consists of:

1. The cost of the investment, plus
2. The investor's cumulative share of the investee's adjusted earnings since the investment was made, minus
3. The investor's cumulative share of dividends from the investee since the shares were purchased.

The difference between the investor's share of the investee's earnings and the dividends received (item 2 less 3, above) is called **unremitted earnings** and increases book value above cost.

Illustration

In its simplest form, the equity method requires that the investment account represent the investor's proportionate share of the acquired value of the investee and that the investment revenue represent the investor's proportionate share of the investee's income. Assume, for initial simplicity, that Teck Computer Company (TCC) makes an investment of $100,000 for 40% of the voting shares of RPP Software (RPP) on 1 January 20X1. In 20X1, RPP has earnings of $30,000 and pays dividends totalling $10,000. If the investment is accounted for by the equity method, TCC will make the following two entries at the end of 20X1:

To record TCC's share of RPP's earnings:

Investment in RPP Software	12,000	
Investment revenue: Share of earnings of associate ($30,000 × 40%)		12,000

To record receipt of dividends from RPP:

Cash ($10,000 × 40%)	4,000	
Investment in RPP Software		4,000

Note that dividends from the associate *are not recorded as investment revenue*. Under the equity method, the investor company records its proportionate share of the associate's earnings as investment revenue and increases its investment account by this amount. When the associate pays dividends, its net worth is reduced, and thus the investment account of the investor is reduced. Dividends are viewed as a *disinvestment*, that is, a return of the investment to the investor, rather than a return *on* the investment.

Following the two entries for 20X1, the investment account for RPP will reflect the following:

Investment in RPP Software, at Equity	
Original investment	$ 100,000
Proportionate share of earnings of associate ($30,000 × 40%)	12,000
Dividends received from associate ($10,000 × 40%)	(4,000)
Ending balance	$108,000

Included in earnings:

Investment revenue: Share of earnings of associate	$12,000

The difference between investment revenue and dividends is the amount of earnings accruing to the investor that the associate retained, or the *unremitted earnings* of the associate. This is $8,000 in this example. Thus, the equity-based investment account is equal to the original investment plus the investor's proportionate share of the associate's unremitted earnings. This is also the *cumulative increase in the associate's retained earnings since the investment was made*. However, the $108,000 asset value no longer reflects the cost of the investment. This $108,000 number is not fair value, either, and is difficult to interpret.

Discontinued Operations

If the investee reports earnings from discontinued operations, the investor company must report its proportionate share of these items in earnings separately, in the same way as if they were incurred by the investor company. However, separate disclosure is needed only if they remain material items in earnings of the investor, which is rare.

Other Comprehensive Income

If the associate reports items in other comprehensive income, the investor company must report its proportionate share of these items in OCI separately.

Equity Method Adjustments

The equity method is typically more complex than this simple example. It is usually necessary to make certain adjustments to the amount of investment revenue that is recorded on the investor's books. Two factors must be considered:

1. When an investor company acquires the equity securities of an investee company, it will usually pay more for the securities than their book value because tangible assets are undervalued or intangible assets are present but not recorded. In this situation, the investor's subsequent proportionate share of the investee's earnings must be adjusted to reflect *depreciation of the underlying fair value of the net assets acquired and impairment of goodwill, if any*. Therefore, it is necessary to:
   a. Measure the book value versus the fair value of net identifiable assets acquired;
   b. Compare the proportionate fair value to the price paid; and
   c. Determine the amount of goodwill, if any.

   The fair values of identifiable assets and goodwill are not explicitly recorded under the equity method, but the investor's share of income must be decreased by appropriate depreciation on the fair values of depreciable assets and any writedown caused by an impairment of goodwill.

2. If the investor and the investee have transactions with each other during the year, there may be *unrealized unconfirmed* profits from these transactions recorded in earnings. For example, assume that the investor sold inventory to the investee at a profit of $25,000. If the investee subsequently sold these goods to a third party, then the intercompany sales price is validated, or realized, in this subsequent transaction, and no particular accounting concerns arise. However, if the inventory is still held by the investee, then the profit is *unrealized* and *unconfirmed* through sale to an independent third party. It is not acceptable to recognize an increase in earnings if all that has happened is a sale to a "customer" that the vendor can significantly influence. Therefore, the investment revenue recognized must be adjusted for *unrealized, unconfirmed intercompany profits of both companies*.

Example: Equity Method

On 2 January 20X1, Giant Company purchased 3,600 shares of the 18,000 outstanding common shares of Small Corporation for $300,000 cash. Two Giant Company senior executives were elected to the Small Corp. board of directors. Giant is deemed to be able to exercise significant influence over Small's operating and financial policies, so the equity method of accounting for the investment is appropriate.

Acquisition

Giant records its investment as follows:

Investment in Small, at equity	300,000	
Cash		300,000

Fair Values and Goodwill

The net assets (assets less liabilities, or equity) of Small at 2 January 20X1, and estimated fair values, are as follows:

	Book Value	Fair Value	Difference
Cash and receivables	$ 500,000	$ 500,000	$ 0
Plant and equipment, net (10-year remaining life)	500,000	700,000	200,000
Land	150,000	170,000	20,000
Total assets	$1,150,000	$1,370,000	
Less: liabilities	(150,000)	(150,000)	0
Net assets; also equal to equity	$1,000,000	$1,220,000	$220,000

Giant bought 20% of Small's shareholders' equity, which has a book value of $200,000 ($1,000,000 × 20%); therefore, $200,000 is the proportion of Small book value purchased by Giant. However, Giant paid $300,000 for its 20% interest in Small. The accounting problem is to determine why Giant paid that much and then to account for the acquisition price accordingly. The $100,000 excess paid over net book value is related to fair-value adjustments, and goodwill.

First, each asset and liability is examined to see if book value properly states fair value. To the extent that some assets were undervalued, the $100,000 excess is explained. If there is a remaining unexplained residual, it is attributed to goodwill. This is based on the assumption any excess paid is because there is an unrecorded intangible asset, which promises future cash flow.

The "difference" column above shows the specific assets whose fair value exceeds book value. Giant acquired a portion (20%) of each of these items, including the amount by which fair value exceeds book value.

	Book Value	Fair Value	Difference	20% of Difference
Plant and equipment (10-year remaining life)	$500,000	$700,000	$200,000	$40,000
Land	150,000	170,000	20,000	4,000
Totals			$220,000	$44,000

Giant, then, has acquired a 20% interest in Small at a cost of $300,000, and the items acquired can be represented as follows:

Purchase price (of 20% interest)	$300,000
20% of the net book value of Small ($1,000,000 × .20)	200,000
Excess relating to fair values and goodwill	100,000

20% of difference between fair value and book value:		
Plant and equipment (20% × $200,000)	$40,000	
Land (20% × $20,000)	4,000	44,000
Goodwill		$ 56,000

Thus, $44,000 of the $100,000 excess purchase price that Giant paid can be identified with specific assets. The remaining difference, $56,000, cannot be specifically identified with any asset and therefore represents goodwill. Goodwill is just the "leftover" but should represent positive cash flows expected from the investment. Goodwill can also be computed as follows:

Computation of Goodwill Purchased by Giant Company		
Purchase price (of 20% interest)		$300,000
Fair value of identifiable assets	$1,370,000	
Less: Fair value of liabilities	(150,000)	
Total	$1,220,000	
Fair value of 20% of identifiable net assets acquired: ($1,220,000 × 20%)		(244,000)
Goodwill		$ 56,000

Subsequent Depreciation

The equity method requires that Giant record its initial $300,000 investment in Small in one investment account, despite the fact that it has many components. No formal recognition is given to the various component parts of the investment. However, the amount of investment revenue recognized annually will be changed as a result of these components.

When Small uses or disposes of any of the fair-valued elements, either in the normal course of business or by asset sale, Giant must record appropriate adjustments to its investment account through the annual entry that recognizes investment revenue. For example, depreciation is too low with reference to fair value. If the plant and equipment has a remaining useful life of 10 years and Small uses straight-line depreciation, Giant needs to increase the depreciation expense for Small by $40,000 divided by 10 years, or $4,000 each year for the next 10 years.

Next, goodwill must be considered. Goodwill is not amortized, but must be evaluated for possible impairment. If there is an impairment, investment revenue must be decreased accordingly. In this example, goodwill has been evaluated for potential impairment, but no writedown is required in 20X1.

No annual adjustment need be made for the excess of fair value over book value for the land. When Small sells the land, an adjustment is then made, showing that the cost of 20% of the land from the Giant perspective is understated by $4,000 on Small's books. Giant's proportionate share of any gain on disposal of the land would be decreased by $4,000.

Unconfirmed Unrealized Profits

In 20X1, Small sold goods to Giant for $46,000, but none has been resold by Giant at year-end. The goods originally cost Small $38,000, and thus Small has recorded an $8,000 profit that has not been confirmed by a transaction with an outside party. Since Giant owns 20% of Small and records only 20% of Small's income, it must eliminate 20% of the gain, or $1,600 of the $8,000 unrealized profit.

Investment Revenue

Giant's revenue from its investment in Small must be calculated with reference to the fair-value items described above. Suppose that for the fiscal year ending 31 December 20X1, Small reports the following:

Net earnings before discontinued operations	$ 73,000
Net earnings from discontinued operations	30,000
Net earnings	$103,000

Cash dividends, paid on 31 December	$ 50,000

Investment revenue is a combination of Giant's share of a variety of items.

Small's net earnings before discontinued operations ($73,000 × 20%)	$14,600
Additional depreciation on plant and equipment fair value ($40,000 ÷ 10)	(4,000)
Elimination of unrealized intercompany profit in inventory ($8,000 × 20%)	(1,600)
Net investment revenue, based on net earnings before discontinued operations	$ 9,000
Giant's share of net earnings from discontinued operations ($30,000 × 20%)	$ 6,000

The investment revenue for 20X1, after all the adjustments, is $9,000 based on net earnings before the discontinued operation and $6,000 of net earnings from discontinued operations. These two items would be shown separately on Giant's statement of comprehensive income.

Investment revenue is a total of $15,000 ($9,000 + $6,000). If no adjustments had been made, Giant would have recorded a total of $20,600 of investment revenue (($73,000 + $30,000) × 20%). This result of the equity method is quite common; less than you might expect is recorded as investment revenue. This happens because the investor very often pays more than book value for its interest in the associate, and the resulting depreciation of fair values reduces earnings. Then, too, intercompany transactions are quite common, and elimination of unrealized profits will also reduce earnings.

Entries

At 31 December, Giant would make the following entries to reflect its interest in the earnings of Small:

Investment in Small, at equity	15,000	
Investment revenue: Share of earnings of associate		9,000
Investment revenue: Share of earnings of associate from discontinued operations		6,000

To record the receipt of cash dividends paid by Small:

Cash ($50,000 × 20%)	10,000	
Investment in Small, at equity		10,000

Balance in Investment Account

After these entries are posted, the balance in the investment account is $305,000.

Beginning balance (acquisition price)	$300,000
Proportionate share of Small's earnings	15,000
Dividends received	(10,000)
Investment account balance, 31 December 20X1	$305,000

The total investment revenue Giant reports from its investment in Small is $15,000. Since Giant received $10,000 of this in the form of cash dividends, the net increase in its investment is the *unremitted earnings* of $5,000.

Unrealized Profit Elimination

The example shown above involved an intercompany unrealized profit that had been recorded by the associate. This is called an **upstream** profit because the transaction went from the bottom of the investment river (the associate) to the top (the investor). Since the investor picks up only its share of the associate's income, it also picks up only a partial, or 20%, elimination of the profit.

Assume instead that the transaction in the Giant example is **downstream**, a sale from the investor to the associate. Again, none of the inventory is sold at year-end. In this case, Giant has recorded, as part of gross profit, an $8,000 amount that has not been confirmed by a sale to an outside party. *No adjustment is made to the investor's sales or gross profit.* Again, investment revenue is reduced by the investor's share of the $8,000 unrealized profit, or $1,600. The rule is that both upstream and downstream profits are *fractionally eliminated* (the investor's share only).

Goodwill Impairment

The procedures for evaluating goodwill for potential impairment were explained in Chapter 10. If goodwill has to be written down, investment revenue is reduced by the amount of the writedown. This may well create an investment loss for the year, and the *investment account* would be reduced as a result. This is the obvious result of a writedown: Assets go down!

CONSOLIDATION

A parent company is required to consolidate its financial statements with those of its subsidiaries when general purpose financial statements are issued. The parent company uses the cost or equity method to account for the investment during the year, but, at the end of the reporting period, must prepare consolidated financial statements for reporting to its shareholders and other financial statement users. Consolidated statements are prepared by combining the separate sets of financial statements into one, which are intended to portray the activities of the whole enterprise. This is an application of *substance over form* because consolidated statements portray the economic entity that exists *in substance* rather than relying on the *legal form* that has been used to organize the activities of an enterprise.

Consolidation is accomplished using the *acquisition method*. The parent and the subsidiary are combined as of the acquisition date. Fair values of the subsidiary's assets are recognized based on this acquisition transaction, including goodwill. Prior results are not combined.

It is important to understand that consolidation *does not happen on any one company's books*. Financial statements from the parent and the subsidiary are imported to a spreadsheet and adjusted, and then the consolidated financial statements are produced.

Consolidation Method

When an investor controls an investee, **consolidation** is required. The parent investor must prepare consolidated statements so that the financial statements reflect the assets, liabilities, revenues, and expenses of the entire economic entity, consisting of the parent and all of its subsidiaries.

When consolidated statements are prepared, the investment account relating to a subsidiary disappears entirely from the statement of financial position. Instead, the subsidiary's assets and liabilities are added to those of the parent and are reported together as a single economic entity. If the parent owns less than 100% of the subsidiary's shares, the equity interest of the minority shareholders is shown as a separate equity account on the parent's consolidated statement of financial position. This is called the **non-controlling interest (NCI)**. In consolidated financial statements, the fair value of the subsidiary's assets is recorded as of the acquisition date and intercompany transactions are eliminated along with other adjustments similar to the equity method described earlier.

Recording versus Reporting

It is very important to make a distinction between the way an investor records investments in its books and the way that the investment is reported in the investor's published financial statements. *Reporting* may involve fair value, equity, or consolidation. *Recording may well be different during the year.*

For example, an investor may account for a strategic investment using the cost method during the year simply because it is the easiest method; this is the investor's *recording method*. When financial statements are prepared, a different *reporting method* (e.g., consolidation) may be required. In that case, the accounts relating to the investment are adjusted by means of a worksheet and/or adjusting entries.

Public companies may prepare nonconsolidated (or separate-entity) statements for specific users, such as their lenders, *as well as* consolidated general purpose statements. Indeed, knowledgeable lenders will insist on seeing a corporation's nonconsolidated statements if they have immediate recourse only to the assets and cash flows of the specific legal entity to which they are making the loan. As well, nonconsolidated statements are essential for income tax purposes because each corporation is taxed separately (with some exceptions), and the corporation's separate-entity financial statements must be attached to the tax return. For nonconsolidated statement purposes, the parent may use cost, the equity method, FVTPL or FVOCI-Equity to account for its investment in a subsidiary.

Cost Method

In the cost method used for equity investments:

- The original investment is recorded at its investment cost. This is book value or carrying value, but it also represents fair value on the purchase date.
- Dividends declared are recorded as investment revenue.
- When an investment is sold, cash increases and the investment decreases. There will be a gain or loss on the sale of shares that is included in earnings.

An example of using the cost method is provided under Accounting Standards for Private Enterprises later in this chapter.

Consolidation Process

Consolidation is mostly an additive process; the financial statements are added together, line by line. Common adjustments include the following:

1. The investment account must be eliminated from the parent company's financial statements, and the corresponding equity accounts must be eliminated from the subsidiary's financial statements. Dividends reported are only those dividends paid by the parent.
2. The net assets of the subsidiary are valued at fair value, not book value, on the date of acquisition. This not only includes all recorded asset and liabilities but also involves valuing elements such as intangible assets that might not be on the subsidiary's books. Most significantly, any goodwill inherent in the purchase price will be recorded. This reflects the fact that the parent has acquired assets, including intangible assets, at fair value.
3. Since fair values are recognized, these values must be depreciated in subsequent years.
4. Goodwill is not amortized. Goodwill is written down if impaired. The impairment test must be done on an annual basis.
5. Any portion of the subsidiary that is consolidated but is owned by a minority (non-controlling) shareholder must be recognized as a separate equity account. The non-controlling interest is assigned a portion of net assets (at fair value at the acquisition date less any subsequent reductions) and a portion of earnings. Two alternative approaches are acceptable to value the non-controlling interest, with the choice focused around goodwill valuation.
6. Intercompany receivables and payables, gains and losses, and revenues and expenses must be eliminated so that the consolidated financial statements reflect only transactions with outsiders.
7. If there are any intercompany unrealized profits at year-end, these must be eliminated so that consolidated earnings are not misstated.

Connection to the Equity Method

The calculations and adjustments that are required for the equity method are also required for consolidation. That is, data must be gathered to establish the fair value of net assets acquired and amount of goodwill. These amounts are recognized and then depreciated or evaluated for impairment. Intercompany unconfirmed profits are eliminated. In consolidation, however, all the different financial statement elements are recognized separately. In the equity method, the net assets are *subsumed in the investment account and the investment revenue line in earnings.*

The exhibit below summarizes the accounting methods used for strategic investments.

EXHIBIT 11-11

ACCOUNTING FOR STRATEGIC INVESTMENTS

Summary of Accounting Methods

Method	Carrying Value	Investment Revenue	Realized Gains and Losses
Equity	Cost plus unremitted earnings to date	Share of investee earnings adjusted for fair-value increments of depreciation and unrealized intercompany profits	Included in earnings; should be rare
Consolidation	Investment account replaced with financial statements elements of investee for reporting	Investment revenue represented through inclusion of investee revenue and expense elements; adjusted for fair-value increments of depreciation and unrealized intercompany profits	Included in earnings or equity and will depend on the proportionate ownership sold

CONCEPT REVIEW

1. An investor owns 40% of the shares of another company. Is this evidence enough to conclude on how the investment should be reported?

2. What adjustments must be made to the investor's share of associate earnings to arrive at equity method investment revenue?

3. Explain what is meant by unrealized profits. Why should they be eliminated when the investor's share of earnings is calculated?

4. Does the balance of the investment account represent fair value if the equity method is used? Explain.

5. Will an investment in a subsidiary (asset) account appear on a set of consolidated financial statements? Explain.

6. Under the equity method, investment revenue is present even if there are no dividends declared. Why is this the case?

RECLASSIFICATION

It happens that circumstances change, and investment classification has to be revisited. *Reclassification should not be common.* Reclassification occurs when the entity's business model for managing the investment has changed. Points to note are as follows:

- Reclassification of AC investments is appropriate only when the objective of the entity's business model for managing the assets is no longer just to receive its cash flows. In these cases, an AC investment could be reclassified as FVOCI-Bond or FVTPL.
- Reclassification of FVOCI-Bond investments is appropriate only when the objective of the entity's business model for managing the assets has changed. In these cases, a FVOCI-Bond investment could be reclassified as AC or FVTPL.
- Classification of a FVOCI-Equity investment may be made only on initial recognition and is irrevocable; transfers to and from this class are not permitted.
- Share investments may move from FVTPL to being strategic investments if control or significant influence is established. Strategic investments may move into FVTPL if control or significant influence is lost.

Reclassifications are primarily driven by the facts of the situation. Sometimes reclassifications are caused by the actions of others; for example, significant influence may be lost if another shareholder becomes dominant. Other times, it is an internal change of business model or intent that changes.

Reclassification of AC or FVOCI-Bond Investments

Reclassification into or out of an AC or a FVOCI-Bond investment portfolio is permitted *only when the objective of the entity's business model for managing those assets has changed.* This type of change would be infrequent. The change would be dictated by senior management in reaction to significant internal or external factors that can be demonstrated to external parties.

One example might be to reclassify an existing portfolio of bonds or loans receivable from FVTPL to AC. Perhaps the portfolio had been held for resale but now is being held to collect the contractual cash flows. The change in business model was dictated because the company acquired the expertise to manage the portfolio internally and changed its strategy accordingly. Alternatively, if an AC bond portfolio is managed not only for cash flows but also for possible sale, then the bond investment would be reclassified out of AC and into FVOCI-Bonds.

Transfer Value

If investments are reclassified, they are transferred to the alternative category at an appropriate value, which is often fair value. For example, if a FVTPL investment is transferred to the associate category, the transfer takes place at the investment's existing carrying value, that is fair value, and the investment is then accounted for using the equity method with fair value as the starting point. A transfer into FVTPL begins with the fair value on the transfer date. Refer to Exhibit 11-12 for examples of reclassification rules.

EXHIBIT 11-12			
EXAMPLES OF RECLASSIFICATION RULES			
Transfer From	**Transfer To**	**Transfer Value**	**Prior Gains and Losses**
Fair value through other comprehensive income – Equity (1)	Transfers not permitted	Transfers not permitted.	—
Amortized cost	FVOCI-Bond	Fair value at reclassification date.	Include cumulative gain or loss to date (fair value less carrying value on date of transfer) in OCI No adjustment for interest revenue or impairment losses
Amortized cost	Fair value through profit or loss	Fair value at reclassification date.	Include cumulative gain or loss to date (fair value less carrying value on date of transfer) in earnings

FVOCI-Bonds	Amortized cost	New amortized cost is fair value at reclassification date plus (minus) accumulated gains (losses) in OCI.	Prior accumulated gains (losses) in OCI are adjusted out of AOCI and do not impact profit or loss. No adjustment for interest revenue or impairment losses.
FVOCI-Bonds	Fair value through profit or loss	Continue to measure at fair value.	Accumulated OCI adjustments are reclassified to profit or loss at reclassification date.
FVTPL	Amortized cost	Fair value at reclassification date is new AC. At this date, the effective interest rate is determined.	
FVTPL	FVOCI-Bonds	Continue to measure at fair value with a new effective interest rate.	
FVTPL	Associate; significant influence established	Existing carrying value (often fair value).	No additional gain or loss recorded; equity method applied to carrying value of investment account as the starting point.

(1) Note: Category open only on initial acquisition of an investment and designation is irrevocable.

DISCLOSURE AND SCF REQUIREMENTS

Current versus Long-Term Investments

Should investments be classified as current or long-term assets in the SFP? The answer will have a significant effect on the current liquidity picture portrayed. An investment is current if it is:

- Classified as a *cash equivalent* (money market financial instruments with an initial term of 90 days or less; see Chapter 5); or
- Expected to be realized during the company's normal operating cycle or within 12 months, or an investment held for trading.

FVTPL investments, FVOCI investments, and AC investments about to mature may all be current. Investments in associates and joint ventures are long-term investments.

Disclosure of Financial Instruments

All AC, FVOCI-Bonds, FVOCI-Equity, and FVTPL investments are financial instruments. Financial instrument disclosure is extensive but should be limited to material areas to avoid overwhelming the financial statement users. The objectives of disclosure are to ensure that information is available to assess the significance of financial instruments for the company's financial position, the nature and extent of risks associated with financial instruments, and how those risks are managed. Some of the disclosures include the following:

1. The important components of each financial statement category (i.e., various types of investments).

2. Information related to value, by category. Methods used to assess fair value and its components must be explained. When a financial instrument has been valued at fair value, detail about the change in fair value is required.

3. Information related to the legal terms of the investments, including maturity dates, interest rates, collateral, and so on.

4. Various revenue and expense amounts and AOCI reserve amounts that must be disclosed separately, including interest revenue, holding gains and losses, and so on.

5. Information on exposure to *credit risk, liquidity risk,* and *market risk,* as appropriate. Objectives, policies, and processes for managing risk must be disclosed. Such disclosure is extensive, and includes both qualitative and quantitative elements.

6. Accounting policy information that is required as a matter of course for all financial statement elements.

Disclosure Example

IFRS 9 was published in 2009, and must be adopted in 2018. It is available for early adoption in the meantime. Refer to Exhibit 11-13, which contains extracts from the 31 December 2014 financial statements of Aston Hill Financial Inc., an early adopter of IFRS 9. Some of its investments are classified as FVTPL and some as FVOCI. At 31 December 2014, the FVTPL investments have fair value estimated through Level 2 approaches.

EXHIBIT 11-13	
FINANCIAL STATEMENT EXTRACTS ASTON HILL FINANCIAL INC.	
Extracts from December 31, 2014 Financial Statements	
Partial extract from the Consolidated Statements of Financial Position:	
	December 31, 2014
Assets	
Current assets	
Cash and cash equivalents	$ 12,209
Trade and other receivables	5,221
Investments at fair value through profit or loss	2,035
Short-term restricted trust units receivable	68
Prepaid expenses	544
	20,077
Property and equipment	996
Prepaid deposits and expenses	1,748
Investments at fair value through other comprehensive income	–
Goodwill	3,946
Intangible assets	67,837
Deferred sales commissions	3,280
Total assets	**$97,884**
Partial extract from Consolidated Statements of Net and Comprehensive Income:	

...

	December 31, 2014
Net income to controlling interest for the year	$ 1,480
Other comprehensive (loss) income ("OCI"):	
Net change in fair value of investments through other comprehensive income (net of tax)	884
Transfer to retained earnings on sale of investments through other comprehensive income (net of tax)	(884)
Other comprehensive (loss) income for the year, net of tax	–
Total comprehensive (loss) income for the year	$ 1,480

5. DETERMINATION OF FAIR VALUES

...

b) Financial assets and liabilities at fair value through profit or loss:

Non-derivative financial assets and liabilities at fair value through profit or loss are classified as, and reported at, fair value through profit or loss. The fair value of a financial instrument is the amount of consideration that would be agreed upon in an arm's length transaction between knowledgeable, willing parties who are under no compulsion to act. The investments held at fair value through profit or loss are valued at each reporting period using the closing price of the reporting period. Any unrealized gains or losses are included in net losses (gains) on investments in net income in the period.

c) Financial assets at fair value through other comprehensive income:

The Company's investment in Journey Energy Inc. ("Journey") was a financial asset reported at fair value through other comprehensive income. The fair value of a financial instrument is the amount of consideration that would be agreed upon in an arm's length transaction between knowledgeable, willing parties who are under no compulsion to act. Estimated fair value was determined on the basis of the expected realizable value of the investments if they were disposed of in an orderly fashion over a reasonable period of time.

The Company used estimation techniques to determine fair value which include using recent arm's length market transactions between knowledgeable, willing parties, if available, reference to the current fair value of another financial instrument that is substantially the same, discounted cash flow analysis, multiple earnings analysis, and reserve based valuations. The investment in Journey was disposed of in June 24, 2014, please refer to note 5(g) for further details.

Comparative figures and references to disclosure notes have been deleted.

Source: Aston Hill Financial Inc., 2014 Annual Financial Statements, pages 4, 5 and 23, www.sedar.com, posted 5 March 2014.

Disclosure of Strategic Investments

There are extensive disclosures relating to strategic investments, that is, associates, subsidiaries, and joint arrangements. The overall objectives of disclosure with respect to strategic investments are to allow financial statements users to evaluate:

- The impact of the investments on financial position, operating results and cash flows; and
- The risks associated with the investments.

There is an extensive array of information required to meet these objectives.

Statement of Cash Flows

Financial instruments that are considered to be *cash equivalents* are included in the definition of cash when the statement of cash flows (SCF) is prepared. Consequently, investments in cash equivalents do not appear on the SCF but instead are included in the cash balance.

For other investments in bond and equity securities, the cash flow impacts occur in three ways:

1. There is a cash outflow when an investment is purchased. The initial cash outflow is reported as an investing activity on the SCF.
2. Cash payments are received by the investor (dividends or interest). This cash flow may be classified in operating activities or investing activities, as we saw in Chapter 5. This is a management choice that must be applied consistently.
3. Cash is received when the investment is sold or is redeemed at maturity. This is an investing cash flow.

When the recorded values of FVOCI investments or FVTPL investments change because of changes in fair value, this is a non-cash event; it does not appear on the statement of cash flows if the direct method is used. If the indirect method is used, gains and losses on FVTPL investments included in earnings are adjusted in operating activities as non-cash amounts. For FVOCI investments, other comprehensive income is affected, and no adjustments are needed to earnings on the SCF.

On sale, the net cash proceeds that the company receives when it sells or redeems an investment security are reported as a positive (inflow) amount in the investing activities section of the SCF. If the indirect method is used, any gain or loss on disposal recognized in profit or loss must be removed from earnings when computing the operating cash flow, since a gain or loss is not cash flow but is merely the difference between the cash proceeds and the investment's carrying value at the time of the sale. Note also that premium or discount amortization in interest revenue on AC investments is a non-cash item and must be included as a reconciliation item in operating activities.

Reporting the periodic cash flows for dividends received on strategic investments presents a somewhat greater challenge. If the investment is being reported on the equity basis, then:

- Cash received as dividends must be reported on the SCF as cash flow in either operating activities or investing activities; and
- The investor's share of the investee's earnings must be removed from earnings when calculating cash flow from operating activities (when using the indirect method).

If the strategic investment gives the investor control over the investee and the parent prepares consolidated statements, the cash flows between the parent and subsidiary are eliminated on consolidation and do not appear on the statement of cash flows at all. A consolidated SCF is prepared.

LOOKING AHEAD

IFRS 9 was issued in 2009 to be effective in 2013, later changed to 2018. Early adoption is allowed, but in the meantime, the classification rules of IAS 39 apply. The following major differences between IAS 39 and IFRS 9 can be highlighted:

1. Certain financial instrument categories have *different names* under the two standards:

Investment Categories	
in IFRS 9	**in IAS 39**
1	Amortized cost	Held-to-maturity
2	Fair-value-through-other-comprehensive-income-Bonds (FVOCI-Bonds)	Available-for-sale

3	Fair-value-through-other-comprehensive income-Equity (FVOCI- Equity)	Available-for-sale
4	Fair-value-through-profit-or-loss (FVTPL)	Fair-value-through-profit-or-loss (FVTPL) (same name)
5	Loans and receivables	Loans and receivables (same name)

2. Investment categories have *different classification criteria* under the two standards; IFRS 9 relies on a *business model* classification for amortized cost and FVOCI-Bond investments, while IAS 39 relies on *positive intent* to hold to maturity. In the fair-value categories, the catch-all is FVTPL under IFRS 9 and is available-for-sale (AFS) for IAS 39. Management designation is required for FVOCI-Equity under IFRS 9, but management designation is the criterion for FVTPL for IAS 39. Remember, though, that an investment in bonds may not be designated as FVOCI-Equity under IFRS 9.

A comparison of the investment classification criteria:

	Investment Classification Criteria	
	IFRS 9	**IAS 39**
1. Amortized cost/ Held-to-maturity	AC investments must meet two tests: • The financial asset must have contractual terms that give rise on specified dates to cash flows that are solely payments of principal and interest on the principal amount. • The asset must be held and managed within a business model whose objective is to hold assets to collect contractual cash flows.	An investment that has a defined maturity date, fixed or determinable payments, and for which there is *positive intent* to hold to maturity.
2. FVOCI-Bonds/Available-for-sale	FVOCI-Bond investments must meet two tests: • The financial asset must have contractual terms that give rise on specified dates to cash flows that are solely payments of principal and interest on the principal amount. • The asset must be held and managed within a	Any investment that is a financial instrument and is not in the other two categories; this is the *catch-all category* of investments.

	business model whose objective is to hold assets to collect contractual cash flows or to sell the asset.	
2. Fair-value through-other-comprehensive-income -Equity/Available-for-sale	An equity investment *designated by management* as fair-value-through-other-comprehensive-income- Equity. Note that: • Only equity investments can be FVOCI-Equity; investments in bonds or loans do not qualify; • The election to classify an investment as FVOCI-Equity must be made when the investment is initially recognized and is irrevocable; and • The investment cannot have been acquired primarily for resale.	Any investment that is a financial instrument and is not in the other two categories; this is the *catch-all category* of investments.
3. Fair-value-through-profit-or-loss	Any investment that is a financial instrument and is not in the other categories; this is the *catch-all category* of investments.	An investment *designated by management* as held for trading; part of a portfolio managed for short-term profit or acquired principally for resale; also certain qualifying financial instruments designated by management as FVTPL.

3. Under IAS 39, the held-to-maturity category is *tainted* if an investment is reclassified out of the category and/or sold prior to maturity. The category is closed as a result of the tainting rule; any other investments in the category are reclassified, and no investments may be classified as held-to-maturity for the two fiscal years after the tainting takes place. *There is no such tainting rule under IFRS 9 in the amortized cost category.*

4. Under IAS 39, when an investment is accounted for as an available-for-sale investment, *OCI amounts are reclassified to earnings when the investment is sold or matures.* Under IFRS 9, FVOCI-Equity category, OCI amounts are *permanently excluded from earnings.* The amounts may be reclassified to another equity account when the investment is sold, but can never be reclassified to earnings. Under IFRS 9, FVOCI-Bonds, OCI amounts are reclassified to earnings on sale of the bond investment.

ACCOUNTING STANDARDS FOR PRIVATE ENTERPRISES

ASPE allows *significantly* different accounting policies for investments compared with IFRS. The accounting policy choice again depends on whether the investment is for passive or for strategic purposes. The definition of passive and strategic investments for ASPE is similar to IFRS.

Passive Investments

Passive investments (i.e., other than strategic investments) are accounted for as follows:

Investment Classification	ASPE	IFRS
Equity securities for which prices are quoted in an active market	Fair value	Classification as FVTPL or FVOCI-Equity
Any other investment, as designated by management; this is irrevocable under ASPE.	Fair value	Classification as AC, FVTPL, or FVOCI-Bonds or FVOCI-Equity
All others	Cost or amortized cost	As above

Essentially, the cost method is permitted, *unless the investment has a fair value established in an active market.* An active market means that the quoted prices for the investment are readily and regularly available. In this case, fair value is both relevant to users and reliably determinable, and therefore it must be reflected in the financial statements. For those investments measured at fair value, unrealized gains and losses are always included in earnings as *there is no other comprehensive income* for private companies and therefore FVOCI is not an option.

Transaction costs incurred at the time of purchase of the investments are expensed only for investments subsequently measured at fair value. For all other investments measured subsequently at cost or amortized cost, the transaction costs are included in the initial cost.

Cost Method for Equity Investments

In the **cost method** used for equity investments:

- The original investment is recorded at its initial investment cost. This is book value or carrying value, but it also represents fair value on the purchase date.
- Transaction costs, such as brokerage fees, are included in acquisition cost and capitalized.
- Dividends declared are recorded as investment revenue.
- When an investment is sold, cash increases and the investment decreases. There will be a gain or loss on the sale of shares that is included in earnings.

Example: Share Investment

To illustrate the cost method for an investment in shares, assume that on 1 November 20X1, Able Company purchases 50,000 shares of Phillips Company common shares for $20 per share. Commissions and legal fees with respect to the purchase are $50,000; these are capitalized.

Note under IFRS, assume that this investment gives Able control of Phillips, and Able will consolidate at year-end. *During the year, however, Able will record the investment using the cost method.*

Acquisition

The entry to record the purchase is as follows:

Investment in Phillips Company common shares	1,050,000	
Cash [(50,000 shares × $20) + $50,000 fees]		1,050,000

Investment Revenue

On 31 December, Phillips declares a dividend of $0.50 per share. The dividend is recorded when declared:

Dividends receivable (50,000 × $0.50)	25,000	
Dividend income		25,000

The dividend is paid on 13 January, and the cash receipt is recorded:

Cash	25,000	
Dividend receivable		25,000

Sale

If the investment is sold, the difference between book value and the selling price, less commissions and other expenses, is recorded as a gain or loss. Assume that the shares of Phillips Company common shares were sold for $2,300,000, less $61,000 of fees and commissions.

Cash ($2,300,000 − $61,000)	2,239,000	
Investment in Phillips Company common shares		1,050,000
Gain on sale of investment		1,189,000

Amortized Cost Method for Bond Investments

Another difference between ASPE and IFRS is found in the application of the amortized cost method. Under ASPE, interest may be recognized using the effective interest rate method (as required by IFRS) or the straight-line method. The straight-line method is demonstrated below.

Example: Straight-Line Method

Using the straight-line method, interest revenue is measured as a constant amount each period. That is, interest revenue is cash received plus the discount amortization, or cash received minus the premium amortization. The investment value changes by the amortization amount, and the investment book value approaches face value at maturity.

Using the same example as used earlier in the chapter, assume that Marcus Corp. purchased Baker Company bonds when the market interest rate was 6%. The Baker bonds had a $500,000 maturity value, paid 5.5% interest semi-annually, and had a five-year life. The fair value is calculated as follows:

Principal $500,000 × (P/F, 3%, 10)	$372,045
Interest $13,750 × (P/A, 3%, 10)	117,290
Fair value (Present value)	$489,335

The straight-line amortization method calculations are illustrated in Exhibit 11-14. Note the following:

- The cash payment, interest revenue, and amortization are constant each period.

- Amortization is obtained by dividing the total discount of $10,665 ($500,000 − $489,335) by 10, which is the number of interest payments.
- Interest revenue is the sum of cash receipts plus amortization, or $13,750 plus $1,067 or $1,066.
- The bond carrying value is increased to par value by the end of the 10-period amortization process.

EXHIBIT 11-14				
STRAIGHT-LINE AMORTIZATION				
Period	**Cash Payment**	**Interest Income**	**Amortization**	**Bond Carrying Value**
0				$489,335
1	$13,750	$14,817	$1,067*	490,402
2	13,750	14,817	1,067	491,469
3	13,750	14,817	1,067	492,536
4	13,750	14,817	1,067	493,603
5	13,750	14,817	1,067	494,670
6	13,750	14,816	1,066	495,736
7	13,750	14,816	1,066	496,802
8	13,750	14,816	1,066	497,868
9	13,750	14,816	1,066	498,934
10	13,750	14,816	1,066	500,000

*($500,000 − $489,335) = $10,665; $10,665/10; rounded

Impairment

Impairment testing and recognition is different under ASPE, which uses the **loss event** approach. Shares accounted for using the cost method and bond investments measured at amortized cost must be regularly evaluated for impairment.

Under ASPE, **impairment** reflects a decline in value below cost that must be recorded in the year. Investments must be reviewed to see if there has been a "loss event," or circumstances that have caused a significant adverse change in the expected timing or amount of future cash flows from the investment. Note that this trigger may result from the combination of circumstances rather than one event. Examples are:

1. Significant financial difficulty of the investee;
2. A breach of contract, such as failure to pay required interest or principal on outstanding debt;
3. Concessions granted by the investor because of financial difficulties;
4. Probable bankruptcy or financial reorganization;
5. Disappearance of an active market for the investment because of financial difficulties;
6. A significant adverse change in the technological, market, economic or legal environment in which the customer or issuer operates; and
7. Adverse national or local economic conditions or adverse changes in industry conditions indicate that there is a decrease in the estimated future cash flows.

If, as a result of this assessment, it is determined that an adverse change in the expected future cash flows has occurred, the carrying amount of the equity or bond investment is reduced to the *highest* of the following three amounts:

- The present value of the cash flows expected discounted using a current market rate of interest for this investment;

- The amount that could be realized if the investment was sold at the balance sheet date;
- In cases where the investment is secured, the amount expected to be realized on exercising rights to the collateral (net of any related costs).

When an impairment loss is recorded, it is measured as the difference between the investment's carrying value and the higher of the above three determined amounts. The carrying amount of the investment can be reduced directly, or an allowance account may be used.

The following is an example of a recognition of an impairment loss.

Example: Impairment Loss

Dionner Inc. owns 2,000 shares in Siqua Inc., a private company, representing a 5% ownership. This investment was purchased in 20X3 for $20,000. It is recorded at cost since there is no quoted price available for these shares. The original investment is recorded at its investment cost of $20,000. This is book value (or carrying value), but it also represents fair value on the purchase date. In late 20X6, Dionner was made aware that Siqua was having financial difficulties due to the introduction of a new competitor's product into its industry and that dividends were now suspended for an indefinite period. At 31 December 20X6, Dionner assessed that this information provided an indication of impairment and that there was an adverse change in the expected future cash flows related to this investment. Dionner determined the following three amounts:

- The present value of the future cash flows expected was $5,000.
- The amount that could be realized on sale of the investment was estimated to be $5,400.
- There is no collateral, so there was nil to be realized for any underlying security.

The highest of these three amounts is $5,400, and accordingly, an impairment loss of $14,600 ($20,000 − $5,400) is recognized as follows:

Impairment loss	14,600	
Investment—Siqua Shares		14,600

Alternatively, an allowance account could be used:

Impairment loss	14,600	
Allowance for impairment: Investment—Siqua Shares		14,600

This impairment loss can be reversed if an event subsequently occurs to indicate a reduction in the impairment previously recognized.

Strategic Investments

For *strategic investments,* the following policies apply:

Investment Classification	ASPE	IFRS
Associate	Cost* or Equity	Equity
Subsidiary	Consolidation or Cost* or Equity	Consolidation
Jointly controlled enterprise	Cost* or Equity	Joint Venture—Equity
Jointly controlled operations or assets	Include share of assets and liabilities	Joint operations—Include share of assets and liabilities
*If share prices are quoted in active markets, cost is not permitted, but fair value is the alternative.		

Note the significant breadth of alternatives allowed for private companies. While private companies can choose the alternative that conforms to IASB standards, ASPE allows major alternatives. This reflects the fact that there are different financial statements users for private companies, and the cost of compliance is high for more complex accounting policies, especially when fair values must be estimated. It is up to each private company to assess its reporting information needs and proceed accordingly.

Joint Arrangements

ASPE recently changed its reporting for joint arrangements, with the new standard to be adopted 1 January 2016. Similar to IFRS, a joint arrangement arises when there is contractual arrangement between two or more investors specifying that control is jointly held by all of the investors. Under ASPE, there are three categories of joint arrangements that determine the appropriate accounting:

- Jointly controlled operations—where each investor uses its own assets for the purpose of the joint arrangement activities. Revenue and expenses of the joint operations are shared by the investors. For this type of investment, the investor recognizes the assets it controls and the liabilities it incurs on its balance sheet. (This is similar to joint operations under IFRS.) The investor's share of revenues and expenses are recognized on its income statement.

- Jointly controlled assets—where investors jointly control and own assets contributed to the joint arrangement or purchased by the joint arrangement. Investors share in the output from these assets and share the costs incurred. For this type of investment, the investor recognizes its share of the assets jointly controlled and the liabilities jointly incurred. The investor's share of revenues and expenses are reported on its income statement.

- Jointly controlled enterprises—where a separate entity is established and each investor owns a share of this enterprise. Each investor has rights to the net assets of the enterprise and is entitled to a share of the net income of the jointly controlled enterprise. Investments where the investor has a right to the net assets are accounted for using either the cost method or the equity method.

Comparison of Equity and Cost Method

Under ASPE, a significant-influence investment may be accounted for using the cost method instead of the equity method. Refer to the Small Company example earlier in this chapter showing the equity method. If Small were accounted for using the cost method, the following entries would be made. The entries are compared to the equity method, side-by-side, for clarity.

Entries	Alternative 1: Cost Method Is Appropriate		Alternative 2: Equity Method Is Appropriate	
a. Entry to date of acquisition:				
Investment in Small	300,000		300,000	
Cash		300,000		300,000
b. Entry at year-end to record earnings reported by Small:	No entry			
Investment in Small			15,000	
Investment revenue, earnings				9,000
Investment revenue, discountinued operations				6,000
c. Entry for a cash dividend:				
Cash	10,000			

Investment revenue	10,000	
Cash		10,000
Investment in Small		10,000
d. Entry to reflect change in fair value	None, unless impairment	None, unless impairment

The two methods are significantly different in how they define investment revenue, whether they recognize underlying net asset fair value and goodwill, treatment of dividends of the associate, and the amount reported for the investment.

Other Differences

Under ASPE, there is no choice for the classification of cash flow from investment revenue. This cash flow must be included in operating activities.

There are a myriad of small differences between ASPE and IFRS, in addition to the major policy differences listed above. For example, under ASPE in the equity method, downstream profits are eliminated *in their entirety*, while under IFRS, such elimination is fractional. And, of course, there are significant differences in the extent and nature of required disclosure.

RELEVANT STANDARDS

CPA Canada Handbook, Part I (IFRS):

- IAS 1, Presentation of Financial Statements
- IAS 21, The Effects of Changes in Foreign Exchange Rates
- IAS 27, Separate Financial Statements
- IAS 28, Investments in Associates and Joint Ventures
- IAS 32, Financial Instruments: Presentation
- IAS 36, Impairment of Assets
- IAS 39, Financial Instruments: Recognition and Measurement
- IFRS 3, Business Combinations
- IFRS 7, Financial Instruments: Disclosure
- IFRS 9, Financial Instruments
- IFRS 10, Consolidated Financial Statements
- IFRS 12, Disclosure of Interests in Other Entities
- IFRS 13, Fair Value Measurement

CPA Canada Handbook, Part II (ASPE):

- Section 1582, Business Combinations
- Section 1590, Subsidiaries
- Section 1600, Consolidated Financial Statements
- Section 1651, Foreign Currency Translation
- Section 3051, Investments
- Section 3056, Interests in Joint Arrangements
- Section 3856, Financial Instruments

SUMMARY OF KEY POINTS

1. Companies invest in the securities of other entities for a variety of reasons, including increasing return on idle funds, managing an active investment portfolio, managing a long-term investment portfolio of loans or equity instruments, creating strategic alliances, and creating appropriate legal vehicles for business activities.

2. Passive bond investments can be classified as amortized cost (AC), fair-value-through-profit-or-loss-bonds (FVOCI-Bond), or fair-value-through-profit-or-loss (FVTPL). Passive equity investments are classified as fair-value-through-profit-or-loss (FVTPL), or an irrevocable election can be made at time of purchase to fair-value-through-other-comprehensive-income-equity (FVOCI-Equity). If the investments are strategic, they are classified as subsidiaries, associates, or joint arrangements.

3. Bond investments are classified as AC only if their cash flows are for principal and interest and they are managed within a business model whose objective is to hold assets to collect contractual cash flows. Bond investments are classified as FVOCI-Bond if their cash flows are for principal and interest only and they are managed within a business model whose objectives are both to collect the contractual cash flows and to sell. In cases where the contractual cash flows represent other than principal and interest return or they are managed with an objective to sell only, these investments are classified as FVTPL.

4. For passive share investments, FVTPL encompasses most investments, and those investments management designates as FVTPL. FVOCI-Equity investments are equity securities designated by management as FVOCI-Equity on initial recognition.

5. Amortized cost investments are recorded at cost and interest revenue is accrued as time passes. Any premium or discount is amortized to income over the life of the investment, using the effective-interest method. Impairment losses for expected credit losses are recognized when credit risk increases. Impairment losses may be reversed when credit risk improves.

6. FVOCI-Bond investments are remeasured at fair value with changes in fair value recognized in OCI. Similar to AC investments, interest revenue is accrued as time passes and any premium or discount is amortized to income over the life of the investment, using the effective-interest method. On sale of the investment, the gains (losses) accumulated in OCI are reclassified to net earnings. Impairment losses for expected credit losses are recognized when credit risk increases. Impairment losses may be reversed when credit risk improves.

7. FVTPL investments are remeasured at fair value at each reporting date. Gains or losses are recognized in earnings. Interest revenue is recognized as time passes and dividends are reported as investment revenue when declared.

8. FVOCI-Equity investments are remeasured to fair value at each reporting date. Gains or losses are recognized in other comprehensive income and accumulated in an equity reserve account (AOCI). These gains and losses may be transferred to another equity account (retained earnings) when realized through sale or may remain in the equity reserve account. Dividends are reported as investment revenue when declared.

9. Strategic equity investments are classified according to the power of the investor within the corporate governance structure of the investee. If the investor controls the investee, the investment is a subsidiary and is consolidated. Consolidation requires combining the financial statements of the parent and the subsidiary at reporting dates. If the investor has some influence but does not have control, the investee is an associate that must be accounted for using the equity method. A joint arrangement is present when power is shared; a joint venture is one that conveys an investment in net assets and is accounted for using the equity method.

10. Under the equity method, the investment is first recorded at cost (initial fair value), but the balance of the investment account changes to reflect the investor's proportionate share of the investee's adjusted earnings less dividends received. Investment revenue includes the investor's share of the investee's profits (or losses) less depreciation of fair values present at acquisition, goodwill impairment, and elimination of unrealized intercompany profits.

11. Certain investments may be reclassified from one category to another. The reclassification generally takes place at fair value, and any gains and losses are subject to specific rules depending on the reclassification category.

12. Investments are classified as current assets if they are a cash equivalent or will be realized in the next year. Otherwise, the investment is long term.

13. Extensive disclosure is needed for investments. Exact disclosures vary, depending on how the investment is classified. The objectives are to provide information on the risks associated with the investments and information regarding the impact/significance of the investments on financial position, operating results, and cash flows.

14. The statement of cash flows reflects cash paid for investments, cash received on sale, and cash received as investment revenue. Investment revenue is either operating or investing, at management's choice. Non-cash items are adjusted in operations when the indirect method of presentation is used.

15. ASPE allows choices for investment accounting. Many investments can be accounted for using the cost method. If investments are equity investments where prices are quoted in an active market, they must be measured at fair value. Strategic investments may be accounted for using the cost, fair value, equity, or consolidation alternatives, depending on the classification and management assessment of reporting objectives.

Key Terms

amortized cost (AC)

associate

cash equivalent

consolidation

control

cost method

credit-impaired

credit losses

discount

downstream

effective-interest method

equity method

expected credit loss approach

expected credit losses

fair value

fair-value method

fair-value-through-other-comprehensive-income-equity (FVOCI-Equity)

fair-value-through-other-comprehensive-income-bonds (FVOCI-Bond)

fair-value-through-profit-or-loss (FVTPL)

holding gains or losses

impairment

joint arrangement (JA)

joint operation (JO)

joint venture (JV)

loss event

non-controlling interest (NCI)

parent company

passive investment

premium

significant influence

straight-line method

strategic investment

subsidiary company

unremitted earnings

upstream

Review Problem 11-1

On 1 January 20X5, Acme Fruit Company has the following investments:

	Net Carrying Value at 1 January 20X5
FVTPL investments:	
Pear (2,000 common shares)	$19,000
Quince (10,000 common shares)	50,000
Cherry (5,000 common shares)	40,000

To date, the company has recognized in earnings a $5,000 holding loss with respect to the Pear shares, a $5,000 holding gain with respect to the Quince shares, and a $2,000 holding gain with respect to the Cherry shares.

The following transactions occur during 20X5:

a. On 1 February 20X5, Acme purchases $30,000 of face amount bonds issued by Plum Inc. for $29,500 plus accrued interest. The bonds have a coupon rate of 8%, pay interest semi-annually on 30 June and 31 December, and mature on 31 December 20X9. The investment is classified as an AC investment.

b. Dividends of $0.75 per share are received on the Pear common shares on 30 May.

c. Interest on the Plum bonds is received on 30 June and 31 December. Total amortization of the discount has been calculated to be $109 in 20X5.

d. On 1 July, the Quince shares are sold for $58,000. The proceeds are used to buy 1,000 Banana Company shares for $40 per share. These shares are classified as FVOCI-Equity.

e. On 1 October, Acme purchased $45,000 of face amount bonds issued by Orange Corp. for $52,130. The bonds have a coupon of 11%, pay interest semi-annually on April 1 and October 1, and mature on 1 October 20X12. The effective interest rate for these bonds is 8%. This investment is classified as FVOCI-Bonds.

f. On 30 November, Pear shares are sold for $21,000.

g. At 31 December, the fair values of the various investments are determined to be as follows:

i. Cherry common	$57,500
ii. Banana common	33,000
iii. Plum bonds (excluding accrued interest)	31,000
iv. Orange bonds (excluding accrued interest)	49,000

h. The Cherry and Banana shares are short-term investments at year-end, while the Plum and Orange bonds are long term.

Required:

1. Prepare the amortization schedule for the Orange bonds for the first two interest payments.

2. What amount of investment revenue or loss, from all sources, is reported in earnings for 20X5?

3. Show the change in other comprehensive income for the year to be included on the SCI, and the cumulative equity reserve account that would be reported on the SFP at the end of 20X5.

4. Show the accounts and amounts related to the investments that are reported as assets at the end of 20X5.

REVIEW PROBLEM 11-1—SOLUTION

1. The amortization schedule for the Orange bonds for the first two interest payments is as follows:

   • The bond carrying value is increased to par value by the end of the 10-period amortization process.

Period	Cash Payment	Interest Income at 4% (8%/2)	Amortization	Bond Carrying Value
1 Oct 20X5				$52,130
1 Apr 20X6	$2,475	$2,085	$390	51,740
1 Oct 20X6	2,475	2,070	405	51,335

2. Investment revenue:

Plum bonds:

Interest: $30,000 × 8% × 11/12	$2,200	
Discount amortization: (given)	109	$ 2,309
Orange bonds: Interest: 2,085 × 3/6		1,043
Pear dividends: 2,000 shares × $0.75		1,500
Holding gain: sale of Quince shares		8,000
Holding gain: sale of Pear shares		2,000
Holding gain: Cherry shares ($57,500 − $40,000)		17,500
Total investment revenue		$32,352

2. Change in other comprehensive income, 20X5:

Holding loss: Investment – FVOCI-E Banana shares ($40,000 − $33,000)	$ 7,000 (dr.)
Holding loss: Investment- FVOCI-B Orange bonds	
($49,000 − ($52,130 − 3/6 (390)))	$ 2,935 (dr.)
Total other comprehensive income	$ 9,935 (dr.)
AOCI: Investments – FVOCI-Equity, 31 December, 20X5	$ 7,000 (dr.)
AOCI: Investments – FVOCI-Bonds, 31 December, 20X5	$ 2,935 (dr.)

3. Investment assets at 31 December 20X5:

Short-term Investments – FVTPL	$57,500
Short-term Investments – FVOCI-Equity	$33,000
Long-term Investments – Amortized cost ($29,500 + $109)	$29,609
Long-term Investments – FVOCI-Bonds	$49,000

CASE 11-1

QUINTER CORP.

Quinter Corp. (QC) was formed in April 20X5 and funded by five shareholders that are public companies. As such, the shareholders are requiring that QC adopt IFRS even though it is a private company. QC was formed to hold a variety of investments. Quinter looks for share and bond investments that are undervalued. Some of the investments are purchased for resale at some future date and others are held to collect cash flows. In its first year of operation, QC made four different investments.

You, the new accountant, have been hired to prepare Quinter's accounting records since prior to this date, accounting information may not have been posted correctly. It is now 5 January 20X6 and Quinter had its first fiscal year-end of 31 December 20X5. You have recently left a meeting with the VP Finance, who is your boss. He has asked you to review the four investments made to date and to prepare a discussion of the choices he is considering for reporting each of these investments. For each investment, discuss the potential impact on the statement of financial position and net profits, along with the impact on the company's ROA (Return on Assets) before income taxes, using the financial information provided. Selected financial data for the forecasted results to 31 December 20X5 has been provided in Exhibit 1. Exhibit 2 summarizes the investments purchased to date.

EXHIBIT 1
SELECTED FINANCIAL INFORMATION

Forecasted amounts to 31 December 20X5

Net earnings before any investment revenue and income taxes	$100,000
Other comprehensive income before any adjustments for investments	nil
Total assets excluding investment assets	$1,000,000

EXHIBIT 2
DETAILS OF INVESTMENTS

1. On 1 July 20X5, purchased $6,000,000 face value bonds of Paper Inc. for $6,634,520. The bonds pay interest at 6% semi-annually. The current market rate for similar bonds at the time of the purchase of the bonds was 4%. The bonds mature on 1 July 20X11. At 31 December 20X5, the bonds had a fair market value of 105. The company is considering whether or not to classify these bonds as AC or FVOCI-Bonds.

2. On 1 August 20X5, purchased $5,000,000 convertible bonds of Book Co. The bonds pay interest at 3% semi-annually and are convertible into 200,000 common shares of Book Co. at a conversion price of $25 per share. The bonds mature in August 20X9. The bonds were purchased for $5,400,000. At 31 December 20X5, these bonds have a market value of $5,700,000.

3. On 30 September 20X5, purchased 40,000 common shares of Wave Corp. for $75.60 each. At 31 December 20X5, the shares were trading at $89.70 each. These shares are held for trading purposes only. Dividends totalling $45,000 were received on December 12, 20X5.

4. On 15 October 20X5, purchased 80,000 preferred shares of Beach Inc. for $55.00 each. The preferred shares have a cumulative annual dividend of $2.50 per share. There were no dividends declared or received during 20X5. At 31 December 20X5, the shares were trading at $52.00 each.

Required:

Prepare the requested report for the VP Finance. He is particularly interested in which classification choices will provide the company with the highest ROA before income taxes. To discuss this, for each investment calculate the closing balance of each investment at 31 December 20X5 and any related income for 20X5 for each alternative discussed. Calculate the ROA for each alternative for each investment. Make a final recommendation.

CASE 11-2

WILD ONES LTD.

In May 20X1, a group of outdoor enthusiasts formed Wild Ones Ltd. (Wild Ones). Wild Ones operates in central Newfoundland and is involved in a variety of outdoor adventure activities. Start-up capital was provided from an inheritance that one of the owners had received and modest savings of the other owners. For the first eight months of operations, co-op students looked after basic financial record keeping. An unaudited balance sheet as of 31 December 20X1 is presented in Exhibit 1.

EXHIBIT 1

WILD ONES LTD.

Balance Sheet, 31 December 20X1

(unaudited)

Assets:	
Cash	$ 4,500
Accounts receivable	42,000
Inventory	84,000
Investment in River Rafters	38,000
Promotional costs	12,000
Total Assets	$180,500
Liabilities:	
Accounts payable	$ 3,200
Loan payable to Regal Bank	9,500
Loan payable to ACOA	150,000
Total Liabilities	$ 162,700
Shareholders' Equity:	
Common shares	$ 2,500
Retained earnings	15,300
Total Equity	$ 17,800
Total Liabilities and Equity	$180,500

It is now 24 January 20X2, and you, an accountant, have just been hired by Wild Ones on a part-time basis to take on financial accounting responsibilities for the company's first fiscal year-end of 30 April 20X2. During its first year of operations, Wild Ones secured financing from the Regal Bank and the Atlantic Canada Opportunities Agency (ACOA), details of which are contained Exhibit 2. The terms of these lending agreements require Wild Ones to prepare its financial statements in accordance with Accounting Standards for Private Enterprises (ASPE) and to have audited financial statements. The firm of Jake and Malachy, public accountants, will be completing the audit of Wild Ones' financial statements.

EXHIBIT 2

WILD ONES LTD.

Events Occurring in the Eight Months Ended 31 December 20X1

1. Shortly after Wild Ones was formed, its owners decided to invest in River Rafters, another privately owned outdoor adventure company operating in central Newfoundland. Wild Ones paid $44,000 in return for 22% of the common shares of River Rafters, a company that has operated in the area for 15 years. The owners of Wild Ones were also given two of the six seats on River Rafter's board of directors.

   Poor weather during 20X1 meant that River Rafters had a particularly unusual and unprofitable year. River Rafter's total net loss for the period of time that Wild Ones has owned shares was $33,000. However, because River Rafters has had such a record of success and has significant cash on hand, it paid its usual dividend to owners this fall. Wild One has recorded its receipt of $6,000 in dividends as a debit to cash and a credit to the asset account, Investment in River Rafters, leaving a balance of $38,000 in the investment account: $44,000 purchase price less $6,000 of dividends received.

2. To gear up for winter operations, in September Wild Ones secured a loan with the Regal Bank. The loan bears interest at 9% and requires end-of-month payments of interest and also a specified principal amount. Wild Ones has made all payments as scheduled. The terms of the loan require Wild Ones to supply the bank with audited financial statements prepared in accordance with ASPE and to not exceed a specified bond-to-equity ratio. If the bond covenant is violated, the loan will become immediately due.

3. On 1 October 20X1, Wild Ones secured $150,000 of financing from the ACOA. The loan requires interest payments of 1% of the loan each 1 October, beginning in 20X2 and going through to 20X5. The principal payment is due in full as one payment of $150,000 at the end of four years (1 October 20X5). Wild One must provide ACOA with audited financial statements prepared in accordance with ASPE within 90 days of its fiscal year-end. No interest has been recorded because none is due at 31 December.

4. The owners tell you that you do not need to make any income tax entries or adjustments at this time.

5. Through the fall, Wild Ones worked on developing a prototype of a new snowshoe design. The company field-tested the prototype with a variety of independent adventure guides in northern Canada. Reviews were favourable, so Wild Ones immediately began manufacturing snowshoes in a rented facility. Sales during December were brisk and profitable. The company has outstanding sales orders for inventory to be delivered in January and is forecasting steady sales through North and South America for at least three years. The co-op student explained that the accounting for this venture was pretty easy. The snowshoe development costs of $81,000 were charged to repairs expense. $12,000 spent on a promotional event in South America in November was capitalized and will be written off over three years of expected sales.

(Judy Cumby, used with permission.)

Wild Ones' owners explain that they want you to analyze the information presented and then:

- Explain the changes you believe are required;
- Prepare any necessary 31 December 20X1 adjusting journal entries; and
- Prepare a revised balance sheet.

Required:

Prepare a report that addresses the requests of the owners.

CASE 11-3

QUINN INC.

Quinn Inc. (QI) was formed in March 20X8 when Devon Goodman, Scott Adams, and Chase Beson pooled their resources and talents to take advantage of a booming economy in Western Canada. The company selected 28 February as the date of its year-end. Beson had been making basic accounting entries for the first 10 months of operation and prepared a draft unaudited statement of financial position as of 31 December 20X8 (Exhibit 1). There is some information provided about the events of the year (Exhibit 2). Beson is entitled to sell his shares in QI to Goodman, based on a multiple of QI's net income for the year ended 28 February 20X9. Goodman now owns 21 shares of QI.

EXHIBIT 1	
QUINN INC.	
Balance Sheet	
31 December	
ASSETS	**Unaudited 20X8**
Cash	$ 7,200
Accounts receivable, net	254,000
Inventory	50,800
Investments	80,000
Investment in Procurement Inc.	375,000
Capital assets, net of depreciation	50,000
TOTAL ASSETS	**$817,000**
LIABILITIES	
Accounts payable	$ 62,900
Loan payable	600,000
	$662,900
SHAREHOLDERS' EQUITY	
Common shares, 41 shares issued	$ 4,100

Reserve: Holding loss	(50,000)
Retained earnings (earnings to date)	200,000
	$154,100
TOTAL ASSETS AND SHAREHOLDERS' EQUITY	**$ 817,000**

QUINN INC.

Events Occurring in the 10 Months Ended 31 December 20X8

1. QI develops and manufactures electronic devices used for personal identification. Operation of the electronic devices depends on two components: the identification cards held by authorized users and a card reader/programming device. If the card reader recognizes the card as legitimate, the cardholder will be granted access (to a building, specific room, etc.). On average, each programming device can process 80 identification cards. QI tells its customers that it will throw in the programming device "for free," but the reality is that the identification cards will not work with any device other than the proprietary technology in QI's programming device.

   QI has sold several sets of electronic cards and programming devices to a number of customers who are quite pleased with the technology's accuracy and speed. However, in mid-December, QI delivered four programming devices and 320 electronic cards to a property management company, SpaceCo Inc. SpaceCo is not satisfied with the programming devices, as there have been a number of access errors. QI loaned SpaceCo some of its demo units until it can get replacement ones manufactured for SpaceCo in March. SpaceCo's personnel are not pleased with the situation and are threatening to not pay the balance of its account when it comes due in early February.

   Beson has recorded journal entries that reflected the sale to SpaceCo:

Unit	Unit Price	Quantity	Total Price
Programming device	$ 0.00	4	$ 0
Electronic cards	$ 543.75	320	$174,000
Total revenue			$174,000

Unit	Unit Cost	Quantity	Total Cost
Programming device	$2,800	4	$ 11,200
Electronic cards	$ 280	320	$ 89,600
Total cost			$100,800

   SpaceCo paid 20% (or $34,800) in cash upfront. QI recorded a receivable for the remaining $139,200.

2. On 1 July, QI paid $300,000 for 40% of the common shares of Procurement Inc., a private company that provides equipment and services to oil exploration companies operating in Alberta. Procurement's business was booming through the summer. In response to falling oil prices and a global credit crunch, many companies started to scale back their oil exploration activities in the fall. However, Procurement's operations were not affected by these factors and the company reported a profit of $75,000 for the six months ended 31 December 20X8. Beson has increased the investment to $375,000 and booked $75,000 investment earnings.

3. QI Inc. decided to take some of its cash and invest it in publicly traded companies to earn short-term profits. On 15 July, QI purchased 5,000 shares of PZQ Ltd., a public company, at $26 per share. Unfortunately, PZQ was hit hard by economic issues and by 31 December 20X8, its shares were trading at $16 per share. Beson recorded the unrealized loss of $50,000 in equity as a reserve.

4. QI did not declare or pay dividends during the year.

It is now 27 January 20X9. Two weeks ago, Goodman hired you, Chen Ngu, an accountant, to be QI's chief financial officer. Goodman has requested a revised statement of financial position as of 31 December 20X8 and revised net earnings for the 10 months ended 31 December 20X8. She also asks that you provide her with journal entries to support adjustments you make to the draft 31 December statement of financial position and earnings figures provided by Beson. She is interested in accounting choices that present QI as a strong company, but she has specified that generally accepted accounting principles must be adopted. QI is not subject to income tax.

Required:

Respond to the requests of Devon Goodman.

(Judy Cumby, used with permission.)

CASE 11-4

NORTHERN ENERGY LTD.

Northern Energy Ltd. (NEL) is a large Canadian private company organized in three operating segments: propane operations, trucking, and mineral explorations. Financial statements have not been audited, and NEL has simply used the cost method for its investments. NEL is now considering issuing bonds in a public offering, which would mean adoption of IFRS. You, an accountant, consulting on reporting issues, have been asked to prepare a report for circulation to the board of directors and shareholders, to help them understand the implications of this potential shift. They specifically wish to understand what financial statement elements might change with revised investment reporting.

Investments reported on the 20X6 statement of financial position:

Investment	Accounting Method	Net Book Value (in thousands)
Nico Investments Ltd., common shares	Cost	$416.3
Canner Ltd., 5% nonvoting preference shares	Cost	174.0
Later Corp., common shares	Cost	675.3
Placement Resources Corp., common shares	Cost	455.2

Trufeld Trucking Ltd., 8% bonds	Cost[*]	266.8
Lu Trucking, common shares	Cost	45.8

*Amortized cost

Additional information is contained in Exhibit 1.

Required

Prepare the report.

EXHIBIT 1

NEL INVESTMENTS

Later Corp., Common Shares

Later Corp. (LC) is a nationwide courier company, whose shares were acquired by NEL in 20X2. NEL purchased 57.4% of the outstanding shares from the founder of LC on his retirement; the remaining shares are owned by management and two family members of the founder. LC had real estate assets that were significantly undervalued in its financial statements, prompting NEL to pay a significant premium over book value for the company.

The LC board of directors consists of 14 members. NEL has the right to appoint eight directors, but to date has nominated only four individuals. The other four slots of NEL are filled by continuing members whom NEL found acceptable.

Nico Investments Ltd.

NEL owns 80% of the common shares of Nico Investments Ltd. (Nico), which manufactures and distributes aluminum wheels. The remaining shares are owned by Frank Nico, the founder. Nico has had persistent challenges with its product and markets and has achieved breakeven results at best since NEL acquired the shares in 20X0, although prospects are positive. Nico reports a deficit on its financial statements but is solvent. Nico has never declared dividends. NEL has guaranteed loans of Nico. Nico has a nine-member board of directors, of which NEL appoints seven members, including the chair, who is Frank Nico. According to the terms of signed shareholder agreements, Mr. Nico can veto certain decisions of the board dealing with operating and financing issues.

Trufeld Trucking Ltd., 8% Bonds

These 8% bonds pay interest semi-annually and mature in 20X14. The par value is $275,000. NEL provided this bond financing to Trufeld, a long-time "friendly" competitor in NEL's trucking business. The two companies often enter joint bids for long-term hauling contracts, and take on freight for the other if overbooked. The bonds are secured against assets in Trufeld's trucking fleet. NEL has one member on the Trufeld board of directors as a result of the bond investment. NEL expects to collect interest and principal on the bond, and will not resell it.

Canner Ltd., 5% Nonvoting Preference Shares

NEL purchased these preferred shares in 20X4, when Canner came to NEL looking for equity financing. NEL purchases product from Canner for its propane operations. Canner is a closely held private company. Money was needed for an expansion, but Canner was unwilling to agree to the terms presented by lenders. Canner is located in a small town, and many of its workers are shareholders and are related through family ties. Canner has a six-member board of directors, and NEL places one member on the board. To date, this has been a positive experience for all concerned, as the Canner board of directors has been receptive to the suggestions of the NEL representative; many improvements and modernization of governance and operations are being considered. Canner pays regular dividends.

Placement Resources Corp., Common Shares

Placement Resources is a mineral exploration company with active exploration going on in Northern Manitoba. NEL owns 10.2% of the common shares. NEL became involved in this company in 20X5, at the suggestion of a major shareholder of NEL. This shareholder owns 14% of NEL and 44% of Placement. After appropriate investigation, NEL purchased a common share interest and has been very pleased with the results. NEL estimates that the shares owned have a current fair value of at least $900 (thousand), although this is an estimate because Placement is traded only over the counter. Placement has had an erratic operating history, with high net income in some years when exploration is successful and losses in other years. In good years, dividend payouts are material. NEL has two members on the 11-member board of directors; the NEL shareholder has four members on the board and is highly influential.

Lu Trucking, Common Shares

The common shares of Lu Trucking represent 24.3% of the voting shares and were purchased in 20X4, when NEL was considering acquiring this rival trucking company. Lu Trucking is a private company. The remaining shareholders of Lu were not enthused about a transfer of ownership. NEL originally had one member on the nine-member board of directors but has ceased to appoint a representative because relations were poor. NEL has attempted to sell these shares several times to other shareholders of Lu, with little success, as they are unable to agree on a price. Lu pays regular, although modest, dividends.

TECHNICAL REVIEW

connect

TR11-1 Amortized Cost; Bond:

On 1 January 20X2, Investor Company purchased $1,000,000 of Operating Corp. 5% bonds, classified as an AC investment. The bonds pay semi-annual interest each 30 June and 31 December. The market interest rate was 6% on the date of purchase. The bonds mature on 30 December 20X11.

Required:

1. Calculate the price paid by Investor.
2. Construct a table that shows interest revenue reported by Investor, and the carrying value of the investment, for the first two interest periods. Use the effective-interest method.
3. Give entries for the first interest payment based on your calculations in requirement 2.

connect

TR11-2 FVOCI-Bond:

On 1 January 20X4, Queen Company purchased $5,000,000 of Sport Corp. 7% bonds, classified as an FVOCI-Bonds investment. The bonds pay semi-annual interest each 30 June and 31 December. The market interest rate was 5% on the date of purchase. The bonds mature on 31 December 20X8.

Required:

1. Calculate the price paid by Queen Company.
2. Construct a table that shows interest revenue reported by Queen, and the carrying value of the investment, for the first two interest periods. Use the effective-interest method.
3. Queen has a June 30 year-end. On June 30, 20X4, the fair value of the investment was $5,240,000. Prepare the journal entries required on June 30 related to this investment.
4. Prepare the journal entry for the second payment of interest received on December 31, 20X4.

connect

TR11-3 FVTPL; Bond:

On 1 January 20X2, Lucky Company purchased $5,000,000 of Fire Corp. 3% bonds, classified as a FVTPL. The bonds pay semi-annual interest each 30 June and 31 December. The market interest rate was 4% on the date of purchase. The bonds mature on 30 December 20X11. At the end of 20X2, the bonds had a fair value of $4,800,000.

Required:

1. Calculate the price paid by Lucky.
2. Give entries for the first year assuming that the investment is classified as FVTPL.

connect

TR11-4 Sale of Bond Classified as FVOCI-Bond:

On 1 January 20X2, Speedy Company purchased $3,000,000 of Wind Corp. 3% bonds, classified as an FVOCI-Bond investment for $2,737,438. The bonds pay semi-annual interest each 30 June and 31 December. The market interest rate was 5% on the date of purchase. The bonds mature on 31 December 20X6. At the end of 20X2, the bonds had a fair value of $2,900,000. On 1 July 20X3, Speedy sold the bonds for $2,950,000.

Required:

1. Construct a table that shows interest revenue reported by Speedy for the first three interest periods. Use the effective-interest method.
2. Give entries for the first year assuming that the investment is classified as FVOCI-Bond.
3. Give entries for the sale of the investment in 20X3.

connect

TR11-5 Impairment—AC Bond:

On 1 July 20X2, King Ltd. purchased $500,000 bonds of Princess Inc. at par. The bonds pay 6% interest annually on June 30. The bonds mature on 30 June 20X9. King has a June 30 year-end. At 30 June 20X3, King assessed that the credit risk of the Princess bonds had significantly increased and that the expected credit losses were estimated to be $22,000.

Required:

1. Prepare journal entries for fiscal 20X3 related to these bonds.
2. At 30 June 20X4, King assessed that the Princess bonds were now credit-impaired due to an adverse change in technology within Princess's industry. The present value of the estimated future cash flows was $425,000. Prepare the journal entries for 20X4.
3. Given the facts in requirement 2, prepare the journal entry to recognize interest revenue for 20X5.

connect

TR11-6 Cost and FVTPL; Shares:

On 30 June 20X2, King Ltd. purchased 10,000 shares of Prince Inc. for $12,000 plus $1,000 in commission. In 20X2, the company received $500 of dividends, and the shares had a fair value of $16,000 at the end of the year. In 20X3, there were no dividends and the shares were sold for $22,000 less a $500 commission.

Required:

1. Prepare journal entries for 20X2 and 20X3:
    a. Assuming King reports under ASPE and has chosen the cost method.
    b. Assuming King reports under IFRS and classified the investment as fair-value-through-profit-or-loss.

connect

TR11-7 FVOCI; Shares:

In 20X1, FYY Ltd. purchased 500 shares of Humor Inc. for $6,000 plus $500 in commission. The shares had a fair value of $19,000 at the end of 20X1, $25,000 at the end of 20X2, and $40,000 at the end of 20X3. In 20X4, the shares were sold for $31,000 less $500 in commission. In each of 20X1, 20X2, and 20X3, dividends of $1,200 were received.

Required:

1. Prepare journal entries for 20X1 to 20X4,
    a. Assuming FYY reports using ASPE and the cost method is used.
    b. Assuming FYY reports using IFRS, and the shares are classified as FVOCI-Equity.

connect

TR11-8 Equity Method:

On 3 January 20X4, Windsor Company purchased 30% of the shares of Brampton for $565,000 cash. Windsor will use the equity method. On this date, Brampton has $2,000,000 of assets, $1,600,000 of liabilities, and $400,000 of equity. Book values reflect fair values except for $800,000 of equipment, which has a five-year life and a fair value of $1,000,000. In 20X4, Brampton pays $30,000 of total dividends and reports earnings of $100,000.

Required:

1. Calculate goodwill on acquisition, and the annual extra depreciation on investee equipment at fair value.
2. Prepare 20X4 journal entries for Windsor Company.
3. At the end of 20X4, what is the balance in the investment account?

connect

TR11-9 Joint Arrangement:

On 3 January 20X5, London Company entered into a joint arrangement with two other investors to develop a gold mine called JDX Gold. Based on the contractual arrangement, London will have rights to the net assets and net income of JDX Gold. London has a 25% interest in JDX Gold. On January 3, 20X5, London contributed $2,500,000 to JDX. Both London and JDX have a December 31 year-end. At 31 December 20X5, JDX reported a net loss of $400,000 and no dividends were declared. For the 20X6 fiscal year-end, JDX reported a net income of $625,000 and dividends of $200,000 were paid.

Required:

1. What type of joint arrangement is this and what is the appropriate accounting method used for this investment?
2. Prepare 20X5 and 20X6 journal entries for London.
3. At the end of 20X5 and 20X6, what is the balance in the investment account? What investment revenue is reported on the Statement of Comprehensive Income (SCI)?

connect

TR11-10 Foreign Exchange:

On 1 July 20X2, a company bought an investment in IBM bonds at par for US$50,000 when the exchange rate was US$1 = Cdn$1.12. The investment is classified as FVTPL. The company paid cash on the acquisition date. At 31 December, the exchange rate was US$1 = Cdn$1.09. The fair value was US$52,000.

Required:

Prepare journal entries to record the purchase of bonds and any adjusting entries at year-end. Disregard any interest accrual.

ASSIGNMENTS

A11-1 Classification:

The following investments are held by investors that are public companies:

a. A $5,000,000 5% publicly traded 10-year bond of Tree Ltd. The bonds are held for short-term capital appreciation, as the investor is expecting interest rates to change.

b. A $4,000,000, 5% publicly traded bond that matures in 10 years. The bond is in a portfolio that is managed with the objective of collecting interest and principal.

c. Common shares of Shrub Ltd., amounting to 30% of the outstanding shares. The remaining shares are equally divided among four other investors. Each investor has two representatives on the 10-member board of directors. All strategic decisions must be unanimously agreed to by the board members.

d. Common shares of Plant Ltd., amounting to 30% of the outstanding shares. The remaining shares are equally divided among 18 other investors. The investor has two seats on the 10-member board of directors.

e. A $4,000,000 4% publicly traded 5-year bond of Maple Inc, The bond is in a portfolio that is managed with the objective of collecting interest and principal or sale.

f. Common shares of Elm Inc., amounting to 5% of the outstanding common shares. Elm is publicly traded. Management wishes gains and losses caused by changes in fair value to bypass earnings.

g. Common shares of Beech Ltd., amounting to 16% of the voting shares. The investor has four members on the 10-member board of directors, and has extensive intercompany transactions with Beech.

h. Common shares of Spruce Corp., amounting to 60% of the common shares of Spruce. The seven-member board of directors consists of four members appointed by the investor.

Required:

How should the investor classify each of the above investments? What accounting method should be used for each?

A11-2 Classification:

For each situation below, indicate how the investment would be classified, and how it would be accounted for. The investor is a public company.

a. Common shares are bought in a public company whose shares are broadly held and widely traded. The company is a supplier of the investor. The investor owns 30% of the voting shares, and puts three people on a 16-member board of directors. The intent is to hold the investment for a considerable period of time because of strategic ties.

b. Twenty-year, fixed rate bonds. Management is holding these bonds with the objective to receive the cash flows. However, management expects interest rates to fall and the price of the bonds to increase significantly over the coming year. If this happens, the investment will be sold.

c. A mining company has been incorporated to develop a mineral reserve. The investor has agreed to contribute equipment and expertise to physically mine the site, in exchange for 55% of the shares and six members on the 10-member board of directors. The remaining shares are held by the company that owned the mineral rights to the property. By contractual arrangement between the two investors, decisions will be made jointly.

d. To invest idle cash, common shares are bought in a large, public company, a tiny fraction of the outstanding common shares. The shares are pledged as collateral against demand bank loans. The fair value of the shares, and market conditions, are regularly evaluated to see if the shares should be held or sold. The investor wishes gains and losses to be excluded from earnings because of volatility.

e. Investment in $8,000,000 of 20-year bonds, part of a portfolio that is held to generate principal and interest cash flows.

f. Common shares are bought in a large public company, whose shares are broadly held and widely traded. The investor owns 5% of the voting shares, sits on the board, and is the largest single shareholder. The fair value of the shares and market conditions are regularly evaluated to see if the shares should be held or sold.

g. Common shares are bought in a small, family-owned business. The investor is the only nonfamily shareholder. The shares constitute 30% of the voting shares, and the investor has one member on an eight-member board of directors, all of the rest of whom are appointed by members of the family investor group. Fair values for the shares are not available as they are rarely sold.

 A11-3 Classification:

Consider the following investment categories:

A. AC investment
B. FVOCI-Bond investment
C. FVTPL investment
D. FVOCI-Equity investment
E. Associate
F. Subsidiary
G. Joint venture

An investor company that is a public company has the following items:

a. SRY Ltd. preferred shares, paying a dividend of $1.25 per share. The shares are not intended to be sold in the near future but are publicly traded.

b. Investment of $10,000,000 in five-year Smith Corp. publicly traded bonds, 8% interest payable semi-annually. The securities will be held as part of a portfolio that is managed for principal and interest cash flows only.

c. Investment in Ng common shares bought with idle cash in expectation that the price per share will rise in the short term. These shares are held for trading purposes.

d. Investment of $2,000,000 in Howard Corp. publicly traded bonds. The securities will be held until the investor needs short-term cash, or until interest rates swing and increase the price of the bonds, whichever comes first. The investor wishes gains and losses to be excluded from earnings because of volatility.

e. Shares in Farmo Company, a supplier. The shares owned amount to 40% of the shares outstanding and allow the investor two seats on the 11-member board of directors and the right to net assets. The other 60% of the shares are owned by the two brothers who started the company. All major decisions must be agreed to unanimously by the three major shareholders.

f. Investment in Goldkam Company, a customer in financial difficulty. The shares owned amount to 15% of the shares outstanding and allow the investor two seats on the 11-member board of directors. The other 85% of the shares are owned by the close-knit family that started the company. Because the investor is a customer, and has provided financing, there is evidence the investor has been influential in board decisions.

g. Shares in Chen Company, a supplier. The shares owned amount to 60% of the shares outstanding and allow the investor six seats on the 11-member board of directors. The investor has never appointed any member of the board because the investor is pleased with the way the company is now run and has been content to be a silent investor.

h. Shares in Kondor Ltd, a customer. The shares owned amount to 5% of the publicly traded shares outstanding. The company has no immediate intention of selling the shares but will do so if the price increases or if the investor needs money for other strategic purposes.

i. Shares in Lin Ltd, a customer. The shares owned amount to 8% of the shares outstanding. Lin is a private company and shares are rarely traded. The company has no immediate intention of selling the shares but will do so if the investment becomes liquid and the shares can be sold at a reasonable price.

Required:

Classify the items above into one of the investment categories, as appropriate. State any assumptions made.

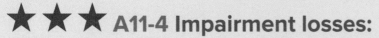 **★ ★ ★ A11-4 Impairment losses:**

Timmins Ltd. owns a number of investments in bonds. Timmins has a 31 December year-end.

Case A $3,000,000 bonds in Lakehead Corp. a publicly traded company. The bonds are currently classified as AC with an amortized cost of $3,250,000 as at December 31 and an effective interest rate of 4%, payable annually on 31 December. At the year-end, the change in credit risk was assessed to be not significant. Expected credit losses are estimated to be $125,000 at the year-end. At the year-end, the fair market value of the bonds is $2,950,000.

Case B $2,000,000 bonds in Guelph Ltd. The bonds are not publicly traded. The bonds are currently classified as FVOCI-Bonds. At the year-end, the amortized cost and carrying amount is $1,890,000 with an effective interest rate of 5% payable annually on 31 December. At the year-end assessment, it was determined that the credit risk of these bonds had changed significantly. Expected credit losses are estimated to be $225,000. The fair value of the bonds is estimated to be $1,530,000 at 31 December.

Case C $7,000,000 bonds in Ajax Corp. The bonds are publicly traded and classified as FVTPL. The bonds pay 3% interest annually on 31 December. The bonds have a current carrying value of $6,750,000 as at December 31. At the year-end assessment, it was determined that the credit risk of these bonds had changed significantly. Expected credit losses are estimated to be $565,000. The fair value of the bonds as at 31 December is $6,122,000.

Required:

In each case, explain the accounting entries required to adjust the value of the investment at 31 December. Also determine the interest income to be recognized the following year.

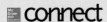

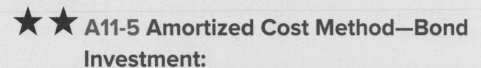 **★ ★ A11-5 Amortized Cost Method—Bond Investment:**

On 1 July 20X8, Sun Company purchased $4,000,000 of Moon Corp. 6.2% bonds, classified as an AC investment. The bonds pay semi-annual interest each 30 June and 31 December. The market interest rate was 6% on the date of purchase. The bonds mature on 30 June 20X13.

Required:

1. Calculate the price paid by Sun Company.

2. Construct a table that shows interest revenue reported by Sun, and the carrying value of the investment, for each interest period for four interest periods. Use the effective-interest method.

3. Give entries for the first two interest periods based on your calculations in requirement 2.

4. How much interest revenue would be reported for the year ended 31 December 20X9? What would the balance of the investment account be at this time?

★ ★ A11-6 FVOCI-Bond Method—Bond Investment:

On 1 June 20X8, Ghana Company purchased $7,000,000 of Monaco Corp. 5.8% bonds, classified as a FVOCI-Bond investment. The bonds pay semi-annual interest each 30 May and 30 November. The market interest rate was 6% on the date of purchase. The bonds mature on 30 May 20X13.

Required:

1. Calculate the price paid by Ghana Company.

2. Construct a table that shows interest revenue reported by Ghana, and the carrying value of the investment, for each interest period for four interest periods. Use the effective-interest method.

3. Give entries for 20X8 and for 20X9, including the year-end accrual, based on your calculations in requirement 2.

4. At the year-end, 31 December 20X8 and 31 December 20X9, the fair value of the bonds was $7,240,000 and $6,755,000 respectively. Give the entries to record the changes in fair value.

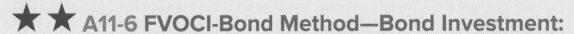

★ ★ A11-7 Amortized Cost Method—Debt Investment:

On 1 July 20X2, New Company purchased $600,000 of Old Corp. 5.5% bonds, classified as an AC investment. The bonds pay semi-annual interest each 30 June and 31 December. The market interest rate was 5% on the date of purchase. The bonds mature on 30 June 20X5.

Required:

1. Calculate the price paid by New Company.

2. Construct a table that shows interest revenue reported by New Company, and the carrying value of the investment, for each interest period to maturity. Use the effective-interest method.

3. Give entries for the first three interest periods based on your calculations in requirement 2.

★ ★ ★ A11-8 Amortized Cost versus FVTPL—Bond Investment:

On 1 January 20X5, Franco Ltd. purchased $400,000 of Gentron Company 5% bonds. The bonds pay semi-annual interest each 30 June and 31 December. The market interest rate was 6% on the date of purchase. The bonds mature on 31 December 20X10.

Required:

1. Calculate the price paid by Franco Ltd.
2. Assume that the bond is classified as an AC investment. Construct a table that shows interest revenue reported by Franco, and the carrying value of the investment, for four interest periods. Use the effective-interest method.
3. Give entries for the first four interest periods based on your calculations in requirement 2.
4. Assume instead that the bond is classified as a FVTPL investment, and the fair value at the end of 20X5 was $385,000, and was $391,500 at the end of 20X6. Give entries for each interest period in 20X5 and 20X6, and adjust the bond to fair value *at the end of each fiscal year*. (That is, the bond is not adjusted to fair value at each interest payment date, just at the reporting date.)
5. Show how the bond would be presented on the statement of financial position at the end of 20X5 and 20X6, if it were (a) AC and (b) FVTPL.

★ ★ ★ A11-9 Amortized Cost versus FVOCI—Bond Investment:

On 1 May 20X7, Bertrum Ltd. purchased $1,000,000 of Fox Corp. 6.2% bonds. The bonds pay semi-annual interest each 1 May and 1 November. The market interest rate was 6% on the date of purchase. The bonds mature on 1 November 20X11.

Required:

1. Calculate the price paid by Bertrum.
2. Construct a table that shows interest revenue reported by Bertrum, and the carrying value of the investment, for each interest period to maturity. Use the effective-interest method.
3. Assuming the bond is classified as AC, prepare the entries for 20X7 and 20X8 for Bertrum, including adjusting entries at the 31 December year-end.
4. Assuming that the bond is classified as AC and that Bertrum sold the bonds on 1 February 20X9, for 99 plus accrued interest. Give the entry to record interest revenue to 1 February, and the entry for the sale.

5. Assume instead that the investment is classified as FVOCI-Bond. Repeat requirements 3 and 4 above and prepare the entries for 20X7, assuming that the fair value of the bond was $1,050,000 on 31 December 20X7 and $1,310,000 on December 31 20X8.

A11-10 FVTPL—Comprehension:

At the end of 20X9, Canfrax Corp. Ltd. reported an unrealized loss on Comet Company shares of $24,600 in earnings. Investments were reported on the statement of financial position as follows:

Long-term assets: investments:	
Star Co. common shares	$1,370,100
Comet Co. common shares	434,700
Shareholders' equity; OCI reserve account:	
Star Co. shares, unrealized gain	$ 150,300

Required:

1. Why are the investments classified as long term? Under what circumstances would they be classified as current?
2. What do the values reported as long-term investments represent? How is this value measured?
3. How have the Star Co. shares been classified? Explain. What criteria must be met for them to be classified in this way? Could the investment have been classified as AC? Explain.
4. Shares were purchased in 20X9. What price would originally have been paid for the Star shares? Comet shares?
5. If the Star shares are sold for $1,500,000, and the Comet shares are sold for $435,000, what gain or loss is included in earnings?

★ ★ A11-11 FVTPL:

On 1 November 20X8, Porter Company acquired the following FVTPL investments:

*   Minto Corp.—2,000 common shares at $15 cash per share
*   Pugwash Corp.—700 preferred shares at $25 cash per share

The annual reporting period ends 31 December. Quoted fair values on 31 December 20X8 were as follows:

*   Minto Corp. common, $12
*   Pugwash Corp. preferred, $27

The following information relates to 20X9:

2 March	Received cash dividends per share as follows: Minto, $2.10; and Pugwash, $1.25.
1 October	Sold 200 shares of Pugwash preferred at $29 per share.
31 December	Fair values were as follows: Minto common, $23, and Pugwash preferred, $26.

Required:

1. Give the entry for Porter to record the purchase of the securities.
2. Give the adjusting entries needed at the end of 20X8.
3. List the amount that would be reported in 20X8 earnings and the asset amounts on the statement of financial position.
4. Give all entries required in 20X9.
5. List the amount that would be reported in 20X9 earnings and the asset amounts on the statement of financial position.
6. Repeat requirement 5, assuming that both the investments were originally designated FVOCI-Equity investments. Include the balance of the AOCI equity reserve for holding gains for the SFP amounts. The holding gain amounts are not reclassified after realization.

★ ★ A11-12 FVTPL:

London Ltd. reported the following transactions and information regarding the shares of Dolma Corp:

- 15 October 20X2, purchased 3,000 shares at $42 per share plus $1,200 commission.
- 1 December 20X2, received $0.50 per share cash dividend.
- 31 December 20X2, fair value is $38 per share.
- 1 December 20X3, received $0.50 per share cash dividend.
- 31 December 20X3, fair value is $45 per share.
- 15 November 20X4, sold 1,000 shares at $41 per share less $450 commission.
- 1 December 20X4, received $0.50 per share cash dividend.
- 31 December 20X4, fair value is $40 per share.

Required:

1. Show the amounts and accounts that would be reported in earnings and the statement of financial position for 20X2, 20X3, and 20X4 if the company uses the:
   a. Cost method.
   b. FVTPL method.
   c. FVOCI-Equity method; realized amounts are transferred to retained earnings.
2. Explain when each of the above methods would be appropriate for this investment.

★ ★ A11-13 FVTPL:

On 30 April 20X2, Marc Company purchased 4,000 shares of Spencer Ltd. for $17 per share plus $400 in commission. In 20X2, the company received a $0.65 per share dividend, and the shares had a fair value of $16 per share at the end of the year. In 20X3, the dividend was $1.05 per share, and the fair value was $20 per share at the end of the year. In 20X4, the shares were sold for $18 per share less a $550 commission.

Required:

1. Show the amounts and accounts that would be reported in earnings and the statement of financial position for 20X2, 20X3, and 20X4 if the company uses the:
   a. Cost method.
   b. FVTPL method.
   c. FVOCI-Equity method; realized amounts are transferred to retained earnings.
2. Explain when each of the above methods would be appropriate for this investment.

★ ★ A11-14 FVTPL:

During 20X2, Morran Company purchased shares in two corporations and bond securities of a third. The share investments are classified as FVOCI-Equity and the bond investment is FVTPL. Transactions in 20X2 include:

a. Purchased 3,000 of the 100,000 common shares outstanding of Front Corp. at $31 per share plus a 4% brokerage fee.
b. Purchased 10,000 of 40,000 outstanding preferred shares (nonvoting) of Ledrow Corp. at $78 per share plus a 3% brokerage fee.
c. Purchased an additional 2,000 common shares of Front Corp. at $35 per share plus a 4% brokerage fee.
d. Purchased $400,000 par value of Container Corp., 9% bonds at 100 (par) plus accrued interest. The purchase is made on 1 November; interest is paid semi-annually on 31 January and 31 July. The bond matures on 31 July 20X7.
e. Received $4 per share cash dividend on the Ledrow Corp. shares.
f. Interest is accrued at the end of 20X2.
g. Fair values at 31 December 20X2: Front shares, $34 per share; Ledrow, $82 per share; Container Corp. bonds, 98.

Required:

1. Give the entries in the accounts of Morran Company for each transaction.
2. Give the items and amounts that would be reported in 20X2 earnings, and all amounts on the statement of financial position.
3. Repeat requirements 1 and 2, assuming that all the investments are FVTPL investments. Note that for FVTPL investments, all acquisition fees are expensed immediately.

★ ★ A11-15 FVTPL:

Cudmore Ltd. had two FVTPL investments at the end of 20X4, disclosed on the SFP as follows:

Kelowna Ltd.	2,000 shares	$ 88,700
Burnaby Corp.	7,200 shares	66,240
		$154,940

By the end of 20X4, unrealized losses of $3,700 related to the Kelowna Ltd. shares and unrealized gains of $15,264 related to the Burnaby Corp. shares had been included in earnings.

During 20X5, Cudmore sold the Kelowna shares after receiving a dividend of $1.30 per share. Cudmore received $82,000 for the shares, less a $1,200 commission. Cudmore also received a dividend of $2 per share on the Burnaby shares, and then sold 2,300 shares for $10.20 per share, less a $700 commission. Cudmore bought 700 Wilton Ltd. shares for $21,000 plus a $630 commission. This is an FVTPL investment.

At the end of the year, the fair value of the Kelowna shares was $84,000, Burnaby shares were $13.58 per share, and Wilton shares had a total fair value of $20,000.

Required:

1. List the items that would be included in 20X5 earnings with respect to the investments.
2. List the items that would appear on the 20X5 statement of financial position with respect to the investments.
3. What criteria would have to be met to show these investments as current assets? Long-term assets?

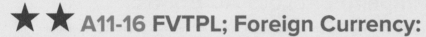 **A11-16 FVTPL; Foreign Currency:**

On 22 May 20X5, Friedland Ltd. purchased 52,000 shares of Gerstan Ltd. for US$13.40 per share, plus US$2,000 in commissions and fees. The shares were purchased from a broker on account, with later cash payment. On 22 May 20X5, the exchange rate was US$1 = Cdn$1.07. The shares were held as a FVTPL investment. The account was settled with the broker on 3 September 20X5, when US$1 = Cdn$1.12.

On 18 June 20X5, Friedland bought a US$1,450,000 six-year bond at par value, when the exchange rate was US$1 = Cdn$1.10. Friedland paid cash on the acquisition date. There was no accrued interest. Management classified this bond as a FVTPL investment.

At 31 December 20X5, Gerstan shares had a quoted fair value of US$15 per share, the bonds were trading at 106, and the exchange rate was US$1 = Cdn$1.05.

Required:

1. Provide the journal entry to record purchase of the bond on 18 June.
2. Provide journal entries to record the acquisition of the Gerstan shares on 22 May, and payment to the broker in September.
3. Provide the 31 December 20X5 adjustment that must be made to reflect fair values and/or exchange rate changes. No interest accrual need be made. Explain the components of the Gerstan adjustment.

 **A11-17 FVTPL; Impairment:**

Lauren Corp. purchased a $728,000 investment in the common shares of Reesh Corp. on 15 May 20X5. The investment is a FVTPL investment. Reesh is a private company and few shares are bought and sold. Lauren was speculating that the value of the Reesh common shares might increase dramatically when a major contract bid was accepted. Unfortunately, the bid was rejected in 20X6, and Lauren management suggested that Reesh shares might be worth only half the price paid. Lauren continued to hold the investment throughout 20X7, waiting for positive developments that would increase share value. There was no re-estimate of fair value in 20X7. The shares were finally sold in 20X8 for $524,300.

Required:

1. Assume that the Reesh Company FVTPL shares are carried at original cost at the end of 20X5. Why might original cost be appropriate? What criteria must be met for a subsequent value lower than cost to be recorded?

2. When the fair value of an investment written down subsequently increases, is the increase in value recorded? Is net income affected? Explain.

3. List the accounts and amounts that would appear in earnings and the statement of financial position for 20X5 to 20X8, inclusive. Assume that the management estimate of fair value was accepted as valid in 20X6. What evidence would be used to establish validity?

4. Repeat requirement 3 assuming that the investment was designated FVOCI-Equity when it was initially acquired.

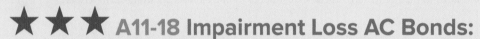

★★★ A11-18 Impairment Loss AC Bonds:

Premium Investments Ltd. bought the following bond investment: $4,000,000 bonds of Trans-BC Operations Ltd.. The bonds were purchased 1 Feb 20X5. Interest at 6% is payable semi-annually on January 31 and July 31. The bonds mature in four years on 31 January 20X9. The current market rate at the time of purchase was 4%. The company has classified these bonds as AC. Premium has a 31 January year-end.

At 31 January 20X6, Premium assessed the credit risk of the Trans-BC bonds to have not changed significantly. They estimated expected credit losses at $65,000.

At the end of 31 January 20X7, the credit risk of Trans-BC bonds was assessed to have changed significantly and the expected credit losses were estimated to be $475,000.

During 20X7, Trans-BC suffered significant losses and contacted Premium about possibly renegotiating its contractual payments. Interest payments were received on July 31 and January 31 as required. Based on discussions with Trans-BC, Premium estimated that future expected cash flows would be as follows: $75,000 paid semi-annually on 31 July and 31 January with a final payment of $3,000,000 on 31 January 31 20X12 as follows:

Period	Cash Payment $
July 31, 20X8	$75,000
Jan 31, 20X9	75,000
July 31, 20X9	75,000
Jan 31, 20X10	75,000
July 31, 20X10	75,000
Jan 31, 20X11	75,000
July 31, 20X11	75,000

Jan 31, 20X12	75,000
Jan 31, 20X12	3,000,000

Required:

1. Calculate the price of Trans-BC bonds paid by Premium. (Round to the nearest 10)

2. Construct a table that shows interest revenue reported by Premium and the carrying value of the investment for each interest period to maturity using the effective interest method.

3. Prepare the journal entries related to the bond for fiscal years 31 January 20X6, 20X7, and 20X8, given the additional information.

4. Prepare the revised amortization schedule based on the revised payments. Prepare the journal entries for the payments received during the fiscal year 31 January 20X9.

 connect

★ ★ A11-19 Equity Method:

On 1 January 20X5, Zan Company purchased 5,000 of the 20,000 outstanding common shares of Woo Computer Corp. (WC) for $120,000 cash. Zan had significant influence as a result of the investment and will use the equity method to account for the investment.

On 1 January 20X5, the statement of financial position of WC showed the following book values (summarized):

Assets not subject to depreciation	$150,000[*]
Assets subject to depreciation (net)	120,000[**]
Liabilities	40,000
Common shares	180,000
Retained earnings	50,000

[*]Fair value, $170,000; difference relates to land.
[**]Fair value, $140,000, estimated remaining life, 5 years.

Assume there is no impairment of goodwill. Additional subsequent data on WC are as follows:

	20X5	20X6
Earnings	$40,000	$65,000
Cash dividends declared and paid	15,000	20,000
Fair value per share	$17	$31

Required:

1. Provide the investor's entries or give the required information for:
   a. Entry at date of acquisition.
   b. Amount of goodwill purchased.
   c. Entries at 31 December 20X5 to recognize investment revenue and dividends.
   d. Entries at 31 December 20X6 to recognize investment revenue and dividends.
2. Are any entries needed to recognize a writedown to fair value at the end of 20X5 or 20X6? Explain.
3. Reconstruct the investment account, showing the opening and closing balances and all changes in the account.
4. How much investment revenue would be reported each year if the cost method was used? What would be the balance in the investment account?

★ ★ A11-20 Equity Method:

On 1 January 20X6, Loffer Ltd. purchased 37% of Ming's common shares for a price of $875,000. The remainder of the shares in Ming are closely held by family members of the founder of the company. Loffer considers this a strategic investment, acquired to get a toehold in a critical consumer goods market. Loffer is a supplier of components to Ming.

On this date, the assets of Ming had a book value of $700,000, liabilities were $200,000, and equity was $500,000. Loffer paid significantly more than book value for its interest because of important patents held by Ming; the fair value of these patents is not recorded on the books. The patents give Ming a distinct competitive advantage, expected to last for at least 10 years before new technologies would develop to provide alternatives for customers. In the meantime, Ming is able to charge premium prices.

Loffer was entitled to place three members on the 11-person board of directors as a result of its investment. Loffer's board members have felt that they were influential throughout 20X6 in strategic decisions. In 20X6, Ming reported earnings of $250,000 and paid dividends of $55,000.

Required:

1. Discuss whether significant influence is present.
2. Assuming that this is an investment in an associate, why is the dividend cash flow not considered the appropriate measure of investment earnings?
3. Will Loffer's share of earnings be calculated as a simple percentage of earnings? Why or why not?
4. What value for the patents is implied by Loffer's purchase price? Why does this impact future earnings?
5. If the investment is accounted for using the equity method, what will be the balance in the investment account at the end of the year? Assume all the excess paid over book value relates to patents and there are no intercompany unconfirmed profits at year-end. Does this balance represent fair value?

★ ★ ★ A11-21 Comprehensive Investments:

Royals Imports is a public company. It reported the following at the end of 20X5:

FVOCI investment, Huebner Co. 20,000 shares ($542,000 cost)		$ 742,000
FVTPL investments		
Adams Co., 28,000 shares	$1,816,000	
Sawicki Co., $150,000 par value, 8% bond, due 31 December 20X7; originally purchased at par	148,000	$ 1,964,000
AC investment		
Duval Co. bonds, $400,000 par value, 9% bond, semi-annual interest; due 30 June 20X8 (the market interest rate was 10% on acquisition)		391,344
Investment in associate, Binod Ltd., 30,000 shares, equity method		2,478,000
Shareholders' equity		
Reserve—unrealized holding gains (re: Huebner Co.)		90,000

The following transactions and events took place in 20X6:

a. Dividends received, Huebner Co, $1.20 per share, Adams Co., $0.80 per share, Binod Ltd., $1.70 per share.

b. Semi-annual interest was received on both bonds on 30 June.

c. Early in July, the Huebner Co. shares were sold for $807,000, and the Adams Co. shares were sold for $63.50 per share. Holding gains and losses in reserves are not reclassified on realization.

d. Three thousand Wong Ltd. shares were acquired for a total of $312,000. This is an FVTPL investment.

e. Royals owns 25% of the voting shares of Binod Ltd. Binod Ltd. reported earnings of $400,000 for 20X6. There was $216,000 of goodwill inherent in the original purchase price, and a fair-value allocation on equipment, on which annual depreciation of $6,800 must be recorded.

f. The Sawicki Co. bond was sold for $142,800 plus accrued interest on 1 November 20X6.

g. Power Co. shares were acquired as a FVTPL investment, 600,000 shares for a total cost of $198,000.

h. Semi-annual interest was received on the Duval Co bond at the end of December.

i. Wong Co. paid a dividend of $0.50 per share.

j. Fair values on 31 December 20X6: Wong Ltd., $99 per share; Power Co., $0.73 per share; Huebner Ltd., $60 per share; Adams Co., $97.

Required:

1. List the accounts and amounts that would appear in earnings. Also calculate the change in accumulated other comprehensive income for the year ended 31 December 20X6.

2. List the accounts and amounts that would appear on the statement of financial position for the year ended 31 December 20X6.

★ A11-22 Consolidation—Explanation:

In 20X1, Pepper Company bought 75% of S Company's common shares, establishing control over the board of directors. Pepper Company used the cost method to account for its investment in S Co. during the year, but prepared consolidated financial statements at the end of the fiscal year, which are shown in summary form:

	Pepper Co.	S Co.	Consolidated
Statement of Financial Position			
Cash	$ 11,000	$ 12,000	$ 23,000
Accounts receivable	22,000	19,000	37,000
Inventory	14,200	9,200	22,400
Capital assets	83,000	64,300	154,000
Investment in S Co.	74,000	—	—
Intangible assets	—	—	4,967
	$204,200	$104,500	$ 241,367
Current liabilities	$ 30,000	$ 9,000	$ 35,000
Long-term liabilities	4,000	2,500	6,500
Non-controlling interest	—	—	25,942
Common shares	100,000	60,000	100,000
Retained earnings	70,200	33,000	73,925
	$204,200	$104,500	$ 241,367
Statement of Earnings and Comprehensive Income			
Sales and other revenue	$ 96,000	$ 63,000	$146,750
Cost of sales	80,500	49,000	120,500
Operating expenses	2,500	4,900	7,533
Net earnings	$ 13,000	$ 9,100	$ 18,717
Non-controlling interest in earnings			1,992
Comprehensive income	$ 13,000	$ 9,100	$ 16,725

Required:

1. Why does the parent company use the cost method during the year?

2. Identify the accounts on the consolidated statements that do not appear on either of the unconsolidated statements. Explain the meaning of each new account.

3. Identify the accounts or amounts that appear on the unconsolidated financial statements that do not carry over to the consolidated amounts. Explain why they have been eliminated.

4. What is the most likely reason that the unconsolidated accounts receivables and current liabilities do not add to the balance shown in the consolidated financial statements?

 A11-23 Reclassification:

On 31 December 20X6, TKB Company's investments in equity securities were as follows:

	Carrying Value	AOCI: Equity Reserve: Holding Gains and Losses (Cumulative)
FVOCI-Equity investment		
Gold Corp., common shares	$763,500	$42,230 loss
FVTPL investment		
MacKinnon Corp., common shares	781,300	
AC investment		
Walsh Ltd. 7% bonds, $300,000 par value	297,000	
Significant-influence investment Orr Ltd.	2,394,000	

Required:

1. Explain what the carrying value for each investment represents.
2. What was the original cost of the FVOCI investment?
3. TKB reclassified the AC investment to a FVTPL investment on this date, when its fair value was $316,000. Explain how the reclassification will be reflected in the financial statements. How is fair value established?
4. TKB reclassifies the Orr common shares as a FVTPL investment when the fair value is $2,519,000. What accounting is required for this reclassification?
5. What is the rule for classifications in and out of the FVOCI-Equity category?

 connect

 A11-24 Statement of Cash Flows:

For each of the following transactions, identify the item(s) that would appear on the statement of cash flows. Assume that the indirect method of presentation is used in the operating activities section, and cash flow from investing revenue is classified in operating activities. Identify the appropriate section (i.e., operating, investing, financing) and whether the item is an inflow or an outflow, or an add-back or deduction in operating activities.

a. Purchased common shares of XTech Ltd. for $130,000, a FVOCI-Equity investment.
b. The common shares in item (a) were revalued to $190,000 fair value at year-end, and $60,000 of unrealized holding gain was recognized in an equity reserve.
c. Guaranteed Investment Certificates (GICs) with a short term were purchased for $250,000, a FVTPL investment that is considered a cash equivalent.

d. The company owns an AC investment of $276,000, a $300,000, eight-year bond bought at a discount in previous years. The bond pays annual interest of 3%, and $6,200 of discount amortization had been recorded in the current year.

e. The company owns 47,000 shares of Apps Co., over which it has significant influence. In the current year, investment revenue of $99,000 was recorded, and cash dividends of $46,000 were received.

f. Common shares of Android Ltd. were purchased for $210,000, a FVTPL investment.

g. The common shares in item (f) were revalued to $175,000 fair value at year-end.

h. The XTech common shares in (a) and (b) were sold for $200,000. A gain of $10,000 was recognized in OCI.

i. The GICs in (c) were sold for $251,000. A gain of $1,000 was recorded.

 A11-25 Statement of Cash Flows:

The following comparative data are available from the 20X4 statement of financial position of Trevor Holdings Ltd:

	20X4	20X3
Current investments:		
FVTPL investments	$ 756,000	$675,000
Long-term investments:		
FVOCI-Equity investments	1,005,000	991,000
Agrium bonds, at amortized cost	551,000	531,300
Investment in Falcon Ltd., at equity	2,011,000	1,649,000
Shareholders' equity:		
Reserves		
Unrealized holding gains	59,300	51,400

In 20X4, the following transactions took place and are properly reflected in the accounts, above.

a. There were no purchases or sales of FVTPL investments during the year.

b. Dividends of $80,000 were received from Falcon Ltd. No shares of Falcon were bought or sold during the year.

c. FVOCI-Equity investments, with a carrying value of $42,800 and cumulative holding gains of $18,000 to date, were sold for $64,400. Holding gains and losses in reserves are not reclassified on sale.

d. FVOCI-Equity investments were purchased during the year.

e. FVTPL and FVOCI-Equity investments were adjusted to fair value at year-end.

Required:

What items would appear on the 20X4 statement of cash flows? Assume the operating section uses the indirect method of presentation. Cash inflow from investment revenue is classified in operating activities.

 A11-26 ASPE—Classification:

Return to the facts of A11-1. Assume now that the investor is a private company that complies with ASPE.

Required:

How should the investor classify each of the investments? What accounting method should be used for each?

 A11-27 ASPE—Classification:

Return to the facts of A11-2. Assume now that the investor is a private company that complies with ASPE.

Required:

How should the investor classify each of the investments? What accounting method should be used for each?

★ ★ **A11-28 ASPE—Amortized Cost Investment:**

Return to the facts of A11-7. Assume now that New Company is a private company that complies with ASPE. Straight-line amortization will be used rather than the effective-interest method.

Required:

1. Calculate the price paid by New Company.
2. Construct a table that shows interest revenue reported by New Company, and the carrying value of the investment, for each interest period to maturity. Use the straight-line method.
3. Give entries for the first three interest periods based on your calculations in requirement 2.

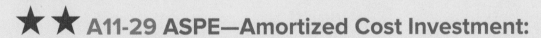

★ ★ **A11-29 ASPE—Amortized Cost Investment:**

On 1 January 20X8, Khalil Ltd. purchased $2,000,000 of six-year, Harvest Ltd. 5.4% bonds. The bonds pay semi-annual interest each 30 June and 31 December. The market interest rate was 6% on the date of purchase. Khalil is a private company that complies with ASPE and uses straight-line amortization.

Required:

1. Calculate the price paid by Khalil Ltd.
2. Construct a table that shows interest revenue reported by Khalil and the carrying value of the investment for four interest periods. Use the straight-line method.
3. Give entries for the first four interest periods based on your calculations in requirement 2.

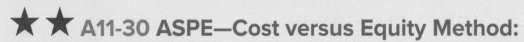

A11-30 ASPE—Cost versus Equity Method:

On 3 January 20X4, TA Company purchased 2,000 shares of the 10,000 outstanding shares of common stock of UK Corp. for $14,600 cash. TA has significant influence as a result of this acquisition. At that date, the statement of financial position of UK Corp. reflected the following:

- Nondepreciable assets, $50,000 (book value is the same as fair value)
- Depreciable assets (net), $30,000 (fair value, $33,000)
- Total liabilities, $20,000 (book value equals fair value)
- Shareholders' equity, $60,000

Assume a 10-year remaining life (straight-line method) for the depreciable assets. Goodwill is not impaired over the time period in question.

Required:

1. Give any required entries for TA's books for each item (a) through (d) below, if applicable, assuming that the cost method is used.
    a. Entry at date of acquisition.
    b. Goodwill purchased—computation only.
    c. Entry on 31 December 20X4 to record $15,000 earnings reported by UK.
    d. Entry on 31 March 20X5 for a cash dividend of $1 per share declared and paid by UK.
2. Repeat requirement 1 above, assuming that the equity method is appropriate.
3. Why might TA use the cost method if it has significant influence?

Fundamentals: The Accounting Information Processing System (AIS)

ACCOUNTS, TRANSACTION RECORDING, AND FINANCIAL STATEMENTS

This Appendix is a review of the mechanics of the accounting information processing system. Transactions and events are recorded in accounts, which describe specific financial statement elements. These elements are reported to investors, creditors, and other interested readers in periodic financial statements.

Accounts

There are eight major types of accounts, grouped under two headings: **permanent accounts** (assets, liabilities, and owners' equity accounts) and **temporary accounts** (revenues, expenses, gains, losses, and dividends). Permanent accounts are also called "**real accounts**," and temporary accounts are also called "**nominal accounts**." The permanent accounts appear on the statement of financial position (SFP). *Temporary* accounts, which are revenues, expenses, gains, and losses, appear on the statement of comprehensive income (SCI) and are closed out at the end of each fiscal year. Dividends are closed directly to retained earnings and reported on the statement of changes in equity.

The **accounting identity** states the relationship between the balances of the permanent accounts:

$$\text{Assets} = \text{Liabilities} + \text{Owners' Equity}$$

Recording Transactions

To maintain the accounting identity, every transaction recorded must affect at least two accounts. This protocol, called the **double-entry system**, records the change in a resource or obligation and the reason for, or source of, the change.

Complementing the double-entry system, the **debit–credit convention** is used as a recording and balancing procedure. This convention divides accounts into two sides. The debit (dr.) side is always the left side, and the credit (cr.) side is always the right side. These terms carry no further meaning and cannot be interpreted as "increases" or "decreases," since, depending on the account type, a debit or a credit can record an increase or decrease to the account balance. This is illustrated in the T-accounts summarized in Exhibit A-1. The **T-account** is a form of account used for demonstrating transactions; its skeletal form takes the shape of the letter T. The T-account reflects the general format of ledger accounts, as we will discuss later.

The debit–credit convention is a convenient way to check for recording errors. When the sums of debits and credits are not equal, an error is evident.

EXHIBIT A-1

DEBIT/CREDIT IMPACT ON T-ACCOUNTS

Permanent Accounts

Assets		=	Liabilities		+	Owners' Equity	
Debit	Credit		Debit	Credit		Debit	Credit
entries	entries		entries	entries		entries	entries
increase	*decrease*		*decrease*	*increase*		*decrease*	*increase*
assets	assets		liabilities	liabilities		owners'	owners'
						equity	equity

Temporary Accounts

Expenses		Revenues		Dividends	
Debit	Credit	Debit	Credit	Debit	Credit
entries	entries	entries	entries	entries	entries
increase	*decrease*	*decrease*	*increase*	*increase*	*decrease*
expenses	expenses	revenues	revenues	dividends	dividends

Losses		Gains	
Debit	Credit	Debit	Credit
entries	entries	entries	entries
increase	*decrease*	*decrease*	*increase*
losses	losses	gains	gains

Financial Statements

At the end of a reporting period, after all transactions and events are recorded in accounts, **financial statements** are prepared. The financial statements report account balances, changes in account balances, and aggregations of account balances, such as earnings and total assets. The financial statements include the *statement of comprehensive income, statement of changes in equity, statement of financial position,* and *statement of cash flows.*

- The statement of comprehensive income (SCI) reports revenues, expenses, gains, and losses and thus shows profit or loss for the year. Items that are specified to be included in other comprehensive income (OCI) are summarized and added to the profit or loss to arrive at comprehensive income.
- Both earnings and other comprehensive income items change equity. The statement of changes in equity shows the opening and closing balances of every equity account for the company, with each change listed separately.
- The statement of financial position (SFP) reports assets, liabilities, and owners' equity. This statement is commonly called a *balance sheet*; the terms are used interchangeably in this text.
- The statement of cash flows (SCF) lists sources and uses of cash.

The steps leading to these financial statements are discussed in the rest of this Appendix.

The AIS and the Accounting Cycle

An **accounting information system** (AIS) is designed to record accurate financial data in a timely and chronological manner, facilitate retrieval of financial data in a form useful to management, and simplify periodic preparation of financial statements for external use. The design of the AIS, to meet the company's information requirements, depends on the firm's size, the nature of its operations, the volume of data, its organizational structure, and government regulation.

The accounting cycle, illustrated in Exhibit A-2, is a series of sequential steps leading to the financial statements. This cycle is repeated each reporting period, normally a year. Companies may combine some of these steps or change their order to suit their specific needs. Depending on the information-processing technology used, certain accounting cycle steps can be combined or in some cases omitted. Most accounting systems are computerized, in whole or in part. The fundamental nature of the process, however, is the same regardless of the technology used.

EXHIBIT A-2

THE ACCOUNTING CYCLE

1. **Identify Transactions or Events to Be Recorded**

   Gather information, generally in the form of source documents, about transactions or events.

2. **Journalize Transactions and Events**

   Identify, assess, and record the economic impact of transactions on the firm in a chronological record (a journal), using journal entries that facilitate transfer to the accounts.

3. **Post from Journal to Ledger**

   Transfer information from the journal to the ledger.

4. **Prepare Unadjusted Trial Balance**

   Provide a convenient listing of ledger accounts to prove debit–credit equality and provide a starting point for adjusting journal entries.

5. **Journalize and Post Adjusting Journal Entries**

   Record accruals, expiration of deferrals, estimations, and other events to ensure the accuracy and completeness of the accounts.

6. **Prepare Adjusted Trial Balance**

   Establish debit–credit equality and simplify preparation of the financial statements.

7. **Prepare Financial Statements**

   Summarize financial information in a form that will be useful to decision makers.

8. **Journalize and Post Closing Entries**

   Close temporary accounts and update retained earnings.

9. **Prepare Post-Closing Trial Balance**

   Establish debit–credit equality after the closing entries.

10. **Journalize and Post Reversing Journal Entries**

    Optional step; simplifies certain subsequent journal entries.

The first three steps in the accounting cycle require the most time and effort. The frequency of posting, Step 3, depends on the volume and nature of transactions and the technology used. For example, on-line systems may update inventory accounts immediately when there is a sale or purchase. Steps 4 through 9 generally occur at the end of the fiscal year. The tenth step, the posting of reversing entries, is optional and occurs at the beginning of the new accounting period.

THE IMPACT OF TECHNOLOGY

Computerized systems have many advantages, including speed and accuracy. The norm is to use a customized or off-the-shelf computer program that will facilitate the following steps in the accounting cycle (refer to Exhibit A-2):

- Journalizing transactions, adjustments, closing, and reversing entries;
- Posting entries;
- Preparing trial balances; and
- Preparing financial statements.

What is left for the accountant to do? First, identification and control of transactions and adjustments is crucial. The accountant manages the entire process, ensuring that information entered is accurate and complete. Second, many elements in financial reporting require the exercise of professional judgement—choice of accounting policy, impairment testing, composition of the notes to the financial statements, and so on. These tasks require qualified decision makers.

Regardless of how the steps in the accounting cycle are performed, they accomplish the same task—posting is manual or computerized. The accountant has to understand this process to manage it.

THE ACCOUNTING CYCLE

The annual accounting cycle includes 10 steps, explained in the following section.

Step 1: Identify Transactions or Events to Be Recorded

The first step is the requirement to identify transactions and events that cause a change in the firm's resources or obligations and to collect relevant economic data about those transactions. Events that change a firm's resources or obligations are categorized into three types:

1. *Exchanges of resources and obligations between the reporting firm and outside parties.* These exchanges are either **reciprocal transfers** or **nonreciprocal transfers**. In a reciprocal transfer, the firm both transfers and receives resources (e.g., sale of goods for cash). In a nonreciprocal transfer, the firm either transfers *or* receives current or future resources (e.g., payment of cash dividends or receipt of a donation). All exchanges require a journal entry.

2. *Internal events within the firm that affect resources or obligations but do not involve outside parties.* Examples are recognition of depreciation of property, plant, and equipment and the use of inventory for production. These events also generally require a journal entry. However, other events, such as increases in the value of the company's brand resulting from superior management and good customer service, are not recorded.

3. *External economic and environmental events beyond the control of the company.* Examples include casualty losses and changes in the fair market value of financial assets and investment properties.

Transactions are events requiring a journal entry. Transactions are often accompanied by a source document, generally a paper record that describes the exchange, the parties involved, the date, and the dollar amount. Examples are sales invoices, freight bills, and cash register receipts. Certain events, such as the accrual of interest, are not signalled by a separate source document. Recording these transactions requires reference to the underlying contract supporting the original exchange of resources. Source documents are essential for the initial recording of transactions in a journal and are also used for subsequent tracing and verification, for evidence in legal proceedings, and for audits of financial statements.

Step 2: Journalize Transactions and Events

Journals

Transactions are recorded chronologically in a **journal**—an organized medium for recording transactions in debit–credit format. A **journal entry** is a debit–credit description of a transaction that includes the date, the accounts and amounts involved, and a brief description. A journal entry is a temporary recording, although journals are retained as part of the audit trail; account balances are not changed until the information is transferred to the ledger accounts in Step 3.

Accounting systems usually have two types of journals: the **general journal** and **special journals**. The general journal has a flexible format and can be used to record any entry. Nonrepetitive entries and entries involving infrequently used accounts are recorded in this journal. To save time and increase accuracy, repetitive entries are recorded in special journals, which have a predetermined, rigid format. If special journals are not used, all transactions are recorded in the general journal. Special journals are discussed later in this Appendix. The general journal is used to illustrate most entries in this text.

The journal entry step is not absolutely essential; transaction data can be recorded directly into the accounts. However, the journal entry step has significant advantages, and it is standard practice to record all transactions first in a journal. Transaction processing is more efficient, and less costly, if transactions are grouped in a journal and processed together. By using journals, review and analysis of transactions is much simpler and the accounts consume less storage space. Also, a chronological list of transactions is provided. Transactions can be difficult to reconstruct without a journal because the debits and credits are located in different accounts. Journals are typically part of the paper trail relied on by auditors. The journal entry also ensures that the debits and credits are balanced prior to posting in the general ledger.

Some companies use computerized systems to bypass the traditional journal entry step. Retailers, for example, record relevant information about a transaction by using bar codes printed on product packages. Optical scanning equipment reads the bar code and the transaction is recorded directly in the relevant ledger accounts.

Exhibit A-3 illustrates an entry in a general journal. This entry records the purchase of equipment financed with cash and debt. Equipment is *debited* and recorded at the value of the resources used to acquire it. The names of the accounts *credited* are listed below and are indented.

EXHIBIT A-3

GENERAL JOURNAL

| | | | Amount | |
| | Accounts and | | | |
Date 20X5	Explanation	Posting Ref.	Debit	Credit
2 Jan.	Equipment	150	15,000	
	Cash	101		5,000
	Notes payable	215		10,000

Purchased equipment for use in the business.

Paid $5,000 cash and gave a $10,000, one-year note with 5% interest payable at maturity.

Step 3: Post from Journal to Ledger

Transferring transaction data from the journal to the ledger is called **posting**. Posting reclassifies the data from the journal's chronological format to an account classification format in the ledger, which is a collection of the formal accounts.

Posting

Exhibit A-4 illustrates a section of a general ledger in T-account form. This ledger depicts three general ledger accounts after posting the journal entry shown in Exhibit A-3. Posting references and page numbers are used in both the journal and the ledger to ensure that an audit trail exists—that is, to indicate where an item in the account ledger came from and to which account the item was posted. Posting references also serve to confirm that an entry was posted.

EXHIBIT A-4				
GENERAL LEDGER (EXCERPTS)				
Cash				Acct. 101
20X5			20X5		
1 Jan.	Balance	18,700	2 Jan.	J-16	5,000
Equipment				Acct. 150
20X5					
1 Jan.	Balance	62,000			
2	J-16	15,000			
Notes Payable				Acct. 215
			20X5		
			2 Jan.	J-16	10,000

When the $5,000 cash credit from the general journal entry of Exhibit A-3 is posted to the cash ledger account, "101" is listed in the journal to indicate the account number *to which* the credit is posted. Similarly, in the cash ledger account, "J-16" indicates the journal page number *from which* this amount is posted. Cross-referencing is especially important when posting large numbers of transactions, detecting and correcting errors, and maintaining an audit trail.

Ledgers

Accounting systems usually have two types of ledgers: the general ledger and subsidiary ledgers. The **general ledger** holds all the accounts, grouped according to the basic elements of financial statements. Subsidiary ledgers support general ledger accounts that comprise many separate individual accounts. For example, a firm with a substantial number of customer accounts receivable will maintain one ledger account per customer, stored in an accounts receivable subsidiary ledger. The individual customer account is called the "subsidiary account." The general ledger holds only the "control account," the balance of which reflects the sum of all the individual customer account balances. Only the control accounts are used in compiling financial statements.

For example, assume that a firm's accounts receivable consists of two individual accounts with a combined balance of $6,000. The firm's general and subsidiary ledgers might show these balances:

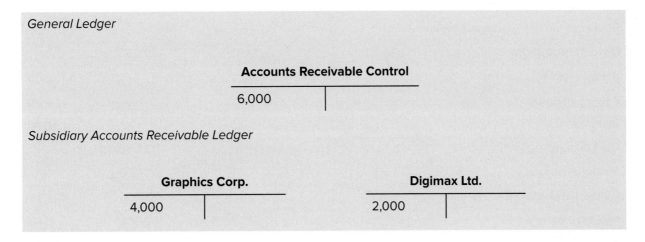

General Ledger

Accounts Receivable Control

6,000

Subsidiary Accounts Receivable Ledger

Graphics Corp.

4,000

Digimax Ltd.

2,000

Step 4: Prepare Unadjusted Trial Balance

An unadjusted trial balance is prepared at the end of the reporting period, after all transaction entries are recorded in the journals and posted to the ledger. The unadjusted trial balance is a list of general ledger accounts and their account balances, in the following order: assets, liabilities, owners' equity, revenues, expenses, gains, and losses. For accounts with subsidiary ledgers, only the control account balances are entered into the trial balance, after reconciliation with the subsidiary ledger.

The unadjusted trial balance is the starting point for developing adjusting entries and for the worksheet, if used. Exhibit A-5 illustrates an unadjusted trial balance for Sonora Ltd., a fictitious retailing company, at the end of the fiscal year. The trial balance reflects Sonora's transaction journal entries recorded during 20X5 and is the basis for the remainder of this accounting cycle illustration.

EXHIBIT A-5		
SONORA LIMITED		
Unadjusted Trial Balance		
31 December 20X5		
Account	**Debit**	**Credit**
Cash	$ 67,300	
Accounts receivable	45,000	
Allowance for doubtful accounts		$ 1,000
Notes receivable	8,000	
Inventory	92,000	
Prepaid insurance	600	
Land	8,000	
Building	160,000	
Accumulated depreciation, building		90,000
Equipment	91,000	
Accumulated depreciation, equipment		27,000
Accounts payable		29,000
Bonds payable, 6%		50,000

Common shares, no par, 15,000 shares		170,000
Retained earnings (1 January balance)		41,500
Dividends declared	10,000	
Sales revenue		325,200
Interest revenue		500
Rent revenue		1,800
Cost of goods sold	115,000	
Selling expenses*	104,000	
General and administrative expenses*	23,600	
Interest expense	2,500	
Loss on discontinued operations	9,000	
Totals	$736,000	$736,000

*These broad categories of expenses are used to simplify presentation.

The unadjusted trial balance is a convenient means for checking that the sum of debit account balances equals the sum of credit account balances. If the sums of debit and credit balances are not equal, the error must be found and corrected. A re-examination of source documents and postings is one way to discover the source of an error. Equality of debits and credits does not, however, imply that the accounts are error-free. A completely unposted journal entry, an incorrectly classified account, and an erroneous journal entry amount are errors that do not cause inequality of total debits and credits.

Sonora uses a **perpetual inventory system**. Under this system, the inventory account balance is updated each time inventory is purchased or sold. Thus, the inventory account balance is up to date at the end of the accounting period, and cost of goods sold will reflect all goods sold to date. The inventory balance must be verified by a physical count, and adjusted to the balance determined by the count.

Alternatively, in a **periodic inventory system**, acquisitions during the period are debited to a *purchases* account, not the inventory account. The inventory account balance remains at the 1 January amount all year, and the cost of goods sold is not readily determinable. Merchandise on hand is counted and costed at the end of each accounting period. The resulting inventory amount is used to update the inventory account balance at the report date and to determine cost of goods sold.

As shown in Exhibit A-5, Sonora's retained earnings account reflects the 1 January 20X5 balance, since no transactions directly affected this account during 20X5. Income tax expense is not listed in the unadjusted trial balance because the corporate income tax liability for the current year is not known until pre-tax income is computed. The loss from discontinued operations also does not yet reflect any tax effect.

Step 5: Journalize and Post Adjusting Journal Entries

Many changes in a firm's economic resources and obligations occur continuously. For example, interest accrues daily on debts, as does rent expense for an office building. Other resources and obligations, such as employee salaries, originate as service is rendered with payment to follow at specified dates. The end of the accounting period generally does not coincide with the receipt or payment of cash associated with these types of resource changes.

Accrual-basis accounting requires the recording of these changes at the end of the accounting period so that financial statements are faithfully represented. **Adjusting journal entries (AJEs)** are used to record such resource changes to ensure the accuracy of the financial statements. In all cases, AJEs are posted to the general ledger accounts.

Classification of AJEs

AJEs generally record a resource or obligation change and usually involve both permanent and temporary accounts. AJEs are recorded and dated as of the last day of the fiscal period. They are recorded in the general journal and posted to the ledger accounts. Source documents from earlier transactions are the primary information sources for AJEs. AJEs may be classified into three categories: deferral-type, accruals, and other AJEs.

Deferral-type entries are recorded for cash flows that occur *before expense and revenue recognition*. These AJEs are recorded when cash is paid for expenses that apply to more than one accounting period or when cash is received for revenue that applies to a later accounting period, in whole or in part. The portion of the expense or revenue that applies to future periods is deferred as a prepaid expense (asset) or unearned revenue (liability). The chart below clarifies the terminology used:

Deferral Type	Cash Timing	Results In
Deferred revenue	Cash received before revenue recognition is appropriate	Deferred revenue (liability) (perhaps as unearned revenue)
Deferred expense	Cash paid before expense recognition is appropriate	Prepaid expense (asset) (perhaps a deferred asset)

The exact AJE required for a deferral-type entry depends on the method used for first recording operational cash payments and receipts. One method, here called the **standard recording method**, records an *asset* upon payment of cash before goods or services are consumed and records a *liability* upon receipt of cash before goods or services are transferred. For example, if an entity prepays two months' rent on 1 July, the standard method debits prepaid rent for that amount. An adjustment later in the year recognizes rent expense and the reduction of prepaid rent.

A second method, here called the **expedient recording method**, records an *expense* upon payment of cash before goods or services are consumed and records a *revenue* upon receipt of cash before goods or services are transferred. In the case of rent paid in advance, the expedient method debits rent expense for two months' rent. This method is expedient because many cash payments and receipts relate to expenses and revenues that apply only to the year in which the cash flow occurs. No AJE is required in this example because rent expense is correctly stated at year-end. If, at the year-end, a portion of the expense or revenue applies to a future accounting period, however, an AJE is required.

Accruals are recorded for cash flows that occur *after expense and revenue recognition*. These AJEs are recorded when cash is to be paid or received in a future accounting period but all or a portion of the future cash flow applies to expenses or revenues of the current period. For example, unpaid wages accrued as wages payable at year-end represent wage costs matched against current year revenues but not to be paid until next year. If the company is a landlord and rents space to tenants, uncollected rent accrued as rent receivable at year-end represents revenue earned in the current year but to be collected next year. In both cases, the expense or revenue is recognized before the cash flow occurs. The chart below clarifies the terminology used:

Accrual Type	Cash Timing	Results In
Accrued revenue	Cash received after revenue recognition is appropriate	Accounts receivable (asset) (perhaps accrued revenue)
Accrued expense	Cash paid after expense recognition is appropriate	Accounts payable (liability) (perhaps an accrued expense)

Other types of journal entries are often recorded at the end of the accounting period and are listed here as adjusting journal entries for completeness. These include:

- Reclassifications of permanent accounts;
- Estimation of expenses (e.g., bad debt expense);
- Cost allocations (e.g., depreciation);
- Recognition of cost of goods sold and inventory losses;
- Remeasurements to fair value (e.g., for financial assets or investment properties); and
- Correction of errors discovered at year-end.

Cash generally is not involved in AJEs because of the purpose of AJEs. However, corrections of errors involving the cash account discovered at the end of the accounting period are recorded as AJEs. Also, the entry required to adjust the cash balance upon receipt of the end-of-year bank statement, which lists service charges and other items unknown until receipt, is recorded as an AJE.

In the following discussion, Sonora's 31 December 20X5 unadjusted trial balance (see Exhibit A-5) and additional information are used to illustrate AJEs.

Deferral-Type Examples

Deferred expenses

Some costs are paid in advance and deferred as assets until they are recognized as an expense. For example, on 1 November 20X5, Sonora paid a six-month insurance premium of $600 in advance for the period 1 November to 30 April 20X6. On that date, the $600 payment is recorded as a debit to prepaid insurance and a credit to cash (the standard method). In the unadjusted trial balance, the full $600 payment is reflected in prepaid insurance. One third of this payment ($200) is applicable to 20X5. A $200 expense, indicating the partial expiration of the asset, must be recognized. Sonora records insurance expense and other similar expenses in the general and administrative expense account. AJE (a) adjusts prepaid insurance and recognizes the expense:

a. 31 December 20X5		
General and administrative expenses	200	
Prepaid insurance		200

The credit to prepaid insurance records the reduction in the asset that took place during the last two months of 20X5 as insurance benefits were used up. The remaining $400 of prepaid insurance reflects insurance coverage for the first four months of 20X6.

Deferred revenue

Some revenues are received in advance and must be deferred as liabilities until they are recognized in earnings. For example, Sonora leased a small office in its building to a tenant on 1 January 20X5. The lease required an initial payment of $1,800 for 18 months' rent, which is recorded as a debit to cash and a credit to rent revenue (the expedient method). On 31 December 20X5, the unadjusted trial balance reports $1,800 in rent revenue, which is overstated by the $600 (one-third) relating to 20X6. AJE (b) is required to reduce the rent revenue recognized in 20X5 from $1,800 to $1,200 and to create a liability equal to the amount of rent revenue relating to 20X6 ($600).

b. 31 December 20X5		
Rent revenue	600	
Rent collected in advance (liability)		600

The result of this adjustment is a liability equal to the resources received for future services.

Accrual Examples

Accrued expenses

Some expenses must be recognized before they are paid, which results in the recognition of a liability. For example, Sonora has issued, at face value, $50,000 of 6% bonds paying interest annually each 31 October. For the current accounting period, a two-month interest obligation accrues between 31 October 20X5 and 31 December 20X5. Sonora must recognize the liability and the resulting expense. The amount for the two-month period is $500 ($50,000 × 6% × 2/12). Therefore, on 31 December 20X5, both the interest expense and the associated payable are recognized in AJE (c):

c. 31 December 20X5		
Interest expense	500	
Interest payable		500

Accrued revenue

Some revenues must be recognized before they are received, which results in the recognition of a receivable. Sonora's unadjusted trial balance lists $8,000 in notes receivable. The interest rate on these notes is 15%, payable each 30 November. As of 31 December 20X5, the payer of the notes is obligated to Sonora for one month's interest of $100 ($8,000 $\times$ 15% $\times$ 1/12). AJE (d) records the resulting receivable and revenue:

d. 31 December 20X5		
Interest receivable	100	
Interest revenue		100

Other Examples

Other common adjusting journal entries are illustrated below.

Depreciation expense

Property, plant, and equipment includes many productive assets with a useful life exceeding one year. The cost of these assets is recognized as an expense over their period of use. *Depreciation* or *amortization* is a systematic and rational allocation of asset cost over a number of accounting periods. The amount of depreciation expense recognized depends on a number of factors:

- The original expenditure and subsequent capitalized expenditures;
- The asset's useful life;
- The method chosen for depreciation measurement; and
- The asset's residual value.

Many methods of depreciation are permitted under GAAP. All entail systematic and rational allocation of the cost of a capital asset over its useful life.

AJE (e) illustrates depreciation recorded for Sonora at the end of 20X5 using the straight-line method. Sonora debits two expense accounts because the company uses the building and equipment assets both for selling and for general and administrative functions. Depreciation is commonly allocated to several functions, including manufacturing operations. The adjusting entry for depreciation is as follows:

e. 31 December 20X5		
Selling expense (depreciation)	8,200	
General and administrative expense (depreciation)	10,800	
Accumulated depreciation, building		10,000
Accumulated depreciation, equipment		9,000

The calculations:

Asset	Cost	Residual Value	Useful Life Years	Proportionate Use by Function	
				Selling Function	G & A* Function
Building	$160,000	$10,000	15	46%	54%
Equipment	91,000	1,000	10	40	60

Computation:

Building:

  [($160,000 − $10,000)/15 yrs.] = $10,000 × 0.46 = $4,600; $10,000 × 0.54 = $5,400

Equipment:

  [($91,000 − $1,000)/10 yrs.]   =   9,000 × 0.40 =   3,600; $9,000 × 0.60 =   5,400

  Totals $19,000 $8,200 $10,800

*General and administrative

AJE (e) reduces the *net book value* of the building and equipment accounts by crediting accumulated depreciation. Accumulated depreciation is a **contra account**, which has the opposite balance of the related asset account. A contra account is always reported on the financial statements along with its main account, producing a net amount for the two accounts taken together. That is, accumulated depreciation is subtracted from the asset value recorded in the building and equipment accounts. The net result is called *net book value*, which is the net undepreciated amount, or cost less accumulated depreciation. Sonora's statement of financial position illustrates this offset.

Bad debt expense

Goods and services are often sold on credit. Accounts that are never collected result in bad debt expense, which is a risk of doing business on credit terms. Firms use a bad debt estimate to reduce earnings and net accounts receivable in the period of sale. This practice prevents overstatement of both earnings and assets and is required whenever bad debts are probable and estimable. Recognition of bad debt expense is accomplished with an AJE that debits bad debt expense and credits the allowance for doubtful accounts, a contra account to the accounts receivable account.

Estimates of uncollectible accounts may be based on credit sales for the period or the year-end accounts receivable balance. Assume that Sonora extends credit on $120,000 of sales during 20X5. Prior experience indicates an expected 1% average bad debt rate on credit sales. Sonora treats bad debt expense as a component of selling expenses and records AJE (f):

f. 31 December 20X5		
Selling expense ($120,000 × .01)	1,200	
Allowance for doubtful accounts		1,200

The credit is made to the allowance account, rather than to accounts receivable, because the amount is still an estimate. Write-off of any particular accounting receivable is still premature.

The $1,200 allowance is the portion of 20X5 credit sales not expected to be collected. Net accounts receivable, the difference between the balance in accounts receivable and the allowance account, is an estimate of the cash ultimately expected to be received from sales on account. Bad debt expense appears on the SCI.

Cost of coods sold—perpetual system

The methodology used to determine cost of goods sold depends on whether a perpetual or a periodic inventory system is used. Sonora uses a perpetual inventory system. As background, recall that a perpetual inventory system maintains an inventory record for each item stocked. This record contains data on each purchase and issue. The cost of each item purchased is debited to the inventory account when it is bought and removed each time goods are sold to maintain a record of inventory on hand. Suppose an item that sells for $300 is carried in inventory at a cost of $180. The sale of this item requires two entries:

Cash (or accounts receivable)	300	
Sales revenue		300
Cost of goods sold	180	
Inventory		180

In a perpetual inventory system, the balance in the inventory account and the balance in cost of goods sold should reflect all transactions to date. A physical count is done to verify the inventory balance. If the result of the physical count is a different inventory amount than that recorded, an adjusting entry to decrease or increase inventory is recorded, with the other side of the entry changing cost of goods sold. For Sorona, a physical count determines that ending inventory is $90,000. The trial balance shows a balance of $92,000 and must be adjusted to the verified balance.

g. *31 December 20X5*		
Cost of goods sold	2,000	
Inventory		2,000

Periodic system

A periodic system does not maintain a current balance in inventory or cost of goods sold. Instead, the physical inventory count at the end of the period is used to determine the balances of these two accounts. The purchases account, rather than the inventory account, is debited for all purchases during the period. In this case, the unadjusted trial balance at the end of an accounting period reflects the beginning inventory, and cost of goods sold does not yet exist as an account. An AJE can be used to set purchases, purchases returns, and other purchase-related accounts to zero (i.e., close these accounts), to replace the beginning inventory amount with the ending inventory amount in the inventory ledger account, and to recognize cost of goods sold for the period.

To illustrate, assume that Sonora had an opening inventory of $75,000, closing inventory of $90,000, and purchases of $132,000. *Opening inventory and purchases* would be listed in the unadjusted trial balance. The cost of goods sold would be recorded only at year-end, as follows:

31. December 20X5		
Inventory (ending)	90,000	
Cost of goods sold ($75,000 + $132,000 − $90,000)	117,000	
Inventory (beginning)		75,000
Purchases		132,000

Alternatively, the accounts related to cost of goods sold may be left in the adjusted trial balance, untouched, and used in detail to create the financial statements. They would then be eliminated in closing entries. Both approaches are widely used in practice and result in the same reported earnings and financial position. It is really a question of which method is preferred by a particular accountant and/or computerized reporting package.

Income tax expense

The recognition of income tax expense is often the final AJE. Many firms accrue and pay estimated income taxes monthly, necessitating an AJE at the end of the accounting period only to record any additional taxes due. For simplicity, assume that Sonora pays its income tax once each year after the end of the full accounting period. Sonora's adjusted income before tax must be calculated to determine tax expense.

Assume that Sonora faces an average income tax rate of 40%, depreciation expense equals tax depreciation, and the losses from discontinued operations and all other expenses are fully tax deductible. Calculation of the $50,000 pre-tax earnings is shown below. AJE (h) recognizes the resulting $20,000 ($50,000 × 40%) income tax expense:

h. 31 December 20X5		
Income tax expense	20,000	
Income tax payable		20,000

Calculation of Pre-Tax Earnings

For the Year Ended 31 December 20X5

Revenues:		
Sales revenue	$325,200	
Interest revenue [$500 + $100 (d)]	600	
Rent revenue [$1,800 − $600 (b)]	1,200	$ 327,000
Expenses and losses:		
Cost of goods sold [$115,000 + $2,000(g)]	117,000	
Selling expenses [$104,000 + $8,200 (e) + $1,200 (f)]	113,400	
General and administrative expenses [$23,600 + $200 (a) + $10,800 (e)]	34,600	
Interest expense [$2,500 + $500 (c)]	3,000	
Discontinued operations (pretax)	9,000	277,000
Pre-tax earnings		$ 50,000
Income tax expense ($50,000 × 0.4)		$ 20,000

For simplicity, the entire income tax expense is recorded in one account. Sonora's statement of comprehensive income (see Exhibit A-7) separates the $3,600 income tax *reduction* associated with the loss from discontinued operations ($9,000 × 40%) from income tax on earnings before the discontinued operation of $23,600. This practice is called *intraperiod tax allocation*.

Step 6: Prepare Adjusted Trial Balance

At this point in the cycle, the transaction journal entries and the AJEs have been journalized and posted, and an adjusted trial balance is prepared. The adjusted trial balance lists all the account balances that will appear in the financial statements, with the exception of retained earnings, which does not reflect the current year's earnings or dividends. The purpose of the adjusted trial balance is to calculate adjusted balances and then confirm debit–credit equality. Exhibit A-6 presents the adjusted trial balance for Sonora.

EXHIBIT A-6		
SONORA LIMITED		
Adjusted Trial Balance		
31 December 20X5		
Account	**Debit**	**Credit**
Cash	$ 67,300	

Accounts receivable	45,000	
Allowance for doubtful accounts		$ 2,200
Notes receivable	8,000	
Interest receivable	100	
Inventory	90,000	
Prepaid insurance	400	
Land	8,000	
Building	160,000	
Accumulated depreciation, building		100,000
Equipment	91,000	
Accumulated depreciation, equipment		36,000
Accounts payable		29,000
Interest payable		500
Rent collected in advance		600
Income tax payable		20,000
Bonds payable, 6%		50,000
Common shares, no par, 15,000 shares		170,000
Retained earnings (1 January balance)		41,500
Dividends declared	10,000	
Sales revenue		325,200
Interest revenue		600
Rent revenue		1,200
Cost of goods sold	117,000	
Selling expenses	113,400	
General and administrative expenses	34,600	
Interest expense	3,000	
Income tax expense	20,000	
Loss on discontinued operations	9,000	
Totals	$776,800	$776,800

New accounts emerge from the adjustment process, while other accounts may disappear. For Sonora, the new accounts are interest receivable, interest payable, rent collected in advance, income tax payable, and income tax expense. The financial statements now can be prepared from the adjusted trial balance.

Step 7: Prepare Financial Statements

The financial statements are the culmination of the accounting cycle. Financial statements can be produced for a period of any duration. However, monthly, quarterly, and annual statements are the most common.

The SCI, statement of changes in equity, and SCF are prepared directly from the adjusted trial balance. The SCI is prepared first because earnings must be known before the statement of changes in equity and then the SFP can be completed. The temporary account balances are transferred to the SCI (except for dividends), and the permanent account balances (except for equity accounts) are transferred to the statement of financial position. Exhibit A-7 illustrates Sonora's 20X5 SCI and statement of changes in equity.

EXHIBIT A-7
SONORA LIMITED
Statement of Comprehensive Income

For the year ended 31 December 20X5

Revenues:		
Sales	$325,200	
Interest	600	
Rent	1,200	
Total revenues		$327,000
Expenses:		
Cost of goods sold	117,000	
Selling	113,400	
General and administrative	34,600	
Interest	3,000	
Total expenses before income tax		268,000
Earnings before tax and discontinued operations		59,000
Income tax on earnings before discontinued operations ($59,000 × 40%)		23,600
Earnings before discontinued operations		35,400
Loss from discontinued operations	9,000	
Less tax savings ($9,000 × 40%)	3,600	5,400
Net earnings and comprehensive income		$ 30,000

Statement of Changes in Equity

For the year ended 31 December 20X5

	Common Shares	Retained Earnings
Opening balance, 1 January 20X5	$170,000	$ 41,500
Net earnings and comprehensive income		30,000
		$ 71,500
Less: dividends declared		10,000
Closing balance, 31 December 20X5	$ 170,000	$ 61,500

Total income tax expense ($20,000) is allocated $23,600 to income before discontinued operations and $3,600 tax *savings* to the loss from discontinued operations. Discontinued operations are disclosed separately at the end of the statement.

The statement of changes in equity includes a column for each equity account. There is no change to the common share account. Retained earnings, however, has increased by earnings and decreased by dividends declared. Dividends are a distribution of capital to shareholders. *They are not an expense and do not belong on the SCI when the corresponding shares are reported as equity.*[1]

Exhibit A-8 illustrates the 20X5 SFP. The ending retained earnings balance is taken from the statement of changes in equity rather than from the adjusted trial balance.

EXHIBIT A-8

SONORA LIMITED

Statement of Financial Position

At 31 December 20X5

Assets			
Current assets:			
Cash			$ 67,300
Accounts receivable		$ 45,000	
Allowance for doubtful accounts		(2,200)	42,800
Notes receivable			8,000
Interest receivable			100
Inventory			90,000
Prepaid insurance			400
Total current assets			208,600
Property, plant and equipment:			
Land		8,000	
Building	$160,000		
Accumulated depreciation, building	(100,000)	60,000	
Equipment	91,000		
Accumulated depreciation, equipment	(36,000)	55,000	
Total capital assets			123,000
Total assets			$331,600
Liabilities			
Current liabilities:			
Accounts payable			$ 29,000
Interest payable			500
Rent collected in advance			600
Income tax payable			20,000
Total current liabilities			50,100
Long-term liabilities:			
Bonds payable, 6%			50,000

---

1. In cases where certain types of preferred shares are recognized as liabilities, the related dividends would be recognized on the SCI.

Total liabilities		100,100
Shareholders' Equity		
Contributed capital:		
Common shares, no par, 15,000 shares issued and outstanding	$170,000	
Retained earnings	61,500	
Total shareholders' equity		231,500
Total liabilities and shareholders' equity		$331,600

Step 8: Journalize and Post Closing Entries

The balances of the revenue, expense, gain, and loss accounts, which are the nominal accounts, are reduced to zero at the end of each accounting period through a transfer to retained earnings. Dividends accounts are also closed. This allows a fresh start for the next fiscal period. Earnings are measured for a specific interval of time, and are not cumulative. Permanent accounts are not closed because they carry over to the next accounting period. Closing entries:

- Reduce to zero (close) the balances of temporary accounts related to earnings measurement and dividends;
- Are recorded in the general journal at the end of the accounting period; and
- Are posted to the ledger accounts.

While some accountants prefer to close temporary accounts directly to retained earnings, it is quite common to use an account called "income summary" to accumulate the balances of temporary accounts in the closing entry process. The income summary is a clearing account—an account used on a short-term basis for a specific purpose. The balances in expenses and losses are reduced to zero and transferred to the income summary by crediting each of those accounts and debiting income summary for the total. Revenues and gains are debited to close them, and the income summary account is credited.

This process leaves a net balance in the income summary account equal to earnings (credit balance if earnings are positive and debit balance if a loss.) The income summary account is then closed by transferring the earnings amount to retained earnings. Sonora makes four closing entries to transfer 20X5 earnings to retained earnings:

31 December 20X5		
1. *To close the revenue and gain accounts to the income summary*		
Sales revenue	325,200	
Interest revenue	600	
Rent revenue	1,200	
Income summary		327,000
2. *To close the expense and loss accounts to the income summary*		
Income summary	297,000	
Cost of goods sold		117,000
Selling expense		113,400
General and administrative expenses		34,600
Interest expense		3,000
Loss from discontinued operations		9,000

	Debit	Credit
Income tax expense		20,000
3. *To close the income summary (i.e., transfer earnings to retained earnings)*		
Income summary	30,000	
Retained earnings		30,000
4. *To close dividends to retained earnings*		
Retained earnings	10,000	
Dividends declared		10,000

After the first two closing entries are recorded and posted, the balance in the income summary equals earnings ($30,000):

Income Summary			
(2)	297,000	(1)	327,000
		Balance	30,000

The temporary accounts now have zero balances and are ready for the next period's accounting cycle. The third entry closes the income summary account and transfers earnings to retained earnings. Finally, dividends declared is closed to retained earnings. The retained earnings account in the ledger now has a balance of $61,500, per the statement of financial position.

Step 9: Prepare Post-Closing Trial Balance

A post-closing trial balance lists only the balances of the permanent accounts after the closing process is finished. The temporary accounts have balances of zero. This step is taken to check for debit–credit equality after the closing entries are posted. Firms with a large number of accounts find this a valuable checking procedure because the chance of error increases with the number of accounts and postings. The retained earnings account is now stated at the correct ending balance and is the only permanent account with a balance different from the one shown in the adjusted trial balance. Exhibit A-9 illustrates the post-closing trial balance.

EXHIBIT A-9		
SONORA LIMITED		
Post-Closing Trial Balance		
31 December 20X5		
Account	**Debit**	**Credit**
Cash	$ 67,300	
Accounts receivable	45,000	
Allowance for doubtful accounts		$ 2,200
Notes receivable	8,000	
Interest receivable	100	
Inventory	90,000	
Prepaid insurance	400	
Land	8,000	
Building	160,000	

Accumulated depreciation, building		100,000
Equipment	91,000	
Accumulated depreciation, equipment		36,000
Accounts payable		29,000
Interest payable		500
Rent collected in advance		600
Income tax payable		20,000
Bonds payable, 6%		50,000
Common shares, no par, 15,000 shares		170,000
Retained earnings (31 December balance)		61,500
Totals	$469,800	$ 469,800

Step 10: Journalize and Post Reversing Journal Entries

Depending on the firm's accounting system and its accounting policies, **reversing journal entries (RJEs)** may be used to simplify certain journal entries in the *next* accounting period. RJEs are optional entries that:

- Are dated the first day of the next accounting period;
- Relate to a specific AJE;
- Use the same accounts and amounts as an AJE but with the debits and credits reversed; and
- Are posted to the ledger.

RJEs are appropriate only for AJEs that defer the recognition of revenue or expense items originally recorded under the expedient method, or entries that accrue revenue or expense items during the current period (e.g., wages expense).

Thus, if a deferral or accrual AJE creates or increases an asset or liability, an RJE is appropriate. RJEs are inappropriate for AJEs that adjust assets and liabilities recorded for cash flows preceding the recognition of revenues and expenses (the standard method) and for some other AJEs, such as reclassifications, error corrections, and estimates.

In the following examples, assume a 31 December year-end.

Deferred item

Assume that on 1 November 20X5, $300 is paid in advance for three months' rent:

1 November 20X5—originating entry		
Rent expense	300	
Cash		300
3. December 20X5—adjusting entry		
Prepaid rent	100	
Rent expense		100

With Reversing Entry				Without Reversing Entry		
1 January 20X6 Reversing entry:	Rent expense	100				
	Prepaid rent		100			
31 January 20X6 Subsequent entry:	*(No entry needed)*					

				Rent expense	100	
				Prepaid rent		100

With or without the RJE, rent expense recorded in 20X6 is $100. Use of the RJE, however, saves the cost and effort of reviewing the relevant accounts and source documents to determine the subsequent year's entry. The RJE makes the necessary adjustments to the accounts while the information used in making the AJE is available.

Now consider the standard method applied to the same example.

1 November 20X5—originating entry		
Prepaid rent	300	
Cash		300
31 December 20X5—adjusting entry		
Rent expense	200	
Prepaid rent		200

The RJE is not appropriate. No purpose is served by reinstating (debiting) prepaid rent $200 because that amount has expired.

Accrued item

Assume that the last payroll for 20X5 is on 28 December. Wages earned through 28 December are included in this payroll. The next payroll period ends 4 January 20X6, at which time $2,800 of wages will be paid. Wages earned for the three-day period ending 31 December 20X5 are $1,500, which will be paid in 20X6. The following AJE is necessary to accrue these wages:

31 December 20X5—adjusting entry		
Wages expense	1,500	
Wages payable		1,500

With Reversing Entry				Without Reversing Entry		
1 January 20X6 Reversing entry:	Wages payable	1,500				
	Wages expense		1,500			
4 January 20X6 Subsequent entry:						
	Wages expense	2,800		Wages expense	1,300	
	Cash		2,800	Wages payable	1,500	
				Cash		2,800

In this example, the RJE simplifies the subsequent payroll entry, which can now be recorded in a manner identical to all other payrolls. With or without reversing entries, total 20X6 wage expense recognized through 4 January 20X6 is $1,300. RJEs often create abnormal short-term account balances. In the above 1 January 20X6 entry, the RJE creates a credit balance in wages expense. The subsequent entry changes the net balance of wages expense to a $1,300 debit.

Some of Sonora's AJEs could be reversed: entry (b) for rent revenue (expedient method—deferred item); entry (c) for interest expense (accrual); entry (d) for interest revenue (accrual); and perhaps entry (h) for income tax expense (accrual).

SUBSIDIARY LEDGERS

Companies typically maintain both *control* and *subsidiary* ledger accounts. **Subsidiary ledgers** are often kept for accounts payable and accounts receivable, and also inventory, although any ledger account can be supported by a subsidiary ledger if size and complexity warrant.

The sum of all account balances in a subsidiary ledger must equal the related control account balance in the general ledger. To ensure that the control account and its subsidiary ledger are equal, frequent reconciliations are made. All posting must be complete, both to the control account and to the subsidiary ledger, before a reconciliation can be accomplished. Postings are made *in total* to the control account and *to individual accounts* in the subsidiary ledger. These postings are described in more depth in the next section.

To illustrate a reconciliation, refer ahead to the accounts receivable subsidiary ledger in Exhibit A-14. A reconciliation for accounts receivable control and the accounts receivable subsidiary ledger based on the information in Exhibit A-14 follows:

RECONCILIATION OF ACCOUNTS RECEIVABLE SUBSIDIARY LEDGER	
At 31 January 20X5	**Amount**
Subsidiary ledger balances	
112.13 Adams Co.	$ 980
112.42 Miller, J. B.	196
112.91 XY Manufacturing Co.	1,960
Total	$3,136
General ledger balance	
Accounts receivable control ($5,000 + $9,360 − $11,224)	$3,136

Subsidiary ledgers contain information that help the company operate efficiently—individual accounts receivable and payable balances are essential information. In smaller companies, subsidiary ledgers can be maintained through a simple filing system. For example, a copy of a sales invoice that is not paid can be kept in a special file until the money is received. At any time, the outstanding receivables are equal to the total of the invoices in the file. The same can be done with accounts payable, if all unpaid bills are kept in an accounts payable file. The point is that formal accounting systems are made necessary by size and complexity, but simple methods in simple situations can be just as effective if efficiently operated.

SPECIAL JOURNALS

Both *general journals* and *special journals* are used in many accounting systems. Even when extensive use is made of special journals, a need exists for a general journal to record the adjusting, closing, reversing, and correcting entries and those transactions that do not apply to any of the special journals. A general journal was illustrated in Exhibit A-3.

A special journal is designed to expedite the recording of similar transactions that occur frequently. Each special journal is constructed specifically to simplify the data-processing tasks involved in journalizing and posting those types of transactions. Special journals can be custom designed to meet the particular needs of the business. Commonly used special journals include:

1. *Sales journal* for recording sales of merchandise *on credit*, and the related cost of goods sold;
2. *Purchases journal* for recording purchases of merchandise inventory *on credit*;
3. *Cash receipts journal* for recording only cash receipts, including cash sales and the related cost of goods sold; and
4. *Cash disbursements journal* for recording only cash payments, including cash purchases of merchandise inventory.

The special journals illustrated in this Appendix carry page numbers preceded by letters indicating the journal name. The S in the page number of Exhibit A-10 denotes the sales journal, for example.

EXHIBIT A-10							
PAGE S-23			**SALES JOURNAL**				
Date 20X5	Sales Invoice No.	Accounts Receivable (name)	Terms	Post. Ref.	Receivable and Sale Amount	Post. Ref.	Cost of Goods Sold and Inventory Amount
2 Jan.	93	Adams Co.	n/30	112.13	$ 980	120.899	$ 410
3	94	Sayre Corp.	n/30	112.80	490	120.113	165
11	95	Cope & Day Co.	net	112.27	5,734	120.189	2,450
27	96	XY Mfg. Co.	n/30	112.91	1,960	120.998	671
30	97	Miller, J. B.	n/30	112.42	196	120.003	57
31	—	Total			$ 9,360		$ 3,753
31	—	Posting			(112/500)		(120/650)

Sales Journal

This special journal is designed to record sales on account, which otherwise would be recorded as follows in a general journal:

2 January 20X5		
Accounts receivable	980	
Sales revenue		980
Cost of goods sold	410	
Inventory		410
(Credit sale to Adams Company; invoice price, $980; terms n/30. The related inventory sold has a cost of $410)		

The sales journal can accommodate any entry that involves a debit to accounts receivable and a credit to sales, along with its related cost of goods sold. However, this is the *only* situation it can record. If the debit is to cash, or notes receivable, another journal must be used. Exhibit A-10 illustrates a typical sales journal for credit sales. The above entry is shown as the first entry in 20X5. The amount of sale, and the cost of goods sold, are each recorded only once. Each entry in the sales journal records the same information found in the traditional debit–credit format.

The posting of amounts from the sales journal to the general and subsidiary ledgers is simplified. The two phases in posting a sales journal are the following:

1. *Daily posting.* The amount of each credit sale is posted daily to the appropriate individual account in the accounts receivable subsidiary ledger. Each reduction to inventory is posted daily to the relevant inventory account in the inventory subsidiary ledger. Posting is indicated by entering the account number in the posting reference column. For example, the number 112.13 entered in the posting reference column in Exhibit A-10 is the account number assigned to Adams Company and shows that $980 is posted as a debit to Adams Company in the subsidiary ledger. The number 112 is the general number used for accounts receivable (see Exhibit A-14). The inventory number has a similar logic. The number would be the SKU, or *stock-keeping unit*, assigned to the inventory item.

2. *Monthly posting.* At the end of each month, the numeric columns are totalled. Two journal entries result in the general ledger. One is a debit to accounts receivable and a credit to sales for $9,360. The other is a debit to cost of goods sold and a credit to inventory for $3,753. Posting to the subsidiary ledgers would be completed prior to this. The T-accounts shown in Exhibit A-14 illustrate how these postings for sales and accounts receivable are reflected in both the general ledger and the subsidiary ledger. The ledgers reference the journal page (S-23) from which each amount is posted.

Purchases Journal

This special journal is designed to accommodate frequent purchases of merchandise inventory on account. Again, there is only one transaction that can go into this journal—a debit to inventory, and a credit to accounts payable. Other entries, including the acquisition of inventory for cash, go elsewhere. Consider the following entry, recorded in general journal format:

3 January 20X5		
Inventory ($1,000 × .99)	990	
Accounts payable (PT Mfg. Co.) (terms 1/20, n/30)		990

Terms of 1/20 mean that if the invoice is paid within 20 days, a 1% discount can be applied to the invoice amount. In this case, the invoice is recorded at its net amount, after the 1% discount. Some companies prefer to record purchase invoices gross and record purchase discounts taken when they record payment. Note also that the entry assumes a perpetual inventory system. Under a periodic inventory system, the debit would always be to the purchases account.

This entry is recorded as the first 20X5 entry in the purchases journal illustrated in Exhibit A-11. The accounting simplifications found in the sales journal are present in the purchases journal as well. Each amount is posted daily as a debit to the individual inventory account in the inventory subsidiary ledger. Each amount is also posted each day as a credit to the account of an individual creditor in the accounts payable subsidiary ledger. At the end of the month, the total of the inventory purchases and payable amount column ($6,760 in Exhibit A-11) is posted to the general ledger as a debit to the inventory account (no. 120) and as a credit to the accounts payable control account (no. 210). Posting references refer to both the subledger for inventory and for accounts payable.

EXHIBIT A-11					
PURCHASES JOURNAL					
Date 20X5	Purchase Order No.	Accounts Payable (name)	Terms	Posting Ref.	Inventory and Payable Amount
				120.998	
3 Jan.	41	PT Mfg. Co.	1/20, n/30	210.61	$ 990
7	42	Able Suppliers Ltd.	net	120.431 210.12	150
31	—	Total	—	—	$6,760
31	—	Postings	—	—	(120/210)

Cash Receipts Journal

A special cash receipts journal is used to accommodate a large volume of cash receipts transactions. This journal can accommodate any entry that involves a debit to cash. Multiple sources of cash (the credits) are accommodated by designing several credit columns for recurring credits, and a miscellaneous accounts column for infrequent credits, as shown in Exhibit A-12. Space is also provided for the names of particular accounts receivable.

				EXHIBIT A-12					
				CASH RECEIPTS JOURNAL					
			Credits						Debit and Credit
Date 20X5	Explanation	Debit Cash	Account Title	Post. Ref.	Accounts Receivable	Sales Revenue	Misc. Accounts	Cost of Goods Sold and Inventory Amount
4 Jan.	Cash sales	$ 11,200		120.431		$11,200		$ 5,998
7	On acct.	4,490	Sayre Corp.	112.80	$ 4,490			
8	Sale of land	10,000	Land	123			$ 4,000	
			Gain on sale of land	510			6,000	
10	On acct.	1,000	Adams Co.	112.13	1,000			
19	Cash sales	43,600		120.875		43,600		24,320
20	On acct.	5,734	Cope & Day Co.	112.27	5,734			
31	Totals	$116,224		—	$11,224	$71,000	$34,000	$32,116
31	Posting	(101)		—	(112)	(500)	(NP)*	(650/120)

*NP—not posted as one total because the individual amounts are posted as indicated in the posting reference column.

During the month, each amount in the accounts receivable column is posted daily as a credit to an individual customer account in the accounts receivable subsidiary ledger. At the end of the month, the individual amounts in the miscellaneous account column are posted as credits to the appropriate general ledger accounts, and the totals for the cash, accounts receivable, and sales revenue columns are posted to the general ledger as indicated by the posting reference. The total of the miscellaneous accounts column is not posted because it consists of changes in different accounts. However, this column is totalled to ascertain overall debit–credit equality.

Cash Disbursements Journal

Most companies use some form of a cash disbursements journal, which is also sometimes called a *cheque register*. This journal can accommodate any entry that involves a credit to cash, and has columns for the common debits and a miscellaneous debits column to make it flexible. Exhibit A-13 illustrates a typical cash disbursements journal. Journalizing and posting follow the same procedures explained for the cash receipts journal.

EXHIBIT A-13

CASH DISBURSEMENTS JOURNAL

Date 20X5	Cheque No.	Explanation	Credit Cash	Account Name	Post. Ref.	Accounts Payable	Inventory	Misc. Accounts
						Debits		
2 Jan.	141	Pur. inv.	$ 3,000		120.899		$ 3,000	
10	142	On acct.	990	PTMfg.Co.	210.61	$ 990		
15	143	Jan. rent	660	Rent exp.	1300			$ 660
16	144	Pur. inv.	1,810		120.351		1,810	
31	—	Totals	$98,400		—	$5,820	$90,980	$1,600
31	—	Posting	(101)		—	(210)	(120)	(NP)

The General Journal

Special journals can be used to record common entries, but there will always be entries that do not fit the format for any special journal and must be recorded in general journal format (Exhibit A-14). Adjusting and reversing entries are prime examples, but unusual operating transactions will also be recorded in this format. The general journal is an essential element of accounting record keeping.

EXHIBIT A-14

GENERAL LEDGER AND SUBSIDIARY LEDGER GENERAL LEDGER (PARTIAL)

			Cash				Acct. 101
20X5				20X5			
1 Jan.	Balance		18,700	31 Jan.	CD-31		98,400
31	CR-19		116,224				

			Accounts Receivable Control				Acct. 112
20X5				20X5			
1 Jan.	Balance		5,000	31 Jan.	CR-19		11,224
31	S-23		9,360				

			Sales Revenue				Acct. 500
				20X5			
				31 Jan.	S-23		9,360
				31	CR-19		71,000

Subsidiary Ledger for Accounts Receivable (Acct. No. 112)

Date 20X5	Post Ref.	Explanation	Debit	Credit	Balance
		Adams Company—Acct. No. 112.13			
1 Jan.		Balance			1,000
2	S-23		980		1,980

10	CR-19			1,000	980
Cope & Day Company—Acct. No. 112.27					
11 Jan.	S-23		5,734		5,734
20	CR-19			5,734	0
Miller, J. B.—Acct. No. 112.42					
30 Jan.	S-23		196		196
Sayre Corporation—Acct. No. 112.80					
1 Jan.		Balance			4,000
3	S-23		490		4,490
7	CR-19			4,490	0
XY Manufacturing Company—Acct. No. 112.91					
27 Jan.	S-23		1,960		1,960

WORKSHEETS

A worksheet is a multicolumn work space that provides an organized format for performing several end-of-period accounting cycle steps and for preparing financial statements before posting AJEs. It also provides evidence, or an audit trail, of an organized and structured accounting process that can be more easily reviewed than other methods of analysis.

Use of a worksheet is always optional. The worksheet is not part of the basic accounting records. Worksheets assist with only a portion of the accounting cycle. Formal AJEs are recorded in the accounts in addition to those entered on the worksheet. Worksheets are also often used in preparing consolidated statements.

Illustration of the Worksheet Approach

Exhibit A-15 illustrates the completed worksheet for Sonora, the company used in this Appendix to present the accounting cycle. The worksheet has a debit and a credit column for each of the following: unadjusted trial balance, AJEs, adjusted trial balance, SCI, retained earnings, and SFP. The worksheet is prepared in four steps:

Step 1   *Enter the unadjusted trial balance in the first set of columns of the worksheet by inserting the year-end balances of all ledger accounts.*

- The retained earnings balance is the beginning-of-year balance because no transactions have yet affected this account.

Step 2   *Enter the adjusting entries.*

- The lowercase letters refer to the same AJEs discussed in this appendix for Sonora.
- The worksheet AJEs are facilitating entries only and are not formally recorded in the general journal at this point. (These entries will be recorded later in the general journal.) If a new account is created by an AJE, it can be inserted in its normal position or at the bottom of the worksheet.
- Determine income tax expense and payable. (Sonora's tax computation was illustrated earlier.) Enter the accounts and the amounts in the AJE columns. Income tax expense (entry [h]) is positioned below the totals of the AJE columns because this reflects its sequence in the adjustment process.

Step 3   *Cross-add.*

- Enter the adjusted trial balance by adding or subtracting across the unadjusted trial balance columns and AJE columns, for each account. For example, the adjusted balance of the allowance for doubtful accounts is the sum of its $1,000 unadjusted balance and the $1,200 increase from AJE (f).

- Confirm the debit–credit equality of all totals.

Step 4   *Extend the adjusted trial balance amounts to the financial statements; complete the worksheet.*

- Each account in the adjusted trial balance is extended to one of the three sets of remaining debit–credit columns. Temporary accounts are sorted to the SCI columns (revenues to the credit column, expenses to the debit column). Permanent accounts are sorted to the SFP columns except for the beginning balance in retained earnings, which is extended to the retained earnings columns. Dividends go in the retained earnings columns in this example.

- Total the SCI columns before income tax expense. Pre-tax income is the difference between the debit and credit column totals. A net credit represents positive earnings; a net debit represents a loss. For Sonora, pre-tax earnings are $50,000 ($327,000 − $277,000). Next, determine earnings after taxes by extending the income tax expense amount ($20,000) into the debit column and again totalling the columns. Net earnings is the difference between the columns, or $30,000 ($327,000 − $297,000).

EXHIBIT A-15

COMPLETED WORKSHEET FOR SONORA LTD.

	Unadjusted Trial Balance Debit	Unadjusted Trial Balance Credit	Adjusting Entries Debit	Adjusting Entries Credit	Adjusted Trial Balance Debit	Adjusted Trial Balance Credit	Statement of Comprehensive Income Debit	Statement of Comprehensive Income Credit	Retained Earnings Debit	Retained Earnings Credit	Statement of Financial Position Debit	Statement of Financial Position Credit
Cash	67,300				67,300						67,300	
Accounts receivable	45,000				45,000						45,000	
Allowance for doubtful accounts		1,000		(f) 1,200		2,200						2,200
Notes receivable	8,000				8,000						8,000	
Interest receivable			(d) 100		100						100	
Inventory	92,000			(g) 2,000	90,000						90,000	
Prepaid insurance	600			(a) 200	400						400	
Land	8,000				8,000						8,000	
Building	160,000				160,000						160,000	
Accumulated depreciation, building		90,000		(e) 10,000		100,000						100,000
Equipment	91,000				91,000						91,000	
Accumulated depreciation, equipment		27,000		(e) 9,000		36,000						36,000
Accounts payable		29,000				29,000						29,000
Interest payable				(c) 500		500						500
Rent collected in advance				(b) 600		600						600
Bonds payable, 6%		50,000				50,000						50,000
Common shares, no par, 15,000 shares		170,000				170,000						170,000
Retained earnings		41,500				41,500				41,500		
Dividends declared	10,000				10,000				10,000			
Sales revenue		325,200				325,200		325,200				
Interest revenue		500		(d) 100		600		600				
Rent revenue		1,800	(b) 600			1,200		1,200				
Cost of goods sold	115,000		(g) 2,000		117,000		117,000					

Account	Trial Balance Dr	Trial Balance Cr	Adjustments (ref) Dr	Adjustments (ref) Cr	Adjusted Trial Balance Dr	Adjusted Trial Balance Cr	Income Statement Dr	Income Statement Cr	Retained Earnings Dr	Retained Earnings Cr	Statement of Financial Position Dr	Statement of Financial Position Cr
Selling expenses	104,000		(e) 8,200		113,400		113,400					
General and administrative expenses	23,600		(f) 1,200; (a) 200		34,600		34,600					
Interest expense	2,500		(e) 10,800	3,000		3,000						
Loss on discontinued operations	9,000		(c) 500	9,000		9,000						
Income tax expense			23,600	23,600	756,800	756,800	277,000					
Income tax payable				(h) 20,000	20,000	20,000	20,000					297,000
Net Earnings to retained earnings			(h) —	20,000	776,800	776,800	327,000		30,000			
Retained earnings to SFP		736,000						61,500		61,500	20,000	
Totals	736,000	736,000	23,600	23,600	327,000	327,000	327,000	71,500	71,500	71,500	469,800	469,800

- Total the retained earnings columns and enter a balancing amount (the ending retained earnings balance) in the appropriate column to achieve debit–credit equality. For Sonora, the balancing amount is a $61,500 debit. Add a line description (retained earnings to SFP) and enter the balancing amount in the appropriate SFP column.
- Total the SFP columns and confirm debit–credit equality.

The worksheet is now complete, and the financial statements are prepared directly from the last three sets of worksheet columns. The formal AJEs are then journalized and posted.

Combined Version

To save space, the retained earnings and SFP columns can be combined. If this is done, the opening retained earnings account and dividends are entered in the SFP columns and the earnings figure is included at the bottom of the SFP columns to balance the worksheet.

Accounting Standards for Private Enterprises

Transaction recording mechanics are the same regardless if the company has adopted ASPE or IFRS. Only the titles and nature of the statements have changed. The basic financial statements are also the same, with ASPE requiring an income statement, balance sheet, and a statement of retained earnings. A retained earnings statement shows the opening retained earnings balance, itemizes each increase and decrease in retained earnings for the year, and then concludes with the closing balance in the account. A statement of changes in equity is not required under ASPE. ASPE also does not have any other comprehensive income items to be reported.

SUMMARY OF KEY POINTS

1. The AIS provides information for daily management information needs and for preparation of financial statements.
2. The SFP discloses the balances of the permanent accounts, which include assets, liabilities, and owners' equity accounts. The SCI includes the preclosing balances of most temporary accounts, which include revenues, gains, expenses, and losses.
3. Transactions are recorded in a double-entry system, where each transaction changes two or more accounts. Debits to assets, expenses, losses, and dividends declared increase those accounts. Credits to liabilities, owners' equity, revenues, and gains increase those accounts.
4. There are 10 steps in the accounting cycle that culminate in the financial statements. Refer to Exhibit A-2.
5. AJEs are required under accrual accounting to complete the measurement and recording of changes in resources and obligations.

6. RJEs are optional entries, dated at the beginning of the accounting period, that reverse certain AJEs from the previous period and are used to facilitate subsequent journal entries.

7. Subsidiary ledgers are used to maintain records on the component elements of ledger control accounts.

8. Special journals are used to record repetitive entries, such as sales, inventory purchases, cash receipts, and cash disbursements. A general journal is used to record entries that do not fit into special journals.

9. A worksheet may be used to organize the adjustment and financial statement preparation phases of the accounting cycle.

Key Terms

accounting identity

accounting information system (AIS)

adjusting journal entries (AJEs)

contra account

debit–credit convention

deferral-type entries

double-entry system

expedient recording method

financial statement

general journal

general ledger

journal

journal entry

nominal accounts

nonreciprocal transfer

periodic inventory system

permanent accounts

perpetual inventory system

posting

real accounts

reciprocal transfer

reversing journal entries (RJEs)

special journal

standard recording method

subsidiary ledger

T-account

temporary accounts

transactions

Review Problem

Bucknell Company developed its unadjusted trial balance dated 31 December 20X5, which appears below. Bucknell uses the expedient recording method whenever possible, adjusts its accounts once per year, records all appropriate RJEs, and uses a perpetual inventory system. Ignore income taxes.

BUCKNELL COMPANY UNADJUSTED TRIAL BALANCE

31 December 20X5	Debit	Credit
Cash	$ 40,000	
Accounts receivable	60,000	
Allowance for doubtful accounts		$ 6,000
Inventory	75,000	
Equipment	780,000	

Accumulated depreciation		100,000
Land	150,000	
Accounts payable		22,000
Notes payable, 8%, due 1 April 20X10		200,000
Common shares, no-par, 60,000 shares		400,000
Retained earnings		50,000
Sales revenue (all on account)		900,000
Subscription revenue		24,000
Cost of goods sold	265,000	
Rent expense	60,000	
Interest expense	12,000	
Selling expense	40,000	
Insurance expense	30,000	
Wages expense	110,000	
General and administrative expense	80,000	
Totals	$1,702,000	$1,702,000

Additional information:

a. Ending inventory by physical count is $70,000.

b. The equipment has a total estimated useful life of 14 years and an estimated residual value of $80,000. Bucknell uses straight-line depreciation and treats depreciation expense as a general and administrative expense.

c. Bad debt expense for 20X5 is estimated to be 1% of sales.

d. The note payable requires interest to be paid semi-annually, every 1 October and 1 April.

e. $5,000 of wages were earned in December but not recorded or paid.

f. The rent expense represents a payment made on 2 January 20X5, for two years' rent (20X5 and 20X6).

g. The insurance expense represents payment made for a one-year policy, paid 30 June 20X5. Coverage began on that date.

h. The subscription revenue represents cash received from several university libraries for an 18-month subscription to a journal published by Bucknell. The subscription period began 1 July 20X5.

Required:

1. Record the required AJEs.
2. Prepare the adjusted trial balance.
3. Prepare an SCI and an SFP for 20X5.
4. Prepare closing entries.
5. Prepare RJEs.

REVIEW PROBLEM—SOLUTION

Requirement 1

a.	Cost of goods sold	5,000	
	Inventory ($75,000 − $70,000)		5,000
b.	General and administrative expense	50,000	
	($780,000 − $80,000)/14		
	Accumulated depreciation		50,000
c.	Bad debt expense (0.01 × $900,000)	9,000	
	Allowance for doubtful accounts		9,000
d.	Interest expense ($200,000 × 0.08 × 3/12)	4,000	
	Interest payable		4,000
e.	Wages expense	5,000	
	Wages payable		5,000
f.	Prepaid rent ($60,000 × 1/2)	30,000	
	Rent expense		30,000
g.	Prepaid insurance ($30,000 × 6/12)	15,000	
	Insurance expense		15,000
h.	Subscription revenue ($24,000 × 12/18)	16,000	
	Unearned subscriptions		16,000

Requirement 2

BUCKNELL COMPANY
ADJUSTED TRIAL BALANCE

31 December 20X5	Debit	Credit
Cash	$ 40,000	
Accounts receivable	60,000	
Allowance for doubtful accounts (9,000 + 6,000 (c))		$ 15,000
Inventory (75,000 − 5,000 (a))	70,000	
Prepaid rent (30,000 (f))	30,000	
Prepaid insurance (15,000 (g))	15,000	
Equipment	780,000	
Accumulated depreciation (100,000 + 50,000 (b))		150,000
Land	150,000	
Accounts payable		22,000
Interest payable (4,000 (d))		4,000
Wages payable (5,000 (e))		5,000
Unearned subscriptions(16,000 (h))		16,000

Notes payable, 8%, due 1 April 20X10		200,000
Common shares, no-par, 60,000 shares		400,000
Retained earnings		50,000
Sales revenue		900,000
Subscription revenue (24,000 − 16,000 (h))		8,000
Cost of goods sold (265,000 + 5,000 (a))	270,000	
Rent expense (60,000-30,000 (f))	30,000	
Interest expense (12,000 + 4,000 (d))	16,000	
Selling expense	40,000	
Insurance expense (30,000-15,000 (g))	15,000	
Wages expense (110,000 + 5,000 (e))	115,000	
Bad debt expense (9,000 (c))	9,000	
General and administrative expense (80,000 + 50,000 (b))	130,000	
Totals	$1,770,000	$1,770,000

Requirement 3

BUCKNELL COMPANY
STATEMENT OF COMPREHENSIVE INCOME

For the year ended 31 December 20X5

Revenues:		
Sales revenue	$900,000	
Subscription revenue	8,000	
Total revenue		$908,000
Expenses:		
Cost of goods sold	270,000	
Rent expense	30,000	
Interest expense	16,000	
Selling expense	40,000	
Insurance expense	15,000	
Wages expense	115,000	
Bad debt expense	9,000	
General and administrative expense	130,000	
Total expenses		625,000
Net earnings and comprehensive income		$283,000

BUCKNELL COMPANY
STATEMENT OF FINANCIAL POSITION

31 December 20X5

Assets			
Current assets			
Cash		$ 40,000	
Accounts receivable	$ 60,000		
Allowance for doubtful accounts	(15,000)	45,000	
Inventory		70,000	
Prepaid rent		30,000	
Prepaid insurance		15,000	
Noncurrent assets			$200,000
Equipment	780,000		
Accumulated depreciation	(150,000)	630,000	
Land		150,000	780,000
Total assets			$980,000
Liabilities			
Current liabilities			
Accounts payable		$ 22,000	
Interest payable		4,000	
Wages payable		5,000	
Unearned subscriptions		16,000	$ 47,000
Noncurrent liabilities			
Notes payable, 8%, due 1 April 20X10			200,000
Total liabilities			$247,000
Owners' Equity			
Common shares, no-par, 60,000 shares outstanding		400,000	
Retained earnings		333,000[*]	
Total owners' equity			733,000
Total liabilities and owners' equity			$980,000

[*]$50,000 + $283,000

Requirement 4

Sales revenue	900,000	
Subscription revenue	8,000	
Income summary		908,000
Income summary	625,000	
Cost of goods sold		270,000
Rent expense		30,000
Interest expense		16,000
Selling expense		40,000
Insurance expense		15,000
Wages expense		115,000
Bad debt expense		9,000
General and administrative expense		130,000
Income summary	283,000	
Retained earnings		283,000

Requirement 5

Interest payable	4,000	
Interest expense		4,000
Wages payable	5,000	
Wages expense		5,000
Rent expense	30,000	
Prepaid rent		30,000
Insurance expense	15,000	
Prepaid insurance		15,000
Unearned subscriptions	16,000	
Subscription revenue		16,000

TECHNICAL REVIEW

connect

TRApp1-1 Deferred Expenses:

On 1 November, a payment of $600 was made for six months' insurance.

Required:

Prepare the journal entries, assuming the standard method is used, to record the payment on November 1 and the year-end adjustment as at 31 December.

connect

TRApp1-2 Deferred Revenue:

On 1 April, cash of $2,400 was received from a customer for a 12-month service contract.

Required:

Prepare the journal entries, assuming the expedient method is used, to record the cash receipt on April 1 and the year-end adjustment as at 31 October.

connect

TRApp1-3 Accrued Expenses and Reversing Journal Entries:

The company has a year-end of 30 April and the last pay period ended 25 April. On 9 May, the payroll was completed, totalling $14,000, and was recorded using the expedient recording method.

Required:

Prepare the journal entries required at the end of April to accrue any wage expense, the reversing journal entry at 1 May, and the payment entry on 9 May. Determine the balance in the wage expense amount on 9 May after these entries. (*Note:* There are 14 days in the pay period).

connect

TRApp1-4 Accrued Revenue and Reversing Journal Entries:

The company has a year-end of 31 August. On August 3, the company sold an old piece of equipment for $10,000. The equipment had a cost of $25,000 and an accumulated depreciation amount of $17,000 at the time of the sale. The cash from this sale was received on 15 September.

Required:

Prepare the journal entries required at the date of sale, 3 August, at the year-end, and on 15 September when the cash was actually received. Assume that the company uses the standard recording method and no reversing journal entry is made.

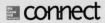 connect

TRApp1-5 Adjusting Journal Entries:

A company has machinery that had an original cost of $250,000, a residual value of $5,000, and a useful life of seven years. The machinery is depreciated on a straight-line basis. The balance in the allowance for doubtful accounts is currently $45,000, but the company has estimated that the amount of receivables that are unlikely to be collected totals $56,000, using the percentage of receivables method.

Required:

Prepare the adjusting journal entries required to record depreciation and the bad debts expense for the year.

connect

TRApp1-6 Adjusting Journal Entries:

USRA Inc. uses the periodic system for recording inventory. Just prior to the year-end inventory count on 30 April 20X2, the company has the following information in its general ledger:

Inventory (beginning)	$572,000 (unchanged from May 1, 20X1)
Purchases	$7,436,000

On April 30, the physical count for the inventory totaled $483,000.

Required:

Prepare the adjusting journal entries required at 30 April 20X2 to adjust the inventory to its correct balance and set up the cost of goods sold for the year.

connect

TRApp1-7 Adjusting Journal Entries:

Kelly Corp. is preparing its financial statements of the year ended 30 November 20X2. It has determined that its earnings before taxes is $346,000. It pays taxes at a rate of 25%. On 29 January 20X3, Kelly paid the income taxes that was owing for 20X2.

Required:

Prepare the adjusting journal entries required at 30 November 20X2 and 29 January 20X3 to record the above information.

TRApp1-8 Closing Entries:

A company has the following SCI for the year ended 31 October 20X4.

Revenues:		$1,082,000
Expenses:		
Cost of goods sold	$350,000	
Rent expense	50,000	
Selling expense	75,000	
Insurance expense	15,000	
Wages expense	295,000	
General and administrative expense	130,000	
Total expenses		$ 915,000
Net earnings and comprehensive income		$ 167,000

Required:

Prepare the closing entries for this company.

TRApp1-9 Adjusted Trial Balance:

At the year-end, the company had $1,567,000 in marketing expenses and $3,670,000 in sales. The following adjusting journal entries were made by the company:

Prepaid advertising	115,000	
Marketing expenses		115,000

To adjust for costs related to advertising brochures to be received next year.

Marketing expenses	92,000	

Sales		92,000

To correct an error made in posting.

Sales	69,000	
Unearned revenue		69,000

To record a customer deposit paid in advance for work to be completed next year.

Required:

Calculate the adjusted balances for marketing expenses and sales after these entries have been posted.

TRApp1-10 Adjusting Entries and Statement of Changes in Equity:

On 28 December 20X5, Lyons Co. declared dividends of $23,000, to be paid on 18 February 20X6. It also issued 100 new common shares for cash of $500,000 on 28 December 20X5. There were no other common shares issued during the year. Net earnings for the year ended 31 December 20X5 are $95,600.

Required:

Prepare the adjusting journal entries to record the transactions occurring on 28 December 20X5. Prepare the statement of changes in equity for the year ended 31 December 20X5, assuming that the opening balance of the retained earnings is $449,000 and the opening balance of the common share capital account is $780,000.

ASSIGNMENTS

★ ★ AApp1-1 Journalize Transactions:

The Fardy Information Management Inc. follows the expedient recording method. It engaged in transactions during the month of May:

a. Paid $8,500 for May rent.

b. Bought $5,300 of office supplies on account.

c. Payroll for May was $72,000. Employees were paid $54,800, and the remainder was payroll deductions (income tax etc.) All payroll deductions were immediately remitted to the Receiver General.

d. Customers were billed $105,400 for completed assignments.

e. Utilities of $3,950 were paid.

f. Declared a cash dividend of $1.70 per preferred share and $0.80 per common share, payable 6 June. There are 60,000 preferred shares and 180,000 common shares outstanding.

g. Sold used computer equipment with an original cost of $53,700 accumulated depreciation to date of $49,200, for $7,000.

h. Paid suppliers $4,000 on account for supplies in (b).

i. Collected $81,900 from customers on account in (d).

Required:

1. Journalize each of the above transactions in general journal form.

2. Which entries would be different if the standard recording method were used? Repeat these entries, using the standard reporting method. Explain how the (eventual) adjusting journal entries for these accounts would be different under this approach.

3. Indicate in which journal each transaction would normally be recorded, assuming that the company keeps a journal for purchases (merchandise for resale/inventory purchases), sales, cash receipts, cash disbursements, and also a general journal.

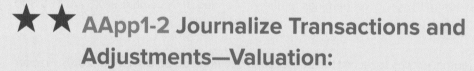

★ ★ AApp1-2 Journalize Transactions and Adjustments—Valuation:

Zfind Corp. reports the following in the month of April:

a. Issued 17,000 no-par common shares for cash, $68,000.

b. Issued 15,000 no-par common shares for a piece of used equipment with an appraised value of $52,000. The equipment had an original cost of $76,000 to the seller three years ago. The net book value (cost less accumulated depreciation) on the books of the seller was $42,900 on the date of sale.

c. Bought land with an appraised value of $70,000. An 8%, three-year note payable was issued in the amount of $50,000, and $20,000 was paid in cash.

d. Bought office supplies on account, $1,200. An asset account is debited.

e. Hired three employees at the beginning of the month. All employees are paid on a monthly basis. Monthly salaries for the three will amount to $8,000. (Two will be paid $3,000 per month each, and one will be paid $2,000 per month.)

f. Three months' rent is paid in advance. The lease calls for $1,000 of rent per month. An asset account is debited.

g. Goods for resale in the amount of $120,000 are bought. Twenty percent of the price is paid in cash, and the rest is on account. These goods are priced to sell at $266,000.

h. Received an order from a customer for goods worth $50,000. The goods will be shipped in the next week (see [j]).

i. Miscellaneous operating expenses are paid in the amount of $14,400, cash.

j. Goods are delivered to customers and they are billed, on account, $245,000. The order, in (h) above, is included in this total. The goods delivered to the customers cost $110,000. There are still goods that cost $10,000, with a retail value of $21,000, in inventory.

k. One month has gone by, and monthly rent expense is recorded.

l. Employee salaries for one month are paid.

m. The board of directors declares, but does not pay, a dividend in the amount of $13,600.

n. Office supplies on hand at year-end, per physical count, are $400.

o. Goods purchased on account in (g) above are paid for in full.

p. Eighty percent of the accounts receivable from customers, as recorded in (j) above, are received.

Required:

1. Journalize the transactions and events listed above. If no journal entry is needed, write "no entry." Zfind uses a perpetual inventory system. If there is a choice of value to use, justify your choice.

2. Which entries recorded are transactions, and which are adjustments? Explain.

★ ★ AApp1-3 Journalize and Post—Unadjusted Trial Balance:

The following selected transactions or events were completed during 20X5 by HUP Inc., a retailer of makeup and skin care products:

a. Issued 25,000 shares of its own no-par common shares for $7 per share and received cash in full.

b. Borrowed $500,000 cash on a 6%, one-year note, interest payable at maturity on 30 April 20X6.

c. Paid $350,000 for leasehold improvements on a shopping mall location that will be the major retail outlet; also paid one year's rent of $100,000 in full.

d. Purchased merchandise inventory for resale at a cash cost of $260,000.

e. Purchased merchandise inventory for resale on credit for $58,800.

f. Sold merchandise that cost $96,000 for $198,000 cash.

g. Paid $87,000 cash for operating expenses.

h. Paid two-thirds of the balance for the merchandise purchased in (e).

i. Paid cash for an insurance premium, $3,600; the premium is for two years' coverage (debit prepaid insurance).

j. Counted inventory and had $219,000 of merchandise on hand.

k. Paid damages to a customer who was injured through use of a company product, $4,000 cash.

Required:

1. Enter transactions in a general journal; use "J1" for the first journal page number. Use the letter of the transaction in place of the date.

2. Set up appropriate T-accounts, and post the journal entries. Use posting reference numbers in your posting. Assign each T-account an appropriate title, and number each account in statement of financial position order followed by the temporary accounts; start with "Cash, No. 101."

3. Prepare an unadjusted trial balance.

 **AApp1-4 Adjusting Entries:**

Manitoba Mini Homes Corp. has annual earnings of $24,600 in its unadjusted trial balance. The company prepares financial statements annually, with adjusting journal entries recorded at year-end. The following items have not yet been addressed for the fiscal period ended 31 December:

a. A 12-month, $1,560 insurance policy that commenced on 1 September was paid on 1 September and debited to prepaid insurance at that time. The prepaid insurance account already had a balance of $960 on 1 September in relation to the prior insurance coverage, which expired on 30 August.

b. The office supplies inventory account had a balance of $1,300 at the beginning of the year. Supplies costing $3,900 were purchased during the year and expensed as bought. There is an inventory of $1,700 physically on hand at the end of the year.

c. Manitoba completed a mini-home sale on the last day of the fiscal year but has not yet recorded the transaction. The mini-home was sold for $56,000, and the proceeds were to be paid in early January. The unit has a cost of $43,100 and was still in inventory on the books as of 31 December.

d. A service charge of $135, a deduction from the cash account per the bank statement for December, has not yet been recorded. Interest on outstanding loans for $560 was also taken out of the bank account in December but is not recorded.

e. A customer paid a $10,000 deposit for repairs in December. This amount was credited to revenue, but the work is not expected to be done until January.

f. A customer paid $5,160 in early November for one year's rent on a mini-home, a rental arrangement effective on 1 November. The cash received was credited to revenue in November.

g. A customer paid $6,000 in early August for one year's rent on a mini-home, a rental arrangement commencing on 1 August. The cash received was credited to unearned revenue in August.

h. A customer who rents a mini-home did not pay her rent in November or December, although the company believes that the amount will be paid in January. Nothing has been recorded for November or December. Monthly rental is $500 on this unit.

Required:

1. Journalize each of the above transactions in general journal form, as needed.
2. Calculate the revised earnings for the period, reflecting the adjustments in requirement 1.

★ **AApp1-5 Adjusting Entries:**

Signal Corp. adjusts and closes its accounts each 30 September. The following situations require adjusting entries at the current year-end:

a. Fuel supplies that cost $12,420 were purchased during the year and debited to fuel inventory. At the year-end, the amount of fuel still on hand was $1,270.

b. Signal sold goods for cash to customers on 30 September for $72,500. These sales have not yet been recorded.

c. Equipment is to be depreciated for a half year. It cost $930,000, and the estimated useful life is 12 years with an estimated residual value of $14,400. Use straight-line depreciation.

d. The allowance for doubtful accounts currently has a balance of $59,700. Signal has estimated the amount of uncollectible customer accounts to be $43,100.

e. Signal signed a maintenance contract for office cleaning for 30 months starting April 1 for $90,000. The entire amount was set up as prepaid maintenance at the time of payment and no amount for the current year has yet been expensed.

f. Late in September, it was found that a posting error had been made. A deposit of $7,100 from a customer had been recorded as other income and should have been recorded as unearned revenue.

g. On September 21, the company received its statement for vehicle insurance, which is for one year commencing October 5. The amount of $7,560 is due on 2 October.

Required:

Prepare adjusting entries in the general journal for each situation. If no entry is required for an item, explain why.

★ ★ AApp1-6 Adjusting Entries:

The following items are independent. Assume that the original transactions have been recorded correctly or as described. Assume a 31 December year-end unless otherwise noted.

a. Prepaid insurance had a debit balance of $18,200 at the beginning of January. This represents the remaining 14 months in an insurance policy that was purchased in a prior year. On 1 April of the current year, a 30-month policy was bought for $50,400, which was debited to prepaid insurance. There were no other entries to the prepaid insurance account during the year. On 1 November, an 18-month policy was bought for $9,360. This policy was debited to insurance expense.

b. Certain invoices had not been recorded at 31 December: a $7,400 bill for power, a $920 phone bill, and a repair bill for $1,350. All these bills are due in January.

c. Salaries payable has a balance of $3,700, unadjusted from the last year-end. There are 14 employees. They were paid up to Friday, 27 December. There were two additional working days prior to the year-end. Three employees earn $600 per (five-day) week each, three earn $500 per week, and eight earn $400 per week.

d. There are two notes payable outstanding. The first is an $890,000, 4% note, issued on 1 September; no interest has been paid to date. The second is a $700,000, 3.5% note issued on 1 April; six months' interest was paid on 1 October. The notes payable themselves were properly recorded on issuance, but interest must be accrued to 31 December, the year-end.

e. There is an unearned revenue account with a balance of $160,000. This includes a $10,000 security deposit from a tenant. This deposit will be returned when the tenant eventually vacates. The remaining $150,000 is six months' rent received, on a lease beginning 1 December, on commercial property.

f. Supplies inventory had a balance of $23,600 at the end of last year. During the year, $69,800 of supplies were purchased, and were debited directly to supplies expense. At year-end, an inventory count was conducted, and the balance was ascertained to be $24,750.

g. Advertising expense of $94,800 includes a $6,300 payment for an advertisement that will run in January of next year.

Required:

1. Prepare adjusting journal entries to reflect the facts above.
2. Prepare reversing entries for adjusting journal entries that must be reversed.

AApp1-7 Adjusting Entries:

Zeonan Inc., an accounting firm, adjusts and closes its accounts each 30 June.

1. On 1 February 20X4, the company collected cash, $15,540, which was for rent collected in advance from a tenant for the next 12 months. Give the adjusting journal entry as at 30 June 20X4 assuming the following at the time of the collection:

   Case A $15,540 was credited to rent revenue.

   Case B $15,540 was credited to rent collected in advance.

2. On 30 June 20X5, the maintenance supplies inventory account showed a balance on hand amounting to $12,100. During 20X6, purchases of maintenance supplies amounted to $24,000. An inventory of maintenance supplies on hand at 30 June 20X6 reflected unused supplies amounting to $6,500. Give the adjusting journal entry that should be made on 30 June 20X6, under the following conditions:

   Case A Purchases were debited to the maintenance supplies inventory account.

   Case B Purchases were debited to maintenance supplies expense.

3. On 30 June 20X5, the prepaid insurance account showed a debit balance of $3,435, which was for coverage for the three months July to September. On 1 September 20X5, the company obtained another policy covering a three-year period from that date. The three-year premium, amounting to $41,472, was paid on 1 September. Give the adjusting journal entry that should be made on 30 June 20X6.

   Case A $41,472 was debited to prepaid insurance.

   Case B $41,472 was debited to insurance expense.

Required:

Provide adjusting journal entries.

 AApp1-8 Adjusting Entries:

Gilby Repairs Ltd. has transactions that can be used to illustrate terminology and also the recording and adjustment decisions in the accounting cycle. The company prepares complete monthly financial statements and uses reversing entries, where appropriate. Four transactions are described below:

Transaction 1

The company received $32,900 in July from a customer for repairs to be done in August. The repairs were completed in August as scheduled. Assume that the standard recording method is used. Prepare an entry to record the cash receipt in July; an adjusting entry at the end of July, if needed; a reversing entry for the first of August, if needed; and an entry for the work done in August, if needed. Repeat these entries, assuming that the expedient recording method is used.

Transaction 2

The company did work worth $105,130 for a customer in September and then delivered and invoiced the job in September. The customer paid in October. Prepare an entry to record the work done in September, if needed; a reversing entry for the first of October, if needed; and the cash transaction in October.

Transaction 3

Gilby began the month of February with a $5,300 balance in the supplies inventory asset account. Gilby purchased $12,600 of supplies in February for cash, and a physical count revealed $4,900 of supplies on hand at the end of the month. Assume that the standard recording method is used. Prepare an entry to record the cash payment in February, an adjusting entry at the end of February, if needed; and a reversing entry for the first of March, if needed. Repeat these entries, assuming that the expedient recording method is used.

Transaction 4

Gilby used $15,030 of services from the Carleton Consulting Company during the month of May. The bill for this was received and paid in June. Prepare entries needed in May, any reversing entry on the first of June, if needed, and any entry needed in June.

Required:

Prepare journal entries as requested in the transactions above.

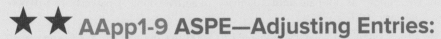 **AApp1-9 ASPE—Adjusting Entries:**

Oliver Trading Corp. has a preliminary figure for earnings of $341,457, for the year ended 31 December 20X5. The company also has provided the following information in relation to its annual financial information:

a. No income tax has been recorded, but the tax rate is 32%.

b. The company has a bank loan outstanding for $180,000, which has been outstanding for the entire year. The interest has not been paid or recorded for the final quarter. Interest is based on an annual rate of 7%.

c. Property taxes of $17,424 were paid in March and were for the 12-month period starting on 1 April. The total amount was expensed in March when paid.

d. Accounts receivable were reviewed for bad debts, and it was determined that $7,500 of the $80,000 owing was unlikely to be collected. At present, there is a balance of $2,850 (debit) in the allowance for doubtful accounts.

e. The merchandise inventory account has a balance of $150,000. The company uses a perpetual inventory system, so cost of goods sold has been recorded as the year has progressed. However, the physical inventory count at the end of the year showed a total of $148,100 of goods on hand. The difference between this and the accounting records was probably due to theft.

f. A customer paid $40,000 on an outstanding account receivable in December. This amount was credited to sales, in error.

g. Depreciation of equipment in the amount of $12,900 has not been recorded.

h. Accounting fees paid, in the amount of $6,400, were debited to dividends instead of an expense account.

i. A customer paid $102,000 as a deposit in June. This was credited to unearned revenue, but the transaction was completed in October, and the goods delivered. Cost of goods sold was correctly recorded at that time, but the unearned revenue was not changed.

j. At the beginning of the year, there was a balance of $2,175 in the prepaid insurance account, for a policy that will expire at the end of March 20X6. During the year, a second policy for different coverage came into effect on August 1. This policy cost $4,152 and covers 24 months. The payment was debited to insurance expense when it was made.

Required:

Journalize each of the above transactions in general journal form.

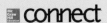

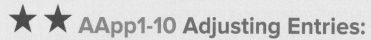 **AApp1-10 Adjusting Entries:**

Triple Y Exports Ltd. uses a perpetual inventory system, recording cost of goods sold each time there is a sale, and updating inventory records for each new purchase of goods. The company has the following transactions and events at 31 December 20X5, the end of the accounting period:

a. On 1 November 20X5, Triple Y invested $75,000 excess cash in an interest-bearing investment for a yield of 4%. Interest will be paid at maturity at the end of April 20X6. The investment has been recorded but the interest for the year has not.

b. Triple Y has a term loan from its bank, of $200,000. Interest at the rate of 6% per annum is paid at the end of each month. Interest for December was not paid until 2 January, in an oversight. A payment of $10,000 principal was also paid on 2 January 20X6.

c. At the beginning of 20X5, office supplies inventory amounted to $600. At the end of 20X5, a count of inventory showed that there was $750 on hand. During 20X5, office supplies amounting to $8,800 were purchased and the inventory account was increased as a result.

d. At the beginning of 20X5, there was a balance of $4,960 in the prepaid insurance account related to a general fire insurance policy that will expire on 1 May 20X6. There was also a prepaid amount of $1,500 relating to vehicle insurance, expiring 28 February 20X5. In 20X5, a six-month vehicle policy costing $4,800 was purchased on March 1, and a further six-month policy costing $5,160 was purchased after the first one expired. The policies purchased in 20X5 were debited to prepaid insurance.

e. A customer returned goods for full credit. The goods have a cost of $1,700 and a retail price of $6,700. The goods had been purchased by the customer on account and correctly recorded on initial sale. When the return was made, inventory was debited and accounts receivable credited for $1,700.

f. The bank statement indicates that the bank, in error, cashed a cheque on the company's bank account in December 20X5 for $4,600. This cheque was written by YYY Exports Ltd., not Triple Y Exports. Triple Y has reported the issue to the bank, and the bank has promised to reverse the amount.

g. The accountant has reviewed the invoices that arrived in early January 20X6. The following items are for goods and services purchased or consumed in December: Target Advertising Limited $3,600, BlueWave Cell Communications, $650, Econ Electricity, $1,200, and Forward Oil, $3,200.

h. The accountant reviewed the invoices that were issued to customers in early January and noted the following sales that took place in December: Customer Lui, $54,000 (cost of goods shipped, $34,600), Customer O'Grady, $75,900 (cost of goods shipped, $54,100); and Customer Sami, $23,400 (cost of goods shipped, $12,900). Neither the sale nor the product removed from inventory was recorded in December.

i. There was a payroll of $45,600 paid on 3 January; this covered the period of 30 December to 3 January.

j. A tenant in the administration building pays $1,350 rent per month. The tenant paid one year's rent on 1 March 20X5. The cash received was credited to rental revenue at that time.

Required:

Give the adjusting entry (or entries) that should be made on 31 December 20X5, for each item. If an adjusting entry is not required, explain why. Prepare any reversing entries that might be appropriate.

connect

 **AApp1-11 Adjusting Entries:**

Set forth below is the adjusted trial balance of the Trough Corp. as of 31 March 20X2:

Account	Debit	Credit
Cash	$ 24,400	
Accounts receivable	71,000	
Merchandise inventory	86,000	
Prepaid rent	8,000	
Equipment	35,200	
Accumulated depreciation		$ 6,500
Accounts payable		40,100
Note payable		40,000
Accrued interest payable		800
Capital stock		10,000
Retained earnings		127,200
	$224,600	$224,600

The following information describes the company's April transactions and provides the data required for month-end adjustments:

- Cash sales were $85,900.
- Sales on account were $78,500.
- Repaid $10,000 of note payable principal on 1 April.
- Operating expenses of $25,000 were paid in cash.
- Collected $41,000 in cash from customers on account.
- Wrote off $2,000 of accounts receivable as uncollectible. No other accounts receivable are in doubt of collection.
- Shareholders invested $20,000 in the business in exchange for 1,000 common shares.
- Bought $82,000 of merchandise on account.
- Ending merchandise inventory was $53,400.
- Paid suppliers $37,000 on account.
- Spent $5,000 for advertising to take place in May 20X2.
- Paid $14,300 in cash for wages, and still owed $2,500 for wages at month-end.
- The rent had previously been paid in advance to 31 July 20X2.
- The equipment has a total useful life of 10 years, and salvage of $4,000. These estimates have not changed since the asset was first acquired.
- The note payable bears an interest rate of 6% per year, and interest is due on 1 May.

Required:

1. Journalize the April transactions and adjusting journal entries.
2. Prepare an SCI and SFP for the month of April.

★ ★ AApp1-12 Entries and Financial Statements:

Provided below is the trial balance for Computer Guru Consulting Ltd., on 31 December 20X2, for the 20X2 fiscal year. No adjustments have been made in 20X2.

Cash	$ 11,300	
Accounts receivable	18,200	
Allowance for doubtful accounts		$ 650
Inventory	94,140	
Equipment	157,500	
Accumulated depreciation, equipment		24,200
Accounts payable		75,200
Unearned revenue		12,000
Note payable		94,000
Common shares		40,000
Retained earnings		96,000
Dividends	18,600	
Sales		850,000
Cost of goods sold	580,000	
Wages	196,000	
Operating expenses	69,800	
Sales salaries	46,510	

Other information:

a. The note payable had an interest rate of 6%. $50,000 was borrowed on 1 February, and the balance was borrowed on 1 June 20X2. No interest was paid in 20X2.

b. An inventory count showed that goods with a cost of $89,200 were on hand at the end of the year.

c. Operating expenses include an insurance policy that was effective on 1 January 20X2 and runs for three years. The policy cost $5,400.

d. An unpaid supplier invoice for heating oil for $3,600 has been recorded for $6,300 in error.

e. A customer paid a $9,000 down payment on a job in December; this amount was credited to unearned revenue. The job is about 50% complete but has not been finished or reviewed with the customer. The remaining $3,000 in unearned revenue is an advance from a customer, for a job that has been cancelled; this amount will be refunded to the customer shortly.

f. Depreciation on equipment has not yet been recorded. The equipment is three years old at the end of 20X2, and estimates of useful life and salvage value have not changed since it was acquired. Depreciation is recorded on a straight-line basis.

g. A review of invoices sent to customers in January 20X3 showed that sales of $41,200 actually took place in December. These sales were connected with goods that cost $13,400. The product had been physically removed from inventory in December, and inventory and cost of sales were properly recorded in December. Sales were not recorded until January.

h. A review of invoices and payments in early January 20X3 showed some expenses that were related to December but not recorded until January: operating expenses, $5,675, and sales salaries, $4,200.

i. A payment for business operating expenses was made by one of the shareholders in 20X2, and he then submitted the $12,500 invoice for payment. When he was reimbursed, the amount was debited to dividends.

j. Accounts receivable were reviewed, and it was determined that $6,500 of accounts receivable are unlikely to be collected, although the company is still making collection attempts. (Percentage of accounts receivable method is used by the company.)

Required:

1. Record adjusting entries, as needed, for the additional information provided above.
2. Calculate the revised earnings for the period, reflecting the adjustments in requirement 1.
3. Record any reversing entries that are appropriate.

★ ★ AApp1-13 Adjustments and Financial Statements:

Dan Richards incorporated an appliance repair shop on 1 January 20X2 and has been quite pleased with the results of his first year. His cash receipts and disbursements are:

Inflows:

Repair revenue received	$49,000
Rent revenue received	6,000
Cash refunds from suppliers, for returned parts	1,200
Cash originally invested by Dan	3,000
Bank loan	18,000
	$77,200

Outflows:

Wages paid	18,000
Dividends paid	3,400
Parts and supplies paid for	9,000
Insurance premiums paid	2,000
Rent paid	12,500
Equipment purchased	9,500
Other operating expenses paid	2,000
	$56,400

Other information:

- Equipment has a 10-year life and a $500 salvage value and is to be depreciated using the declining-balance method, using a rate of 20%.
- Parts still on hand amount to $2,760.
- The insurance premium was paid on 1 August for an eight-month policy.
- Rental revenue is from a tenant who rents excess space. She paid 12 months rent on 1 April when she moved in.

- Dan owes his workers another $1,200 in wages, and customers owe him $7,560 for repair work done.
- Dan owes his suppliers $1,490 for parts.
- The bank loan was taken out on 1 March and has an interest rate of 12%.
- Bad debts are likely 4% of repair revenue.
- Rent paid was for the 12-month calendar year of 20X2. Dan must also pay 1% of repair revenue to his landlord but has not done this yet.
- For simplicity, assume that there are no income taxes.

Required:

1. Prepare an SCI for Dan for the year ended 31 December 20X2.
2. Prepare an SFP as of 31 December 20X2.

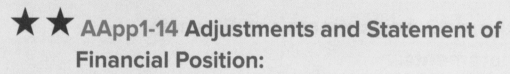

★ ★ AApp1-14 Adjustments and Statement of Financial Position:

On 31 December 20X5, the Hearth & Stove Corp. is preparing financial statements. The following unadjusted trial balance has been prepared:

HEARTH & STOVE CORP.
Trial Balance

	Debit	Credit
Accounts payable		$ 66,450
Accounts receivable	$ 316,635	
Advertising expense	19,200	
Accumulated depreciation—office equipment		59,700
Allowance for doubtful accounts		6,750
Cash	25,200	
Cost of goods sold	990,000	
Common shares		67,500
Dividends declared	15,600	
Insurance expense	2,700	
Interest expense	3,960	
Interest revenue		1,260
Inventory	75,000	
Land	217,500	
Long-term investments	468,900	
Mortgage payable		445,500
Notes payable—short term		16,200

Office equipment	108,000	
Office expense	19,650	
Prepaid insurance	0	
Retained earnings, opening		68,730
Revenue received in advance		52,200
Sales		1,833,000
Supplies inventory	600	
Supplies expense	6,300	
Miscellaneous expense	23,145	
Rent expense	108,000	
Wages expense	216,900	
	$2,617,290	$2,617,290

The following facts are also available at the end of 20X5:

a. The inventory on hand is $70,050 according to the physical count.

b. The allowance for doubtful accounts should have a balance of $8,400.

c. The office equipment is depreciated at a rate of 8% per year (straight-line).

d. There are supplies of $1,800 on hand.

e. On 31 March of this year, the company bought a $2,700 insurance policy with a 12-month term.

f. Customers have not yet been billed for products delivered on the last day of the year. The products have a retail value of $81,000. The cost of goods sold for this transaction was properly recorded.

g. Income tax is estimated to be 30% of all earnings before income tax. No income tax has been recorded or paid.

Required:

1. Prepare adjusting journal entries to reflect the information in (a) to (g) above.

2. Prepare a statement of changes in equity in good form that reflects the trial balance above and your journal entries. There were no changes to common shares during the year.

3. Prepare a classified SFP in good form that reflects the trial balance above and your journal entries.

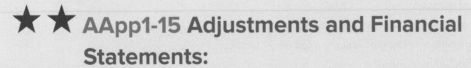

★ ★ AApp1-15 Adjustments and Financial Statements:

Toronado Ltd. reported the following items in its unadjusted trial balance as of 31 December 20X4 for the 20X4 fiscal year. This trial balance is listed in alphabetical order. Note that this is a *partial* trial balance and does not include all accounts. Accounts have normal (debit or credit) balances.

Administration expense	$235,700
Accounts payable	76,800
Accounts receivable	99,800
Allowance for doubtful accounts (credit)	2,000
Cash dividends declared	31,000
Freight-out (delivery to customers)	26,900
Gain on sale of automobile	1,400
Insurance expense	38,400
Interest expense	27,100
Loans receivable, 8%	75,000
Merchandise inventory, 1 January	89,400
Notes payable, 6%	500,000
Purchases	560,300
Salaries and employee benefits	120,900
Sales returns and allowances	42,100
Sales revenues	1,876,000
Selling expense	34,000
Supplies expense	45,900
Supplies inventory	600
Retained earnings, 1 January	568,300
Unearned revenue	32,000
Utilities expense	65,400

Other information:

- The tax rate is 30%, but no tax has yet been recorded.
- Closing merchandise inventory is $76,500. Closing supplies inventory is $1,300.
- The insurance expense represents a payment made on 1 May for a 24-month fire insurance policy.
- Customers owe $53,000 for goods delivered on 31 December; this amount has not yet been recorded.
- All sales are on account, except those that are prepaid.
- Unearned revenue represents all customer deposits received during the year. Of this amount, 60% is still unearned at the end of the year.
- Bad debt expense is to be recognized as 1% of total sales.
- Interest on the note payable was last paid and recorded on 31 October.
- The company owes $3,200 in utilities.
- Interest on the loan receivable has not been paid or recorded all year.

Required:

1. Prepare journal entries to reflect the required adjustments. Round adjustments to the nearest $100, if necessary.
2. Prepare an SCI based on the adjusted balances.
3. Prepare a statement of changes in equity (for retained earnings only) based on the adjusted balances.

★ AApp1-16 Preparing a Statement of Financial Position:

Your assistant has prepared the following *partial* adjusted trial balance data for the Green Solutions Cleaning Products Corp. as of 31 December 20X8. The accounts are arranged in alphabetical order; unfortunately, the debit and credit balances have been listed in the same column. Some revenue, expense, gain or loss accounts may be missing.

Accounts payable	$288,000
Accounts receivable	537,600
Accumulated depreciation—buildings	158,400
Accumulated depreciation—equipment	80,000
Advertising expense	38,400
Bonds payable	1,320,000
Buildings	576,000
Capital stock	428,000
Cash	96,000
Depreciation expense—buildings	64,000
Depreciation expense—equipment	12,000
Dividends declared	115,200
Dividends payable	50,000
Equipment	434,240
Expired insurance	11,600
Interest earned	4,590
Interest receivable	2,400
Inventory (merchandise) (closing balance)	484,800
Land	556,800
Long-term investments	436,800
Mortgage payable	384,000
Notes payable—short term	120,000
Office expenses	128,160
Premium on bonds payable	10,000

Prepaid insurance	6,000
Property tax expense	60,960
Retained earnings—31 December 20X7	78,720
Sales	1,968,000
Supplies on hand	6,500
Unearned revenue	12,400

Required:

Prepare the 31 December 20X8 SFP. For the closing retained earnings, use the value that will make the statement balance.

★ ★ AApp1-17 ASPE—Preparing Financial Statements:

The following trial balance for Falcon Corp. is in alphabetical order.

31 December 20X7	Debit	Credit
Accounts payable		235,900
Accounts receivable	344,000	
Accumulated amortization, building		200,700
Allowance for doubtful accounts		46,200
Bank loans payable—short term		460,000
Building	456,000	
Cash	26,500	
Common shares		170,000
Cost of goods sold	933,100	
Dividends	24,000	
Income tax expense	116,000	
Interest expense	52,100	
Inventory, 31 December 20X7	291,700	
Land	36,000	
Long-term bond payable		120,000
Long-term investments	230,000	
Notes receivable—short term	100,000	

Office supplies	3,600	
Operating expenses	458,000	
Operating expenses payable		48,900
Prepaid insurance	1,500	
Rent revenue		24,700
Retained earnings (1 January 20X7)		44,300
Sales		1,822,200
Selling expenses	107,800	
Unearned revenue		4,000
Wages payable		3,400
	$3,180,300	$3,180,300

Required:

1. Prepare an income statement from the information given.
2. Prepare a balance sheet and a statement of retained earnings.

★ ★ AApp1-18 Entries and Worksheet:

Pinehill Ltd. is a retail operation that uses a perpetual inventory system. The unadjusted trial balance for the year ended 31 December 20X5 follows:

PINEHILL LTD.

Unadjusted Trial Balance

Cash	$ 65,000	
Accounts receivable	112,000	
Allowance for doubtful accounts		$ 17,000
Merchandise inventory	440,000	
Store equipment	230,000	
Accumulated depreciation, store equipment		57,500
Accounts payable		164,000
Loan payable—long term		92,000
Common shares		200,000
Retained earnings		238,500
Sales revenue		1,600,000
Sales returns and allowances	41,000	
Cost of goods sold	978,000	

Selling expenses	453,000	
Administrative expenses	50,000	
	$2,369,000	$2,369,000

Additional information:

- The allowance for doubtful accounts should have a balance of $19,000. This is a selling expense.
- The company uses a perpetual inventory system, but the closing inventory is verified by physical count. This count showed that the correct balance for closing inventory is $415,000.
- No depreciation has been recorded for 20X5. The store equipment is being amortized using the straight-line method over an estimated useful life of 20 years with no residual value. This is a selling expense.
- The long-term loan was a two-year loan from a local bank. The interest rate is 7%, payable at the end of each 12-month period. The money was borrowed on 1 April 20X5. This is an administrative expense.
- The income tax rate is 30%; no tax has yet been paid or recorded.

Required:

1. Prepare adjusting entries for the year ended 31 December 20X5.
2. Complete the year-end worksheet. Combine the SFP and retained earnings columns.

★ ★ AApp1-19 Entries and Worksheet:

The following information pertains to the first year of operations for Carmen Corp.:

CARMEN CORP.		
Unadjusted Trial Balance		
31 December 20X6	**Debit**	**Credit**
Cash	$ 5,100	
Accounts receivable	11,700	
Office equipment	6,900	
Computer equipment	5,400	
Accounts payable		7,550
Loan payable—long term		30,000
Common shares		70
Sales revenue		36,300
Rent expense	12,000	
Supplies inventory	18,100	
Interest expense	2,100	
Insurance expense	1,320	
Miscellaneous expense	11,300	
	$73,920	$73,920

Additional information:

a. On 1 July, the company signed a five-year lease for office space in a new industrial park. The company moved immediately. Rent is $1,500 per month and some rent was paid upfront as a deposit.

b. On 15 June, the company borrowed $30,000 from the bank. Interest at 14% is payable at the middle of every month. Payments have been made to date.

c. Leasehold improvements were made to the rented premises. Total cost for things such as partitions, painting, and wiring was $8,000 and was charged to miscellaneous expense.

d. Used computer equipment was purchased at an auction for $5,400. It was worth $9,000.

e. There was one job completed at year-end but not billed in the amount of $10,000.

f. Bad debts relating to the year-end accounts receivable are expected to be $350.

g. Year-end accounting fees are estimated to be $1,800.

h. On 1 October the company bought a used car for $7,600. Although the vehicle was to be used primarily on company business, the owner/manager used personal funds to pay for it. Consequently no entry was made in the books of the company. The company will repay the owner/manager when there is enough money.

i. The following depreciation and amortization policies are to be used; a full year of depreciation is charged in the first year of ownership. There are no residual values.

> Office and computer equipment: 5 years straight-line
>
> Vehicles: 8 years straight-line
>
> Leasehold improvements: 5 years straight-line

j. Supplies inventory was $3,000 at the year-end count.

k. The effective tax rate for the company is 25%.

Required:

1. Prepare the adjusting journal entries required at year-end (31 December 20X6).
2. Complete the year-end worksheet. Combine the retained earnings and SFP columns.

★ ★ ★ AApp1-20 ASPE—The Accounting Cycle:

At 31 December 20X5, the post-closing trial balance of Fox Ltd., a retailer of health food supplements, reflects the following:

Acct. No.	Account	Debit	Credit
101	Cash	$81,000	
102	Accounts receivable	63,000	
103	Allowance for doubtful accounts		$ 3,000
104	Inventory (perpetual inventory system)	105,000	
105	Prepaid insurance (20 months remaining at 1 January)	2,700	
200	Equipment (20-year estimated life, no residual value)	150,000	

201	Accumulated amortization, equipment		67,500
300	Accounts payable		22,500
301	Wages payable		—
302	Income taxes payable (for 20X5)		12,000
400	Common shares, no-par, 100,000 shares		240,000
401	Retained earnings		56,700
500	Sales revenue		—
600	Cost of goods sold	—	
601	Operating expenses	—	
602	Income tax expense	—	
700	Income summary	—	
		$401,700	$401,700

The following transactions occurred during 20X6 in the order given (use the letter at the left in place of date):

a. Sales revenue of $90,000, of which $30,000 was on credit; cost of goods sold, provided by perpetual inventory record, $58,500. (*Note:* When the perpetual system is used, make two entries to record a sale: *first*, debit cash or accounts receivable and credit sales revenue; *second*, debit cost of goods sold and credit inventory.)

b. Collected $51,000 on accounts receivable.

c. Paid income taxes payable (20X5), $12,000.

d. Purchased merchandise, $120,000, of which $24,000 was on credit.

e. Paid accounts payable, $18,000.

f. Sales revenue of $216,000 (in cash); cost of goods sold, $140,400.

g. Paid operating expenses, $57,000.

h. Issued 1,000 common shares for $3,000 cash.

i. Purchased merchandise, $300,000, of which $81,000 was on credit.

j. Sales revenue of $294,000, of which $90,000 was on credit; cost of goods sold, $191,100.

k. Collected cash on accounts receivable, $78,000.

l. Paid accounts payable, $84,000.

m. Paid various operating expenses in cash, $54,000.

Required:

1. Journalize each of the transactions listed above for 20X6; use only a general journal.

2. Set up T-accounts in the general ledger for each of the accounts listed in the above trial balance, and enter the account number and 31 December 20X5 balance.

3. Post the journal entries; use posting reference numbers.

4. Prepare an unadjusted trial balance.

5. Journalize the adjusting entries and post them to the ledger. Assume a bad debt rate of 0.5% of credit sales for the period at 31 December 20X6; accrued wages were $900. The average income tax rate was 40%. Record

straight-line amortization and insurance expense. Debit expenses to the operating expense account. (Check your work: Income tax expense is $35,352.)

6. Prepare an adjusted trial balance.

7. Prepare the income statement and balance sheet.

8. Journalize and post the closing entries.

9. Prepare a post-closing trial balance.

★ ★ ★ AApp1-21 The Accounting Cycle:

The post-closing trial balance of Gensing Enterprises Ltd., a farming operation, at 31 December 20X6, reflects the following:

Acct. No.	Account	Debit	Credit
101	Cash	$ 42,000	
102	Accounts receivable	35,800	
103	Allowance for doubtful accounts		$ 2,000
104	Inventory, 31 December 20X6	46,000	
105	Fertilizer and supplies inventory	6,700	
106	Prepaid insurance (expires at the end of November 20X7)	9,000	
200	Equipment	344,800	
201	Accumulated depreciation, equipment		124,600
202	Land	682,000	
300	Accounts payable		67,500
301	Unearned revenue		32,000
302	Notes payable		75,000
400	Common shares		400,000
401	Retained earnings		465,200
500	Sales revenue		—
600	Cost of goods sold	—	
601	Operating expenses	—	
700	Income summary		
		$1,166,300	$1,166,300

Various transactions occurred in 20X7:

a. Sales amounted to $767,000. Cash sales were 25% of the total, and the rest was on account.

b. At the beginning of the year, there was unearned revenue. This revenue was earned in 20X7, in addition to the sales transactions in part (a).

c. Operating expenses of $67,200 were paid in cash.

d. Fertilizer and other supplies were bought for $46,900, on credit.

e. Harvesting costs of $244,200 were paid. Harvesting costs of the crop are debited to inventory.

f. The cost of all goods sold for the period was $281,400. This should be recorded as a journal entry that increases cost of goods sold and reduces the inventory account.

g. The opening accounts receivable were collected in the amount of $31,000. No accounts were written off. Seventy percent of the current year sales on account were also collected.

h. The opening balance of accounts payable was paid in full.

i. Ninety percent of the fertilizer and other supplies, bought on credit, were paid for.

j. Paid dividends of $22,000.

k. A $10,800, 12-month insurance policy was paid on 1 December. The amount was debited to prepaid insurance.

l. A contract was signed with a customer for a certain quantity of next year's crop. The customer paid the full $50,000 price in cash in advance.

m. The note payable was partially repaid at the end of November, in the amount of $50,000. Interest of $5,500 was also paid on the entire note, all pertaining to 20X7. The remaining $25,000 balance of the note payable has an interest rate of 12% per annum. Interest must be accrued for the month of December 20X7 in requirement (5). The $25,000 balance is long term.

Required:

1. Journalize the transactions for 20X7. Use only a general journal. Debit all operating expenses to a general "operating expense" account, for simplicity. Add other accounts if needed. Interest expense is recorded in a separate account.

2. Set up T-accounts in the general ledger for each of the accounts listed in the above trial balance, and enter the account number and the 31 December balance.

3. Post the journal entries; use posting reference numbers. Assign new account numbers as needed.

4. Prepare an unadjusted trial balance.

5. Journalize and post the following adjusting journal entries:
   a. Depreciation for the year, $45,000.
   b. Bad debts are expected to be 2% of credit sales.
   c. Inventory of fertilizer and other supplies was $7,600 at year-end.
   d. Interest expense was accrued for December 20X7.
   e. Prepaid insurance expired.
   f. Wages earned but unpaid at year-end, $5,000.

   Debit expenses other than interest to operating expenses, and payables to accounts payable, for simplicity. There is no income tax.

6. Prepare an adjusted trial balance.

7. Prepare the SCI and SFP.

8. Journalize and post the closing entries.

9. Prepare a post-closing trial balance.

10. For which adjusting journal entries in requirement 5 above would reversing entries be appropriate? Explain.

★ ★ ★ AApp1-22 Worksheet, Adjusting and Closing Entries, Statements:

Darma Corp. is currently completing the end-of-the-period accounting process. At 31 December 20X5, the following unadjusted trial balance was developed from the general ledger:

Account	Debit	Credit
Cash	$ 120,520	
Accounts receivable	76,000	
Allowance for doubtful accounts		$ 4,000
Interest receivable	0	
Inventory (perpetual inventory system)	210,000	
Sales supplies inventory	1,800	
Long-term note receivable, 14%	24,000	
Equipment	360,000	
Accumulated depreciation, equipment		128,000
Patent (net)	16,800	
Accounts payable		46,000
Interest payable		0
Property tax payable		0
Rent collected in advance		0
Mortgage payable, 12%		120,000
Common shares, no-par, 10,000 shares		230,000
Retained earnings		64,880
Sales revenue		1,400,000
Investment revenue		2,240
Rent revenue		6,000
Cost of goods sold	760,000	
Selling expenses	328,800	
General and administrative expenses	110,000	
Interest expense	13,200	
Discontinued operations gain (pretax)		20,000
	$2,021,120	$2,021,120

Additional data for adjustments and other purposes:

a. Estimated bad debt loss rate is 0.25% of credit sales. Credit sales for the year amounted to $400,000; classify as a selling expense.

b. Interest on the long-term note receivable was last collected and recorded on 31 August 20X5.

c. Estimated useful life of the equipment is 10 years; residual value, $40,000. Allocate 10% of depreciation expense to general and administrative expense and the balance to selling expense to reflect proportionate use. Use straight-line depreciation.

d. Estimated remaining economic life of the patent is 14 years (from 1 January 20X5) with no residual value. Use straight-line depreciation, and classify as selling expense (used in sales promotion).

e. Interest on the mortgage payable was last paid and recorded on 30 November 20X5.

f. On 1 June 20X5, the company rented office space to a tenant for one year and collected $6,000 rent in advance for the year; the entire amount was credited to rent revenue on this date.

g. On 31 December 20X5, the company received a statement for calendar-year 20X5 property taxes amounting to $2,600. The payment is due 15 February 20X6. Classify the adjustment as a selling expense.

h. Sales supplies on hand at 31 December 20X5 amounted to $600; classify as a selling expense.

i. Assume an average 40% corporate income tax rate on all items including the discontinued operations gain. (Check your work: Total income tax expense is $70,264.)

Required:

1. Enter the above unadjusted trial balance on a worksheet.
2. Complete the worksheet.
3. Prepare the SCI and SFP.
4. Journalize the closing entries.

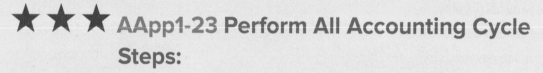

★ ★ ★ AApp1-23 Perform All Accounting Cycle Steps:

Construction Resources Ltd. (CRL), a calendar-year firm, began operations as a retailer in January 20X5.

Information about transactions and adjustments in 20X5:

1. Investors contributed $500,000 in exchange for 70,000 shares of no-par common shares.

2. CRL obtained a 6%, $500,000 bank loan on 1 February. This loan is evidenced by a signed promissory note calling for interest payments every 1 February. The note is due in full on 31 January 20X9.

3. A rental contract for production and office facilities was signed on 1 February, which required $12,000 immediate payment covering both the first month's rent and a $7,000 deposit refundable in three years or upon termination of the contract, whichever occurs first. Monthly rent is $5,000. As an added incentive to pay rent in advance, CRL accepted an offer to maintain rent at $5,000 per month for the first three years if CRL paid the 2nd through the 13th (March 20X5 through February 20X6) months' rent immediately. In all, CRL paid $72,000 for rent on 1 February. CRL intends to occupy the facilities for at least three years.

4. Equipment costing $350,000 was purchased for cash in early February. It has an estimated residual value of $35,000 and a six-year useful life. CRL uses the straight-line method of depreciation. A full year of depreciation is recorded in the year of acquisition.

5. CRL recognized various cash operating expenses for the year, including the following:

Wages	$310,000
Utilities	47,000
Selling	92,000
General and administrative	198,000

6. Total merchandise inventory purchases for the year, on account, amounted to $4,815,000.

7. All suppliers were paid for except for $90,000 outstanding at year-end.

8. All sales are made on credit and totalled $5,900,000 in 20X5; $4,925,000 was collected on account during the year. CRL estimates that 0.5% of total sales will be uncollectible and has written off $12,000 of accounts. The inventory sold had a cost of $4,447,000.

9. CRL declared a cash dividend of $114,000, payable in January 20X6.

10. Income tax expense is $342,000. All taxes for a fiscal year are payable in April of the following year.

Required:

Perform the 10 accounting cycle steps for CRL for 20X5. Worksheets, special journals, and subsidiary ledgers are not required. Prepare journal entries in summary (for the year) form. Post to T-accounts. CRL uses the expedient recording system and records reversing entries, whenever appropriate. CRL uses a perpetual inventory system.

 AApp1-24 Special Journals:

Imported Delights Ltd. had the following transactions in April 20X5:

April

4	Sold goods to customers on account, $46,280. The cost of these goods was $19,880.
9	Sold goods to customers for cash, $156,400. The cost of these goods was $44,460.
10	Paid electricity bill, $4,200.
14	Received payment from customers for 70% of 4 April sale.
14	Sold goods to customer on account, $161,120. The cost of these goods was $88,230.
15	Repaid note payable of $70,000, borrowed and properly recorded in January, plus $656 interest.
16	Received goods back from customer of 4 April and issued a credit note for $2,900. The cost of these goods was $1,300.
16	Bought merchandise inventory from a supplier on credit, $45,700.
17	Returned merchandise inventory to supplier from order of 16 April and got a credit note of $5,100.
22	Paid wages and salaries, $72,800.

22	Board of directors declared a $10,000 dividend. The dividend was both recorded and paid on this date.
24	Purchased merchandise inventory from a supplier on credit, $63,500.
25	Purchased merchandise inventory with cash, $9,350.
26	Borrowed $120,000 from the bank, and signed a 80-day, 7% note payable.
28	Bought office supplies on credit, $4,110.
29	Bought machinery, and issued a 90-day, 14% note payable for the full amount of $126,000.
30	Paid net amount due to supplier for goods purchased on 16 April.
31	Recorded depreciation expense on plant machinery of $5,400 for the month of April.

Required:

1. Draft special journals for cash receipts, cash disbursements, sales, and purchases. Also open a general journal.
2. Record the transactions in the appropriate journal. Leave the column blank if details (e.g., name or account number) are not available. There are no discounts offered to or by the company, so all sales and purchases are recorded gross.

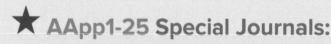

★ AApp1-25 Special Journals:

Gagetron Ltd. uses a perpetual inventory system. The company maintains special journals:

- Purchases (merchandise inventory for resale);
- Sales (sales on account and the related cost of goods sold);
- Cash receipts (all cash receipts, including payment by customers on account, and cash sales and the related cost of goods sold, but also miscellaneous receipts); and
- Cash disbursements (payments to suppliers on account, but also miscellaneous payments).

The company also maintains a general journal.

The company has the following transactions during the year:

a. Collected $99,800 from customers on account.
b. Collected $67,800 from customers for cash sales; these goods had a cost of $40,700.
c. Sold merchandise on account, $84,800; these goods had a cost of $51,000.
d. Bought merchandise inventory on credit, $395,600.
e. Paid $56,000 for dividends to common shareholders.
f. Paid $12,800 for rent.
g. Borrowed $50,000 from the bank.
h. Accepted a return from a customer and cancelled the related $10,700 sale. These goods had a cost of $6,200.

i. Paid for $272,800 of the inventory previously bought on credit.

j. Return merchandise inventory purchased on credit to the supplier, in the amount of $14,600.

Required:

Indicate the journal in which each of the above transactions would be recorded.

★ ★ AApp1-26 Special Journals:

Solid Fields Ltd. had transactions in August 20X5 as follows:

August

| 3 | Sold merchandise on account to Duane Kennerly, Invoice No. 902, $44,300. (Terms of all credit sales are 2/10, n/30 and sales are recorded at the gross amount.) The inventory sold cost $16,100. |

3   Issued cheque No. 546 to Downtown Property Management Ltd. for rent, $2,175.

3   Issued cheque No. 547 to Charles Milbury for travel costs, $511.

3   Received merchandise and an invoice dated 31 July, terms n/15, from Worthy Company, $97,800.

3   Purchased office equipment on account from Dee Ltd. Company, invoice dated 3 August, terms n/10 EOM, $62,625.

8   Issued cheque No. 548 to *The Chronicle News* for advertising, $975.

10   Issued cheque No. 549 to Worthy Company in payment of its 31 July invoice.

11   Sold unneeded office supplies at cost for cash, $160.

16   Sold merchandise on account to Sally Gunz, invoice No. 903, $10,735. The inventory sold cost $5,400.

18   Received payment from Duane Kennerly for the sale of 3 August.

20   Received merchandise and an invoice dated 18 August, terms n/60, from WayMobile Company, $47,500.

21   Issued a credit memorandum to Sally Gunz for defective merchandise sold on 16 August and returned for credit, $3,835. The merchandise returned was not saleable and was destroyed.

24   Received a $4,700 credit memorandum from WayMobile Company for defective merchandise received on 20 August and returned for credit.

25   Purchased on account from The Office Stop, merchandise inventory, $42,500, invoice dated 25 August, terms n/10 EOM.

26   Received payment from Sally Gunz for the 16 August sale. She paid the net amount due within the discount period and deducted 2% from the amount owing.

28   Issued cheque No. 550 to WayMobile Company in payment of its 20 August invoice, less the purchase return.

30   Cash sales for the month ended 30 August were $61,230. The inventory sold cost $9,600.

Required:

1. Draft special journals for cash receipts, cash disbursements, sales, and purchases. The company also maintains a general journal.
2. Record the transactions in the appropriate journal. Leave columns blank if details (e.g., account numbers) are not available. Sales are recorded at the gross amount.

 AApp1-27 Special Journals:

Calm Seas Ltd. had the following transactions in September 20X5:

Sept.

1   Purchased inventory for cash, $5,600.

1   Purchased inventory from a supplier on credit, terms 2/10, n/30, $13,400.

2   Purchased $35,000 of automotive equipment for cash.

2   Purchased office equipment by issuing a note payable, $15,700.

5   Purchased inventory of $54,300 on account, terms 1/15, n/30.

10   Sold merchandise for $16,900 to a customer on account, terms 2/10, n/30. The inventory sold cost $7,600. Sales are recorded at the gross amount.

12   Received a credit memo from the supplier re: the inventory acquired on 5 September, $3,200 gross ($3,168 net).

12   Borrowed $70,000 from the bank at an interest rate of 4%.

13   Paid the supplier for the net purchase of 5 September.

22   Received payment from the customer re: sale on 10 September. This cheque was issued within the discount period.

25   Paid salaries of $6,200.

29   Cash sales for the month of September amounted to $97,250. The inventory sold cost $42,160.

Required:

1. Draft special journals for cash receipts, cash disbursements, sales, and purchases. The company also maintains a general journal.

2. Record the transactions in the appropriate journal. Leave columns blank if details (e.g., account numbers) are not available. Inventory and sales are recorded at the net amount.

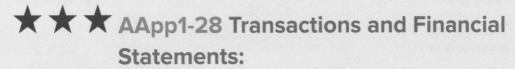

★ ★ ★ AApp1-28 Transactions and Financial Statements:

Multimedia Inc., a producer of graphics and artwork for movie theatres and other media distributors, provided the following information for 20X5:

Selected Accounts from the Statement of Financial Position, as of 1 January 20X5

Accounts receivable	$ 10,000
Prepaid insurance	20,000
Supplies	5,000
Equipment (net)	80,000
Accounts payable (suppliers)	40,000*
Unearned rent	13,000
Wages payable	7,000
Common shares	27,000
Retained earnings	50,000

*The 31 December 20X5 balance is $50,000.

Statement of Comprehensive Income, year ended 31 December 20X5

Sales	$ 200,000
Insurance expense	(15,000)
Depreciation expense	(10,000)
Supplies expense	(30,000)
Wages expense	(60,000)
Rent revenue	—
	12,000
Net earnings and comprehensive income	$ 97,000

Statement of Cash Flows, year ended 31 December 20X5

Operating activities:

Collections from customers	$ 90,000
Insurance payments	(25,000)

Payments to suppliers	(45,000)
Payments to employees	(52,000)
Rental receipts	—
	19,000
Net operating cash flow	$ (13,000)
Cash balance, 1 January 20X5	—
Cash balance, 1 January 20X5	22,000
Cash balance, 31 December 20X5*	$ 9,000

*No investing or financing cash flows.

Required:

Prepare the 31 December 20X5 SCF for Multimedia.

 AApp1-29 Transactions and Financial Statements:

During the first week of January 20X5, Nick Power began an energy-efficiency consulting company, Power Smart Ltd. He kept no formal accounting records; however, his record of cash receipts and disbursements was accurate. The business got off to a strong start, but Nick soon needed financing for day-to-day expenses. He approached his bank for a $60,000 loan and was told that he needed accrual-based SCI and SFP before he would be approved. Knowing very little about accounting, he engaged you to prepare statements requested by the bank. He supplies you with the following information:

	Receipts	Disbursements
Investment	$ 60,000	
Computer and office equipment		$ 150,400
Operating expenses		31,400
Supplies		25,400
Rent payments		25,200
Insurance premium		10,800
Advertising—all ads complete		19,600
Wages of assistant		92,400
Telephone		25,880
Payments to James Kenna		174,000
Received from customers	509,000	
Cash balance		13,920
	$569,000	$569,000

Additional information:

- Equipment purchased includes a $4,000 computer purchased for Nick's son, for school projects.
- The amount received from customers includes a $10,000 deposit on a project to be done in January 20X6, but not yet started.
- Rent payments included $1,800 per month rental and $3,600 deposit.
- The equipment has an estimated five-year life and $2,400 salvage value.
- Supplies on hand 31 December 20X5 were $11,800.
- There were unpaid bills of $500 for cell phone, $1,080 for electricity, and $760 for travel at December 20X5.
- Insurance premium was for a three-year policy that expires on 31 December 20X7.
- Wages earned in the last week of December 20X5 to be paid in January 20X6 amounted to $1,800.
- Design revenue earned but not yet collected amounted to $82,800.
- The organization is set up as a company; the $174,000 withdrawn by Nick is $148,000 salary and $26,000 dividends.

Required:

Prepare the financial statements as requested.

(CGA-Canada, adapted)

★ ★ AApp1-30 Transactions and Financial Statements:

Shirt Shack Ltd. is a retail store operating in a downtown shopping mall. On 1 January 20X8, it reported the following:

SHIRT SHACK LTD.	
Statement of Financial Position	
As of 1 January 20X8	
Cash	$ 4,000
Accounts receivable (net of allowance of $2,000)	28,000
Prepaid rent (rental deposit)	1,000
Inventory	36,000
Leasehold improvements (net)	16,000
Total assets	$85,000
Accounts payable	$32,000
Accrued wages payable	3,500
Accrued interest payable	200
Accrued rent payable	0

Notes payable, 10%	14,800
Common shares	10,000
Retained earnings	24,500
Total liabilities plus equity	$85,000

During 20X8, the company reported the following:

a. Cash paid to employees (salaries and commissions), $67,000. Cash paid to suppliers' for payment of accounts payable, $90,000 (Note payables to all suppliers are for inventory purchases.)

b. Cash collected on customer accounts receivable accounts, $220,000.

c. On 31 December 20X8, a physical inventory count revealed that inventory was $42,000. The company uses the periodic inventory system.

d. At 31 December 20X8, customers owed Shirt Shack $35,000, and the company owed its suppliers for inventory purchases $14,000. Of the accounts receivable, aging analysis indicated that $4,000 was expected to be uncollectible. No accounts were written off in 20X8.

e. Cash paid to landlord, $12,000 ($1,000 per month for 12 months). Shirt Shack is required to pay monthly rent and, at year-end, make an additional payment to bring the total rent expense up to 10% of sales. This payment will be made in January 20X9.

f. Cash paid for miscellaneous operating expenses, $6,000.

g. Cash paid in dividends, $14,500; in interest, $1,680. No interest is owing at 31 December 20X8.

h. Shirt Shack owed employees $500 in wages and $1,000 in commissions at year-end.

i. The leasehold improvements were acquired on 1 January 20X7. They had an expected life of 10 years and were installed in leased premises that had a five-year lease on 1 January 20X7.

Required:

1. Prepare journal entries for all transactions and needed adjustments.

2. Prepare an SCI for the year ended 31 December 20X8. Ignore income tax.

3. Show all calculations.

COMPOUND INTEREST TABLES AND FORMULAE

Table I-1: Present value of 1: (P/F, *i*, *n*)

$$P/F = \frac{1}{(1+i)^n}$$

n	2%	2.5%	3%	4%	5%	6%	7%	8%	9%	10%	11%	12%	14%	15%
1	0.98039	0.97561	0.97087	0.96154	0.95238	0.94340	0.93458	0.92593	0.91743	0.90909	0.90090	0.89286	0.87719	0.86957
2	0.96117	0.95181	0.94260	0.92456	0.90703	0.89000	0.87344	0.85734	0.84168	0.82645	0.81162	0.79719	0.76947	0.75614
3	0.94232	0.92860	0.91514	0.88900	0.86384	0.83962	0.81630	0.79383	0.77218	0.75131	0.73119	0.71178	0.67497	0.65752
4	0.92385	0.90595	0.88849	0.85480	0.82270	0.79209	0.76290	0.73503	0.70843	0.68301	0.65873	0.63552	0.59208	0.57175
5	0.90573	0.88385	0.86261	0.82193	0.78353	0.74726	0.71299	0.68058	0.64993	0.62092	0.59345	0.56743	0.51937	0.49718
6	0.88797	0.86230	0.83748	0.79031	0.74622	0.70496	0.66634	0.63017	0.59627	0.56447	0.53464	0.50663	0.45559	0.43233
7	0.87056	0.84127	0.81309	0.75992	0.71068	0.66506	0.62275	0.58349	0.54703	0.51316	0.48166	0.45235	0.39964	0.37594
8	0.85349	0.82075	0.78941	0.73069	0.67684	0.62741	0.58201	0.54027	0.50187	0.46651	0.43393	0.40388	0.35056	0.32690
9	0.83676	0.80073	0.76642	0.70259	0.64461	0.59190	0.54393	0.50025	0.46043	0.42410	0.39092	0.36061	0.30751	0.28426
10	0.82035	0.78120	0.74409	0.67556	0.61391	0.55839	0.50835	0.46319	0.42241	0.38554	0.35218	0.32197	0.26974	0.24718
11	0.80426	0.76214	0.72242	0.64958	0.58468	0.52679	0.47509	0.42888	0.38753	0.35049	0.31728	0.28748	0.23662	0.21494
12	0.78849	0.74356	0.70138	0.62460	0.55684	0.49697	0.44401	0.39711	0.35553	0.31863	0.28584	0.25668	0.20756	0.18691
13	0.77303	0.72542	0.68095	0.60057	0.53032	0.46884	0.41496	0.36770	0.32618	0.28966	0.25751	0.22917	0.18207	0.16253
14	0.75788	0.70773	0.66112	0.57748	0.50507	0.44230	0.38782	0.34046	0.29925	0.26333	0.23199	0.20462	0.15971	0.14133
15	0.74301	0.69047	0.64186	0.55526	0.48102	0.41727	0.36245	0.31524	0.27454	0.23939	0.20900	0.18270	0.14010	0.12289
16	0.72845	0.67362	0.62317	0.53391	0.45811	0.39365	0.33873	0.29189	0.25187	0.21763	0.18829	0.16312	0.12289	0.10686
17	0.71416	0.65720	0.60502	0.51337	0.43630	0.37136	0.31657	0.27027	0.23107	0.19784	0.16963	0.14564	0.10780	0.09293
18	0.70016	0.64117	0.58739	0.49363	0.41552	0.35034	0.29586	0.25025	0.21199	0.17986	0.15282	0.13004	0.09456	0.08081
19	0.68643	0.62553	0.57029	0.47464	0.39573	0.33051	0.27651	0.23171	0.19449	0.16361	0.13768	0.11611	0.08295	0.07027
20	0.67297	0.61027	0.55368	0.45639	0.37689	0.31180	0.25842	0.21455	0.17843	0.14864	0.12403	0.10367	0.07276	0.06110
21	0.65978	0.59539	0.53755	0.43883	0.35894	0.29416	0.24151	0.19866	0.16370	0.13513	0.11174	0.09256	0.06383	0.05313
22	0.64684	0.58086	0.52189	0.42196	0.34185	0.27751	0.22571	0.18394	0.15018	0.12285	0.10067	0.08264	0.05599	0.04620
23	0.63416	0.56670	0.50669	0.40573	0.32557	0.26180	0.21095	0.17032	0.13778	0.11168	0.09069	0.07379	0.04911	0.04017
24	0.62172	0.55288	0.49193	0.39012	0.31007	0.24698	0.19715	0.15770	0.12640	0.10153	0.08170	0.06588	0.04308	0.03493
25	0.60953	0.53939	0.47761	0.37512	0.29530	0.23300	0.18425	0.14602	0.11597	0.09230	0.07361	0.05882	0.03779	0.03038
26	0.59758	0.52623	0.46369	0.36069	0.28124	0.21981	0.17220	0.13520	0.10639	0.08391	0.06631	0.05252	0.03315	0.02642

27	0.58586	0.51340	0.45019	0.34682	0.26785	0.20737	0.16093	0.12519	0.09761	0.07628	0.05974	0.04689	0.02908	0.02297
28	0.57437	0.50088	0.43708	0.33348	0.25509	0.19563	0.15040	0.11591	0.08955	0.06934	0.05382	0.04187	0.02551	0.01997
29	0.56311	0.48866	0.42435	0.32065	0.24295	0.18456	0.14056	0.10733	0.08215	0.06304	0.04849	0.03738	0.02237	0.01737
30	0.55207	0.47674	0.41199	0.30832	0.23138	0.17411	0.13137	0.09938	0.07537	0.05731	0.04368	0.03338	0.01963	0.01510
31	0.54125	0.46511	0.39999	0.29646	0.22036	0.16425	0.12277	0.09202	0.06915	0.05210	0.03935	0.02980	0.01722	0.01313
32	0.53063	0.45377	0.38834	0.28506	0.20987	0.15496	0.11474	0.08520	0.06344	0.04736	0.03545	0.02661	0.01510	0.01142
33	0.52023	0.44270	0.37703	0.27409	0.19987	0.14619	0.10723	0.07889	0.05820	0.04306	0.03194	0.02376	0.01325	0.00993
34	0.51003	0.43191	0.36604	0.26355	0.19035	0.13791	0.10022	0.07305	0.05339	0.03914	0.02878	0.02121	0.01162	0.00864
35	0.50003	0.42137	0.35538	0.25342	0.18129	0.13011	0.09366	0.06763	0.04899	0.03558	0.02592	0.01894	0.01019	0.00751
36	0.49022	0.41109	0.34503	0.24367	0.17266	0.12274	0.08754	0.06262	0.04494	0.03235	0.02335	0.01691	0.00894	0.00653
37	0.48061	0.40107	0.33498	0.23430	0.16444	0.11579	0.08181	0.05799	0.04123	0.02941	0.02104	0.01510	0.00784	0.00568
38	0.47119	0.39128	0.32523	0.22529	0.15661	0.10924	0.07646	0.05369	0.03783	0.02673	0.01896	0.01348	0.00688	0.00494
39	0.46195	0.38174	0.31575	0.21662	0.14915	0.10306	0.07146	0.04971	0.03470	0.02430	0.01708	0.01204	0.00604	0.00429
40	0.45289	0.37243	0.30656	0.20829	0.14205	0.09722	0.06678	0.04603	0.03184	0.02209	0.01538	0.01075	0.00529	0.00373
45	0.41020	0.32917	0.26444	0.17120	0.11130	0.07265	0.04761	0.03133	0.02069	0.01372	0.00913	0.00610	0.00275	0.00186
50	0.37153	0.29094	0.22811	0.14071	0.08720	0.05429	0.03395	0.02132	0.01345	0.00852	0.00542	0.00346	0.00143	0.00092

Table I-2: Present value of an ordinary annuity of n payments of 1: (P/A, i, n)

$$P/A = \frac{1 - \frac{1}{(1+i)^n}}{i}$$

n	2%	2.5%	3%	4%	5%	6%	7%	8%	9%	10%	11%	12%	14%	15%
1	0.98039	0.97561	0.97087	0.96154	0.95238	0.94340	0.93458	0.92593	0.91743	0.90909	0.90090	0.89286	0.87719	0.86957
2	1.94156	1.92742	1.91347	1.88609	1.85941	1.83339	1.80802	1.78326	1.75911	1.73554	1.71252	1.69005	1.64666	1.62571
3	2.88388	2.85602	2.82861	2.77509	2.72325	2.67301	2.62432	2.57710	2.53129	2.48685	2.44371	2.40183	2.32163	2.28323
4	3.80773	3.76197	3.71710	3.62990	3.54595	3.46511	3.38721	3.31213	3.23972	3.16987	3.10245	3.03735	2.91371	2.85498
5	4.71346	4.64583	4.57971	4.45182	4.32948	4.21236	4.10020	3.99271	3.88965	3.79079	3.69590	3.60478	3.43308	3.35216
6	5.60143	5.50813	5.41719	5.24214	5.07569	4.91732	4.76654	4.62288	4.48592	4.35526	4.23054	4.11141	3.88867	3.78448
7	6.47199	6.34939	6.23028	6.00205	5.78637	5.58238	5.38929	5.20637	5.03295	4.86842	4.71220	4.56376	4.28830	4.16042
8	7.32548	7.17014	7.01969	6.73274	6.46321	6.20979	5.97130	5.74664	5.53482	5.33493	5.14612	4.96764	4.63886	4.48732
9	8.16224	7.97087	7.78611	7.43533	7.10782	6.80169	6.51523	6.24689	5.99525	5.75902	5.53705	5.32825	4.94637	4.77158
10	8.98259	8.75206	8.53020	8.11090	7.72173	7.36009	7.02358	6.71008	6.41766	6.14457	5.88923	5.65022	5.21612	5.01877
11	9.78685	9.51421	9.25262	8.76048	8.30641	7.88687	7.49867	7.13896	6.80519	6.49506	6.20652	5.93770	5.45273	5.23371
12	10.57534	10.25776	9.95400	9.38507	8.86325	8.38384	7.94269	7.53608	7.16073	6.81369	6.49236	6.19437	5.66029	5.42062
13	11.34837	10.98318	10.63496	9.98565	9.39357	8.85268	8.35765	7.90378	7.48690	7.10336	6.74987	6.42355	5.84236	5.58315
14	12.10625	11.69091	11.29607	10.56312	9.89864	9.29498	8.74547	8.24424	7.78615	7.36669	6.98187	6.62817	6.00207	5.72448
15	12.84926	12.38138	11.93794	11.11839	10.37966	9.71225	9.10791	8.55948	8.06069	7.60608	7.19087	6.81086	6.14217	5.84737
16	13.57771	13.05500	12.56110	11.65230	10.83777	10.10590	9.44665	8.85137	8.31256	7.82371	7.37916	6.97399	6.26506	5.95423
17	14.29187	13.71220	13.16612	12.16567	11.27407	10.47726	9.76322	9.12164	8.54363	8.02155	7.54879	7.11963	6.37286	6.04716
18	14.99203	14.35336	13.75351	12.65930	11.68959	10.82760	10.05909	9.37189	8.75563	8.20141	7.70162	7.24967	6.46742	6.12797
19	15.67846	14.97889	14.32380	13.13394	12.08532	11.15812	10.33560	9.60360	8.95011	8.36492	7.83929	7.36578	6.55037	6.19823
20	16.35143	15.58916	14.87747	13.59033	12.46221	11.46992	10.59401	9.81815	9.12855	8.51356	7.96333	7.46944	6.62313	6.25933
21	17.01121	16.18455	15.41502	14.02916	12.82115	11.76408	10.83553	10.01680	9.29224	8.64869	8.07507	7.56200	6.68696	6.31246
22	17.65805	16.76541	15.93692	14.45112	13.16300	12.04158	11.06124	10.20074	9.44243	8.77154	8.17574	7.64465	6.74294	6.35866
23	18.29220	17.33211	16.44361	14.85684	13.48857	12.30338	11.27219	10.37106	9.58021	8.88322	8.26643	7.71843	6.79206	6.39884
24	18.91393	17.88499	16.93554	15.24696	13.79864	12.55036	11.46933	10.52876	9.70661	8.98474	8.34814	7.78432	6.83514	6.43377
25	19.52346	18.42438	17.41315	15.62208	14.09394	12.78336	11.65358	10.67478	9.82258	9.07704	8.42174	7.84314	6.87293	6.46415

n														
26	20.12104	18.95061	17.87684	15.98277	14.37519	13.00317	11.82578	10.80998	9.92897	9.16095	8.48806	7.89566	6.90608	6.49056
27	20.70690	19.46401	18.32703	16.32959	14.64303	13.21053	11.98671	10.93516	10.02658	9.23722	8.54780	7.94255	6.93515	6.51353
28	21.28127	19.96489	18.76411	16.66306	14.89813	13.40616	12.13711	11.05108	10.11613	9.30657	8.60162	7.98442	6.96066	6.53351
29	21.84438	20.45355	19.18845	16.98371	15.14107	13.59072	12.27767	11.15841	10.19828	9.36961	8.65011	8.02181	6.98304	6.55088
30	22.39646	20.93029	19.60044	17.29203	15.37245	13.76483	12.40904	11.25778	10.27365	9.42691	8.69379	8.05518	7.00266	6.56598
31	22.93770	21.39541	20.00043	17.58849	15.59281	13.92909	12.53181	11.34980	10.34280	9.47901	8.73315	8.08499	7.01988	6.57911
32	23.46833	21.84918	20.38877	17.87355	15.80268	14.08404	12.64656	11.43500	10.40624	9.52638	8.76860	8.11159	7.03498	6.59053
33	23.98856	22.29188	20.76579	18.14765	16.00255	14.23023	12.75379	11.51389	10.46444	9.56943	8.80054	8.13535	7.04823	6.60046
34	24.49859	22.72379	21.13184	18.41120	16.19290	14.36814	12.85401	11.58693	10.51784	9.60857	8.82932	8.15656	7.05985	6.60910
35	24.99862	23.14516	21.48722	18.66461	16.37419	14.49825	12.94767	11.65457	10.56682	9.64416	8.85524	8.17550	7.07005	6.61661
36	25.48884	23.55625	21.83225	18.90828	16.54685	14.62099	13.03521	11.71719	10.61176	9.67651	8.87859	8.19241	7.07899	6.62314
37	25.96945	23.95732	22.16724	19.14258	16.71129	14.73678	13.11702	11.77518	10.65299	9.70592	8.89963	8.20751	7.08683	6.62881
38	26.44064	24.34860	22.49246	19.36786	16.86789	14.84602	13.19347	11.82887	10.69082	9.73265	8.91859	8.22099	7.09371	6.63375
39	26.90259	24.73034	22.80822	19.58448	17.01704	14.94907	13.26493	11.87858	10.72552	9.75696	8.93567	8.23303	7.09975	6.63805
40	27.35548	25.10278	23.11477	19.79277	17.15909	15.04630	13.33171	11.92461	10.75736	9.77905	8.95105	8.24378	7.10504	6.64178
45	29.49016	26.83302	24.51871	20.72004	17.77407	15.45583	13.60552	12.10840	10.88120	9.86281	9.00791	8.28252	7.12322	6.65429
50	31.42361	28.36231	25.72976	21.48218	18.25593	15.76186	13.80075	12.23348	10.96168	9.91481	9.04165	8.30450	7.13266	6.66051

Table I-3: Present value of an annuity due of n payments of 1: (P/AD, i, n)

$$P/AD = \left[\dfrac{1 - \dfrac{1}{(1+i)^n}}{i} \right] \times (1+i)$$

n	2%	2.5%	3%	4%	5%	6%	7%	8%	9%	10%	11%	12%	14%	15%
1	1.00000	1.00000	1.00000	1.00000	1.00000	1.00000	1.00000	1.00000	1.00000	1.00000	1.00000	1.00000	1.00000	1.00000
2	1.98039	1.97561	1.97087	1.96154	1.95238	1.94340	1.93458	1.92593	1.91743	1.90909	1.90090	1.89286	1.87719	1.86957
3	2.94156	2.92742	2.91347	2.88609	2.85941	2.83339	2.80302	2.78326	2.75911	2.73554	2.71252	2.69005	2.64666	2.62571
4	3.88388	3.85602	3.82861	3.77509	3.72325	3.67301	3.62432	3.57710	3.53129	3.48685	3.44371	3.40183	3.32163	3.28323
5	4.80773	4.76197	4.71710	4.62990	4.54595	4.46511	4.38721	4.31213	4.23972	4.16987	4.10245	4.03735	3.91371	3.85498
6	5.71346	5.64583	5.57971	5.45182	5.32948	5.21236	5.10020	4.99271	4.88965	4.79079	4.69590	4.60478	4.43308	4.35216
7	6.60143	6.50813	6.41719	6.24214	6.07569	5.91732	5.76654	5.62288	5.48592	5.35526	5.23054	5.11141	4.88867	4.78448
8	7.47199	7.34939	7.23028	7.00205	6.78637	6.58238	6.38929	6.20637	6.03295	5.86842	5.71220	5.56376	5.28830	5.16042
9	8.32548	8.17014	8.01969	7.73274	7.46321	7.20979	6.97130	6.74664	6.53482	6.33493	6.14612	5.96764	5.63886	5.48732
10	9.16224	8.97087	8.78611	8.43533	8.10732	7.80169	7.51523	7.24689	6.99525	6.75902	6.53705	6.32825	5.94637	5.77158
11	9.98259	9.75206	9.53020	9.11090	8.72173	8.36009	8.02358	7.71008	7.41766	7.14457	6.88923	6.65022	6.21612	6.01877
12	10.78685	10.51421	10.25262	9.76048	9.30641	8.88687	8.49867	8.13896	7.80519	7.49506	7.20652	6.93770	6.45273	6.23371
13	11.57534	11.25776	10.95400	10.38507	9.86325	9.38384	8.94269	8.53608	8.16073	7.81369	7.49236	7.19437	6.66029	6.42062
14	12.34837	11.98318	11.63496	10.98565	10.39357	9.85268	9.35765	8.90378	8.48690	8.10336	7.74987	7.42355	6.84236	6.58315
15	13.10625	12.69091	12.29607	11.56312	10.89864	10.29498	9.74547	9.24424	8.78615	8.36669	7.98187	7.62817	7.00207	6.72448
16	13.84926	13.38138	12.93794	12.11839	11.37966	10.71225	10.10791	9.55948	9.06069	8.60608	8.19087	7.81086	7.14217	6.84737
17	14.57771	14.05500	13.56110	12.65230	11.83777	11.10590	10.44665	9.85137	9.31256	8.82371	8.37916	7.97399	7.26506	6.95423
18	15.29187	14.71220	14.16612	13.16567	12.27407	11.47726	10.76322	10.12164	9.54363	9.02155	8.54879	8.11963	7.3726	7.04716
19	15.99203	15.35336	14.75351	13.65930	12.68959	11.82760	11.05909	10.37189	9.75563	9.20141	8.70162	8.24967	7.46742	7.12797
20	16.67846	15.97889	15.32380	14.13394	13.08532	12.15812	11.33560	10.60360	9.95011	9.36492	8.83929	8.36578	7.55037	7.19823
21	17.35143	16.58916	15.87747	14.59033	13.46221	12.46992	11.59401	10.81815	10.12855	9.51356	8.96333	8.46944	7.62313	7.25933
22	18.01121	17.18455	16.41502	15.02916	13.82115	12.76408	11.83553	11.01680	10.29224	9.64869	9.07507	8.56200	7.68696	7.31246
23	18.65805	17.76541	16.93692	15.45112	14.16300	13.04158	12.06124	11.20074	10.44243	9.77154	9.17574	8.64465	7.74294	7.35866
24	19.29220	18.33211	17.44361	15.85684	14.48857	13.30338	12.27219	11.37106	10.58021	9.88322	9.26643	8.71843	7.79206	7.39884
25	19.91393	18.88499	17.93554	16.24696	14.79864	13.55036	12.46933	11.52876	10.70661	9.98474	9.34814	8.78432	7.83514	7.43377

n														
26	7.46415	7.87293	8.84314	9.42174	10.07704	10.82258	11.67478	12.65358	13.78336	15.09394	16.62208	18.41315		21.12104
27	7.49056	7.90608	8.89566	9.48806	10.16095	10.92897	11.80998	12.82578	14.00317	15.37519	16.98277	18.87684	19.95061	21.70690
28	7.51353	7.93515	8.94255	9.54780	10.23722	11.02658	11.98516	12.98671	14.21053	15.64303	17.32959	19.32703	20.46401	22.28127
29	7.53351	7.96066	8.98442	9.60162	10.30657	11.11613	12.05108	13.13711	14.40616	15.89813	17.66306	19.76411	20.96489	22.84438
30	7.55088	7.98304	9.02181	9.65011	10.36961	11.19828	12.15841	13.27767	14.59072	16.14107	17.98371	20.18845	21.45355	
31	7.56598	8.00266	9.05518	9.69379	10.42691	11.27365	12.25778	13.40904	14.76483	16.37245	18.29203	20.60044	21.93029	23.39646
32	7.57911	8.01988	9.08499	9.73315	10.47901	11.34280	12.34980	13.53181	14.92909	16.59281	18.58849	21.00043	22.39541	23.93770
33	7.59053	8.03498	9.11159	9.76860	10.52638	11.40624	12.43500	13.64656	15.08404	16.80268	18.87355	21.38877	22.34918	24.46833
34	7.60046	8.04823	9.13535	9.80054	10.56943	11.46444	12.51389	13.75379	15.23023	17.00255	19.14765	21.76579	23.29188	24.98856
35	7.60910	8.05985	9.15656	9.82932	10.60857	11.51784	12.58693	13.85401	15.36814	17.19290	19.41120	22.13184	23.72379	25.49859
36	7.61661	8.07005	9.17550	9.85524	10.64416	11.56682	12.65457	13.94767	15.49325	17.37419	19.66461	22.48722	24.14516	25.99862
37	7.62314	8.07899	9.19241	9.87859	10.67651	11.61176	12.71719	14.03521	15.62099	17.54685	19.90828	22.83225	24.55625	26.48884
38	7.62881	8.08683	9.20751	9.89963	10.70592	11.65299	12.77518	14.11702	15.73673	17.71129	20.14258	23.16724	24.95732	26.96945
39	7.63375	8.09371	9.22099	9.91859	10.73265	11.69082	12.82837	14.19347	15.34602	17.86789	20.36786	23.49246	25.34860	27.44064
40	7.63805	8.09975	9.23303	9.93567	10.75696	11.72552	12.87853	14.26493	15.94907	18.01704	20.58448	23.80822	25.73034	27.90259
45	7.65244	8.12047	9.27642	9.99878	10.84909	11.86051	13.07707	14.55791	16.38318	18.66277	21.54884	25.25427	27.50385	30.07996
50	7.65959	8.13123	9.30104	10.03624	10.90630	11.94823	13.21216	14.76680	16.70757	19.16872	22.34147	26.50166	29.07137	32.05208